SHOWCASE PRESENTS
GREEN LANTERN
VOLUME TWO

Dan DiDio Senior VP-Executive Editor

Julius Schwartz Editor-original series

Peter Hamboussi Editor-collected edition

Robbin Brosterman Senior Art Director

Paul Levitz President & Publisher

Georg Brewer VP-Design & DC Direct Creative

Richard Bruning Senior VP-Creative Director

Patrick Caldon Executive VP-Finance & Operations

Chris Caramalis VP-Finance

John Cunningham VP-Marketing

Terri Cunningham VP-Managing Editor

Stephanie Fierman Senior VP-Sales & Marketing

Alison Gill VP-Manufacturing

Hank Kanalz VP-General Manager, WildStorm

Jim Lee Editorial Director-WildStorm

Paula Lowitt Senior VP-Business & Legal Affairs

MaryEllen McLaughlin VP-Advertising & Custom Publishing

John Nee VP-Business Development

Gregory Noveck Senior VP-Creative Affairs

Cheryl Rubin Senior VP-Brand Management

Jeff Trojan VP-Business Development, DC Direct

Bob Wayne VP-Sales

Cover illustration by Gil Kane & Murphy Anderson.
Front cover colored by Alex Sinclair.

SHOWCASE PRESENTS GREEN LANTERN VOL. TWO
Published by DC Comics. Cover and compilation
copyright © 2007 DC Comics. All Rights Reserved.

Originally published in single magazine form in GREEN LANTERN 18-38 © 1963, 1964, 1965. DC Comics. All Rights Reserved. All characters, their distinctive likenesses and related elements featured in this publication are trademarks of DC Comics.

DC Comics, 1700 Broadway, New York, NY 10019
A Warner Bros. Entertainment Company
Printed in Canada. First Printing.
ISBN: 1-4012-1264-6
ISBN 13: 978-1-4012-1264-3

TABLE OF CONTENTS

ALL COVERS AND STORIES PENCILLED BY **GIL KANE** UNLESS OTHERWISE NOTED.

UNTIL THE 1970s IT WAS NOT COMMON PRACTICE IN THE COMIC BOOK INDUSTRY TO CREDIT ALL STORIES. IN THE PREPARATION OF THIS COLLECTION WE HAVE USED OUR BEST EFFORTS TO REVIEW ANY SURVIVING RECORDS AND CONSULT ANY AVAILABLE DATABASES AND KNOWLEDGEABLE PARTIES. WE REGRET THE INNATE LIMITATIONS OF THIS PROCESS AND ANY MISSING OR MISASSIGNED ATTRIBUTIONS THAT MAY OCCUR. ANY ADDITIONAL INFORMATION ON CREDITS SHOULD BE DIRECTED TO: EDITOR, COLLECTED EDITIONS, C/O DC COMICS.

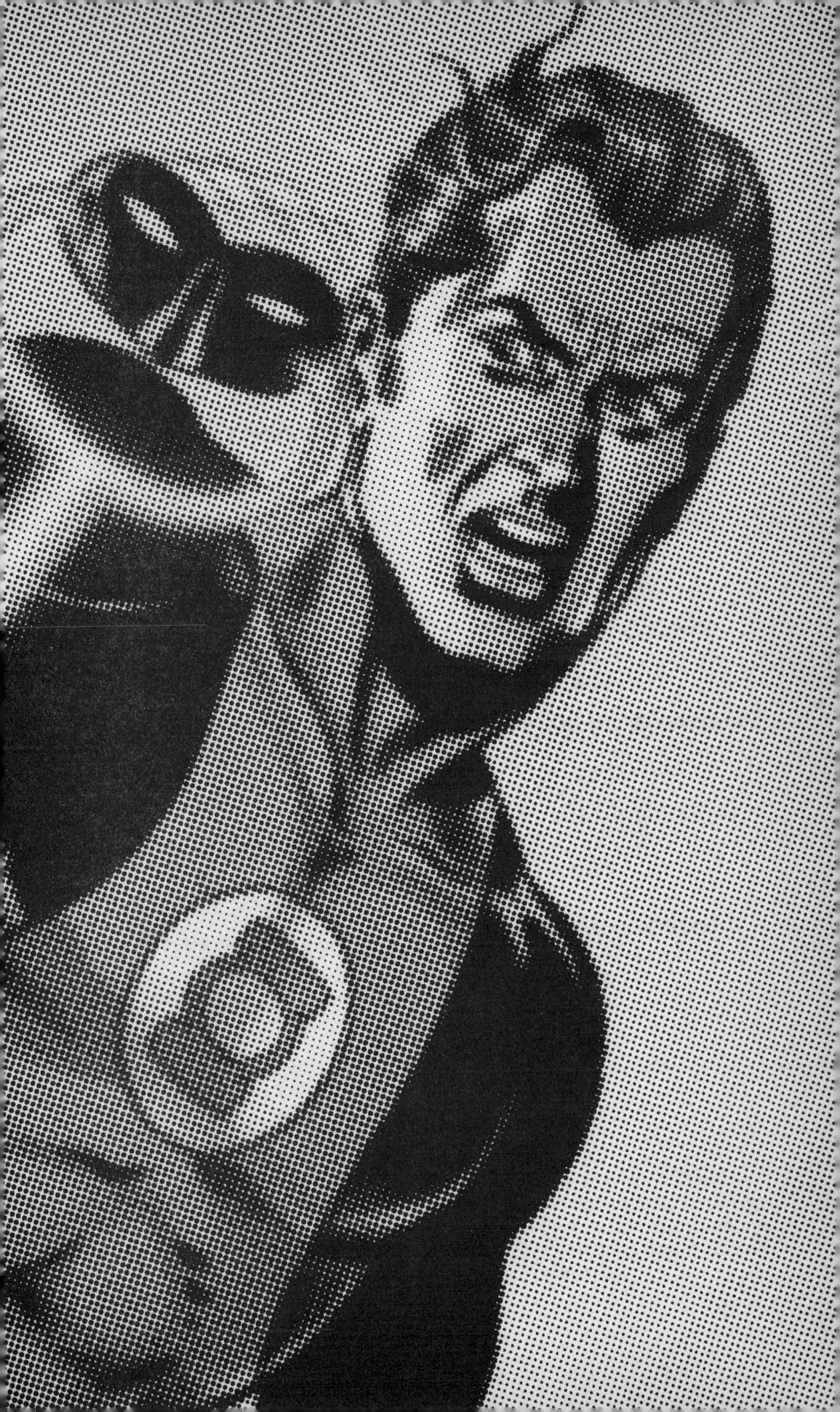

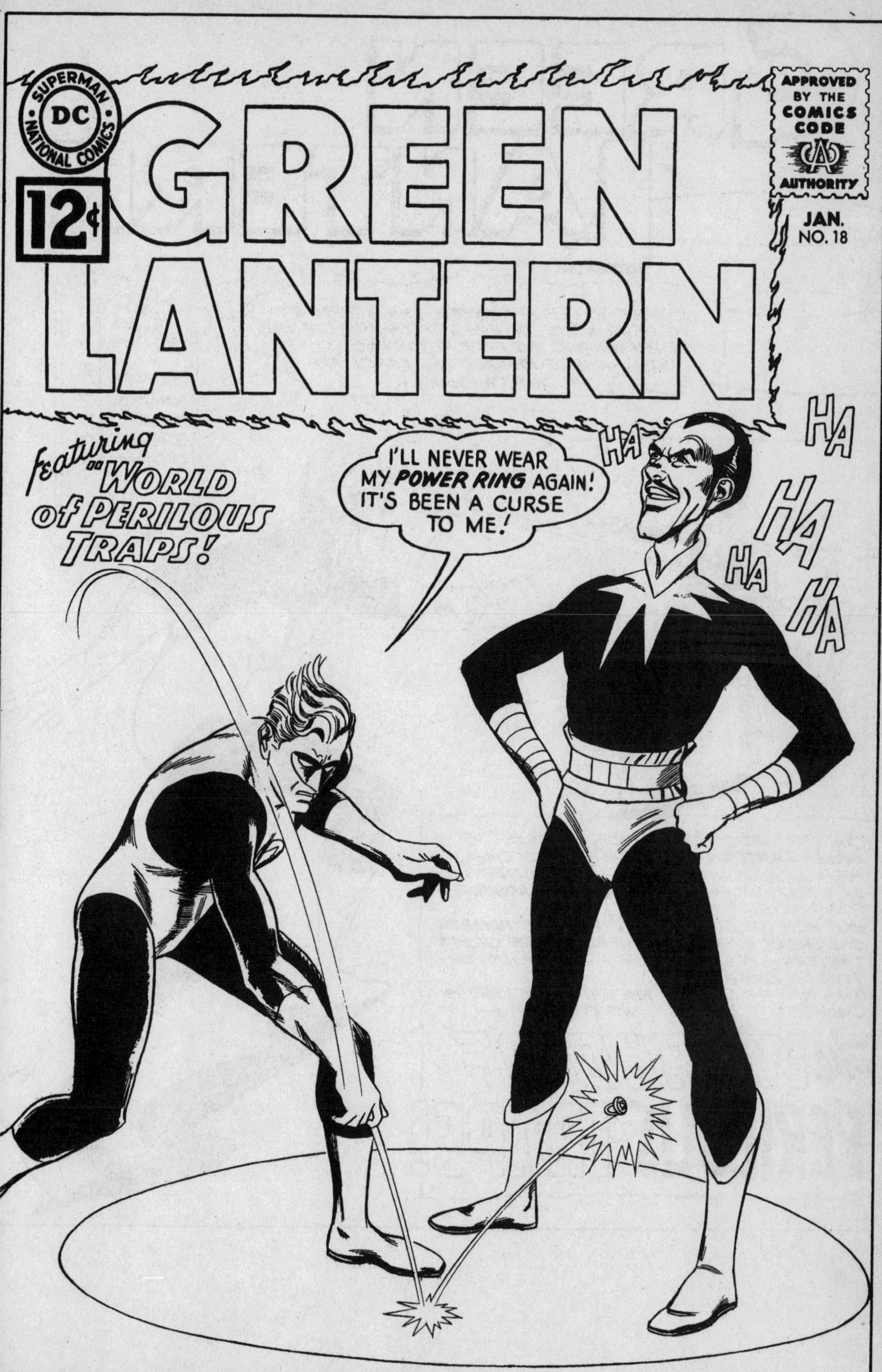
SUPERMAN
DC
NATIONAL COMICS
12¢
GREEN LANTERN
APPROVED BY THE COMICS CODE AUTHORITY
JAN.
NO. 18
featuring "WORLD of PERILOUS TRAPS!"
I'LL NEVER WEAR MY POWER RING AGAIN! IT'S BEEN A CURSE TO ME!
HA HA HA HA HA HA

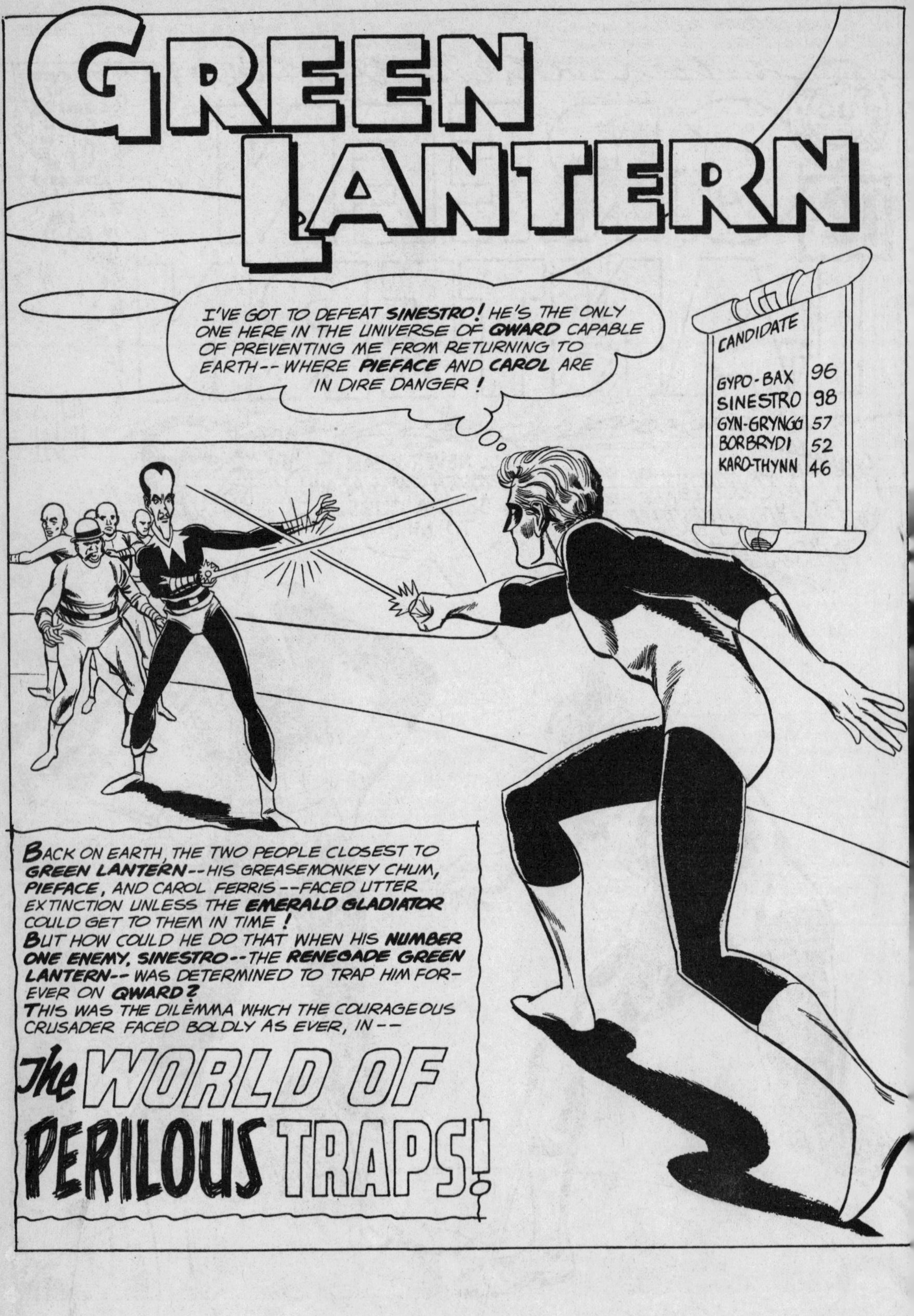
GREEN LANTERN
I'VE GOT TO DEFEAT SINESTRO! HE'S THE ONLY ONE HERE IN THE UNIVERSE OF QWARD CAPABLE OF PREVENTING ME FROM RETURNING TO EARTH--WHERE PIEFACE AND CAROL ARE IN DIRE DANGER!
CANDIDATE
GYPO-BAX 96
SINESTRO 98
GYN-GRYNGG 57
BORBRYDI 52
KARO-THYNN 46
BACK ON EARTH, THE TWO PEOPLE CLOSEST TO GREEN LANTERN--HIS GREASEMONKEY CHUM, PIEFACE, AND CAROL FERRIS--FACED UTTER EXTINCTION UNLESS THE EMERALD GLADIATOR COULD GET TO THEM IN TIME!
BUT HOW COULD HE DO THAT WHEN HIS NUMBER ONE ENEMY, SINESTRO--THE RENEGADE GREEN LANTERN--WAS DETERMINED TO TRAP HIM FOREVER ON QWARD?
THIS WAS THE DILEMMA WHICH THE COURAGEOUS CRUSADER FACED BOLDLY AS EVER, IN--
The WORLD OF PERILOUS TRAPS!

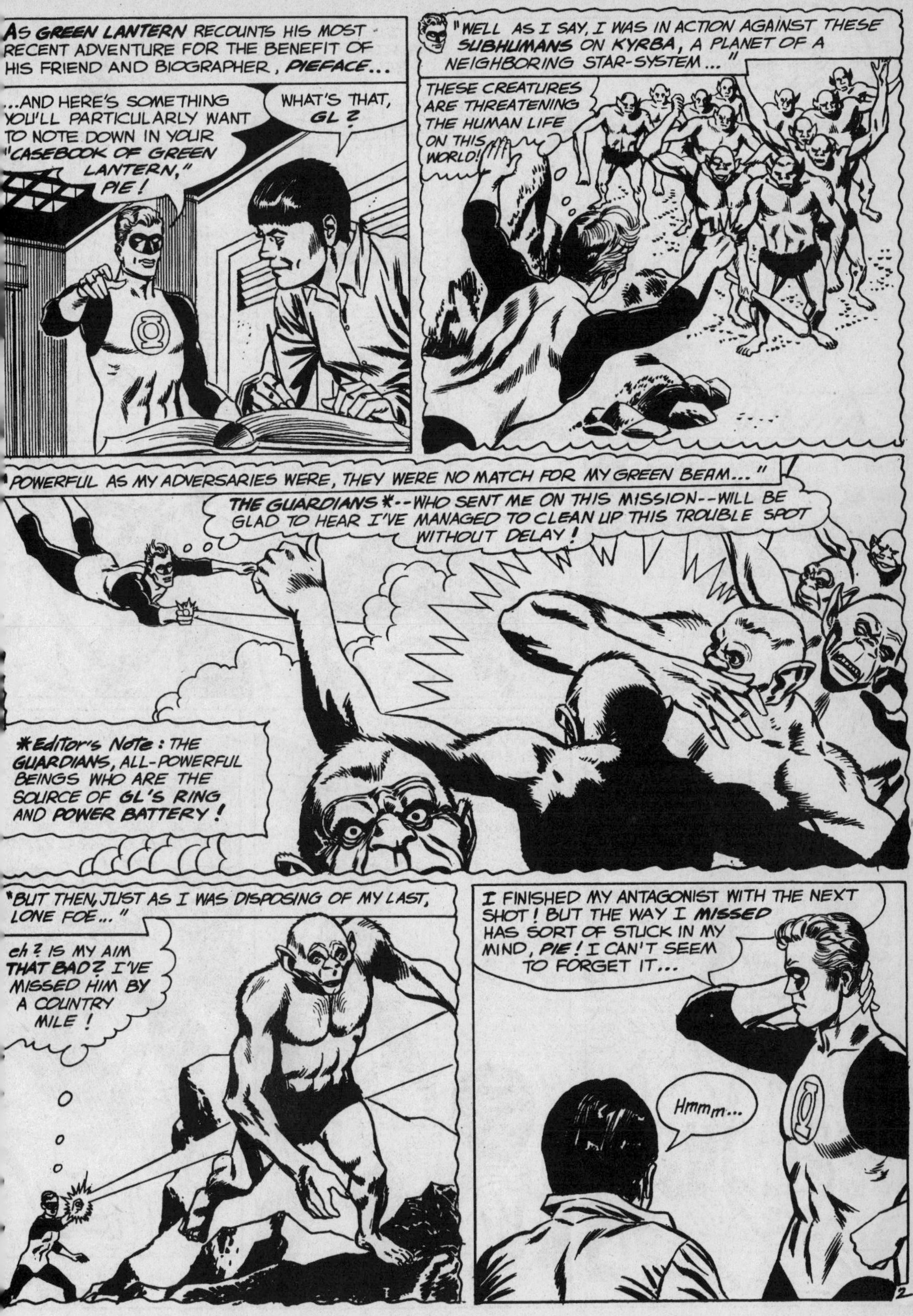
AS GREEN LANTERN RECOUNTS HIS MOST RECENT ADVENTURE FOR THE BENEFIT OF HIS FRIEND AND BIOGRAPHER, PIEFACE...
...AND HERE'S SOMETHING YOU'LL PARTICULARLY WANT TO NOTE DOWN IN YOUR "CASEBOOK OF GREEN LANTERN," PIE!
WHAT'S THAT, GL?
"WELL AS I SAY, I WAS IN ACTION AGAINST THESE SUBHUMANS ON KYRBA, A PLANET OF A NEIGHBORING STAR-SYSTEM..."
THESE CREATURES ARE THREATENING THE HUMAN LIFE ON THIS WORLD!
"POWERFUL AS MY ADVERSARIES WERE, THEY WERE NO MATCH FOR MY GREEN BEAM..."
THE GUARDIANS*--WHO SENT ME ON THIS MISSION--WILL BE GLAD TO HEAR I'VE MANAGED TO CLEAN UP THIS TROUBLE SPOT WITHOUT DELAY!
*Editor's Note: THE GUARDIANS, ALL-POWERFUL BEINGS WHO ARE THE SOURCE OF GL'S RING AND POWER BATTERY!
"BUT THEN, JUST AS I WAS DISPOSING OF MY LAST, LONE FOE..."
eh? IS MY AIM THAT BAD? I'VE MISSED HIM BY A COUNTRY MILE!
I FINISHED MY ANTAGONIST WITH THE NEXT SHOT! BUT THE WAY I MISSED HAS SORT OF STUCK IN MY MIND, PIE! I CAN'T SEEM TO FORGET IT...
Hmmm...
2

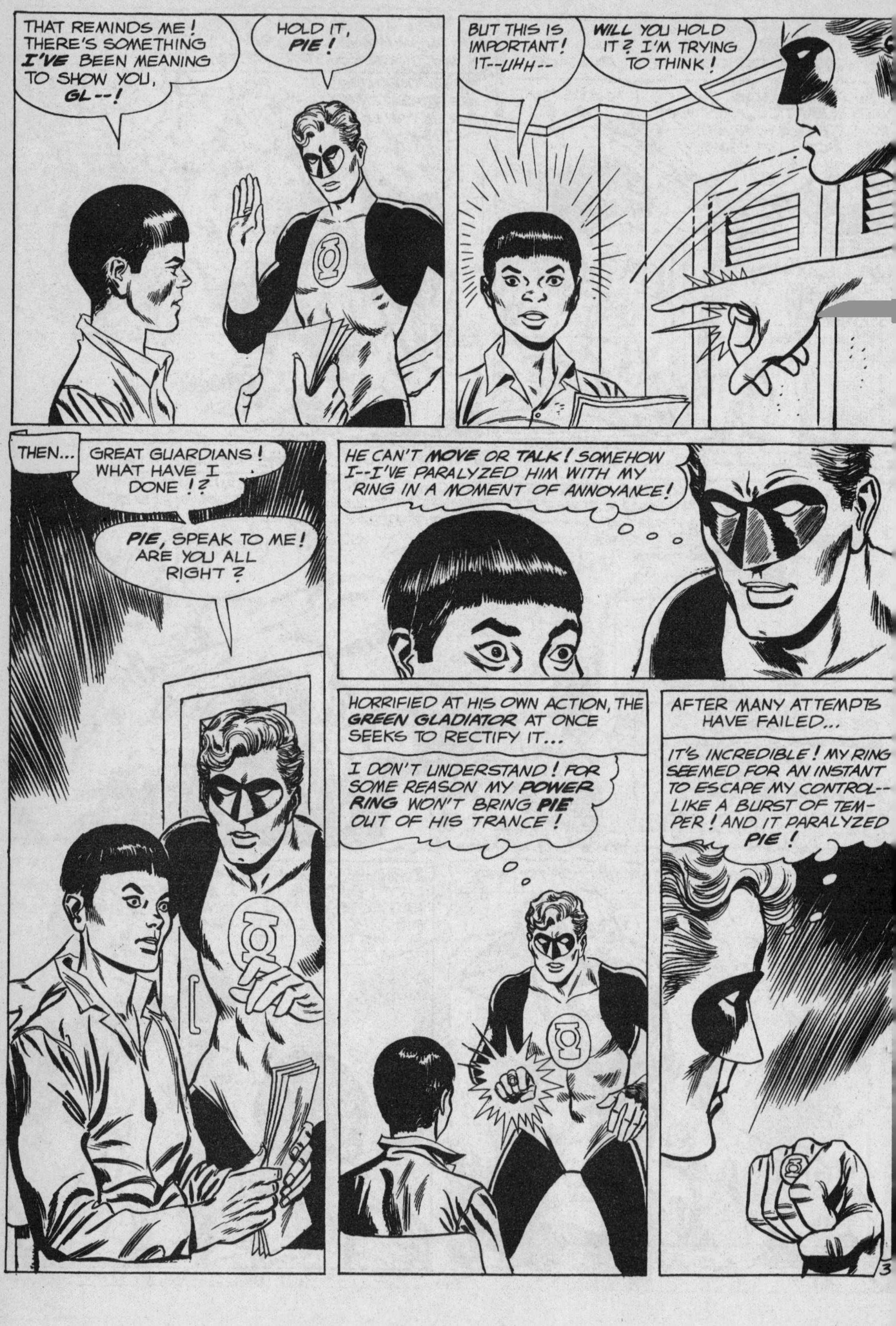
THAT REMINDS ME! THERE'S SOMETHING I'VE BEEN MEANING TO SHOW YOU, GL--!
HOLD IT, PIE!
BUT THIS IS IMPORTANT! IT--UHH--
WILL YOU HOLD IT? I'M TRYING TO THINK!
THEN...
GREAT GUARDIANS! WHAT HAVE I DONE!?
PIE, SPEAK TO ME! ARE YOU ALL RIGHT?
HE CAN'T MOVE OR TALK! SOMEHOW I--I'VE PARALYZED HIM WITH MY RING IN A MOMENT OF ANNOYANCE!
HORRIFIED AT HIS OWN ACTION, THE GREEN GLADIATOR AT ONCE SEEKS TO RECTIFY IT...
I DON'T UNDERSTAND! FOR SOME REASON MY POWER RING WON'T BRING PIE OUT OF HIS TRANCE!
AFTER MANY ATTEMPTS HAVE FAILED...
IT'S INCREDIBLE! MY RING SEEMED FOR AN INSTANT TO ESCAPE MY CONTROL--LIKE A BURST OF TEMPER! AND IT PARALYZED PIE!
3

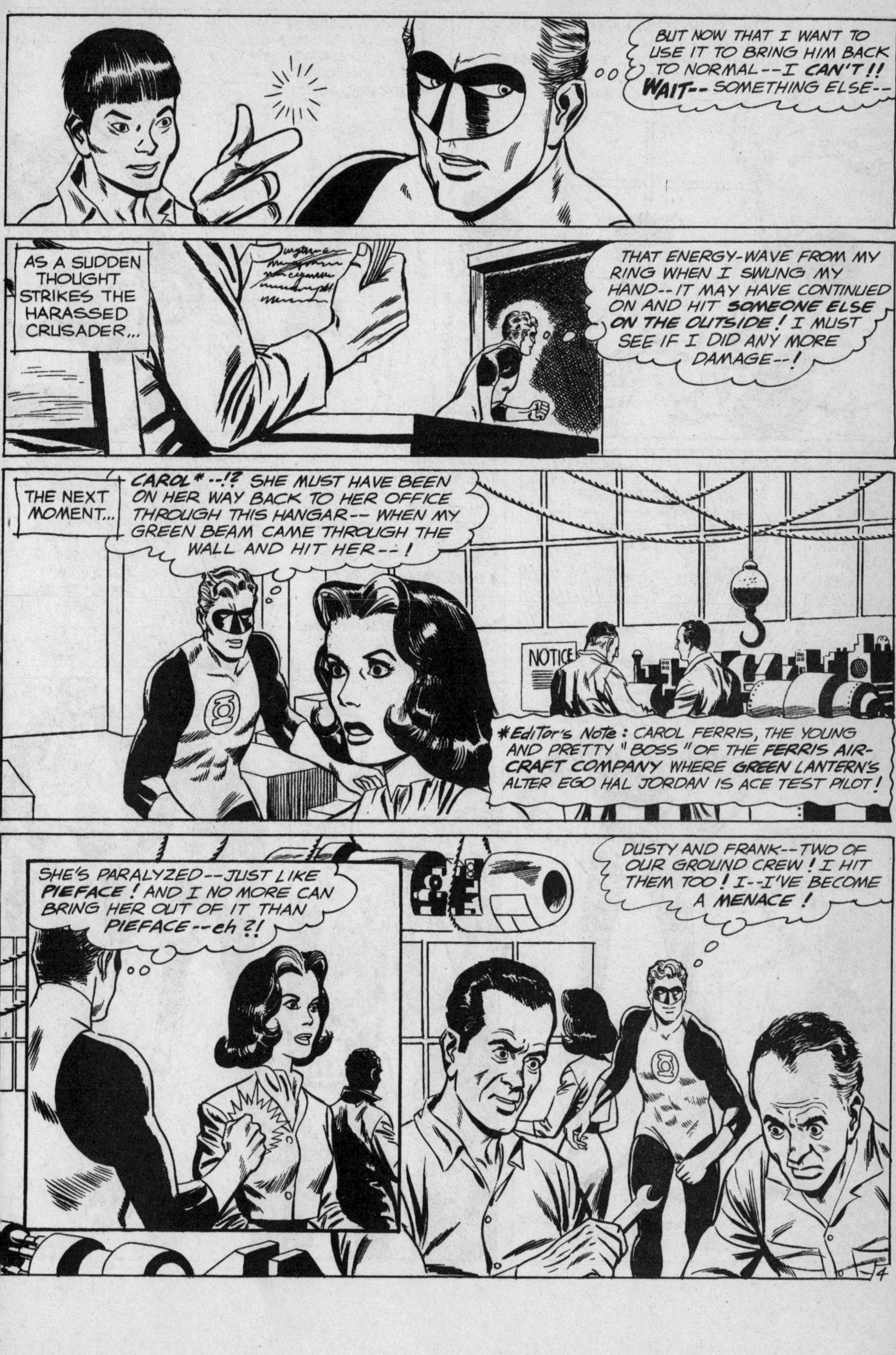
BUT NOW THAT I WANT TO USE IT TO BRING HIM BACK TO NORMAL--I CAN'T!! WAIT-- SOMETHING ELSE--
AS A SUDDEN THOUGHT STRIKES THE HARASSED CRUSADER...
THAT ENERGY-WAVE FROM MY RING WHEN I SWUNG MY HAND--IT MAY HAVE CONTINUED ON AND HIT SOMEONE ELSE ON THE OUTSIDE! I MUST SEE IF I DID ANY MORE DAMAGE--!
THE NEXT MOMENT...
CAROL* --!? SHE MUST HAVE BEEN ON HER WAY BACK TO HER OFFICE THROUGH THIS HANGAR-- WHEN MY GREEN BEAM CAME THROUGH THE WALL AND HIT HER--!
NOTICE
*EdiTor's Note: CAROL FERRIS, THE YOUNG AND PRETTY "BOSS" OF THE FERRIS AIRCRAFT COMPANY WHERE GREEN LANTERN'S ALTER EGO HAL JORDAN IS ACE TEST PILOT!
SHE'S PARALYZED--JUST LIKE PIEFACE! AND I NO MORE CAN BRING HER OUT OF IT THAN PIEFACE--eh?!
DUSTY AND FRANK--TWO OF OUR GROUND CREW! I HIT THEM TOO! I--I'VE BECOME A MENACE!
4

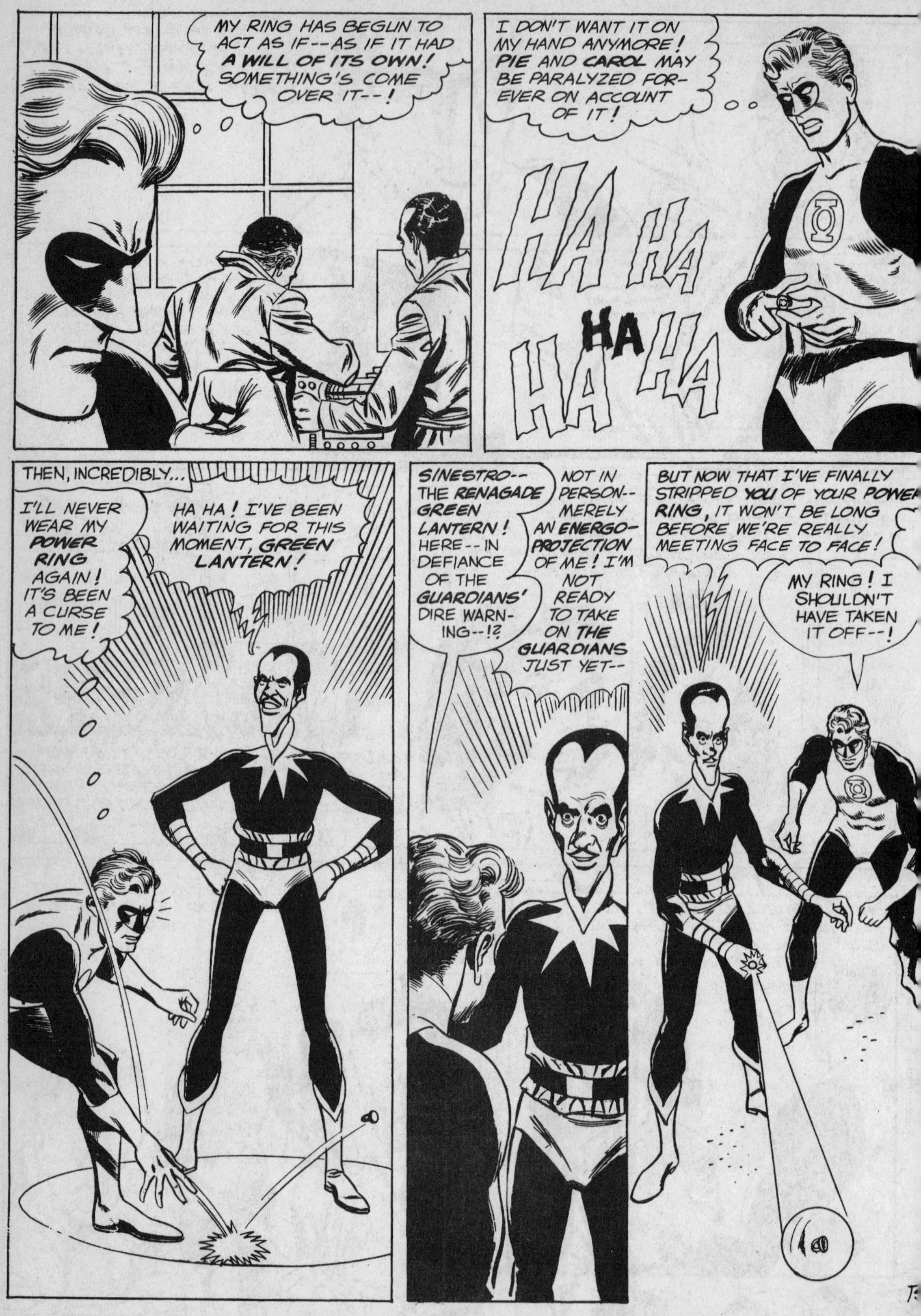
MY RING HAS BEGUN TO ACT AS IF--AS IF IT HAD A WILL OF ITS OWN! SOMETHING'S COME OVER IT--!
I DON'T WANT IT ON MY HAND ANYMORE! PIE AND CAROL MAY BE PARALYZED FOREVER ON ACCOUNT OF IT!
HA HA HA HA HA HA
THEN, INCREDIBLY...
I'LL NEVER WEAR MY POWER RING AGAIN! IT'S BEEN A CURSE TO ME!
HA HA! I'VE BEEN WAITING FOR THIS MOMENT, GREEN LANTERN!
SINESTRO--THE RENAGADE GREEN LANTERN! HERE--IN DEFIANCE OF THE GUARDIANS' DIRE WARNING--!?
NOT IN PERSON--MERELY AN ENERGO-PROJECTION OF ME! I'M NOT READY TO TAKE ON THE GUARDIANS JUST YET--
BUT NOW THAT I'VE FINALLY STRIPPED YOU OF YOUR POWER RING, IT WON'T BE LONG BEFORE WE'RE REALLY MEETING FACE TO FACE!
MY RING! I SHOULDN'T HAVE TAKEN IT OFF--!

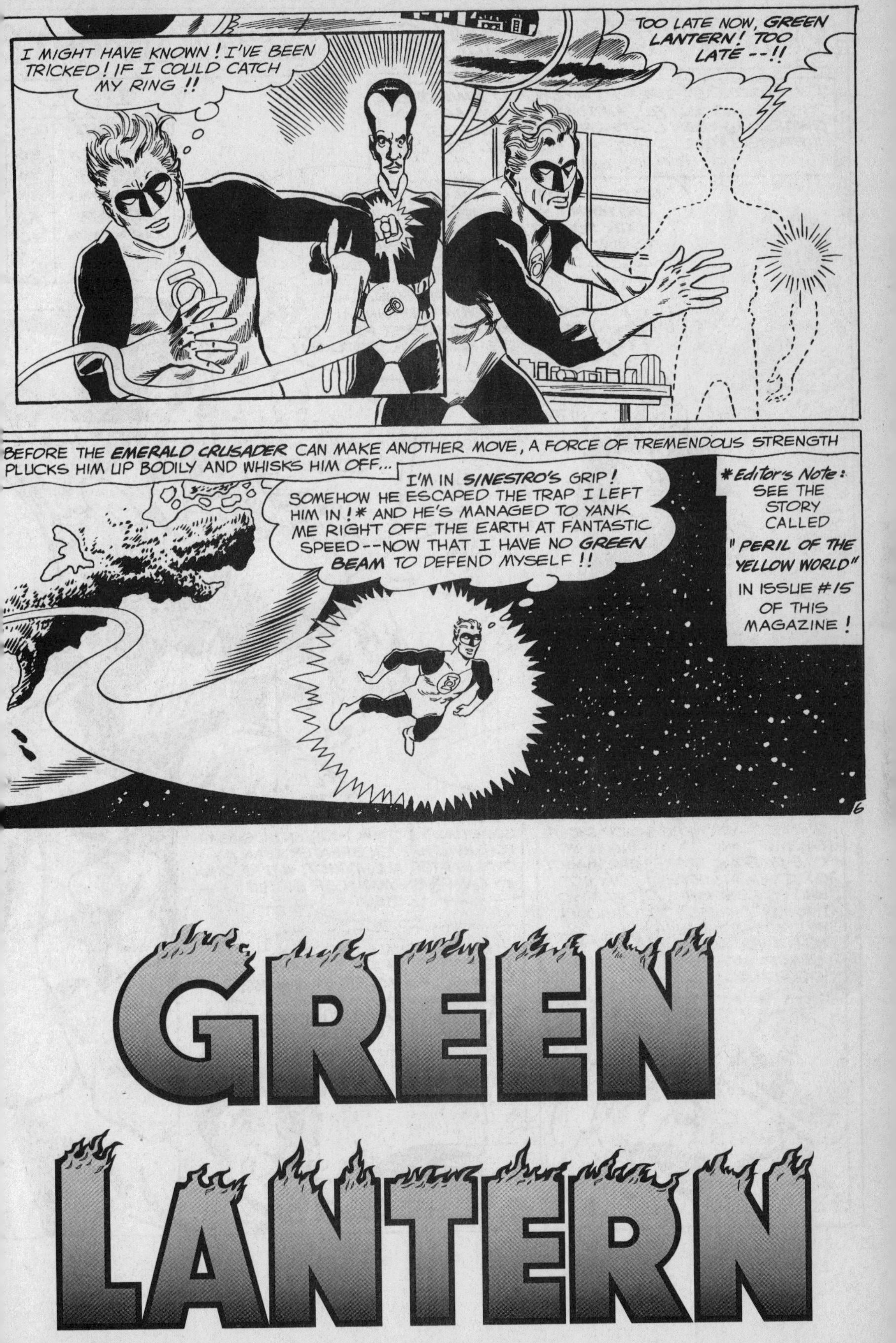
I MIGHT HAVE KNOWN! I'VE BEEN TRICKED! IF I COULD CATCH MY RING!!
TOO LATE NOW, GREEN LANTERN! TOO LATE--!!
BEFORE THE EMERALD CRUSADER CAN MAKE ANOTHER MOVE, A FORCE OF TREMENDOUS STRENGTH PLUCKS HIM UP BODILY AND WHISKS HIM OFF...
I'M IN SINESTRO'S GRIP! SOMEHOW HE ESCAPED THE TRAP I LEFT HIM IN!* AND HE'S MANAGED TO YANK ME RIGHT OFF THE EARTH AT FANTASTIC SPEED--NOW THAT I HAVE NO GREEN BEAM TO DEFEND MYSELF!!
*Editor's Note: SEE THE STORY CALLED "PERIL OF THE YELLOW WORLD" IN ISSUE #15 OF THIS MAGAZINE!
6

GREEN LANTERN

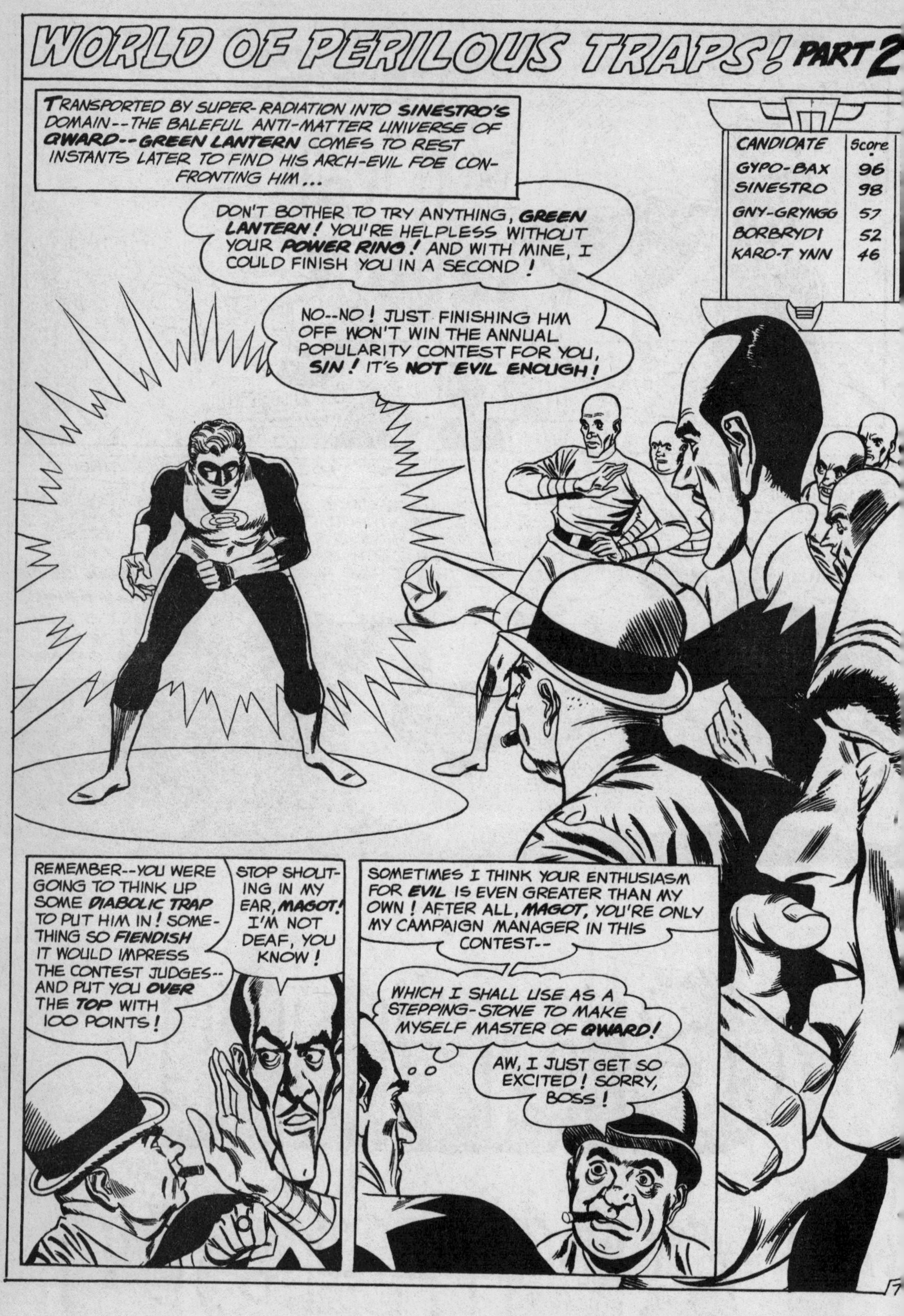
WORLD OF PERILOUS TRAPS! PART 2
TRANSPORTED BY SUPER-RADIATION INTO SINESTRO'S DOMAIN--THE BALEFUL ANTI-MATTER UNIVERSE OF QWARD--GREEN LANTERN COMES TO REST INSTANTS LATER TO FIND HIS ARCH-EVIL FOE CONFRONTING HIM...
CANDIDATE Score
GYPO-BAX 96
SINESTRO 98
GNY-GRYNGG 57
BORBRYDI 52
KARO-T YNN 46
DON'T BOTHER TO TRY ANYTHING, GREEN LANTERN! YOU'RE HELPLESS WITHOUT YOUR POWER RING! AND WITH MINE, I COULD FINISH YOU IN A SECOND!
NO--NO! JUST FINISHING HIM OFF WON'T WIN THE ANNUAL POPULARITY CONTEST FOR YOU, SIN! IT'S NOT EVIL ENOUGH!
REMEMBER--YOU WERE GOING TO THINK UP SOME DIABOLIC TRAP TO PUT HIM IN! SOMETHING SO FIENDISH IT WOULD IMPRESS THE CONTEST JUDGES--AND PUT YOU OVER THE TOP WITH 100 POINTS!
STOP SHOUTING IN MY EAR, MAGOT! I'M NOT DEAF, YOU KNOW!
SOMETIMES I THINK YOUR ENTHUSIASM FOR EVIL IS EVEN GREATER THAN MY OWN! AFTER ALL, MAGOT, YOU'RE ONLY MY CAMPAIGN MANAGER IN THIS CONTEST--
WHICH I SHALL USE AS A STEPPING-STONE TO MAKE MYSELF MASTER OF QWARD!
AW, I JUST GET SO EXCITED! SORRY, BOSS!

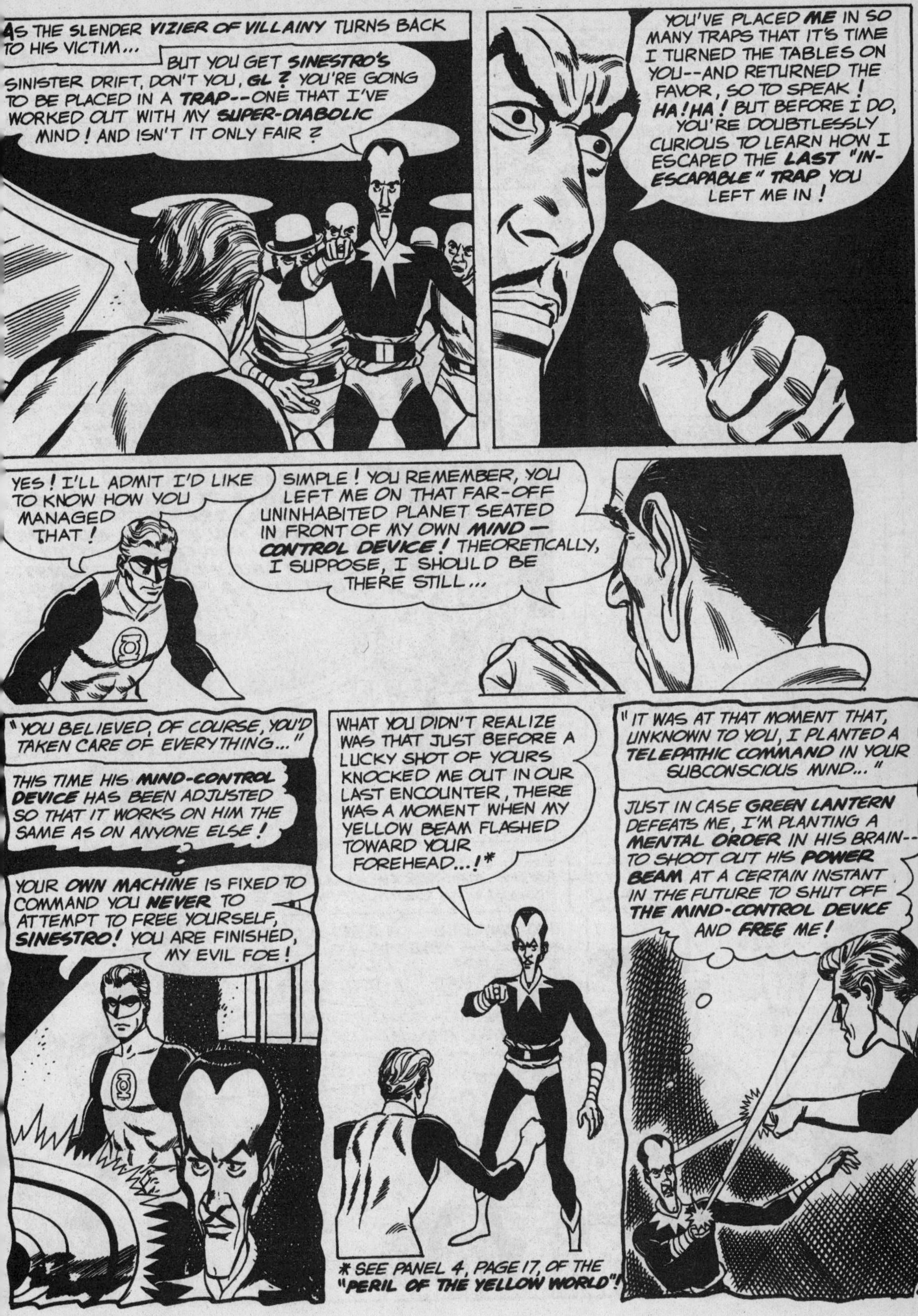
AS THE SLENDER VIZIER OF VILLAINY TURNS BACK TO HIS VICTIM...
BUT YOU GET SINESTRO'S SINISTER DRIFT, DON'T YOU, GL? YOU'RE GOING TO BE PLACED IN A TRAP--ONE THAT I'VE WORKED OUT WITH MY SUPER-DIABOLIC MIND! AND ISN'T IT ONLY FAIR?
YOU'VE PLACED ME IN SO MANY TRAPS THAT IT'S TIME I TURNED THE TABLES ON YOU--AND RETURNED THE FAVOR, SO TO SPEAK! HA! HA! BUT BEFORE I DO, YOU'RE DOUBTLESSLY CURIOUS TO LEARN HOW I ESCAPED THE LAST "IN-ESCAPABLE" TRAP YOU LEFT ME IN!
YES! I'LL ADMIT I'D LIKE TO KNOW HOW YOU MANAGED THAT!
SIMPLE! YOU REMEMBER, YOU LEFT ME ON THAT FAR-OFF UNINHABITED PLANET SEATED IN FRONT OF MY OWN MIND-CONTROL DEVICE! THEORETICALLY, I SUPPOSE, I SHOULD BE THERE STILL...
"YOU BELIEVED, OF COURSE, YOU'D TAKEN CARE OF EVERYTHING..."
THIS TIME HIS MIND-CONTROL DEVICE HAS BEEN ADJUSTED SO THAT IT WORKS ON HIM THE SAME AS ON ANYONE ELSE!
YOUR OWN MACHINE IS FIXED TO COMMAND YOU NEVER TO ATTEMPT TO FREE YOURSELF, SINESTRO! YOU ARE FINISHED, MY EVIL FOE!
WHAT YOU DIDN'T REALIZE WAS THAT JUST BEFORE A LUCKY SHOT OF YOURS KNOCKED ME OUT IN OUR LAST ENCOUNTER, THERE WAS A MOMENT WHEN MY YELLOW BEAM FLASHED TOWARD YOUR FOREHEAD...!*
* SEE PANEL 4, PAGE 17, OF THE "PERIL OF THE YELLOW WORLD"!
"IT WAS AT THAT MOMENT THAT, UNKNOWN TO YOU, I PLANTED A TELEPATHIC COMMAND IN YOUR SUBCONSCIOUS MIND..."
JUST IN CASE GREEN LANTERN DEFEATS ME, I'M PLANTING A MENTAL ORDER IN HIS BRAIN--TO SHOOT OUT HIS POWER BEAM AT A CERTAIN INSTANT IN THE FUTURE TO SHUT OFF THE MIND-CONTROL DEVICE AND FREE ME!
8

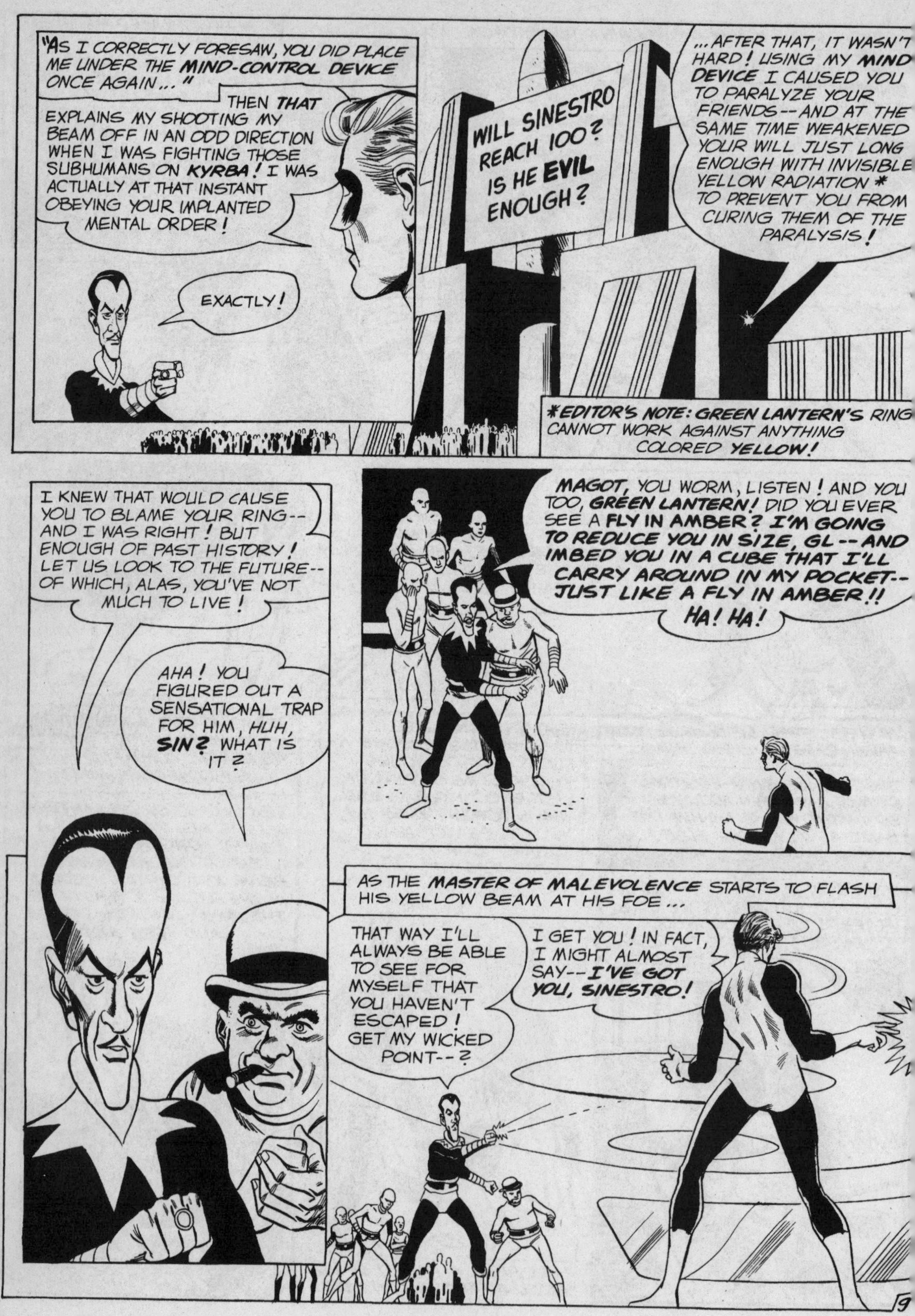
"AS I CORRECTLY FORESAW, YOU DID PLACE ME UNDER THE MIND-CONTROL DEVICE ONCE AGAIN..."
THEN THAT EXPLAINS MY SHOOTING MY BEAM OFF IN AN ODD DIRECTION WHEN I WAS FIGHTING THOSE SUBHUMANS ON KYRBA! I WAS ACTUALLY AT THAT INSTANT OBEYING YOUR IMPLANTED MENTAL ORDER!
EXACTLY!
WILL SINESTRO REACH 100? IS HE EVIL ENOUGH?
...AFTER THAT, IT WASN'T HARD! USING MY MIND DEVICE I CAUSED YOU TO PARALYZE YOUR FRIENDS--AND AT THE SAME TIME WEAKENED YOUR WILL JUST LONG ENOUGH WITH INVISIBLE YELLOW RADIATION * TO PREVENT YOU FROM CURING THEM OF THE PARALYSIS!
*EDITOR'S NOTE: GREEN LANTERN'S RING CANNOT WORK AGAINST ANYTHING COLORED YELLOW!
I KNEW THAT WOULD CAUSE YOU TO BLAME YOUR RING--AND I WAS RIGHT! BUT ENOUGH OF PAST HISTORY! LET US LOOK TO THE FUTURE--OF WHICH, ALAS, YOU'VE NOT MUCH TO LIVE!
AHA! YOU FIGURED OUT A SENSATIONAL TRAP FOR HIM, HUH, SIN? WHAT IS IT?
MAGOT, YOU WORM, LISTEN! AND YOU TOO, GREEN LANTERN! DID YOU EVER SEE A FLY IN AMBER? I'M GOING TO REDUCE YOU IN SIZE, GL--AND IMBED YOU IN A CUBE THAT I'LL CARRY AROUND IN MY POCKET--JUST LIKE A FLY IN AMBER!! HA! HA!
AS THE MASTER OF MALEVOLENCE STARTS TO FLASH HIS YELLOW BEAM AT HIS FOE...
THAT WAY I'LL ALWAYS BE ABLE TO SEE FOR MYSELF THAT YOU HAVEN'T ESCAPED! GET MY WICKED POINT--?
I GET YOU! IN FACT, I MIGHT ALMOST SAY--I'VE GOT YOU, SINESTRO!
9

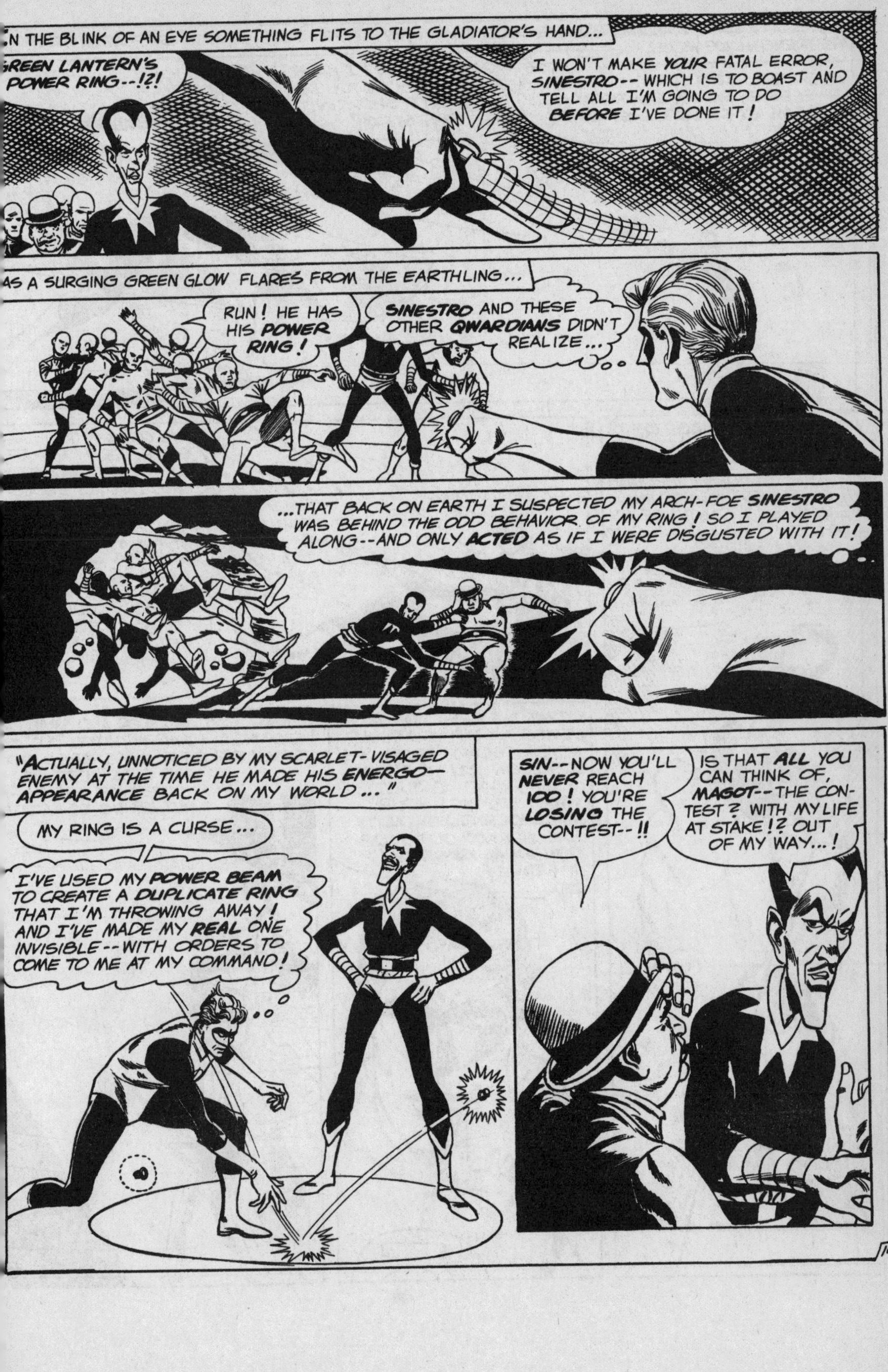
IN THE BLINK OF AN EYE SOMETHING FLITS TO THE GLADIATOR'S HAND...
GREEN LANTERN'S POWER RING--!?!
I WON'T MAKE YOUR FATAL ERROR, SINESTRO-- WHICH IS TO BOAST AND TELL ALL I'M GOING TO DO BEFORE I'VE DONE IT!
AS A SURGING GREEN GLOW FLARES FROM THE EARTHLING...
RUN! HE HAS HIS POWER RING!
SINESTRO AND THESE OTHER QWARDIANS DIDN'T REALIZE...
...THAT BACK ON EARTH I SUSPECTED MY ARCH-FOE SINESTRO WAS BEHIND THE ODD BEHAVIOR OF MY RING! SO I PLAYED ALONG--AND ONLY ACTED AS IF I WERE DISGUSTED WITH IT!
"ACTUALLY, UNNOTICED BY MY SCARLET-VISAGED ENEMY AT THE TIME HE MADE HIS ENERGO-APPEARANCE BACK ON MY WORLD..."
MY RING IS A CURSE...
I'VE USED MY POWER BEAM TO CREATE A DUPLICATE RING THAT I'M THROWING AWAY! AND I'VE MADE MY REAL ONE INVISIBLE--WITH ORDERS TO COME TO ME AT MY COMMAND!
SIN--NOW YOU'LL NEVER REACH 100! YOU'RE LOSING THE CONTEST--!!
IS THAT ALL YOU CAN THINK OF, MAGOT--THE CONTEST? WITH MY LIFE AT STAKE!? OUT OF MY WAY...!
10

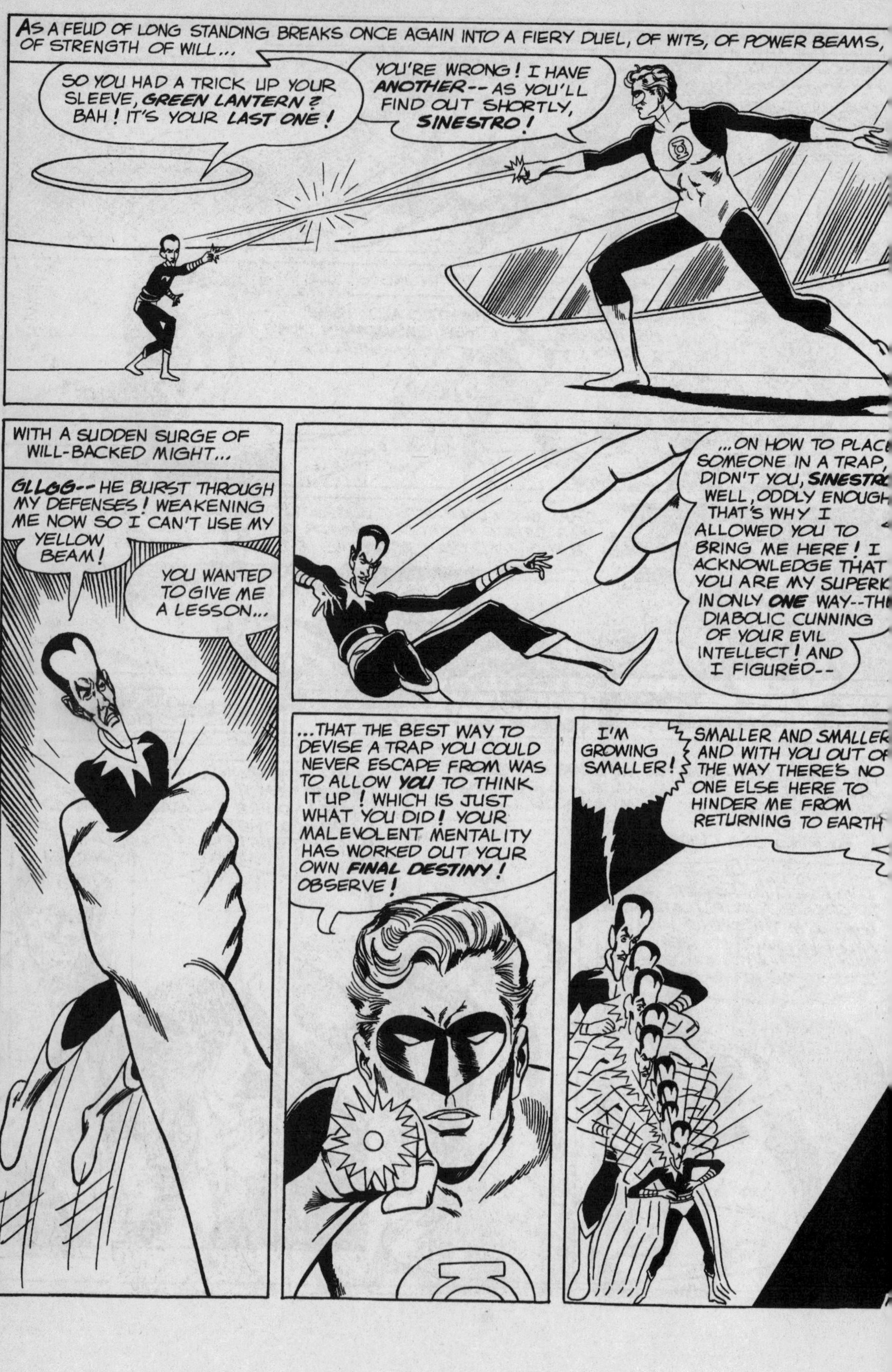
AS A FEUD OF LONG STANDING BREAKS ONCE AGAIN INTO A FIERY DUEL, OF WITS, OF POWER BEAMS, OF STRENGTH OF WILL...
SO YOU HAD A TRICK UP YOUR SLEEVE, GREEN LANTERN? BAH! IT'S YOUR LAST ONE!
YOU'RE WRONG! I HAVE ANOTHER-- AS YOU'LL FIND OUT SHORTLY, SINESTRO!
WITH A SUDDEN SURGE OF WILL-BACKED MIGHT...
GLLGG-- HE BURST THROUGH MY DEFENSES! WEAKENING ME NOW SO I CAN'T USE MY YELLOW BEAM!
YOU WANTED TO GIVE ME A LESSON...
...ON HOW TO PLAC SOMEONE IN A TRAP, DIDN'T YOU, SINESTR WELL, ODDLY ENOUGH THAT'S WHY I ALLOWED YOU TO BRING ME HERE! I ACKNOWLEDGE THAT YOU ARE MY SUPER IN ONLY ONE WAY--TH DIABOLIC CUNNING OF YOUR EVIL INTELLECT! AND I FIGURED--
...THAT THE BEST WAY TO DEVISE A TRAP YOU COULD NEVER ESCAPE FROM WAS TO ALLOW YOU TO THINK IT UP! WHICH IS JUST WHAT YOU DID! YOUR MALEVOLENT MENTALITY HAS WORKED OUT YOUR OWN FINAL DESTINY! OBSERVE!
I'M GROWING SMALLER!
SMALLER AND SMALLER AND WITH YOU OUT OF THE WAY THERE'S NO ONE ELSE HERE TO HINDER ME FROM RETURNING TO EARTH

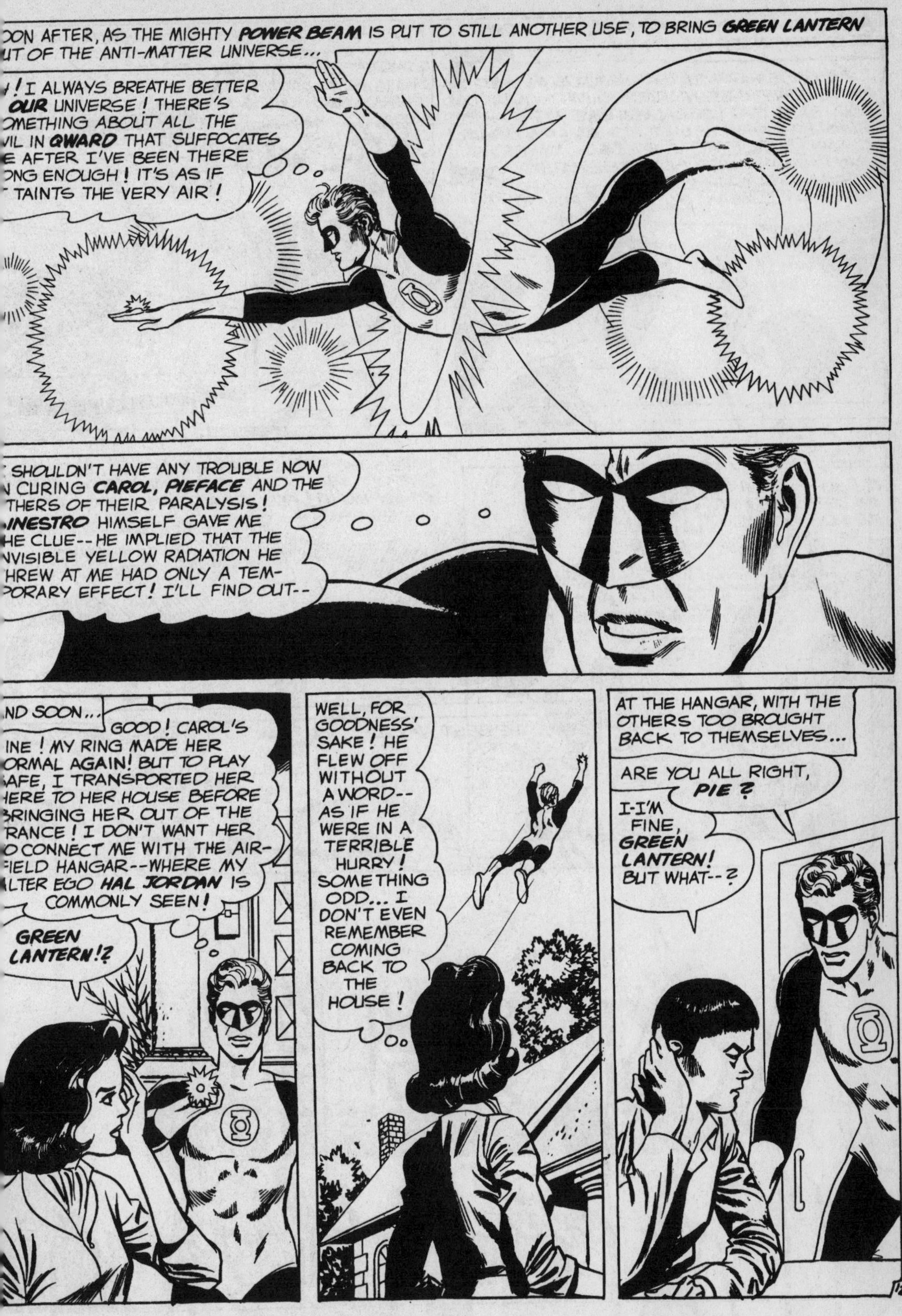
OON AFTER, AS THE MIGHTY POWER BEAM IS PUT TO STILL ANOTHER USE, TO BRING GREEN LANTERN UT OF THE ANTI-MATTER UNIVERSE...
! I ALWAYS BREATHE BETTER OUR UNIVERSE! THERE'S OMETHING ABOUT ALL THE VIL IN QWARD THAT SUFFOCATES E AFTER I'VE BEEN THERE ONG ENOUGH! IT'S AS IF TAINTS THE VERY AIR!
SHOULDN'T HAVE ANY TROUBLE NOW CURING CAROL, PIEFACE AND THE THERS OF THEIR PARALYSIS! INESTRO HIMSELF GAVE ME HE CLUE--HE IMPLIED THAT THE NVISIBLE YELLOW RADIATION HE HREW AT ME HAD ONLY A TEM-PORARY EFFECT! I'LL FIND OUT--
ND SOON...
GOOD! CAROL'S INE! MY RING MADE HER ORMAL AGAIN! BUT TO PLAY AFE, I TRANSPORTED HER HERE TO HER HOUSE BEFORE BRINGING HER OUT OF THE RANCE! I DON'T WANT HER O CONNECT ME WITH THE AIR-FIELD HANGAR--WHERE MY LTER EGO HAL JORDAN IS COMMONLY SEEN!
GREEN LANTERN!?
WELL, FOR GOODNESS' SAKE! HE FLEW OFF WITHOUT A WORD--AS IF HE WERE IN A TERRIBLE HURRY! SOMETHING ODD... I DON'T EVEN REMEMBER COMING BACK TO THE HOUSE!
AT THE HANGAR, WITH THE OTHERS TOO BROUGHT BACK TO THEMSELVES...
ARE YOU ALL RIGHT, PIE?
I-I'M FINE, GREEN LANTERN! BUT WHAT--?
12

AFTER **GL** HAS REVEALED THAT HE ACCIDEN-- TALLY PARALYZED HIS ESKIMO PAL ...

JUMPING FISHHOOKS! THAT REMINDS ME--I REMEMBER WHAT I WANTED TO WARN YOU ABOUT! IN THAT LAST ADVENTURE WITH **SINESTRO**-- WHEN HE SHOT HIS **YELLOW BEAM** TOWARD YOUR FOREHEAD-- WELL, MAYBE HE MAY HAVE PLANTED SOME TELEPATHIC COMMAND IN YOUR MIND--! SEE WHAT I MEAN, **GL**?

PIE, YOU'RE A GENIUS! THAT'S EXACTLY WHAT HAPPENED!

WITH THE ENTIRE ADVENTURE LAID BARE TO **PIEF**

...AND AFTER **SINESTRO** ESCAPED, HE USED THE SAME **MIND-CONTROL DEVICE**-- SETTING IT TO ULTRA-LONG-RANGE FREQUENCY-- TO REACH ME AND TO CAUSE ME NEARLY TO GO BERSERK HERE!

WON--EEE! THERE'S NO LIMIT TO HIS VICIOUSNESS, IS THERE?

NO, BUT I DON'T THINK WE'RE GOING TO HAVE TO WORRY ABOUT HIM ANYMORE, **PIE**!

WHY DO YOU SAY THAT, **GL**? AN **ESCAPE ARTIST** LIKE HIM! HOW CAN YOU BE SURE?

HERE'S THE REASON, **PIEFACE**! FROM HERE ON IN I'VE GOT MR. WICKED-MAN **SINESTRO** IN THE PA**
OF MY HAND**! AND I'M NOT LETTING GO OF HIM EVER AGAIN!

JUMPING FISHHOOKS!

The End

GREEN
LANTERN

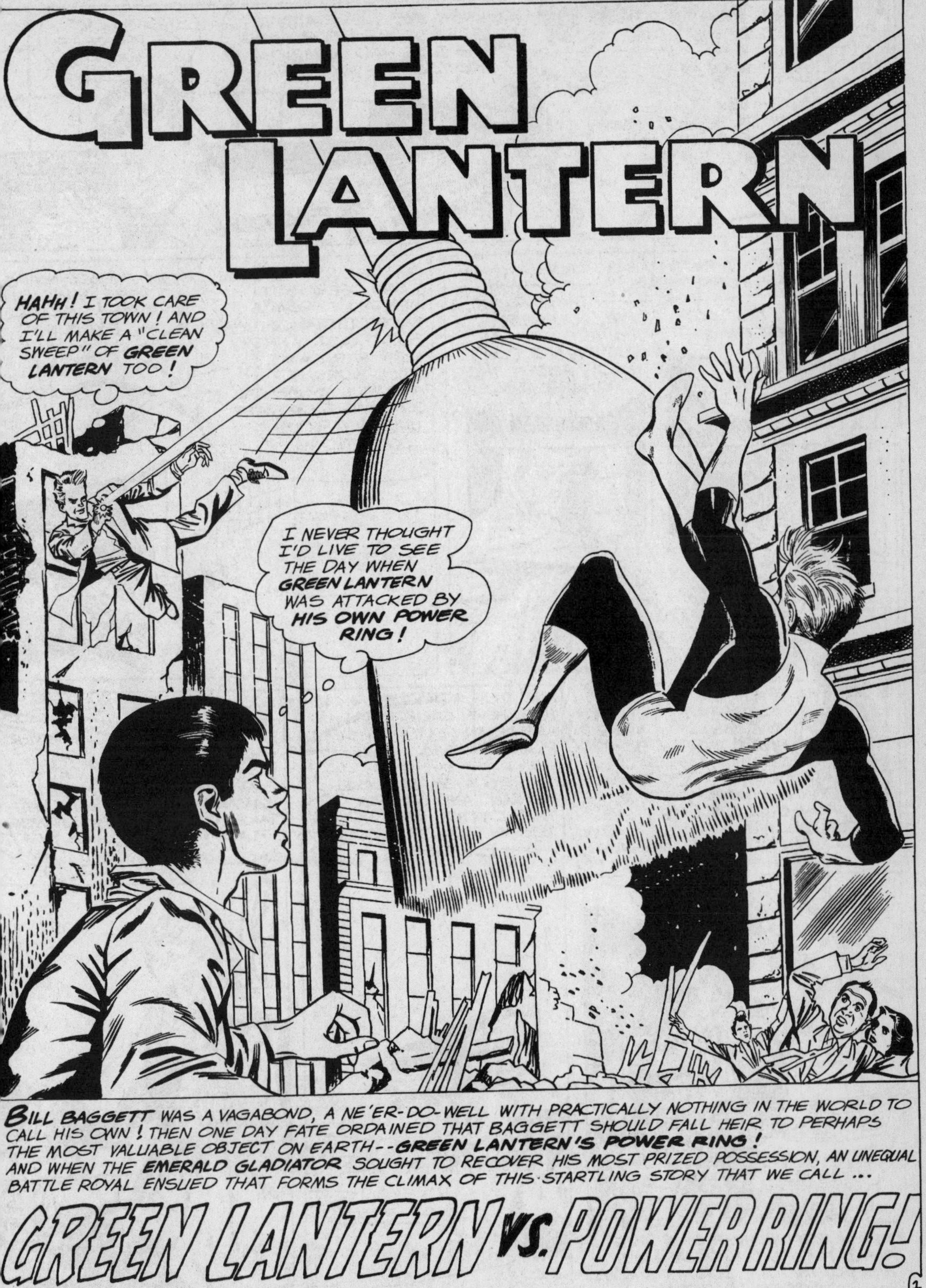
GREEN LANTERN
HAHH! I TOOK CARE OF THIS TOWN! AND I'LL MAKE A "CLEAN SWEEP" OF GREEN LANTERN TOO!
I NEVER THOUGHT I'D LIVE TO SEE THE DAY WHEN GREEN LANTERN WAS ATTACKED BY HIS OWN POWER RING!
BILL BAGGETT WAS A VAGABOND, A NE'ER-DO-WELL WITH PRACTICALLY NOTHING IN THE WORLD TO CALL HIS OWN! THEN ONE DAY FATE ORDAINED THAT BAGGETT SHOULD FALL HEIR TO PERHAPS THE MOST VALUABLE OBJECT ON EARTH--GREEN LANTERN'S POWER RING! AND WHEN THE EMERALD GLADIATOR SOUGHT TO RECOVER HIS MOST PRIZED POSSESSION, AN UNEQUAL BATTLE ROYAL ENSUED THAT FORMS THE CLIMAX OF THIS STARTLING STORY THAT WE CALL ...
GREEN LANTERN VS. POWER RING!
1

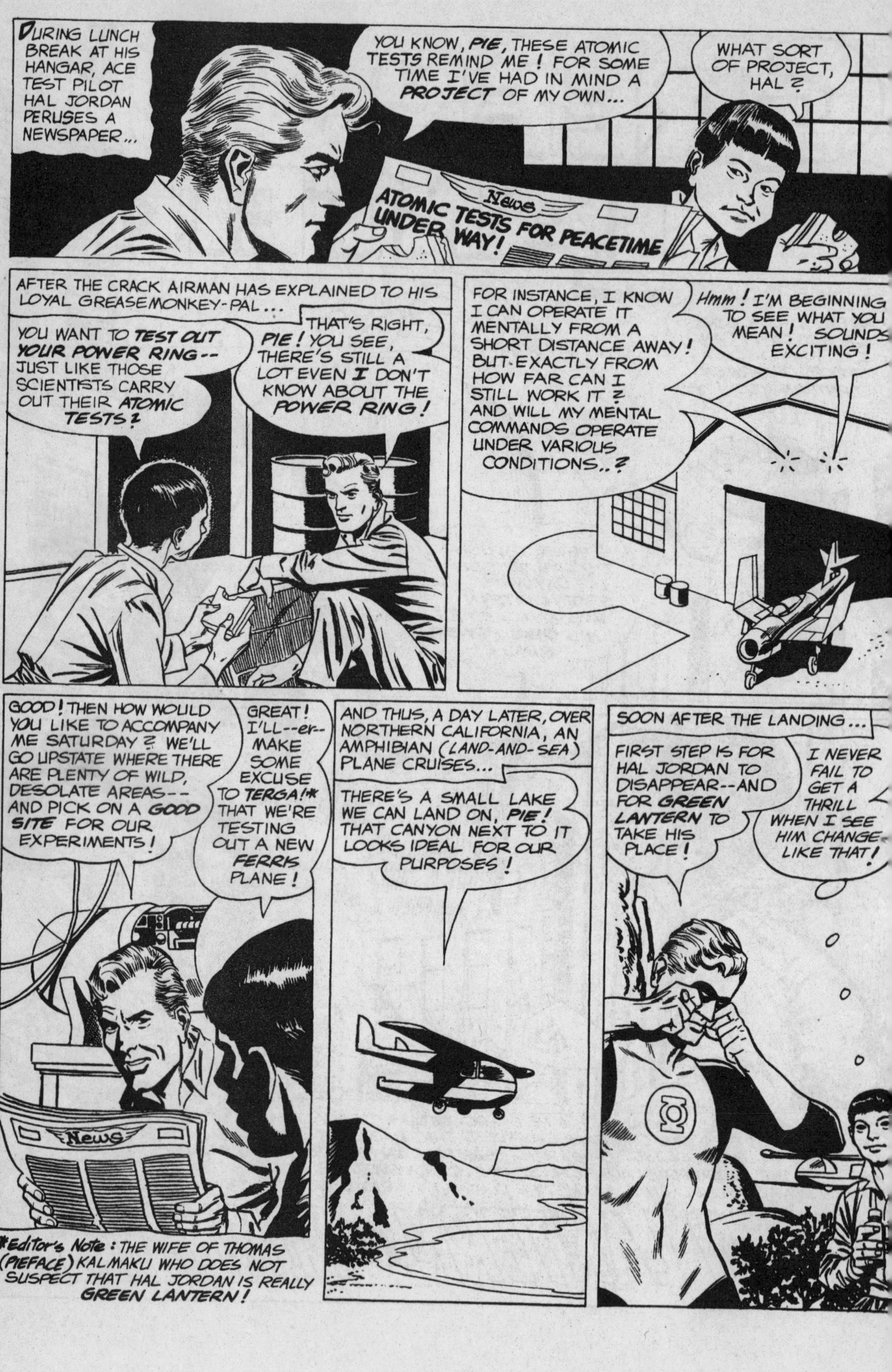
DURING LUNCH BREAK AT HIS HANGAR, ACE TEST PILOT HAL JORDAN PERUSES A NEWSPAPER...
YOU KNOW, PIE, THESE ATOMIC TESTS REMIND ME! FOR SOME TIME I'VE HAD IN MIND A PROJECT OF MY OWN...
WHAT SORT OF PROJECT, HAL?
News
ATOMIC TESTS FOR PEACETIME UNDER WAY!
AFTER THE CRACK AIRMAN HAS EXPLAINED TO HIS LOYAL GREASEMONKEY-PAL...
YOU WANT TO TEST OUT YOUR POWER RING-- JUST LIKE THOSE SCIENTISTS CARRY OUT THEIR ATOMIC TESTS?
THAT'S RIGHT, PIE! YOU SEE, THERE'S STILL A LOT EVEN I DON'T KNOW ABOUT THE POWER RING!
FOR INSTANCE, I KNOW I CAN OPERATE IT MENTALLY FROM A SHORT DISTANCE AWAY! BUT EXACTLY FROM HOW FAR CAN I STILL WORK IT? AND WILL MY MENTAL COMMANDS OPERATE UNDER VARIOUS CONDITIONS..?
Hmm! I'M BEGINNING TO SEE WHAT YOU MEAN! SOUNDS EXCITING!
GOOD! THEN HOW WOULD YOU LIKE TO ACCOMPANY ME SATURDAY? WE'LL GO UPSTATE WHERE THERE ARE PLENTY OF WILD, DESOLATE AREAS-- AND PICK ON A GOOD SITE FOR OUR EXPERIMENTS!
GREAT! I'LL--er-- MAKE SOME EXCUSE TO TERGA!* THAT WE'RE TESTING OUT A NEW FERRIS PLANE!
News
*Editor's Note: THE WIFE OF THOMAS (PIEFACE) KALMAKU WHO DOES NOT SUSPECT THAT HAL JORDAN IS REALLY GREEN LANTERN!
AND THUS, A DAY LATER, OVER NORTHERN CALIFORNIA, AN AMPHIBIAN (LAND-AND-SEA) PLANE CRUISES...
THERE'S A SMALL LAKE WE CAN LAND ON, PIE! THAT CANYON NEXT TO IT LOOKS IDEAL FOR OUR PURPOSES!
SOON AFTER THE LANDING...
FIRST STEP IS FOR HAL JORDAN TO DISAPPEAR--AND FOR GREEN LANTERN TO TAKE HIS PLACE!
I NEVER FAIL TO GET A THRILL WHEN I SEE HIM CHANGE LIKE THAT!

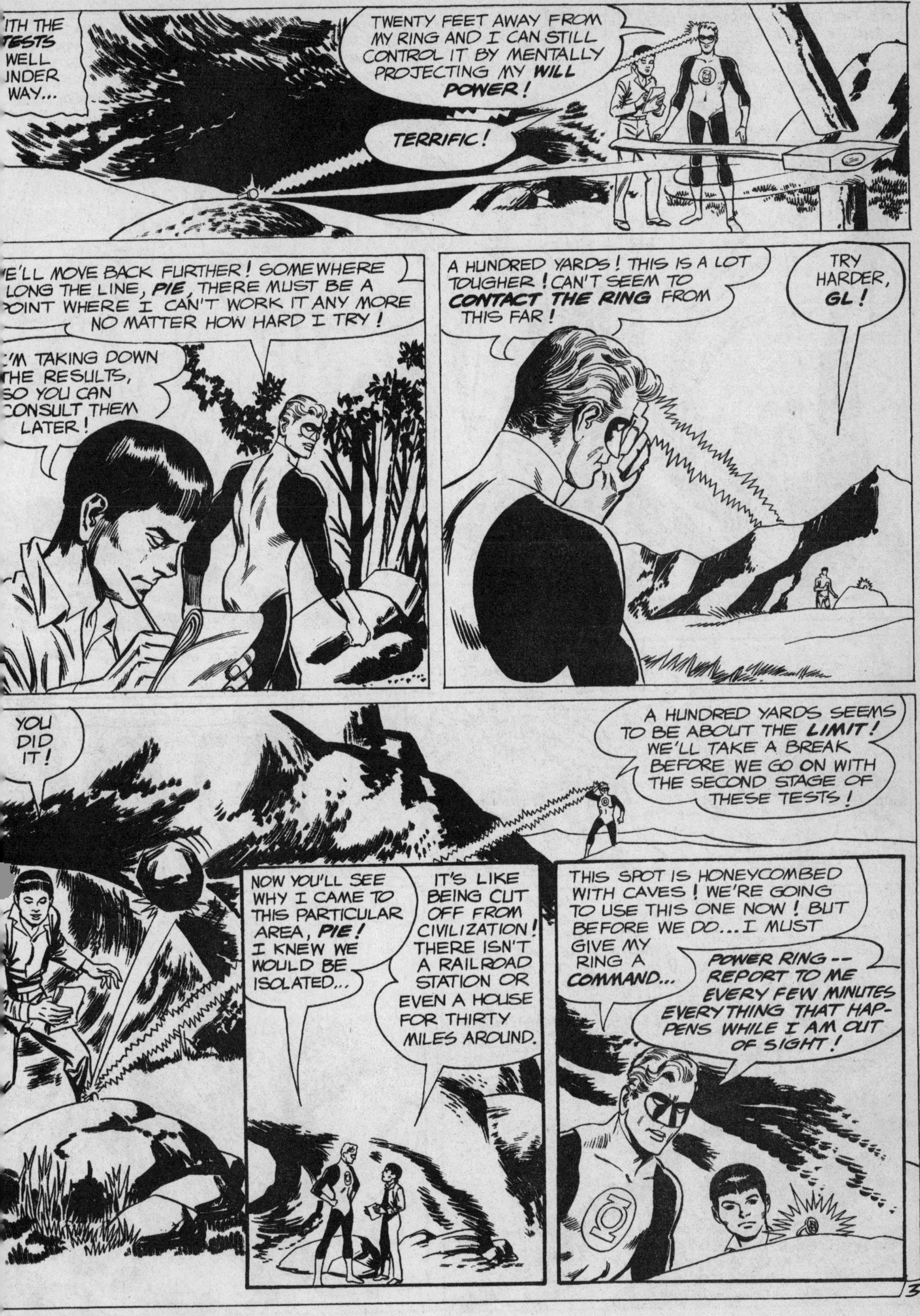
ITH THE TESTS WELL UNDER WAY...
TWENTY FEET AWAY FROM MY RING AND I CAN STILL CONTROL IT BY MENTALLY PROJECTING MY WILL POWER!
TERRIFIC!
E'LL MOVE BACK FURTHER! SOMEWHERE LONG THE LINE, PIE, THERE MUST BE A POINT WHERE I CAN'T WORK IT ANY MORE NO MATTER HOW HARD I TRY!
I'M TAKING DOWN THE RESULTS, SO YOU CAN CONSULT THEM LATER!
A HUNDRED YARDS! THIS IS A LOT TOUGHER! CAN'T SEEM TO CONTACT THE RING FROM THIS FAR!
TRY HARDER, GL!
YOU DID IT!
A HUNDRED YARDS SEEMS TO BE ABOUT THE LIMIT! WE'LL TAKE A BREAK BEFORE WE GO ON WITH THE SECOND STAGE OF THESE TESTS!
NOW YOU'LL SEE WHY I CAME TO THIS PARTICULAR AREA, PIE! I KNEW WE WOULD BE ISOLATED...
IT'S LIKE BEING CUT OFF FROM CIVILIZATION! THERE ISN'T A RAILROAD STATION OR EVEN A HOUSE FOR THIRTY MILES AROUND.
THIS SPOT IS HONEYCOMBED WITH CAVES! WE'RE GOING TO USE THIS ONE NOW! BUT BEFORE WE DO... I MUST GIVE MY RING A COMMAND...
POWER RING -- REPORT TO ME EVERY FEW MINUTES EVERYTHING THAT HAPPENS WHILE I AM OUT OF SIGHT!
3

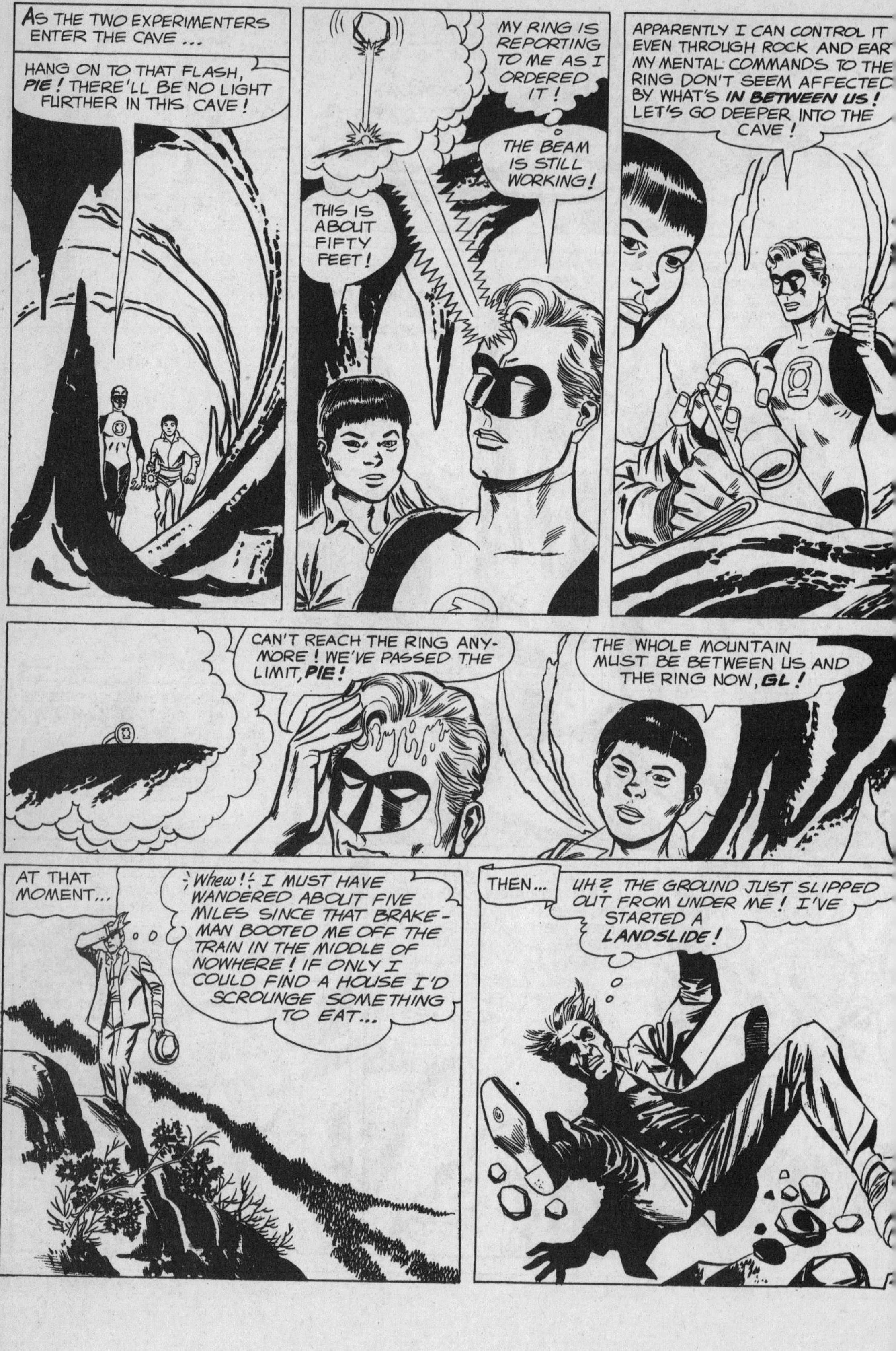
AS THE TWO EXPERIMENTERS ENTER THE CAVE ...
HANG ON TO THAT FLASH, PIE! THERE'LL BE NO LIGHT FURTHER IN THIS CAVE!
MY RING IS REPORTING TO ME AS I ORDERED IT!
THE BEAM IS STILL WORKING!
THIS IS ABOUT FIFTY FEET!
APPARENTLY I CAN CONTROL IT EVEN THROUGH ROCK AND EAR MY MENTAL COMMANDS TO THE RING DON'T SEEM AFFECTED BY WHAT'S IN BETWEEN US! LET'S GO DEEPER INTO THE CAVE!
CAN'T REACH THE RING ANY-MORE! WE'VE PASSED THE LIMIT, PIE!
THE WHOLE MOUNTAIN MUST BE BETWEEN US AND THE RING NOW, GL!
AT THAT MOMENT...
Whew! I MUST HAVE WANDERED ABOUT FIVE MILES SINCE THAT BRAKE-MAN BOOTED ME OFF THE TRAIN IN THE MIDDLE OF NOWHERE! IF ONLY I COULD FIND A HOUSE I'D SCROUNGE SOMETHING TO EAT...
THEN...
UH? THE GROUND JUST SLIPPED OUT FROM UNDER ME! I'VE STARTED A LANDSLIDE!

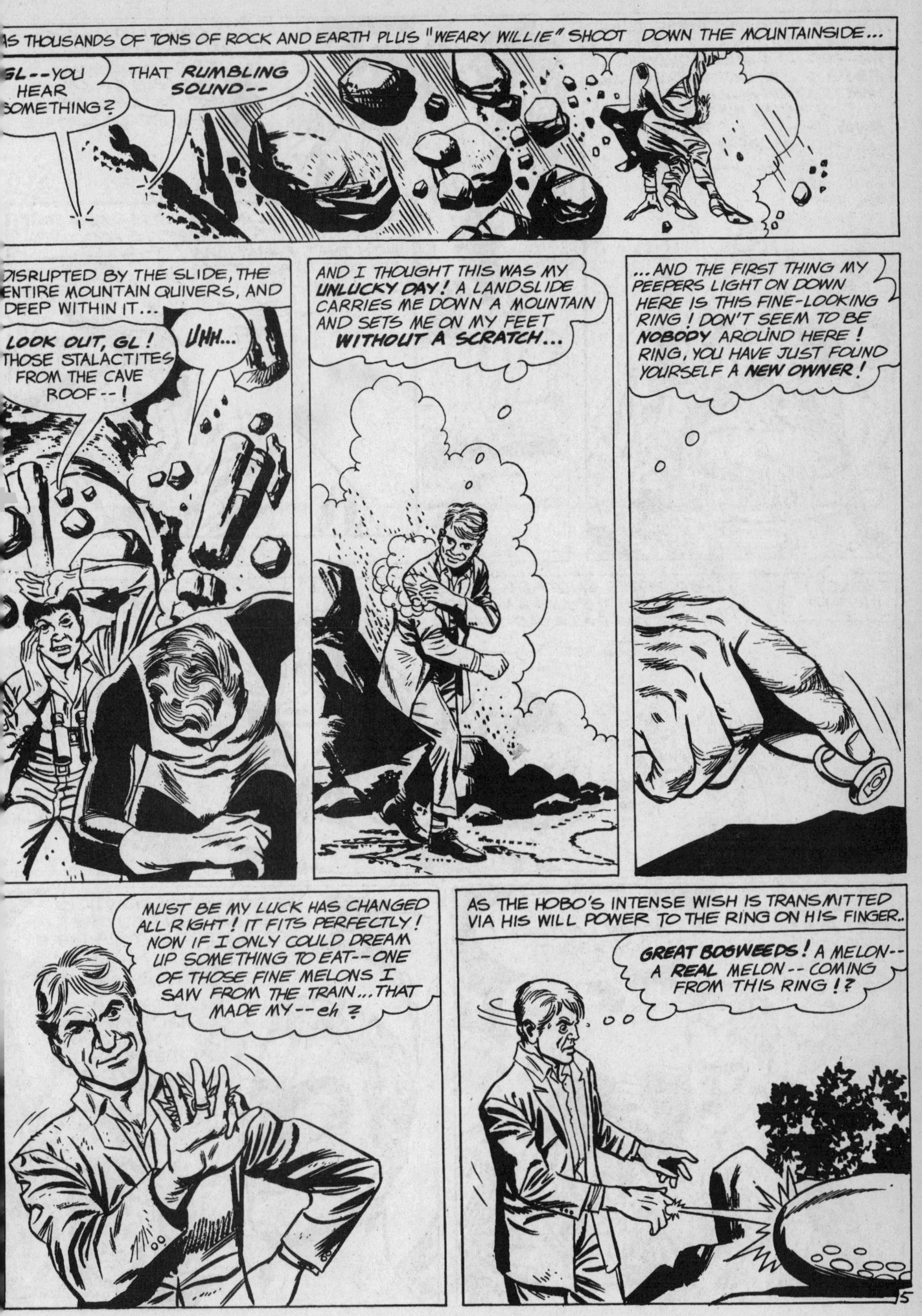
AS THOUSANDS OF TONS OF ROCK AND EARTH PLUS "WEARY WILLIE" SHOOT DOWN THE MOUNTAINSIDE...
GL--YOU HEAR SOMETHING?
THAT RUMBLING SOUND--
DISRUPTED BY THE SLIDE, THE ENTIRE MOUNTAIN QUIVERS, AND DEEP WITHIN IT...
LOOK OUT, GL! THOSE STALACTITES FROM THE CAVE ROOF--!
UHH...
AND I THOUGHT THIS WAS MY UNLUCKY DAY! A LANDSLIDE CARRIES ME DOWN A MOUNTAIN AND SETS ME ON MY FEET WITHOUT A SCRATCH...
...AND THE FIRST THING MY PEEPERS LIGHT ON DOWN HERE IS THIS FINE-LOOKING RING! DON'T SEEM TO BE NOBODY AROUND HERE! RING, YOU HAVE JUST FOUND YOURSELF A NEW OWNER!
MUST BE MY LUCK HAS CHANGED ALL RIGHT! IT FITS PERFECTLY! NOW IF I ONLY COULD DREAM UP SOMETHING TO EAT--ONE OF THOSE FINE MELONS I SAW FROM THE TRAIN...THAT MADE MY--eh?
AS THE HOBO'S INTENSE WISH IS TRANSMITTED VIA HIS WILL POWER TO THE RING ON HIS FINGER..
GREAT BOSWEEDS! A MELON--A REAL MELON--COMING FROM THIS RING!?
5

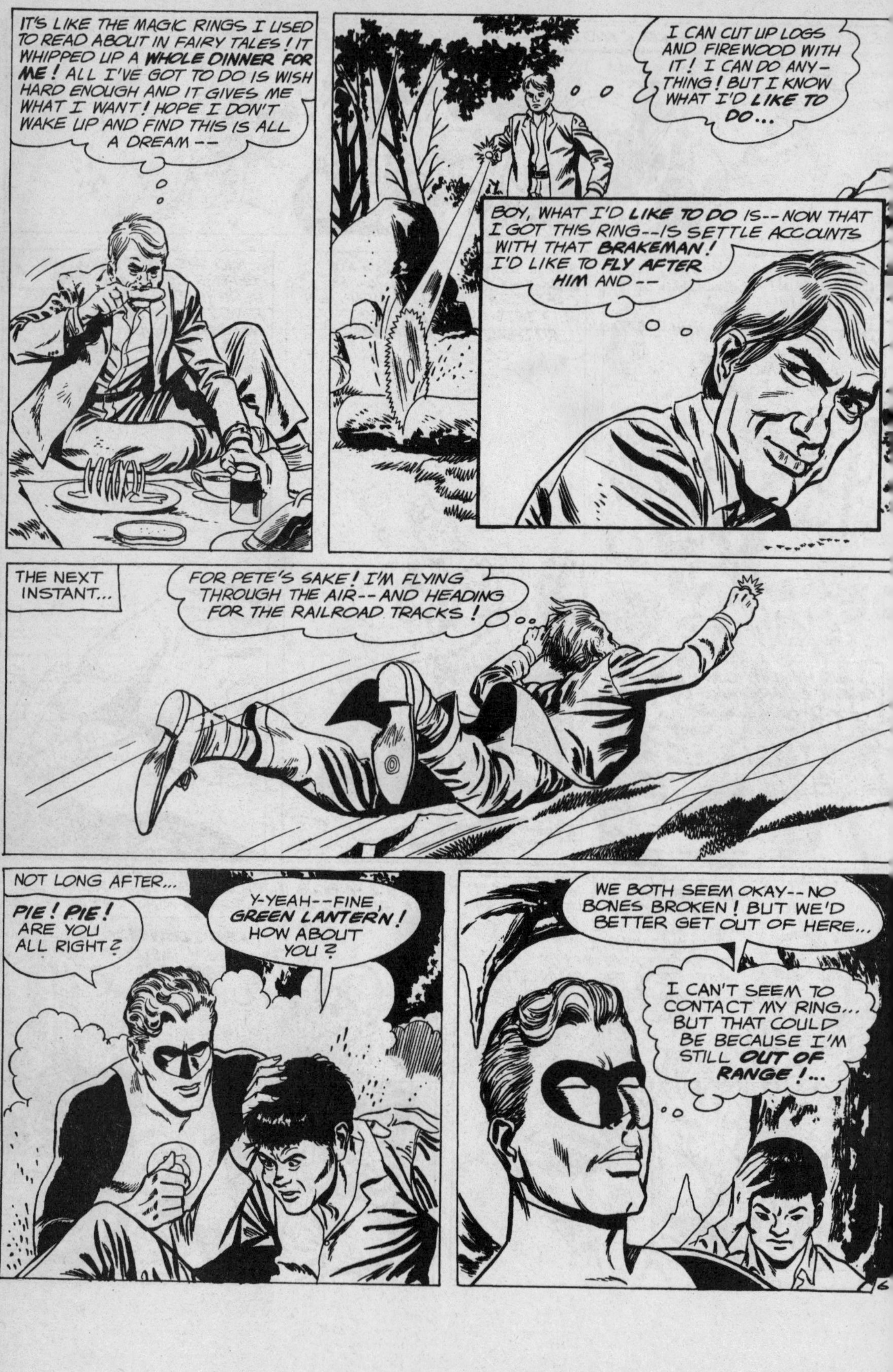
IT'S LIKE THE MAGIC RINGS I USED TO READ ABOUT IN FAIRY TALES! IT WHIPPED UP A WHOLE DINNER FOR ME! ALL I'VE GOT TO DO IS WISH HARD ENOUGH AND IT GIVES ME WHAT I WANT! HOPE I DON'T WAKE UP AND FIND THIS IS ALL A DREAM --
I CAN CUT UP LOGS AND FIREWOOD WITH IT! I CAN DO ANYTHING! BUT I KNOW WHAT I'D LIKE TO DO...
BOY, WHAT I'D LIKE TO DO IS-- NOW THAT I GOT THIS RING--IS SETTLE ACCOUNTS WITH THAT BRAKEMAN! I'D LIKE TO FLY AFTER HIM AND --
THE NEXT INSTANT...
FOR PETE'S SAKE! I'M FLYING THROUGH THE AIR-- AND HEADING FOR THE RAILROAD TRACKS!
NOT LONG AFTER...
PIE! PIE! ARE YOU ALL RIGHT?
Y-YEAH--FINE, GREEN LANTERN! HOW ABOUT YOU?
WE BOTH SEEM OKAY-- NO BONES BROKEN! BUT WE'D BETTER GET OUT OF HERE...
I CAN'T SEEM TO CONTACT MY RING... BUT THAT COULD BE BECAUSE I'M STILL OUT OF RANGE!...
6

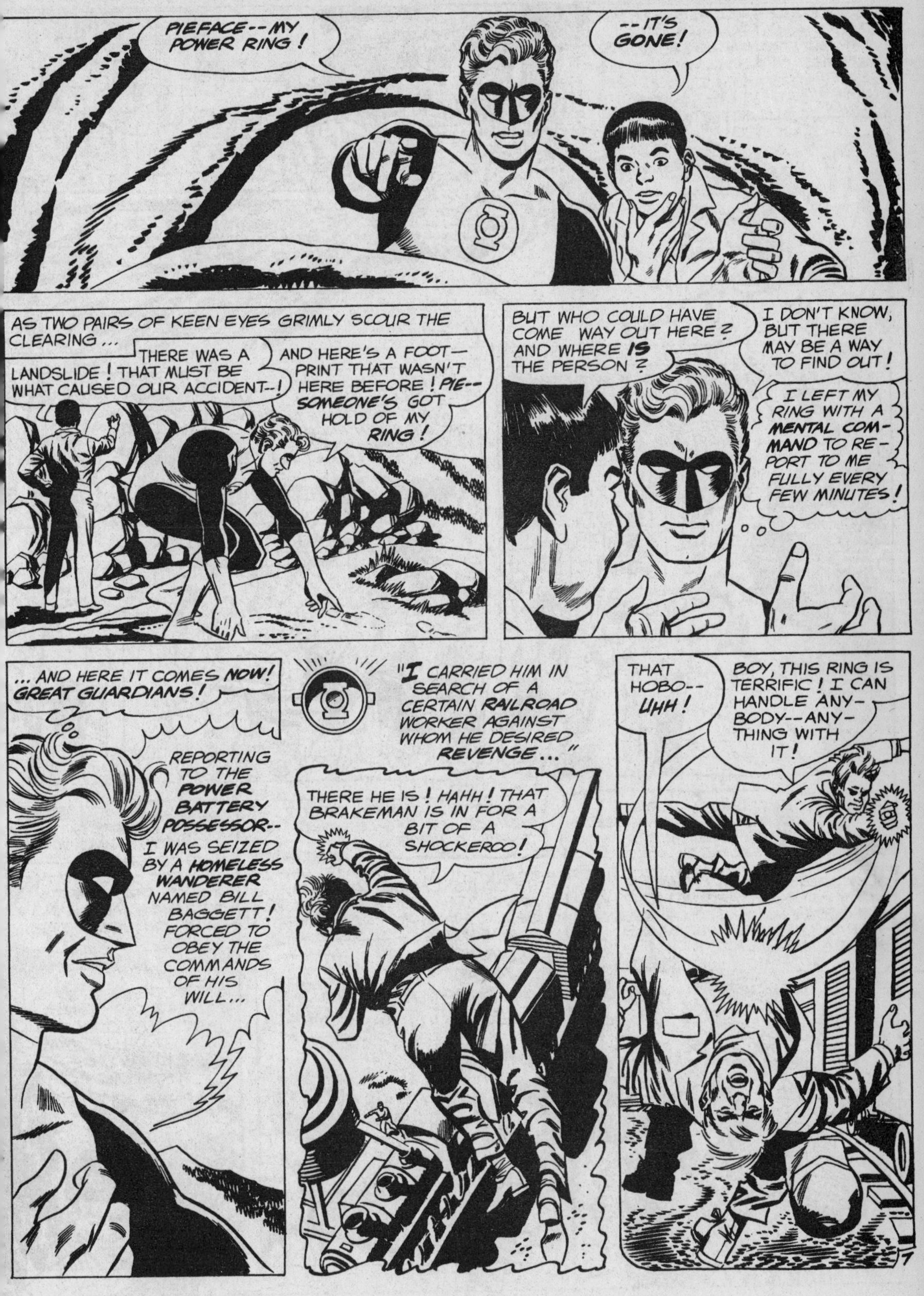
PIEFACE--MY POWER RING!
--IT'S GONE!
AS TWO PAIRS OF KEEN EYES GRIMLY SCOUR THE CLEARING...
THERE WAS A LANDSLIDE! THAT MUST BE WHAT CAUSED OUR ACCIDENT--!
AND HERE'S A FOOT-PRINT THAT WASN'T HERE BEFORE! PIE--SOMEONE'S GOT HOLD OF MY RING!
BUT WHO COULD HAVE COME WAY OUT HERE? AND WHERE IS THE PERSON?
I DON'T KNOW, BUT THERE MAY BE A WAY TO FIND OUT!
I LEFT MY RING WITH A MENTAL COMMAND TO REPORT TO ME FULLY EVERY FEW MINUTES!
...AND HERE IT COMES NOW! GREAT GUARDIANS!
REPORTING TO THE POWER BATTERY POSSESSOR--I WAS SEIZED BY A HOMELESS WANDERER NAMED BILL BAGGETT! FORCED TO OBEY THE COMMANDS OF HIS WILL...
"I CARRIED HIM IN SEARCH OF A CERTAIN RAILROAD WORKER AGAINST WHOM HE DESIRED REVENGE..."
THERE HE IS! HAHH! THAT BRAKEMAN IS IN FOR A BIT OF A SHOCKEROO!
THAT HOBO--UHH!
BOY, THIS RING IS TERRIFIC! I CAN HANDLE ANYBODY--ANYTHING WITH IT!
7

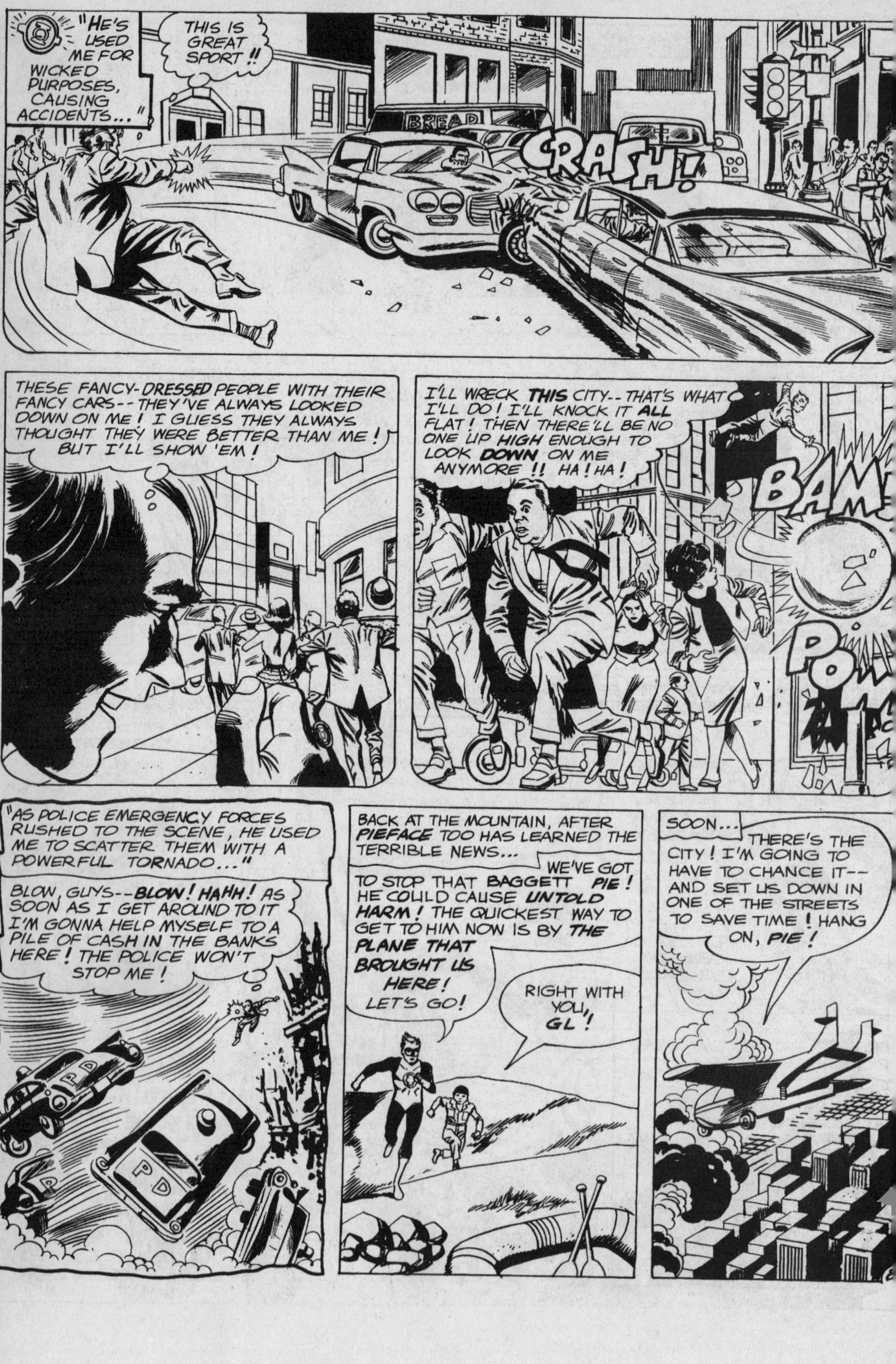
"HE'S USED ME FOR WICKED PURPOSES, CAUSING ACCIDENTS..."
THIS IS GREAT SPORT!!
BREAD
CRASH!
THESE FANCY-DRESSED PEOPLE WITH THEIR FANCY CARS--THEY'VE ALWAYS LOOKED DOWN ON ME! I GUESS THEY ALWAYS THOUGHT THEY WERE BETTER THAN ME! BUT I'LL SHOW 'EM!
I'LL WRECK THIS CITY--THAT'S WHAT I'LL DO! I'LL KNOCK IT ALL FLAT! THEN THERE'LL BE NO ONE UP HIGH ENOUGH TO LOOK DOWN ON ME ANYMORE!! HA! HA!
"AS POLICE EMERGENCY FORCES RUSHED TO THE SCENE, HE USED ME TO SCATTER THEM WITH A POWERFUL TORNADO..."
BLOW, GUYS--BLOW! HAHH! AS SOON AS I GET AROUND TO IT I'M GONNA HELP MYSELF TO A PILE OF CASH IN THE BANKS HERE! THE POLICE WON'T STOP ME!
PD
PD
BACK AT THE MOUNTAIN, AFTER PIEFACE TOO HAS LEARNED THE TERRIBLE NEWS...
WE'VE GOT TO STOP THAT BAGGETT PIE! HE COULD CAUSE UNTOLD HARM! THE QUICKEST WAY TO GET TO HIM NOW IS BY THE PLANE THAT BROUGHT US HERE! LET'S GO!
RIGHT WITH YOU, GL!
SOON...
THERE'S THE CITY! I'M GOING TO HAVE TO CHANCE IT--AND SET US DOWN IN ONE OF THE STREETS TO SAVE TIME! HANG ON, PIE!

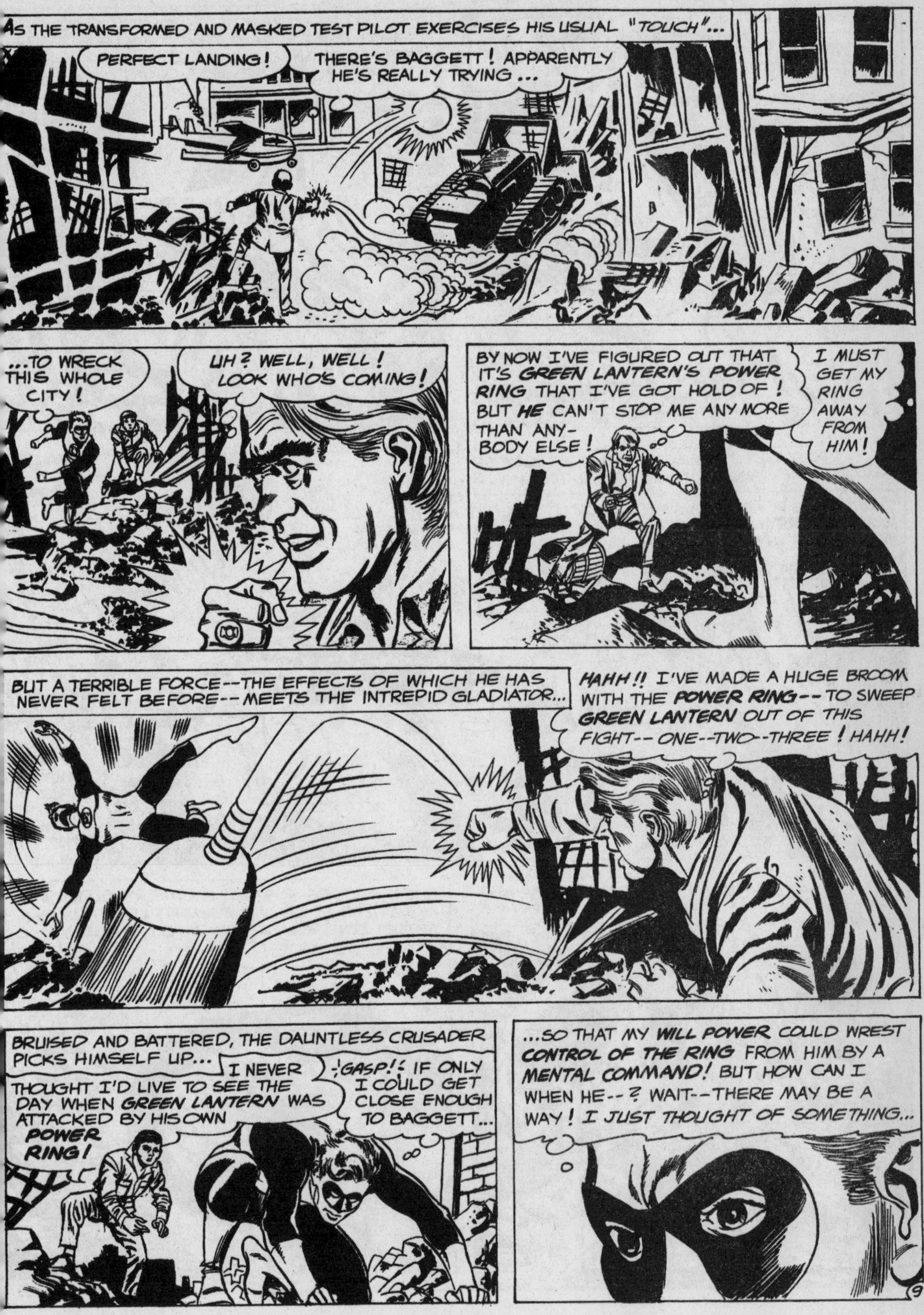
AS THE TRANSFORMED AND MASKED TEST PILOT EXERCISES HIS USUAL "TOUCH"...
PERFECT LANDING!
THERE'S BAGGETT! APPARENTLY HE'S REALLY TRYING ...
...TO WRECK THIS WHOLE CITY!
UH? WELL, WELL! LOOK WHO'S COMING!
BY NOW I'VE FIGURED OUT THAT IT'S GREEN LANTERN'S POWER RING THAT I'VE GOT HOLD OF! BUT HE CAN'T STOP ME ANY MORE THAN ANYBODY ELSE!
I MUST GET MY RING AWAY FROM HIM!
BUT A TERRIBLE FORCE--THE EFFECTS OF WHICH HE HAS NEVER FELT BEFORE--MEETS THE INTREPID GLADIATOR...
HAHH!! I'VE MADE A HUGE BROOM WITH THE POWER RING--TO SWEEP GREEN LANTERN OUT OF THIS FIGHT--ONE--TWO--THREE! HAHH!
BRUISED AND BATTERED, THE DAUNTLESS CRUSADER PICKS HIMSELF UP...
I NEVER THOUGHT I'D LIVE TO SEE THE DAY WHEN GREEN LANTERN WAS ATTACKED BY HIS OWN POWER RING!
GASP! IF ONLY I COULD GET CLOSE ENOUGH TO BAGGETT...
...SO THAT MY WILL POWER COULD WREST CONTROL OF THE RING FROM HIM BY A MENTAL COMMAND! BUT HOW CAN I WHEN HE--? WAIT--THERE MAY BE A WAY! I JUST THOUGHT OF SOMETHING...
9

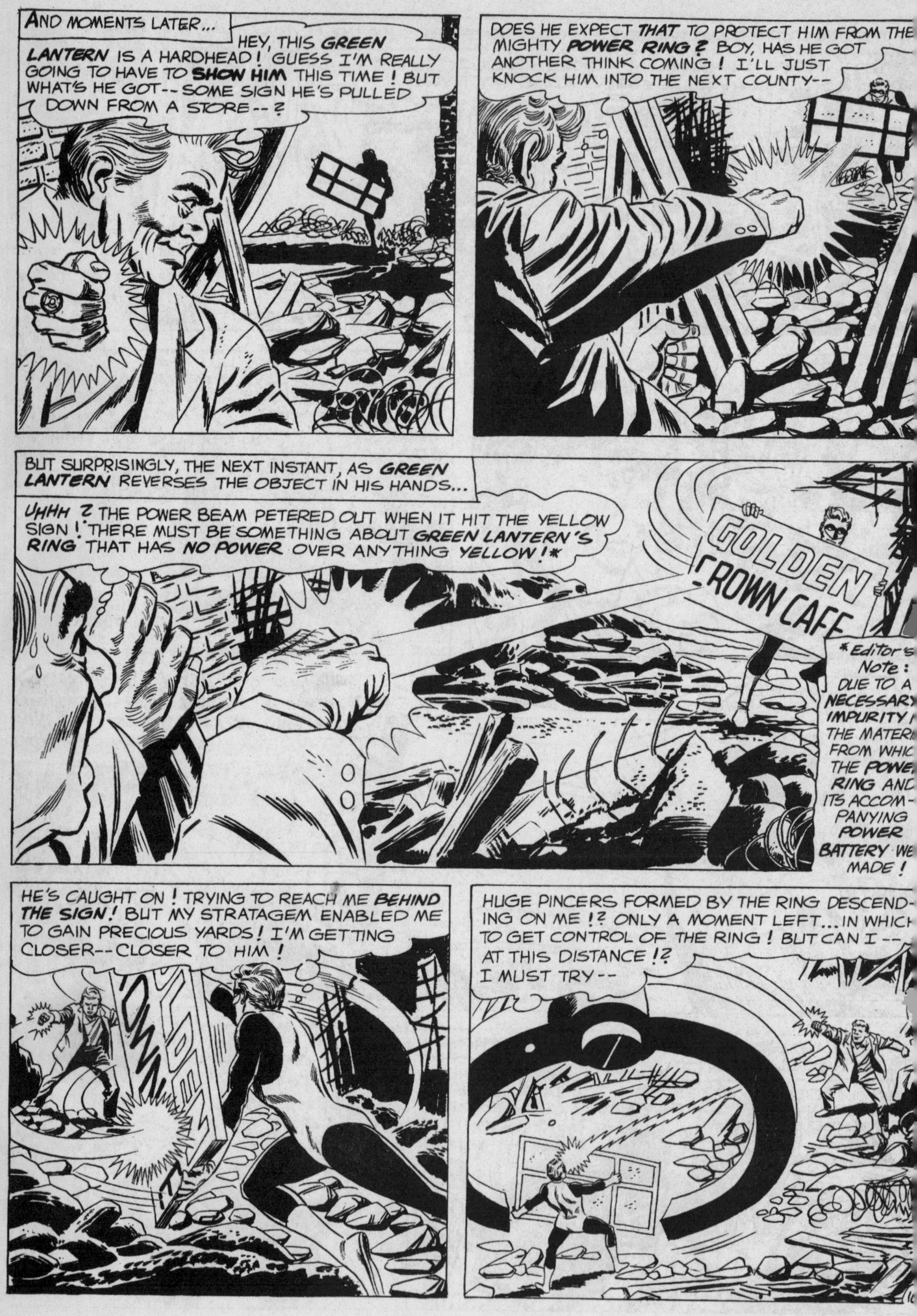
AND MOMENTS LATER...
HEY, THIS GREEN LANTERN IS A HARDHEAD! GUESS I'M REALLY GOING TO HAVE TO SHOW HIM THIS TIME! BUT WHAT'S HE GOT-- SOME SIGN HE'S PULLED DOWN FROM A STORE--?
DOES HE EXPECT THAT TO PROTECT HIM FROM THE MIGHTY POWER RING? BOY, HAS HE GOT ANOTHER THINK COMING! I'LL JUST KNOCK HIM INTO THE NEXT COUNTY--
BUT SURPRISINGLY, THE NEXT INSTANT, AS GREEN LANTERN REVERSES THE OBJECT IN HIS HANDS...
UHHH? THE POWER BEAM PETERED OUT WHEN IT HIT THE YELLOW SIGN! THERE MUST BE SOMETHING ABOUT GREEN LANTERN'S RING THAT HAS NO POWER OVER ANYTHING YELLOW!*
GOLDEN CROWN CAFE
*Editor's Note: DUE TO A NECESSARY IMPURITY THE MATER FROM WHIC THE POWE RING AND ITS ACCOM-PANYING POWER BATTERY WE MADE!
HE'S CAUGHT ON! TRYING TO REACH ME BEHIND THE SIGN! BUT MY STRATAGEM ENABLED ME TO GAIN PRECIOUS YARDS! I'M GETTING CLOSER-- CLOSER TO HIM!
HUGE PINCERS FORMED BY THE RING DESCEND-ING ON ME!? ONLY A MOMENT LEFT... IN WHICH TO GET CONTROL OF THE RING! BUT CAN I -- AT THIS DISTANCE!?
I MUST TRY--

ABRUPTLY, A STRANGE CONTEST ENSUES, A CONTEST OF WILLS MADE UN-EQUAL BY *GL'S* GREATER DISTANCE FROM THE *POWER RING*...

THE RING--I'M HAVING TROUBLE GETTING IT TO DO WHAT I WANT! GOT TO CON-CENTRATE HARDER!

I'VE GOT TO POUR *WILL POWER* OUT LIKE I NEVER DID BEFORE!

LITTLE BY LITTLE THE DUEL TAKES THE FORM OF GIANT GREEN HANDS GRAPPLING FOR MASTERY...

THE RING IS RESPONDING TO MY THOUGHT-IMPULSES--BUT IT ALSO IS RESPONDING TO BAGGETT'S WILL! THE QUESTION IS--WHICH OF US CAN *"OVERPOWER"* THE OTHER? HE'S APPLYING CRUSHING FORCE...

...BUT EVEN THOUGH HIS TASK IS EASIER THAN MINE... BEING CLOSER TO THE RING...EVEN SO...I'VE SUCCEEDED IN EQUALIZING MATTERS! HE HAD ME ON THE DEFENSIVE! NOW IT'S *MY TURN*...

THEN, WITH CONVINCING FORCE...

THATAWAY, GL--! YOU KAYOED HIM WITH HIS OWN HAND!

AND THE NEXT MOMENT...

AT LAST--I'VE GOT BACK MY RING!

ON YOUR FEET, BAGGETT! YOU'VE GOT A DATE WITH THE POLICE DEPARTMENT HERE!

GULP! YOU TRICKED ME--THAT YELLOW SIGN...

11

LATER, WITH THE VAGABOND SAFELY BEHIND BARS...

THERE, *PIE!* I GUESS THAT ABOUT DOES IT!

SURE DOES, *GL!* YOUR RING HAS REPAIRED EVERY BIT OF DAMAGE BAGGETT DID! WHEW! I GUESS WE CAN RELAX NOW!

THAT NIGHT IN HAL'S DRESSING ROOM AT THE HANGAR...

WELL, WE'VE FINISHED THE RESULTS OF OUR *TESTS, PIE!* FOR ONE THING, THEY TAUGHT ME I MUST NEVER TAKE THE CHANCE OF MY RING FALLING INTO THE *WRONG HANDS* AGAIN! IT'S TOO DANGEROUS! BUT IN ADDITION THERE WERE PRACTICAL RESULTS...

ACCORDING TO THESE FIGURES, I CAN CONTROL THE *POWER RING* UP TO ABOUT A HUNDRED YARDS...BUT THE *DEGREE OF CONTROL* DECREASES AS THE DISTANCE INCREASES! AND ALSO THE TESTS GAVE ME PRACTICE IN *MENTAL CONTROL* OVER THE RING AT A DISTANCE...

...PRACTICE WHICH I PUT TO GOOD USE ALMOST AT ONCE IN HANDLING BAGGETT!

AND YOU SURE "HANDLED" HIM, *GL*— WITH A *KING-SIZE HAND* MADE BY YOUR RING!

The End

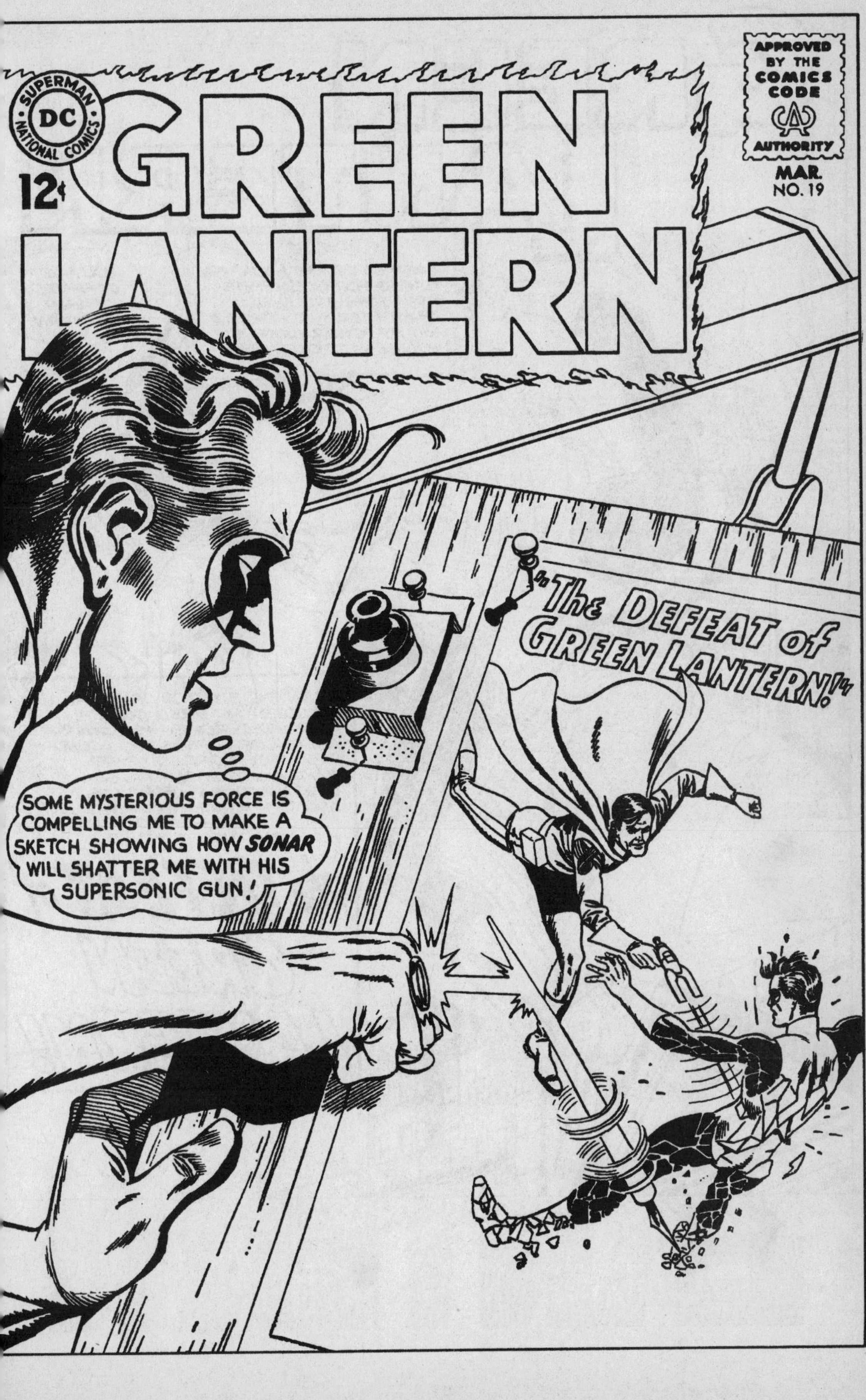
SUPERMAN DC NATIONAL COMICS
12¢
GREEN LANTERN
APPROVED BY THE COMICS CODE AUTHORITY
MAR. NO. 19
"The DEFEAT of GREEN LANTERN!"
SOME MYSTERIOUS FORCE IS COMPELLING ME TO MAKE A SKETCH SHOWING HOW SONAR WILL SHATTER ME WITH HIS SUPERSONIC GUN!

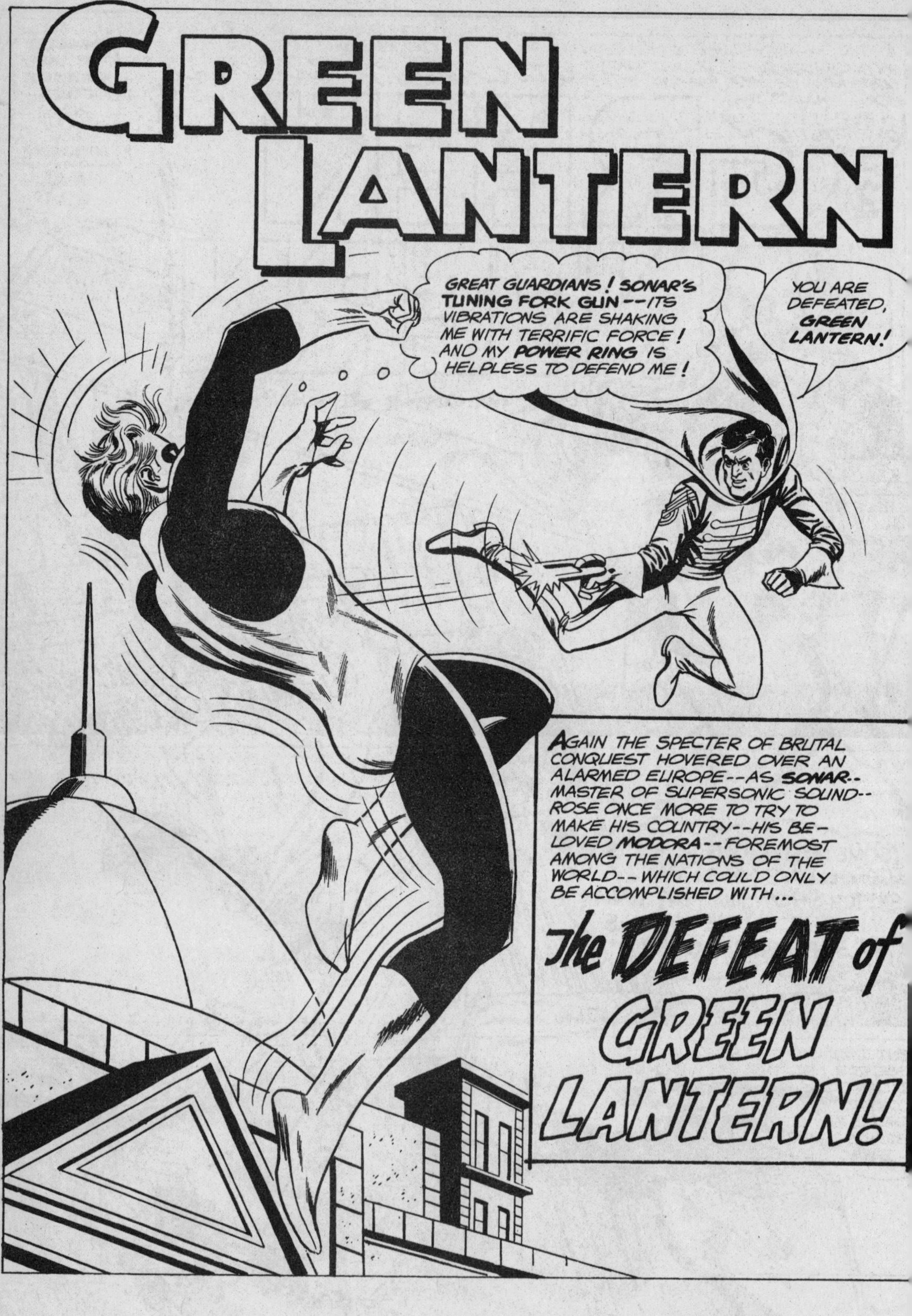
GREEN LANTERN
GREAT GUARDIANS! SONAR'S TUNING FORK GUN--ITS VIBRATIONS ARE SHAKING ME WITH TERRIFIC FORCE! AND MY POWER RING IS HELPLESS TO DEFEND ME!
YOU ARE DEFEATED, GREEN LANTERN!
AGAIN THE SPECTER OF BRUTAL CONQUEST HOVERED OVER AN ALARMED EUROPE--AS SONAR--MASTER OF SUPERSONIC SOUND--ROSE ONCE MORE TO TRY TO MAKE HIS COUNTRY--HIS BE-LOVED MODORA--FOREMOST AMONG THE NATIONS OF THE WORLD--WHICH COULD ONLY BE ACCOMPLISHED WITH...
The DEFEAT of GREEN LANTERN!

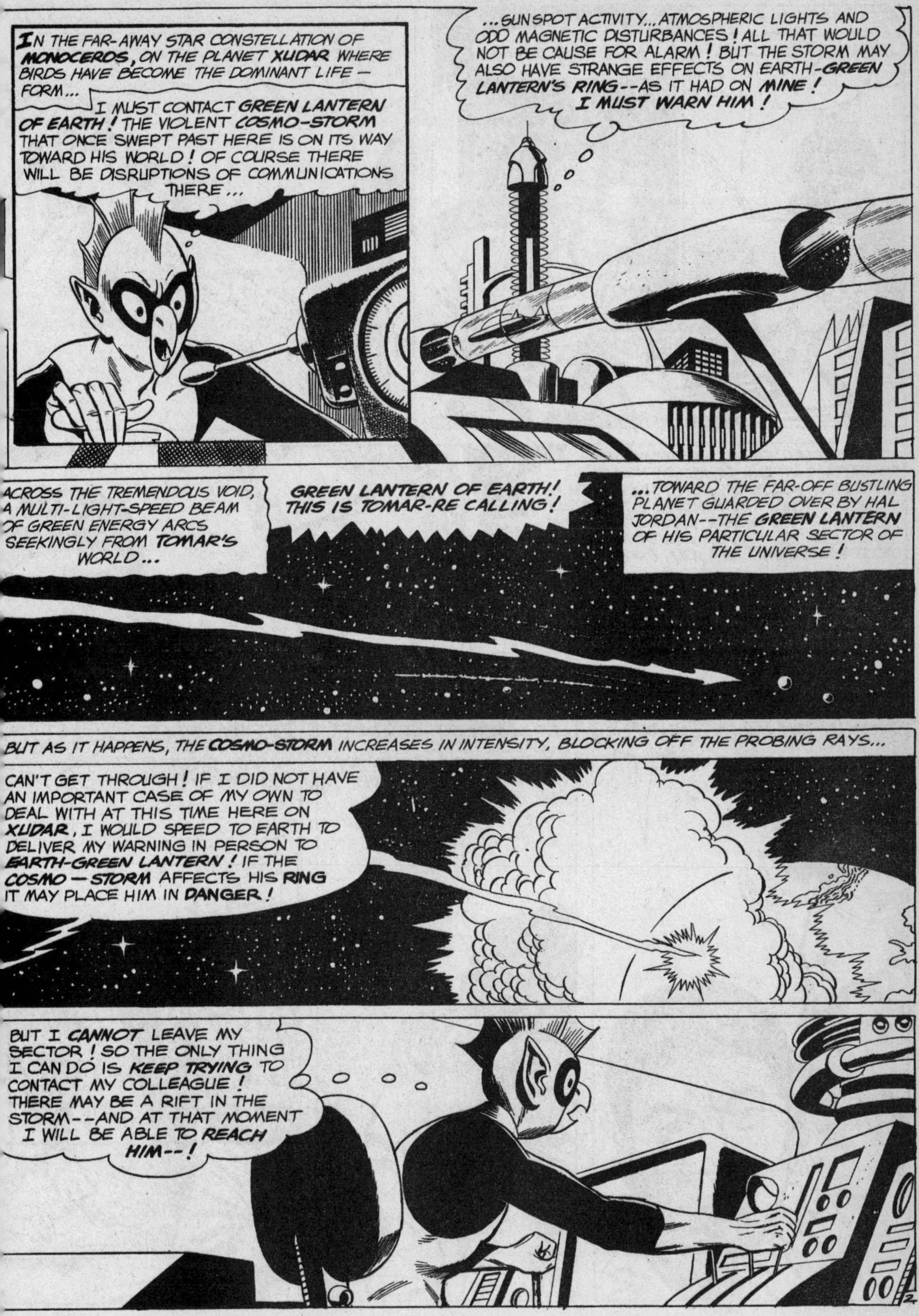
IN THE FAR-AWAY STAR CONSTELLATION OF MONOCEROS, ON THE PLANET XUDAR WHERE BIRDS HAVE BECOME THE DOMINANT LIFE-FORM...
I MUST CONTACT GREEN LANTERN OF EARTH! THE VIOLENT COSMO-STORM THAT ONCE SWEPT PAST HERE IS ON ITS WAY TOWARD HIS WORLD! OF COURSE THERE WILL BE DISRUPTIONS OF COMMUNICATIONS THERE...
...SUNSPOT ACTIVITY... ATMOSPHERIC LIGHTS AND ODD MAGNETIC DISTURBANCES! ALL THAT WOULD NOT BE CAUSE FOR ALARM! BUT THE STORM MAY ALSO HAVE STRANGE EFFECTS ON EARTH-GREEN LANTERN'S RING--AS IT HAD ON MINE! I MUST WARN HIM!
ACROSS THE TREMENDOUS VOID, A MULTI-LIGHT-SPEED BEAM OF GREEN ENERGY ARCS SEEKINGLY FROM TOMAR'S WORLD...
GREEN LANTERN OF EARTH! THIS IS TOMAR-RE CALLING!
...TOWARD THE FAR-OFF BUSTLING PLANET GUARDED OVER BY HAL JORDAN--THE GREEN LANTERN OF HIS PARTICULAR SECTOR OF THE UNIVERSE!
BUT AS IT HAPPENS, THE COSMO-STORM INCREASES IN INTENSITY, BLOCKING OFF THE PROBING RAYS...
CAN'T GET THROUGH! IF I DID NOT HAVE AN IMPORTANT CASE OF MY OWN TO DEAL WITH AT THIS TIME HERE ON XUDAR, I WOULD SPEED TO EARTH TO DELIVER MY WARNING IN PERSON TO EARTH-GREEN LANTERN! IF THE COSMO-STORM AFFECTS HIS RING IT MAY PLACE HIM IN DANGER!
BUT I CANNOT LEAVE MY SECTOR! SO THE ONLY THING I CAN DO IS KEEP TRYING TO CONTACT MY COLLEAGUE! THERE MAY BE A RIFT IN THE STORM--AND AT THAT MOMENT I WILL BE ABLE TO REACH HIM--!
2

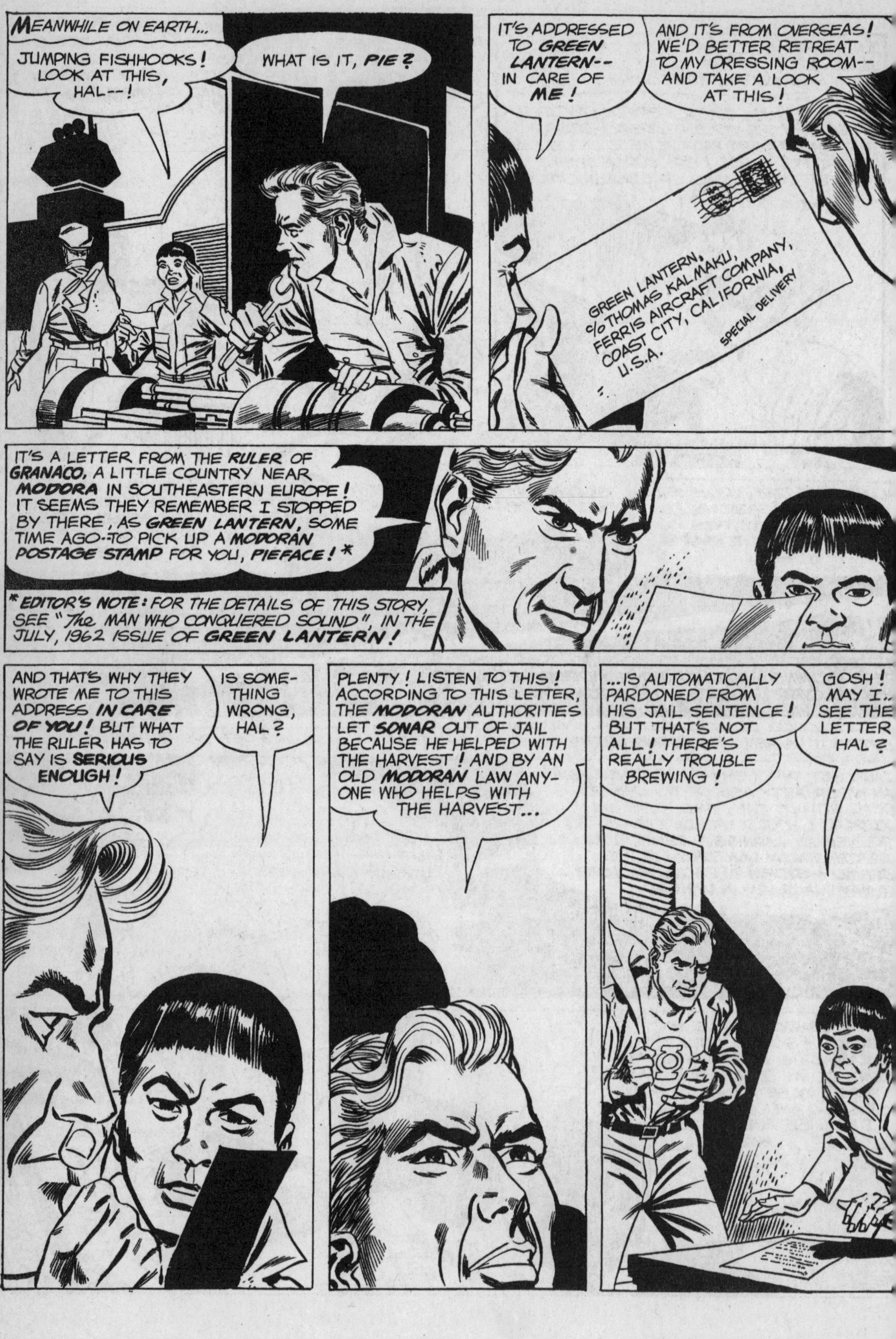
MEANWHILE ON EARTH...
JUMPING FISHHOOKS! LOOK AT THIS, HAL--!
WHAT IS IT, PIE?
IT'S ADDRESSED TO GREEN LANTERN-- IN CARE OF ME!
AND IT'S FROM OVERSEAS! WE'D BETTER RETREAT TO MY DRESSING ROOM-- AND TAKE A LOOK AT THIS!
GREEN LANTERN,
c/o THOMAS KALMAKU,
FERRIS AIRCRAFT COMPANY,
COAST CITY, CALIFORNIA,
U.S.A.
SPECIAL DELIVERY
IT'S A LETTER FROM THE RULER OF GRANACO, A LITTLE COUNTRY NEAR MODORA IN SOUTHEASTERN EUROPE! IT SEEMS THEY REMEMBER I STOPPED BY THERE, AS GREEN LANTERN, SOME TIME AGO--TO PICK UP A MODORAN POSTAGE STAMP FOR YOU, PIEFACE! *
* EDITOR'S NOTE: FOR THE DETAILS OF THIS STORY, SEE "The MAN WHO CONQUERED SOUND", IN THE JULY, 1962 ISSUE OF GREEN LANTERN!
AND THAT'S WHY THEY WROTE ME TO THIS ADDRESS IN CARE OF YOU! BUT WHAT THE RULER HAS TO SAY IS SERIOUS ENOUGH!
IS SOMETHING WRONG, HAL?
PLENTY! LISTEN TO THIS! ACCORDING TO THIS LETTER, THE MODORAN AUTHORITIES LET SONAR OUT OF JAIL BECAUSE HE HELPED WITH THE HARVEST! AND BY AN OLD MODORAN LAW ANYONE WHO HELPS WITH THE HARVEST...
...IS AUTOMATICALLY PARDONED FROM HIS JAIL SENTENCE! BUT THAT'S NOT ALL! THERE'S REALLY TROUBLE BREWING!
GOSH! MAY I.. SEE THE LETTER HAL?

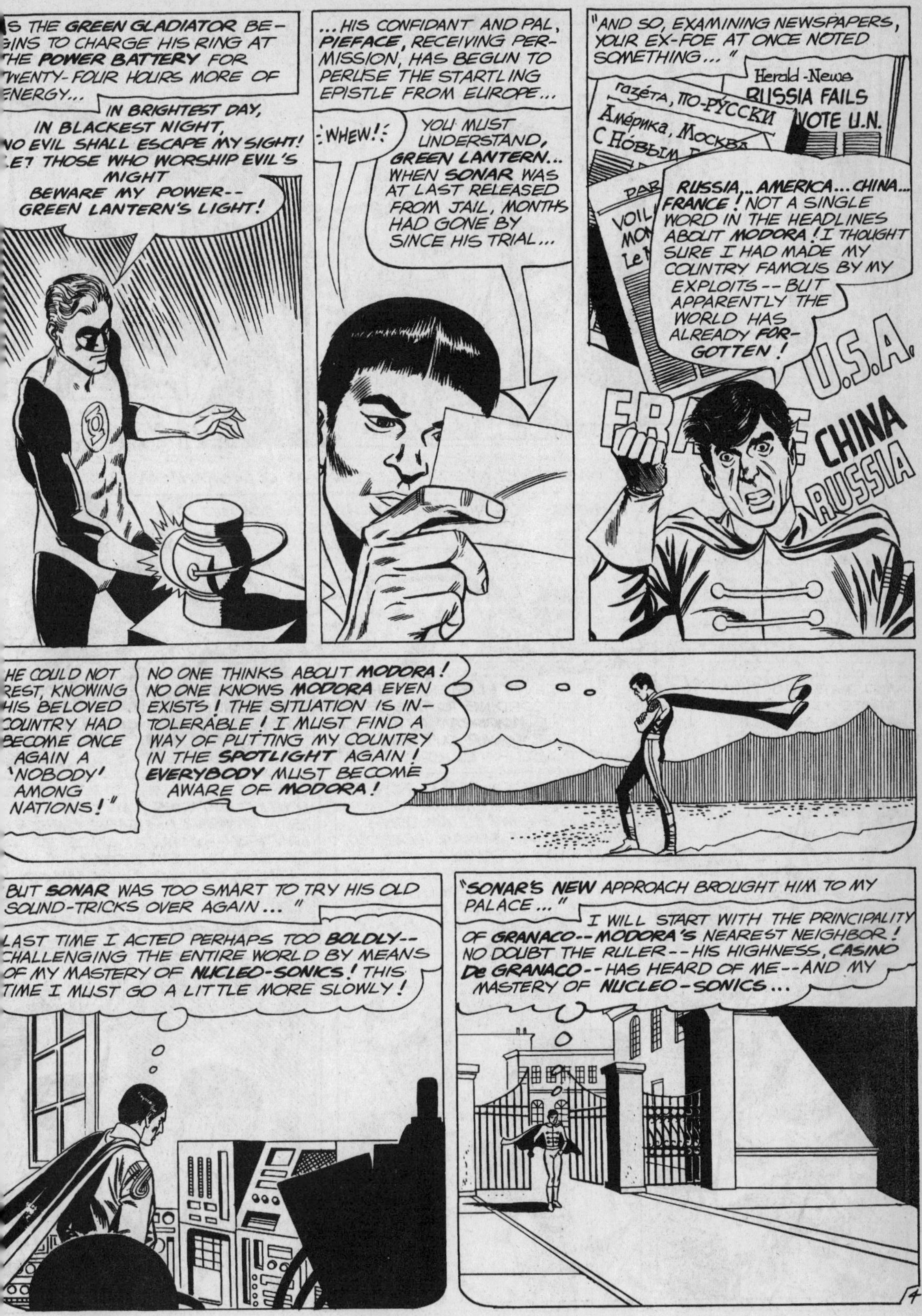
S THE GREEN GLADIATOR BEGINS TO CHARGE HIS RING AT THE POWER BATTERY FOR TWENTY-FOUR HOURS MORE OF ENERGY...
IN BRIGHTEST DAY, IN BLACKEST NIGHT, NO EVIL SHALL ESCAPE MY SIGHT! LET THOSE WHO WORSHIP EVIL'S MIGHT BEWARE MY POWER-- GREEN LANTERN'S LIGHT!
...HIS CONFIDANT AND PAL, PIEFACE, RECEIVING PERMISSION, HAS BEGUN TO PERUSE THE STARTLING EPISTLE FROM EUROPE...
WHEW!
YOU MUST UNDERSTAND, GREEN LANTERN... WHEN SONAR WAS AT LAST RELEASED FROM JAIL, MONTHS HAD GONE BY SINCE HIS TRIAL...
"AND SO, EXAMINING NEWSPAPERS, YOUR EX-FOE AT ONCE NOTED SOMETHING..."
Herald-News
RUSSIA FAILS
VOTE U.N.
газéта, по-русски
Амéрика, Москва
С Нóвым
RUSSIA... AMERICA... CHINA... FRANCE! NOT A SINGLE WORD IN THE HEADLINES ABOUT MODORA! I THOUGHT SURE I HAD MADE MY COUNTRY FAMOUS BY MY EXPLOITS--BUT APPARENTLY THE WORLD HAS ALREADY FORGOTTEN!
U.S.A.
CHINA
RUSSIA
HE COULD NOT REST, KNOWING HIS BELOVED COUNTRY HAD BECOME ONCE AGAIN A 'NOBODY' AMONG NATIONS!"
NO ONE THINKS ABOUT MODORA! NO ONE KNOWS MODORA EVEN EXISTS! THE SITUATION IS INTOLERABLE! I MUST FIND A WAY OF PUTTING MY COUNTRY IN THE SPOTLIGHT AGAIN! EVERYBODY MUST BECOME AWARE OF MODORA!
BUT SONAR WAS TOO SMART TO TRY HIS OLD SOUND-TRICKS OVER AGAIN..."
LAST TIME I ACTED PERHAPS TOO BOLDLY--CHALLENGING THE ENTIRE WORLD BY MEANS OF MY MASTERY OF NUCLEO-SONICS! THIS TIME I MUST GO A LITTLE MORE SLOWLY!
"SONAR'S NEW APPROACH BROUGHT HIM TO MY PALACE..."
I WILL START WITH THE PRINCIPALITY OF GRANACO--MODORA'S NEAREST NEIGHBOR! NO DOUBT THE RULER--HIS HIGHNESS, CASINO De GRANACO--HAS HEARD OF ME--AND MY MASTERY OF NUCLEO-SONICS...
4

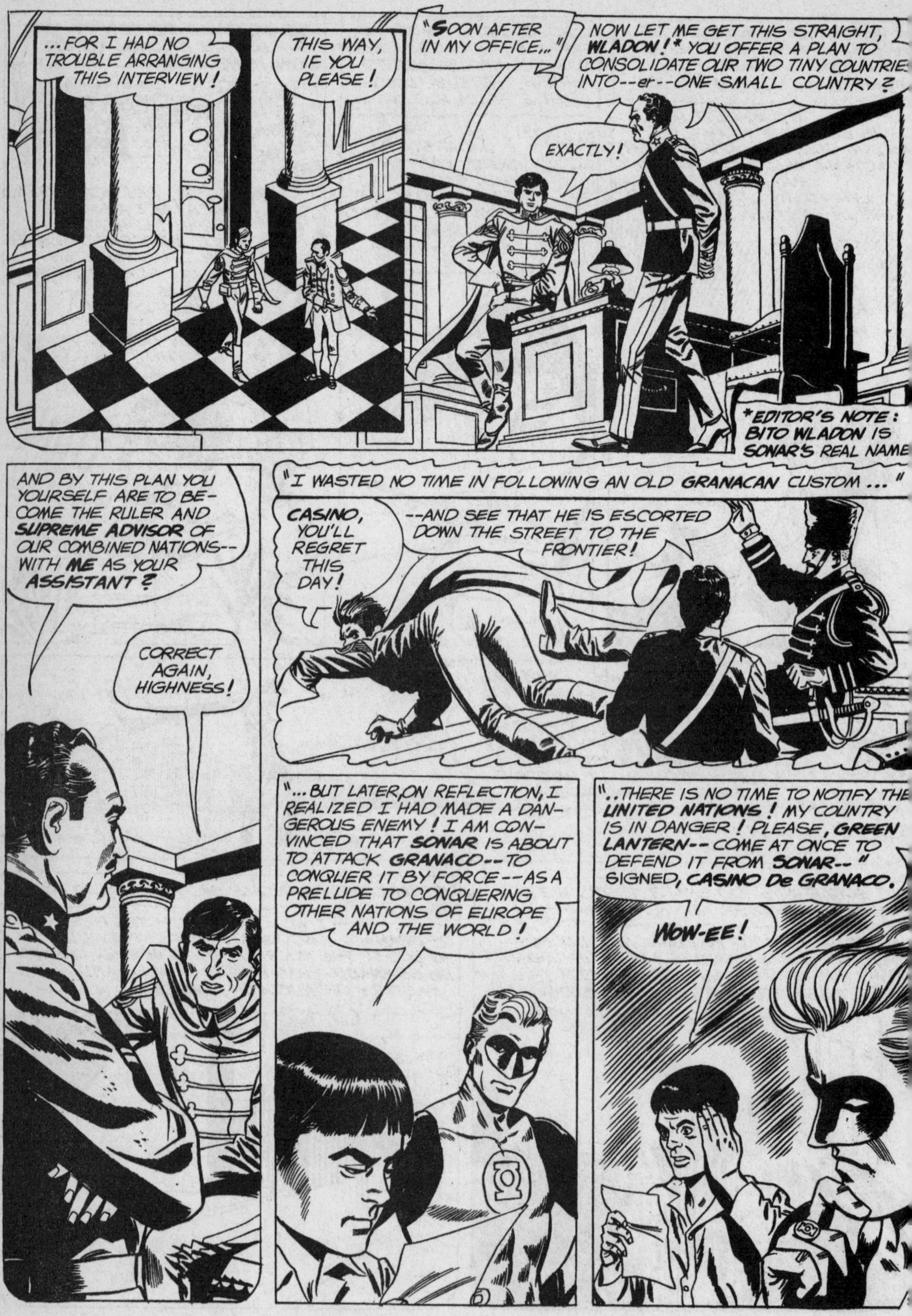
...FOR I HAD NO TROUBLE ARRANGING THIS INTERVIEW!
THIS WAY, IF YOU PLEASE!
"SOON AFTER IN MY OFFICE..."
NOW LET ME GET THIS STRAIGHT, WLADON!* YOU OFFER A PLAN TO CONSOLIDATE OUR TWO TINY COUNTRIES INTO--er--ONE SMALL COUNTRY?
EXACTLY!
*EDITOR'S NOTE: BITO WLADON IS SONAR'S REAL NAME
AND BY THIS PLAN YOU YOURSELF ARE TO BECOME THE RULER AND SUPREME ADVISOR OF OUR COMBINED NATIONS--WITH ME AS YOUR ASSISTANT?
CORRECT AGAIN, HIGHNESS!
"I WASTED NO TIME IN FOLLOWING AN OLD GRANACAN CUSTOM..."
CASINO, YOU'LL REGRET THIS DAY!
--AND SEE THAT HE IS ESCORTED DOWN THE STREET TO THE FRONTIER!
"...BUT LATER, ON REFLECTION, I REALIZED I HAD MADE A DANGEROUS ENEMY! I AM CONVINCED THAT SONAR IS ABOUT TO ATTACK GRANACO--TO CONQUER IT BY FORCE--AS A PRELUDE TO CONQUERING OTHER NATIONS OF EUROPE AND THE WORLD!
"..THERE IS NO TIME TO NOTIFY THE UNITED NATIONS! MY COUNTRY IS IN DANGER! PLEASE, GREEN LANTERN--COME AT ONCE TO DEFEND IT FROM SONAR--" SIGNED, CASINO De GRANACO.
WOW-EE!

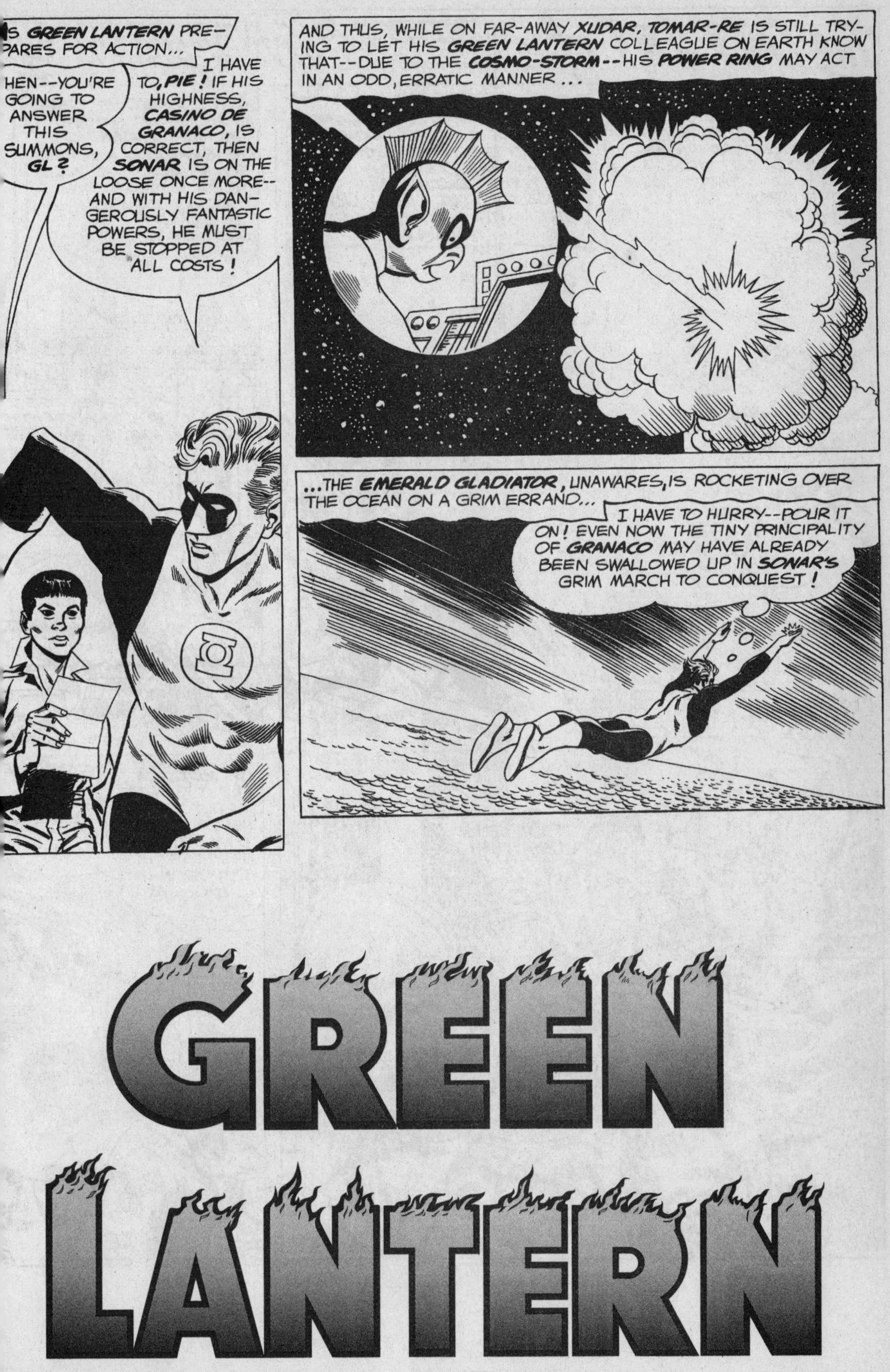
S GREEN LANTERN PRE-PARES FOR ACTION...
HEN--YOU'RE GOING TO ANSWER THIS SUMMONS, GL?
I HAVE TO, PIE! IF HIS HIGHNESS, CASINO DE GRANACO, IS CORRECT, THEN SONAR IS ON THE LOOSE ONCE MORE--AND WITH HIS DANGEROUSLY FANTASTIC POWERS, HE MUST BE STOPPED AT ALL COSTS!
AND THUS, WHILE ON FAR-AWAY XUDAR, TOMAR-RE IS STILL TRYING TO LET HIS GREEN LANTERN COLLEAGUE ON EARTH KNOW THAT--DUE TO THE COSMO-STORM--HIS POWER RING MAY ACT IN AN ODD, ERRATIC MANNER...
...THE EMERALD GLADIATOR, UNAWARES, IS ROCKETING OVER THE OCEAN ON A GRIM ERRAND...
I HAVE TO HURRY--POUR IT ON! EVEN NOW THE TINY PRINCIPALITY OF GRANACO MAY HAVE ALREADY BEEN SWALLOWED UP IN SONAR'S GRIM MARCH TO CONQUEST!

GREEN LANTERN

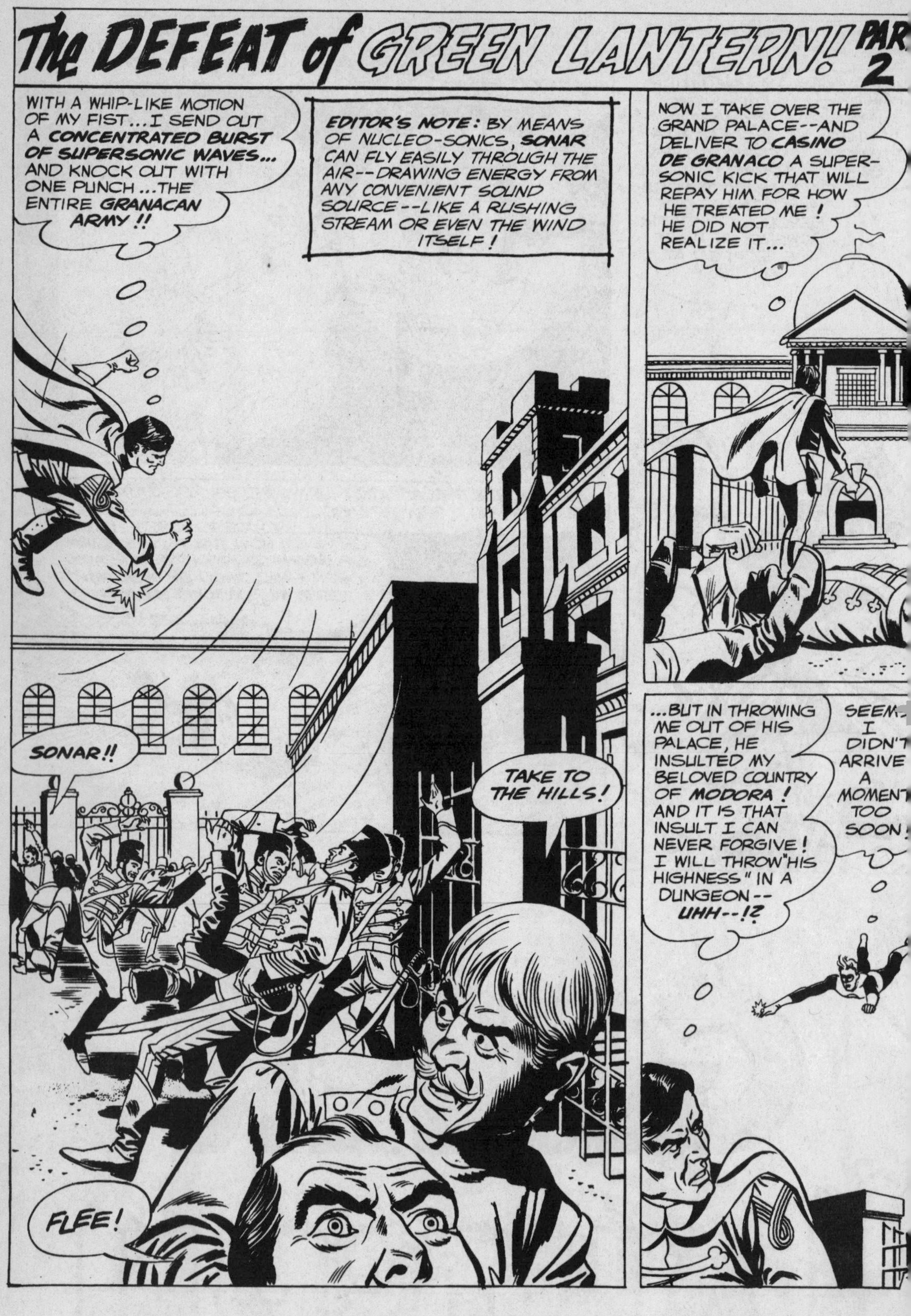
The DEFEAT of GREEN LANTERN! PAR
2
WITH A WHIP-LIKE MOTION OF MY FIST... I SEND OUT A CONCENTRATED BURST OF SUPERSONIC WAVES... AND KNOCK OUT WITH ONE PUNCH ... THE ENTIRE GRANACAN ARMY !!
EDITOR'S NOTE: BY MEANS OF NUCLEO-SONICS, SONAR CAN FLY EASILY THROUGH THE AIR--DRAWING ENERGY FROM ANY CONVENIENT SOUND SOURCE--LIKE A RUSHING STREAM OR EVEN THE WIND ITSELF!
SONAR!!
TAKE TO THE HILLS!
FLEE!
NOW I TAKE OVER THE GRAND PALACE--AND DELIVER TO CASINO DE GRANACO A SUPER-SONIC KICK THAT WILL REPAY HIM FOR HOW HE TREATED ME! HE DID NOT REALIZE IT...
...BUT IN THROWING ME OUT OF HIS PALACE, HE INSULTED MY BELOVED COUNTRY OF MODORA! AND IT IS THAT INSULT I CAN NEVER FORGIVE! I WILL THROW "HIS HIGHNESS" IN A DUNGEON -- UHH--!?
SEEM I DIDN'T ARRIVE A MOMENT TOO SOON

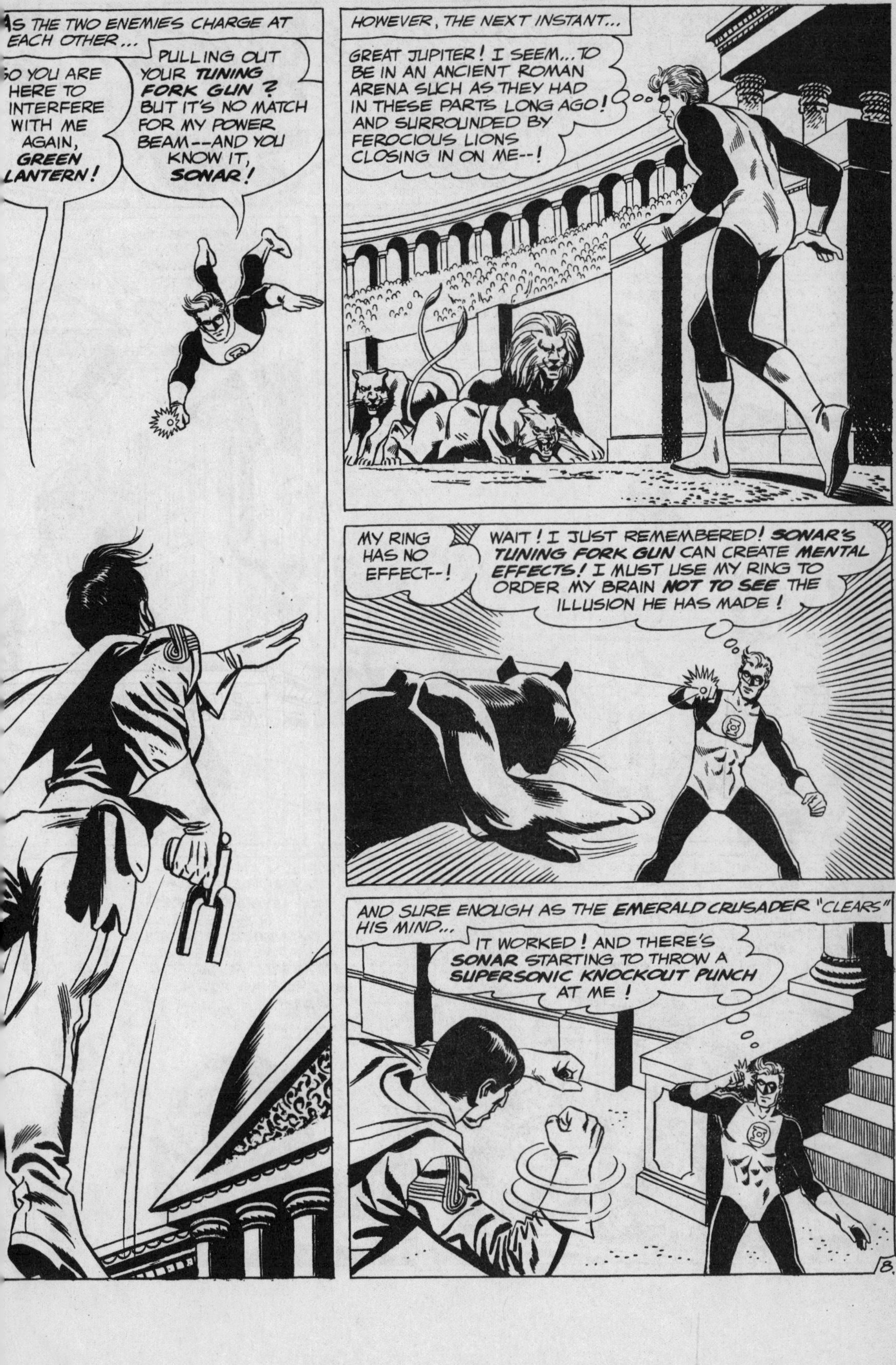
AS THE TWO ENEMIES CHARGE AT EACH OTHER...
SO YOU ARE HERE TO INTERFERE WITH ME AGAIN, GREEN LANTERN!
PULLING OUT YOUR TUNING FORK GUN? BUT IT'S NO MATCH FOR MY POWER BEAM--AND YOU KNOW IT, SONAR!
HOWEVER, THE NEXT INSTANT...
GREAT JUPITER! I SEEM... TO BE IN AN ANCIENT ROMAN ARENA SUCH AS THEY HAD IN THESE PARTS LONG AGO! AND SURROUNDED BY FEROCIOUS LIONS CLOSING IN ON ME--!
MY RING HAS NO EFFECT--!
WAIT! I JUST REMEMBERED! SONAR'S TUNING FORK GUN CAN CREATE MENTAL EFFECTS! I MUST USE MY RING TO ORDER MY BRAIN NOT TO SEE THE ILLUSION HE HAS MADE!
AND SURE ENOUGH AS THE EMERALD CRUSADER "CLEARS" HIS MIND...
IT WORKED! AND THERE'S SONAR STARTING TO THROW A SUPERSONIC KNOCKOUT PUNCH AT ME!
8.

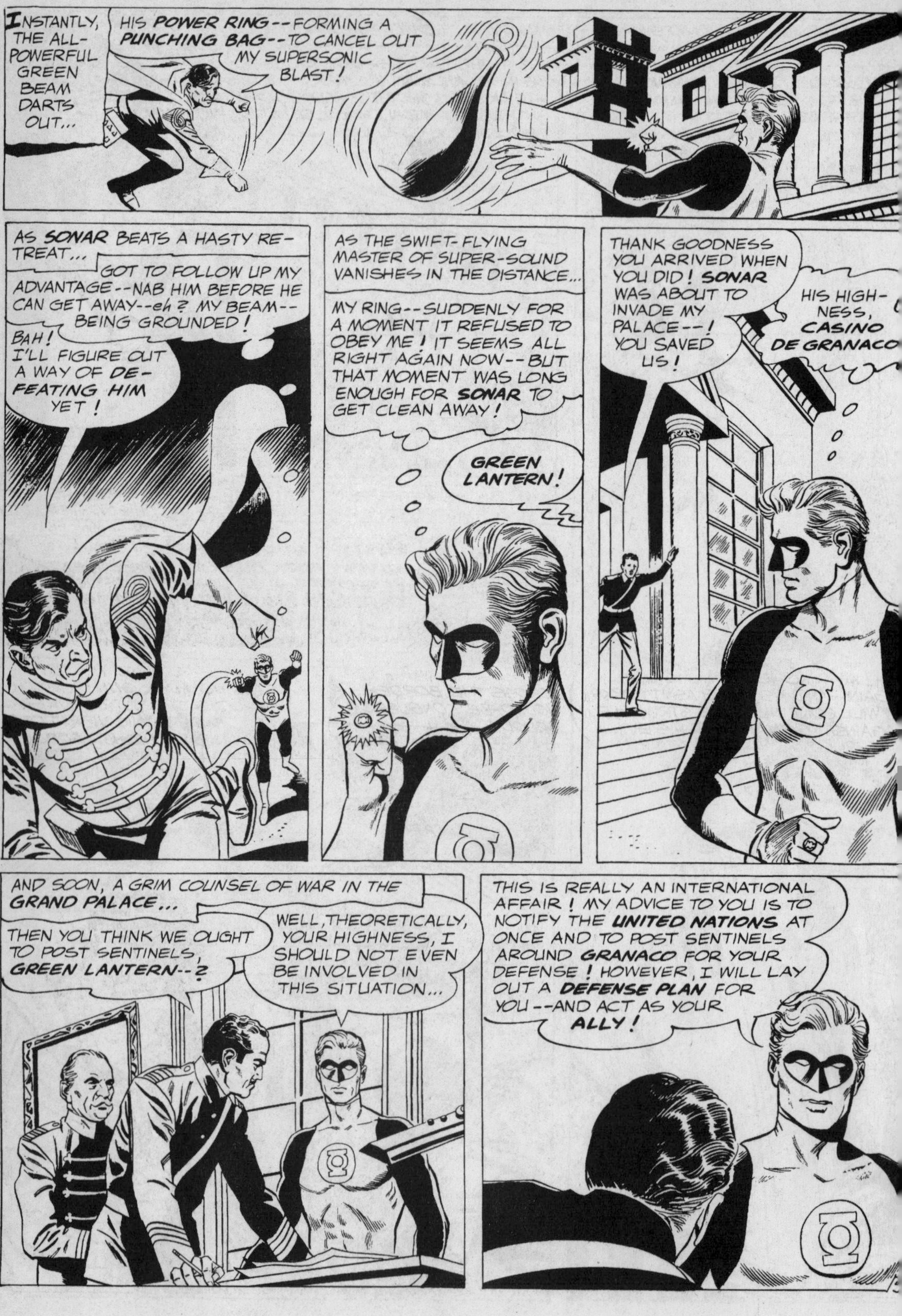
INSTANTLY, THE ALL-POWERFUL GREEN BEAM DARTS OUT...
HIS POWER RING--FORMING A PUNCHING BAG--TO CANCEL OUT MY SUPERSONIC BLAST!
AS SONAR BEATS A HASTY RETREAT...
GOT TO FOLLOW UP MY ADVANTAGE--NAB HIM BEFORE HE CAN GET AWAY--eh? MY BEAM--BEING GROUNDED!
BAH! I'LL FIGURE OUT A WAY OF DEFEATING HIM YET!
AS THE SWIFT-FLYING MASTER OF SUPER-SOUND VANISHES IN THE DISTANCE...
MY RING--SUDDENLY FOR A MOMENT IT REFUSED TO OBEY ME! IT SEEMS ALL RIGHT AGAIN NOW--BUT THAT MOMENT WAS LONG ENOUGH FOR SONAR TO GET CLEAN AWAY!
GREEN LANTERN!
THANK GOODNESS YOU ARRIVED WHEN YOU DID! SONAR WAS ABOUT TO INVADE MY PALACE--! YOU SAVED US!
HIS HIGHNESS, CASINO DE GRANACO
AND SOON, A GRIM COUNSEL OF WAR IN THE GRAND PALACE...
THEN YOU THINK WE OUGHT TO POST SENTINELS, GREEN LANTERN--?
WELL, THEORETICALLY, YOUR HIGHNESS, I SHOULD NOT EVEN BE INVOLVED IN THIS SITUATION...
THIS IS REALLY AN INTERNATIONAL AFFAIR! MY ADVICE TO YOU IS TO NOTIFY THE UNITED NATIONS AT ONCE AND TO POST SENTINELS AROUND GRANACO FOR YOUR DEFENSE! HOWEVER, I WILL LAY OUT A DEFENSE PLAN FOR YOU--AND ACT AS YOUR ALLY!

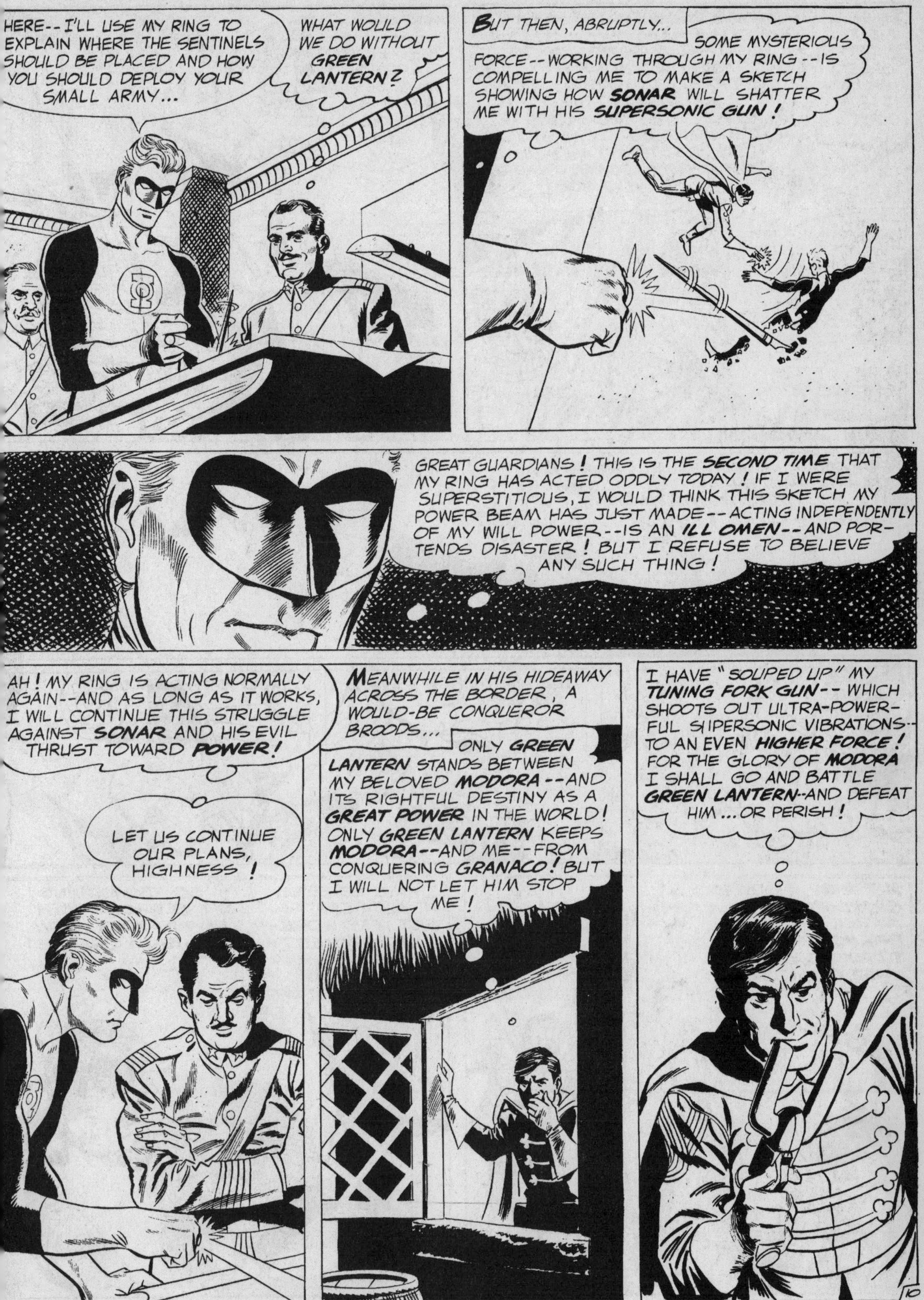
HERE--I'LL USE MY RING TO EXPLAIN WHERE THE SENTINELS SHOULD BE PLACED AND HOW YOU SHOULD DEPLOY YOUR SMALL ARMY...
WHAT WOULD WE DO WITHOUT GREEN LANTERN?
BUT THEN, ABRUPTLY...
SOME MYSTERIOUS FORCE--WORKING THROUGH MY RING--IS COMPELLING ME TO MAKE A SKETCH SHOWING HOW SONAR WILL SHATTER ME WITH HIS SUPERSONIC GUN!
GREAT GUARDIANS! THIS IS THE SECOND TIME THAT MY RING HAS ACTED ODDLY TODAY! IF I WERE SUPERSTITIOUS, I WOULD THINK THIS SKETCH MY POWER BEAM HAS JUST MADE--ACTING INDEPENDENTLY OF MY WILL POWER--IS AN ILL OMEN--AND PORTENDS DISASTER! BUT I REFUSE TO BELIEVE ANY SUCH THING!
AH! MY RING IS ACTING NORMALLY AGAIN--AND AS LONG AS IT WORKS, I WILL CONTINUE THIS STRUGGLE AGAINST SONAR AND HIS EVIL THRUST TOWARD POWER!
LET US CONTINUE OUR PLANS, HIGHNESS!
MEANWHILE IN HIS HIDEAWAY ACROSS THE BORDER, A WOULD-BE CONQUEROR BROODS...
ONLY GREEN LANTERN STANDS BETWEEN MY BELOVED MODORA--AND ITS RIGHTFUL DESTINY AS A GREAT POWER IN THE WORLD! ONLY GREEN LANTERN KEEPS MODORA--AND ME--FROM CONQUERING GRANACO! BUT I WILL NOT LET HIM STOP ME!
I HAVE "SOUPED UP" MY TUNING FORK GUN--WHICH SHOOTS OUT ULTRA-POWERFUL SUPERSONIC VIBRATIONS--TO AN EVEN HIGHER FORCE! FOR THE GLORY OF MODORA I SHALL GO AND BATTLE GREEN LANTERN--AND DEFEAT HIM...OR PERISH!
10

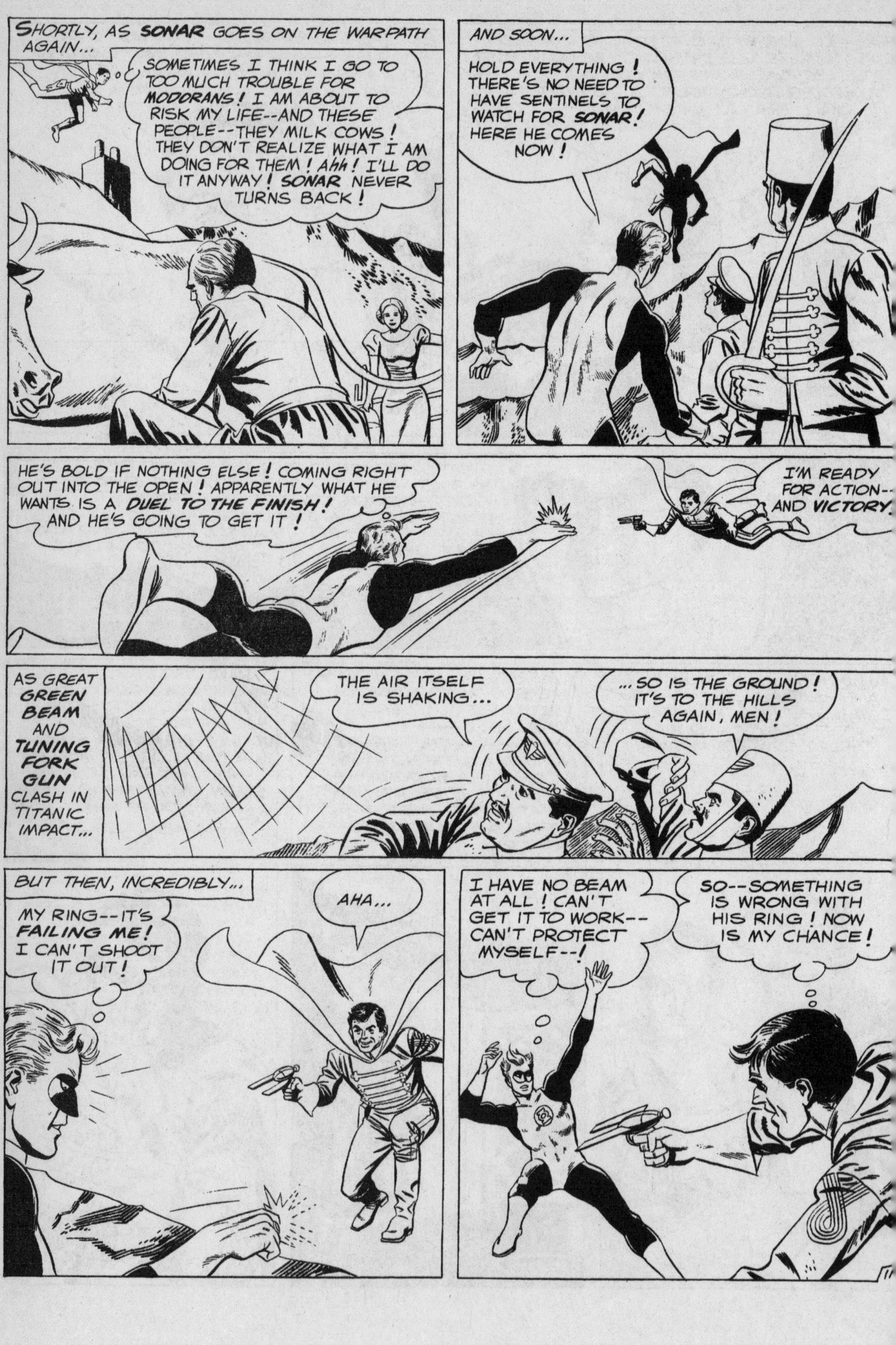
SHORTLY, AS SONAR GOES ON THE WARPATH AGAIN...
SOMETIMES I THINK I GO TO TOO MUCH TROUBLE FOR MODORANS! I AM ABOUT TO RISK MY LIFE--AND THESE PEOPLE--THEY MILK COWS! THEY DON'T REALIZE WHAT I AM DOING FOR THEM! Ahh! I'LL DO IT ANYWAY! SONAR NEVER TURNS BACK!
AND SOON...
HOLD EVERYTHING! THERE'S NO NEED TO HAVE SENTINELS TO WATCH FOR SONAR! HERE HE COMES NOW!
HE'S BOLD IF NOTHING ELSE! COMING RIGHT OUT INTO THE OPEN! APPARENTLY WHAT HE WANTS IS A DUEL TO THE FINISH! AND HE'S GOING TO GET IT!
I'M READY FOR ACTION--AND VICTORY!
AS GREAT GREEN BEAM AND TUNING FORK GUN CLASH IN TITANIC IMPACT...
THE AIR ITSELF IS SHAKING...
...SO IS THE GROUND! IT'S TO THE HILLS AGAIN, MEN!
BUT THEN, INCREDIBLY...
MY RING--IT'S FAILING ME! I CAN'T SHOOT IT OUT!
AHA...
I HAVE NO BEAM AT ALL! CAN'T GET IT TO WORK--CAN'T PROTECT MYSELF--!
SO--SOMETHING IS WRONG WITH HIS RING! NOW IS MY CHANCE!
11

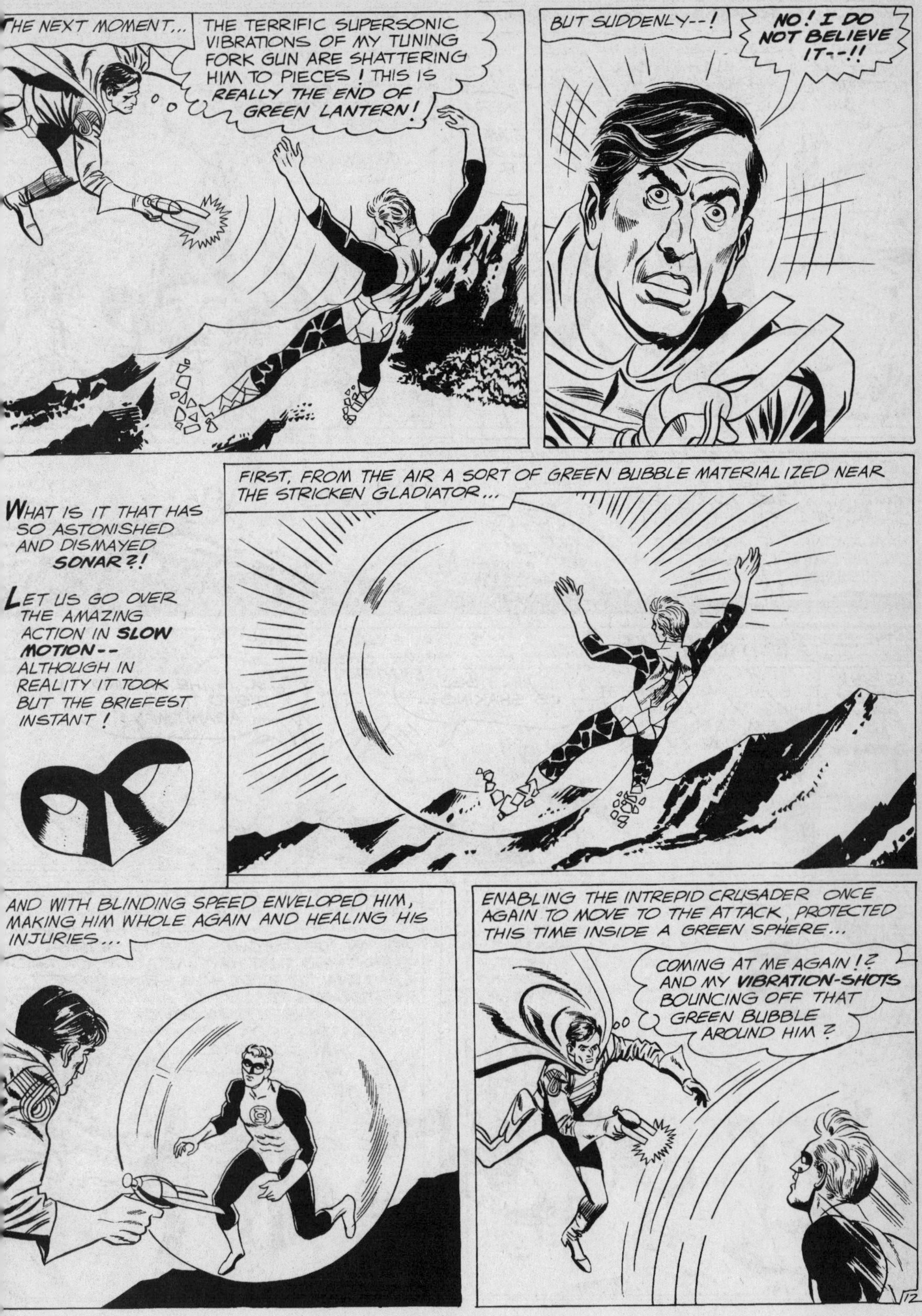
THE NEXT MOMENT...
THE TERRIFIC SUPERSONIC VIBRATIONS OF MY TUNING FORK GUN ARE SHATTERING HIM TO PIECES! THIS IS REALLY THE END OF GREEN LANTERN!
BUT SUDDENLY--!
NO! I DO NOT BELIEVE IT--!!
WHAT IS IT THAT HAS SO ASTONISHED AND DISMAYED SONAR?!
LET US GO OVER THE AMAZING ACTION IN SLOW MOTION--ALTHOUGH IN REALITY IT TOOK BUT THE BRIEFEST INSTANT!
FIRST, FROM THE AIR A SORT OF GREEN BUBBLE MATERIALIZED NEAR THE STRICKEN GLADIATOR...
AND WITH BLINDING SPEED ENVELOPED HIM, MAKING HIM WHOLE AGAIN AND HEALING HIS INJURIES...
ENABLING THE INTREPID CRUSADER ONCE AGAIN TO MOVE TO THE ATTACK, PROTECTED THIS TIME INSIDE A GREEN SPHERE...
COMING AT ME AGAIN!? AND MY VIBRATION-SHOTS BOUNCING OFF THAT GREEN BUBBLE AROUND HIM?
12

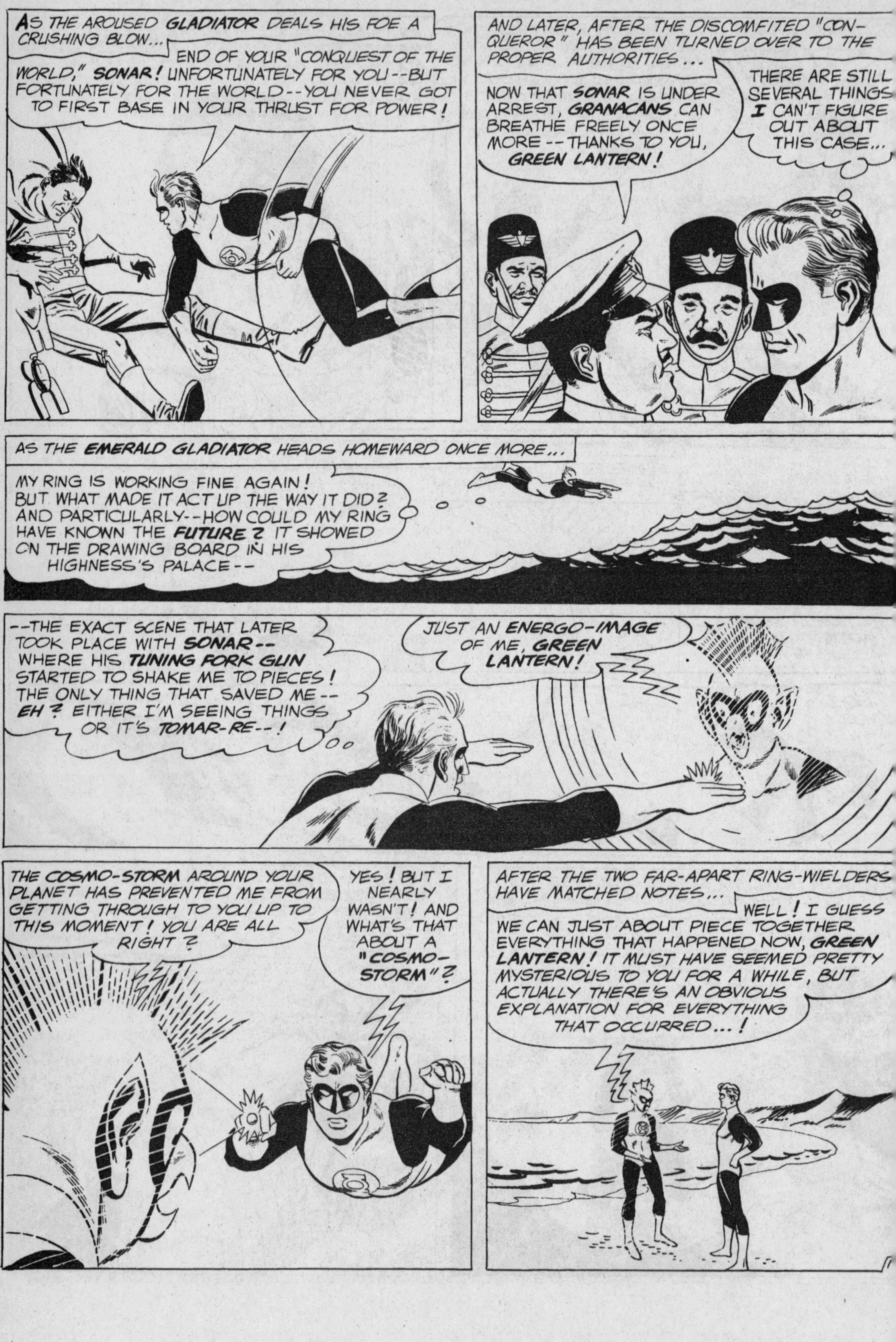
AS THE AROUSED GLADIATOR DEALS HIS FOE A CRUSHING BLOW...
END OF YOUR "CONQUEST OF THE WORLD," SONAR! UNFORTUNATELY FOR YOU--BUT FORTUNATELY FOR THE WORLD--YOU NEVER GOT TO FIRST BASE IN YOUR THRUST FOR POWER!
AND LATER, AFTER THE DISCOMFITED "CONQUEROR" HAS BEEN TURNED OVER TO THE PROPER AUTHORITIES...
NOW THAT SONAR IS UNDER ARREST, GRANACANS CAN BREATHE FREELY ONCE MORE--THANKS TO YOU, GREEN LANTERN!
THERE ARE STILL SEVERAL THINGS I CAN'T FIGURE OUT ABOUT THIS CASE...
AS THE EMERALD GLADIATOR HEADS HOMEWARD ONCE MORE...
MY RING IS WORKING FINE AGAIN! BUT WHAT MADE IT ACT UP THE WAY IT DID? AND PARTICULARLY--HOW COULD MY RING HAVE KNOWN THE FUTURE? IT SHOWED ON THE DRAWING BOARD IN HIS HIGHNESS'S PALACE--
--THE EXACT SCENE THAT LATER TOOK PLACE WITH SONAR--WHERE HIS TUNING FORK GUN STARTED TO SHAKE ME TO PIECES! THE ONLY THING THAT SAVED ME--EH? EITHER I'M SEEING THINGS OR IT'S TOMAR-RE--!
JUST AN ENERGO-IMAGE OF ME, GREEN LANTERN!
THE COSMO-STORM AROUND YOUR PLANET HAS PREVENTED ME FROM GETTING THROUGH TO YOU UP TO THIS MOMENT! YOU ARE ALL RIGHT?
YES! BUT I NEARLY WASN'T! AND WHAT'S THAT ABOUT A "COSMO-STORM"?
AFTER THE TWO FAR-APART RING-WIELDERS HAVE MATCHED NOTES...
WELL! I GUESS WE CAN JUST ABOUT PIECE TOGETHER EVERYTHING THAT HAPPENED NOW, GREEN LANTERN! IT MUST HAVE SEEMED PRETTY MYSTERIOUS TO YOU FOR A WHILE, BUT ACTUALLY THERE'S AN OBVIOUS EXPLANATION FOR EVERYTHING THAT OCCURRED...!

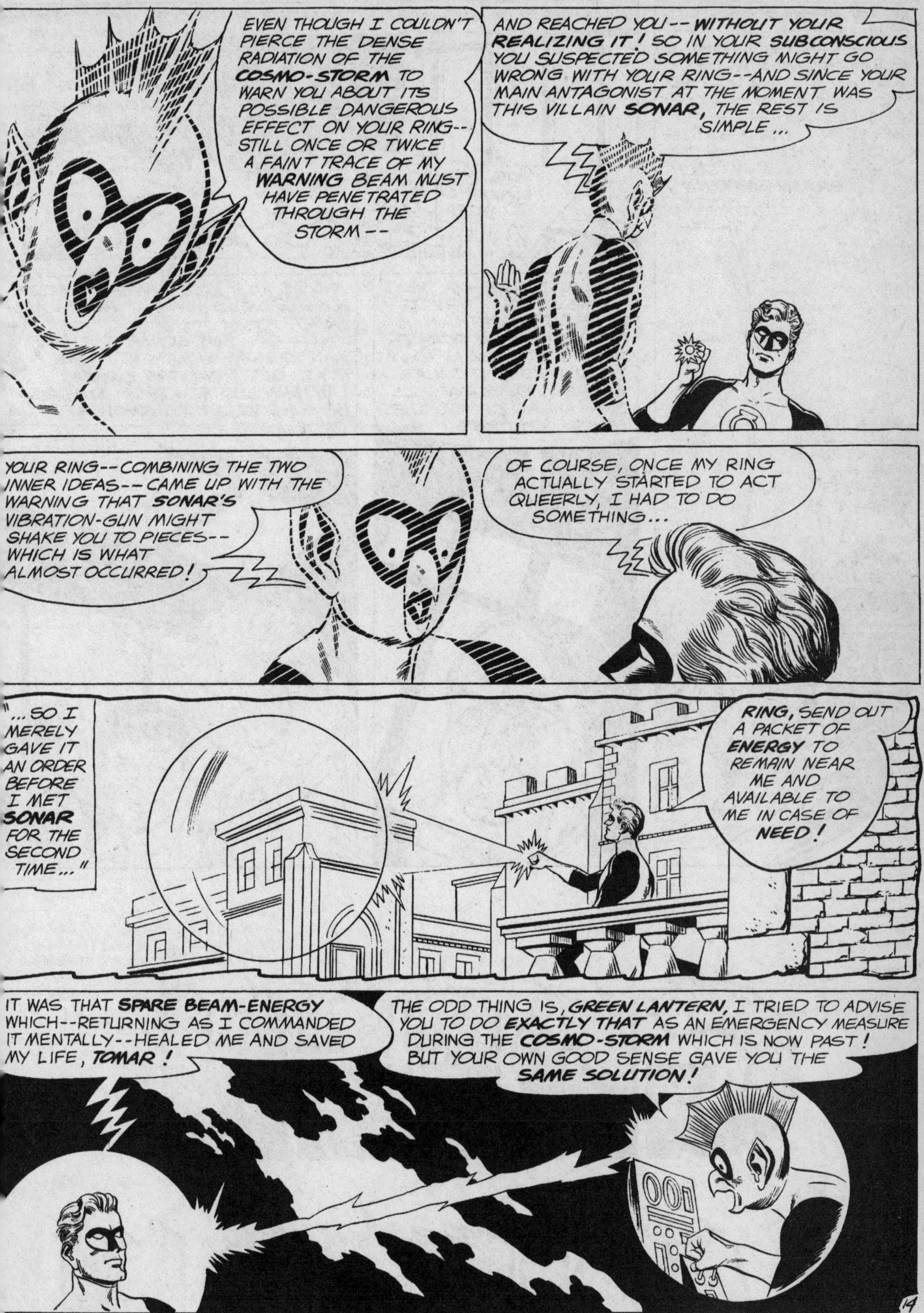
EVEN THOUGH I COULDN'T PIERCE THE DENSE RADIATION OF THE COSMO-STORM TO WARN YOU ABOUT ITS POSSIBLE DANGEROUS EFFECT ON YOUR RING--STILL ONCE OR TWICE A FAINT TRACE OF MY WARNING BEAM MUST HAVE PENETRATED THROUGH THE STORM--
AND REACHED YOU--WITHOUT YOUR REALIZING IT! SO IN YOUR SUBCONSCIOUS YOU SUSPECTED SOMETHING MIGHT GO WRONG WITH YOUR RING--AND SINCE YOUR MAIN ANTAGONIST AT THE MOMENT WAS THIS VILLAIN SONAR, THE REST IS SIMPLE...
YOUR RING--COMBINING THE TWO INNER IDEAS--CAME UP WITH THE WARNING THAT SONAR'S VIBRATION-GUN MIGHT SHAKE YOU TO PIECES--WHICH IS WHAT ALMOST OCCURRED!
OF COURSE, ONCE MY RING ACTUALLY STARTED TO ACT QUEERLY, I HAD TO DO SOMETHING...
"...SO I MERELY GAVE IT AN ORDER BEFORE I MET SONAR FOR THE SECOND TIME..."
RING, SEND OUT A PACKET OF ENERGY TO REMAIN NEAR ME AND AVAILABLE TO ME IN CASE OF NEED!
IT WAS THAT SPARE BEAM-ENERGY WHICH--RETURNING AS I COMMANDED IT MENTALLY--HEALED ME AND SAVED MY LIFE, TOMAR!
THE ODD THING IS, GREEN LANTERN, I TRIED TO ADVISE YOU TO DO EXACTLY THAT AS AN EMERGENCY MEASURE DURING THE COSMO-STORM WHICH IS NOW PAST! BUT YOUR OWN GOOD SENSE GAVE YOU THE SAME SOLUTION!
14

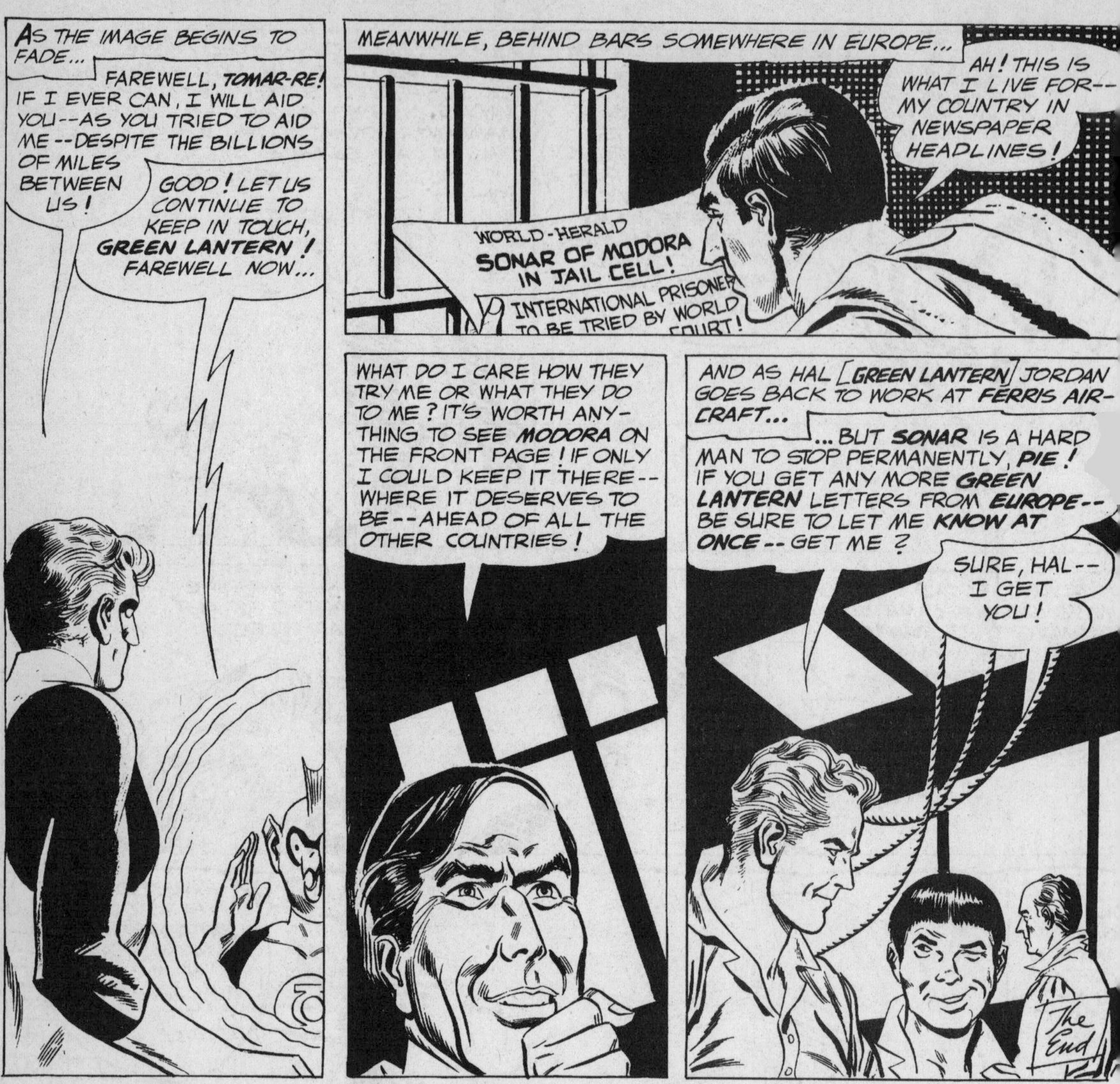
AS THE IMAGE BEGINS TO FADE...
FAREWELL, TOMAR-RE! IF I EVER CAN, I WILL AID YOU--AS YOU TRIED TO AID ME--DESPITE THE BILLIONS OF MILES BETWEEN US!
GOOD! LET US CONTINUE TO KEEP IN TOUCH, GREEN LANTERN! FAREWELL NOW...
MEANWHILE, BEHIND BARS SOMEWHERE IN EUROPE...
AH! THIS IS WHAT I LIVE FOR--MY COUNTRY IN NEWSPAPER HEADLINES!
WORLD-HERALD
SONAR OF MODORA IN JAIL CELL!
INTERNATIONAL PRISONER TO BE TRIED BY WORLD COURT!
WHAT DO I CARE HOW THEY TRY ME OR WHAT THEY DO TO ME? IT'S WORTH ANYTHING TO SEE MODORA ON THE FRONT PAGE! IF ONLY I COULD KEEP IT THERE--WHERE IT DESERVES TO BE--AHEAD OF ALL THE OTHER COUNTRIES!
AND AS HAL [GREEN LANTERN] JORDAN GOES BACK TO WORK AT FERRIS AIRCRAFT...
...BUT SONAR IS A HARD MAN TO STOP PERMANENTLY, PIE! IF YOU GET ANY MORE GREEN LANTERN LETTERS FROM EUROPE--BE SURE TO LET ME KNOW AT ONCE--GET ME?
SURE, HAL--I GET YOU!
The End

GREEN LANTERN

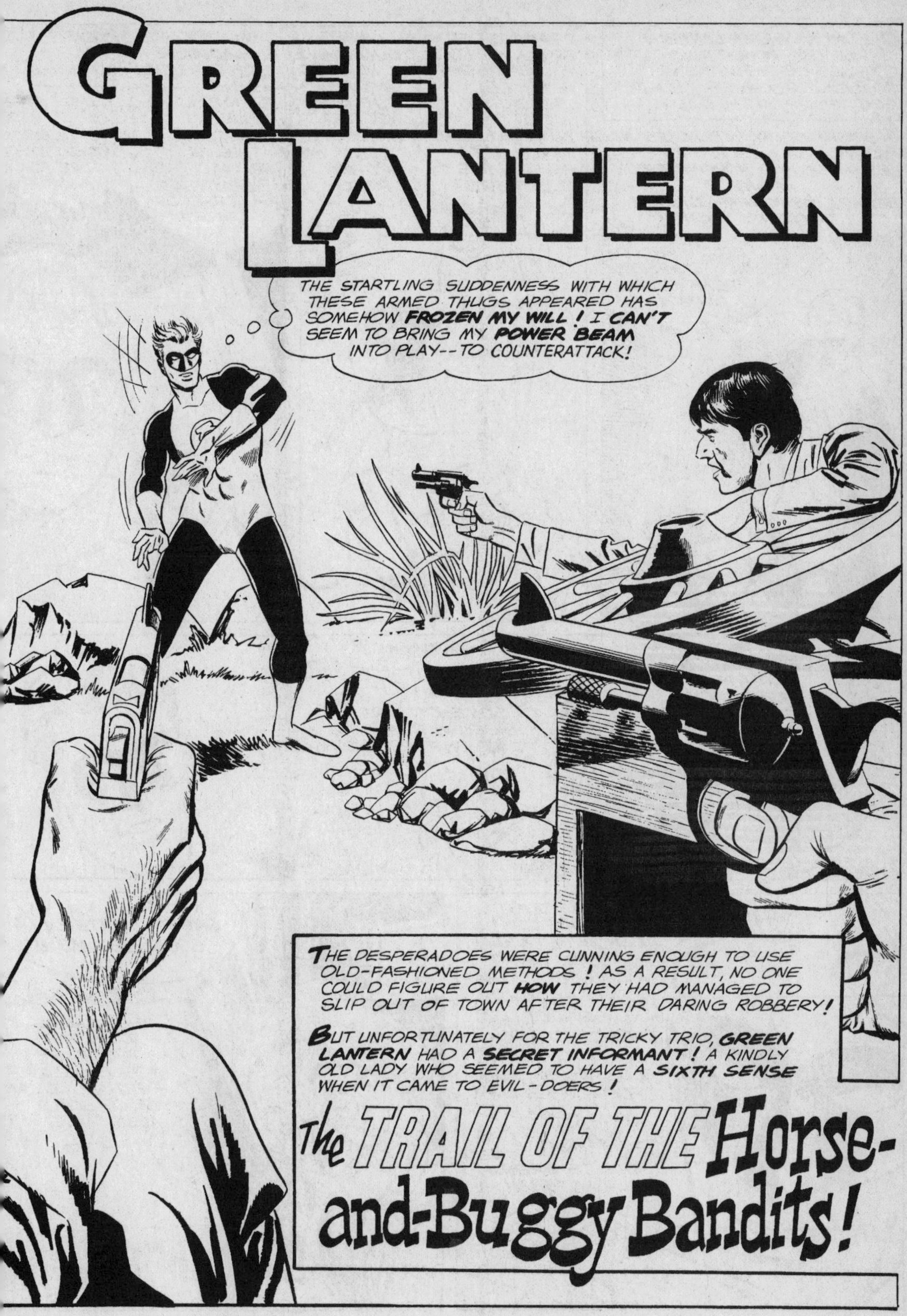
GREEN LANTERN
THE STARTLING SUDDENNESS WITH WHICH THESE ARMED THUGS APPEARED HAS SOMEHOW FROZEN MY WILL! I CAN'T SEEM TO BRING MY POWER BEAM INTO PLAY--TO COUNTERATTACK!
THE DESPERADOES WERE CUNNING ENOUGH TO USE OLD-FASHIONED METHODS! AS A RESULT, NO ONE COULD FIGURE OUT HOW THEY HAD MANAGED TO SLIP OUT OF TOWN AFTER THEIR DARING ROBBERY!
BUT UNFORTUNATELY FOR THE TRICKY TRIO, GREEN LANTERN HAD A SECRET INFORMANT! A KINDLY OLD LADY WHO SEEMED TO HAVE A SIXTH SENSE WHEN IT CAME TO EVIL-DOERS!
The TRAIL OF THE Horse-and-Buggy Bandits!

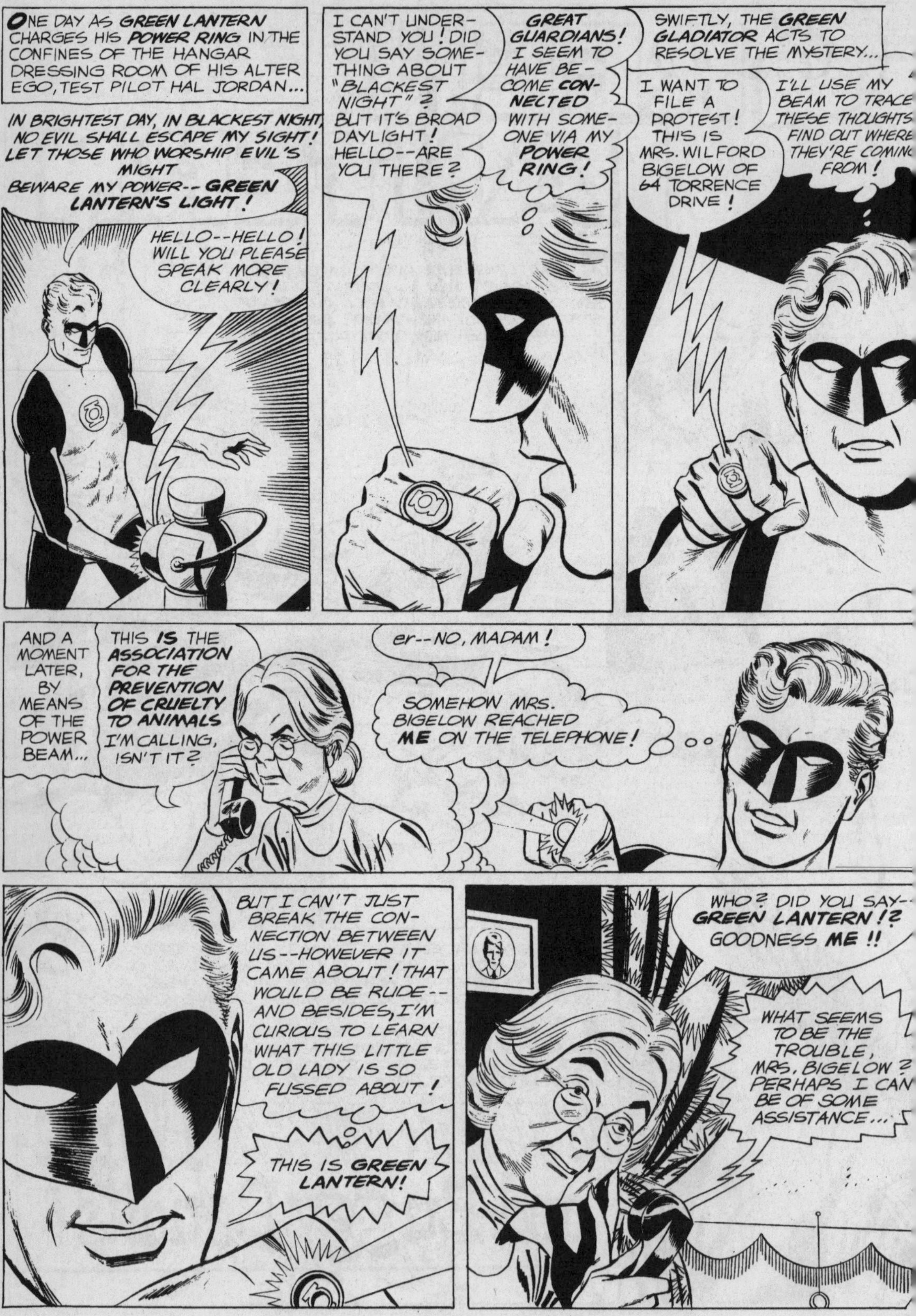
ONE DAY AS GREEN LANTERN CHARGES HIS POWER RING IN THE CONFINES OF THE HANGAR DRESSING ROOM OF HIS ALTER EGO, TEST PILOT HAL JORDAN...
IN BRIGHTEST DAY, IN BLACKEST NIGHT, NO EVIL SHALL ESCAPE MY SIGHT! LET THOSE WHO WORSHIP EVIL'S MIGHT BEWARE MY POWER-- GREEN LANTERN'S LIGHT!
HELLO--HELLO! WILL YOU PLEASE SPEAK MORE CLEARLY!
I CAN'T UNDERSTAND YOU! DID YOU SAY SOMETHING ABOUT "BLACKEST NIGHT"? BUT IT'S BROAD DAYLIGHT! HELLO--ARE YOU THERE?
GREAT GUARDIANS! I SEEM TO HAVE BECOME CONNECTED WITH SOMEONE VIA MY POWER RING!
SWIFTLY, THE GREEN GLADIATOR ACTS TO RESOLVE THE MYSTERY...
I WANT TO FILE A PROTEST! THIS IS MRS. WILFORD BIGELOW OF 64 TORRENCE DRIVE!
I'LL USE MY BEAM TO TRACE THESE THOUGHTS FIND OUT WHERE THEY'RE COMING FROM!
AND A MOMENT LATER, BY MEANS OF THE POWER BEAM...
THIS IS THE ASSOCIATION FOR THE PREVENTION OF CRUELTY TO ANIMALS I'M CALLING, ISN'T IT?
er--NO, MADAM!
SOMEHOW MRS. BIGELOW REACHED ME ON THE TELEPHONE!
BUT I CAN'T JUST BREAK THE CONNECTION BETWEEN US--HOWEVER IT CAME ABOUT! THAT WOULD BE RUDE--AND BESIDES, I'M CURIOUS TO LEARN WHAT THIS LITTLE OLD LADY IS SO FUSSED ABOUT!
THIS IS GREEN LANTERN!
WHO? DID YOU SAY--GREEN LANTERN!? GOODNESS ME!!
WHAT SEEMS TO BE THE TROUBLE, MRS. BIGELOW? PERHAPS I CAN BE OF SOME ASSISTANCE...

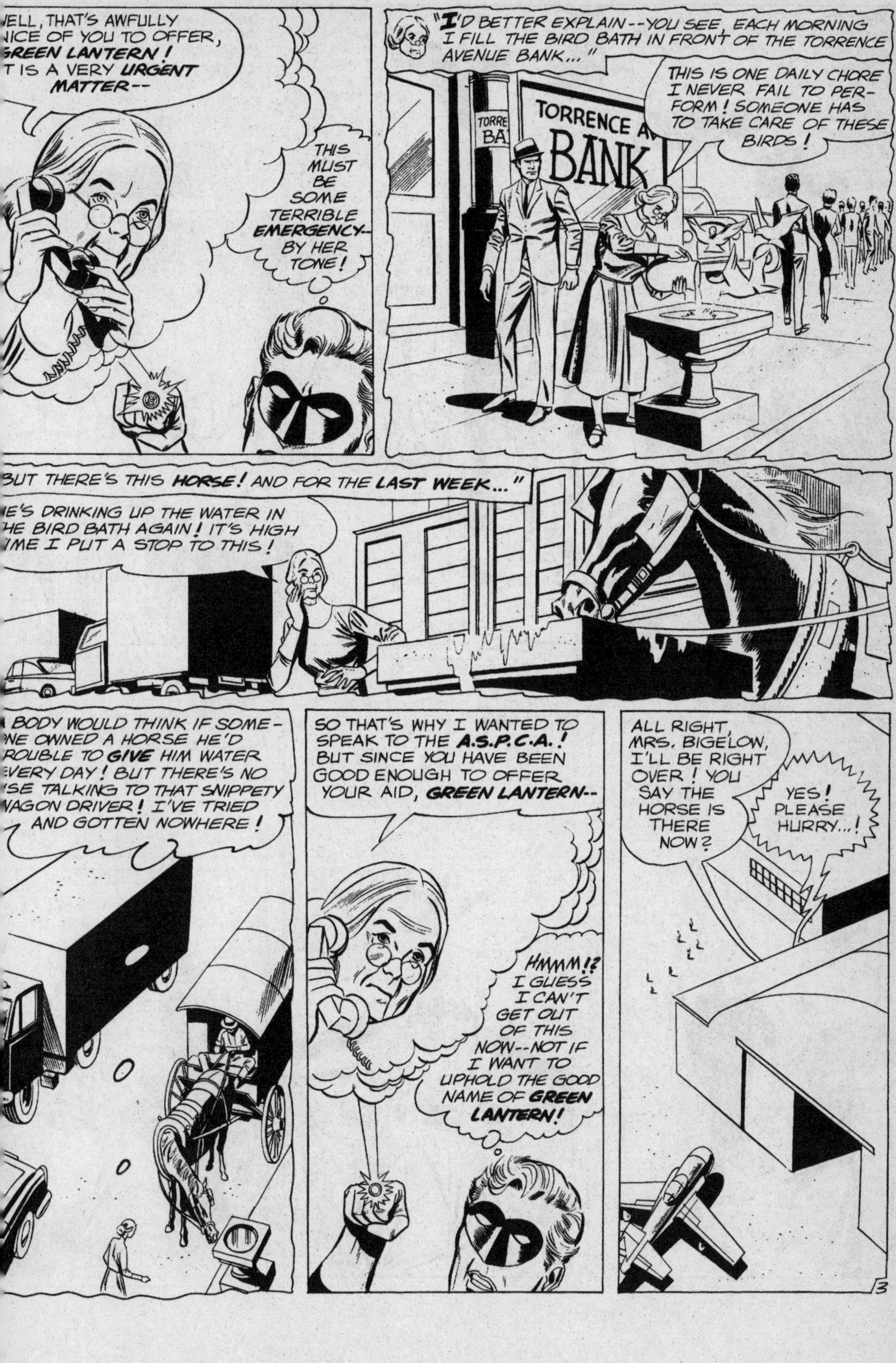
WELL, THAT'S AWFULLY NICE OF YOU TO OFFER, GREEN LANTERN! IT IS A VERY URGENT MATTER--
THIS MUST BE SOME TERRIBLE EMERGENCY-- BY HER TONE!
"I'D BETTER EXPLAIN--YOU SEE, EACH MORNING I FILL THE BIRD BATH IN FRONT OF THE TORRENCE AVENUE BANK..."
TORRENCE AV BANK
TORRE BA
THIS IS ONE DAILY CHORE I NEVER FAIL TO PERFORM! SOMEONE HAS TO TAKE CARE OF THESE BIRDS!
"BUT THERE'S THIS HORSE! AND FOR THE LAST WEEK..."
HE'S DRINKING UP THE WATER IN THE BIRD BATH AGAIN! IT'S HIGH TIME I PUT A STOP TO THIS!
A BODY WOULD THINK IF SOMEONE OWNED A HORSE HE'D TROUBLE TO GIVE HIM WATER EVERY DAY! BUT THERE'S NO USE TALKING TO THAT SNIPPETY WAGON DRIVER! I'VE TRIED AND GOTTEN NOWHERE!
SO THAT'S WHY I WANTED TO SPEAK TO THE A.S.P.C.A.! BUT SINCE YOU HAVE BEEN GOOD ENOUGH TO OFFER YOUR AID, GREEN LANTERN--
HMMM!? I GUESS I CAN'T GET OUT OF THIS NOW--NOT IF I WANT TO UPHOLD THE GOOD NAME OF GREEN LANTERN!
ALL RIGHT, MRS. BIGELOW, I'LL BE RIGHT OVER! YOU SAY THE HORSE IS THERE NOW?
YES! PLEASE HURRY...!
3

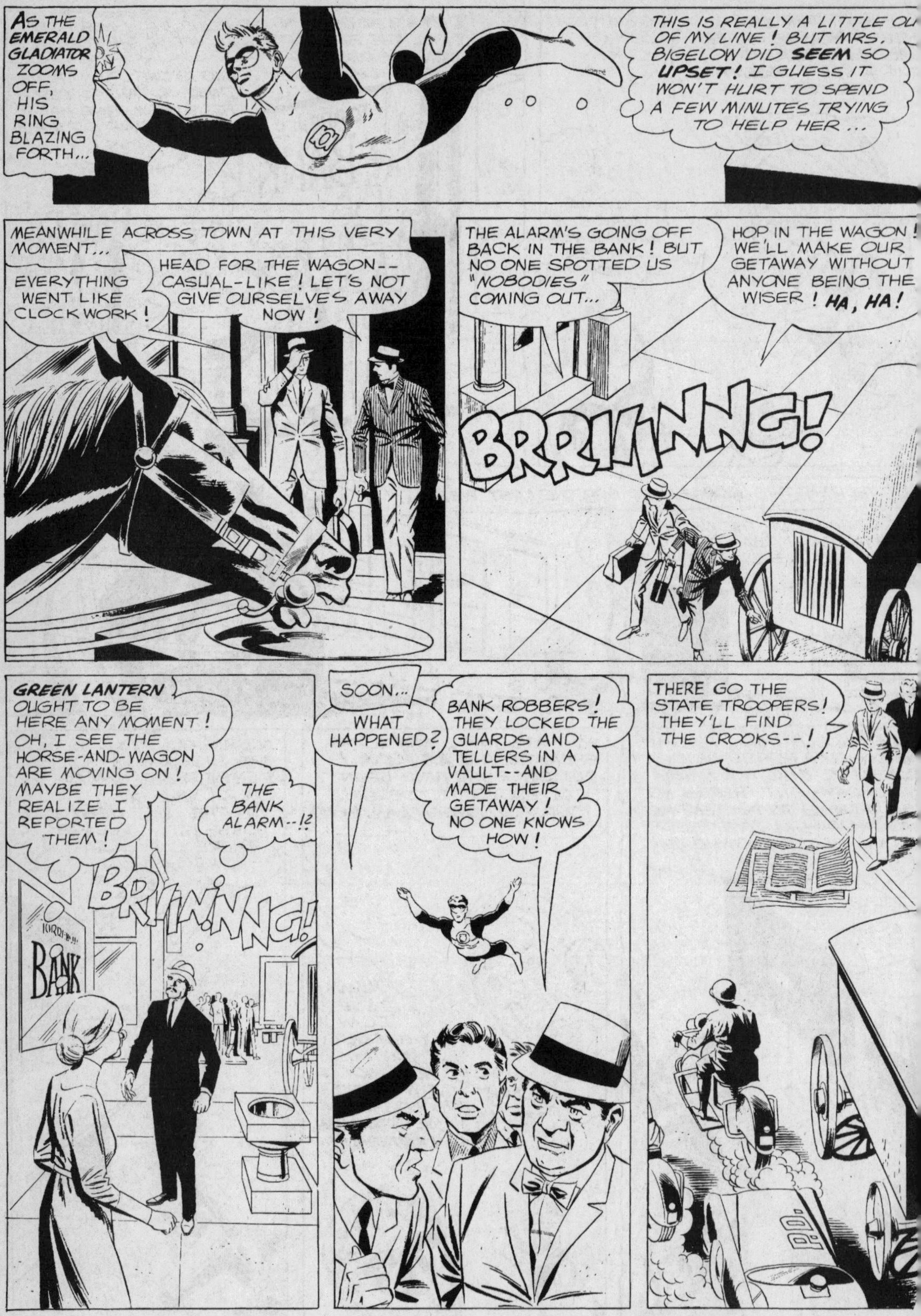
AS THE EMERALD GLADIATOR ZOOMS OFF, HIS RING BLAZING FORTH...
THIS IS REALLY A LITTLE OU OF MY LINE! BUT MRS. BIGELOW DID SEEM SO UPSET! I GUESS IT WON'T HURT TO SPEND A FEW MINUTES TRYING TO HELP HER...
MEANWHILE ACROSS TOWN AT THIS VERY MOMENT...
EVERYTHING WENT LIKE CLOCKWORK!
HEAD FOR THE WAGON-- CASUAL-LIKE! LET'S NOT GIVE OURSELVES AWAY NOW!
THE ALARM'S GOING OFF BACK IN THE BANK! BUT NO ONE SPOTTED US "NOBODIES" COMING OUT...
HOP IN THE WAGON! WE'LL MAKE OUR GETAWAY WITHOUT ANYONE BEING THE WISER! HA, HA!
BRRIIINNG!
GREEN LANTERN OUGHT TO BE HERE ANY MOMENT! OH, I SEE THE HORSE-AND-WAGON ARE MOVING ON! MAYBE THEY REALIZE I REPORTED THEM!
THE BANK ALARM--!?
BRIIINNG!
BANK
SOON...
WHAT HAPPENED?
BANK ROBBERS! THEY LOCKED THE GUARDS AND TELLERS IN A VAULT--AND MADE THEIR GETAWAY! NO ONE KNOWS HOW!
THERE GO THE STATE TROOPERS! THEY'LL FIND THE CROOKS--!

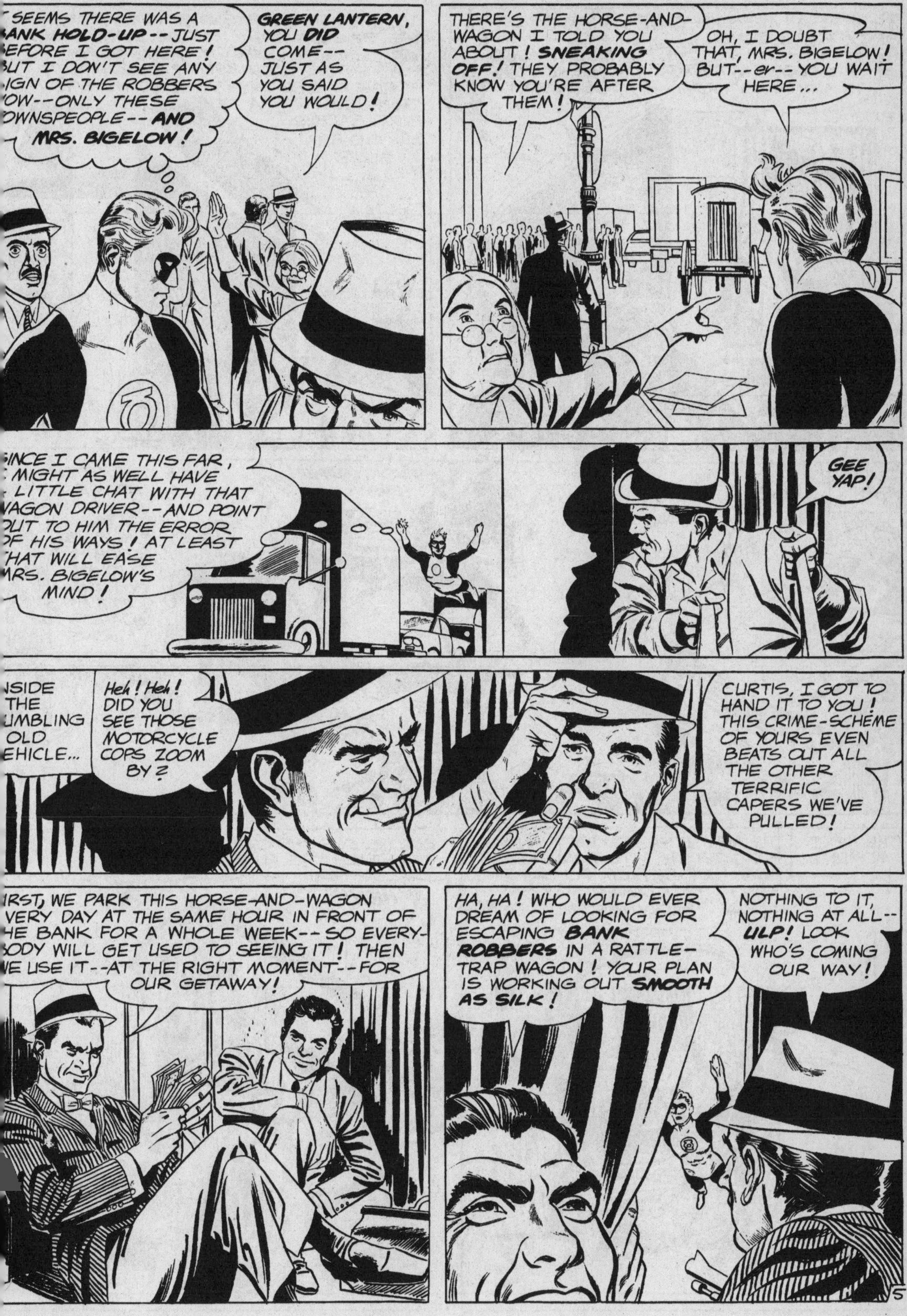
T SEEMS THERE WAS A BANK HOLD-UP--JUST BEFORE I GOT HERE! BUT I DON'T SEE ANY SIGN OF THE ROBBERS NOW--ONLY THESE TOWNSPEOPLE--AND MRS. BIGELOW!
GREEN LANTERN, YOU DID COME--JUST AS YOU SAID YOU WOULD!
THERE'S THE HORSE-AND-WAGON I TOLD YOU ABOUT! SNEAKING OFF! THEY PROBABLY KNOW YOU'RE AFTER THEM!
OH, I DOUBT THAT, MRS. BIGELOW! BUT--er--YOU WAIT HERE...
SINCE I CAME THIS FAR, I MIGHT AS WELL HAVE A LITTLE CHAT WITH THAT WAGON DRIVER--AND POINT OUT TO HIM THE ERROR OF HIS WAYS! AT LEAST THAT WILL EASE MRS. BIGELOW'S MIND!
GEE YAP!
INSIDE THE RUMBLING OLD VEHICLE...
Heh! Heh! DID YOU SEE THOSE MOTORCYCLE COPS ZOOM BY?
CURTIS, I GOT TO HAND IT TO YOU! THIS CRIME-SCHEME OF YOURS EVEN BEATS OUT ALL THE OTHER TERRIFIC CAPERS WE'VE PULLED!
FIRST, WE PARK THIS HORSE-AND-WAGON EVERY DAY AT THE SAME HOUR IN FRONT OF THE BANK FOR A WHOLE WEEK--SO EVERYBODY WILL GET USED TO SEEING IT! THEN WE USE IT--AT THE RIGHT MOMENT--FOR OUR GETAWAY!
HA, HA! WHO WOULD EVER DREAM OF LOOKING FOR ESCAPING BANK ROBBERS IN A RATTLE-TRAP WAGON! YOUR PLAN IS WORKING OUT SMOOTH AS SILK!
NOTHING TO IT, NOTHING AT ALL--ULP! LOOK WHO'S COMING OUR WAY!
5

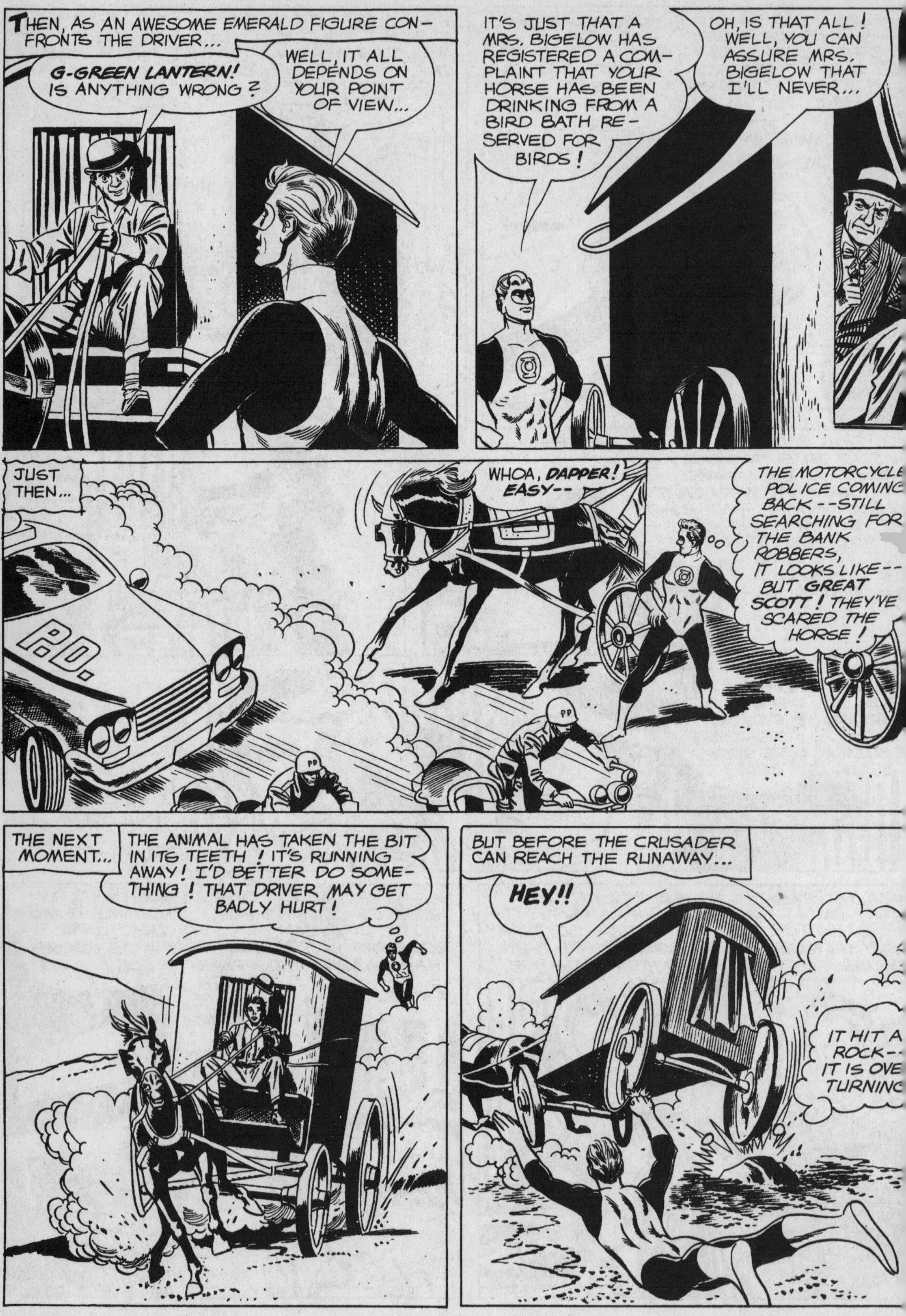
THEN, AS AN AWESOME EMERALD FIGURE CONFRONTS THE DRIVER...
G-GREEN LANTERN! IS ANYTHING WRONG?
WELL, IT ALL DEPENDS ON YOUR POINT OF VIEW...
IT'S JUST THAT A MRS. BIGELOW HAS REGISTERED A COMPLAINT THAT YOUR HORSE HAS BEEN DRINKING FROM A BIRD BATH RESERVED FOR BIRDS!
OH, IS THAT ALL! WELL, YOU CAN ASSURE MRS. BIGELOW THAT I'LL NEVER...
JUST THEN...
WHOA, DAPPER! EASY--
THE MOTORCYCLE POLICE COMING BACK--STILL SEARCHING FOR THE BANK ROBBERS, IT LOOKS LIKE--BUT GREAT SCOTT! THEY'VE SCARED THE HORSE!
P.D.
THE NEXT MOMENT...
THE ANIMAL HAS TAKEN THE BIT IN ITS TEETH! IT'S RUNNING AWAY! I'D BETTER DO SOMETHING! THAT DRIVER MAY GET BADLY HURT!
BUT BEFORE THE CRUSADER CAN REACH THE RUNAWAY...
HEY!!
IT HIT A ROCK--IT IS OVE TURNING

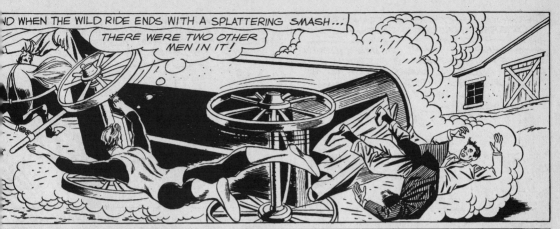

...ND WHEN THE WILD RIDE ENDS WITH A SPLATTERING SMASH...

THERE WERE TWO OTHER MEN IN IT!

...ITHOUT DELAY, THE SCATTERED CROOKS OPEN FIRE ON A TOTALLY-UNSUSPECTING **GREEN LANTERN**...

FIRING AT ME-- ...ROM THREE DIFFERENT DIRECTIONS! HH--! THE SUDDENNESS OF IT-- ...AVING A **PARALYZING EFFECT** ...N MY WILL! I CAN'T SEEM TO ...ET MY RING INTO ACTION TO ...EFEND MYSELF--!

POW! POW! POW!

...J A SPLIT ...ECOND, THE ...SUALLY- ...ASTERFUL ...LADIATOR SEES DEATH ...LINGING AT HIM...

I KNOW NOW WHAT PEOPLE MEAN WHEN THEY SAY THEY "FROZE IN PLACE" FACING A MENACE! I--I SEEM ABSOLUTELY TURNED TO **STONE!** AND NO TIME TO BREAK THE SPELL --

ZIIP!

VIIP!

ZING!

...HEN, WITH BLINDING SPEED, INCREDIBLY...

...whew!! I ALMOST FORGOT...THAT AS LONG ...S IT'S **CHARGED**... MY **POWER RING** IN AN ...MERGENCY WILL ACT BY **ITSELF** TO PRO-TECT ME FROM **FATAL HARM**...

VVIP! SPLAT! VIIP!

MY RING CREATED THAT **CONCRETE-BLOCK BARRICADE** IN THE NICK OF TIME! BUT I DON'T NEED IT ANYMORE! THE PARALYSIS IS GONE! I CAN MOVE AGAIN-- AS THOSE THUGS ARE ABOUT TO FIND OUT!

MAKE A DASH FOR THAT BARN!

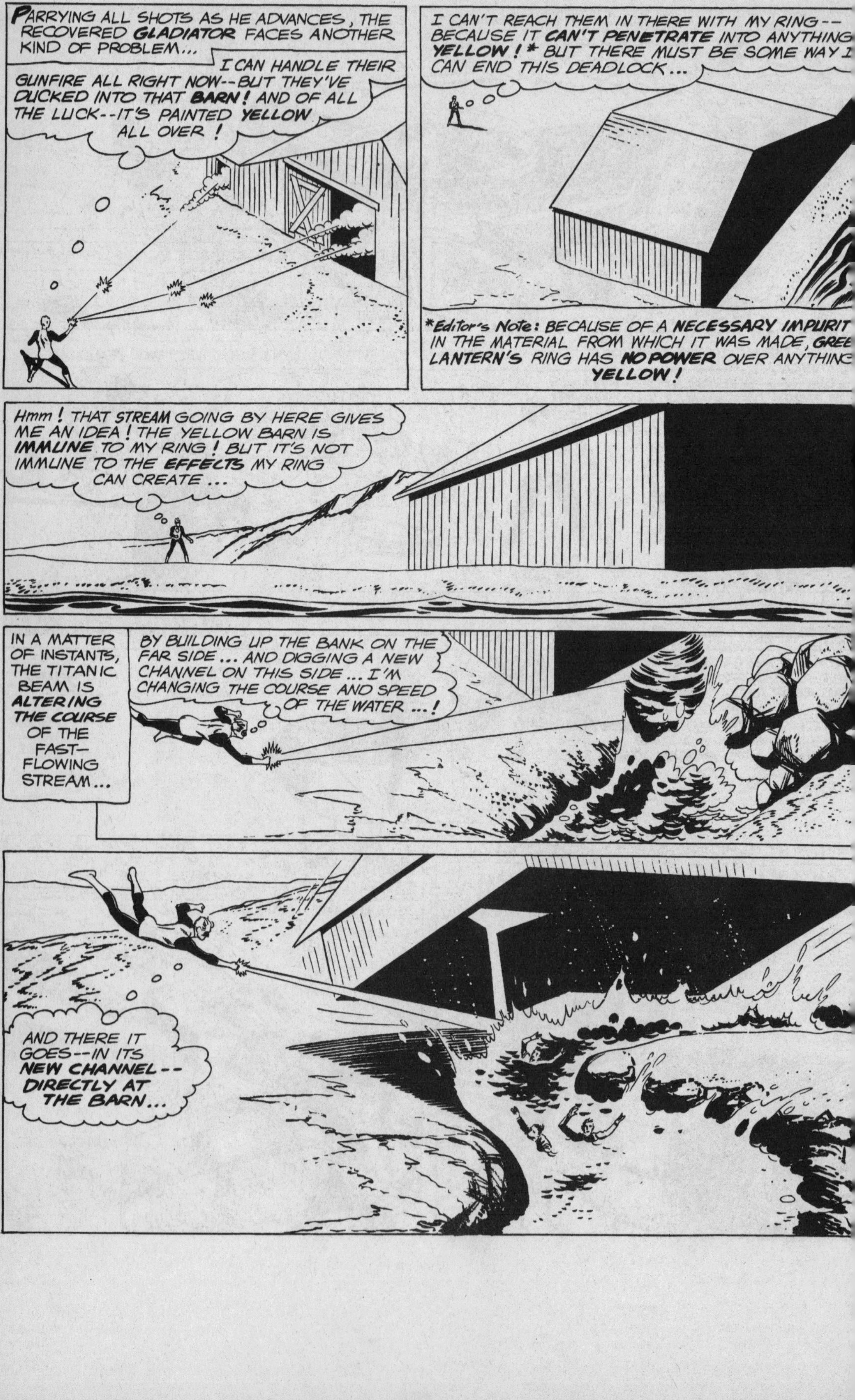

PARRYING ALL SHOTS AS HE ADVANCES, THE RECOVERED GLADIATOR FACES ANOTHER KIND OF PROBLEM...
I CAN HANDLE THEIR GUNFIRE ALL RIGHT NOW--BUT THEY'VE DUCKED INTO THAT BARN! AND OF ALL THE LUCK--IT'S PAINTED YELLOW ALL OVER!
I CAN'T REACH THEM IN THERE WITH MY RING--BECAUSE IT CAN'T PENETRATE INTO ANYTHING YELLOW!* BUT THERE MUST BE SOME WAY I CAN END THIS DEADLOCK...
*Editor's Note: BECAUSE OF A NECESSARY IMPURIT IN THE MATERIAL FROM WHICH IT WAS MADE, GREE LANTERN'S RING HAS NO POWER OVER ANYTHIN YELLOW!
Hmm! THAT STREAM GOING BY HERE GIVES ME AN IDEA! THE YELLOW BARN IS IMMUNE TO MY RING! BUT IT'S NOT IMMUNE TO THE EFFECTS MY RING CAN CREATE...
IN A MATTER OF INSTANTS, THE TITANIC BEAM IS ALTERING THE COURSE OF THE FAST-FLOWING STREAM...
BY BUILDING UP THE BANK ON THE FAR SIDE... AND DIGGING A NEW CHANNEL ON THIS SIDE... I'M CHANGING THE COURSE AND SPEED OF THE WATER...!
AND THERE IT GOES--IN ITS NEW CHANNEL--DIRECTLY AT THE BARN...

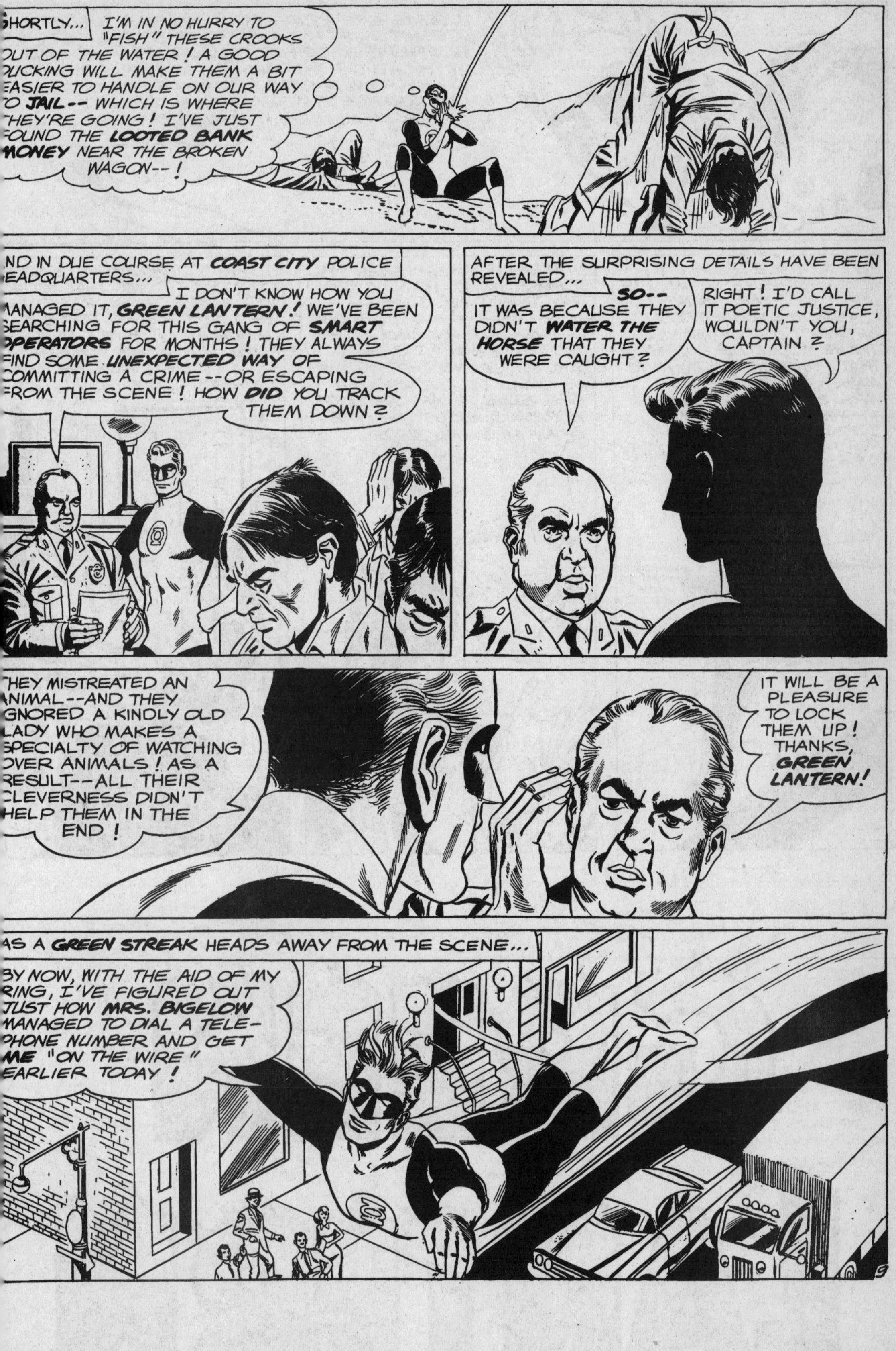
SHORTLY...
I'M IN NO HURRY TO "FISH" THESE CROOKS OUT OF THE WATER! A GOOD DUCKING WILL MAKE THEM A BIT EASIER TO HANDLE ON OUR WAY TO JAIL-- WHICH IS WHERE THEY'RE GOING! I'VE JUST FOUND THE LOOTED BANK MONEY NEAR THE BROKEN WAGON--!
AND IN DUE COURSE AT COAST CITY POLICE HEADQUARTERS...
I DON'T KNOW HOW YOU MANAGED IT, GREEN LANTERN! WE'VE BEEN SEARCHING FOR THIS GANG OF SMART OPERATORS FOR MONTHS! THEY ALWAYS FIND SOME UNEXPECTED WAY OF COMMITTING A CRIME--OR ESCAPING FROM THE SCENE! HOW DID YOU TRACK THEM DOWN?
AFTER THE SURPRISING DETAILS HAVE BEEN REVEALED...
SO-- IT WAS BECAUSE THEY DIDN'T WATER THE HORSE THAT THEY WERE CAUGHT?
RIGHT! I'D CALL IT POETIC JUSTICE, WOULDN'T YOU, CAPTAIN?
THEY MISTREATED AN ANIMAL--AND THEY IGNORED A KINDLY OLD LADY WHO MAKES A SPECIALTY OF WATCHING OVER ANIMALS! AS A RESULT--ALL THEIR CLEVERNESS DIDN'T HELP THEM IN THE END!
IT WILL BE A PLEASURE TO LOCK THEM UP! THANKS, GREEN LANTERN!
AS A GREEN STREAK HEADS AWAY FROM THE SCENE...
BY NOW, WITH THE AID OF MY RING, I'VE FIGURED OUT JUST HOW MRS. BIGELOW MANAGED TO DIAL A TELEPHONE NUMBER AND GET ME "ON THE WIRE" EARLIER TODAY!
9

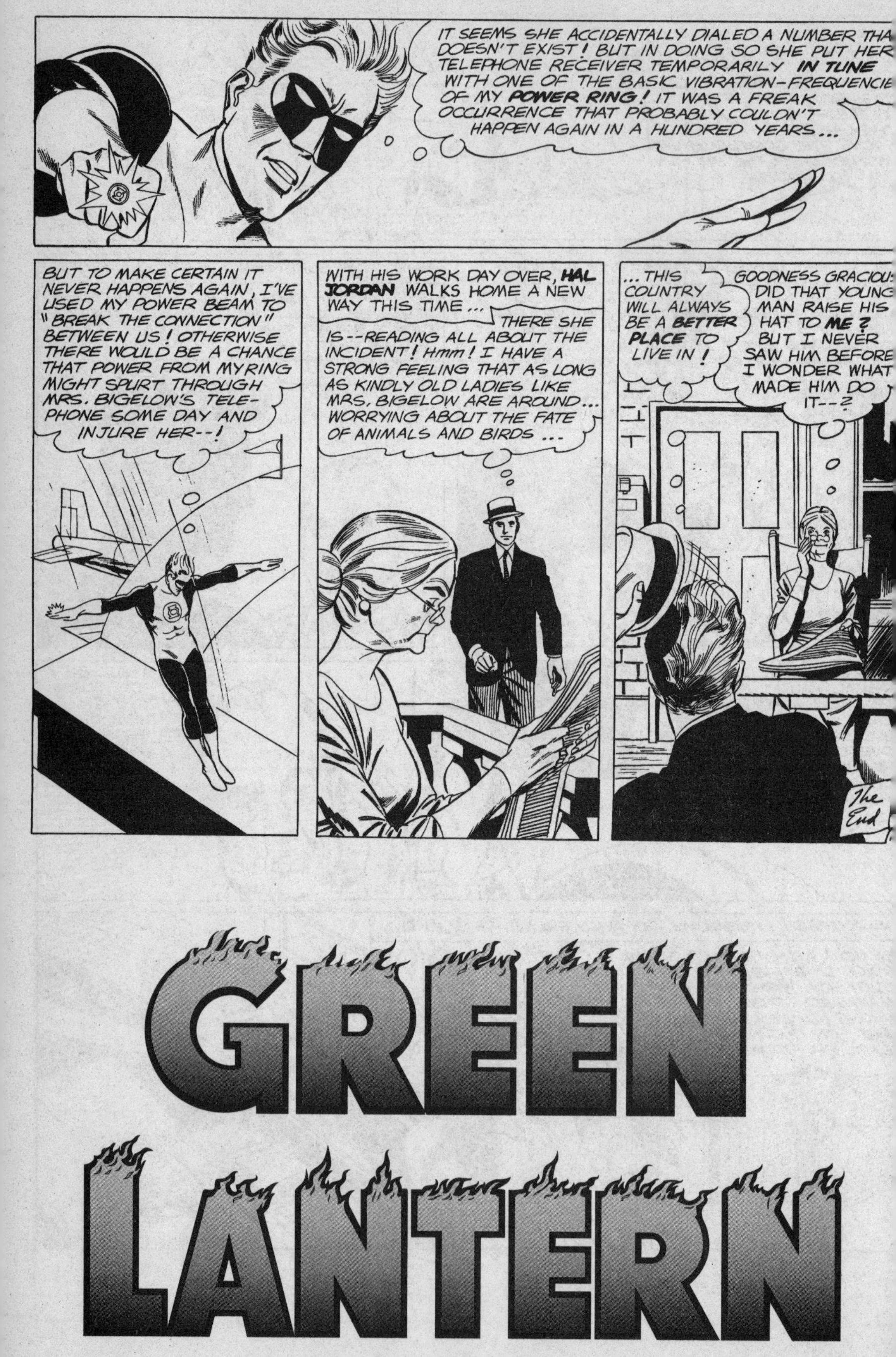
IT SEEMS SHE ACCIDENTALLY DIALED A NUMBER THA
DOESN'T EXIST! BUT IN DOING SO SHE PUT HER
TELEPHONE RECEIVER TEMPORARILY IN TUNE
WITH ONE OF THE BASIC VIBRATION-FREQUENCIE
OF MY POWER RING! IT WAS A FREAK
OCCURRENCE THAT PROBABLY COULDN'T
HAPPEN AGAIN IN A HUNDRED YEARS...
BUT TO MAKE CERTAIN IT NEVER HAPPENS AGAIN, I'VE USED MY POWER BEAM TO "BREAK THE CONNECTION" BETWEEN US! OTHERWISE THERE WOULD BE A CHANCE THAT POWER FROM MY RING MIGHT SPURT THROUGH MRS. BIGELOW'S TELE-PHONE SOME DAY AND INJURE HER--!
WITH HIS WORK DAY OVER, HAL JORDAN WALKS HOME A NEW WAY THIS TIME...
THERE SHE IS--READING ALL ABOUT THE INCIDENT! Hmm! I HAVE A STRONG FEELING THAT AS LONG AS KINDLY OLD LADIES LIKE MRS. BIGELOW ARE AROUND... WORRYING ABOUT THE FATE OF ANIMALS AND BIRDS...
...THIS COUNTRY WILL ALWAYS BE A BETTER PLACE TO LIVE IN!
GOODNESS GRACIOU DID THAT YOUNG MAN RAISE HIS HAT TO ME? BUT I NEVER SAW HIM BEFORE I WONDER WHAT MADE HIM DO IT--?
The End

GREEN LANTERN

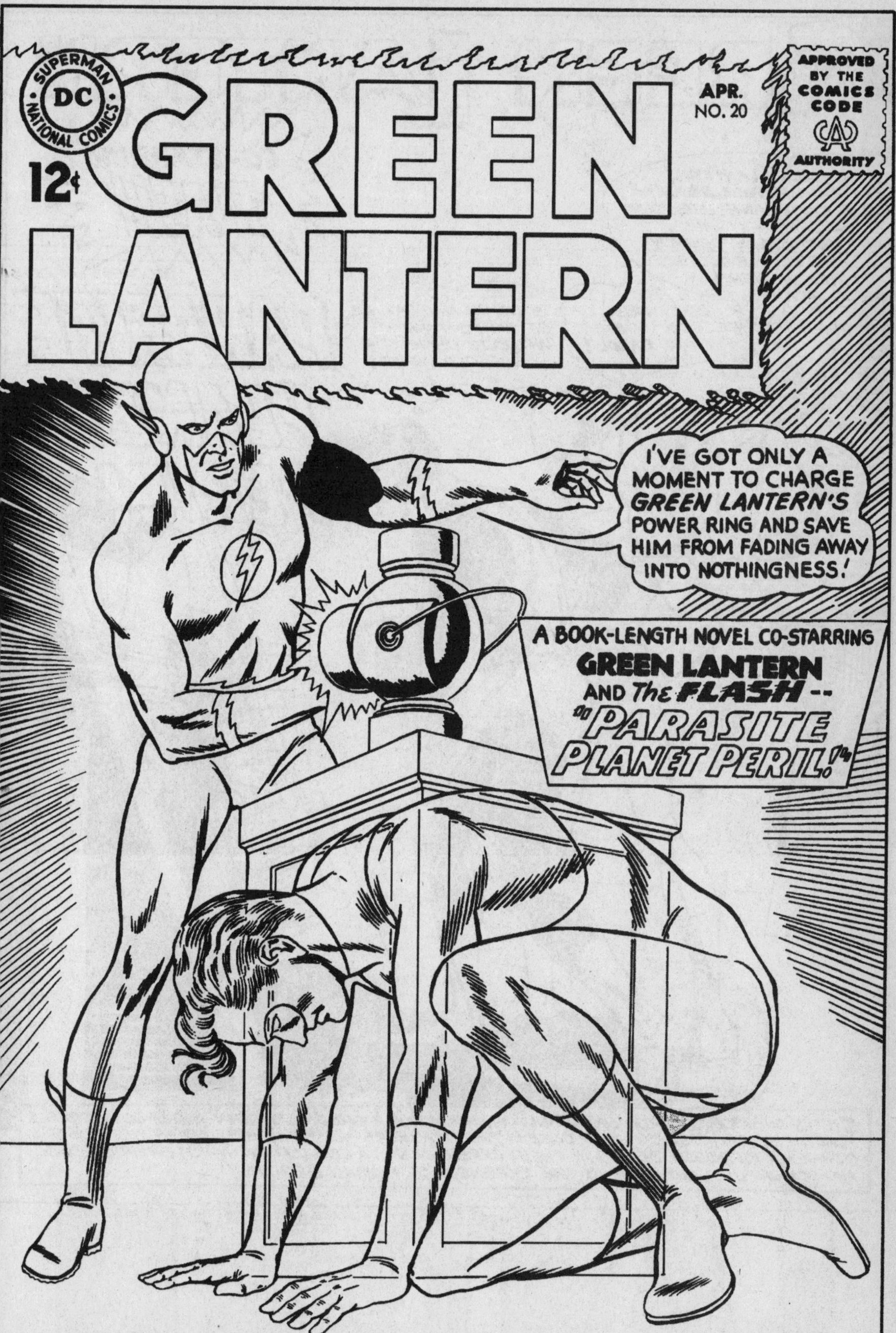
SUPERMAN DC NATIONAL COMICS
12¢
GREEN LANTERN
APR. NO. 20
APPROVED BY THE COMICS CODE AUTHORITY
I'VE GOT ONLY A MOMENT TO CHARGE GREEN LANTERN'S POWER RING AND SAVE HIM FROM FADING AWAY INTO NOTHINGNESS!
A BOOK-LENGTH NOVEL CO-STARRING GREEN LANTERN AND The FLASH -- "PARASITE PLANET PERIL!"

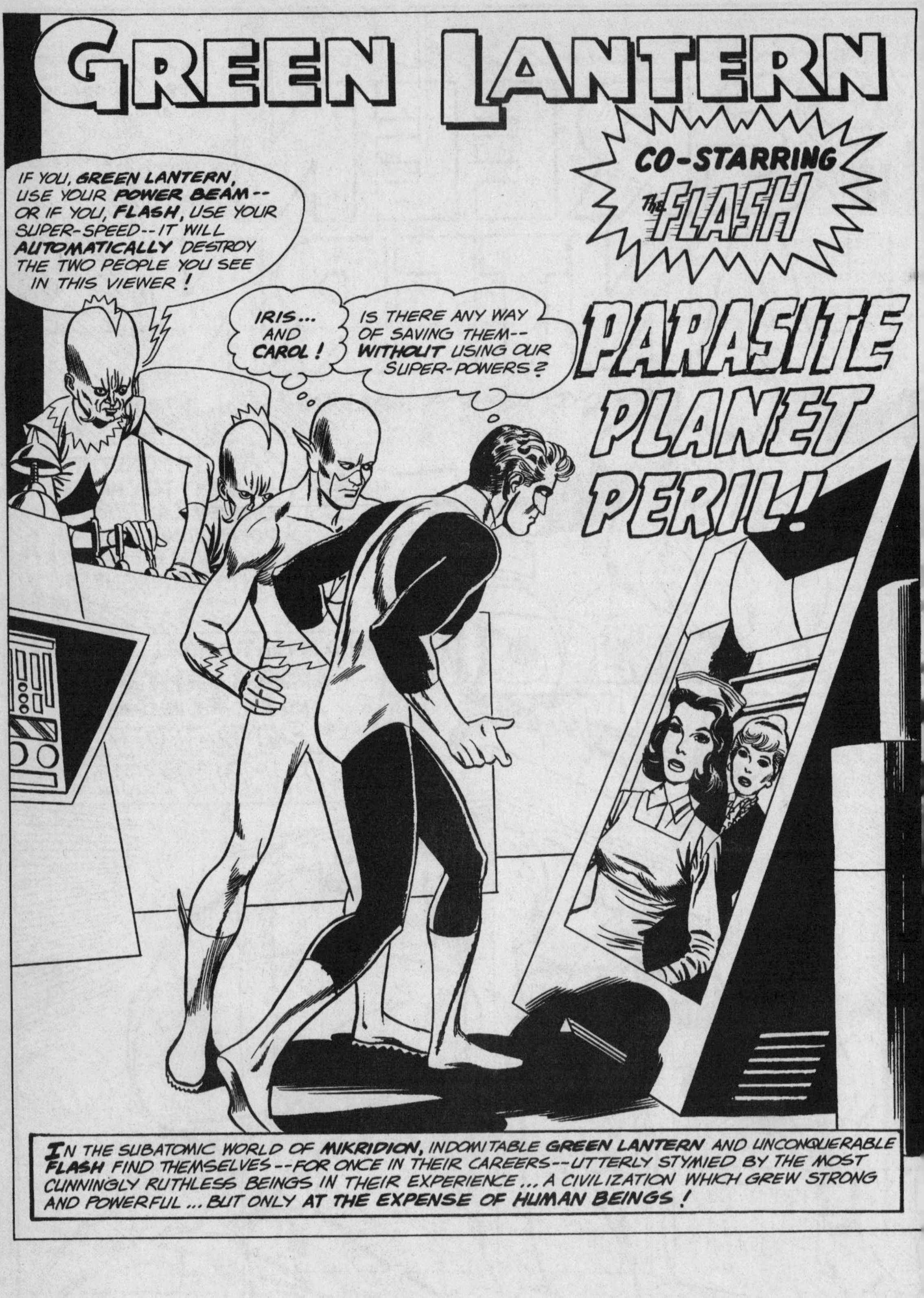
GREEN LANTERN
CO-STARRING The FLASH
PARASITE PLANET PERIL!
IF YOU, GREEN LANTERN, USE YOUR POWER BEAM-- OR IF YOU, FLASH, USE YOUR SUPER-SPEED--IT WILL AUTOMATICALLY DESTROY THE TWO PEOPLE YOU SEE IN THIS VIEWER!
IRIS... AND CAROL!
IS THERE ANY WAY OF SAVING THEM-- WITHOUT USING OUR SUPER-POWERS?
IN THE SUBATOMIC WORLD OF MIKRIDION, INDOMITABLE GREEN LANTERN AND UNCONQUERABLE FLASH FIND THEMSELVES--FOR ONCE IN THEIR CAREERS--UTTERLY STYMIED BY THE MOST CUNNINGLY RUTHLESS BEINGS IN THEIR EXPERIENCE... A CIVILIZATION WHICH GREW STRONG AND POWERFUL... BUT ONLY AT THE EXPENSE OF HUMAN BEINGS!

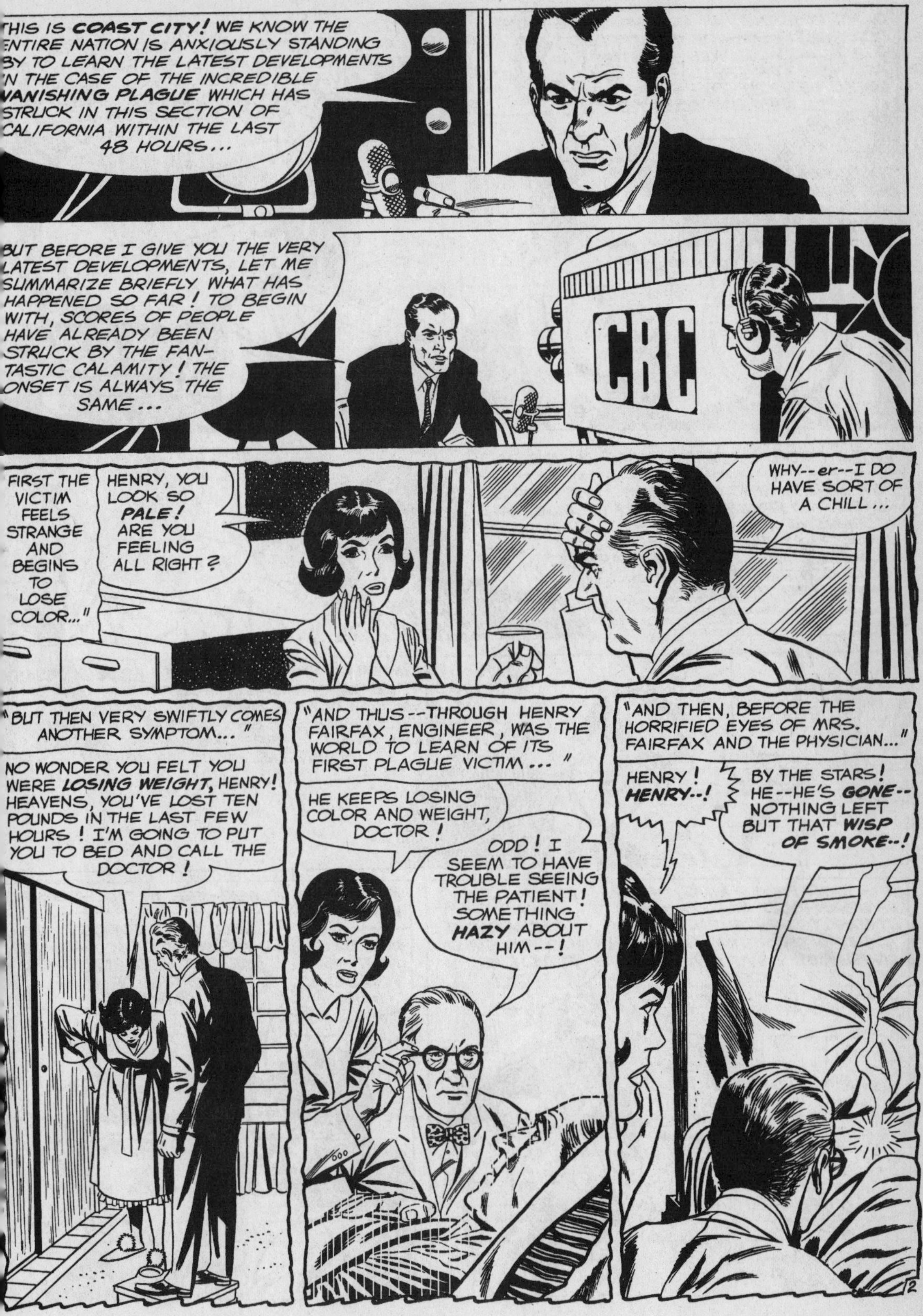
THIS IS COAST CITY! WE KNOW THE ENTIRE NATION IS ANXIOUSLY STANDING BY TO LEARN THE LATEST DEVELOPMENTS IN THE CASE OF THE INCREDIBLE VANISHING PLAGUE WHICH HAS STRUCK IN THIS SECTION OF CALIFORNIA WITHIN THE LAST 48 HOURS...
BUT BEFORE I GIVE YOU THE VERY LATEST DEVELOPMENTS, LET ME SUMMARIZE BRIEFLY WHAT HAS HAPPENED SO FAR! TO BEGIN WITH, SCORES OF PEOPLE HAVE ALREADY BEEN STRUCK BY THE FANTASTIC CALAMITY! THE ONSET IS ALWAYS THE SAME...
CBC
FIRST THE VICTIM FEELS STRANGE AND BEGINS TO LOSE COLOR..."
HENRY, YOU LOOK SO PALE! ARE YOU FEELING ALL RIGHT?
WHY--er--I DO HAVE SORT OF A CHILL...
"BUT THEN VERY SWIFTLY COMES ANOTHER SYMPTOM..."
NO WONDER YOU FELT YOU WERE LOSING WEIGHT, HENRY! HEAVENS, YOU'VE LOST TEN POUNDS IN THE LAST FEW HOURS! I'M GOING TO PUT YOU TO BED AND CALL THE DOCTOR!
"AND THUS--THROUGH HENRY FAIRFAX, ENGINEER, WAS THE WORLD TO LEARN OF ITS FIRST PLAGUE VICTIM..."
HE KEEPS LOSING COLOR AND WEIGHT, DOCTOR!
ODD! I SEEM TO HAVE TROUBLE SEEING THE PATIENT! SOMETHING HAZY ABOUT HIM--!
"AND THEN, BEFORE THE HORRIFIED EYES OF MRS. FAIRFAX AND THE PHYSICIAN..."
HENRY! HENRY--!
BY THE STARS! HE--HE'S GONE--NOTHING LEFT BUT THAT WISP OF SMOKE--!
2

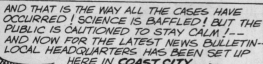

AND THAT IS THE WAY ALL THE CASES HAVE OCCURRED! SCIENCE IS BAFFLED! BUT THE PUBLIC IS CAUTIONED TO STAY CALM!-- AND NOW FOR THE LATEST NEWS BULLETIN-- LOCAL HEADQUARTERS HAS BEEN SET UP HERE IN **COAST CITY...**

...TO DIRECT THE FIGHT AGAINST THE MYSTERIC CALAMITY! AMONG THOSE WHO HAVE RE- SPONDED TO THE APPEAL FOR HELP IN THIS GRAVE EMERGENCY ARE NONE OTHER THAN **GREEN LANTERN** AND **FLASH**... READY AS ALWAYS TO AID IN A GOOD CAUSE...!

IN THE LOCAL HOSPITAL HEADQUARTERS...

NOW HERE'S WHAT OUR COMMITTEE PROPOSES, **FLASH** AND **GREEN LANTERN**! WE WILL HAVE TELEPHONE GIRLS ON 24-HOUR DUTY HERE! AS SOON AS WORD COMES IN THAT SOMEONE IN THE CITY APPEARS TO HAVE CONTRACTED THE **VANISHING PLAGUE**...

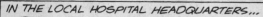

...THE INFORMATION WILL BE GIVEN TO **YOU, FLASH** AND AT SUPER-SPEED--WITHOUT WASTING A MOMENT-- YOU WILL BRING THE VICTIM TO THE WING OF THIS HOSPITAL THAT WE HAVE TAKEN OVER! HERE THE LATEST MEDICAL TECHNIQUES WILL BE TRIED!

WITH YOUR **POWER RING, GREEN LANTERN,** YOU WILL DO YOUR UTMOST TO PREVENT THE HOSPITALIZED VICTIM FROM VANISHING... OR AT LEAST TO DELAY THE PROCESS! THAT SEEMS TO BE ALL WE CAN DO AT PRESENT...

CHECK! I'M READY, MR. CHAIRMAN... AND I'M SURE **FLASH** IS TOO!

MEANWHILE, ELSEWHERE IN THE HOSPITAL WING...

IRIS WEST! WHAT ARE **YOU** DOING HERE?

WELL, CAROL FERRIS! THIS I$ A SURPRISE! MY PAPER SEN ME OUT HERE TO COVER THE STORY OF THIS **PLAGUE**...

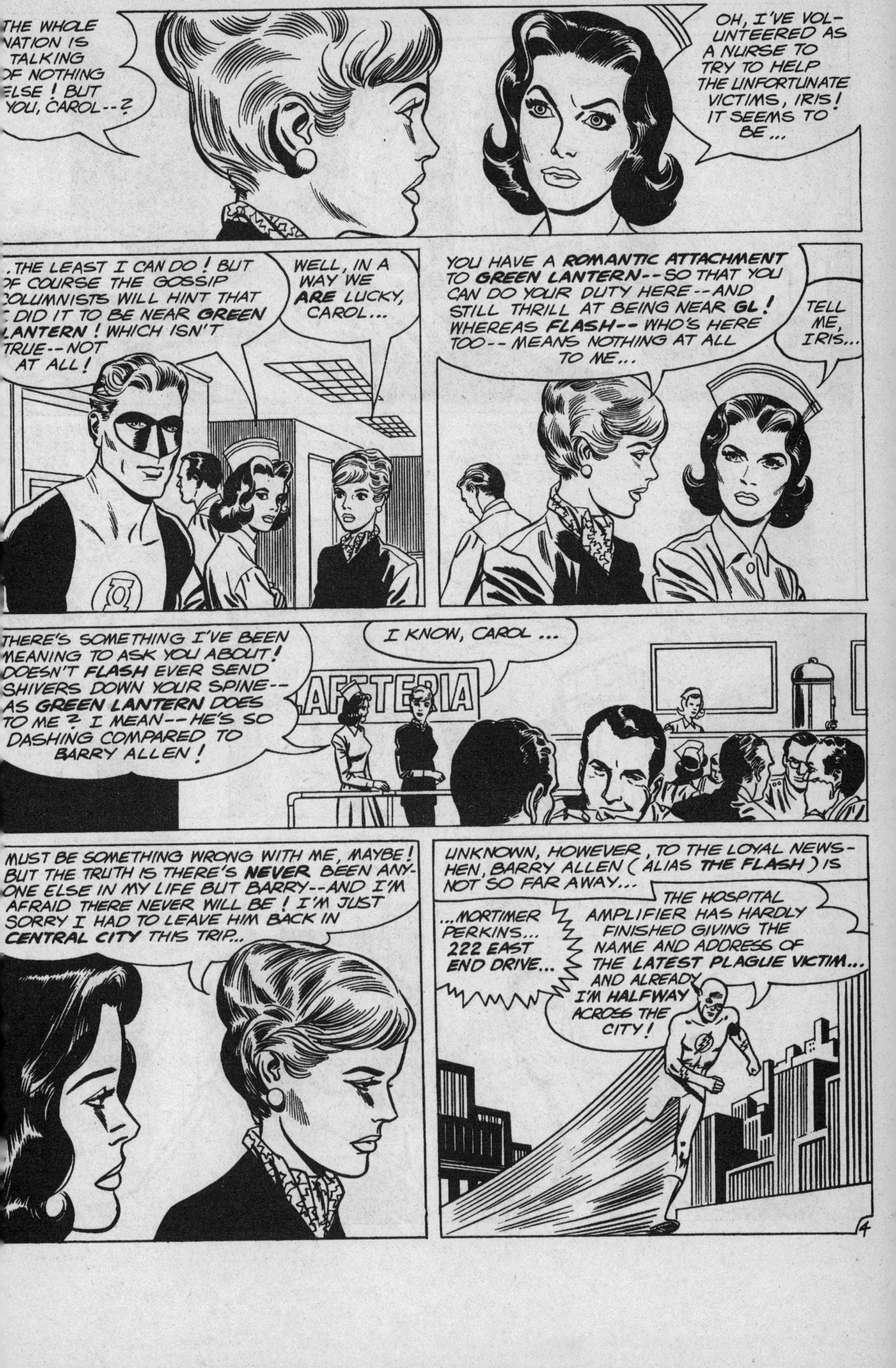
THE WHOLE NATION IS TALKING OF NOTHING ELSE! BUT YOU, CAROL--?
OH, I'VE VOLUNTEERED AS A NURSE TO TRY TO HELP THE UNFORTUNATE VICTIMS, IRIS! IT SEEMS TO BE...
...THE LEAST I CAN DO! BUT OF COURSE THE GOSSIP COLUMNISTS WILL HINT THAT I DID IT TO BE NEAR GREEN LANTERN! WHICH ISN'T TRUE--NOT AT ALL!
WELL, IN A WAY WE ARE LUCKY, CAROL...
YOU HAVE A ROMANTIC ATTACHMENT TO GREEN LANTERN--SO THAT YOU CAN DO YOUR DUTY HERE--AND STILL THRILL AT BEING NEAR GL! WHEREAS FLASH--WHO'S HERE TOO--MEANS NOTHING AT ALL TO ME...
TELL ME, IRIS...
THERE'S SOMETHING I'VE BEEN MEANING TO ASK YOU ABOUT! DOESN'T FLASH EVER SEND SHIVERS DOWN YOUR SPINE--AS GREEN LANTERN DOES TO ME? I MEAN--HE'S SO DASHING COMPARED TO BARRY ALLEN!
I KNOW, CAROL...
CAFETERIA
MUST BE SOMETHING WRONG WITH ME, MAYBE! BUT THE TRUTH IS THERE'S NEVER BEEN ANYONE ELSE IN MY LIFE BUT BARRY--AND I'M AFRAID THERE NEVER WILL BE! I'M JUST SORRY I HAD TO LEAVE HIM BACK IN CENTRAL CITY THIS TRIP...
UNKNOWN, HOWEVER, TO THE LOYAL NEWSHEN, BARRY ALLEN (ALIAS THE FLASH) IS NOT SO FAR AWAY...
...MORTIMER PERKINS... 222 EAST END DRIVE...
THE HOSPITAL AMPLIFIER HAS HARDLY FINISHED GIVING THE NAME AND ADDRESS OF THE LATEST PLAGUE VICTIM... AND ALREADY I'M HALFWAY ACROSS THE CITY!
4

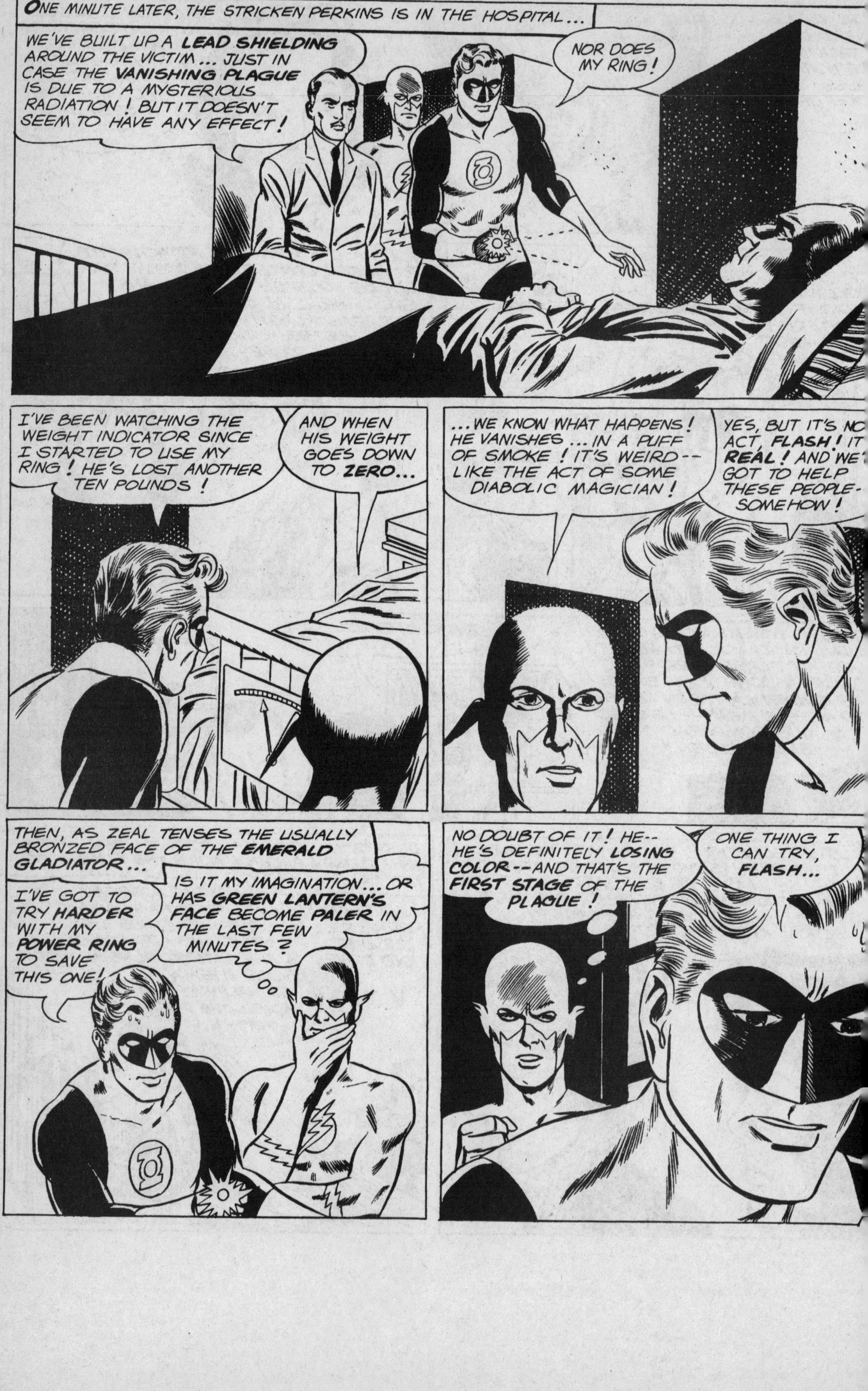
ONE MINUTE LATER, THE STRICKEN PERKINS IS IN THE HOSPITAL...
WE'VE BUILT UP A LEAD SHIELDING AROUND THE VICTIM... JUST IN CASE THE VANISHING PLAGUE IS DUE TO A MYSTERIOUS RADIATION! BUT IT DOESN'T SEEM TO HAVE ANY EFFECT!
NOR DOES MY RING!
I'VE BEEN WATCHING THE WEIGHT INDICATOR SINCE I STARTED TO USE MY RING! HE'S LOST ANOTHER TEN POUNDS!
AND WHEN HIS WEIGHT GOES DOWN TO ZERO...
...WE KNOW WHAT HAPPENS! HE VANISHES... IN A PUFF OF SMOKE! IT'S WEIRD-- LIKE THE ACT OF SOME DIABOLIC MAGICIAN!
YES, BUT IT'S NO ACT, FLASH! IT REAL! AND WE GOT TO HELP THESE PEOPLE-SOMEHOW!
THEN, AS ZEAL TENSES THE USUALLY BRONZED FACE OF THE EMERALD GLADIATOR...
I'VE GOT TO TRY HARDER WITH MY POWER RING TO SAVE THIS ONE!
IS IT MY IMAGINATION... OR HAS GREEN LANTERN'S FACE BECOME PALER IN THE LAST FEW MINUTES?
NO DOUBT OF IT! HE-- HE'S DEFINITELY LOSING COLOR--AND THAT'S THE FIRST STAGE OF THE PLAGUE!
ONE THING I CAN TRY, FLASH...

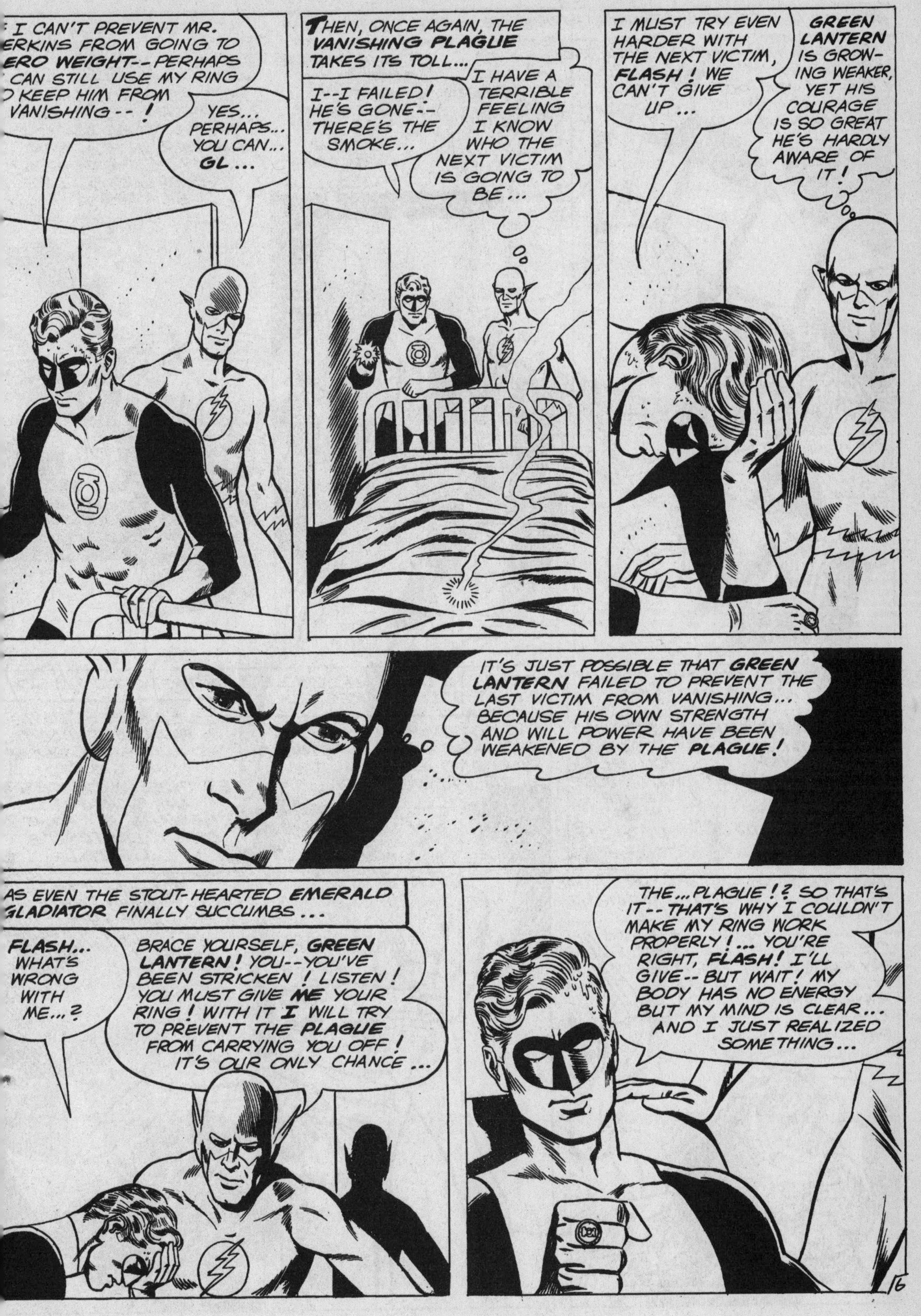
F I CAN'T PREVENT MR. ERKINS FROM GOING TO ERO WEIGHT--PERHAPS CAN STILL USE MY RING O KEEP HIM FROM VANISHING--!
YES... PERHAPS... YOU CAN... GL...
THEN, ONCE AGAIN, THE VANISHING PLAGUE TAKES ITS TOLL...
I--I FAILED! HE'S GONE--THERE'S THE SMOKE...
I HAVE A TERRIBLE FEELING I KNOW WHO THE NEXT VICTIM IS GOING TO BE...
I MUST TRY EVEN HARDER WITH THE NEXT VICTIM, FLASH! WE CAN'T GIVE UP...
GREEN LANTERN IS GROWING WEAKER, YET HIS COURAGE IS SO GREAT HE'S HARDLY AWARE OF IT!
IT'S JUST POSSIBLE THAT GREEN LANTERN FAILED TO PREVENT THE LAST VICTIM FROM VANISHING... BECAUSE HIS OWN STRENGTH AND WILL POWER HAVE BEEN WEAKENED BY THE PLAGUE!
AS EVEN THE STOUT-HEARTED EMERALD GLADIATOR FINALLY SUCCUMBS...
FLASH... WHAT'S WRONG WITH ME...?
BRACE YOURSELF, GREEN LANTERN! YOU--YOU'VE BEEN STRICKEN! LISTEN! YOU MUST GIVE ME YOUR RING! WITH IT I WILL TRY TO PREVENT THE PLAGUE FROM CARRYING YOU OFF! IT'S OUR ONLY CHANCE...
THE... PLAGUE!? SO THAT'S IT--THAT'S WHY I COULDN'T MAKE MY RING WORK PROPERLY!... YOU'RE RIGHT, FLASH! I'LL GIVE--BUT WAIT! MY BODY HAS NO ENERGY BUT MY MIND IS CLEAR... AND I JUST REALIZED SOMETHING...
16

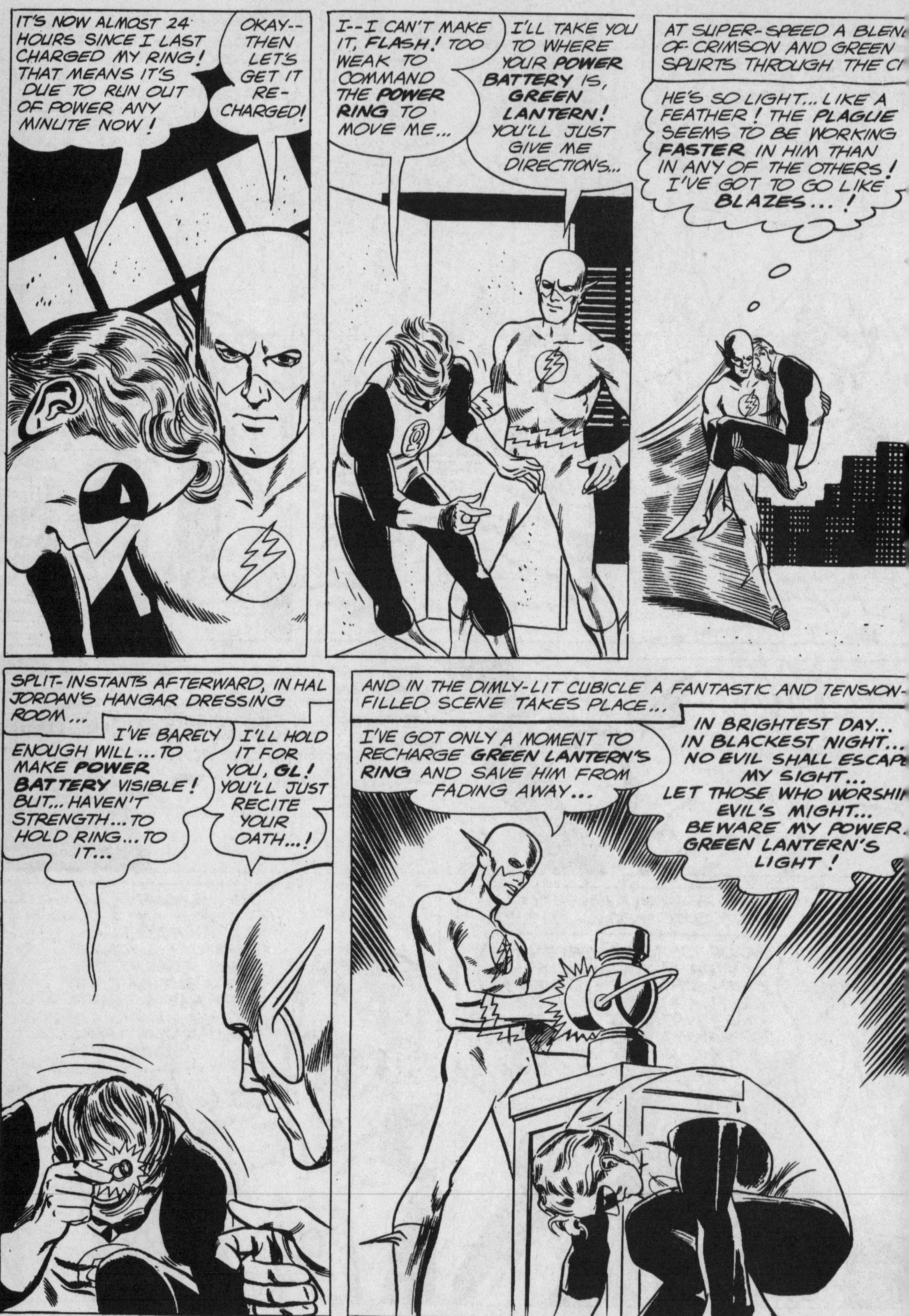
IT'S NOW ALMOST 24 HOURS SINCE I LAST CHARGED MY RING! THAT MEANS IT'S DUE TO RUN OUT OF POWER ANY MINUTE NOW!
OKAY-- THEN LET'S GET IT RE-CHARGED!
I--I CAN'T MAKE IT, FLASH! TOO WEAK TO COMMAND THE POWER RING TO MOVE ME...
I'LL TAKE YOU TO WHERE YOUR POWER BATTERY IS, GREEN LANTERN! YOU'LL JUST GIVE ME DIRECTIONS...
AT SUPER-SPEED A BLEN OF CRIMSON AND GREEN SPURTS THROUGH THE C
HE'S SO LIGHT... LIKE A FEATHER! THE PLAGUE SEEMS TO BE WORKING FASTER IN HIM THAN IN ANY OF THE OTHERS! I'VE GOT TO GO LIKE BLAZES...!
SPLIT-INSTANTS AFTERWARD, IN HAL JORDAN'S HANGAR DRESSING ROOM...
I'VE BARELY ENOUGH WILL... TO MAKE POWER BATTERY VISIBLE! BUT... HAVEN'T STRENGTH... TO HOLD RING... TO IT...
I'LL HOLD IT FOR YOU, GL! YOU'LL JUST RECITE YOUR OATH...!
AND IN THE DIMLY-LIT CUBICLE A FANTASTIC AND TENSION-FILLED SCENE TAKES PLACE...
I'VE GOT ONLY A MOMENT TO RECHARGE GREEN LANTERN'S RING AND SAVE HIM FROM FADING AWAY...
IN BRIGHTEST DAY... IN BLACKEST NIGHT... NO EVIL SHALL ESCAPE MY SIGHT... LET THOSE WHO WORSHI EVIL'S MIGHT... BEWARE MY POWER. GREEN LANTERN'S LIGHT!

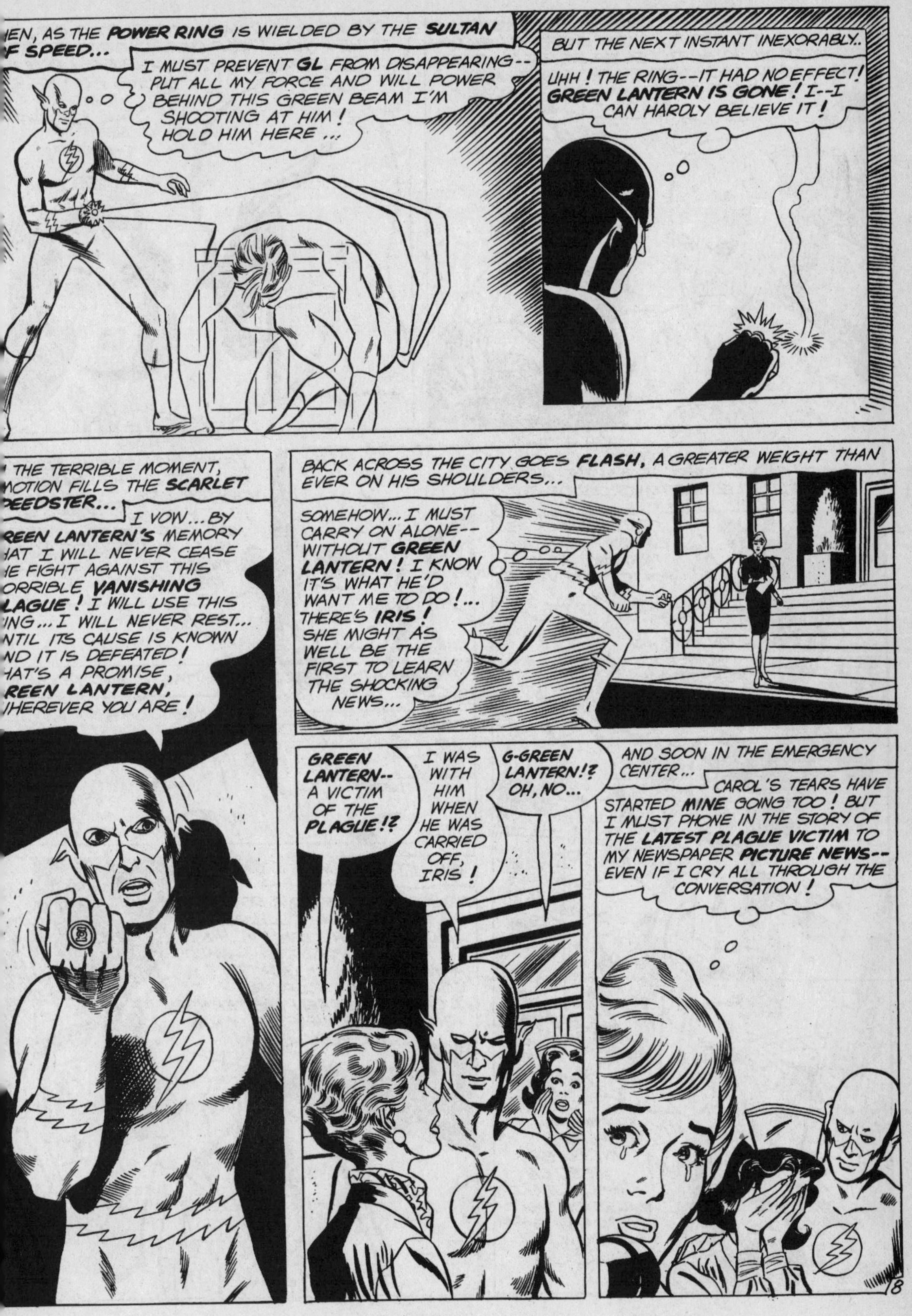
HEN, AS THE POWER RING IS WIELDED BY THE SULTAN F SPEED...
I MUST PREVENT GL FROM DISAPPEARING-- PUT ALL MY FORCE AND WILL POWER BEHIND THIS GREEN BEAM I'M SHOOTING AT HIM! HOLD HIM HERE ...
BUT THE NEXT INSTANT INEXORABLY..
UHH! THE RING--IT HAD NO EFFECT! GREEN LANTERN IS GONE! I--I CAN HARDLY BELIEVE IT!
THE TERRIBLE MOMENT, MOTION FILLS THE SCARLET PEEDSTER...
I VOW...BY REEN LANTERN'S MEMORY HAT I WILL NEVER CEASE HE FIGHT AGAINST THIS ORRIBLE VANISHING LAGUE! I WILL USE THIS ING...I WILL NEVER REST... NTIL ITS CAUSE IS KNOWN ND IT IS DEFEATED! HAT'S A PROMISE, REEN LANTERN, HEREVER YOU ARE!
BACK ACROSS THE CITY GOES FLASH, A GREATER WEIGHT THAN EVER ON HIS SHOULDERS...
SOMEHOW... I MUST CARRY ON ALONE-- WITHOUT GREEN LANTERN! I KNOW IT'S WHAT HE'D WANT ME TO DO!... THERE'S IRIS! SHE MIGHT AS WELL BE THE FIRST TO LEARN THE SHOCKING NEWS...
GREEN LANTERN-- A VICTIM OF THE PLAGUE!?
I WAS WITH HIM WHEN HE WAS CARRIED OFF, IRIS!
G-GREEN LANTERN!? OH, NO...
AND SOON IN THE EMERGENCY CENTER...
CAROL'S TEARS HAVE STARTED MINE GOING TOO! BUT I MUST PHONE IN THE STORY OF THE LATEST PLAGUE VICTIM TO MY NEWSPAPER PICTURE NEWS-- EVEN IF I CRY ALL THROUGH THE CONVERSATION!
8

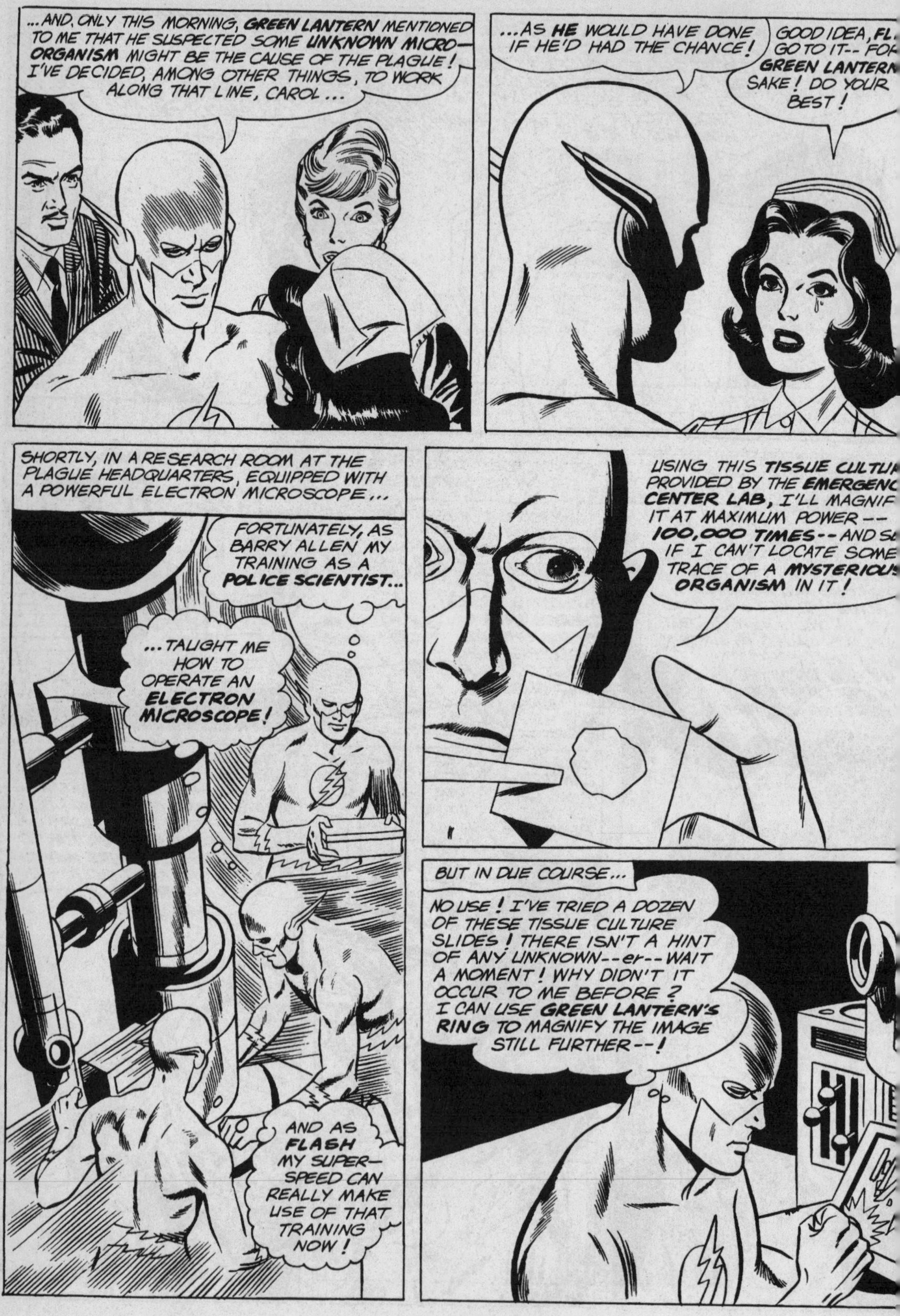
...AND, ONLY THIS MORNING, GREEN LANTERN MENTIONED TO ME THAT HE SUSPECTED SOME UNKNOWN MICRO-ORGANISM MIGHT BE THE CAUSE OF THE PLAGUE! I'VE DECIDED, AMONG OTHER THINGS, TO WORK ALONG THAT LINE, CAROL...
...AS HE WOULD HAVE DONE IF HE'D HAD THE CHANCE!
GOOD IDEA, FL GO TO IT-- FOR GREEN LANTERN SAKE! DO YOUR BEST!
SHORTLY, IN A RESEARCH ROOM AT THE PLAGUE HEADQUARTERS, EQUIPPED WITH A POWERFUL ELECTRON MICROSCOPE...
FORTUNATELY, AS BARRY ALLEN MY TRAINING AS A POLICE SCIENTIST...
...TAUGHT ME HOW TO OPERATE AN ELECTRON MICROSCOPE!
AND AS FLASH MY SUPER-SPEED CAN REALLY MAKE USE OF THAT TRAINING NOW!
USING THIS TISSUE CULTU PROVIDED BY THE EMERGENC CENTER LAB, I'LL MAGNIF IT AT MAXIMUM POWER -- 100,000 TIMES-- AND SE IF I CAN'T LOCATE SOME TRACE OF A MYSTERIOUS ORGANISM IN IT!
BUT IN DUE COURSE...
NO USE! I'VE TRIED A DOZEN OF THESE TISSUE CULTURE SLIDES! THERE ISN'T A HINT OF ANY UNKNOWN--er--WAIT A MOMENT! WHY DIDN'T IT OCCUR TO ME BEFORE? I CAN USE GREEN LANTERN'S RING TO MAGNIFY THE IMAGE STILL FURTHER--!

L ONCE EXPLAINED TO ME THAT HE COULD DO ANYTHING WITH HIS RING * IF HE BACKED IT ITH SUFFICIENT **STRENGTH OF WILL**! I FEEL E'S BEHIND ME NOW--HELPING ME DO WHAT HAVE TO DO--REALLY **MAGNIFY THAT IMAGE**--!

AS THE GREAT **GREEN BEAM** UNDER **NEW GUIDANCE** SHOOTS OUT OBEDIENTLY...

...THIS ISN'T EASY! I--I CAN FEEL THE TENSION! I'VE GOT THE MAGNIFICATION UP TO **300,000** NOW!... THERE IT IS AT...**400,000**!... AND STILL NO SIGN OF ANY LIVING PARTICLE... ANY VICIOUS VIRUS...!

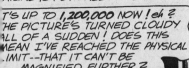

EDITOR'S NOTE: ANYTHING--EXCEPT HAVE AN EFFECT N A **YELLOW-COLORED** OBJECT! THE RING BY ITS ATURE IS POWERLESS TO DO THAT!

T'S UP TO **1,200,000** NOW! eh? THE PICTURE'S TURNED CLOUDY ALL OF A SUDDEN! DOES THIS MEAN I'VE REACHED THE PHYSICAL LIMIT--THAT IT CAN'T BE MAGNIFIED FURTHER?

BUT THE NEXT INSTANT, FANTASTICALLY...

WHAT'S THAT!? SUDDENLY THE CLOUD CLEARED AND--THAT **CREATURE** POPPED INTO VIEW--! I GET THE ODDEST FEELING--

--THAT HE'S **AWARE OF ME**-- IN AN **EVIL** KIND OF WAY! THAT HE KNOWS I AM LOOKING AT HIM! BUT--WHAT'S HE DOING NOW--MOVING ABOUT--?

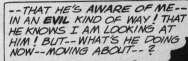

10

ABRUPTLY... GONE! THE VIEWER IS DARK--AND I CAN'T MAKE IT LIGHT UP! IT'S AS IF THAT INCREDIBLE BEING SOMEHOW CUT HIMSELF OFF FROM MY SIGHT--AS IF HE SNAPPED A SWITCH! BUT I KNOW WHAT I MUST DO... I KNOW WHAT GL WOULD DO...!

I MUST USE THIS POWER BEAM TO INVESTIGATE THE SCENE I JUST SAW! NOW I'VE REALLY GOT TO PUT GREEN LANTERN'S POWER RING TO WORK-- TO REDUCE ME IN SIZE TO AN INCREDIBLE DEGREE...

...AND AT THE SAME TIME REDUCE ITSELF TOO...SO THAT I CAN CONTINUE TO WEAR THE RING AND USE IT! I'M GOING DOWN FAST...BUT I'VE GOT A LONG WAY TO TRAVEL...CAN THAT CREATURE HAVE ANY-THING TO DO WITH THE VANISHING PLAGUE?

...THAT'S WHAT I MUST FIND OUT!...I'M DOWN TO 800,000 TIMES SMALLER THAN NORMAL SIZE!... 900,000 TIMES... AND STILL GOING STRONG..!

BUT THEN WITH BREATHTAKING SWIFTNESS, THE RAPIDLY-DWINDLING SCARLET SPEEDSTER SUDDENLY VANISHES ALTOGETHER!

HAS FLASH TOO JOINED THE RANKS OF THE VICTIMS WHO HAVE DISAPPEARED? WHAT HAS HAPPENED TO HIM?

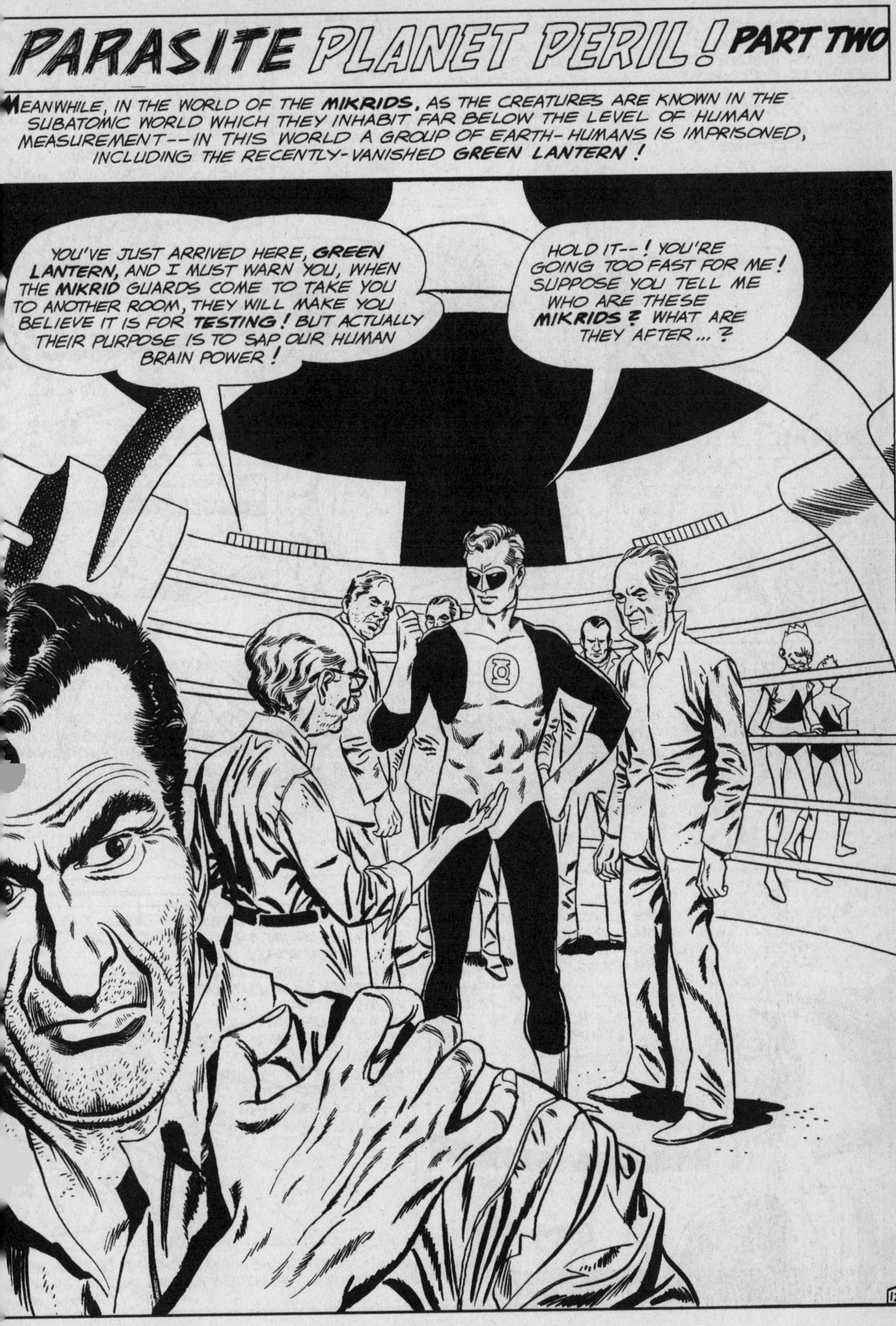
PARASITE PLANET PERIL! PART TWO
MEANWHILE, IN THE WORLD OF THE MIKRIDS, AS THE CREATURES ARE KNOWN IN THE SUBATOMIC WORLD WHICH THEY INHABIT FAR BELOW THE LEVEL OF HUMAN MEASUREMENT--IN THIS WORLD A GROUP OF EARTH-HUMANS IS IMPRISONED, INCLUDING THE RECENTLY-VANISHED GREEN LANTERN!
YOU'VE JUST ARRIVED HERE, GREEN LANTERN, AND I MUST WARN YOU, WHEN THE MIKRID GUARDS COME TO TAKE YOU TO ANOTHER ROOM, THEY WILL MAKE YOU BELIEVE IT IS FOR TESTING! BUT ACTUALLY THEIR PURPOSE IS TO SAP OUR HUMAN BRAIN POWER!
HOLD IT--! YOU'RE GOING TOO FAST FOR ME! SUPPOSE YOU TELL ME WHO ARE THESE MIKRIDS? WHAT ARE THEY AFTER...?
12

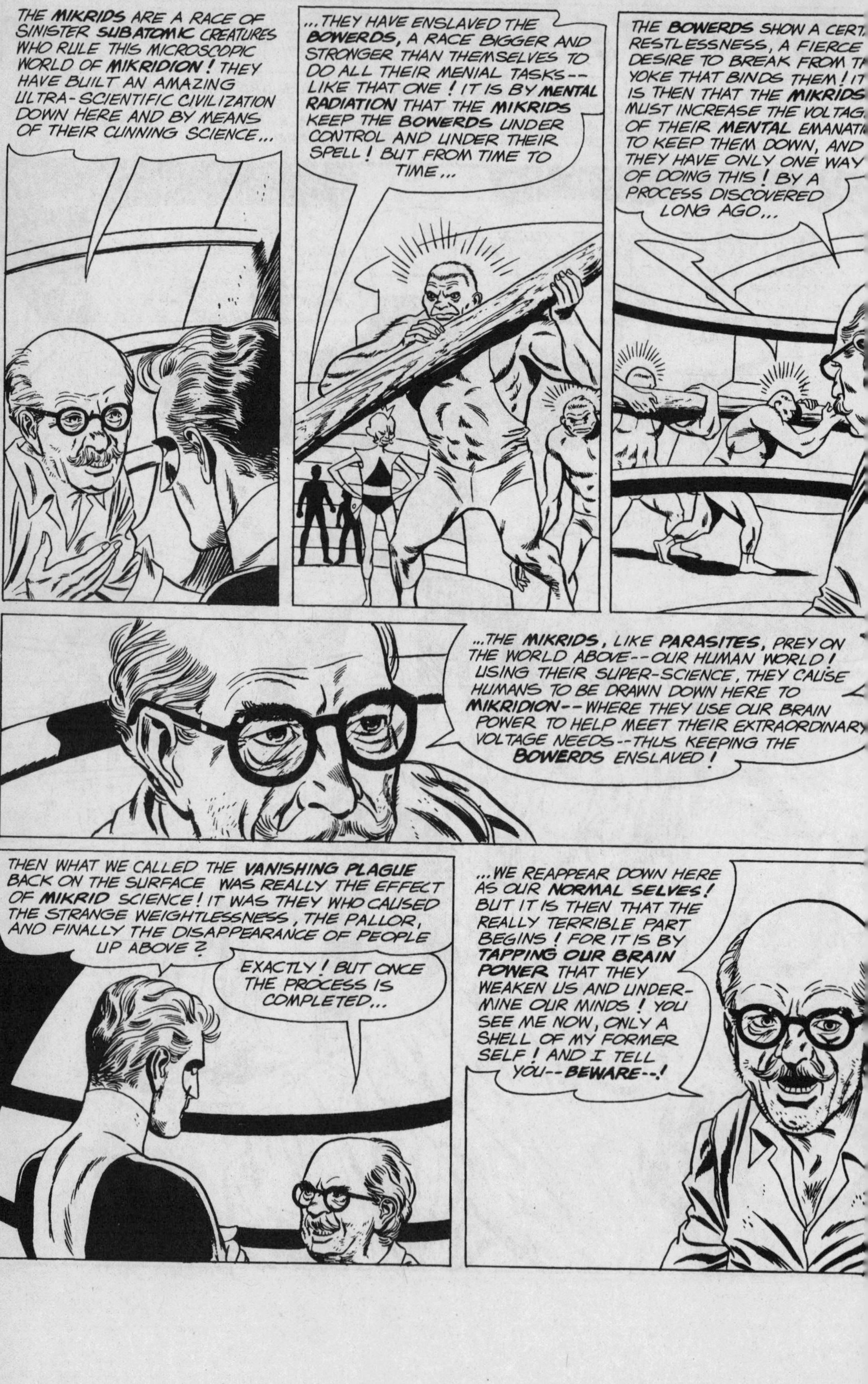
THE MIKRIDS ARE A RACE OF SINISTER SUBATOMIC CREATURES WHO RULE THIS MICROSCOPIC WORLD OF MIKRIDION! THEY HAVE BUILT AN AMAZING ULTRA-SCIENTIFIC CIVILIZATION DOWN HERE AND BY MEANS OF THEIR CUNNING SCIENCE...
...THEY HAVE ENSLAVED THE BOWERDS, A RACE BIGGER AND STRONGER THAN THEMSELVES TO DO ALL THEIR MENIAL TASKS--LIKE THAT ONE! IT IS BY MENTAL RADIATION THAT THE MIKRIDS KEEP THE BOWERDS UNDER CONTROL AND UNDER THEIR SPELL! BUT FROM TIME TO TIME...
THE BOWERDS SHOW A CERT RESTLESSNESS, A FIERCE DESIRE TO BREAK FROM T YOKE THAT BINDS THEM! IT IS THEN THAT THE MIKRIDS MUST INCREASE THE VOLTAG OF THEIR MENTAL EMANATI TO KEEP THEM DOWN, AND THEY HAVE ONLY ONE WAY OF DOING THIS! BY A PROCESS DISCOVERED LONG AGO...
...THE MIKRIDS, LIKE PARASITES, PREY ON THE WORLD ABOVE--OUR HUMAN WORLD! USING THEIR SUPER-SCIENCE, THEY CAUSE HUMANS TO BE DRAWN DOWN HERE TO MIKRIDION--WHERE THEY USE OUR BRAIN POWER TO HELP MEET THEIR EXTRAORDINARY VOLTAGE NEEDS--THUS KEEPING THE BOWERDS ENSLAVED!
THEN WHAT WE CALLED THE VANISHING PLAGUE BACK ON THE SURFACE WAS REALLY THE EFFECT OF MIKRID SCIENCE! IT WAS THEY WHO CAUSED THE STRANGE WEIGHTLESSNESS, THE PALLOR, AND FINALLY THE DISAPPEARANCE OF PEOPLE UP ABOVE?
EXACTLY! BUT ONCE THE PROCESS IS COMPLETED...
...WE REAPPEAR DOWN HERE AS OUR NORMAL SELVES! BUT IT IS THEN THAT THE REALLY TERRIBLE PART BEGINS! FOR IT IS BY TAPPING OUR BRAIN POWER THAT THEY WEAKEN US AND UNDERMINE OUR MINDS! YOU SEE ME NOW, ONLY A SHELL OF MY FORMER SELF! AND I TELL YOU--BEWARE--!

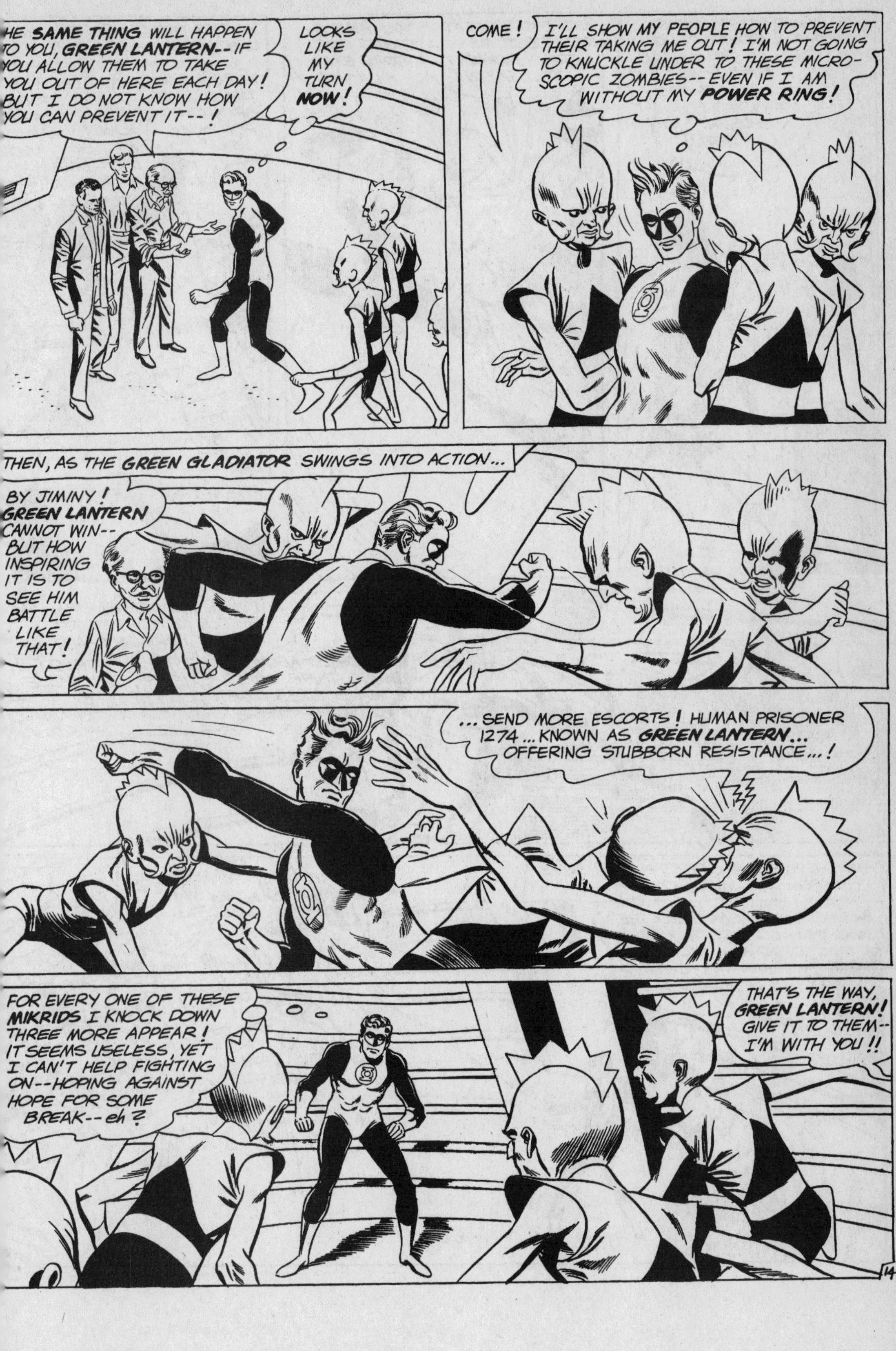
HE SAME THING WILL HAPPEN TO YOU, GREEN LANTERN-- IF YOU ALLOW THEM TO TAKE YOU OUT OF HERE EACH DAY! BUT I DO NOT KNOW HOW YOU CAN PREVENT IT--!
LOOKS LIKE MY TURN NOW!
COME!
I'LL SHOW MY PEOPLE HOW TO PREVENT THEIR TAKING ME OUT! I'M NOT GOING TO KNUCKLE UNDER TO THESE MICRO-SCOPIC ZOMBIES-- EVEN IF I AM WITHOUT MY POWER RING!
THEN, AS THE GREEN GLADIATOR SWINGS INTO ACTION...
BY JIMINY! GREEN LANTERN CANNOT WIN-- BUT HOW INSPIRING IT IS TO SEE HIM BATTLE LIKE THAT!
...SEND MORE ESCORTS! HUMAN PRISONER 1274... KNOWN AS GREEN LANTERN... OFFERING STUBBORN RESISTANCE...!
FOR EVERY ONE OF THESE MIKRIDS I KNOCK DOWN THREE MORE APPEAR! IT SEEMS USELESS, YET I CAN'T HELP FIGHTING ON--HOPING AGAINST HOPE FOR SOME BREAK-- eh?
THAT'S THE WAY, GREEN LANTERN! GIVE IT TO THEM-- I'M WITH YOU!!
14

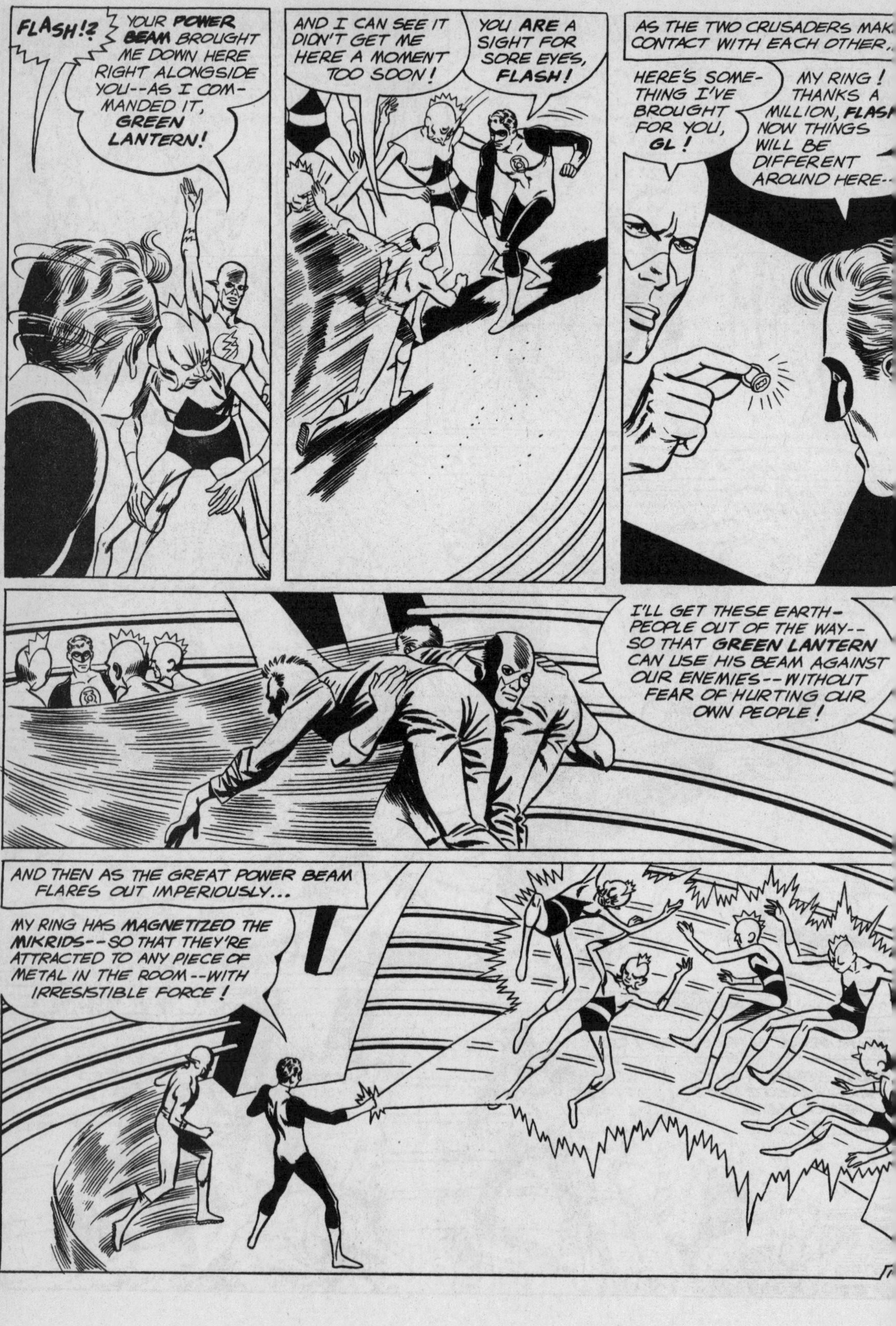
FLASH!?
YOUR POWER BEAM BROUGHT ME DOWN HERE RIGHT ALONGSIDE YOU--AS I COMMANDED IT, GREEN LANTERN!
AND I CAN SEE IT DIDN'T GET ME HERE A MOMENT TOO SOON!
YOU ARE A SIGHT FOR SORE EYES, FLASH!
AS THE TWO CRUSADERS MAK CONTACT WITH EACH OTHER...
HERE'S SOMETHING I'VE BROUGHT FOR YOU, GL!
MY RING! THANKS A MILLION, FLAS NOW THINGS WILL BE DIFFERENT AROUND HERE--
I'LL GET THESE EARTH-PEOPLE OUT OF THE WAY--SO THAT GREEN LANTERN CAN USE HIS BEAM AGAINST OUR ENEMIES--WITHOUT FEAR OF HURTING OUR OWN PEOPLE!
AND THEN AS THE GREAT POWER BEAM FLARES OUT IMPERIOUSLY...
MY RING HAS MAGNETIZED THE MIKRIDS--SO THAT THEY'RE ATTRACTED TO ANY PIECE OF METAL IN THE ROOM--WITH IRRESISTIBLE FORCE!

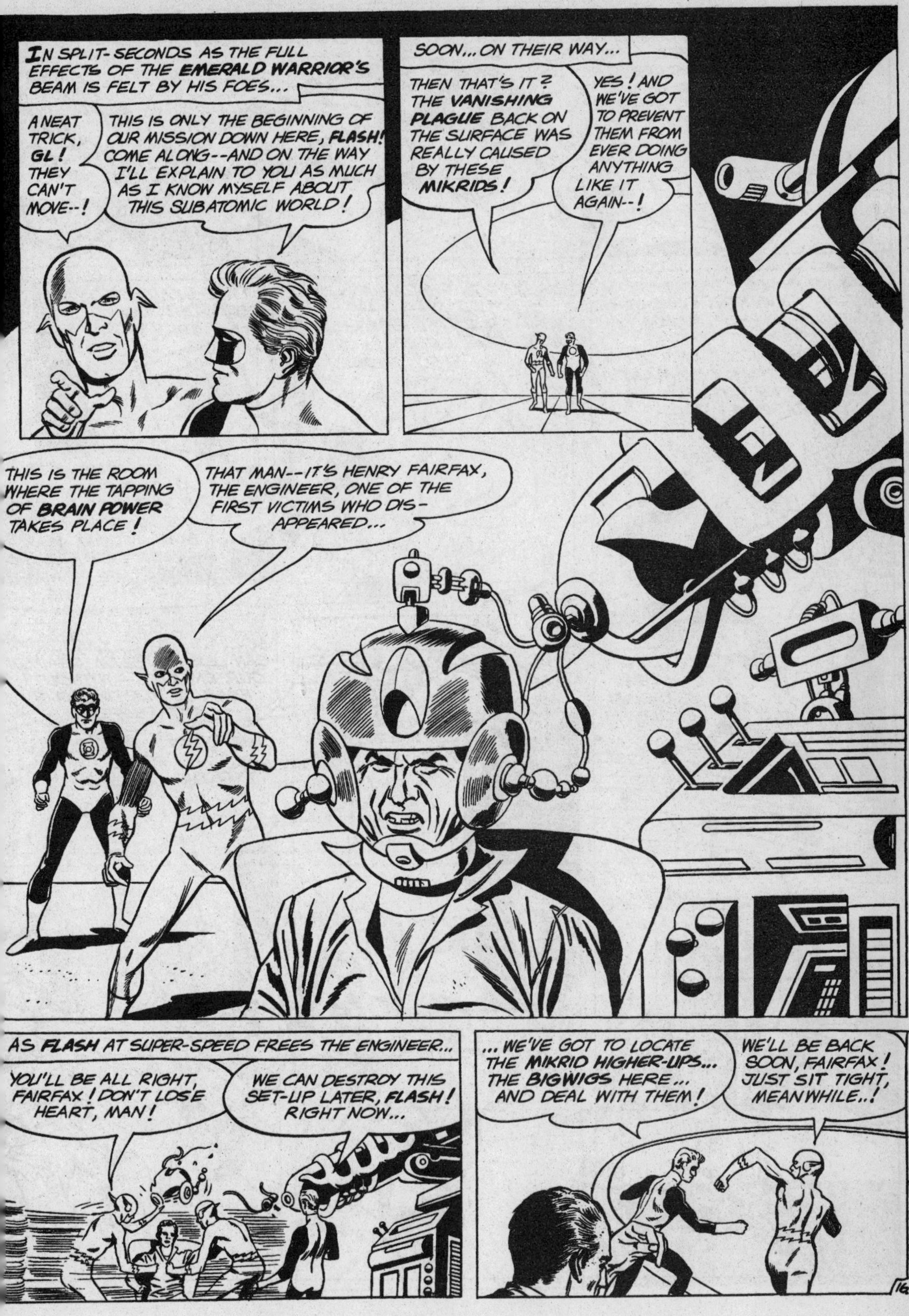
IN SPLIT-SECONDS AS THE FULL EFFECTS OF THE EMERALD WARRIOR'S BEAM IS FELT BY HIS FOES...
A NEAT TRICK, GL! THEY CAN'T MOVE--!
THIS IS ONLY THE BEGINNING OF OUR MISSION DOWN HERE, FLASH! COME ALONG--AND ON THE WAY I'LL EXPLAIN TO YOU AS MUCH AS I KNOW MYSELF ABOUT THIS SUBATOMIC WORLD!
SOON... ON THEIR WAY...
THEN THAT'S IT? THE VANISHING PLAGUE BACK ON THE SURFACE WAS REALLY CAUSED BY THESE MIKRIDS!
YES! AND WE'VE GOT TO PREVENT THEM FROM EVER DOING ANYTHING LIKE IT AGAIN--!
THIS IS THE ROOM WHERE THE TAPPING OF BRAIN POWER TAKES PLACE!
THAT MAN--IT'S HENRY FAIRFAX, THE ENGINEER, ONE OF THE FIRST VICTIMS WHO DIS-APPEARED...
AS FLASH AT SUPER-SPEED FREES THE ENGINEER...
YOU'LL BE ALL RIGHT, FAIRFAX! DON'T LOSE HEART, MAN!
WE CAN DESTROY THIS SET-UP LATER, FLASH! RIGHT NOW...
... WE'VE GOT TO LOCATE THE MIKRID HIGHER-UPS... THE BIGWIGS HERE... AND DEAL WITH THEM!
WE'LL BE BACK SOON, FAIRFAX! JUST SIT TIGHT, MEANWHILE..!
16

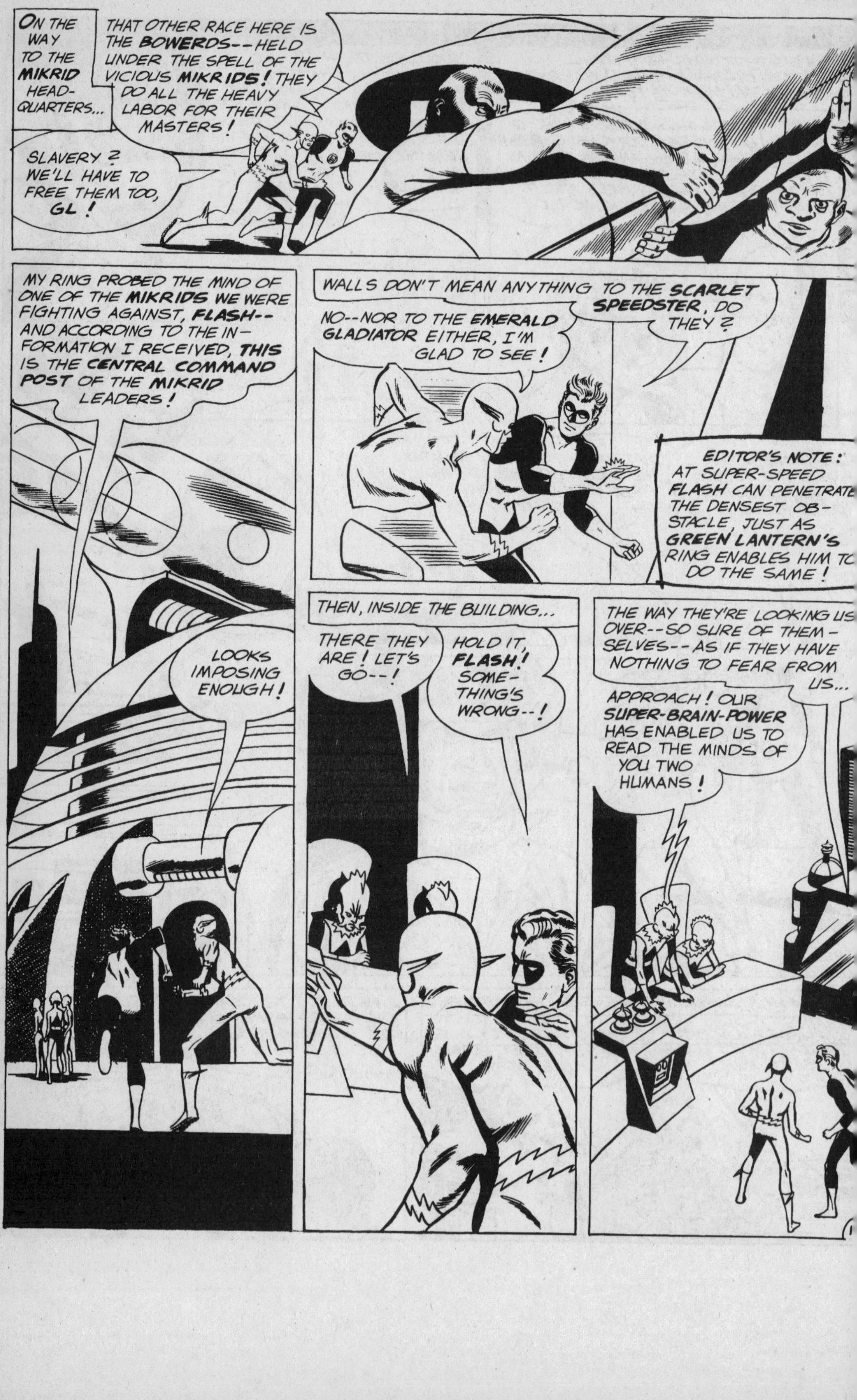
ON THE WAY TO THE MIKRID HEAD-QUARTERS...
THAT OTHER RACE HERE IS THE BOWERDS--HELD UNDER THE SPELL OF THE VICIOUS MIKRIDS! THEY DO ALL THE HEAVY LABOR FOR THEIR MASTERS!
SLAVERY? WE'LL HAVE TO FREE THEM TOO, GL!
MY RING PROBED THE MIND OF ONE OF THE MIKRIDS WE WERE FIGHTING AGAINST, FLASH-- AND ACCORDING TO THE INFORMATION I RECEIVED, THIS IS THE CENTRAL COMMAND POST OF THE MIKRID LEADERS!
LOOKS IMPOSING ENOUGH!
WALLS DON'T MEAN ANYTHING TO THE SCARLET SPEEDSTER, DO THEY?
NO--NOR TO THE EMERALD GLADIATOR EITHER, I'M GLAD TO SEE!
EDITOR'S NOTE: AT SUPER-SPEED FLASH CAN PENETRATE THE DENSEST OBSTACLE, JUST AS GREEN LANTERN'S RING ENABLES HIM TO DO THE SAME!
THEN, INSIDE THE BUILDING...
THERE THEY ARE! LET'S GO--!
HOLD IT, FLASH! SOMETHING'S WRONG--!
THE WAY THEY'RE LOOKING US OVER--SO SURE OF THEMSELVES--AS IF THEY HAVE NOTHING TO FEAR FROM US...
APPROACH! OUR SUPER-BRAIN-POWER HAS ENABLED US TO READ THE MINDS OF YOU TWO HUMANS!

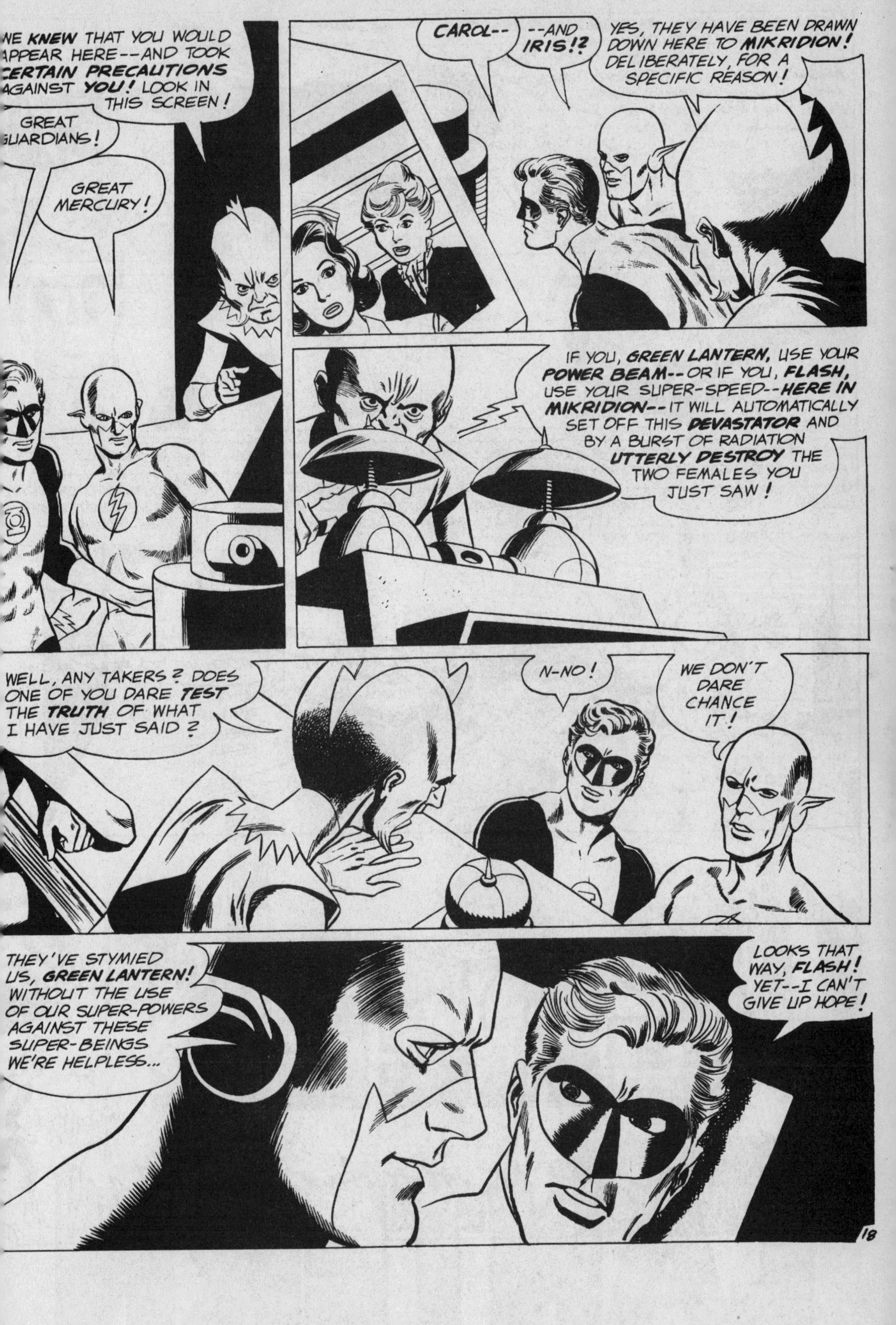
WE KNEW THAT YOU WOULD APPEAR HERE--AND TOOK CERTAIN PRECAUTIONS AGAINST YOU! LOOK IN THIS SCREEN!
GREAT GUARDIANS!
GREAT MERCURY!
CAROL--
--AND IRIS!?
YES, THEY HAVE BEEN DRAWN DOWN HERE TO MIKRIDION! DELIBERATELY, FOR A SPECIFIC REASON!
IF YOU, GREEN LANTERN, USE YOUR POWER BEAM--OR IF YOU, FLASH, USE YOUR SUPER-SPEED--HERE IN MIKRIDION--IT WILL AUTOMATICALLY SET OFF THIS DEVASTATOR AND BY A BURST OF RADIATION UTTERLY DESTROY THE TWO FEMALES YOU JUST SAW!
WELL, ANY TAKERS? DOES ONE OF YOU DARE TEST THE TRUTH OF WHAT I HAVE JUST SAID?
N-NO!
WE DON'T DARE CHANCE IT!
THEY'VE STYMIED US, GREEN LANTERN! WITHOUT THE USE OF OUR SUPER-POWERS AGAINST THESE SUPER-BEINGS WE'RE HELPLESS...
LOOKS THAT WAY, FLASH! YET--I CAN'T GIVE UP HOPE!
18

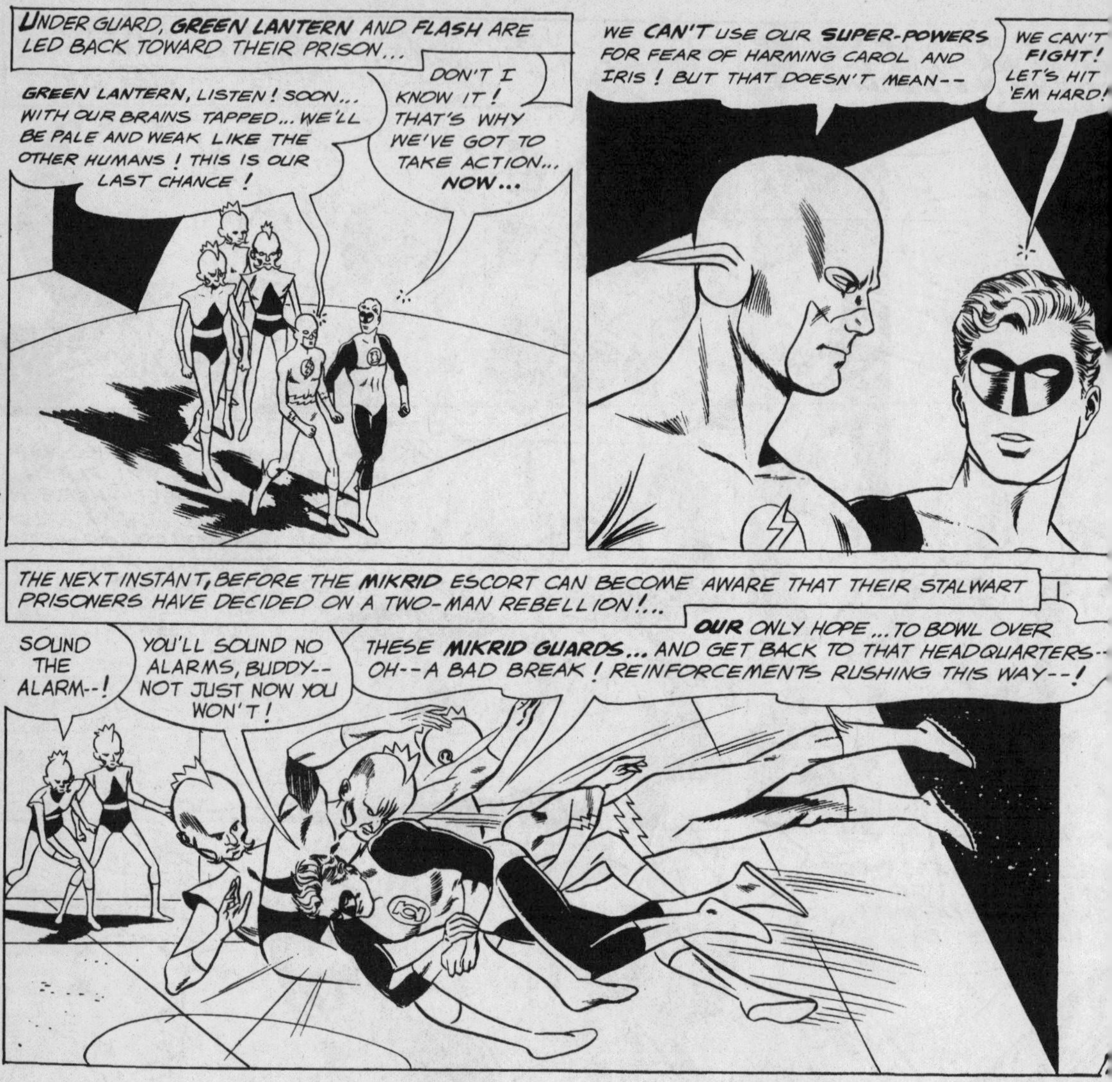
UNDER GUARD, GREEN LANTERN AND FLASH ARE LED BACK TOWARD THEIR PRISON...
GREEN LANTERN, LISTEN! SOON... WITH OUR BRAINS TAPPED... WE'LL BE PALE AND WEAK LIKE THE OTHER HUMANS! THIS IS OUR LAST CHANCE!
DON'T I KNOW IT! THAT'S WHY WE'VE GOT TO TAKE ACTION... NOW...
WE CAN'T USE OUR SUPER-POWERS FOR FEAR OF HARMING CAROL AND IRIS! BUT THAT DOESN'T MEAN--
WE CAN'T FIGHT! LET'S HIT 'EM HARD!
THE NEXT INSTANT, BEFORE THE MIKRID ESCORT CAN BECOME AWARE THAT THEIR STALWART PRISONERS HAVE DECIDED ON A TWO-MAN REBELLION!...
SOUND THE ALARM--!
YOU'LL SOUND NO ALARMS, BUDDY-- NOT JUST NOW YOU WON'T!
OUR ONLY HOPE... TO BOWL OVER THESE MIKRID GUARDS... AND GET BACK TO THAT HEADQUARTERS-- OH-- A BAD BREAK! REINFORCEMENTS RUSHING THIS WAY--!

GREEN LANTERN

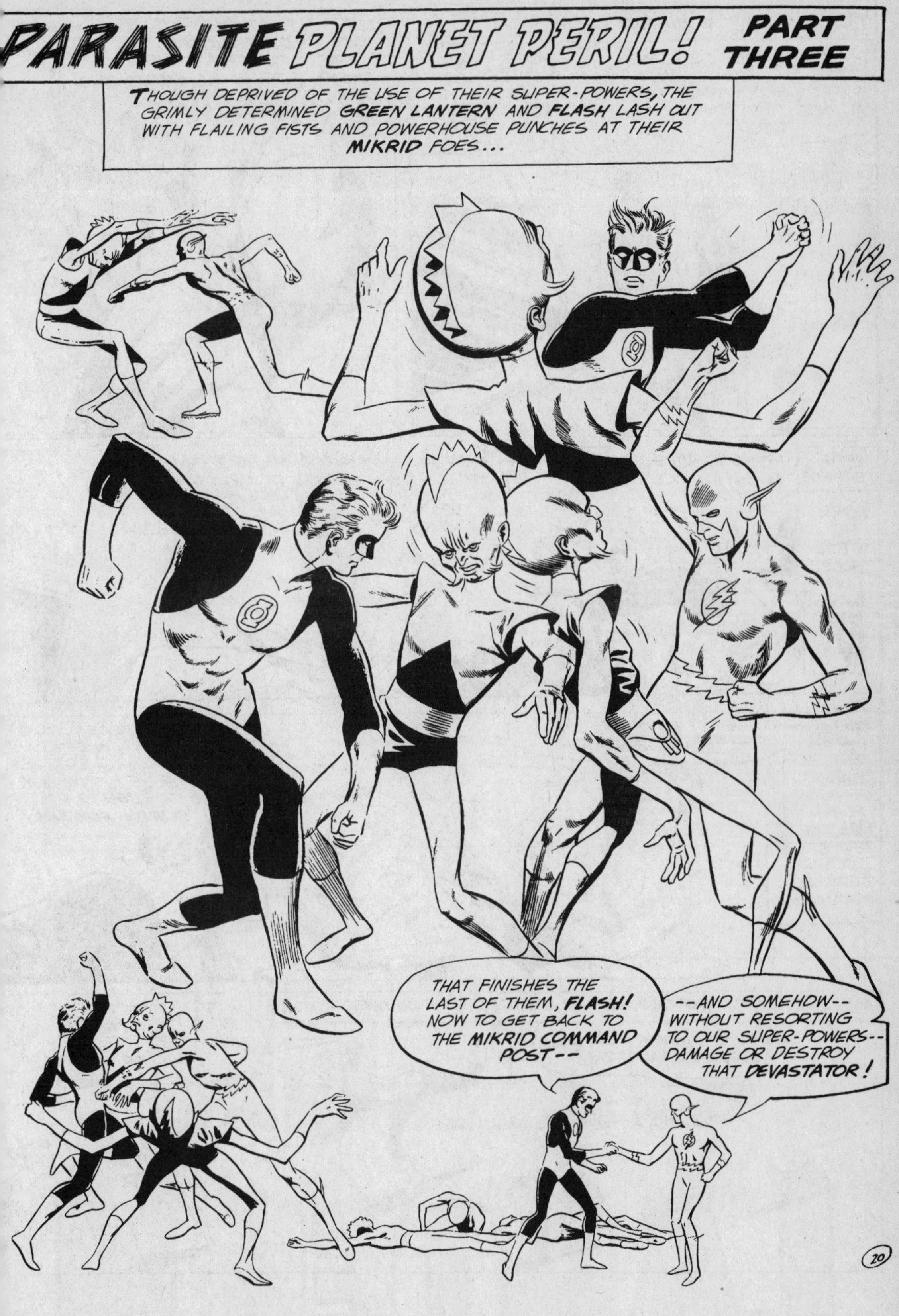
PARASITE PLANET PERIL! PART THREE
THOUGH DEPRIVED OF THE USE OF THEIR SUPER-POWERS, THE GRIMLY DETERMINED GREEN LANTERN AND FLASH LASH OUT WITH FLAILING FISTS AND POWERHOUSE PUNCHES AT THEIR MIKRID FOES...
THAT FINISHES THE LAST OF THEM, FLASH! NOW TO GET BACK TO THE MIKRID COMMAND POST--
--AND SOMEHOW--WITHOUT RESORTING TO OUR SUPER-POWERS--DAMAGE OR DESTROY THAT DEVASTATOR!
20

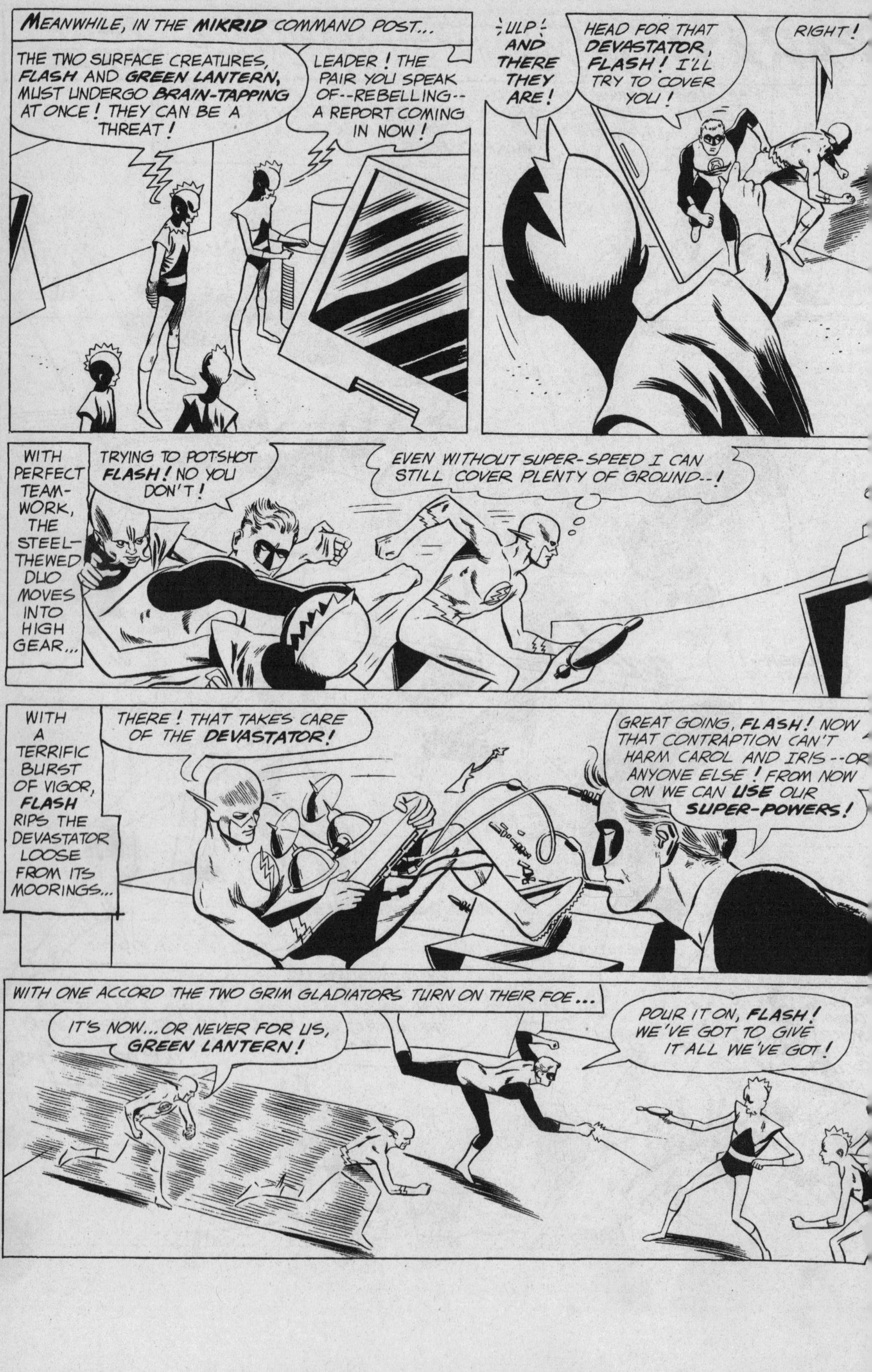
MEANWHILE, IN THE MIKRID COMMAND POST...
THE TWO SURFACE CREATURES, FLASH AND GREEN LANTERN, MUST UNDERGO BRAIN-TAPPING AT ONCE! THEY CAN BE A THREAT!
LEADER! THE PAIR YOU SPEAK OF--REBELLING--A REPORT COMING IN NOW!
ULP! AND THERE THEY ARE!
HEAD FOR THAT DEVASTATOR, FLASH! I'LL TRY TO COVER YOU!
RIGHT!
WITH PERFECT TEAM-WORK, THE STEEL-THEWED DUO MOVES INTO HIGH GEAR...
TRYING TO POTSHOT FLASH! NO YOU DON'T!
EVEN WITHOUT SUPER-SPEED I CAN STILL COVER PLENTY OF GROUND--!
WITH A TERRIFIC BURST OF VIGOR, FLASH RIPS THE DEVASTATOR LOOSE FROM ITS MOORINGS...
THERE! THAT TAKES CARE OF THE DEVASTATOR!
GREAT GOING, FLASH! NOW THAT CONTRAPTION CAN'T HARM CAROL AND IRIS--OR ANYONE ELSE! FROM NOW ON WE CAN USE OUR SUPER-POWERS!
WITH ONE ACCORD THE TWO GRIM GLADIATORS TURN ON THEIR FOE...
IT'S NOW...OR NEVER FOR US, GREEN LANTERN!
POUR IT ON, FLASH! WE'VE GOT TO GIVE IT ALL WE'VE GOT!

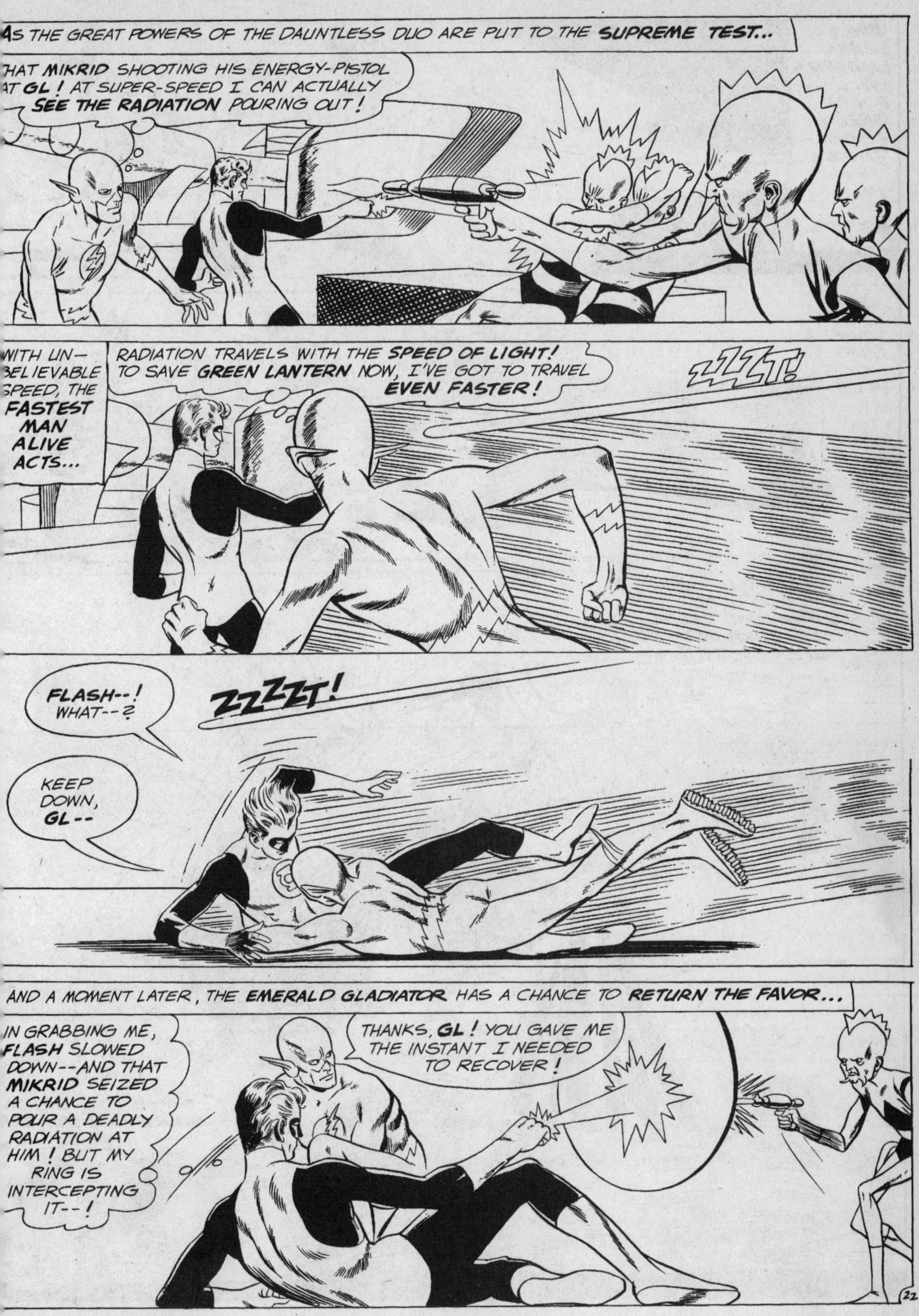
AS THE GREAT POWERS OF THE DAUNTLESS DUO ARE PUT TO THE SUPREME TEST...
THAT MIKRID SHOOTING HIS ENERGY-PISTOL AT GL! AT SUPER-SPEED I CAN ACTUALLY SEE THE RADIATION POURING OUT!
WITH UNBELIEVABLE SPEED, THE FASTEST MAN ALIVE ACTS...
RADIATION TRAVELS WITH THE SPEED OF LIGHT! TO SAVE GREEN LANTERN NOW, I'VE GOT TO TRAVEL EVEN FASTER!
ZZZT!
FLASH--! WHAT--?
ZZZZT!
KEEP DOWN, GL--
AND A MOMENT LATER, THE EMERALD GLADIATOR HAS A CHANCE TO RETURN THE FAVOR...
IN GRABBING ME, FLASH SLOWED DOWN--AND THAT MIKRID SEIZED A CHANCE TO POUR A DEADLY RADIATION AT HIM! BUT MY RING IS INTERCEPTING IT--!
THANKS, GL! YOU GAVE ME THE INSTANT I NEEDED TO RECOVER!
22

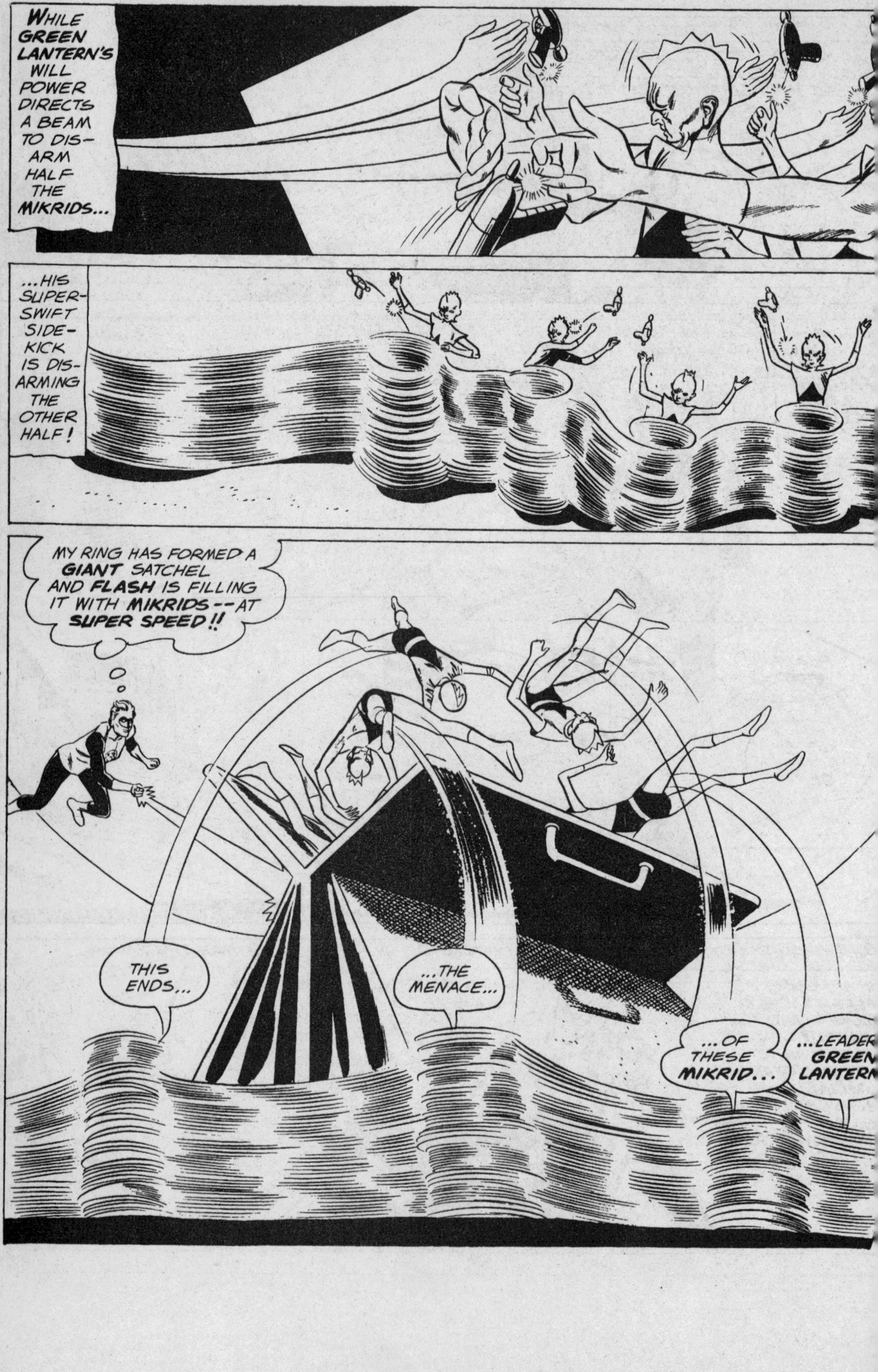
WHILE GREEN LANTERN'S WILL POWER DIRECTS A BEAM TO DIS-ARM HALF THE MIKRIDS...
...HIS SUPER-SWIFT SIDE-KICK IS DIS-ARMING THE OTHER HALF!
MY RING HAS FORMED A GIANT SATCHEL AND FLASH IS FILLING IT WITH MIKRIDS--AT SUPER SPEED!!
THIS ENDS...
...THE MENACE...
...OF THESE MIKRID...
...LEADER GREEN LANTERN

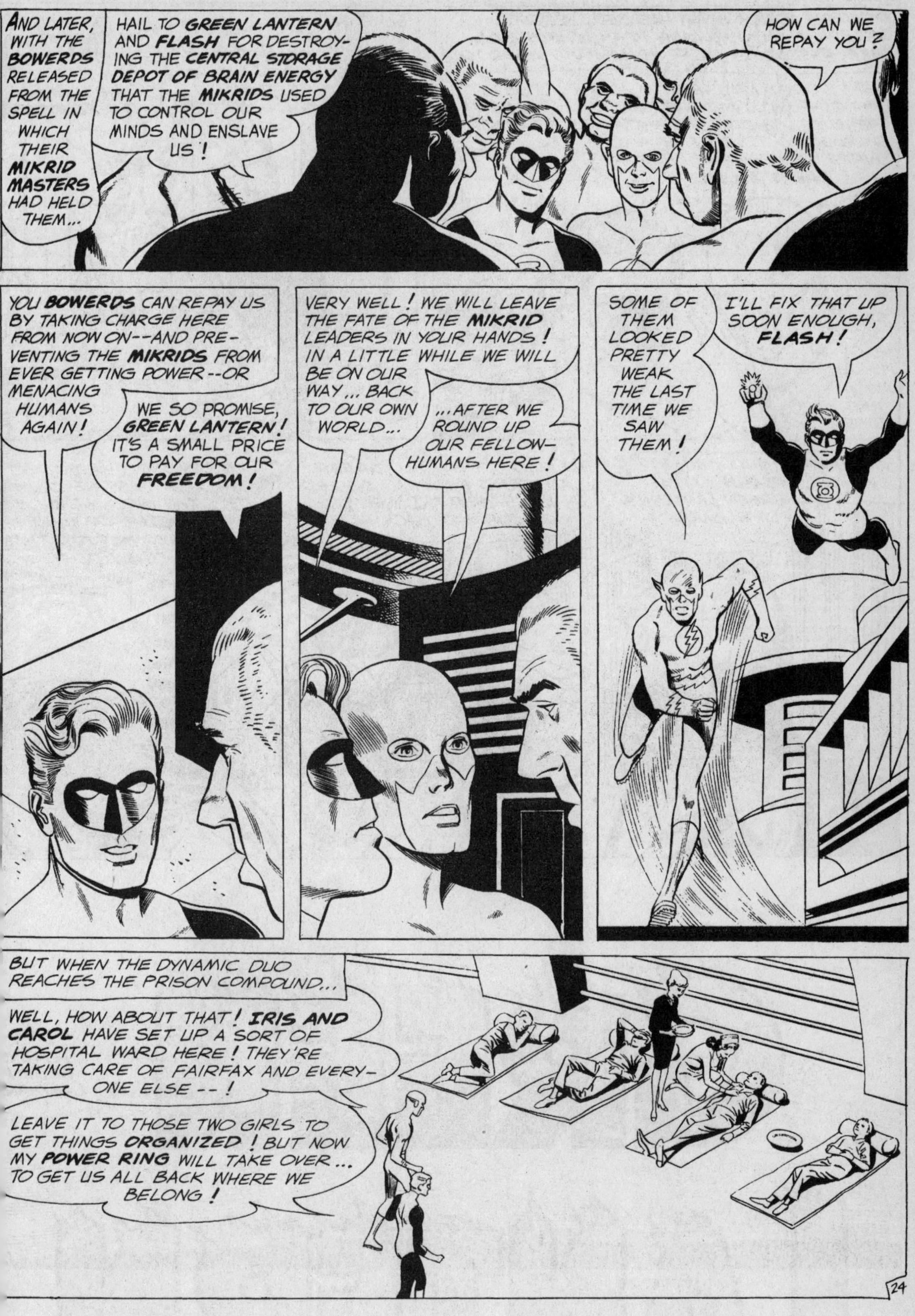
AND LATER, WITH THE BOWERDS RELEASED FROM THE SPELL IN WHICH THEIR MIKRID MASTERS HAD HELD THEM...
HAIL TO GREEN LANTERN AND FLASH FOR DESTROYING THE CENTRAL STORAGE DEPOT OF BRAIN ENERGY THAT THE MIKRIDS USED TO CONTROL OUR MINDS AND ENSLAVE US!
HOW CAN WE REPAY YOU?
YOU BOWERDS CAN REPAY US BY TAKING CHARGE HERE FROM NOW ON--AND PREVENTING THE MIKRIDS FROM EVER GETTING POWER--OR MENACING HUMANS AGAIN!
WE SO PROMISE, GREEN LANTERN! IT'S A SMALL PRICE TO PAY FOR OUR FREEDOM!
VERY WELL! WE WILL LEAVE THE FATE OF THE MIKRID LEADERS IN YOUR HANDS! IN A LITTLE WHILE WE WILL BE ON OUR WAY... BACK TO OUR OWN WORLD...
...AFTER WE ROUND UP OUR FELLOW-HUMANS HERE!
SOME OF THEM LOOKED PRETTY WEAK THE LAST TIME WE SAW THEM!
I'LL FIX THAT UP SOON ENOUGH, FLASH!
BUT WHEN THE DYNAMIC DUO REACHES THE PRISON COMPOUND...
WELL, HOW ABOUT THAT! IRIS AND CAROL HAVE SET UP A SORT OF HOSPITAL WARD HERE! THEY'RE TAKING CARE OF FAIRFAX AND EVERYONE ELSE--!
LEAVE IT TO THOSE TWO GIRLS TO GET THINGS ORGANIZED! BUT NOW MY POWER RING WILL TAKE OVER... TO GET US ALL BACK WHERE WE BELONG!
24

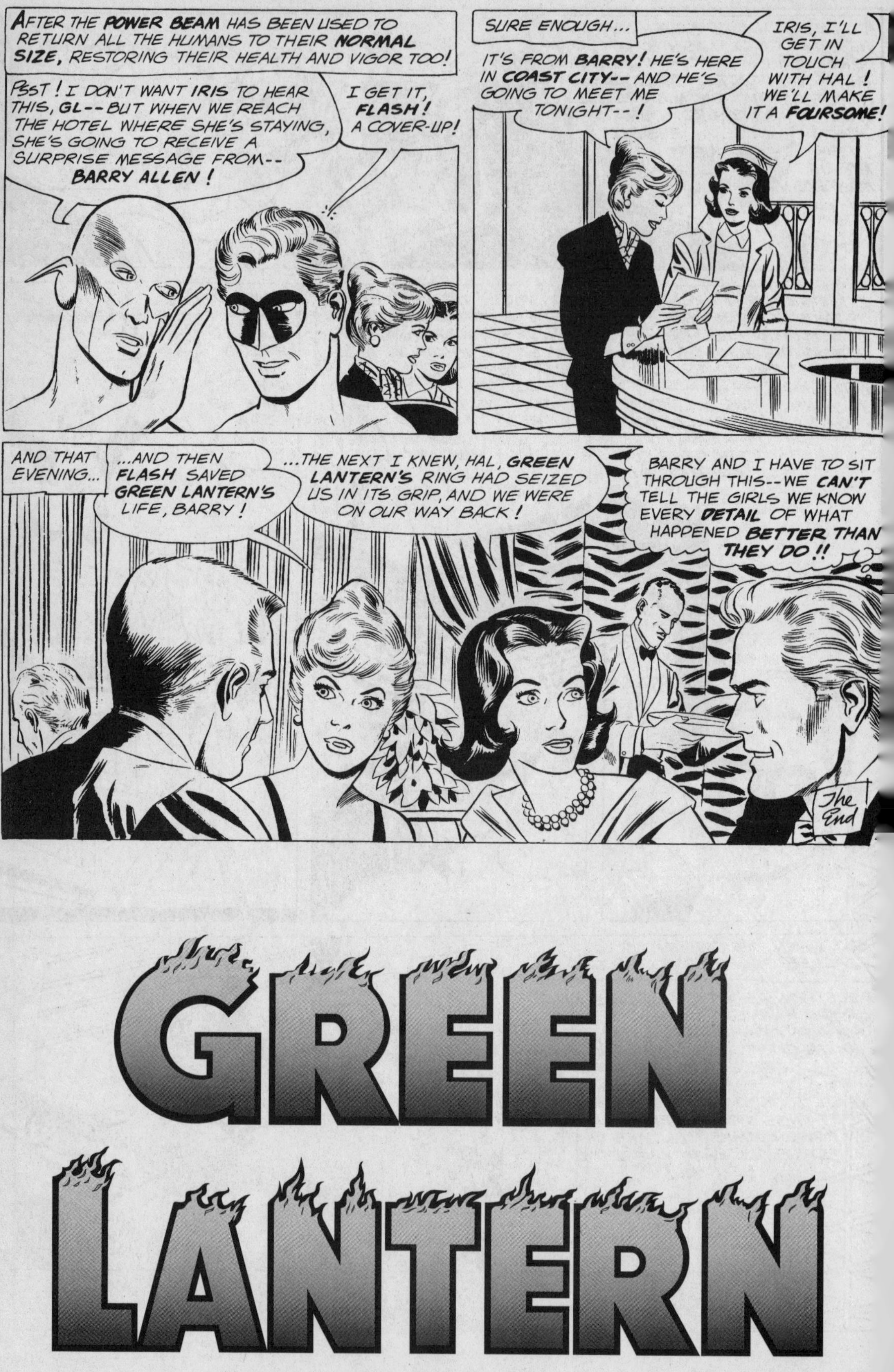
AFTER THE POWER BEAM HAS BEEN USED TO RETURN ALL THE HUMANS TO THEIR NORMAL SIZE, RESTORING THEIR HEALTH AND VIGOR TOO!
PSST! I DON'T WANT IRIS TO HEAR THIS, GL--BUT WHEN WE REACH THE HOTEL WHERE SHE'S STAYING, SHE'S GOING TO RECEIVE A SURPRISE MESSAGE FROM-- BARRY ALLEN!
I GET IT, FLASH! A COVER-UP!
SURE ENOUGH...
IT'S FROM BARRY! HE'S HERE IN COAST CITY-- AND HE'S GOING TO MEET ME TONIGHT--!
IRIS, I'LL GET IN TOUCH WITH HAL! WE'LL MAKE IT A FOURSOME!
AND THAT EVENING...
...AND THEN FLASH SAVED GREEN LANTERN'S LIFE, BARRY!
...THE NEXT I KNEW, HAL, GREEN LANTERN'S RING HAD SEIZED US IN ITS GRIP, AND WE WERE ON OUR WAY BACK!
BARRY AND I HAVE TO SIT THROUGH THIS--WE CAN'T TELL THE GIRLS WE KNOW EVERY DETAIL OF WHAT HAPPENED BETTER THAN THEY DO!!
The End

GREEN LANTERN

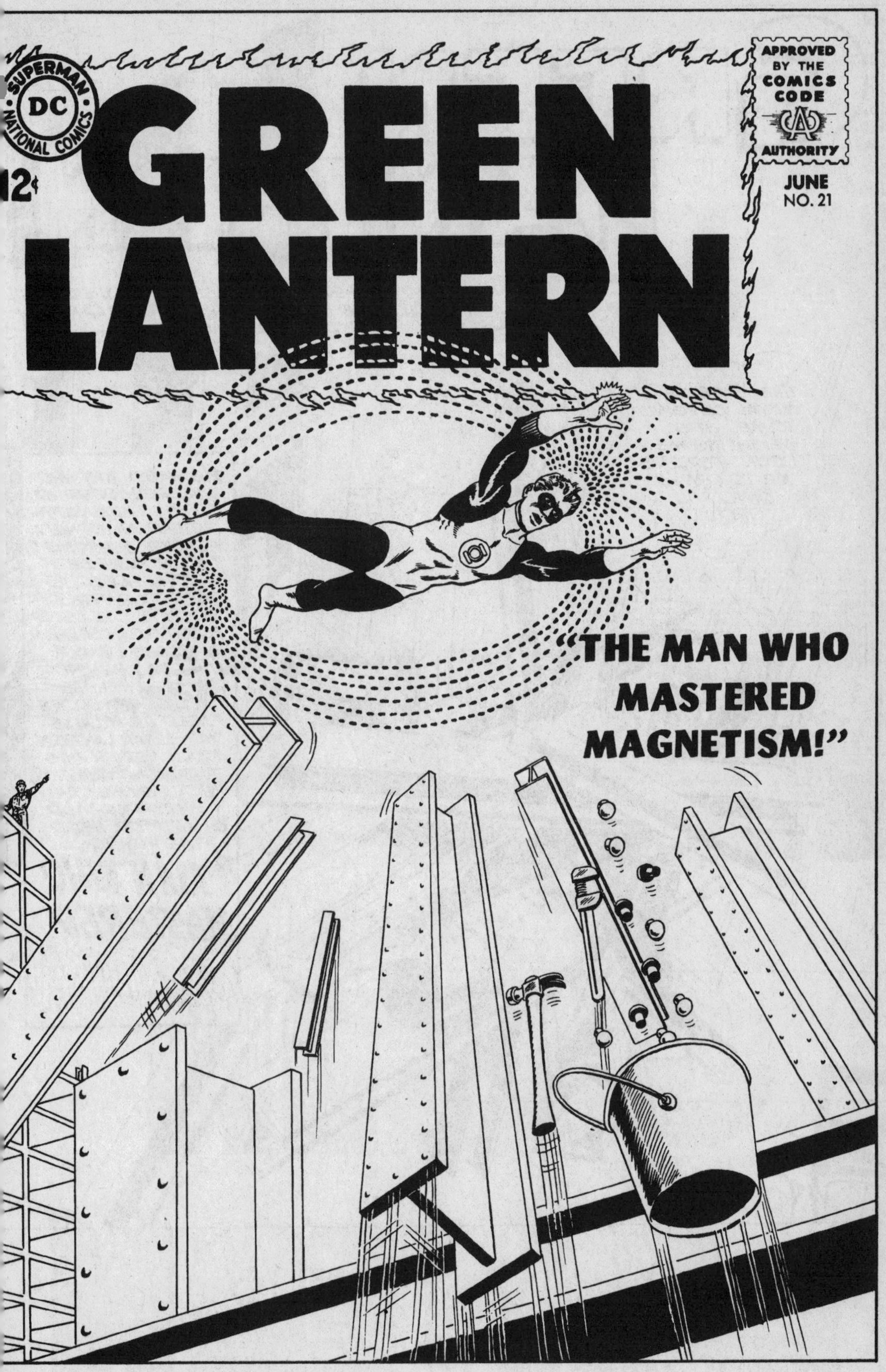
SUPERMAN
DC
NATIONAL COMICS
12¢
GREEN LANTERN
APPROVED BY THE COMICS CODE AUTHORITY
JUNE
NO. 21
"THE MAN WHO MASTERED MAGNETISM!"

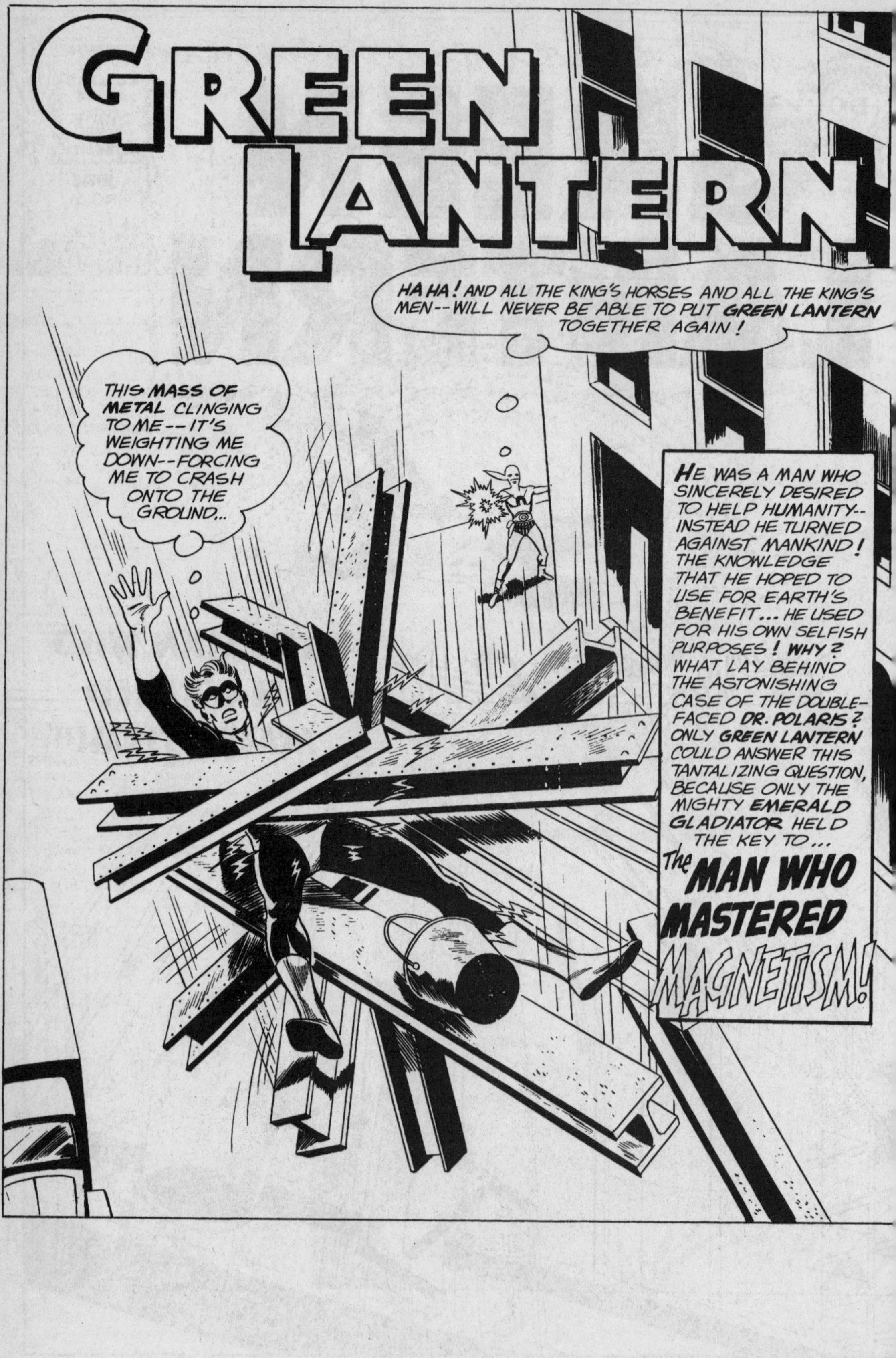
GREEN LANTERN
HA HA! AND ALL THE KING'S HORSES AND ALL THE KING'S MEN--WILL NEVER BE ABLE TO PUT GREEN LANTERN TOGETHER AGAIN!
THIS MASS OF METAL CLINGING TO ME--IT'S WEIGHTING ME DOWN--FORCING ME TO CRASH ONTO THE GROUND...
HE WAS A MAN WHO SINCERELY DESIRED TO HELP HUMANITY--INSTEAD HE TURNED AGAINST MANKIND! THE KNOWLEDGE THAT HE HOPED TO USE FOR EARTH'S BENEFIT... HE USED FOR HIS OWN SELFISH PURPOSES! WHY? WHAT LAY BEHIND THE ASTONISHING CASE OF THE DOUBLE-FACED DR. POLARIS? ONLY GREEN LANTERN COULD ANSWER THIS TANTALIZING QUESTION, BECAUSE ONLY THE MIGHTY EMERALD GLADIATOR HELD THE KEY TO...
The MAN WHO MASTERED MAGNETISM!

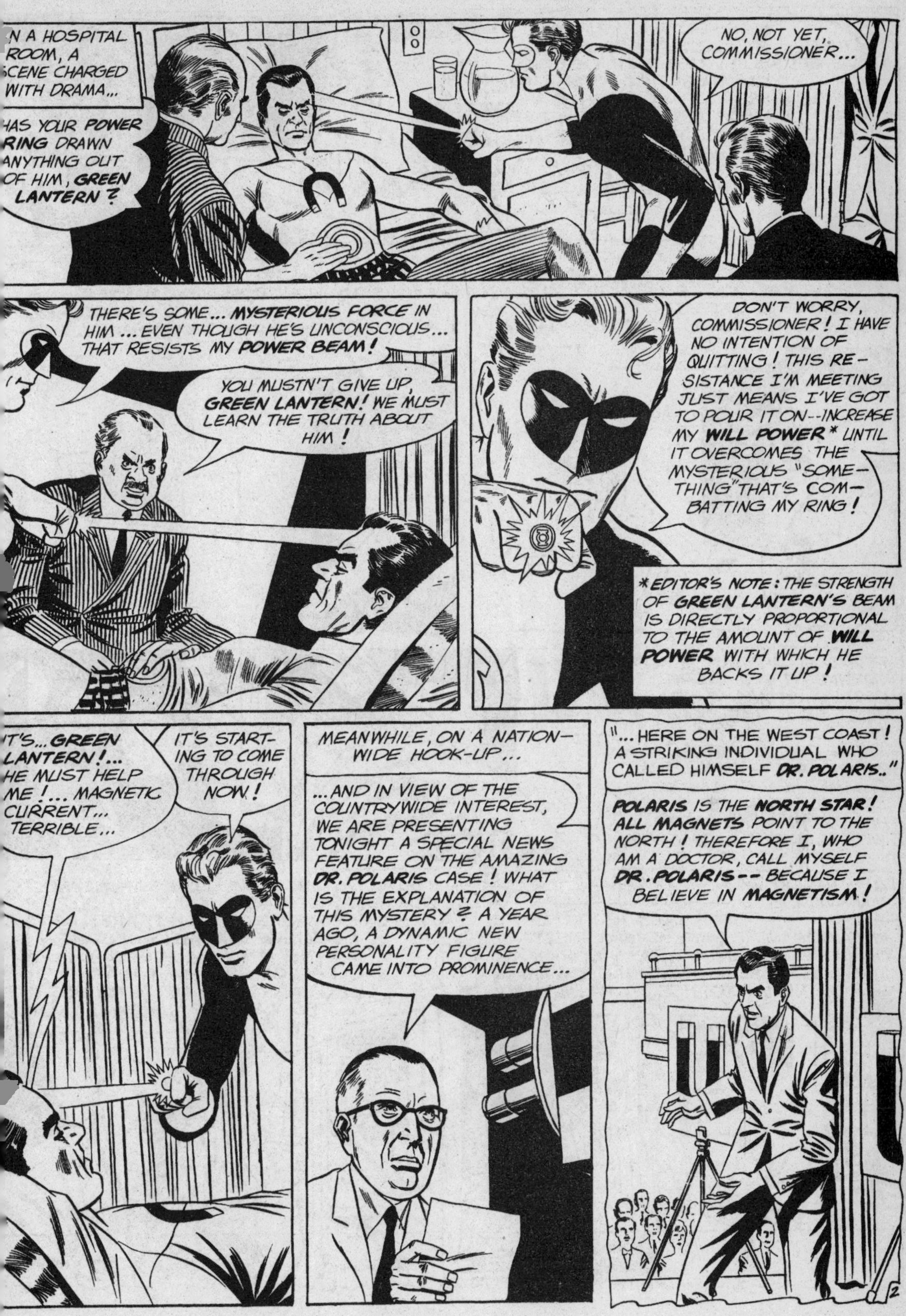
N A HOSPITAL ROOM, A SCENE CHARGED WITH DRAMA...
HAS YOUR POWER RING DRAWN ANYTHING OUT OF HIM, GREEN LANTERN?
NO, NOT YET, COMMISSIONER...
THERE'S SOME... MYSTERIOUS FORCE IN HIM ... EVEN THOUGH HE'S UNCONSCIOUS... THAT RESISTS MY POWER BEAM!
YOU MUSTN'T GIVE UP, GREEN LANTERN! WE MUST LEARN THE TRUTH ABOUT HIM!
DON'T WORRY, COMMISSIONER! I HAVE NO INTENTION OF QUITTING! THIS RESISTANCE I'M MEETING JUST MEANS I'VE GOT TO POUR IT ON--INCREASE MY WILL POWER* UNTIL IT OVERCOMES THE MYSTERIOUS "SOMETHING" THAT'S COMBATTING MY RING!
*EDITOR'S NOTE: THE STRENGTH OF GREEN LANTERN'S BEAM IS DIRECTLY PROPORTIONAL TO THE AMOUNT OF WILL POWER WITH WHICH HE BACKS IT UP!
IT'S... GREEN LANTERN!... HE MUST HELP ME!... MAGNETIC CURRENT... TERRIBLE...
IT'S STARTING TO COME THROUGH NOW!
MEANWHILE, ON A NATION-WIDE HOOK-UP...
...AND IN VIEW OF THE COUNTRYWIDE INTEREST, WE ARE PRESENTING TONIGHT A SPECIAL NEWS FEATURE ON THE AMAZING DR. POLARIS CASE! WHAT IS THE EXPLANATION OF THIS MYSTERY? A YEAR AGO, A DYNAMIC NEW PERSONALITY FIGURE CAME INTO PROMINENCE...
"...HERE ON THE WEST COAST! A STRIKING INDIVIDUAL WHO CALLED HIMSELF DR. POLARIS.."
POLARIS IS THE NORTH STAR! ALL MAGNETS POINT TO THE NORTH! THEREFORE I, WHO AM A DOCTOR, CALL MYSELF DR. POLARIS-- BECAUSE I BELIEVE IN MAGNETISM!
2

"HIS LECTURES ON 'HEALTH VIA MAGNETISM' WERE FILLED TO OVERFLOWING! PEOPLE DRANK IN HIS WORDS..."

YOUR HEALTH IS YOUR MOST PRECIOUS POSSESSION! BUT YOUR HEALTH DEPENDS ON MAGNETISM! TOO MANY PEOPLE HAVE IGNORED THE IMPORTANCE OF MAGNETISM FOR TOO LONG--AND THERE HAS BEEN MUCH SICKNESS! I WILL CORRECT THAT! LISTEN--

MAGNETISM WILL HELP YOU WHILE YOU SLEEP! BUT YOUR BED MUST BE PLACED SO THAT THE MAGNETIC LINES OF FORCE IN THE EARTH TRAVEL ALONG YOUR BODY FROM HEAD TO TOE!

HOWEVER, IF THE MAGNA-FORCE TRAVERSES YOUR BODY IN A CROSSWISE MANNER--AS PICTURED HERE--IT SETS UP DISORDERLY ACTIVITY IN THE BODY CELLS--AND LEADS TO BAD HEALTH!

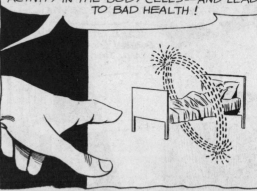

HE HAD MUCH OTHER ADVICE TO GIVE! THERE WERE CERTAIN METALS THAT ALL MUST AVOID--AS DRAWING HARMFUL FORMS OF MAGNETISM TO THEM! DR. POLARIS'S OWN VIBRANT DYNAMIC HEALTH WAS HIS BEST ADVERTISEMENT! HE LITERALLY VIBRATED WITH MYSTERIOUS ENERGY!

"MANY NAMED HIM A GREAT BENEFACTOR OF MANKIND...!"

DR. POLARIS HELPED ME! MY FAMILY AND I HAVE NEVER CEASED TO THANK HIM! I CAN DO A DAY'S WORK NOW LIKE ANYONE ELSE--BECAUSE I'M AWARE OF THE IMPORTANCE OF MAGNETISM!

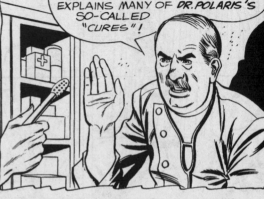

"BUT OTHERS..."

MEDICINE CURES THOUSANDS OF CASES DAILY WITHOUT MAGNETISM! BUT WHEN PEOPLE BELIEVE STRONGLY IN SOMETHING IT HAS A POWERFUL EFFECT ON THEM! THAT EXPLAINS MANY OF DR. POLARIS'S SO-CALLED "CURES"!

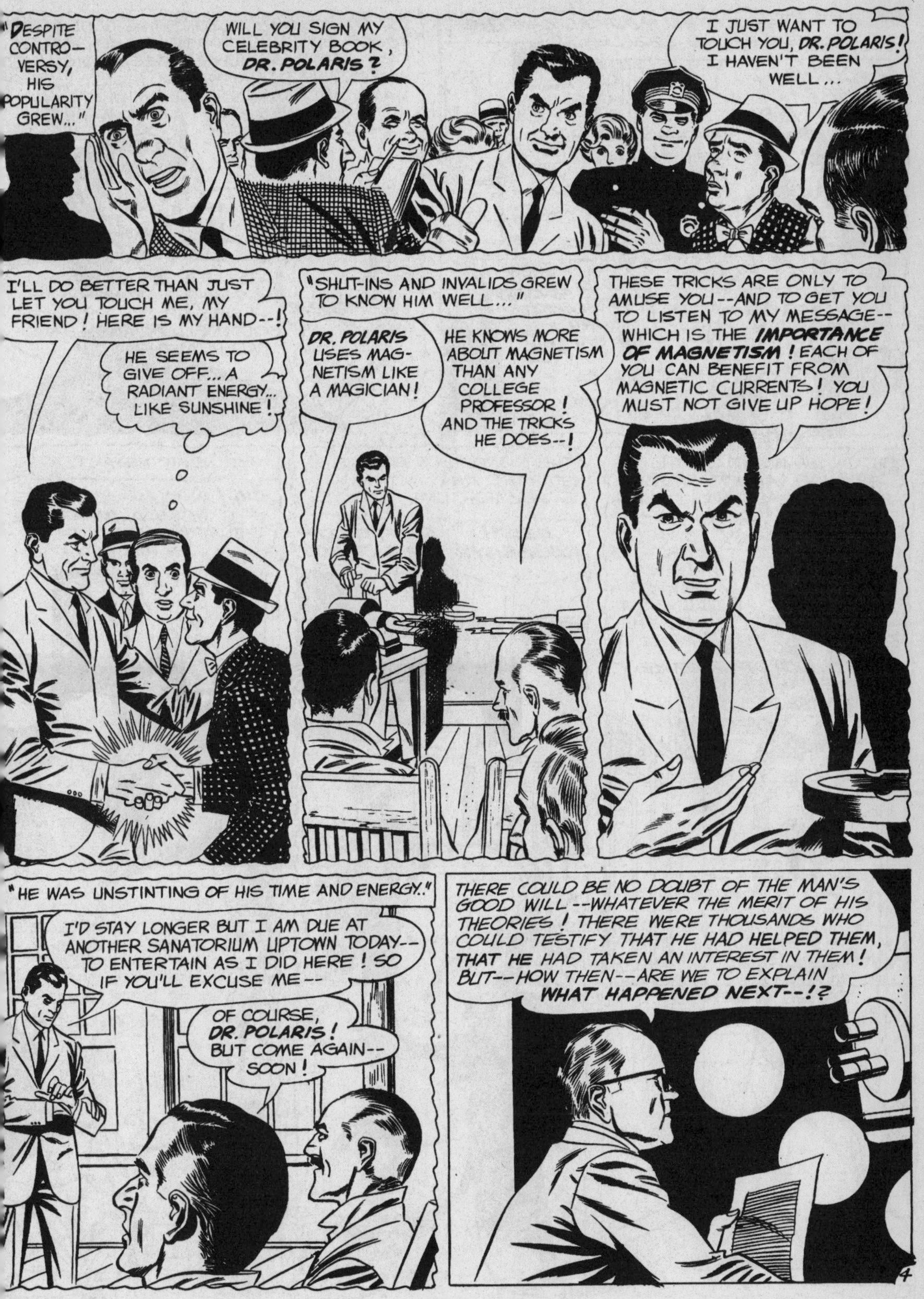
"DESPITE CONTROVERSY, HIS POPULARITY GREW..."
WILL YOU SIGN MY CELEBRITY BOOK, DR. POLARIS?
I JUST WANT TO TOUCH YOU, DR. POLARIS! I HAVEN'T BEEN WELL...
I'LL DO BETTER THAN JUST LET YOU TOUCH ME, MY FRIEND! HERE IS MY HAND--!
HE SEEMS TO GIVE OFF... A RADIANT ENERGY... LIKE SUNSHINE!
"SHUT-INS AND INVALIDS GREW TO KNOW HIM WELL..."
DR. POLARIS USES MAGNETISM LIKE A MAGICIAN!
HE KNOWS MORE ABOUT MAGNETISM THAN ANY COLLEGE PROFESSOR! AND THE TRICKS HE DOES--!
THESE TRICKS ARE ONLY TO AMUSE YOU--AND TO GET YOU TO LISTEN TO MY MESSAGE--WHICH IS THE IMPORTANCE OF MAGNETISM! EACH OF YOU CAN BENEFIT FROM MAGNETIC CURRENTS! YOU MUST NOT GIVE UP HOPE!
"HE WAS UNSTINTING OF HIS TIME AND ENERGY."
I'D STAY LONGER BUT I AM DUE AT ANOTHER SANATORIUM UPTOWN TODAY--TO ENTERTAIN AS I DID HERE! SO IF YOU'LL EXCUSE ME--
OF COURSE, DR. POLARIS! BUT COME AGAIN--SOON!
THERE COULD BE NO DOUBT OF THE MAN'S GOOD WILL--WHATEVER THE MERIT OF HIS THEORIES! THERE WERE THOUSANDS WHO COULD TESTIFY THAT HE HAD HELPED THEM, THAT HE HAD TAKEN AN INTEREST IN THEM! BUT--HOW THEN--ARE WE TO EXPLAIN WHAT HAPPENED NEXT--!?
4

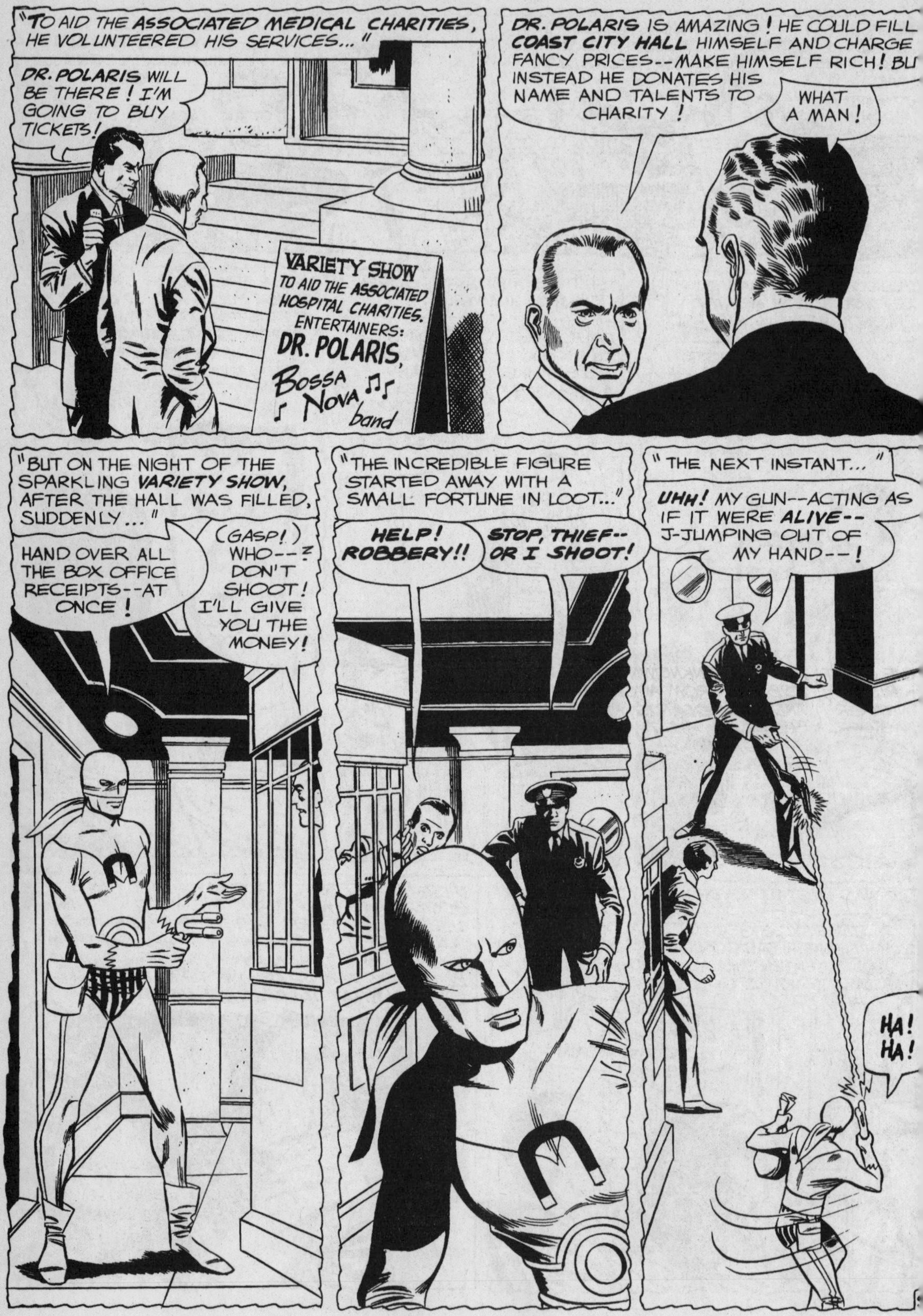
"TO AID THE ASSOCIATED MEDICAL CHARITIES, HE VOLUNTEERED HIS SERVICES..."
DR. POLARIS WILL BE THERE! I'M GOING TO BUY TICKETS!
VARIETY SHOW TO AID THE ASSOCIATED HOSPITAL CHARITIES. ENTERTAINERS: DR. POLARIS, Bossa Nova band
DR. POLARIS IS AMAZING! HE COULD FILL COAST CITY HALL HIMSELF AND CHARGE FANCY PRICES--MAKE HIMSELF RICH! BU
INSTEAD HE DONATES HIS NAME AND TALENTS TO CHARITY!
WHAT A MAN!
"BUT ON THE NIGHT OF THE SPARKLING VARIETY SHOW, AFTER THE HALL WAS FILLED, SUDDENLY..."
HAND OVER ALL THE BOX OFFICE RECEIPTS--AT ONCE!
(GASP!) WHO--? DON'T SHOOT! I'LL GIVE YOU THE MONEY!
"THE INCREDIBLE FIGURE STARTED AWAY WITH A SMALL FORTUNE IN LOOT..."
HELP! ROBBERY!!
STOP, THIEF--OR I SHOOT!
"THE NEXT INSTANT..."
UHH! MY GUN--ACTING AS IF IT WERE ALIVE--J-JUMPING OUT OF MY HAND--!
HA! HA!

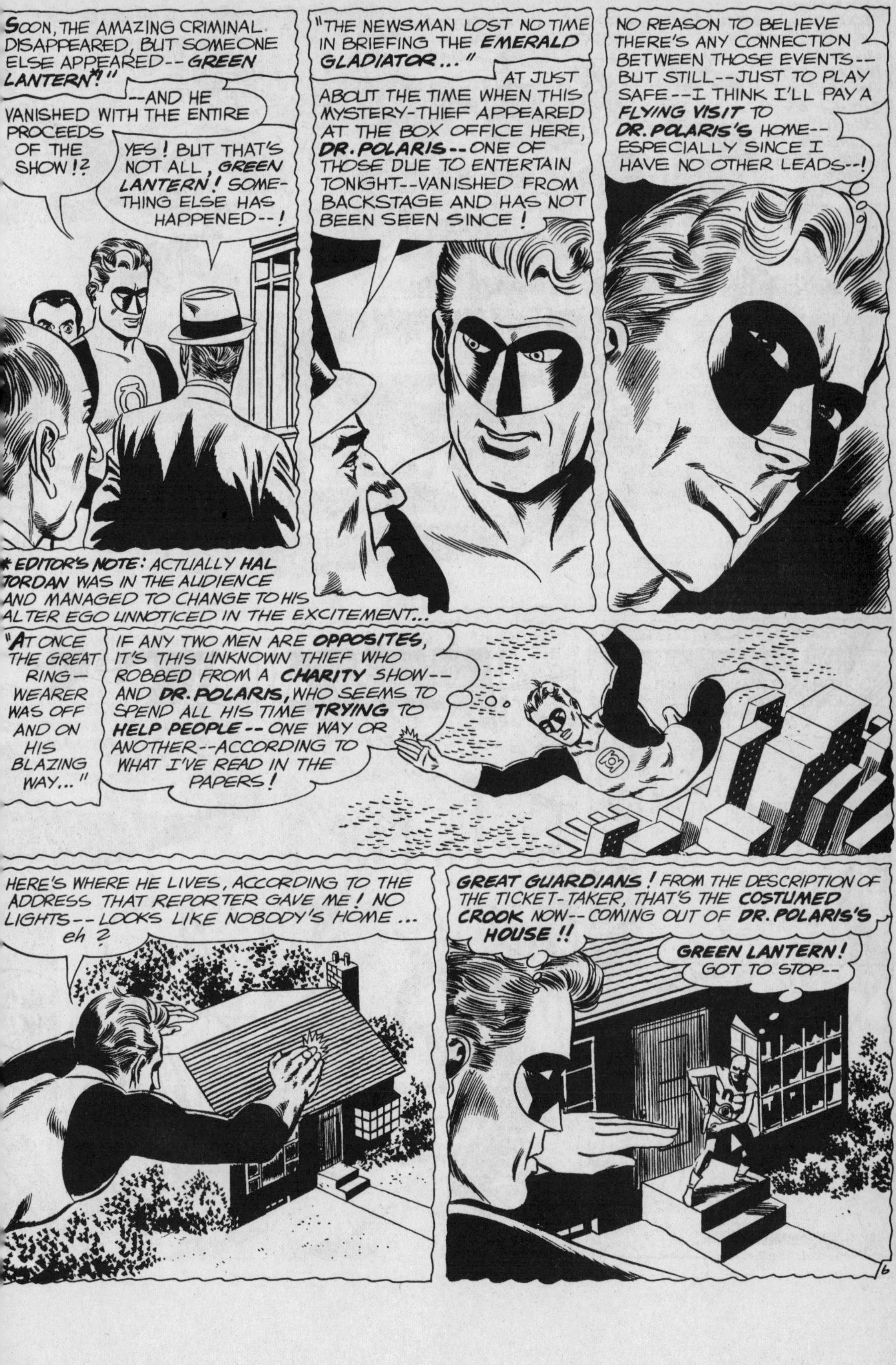
SOON, THE AMAZING CRIMINAL DISAPPEARED, BUT SOMEONE ELSE APPEARED-- GREEN LANTERN*!"
--AND HE VANISHED WITH THE ENTIRE PROCEEDS OF THE SHOW!?
YES! BUT THAT'S NOT ALL, GREEN LANTERN! SOMETHING ELSE HAS HAPPENED--!
"THE NEWSMAN LOST NO TIME IN BRIEFING THE EMERALD GLADIATOR..."
AT JUST ABOUT THE TIME WHEN THIS MYSTERY-THIEF APPEARED AT THE BOX OFFICE HERE, DR. POLARIS--ONE OF THOSE DUE TO ENTERTAIN TONIGHT--VANISHED FROM BACKSTAGE AND HAS NOT BEEN SEEN SINCE!
NO REASON TO BELIEVE THERE'S ANY CONNECTION BETWEEN THOSE EVENTS--BUT STILL--JUST TO PLAY SAFE--I THINK I'LL PAY A FLYING VISIT TO DR. POLARIS'S HOME--ESPECIALLY SINCE I HAVE NO OTHER LEADS--!
* EDITOR'S NOTE: ACTUALLY HAL JORDAN WAS IN THE AUDIENCE AND MANAGED TO CHANGE TO HIS ALTER EGO UNNOTICED IN THE EXCITEMENT...
"AT ONCE THE GREAT RING-WEARER WAS OFF AND ON HIS BLAZING WAY..."
IF ANY TWO MEN ARE OPPOSITES, IT'S THIS UNKNOWN THIEF WHO ROBBED FROM A CHARITY SHOW--AND DR. POLARIS, WHO SEEMS TO SPEND ALL HIS TIME TRYING TO HELP PEOPLE--ONE WAY OR ANOTHER--ACCORDING TO WHAT I'VE READ IN THE PAPERS!
HERE'S WHERE HE LIVES, ACCORDING TO THE ADDRESS THAT REPORTER GAVE ME! NO LIGHTS--LOOKS LIKE NOBODY'S HOME... eh?
GREAT GUARDIANS! FROM THE DESCRIPTION OF THE TICKET-TAKER, THAT'S THE COSTUMED CROOK NOW--COMING OUT OF DR. POLARIS'S HOUSE!!
GREEN LANTERN! GOT TO STOP--
6

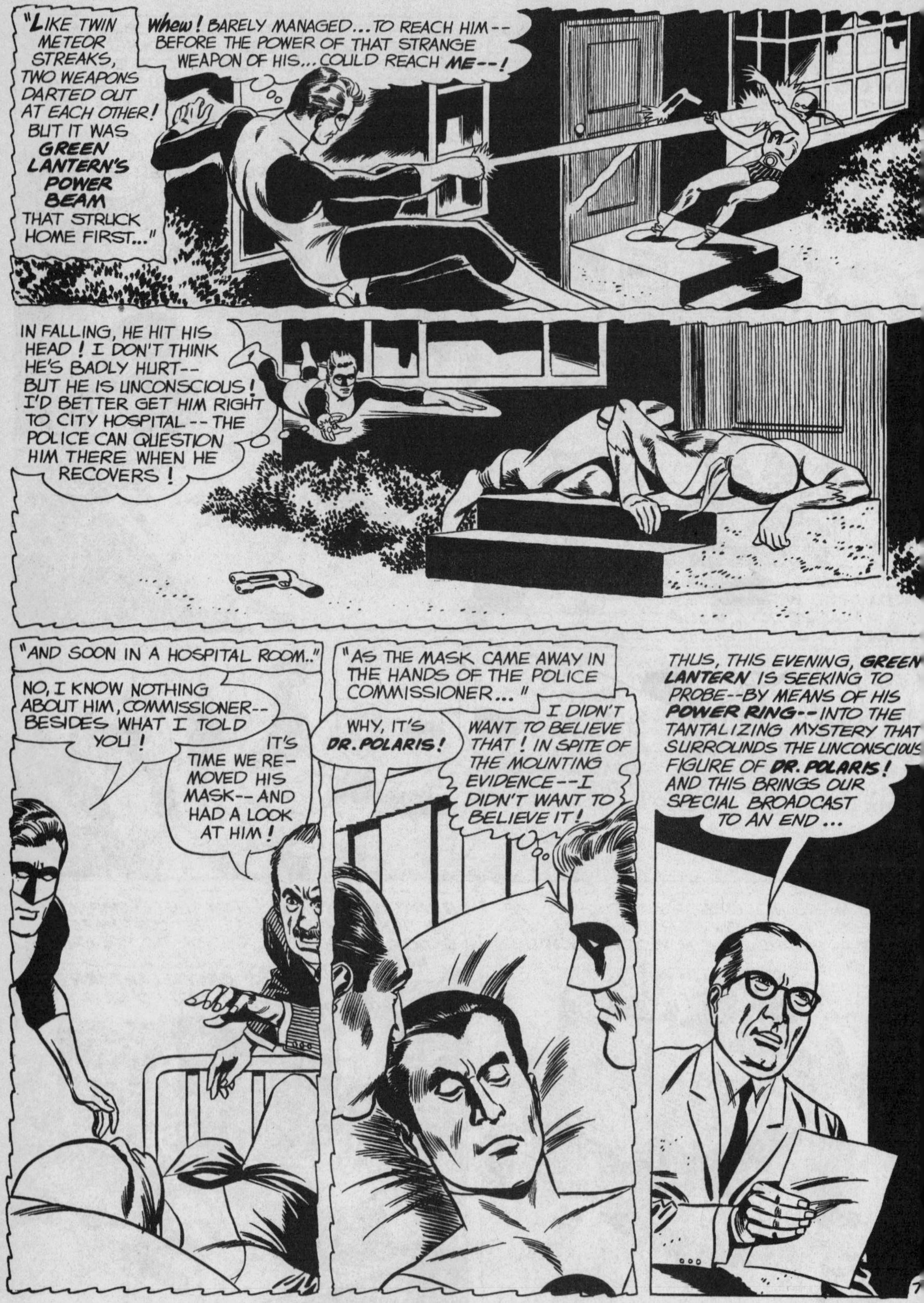
"LIKE TWIN METEOR STREAKS, TWO WEAPONS DARTED OUT AT EACH OTHER! BUT IT WAS GREEN LANTERN'S POWER BEAM THAT STRUCK HOME FIRST..."
Whew! BARELY MANAGED... TO REACH HIM-- BEFORE THE POWER OF THAT STRANGE WEAPON OF HIS... COULD REACH ME--!
IN FALLING, HE HIT HIS HEAD! I DON'T THINK HE'S BADLY HURT-- BUT HE IS UNCONSCIOUS! I'D BETTER GET HIM RIGHT TO CITY HOSPITAL -- THE POLICE CAN QUESTION HIM THERE WHEN HE RECOVERS!
"AND SOON IN A HOSPITAL ROOM.."
NO, I KNOW NOTHING ABOUT HIM, COMMISSIONER-- BESIDES WHAT I TOLD YOU!
IT'S TIME WE REMOVED HIS MASK-- AND HAD A LOOK AT HIM!
"AS THE MASK CAME AWAY IN THE HANDS OF THE POLICE COMMISSIONER..."
WHY, IT'S DR. POLARIS!
I DIDN'T WANT TO BELIEVE THAT! IN SPITE OF THE MOUNTING EVIDENCE--I DIDN'T WANT TO BELIEVE IT!
THUS, THIS EVENING, GREEN LANTERN IS SEEKING TO PROBE--BY MEANS OF HIS POWER RING--INTO THE TANTALIZING MYSTERY THAT SURROUNDS THE UNCONSCIOUS FIGURE OF DR. POLARIS! AND THIS BRINGS OUR SPECIAL BROADCAST TO AN END...

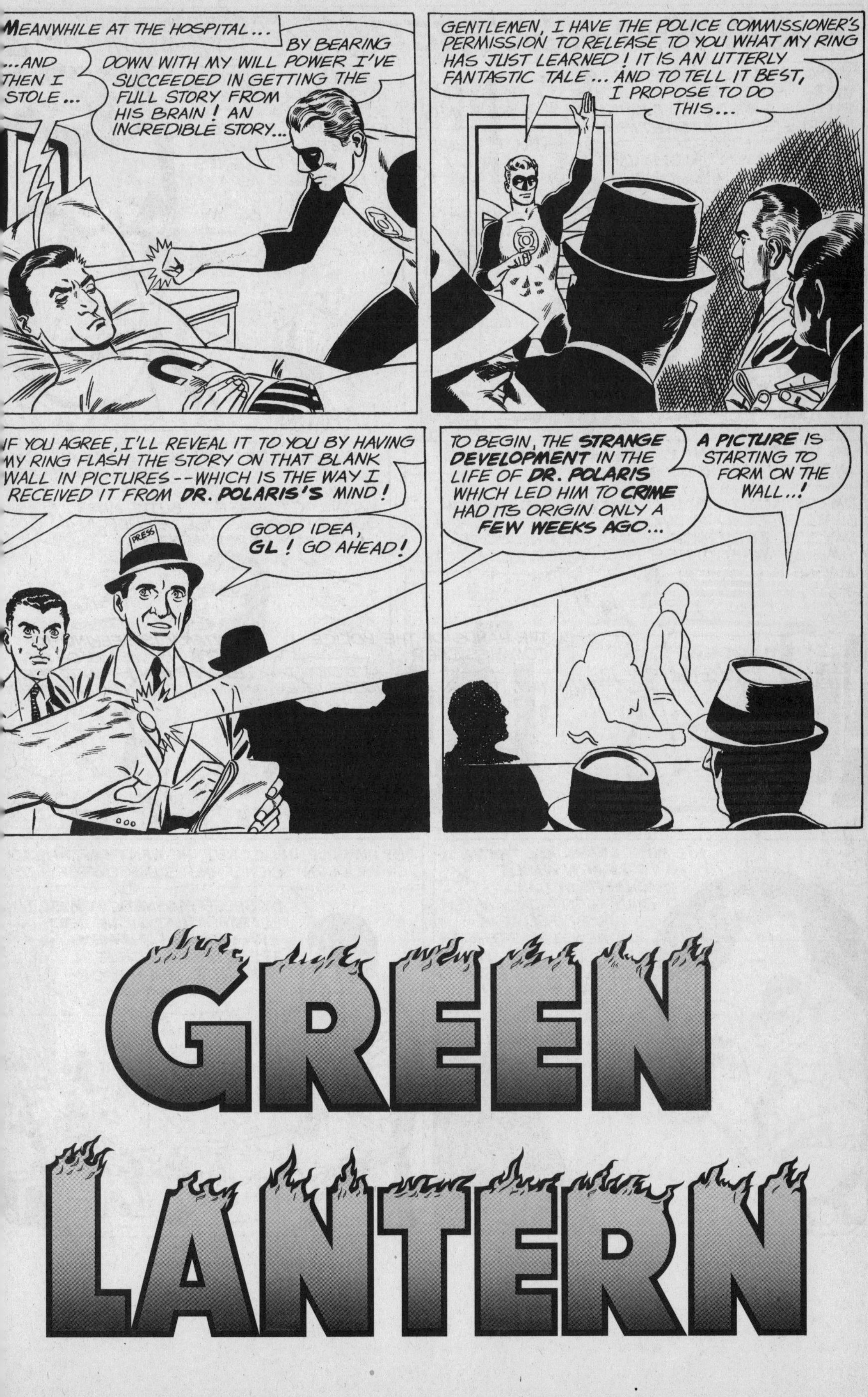
MEANWHILE AT THE HOSPITAL ...
...AND THEN I STOLE ...
BY BEARING DOWN WITH MY WILL POWER I'VE SUCCEEDED IN GETTING THE FULL STORY FROM HIS BRAIN ! AN INCREDIBLE STORY...
GENTLEMEN, I HAVE THE POLICE COMMISSIONER'S PERMISSION TO RELEASE TO YOU WHAT MY RING HAS JUST LEARNED ! IT IS AN UTTERLY FANTASTIC TALE ... AND TO TELL IT BEST, I PROPOSE TO DO THIS...
IF YOU AGREE, I'LL REVEAL IT TO YOU BY HAVING MY RING FLASH THE STORY ON THAT BLANK WALL IN PICTURES--WHICH IS THE WAY I RECEIVED IT FROM DR. POLARIS'S MIND !
PRESS
GOOD IDEA, GL ! GO AHEAD!
TO BEGIN, THE STRANGE DEVELOPMENT IN THE LIFE OF DR. POLARIS WHICH LED HIM TO CRIME HAD ITS ORIGIN ONLY A FEW WEEKS AGO...
A PICTURE IS STARTING TO FORM ON THE WALL...!

GREEN LANTERN

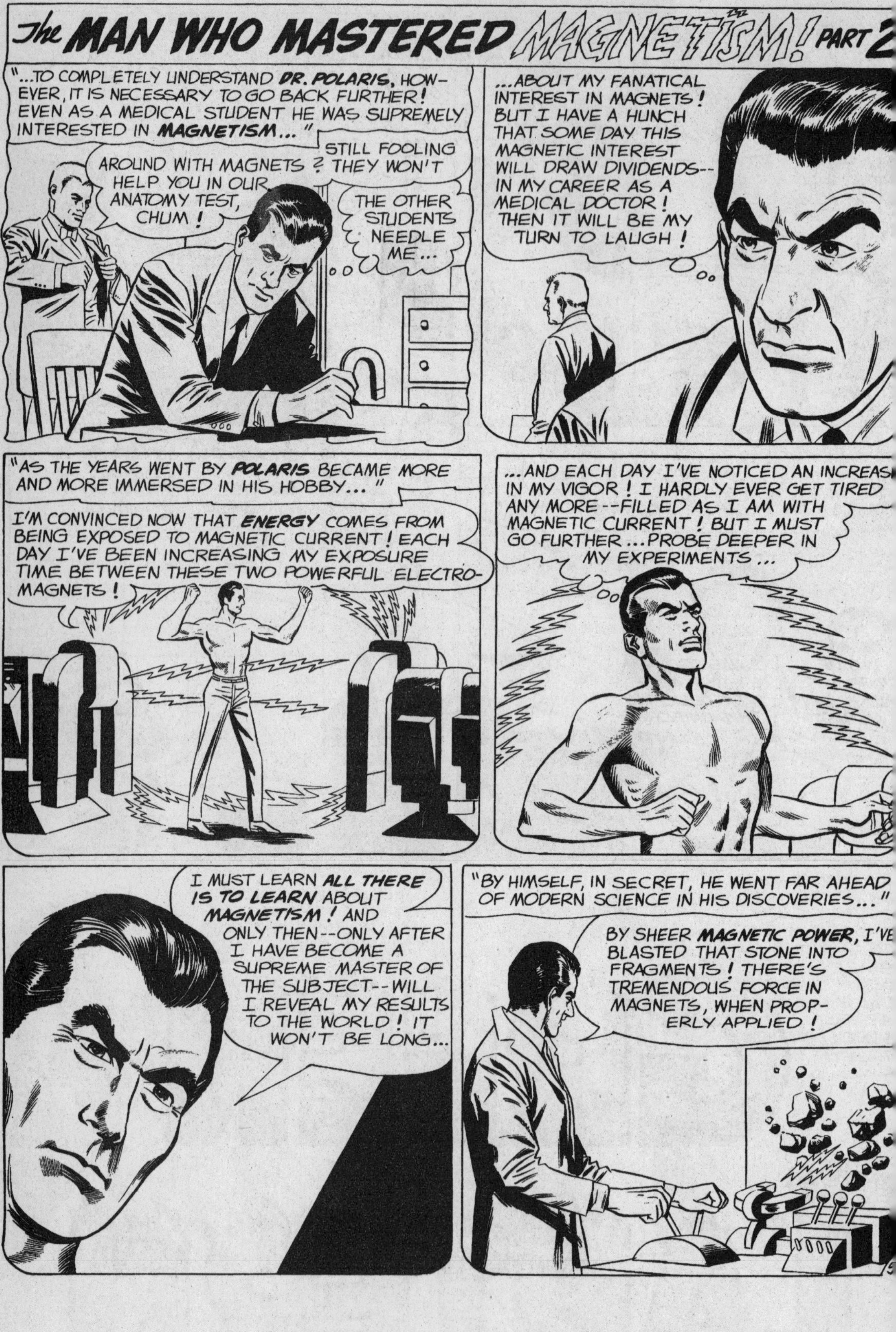
The MAN WHO MASTERED MAGNETISM! PART 2
"...TO COMPLETELY UNDERSTAND DR. POLARIS, HOWEVER, IT IS NECESSARY TO GO BACK FURTHER! EVEN AS A MEDICAL STUDENT HE WAS SUPREMELY INTERESTED IN MAGNETISM..."
STILL FOOLING AROUND WITH MAGNETS? THEY WON'T HELP YOU IN OUR ANATOMY TEST, CHUM!
THE OTHER STUDENTS NEEDLE ME...
...ABOUT MY FANATICAL INTEREST IN MAGNETS! BUT I HAVE A HUNCH THAT SOME DAY THIS MAGNETIC INTEREST WILL DRAW DIVIDENDS--IN MY CAREER AS A MEDICAL DOCTOR! THEN IT WILL BE MY TURN TO LAUGH!
"AS THE YEARS WENT BY POLARIS BECAME MORE AND MORE IMMERSED IN HIS HOBBY..."
I'M CONVINCED NOW THAT ENERGY COMES FROM BEING EXPOSED TO MAGNETIC CURRENT! EACH DAY I'VE BEEN INCREASING MY EXPOSURE TIME BETWEEN THESE TWO POWERFUL ELECTRO-MAGNETS!
...AND EACH DAY I'VE NOTICED AN INCREAS IN MY VIGOR! I HARDLY EVER GET TIRED ANY MORE--FILLED AS I AM WITH MAGNETIC CURRENT! BUT I MUST GO FURTHER...PROBE DEEPER IN MY EXPERIMENTS...
I MUST LEARN ALL THERE IS TO LEARN ABOUT MAGNETISM! AND ONLY THEN--ONLY AFTER I HAVE BECOME A SUPREME MASTER OF THE SUBJECT--WILL I REVEAL MY RESULTS TO THE WORLD! IT WON'T BE LONG...
"BY HIMSELF, IN SECRET, HE WENT FAR AHEAD OF MODERN SCIENCE IN HIS DISCOVERIES..."
BY SHEER MAGNETIC POWER, I'VE BLASTED THAT STONE INTO FRAGMENTS! THERE'S TREMENDOUS FORCE IN MAGNETS, WHEN PROPERLY APPLIED!

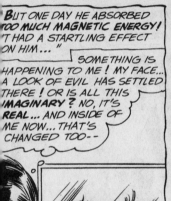

"BUT ONE DAY HE ABSORBED TOO MUCH MAGNETIC ENERGY! IT HAD A STARTLING EFFECT ON HIM..."

SOMETHING IS HAPPENING TO ME! MY FACE... A LOOK OF EVIL HAS SETTLED THERE! OR IS ALL THIS IMAGINARY? NO, IT'S REAL... AND INSIDE OF ME NOW...THAT'S CHANGED TOO--

I ALWAYS WANTED TO HELP PEOPLE--BUT NOW I FEEL I ONLY WANT POWER...WEALTH... FOR MYSELF! AND I CAN GET THEM--BY USING MAGNETISM FOR MY OWN BENEFIT! GOOD GOSH--THIS IS AWFUL! THESE THOUGHTS, THEY'RE BAD-- WRONG--I MUST STOP MYSELF...

I HAVE AN IDEA! PERHAPS I CAN DRAIN THE EXCESS OF MAGNETISM IN ME--IT MUST BE THAT WHICH HAS CHANGED ME! YES, I'LL DO IT! BY REVERSING MY MAGNET I'LL DRAIN OFF SOME OF MY MAGNA-FORCE! I'LL BECOME MY NORMAL SELF AGAIN--

"A BATTLE RAGED INSIDE DR. POLARIS... BUT IT WENT AGAINST HIS GOOD INTENTIONS.."

I--I DON'T WANT TO COMMIT CRIMES! YET I WAS TOO WEAK TO STOP MYSELF FROM DESIGNING THIS UNIFORM-- AND MASK! WHAT IS DRIVING ME ON--?

TONIGHT IS THE NIGHT OF THE CHARITY SHOW-- WHERE I'M DUE TO PERFORM ON STAGE! IT WILL BE MY OPPORTUNITY-- I'LL MAKE A PUBLIC APPEAL FOR GREEN LANTERN TO HELP ME!

I CAN'T STOP MYSELF-- BUT GREEN LANTERN'S POWER RING MAY BE ABLE TO COUNTERACT THE EVIL FORCE THAT HAS SEIZED HOLD OF ME! I'M SURE HE'LL TRY TO HELP ME!

10

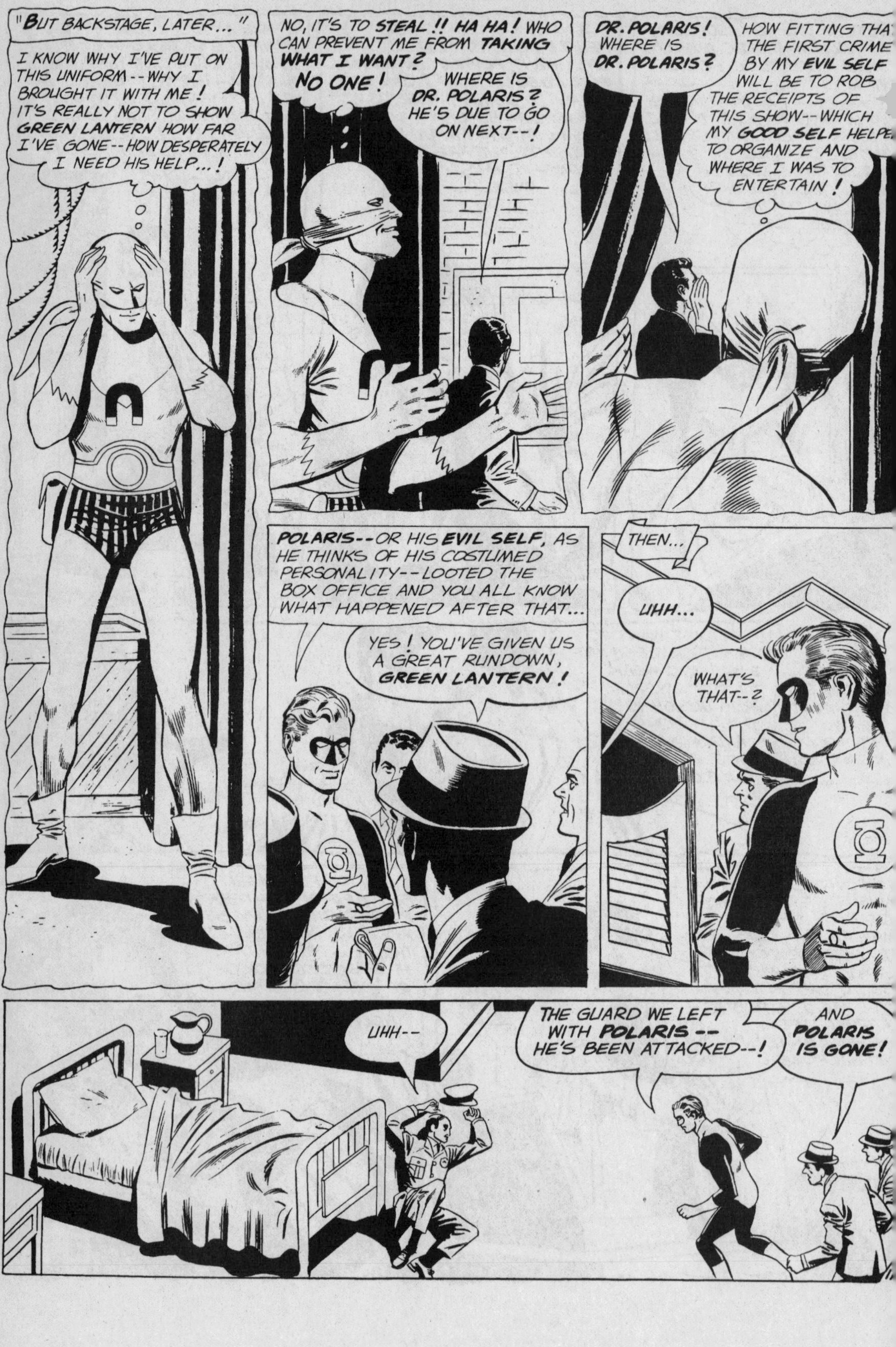
"BUT BACKSTAGE, LATER..."
I KNOW WHY I'VE PUT ON THIS UNIFORM--WHY I BROUGHT IT WITH ME! IT'S REALLY NOT TO SHOW GREEN LANTERN HOW FAR I'VE GONE--HOW DESPERATELY I NEED HIS HELP...!
NO, IT'S TO STEAL!! HA HA! WHO CAN PREVENT ME FROM TAKING WHAT I WANT? NO ONE!
WHERE IS DR. POLARIS? HE'S DUE TO GO ON NEXT--!
DR. POLARIS! WHERE IS DR. POLARIS?
HOW FITTING THA THE FIRST CRIME BY MY EVIL SELF WILL BE TO ROB THE RECEIPTS OF THIS SHOW--WHICH MY GOOD SELF HELPE TO ORGANIZE AND WHERE I WAS TO ENTERTAIN!
POLARIS--OR HIS EVIL SELF, AS HE THINKS OF HIS COSTUMED PERSONALITY--LOOTED THE BOX OFFICE AND YOU ALL KNOW WHAT HAPPENED AFTER THAT...
YES! YOU'VE GIVEN US A GREAT RUNDOWN, GREEN LANTERN!
THEN...
UHH...
WHAT'S THAT--?
UHH--
THE GUARD WE LEFT WITH POLARIS--HE'S BEEN ATTACKED--!
AND POLARIS IS GONE!

IN DUE COURSE... I'VE HUNTED FOR **POLARIS** EVERYWHERE--RIGHT THROUGH THE NIGHT! IT'S DAY NOW--BUT STILL NO SIGN OF HIM! YET I CAN'T STOP SEARCHING...

ANYONE WITH THE TREMENDOUS **MAGNETISM POWER** THAT **DR. POLARIS** HAS UNLEASHED IS TOO DANGEROUS TO BE ALLOWED TO RUN AROUND LOOSE! THERE'S NO TELLING WHAT HE--OR HIS **EVIL SELF** MIGHT DO--WHAT HARM HE MIGHT CAUSE! I'VE GOT TO TRACK HIM DOWN!

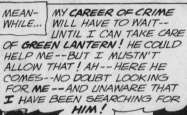

MEANWHILE... MY **CAREER OF CRIME** WILL HAVE TO WAIT-- UNTIL I CAN TAKE CARE OF **GREEN LANTERN**! HE COULD HELP ME--BUT I MUSTN'T ALLOW THAT! AH--HERE HE COMES--NO DOUBT LOOKING FOR **ME**--AND UNAWARE THAT **I** HAVE BEEN SEARCHING FOR **HIM**!

THE BEST PART ABOUT THIS **MAGNETIC METHOD** OF GETTING RID OF **GREEN LANTERN** IS THAT HE WON'T KNOW WHAT HIT HIM--UNTIL IT'S TOO LATE! BUT I MUSTN'T MISS--AND HE'S NOT AN EASY TARGET...!

THERE! GOT HIM FROM HEAD TO FOOT! FROM NOW ON IT'S ONLY A MATTER OF MOMENTS! I MIGHT AS WELL WAIT... AND WATCH THE MAGNETIC DOOM OF **GREEN LANTERN**!

THEN... **GREAT XUDAR!** WHAT IS HAPPENING TO ME?

12

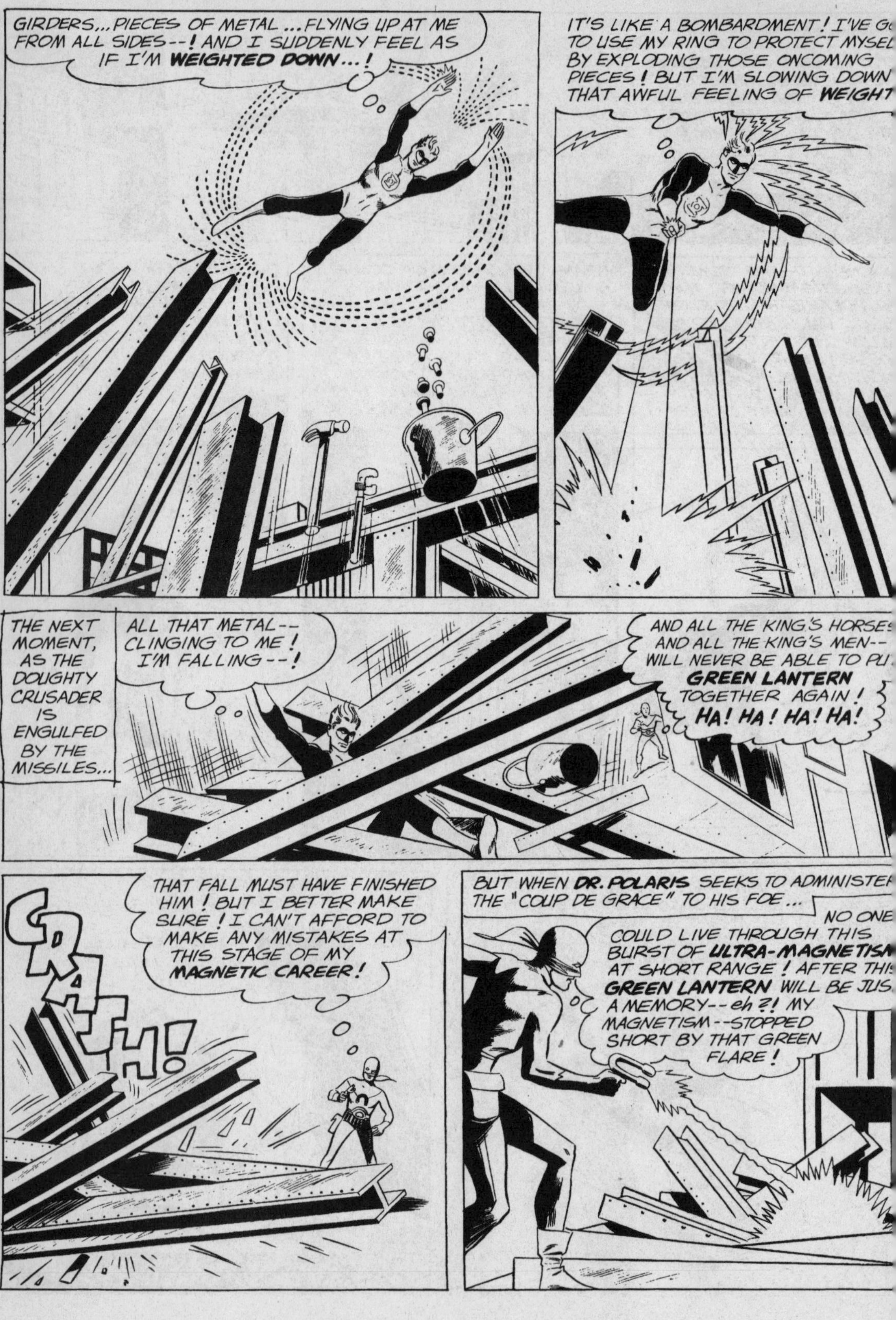
GIRDERS,.. PIECES OF METAL ...FLYING UP AT ME FROM ALL SIDES--! AND I SUDDENLY FEEL AS IF I'M WEIGHTED DOWN...!
IT'S LIKE A BOMBARDMENT! I'VE GO TO USE MY RING TO PROTECT MYSEL BY EXPLODING THOSE ONCOMING PIECES! BUT I'M SLOWING DOWN THAT AWFUL FEELING OF WEIGHT
THE NEXT MOMENT, AS THE DOUGHTY CRUSADER IS ENGULFED BY THE MISSILES...
ALL THAT METAL-- CLINGING TO ME! I'M FALLING--!
AND ALL THE KING'S HORSES AND ALL THE KING'S MEN-- WILL NEVER BE ABLE TO PU GREEN LANTERN TOGETHER AGAIN! HA! HA! HA! HA!
CRASH!
THAT FALL MUST HAVE FINISHED HIM! BUT I BETTER MAKE SURE! I CAN'T AFFORD TO MAKE ANY MISTAKES AT THIS STAGE OF MY MAGNETIC CAREER!
BUT WHEN DR. POLARIS SEEKS TO ADMINISTER THE "COUP DE GRACE" TO HIS FOE...
NO ONE COULD LIVE THROUGH THIS BURST OF ULTRA-MAGNETISM AT SHORT RANGE! AFTER THIS GREEN LANTERN WILL BE JUS A MEMORY--eh?! MY MAGNETISM--STOPPED SHORT BY THAT GREEN FLARE!

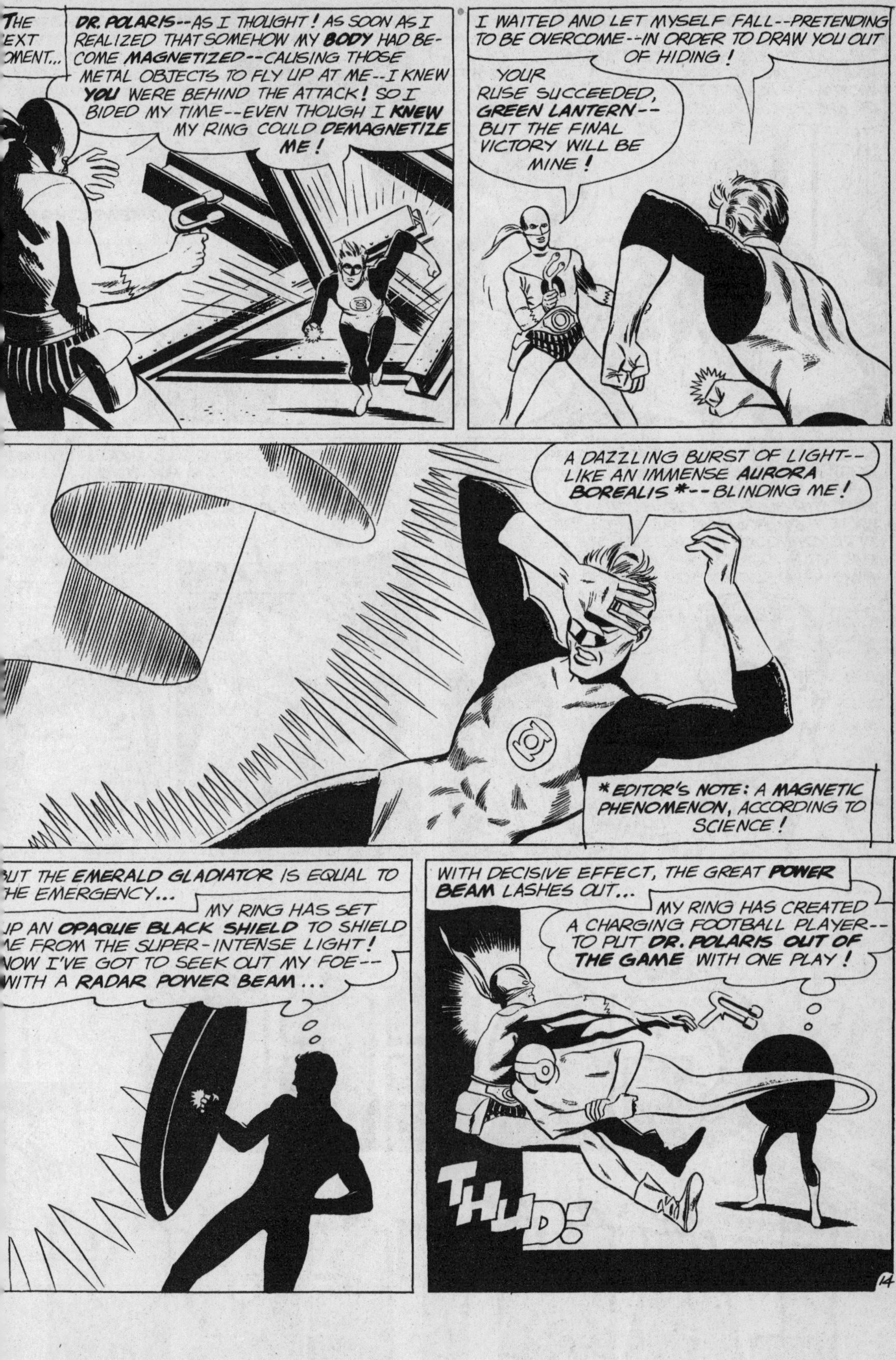
THE
EXT
OMENT...
DR. POLARIS--AS I THOUGHT! AS SOON AS I REALIZED THAT SOMEHOW MY BODY HAD BECOME MAGNETIZED--CAUSING THOSE METAL OBJECTS TO FLY UP AT ME--I KNEW YOU WERE BEHIND THE ATTACK! SO I BIDED MY TIME--EVEN THOUGH I KNEW MY RING COULD DEMAGNETIZE ME!
I WAITED AND LET MYSELF FALL--PRETENDING TO BE OVERCOME--IN ORDER TO DRAW YOU OUT OF HIDING!
YOUR RUSE SUCCEEDED, GREEN LANTERN--BUT THE FINAL VICTORY WILL BE MINE!
A DAZZLING BURST OF LIGHT--LIKE AN IMMENSE AURORA BOREALIS*--BLINDING ME!
*EDITOR'S NOTE: A MAGNETIC PHENOMENON, ACCORDING TO SCIENCE!
BUT THE EMERALD GLADIATOR IS EQUAL TO THE EMERGENCY...
MY RING HAS SET UP AN OPAQUE BLACK SHIELD TO SHIELD ME FROM THE SUPER-INTENSE LIGHT! NOW I'VE GOT TO SEEK OUT MY FOE--WITH A RADAR POWER BEAM...
WITH DECISIVE EFFECT, THE GREAT POWER BEAM LASHES OUT...
MY RING HAS CREATED A CHARGING FOOTBALL PLAYER--TO PUT DR. POLARIS OUT OF THE GAME WITH ONE PLAY!
THUD!
14

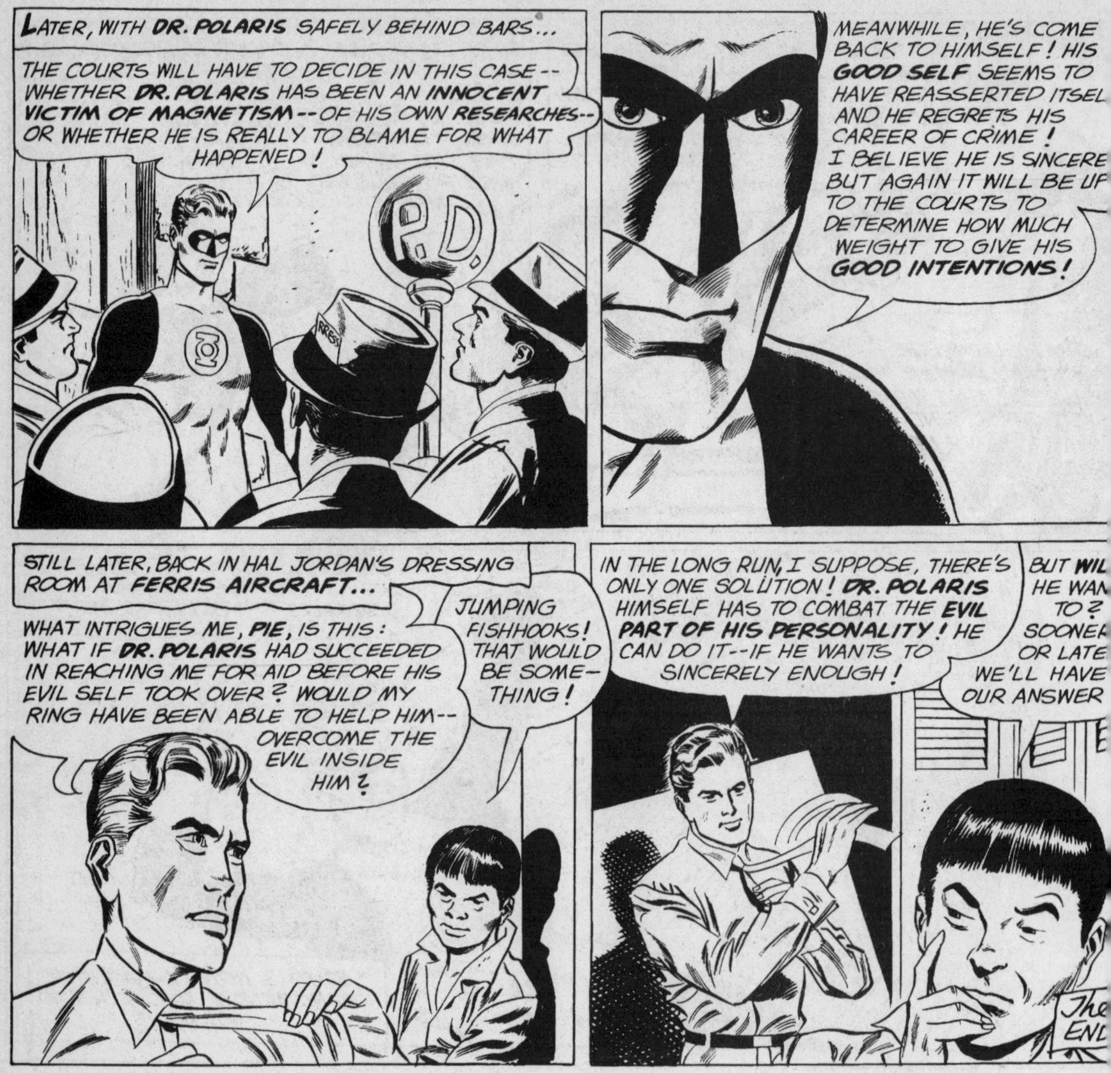
LATER, WITH DR. POLARIS SAFELY BEHIND BARS...
THE COURTS WILL HAVE TO DECIDE IN THIS CASE -- WHETHER DR. POLARIS HAS BEEN AN INNOCENT VICTIM OF MAGNETISM -- OF HIS OWN RESEARCHES -- OR WHETHER HE IS REALLY TO BLAME FOR WHAT HAPPENED!
P.D.
MEANWHILE, HE'S COME BACK TO HIMSELF! HIS GOOD SELF SEEMS TO HAVE REASSERTED ITSEL AND HE REGRETS HIS CAREER OF CRIME! I BELIEVE HE IS SINCERE BUT AGAIN IT WILL BE UP TO THE COURTS TO DETERMINE HOW MUCH WEIGHT TO GIVE HIS GOOD INTENTIONS!
STILL LATER, BACK IN HAL JORDAN'S DRESSING ROOM AT FERRIS AIRCRAFT...
WHAT INTRIGUES ME, PIE, IS THIS: WHAT IF DR. POLARIS HAD SUCCEEDED IN REACHING ME FOR AID BEFORE HIS EVIL SELF TOOK OVER? WOULD MY RING HAVE BEEN ABLE TO HELP HIM -- OVERCOME THE EVIL INSIDE HIM?
JUMPING FISHHOOKS! THAT WOULD BE SOME-THING!
IN THE LONG RUN, I SUPPOSE, THERE'S ONLY ONE SOLUTION! DR. POLARIS HIMSELF HAS TO COMBAT THE EVIL PART OF HIS PERSONALITY! HE CAN DO IT -- IF HE WANTS TO SINCERELY ENOUGH!
BUT WIL HE WAN TO? SOONEF OR LATE WE'LL HAVE OUR ANSWER
The EN

GREEN LANTERN

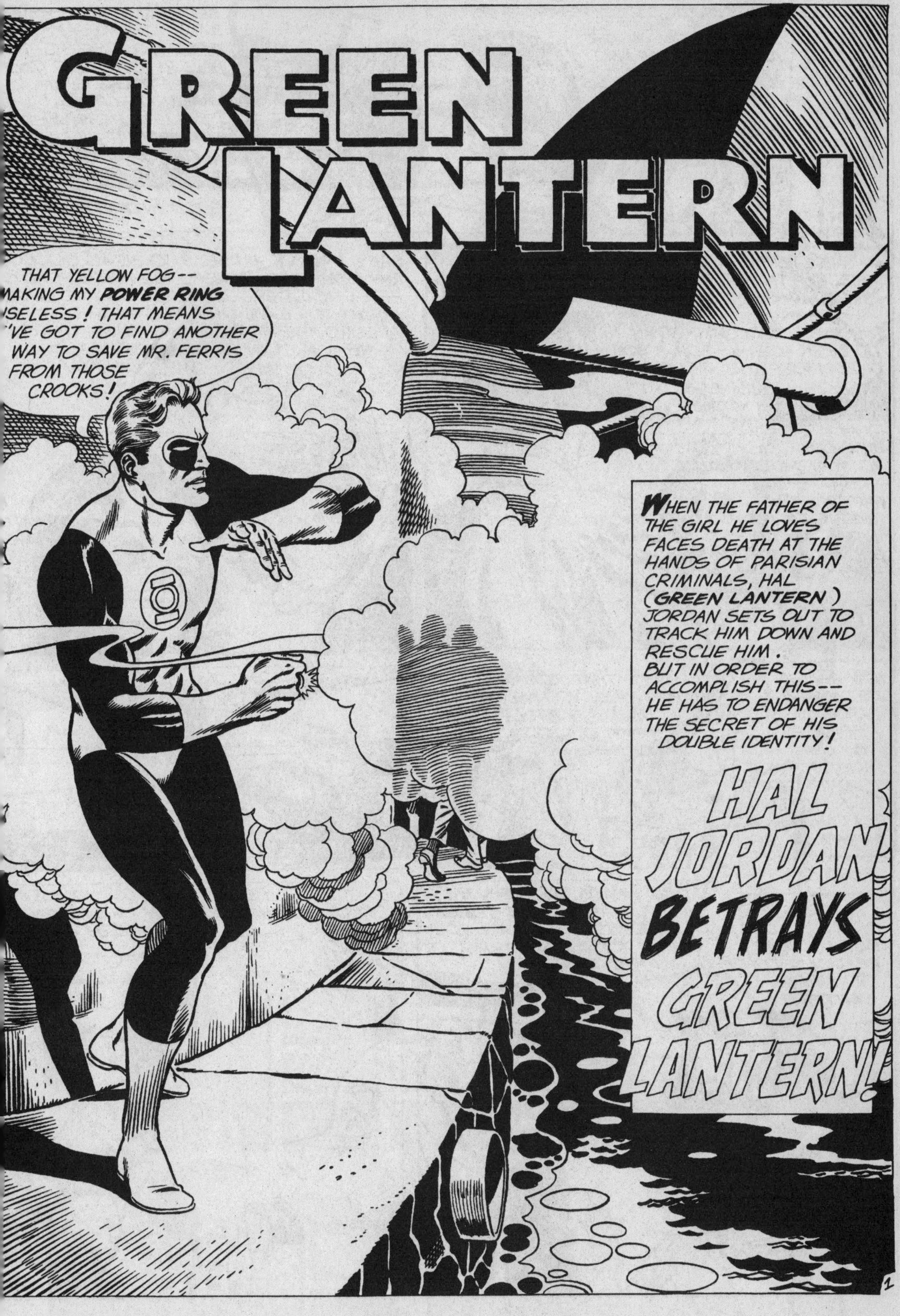
GREEN LANTERN
THAT YELLOW FOG-- MAKING MY POWER RING SELESS! THAT MEANS 'VE GOT TO FIND ANOTHER WAY TO SAVE MR. FERRIS FROM THOSE CROOKS!
WHEN THE FATHER OF THE GIRL HE LOVES FACES DEATH AT THE HANDS OF PARISIAN CRIMINALS, HAL (GREEN LANTERN) JORDAN SETS OUT TO TRACK HIM DOWN AND RESCUE HIM. BUT IN ORDER TO ACCOMPLISH THIS-- HE HAS TO ENDANGER THE SECRET OF HIS DOUBLE IDENTITY!
HAL JORDAN BETRAYS GREEN LANTERN!

A JET STRATO-CRUISER ROARS IN FOR A LANDING ON THE PRIVATE AIRSTRIP OF THE FERRIS AIRCRAFT COMPANY..

HERE COME MOTHER AND DAD NOW--AFTER AN ABSENCE OF TWO YEARS ON THEIR TRIP AROUND THE WORLD!

AS CAROL FERRIS' MIND DRIFTS BACK TWO YEARS, WHEN HER FATHER TURNED OVER CONTROL OF FERRIS AIRCRAFT TO HIS DAUGHTER...

HAL, WHEN CAROL WAS BORN I'D BEEN HOPING FOR A SON-- CARL FERRIS, JR.--TO TAKE OVER THIS BUSINESS. BUT INSTEAD OF ANOTHER CARL... WE HAD A CAROL...

SHE'S PROVEN HERSELF TO BE AS GOOD AS ANY SON--WITH A REAL BUSINESS HEAD ON HER SHOULDERS. MRS. FERRIS AND I ARE ABOUT TO LEAVE ON A TWO-YEAR TRIP AROUND THE WORLD--AND WHILE WE'RE GONE, CAROL WILL BE IN CHARGE OF THE COMPANY!

NOW AS THE JET LANDS, CAROL IS EMBRACED BY HER PARENTS, WHILE TO ONE SIDE THEIR PILOT, HAL JORDAN, WALKS AWAY WITH HIS ESKIMO PAL, PIEFACE...

HOW'S THAT ROMANCE BETWEEN YOU AND HAL COMING, HONEY?

I'M VERY FOND OF HAL, DAD-- BUT MY HEART REALLY BELONGS TO GREEN LANTERN!

THEN WHAT'S THE PROBLEM? IF YOU WANT TO BE GREEN LANTERN'S WIFE--ALL YOU HAVE TO DO IS MARRY HAL JORDAN!

I--I DON'T UNDER-STAND, FATHER...

IT'S VERY SIMPLE. YOU SEE, HAL JORDAN IS GREEN LANTERN!

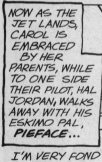

I CAN HARDLY BELIEVE THAT, FATHER! HOW COULD YOU POSSIBLY KNOW SUCH THING?

FROM WHAT JUST HAPPENED IN PARIS! THERE'S NO DOUBT THAT HE AND GREEN LANTERN ARE ONE AND THE SAME MAN! LISTEN AND I'LL TELL YOU ABOUT IT...

EVEN AS CARL FERRIS BEGINS HIS STORY, HIS PILOT HAL (GREEN LANTERN) JORDAN IS IN THE HANGAR, RECHARGING HIS POWER RING...

...LET THOSE WHO WORSHIP EVIL'S MIGHT BEWARE MY POWER, GREEN LANTERN'S LIGHT!

PIE--I'M ON A SPOT! I THINK I'VE BETRAYED THE SECRET OF MY DOUBLE IDENTITY! I'LL TELL YOU ALL ABOUT IT ON THE WAY HOME...

"SOME OF IT I HAD TO PIECE TOGETHER FROM WHAT I LEARNED LATER, BUT IT BEGAN THE OTHER DAY IN A PARISIAN ART SHOP IN MONTARTRE..."

AH--A RENOIR! MAY I TAKE A CLOSER LOOK AT IT?

CARL FERRIS WAS DOING SOME VERY SPECIAL SHOPPING...

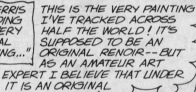

THIS IS THE VERY PAINTING I'VE TRACKED ACROSS HALF THE WORLD! IT'S SUPPOSED TO BE AN ORIGINAL RENOIR--BUT AS AN AMATEUR ART EXPERT I BELIEVE THAT UNDER IT IS AN ORIGINAL REMBRANDT!

UNSEEN BY ANYONE, HIS FINGERNAIL CUT INTO THE WOOD OF THE FRAME BEHIND THE PAINTING, LEAVING A TINY, IDENTIFYING MARK..."

I'LL KNOW THIS OIL PAINTING WHEN I SEE IT AGAIN BY MY "BRAND"!

"THEN HE PRICED THE PICTURE..."

ZE PAINTING EES FEEFTY THOUSAN' DOLLAIRE, M'SIEU...

I'LL BUY IT! I'LL RETURN LATER WITH A CERTIFIED CHECK FOR THAT AMOUNT, LESS THE DEPOSIT I LEAVE TO BIND THE SALE!

3

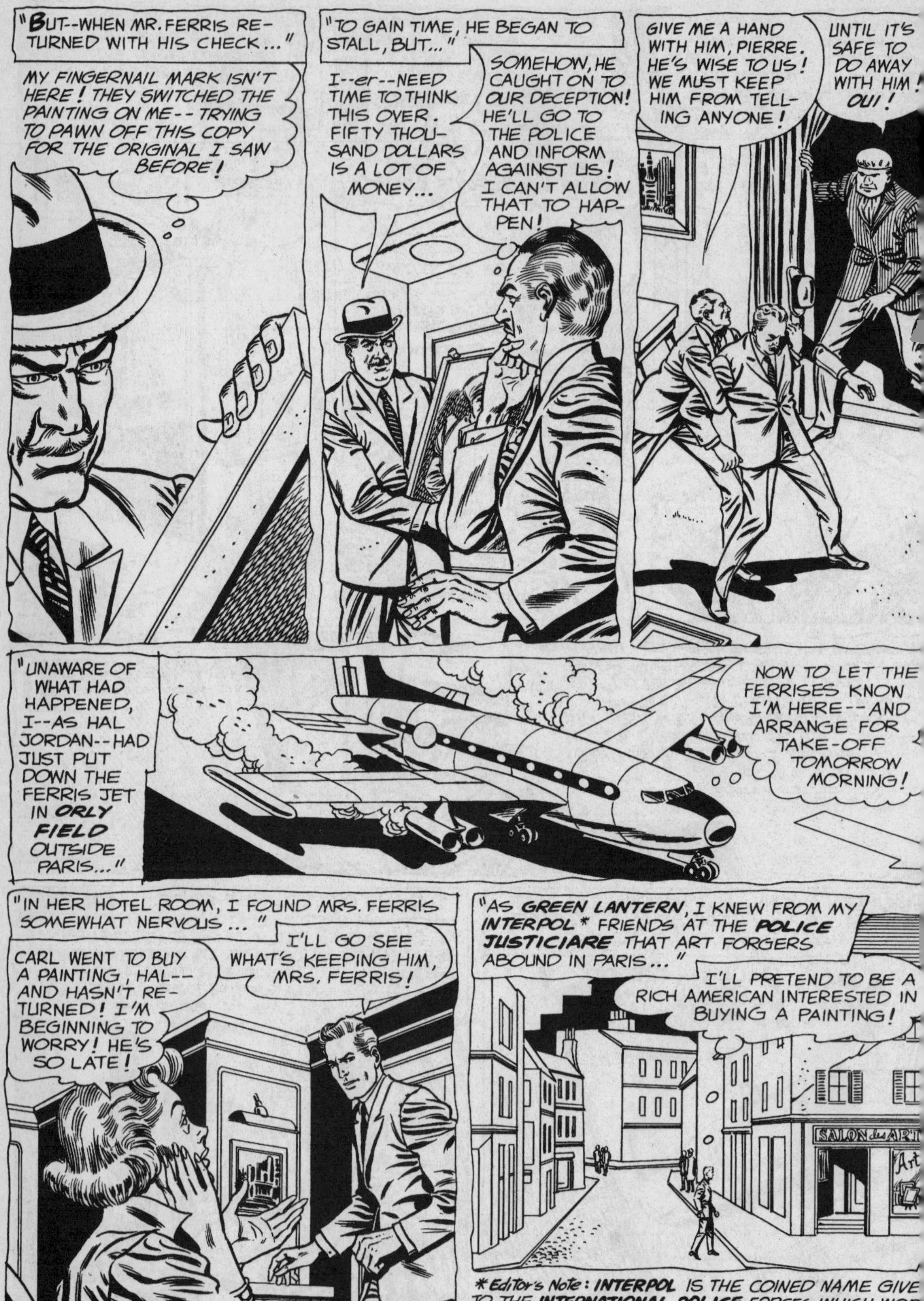
"BUT--WHEN MR. FERRIS RETURNED WITH HIS CHECK..."
MY FINGERNAIL MARK ISN'T HERE! THEY SWITCHED THE PAINTING ON ME--TRYING TO PAWN OFF THIS COPY FOR THE ORIGINAL I SAW BEFORE!
"TO GAIN TIME, HE BEGAN TO STALL, BUT..."
I--er--NEED TIME TO THINK THIS OVER. FIFTY THOUSAND DOLLARS IS A LOT OF MONEY...
SOMEHOW, HE CAUGHT ON TO OUR DECEPTION! HE'LL GO TO THE POLICE AND INFORM AGAINST US! I CAN'T ALLOW THAT TO HAPPEN!
GIVE ME A HAND WITH HIM, PIERRE. HE'S WISE TO US! WE MUST KEEP HIM FROM TELLING ANYONE!
UNTIL IT'S SAFE TO DO AWAY WITH HIM! OUI!
"UNAWARE OF WHAT HAD HAPPENED, I--AS HAL JORDAN--HAD JUST PUT DOWN THE FERRIS JET IN ORLY FIELD OUTSIDE PARIS..."
NOW TO LET THE FERRISES KNOW I'M HERE--AND ARRANGE FOR TAKE-OFF TOMORROW MORNING!
"IN HER HOTEL ROOM, I FOUND MRS. FERRIS SOMEWHAT NERVOUS..."
CARL WENT TO BUY A PAINTING, HAL--AND HASN'T RETURNED! I'M BEGINNING TO WORRY! HE'S SO LATE!
I'LL GO SEE WHAT'S KEEPING HIM, MRS. FERRIS!
"AS GREEN LANTERN, I KNEW FROM MY INTERPOL* FRIENDS AT THE POLICE JUSTICIARE THAT ART FORGERS ABOUND IN PARIS..."
I'LL PRETEND TO BE A RICH AMERICAN INTERESTED IN BUYING A PAINTING!
SALON des ART
*Editor's Note: INTERPOL IS THE COINED NAME GIVE TO THE INTERNATIONAL POLICE FORCES WHICH WOR TOGETHER TO STOP CRIME.

"FROM MRS. FERRIS' DESCRIPTION OF THE PAINTING HER HUSBAND WANTED TO BUY, QUICKLY RECOGNIZED IT..."

I MIGHT BUY IT. ARE YOU SURE NO ONE ELSE IS INTERESTED IN OBTAINING IT?

BUT NO, M'SIEU! WE JUST TOOK EET OUT OF STORAGE. NO ONE HAS SEEN EET IN MONTHS!

"THAT WAS AN OUT-AND-OUT LIE! CARL FERRIS HAD SEEN IT *YESTERDAY!* SO MY SUSPICIONS WERE AROUSED..."

WHEN I LEAVE--I'LL LEAVE MY *INVISIBLE POWER RING* BEHIND-- WITH THE COMMAND TO FOLLOW THE ART DEALER AROUND! I'LL ALSO WILL IT--AS SOON AS IT SEES CARL FERRIS--TO BRING *GREEN LANTERN* TO IT!

"I LEFT THE ART STORE AND WENT BACK TO MY HOTEL ROOM WHERE I CHANGED INTO MY *GREEN LANTERN* OUTFIT..."

THE *RING* HAD BETTER BRING ME SOON--BEFORE IT LOSES ITS POWER! I CHARGED IT BEFORE LEAVING--BUT THAT WAS A GOOD *20* HOURS AGO! THERE'S ONLY *4* HOURS OF CHARGE LEFT...

"ALL I COULD DO WAS PACE THE ROOM...AND WAIT AS PRECIOUS MINUTES WENT BY..."

THERE'S LESS THAN AN HOUR LEFT! IF CARL FERRIS DOESN'T APPEAR BEFORE THEN AND THE RING FAILS TO BRING ME THERE--ALL MAY BE LOST!

"THEN FROM NOWHERE, A GREEN HAND REACHED INTO THE ROOM..."

AH--AT LAST! HERE I GO--!

"I ASSUMED LATER THAT THE ART DEALER WHOM THE RING FOLLOWED HAD CONTACTED HIS PARTNER WHO HAD GRABBED MR. FERRIS AND WAS LEADING HIM THROUGH THE SEWERS OF PARIS..."

THERE THEY ARE--UP AHEAD OF ME! THEY MUST BE PLANNING TO DISPOSE OF MR. FERRIS!

5

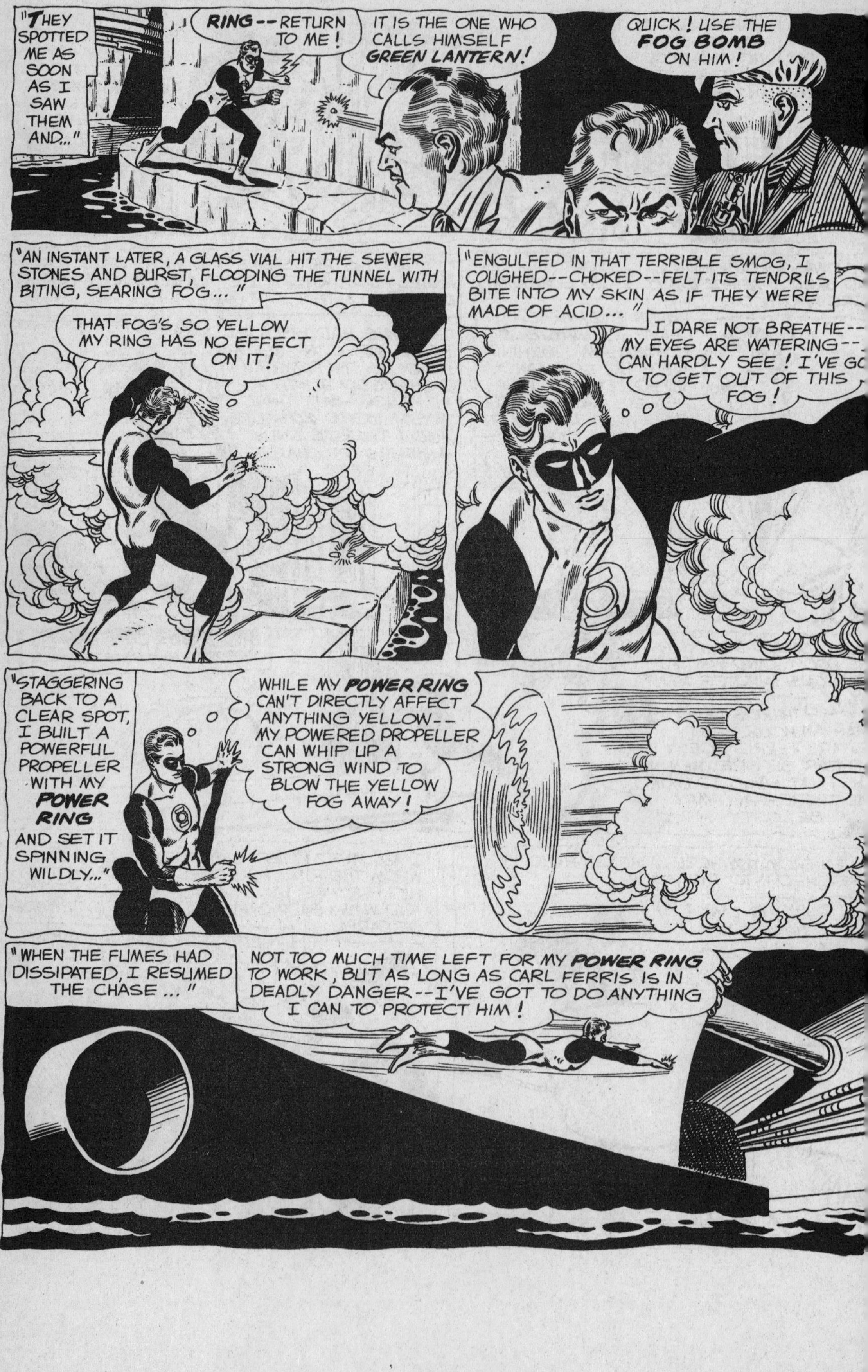
"THEY SPOTTED ME AS SOON AS I SAW THEM AND..."
RING--RETURN TO ME!
IT IS THE ONE WHO CALLS HIMSELF GREEN LANTERN!
QUICK! USE THE FOG BOMB ON HIM!
"AN INSTANT LATER, A GLASS VIAL HIT THE SEWER STONES AND BURST, FLOODING THE TUNNEL WITH BITING, SEARING FOG..."
THAT FOG'S SO YELLOW MY RING HAS NO EFFECT ON IT!
"ENGULFED IN THAT TERRIBLE SMOG, I COUGHED--CHOKED--FELT ITS TENDRILS BITE INTO MY SKIN AS IF THEY WERE MADE OF ACID..."
I DARE NOT BREATHE-- MY EYES ARE WATERING-- CAN HARDLY SEE! I'VE GO TO GET OUT OF THIS FOG!
"STAGGERING BACK TO A CLEAR SPOT, I BUILT A POWERFUL PROPELLER WITH MY POWER RING AND SET IT SPINNING WILDLY..."
WHILE MY POWER RING CAN'T DIRECTLY AFFECT ANYTHING YELLOW-- MY POWERED PROPELLER CAN WHIP UP A STRONG WIND TO BLOW THE YELLOW FOG AWAY!
"WHEN THE FUMES HAD DISSIPATED, I RESUMED THE CHASE..."
NOT TOO MUCH TIME LEFT FOR MY POWER RING TO WORK, BUT AS LONG AS CARL FERRIS IS IN DEADLY DANGER--I'VE GOT TO DO ANYTHING I CAN TO PROTECT HIM!

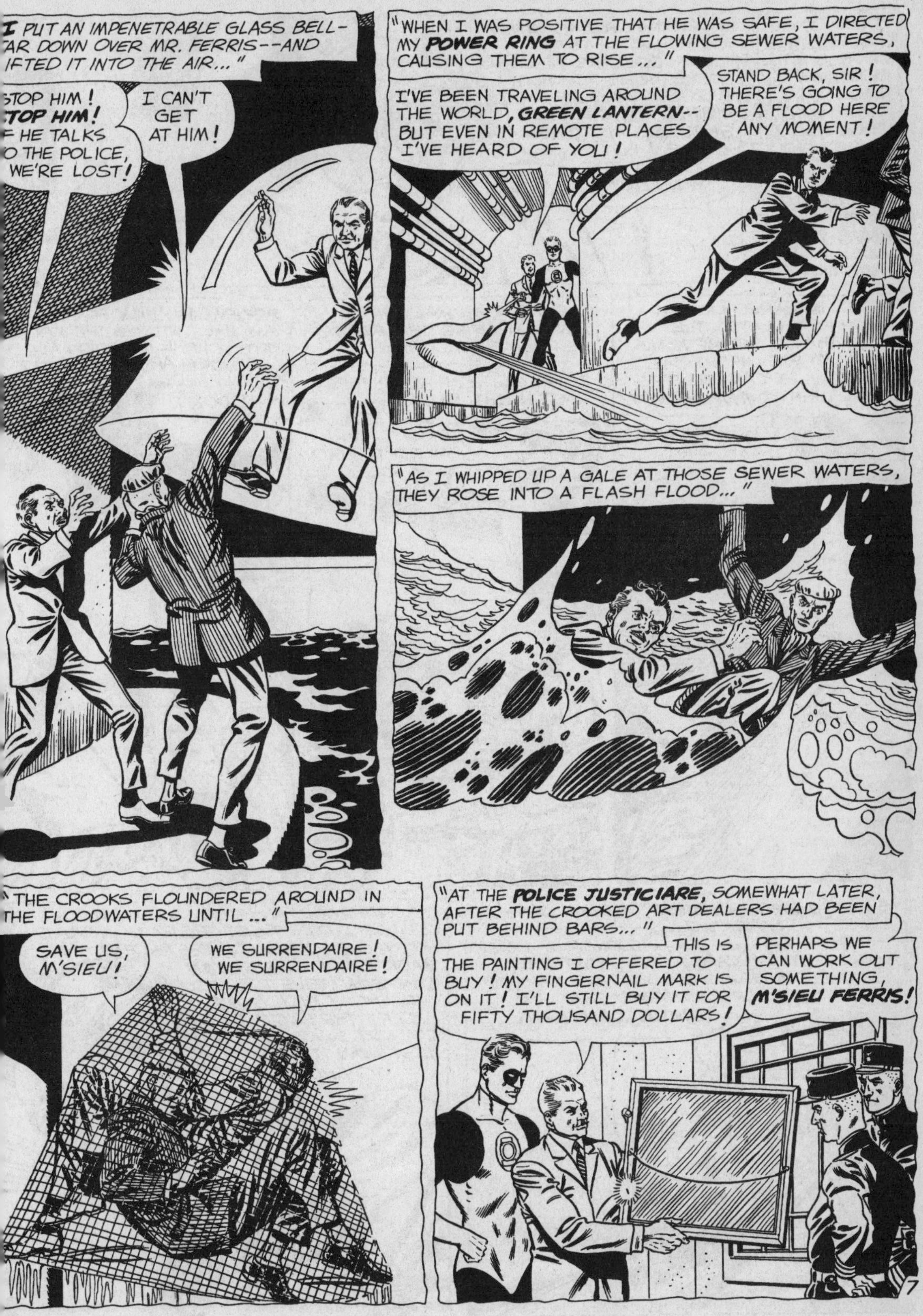
"I PUT AN IMPENETRABLE GLASS BELL-JAR DOWN OVER MR. FERRIS--AND LIFTED IT INTO THE AIR..."
STOP HIM! STOP HIM! IF HE TALKS TO THE POLICE, WE'RE LOST!
I CAN'T GET AT HIM!
"WHEN I WAS POSITIVE THAT HE WAS SAFE, I DIRECTED MY POWER RING AT THE FLOWING SEWER WATERS, CAUSING THEM TO RISE..."
I'VE BEEN TRAVELING AROUND THE WORLD, GREEN LANTERN-- BUT EVEN IN REMOTE PLACES I'VE HEARD OF YOU!
STAND BACK, SIR! THERE'S GOING TO BE A FLOOD HERE ANY MOMENT!
"AS I WHIPPED UP A GALE AT THOSE SEWER WATERS, THEY ROSE INTO A FLASH FLOOD..."
"THE CROOKS FLOUNDERED AROUND IN THE FLOODWATERS UNTIL ..."
SAVE US, M'SIEU!
WE SURRENDAIRE! WE SURRENDAIRE!
"AT THE POLICE JUSTICIARE, SOMEWHAT LATER, AFTER THE CROOKED ART DEALERS HAD BEEN PUT BEHIND BARS..."
THIS IS THE PAINTING I OFFERED TO BUY! MY FINGERNAIL MARK IS ON IT! I'LL STILL BUY IT FOR FIFTY THOUSAND DOLLARS!
PERHAPS WE CAN WORK OUT SOMETHING, M'SIEU FERRIS!
7

"I COULD HAVE EXAMINED THE PAINTING WITH MY *POWER RING*, BUT HAVING LOST ITS CHARGE, I ADVISED CARL FERRIS TO TAKE HIS PAINTING TO A LABORATORY WHERE, WHEN IT WAS EXAMINED UNDER INFRA-- RED LIGHT..."

AN ORIGINAL *REMBRANDT* IS WORTH AT LEAST A MILLION DOLLARS! THOSE CROOKS TRIED TO CHEAT ME BY SHOWING ME AN ORIGINAL *RENOIR*, THEN SWITCHING PICTURES ON ME! BUT I WOUND UP THE WINNER!

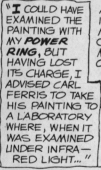

UNDER INFRARED LIGHT-- WHICH PENETRATES THE PAINT GLAZE AND REVEALS THE SURFACE OF THE BASIC PAINTING--I CAN TELL THIS IS AUTHENTIC *REMBRANDT!*

CONGRATULATIONS, SIR!

"NEXT DAY, AS *HAL JORDAN*, I WAS PILOTING THE *FERRIS* JET HOMEWARD WHEN..."

I HAD QUITE AN ADVENTURE LAST NIGHT, HAL!

I'M SORRY I--er-- FAILED TO FIND YOU...

GREEN LANTERN DID AND-- WHY, HAL! WHAT'S THE MATTER WITH YOUR FACE? IT'S ALL BROKEN OUT IN A RASH!

er--I DON'T KNOW, SIR!

AS HAL (*GREEN LANTERN*) JORDAN CON-CLUDES HIS NARRATIVE...

SOONER OR LATER IT WILL DAWN ON CARL FERRIS THAT THE YELLOW FOG STUNG MY SKIN AND CAUSED THE RASH--A SURE GIVEAWAY THAT I'M *GREEN LANTERN*...

BUT THERE'S NO FACE-RASH NOW...

IT LASTED ONLY AN HOUR OR SO. AND OF COURSE I DIDN'T GET THE RASH AROUND MY EYES BECAUSE OF THE PROTECTIVE MASK I WORE AS *GREEN LANTERN*! I'VE TOLD YOU THE WHOLE STORY, *PIE*-- EXCEPT THE ENDING! I'M NOT EXACTLY SURE JUST *HOW* IT'S GOING TO END!

S HAL AND HIS GREASEMONKEY CONFIDANT ENTER THE JORDAN HOME...

FERRIS TUMBLES TO THE FACT THAT I'M *GREEN LANTERN*, THERE'LL BE SOME INTERESTING DEVELOPMENTS! *CAROL* WILL PHONE AND--

ONCE CARL

AS *PIEFACE* LISTENS WORRIEDLY, HAL ANSWERS HIS PHONE...

POOR HAL! HE WANTS TO WIN CAROL'S LOVE AS *HAL JORDAN*-- NOT BECAUSE HE'S THE CELE-BRATED *GREEN LANTERN!*

YES, CAROL. I'LL BE GLAD TO COME TO DINNER. JUST THE TWO OF US. TONIGHT AT EIGHT. RIGHT.

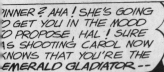

DINNER? AHA! SHE'S GOING O GET YOU IN THE MOOD O PROPOSE, HAL! SURE AS SHOOTING CAROL NOW KNOWS THAT YOU'RE THE EMERALD GLADIATOR--

--AND THE TRAP IS BEING SET! YES SIRREEE, THIS PROMISES TO BE A MOST INTERESTING DINNER...

AT EIGHT O'CLOCK, HAL VISITS HIS SWEET-HEART'S HOUSE, WHERE...

I'VE PREPARED A SPECIAL FRENCH-STYLE DINNER, HAL! I WANT YOU TO BE THE FIRST TO KNOW THAT FATHER'S DECIDED TO RETIRE AND TURN OVER *FERRIS AIRCRAFT* TO ME ...

WHAT A CATCH I'LL BE AS A WIFE--FOR SOME LUCKY FELLOW!

WOO--EE! SHE'S STARTING TO GIVE ME THE BUSINESS-- USING ALL HER FEMININE WILES TO GET ME TO PROPOSE TO HER!

LATER, TOWARD THE END OF THE DINNER ...

AND HERE, HAL, IS MY *PIÈCE DE RÉSISTANCE*-- *CRÊPES SUZETTE!* THE MAN WHO MARRIES ME IS GOING TO BE WELL FED...

OH, BOY, THE TRAP IS ABOUT TO BE SPRUNG! IT'S TIME FOR ME TO MAKE *MY* MOVE--AND SEE WHETHER IT'S *HAL JORDAN* CAROL IS AFTER--OR *GREEN LANTERN!*

9

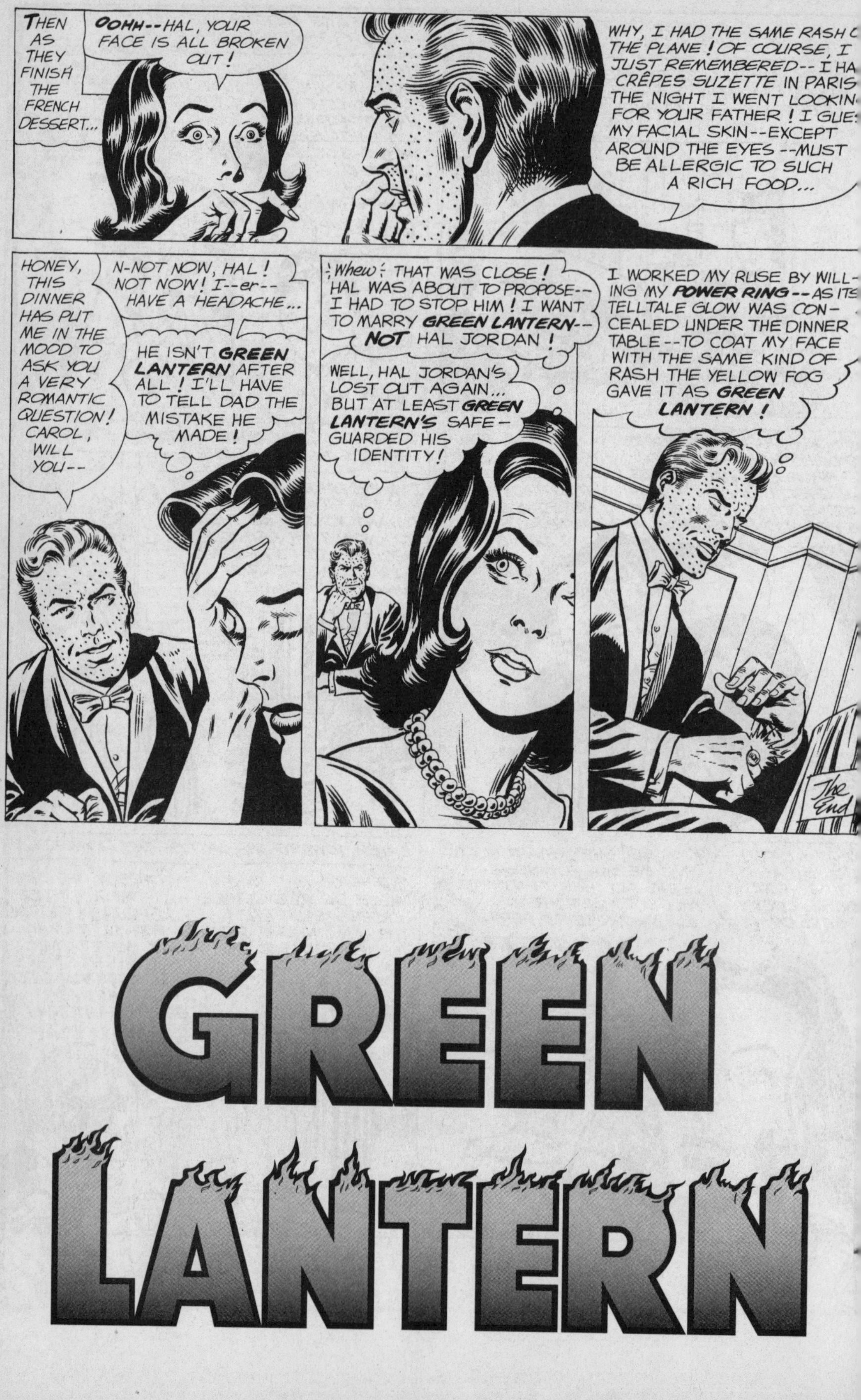
THEN AS THEY FINISH THE FRENCH DESSERT...
OOHH--HAL, YOUR FACE IS ALL BROKEN OUT!
WHY, I HAD THE SAME RASH C THE PLANE! OF COURSE, I JUST REMEMBERED--I HA CRÊPES SUZETTE IN PARIS THE NIGHT I WENT LOOKIN FOR YOUR FATHER! I GUE MY FACIAL SKIN--EXCEPT AROUND THE EYES--MUST BE ALLERGIC TO SUCH A RICH FOOD...
HONEY, THIS DINNER HAS PUT ME IN THE MOOD TO ASK YOU A VERY ROMANTIC QUESTION! CAROL, WILL YOU--
N-NOT NOW, HAL! NOT NOW! I--er--HAVE A HEADACHE...
HE ISN'T GREEN LANTERN AFTER ALL! I'LL HAVE TO TELL DAD THE MISTAKE HE MADE!
Whew! THAT WAS CLOSE! HAL WAS ABOUT TO PROPOSE--I HAD TO STOP HIM! I WANT TO MARRY GREEN LANTERN--NOT HAL JORDAN!
WELL, HAL JORDAN'S LOST OUT AGAIN... BUT AT LEAST GREEN LANTERN'S SAFE-GUARDED HIS IDENTITY!
I WORKED MY RUSE BY WILL-ING MY POWER RING--AS ITS TELLTALE GLOW WAS CON-CEALED UNDER THE DINNER TABLE--TO COAT MY FACE WITH THE SAME KIND OF RASH THE YELLOW FOG GAVE IT AS GREEN LANTERN!
The End

GREEN LANTERN

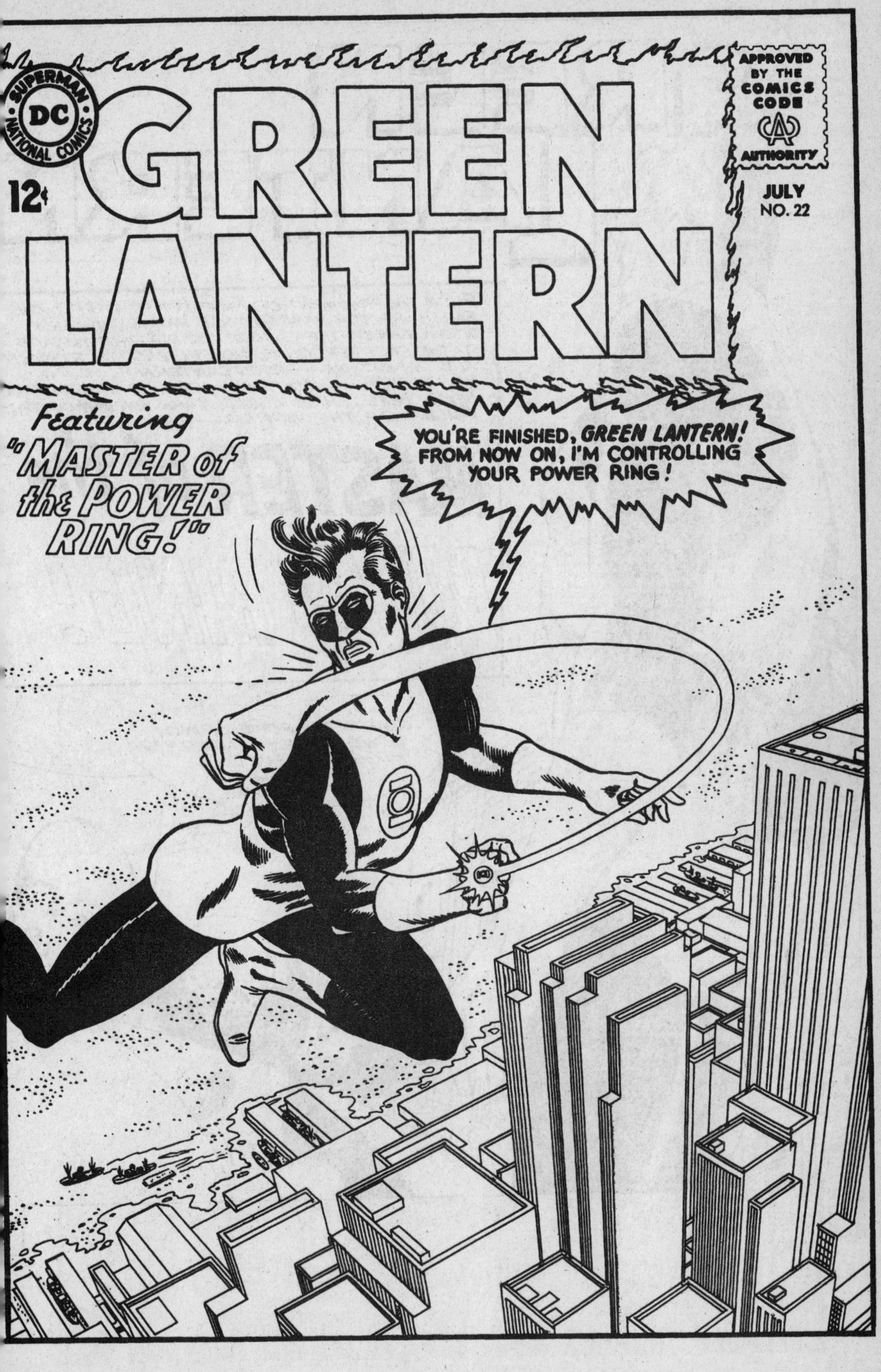
GREEN LANTERN
SUPERMAN DC NATIONAL COMICS
12¢
APPROVED BY THE COMICS CODE AUTHORITY
JULY NO. 22
Featuring "MASTER of the POWER RING!"
YOU'RE FINISHED, GREEN LANTERN! FROM NOW ON, I'M CONTROLLING YOUR POWER RING!

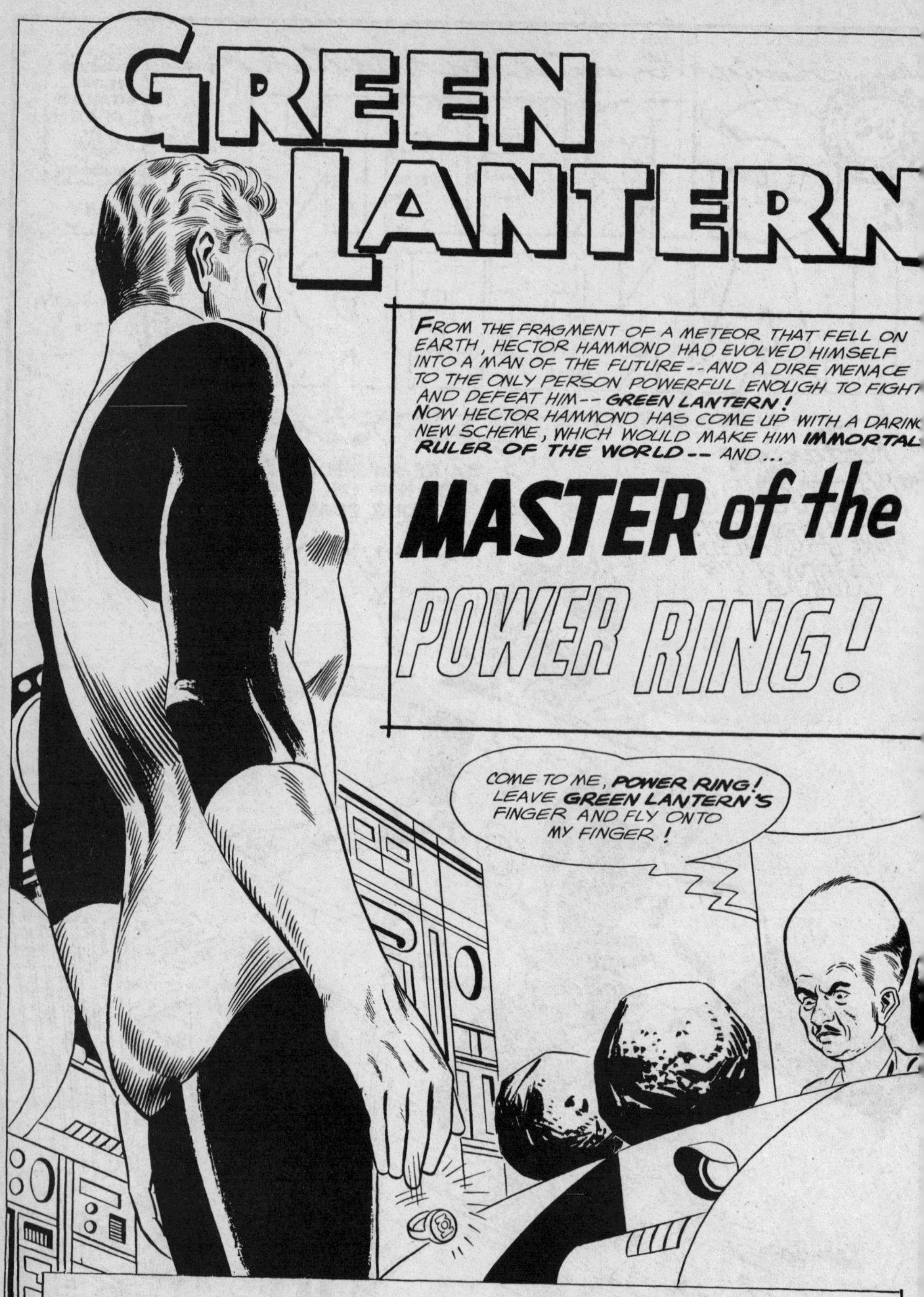
GREEN LANTERN
FROM THE FRAGMENT OF A METEOR THAT FELL ON EARTH, HECTOR HAMMOND HAD EVOLVED HIMSELF INTO A MAN OF THE FUTURE--AND A DIRE MENACE TO THE ONLY PERSON POWERFUL ENOUGH TO FIGHT AND DEFEAT HIM--GREEN LANTERN! NOW HECTOR HAMMOND HAS COME UP WITH A DARING NEW SCHEME, WHICH WOULD MAKE HIM IMMORTAL RULER OF THE WORLD-- AND...
MASTER of the POWER RING!
COME TO ME, POWER RING! LEAVE GREEN LANTERN'S FINGER AND FLY ONTO MY FINGER!

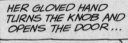
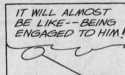
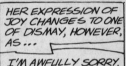

HUMMING TO HERSELF, PRETTY CAROL FERRIS MOVES TOWARD AN OFFICE DOOR IN A COAST CITY SKYSCRAPER...

CAN'T BELIEVE I'M SUCH A LUCKY GIRL!

CONSOLIDATED CHARITIES

HER GLOVED HAND TURNS THE KNOB AND OPENS THE DOOR...

I'M CHAIRLADY OF THIS YEAR'S CHARITY BAZAAR--AND GREEN LANTERN IS CHAIRMAN! I'M GOING TO BE SPENDING PLENTY OF TIME WITH HIM THE NEXT FEW DAYS!

IT WILL ALMOST BE LIKE--BEING ENGAGED TO HIM!

HER EXPRESSION OF JOY CHANGES TO ONE OF DISMAY, HOWEVER, AS...

I'M AWFULLY SORRY, CAROL--BUT I'VE GOT TO LEAVE!

OH, NO'!

I JUST GOT A CALL FROM A UNITED NATIONS REPRESENTATIVE ASKING FOR MY HELP! THERE'S A TERRIBLE SANDSTORM WHIPPING IN FROM THE KALAHARI DESERT--THREATENING TO DESTROY SEVERAL TOWNS IN BECH-UANALAND!

IF I EVER WERE MARRIED TO HIM--IT WOULD BE LIKE BEING MARRIED TO A DOCTOR-- ALWAYS ON CALL FOR EMERGENCIES!

I'LL TRY AND GET BACK FOR OUR DINNER DATE TONIGHT!

HIS POWER RING GLOWING WITH TREMENDOUS POWER, THE EMERALD GLADIATOR WILLS HIS WAY SWIFTLY ACROSS THE ATLANTIC OCEAN...

I WAS LOOKING FORWARD TO BEING WITH CAROL MYSELF THIS WEEK. BUT DUTY COMES BEFORE PLEASURE.

2

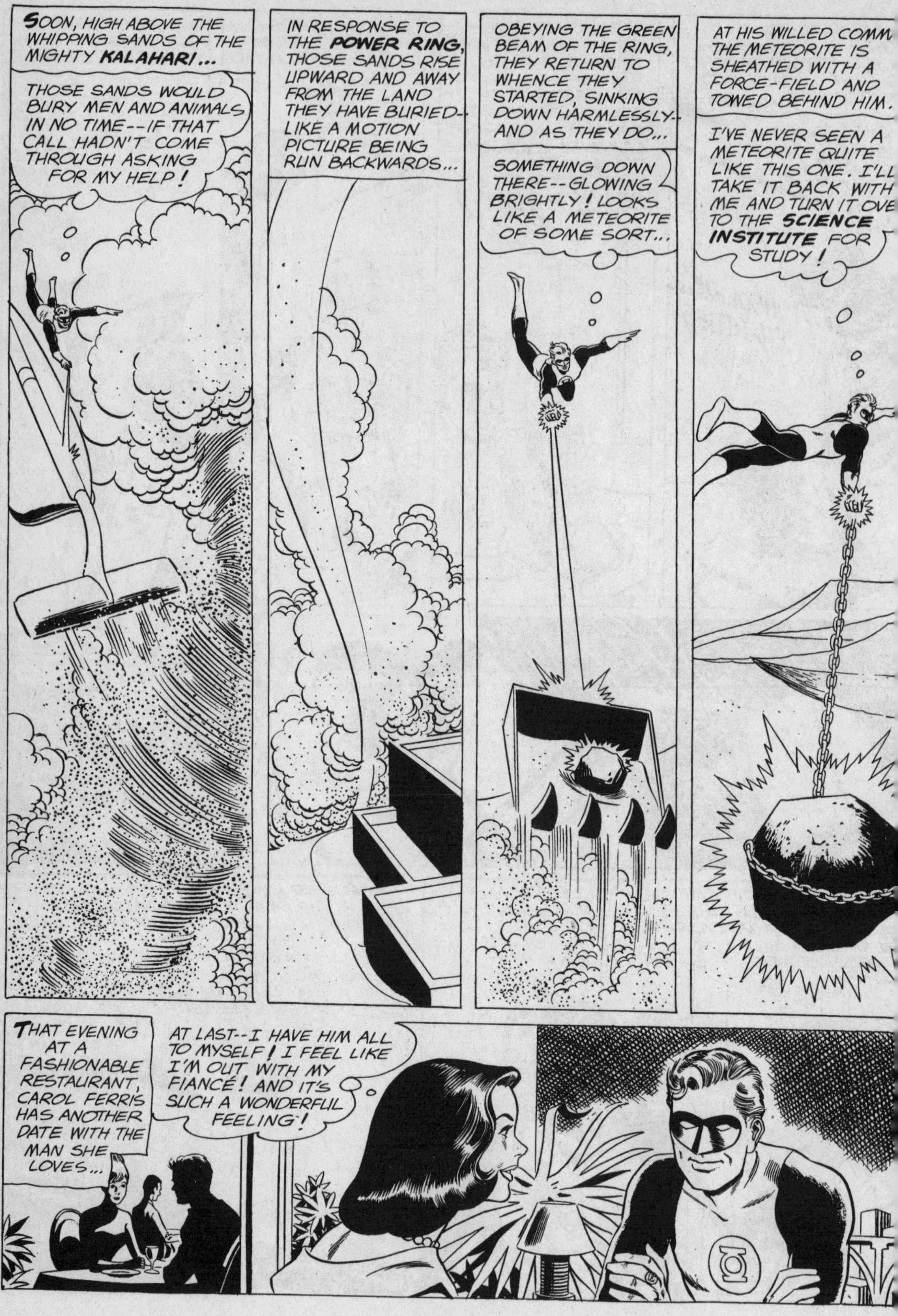
SOON, HIGH ABOVE THE WHIPPING SANDS OF THE MIGHTY KALAHARI...
THOSE SANDS WOULD BURY MEN AND ANIMALS IN NO TIME--IF THAT CALL HADN'T COME THROUGH ASKING FOR MY HELP!
IN RESPONSE TO THE POWER RING, THOSE SANDS RISE UPWARD AND AWAY FROM THE LAND THEY HAVE BURIED-- LIKE A MOTION PICTURE BEING RUN BACKWARDS...
OBEYING THE GREEN BEAM OF THE RING, THEY RETURN TO WHENCE THEY STARTED, SINKING DOWN HARMLESSLY-- AND AS THEY DO...
SOMETHING DOWN THERE--GLOWING BRIGHTLY! LOOKS LIKE A METEORITE OF SOME SORT...
AT HIS WILLED COMM THE METEORITE IS SHEATHED WITH A FORCE-FIELD AND TOWED BEHIND HIM.
I'VE NEVER SEEN A METEORITE QUITE LIKE THIS ONE. I'LL TAKE IT BACK WITH ME AND TURN IT OVE TO THE SCIENCE INSTITUTE FOR STUDY!
THAT EVENING AT A FASHIONABLE RESTAURANT, CAROL FERRIS HAS ANOTHER DATE WITH THE MAN SHE LOVES...
AT LAST--I HAVE HIM ALL TO MYSELF! I FEEL LIKE I'M OUT WITH MY FIANCÉ! AND IT'S SUCH A WONDERFUL FEELING!

...HE MOON HAS LONG BEEN A SYMBOL OF ROMANCE--BUT NOW AS CAROL GLANCES UP AT IT...

OHH! *GREEN LANTERN*, IS IT MY IMAGINATION--OR IS THE MOON REALLY WOBBLING A LITTLE?

YOU'RE RIGHT, CAROL--IT *IS* WOBBLING! DANGEROUSLY SO! IF THAT WOBBLE GROWS WORSE, THE MOON COULD SHAKE ITSELF OUT OF ORBIT--AND PLUNGE DOWN ONTO THE EARTH!

I'M SORRY. I HAVE TO GO TO THE MOON AND STOP THAT WOBBLE! I HOPE YOU UNDERSTAND!

I *DO* UNDERSTAND, *GREEN LANTERN.* I'LL TRY NOT TO MIND--TOO MUCH!

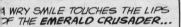

A WRY SMILE TOUCHES THE LIPS OF THE *EMERALD CRUSADER*...

MAYBE THIS WILL CONVINCE YOU THAT YOU AND I CAN NEVER MARRY! I'D ALWAYS BE DASHING OFF SOMEWHERE TO FIGHT A NEW MENACE!

ON THE CONTRARY! I LOOK ON YOU AS A DOCTOR. AN ORDINARY DOCTOR TREATS PEOPLE'S ILLS. YOU TREAT THE ILLS OF THE WHOLE WORLD!

SHORTLY THEREAFTER, *GREEN LANTERN* IS FLYING UPWARD AND OUTWARD THROUGH SPACE TOWARD THE LUNAR ORB...

I'M GLAD CAROL LOOKS AT THIS SENSIBLY--BUT I'D RATHER WIN HER LOVE AS *HAL JORDAN*, TEST PILOT-- THAN AS A SUPER-HERO!

AS HE NEARS THE MOON, HE USES THE *POWER RING* TO FORM A GIANT HAND...

THE MOON IS DEFINITELY WOBBLING, ALL RIGHT! I'VE GOT TO STOP IT-- STEADY IT--THEN HUNT AROUND FOR THE CAUSE!

4

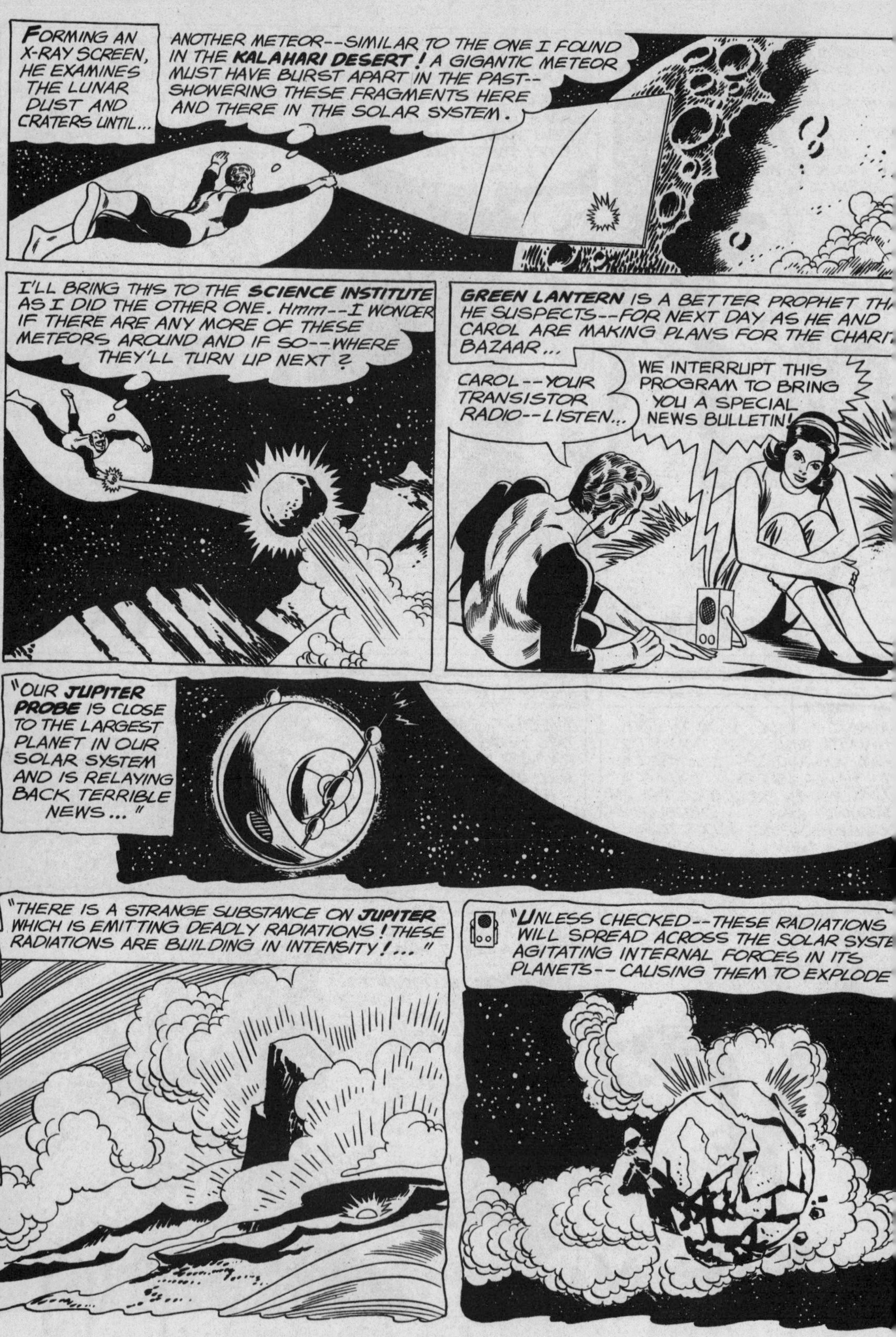
FORMING AN X-RAY SCREEN, HE EXAMINES THE LUNAR DUST AND CRATERS UNTIL...
ANOTHER METEOR--SIMILAR TO THE ONE I FOUND IN THE KALAHARI DESERT! A GIGANTIC METEOR MUST HAVE BURST APART IN THE PAST--SHOWERING THESE FRAGMENTS HERE AND THERE IN THE SOLAR SYSTEM.
I'LL BRING THIS TO THE SCIENCE INSTITUTE AS I DID THE OTHER ONE. Hmm--I WONDER IF THERE ARE ANY MORE OF THESE METEORS AROUND AND IF SO--WHERE THEY'LL TURN UP NEXT?
GREEN LANTERN IS A BETTER PROPHET TH HE SUSPECTS--FOR NEXT DAY AS HE AND CAROL ARE MAKING PLANS FOR THE CHARI BAZAAR...
CAROL--YOUR TRANSISTOR RADIO--LISTEN...
WE INTERRUPT THIS PROGRAM TO BRING YOU A SPECIAL NEWS BULLETIN!
"OUR JUPITER PROBE IS CLOSE TO THE LARGEST PLANET IN OUR SOLAR SYSTEM AND IS RELAYING BACK TERRIBLE NEWS..."
"THERE IS A STRANGE SUBSTANCE ON JUPITER WHICH IS EMITTING DEADLY RADIATIONS! THESE RADIATIONS ARE BUILDING IN INTENSITY!..."
"UNLESS CHECKED--THESE RADIATIONS WILL SPREAD ACROSS THE SOLAR SYSTE AGITATING INTERNAL FORCES IN ITS PLANETS--CAUSING THEM TO EXPLODE

FIGURED THAT BY PICNICKING ON THIS BEACH
E'D HAVE A FEW HOURS TOGETHER--BUT I
AVE NO TIME TO WASTE. I MUST GO TO
UPITER AND--STOP THAT DEADLY RADIATION!
I UNDERSTAND, NATURALLY! IT'S YOUR DUTY TO GO!
I DON'T MIND HIS GOING. NOT REALLY! BUT I DO WISH -Sigh- THAT HE WEREN'T QUITE SO BUSY!
I'LL BE BACK--AS SOON AS I CAN!
AR OUT IN PACE BE-YOND THE ASTEROID BELT AND CLOSE TO HE GIANT OF THE SOLAR SYSTEM...
I'LL COVER THE PLANET WITH A MESH TO PRE-VENT ANY MORE RADIATION LEAVING IT!
HE POWER RING THRUSTS DEEPER INTO UPITER, PROBING, HUNTING...
THERE'S THE GLOWING SPOT THAT'S CAUSING ALL THE TROUBLE! NOW TO GRASP WHAT IT IS AND--EXTRACT IT!
6

GREEN LANTERN

MASTER OF THE POWER RING! PART 2

AS THE GREEN FORCEPS LIFTS THE GLOWING THREAT TO THE SOLAR SYSTEM...

ANOTHER METEOR! WELL, THEY SAY THINGS HAPPEN IN THREES--BUT THIS IS BEGINNING TO SHAPE UP AS MORE THAN JUST AN ODD COINCIDENCE!

INDEED THIS IS NO ODD COINCIDENCE--FOR EVEN AS **GREEN LANTERN** IS SHEATHING THE THIRD METEOR IN A FORCE-FIELD AND BRINGING IT TO THE **SCIENCE INSTITUTE**-- IN A REMOTE PART OF **COAST CITY**...

HA,HA! **GREEN LANTERN** IS DOING JUST WHAT I ARRANGED FOR HIM TO DO!

HE IS BRINGING THOSE THREE METEORS TO THE **SCIENCE INSTITUTE** IN **COAST CITY**-- WHERE I CAN GAIN POSSESSION OF THEM! EVER SINCE I FIRST DISCOVERED THE METEORITE THAT ENABLED ME TO EVOLVE PEOPLE AND OTHER LIVING THINGS INTO THEIR FUTURE COUNTERPARTS--I REALIZED THERE WERE THREE OTHER PARTS TO IT!

WHO IS THIS STRANGE, HUGE-HEADED PERSON? HE IS CHANGED BUT--IF **GREEN LANTERN** WERE HERE--HE WOULD RECOGNIZE HIM AS **HECTOR HAMMOND**!*...

I'VE BEEN SEARCHING FOR THOSE METEORS EVER SINCE I FIRST EVOLVED THOSE FOUR SCIENTISTS AND TRIED TO MASTER ALL KNOWLEDGE*!

"LATER, AFTER MY ALLIANCE WITH **MISTER MEMORY**, THE **PIED PIPER**, **ANGLE MAN**, THE **SEA THIEF** AND **DOCTOR DAVIS*** FAILED--I VOWED I WOULD USE MY METEOR TO MAKE MYSELF IMMORTAL..."

MY FUTURE-BRAIN WILL ENABLE ME TO THINK OF A WAY TO ESCAPE FROM THIS PRISON-- AND AFTER I DO, I'LL SET INTO OPERATION PLANS TO BE- COME THE IMMORTAL MASTER OF THE WORLD!

"THIS I DID--ALTERING MY BODY BY MEANS OF THE EVOLUTION-METEOR I DIS- COVERED--BUT AFTER I BATHED IN ITS RAYS, AN UN- FORESEEN DEVELOPMENT OCCURRED!..."

I CANNOT MOVE! I HAVE MADE MYSELF IMMORTAL--AT THE COST OF LOSING MY MOBILITY! AND UNLESS I CAN MOVE ABOUT WHAT GOOD IS IMMORTALITY?

*EDITOR'S NOTE: SEE GREEN LANTERN #5: "THE POWER RING THAT VANISHED!"

*EDITOR'S NOTE: SEE JUSTICE LEAGUE OF AMERICA #14: "MENACE OF THE ATOM BOMB!"

PUT MY FUTURISTIC BRAIN TO PROBLEM OF FIGURING OUT ERE THE MISSING FRAG- NTS OF THE ORIGINAL METEOR RE TO BE FOUND ... "

LY ONE MAN--*GREEN LANTERN!*--CAN BRING OSE MISSING METEORS O ME --WHICH WILL ENABLE E TO REGAIN THE POWER TO MOVE ABOUT !

WITH MY TREMENDOUS *WILL POWER* I COULD TAKE HIS *POWER RING* AWAY FROM HIM AND USE IT MYSELF--BUT I DON'T KNOW WHEN IT HAS TO BE RECHARGED--OR HOW ! I'VE TRIED AND FAILED TO GET THE METEORS BY MY MENTAL POWERS ALONE . BUT THE METEORS RESIST MY TELEPATHIC CONTROL TO COME TO ME ...

"*AND SO I MADE MY PLANS...*"

I'LL CAUSE A DISTURBANCE NEAR THE METEORITE IN THE *KALAHARI DESERT*, THEN TELEPATHICALLY DIRECT THE *UNITED NATIONS* REPRESENT- ATIVE TO CALL *GREEN LANTERN* FOR HELP! I'LL PUT THE IDEA IN *GREEN LANTERN'S* MIND TO BRING THE METEORITE TO THE *SCIENCE INSTITUTE!*

"AS I DID WITH ONE , SO I DID WITH THE OTHER TWO, MAKING SURE *GREEN LANTERN* WOULD LEARN OF THE THREATS OF THE METEORS AND GO TO STOP THEM ... "

FOR THE MOMENT, I MUST BE CAREFUL NOT TO EXERT ANY DIRECT CONTROL OVER THE *POWER RING !* BY ACTIVATING IT, ITS TELL TALE GLOW WOULD ALERT *GREEN LANTERN* THAT SOMETHING WAS WRONG . SO I'LL *MAKE* HIM GET THE METEORS FOR ME !

NOW THE FUTURISTIC BRAIN OF HECTOR HAMMOND SENDS OUT MORE TELEPATHIC COMMANDS, AND IN A SLUM AREA DINER...

COME ON ! WE'VE GOT A JOB TO DO !

8

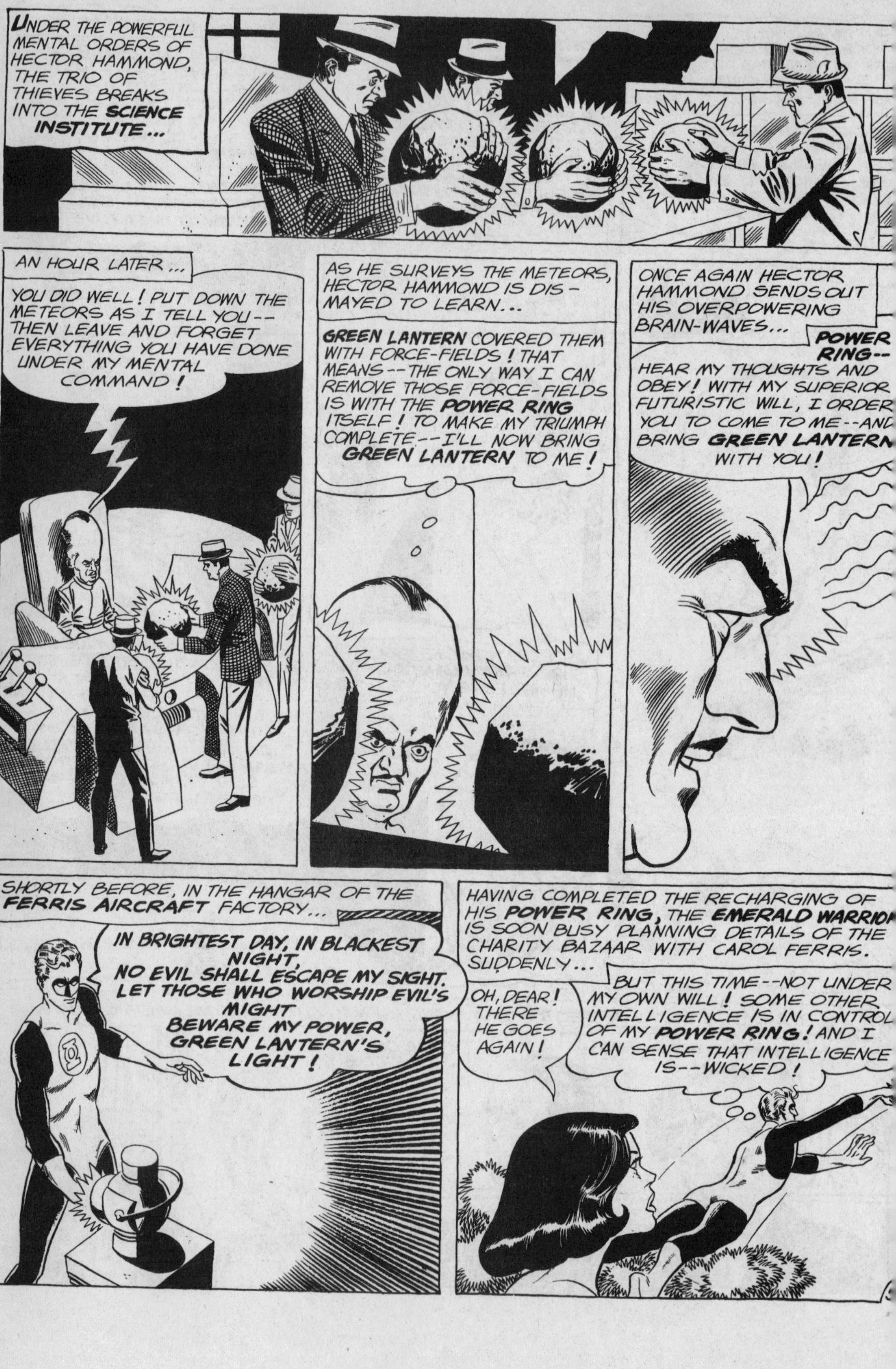
UNDER THE POWERFUL MENTAL ORDERS OF HECTOR HAMMOND, THE TRIO OF THIEVES BREAKS INTO THE SCIENCE INSTITUTE...
AN HOUR LATER...
YOU DID WELL! PUT DOWN THE METEORS AS I TELL YOU--THEN LEAVE AND FORGET EVERYTHING YOU HAVE DONE UNDER MY MENTAL COMMAND!
AS HE SURVEYS THE METEORS, HECTOR HAMMOND IS DISMAYED TO LEARN...
GREEN LANTERN COVERED THEM WITH FORCE-FIELDS! THAT MEANS--THE ONLY WAY I CAN REMOVE THOSE FORCE-FIELDS IS WITH THE POWER RING ITSELF! TO MAKE MY TRIUMPH COMPLETE--I'LL NOW BRING GREEN LANTERN TO ME!
ONCE AGAIN HECTOR HAMMOND SENDS OUT HIS OVERPOWERING BRAIN-WAVES...
POWER RING--HEAR MY THOUGHTS AND OBEY! WITH MY SUPERIOR FUTURISTIC WILL, I ORDER YOU TO COME TO ME--AND BRING GREEN LANTERN WITH YOU!
SHORTLY BEFORE, IN THE HANGAR OF THE FERRIS AIRCRAFT FACTORY...
IN BRIGHTEST DAY, IN BLACKEST NIGHT, NO EVIL SHALL ESCAPE MY SIGHT. LET THOSE WHO WORSHIP EVIL'S MIGHT BEWARE MY POWER, GREEN LANTERN'S LIGHT!
HAVING COMPLETED THE RECHARGING OF HIS POWER RING, THE EMERALD WARRIOR IS SOON BUSY PLANNING DETAILS OF THE CHARITY BAZAAR WITH CAROL FERRIS. SUDDENLY...
OH, DEAR! THERE HE GOES AGAIN!
BUT THIS TIME--NOT UNDER MY OWN WILL! SOME OTHER INTELLIGENCE IS IN CONTROL OF MY POWER RING! AND I CAN SENSE THAT INTELLIGENCE IS--WICKED!

AS HE IS CARRIED SWIFTLY THROUGH THE AIR HIGH ABOVE THE CITY...

I'VE GOT TO FIGHT BACK--PREVENT THIS INTELLIGENCE FROM OVERPOWERING ME! I CAN FEEL ITS WICKEDNESS ALMOST LIKE A TANGIBLE FORCE!

STRONG IS THE FUTURISTIC WILL OF **HECTOR HAMMOND**, BUT STRONG ALSO IS THE TRAINED WILL OF **GREEN LANTERN**, SO THAT...

I'VE FOUGHT IT TO A STAND-STILL! I'VE COME TO A DEAD STOP! I CAN'T MOVE BACKWARD--BUT NEITHER CAN THAT INTELLIGENCE MOVE ME FORWARD!

WITH AN EXTRAORDINARY EFFORT, HECTOR HAMMOND COMMANDS THE **POWER RING** TO SHOOT OUT A MIGHTY FIST AND...

YOU ARE FINISHED, **GREEN LANTERN!** FROM NOW ON I'M CONTROLLING YOUR **POWER RING!**

DAZED AND ONLY HALF CONSCIOUS, THE **GREEN GLADIATOR** IS BORNE SWIFTLY TO A REMOTE CORNER OF **COAST CITY**--AND THROUGH A LABORATORY WALL...

MY FUTURISTIC MENTAL POWERS PROVED TOO MUCH FOR YOU! I HAVE NOW MADE MYSELF MASTER OF YOUR **POWER RING!**

ON THE VERGE OF VICTORY, HECTOR HAMMOND CHUCKLES INWARDLY WITH WICKED GLEE...

IT DOES ME GOOD TO SEE YOU SO HELPLESS, **GREEN LANTERN!** LET ME ASK YOU--WHEN DID YOU LAST CHARGE THE **POWER RING?**

TWO HOURS AGO,...

AN OVERPOWERING MENTAL FORCE -- MAKING ME ANSWER HIM!

10

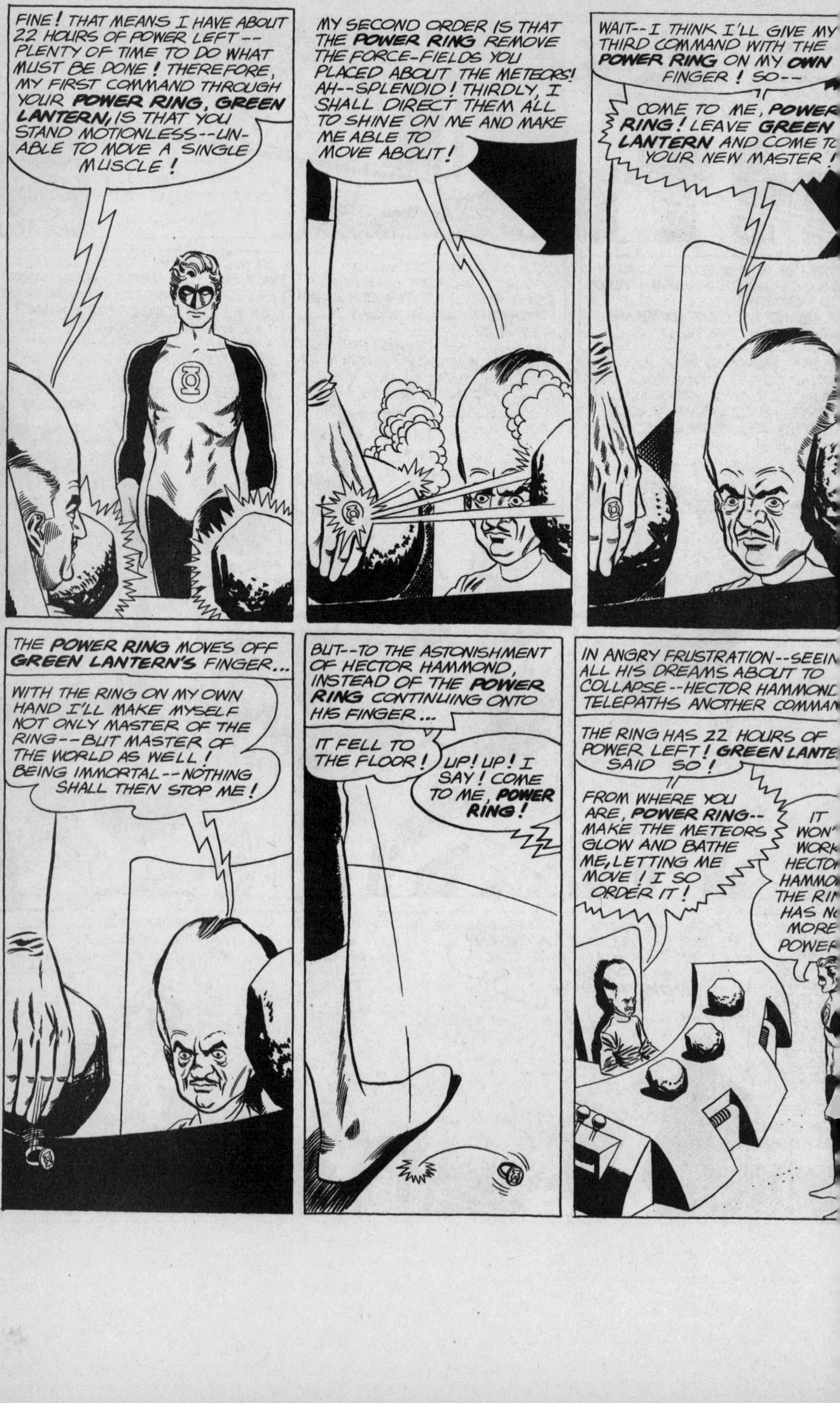
FINE! THAT MEANS I HAVE ABOUT 22 HOURS OF POWER LEFT-- PLENTY OF TIME TO DO WHAT MUST BE DONE! THEREFORE, MY FIRST COMMAND THROUGH YOUR POWER RING, GREEN LANTERN, IS THAT YOU STAND MOTIONLESS--UNABLE TO MOVE A SINGLE MUSCLE!
MY SECOND ORDER IS THAT THE POWER RING REMOVE THE FORCE-FIELDS YOU PLACED ABOUT THE METEORS! AH--SPLENDID! THIRDLY, I SHALL DIRECT THEM ALL TO SHINE ON ME AND MAKE ME ABLE TO MOVE ABOUT!
WAIT--I THINK I'LL GIVE MY THIRD COMMAND WITH THE POWER RING ON MY OWN FINGER! SO--
COME TO ME, POWER RING! LEAVE GREEN LANTERN AND COME TO YOUR NEW MASTER!
THE POWER RING MOVES OFF GREEN LANTERN'S FINGER...
WITH THE RING ON MY OWN HAND I'LL MAKE MYSELF NOT ONLY MASTER OF THE RING--BUT MASTER OF THE WORLD AS WELL! BEING IMMORTAL--NOTHING SHALL THEN STOP ME!
BUT--TO THE ASTONISHMENT OF HECTOR HAMMOND, INSTEAD OF THE POWER RING CONTINUING ONTO HIS FINGER...
IT FELL TO THE FLOOR!
UP! UP! I SAY! COME TO ME, POWER RING!
IN ANGRY FRUSTRATION--SEEIN ALL HIS DREAMS ABOUT TO COLLAPSE--HECTOR HAMMOND TELEPATHS ANOTHER COMMAN
THE RING HAS 22 HOURS OF POWER LEFT! GREEN LANTE SAID SO!
FROM WHERE YOU ARE, POWER RING-- MAKE THE METEORS GLOW AND BATHE ME, LETTING ME MOVE! I SO ORDER IT!
IT WON' WORK HECTO HAMMO THE RI HAS N MORE POWER

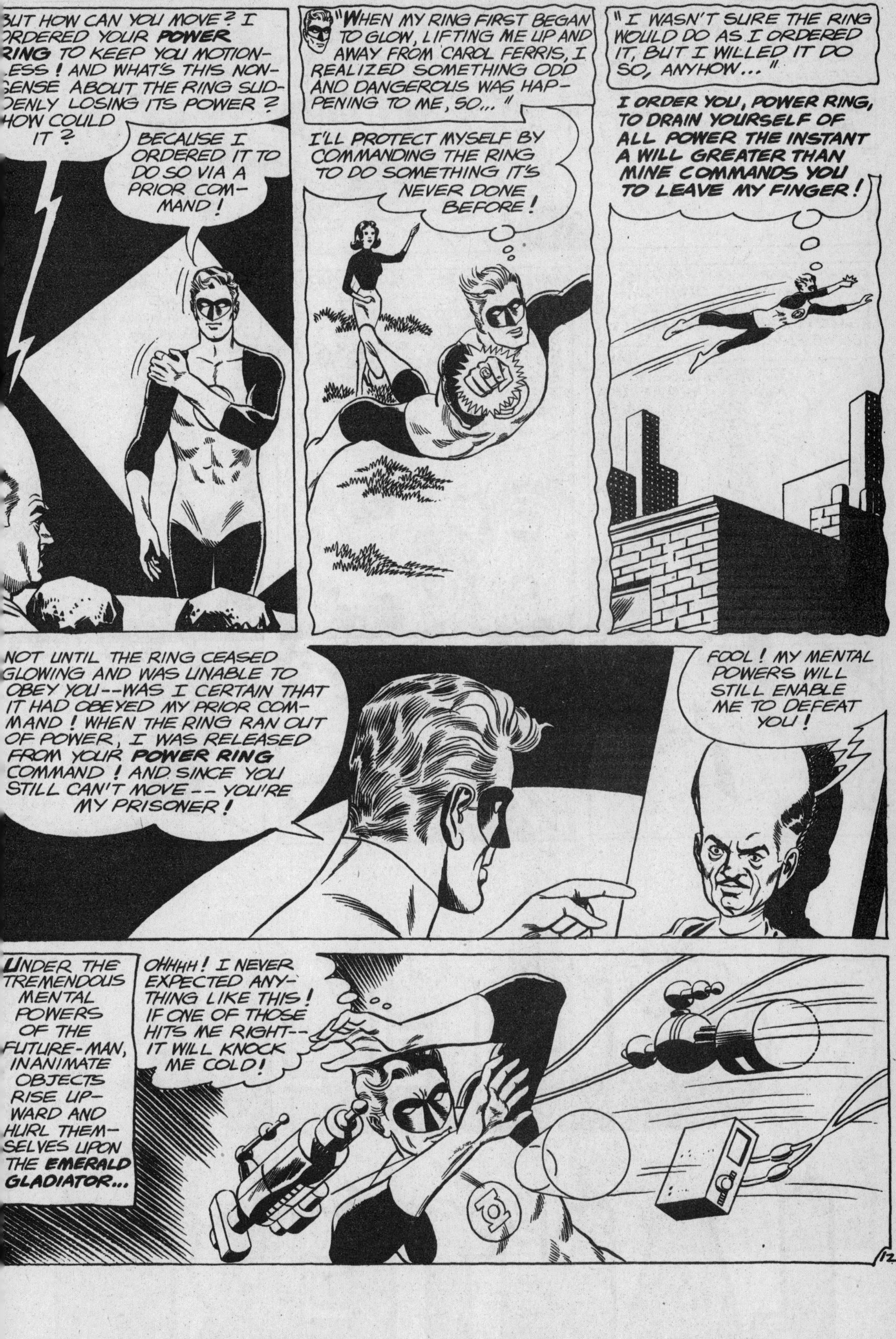
BUT HOW CAN YOU MOVE? I ORDERED YOUR POWER RING TO KEEP YOU MOTIONLESS! AND WHAT'S THIS NONSENSE ABOUT THE RING SUDDENLY LOSING ITS POWER? HOW COULD IT?
BECAUSE I ORDERED IT TO DO SO VIA A PRIOR COMMAND!
"WHEN MY RING FIRST BEGAN TO GLOW, LIFTING ME UP AND AWAY FROM CAROL FERRIS, I REALIZED SOMETHING ODD AND DANGEROUS WAS HAPPENING TO ME, SO..."
I'LL PROTECT MYSELF BY COMMANDING THE RING TO DO SOMETHING IT'S NEVER DONE BEFORE!
"I WASN'T SURE THE RING WOULD DO AS I ORDERED IT, BUT I WILLED IT DO SO, ANYHOW..."
I ORDER YOU, POWER RING, TO DRAIN YOURSELF OF ALL POWER THE INSTANT A WILL GREATER THAN MINE COMMANDS YOU TO LEAVE MY FINGER!
NOT UNTIL THE RING CEASED GLOWING AND WAS UNABLE TO OBEY YOU--WAS I CERTAIN THAT IT HAD OBEYED MY PRIOR COMMAND! WHEN THE RING RAN OUT OF POWER, I WAS RELEASED FROM YOUR POWER RING COMMAND! AND SINCE YOU STILL CAN'T MOVE-- YOU'RE MY PRISONER!
FOOL! MY MENTAL POWERS WILL STILL ENABLE ME TO DEFEAT YOU!
UNDER THE TREMENDOUS MENTAL POWERS OF THE FUTURE-MAN, INANIMATE OBJECTS RISE UPWARD AND HURL THEMSELVES UPON THE EMERALD GLADIATOR...
OHHHH! I NEVER EXPECTED ANYTHING LIKE THIS! IF ONE OF THOSE HITS ME RIGHT-- IT WILL KNOCK ME COLD!
12

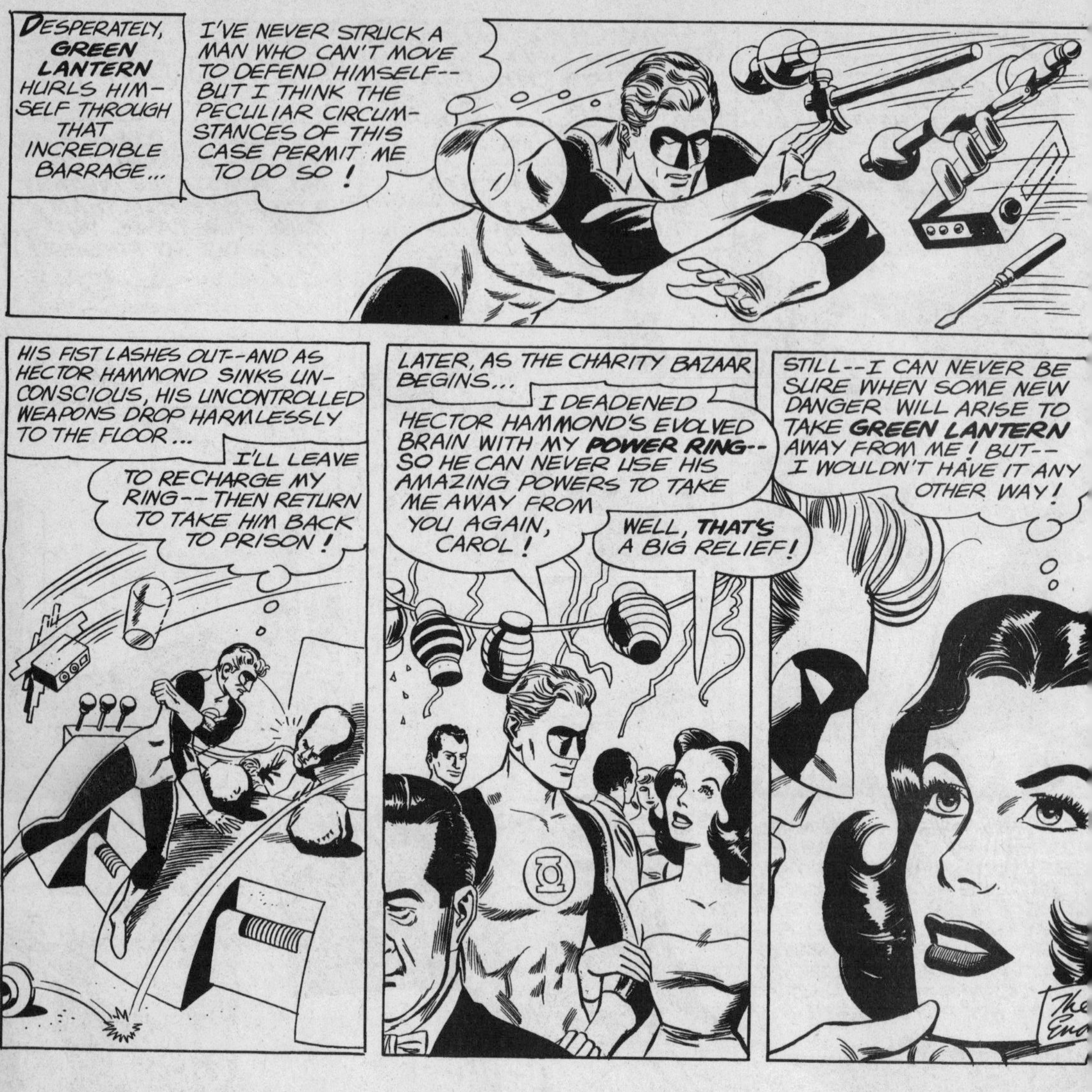
DESPERATELY, GREEN LANTERN HURLS HIMSELF THROUGH THAT INCREDIBLE BARRAGE...
I'VE NEVER STRUCK A MAN WHO CAN'T MOVE TO DEFEND HIMSELF-- BUT I THINK THE PECULIAR CIRCUMSTANCES OF THIS CASE PERMIT ME TO DO SO!
HIS FIST LASHES OUT--AND AS HECTOR HAMMOND SINKS UNCONSCIOUS, HIS UNCONTROLLED WEAPONS DROP HARMLESSLY TO THE FLOOR...
I'LL LEAVE TO RECHARGE MY RING-- THEN RETURN TO TAKE HIM BACK TO PRISON!
LATER, AS THE CHARITY BAZAAR BEGINS...
I DEADENED HECTOR HAMMOND'S EVOLVED BRAIN WITH MY POWER RING-- SO HE CAN NEVER USE HIS AMAZING POWERS TO TAKE ME AWAY FROM YOU AGAIN, CAROL!
WELL, THAT'S A BIG RELIEF!
STILL--I CAN NEVER BE SURE WHEN SOME NEW DANGER WILL ARISE TO TAKE GREEN LANTERN AWAY FROM ME! BUT-- I WOULDN'T HAVE IT ANY OTHER WAY!

GREEN LANTERN

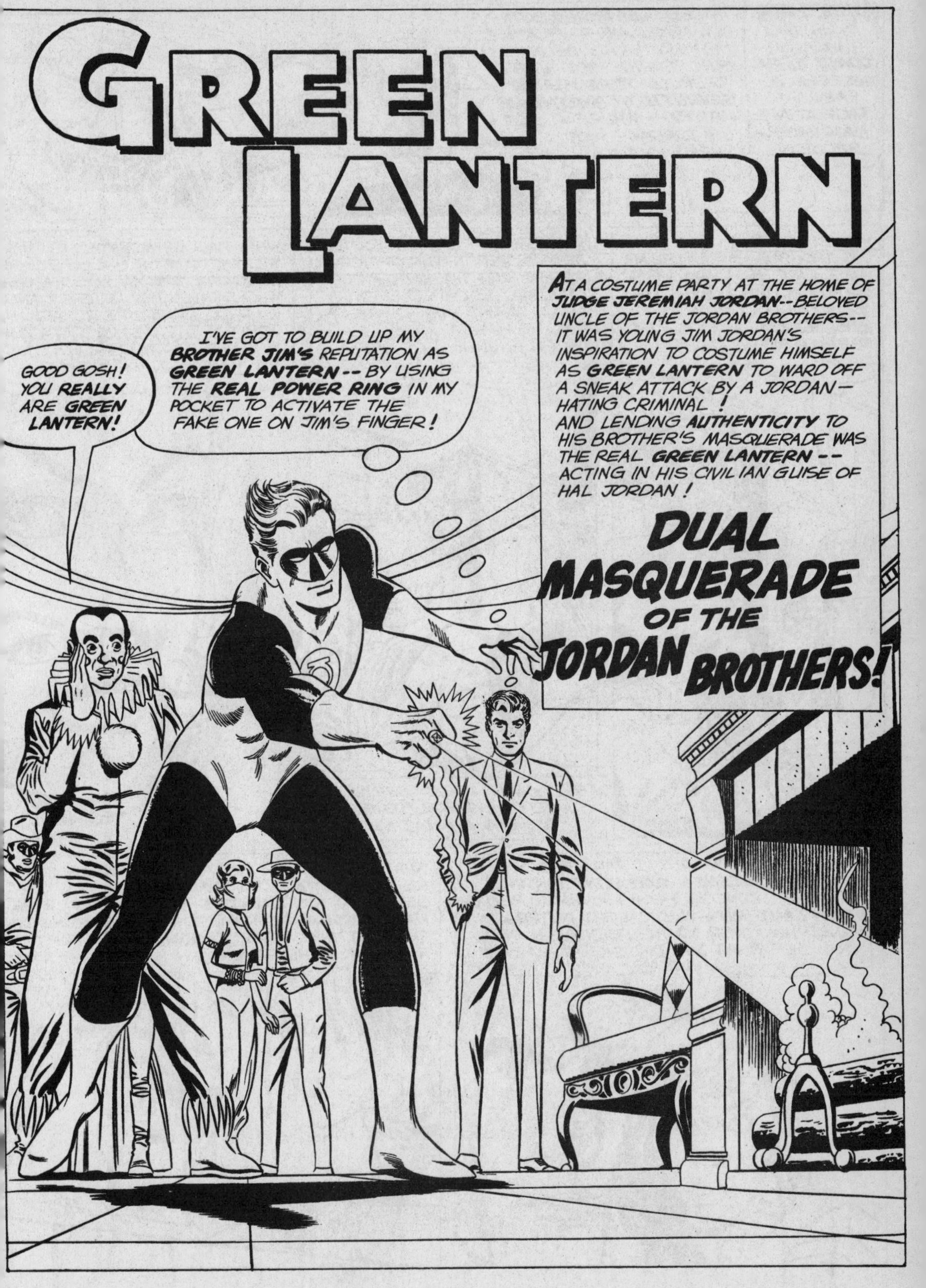
GREEN LANTERN
AT A COSTUME PARTY AT THE HOME OF JUDGE JEREMIAH JORDAN--BELOVED UNCLE OF THE JORDAN BROTHERS--IT WAS YOUNG JIM JORDAN'S INSPIRATION TO COSTUME HIMSELF AS GREEN LANTERN TO WARD OFF A SNEAK ATTACK BY A JORDAN-HATING CRIMINAL! AND LENDING AUTHENTICITY TO HIS BROTHER'S MASQUERADE WAS THE REAL GREEN LANTERN--ACTING IN HIS CIVILIAN GUISE OF HAL JORDAN!
DUAL MASQUERADE OF THE JORDAN BROTHERS!
GOOD GOSH! YOU REALLY ARE GREEN LANTERN!
I'VE GOT TO BUILD UP MY BROTHER JIM'S REPUTATION AS GREEN LANTERN -- BY USING THE REAL POWER RING IN MY POCKET TO ACTIVATE THE FAKE ONE ON JIM'S FINGER!

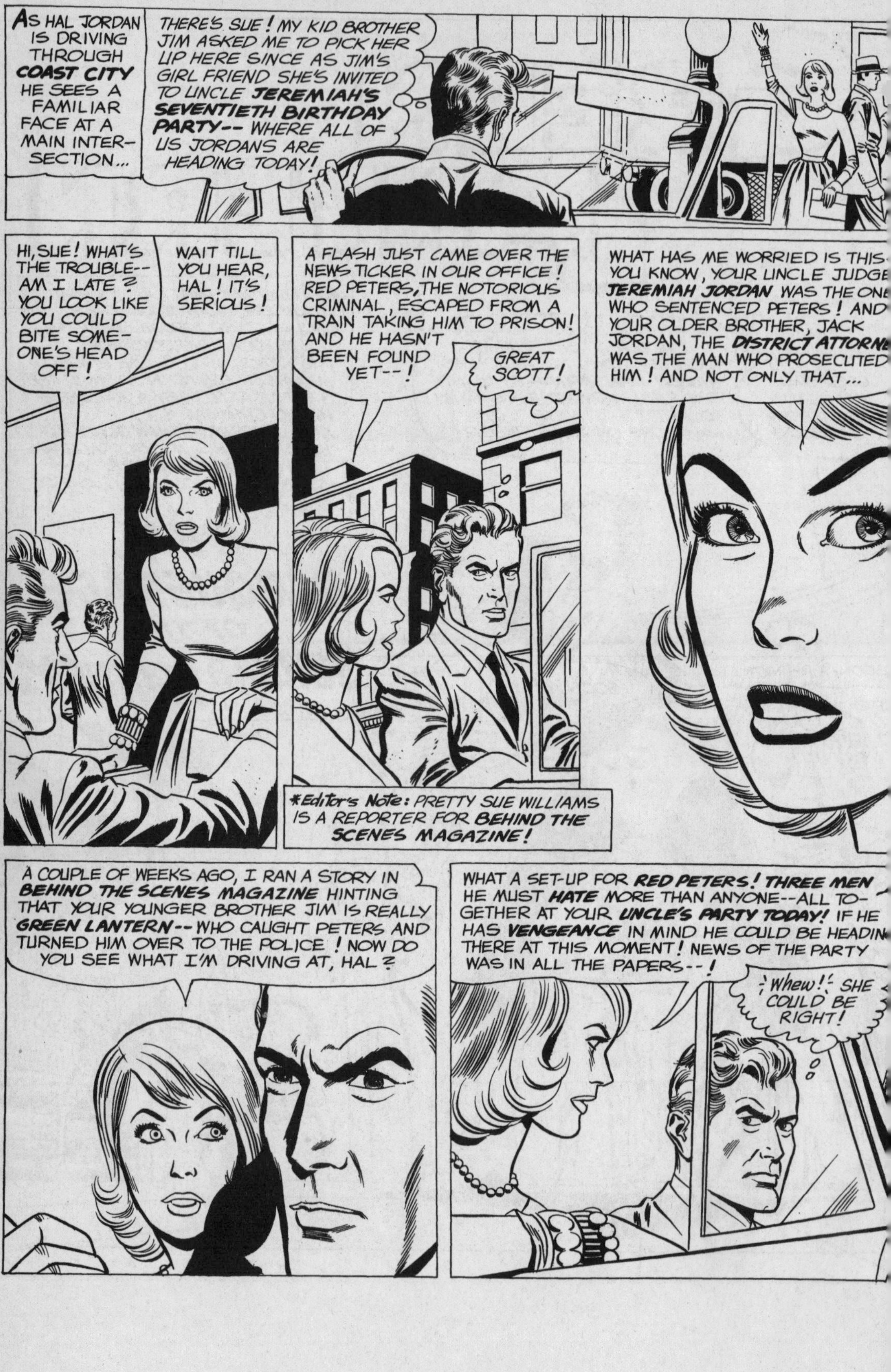
AS HAL JORDAN IS DRIVING THROUGH COAST CITY HE SEES A FAMILIAR FACE AT A MAIN INTER-SECTION...
THERE'S SUE! MY KID BROTHER JIM ASKED ME TO PICK HER UP HERE SINCE AS JIM'S GIRL FRIEND SHE'S INVITED TO UNCLE JEREMIAH'S SEVENTIETH BIRTHDAY PARTY-- WHERE ALL OF US JORDANS ARE HEADING TODAY!
HI, SUE! WHAT'S THE TROUBLE-- AM I LATE? YOU LOOK LIKE YOU COULD BITE SOME-ONE'S HEAD OFF!
WAIT TILL YOU HEAR, HAL! IT'S SERIOUS!
A FLASH JUST CAME OVER THE NEWS TICKER IN OUR OFFICE! RED PETERS, THE NOTORIOUS CRIMINAL, ESCAPED FROM A TRAIN TAKING HIM TO PRISON! AND HE HASN'T BEEN FOUND YET--!
GREAT SCOTT!
*Editor's Note: PRETTY SUE WILLIAMS IS A REPORTER FOR BEHIND THE SCENES MAGAZINE!
WHAT HAS ME WORRIED IS THIS- YOU KNOW, YOUR UNCLE JUDGE JEREMIAH JORDAN WAS THE ONE WHO SENTENCED PETERS! AND YOUR OLDER BROTHER, JACK JORDAN, THE DISTRICT ATTORNE WAS THE MAN WHO PROSECUTED HIM! AND NOT ONLY THAT...
A COUPLE OF WEEKS AGO, I RAN A STORY IN BEHIND THE SCENES MAGAZINE HINTING THAT YOUR YOUNGER BROTHER JIM IS REALLY GREEN LANTERN-- WHO CAUGHT PETERS AND TURNED HIM OVER TO THE POLICE! NOW DO YOU SEE WHAT I'M DRIVING AT, HAL?
WHAT A SET-UP FOR RED PETERS! THREE MEN HE MUST HATE MORE THAN ANYONE--ALL TO-GETHER AT YOUR UNCLE'S PARTY TODAY! IF HE HAS VENGEANCE IN MIND HE COULD BE HEADIN THERE AT THIS MOMENT! NEWS OF THE PARTY WAS IN ALL THE PAPERS--!
Whew! SHE COULD BE RIGHT!

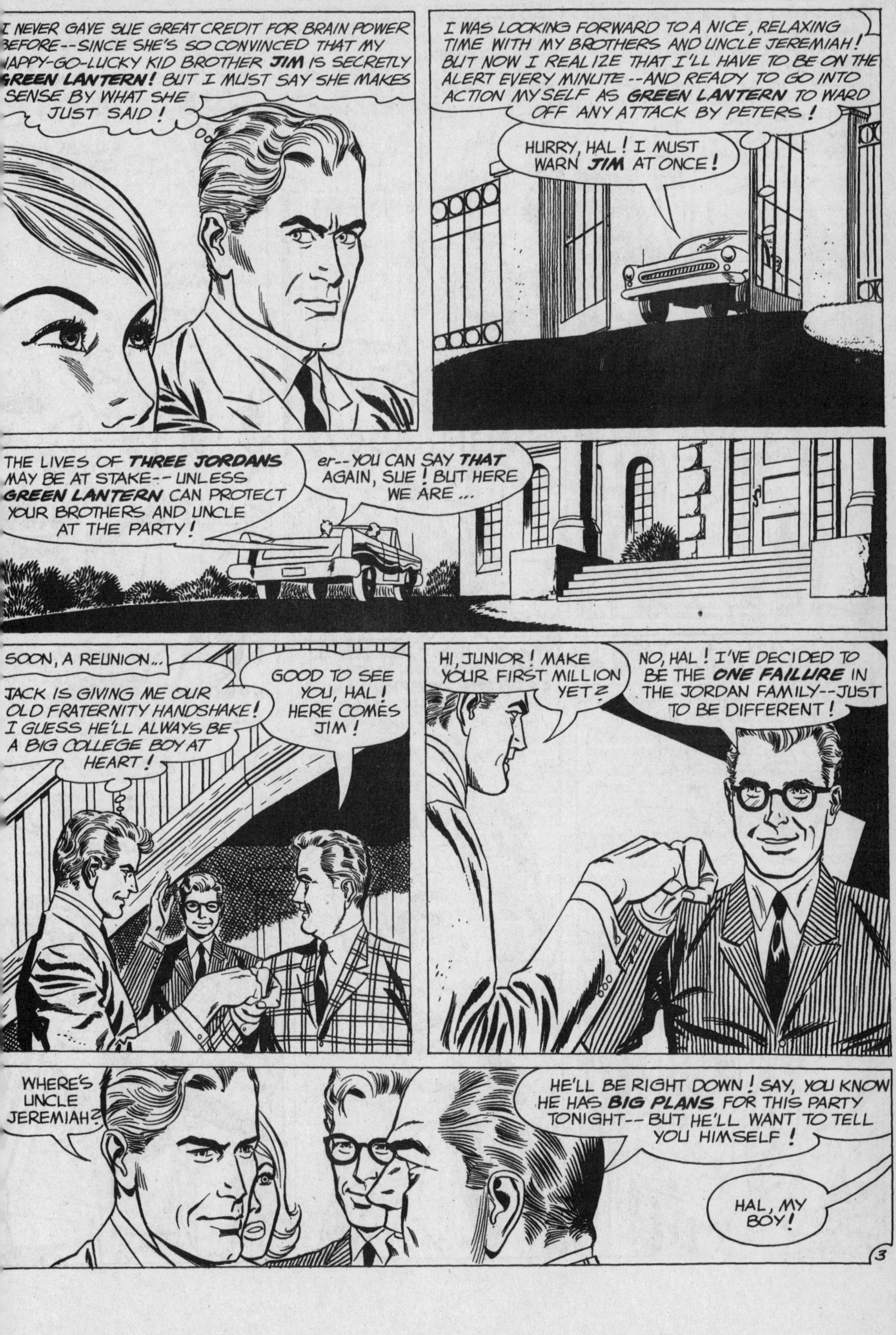
I NEVER GAVE SUE GREAT CREDIT FOR BRAIN POWER BEFORE--SINCE SHE'S SO CONVINCED THAT MY HAPPY-GO-LUCKY KID BROTHER JIM IS SECRETLY GREEN LANTERN! BUT I MUST SAY SHE MAKES SENSE BY WHAT SHE JUST SAID!
I WAS LOOKING FORWARD TO A NICE, RELAXING TIME WITH MY BROTHERS AND UNCLE JEREMIAH! BUT NOW I REALIZE THAT I'LL HAVE TO BE ON THE ALERT EVERY MINUTE--AND READY TO GO INTO ACTION MYSELF AS GREEN LANTERN TO WARD OFF ANY ATTACK BY PETERS!
HURRY, HAL! I MUST WARN JIM AT ONCE!
THE LIVES OF THREE JORDANS MAY BE AT STAKE--UNLESS GREEN LANTERN CAN PROTECT YOUR BROTHERS AND UNCLE AT THE PARTY!
er--YOU CAN SAY THAT AGAIN, SUE! BUT HERE WE ARE...
SOON, A REUNION...
JACK IS GIVING ME OUR OLD FRATERNITY HANDSHAKE! I GUESS HE'LL ALWAYS BE A BIG COLLEGE BOY AT HEART!
GOOD TO SEE YOU, HAL! HERE COMES JIM!
HI, JUNIOR! MAKE YOUR FIRST MILLION YET?
NO, HAL! I'VE DECIDED TO BE THE ONE FAILURE IN THE JORDAN FAMILY--JUST TO BE DIFFERENT!
WHERE'S UNCLE JEREMIAH?
HE'LL BE RIGHT DOWN! SAY, YOU KNOW HE HAS BIG PLANS FOR THIS PARTY TONIGHT--BUT HE'LL WANT TO TELL YOU HIMSELF!
HAL, MY BOY!
3

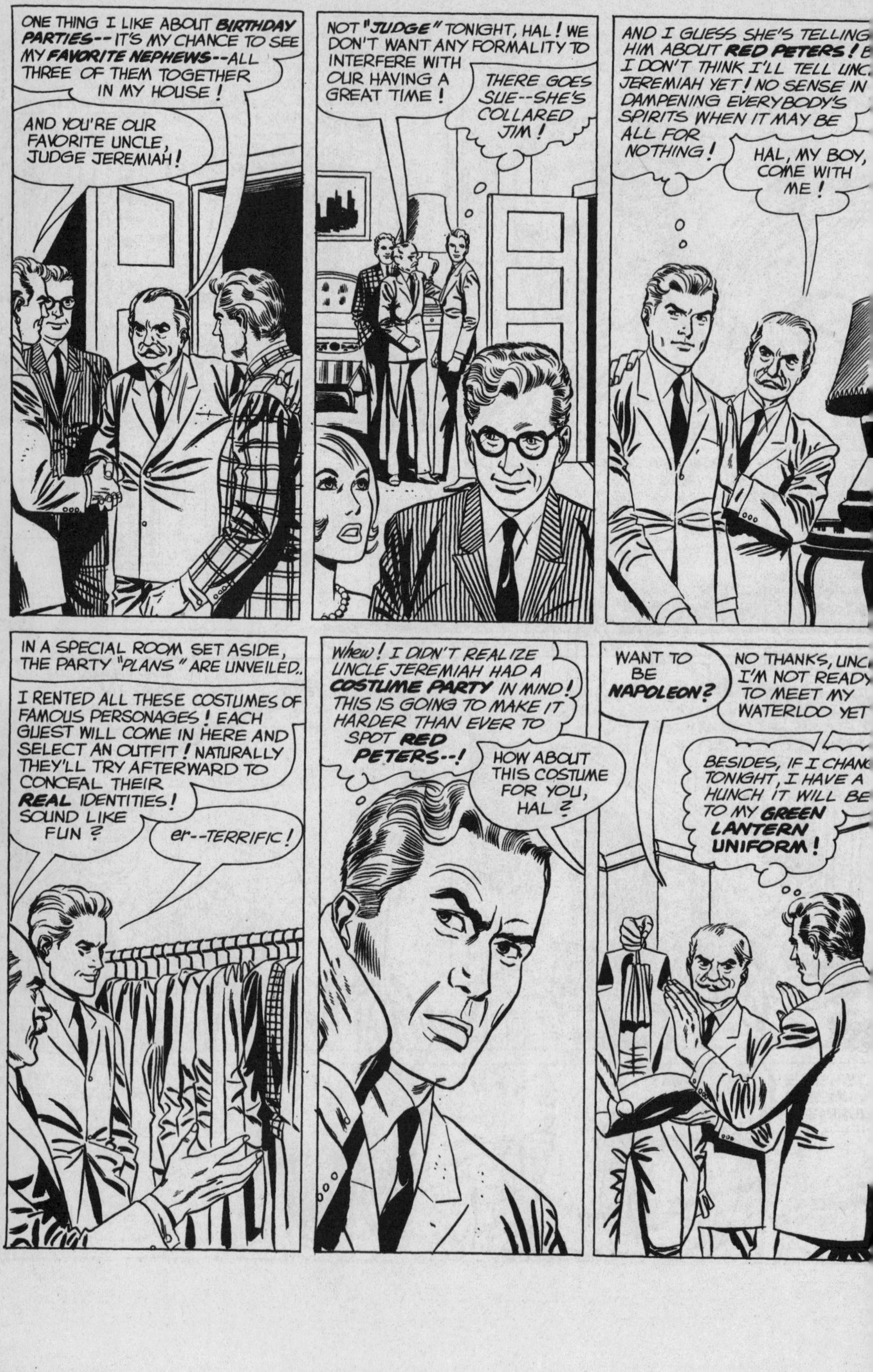
ONE THING I LIKE ABOUT BIRTHDAY PARTIES-- IT'S MY CHANCE TO SEE MY FAVORITE NEPHEWS--ALL THREE OF THEM TOGETHER IN MY HOUSE!
AND YOU'RE OUR FAVORITE UNCLE, JUDGE JEREMIAH!
NOT "JUDGE" TONIGHT, HAL! WE DON'T WANT ANY FORMALITY TO INTERFERE WITH OUR HAVING A GREAT TIME!
THERE GOES SUE--SHE'S COLLARED JIM!
AND I GUESS SHE'S TELLING HIM ABOUT RED PETERS! I DON'T THINK I'LL TELL UNC JEREMIAH YET! NO SENSE IN DAMPENING EVERYBODY'S SPIRITS WHEN IT MAY BE ALL FOR NOTHING!
HAL, MY BOY, COME WITH ME!
IN A SPECIAL ROOM SET ASIDE, THE PARTY "PLANS" ARE UNVEILED.
I RENTED ALL THESE COSTUMES OF FAMOUS PERSONAGES! EACH GUEST WILL COME IN HERE AND SELECT AN OUTFIT! NATURALLY THEY'LL TRY AFTERWARD TO CONCEAL THEIR REAL IDENTITIES! SOUND LIKE FUN?
er--TERRIFIC!
Whew! I DIDN'T REALIZE UNCLE JEREMIAH HAD A COSTUME PARTY IN MIND! THIS IS GOING TO MAKE IT HARDER THAN EVER TO SPOT RED PETERS--!
HOW ABOUT THIS COSTUME FOR YOU, HAL?
WANT TO BE NAPOLEON?
NO THANKS, UNC I'M NOT READY TO MEET MY WATERLOO YET
BESIDES, IF I CHANG TONIGHT, I HAVE A HUNCH IT WILL BE TO MY GREEN LANTERN UNIFORM!

MEANWHILE, IN ANOTHER ROOM OF THE SPACIOUS HOUSE...

RED PETERS IS ON THE LOOSE, SUE? SEEMS TO ME I'VE HEARD THE NAME, BUT--

YOU'VE HEARD THE *NAME*!? JIM JORDAN, YOU'RE *IMPOSSIBLE*!

WHY DO YOU HAVE TO KEEP UP THE PRETENSE EVEN WHEN WE'RE ALONE? I KNOW THAT SECRETLY YOU'RE *GREEN LANTERN*--AND YOU KNOW THAT I KNOW IT! AND WE BOTH KNOW THAT IT WAS *YOU* WHO CAUGHT *RED PETERS* JUST A MONTH AGO!

BUT WHILE YOU'RE PUTTING ON THIS SILLY ACT, YOUR BROTHER *JACK* AND YOUR UNCLE THE JUDGE MAY BOTH BE IN DANGER! YOU'VE GOT TO CHANGE INTO *GREEN LANTERN* AT ONCE--AND GET INTO ACTION!

NO SENSE IN TRYING TO CONVINCE SUE...

...THAT I'M *NOT GREEN LANTERN*! SHE JUST WON'T ACCEPT THE TRUTH NO MATTER WHAT I SAY! BUT WAIT A SECOND...

NOW I REMEMBER *RED PETERS*! ISN'T HE THE ONE WHO RODE A HORSE--

--AND DRESSED LIKE AN *ANCIENT BRITISH HIGHWAYMAN* DUE TO SOME QUEER QUIRK IN HIS BRAIN?

AS IF YOU DIDN'T KNOW! TALK ABOUT BRAIN QUIRKS IN OTHER PEOPLE--!

ARE YOU GOING TO CHANGE TO YOUR *GREEN LANTERN* IDENTITY-- OR NOT!?

HOLD IT, SUE! I'VE GOT AN IDEA THAT MAY STOP THIS *RED PETERS* AND PREVENT HIM FROM HARMING ANYONE--!

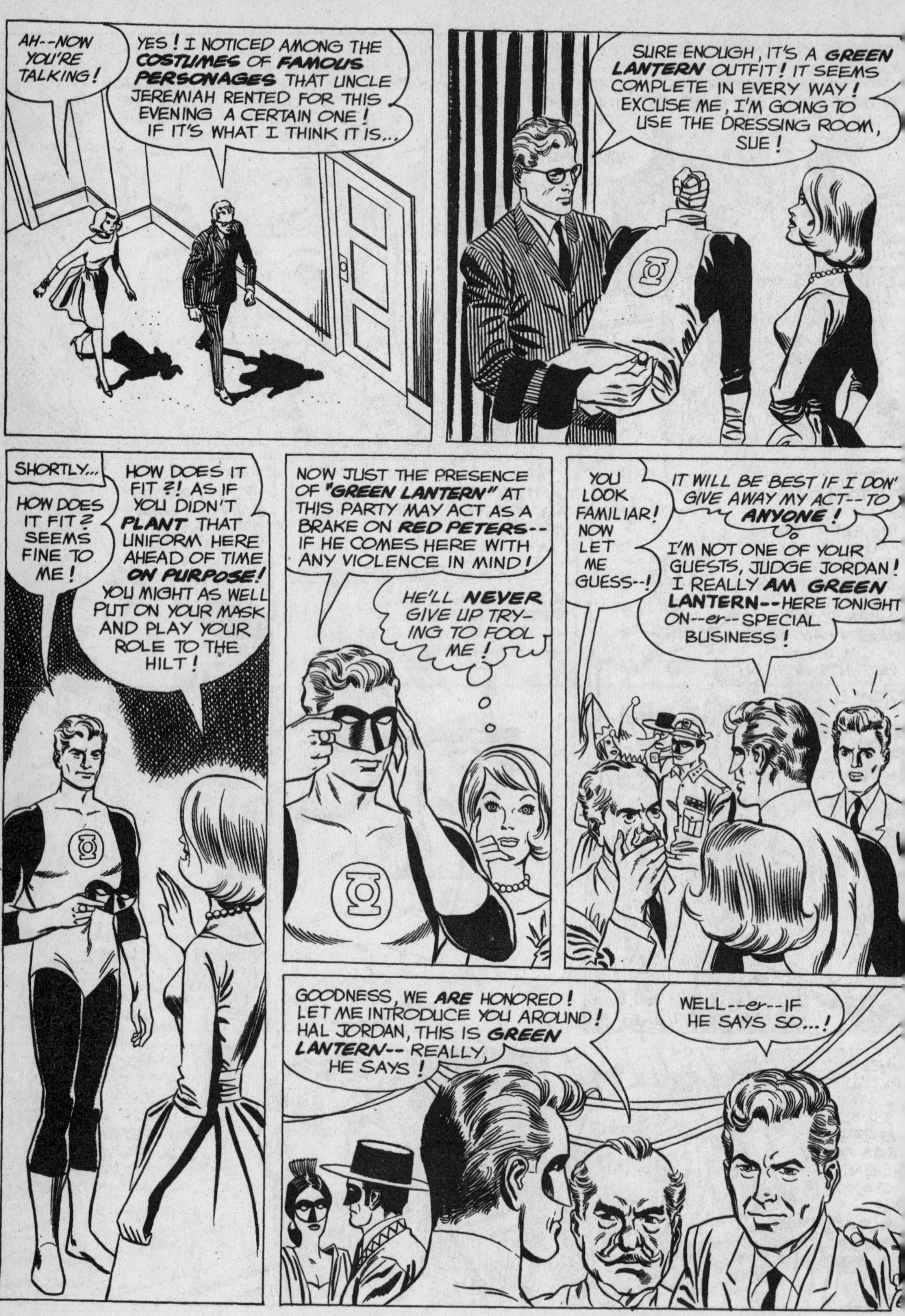
AH--NOW YOU'RE TALKING!
YES! I NOTICED AMONG THE COSTUMES OF FAMOUS PERSONAGES THAT UNCLE JEREMIAH RENTED FOR THIS EVENING A CERTAIN ONE! IF IT'S WHAT I THINK IT IS...
SURE ENOUGH, IT'S A GREEN LANTERN OUTFIT! IT SEEMS COMPLETE IN EVERY WAY! EXCUSE ME, I'M GOING TO USE THE DRESSING ROOM, SUE!
SHORTLY...
HOW DOES IT FIT? SEEMS FINE TO ME!
HOW DOES IT FIT ?! AS IF YOU DIDN'T PLANT THAT UNIFORM HERE AHEAD OF TIME ON PURPOSE! YOU MIGHT AS WELL PUT ON YOUR MASK AND PLAY YOUR ROLE TO THE HILT!
NOW JUST THE PRESENCE OF "GREEN LANTERN" AT THIS PARTY MAY ACT AS A BRAKE ON RED PETERS--IF HE COMES HERE WITH ANY VIOLENCE IN MIND!
HE'LL NEVER GIVE UP TRYING TO FOOL ME!
YOU LOOK FAMILIAR! NOW LET ME GUESS--!
IT WILL BE BEST IF I DON' GIVE AWAY MY ACT--TO ANYONE!
I'M NOT ONE OF YOUR GUESTS, JUDGE JORDAN! I REALLY AM GREEN LANTERN--HERE TONIGHT ON--er--SPECIAL BUSINESS!
GOODNESS, WE ARE HONORED! LET ME INTRODUCE YOU AROUND! HAL JORDAN, THIS IS GREEN LANTERN-- REALLY, HE SAYS!
WELL--er--IF HE SAYS SO...!

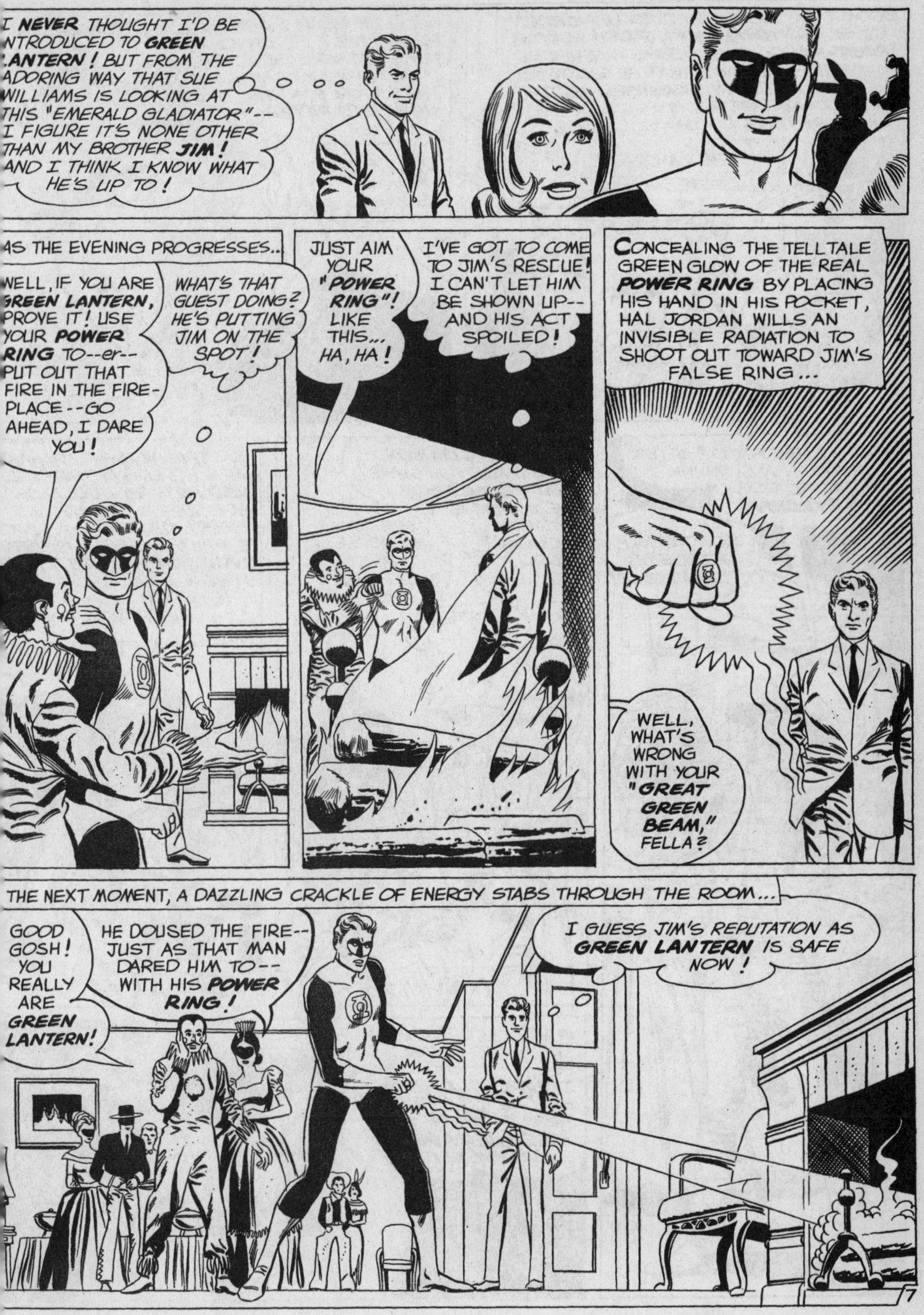
I NEVER THOUGHT I'D BE INTRODUCED TO GREEN LANTERN! BUT FROM THE ADORING WAY THAT SUE WILLIAMS IS LOOKING AT THIS "EMERALD GLADIATOR"-- I FIGURE IT'S NONE OTHER THAN MY BROTHER JIM! AND I THINK I KNOW WHAT HE'S UP TO!
AS THE EVENING PROGRESSES...
WELL, IF YOU ARE GREEN LANTERN, PROVE IT! USE YOUR POWER RING TO--er-- PUT OUT THAT FIRE IN THE FIRE-PLACE--GO AHEAD, I DARE YOU!
WHAT'S THAT GUEST DOING? HE'S PUTTING JIM ON THE SPOT!
JUST AIM YOUR "POWER RING"! LIKE THIS... HA, HA!
I'VE GOT TO COME TO JIM'S RESCUE! I CAN'T LET HIM BE SHOWN UP-- AND HIS ACT SPOILED!
CONCEALING THE TELLTALE GREEN GLOW OF THE REAL POWER RING BY PLACING HIS HAND IN HIS POCKET, HAL JORDAN WILLS AN INVISIBLE RADIATION TO SHOOT OUT TOWARD JIM'S FALSE RING...
WELL, WHAT'S WRONG WITH YOUR "GREAT GREEN BEAM," FELLA?
THE NEXT MOMENT, A DAZZLING CRACKLE OF ENERGY STABS THROUGH THE ROOM...
GOOD GOSH! YOU REALLY ARE GREEN LANTERN!
HE DOUSED THE FIRE-- JUST AS THAT MAN DARED HIM TO-- WITH HIS POWER RING!
I GUESS JIM'S REPUTATION AS GREEN LANTERN IS SAFE NOW!
7

SOON... MAYBE WE OUGHT TO LET *GREEN LANTERN* KNOW, JACK! *MAYOR POST*-- WHO LOVES A JOKE--CONFIDED TO ME THIS MORNING THAT HE'S COMING HERE TO MY PARTY DISGUISED AS THAT INFAMOUS SCOUNDREL *RED PETERS*!

THE MAYOR--!?

WELL, I'M GLAD I OVER-HEARD *THAT* BIT OF NEWS! OTHERWISE I MIGHT HAVE MISTAKEN THE MAYOR FOR THE REAL *RED PETERS*-- eh?

OUT OF MY WAY, YE SCURVY KNAVES!

WHERE'S THE FOOD? AFTER I'VE EATEN AND DRUNK I INTEND TO ROB *EVERYBODY*!

GOODNESS! HE SEEMS SO *FIERCE*!

I CAN SEE I COULDN'T HAVE MADE A MISTAKE! THAT *FALSE FACE* THE MAYOR IS WEARING WOULDN'T FOOL A CHILD!

SEE TO MY HORSE, YARLET! OFF WITH YE!

BUT THIS INCIDENT HAS MA... ME A BIT EDGY! THE REAL *RED PETERS* COULD BE MASQUERADING AROUND HERE! JUST TO PLAY SAF... I THINK THE REAL *GREEN LANTERN* HAD BETTER ... HAVE A LOOK AROUND THE HOUSE AND GROUNDS RIGHT NOW!

IN AN UNOCCUPIED ROOM MOMENTS LATER...

I CHARGED MY RING BEFORE I LEFT, SO HERE'S WHERE I *MASQUERADE*... AS MYSELF!

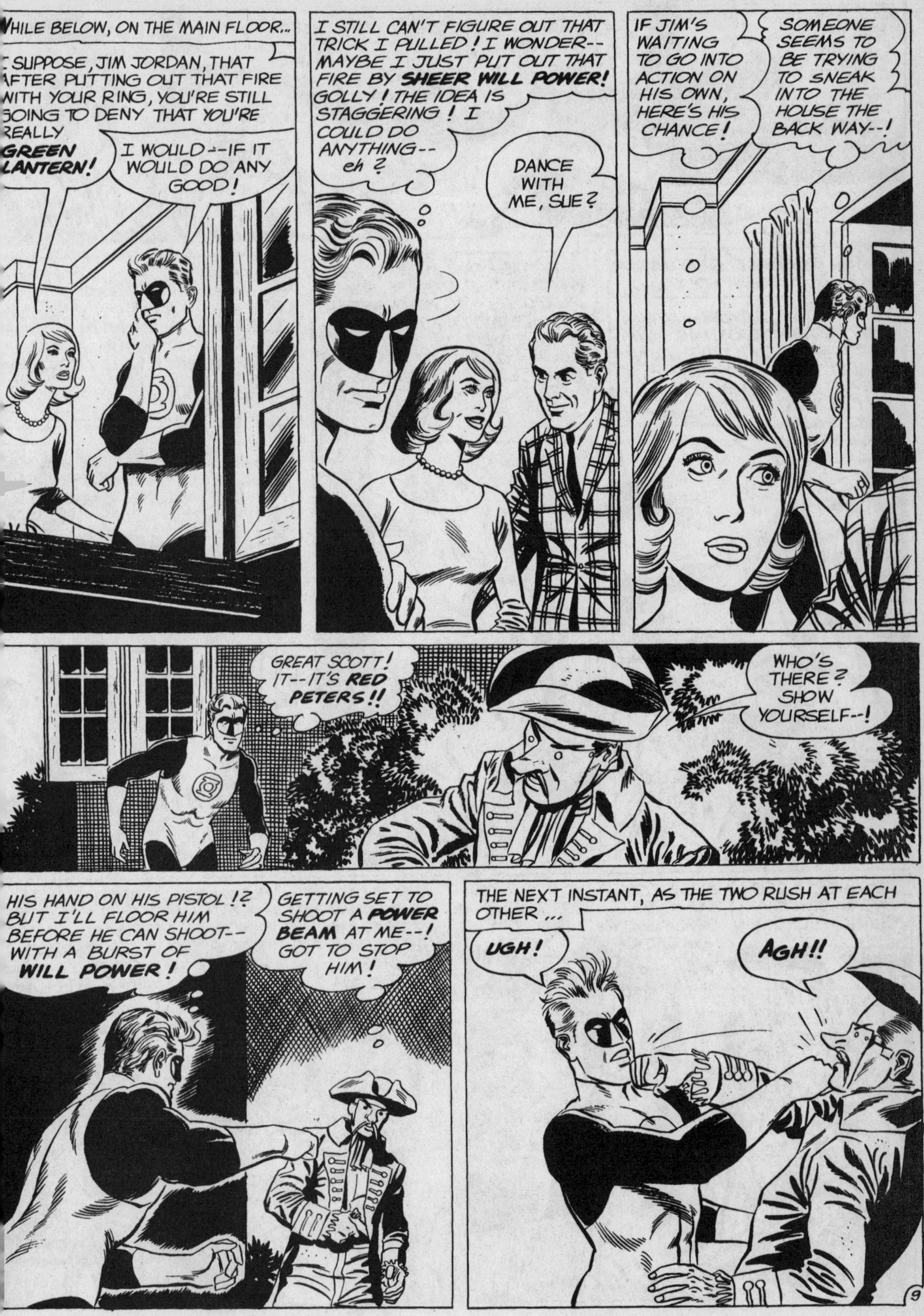
WHILE BELOW, ON THE MAIN FLOOR...
I SUPPOSE, JIM JORDAN, THAT AFTER PUTTING OUT THAT FIRE WITH YOUR RING, YOU'RE STILL GOING TO DENY THAT YOU'RE REALLY GREEN LANTERN!
I WOULD--IF IT WOULD DO ANY GOOD!
I STILL CAN'T FIGURE OUT THAT TRICK I PULLED! I WONDER-- MAYBE I JUST PUT OUT THAT FIRE BY SHEER WILL POWER! GOLLY! THE IDEA IS STAGGERING! I COULD DO ANYTHING-- eh?
DANCE WITH ME, SUE?
IF JIM'S WAITING TO GO INTO ACTION ON HIS OWN, HERE'S HIS CHANCE!
SOMEONE SEEMS TO BE TRYING TO SNEAK INTO THE HOUSE THE BACK WAY--!
GREAT SCOTT! IT--IT'S RED PETERS!!
WHO'S THERE? SHOW YOURSELF--!
HIS HAND ON HIS PISTOL!? BUT I'LL FLOOR HIM BEFORE HE CAN SHOOT-- WITH A BURST OF WILL POWER!
GETTING SET TO SHOOT A POWER BEAM AT ME--! GOT TO STOP HIM!
THE NEXT INSTANT, AS THE TWO RUSH AT EACH OTHER ...
UGH!
AGH!!
9

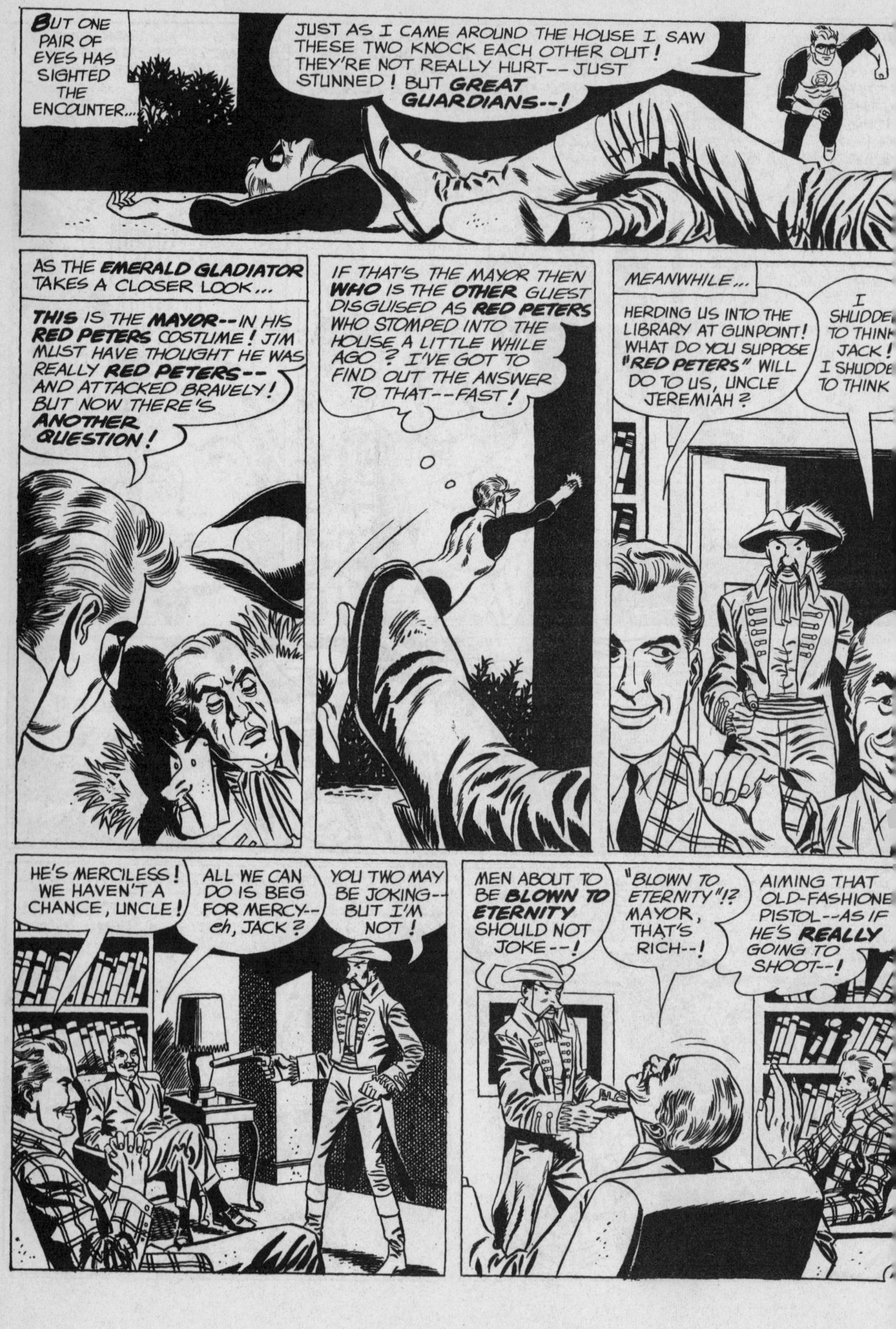
BUT ONE PAIR OF EYES HAS SIGHTED THE ENCOUNTER...
JUST AS I CAME AROUND THE HOUSE I SAW THESE TWO KNOCK EACH OTHER OUT! THEY'RE NOT REALLY HURT-- JUST STUNNED! BUT GREAT GUARDIANS--!
AS THE EMERALD GLADIATOR TAKES A CLOSER LOOK...
THIS IS THE MAYOR--IN HIS RED PETERS COSTUME! JIM MUST HAVE THOUGHT HE WAS REALLY RED PETERS-- AND ATTACKED BRAVELY! BUT NOW THERE'S ANOTHER QUESTION!
IF THAT'S THE MAYOR THEN WHO IS THE OTHER GUEST DISGUISED AS RED PETERS WHO STOMPED INTO THE HOUSE A LITTLE WHILE AGO? I'VE GOT TO FIND OUT THE ANSWER TO THAT--FAST!
MEANWHILE...
HERDING US INTO THE LIBRARY AT GUNPOINT! WHAT DO YOU SUPPOSE "RED PETERS" WILL DO TO US, UNCLE JEREMIAH?
I SHUDDE TO THINK JACK! I SHUDDE TO THINK
HE'S MERCILESS! WE HAVEN'T A CHANCE, UNCLE!
ALL WE CAN DO IS BEG FOR MERCY-- eh, JACK?
YOU TWO MAY BE JOKING-- BUT I'M NOT!
MEN ABOUT TO BE BLOWN TO ETERNITY SHOULD NOT JOKE--!
"BLOWN TO ETERNITY"!? MAYOR, THAT'S RICH--!
AIMING THAT OLD-FASHIONE PISTOL--AS IF HE'S REALLY GOING TO SHOOT--!

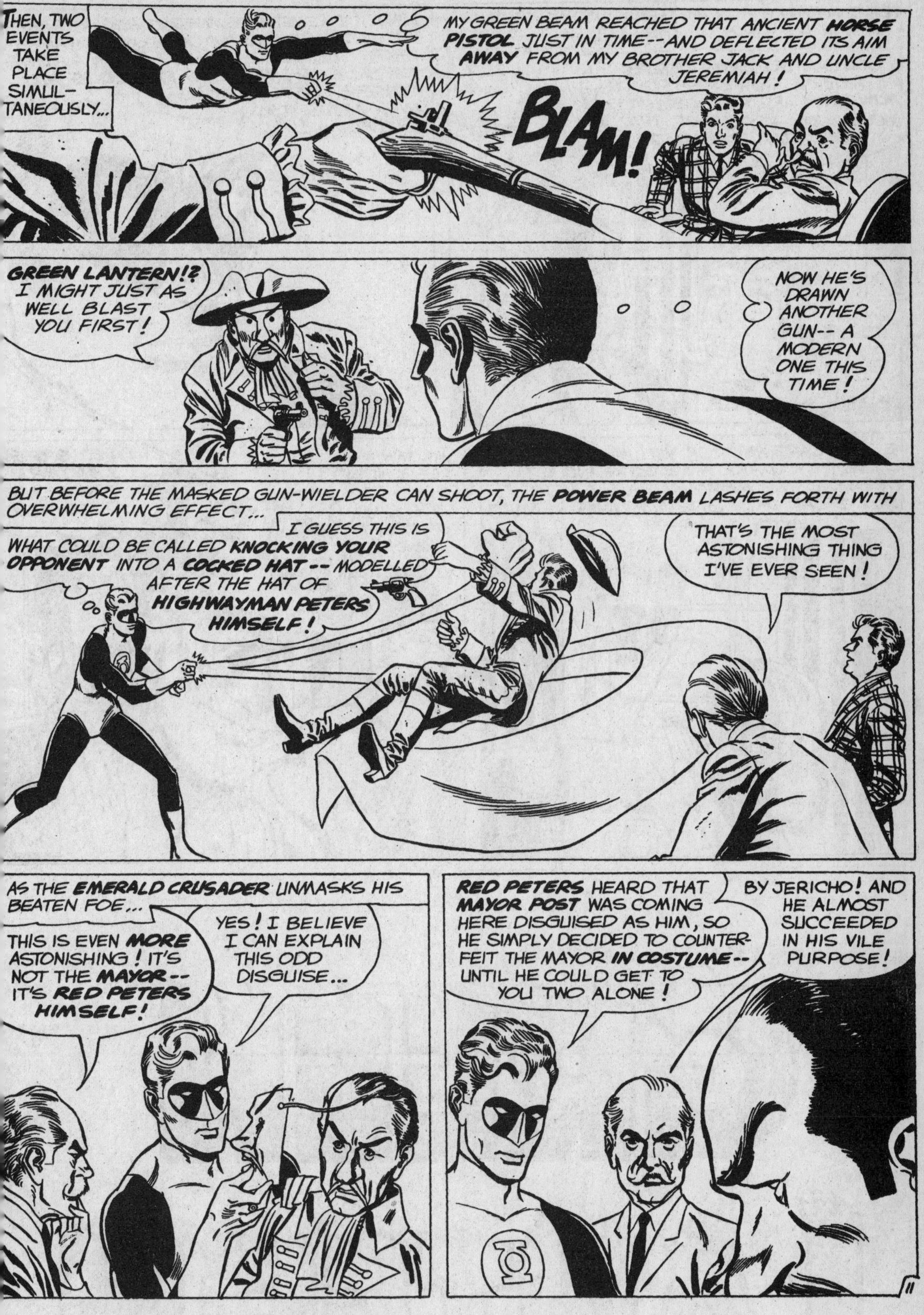
THEN, TWO EVENTS TAKE PLACE SIMUL-TANEOUSLY...
MY GREEN BEAM REACHED THAT ANCIENT HORSE PISTOL JUST IN TIME-- AND DEFLECTED ITS AIM AWAY FROM MY BROTHER JACK AND UNCLE JEREMIAH!
BLAM!
GREEN LANTERN!? I MIGHT JUST AS WELL BLAST YOU FIRST!
NOW HE'S DRAWN ANOTHER GUN-- A MODERN ONE THIS TIME!
BUT BEFORE THE MASKED GUN-WIELDER CAN SHOOT, THE POWER BEAM LASHES FORTH WITH OVERWHELMING EFFECT...
I GUESS THIS IS WHAT COULD BE CALLED KNOCKING YOUR OPPONENT INTO A COCKED HAT -- MODELLED AFTER THE HAT OF HIGHWAYMAN PETERS HIMSELF!
THAT'S THE MOST ASTONISHING THING I'VE EVER SEEN!
AS THE EMERALD CRUSADER UNMASKS HIS BEATEN FOE...
THIS IS EVEN MORE ASTONISHING! IT'S NOT THE MAYOR-- IT'S RED PETERS HIMSELF!
YES! I BELIEVE I CAN EXPLAIN THIS ODD DISGUISE...
RED PETERS HEARD THAT MAYOR POST WAS COMING HERE DISGUISED AS HIM, SO HE SIMPLY DECIDED TO COUNTER-FEIT THE MAYOR IN COSTUME-- UNTIL HE COULD GET TO YOU TWO ALONE!
BY JERICHO! AND HE ALMOST SUCCEEDED IN HIS VILE PURPOSE!
11

NOT LONG AFTER, WITH THE DISCOMFITED CRIMINAL BACK IN THE HANDS OF THE LAW...

SO YOU CAPTURED *RED PETERS* AND RETURNED HIM TO THE POLICE! *NOW HOW* ARE YOU GOING TO WORM YOUR WAY OUT OF THAT ONE, *JIM JORDAN?*

MY JAW HURTS!

FUNNY! I REMEMBER MEETING *RED PETERS*-- BUT NOT CAPTURING HIM OR TAKING HIM ANY-WHERE! YET-- I MUST HAVE BEEN IN A FIGHT- I'M BRUISED! MAYBE MY *FABULOUS WILL POWER* KEEPS WORKING -- EVEN AFTER I'M UNCONSCIOUS!

I DON'T CARE WHETHER YOU WILL ADMIT IT OR NOT! YOU ARE A *HERO* -- AND YOU DESERVE THE *REWARDS* OF A HERO! BUT I CAN ONLY GIVE YOU *ONE* REWARD...

MY JAW IS RESPONDING FAST-- TO THIS KIND OF TREAT-MENT!

I SEE *GREEN LANTERN* TAKES CARE OF EVERYTHING

The End

GREEN LANTERN

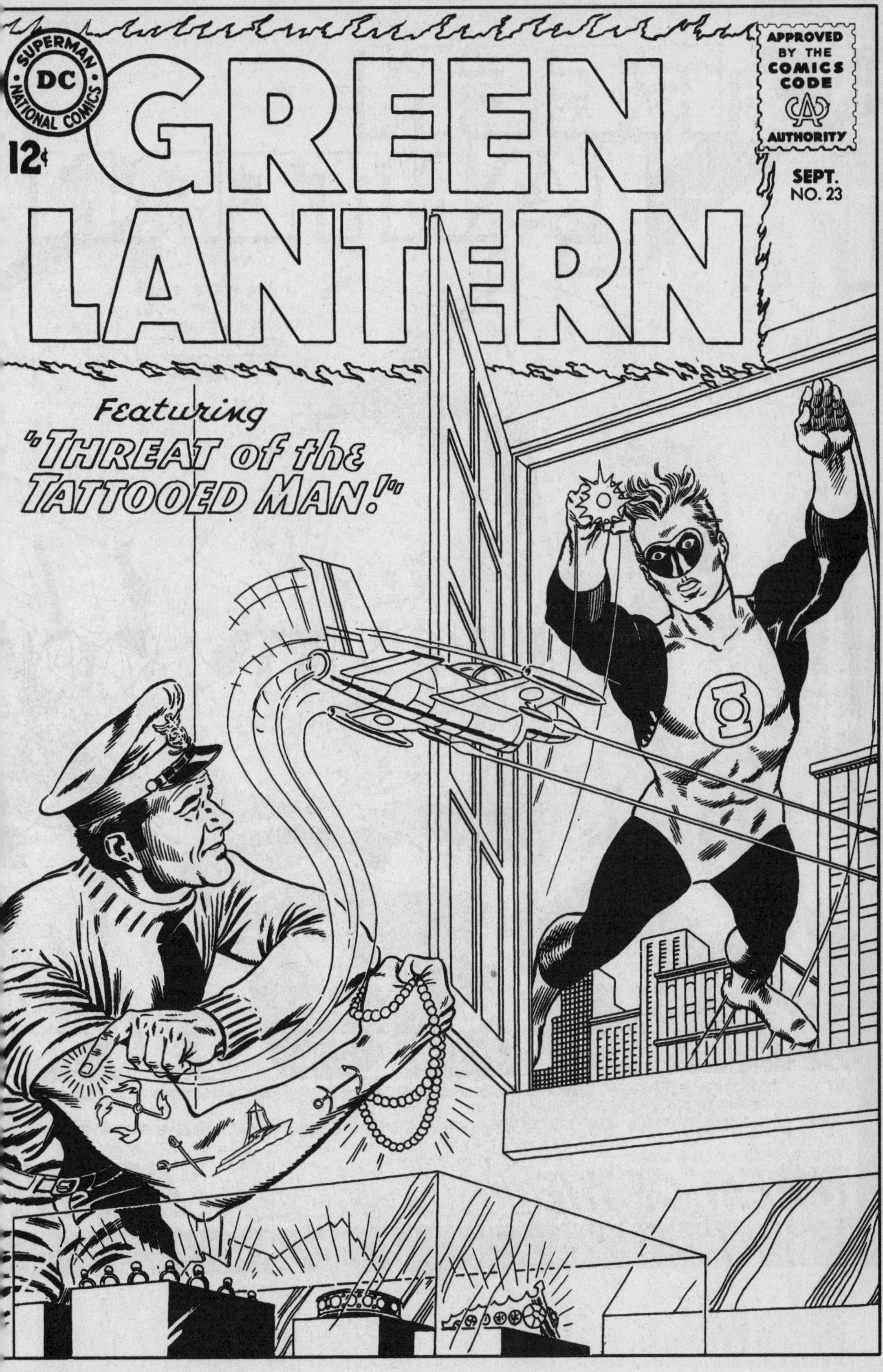
SUPERMAN DC NATIONAL COMICS
12¢
GREEN LANTERN
APPROVED BY THE COMICS CODE AUTHORITY
SEPT. NO. 23
Featuring "THREAT of the TATTOOED MAN!"

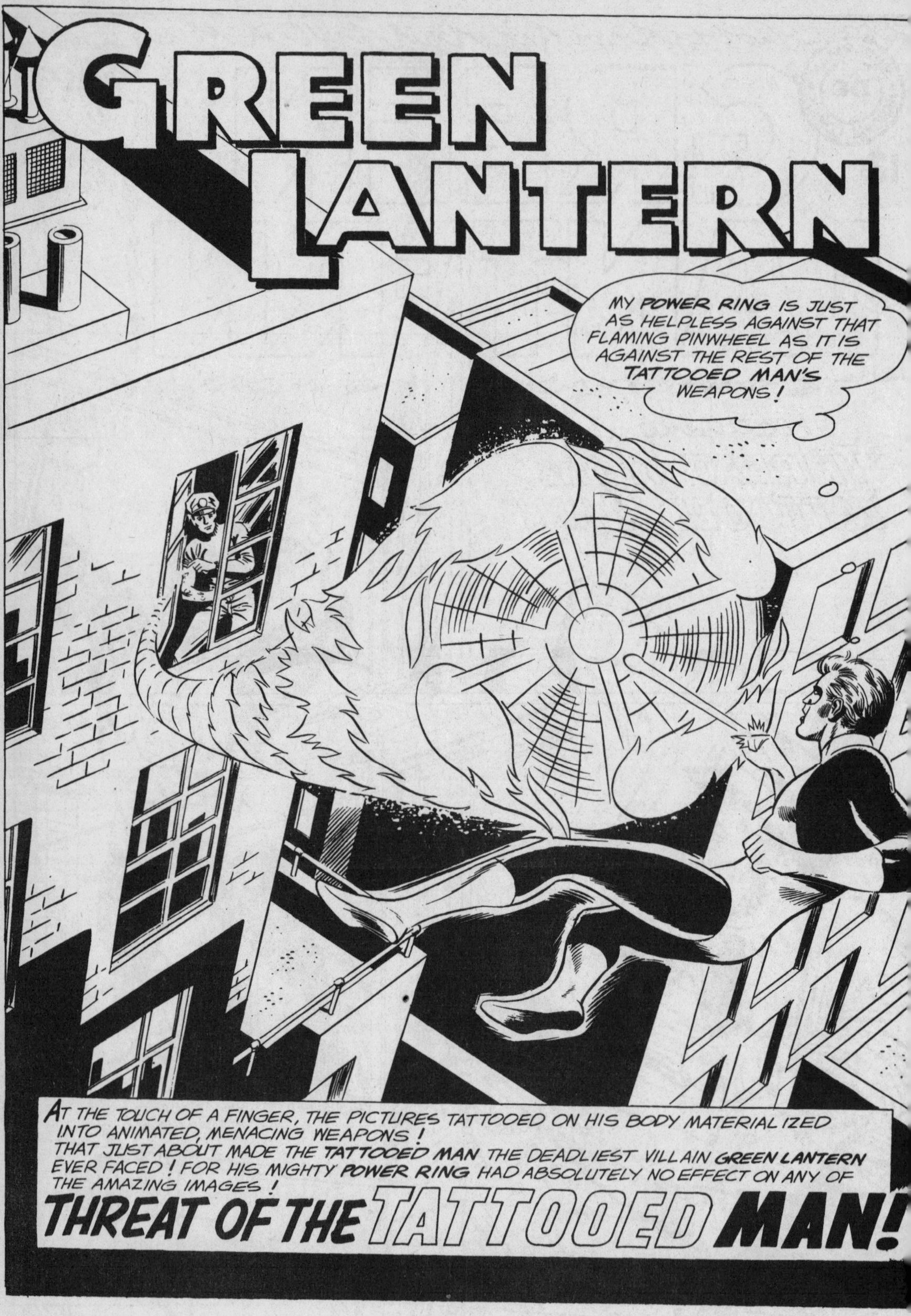
GREEN LANTERN
MY POWER RING IS JUST AS HELPLESS AGAINST THAT FLAMING PINWHEEL AS IT IS AGAINST THE REST OF THE TATTOOED MAN'S WEAPONS!
AT THE TOUCH OF A FINGER, THE PICTURES TATTOOED ON HIS BODY MATERIALIZED INTO ANIMATED, MENACING WEAPONS! THAT JUST ABOUT MADE THE TATTOOED MAN THE DEADLIEST VILLAIN GREEN LANTERN EVER FACED! FOR HIS MIGHTY POWER RING HAD ABSOLUTELY NO EFFECT ON ANY OF THE AMAZING IMAGES!
THREAT OF THE TATTOOED MAN!

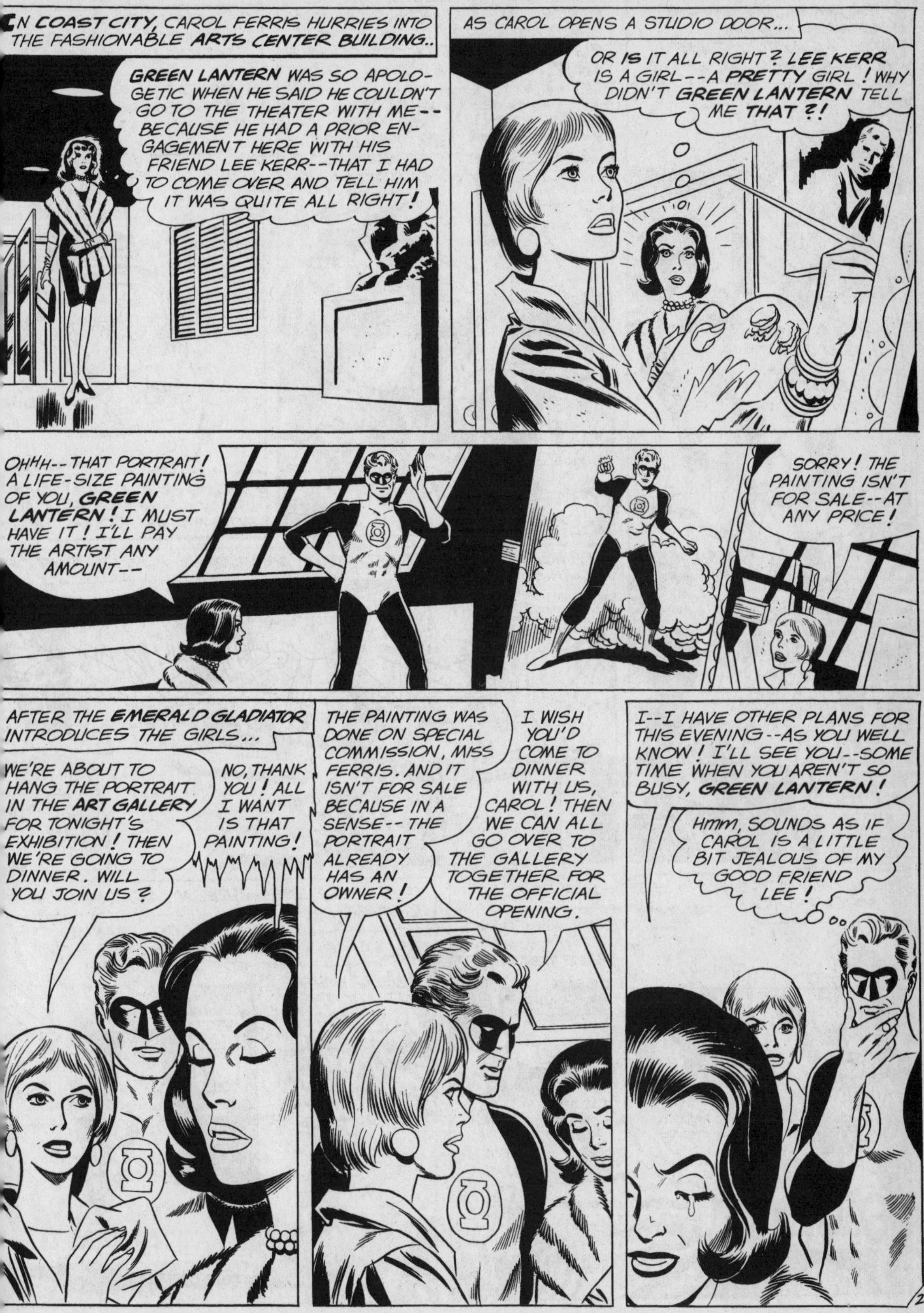
IN COAST CITY, CAROL FERRIS HURRIES INTO THE FASHIONABLE ARTS CENTER BUILDING..
GREEN LANTERN WAS SO APOLOGETIC WHEN HE SAID HE COULDN'T GO TO THE THEATER WITH ME-- BECAUSE HE HAD A PRIOR ENGAGEMENT HERE WITH HIS FRIEND LEE KERR--THAT I HAD TO COME OVER AND TELL HIM IT WAS QUITE ALL RIGHT!
AS CAROL OPENS A STUDIO DOOR...
OR IS IT ALL RIGHT? LEE KERR IS A GIRL--A PRETTY GIRL! WHY DIDN'T GREEN LANTERN TELL ME THAT?!
OHHH--THAT PORTRAIT! A LIFE-SIZE PAINTING OF YOU, GREEN LANTERN! I MUST HAVE IT! I'LL PAY THE ARTIST ANY AMOUNT--
SORRY! THE PAINTING ISN'T FOR SALE--AT ANY PRICE!
AFTER THE EMERALD GLADIATOR INTRODUCES THE GIRLS...
WE'RE ABOUT TO HANG THE PORTRAIT IN THE ART GALLERY FOR TONIGHT'S EXHIBITION! THEN WE'RE GOING TO DINNER. WILL YOU JOIN US?
NO, THANK YOU! ALL I WANT IS THAT PAINTING!
THE PAINTING WAS DONE ON SPECIAL COMMISSION, MISS FERRIS. AND IT ISN'T FOR SALE BECAUSE IN A SENSE--THE PORTRAIT ALREADY HAS AN OWNER!
I WISH YOU'D COME TO DINNER WITH US, CAROL! THEN WE CAN ALL GO OVER TO THE GALLERY TOGETHER FOR THE OFFICIAL OPENING.
I--I HAVE OTHER PLANS FOR THIS EVENING--AS YOU WELL KNOW! I'LL SEE YOU--SOME TIME WHEN YOU AREN'T SO BUSY, GREEN LANTERN!
Hmm, SOUNDS AS IF CAROL IS A LITTLE BIT JEALOUS OF MY GOOD FRIEND LEE!
2

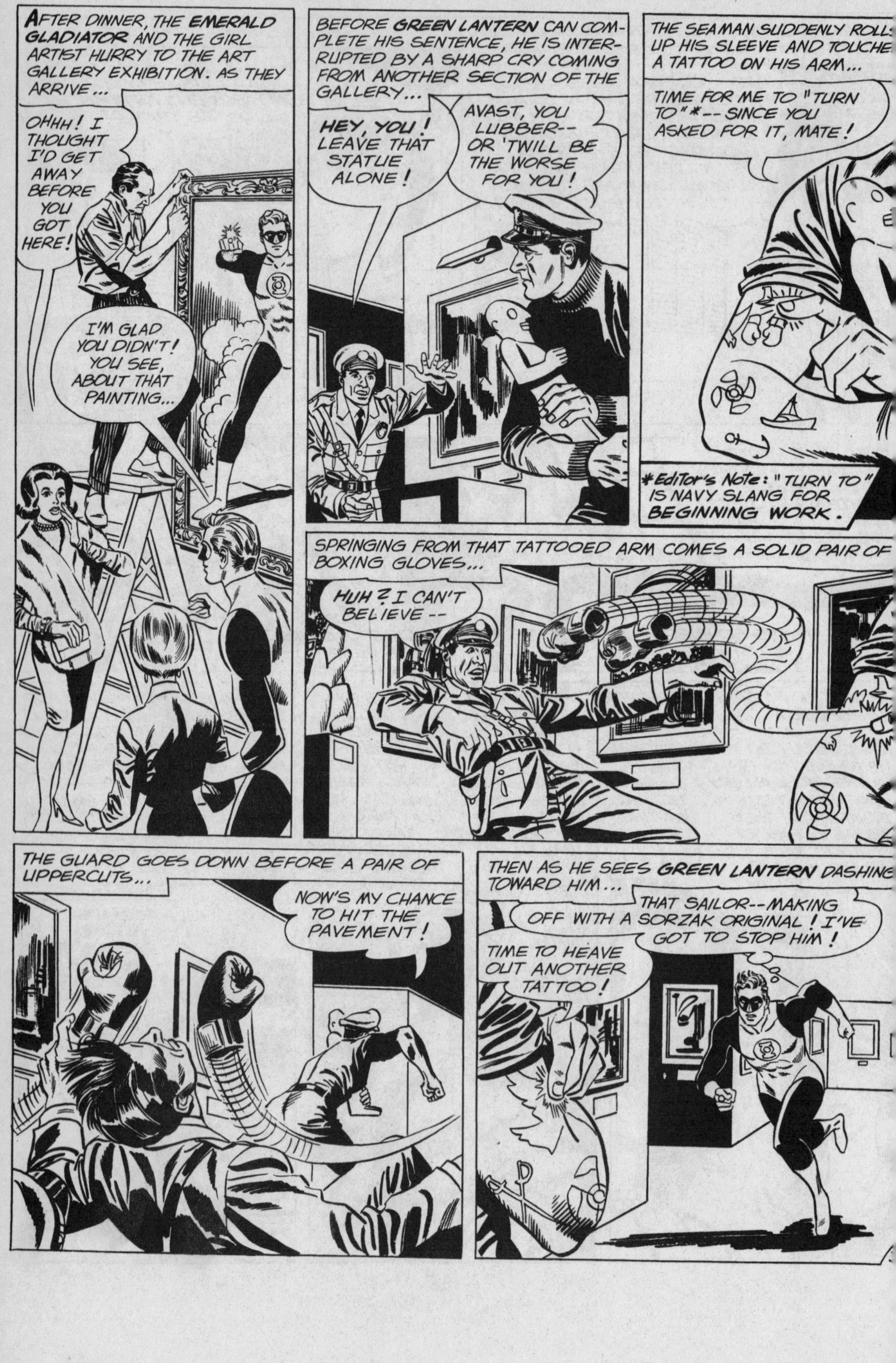
AFTER DINNER, THE EMERALD GLADIATOR AND THE GIRL ARTIST HURRY TO THE ART GALLERY EXHIBITION. AS THEY ARRIVE...
OHHH! I THOUGHT I'D GET AWAY BEFORE YOU GOT HERE!
I'M GLAD YOU DIDN'T! YOU SEE, ABOUT THAT PAINTING...
BEFORE GREEN LANTERN CAN COMPLETE HIS SENTENCE, HE IS INTERRUPTED BY A SHARP CRY COMING FROM ANOTHER SECTION OF THE GALLERY...
HEY, YOU! LEAVE THAT STATUE ALONE!
AVAST, YOU LUBBER-- OR 'TWILL BE THE WORSE FOR YOU!
THE SEAMAN SUDDENLY ROLLS UP HIS SLEEVE AND TOUCHES A TATTOO ON HIS ARM...
TIME FOR ME TO "TURN TO"*-- SINCE YOU ASKED FOR IT, MATE!
*Editor's Note: "TURN TO" IS NAVY SLANG FOR BEGINNING WORK.
SPRINGING FROM THAT TATTOOED ARM COMES A SOLID PAIR OF BOXING GLOVES...
HUH? I CAN'T BELIEVE --
THE GUARD GOES DOWN BEFORE A PAIR OF UPPERCUTS...
NOW'S MY CHANCE TO HIT THE PAVEMENT!
THEN AS HE SEES GREEN LANTERN DASHING TOWARD HIM...
THAT SAILOR--MAKING OFF WITH A SORZAK ORIGINAL! I'VE GOT TO STOP HIM!
TIME TO HEAVE OUT ANOTHER TATTOO!

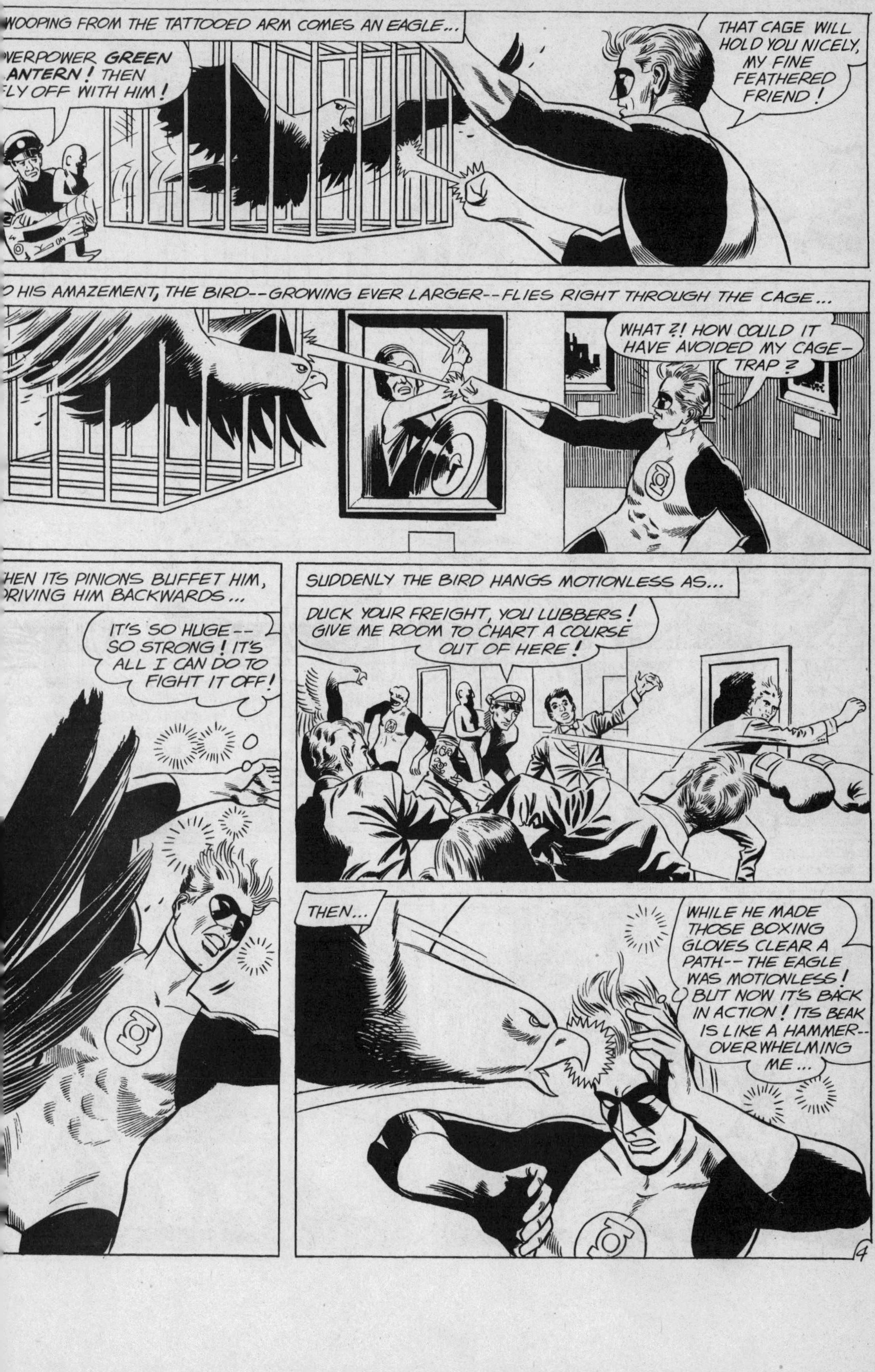
WOOPING FROM THE TATTOOED ARM COMES AN EAGLE...
VERPOWER GREEN ANTERN! THEN FLY OFF WITH HIM!
THAT CAGE WILL HOLD YOU NICELY, MY FINE FEATHERED FRIEND!
O HIS AMAZEMENT, THE BIRD--GROWING EVER LARGER--FLIES RIGHT THROUGH THE CAGE...
WHAT ?! HOW COULD IT HAVE AVOIDED MY CAGE-TRAP ?
HEN ITS PINIONS BUFFET HIM, DRIVING HIM BACKWARDS...
IT'S SO HUGE-- SO STRONG! IT'S ALL I CAN DO TO FIGHT IT OFF!
SUDDENLY THE BIRD HANGS MOTIONLESS AS...
DUCK YOUR FREIGHT, YOU LUBBERS! GIVE ME ROOM TO CHART A COURSE OUT OF HERE!
THEN...
WHILE HE MADE THOSE BOXING GLOVES CLEAR A PATH-- THE EAGLE WAS MOTIONLESS! BUT NOW IT'S BACK IN ACTION! ITS BEAK IS LIKE A HAMMER-- OVERWHELMING ME...
4

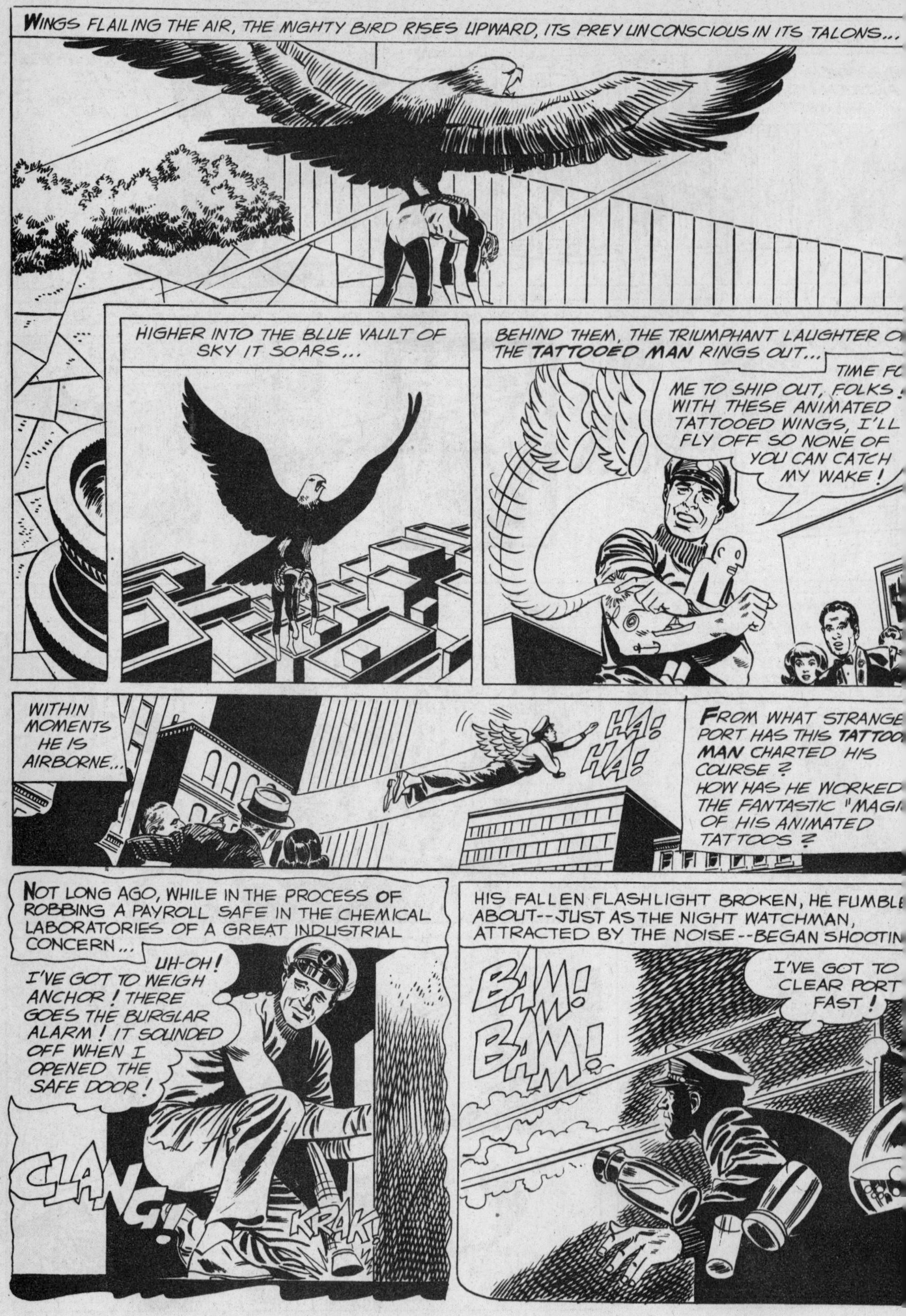
WINGS FLAILING THE AIR, THE MIGHTY BIRD RISES UPWARD, ITS PREY UNCONSCIOUS IN ITS TALONS...
HIGHER INTO THE BLUE VAULT OF SKY IT SOARS...
BEHIND THEM, THE TRIUMPHANT LAUGHTER O THE TATTOOED MAN RINGS OUT...
TIME F ME TO SHIP OUT, FOLKS WITH THESE ANIMATED TATTOOED WINGS, I'LL FLY OFF SO NONE OF YOU CAN CATCH MY WAKE!
WITHIN MOMENTS HE IS AIRBORNE...
HA! HA!
FROM WHAT STRANGE PORT HAS THIS TATTOO MAN CHARTED HIS COURSE? HOW HAS HE WORKED THE FANTASTIC "MAGI OF HIS ANIMATED TATTOOS?
NOT LONG AGO, WHILE IN THE PROCESS OF ROBBING A PAYROLL SAFE IN THE CHEMICAL LABORATORIES OF A GREAT INDUSTRIAL CONCERN...
UH-OH! I'VE GOT TO WEIGH ANCHOR! THERE GOES THE BURGLAR ALARM! IT SOUNDED OFF WHEN I OPENED THE SAFE DOOR!
CLANG!
KRAK!
HIS FALLEN FLASHLIGHT BROKEN, HE FUMBLE ABOUT--JUST AS THE NIGHT WATCHMAN, ATTRACTED BY THE NOISE--BEGAN SHOOTIN
BAM! BAM!
I'VE GOT TO CLEAR PORT FAST!

NEXT MOMENT, IN THE DARKNESS..

UH? THOSE CHEMICALS-- SPILLED--RUNNING TOGETHER ALL OVER THE FLOOR...

CRASH!

DESPERATE, THE SAILOR FIRED RECKLESSLY--EMPTYING HIS GUN...

I'VE EMPTIED MY CANNON! NOW I'M REALLY IN THE DOLDRUMS! UNLESS-- WHY, THERE'S A *BOMB* ON THE FLOOR! I'LL USE IT TO BLAST OUT THE REAR WALL!

BUT AS HIS FINGERS REACHED FOR THE "BOMB"...

AH, IT'S ONLY A BLOB OF CHEMICALS THAT *LOOKS* LIKE A BOMB! BUT, BY NEPTUNE, IF IT WERE A BOMB-- A *REAL BOMB*...

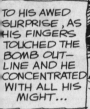

TO HIS AWED SURPRISE, AS HIS FINGERS TOUCHED THE BOMB OUT- LINE AND HE CONCENTRATED WITH ALL HIS MIGHT...

IT--TURNED INTO A *REAL, SOLID* BOMB! I DON'T KNOW HOW IT HAPPENED-- AND I'M NOT GOING TO ASK QUESTIONS! I'LL JUST-- USE IT!

SPRINGING TO THE DOOR THROUGH WHICH THE WATCHMAN WAS SHOOTING--EVEN AS THE THIEF HEARD THE WAIL OF POLICE SIRENS-- HE SLAMMED IT SHUT...

VREEEE!

THIS IS NO PLACE TO GET BUNK FATIGUE! I'VE GOT TO ACT FAST!

I LIGHTED ITS FUSE! WHEN IT GOES OFF-- IT'LL BLAST AN ESCAPE HATCH FOR ME OUT OF THIS STONE FRIGATE!

BUT TO HIS DISMAY THE BOMB FAILED TO FUNCTION...

COME ON! COME ON! BLAST YOUR TIMBERS-- GO OFF! **GO OFF!**

DESPERATELY HE CONCENTRATED ON THE BOMB-- EXPLOSION UNTIL...

VAROOO!

AN INSTANT LATER...

ONE THING'S CERTAIN ABOUT THIS UNCERTAIN HAPPENING! I'VE GOT TO COME BACK HERE-- GET SOME OF THOSE WONDER CHEMICALS! I WANT TO LEARN WHAT MADE THAT MIXTURE ACT THE WAY IT DID!

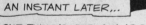

NEXT DAY, POSING AS A RE-PORTER, THE SAILOR--NAMED ABEL TARRANT--RETURNED TO THE LABORATORY.... .

THESE SPONGES WILL SOP UP ENOUGH CHEMICALS FOR ME TO STUDY!

ALONE IN HIS BOARDING HOUSE ROOM, BY TRIAL AND ERROR, THE SAILOR UN--RAVELED THE STRANGE SECRET HE HAD STUMBLED ONTO...

IN ORDER TO MAKE AN OBJECT MATERIALIZE-- I MUST DRAW ITS EXACT OUT-LINE! OTHERWISE, NOTHING HAPPENS! THE CHEMICALS DON'T WORK UNLESS THEY FIRST FORM A PICTURE-- LIKE THIS BASEBALL!

THEN I MUST *TOUCH* THE CHEMICALS AND *CONCENTRATE--BASEBALL MATERIALIZE-- AND RISE INTO THE AIR!* --WHEREUPON THE PICTURE FORMS INTO SOMETHING TANGIBLE OVER WHICH, BY FURTHER CONCENTRATION-- I HAVE FULL MENTAL CONTROL!

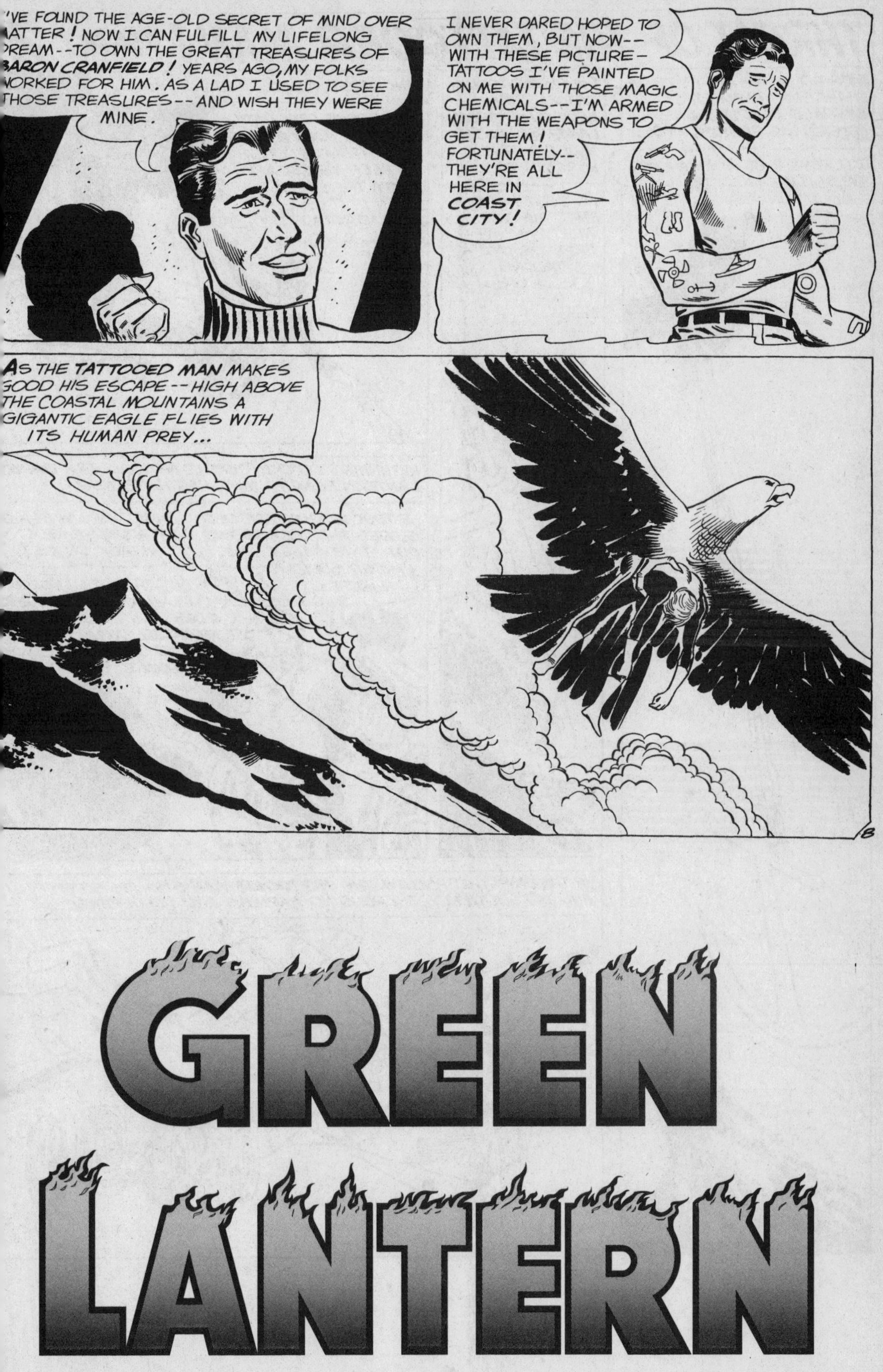
'VE FOUND THE AGE-OLD SECRET OF MIND OVER ATTER! NOW I CAN FULFILL MY LIFELONG REAM--TO OWN THE GREAT TREASURES OF BARON CRANFIELD! YEARS AGO, MY FOLKS ORKED FOR HIM. AS A LAD I USED TO SEE THOSE TREASURES--AND WISH THEY WERE MINE.
I NEVER DARED HOPED TO OWN THEM, BUT NOW--WITH THESE PICTURE-TATTOOS I'VE PAINTED ON ME WITH THOSE MAGIC CHEMICALS--I'M ARMED WITH THE WEAPONS TO GET THEM! FORTUNATELY--THEY'RE ALL HERE IN COAST CITY!
AS THE TATTOOED MAN MAKES GOOD HIS ESCAPE--HIGH ABOVE THE COASTAL MOUNTAINS A GIGANTIC EAGLE FLIES WITH ITS HUMAN PREY...
8

GREEN LANTERN

THREAT OF THE TATTOOED MAN! PART 2

GRIPPED BY THE MIGHTY TALONS OF THE GIANT EAGLE, THE *EMERALD GLADIATOR* RE-COVERS HIS SENSES AND...

I'LL POWER-BEAM AN ANCHOR-CATCH IT AGAINST THE MOUNTAIN PEAK!

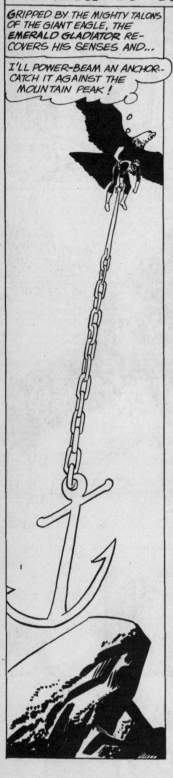

THE FLUKE HOOKS ONTO A ROCK LEDGE AND *GREEN LANTERN* BRACES HIMSELF FOR A FURIOUS TUG...

MY BEST HOPE IS THAT THE JAR WILL YANK ME FREE OF ITS TALONS!

AND AFTER A BRIEF "TUG-OF-WAR"...

AH! BROKE FREE! AT LEAST MY *POWER RING* WAS STRONG ENOUGH TO HELP ME ESCAPE FROM THE EAGLE-- EVEN IF IT COULDN'T OVERCOME IT!

RETURNING QUICKLY TO THE ART GALLERY, *GREEN LANTERN* LEARNS WHAT HAS HAPPENED...

HE TOUCHED HIS TATTOOED GLOVES AND THEY SPRANG OUT AT ME! THEY SURE LANDED SOLID PUNCHES!

THAT JIBES WITH HIS TATTOOED-EAGLE ATTACK ON ME!

BUT THAT STILL DOESN'T EXPLAIN WHY THE *POWER RING* DIDN'T WORK ON THE ANIMATED TATTOO! THERE WAS NO DISCERNIBLE *YELLOW* TO STOP IT--

IN THE DAYS THAT FOLLOW, THE *TATTOOED MAN* STRIKES SO SWIFTLY AND SO SUDDENLY, THERE IS NO WARNING AND NO DEFENSE...

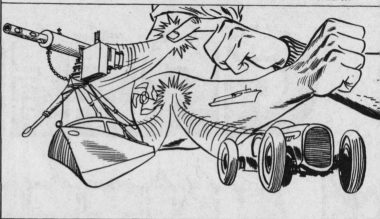

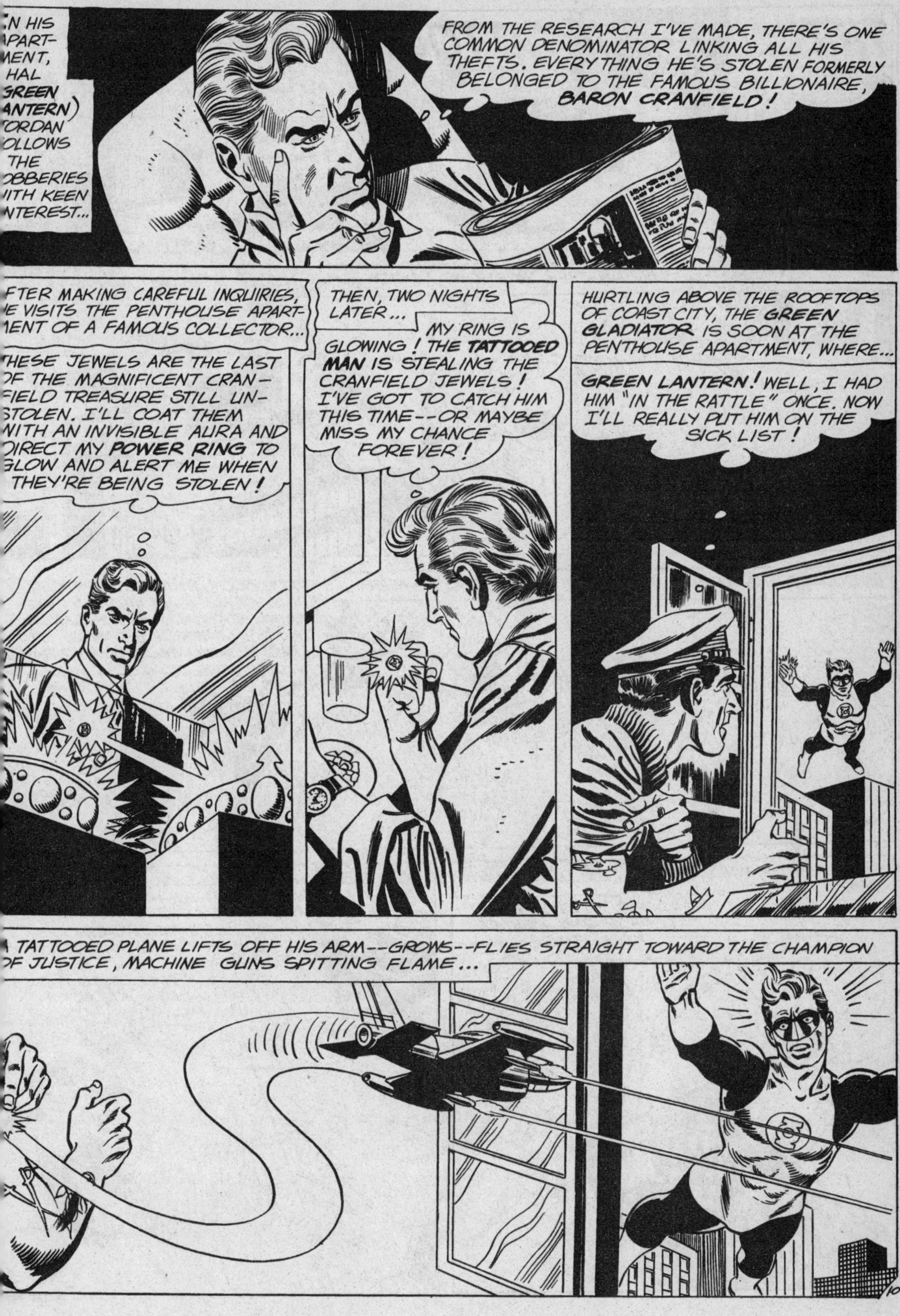

IN HIS APARTMENT, HAL (GREEN LANTERN) JORDAN FOLLOWS THE ROBBERIES WITH KEEN INTEREST...
FROM THE RESEARCH I'VE MADE, THERE'S ONE COMMON DENOMINATOR LINKING ALL HIS THEFTS. EVERYTHING HE'S STOLEN FORMERLY BELONGED TO THE FAMOUS BILLIONAIRE, BARON CRANFIELD!
AFTER MAKING CAREFUL INQUIRIES, HE VISITS THE PENTHOUSE APARTMENT OF A FAMOUS COLLECTOR...
THESE JEWELS ARE THE LAST OF THE MAGNIFICENT CRANFIELD TREASURE STILL UNSTOLEN. I'LL COAT THEM WITH AN INVISIBLE AURA AND DIRECT MY POWER RING TO GLOW AND ALERT ME WHEN THEY'RE BEING STOLEN!
THEN, TWO NIGHTS LATER...
MY RING IS GLOWING! THE TATTOOED MAN IS STEALING THE CRANFIELD JEWELS! I'VE GOT TO CATCH HIM THIS TIME--OR MAYBE MISS MY CHANCE FOREVER!
HURTLING ABOVE THE ROOFTOPS OF COAST CITY, THE GREEN GLADIATOR IS SOON AT THE PENTHOUSE APARTMENT, WHERE...
GREEN LANTERN! WELL, I HAD HIM "IN THE RATTLE" ONCE. NOW I'LL REALLY PUT HIM ON THE SICK LIST!
A TATTOOED PLANE LIFTS OFF HIS ARM--GROWS--FLIES STRAIGHT TOWARD THE CHAMPION OF JUSTICE, MACHINE GUNS SPITTING FLAME...
10

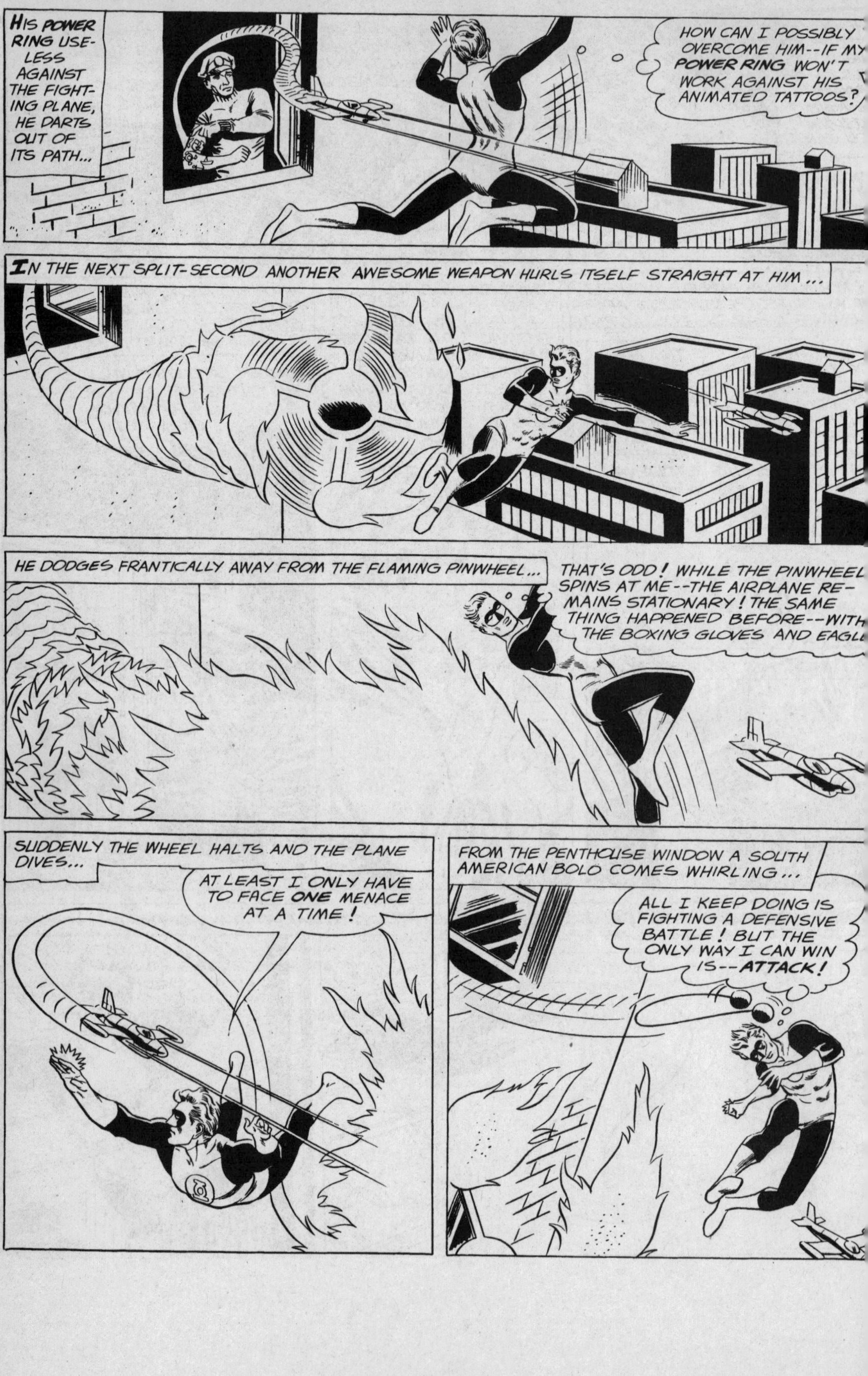
HIS POWER RING USELESS AGAINST THE FIGHTING PLANE, HE DARTS OUT OF ITS PATH...
HOW CAN I POSSIBLY OVERCOME HIM--IF MY POWER RING WON'T WORK AGAINST HIS ANIMATED TATTOOS?
IN THE NEXT SPLIT-SECOND ANOTHER AWESOME WEAPON HURLS ITSELF STRAIGHT AT HIM...
HE DODGES FRANTICALLY AWAY FROM THE FLAMING PINWHEEL...
THAT'S ODD! WHILE THE PINWHEEL SPINS AT ME--THE AIRPLANE REMAINS STATIONARY! THE SAME THING HAPPENED BEFORE--WITH THE BOXING GLOVES AND EAGLE
SUDDENLY THE WHEEL HALTS AND THE PLANE DIVES...
AT LEAST I ONLY HAVE TO FACE ONE MENACE AT A TIME!
FROM THE PENTHOUSE WINDOW A SOUTH AMERICAN BOLO COMES WHIRLING...
ALL I KEEP DOING IS FIGHTING A DEFENSIVE BATTLE! BUT THE ONLY WAY I CAN WIN IS--ATTACK!

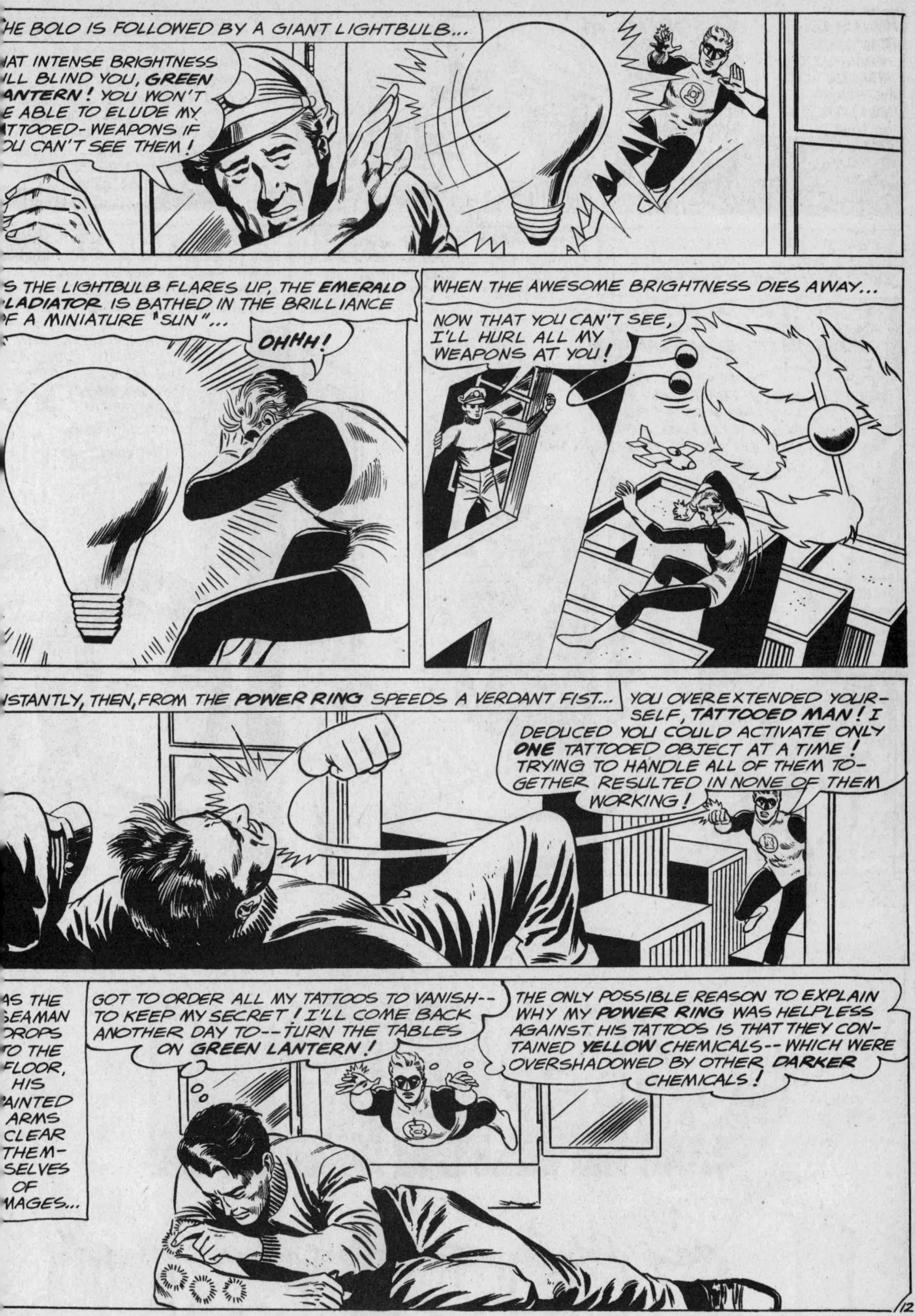
HE BOLO IS FOLLOWED BY A GIANT LIGHTBULB...
IAT INTENSE BRIGHTNESS ILL BLIND YOU, GREEN ANTERN! YOU WON'T E ABLE TO ELUDE MY TTOOED-WEAPONS IF OU CAN'T SEE THEM!
S THE LIGHTBULB FLARES UP, THE EMERALD LADIATOR IS BATHED IN THE BRILLIANCE F A MINIATURE "SUN"...
OHHH!
WHEN THE AWESOME BRIGHTNESS DIES AWAY...
NOW THAT YOU CAN'T SEE, I'LL HURL ALL MY WEAPONS AT YOU!
ISTANTLY, THEN, FROM THE POWER RING SPEEDS A VERDANT FIST...
YOU OVEREXTENDED YOURSELF, TATTOOED MAN! I DEDUCED YOU COULD ACTIVATE ONLY ONE TATTOOED OBJECT AT A TIME! TRYING TO HANDLE ALL OF THEM TOGETHER RESULTED IN NONE OF THEM WORKING!
AS THE SEAMAN DROPS TO THE FLOOR, HIS PAINTED ARMS CLEAR THEMSELVES OF MAGES...
GOT TO ORDER ALL MY TATTOOS TO VANISH-- TO KEEP MY SECRET! I'LL COME BACK ANOTHER DAY TO--TURN THE TABLES ON GREEN LANTERN!
THE ONLY POSSIBLE REASON TO EXPLAIN WHY MY POWER RING WAS HELPLESS AGAINST HIS TATTOOS IS THAT THEY CONTAINED YELLOW CHEMICALS-- WHICH WERE OVERSHADOWED BY OTHER DARKER CHEMICALS!
12

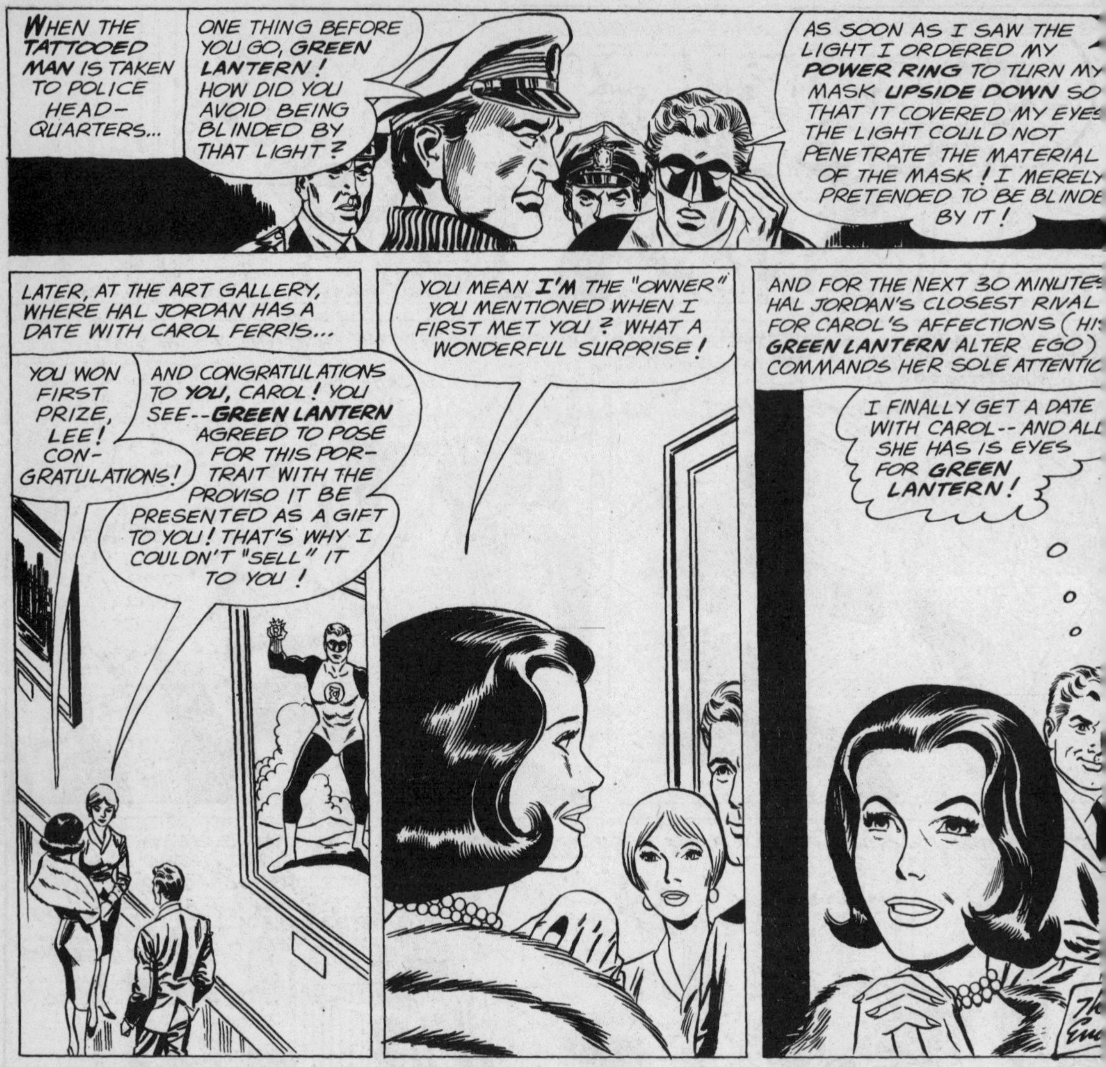
WHEN THE TATTOOED MAN IS TAKEN TO POLICE HEAD-QUARTERS...
ONE THING BEFORE YOU GO, GREEN LANTERN! HOW DID YOU AVOID BEING BLINDED BY THAT LIGHT?
AS SOON AS I SAW THE LIGHT I ORDERED MY POWER RING TO TURN MY MASK UPSIDE DOWN SO THAT IT COVERED MY EYES THE LIGHT COULD NOT PENETRATE THE MATERIAL OF THE MASK! I MERELY PRETENDED TO BE BLINDE BY IT!
LATER, AT THE ART GALLERY, WHERE HAL JORDAN HAS A DATE WITH CAROL FERRIS...
YOU WON FIRST PRIZE, LEE! CON-GRATULATIONS!
AND CONGRATULATIONS TO YOU, CAROL! YOU SEE--GREEN LANTERN AGREED TO POSE FOR THIS POR-TRAIT WITH THE PROVISO IT BE PRESENTED AS A GIFT TO YOU! THAT'S WHY I COULDN'T "SELL" IT TO YOU!
YOU MEAN I'M THE "OWNER" YOU MENTIONED WHEN I FIRST MET YOU? WHAT A WONDERFUL SURPRISE!
AND FOR THE NEXT 30 MINUTES HAL JORDAN'S CLOSEST RIVAL FOR CAROL'S AFFECTIONS (HIS GREEN LANTERN ALTER EGO) COMMANDS HER SOLE ATTENTIO
I FINALLY GET A DATE WITH CAROL--AND ALL SHE HAS IS EYES FOR GREEN LANTERN!

GREEN LANTERN

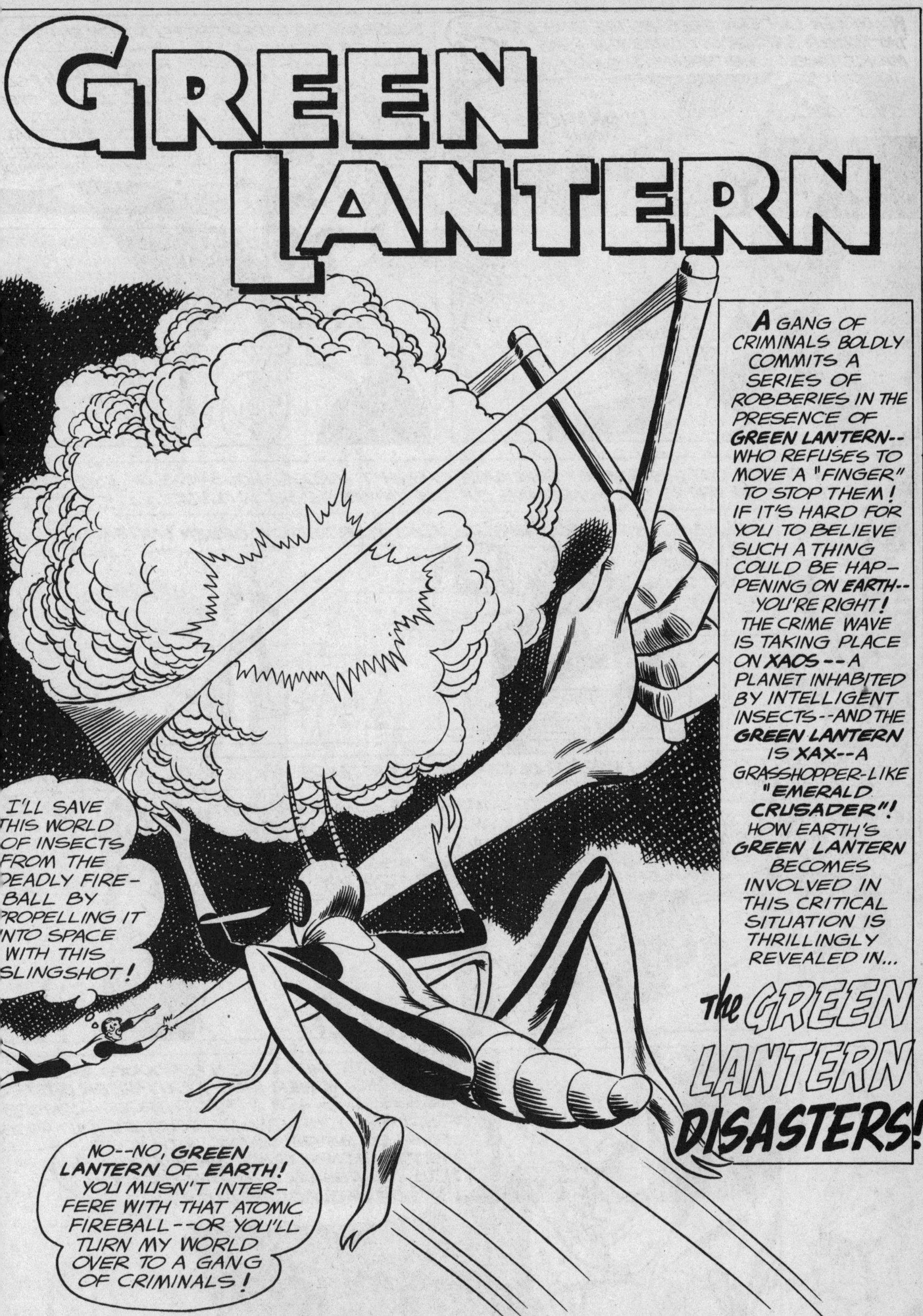
GREEN LANTERN
A GANG OF CRIMINALS BOLDLY COMMITS A SERIES OF ROBBERIES IN THE PRESENCE OF GREEN LANTERN-- WHO REFUSES TO MOVE A "FINGER" TO STOP THEM! IF IT'S HARD FOR YOU TO BELIEVE SUCH A THING COULD BE HAPPENING ON EARTH-- YOU'RE RIGHT! THE CRIME WAVE IS TAKING PLACE ON XAOS--A PLANET INHABITED BY INTELLIGENT INSECTS--AND THE GREEN LANTERN IS XAX--A GRASSHOPPER-LIKE "EMERALD CRUSADER"! HOW EARTH'S GREEN LANTERN BECOMES INVOLVED IN THIS CRITICAL SITUATION IS THRILLINGLY REVEALED IN...
I'LL SAVE THIS WORLD OF INSECTS FROM THE DEADLY FIRE-BALL BY PROPELLING IT INTO SPACE WITH THIS SLINGSHOT!
The GREEN LANTERN DISASTERS!
NO--NO, GREEN LANTERN OF EARTH! YOU MUSN'T INTER-FERE WITH THAT ATOMIC FIREBALL--OR YOU'LL TURN MY WORLD OVER TO A GANG OF CRIMINALS!

As GREEN LANTERN presses his ring against the POWER BATTERY--giving the ring a 24-hour charge...He begins his solemn oath...

IN BRIGHTEST DAY...

Suddenly, he experiences a moment of intense dizziness...

--IN BLACKEST NIGHT...

THAT FAMILIAR SENSATIC MEANS I'M BEING CONTACTED BY THE GUARDIA

In that instant of time, his ENERGY DUPLICATE is swept across thousands of light-year to the planet OA where the GUARDIANS OF THE UNIVERSE sit in council...

NO EVIL SHALL ESCAPE MY SIGHT--

WE HAVE SUMMONED YOU HERE BECAUSE YOUR FELLOW GREEN LANTERN, XAX OF XAOS, HAS NEGLECTED TO REPORT TO US IN SOME TIME!

This astral self of Earth's EMERALD GLADIATOR understands all he sees and hears while on the GUARDIANS' planet...

LET THOSE WHO WORSHIP EVIL'S MIGHT...

A BAND OF CRIMINALS IS RUNNING RAMPANT ON HIS PLANET--YET XAX AVOIDS USING HIS POWER RING TO STOP THEM! YOU ARE ABOUT TO HEAD INTO SPACE ON A MISSION. WHEN THAT MISSION IS COMPLETED--MAKE A DETOUR TO XAOS...

BEWARE MY POWER--

INVESTIGATE THE REASON FOR XAX'S RELUCTAN TO USE HIS POWER RING! YOU POWER BATTER POSSESSORS ARE A PROUD GROUP--CONFIDEN OF SOLVING YOUR OWN DIFFICULTIES AND PROB LEMS! SO BE DIPLOMATIC WITH YOUR INVESTIGATION--DO NOT MAKE XAX FEEL HE IS NECESSARILY UNDER SUSPICION OF NEGLECT OF DUTY...

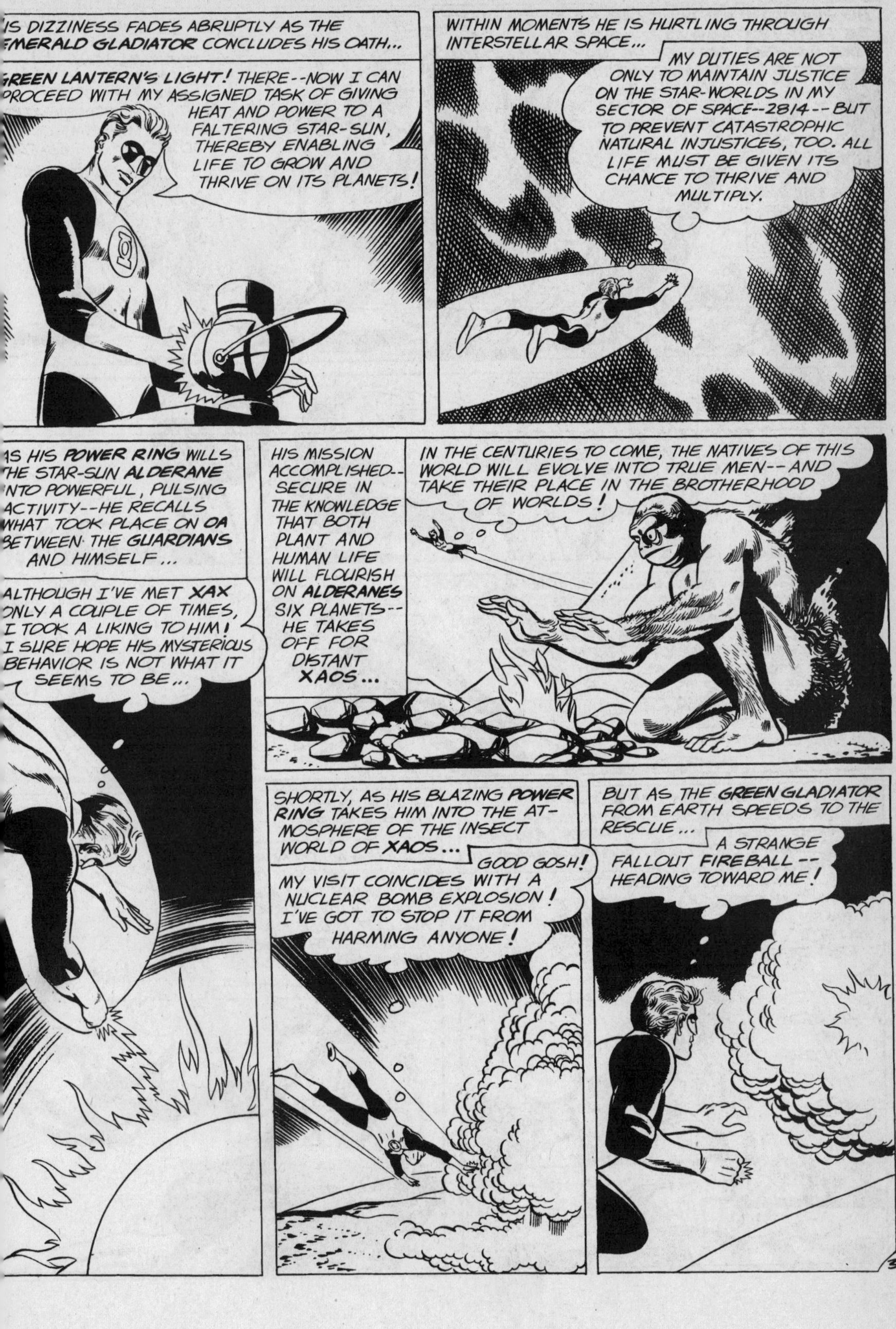
IS DIZZINESS FADES ABRUPTLY AS THE EMERALD GLADIATOR CONCLUDES HIS OATH...
GREEN LANTERN'S LIGHT! THERE--NOW I CAN ROCEED WITH MY ASSIGNED TASK OF GIVING HEAT AND POWER TO A FALTERING STAR-SUN, THEREBY ENABLING LIFE TO GROW AND THRIVE ON ITS PLANETS!
WITHIN MOMENTS HE IS HURTLING THROUGH INTERSTELLAR SPACE...
MY DUTIES ARE NOT ONLY TO MAINTAIN JUSTICE ON THE STAR-WORLDS IN MY SECTOR OF SPACE--2814--BUT TO PREVENT CATASTROPHIC NATURAL INJUSTICES, TOO. ALL LIFE MUST BE GIVEN ITS CHANCE TO THRIVE AND MULTIPLY.
AS HIS POWER RING WILLS THE STAR-SUN ALDERANE INTO POWERFUL, PULSING ACTIVITY--HE RECALLS WHAT TOOK PLACE ON OA BETWEEN THE GUARDIANS AND HIMSELF...
ALTHOUGH I'VE MET XAX ONLY A COUPLE OF TIMES, I TOOK A LIKING TO HIM! I SURE HOPE HIS MYSTERIOUS BEHAVIOR IS NOT WHAT IT SEEMS TO BE...
HIS MISSION ACCOMPLISHED--SECURE IN THE KNOWLEDGE THAT BOTH PLANT AND HUMAN LIFE WILL FLOURISH ON ALDERANES SIX PLANETS--HE TAKES OFF FOR DISTANT XAOS...
IN THE CENTURIES TO COME, THE NATIVES OF THIS WORLD WILL EVOLVE INTO TRUE MEN--AND TAKE THEIR PLACE IN THE BROTHERHOOD OF WORLDS!
SHORTLY, AS HIS BLAZING POWER RING TAKES HIM INTO THE ATMOSPHERE OF THE INSECT WORLD OF XAOS...
GOOD GOSH! MY VISIT COINCIDES WITH A NUCLEAR BOMB EXPLOSION! I'VE GOT TO STOP IT FROM HARMING ANYONE!
BUT AS THE GREEN GLADIATOR FROM EARTH SPEEDS TO THE RESCUE...
A STRANGE FALLOUT FIREBALL--HEADING TOWARD ME!
3

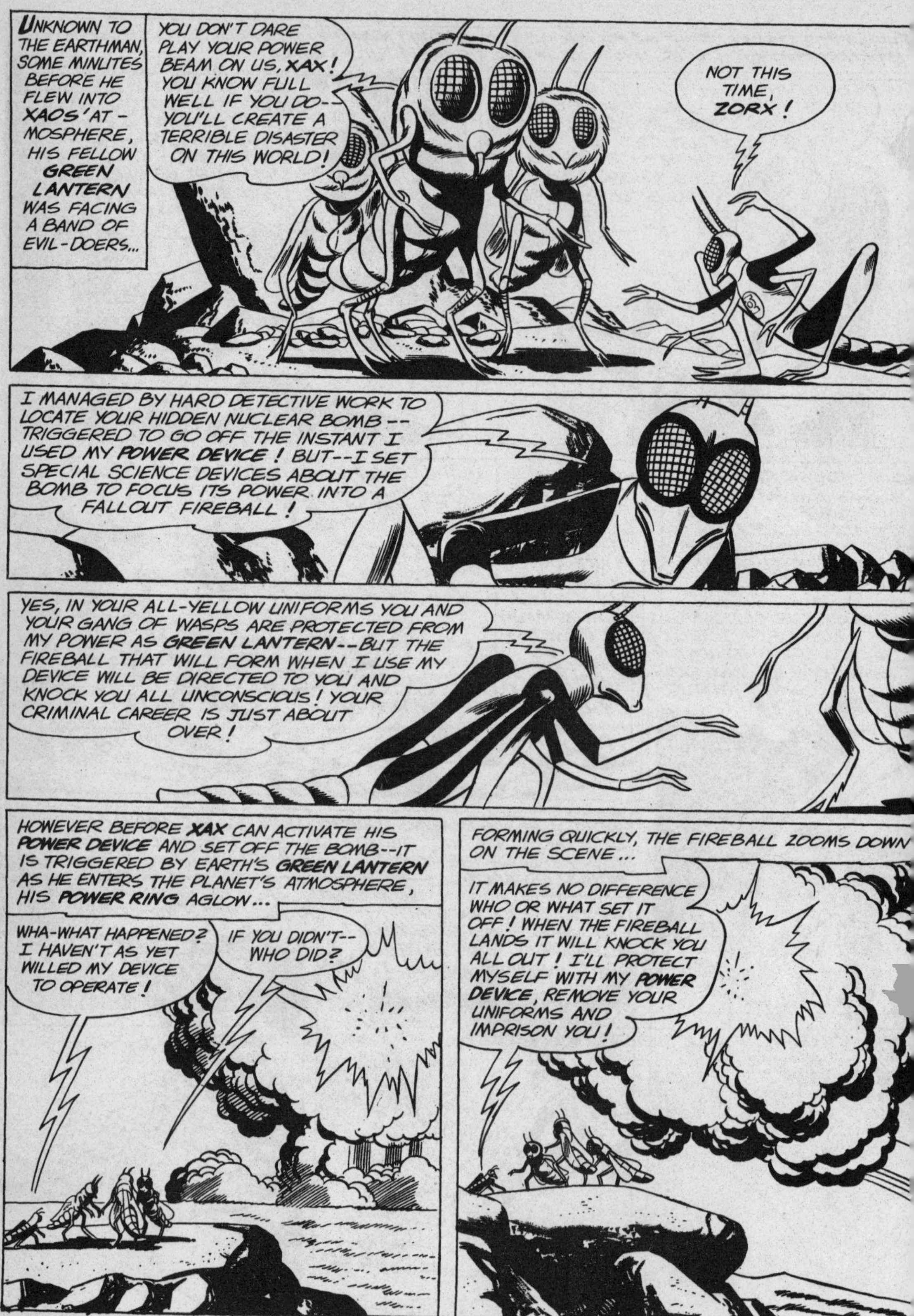
UNKNOWN TO THE EARTHMAN, SOME MINUTES BEFORE HE FLEW INTO XAOS' AT-MOSPHERE, HIS FELLOW GREEN LANTERN WAS FACING A BAND OF EVIL-DOERS...
YOU DON'T DARE PLAY YOUR POWER BEAM ON US, XAX! YOU KNOW FULL WELL IF YOU DO--YOU'LL CREATE A TERRIBLE DISASTER ON THIS WORLD!
NOT THIS TIME, ZORX!
I MANAGED BY HARD DETECTIVE WORK TO LOCATE YOUR HIDDEN NUCLEAR BOMB -- TRIGGERED TO GO OFF THE INSTANT I USED MY POWER DEVICE! BUT--I SET SPECIAL SCIENCE DEVICES ABOUT THE BOMB TO FOCUS ITS POWER INTO A FALLOUT FIREBALL!
YES, IN YOUR ALL-YELLOW UNIFORMS YOU AND YOUR GANG OF WASPS ARE PROTECTED FROM MY POWER AS GREEN LANTERN--BUT THE FIREBALL THAT WILL FORM WHEN I USE MY DEVICE WILL BE DIRECTED TO YOU AND KNOCK YOU ALL UNCONSCIOUS! YOUR CRIMINAL CAREER IS JUST ABOUT OVER!
HOWEVER BEFORE XAX CAN ACTIVATE HIS POWER DEVICE AND SET OFF THE BOMB--IT IS TRIGGERED BY EARTH'S GREEN LANTERN AS HE ENTERS THE PLANET'S ATMOSPHERE, HIS POWER RING AGLOW...
WHA-WHAT HAPPENED? I HAVEN'T AS YET WILLED MY DEVICE TO OPERATE!
IF YOU DIDN'T--WHO DID?
FORMING QUICKLY, THE FIREBALL ZOOMS DOWN ON THE SCENE...
IT MAKES NO DIFFERENCE WHO OR WHAT SET IT OFF! WHEN THE FIREBALL LANDS IT WILL KNOCK YOU ALL OUT! I'LL PROTECT MYSELF WITH MY POWER DEVICE, REMOVE YOUR UNIFORMS AND IMPRISON YOU!

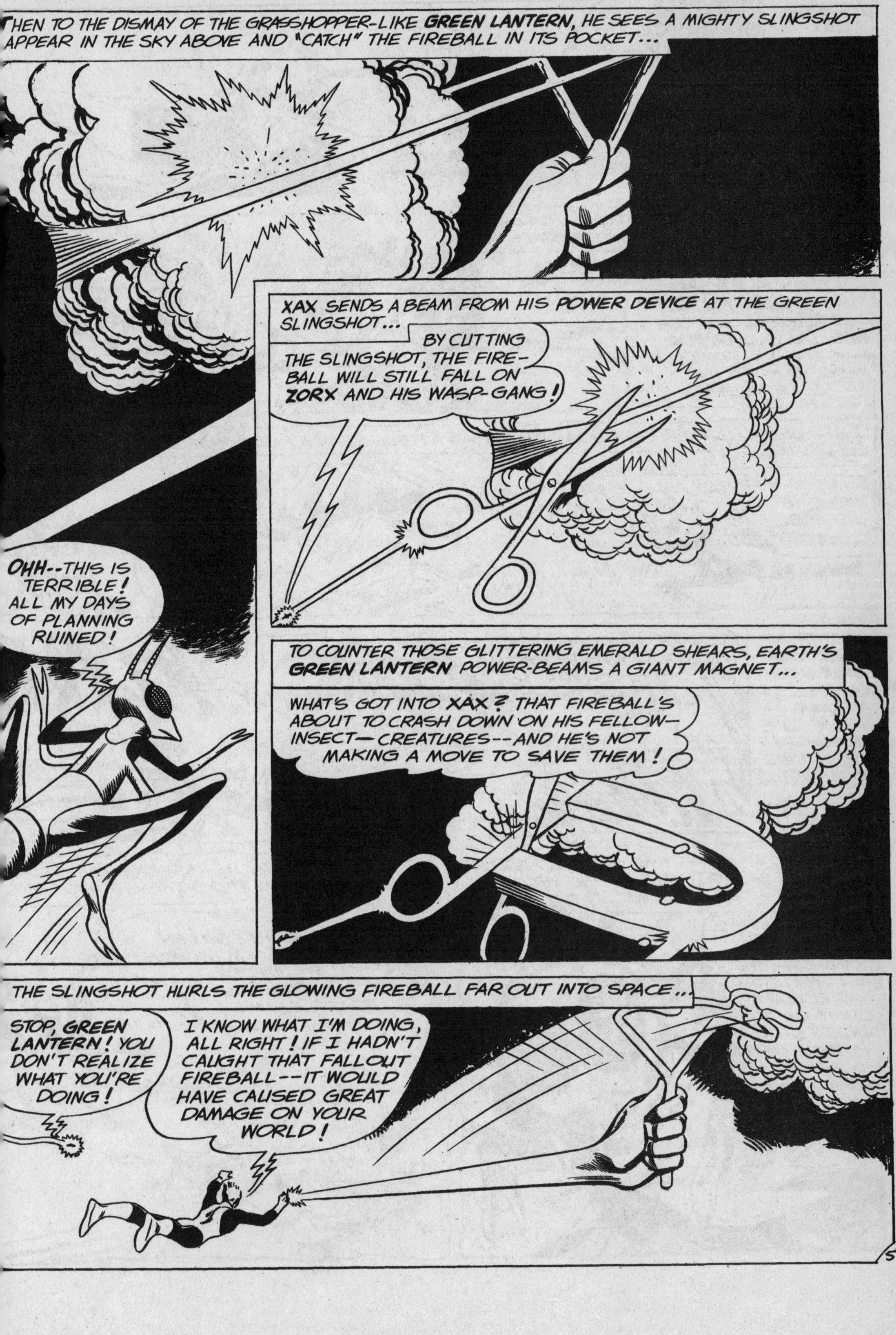
THEN TO THE DISMAY OF THE GRASSHOPPER-LIKE GREEN LANTERN, HE SEES A MIGHTY SLINGSHOT APPEAR IN THE SKY ABOVE AND "CATCH" THE FIREBALL IN ITS POCKET...
XAX SENDS A BEAM FROM HIS POWER DEVICE AT THE GREEN SLINGSHOT...
BY CUTTING THE SLINGSHOT, THE FIRE-BALL WILL STILL FALL ON ZORX AND HIS WASP-GANG!
OHH--THIS IS TERRIBLE! ALL MY DAYS OF PLANNING RUINED!
TO COUNTER THOSE GLITTERING EMERALD SHEARS, EARTH'S GREEN LANTERN POWER-BEAMS A GIANT MAGNET...
WHAT'S GOT INTO XAX? THAT FIREBALL'S ABOUT TO CRASH DOWN ON HIS FELLOW-INSECT-CREATURES--AND HE'S NOT MAKING A MOVE TO SAVE THEM!
THE SLINGSHOT HURLS THE GLOWING FIREBALL FAR OUT INTO SPACE...
STOP, GREEN LANTERN! YOU DON'T REALIZE WHAT YOU'RE DOING!
I KNOW WHAT I'M DOING, ALL RIGHT! IF I HADN'T CAUGHT THAT FALLOUT FIREBALL--IT WOULD HAVE CAUSED GREAT DAMAGE ON YOUR WORLD!
5

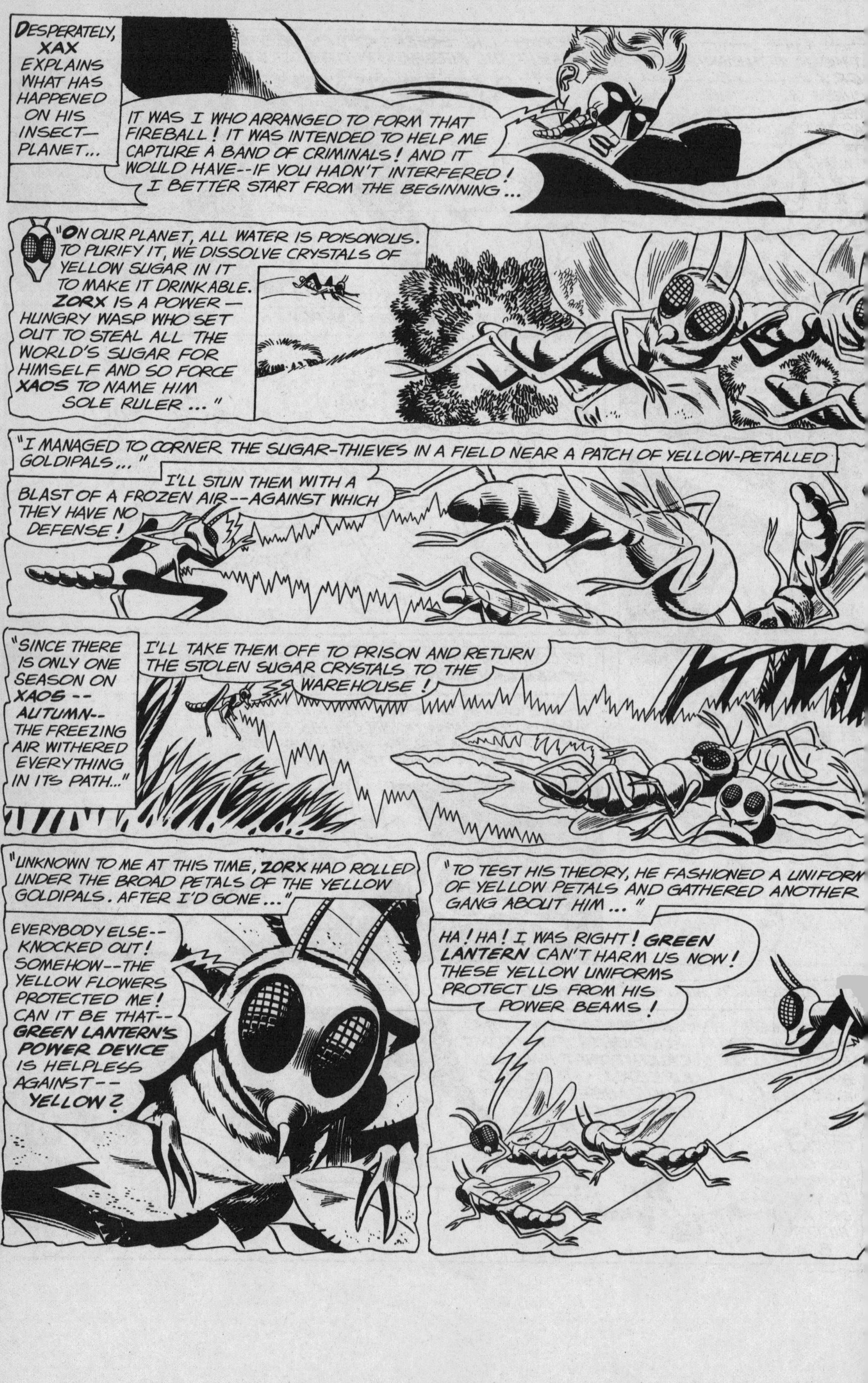
DESPERATELY, XAX EXPLAINS WHAT HAS HAPPENED ON HIS INSECT-PLANET...
IT WAS I WHO ARRANGED TO FORM THAT FIREBALL! IT WAS INTENDED TO HELP ME CAPTURE A BAND OF CRIMINALS! AND IT WOULD HAVE--IF YOU HADN'T INTERFERED! I BETTER START FROM THE BEGINNING...
"ON OUR PLANET, ALL WATER IS POISONOUS. TO PURIFY IT, WE DISSOLVE CRYSTALS OF YELLOW SUGAR IN IT TO MAKE IT DRINKABLE. ZORX IS A POWER-HUNGRY WASP WHO SET OUT TO STEAL ALL THE WORLD'S SUGAR FOR HIMSELF AND SO FORCE XAOS TO NAME HIM SOLE RULER..."
"I MANAGED TO CORNER THE SUGAR-THIEVES IN A FIELD NEAR A PATCH OF YELLOW-PETALLED GOLDIPALS..."
I'LL STUN THEM WITH A BLAST OF A FROZEN AIR--AGAINST WHICH THEY HAVE NO DEFENSE!
"SINCE THERE IS ONLY ONE SEASON ON XAOS--AUTUMN--THE FREEZING AIR WITHERED EVERYTHING IN ITS PATH..."
I'LL TAKE THEM OFF TO PRISON AND RETURN THE STOLEN SUGAR CRYSTALS TO THE WAREHOUSE!
"UNKNOWN TO ME AT THIS TIME, ZORX HAD ROLLED UNDER THE BROAD PETALS OF THE YELLOW GOLDIPALS. AFTER I'D GONE..."
EVERYBODY ELSE--KNOCKED OUT! SOMEHOW--THE YELLOW FLOWERS PROTECTED ME! CAN IT BE THAT--GREEN LANTERN'S POWER DEVICE IS HELPLESS AGAINST--YELLOW?
"TO TEST HIS THEORY, HE FASHIONED A UNIFORM OF YELLOW PETALS AND GATHERED ANOTHER GANG ABOUT HIM..."
HA! HA! I WAS RIGHT! GREEN LANTERN CAN'T HARM US NOW! THESE YELLOW UNIFORMS PROTECT US FROM HIS POWER BEAMS!

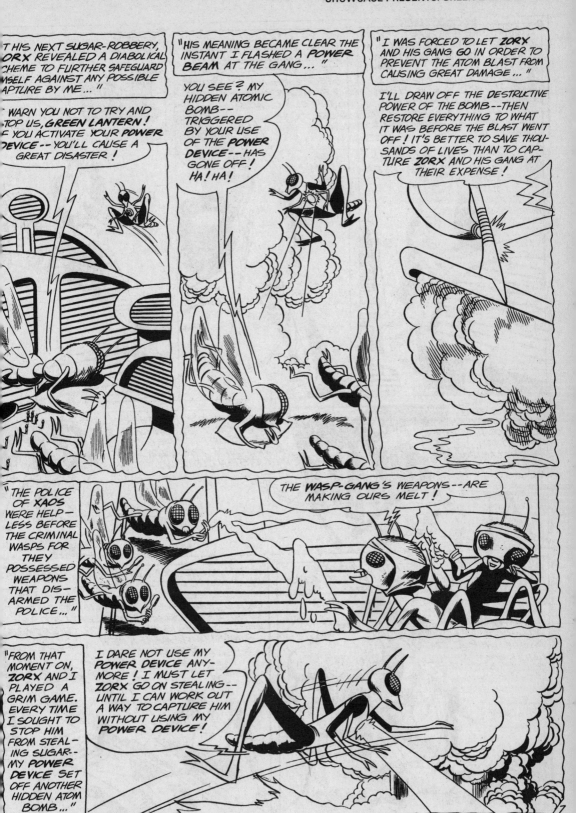

"THIS NEXT SUGAR-ROBBERY, ZORX REVEALED A DIABOLICAL SCHEME TO FURTHER SAFEGUARD HIMSELF AGAINST ANY POSSIBLE CAPTURE BY ME..."

"I WARN YOU NOT TO TRY AND STOP US, GREEN LANTERN! IF YOU ACTIVATE YOUR POWER DEVICE -- YOU'LL CAUSE A GREAT DISASTER!

"HIS MEANING BECAME CLEAR THE INSTANT I FLASHED A POWER BEAM AT THE GANG..."

YOU SEE? MY HIDDEN ATOMIC BOMB-- TRIGGERED BY YOUR USE OF THE POWER DEVICE-- HAS GONE OFF! HA! HA!

"I WAS FORCED TO LET ZORX AND HIS GANG GO IN ORDER TO PREVENT THE ATOM BLAST FROM CAUSING GREAT DAMAGE..."

I'LL DRAW OFF THE DESTRUCTIVE POWER OF THE BOMB--THEN RESTORE EVERYTHING TO WHAT IT WAS BEFORE THE BLAST WENT OFF! IT'S BETTER TO SAVE THOUSANDS OF LIVES THAN TO CAPTURE ZORX AND HIS GANG AT THEIR EXPENSE!

"THE POLICE OF XAOS WERE HELP-LESS BEFORE THE CRIMINAL WASPS FOR THEY POSSESSED WEAPONS THAT DIS-ARMED THE POLICE..."

THE WASP-GANG'S WEAPONS--ARE MAKING OURS MELT!

"FROM THAT MOMENT ON, ZORX AND I PLAYED A GRIM GAME. EVERY TIME I SOUGHT TO STOP HIM FROM STEAL-ING SUGAR-- MY POWER DEVICE SET OFF ANOTHER HIDDEN ATOM BOMB..."

I DARE NOT USE MY POWER DEVICE ANY-MORE! I MUST LET ZORX GO ON STEALING-- UNTIL I CAN WORK OUT A WAY TO CAPTURE HIM WITHOUT USING MY POWER DEVICE!

7

LOCATING ONE OF THE HIDDEN ATOM BOMBS, I RIGGED IT SO THE FIREBALL WOULD FALL ON **ZORX** AND HIS GANG, KNOCKING THEM OUT! THEN-- YOU CAME ALONG...

...AND SPOILED YOUR CLEVER PLAN! I'M SORRY, **XAX**! AND NOW I REALIZE WHY YOU DIDN'T REPORT TO THE **GUARDIANS**...

YES, TO DO SO WOULD HAVE MEANT ACTIVATING MY **POWER DEVICE**--AND THUS SETTING OFF ANOTHER OF THOSE BOMBS! BESIDES, WHEN I DID REPORT, I WANTED TO HAVE THIS DIFFICULTY CLEARED UP!

THERE IS ONLY ONE SUGAR-WAREHOUSE LEFT--AND WHEN **ZORX** TAKES THAT SUGAR, WE'LL BE AT HIS MERCY! TO LIVE, WE'LL HAVE TO MAKE HIM RULER OF OUR WORLD!

PERHA... NOT! FR... SOMETH... YOU SA... YOU G... ME A... IDEA...

AS THE INSECT **GREEN LANTERN** CHARGES HIS RING, EARTH'S **GREEN LANTERN** REVEALS HIS PLAN...

YOU MENTIONED THAT THERE IS ONLY ONE SEASON ON THIS WORLD! IT GIVES US A CHANCE TO TRICK **ZORX**! LISTEN CLOSELY...

SHORTLY THEREAFTER, EARTH'S **GREEN LANTERN** CHARGES HIS OWN **POWER RING** WITH **XAX'S** **POWER BATTERY**...

YOUR SCHEME MAY WORK, **GREEN LANTERN**! I'LL MAKE READY THE ROCKETSHIP AT ONCE!

WITHIN MINUTES, **XAX** IS HURTLING SPACEWARD IN AN INSECT ROCKETSHIP...

WHILE **XAX** IS ON HIS ERRAND--I'LL KEEP AN EYE ON THAT LAST SUGAR-STOREHOUSE LEFT! TOO BAD T... INSECT SUGAR IS **YELLOW**-- OR OUR **POWER RINGS** COULD MAKE A NEW SUPPLY OF IT!

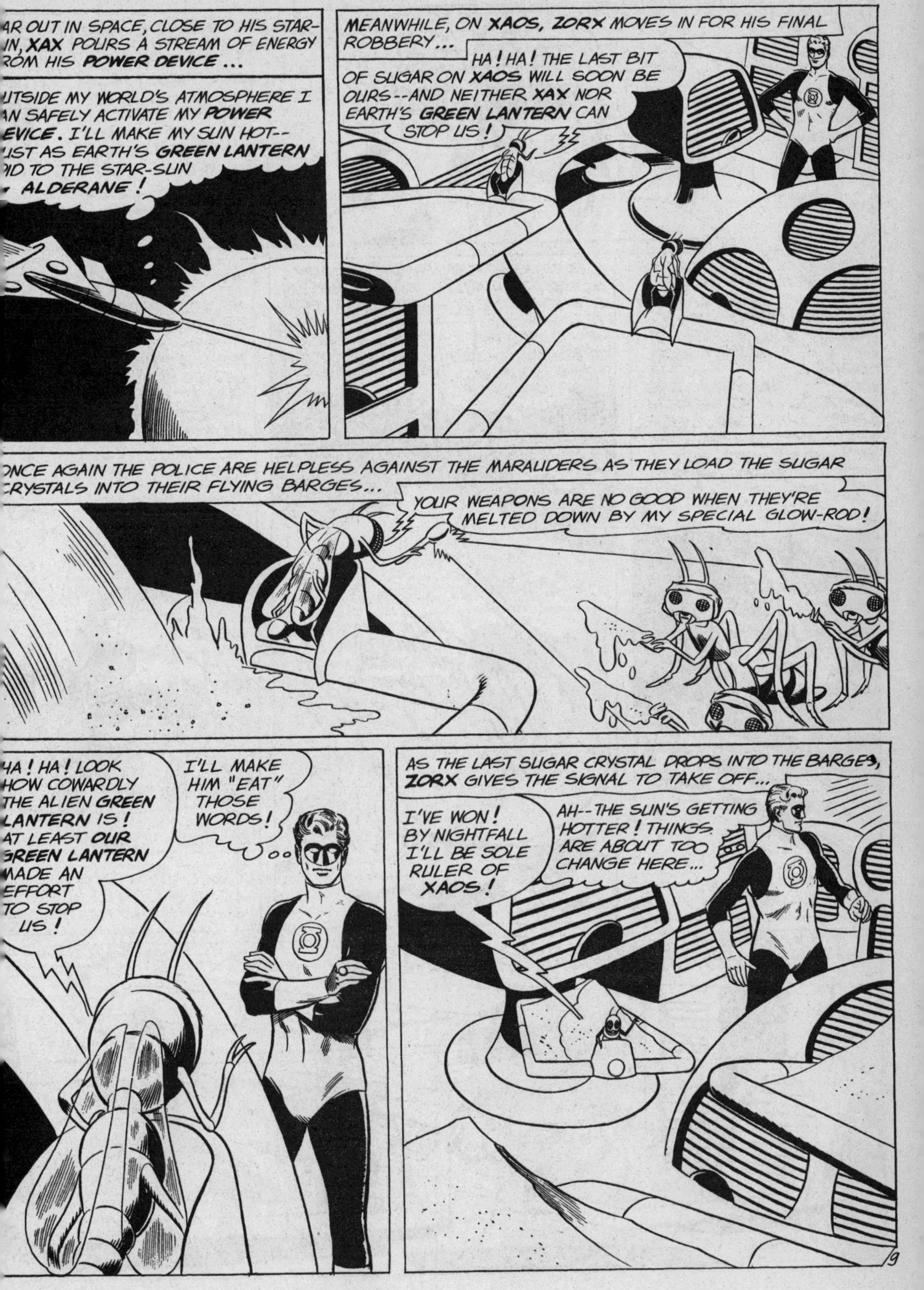
AR OUT IN SPACE, CLOSE TO HIS STAR-UN, XAX POURS A STREAM OF ENERGY ROM HIS POWER DEVICE ...
UTSIDE MY WORLD'S ATMOSPHERE I AN SAFELY ACTIVATE MY POWER EVICE. I'LL MAKE MY SUN HOT-- UST AS EARTH'S GREEN LANTERN DID TO THE STAR-SUN ALDERANE!
MEANWHILE, ON XAOS, ZORX MOVES IN FOR HIS FINAL ROBBERY...
HA! HA! THE LAST BIT OF SUGAR ON XAOS WILL SOON BE OURS--AND NEITHER XAX NOR EARTH'S GREEN LANTERN CAN STOP US!
ONCE AGAIN THE POLICE ARE HELPLESS AGAINST THE MARAUDERS AS THEY LOAD THE SUGAR CRYSTALS INTO THEIR FLYING BARGES...
YOUR WEAPONS ARE NO GOOD WHEN THEY'RE MELTED DOWN BY MY SPECIAL GLOW-ROD!
HA! HA! LOOK HOW COWARDLY THE ALIEN GREEN LANTERN IS! AT LEAST OUR GREEN LANTERN MADE AN EFFORT TO STOP US!
I'LL MAKE HIM "EAT" THOSE WORDS!
AS THE LAST SUGAR CRYSTAL DROPS INTO THE BARGES, ZORX GIVES THE SIGNAL TO TAKE OFF...
I'VE WON! BY NIGHTFALL I'LL BE SOLE RULER OF XAOS!
AH--THE SUN'S GETTING HOTTER! THINGS ARE ABOUT TOO CHANGE HERE...
9

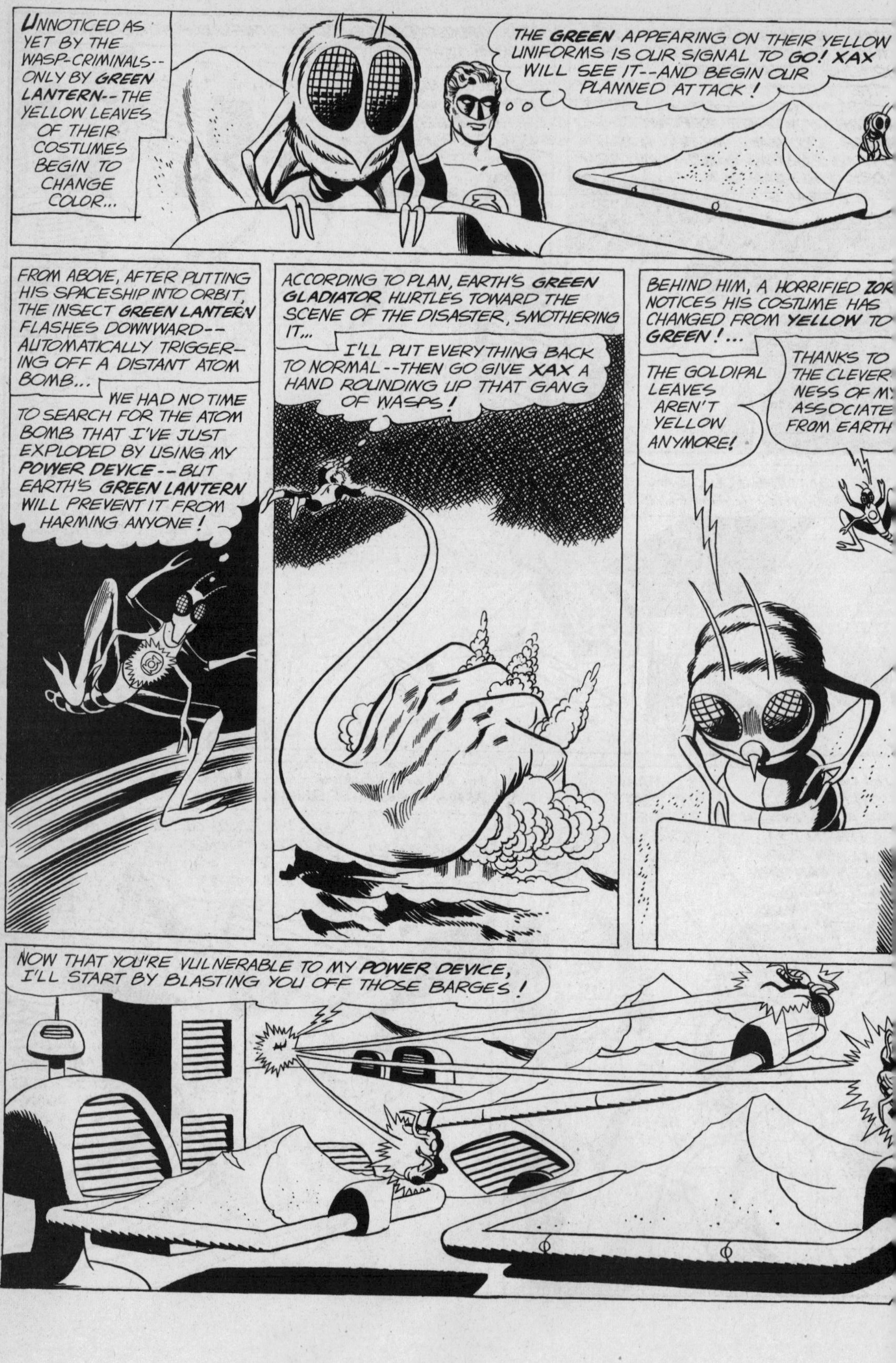
UNNOTICED AS YET BY THE WASP-CRIMINALS--ONLY BY GREEN LANTERN--THE YELLOW LEAVES OF THEIR COSTUMES BEGIN TO CHANGE COLOR...
THE GREEN APPEARING ON THEIR YELLOW UNIFORMS IS OUR SIGNAL TO GO! XAX WILL SEE IT--AND BEGIN OUR PLANNED ATTACK!
FROM ABOVE, AFTER PUTTING HIS SPACESHIP INTO ORBIT, THE INSECT GREEN LANTERN FLASHES DOWNWARD--AUTOMATICALLY TRIGGERING OFF A DISTANT ATOM BOMB...
WE HAD NO TIME TO SEARCH FOR THE ATOM BOMB THAT I'VE JUST EXPLODED BY USING MY POWER DEVICE--BUT EARTH'S GREEN LANTERN WILL PREVENT IT FROM HARMING ANYONE!
ACCORDING TO PLAN, EARTH'S GREEN GLADIATOR HURTLES TOWARD THE SCENE OF THE DISASTER, SMOTHERING IT...
I'LL PUT EVERYTHING BACK TO NORMAL--THEN GO GIVE XAX A HAND ROUNDING UP THAT GANG OF WASPS!
BEHIND HIM, A HORRIFIED ZOR NOTICES HIS COSTUME HAS CHANGED FROM YELLOW TO GREEN!...
THE GOLDIPAL LEAVES AREN'T YELLOW ANYMORE!
THANKS TO THE CLEVERNESS OF MY ASSOCIATE FROM EARTH
NOW THAT YOU'RE VULNERABLE TO MY POWER DEVICE, I'LL START BY BLASTING YOU OFF THOSE BARGES!

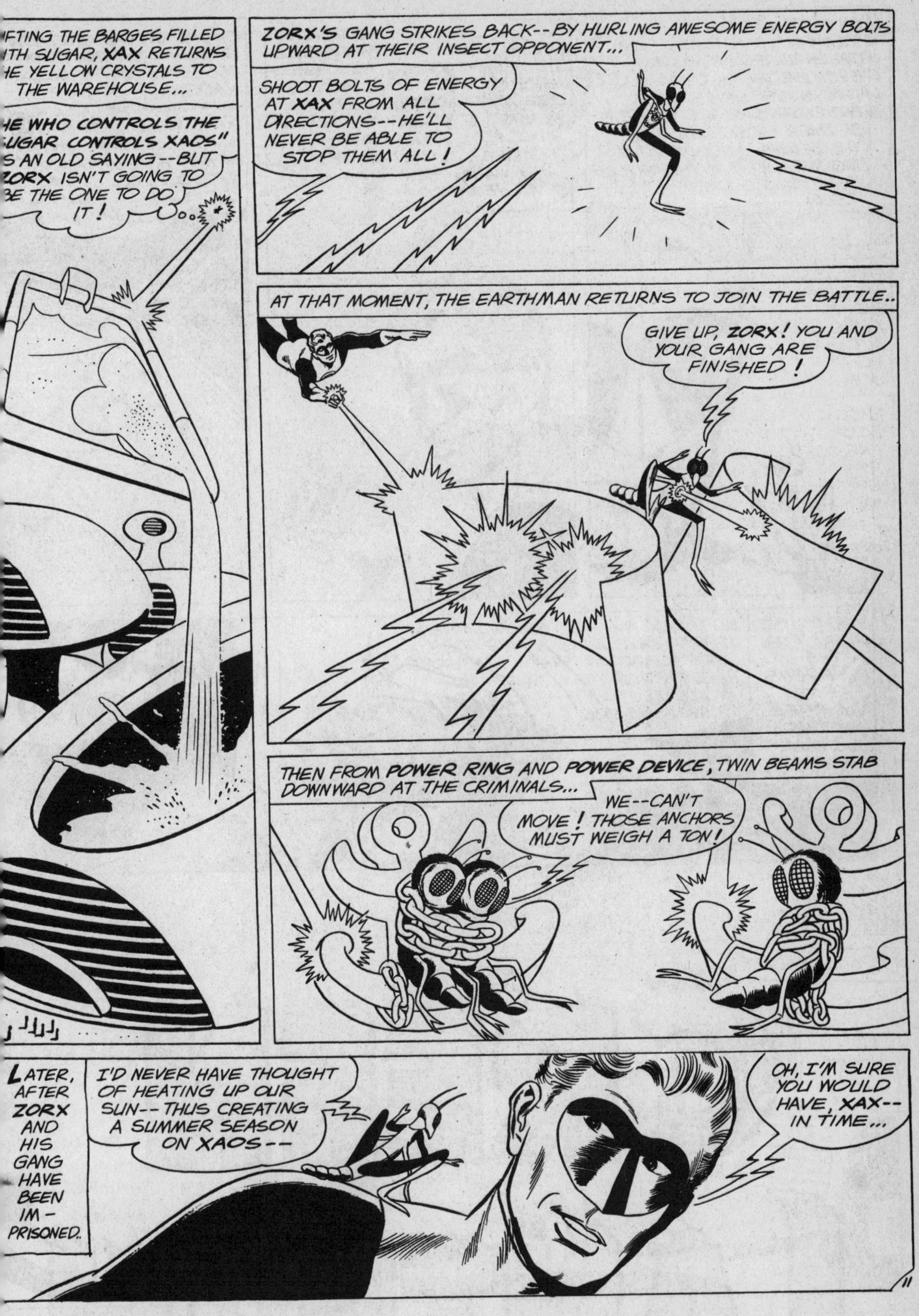

IFTING THE BARGES FILLED WITH SUGAR, XAX RETURNS THE YELLOW CRYSTALS TO THE WAREHOUSE...
"HE WHO CONTROLS THE SUGAR CONTROLS XAOS" IS AN OLD SAYING--BUT ZORX ISN'T GOING TO BE THE ONE TO DO IT!
ZORX'S GANG STRIKES BACK--BY HURLING AWESOME ENERGY BOLTS UPWARD AT THEIR INSECT OPPONENT...
SHOOT BOLTS OF ENERGY AT XAX FROM ALL DIRECTIONS--HE'LL NEVER BE ABLE TO STOP THEM ALL!
AT THAT MOMENT, THE EARTHMAN RETURNS TO JOIN THE BATTLE..
GIVE UP, ZORX! YOU AND YOUR GANG ARE FINISHED!
THEN FROM POWER RING AND POWER DEVICE, TWIN BEAMS STAB DOWNWARD AT THE CRIMINALS...
WE--CAN'T MOVE! THOSE ANCHORS MUST WEIGH A TON!
LATER, AFTER ZORX AND HIS GANG HAVE BEEN IM-PRISONED.
I'D NEVER HAVE THOUGHT OF HEATING UP OUR SUN--THUS CREATING A SUMMER SEASON ON XAOS--
OH, I'M SURE YOU WOULD HAVE, XAX--IN TIME...
11

ON EARTH, LEAVES CHANGE COLOR IN THE AUTUMN-- FROM GREEN TO RED OR YELLOW-- BECAUSE THE CHLOROPHYLL THAT GIVES LEAVES THEIR GREEN APPEARANCE IN THE SUMMER FADES OUT. THEN THE LEAVES' *YELLOW* COLORING MATTER--*XANTHOPHYLL*-- TAKES OVER.

SINCE ALL LEAVES CONTAIN BOTH *CHLOROPHYLL* AND *XANTHOPHYLL*-- I SIMPLY REVERSED THE PROCESS HERE ON *XAOS* TO ALLOW THE *GREEN CHLOROPHYLL* TO RE-PLACE THE *YELLOW XANTHO-PHYLL*! THUS, THE WASP-GANG'S COSTUMES TURNED GREEN AND MADE THEM VULNERABLE!

ON HIS RETURN TO EARTH, *GREEN LANTERN* SENDS COOL-RAY AT THE SUN OF *XAOS* ...

THIS WILL ALLOW XAOS TO RETURN TO ITS NORMAL AUTUMN TIME. IF XAX HAS ANY FURTHER TROUBLE, ALL HE HAS TO DO IS MAKE IT SUMMER AGAIN!

AND ON THE PLANET OA, THE *GUARDIANS OF THE UNIVERSE* BREATHE A SIGH OF RELIEF...

BOTH *XAX* AND HAL (*GREEN LANTERN*) JORDAN HAVE DONE A FINE JOB! ONCE AGAIN OUR *GREEN LANTERNS* HAVE PROVED THEIR WORTH TO INTELLIGENT LIFE-- EVERYWHERE!

GREEN LANTERN

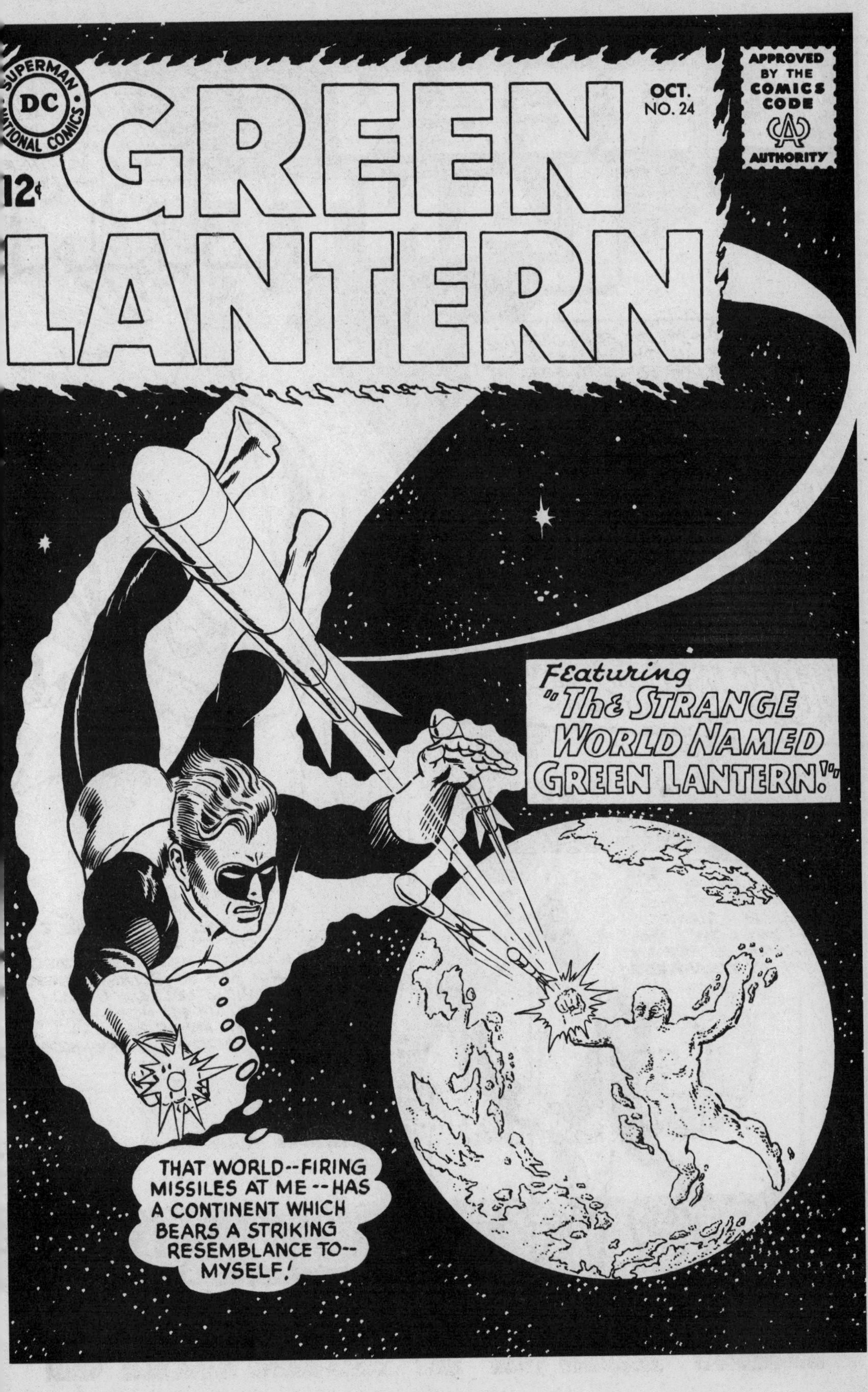
SUPERMAN DC NATIONAL COMICS
12¢
GREEN LANTERN
OCT. NO. 24
APPROVED BY THE COMICS CODE AUTHORITY
Featuring "The STRANGE WORLD NAMED GREEN LANTERN!"
THAT WORLD--FIRING MISSILES AT ME--HAS A CONTINENT WHICH BEARS A STRIKING RESEMBLANCE TO--MYSELF!

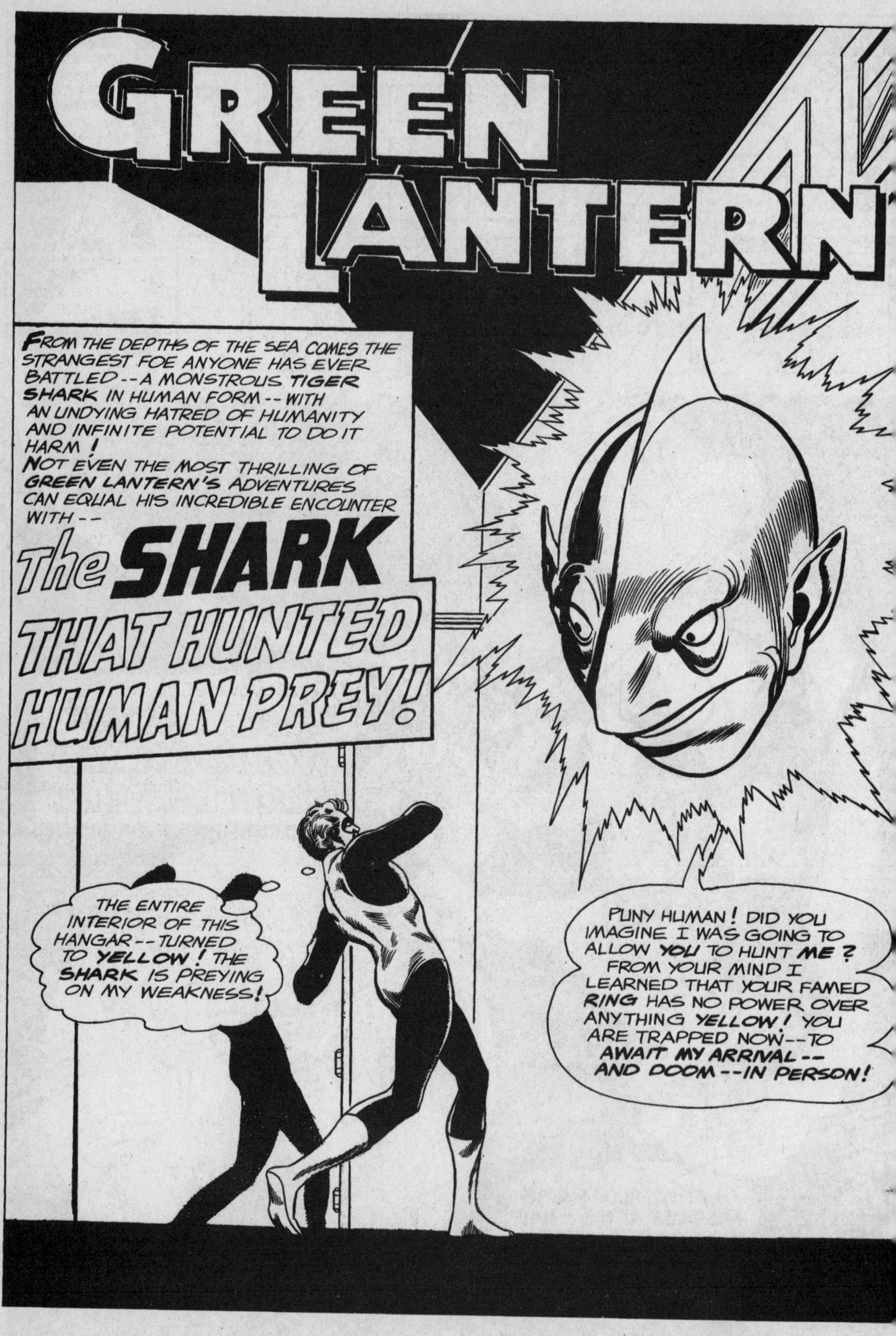
GREEN LANTERN
FROM THE DEPTHS OF THE SEA COMES THE STRANGEST FOE ANYONE HAS EVER BATTLED -- A MONSTROUS TIGER SHARK IN HUMAN FORM -- WITH AN UNDYING HATRED OF HUMANITY AND INFINITE POTENTIAL TO DO IT HARM! NOT EVEN THE MOST THRILLING OF GREEN LANTERN'S ADVENTURES CAN EQUAL HIS INCREDIBLE ENCOUNTER WITH --
The SHARK THAT HUNTED HUMAN PREY!
THE ENTIRE INTERIOR OF THIS HANGAR -- TURNED TO YELLOW! THE SHARK IS PREYING ON MY WEAKNESS!
PUNY HUMAN! DID YOU IMAGINE I WAS GOING TO ALLOW YOU TO HUNT ME? FROM YOUR MIND I LEARNED THAT YOUR FAMED RING HAS NO POWER OVER ANYTHING YELLOW! YOU ARE TRAPPED NOW -- TO AWAIT MY ARRIVAL -- AND DOOM -- IN PERSON!

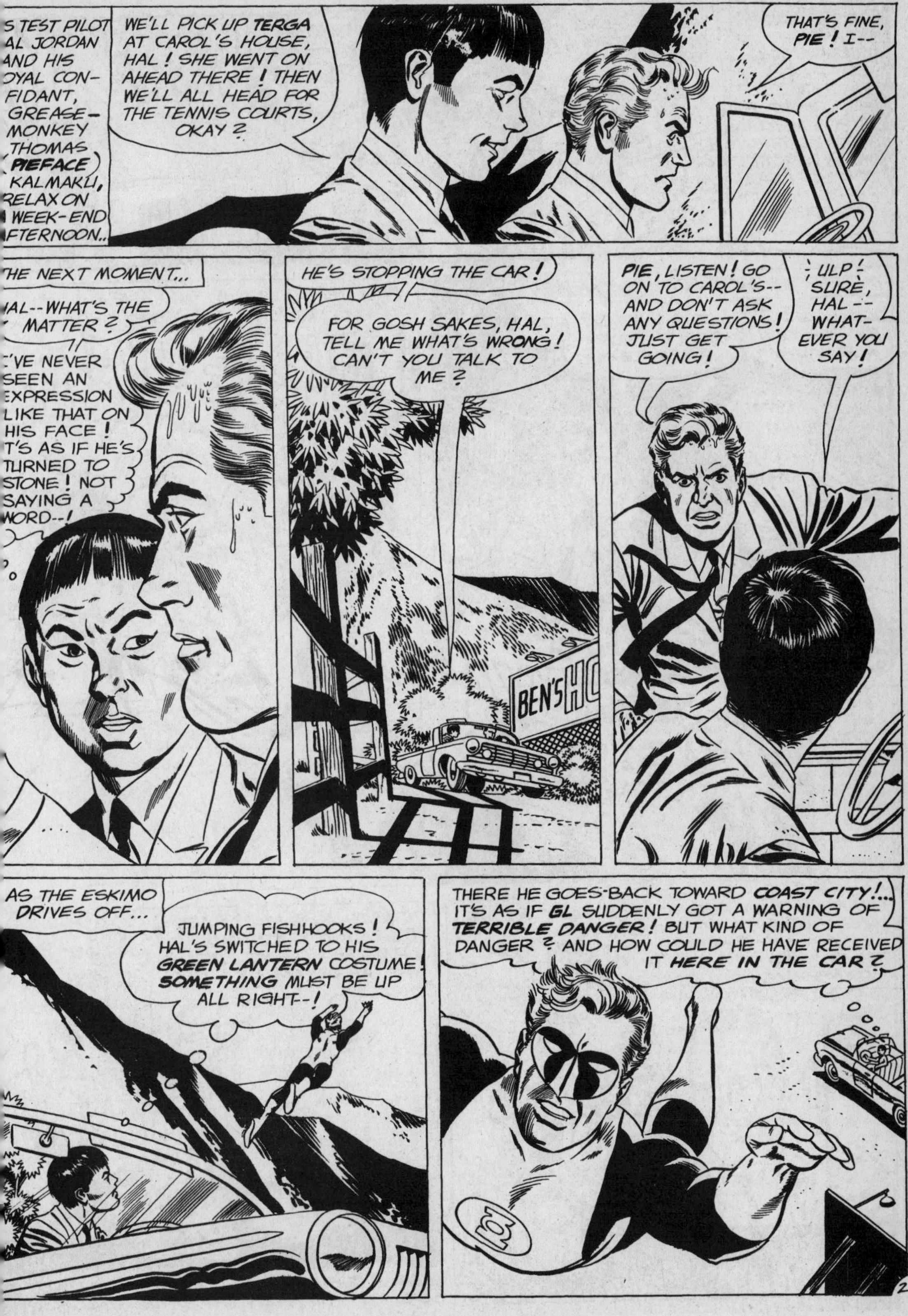
S TEST PILOT AL JORDAN AND HIS OYAL CONFIDANT, GREASE-MONKEY THOMAS (PIEFACE) KALMAKU, RELAX ON WEEK-END AFTERNOON..
WE'LL PICK UP TERGA AT CAROL'S HOUSE, HAL! SHE WENT ON AHEAD THERE! THEN WE'LL ALL HEAD FOR THE TENNIS COURTS, OKAY?
THAT'S FINE, PIE! I--
THE NEXT MOMENT...
HAL--WHAT'S THE MATTER?
'VE NEVER SEEN AN EXPRESSION LIKE THAT ON HIS FACE! T'S AS IF HE'S TURNED TO STONE! NOT SAYING A WORD--!
HE'S STOPPING THE CAR!
FOR GOSH SAKES, HAL, TELL ME WHAT'S WRONG! CAN'T YOU TALK TO ME?
BEN'S H
PIE, LISTEN! GO ON TO CAROL'S--AND DON'T ASK ANY QUESTIONS! JUST GET GOING!
ULP! SURE, HAL-- WHAT-EVER YOU SAY!
AS THE ESKIMO DRIVES OFF...
JUMPING FISHHOOKS! HAL'S SWITCHED TO HIS GREEN LANTERN COSTUME! SOMETHING MUST BE UP ALL RIGHT--!
THERE HE GOES-BACK TOWARD COAST CITY!... IT'S AS IF GL SUDDENLY GOT A WARNING OF TERRIBLE DANGER! BUT WHAT KIND OF DANGER? AND HOW COULD HE HAVE RECEIVED IT HERE IN THE CAR?
2

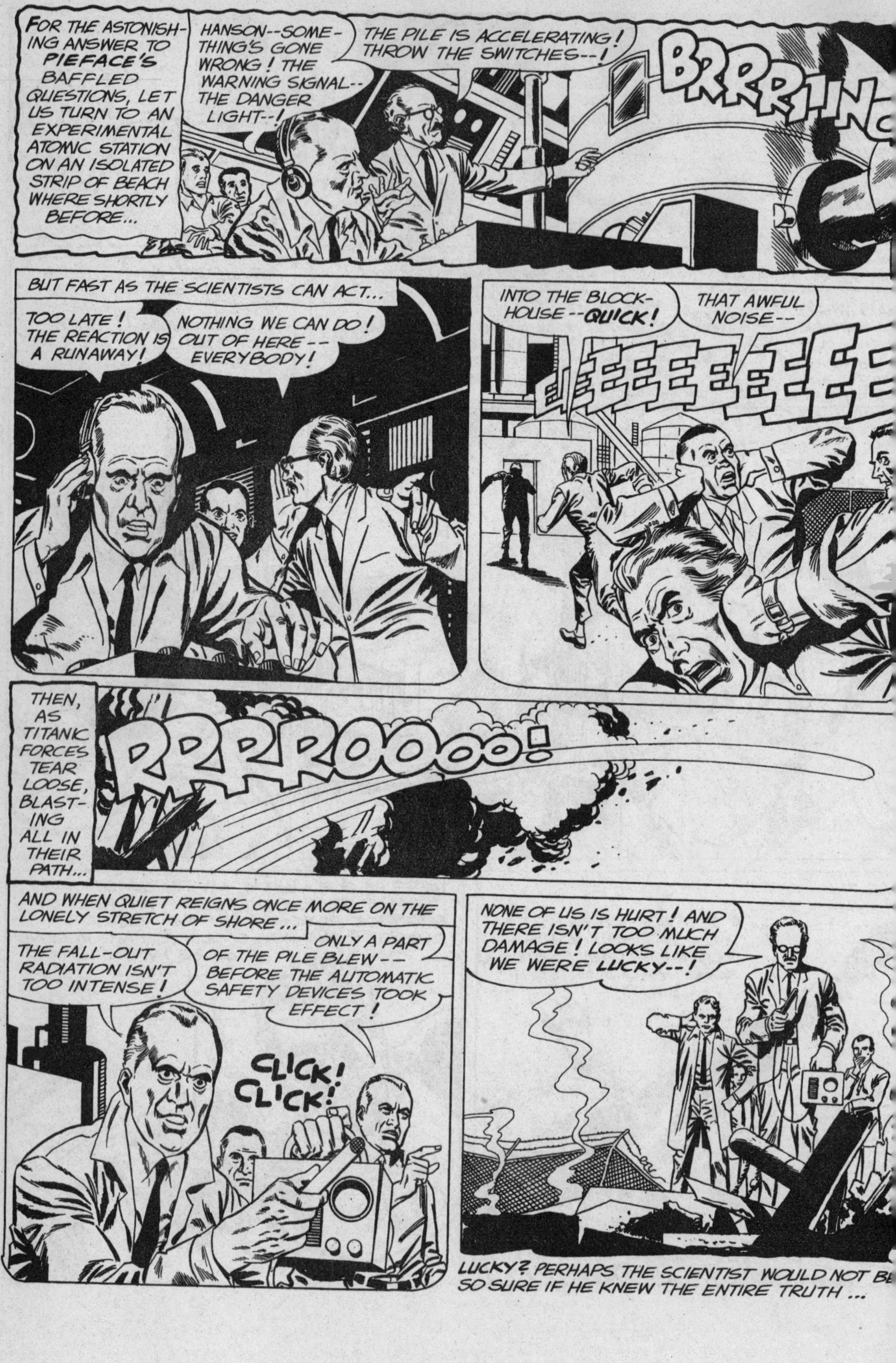
FOR THE ASTONISHING ANSWER TO PIEFACE'S BAFFLED QUESTIONS, LET US TURN TO AN EXPERIMENTAL ATOMIC STATION ON AN ISOLATED STRIP OF BEACH WHERE SHORTLY BEFORE...
HANSON--SOMETHING'S GONE WRONG! THE WARNING SIGNAL--THE DANGER LIGHT--!
THE PILE IS ACCELERATING! THROW THE SWITCHES--!
BRRRIING
BUT FAST AS THE SCIENTISTS CAN ACT...
TOO LATE! THE REACTION IS A RUNAWAY!
NOTHING WE CAN DO! OUT OF HERE--EVERYBODY!
INTO THE BLOCK-HOUSE--QUICK!
THAT AWFUL NOISE--
EEEEEEEEE
THEN, AS TITANIC FORCES TEAR LOOSE, BLASTING ALL IN THEIR PATH...
RRRROOOOO!
AND WHEN QUIET REIGNS ONCE MORE ON THE LONELY STRETCH OF SHORE...
THE FALL-OUT RADIATION ISN'T TOO INTENSE!
ONLY A PART OF THE PILE BLEW--BEFORE THE AUTOMATIC SAFETY DEVICES TOOK EFFECT!
CLICK! CLICK!
NONE OF US IS HURT! AND THERE ISN'T TOO MUCH DAMAGE! LOOKS LIKE WE WERE LUCKY--!
LUCKY? PERHAPS THE SCIENTIST WOULD NOT BE SO SURE IF HE KNEW THE ENTIRE TRUTH ...

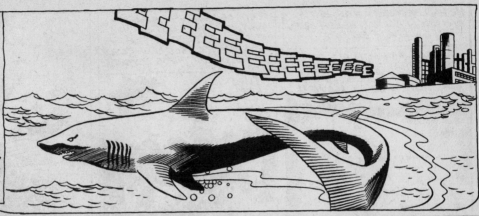

OR ACTUALLY, JUST BEFORE THE FLASH-EXPLOSION, ONE OF THE MOST MONSTROUS DENIZENS OF THE DEEP, A TIGER SHARK, HAD WANDERED IN CLOSE TO SHORE IN HIS CEASELESS SEARCH FOR PREY...

THE FULL FORCE OF THE PRODIGIOUS BLAST STRUCK THE HUGE CREATURE SQUARELY, PENETRATING DEEPLY INTO HIS BRAIN AND NERVE CENTERS ...

... AND PRODUCING A FANTASTIC EFFECT, SENDING THE GIANT CREATURE INTO AN UNCANNY...

...ACCELERATING EVOLUTIONARY SPIRAL...

UNSEEN BY ANY HUMAN EYE, THE CREATURE MANAGED TO REACH THE SHORE, WHERE HE TRAVERSED EVOLUTIONARY EONS IN A MATTER OF MINUTES...

...BECAME MAN AND EVOLVED PAST MAN! BECAME MAN OF A MILLION YEARS FROM NOW...

...WHERE FINALLY THE PROCESS SLOWED... AND CEASED!

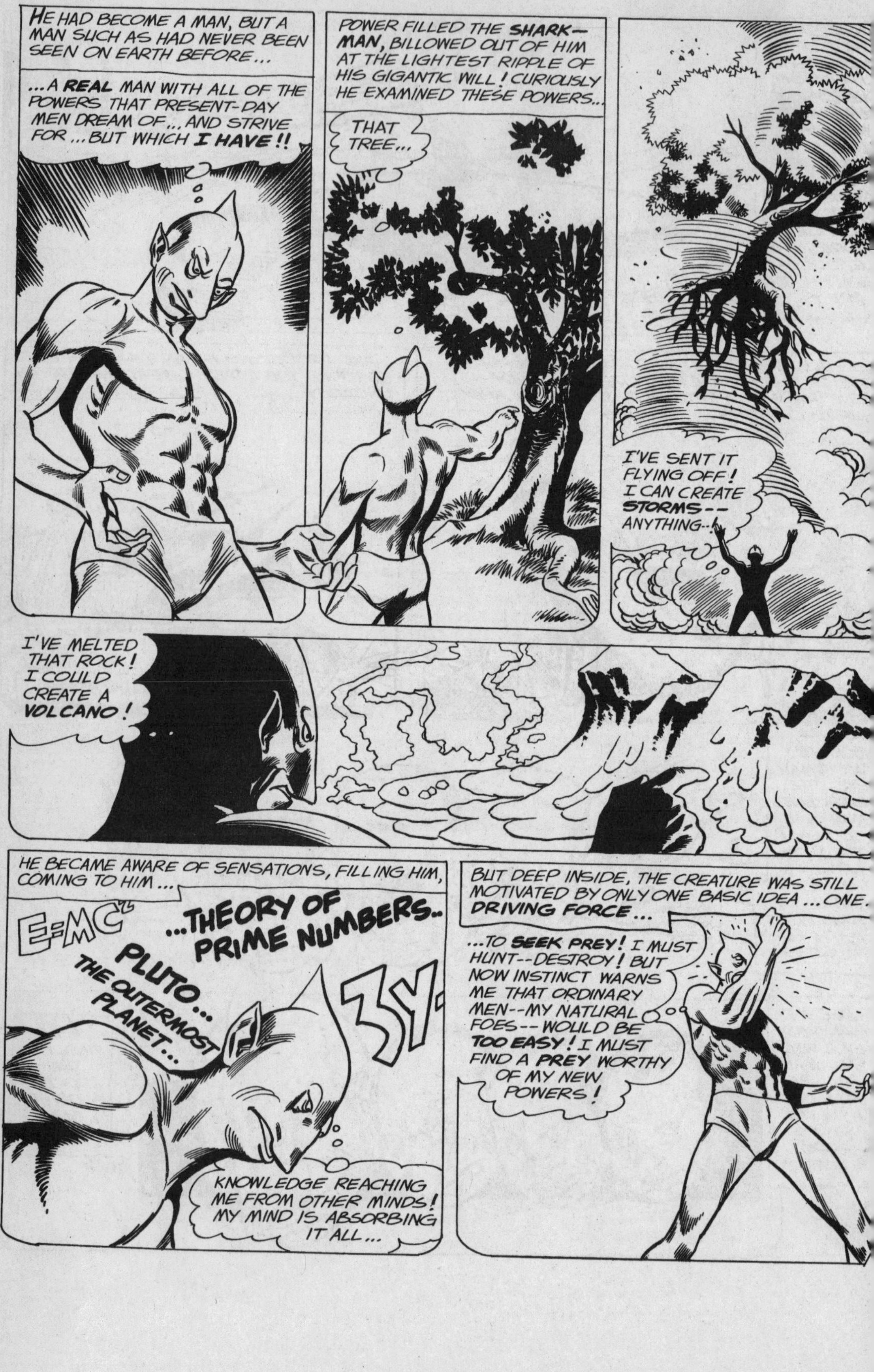
HE HAD BECOME A MAN, BUT A MAN SUCH AS HAD NEVER BEEN SEEN ON EARTH BEFORE...
...A REAL MAN WITH ALL OF THE POWERS THAT PRESENT-DAY MEN DREAM OF..., AND STRIVE FOR ...BUT WHICH I HAVE!!
POWER FILLED THE SHARK-MAN, BILLOWED OUT OF HIM AT THE LIGHTEST RIPPLE OF HIS GIGANTIC WILL! CURIOUSLY HE EXAMINED THESE POWERS...
THAT TREE...
I'VE SENT IT FLYING OFF! I CAN CREATE STORMS-- ANYTHING..!
I'VE MELTED THAT ROCK! I COULD CREATE A VOLCANO!
HE BECAME AWARE OF SENSATIONS, FILLING HIM, COMING TO HIM...
E=MC²
...THEORY OF PRIME NUMBERS..
PLUTO... THE OUTERMOST PLANET...
KNOWLEDGE REACHING ME FROM OTHER MINDS! MY MIND IS ABSORBING IT ALL...
BUT DEEP INSIDE, THE CREATURE WAS STILL MOTIVATED BY ONLY ONE BASIC IDEA ...ONE DRIVING FORCE...
...TO SEEK PREY! I MUST HUNT--DESTROY! BUT NOW INSTINCT WARNS ME THAT ORDINARY MEN--MY NATURAL FOES--WOULD BE TOO EASY! I MUST FIND A PREY WORTHY OF MY NEW POWERS!

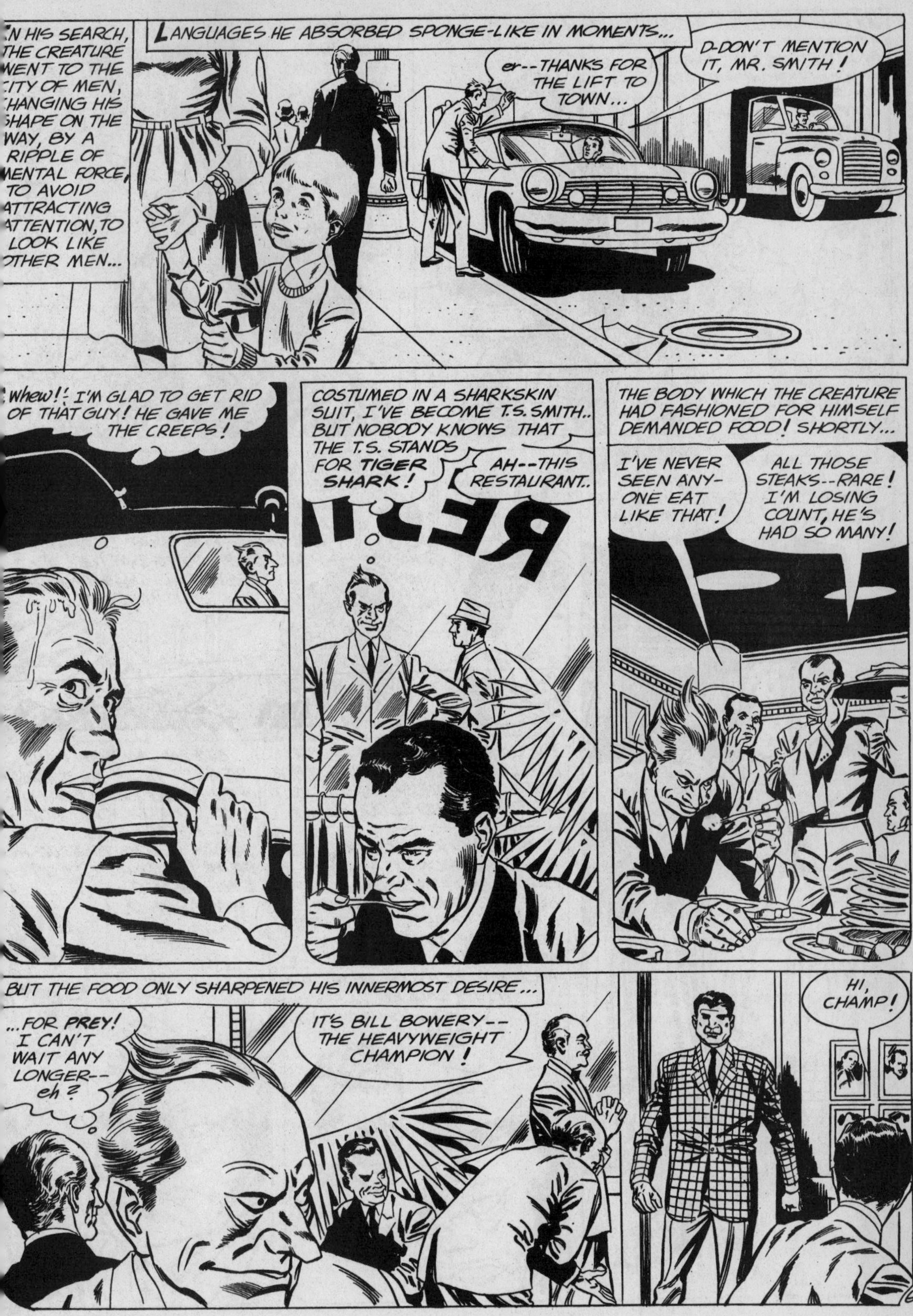
IN HIS SEARCH, THE CREATURE WENT TO THE CITY OF MEN, CHANGING HIS SHAPE ON THE WAY, BY A RIPPLE OF MENTAL FORCE, TO AVOID ATTRACTING ATTENTION, TO LOOK LIKE OTHER MEN...
LANGUAGES HE ABSORBED SPONGE-LIKE IN MOMENTS...
er--THANKS FOR THE LIFT TO TOWN...
D-DON'T MENTION IT, MR. SMITH!
Whew!-I'M GLAD TO GET RID OF THAT GUY! HE GAVE ME THE CREEPS!
COSTUMED IN A SHARKSKIN SUIT, I'VE BECOME T.S. SMITH.. BUT NOBODY KNOWS THAT THE T.S. STANDS FOR TIGER SHARK!
AH--THIS RESTAURANT..
THE BODY WHICH THE CREATURE HAD FASHIONED FOR HIMSELF DEMANDED FOOD! SHORTLY...
I'VE NEVER SEEN ANYONE EAT LIKE THAT!
ALL THOSE STEAKS--RARE! I'M LOSING COUNT, HE'S HAD SO MANY!
BUT THE FOOD ONLY SHARPENED HIS INNERMOST DESIRE...
...FOR PREY! I CAN'T WAIT ANY LONGER--eh?
IT'S BILL BOWERY--THE HEAVYWEIGHT CHAMPION!
HI, CHAMP!
6

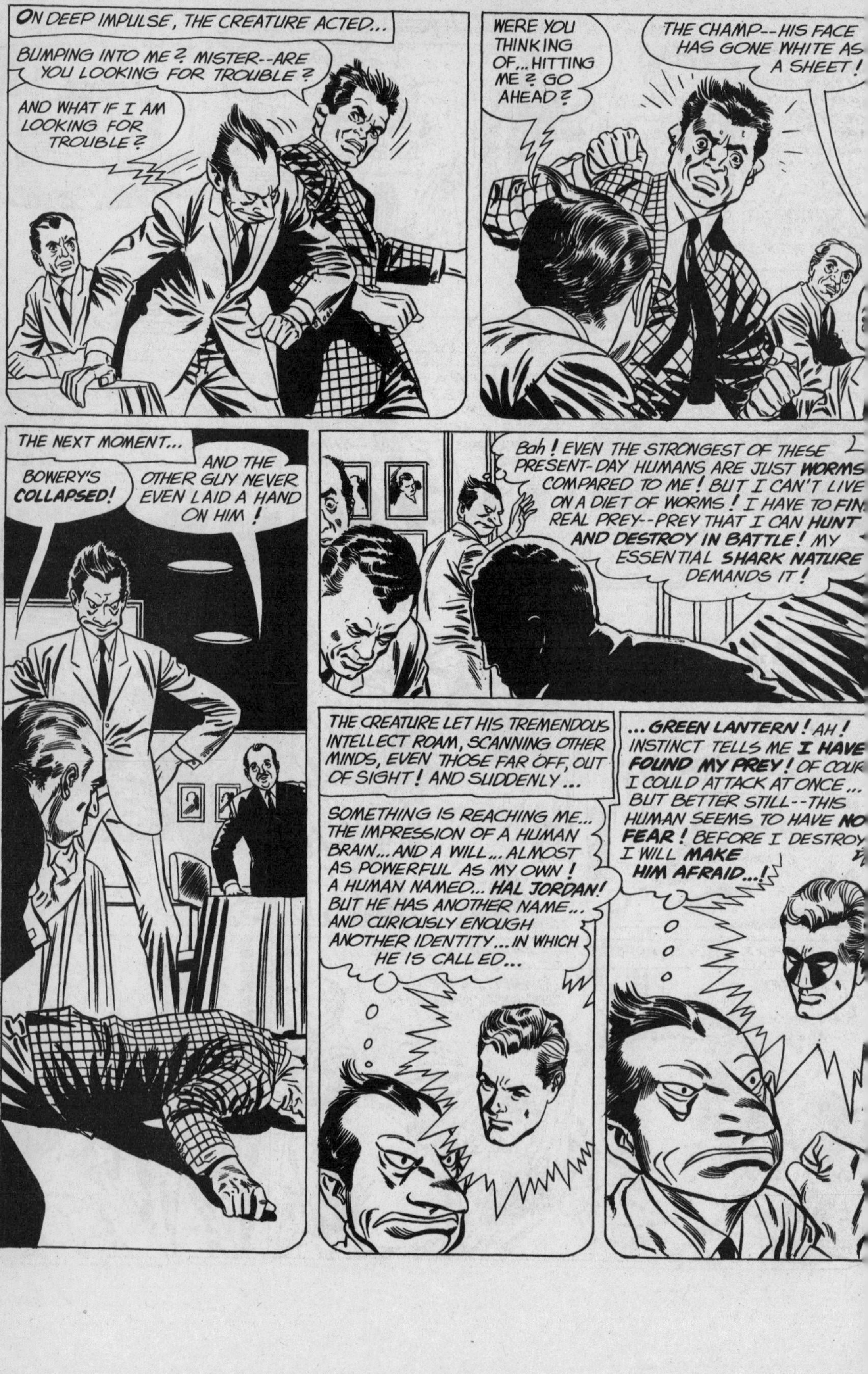
ON DEEP IMPULSE, THE CREATURE ACTED...
BUMPING INTO ME? MISTER--ARE YOU LOOKING FOR TROUBLE?
AND WHAT IF I AM LOOKING FOR TROUBLE?
WERE YOU THINKING OF... HITTING ME? GO AHEAD?
THE CHAMP--HIS FACE HAS GONE WHITE AS A SHEET!
THE NEXT MOMENT...
BOWERY'S COLLAPSED!
AND THE OTHER GUY NEVER EVEN LAID A HAND ON HIM!
Bah! EVEN THE STRONGEST OF THESE PRESENT-DAY HUMANS ARE JUST WORMS COMPARED TO ME! BUT I CAN'T LIVE ON A DIET OF WORMS! I HAVE TO FIN REAL PREY--PREY THAT I CAN HUNT AND DESTROY IN BATTLE! MY ESSENTIAL SHARK NATURE DEMANDS IT!
THE CREATURE LET HIS TREMENDOUS INTELLECT ROAM, SCANNING OTHER MINDS, EVEN THOSE FAR OFF, OUT OF SIGHT! AND SUDDENLY...
SOMETHING IS REACHING ME... THE IMPRESSION OF A HUMAN BRAIN... AND A WILL... ALMOST AS POWERFUL AS MY OWN! A HUMAN NAMED... HAL JORDAN! BUT HE HAS ANOTHER NAME... AND CURIOUSLY ENOUGH ANOTHER IDENTITY... IN WHICH HE IS CALLED...
...GREEN LANTERN! AH! INSTINCT TELLS ME I HAVE FOUND MY PREY! OF COUR I COULD ATTACK AT ONCE... BUT BETTER STILL--THIS HUMAN SEEMS TO HAVE NO FEAR! BEFORE I DESTROY I WILL MAKE HIM AFRAID...!

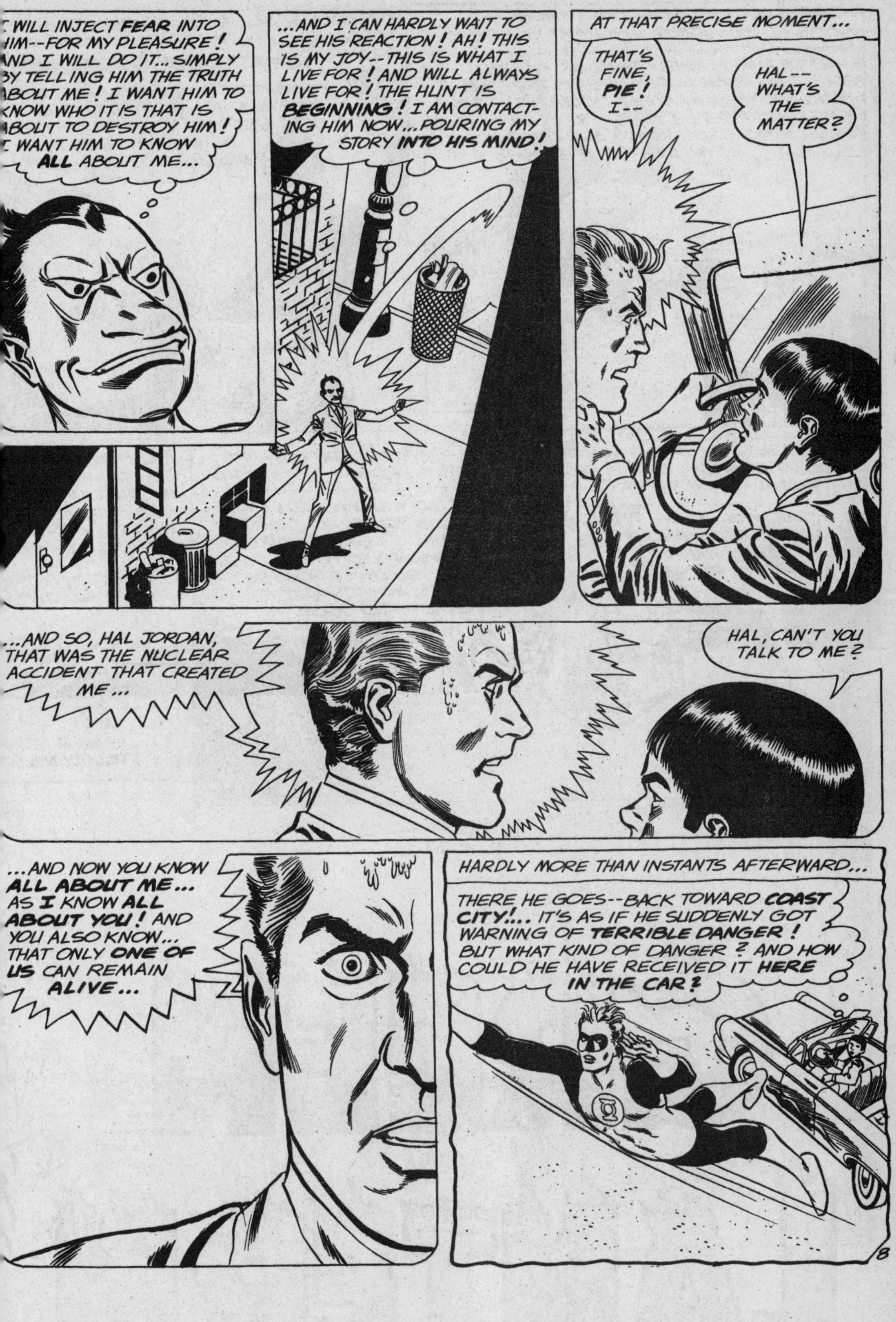
I WILL INJECT FEAR INTO HIM--FOR MY PLEASURE! AND I WILL DO IT... SIMPLY BY TELLING HIM THE TRUTH ABOUT ME! I WANT HIM TO KNOW WHO IT IS THAT IS ABOUT TO DESTROY HIM! I WANT HIM TO KNOW ALL ABOUT ME...
...AND I CAN HARDLY WAIT TO SEE HIS REACTION! AH! THIS IS MY JOY--THIS IS WHAT I LIVE FOR! AND WILL ALWAYS LIVE FOR! THE HUNT IS BEGINNING! I AM CONTACTING HIM NOW... POURING MY STORY INTO HIS MIND!
AT THAT PRECISE MOMENT...
THAT'S FINE, PIE! I--
HAL--WHAT'S THE MATTER?
...AND SO, HAL JORDAN, THAT WAS THE NUCLEAR ACCIDENT THAT CREATED ME...
HAL, CAN'T YOU TALK TO ME?
...AND NOW YOU KNOW ALL ABOUT ME... AS I KNOW ALL ABOUT YOU! AND YOU ALSO KNOW... THAT ONLY ONE OF US CAN REMAIN ALIVE...
HARDLY MORE THAN INSTANTS AFTERWARD...
THERE HE GOES--BACK TOWARD COAST CITY!... IT'S AS IF HE SUDDENLY GOT WARNING OF TERRIBLE DANGER! BUT WHAT KIND OF DANGER? AND HOW COULD HE HAVE RECEIVED IT HERE IN THE CAR?
8

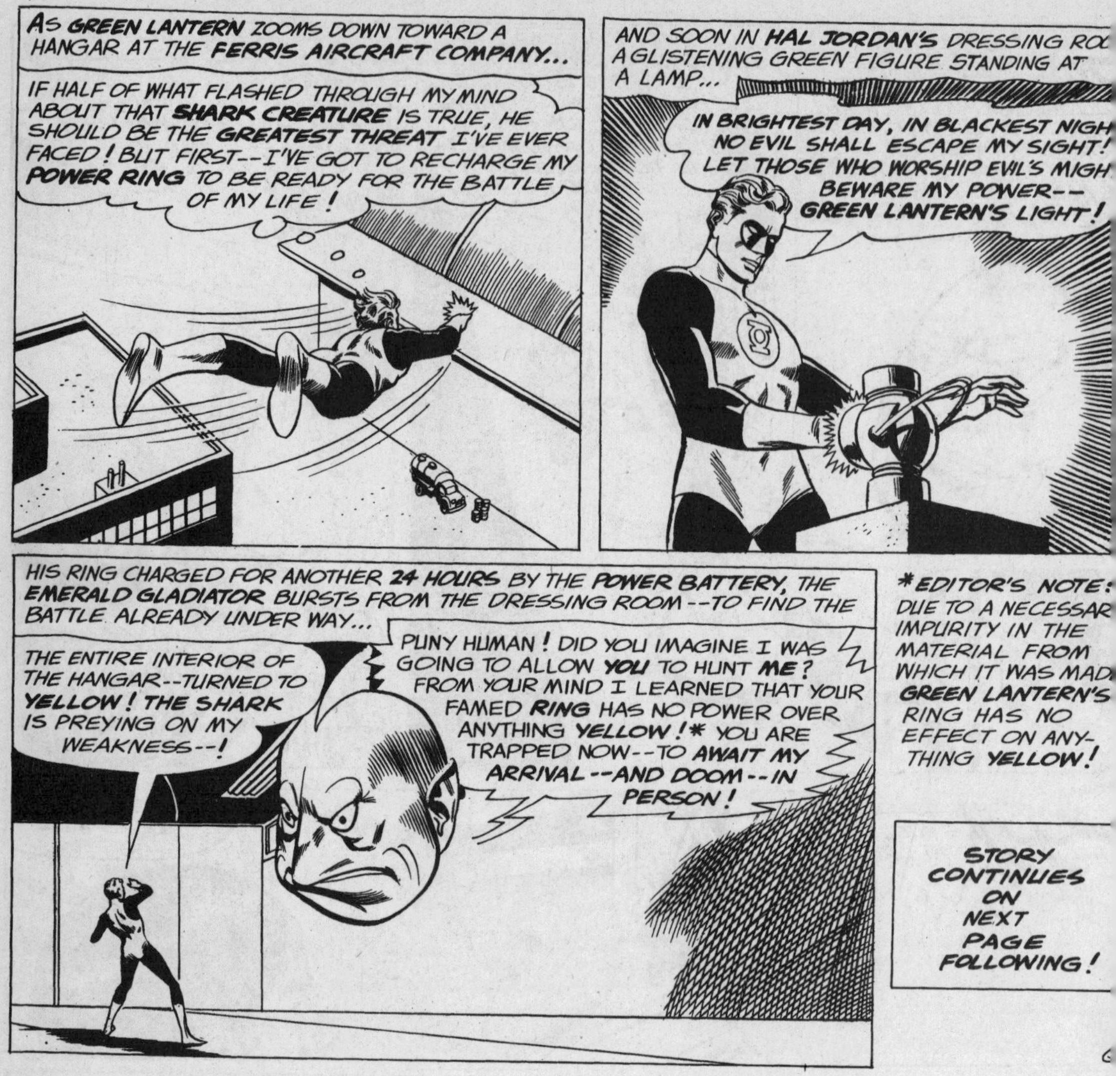
AS GREEN LANTERN ZOOMS DOWN TOWARD A HANGAR AT THE FERRIS AIRCRAFT COMPANY...
IF HALF OF WHAT FLASHED THROUGH MY MIND ABOUT THAT SHARK CREATURE IS TRUE, HE SHOULD BE THE GREATEST THREAT I'VE EVER FACED! BUT FIRST--I'VE GOT TO RECHARGE MY POWER RING TO BE READY FOR THE BATTLE OF MY LIFE!
AND SOON IN HAL JORDAN'S DRESSING RO
A GLISTENING GREEN FIGURE STANDING AT A LAMP...
IN BRIGHTEST DAY, IN BLACKEST NIGH NO EVIL SHALL ESCAPE MY SIGHT! LET THOSE WHO WORSHIP EVIL'S MIGH BEWARE MY POWER-- GREEN LANTERN'S LIGHT!
HIS RING CHARGED FOR ANOTHER 24 HOURS BY THE POWER BATTERY, THE EMERALD GLADIATOR BURSTS FROM THE DRESSING ROOM --TO FIND THE BATTLE ALREADY UNDER WAY...
THE ENTIRE INTERIOR OF THE HANGAR--TURNED TO YELLOW! THE SHARK IS PREYING ON MY WEAKNESS--!
PUNY HUMAN! DID YOU IMAGINE I WAS GOING TO ALLOW YOU TO HUNT ME? FROM YOUR MIND I LEARNED THAT YOUR FAMED RING HAS NO POWER OVER ANYTHING YELLOW!* YOU ARE TRAPPED NOW--TO AWAIT MY ARRIVAL--AND DOOM--IN PERSON!
*EDITOR'S NOTE: DUE TO A NECESSAR IMPURITY IN THE MATERIAL FROM WHICH IT WAS MAD GREEN LANTERN'S RING HAS NO EFFECT ON ANYTHING YELLOW!
STORY CONTINUES ON NEXT PAGE FOLLOWING!

GREEN LANTERN

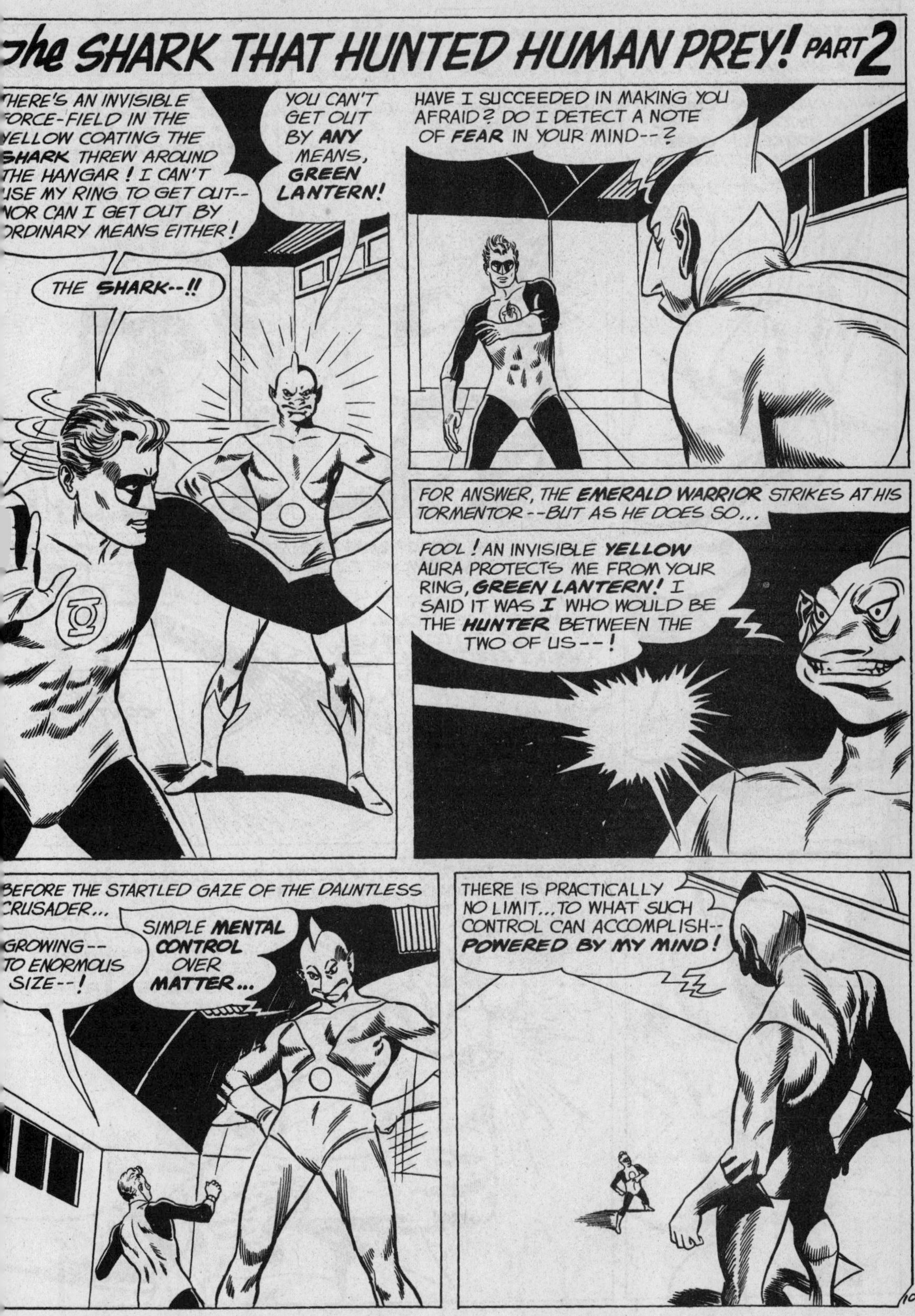

The SHARK THAT HUNTED HUMAN PREY! PART 2
THERE'S AN INVISIBLE FORCE-FIELD IN THE YELLOW COATING THE SHARK THREW AROUND THE HANGAR! I CAN'T USE MY RING TO GET OUT-- NOR CAN I GET OUT BY ORDINARY MEANS EITHER!
YOU CAN'T GET OUT BY ANY MEANS, GREEN LANTERN!
THE SHARK--!!
HAVE I SUCCEEDED IN MAKING YOU AFRAID? DO I DETECT A NOTE OF FEAR IN YOUR MIND--?
FOR ANSWER, THE EMERALD WARRIOR STRIKES AT HIS TORMENTOR--BUT AS HE DOES SO...
FOOL! AN INVISIBLE YELLOW AURA PROTECTS ME FROM YOUR RING, GREEN LANTERN! I SAID IT WAS I WHO WOULD BE THE HUNTER BETWEEN THE TWO OF US--!
BEFORE THE STARTLED GAZE OF THE DAUNTLESS CRUSADER...
GROWING-- TO ENORMOUS SIZE--!
SIMPLE MENTAL CONTROL OVER MATTER...
THERE IS PRACTICALLY NO LIMIT...TO WHAT SUCH CONTROL CAN ACCOMPLISH-- POWERED BY MY MIND!
10

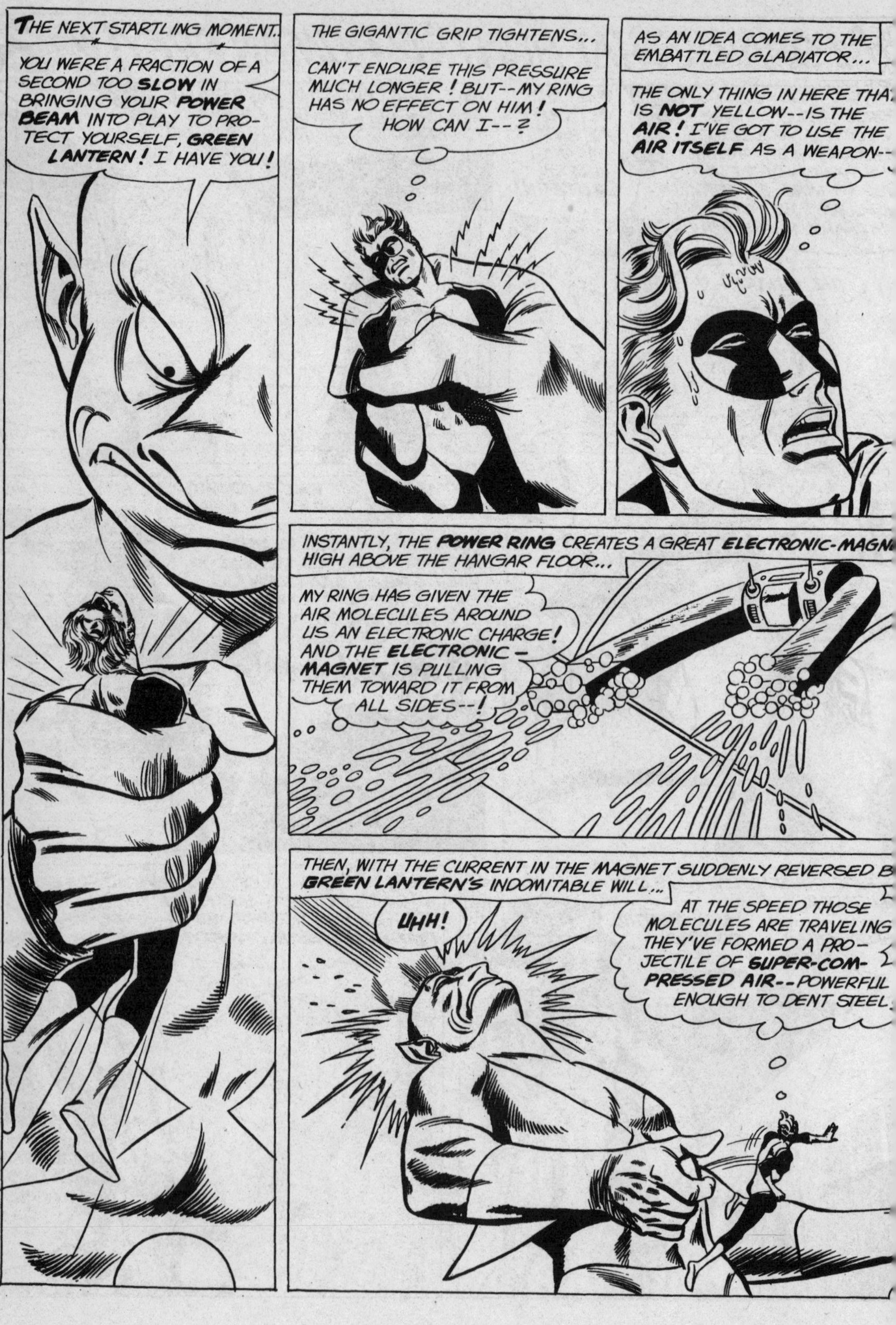
THE NEXT STARTLING MOMENT...
YOU WERE A FRACTION OF A SECOND TOO SLOW IN BRINGING YOUR POWER BEAM INTO PLAY TO PROTECT YOURSELF, GREEN LANTERN! I HAVE YOU!
THE GIGANTIC GRIP TIGHTENS...
CAN'T ENDURE THIS PRESSURE MUCH LONGER! BUT--MY RING HAS NO EFFECT ON HIM! HOW CAN I--?
AS AN IDEA COMES TO THE EMBATTLED GLADIATOR...
THE ONLY THING IN HERE THA IS NOT YELLOW--IS THE AIR! I'VE GOT TO USE THE AIR ITSELF AS A WEAPON--
INSTANTLY, THE POWER RING CREATES A GREAT ELECTRONIC-MAGN HIGH ABOVE THE HANGAR FLOOR...
MY RING HAS GIVEN THE AIR MOLECULES AROUND US AN ELECTRONIC CHARGE! AND THE ELECTRONIC-MAGNET IS PULLING THEM TOWARD IT FROM ALL SIDES--!
THEN, WITH THE CURRENT IN THE MAGNET SUDDENLY REVERSED B GREEN LANTERN'S INDOMITABLE WILL...
UHH!
AT THE SPEED THOSE MOLECULES ARE TRAVELING THEY'VE FORMED A PROJECTILE OF SUPER-COMPRESSED AIR--POWERFUL ENOUGH TO DENT STEEL

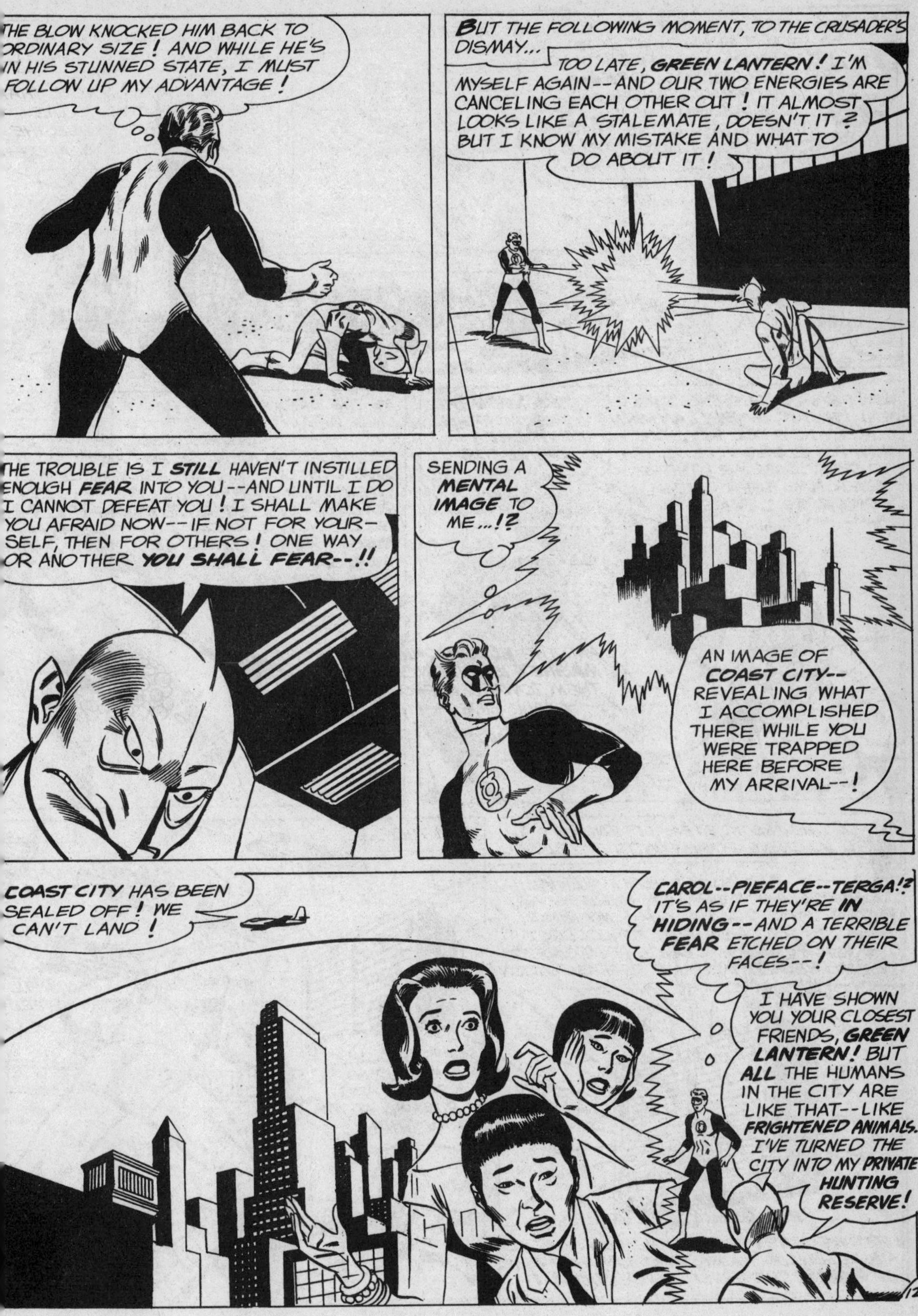
THE BLOW KNOCKED HIM BACK TO ORDINARY SIZE! AND WHILE HE'S IN HIS STUNNED STATE, I MUST FOLLOW UP MY ADVANTAGE!
BUT THE FOLLOWING MOMENT, TO THE CRUSADER'S DISMAY...
TOO LATE, GREEN LANTERN! I'M MYSELF AGAIN--AND OUR TWO ENERGIES ARE CANCELING EACH OTHER OUT! IT ALMOST LOOKS LIKE A STALEMATE, DOESN'T IT? BUT I KNOW MY MISTAKE AND WHAT TO DO ABOUT IT!
THE TROUBLE IS I STILL HAVEN'T INSTILLED ENOUGH FEAR INTO YOU--AND UNTIL I DO I CANNOT DEFEAT YOU! I SHALL MAKE YOU AFRAID NOW--IF NOT FOR YOURSELF, THEN FOR OTHERS! ONE WAY OR ANOTHER YOU SHALL FEAR--!!
SENDING A MENTAL IMAGE TO ME...!?
AN IMAGE OF COAST CITY--REVEALING WHAT I ACCOMPLISHED THERE WHILE YOU WERE TRAPPED HERE BEFORE MY ARRIVAL--!
COAST CITY HAS BEEN SEALED OFF! WE CAN'T LAND!
CAROL--PIEFACE--TERGA!? IT'S AS IF THEY'RE IN HIDING--AND A TERRIBLE FEAR ETCHED ON THEIR FACES--!
I HAVE SHOWN YOU YOUR CLOSEST FRIENDS, GREEN LANTERN! BUT ALL THE HUMANS IN THE CITY ARE LIKE THAT--LIKE FRIGHTENED ANIMALS. I'VE TURNED THE CITY INTO MY PRIVATE HUNTING RESERVE!
12

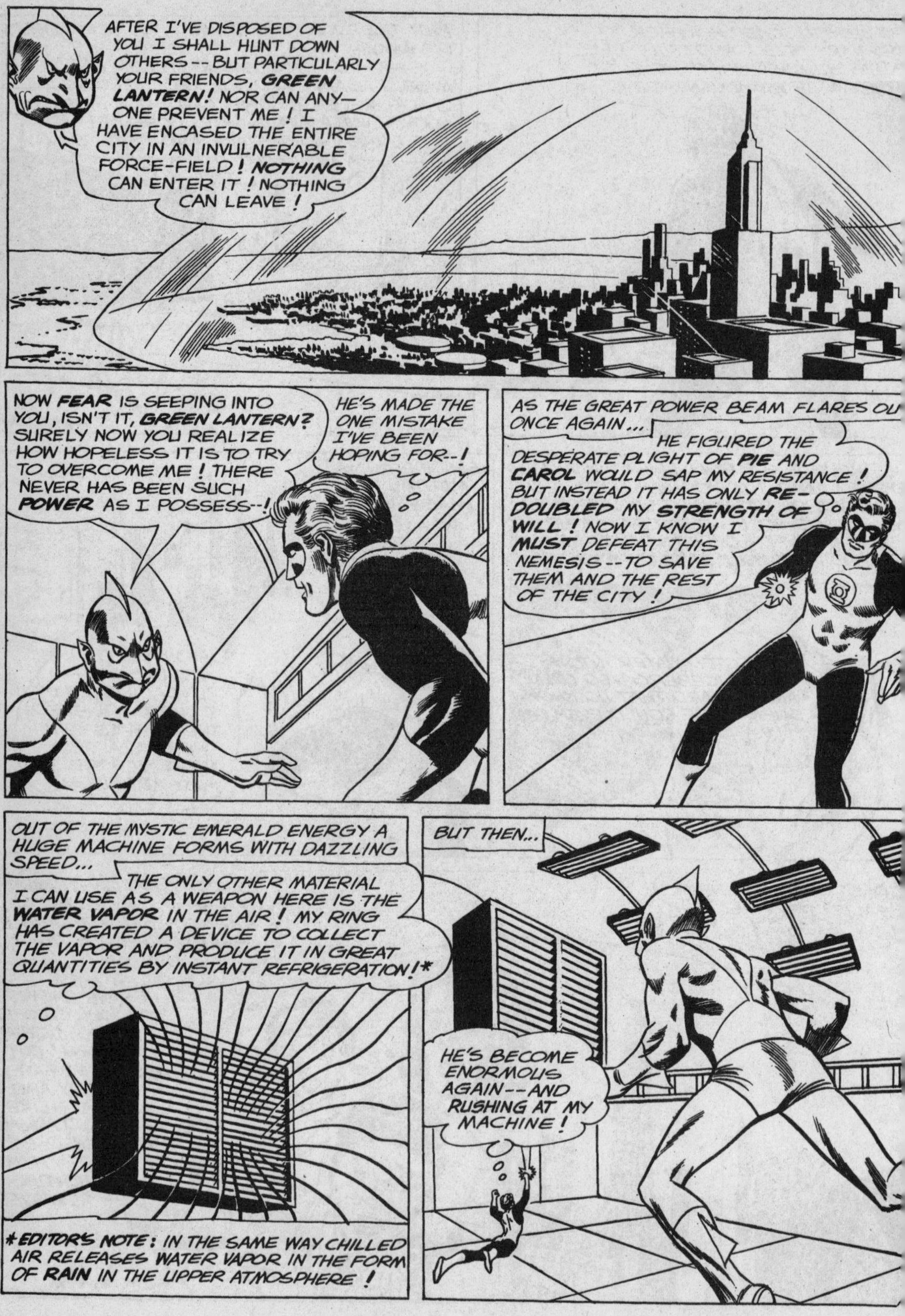
AFTER I'VE DISPOSED OF YOU I SHALL HUNT DOWN OTHERS -- BUT PARTICULARLY YOUR FRIENDS, GREEN LANTERN! NOR CAN ANY-ONE PREVENT ME! I HAVE ENCASED THE ENTIRE CITY IN AN INVULNERABLE FORCE-FIELD! NOTHING CAN ENTER IT! NOTHING CAN LEAVE!
NOW FEAR IS SEEPING INTO YOU, ISN'T IT, GREEN LANTERN? SURELY NOW YOU REALIZE HOW HOPELESS IT IS TO TRY TO OVERCOME ME! THERE NEVER HAS BEEN SUCH POWER AS I POSSESS--!
HE'S MADE THE ONE MISTAKE I'VE BEEN HOPING FOR--!
AS THE GREAT POWER BEAM FLARES OU ONCE AGAIN...
HE FIGURED THE DESPERATE PLIGHT OF PIE AND CAROL WOULD SAP MY RESISTANCE! BUT INSTEAD IT HAS ONLY RE-DOUBLED MY STRENGTH OF WILL! NOW I KNOW I MUST DEFEAT THIS NEMESIS--TO SAVE THEM AND THE REST OF THE CITY!
OUT OF THE MYSTIC EMERALD ENERGY A HUGE MACHINE FORMS WITH DAZZLING SPEED...
THE ONLY OTHER MATERIAL I CAN USE AS A WEAPON HERE IS THE WATER VAPOR IN THE AIR! MY RING HAS CREATED A DEVICE TO COLLECT THE VAPOR AND PRODUCE IT IN GREAT QUANTITIES BY INSTANT REFRIGERATION!*
*EDITOR'S NOTE: IN THE SAME WAY CHILLED AIR RELEASES WATER VAPOR IN THE FORM OF RAIN IN THE UPPER ATMOSPHERE!
BUT THEN...
HE'S BECOME ENORMOUS AGAIN--AND RUSHING AT MY MACHINE!

AS HIS MONSTROUS FOE LUNGES FORWARD, GREEN LANTERN BARELY HAS THE MOMENT HE NEEDS TO CARRY OUT HIS PLAN...

MY RING TURNED THE COLLECTED WATER INTO A GREAT ICEBERG--SO COLD AND SO HARD THAT NO KNOWN SUBSTANCE COULD EVEN DENT IT! AND AS THE SHARK SPRANG AT IT, I MOVED THE ICEBERG AT HIM-- WITH EVERY OUNCE OF MY POWER BEHIND IT!

HE'S BACK TO HIS FORMER SIZE AGAIN--AND UNCONSCIOUS! I'VE GOT TO ACT FAST--FIND A WAY OF RENDERING HIM HELP- LESS--BEFORE HE CAN COME TO!

MY RING CAN HANDLE HIM NOW! APPARENTLY THAT INVISIBLE YELLOW AURA THAT PROTECTED HIM FROM ME IS ACTIVATED BY HIS MENTAL ENERGY--AND HE CAN'T SUSTAIN IT WHILE HE'S UNCONSCIOUS! BUT THAT STILL DOESN'T TELL ME HOW TO SECURE HIM PERMANENTLY--!

THEN, AN INSPIRATION COMES TO THE GRIM GLADIATOR...

BY USING MY POWER BEAM TO PENETRATE HIS MIND, I'VE LEARNED THE ANSWER--BURIED DEEP IN HIS BRAIN! THERE IS ONE FORM IN WHICH MY FOE WOULD BE HELPLESS-- AND NEVER AGAIN CAPABLE OF MENACING ANYONE ON EARTH--

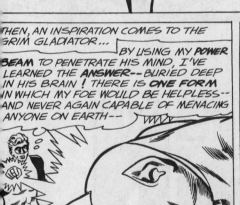

--HIS ORIGINAL SHAPE OF A TIGER SHARK! THE SHAPE FROM WHICH HE STARTED HIS WILD EVOLUTIONARY ASCENT!

IN A TWINKLING THE GREEN RAY HAS TURNED THE DAZED MAN-THING BACK INTO A TIGER SHARK!

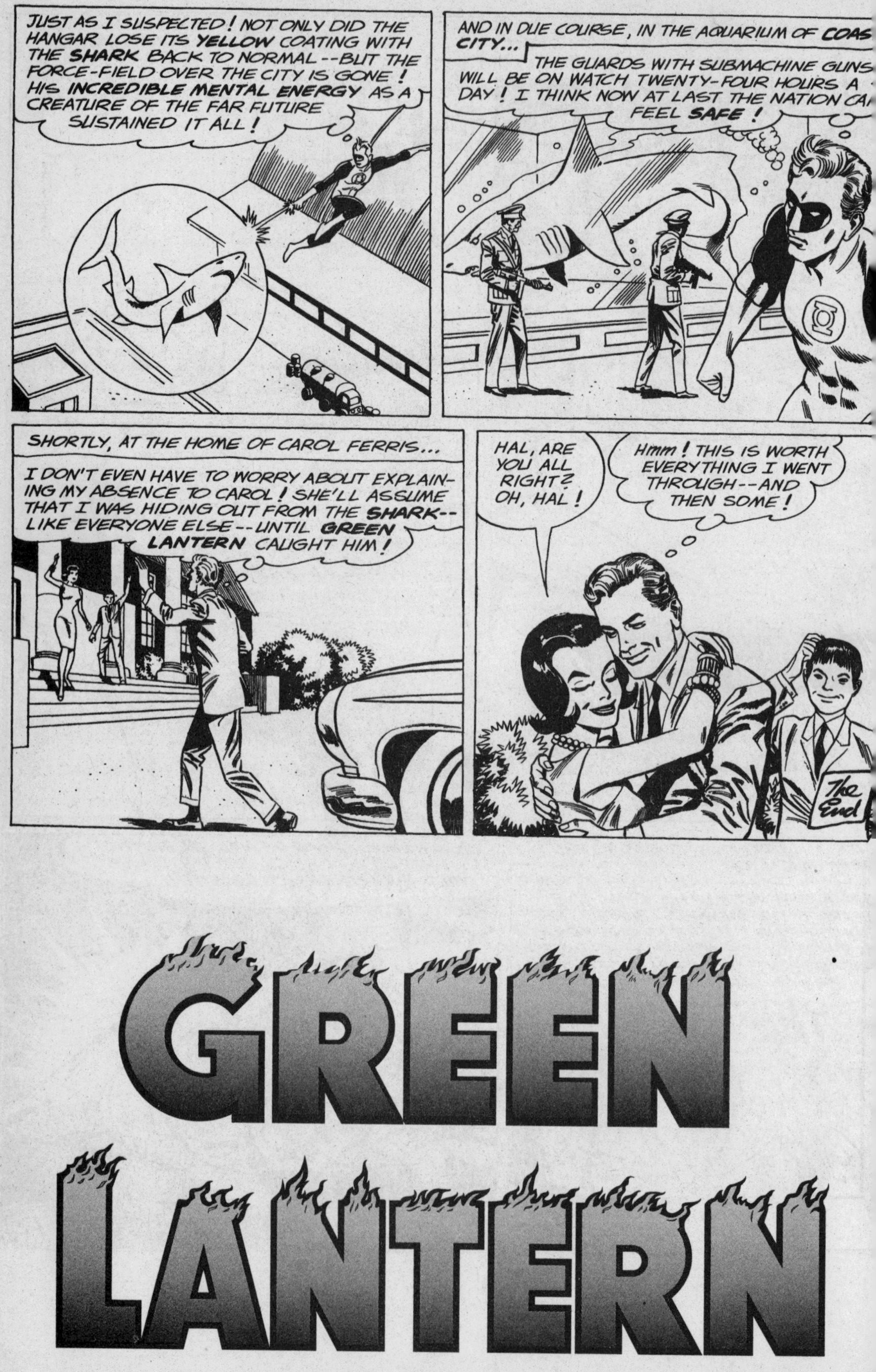
JUST AS I SUSPECTED! NOT ONLY DID THE HANGAR LOSE ITS YELLOW COATING WITH THE SHARK BACK TO NORMAL--BUT THE FORCE-FIELD OVER THE CITY IS GONE! HIS INCREDIBLE MENTAL ENERGY AS A CREATURE OF THE FAR FUTURE SUSTAINED IT ALL!
AND IN DUE COURSE, IN THE AQUARIUM OF COAS CITY...
THE GUARDS WITH SUBMACHINE GUNS WILL BE ON WATCH TWENTY-FOUR HOURS A DAY! I THINK NOW AT LAST THE NATION CA FEEL SAFE!
SHORTLY, AT THE HOME OF CAROL FERRIS...
I DON'T EVEN HAVE TO WORRY ABOUT EXPLAINING MY ABSENCE TO CAROL! SHE'LL ASSUME THAT I WAS HIDING OUT FROM THE SHARK--LIKE EVERYONE ELSE--UNTIL GREEN LANTERN CAUGHT HIM!
HAL, ARE YOU ALL RIGHT? OH, HAL!
Hmm! THIS IS WORTH EVERYTHING I WENT THROUGH--AND THEN SOME!
The End

GREEN LANTERN

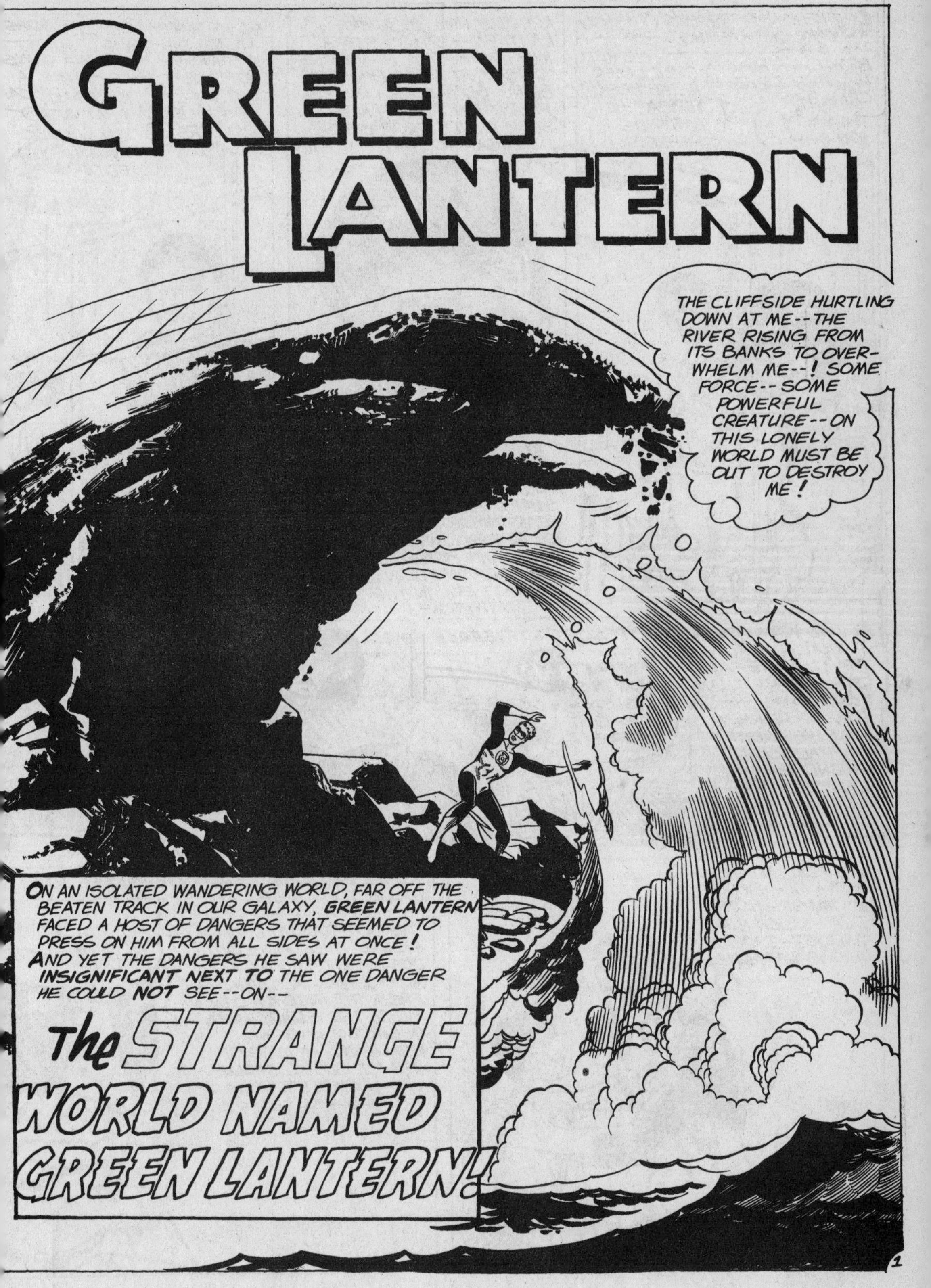
GREEN LANTERN
THE CLIFFSIDE HURTLING DOWN AT ME--THE RIVER RISING FROM ITS BANKS TO OVER-WHELM ME--! SOME FORCE--SOME POWERFUL CREATURE--ON THIS LONELY WORLD MUST BE OUT TO DESTROY ME!
ON AN ISOLATED WANDERING WORLD, FAR OFF THE BEATEN TRACK IN OUR GALAXY, GREEN LANTERN FACED A HOST OF DANGERS THAT SEEMED TO PRESS ON HIM FROM ALL SIDES AT ONCE! AND YET THE DANGERS HE SAW WERE INSIGNIFICANT NEXT TO THE ONE DANGER HE COULD NOT SEE--ON--
The STRANGE WORLD NAMED GREEN LANTERN!
1

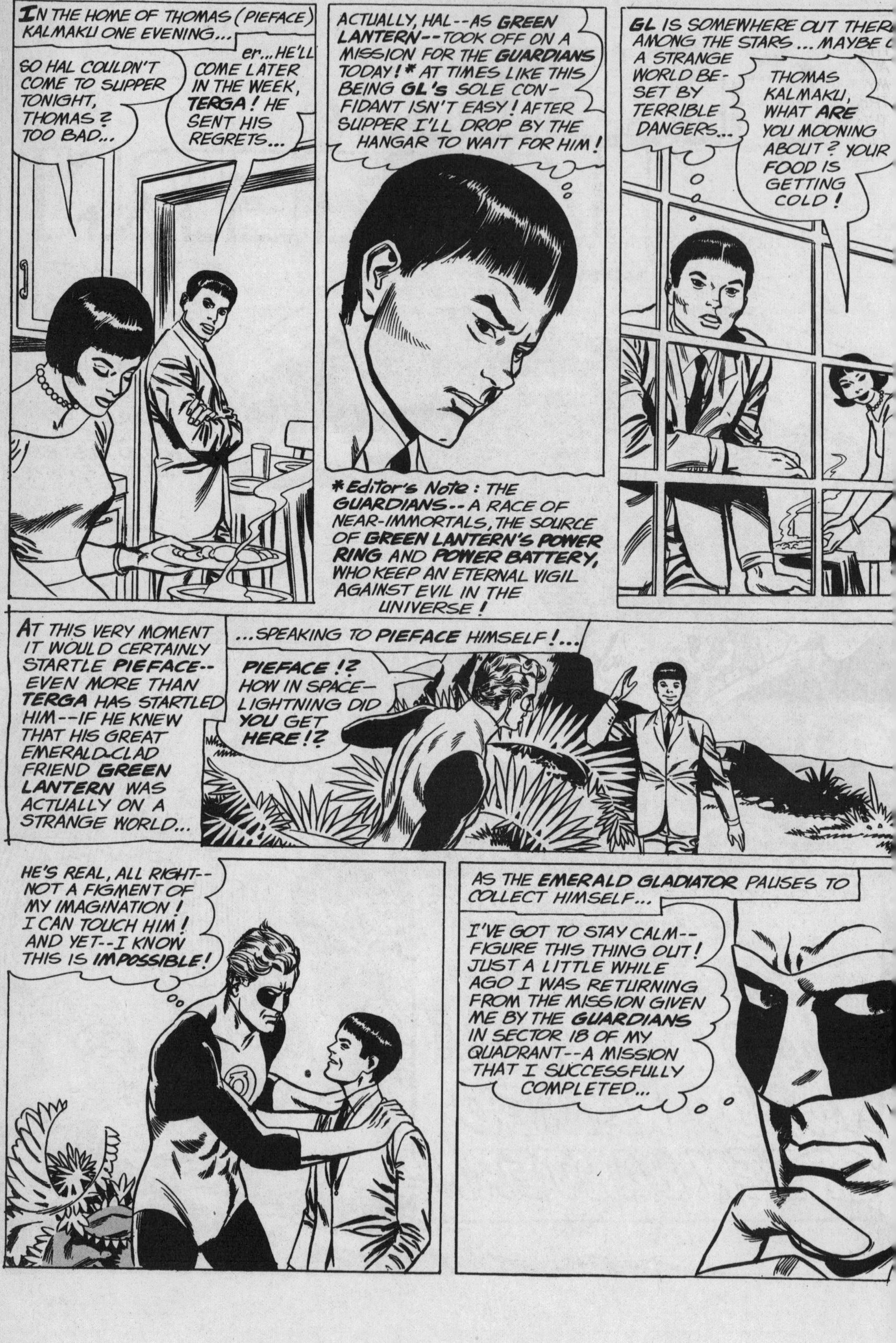
IN THE HOME OF THOMAS (PIEFACE) KALMAKU ONE EVENING...
SO HAL COULDN'T COME TO SUPPER TONIGHT, THOMAS? TOO BAD...
er... HE'LL COME LATER IN THE WEEK, TERGA! HE SENT HIS REGRETS...
ACTUALLY, HAL--AS GREEN LANTERN--TOOK OFF ON A MISSION FOR THE GUARDIANS TODAY!* AT TIMES LIKE THIS BEING GL's SOLE CONFIDANT ISN'T EASY! AFTER SUPPER I'LL DROP BY THE HANGAR TO WAIT FOR HIM!
*Editor's Note: THE GUARDIANS--A RACE OF NEAR-IMMORTALS, THE SOURCE OF GREEN LANTERN'S POWER RING AND POWER BATTERY, WHO KEEP AN ETERNAL VIGIL AGAINST EVIL IN THE UNIVERSE!
GL IS SOMEWHERE OUT THER AMONG THE STARS... MAYBE A STRANGE WORLD BESET BY TERRIBLE DANGERS...
THOMAS KALMAKU, WHAT ARE YOU MOONING ABOUT? YOUR FOOD IS GETTING COLD!
AT THIS VERY MOMENT IT WOULD CERTAINLY STARTLE PIEFACE--EVEN MORE THAN TERGA HAS STARTLED HIM--IF HE KNEW THAT HIS GREAT EMERALD-CLAD FRIEND GREEN LANTERN WAS ACTUALLY ON A STRANGE WORLD...
...SPEAKING TO PIEFACE HIMSELF!...
PIEFACE!? HOW IN SPACE-LIGHTNING DID YOU GET HERE!?
HE'S REAL, ALL RIGHT--NOT A FIGMENT OF MY IMAGINATION! I CAN TOUCH HIM! AND YET--I KNOW THIS IS IMPOSSIBLE!
AS THE EMERALD GLADIATOR PAUSES TO COLLECT HIMSELF...
I'VE GOT TO STAY CALM--FIGURE THIS THING OUT! JUST A LITTLE WHILE AGO I WAS RETURNING FROM THE MISSION GIVEN ME BY THE GUARDIANS IN SECTOR 18 OF MY QUADRANT--A MISSION THAT I SUCCESSFULLY COMPLETED...

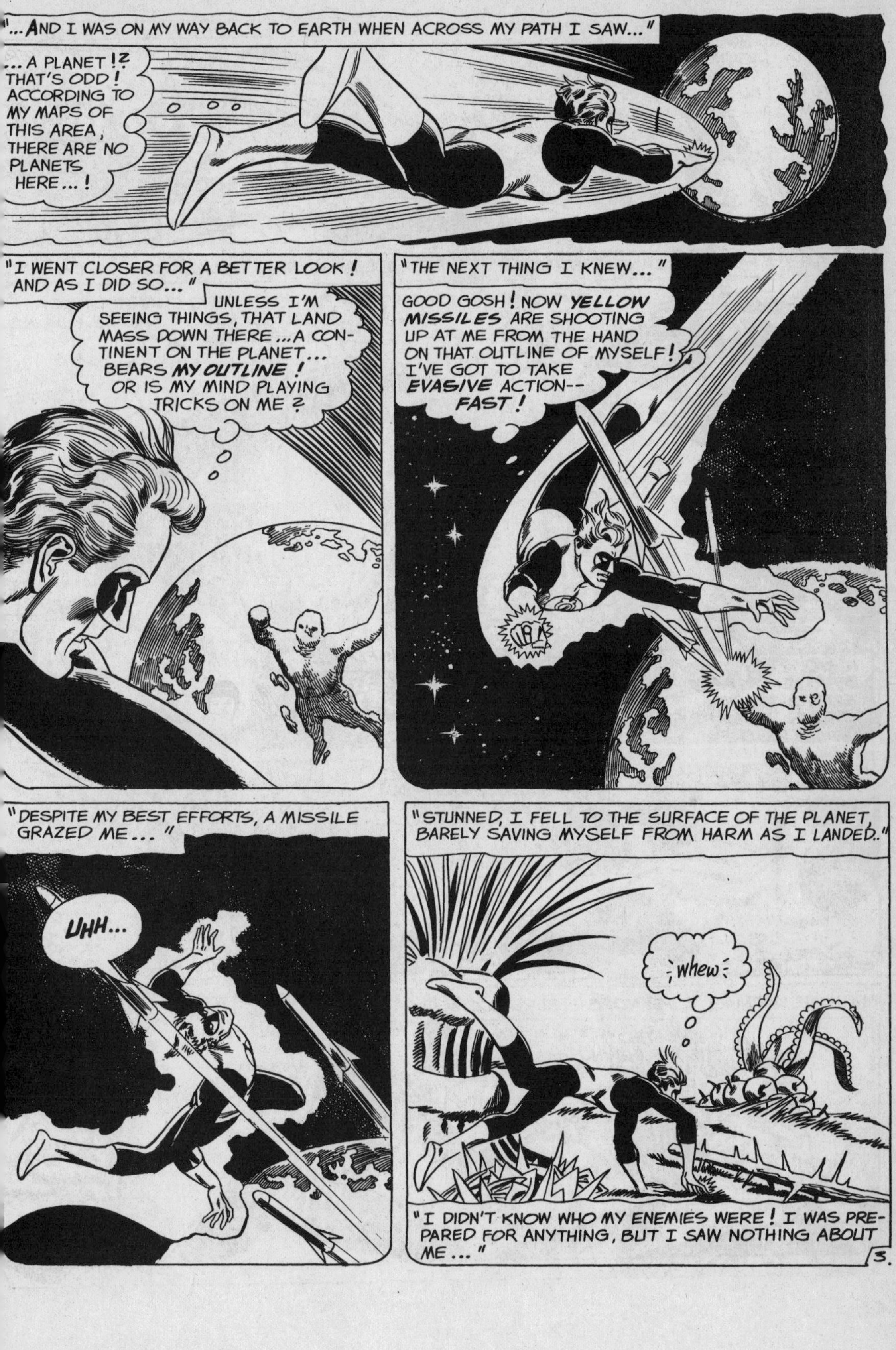
"...AND I WAS ON MY WAY BACK TO EARTH WHEN ACROSS MY PATH I SAW..."
...A PLANET !? THAT'S ODD! ACCORDING TO MY MAPS OF THIS AREA, THERE ARE NO PLANETS HERE...!
"I WENT CLOSER FOR A BETTER LOOK! AND AS I DID SO..."
UNLESS I'M SEEING THINGS, THAT LAND MASS DOWN THERE...A CONTINENT ON THE PLANET... BEARS MY OUTLINE! OR IS MY MIND PLAYING TRICKS ON ME?
"THE NEXT THING I KNEW..."
GOOD GOSH! NOW YELLOW MISSILES ARE SHOOTING UP AT ME FROM THE HAND ON THAT OUTLINE OF MYSELF! I'VE GOT TO TAKE EVASIVE ACTION-- FAST!
"DESPITE MY BEST EFFORTS, A MISSILE GRAZED ME..."
UHH...
"STUNNED, I FELL TO THE SURFACE OF THE PLANET, BARELY SAVING MYSELF FROM HARM AS I LANDED.."
whew
"I DIDN'T KNOW WHO MY ENEMIES WERE! I WAS PREPARED FOR ANYTHING, BUT I SAW NOTHING ABOUT ME..."
3.

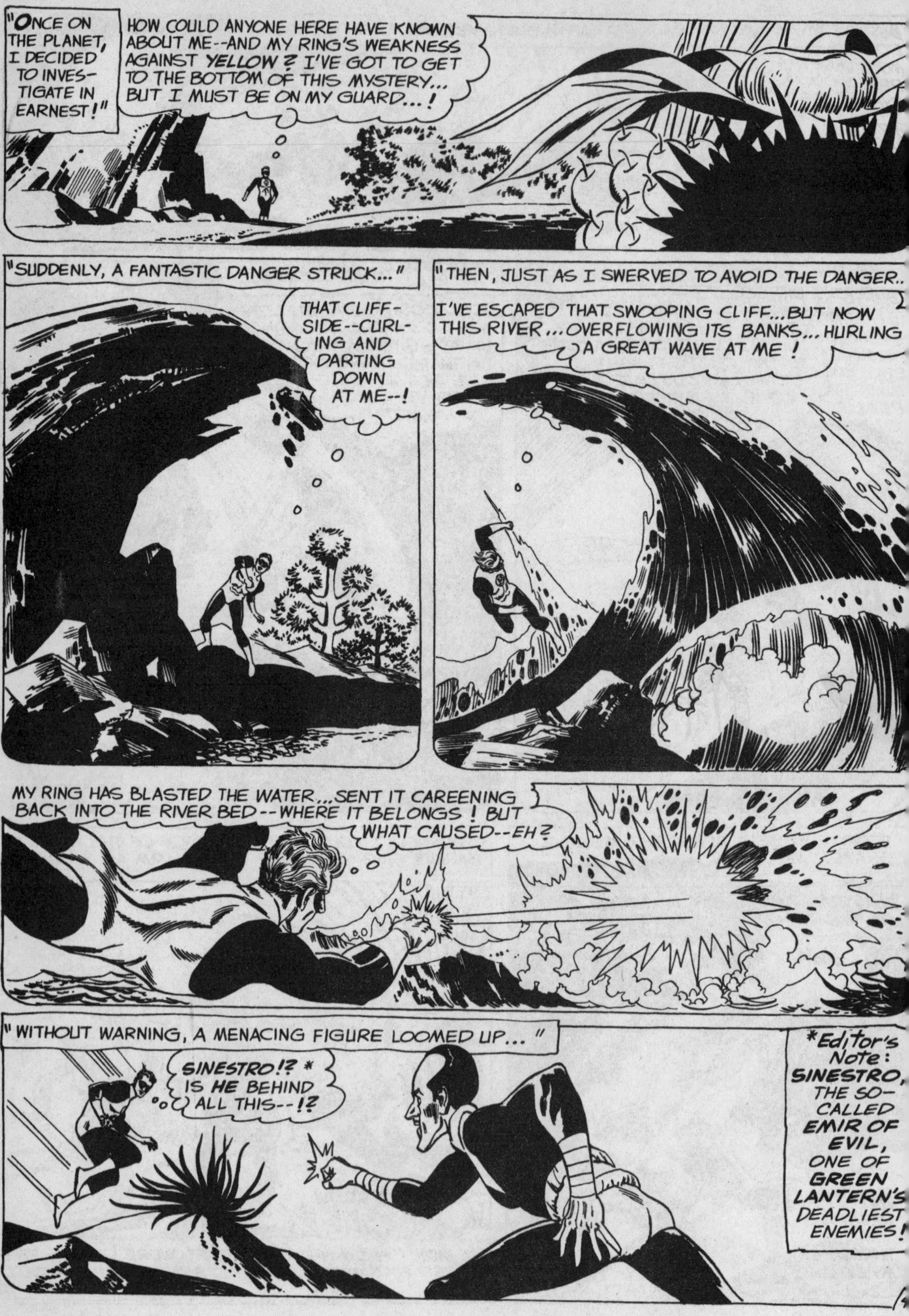
"ONCE ON THE PLANET, I DECIDED TO INVESTIGATE IN EARNEST!"
HOW COULD ANYONE HERE HAVE KNOWN ABOUT ME--AND MY RING'S WEAKNESS AGAINST YELLOW? I'VE GOT TO GET TO THE BOTTOM OF THIS MYSTERY... BUT I MUST BE ON MY GUARD...!
"SUDDENLY, A FANTASTIC DANGER STRUCK..."
THAT CLIFF-SIDE--CURLING AND DARTING DOWN AT ME--!
"THEN, JUST AS I SWERVED TO AVOID THE DANGER..
I'VE ESCAPED THAT SWOOPING CLIFF... BUT NOW THIS RIVER... OVERFLOWING ITS BANKS... HURLING A GREAT WAVE AT ME!
MY RING HAS BLASTED THE WATER... SENT IT CAREENING BACK INTO THE RIVER BED--WHERE IT BELONGS! BUT WHAT CAUSED--EH?
"WITHOUT WARNING, A MENACING FIGURE LOOMED UP..."
SINESTRO!? * IS HE BEHIND ALL THIS--!?
*Editor's Note: SINESTRO, THE SO-CALLED EMIR OF EVIL, ONE OF GREEN LANTERN'S DEADLIEST ENEMIES!

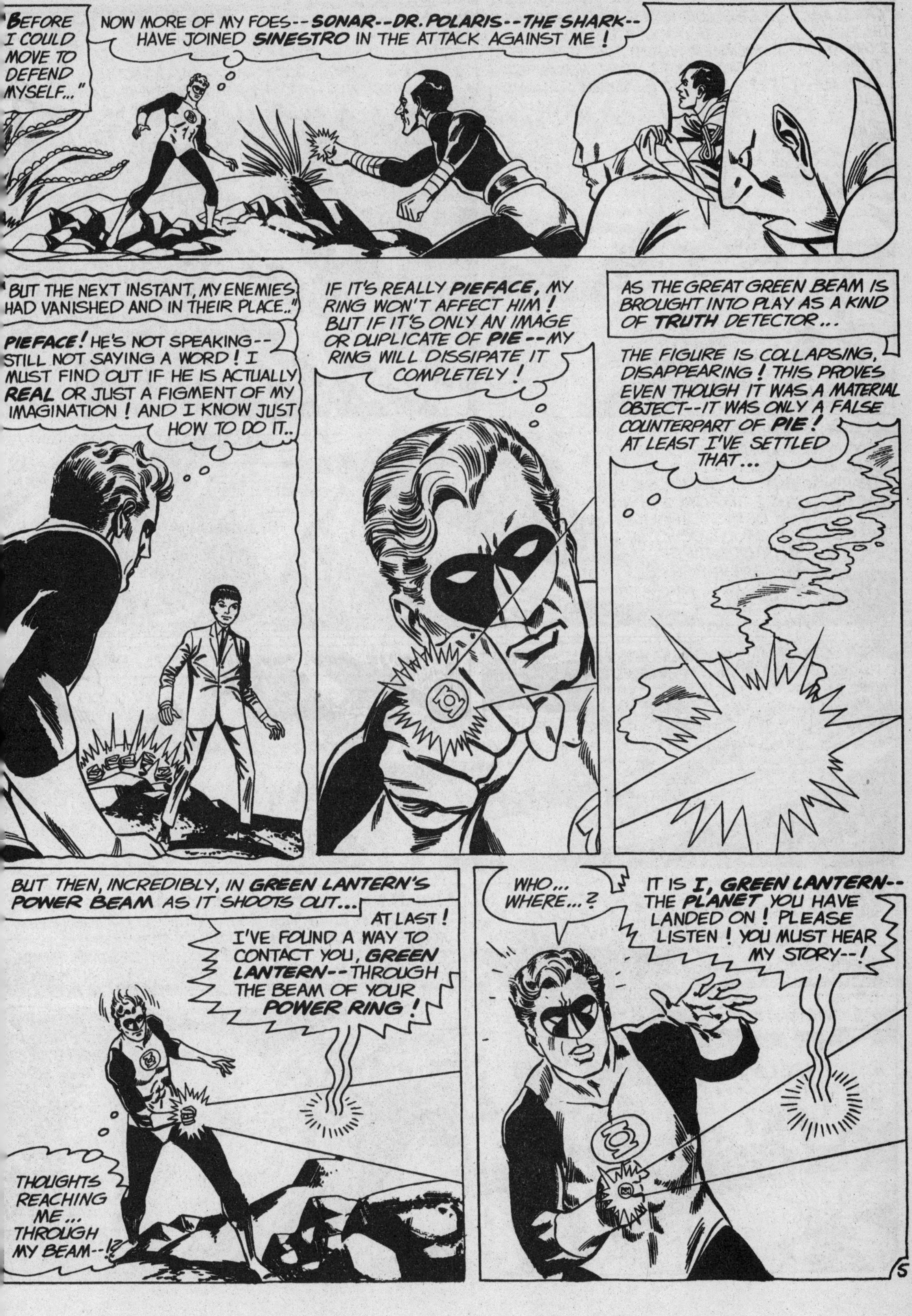
"BEFORE I COULD MOVE TO DEFEND MYSELF..."
NOW MORE OF MY FOES--SONAR--DR. POLARIS--THE SHARK--HAVE JOINED SINESTRO IN THE ATTACK AGAINST ME!
"BUT THE NEXT INSTANT, MY ENEMIES HAD VANISHED AND IN THEIR PLACE.."
PIEFACE! HE'S NOT SPEAKING--STILL NOT SAYING A WORD! I MUST FIND OUT IF HE IS ACTUALLY REAL OR JUST A FIGMENT OF MY IMAGINATION! AND I KNOW JUST HOW TO DO IT..
IF IT'S REALLY PIEFACE, MY RING WON'T AFFECT HIM! BUT IF IT'S ONLY AN IMAGE OR DUPLICATE OF PIE--MY RING WILL DISSIPATE IT COMPLETELY!
AS THE GREAT GREEN BEAM IS BROUGHT INTO PLAY AS A KIND OF TRUTH DETECTOR...
THE FIGURE IS COLLAPSING, DISAPPEARING! THIS PROVES EVEN THOUGH IT WAS A MATERIAL OBJECT--IT WAS ONLY A FALSE COUNTERPART OF PIE! AT LEAST I'VE SETTLED THAT...
BUT THEN, INCREDIBLY, IN GREEN LANTERN'S POWER BEAM AS IT SHOOTS OUT...
AT LAST! I'VE FOUND A WAY TO CONTACT YOU, GREEN LANTERN--THROUGH THE BEAM OF YOUR POWER RING!
THOUGHTS REACHING ME... THROUGH MY BEAM--!?
WHO... WHERE...?
IT IS I, GREEN LANTERN--THE PLANET YOU HAVE LANDED ON! PLEASE LISTEN! YOU MUST HEAR MY STORY--!
5

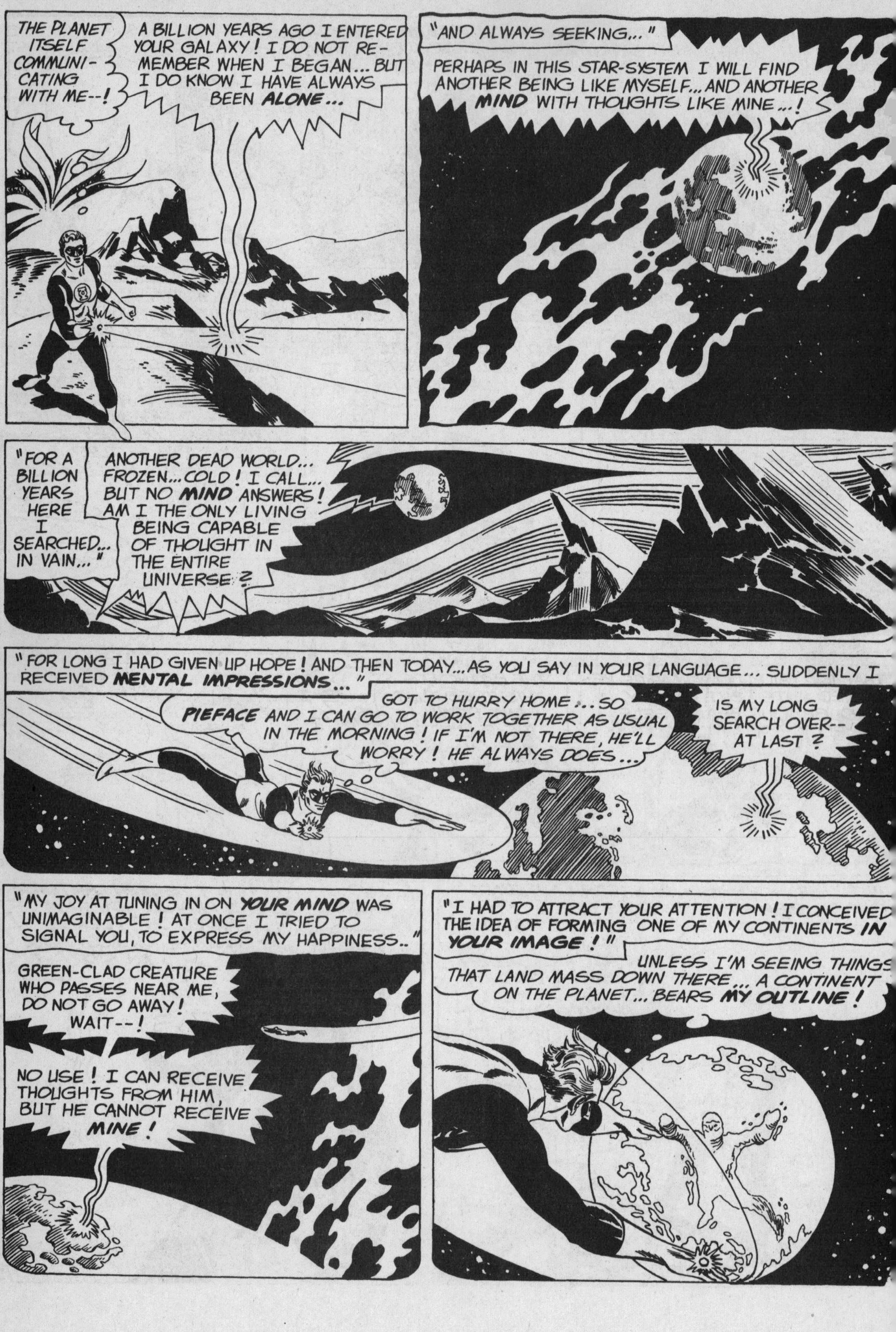
THE PLANET ITSELF COMMUNICATING WITH ME--!
A BILLION YEARS AGO I ENTERED YOUR GALAXY! I DO NOT REMEMBER WHEN I BEGAN... BUT I DO KNOW I HAVE ALWAYS BEEN ALONE...
"AND ALWAYS SEEKING..."
PERHAPS IN THIS STAR-SYSTEM I WILL FIND ANOTHER BEING LIKE MYSELF... AND ANOTHER MIND WITH THOUGHTS LIKE MINE...!
"FOR A BILLION YEARS HERE I SEARCHED... IN VAIN..."
ANOTHER DEAD WORLD... FROZEN... COLD! I CALL... BUT NO MIND ANSWERS! AM I THE ONLY LIVING BEING CAPABLE OF THOUGHT IN THE ENTIRE UNIVERSE?
"FOR LONG I HAD GIVEN UP HOPE! AND THEN TODAY... AS YOU SAY IN YOUR LANGUAGE... SUDDENLY I RECEIVED MENTAL IMPRESSIONS..."
GOT TO HURRY HOME... SO PIEFACE AND I CAN GO TO WORK TOGETHER AS USUAL IN THE MORNING! IF I'M NOT THERE, HE'LL WORRY! HE ALWAYS DOES...
IS MY LONG SEARCH OVER-- AT LAST?
"MY JOY AT TUNING IN ON YOUR MIND WAS UNIMAGINABLE! AT ONCE I TRIED TO SIGNAL YOU, TO EXPRESS MY HAPPINESS.."
GREEN-CLAD CREATURE WHO PASSES NEAR ME, DO NOT GO AWAY! WAIT--!
NO USE! I CAN RECEIVE THOUGHTS FROM HIM, BUT HE CANNOT RECEIVE MINE!
"I HAD TO ATTRACT YOUR ATTENTION! I CONCEIVED THE IDEA OF FORMING ONE OF MY CONTINENTS IN YOUR IMAGE!"
UNLESS I'M SEEING THINGS THAT LAND MASS DOWN THERE... A CONTINENT ON THE PLANET... BEARS MY OUTLINE!

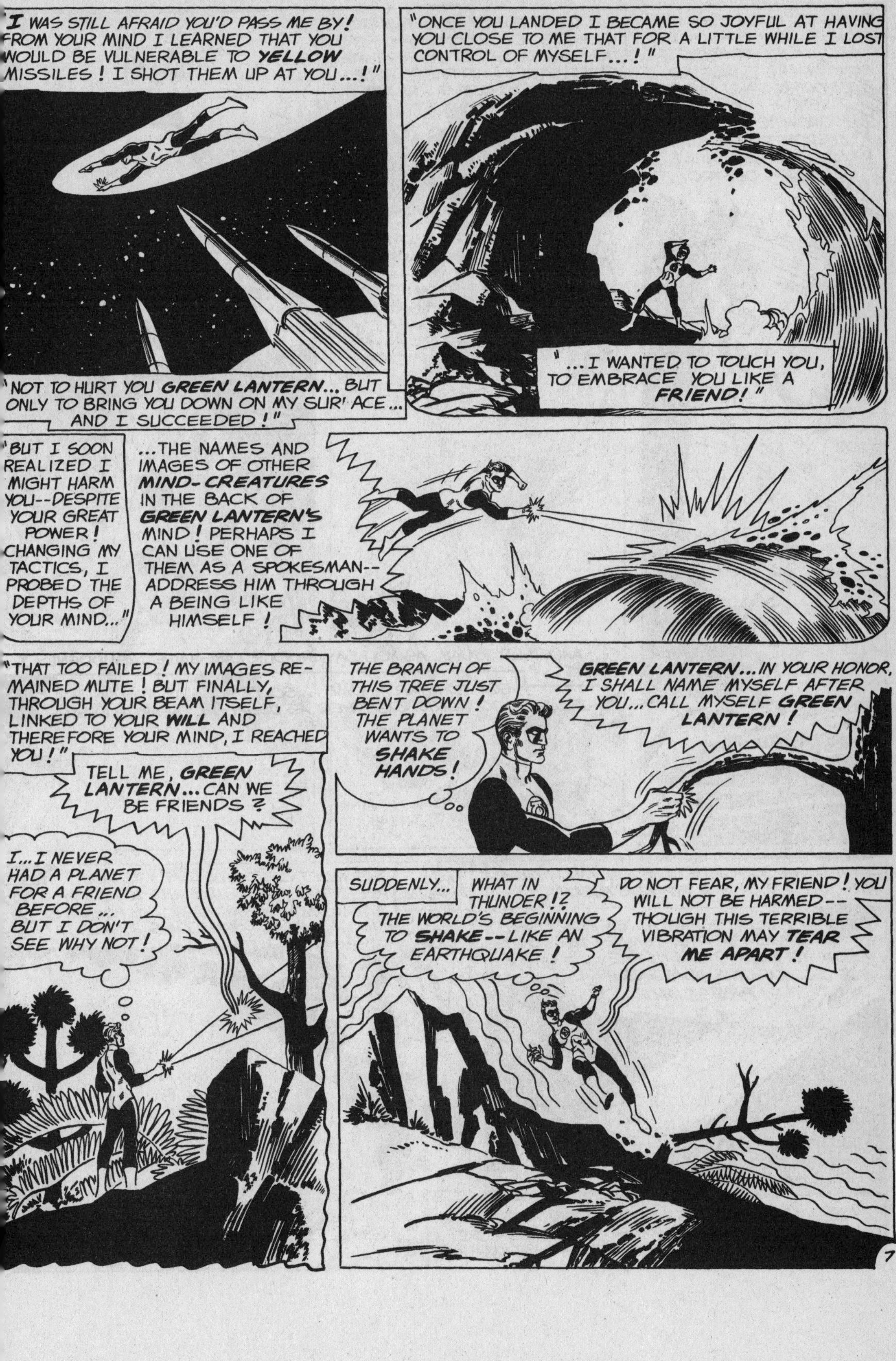
"I WAS STILL AFRAID YOU'D PASS ME BY! FROM YOUR MIND I LEARNED THAT YOU WOULD BE VULNERABLE TO YELLOW MISSILES! I SHOT THEM UP AT YOU...!"
"NOT TO HURT YOU GREEN LANTERN... BUT ONLY TO BRING YOU DOWN ON MY SURFACE... AND I SUCCEEDED!"
"ONCE YOU LANDED I BECAME SO JOYFUL AT HAVING YOU CLOSE TO ME THAT FOR A LITTLE WHILE I LOST CONTROL OF MYSELF...!"
"...I WANTED TO TOUCH YOU, TO EMBRACE YOU LIKE A FRIEND!"
"BUT I SOON REALIZED I MIGHT HARM YOU--DESPITE YOUR GREAT POWER! CHANGING MY TACTICS, I PROBED THE DEPTHS OF YOUR MIND..."
...THE NAMES AND IMAGES OF OTHER MIND-CREATURES IN THE BACK OF GREEN LANTERN'S MIND! PERHAPS I CAN USE ONE OF THEM AS A SPOKESMAN--ADDRESS HIM THROUGH A BEING LIKE HIMSELF!
"THAT TOO FAILED! MY IMAGES REMAINED MUTE! BUT FINALLY, THROUGH YOUR BEAM ITSELF, LINKED TO YOUR WILL AND THEREFORE YOUR MIND, I REACHED YOU!"
TELL ME, GREEN LANTERN... CAN WE BE FRIENDS?
I...I NEVER HAD A PLANET FOR A FRIEND BEFORE... BUT I DON'T SEE WHY NOT!
THE BRANCH OF THIS TREE JUST BENT DOWN! THE PLANET WANTS TO SHAKE HANDS!
GREEN LANTERN...IN YOUR HONOR, I SHALL NAME MYSELF AFTER YOU...CALL MYSELF GREEN LANTERN!
SUDDENLY...
WHAT IN THUNDER!? THE WORLD'S BEGINNING TO SHAKE--LIKE AN EARTHQUAKE!
DO NOT FEAR, MY FRIEND! YOU WILL NOT BE HARMED--THOUGH THIS TERRIBLE VIBRATION MAY TEAR ME APART!
7

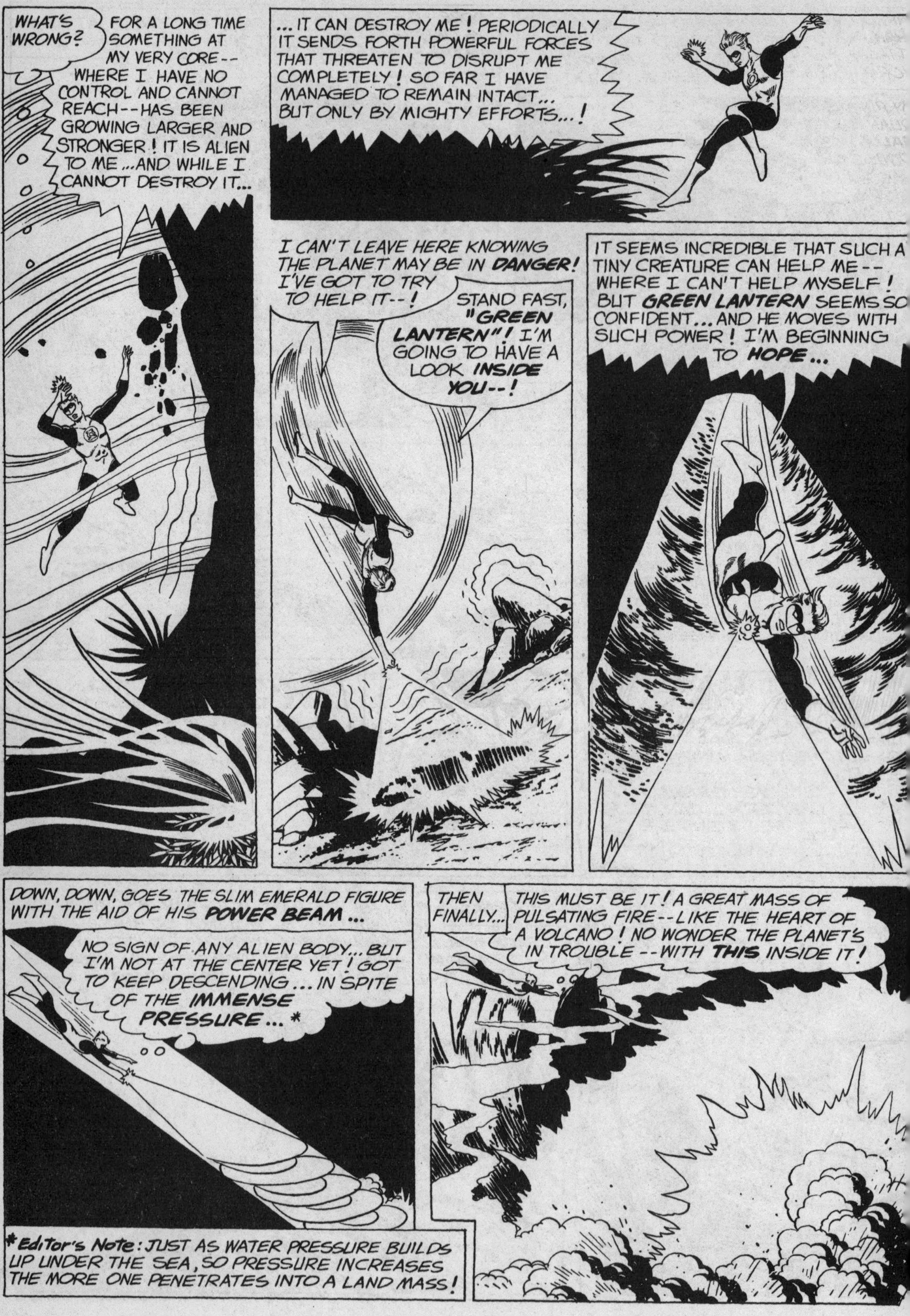
WHAT'S WRONG?
FOR A LONG TIME SOMETHING AT MY VERY CORE--WHERE I HAVE NO CONTROL AND CANNOT REACH--HAS BEEN GROWING LARGER AND STRONGER! IT IS ALIEN TO ME...AND WHILE I CANNOT DESTROY IT...
...IT CAN DESTROY ME! PERIODICALLY IT SENDS FORTH POWERFUL FORCES THAT THREATEN TO DISRUPT ME COMPLETELY! SO FAR I HAVE MANAGED TO REMAIN INTACT... BUT ONLY BY MIGHTY EFFORTS...!
I CAN'T LEAVE HERE KNOWING THE PLANET MAY BE IN DANGER! I'VE GOT TO TRY TO HELP IT--!
STAND FAST, "GREEN LANTERN"! I'M GOING TO HAVE A LOOK INSIDE YOU--!
IT SEEMS INCREDIBLE THAT SUCH A TINY CREATURE CAN HELP ME--WHERE I CAN'T HELP MYSELF! BUT GREEN LANTERN SEEMS SO CONFIDENT...AND HE MOVES WITH SUCH POWER! I'M BEGINNING TO HOPE...
DOWN, DOWN, GOES THE SLIM EMERALD FIGURE WITH THE AID OF HIS POWER BEAM...
NO SIGN OF ANY ALIEN BODY... BUT I'M NOT AT THE CENTER YET! GOT TO KEEP DESCENDING... IN SPITE OF THE IMMENSE PRESSURE...*
*Editor's Note: JUST AS WATER PRESSURE BUILDS UP UNDER THE SEA, SO PRESSURE INCREASES THE MORE ONE PENETRATES INTO A LAND MASS!
THEN FINALLY...
THIS MUST BE IT! A GREAT MASS OF PULSATING FIRE--LIKE THE HEART OF A VOLCANO! NO WONDER THE PLANET'S IN TROUBLE--WITH THIS INSIDE IT!

UNHESITATINGLY, THE **EMERALD CHAMPION** PLUNGES IN TO THE ATTACK, HIS GREEN BEAM WORKING AT FULL THROTTLE...

MY RING IS POURING OUT A QUANTITY OF WATER LIKE **NIAGARA FALLS** -- BUT I CAN'T SEEM TO DOUSE THE FIRE! THE THING HAS A KIND OF LIFE -- IT'S RESISTING MY EFFORTS TO DESTROY IT!

AND WHAT'S MORE -- IT'S FIGHTING BACK! WHEW! THIS IS LIKE BEING ATTACKED BY A **GIGANTIC FLAME-THROWER!**

BUT MY BEAM CAN HANDLE THE FLAME-SPURTS! AND THAT GIVES ME AN IDEA! IF I CAN'T PUT OUT THE FIRE, THERE MAY BE **ANOTHER** WAY TO HELP THE PLANETARY **GREEN LANTERN!**

BACKING HIS RING WITH ALL HIS DETERMINED WILL POWER, THE **CRUSADER** FROM EARTH SHOOTS OUT HIS **POWER RAY...**

MY GREEN BEAM HAS FORMED HUGE TONGS... I'M GRIPPING THE ALIEN MASS... AND IT CAN'T STOP ME! ITS WEIGHT IS ENORMOUS...

...BUT THERE'S **NO LIMIT** TO WHAT MY BEAM CAN LIFT -- PROVIDING IT'S **NOT** YELLOW...! NOW TO GO BACK UP... THE WAY I CAME... BY INCREASING THE SIZE OF THE PASSAGE TO THE SURFACE!

9

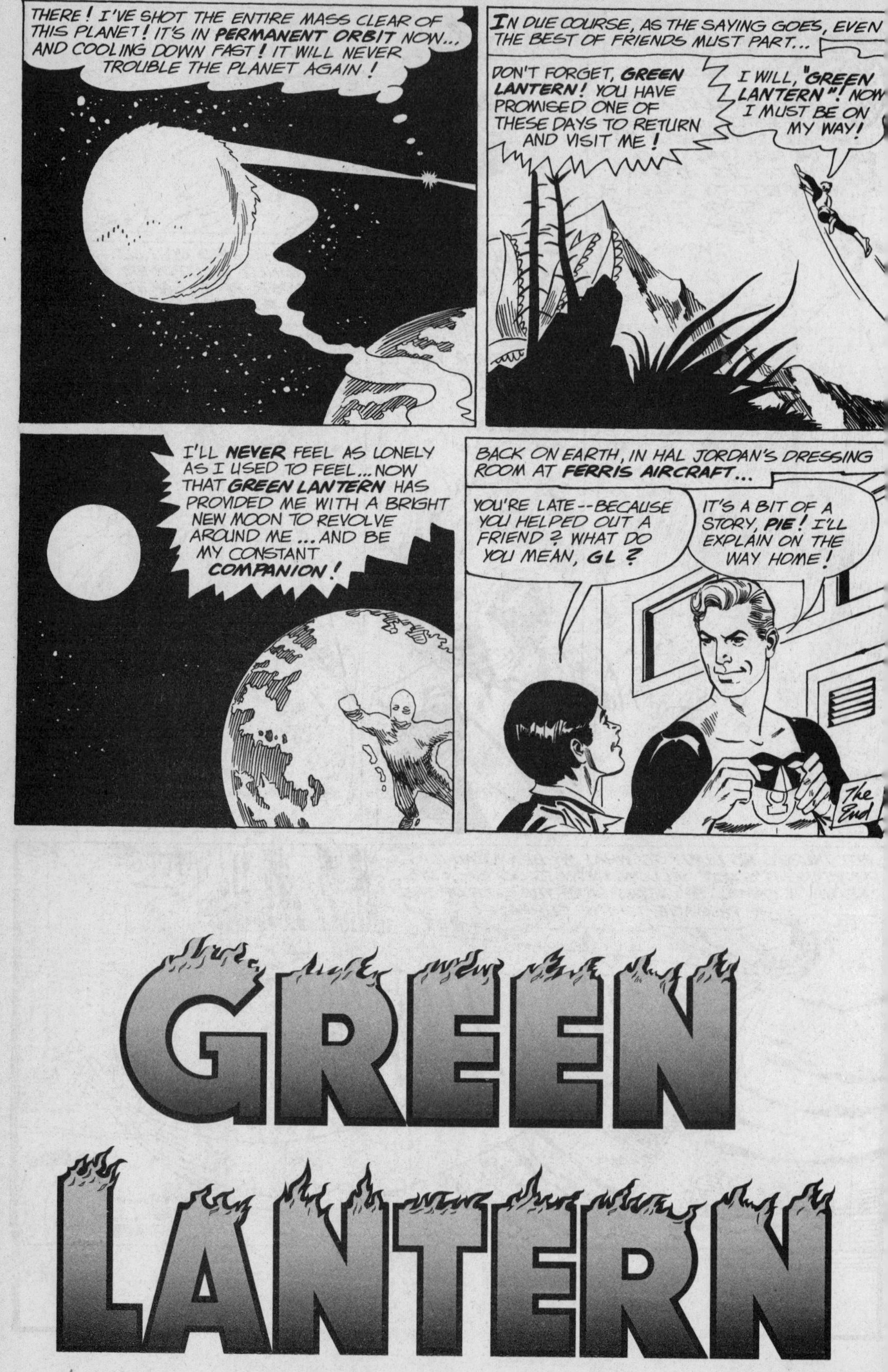
THERE! I'VE SHOT THE ENTIRE MASS CLEAR OF THIS PLANET! IT'S IN PERMANENT ORBIT NOW... AND COOLING DOWN FAST! IT WILL NEVER TROUBLE THE PLANET AGAIN!
IN DUE COURSE, AS THE SAYING GOES, EVEN THE BEST OF FRIENDS MUST PART...
DON'T FORGET, GREEN LANTERN! YOU HAVE PROMISED ONE OF THESE DAYS TO RETURN AND VISIT ME!
I WILL, "GREEN LANTERN"! NOW I MUST BE ON MY WAY!
I'LL NEVER FEEL AS LONELY AS I USED TO FEEL... NOW THAT GREEN LANTERN HAS PROVIDED ME WITH A BRIGHT NEW MOON TO REVOLVE AROUND ME ... AND BE MY CONSTANT COMPANION!
BACK ON EARTH, IN HAL JORDAN'S DRESSING ROOM AT FERRIS AIRCRAFT...
YOU'RE LATE--BECAUSE YOU HELPED OUT A FRIEND? WHAT DO YOU MEAN, GL?
IT'S A BIT OF A STORY, PIE! I'LL EXPLAIN ON THE WAY HOME!
The End

GREEN LANTERN

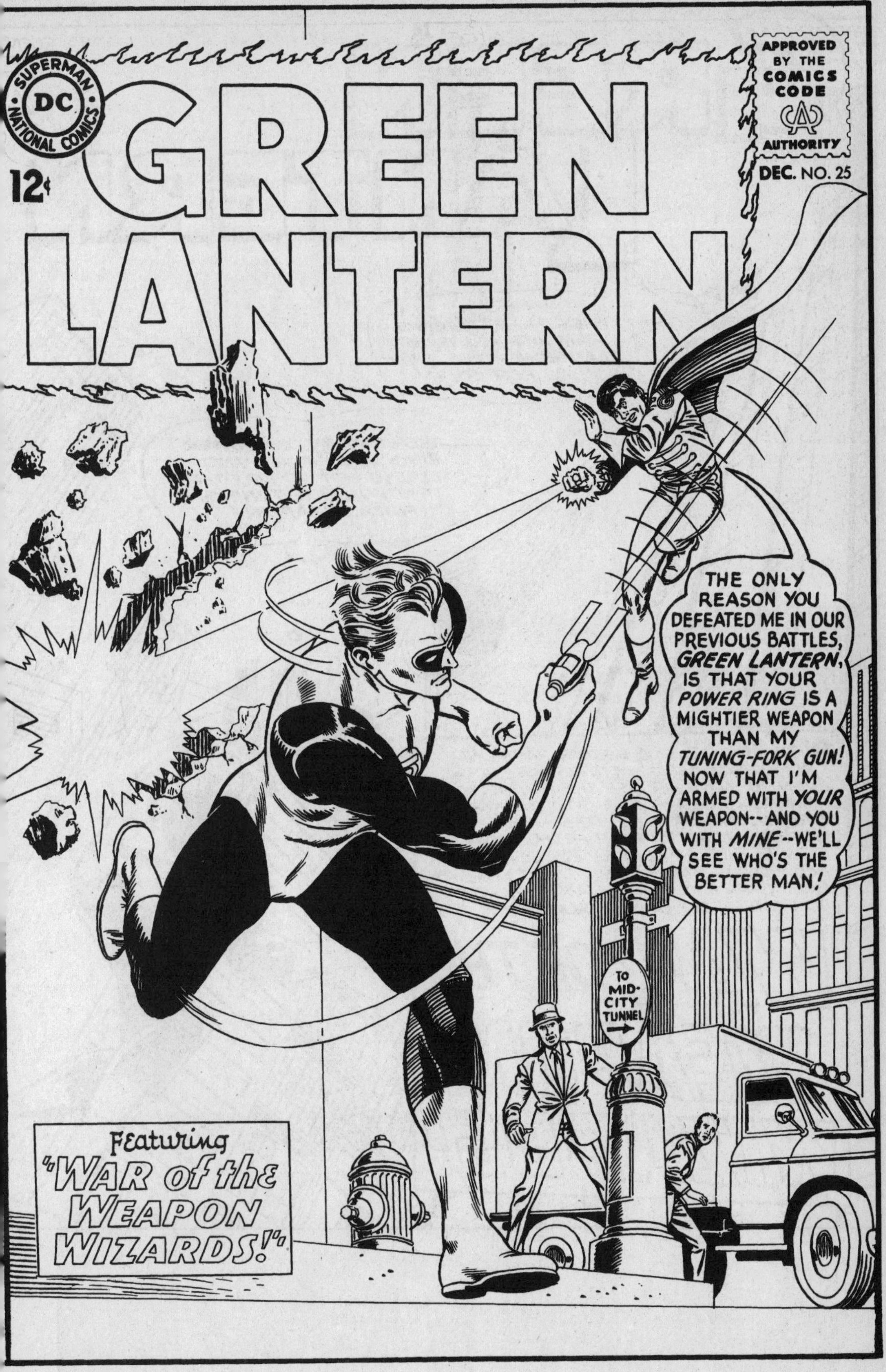
SUPERMAN DC NATIONAL COMICS
12¢
GREEN LANTERN
APPROVED BY THE COMICS CODE AUTHORITY
DEC. NO. 25
THE ONLY REASON YOU DEFEATED ME IN OUR PREVIOUS BATTLES, GREEN LANTERN, IS THAT YOUR POWER RING IS A MIGHTIER WEAPON THAN MY TUNING-FORK GUN! NOW THAT I'M ARMED WITH YOUR WEAPON--AND YOU WITH MINE--WE'LL SEE WHO'S THE BETTER MAN!
TO MID-CITY TUNNEL
Featuring "WAR of the WEAPON WIZARDS!"

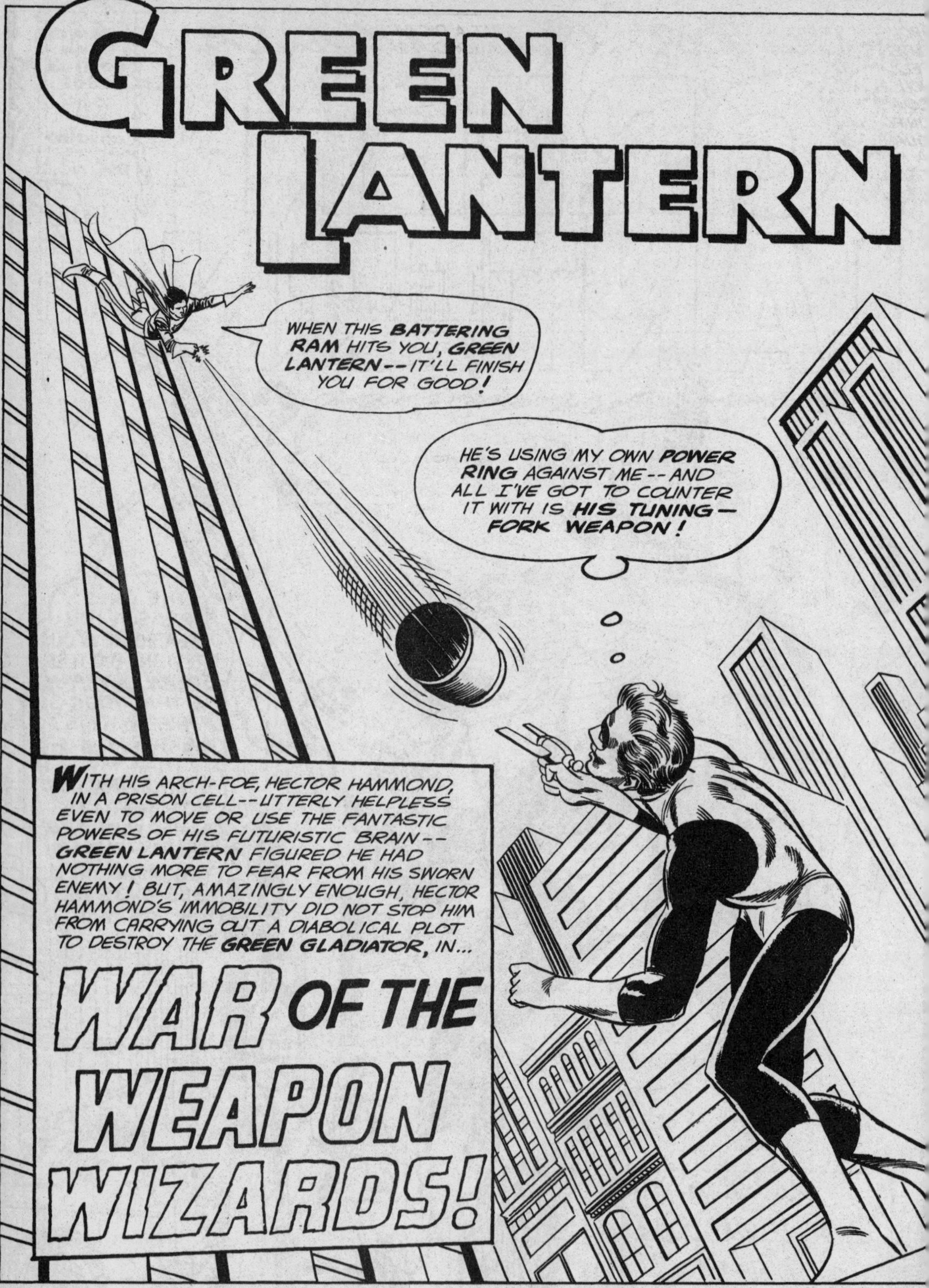
GREEN LANTERN
WHEN THIS BATTERING RAM HITS YOU, GREEN LANTERN--IT'LL FINISH YOU FOR GOOD!
HE'S USING MY OWN POWER RING AGAINST ME--AND ALL I'VE GOT TO COUNTER IT WITH IS HIS TUNING-FORK WEAPON!
WITH HIS ARCH-FOE, HECTOR HAMMOND, IN A PRISON CELL--UTTERLY HELPLESS EVEN TO MOVE OR USE THE FANTASTIC POWERS OF HIS FUTURISTIC BRAIN--GREEN LANTERN FIGURED HE HAD NOTHING MORE TO FEAR FROM HIS SWORN ENEMY! BUT, AMAZINGLY ENOUGH, HECTOR HAMMOND'S IMMOBILITY DID NOT STOP HIM FROM CARRYING OUT A DIABOLICAL PLOT TO DESTROY THE GREEN GLADIATOR, IN...
WAR OF THE WEAPON WIZARDS!

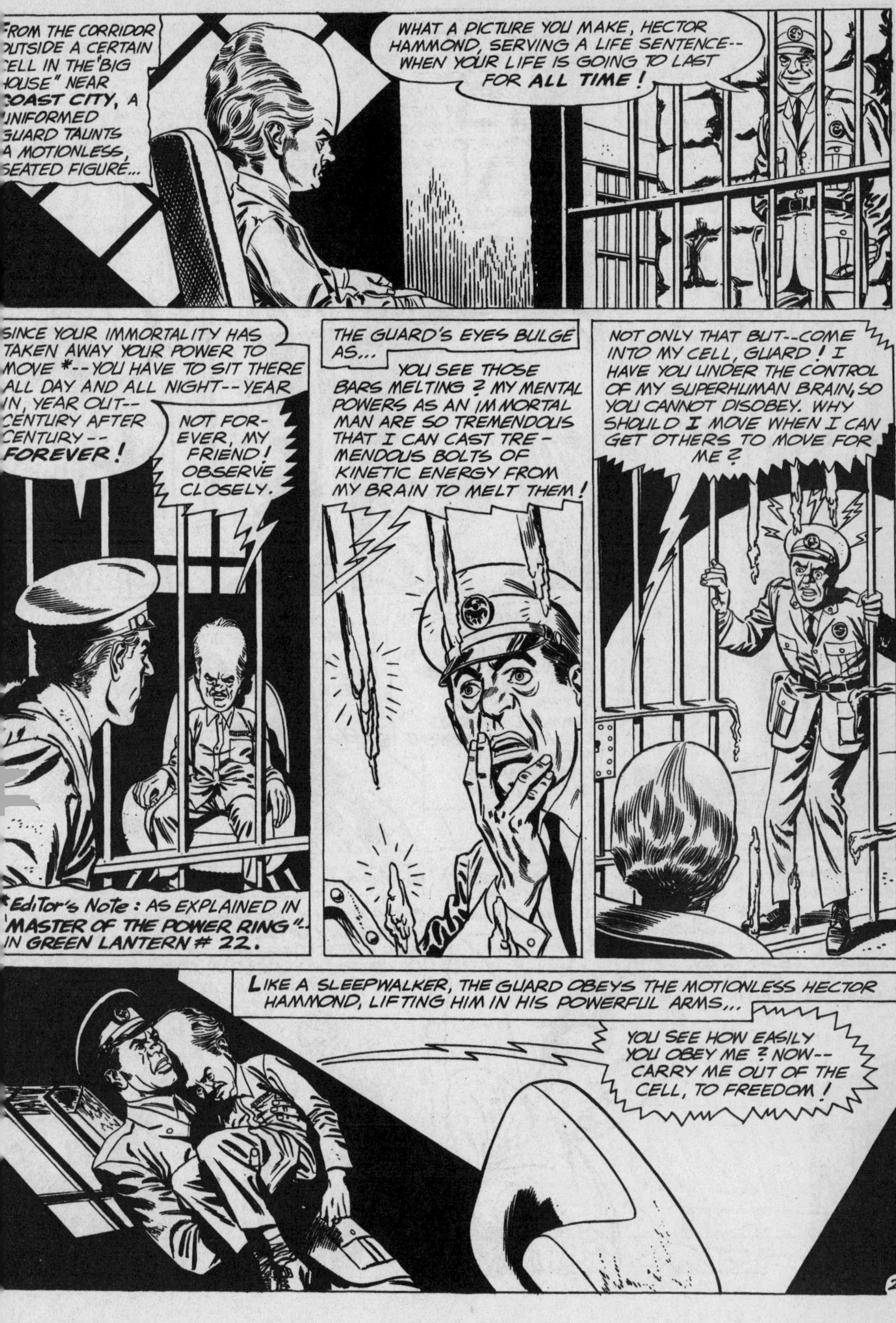
FROM THE CORRIDOR OUTSIDE A CERTAIN CELL IN THE "BIG HOUSE" NEAR COAST CITY, A UNIFORMED GUARD TAUNTS A MOTIONLESS, SEATED FIGURE...
WHAT A PICTURE YOU MAKE, HECTOR HAMMOND, SERVING A LIFE SENTENCE-- WHEN YOUR LIFE IS GOING TO LAST FOR ALL TIME!
SINCE YOUR IMMORTALITY HAS TAKEN AWAY YOUR POWER TO MOVE *--YOU HAVE TO SIT THERE ALL DAY AND ALL NIGHT--YEAR IN, YEAR OUT--CENTURY AFTER CENTURY--FOREVER!
NOT FOREVER, MY FRIEND! OBSERVE CLOSELY.
*EDITOR'S NOTE: AS EXPLAINED IN "MASTER OF THE POWER RING"-- IN GREEN LANTERN #22.
THE GUARD'S EYES BULGE AS...
YOU SEE THOSE BARS MELTING? MY MENTAL POWERS AS AN IMMORTAL MAN ARE SO TREMENDOUS THAT I CAN CAST TREMENDOUS BOLTS OF KINETIC ENERGY FROM MY BRAIN TO MELT THEM!
NOT ONLY THAT BUT--COME INTO MY CELL, GUARD! I HAVE YOU UNDER THE CONTROL OF MY SUPERHUMAN BRAIN, SO YOU CANNOT DISOBEY. WHY SHOULD I MOVE WHEN I CAN GET OTHERS TO MOVE FOR ME?
LIKE A SLEEPWALKER, THE GUARD OBEYS THE MOTIONLESS HECTOR HAMMOND, LIFTING HIM IN HIS POWERFUL ARMS...
YOU SEE HOW EASILY YOU OBEY ME? NOW--CARRY ME OUT OF THE CELL, TO FREEDOM!
2

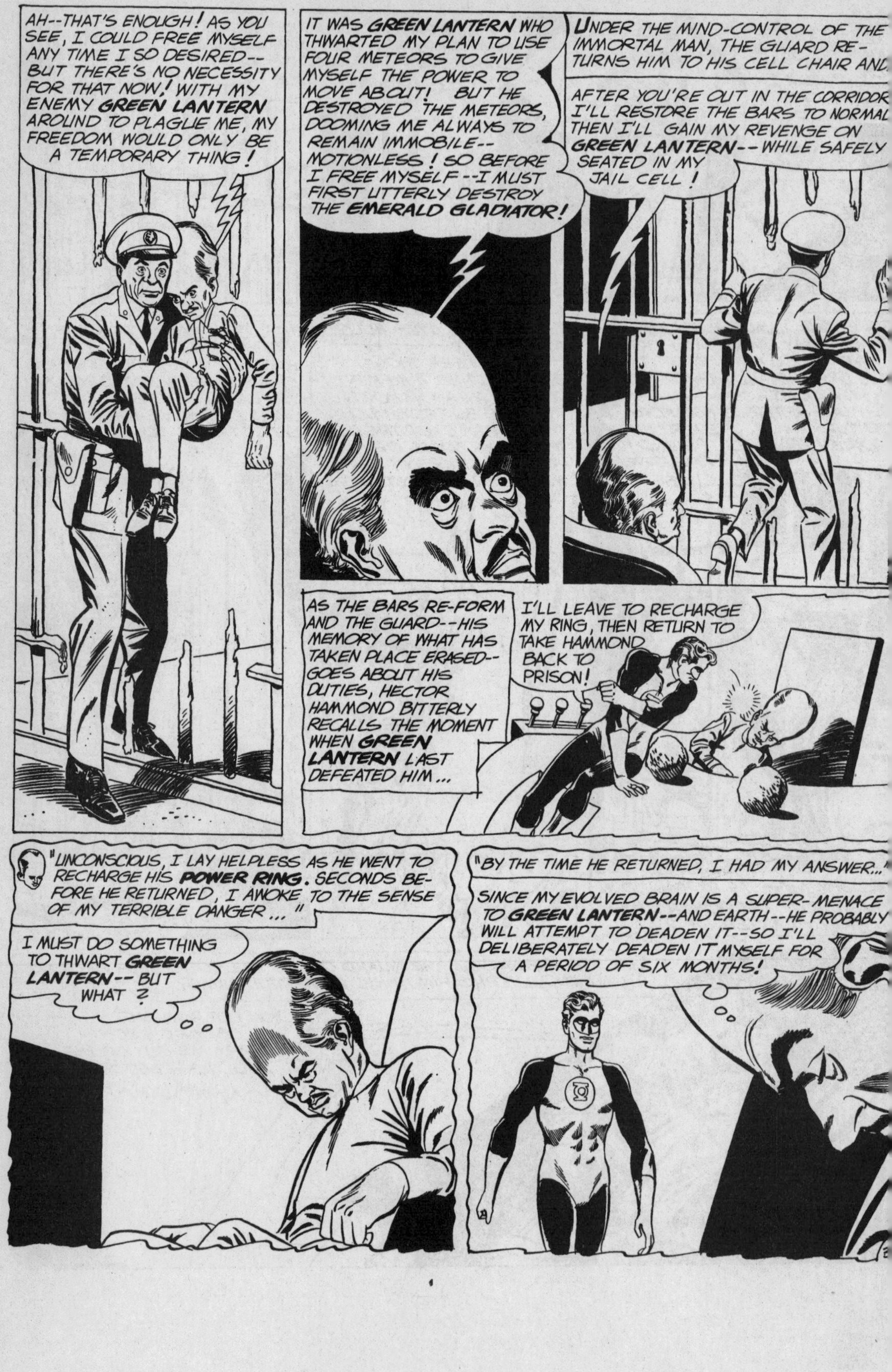
AH--THAT'S ENOUGH! AS YOU SEE, I COULD FREE MYSELF ANY TIME I SO DESIRED-- BUT THERE'S NO NECESSITY FOR THAT NOW! WITH MY ENEMY GREEN LANTERN AROUND TO PLAGUE ME, MY FREEDOM WOULD ONLY BE A TEMPORARY THING!
IT WAS GREEN LANTERN WHO THWARTED MY PLAN TO USE FOUR METEORS TO GIVE MYSELF THE POWER TO MOVE ABOUT! BUT HE DESTROYED THE METEORS, DOOMING ME ALWAYS TO REMAIN IMMOBILE-- MOTIONLESS! SO BEFORE I FREE MYSELF--I MUST FIRST UTTERLY DESTROY THE EMERALD GLADIATOR!
UNDER THE MIND-CONTROL OF THE IMMORTAL MAN, THE GUARD RE-TURNS HIM TO HIS CELL CHAIR AND
AFTER YOU'RE OUT IN THE CORRIDOR I'LL RESTORE THE BARS TO NORMAL THEN I'LL GAIN MY REVENGE ON GREEN LANTERN--WHILE SAFELY SEATED IN MY JAIL CELL!
AS THE BARS RE-FORM AND THE GUARD--HIS MEMORY OF WHAT HAS TAKEN PLACE ERASED-- GOES ABOUT HIS DUTIES, HECTOR HAMMOND BITTERLY RECALLS THE MOMENT WHEN GREEN LANTERN LAST DEFEATED HIM...
I'LL LEAVE TO RECHARGE MY RING, THEN RETURN TO TAKE HAMMOND BACK TO PRISON!
"UNCONSCIOUS, I LAY HELPLESS AS HE WENT TO RECHARGE HIS POWER RING. SECONDS BE-FORE HE RETURNED, I AWOKE TO THE SENSE OF MY TERRIBLE DANGER..."
I MUST DO SOMETHING TO THWART GREEN LANTERN-- BUT WHAT?
"BY THE TIME HE RETURNED, I HAD MY ANSWER..."
SINCE MY EVOLVED BRAIN IS A SUPER-MENACE TO GREEN LANTERN--AND EARTH--HE PROBABLY WILL ATTEMPT TO DEADEN IT--SO I'LL DELIBERATELY DEADEN IT MYSELF FOR A PERIOD OF SIX MONTHS!

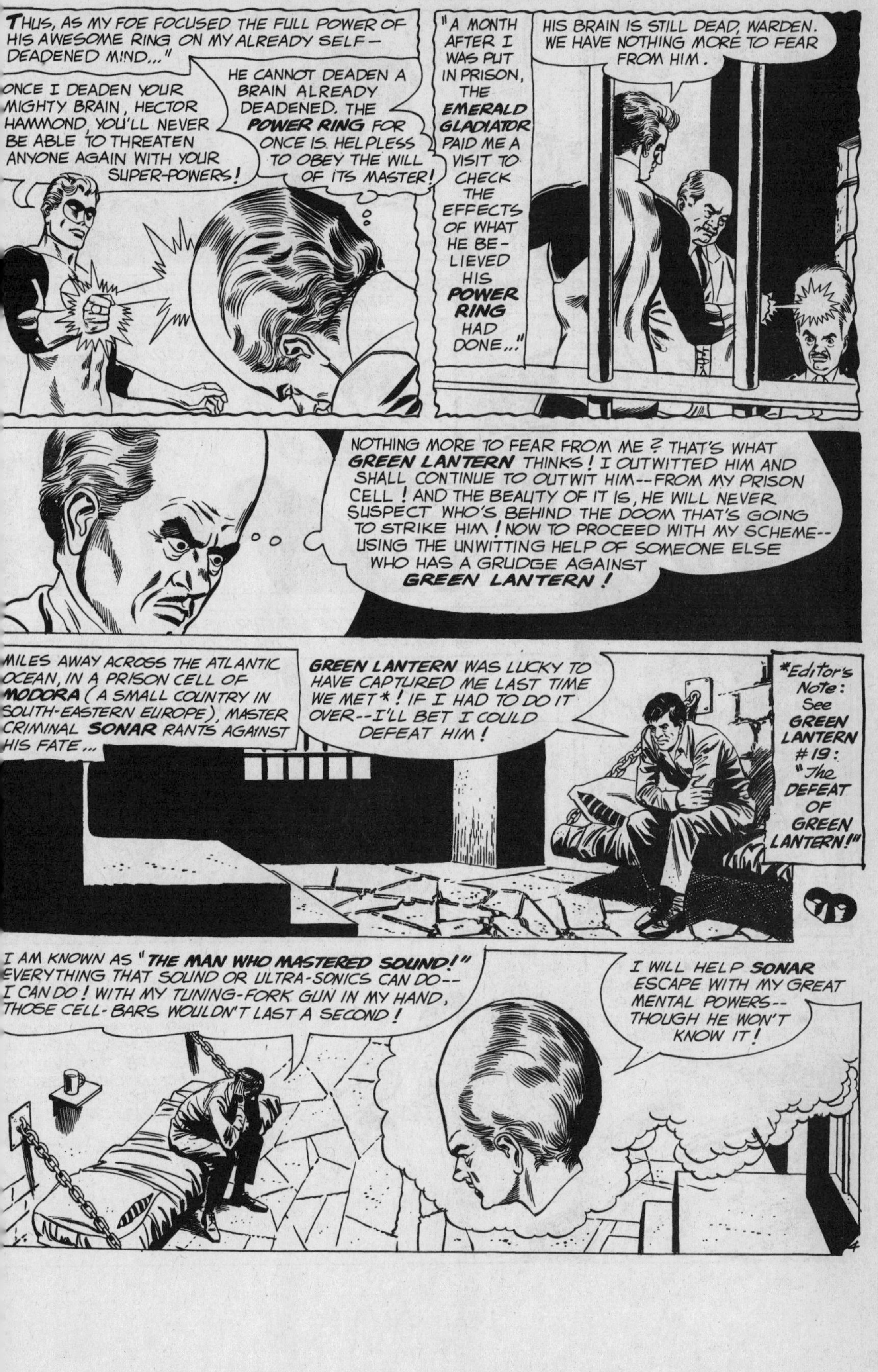
THUS, AS MY FOE FOCUSED THE FULL POWER OF HIS AWESOME RING ON MY ALREADY SELF-DEADENED MIND..."
ONCE I DEADEN YOUR MIGHTY BRAIN, HECTOR HAMMOND, YOU'LL NEVER BE ABLE TO THREATEN ANYONE AGAIN WITH YOUR SUPER-POWERS!
HE CANNOT DEADEN A BRAIN ALREADY DEADENED. THE POWER RING FOR ONCE IS HELPLESS TO OBEY THE WILL OF ITS MASTER!
"A MONTH AFTER I WAS PUT IN PRISON, THE EMERALD GLADIATOR PAID ME A VISIT TO CHECK THE EFFECTS OF WHAT HE BELIEVED HIS POWER RING HAD DONE..."
HIS BRAIN IS STILL DEAD, WARDEN. WE HAVE NOTHING MORE TO FEAR FROM HIM.
NOTHING MORE TO FEAR FROM ME? THAT'S WHAT GREEN LANTERN THINKS! I OUTWITTED HIM AND SHALL CONTINUE TO OUTWIT HIM--FROM MY PRISON CELL! AND THE BEAUTY OF IT IS, HE WILL NEVER SUSPECT WHO'S BEHIND THE DOOM THAT'S GOING TO STRIKE HIM! NOW TO PROCEED WITH MY SCHEME--USING THE UNWITTING HELP OF SOMEONE ELSE WHO HAS A GRUDGE AGAINST GREEN LANTERN!
MILES AWAY ACROSS THE ATLANTIC OCEAN, IN A PRISON CELL OF MODORA (A SMALL COUNTRY IN SOUTH-EASTERN EUROPE), MASTER CRIMINAL SONAR RANTS AGAINST HIS FATE...
GREEN LANTERN WAS LUCKY TO HAVE CAPTURED ME LAST TIME WE MET*! IF I HAD TO DO IT OVER--I'LL BET I COULD DEFEAT HIM!
*Editor's Note: See GREEN LANTERN #19: "The DEFEAT OF GREEN LANTERN!"
I AM KNOWN AS "THE MAN WHO MASTERED SOUND!" EVERYTHING THAT SOUND OR ULTRA-SONICS CAN DO--I CAN DO! WITH MY TUNING-FORK GUN IN MY HAND, THOSE CELL-BARS WOULDN'T LAST A SECOND!
I WILL HELP SONAR ESCAPE WITH MY GREAT MENTAL POWERS--THOUGH HE WON'T KNOW IT!
4

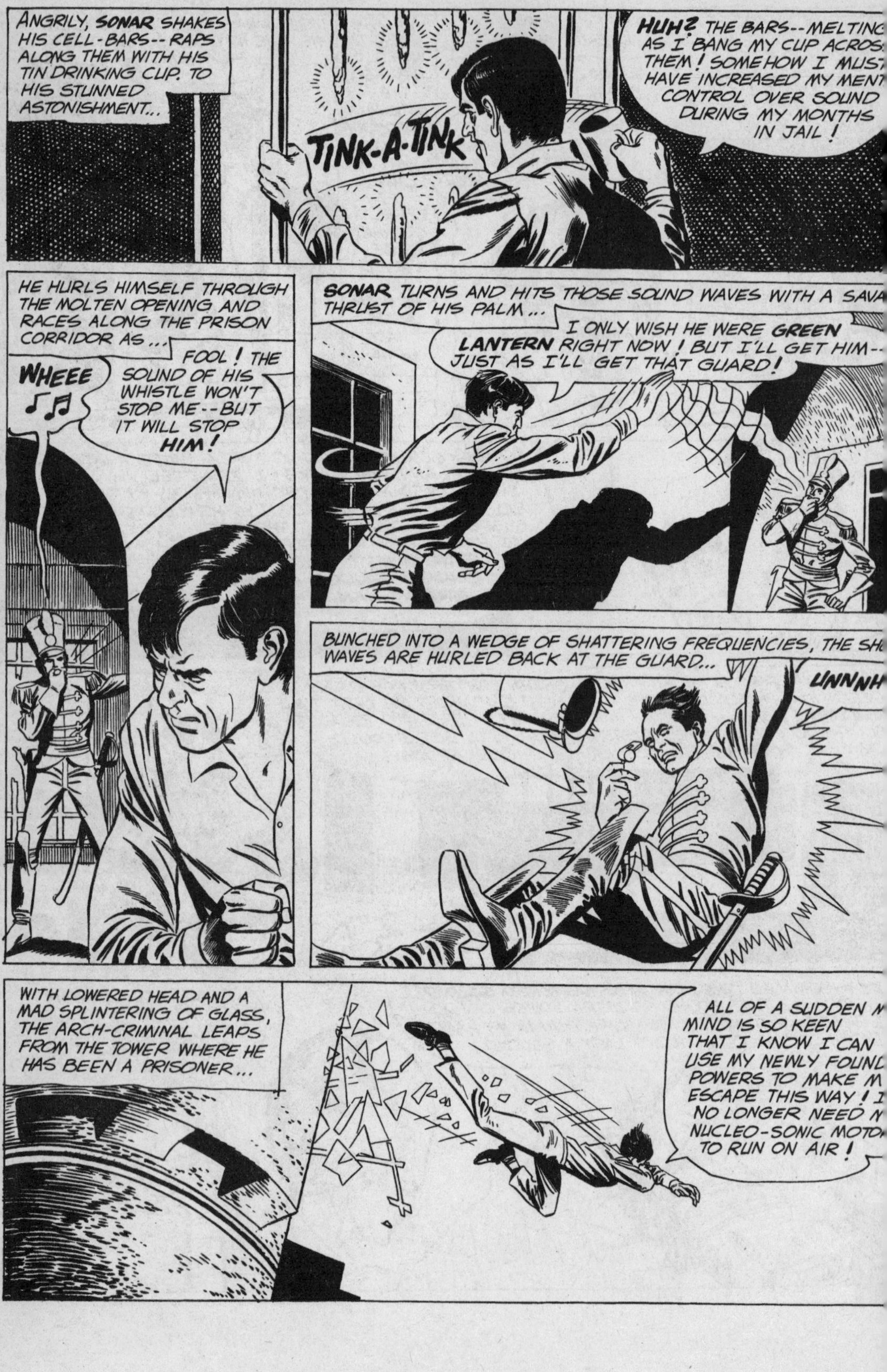
ANGRILY, SONAR SHAKES HIS CELL-BARS-- RAPS ALONG THEM WITH HIS TIN DRINKING CUP. TO HIS STUNNED ASTONISHMENT...
HUH? THE BARS--MELTING AS I BANG MY CUP ACROSS THEM! SOMEHOW I MUST HAVE INCREASED MY MENT CONTROL OVER SOUND DURING MY MONTHS IN JAIL!
TINK-A-TINK
HE HURLS HIMSELF THROUGH THE MOLTEN OPENING AND RACES ALONG THE PRISON CORRIDOR AS...
WHEEE
FOOL! THE SOUND OF HIS WHISTLE WON'T STOP ME--BUT IT WILL STOP HIM!
SONAR TURNS AND HITS THOSE SOUND WAVES WITH A SAVA THRUST OF HIS PALM...
I ONLY WISH HE WERE GREEN LANTERN RIGHT NOW! BUT I'LL GET HIM-- JUST AS I'LL GET THAT GUARD!
BUNCHED INTO A WEDGE OF SHATTERING FREQUENCIES, THE SH WAVES ARE HURLED BACK AT THE GUARD...
UNNNH
WITH LOWERED HEAD AND A MAD SPLINTERING OF GLASS, THE ARCH-CRIMINAL LEAPS FROM THE TOWER WHERE HE HAS BEEN A PRISONER...
ALL OF A SUDDEN M MIND IS SO KEEN THAT I KNOW I CAN USE MY NEWLY FOUND POWERS TO MAKE M ESCAPE THIS WAY! I NO LONGER NEED M NUCLEO-SONIC MOTO TO RUN ON AIR!

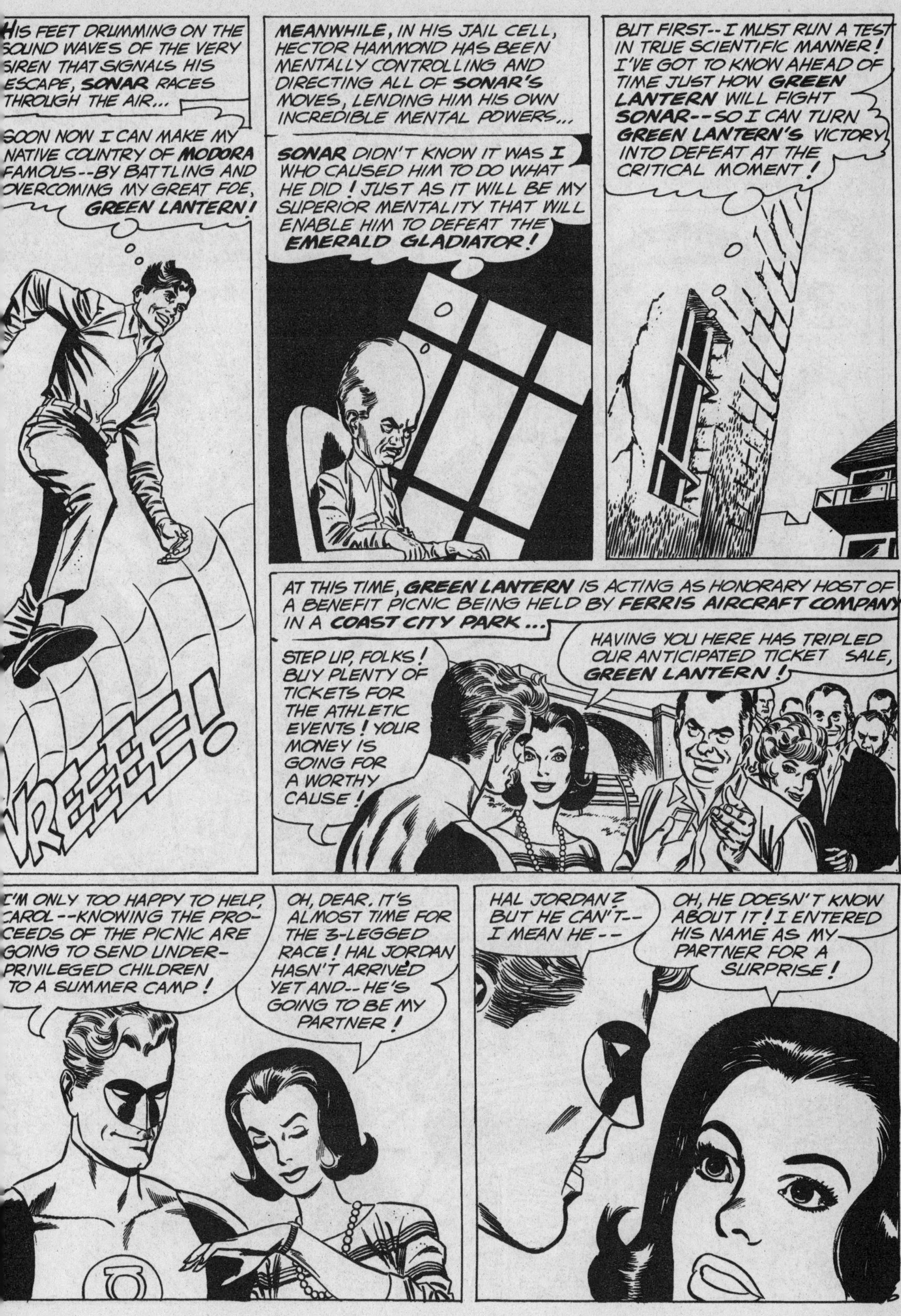
HIS FEET DRUMMING ON THE SOUND WAVES OF THE VERY SIREN THAT SIGNALS HIS ESCAPE, SONAR RACES THROUGH THE AIR...
SOON NOW I CAN MAKE MY NATIVE COUNTRY OF MODORA FAMOUS--BY BATTLING AND OVERCOMING MY GREAT FOE, GREEN LANTERN!
VREEEEE!
MEANWHILE, IN HIS JAIL CELL, HECTOR HAMMOND HAS BEEN MENTALLY CONTROLLING AND DIRECTING ALL OF SONAR'S MOVES, LENDING HIM HIS OWN INCREDIBLE MENTAL POWERS...
SONAR DIDN'T KNOW IT WAS I WHO CAUSED HIM TO DO WHAT HE DID! JUST AS IT WILL BE MY SUPERIOR MENTALITY THAT WILL ENABLE HIM TO DEFEAT THE EMERALD GLADIATOR!
BUT FIRST--I MUST RUN A TEST IN TRUE SCIENTIFIC MANNER! I'VE GOT TO KNOW AHEAD OF TIME JUST HOW GREEN LANTERN WILL FIGHT SONAR--SO I CAN TURN GREEN LANTERN'S VICTORY INTO DEFEAT AT THE CRITICAL MOMENT!
AT THIS TIME, GREEN LANTERN IS ACTING AS HONORARY HOST OF A BENEFIT PICNIC BEING HELD BY FERRIS AIRCRAFT COMPANY IN A COAST CITY PARK...
STEP UP, FOLKS! BUY PLENTY OF TICKETS FOR THE ATHLETIC EVENTS! YOUR MONEY IS GOING FOR A WORTHY CAUSE!
HAVING YOU HERE HAS TRIPLED OUR ANTICIPATED TICKET SALE, GREEN LANTERN!
I'M ONLY TOO HAPPY TO HELP, CAROL--KNOWING THE PROCEEDS OF THE PICNIC ARE GOING TO SEND UNDER-PRIVILEGED CHILDREN TO A SUMMER CAMP!
OH, DEAR. IT'S ALMOST TIME FOR THE 3-LEGGED RACE! HAL JORDAN HASN'T ARRIVED YET AND--HE'S GOING TO BE MY PARTNER!
HAL JORDAN? BUT HE CAN'T--I MEAN HE--
OH, HE DOESN'T KNOW ABOUT IT! I ENTERED HIS NAME AS MY PARTNER FOR A SURPRISE!

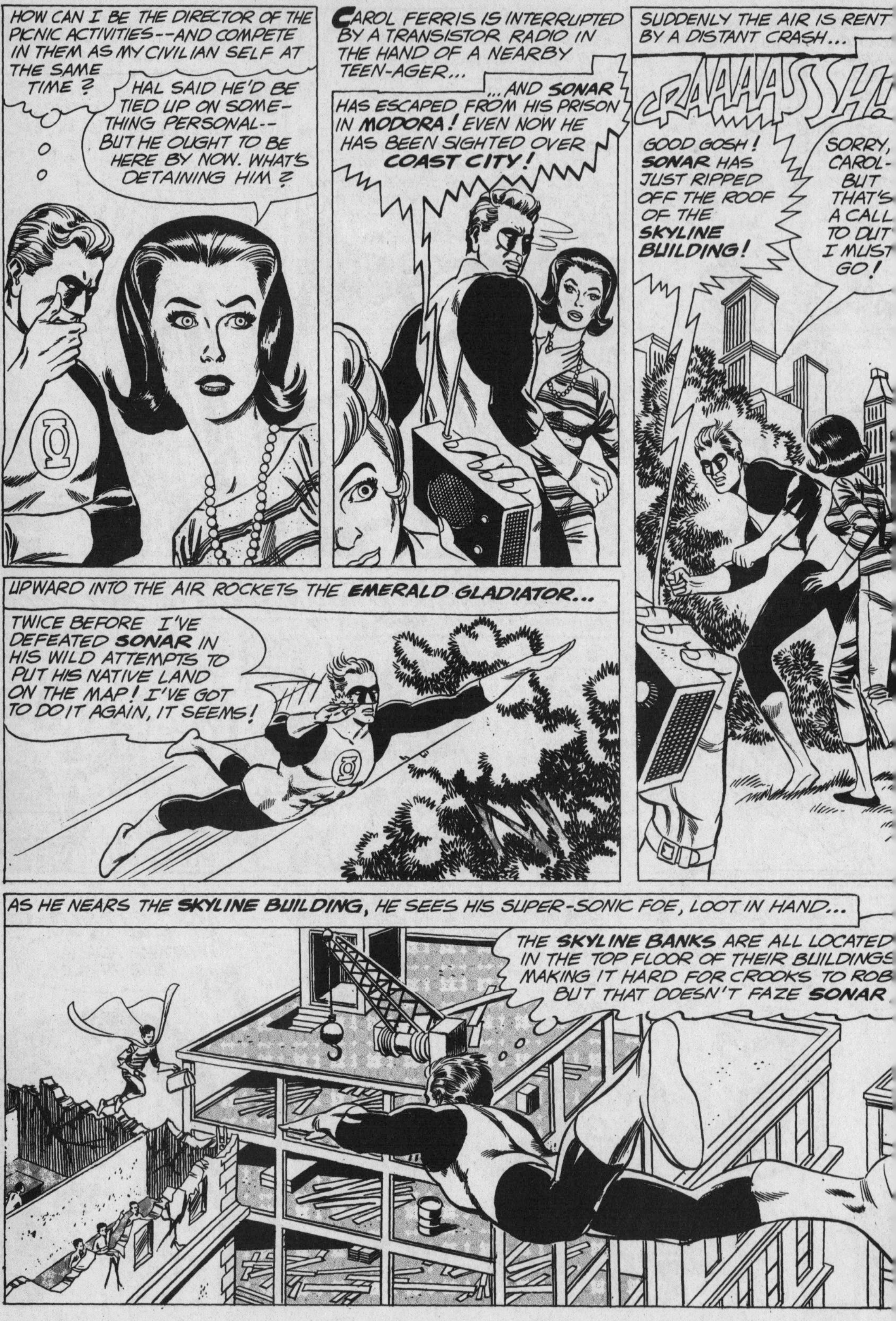

HOW CAN I BE THE DIRECTOR OF THE PICNIC ACTIVITIES--AND COMPETE IN THEM AS MY CIVILIAN SELF AT THE SAME TIME ?
HAL SAID HE'D BE TIED UP ON SOME-THING PERSONAL--BUT HE OUGHT TO BE HERE BY NOW. WHAT'S DETAINING HIM ?
CAROL FERRIS IS INTERRUPTED BY A TRANSISTOR RADIO IN THE HAND OF A NEARBY TEEN-AGER...
...AND SONAR HAS ESCAPED FROM HIS PRISON IN MODORA! EVEN NOW HE HAS BEEN SIGHTED OVER COAST CITY!
SUDDENLY THE AIR IS RENT BY A DISTANT CRASH...
CRAAAAASSH!
GOOD GOSH! SONAR HAS JUST RIPPED OFF THE ROOF OF THE SKYLINE BUILDING!
SORRY, CAROL-BUT THAT'S A CALL TO DUT I MUST GO!
UPWARD INTO THE AIR ROCKETS THE EMERALD GLADIATOR...
TWICE BEFORE I'VE DEFEATED SONAR IN HIS WILD ATTEMPTS TO PUT HIS NATIVE LAND ON THE MAP! I'VE GOT TO DO IT AGAIN, IT SEEMS!
AS HE NEARS THE SKYLINE BUILDING, HE SEES HIS SUPER-SONIC FOE, LOOT IN HAND...
THE SKYLINE BANKS ARE ALL LOCATED IN THE TOP FLOOR OF THEIR BUILDINGS MAKING IT HARD FOR CROOKS TO ROB BUT THAT DOESN'T FAZE SONAR

SUDDENLY SONAR WHIRLS-- AND SENDS SERIES OF SOUND WAVES AT THE STEEL GIRDERS OF A NEARBY BUILDING UNDER CONSTRUCTION...

I APPRECIATE YOUR PROMPT ARRIVAL, *GREEN LANTERN*-- FOR I'VE PREPARED A GREETING FOR YOU!

MADE ALMOST LIFE-LIKE BY THE TUNING FORK'S ULTRA-SONIC VIBRATIONS THAT MOVE TO AND FRO OVER THEM-- THE STEEL GIRDERS DART OUT AND WRAP ABOUT THE *EMERALD GLADIATOR*...

NOW THAT YOU'VE BEEN TURNED INTO A TARGET, I'LL FASHION AN OBJECT TO SHOOT AT YOU!

I'M CAUGHT FAST!

THE NEXT MOMENT, A SOUND-DIRECTED GIRDER FLIPS STRAIGHT AT THE CRUSADER...

SORRY, *GREEN LANTERN*-- BUT I'M ONLY DOING MY PATRIOTIC DUTY!

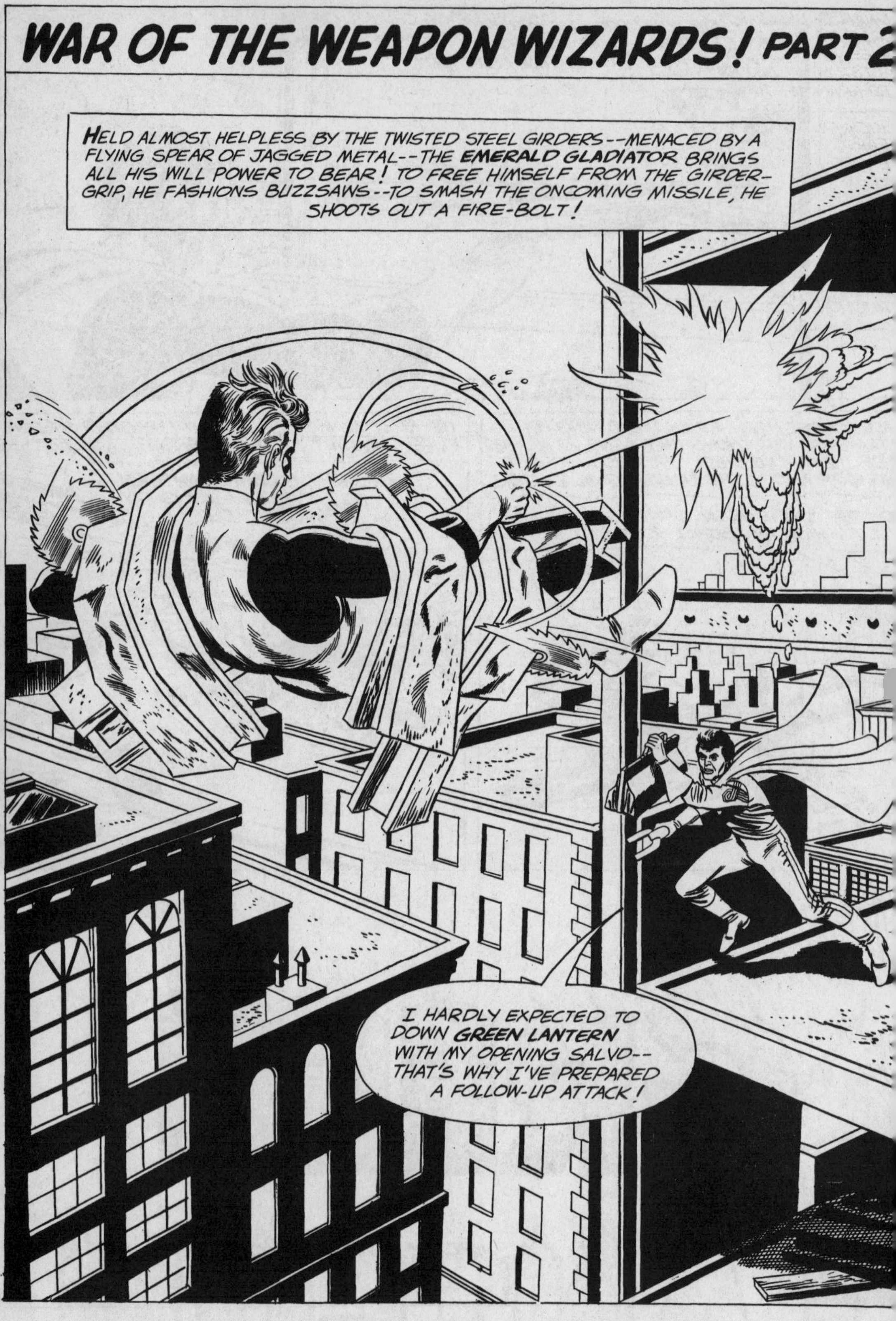
WAR OF THE WEAPON WIZARDS! PART 2
HELD ALMOST HELPLESS BY THE TWISTED STEEL GIRDERS--MENACED BY A FLYING SPEAR OF JAGGED METAL--THE EMERALD GLADIATOR BRINGS ALL HIS WILL POWER TO BEAR! TO FREE HIMSELF FROM THE GIRDER-GRIP, HE FASHIONS BUZZSAWS--TO SMASH THE ONCOMING MISSILE, HE SHOOTS OUT A FIRE-BOLT!
I HARDLY EXPECTED TO DOWN GREEN LANTERN WITH MY OPENING SALVO--THAT'S WHY I'VE PREPARED A FOLLOW-UP ATTACK!

SONAR'S TUNING-FORK GUN HURLS A BATTERY OF SHOCK WAVES AT A NEARBY SKYSCRAPER-- SHATTERING IT UNTIL IT SHATTERS INTO FRAGMENTS...

I'M GETTING A KICK OUT OF THIS WAR OF WEAPONS AND COUNTER-- WEAPONS, *GREEN LANTERN...*

A CANNONADE OF CHUNKS OF STEEL AND CONCRETE BOMBARDS THE FLYING GLADIATOR...

BUT LET'S SEE WHAT YOU DO AGAINST THIS BOM- BARDMENT--COMING AT YOU WITH THE SPEED OF SOUND ITSELF!

UP LIFTS THE *POWER RING!* FROM IT SPURTS A BEAM OF EMERALD LIGHT--THAT FORMS A PROTECTIVE UMBRELLA UNDER- NEATH THAT TERRIBLE RAIN OF DESTRUCTION...

EFFECTIVE--BUT NOT VERY IMAGINATIVE!

EVEN AS *GREEN LANTERN'S* ATTENTION IS FOCUSED ON WARDING OFF THE DEADLY SHOWER...

YOU'RE ALWAYS FIGHTING FOR JUSTICE, *GL*-- IT'S ABOUT TIME YOU FOUGHT *AGAINST* IT, AS REPRESENTED BY THIS STATUE!

10

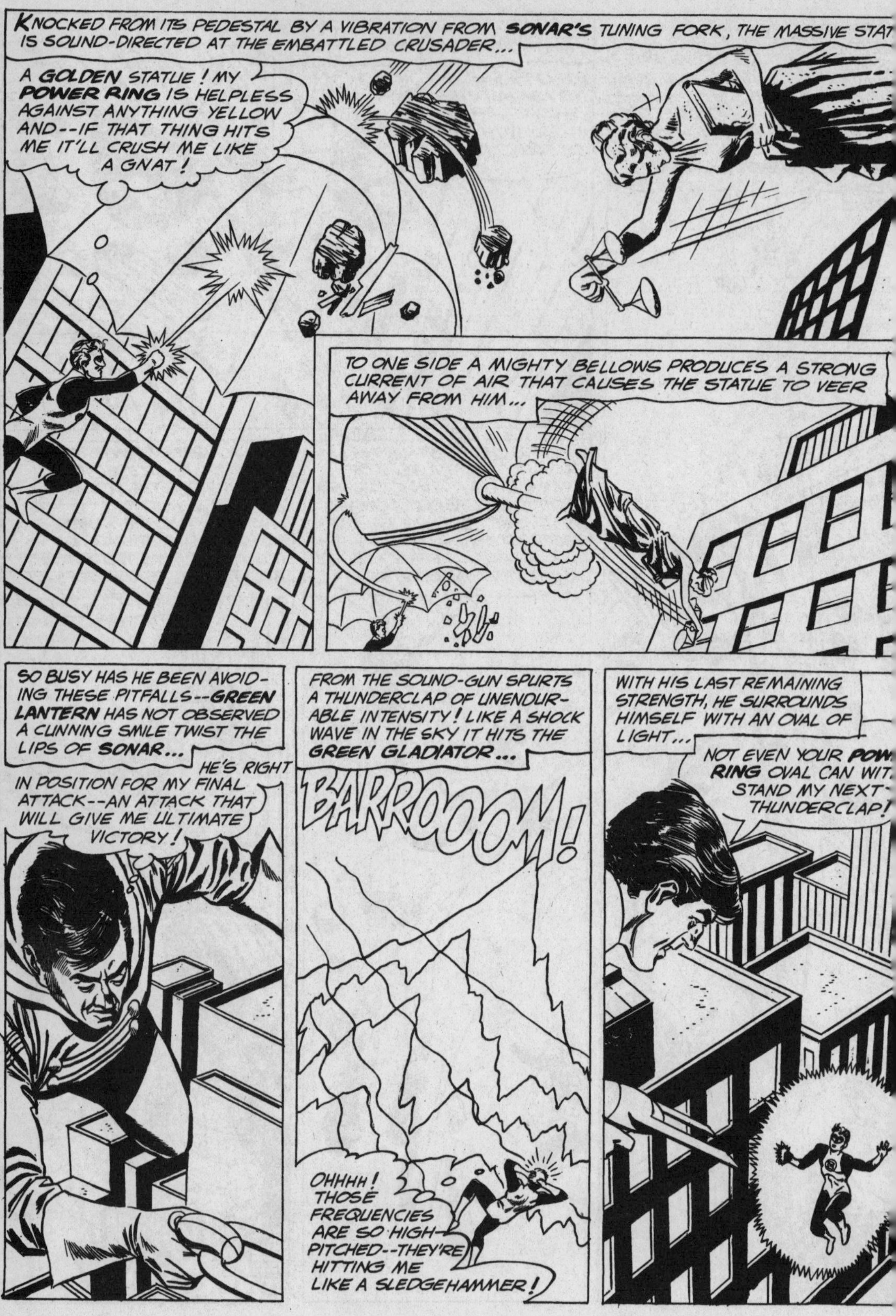
KNOCKED FROM ITS PEDESTAL BY A VIBRATION FROM SONAR'S TUNING FORK, THE MASSIVE STAT
IS SOUND-DIRECTED AT THE EMBATTLED CRUSADER...
A GOLDEN STATUE! MY POWER RING IS HELPLESS AGAINST ANYTHING YELLOW AND--IF THAT THING HITS ME IT'LL CRUSH ME LIKE A GNAT!
TO ONE SIDE A MIGHTY BELLOWS PRODUCES A STRONG CURRENT OF AIR THAT CAUSES THE STATUE TO VEER AWAY FROM HIM...
SO BUSY HAS HE BEEN AVOIDING THESE PITFALLS--GREEN LANTERN HAS NOT OBSERVED A CUNNING SMILE TWIST THE LIPS OF SONAR...
HE'S RIGHT IN POSITION FOR MY FINAL ATTACK--AN ATTACK THAT WILL GIVE ME ULTIMATE VICTORY!
FROM THE SOUND-GUN SPURTS A THUNDERCLAP OF UNENDURABLE INTENSITY! LIKE A SHOCK WAVE IN THE SKY IT HITS THE GREEN GLADIATOR...
BARROOOM!
OHHHH! THOSE FREQUENCIES ARE SO HIGH-PITCHED--THEY'RE HITTING ME LIKE A SLEDGEHAMMER!
WITH HIS LAST REMAINING STRENGTH, HE SURROUNDS HIMSELF WITH AN OVAL OF LIGHT...
NOT EVEN YOUR POW RING OVAL CAN WIT STAND MY NEXT THUNDERCLAP!

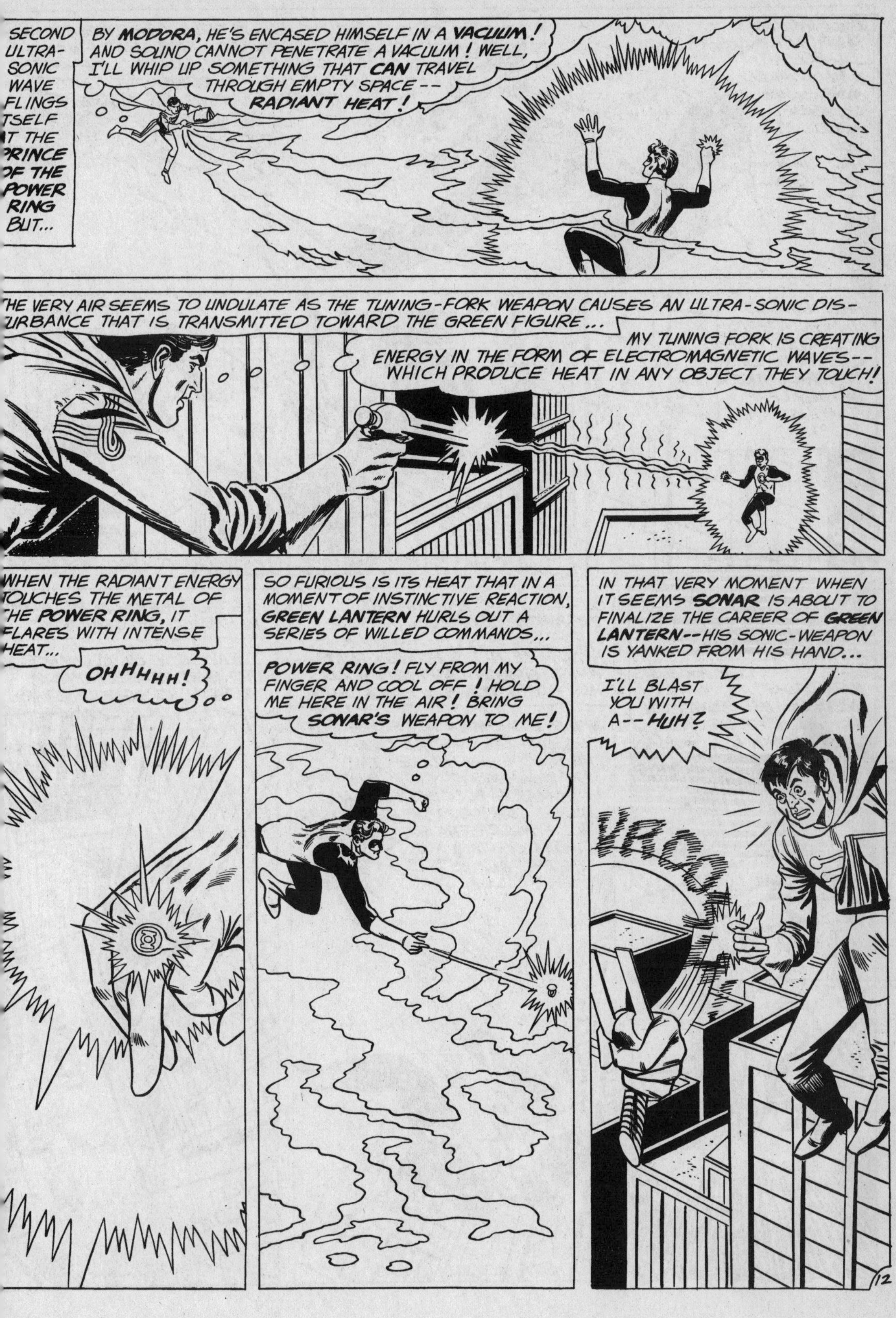
SECOND ULTRA-SONIC WAVE FLINGS TSELF T THE PRINCE OF THE POWER RING BUT...
BY MODORA, HE'S ENCASED HIMSELF IN A VACUUM! AND SOUND CANNOT PENETRATE A VACUUM! WELL, I'LL WHIP UP SOMETHING THAT CAN TRAVEL THROUGH EMPTY SPACE -- RADIANT HEAT!
THE VERY AIR SEEMS TO UNDULATE AS THE TUNING-FORK WEAPON CAUSES AN ULTRA-SONIC DIS-URBANCE THAT IS TRANSMITTED TOWARD THE GREEN FIGURE...
MY TUNING FORK IS CREATING ENERGY IN THE FORM OF ELECTROMAGNETIC WAVES-- WHICH PRODUCE HEAT IN ANY OBJECT THEY TOUCH!
WHEN THE RADIANT ENERGY TOUCHES THE METAL OF THE POWER RING, IT FLARES WITH INTENSE HEAT...
OHHHHH!
SO FURIOUS IS ITS HEAT THAT IN A MOMENT OF INSTINCTIVE REACTION, GREEN LANTERN HURLS OUT A SERIES OF WILLED COMMANDS...
POWER RING! FLY FROM MY FINGER AND COOL OFF! HOLD ME HERE IN THE AIR! BRING SONAR'S WEAPON TO ME!
IN THAT VERY MOMENT WHEN IT SEEMS SONAR IS ABOUT TO FINALIZE THE CAREER OF GREEN LANTERN--HIS SONIC-WEAPON IS YANKED FROM HIS HAND...
I'LL BLAST YOU WITH A--HUH?
VROOO
12

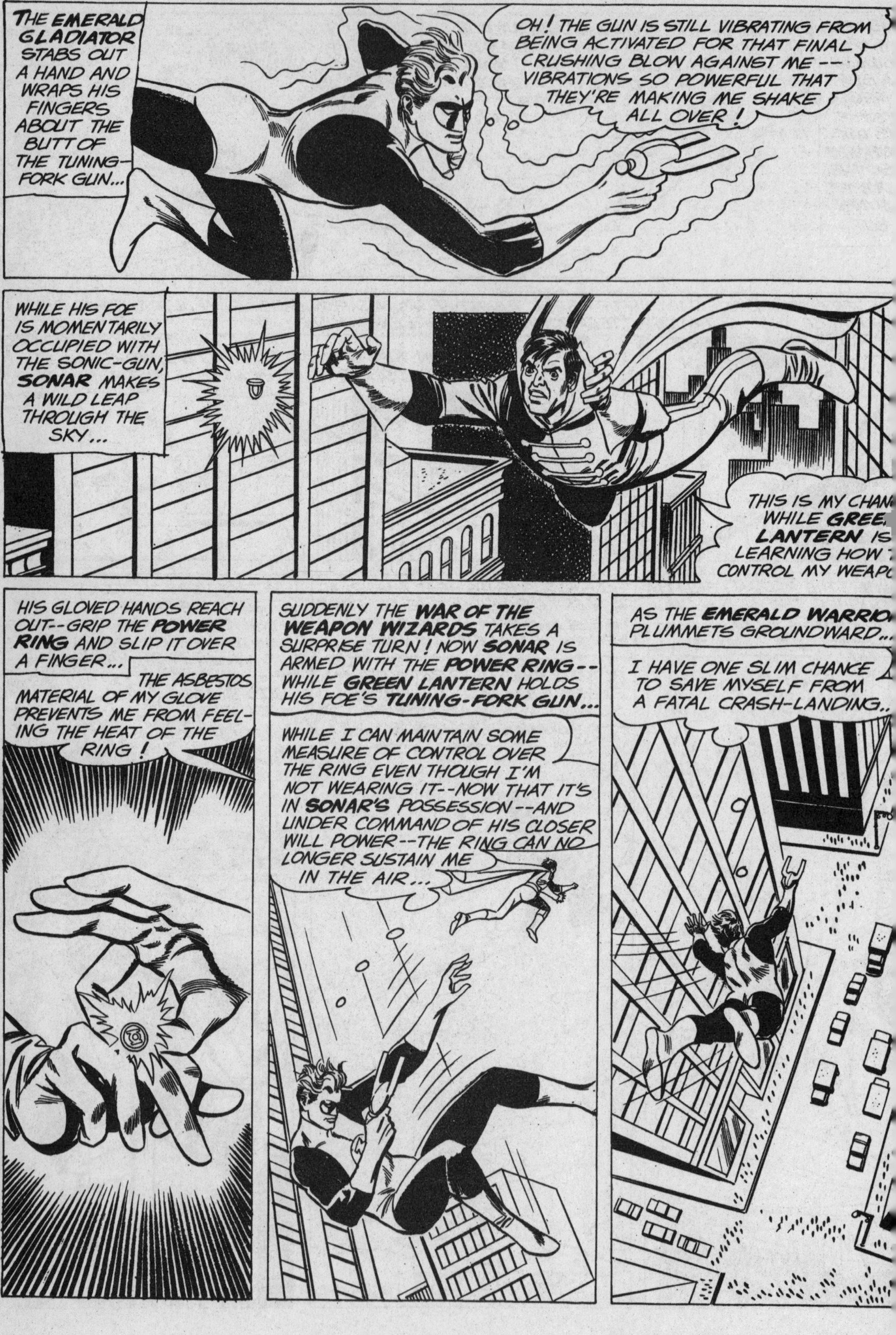
THE EMERALD GLADIATOR STABS OUT A HAND AND WRAPS HIS FINGERS ABOUT THE BUTT OF THE TUNING-FORK GUN...
OH! THE GUN IS STILL VIBRATING FROM BEING ACTIVATED FOR THAT FINAL CRUSHING BLOW AGAINST ME -- VIBRATIONS SO POWERFUL THAT THEY'RE MAKING ME SHAKE ALL OVER!
WHILE HIS FOE IS MOMENTARILY OCCUPIED WITH THE SONIC-GUN, SONAR MAKES A WILD LEAP THROUGH THE SKY...
HIS GLOVED HANDS REACH OUT--GRIP THE POWER RING AND SLIP IT OVER A FINGER...
THE ASBESTOS MATERIAL OF MY GLOVE PREVENTS ME FROM FEELING THE HEAT OF THE RING!
SUDDENLY THE WAR OF THE WEAPON WIZARDS TAKES A SURPRISE TURN! NOW SONAR IS ARMED WITH THE POWER RING--WHILE GREEN LANTERN HOLDS HIS FOE'S TUNING-FORK GUN...
WHILE I CAN MAINTAIN SOME MEASURE OF CONTROL OVER THE RING EVEN THOUGH I'M NOT WEARING IT--NOW THAT IT'S IN SONAR'S POSSESSION--AND UNDER COMMAND OF HIS CLOSER WILL POWER--THE RING CAN NO LONGER SUSTAIN ME IN THE AIR...
I HAVE ONE SLIM CHANCE TO SAVE MYSELF FROM A FATAL CRASH-LANDING...

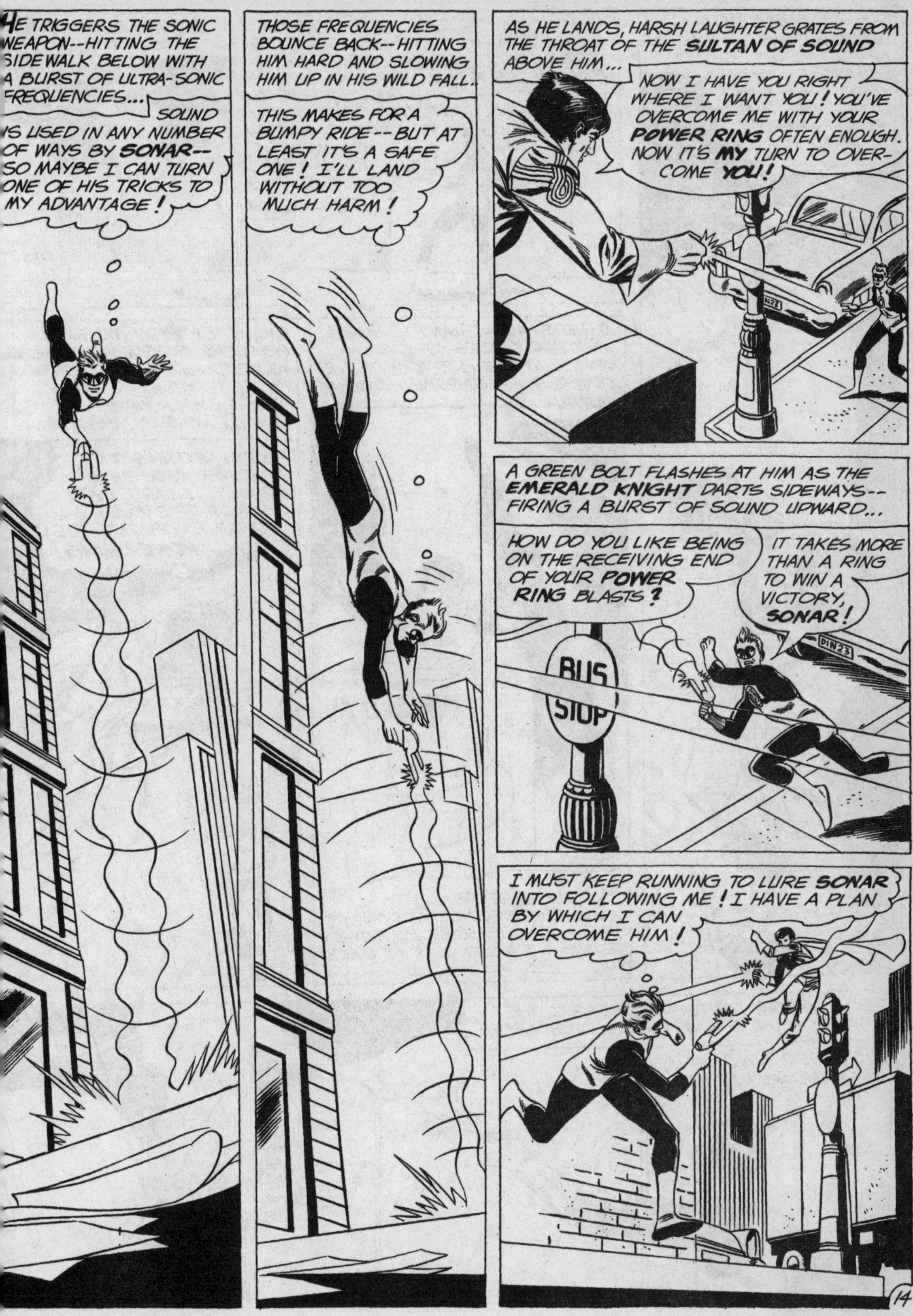
HE TRIGGERS THE SONIC WEAPON--HITTING THE SIDEWALK BELOW WITH A BURST OF ULTRA-SONIC FREQUENCIES...
SOUND IS USED IN ANY NUMBER OF WAYS BY SONAR-- SO MAYBE I CAN TURN ONE OF HIS TRICKS TO MY ADVANTAGE!
THOSE FREQUENCIES BOUNCE BACK--HITTING HIM HARD AND SLOWING HIM UP IN HIS WILD FALL.
THIS MAKES FOR A BUMPY RIDE--BUT AT LEAST IT'S A SAFE ONE! I'LL LAND WITHOUT TOO MUCH HARM!
AS HE LANDS, HARSH LAUGHTER GRATES FROM THE THROAT OF THE SULTAN OF SOUND ABOVE HIM...
NOW I HAVE YOU RIGHT WHERE I WANT YOU! YOU'VE OVERCOME ME WITH YOUR POWER RING OFTEN ENOUGH. NOW IT'S MY TURN TO OVERCOME YOU!
A GREEN BOLT FLASHES AT HIM AS THE EMERALD KNIGHT DARTS SIDEWAYS-- FIRING A BURST OF SOUND UPWARD...
HOW DO YOU LIKE BEING ON THE RECEIVING END OF YOUR POWER RING BLASTS?
IT TAKES MORE THAN A RING TO WIN A VICTORY, SONAR!
DIN23
BUS STOP
I MUST KEEP RUNNING TO LURE SONAR INTO FOLLOWING ME! I HAVE A PLAN BY WHICH I CAN OVERCOME HIM!
14

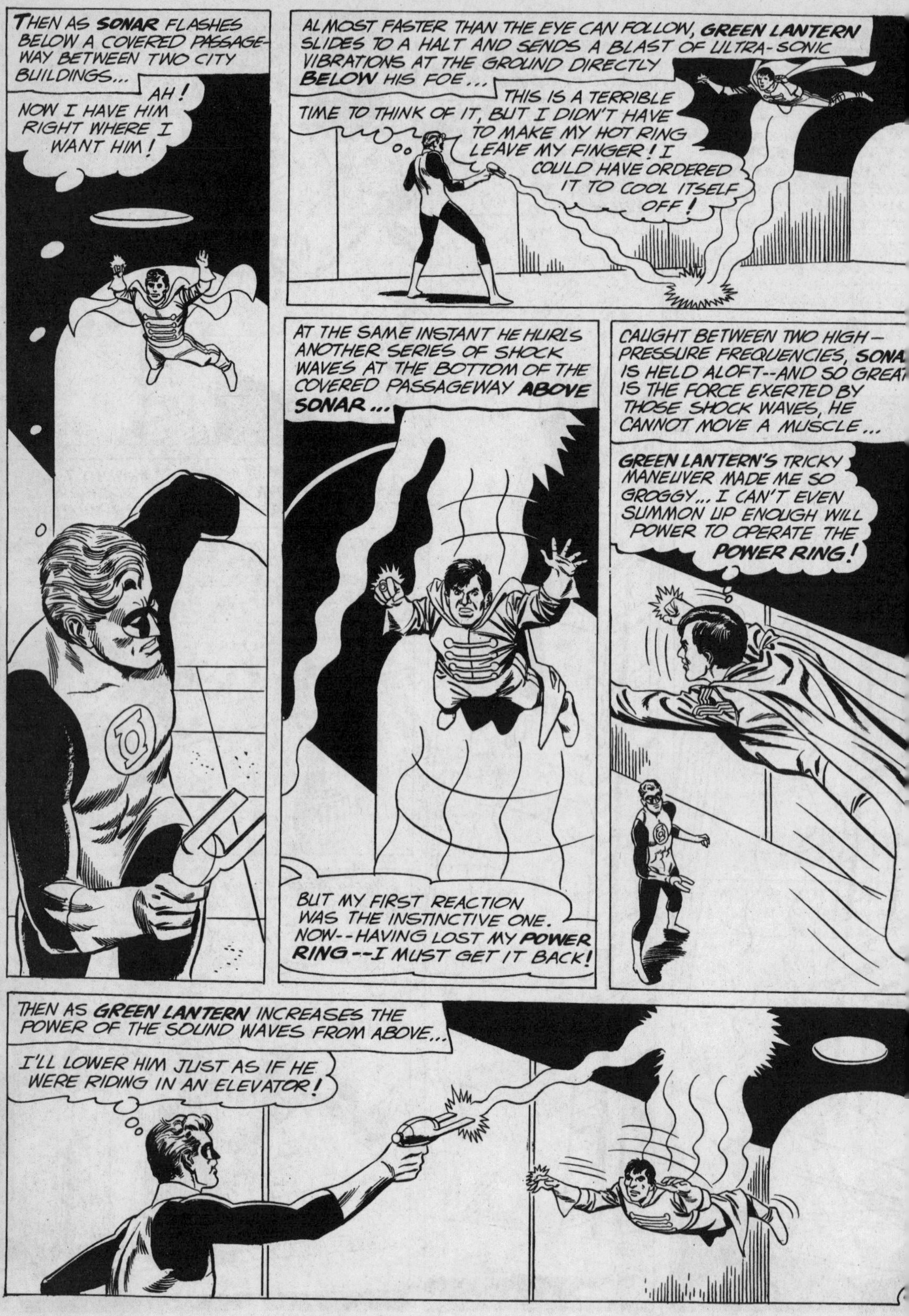
THEN AS SONAR FLASHES BELOW A COVERED PASSAGEWAY BETWEEN TWO CITY BUILDINGS...
AH! NOW I HAVE HIM RIGHT WHERE I WANT HIM!
ALMOST FASTER THAN THE EYE CAN FOLLOW, GREEN LANTERN SLIDES TO A HALT AND SENDS A BLAST OF ULTRA-SONIC VIBRATIONS AT THE GROUND DIRECTLY BELOW HIS FOE...
THIS IS A TERRIBLE TIME TO THINK OF IT, BUT I DIDN'T HAVE TO MAKE MY HOT RING LEAVE MY FINGER! I COULD HAVE ORDERED IT TO COOL ITSELF OFF!
AT THE SAME INSTANT HE HURLS ANOTHER SERIES OF SHOCK WAVES AT THE BOTTOM OF THE COVERED PASSAGEWAY ABOVE SONAR...
BUT MY FIRST REACTION WAS THE INSTINCTIVE ONE. NOW--HAVING LOST MY POWER RING--I MUST GET IT BACK!
CAUGHT BETWEEN TWO HIGH-PRESSURE FREQUENCIES, SONA IS HELD ALOFT--AND SO GREAT IS THE FORCE EXERTED BY THOSE SHOCK WAVES, HE CANNOT MOVE A MUSCLE...
GREEN LANTERN'S TRICKY MANEUVER MADE ME SO GROGGY... I CAN'T EVEN SUMMON UP ENOUGH WILL POWER TO OPERATE THE POWER RING!
THEN AS GREEN LANTERN INCREASES THE POWER OF THE SOUND WAVES FROM ABOVE...
I'LL LOWER HIM JUST AS IF HE WERE RIDING IN AN ELEVATOR!

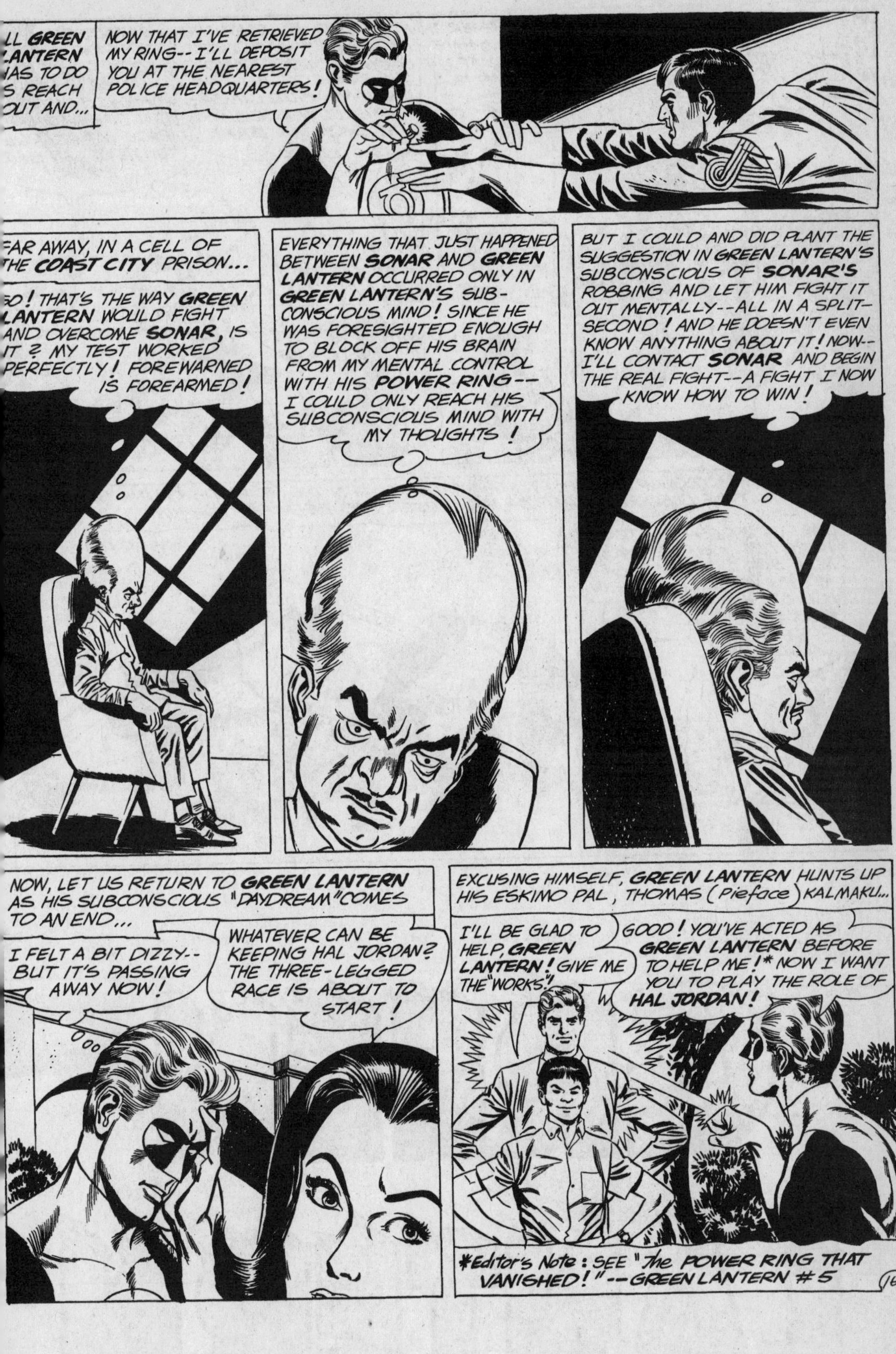
LL GREEN LANTERN HAS TO DO IS REACH OUT AND...
NOW THAT I'VE RETRIEVED MY RING-- I'LL DEPOSIT YOU AT THE NEAREST POLICE HEADQUARTERS!
FAR AWAY, IN A CELL OF THE COAST CITY PRISON...
SO! THAT'S THE WAY GREEN LANTERN WOULD FIGHT AND OVERCOME SONAR, IS IT? MY TEST WORKED PERFECTLY! FOREWARNED IS FOREARMED!
EVERYTHING THAT JUST HAPPENED BETWEEN SONAR AND GREEN LANTERN OCCURRED ONLY IN GREEN LANTERN'S SUB-CONSCIOUS MIND! SINCE HE WAS FORESIGHTED ENOUGH TO BLOCK OFF HIS BRAIN FROM MY MENTAL CONTROL WITH HIS POWER RING-- I COULD ONLY REACH HIS SUBCONSCIOUS MIND WITH MY THOUGHTS!
BUT I COULD AND DID PLANT THE SUGGESTION IN GREEN LANTERN'S SUBCONSCIOUS OF SONAR'S ROBBING AND LET HIM FIGHT IT OUT MENTALLY--ALL IN A SPLIT-SECOND! AND HE DOESN'T EVEN KNOW ANYTHING ABOUT IT! NOW-- I'LL CONTACT SONAR AND BEGIN THE REAL FIGHT--A FIGHT I NOW KNOW HOW TO WIN!
NOW, LET US RETURN TO GREEN LANTERN AS HIS SUBCONSCIOUS "DAYDREAM" COMES TO AN END...
I FELT A BIT DIZZY-- BUT IT'S PASSING AWAY NOW!
WHATEVER CAN BE KEEPING HAL JORDAN? THE THREE-LEGGED RACE IS ABOUT TO START!
EXCUSING HIMSELF, GREEN LANTERN HUNTS UP HIS ESKIMO PAL, THOMAS (Pieface) KALMAKU...
I'LL BE GLAD TO HELP, GREEN LANTERN! GIVE ME THE "WORKS"!
GOOD! YOU'VE ACTED AS GREEN LANTERN BEFORE TO HELP ME!* NOW I WANT YOU TO PLAY THE ROLE OF HAL JORDAN!
*Editor's Note: SEE "The POWER RING THAT VANISHED!" --GREEN LANTERN #5
16

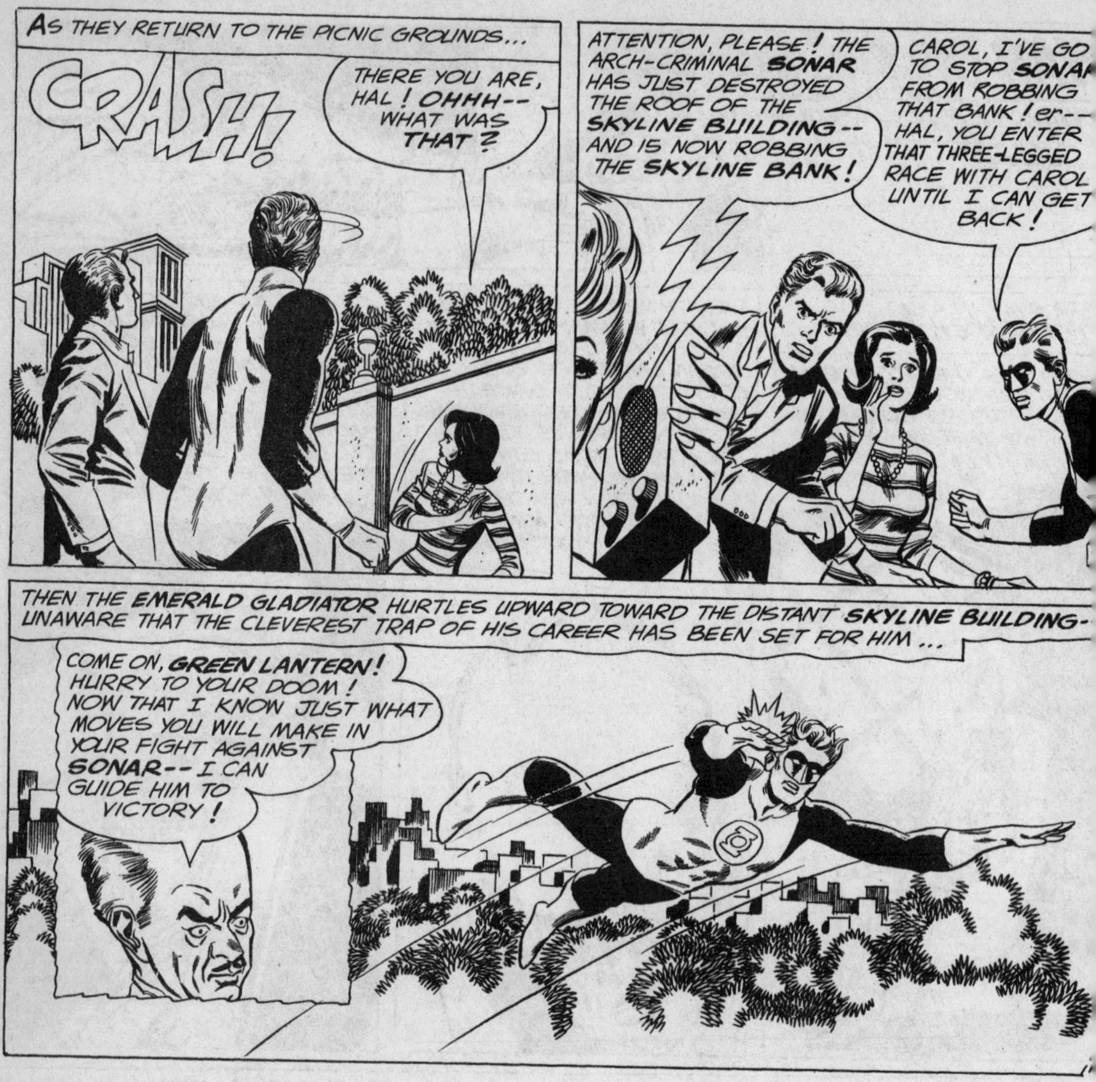

AS THEY RETURN TO THE PICNIC GROUNDS...
CRASH!
THERE YOU ARE, HAL! OHHH-- WHAT WAS THAT?
ATTENTION, PLEASE! THE ARCH-CRIMINAL SONAR HAS JUST DESTROYED THE ROOF OF THE SKYLINE BUILDING-- AND IS NOW ROBBING THE SKYLINE BANK!
CAROL, I'VE GO TO STOP SONA FROM ROBBING THAT BANK! er-- HAL, YOU ENTER THAT THREE-LEGGED RACE WITH CAROL UNTIL I CAN GET BACK!
THEN THE EMERALD GLADIATOR HURTLES UPWARD TOWARD THE DISTANT SKYLINE BUILDING-- UNAWARE THAT THE CLEVEREST TRAP OF HIS CAREER HAS BEEN SET FOR HIM...
COME ON, GREEN LANTERN! HURRY TO YOUR DOOM! NOW THAT I KNOW JUST WHAT MOVES YOU WILL MAKE IN YOUR FIGHT AGAINST SONAR-- I CAN GUIDE HIM TO VICTORY!

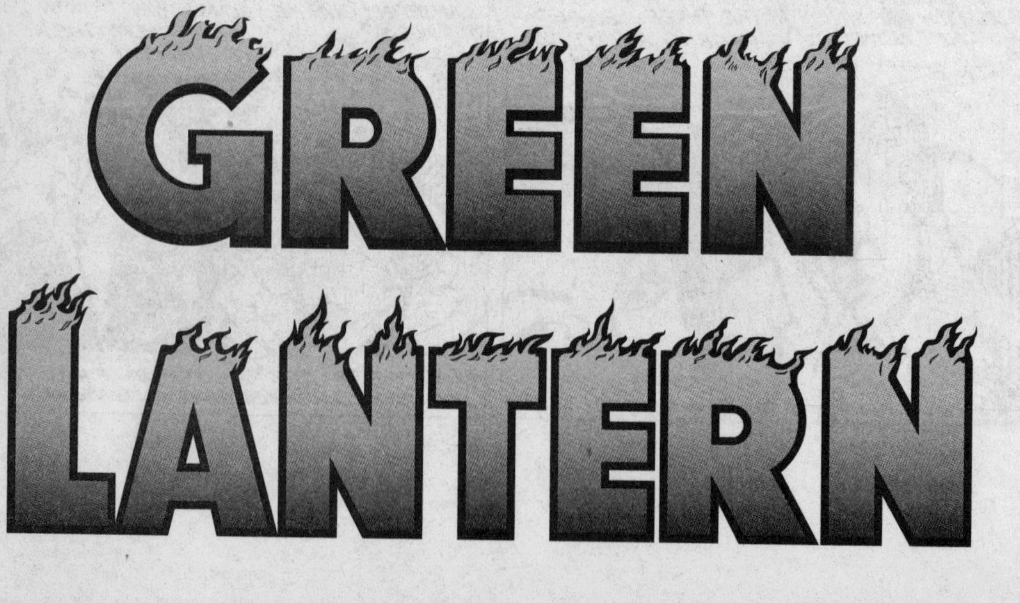

GREEN
LANTERN

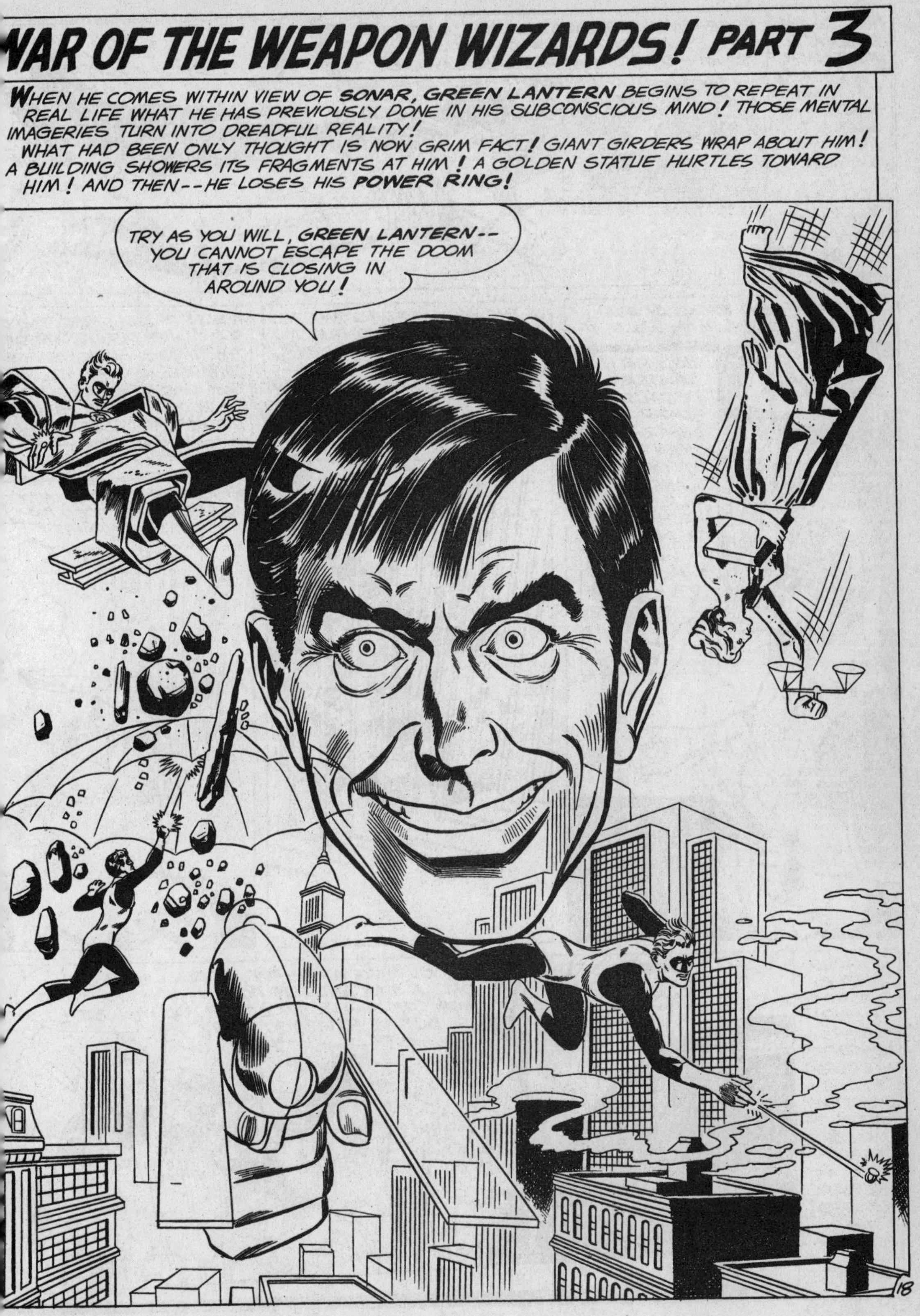
WAR OF THE WEAPON WIZARDS! PART 3
WHEN HE COMES WITHIN VIEW OF SONAR, GREEN LANTERN BEGINS TO REPEAT IN REAL LIFE WHAT HE HAS PREVIOUSLY DONE IN HIS SUBCONSCIOUS MIND! THOSE MENTAL IMAGERIES TURN INTO DREADFUL REALITY!
WHAT HAD BEEN ONLY THOUGHT IS NOW GRIM FACT! GIANT GIRDERS WRAP ABOUT HIM! A BUILDING SHOWERS ITS FRAGMENTS AT HIM! A GOLDEN STATUE HURTLES TOWARD HIM! AND THEN--HE LOSES HIS POWER RING!
TRY AS YOU WILL, GREEN LANTERN--YOU CANNOT ESCAPE THE DOOM THAT IS CLOSING IN AROUND YOU!
18

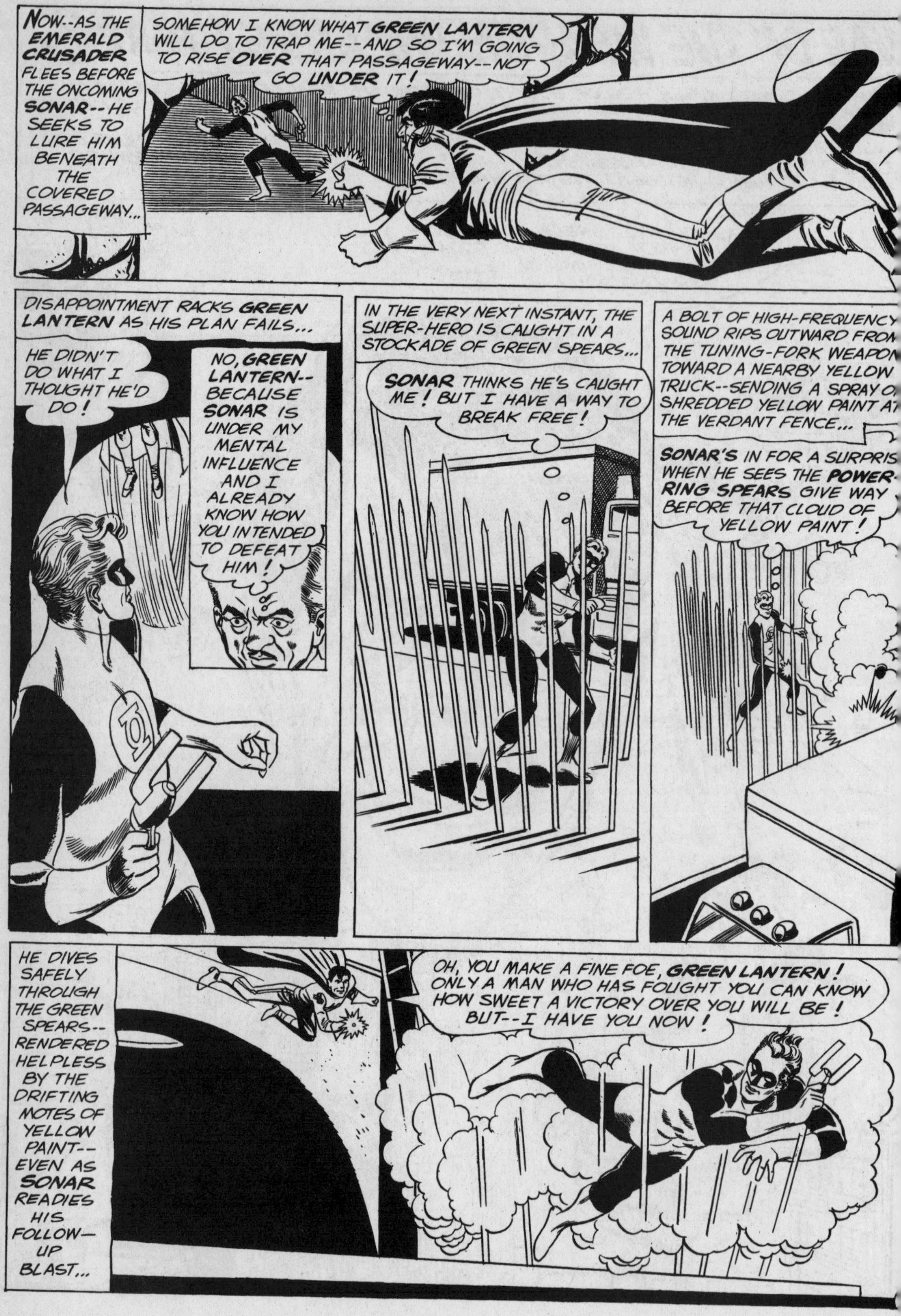
NOW--AS THE EMERALD CRUSADER FLEES BEFORE THE ONCOMING SONAR--HE SEEKS TO LURE HIM BENEATH THE COVERED PASSAGEWAY...
SOMEHOW I KNOW WHAT GREEN LANTERN WILL DO TO TRAP ME--AND SO I'M GOING TO RISE OVER THAT PASSAGEWAY--NOT GO UNDER IT!
DISAPPOINTMENT RACKS GREEN LANTERN AS HIS PLAN FAILS...
HE DIDN'T DO WHAT I THOUGHT HE'D DO!
NO, GREEN LANTERN--BECAUSE SONAR IS UNDER MY MENTAL INFLUENCE AND I ALREADY KNOW HOW YOU INTENDED TO DEFEAT HIM!
IN THE VERY NEXT INSTANT, THE SUPER-HERO IS CAUGHT IN A STOCKADE OF GREEN SPEARS...
SONAR THINKS HE'S CAUGHT ME! BUT I HAVE A WAY TO BREAK FREE!
A BOLT OF HIGH-FREQUENCY SOUND RIPS OUTWARD FROM THE TUNING-FORK WEAPON TOWARD A NEARBY YELLOW TRUCK--SENDING A SPRAY OF SHREDDED YELLOW PAINT AT THE VERDANT FENCE...
SONAR'S IN FOR A SURPRISE WHEN HE SEES THE POWER-RING SPEARS GIVE WAY BEFORE THAT CLOUD OF YELLOW PAINT!
HE DIVES SAFELY THROUGH THE GREEN SPEARS--RENDERED HELPLESS BY THE DRIFTING MOTES OF YELLOW PAINT--EVEN AS SONAR READIES HIS FOLLOW-UP BLAST...
OH, YOU MAKE A FINE FOE, GREEN LANTERN! ONLY A MAN WHO HAS FOUGHT YOU CAN KNOW HOW SWEET A VICTORY OVER YOU WILL BE! BUT--I HAVE YOU NOW!

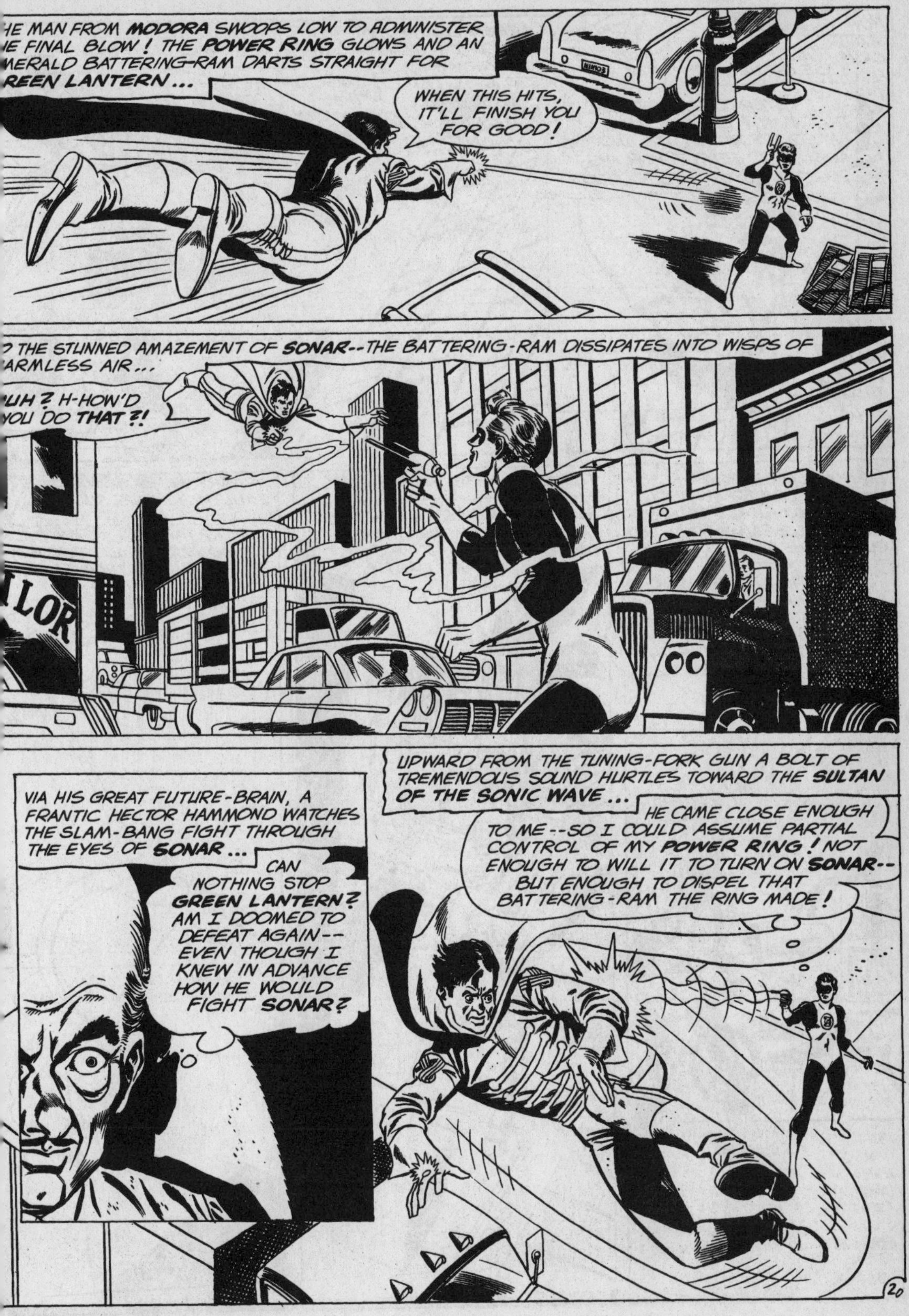
HE MAN FROM MODORA SWOOPS LOW TO ADMINISTER HE FINAL BLOW! THE POWER RING GLOWS AND AN MERALD BATTERING-RAM DARTS STRAIGHT FOR REEN LANTERN...
WHEN THIS HITS, IT'LL FINISH YOU FOR GOOD!
THE STUNNED AMAZEMENT OF SONAR--THE BATTERING-RAM DISSIPATES INTO WISPS OF ARMLESS AIR...
UH? H-HOW'D YOU DO THAT?!
ILOR
VIA HIS GREAT FUTURE-BRAIN, A FRANTIC HECTOR HAMMOND WATCHES THE SLAM-BANG FIGHT THROUGH THE EYES OF SONAR...
CAN NOTHING STOP GREEN LANTERN? AM I DOOMED TO DEFEAT AGAIN--EVEN THOUGH I KNEW IN ADVANCE HOW HE WOULD FIGHT SONAR?
UPWARD FROM THE TUNING-FORK GUN A BOLT OF TREMENDOUS SOUND HURTLES TOWARD THE SULTAN OF THE SONIC WAVE...
HE CAME CLOSE ENOUGH TO ME--SO I COULD ASSUME PARTIAL CONTROL OF MY POWER RING! NOT ENOUGH TO WILL IT TO TURN ON SONAR--BUT ENOUGH TO DISPEL THAT BATTERING-RAM THE RING MADE!
20

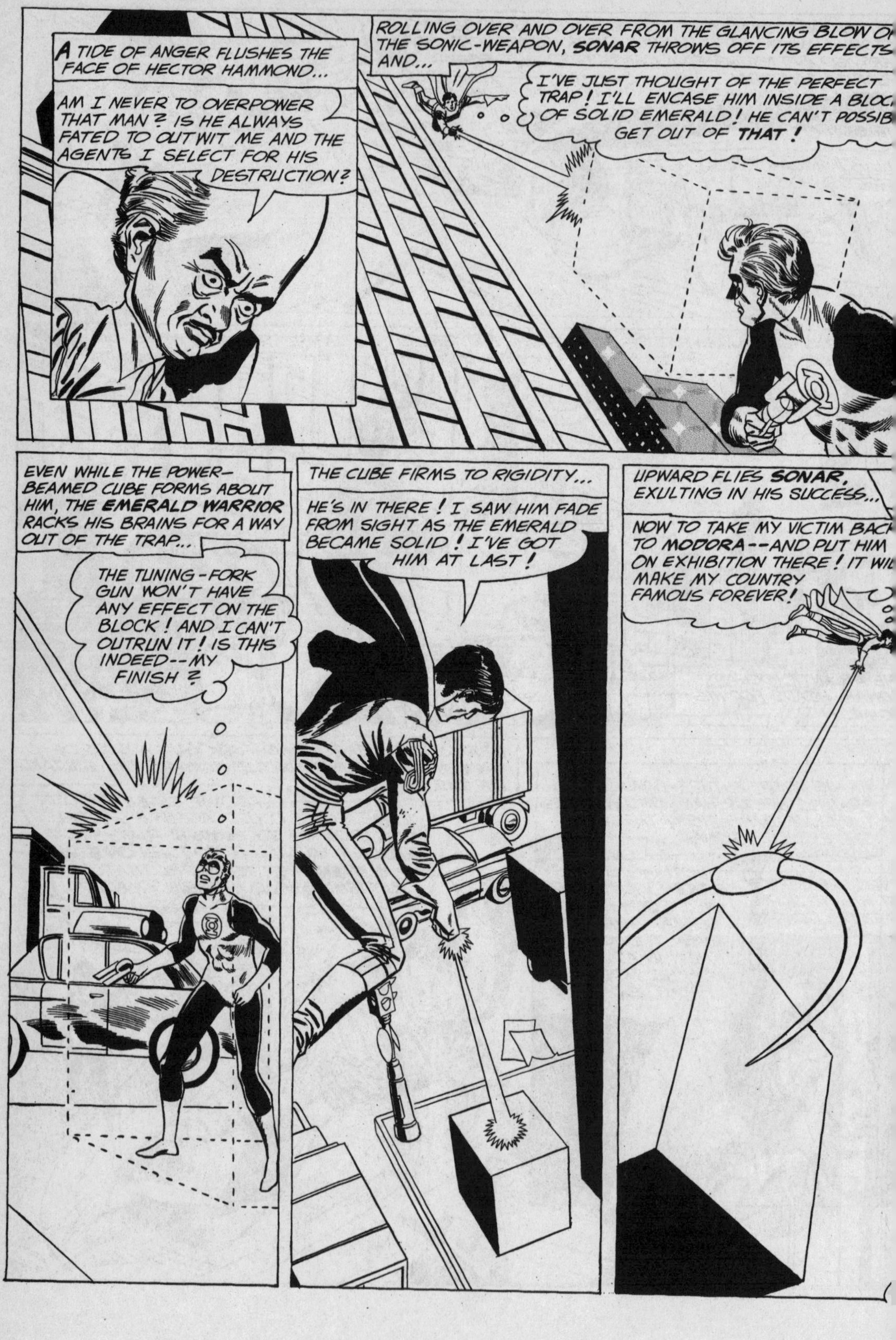
A TIDE OF ANGER FLUSHES THE FACE OF HECTOR HAMMOND...
AM I NEVER TO OVERPOWER THAT MAN? IS HE ALWAYS FATED TO OUTWIT ME AND THE AGENTS I SELECT FOR HIS DESTRUCTION?
ROLLING OVER AND OVER FROM THE GLANCING BLOW OF THE SONIC-WEAPON, SONAR THROWS OFF ITS EFFECTS AND...
I'VE JUST THOUGHT OF THE PERFECT TRAP! I'LL ENCASE HIM INSIDE A BLOC OF SOLID EMERALD! HE CAN'T POSSIB GET OUT OF THAT!
EVEN WHILE THE POWER-BEAMED CUBE FORMS ABOUT HIM, THE EMERALD WARRIOR RACKS HIS BRAINS FOR A WAY OUT OF THE TRAP...
THE TUNING-FORK GUN WON'T HAVE ANY EFFECT ON THE BLOCK! AND I CAN'T OUTRUN IT! IS THIS INDEED--MY FINISH?
THE CUBE FIRMS TO RIGIDITY...
HE'S IN THERE! I SAW HIM FADE FROM SIGHT AS THE EMERALD BECAME SOLID! I'VE GOT HIM AT LAST!
UPWARD FLIES SONAR, EXULTING IN HIS SUCCESS...
NOW TO TAKE MY VICTIM BACK TO MODORA--AND PUT HIM ON EXHIBITION THERE! IT WI MAKE MY COUNTRY FAMOUS FOREVER!

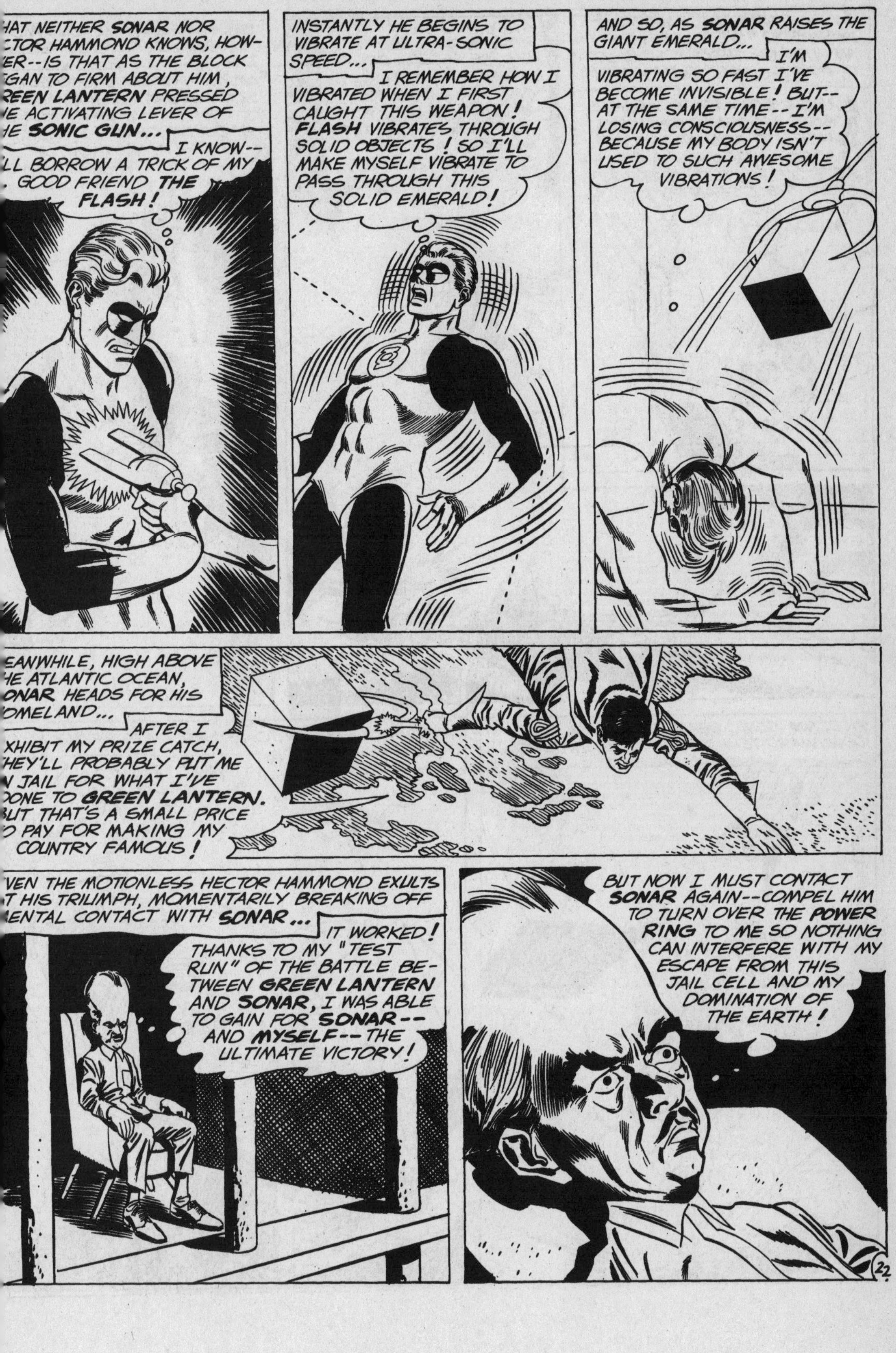
HAT NEITHER SONAR NOR
CTOR HAMMOND KNOWS, HOW-
ER--IS THAT AS THE BLOCK
EGAN TO FIRM ABOUT HIM,
REEN LANTERN PRESSED
HE ACTIVATING LEVER OF
HE SONIC GUN...
I KNOW--
LL BORROW A TRICK OF MY
GOOD FRIEND THE
FLASH!
INSTANTLY HE BEGINS TO VIBRATE AT ULTRA-SONIC SPEED...
I REMEMBER HOW I VIBRATED WHEN I FIRST CAUGHT THIS WEAPON! FLASH VIBRATES THROUGH SOLID OBJECTS! SO I'LL MAKE MYSELF VIBRATE TO PASS THROUGH THIS SOLID EMERALD!
AND SO, AS SONAR RAISES THE GIANT EMERALD...
I'M VIBRATING SO FAST I'VE BECOME INVISIBLE! BUT-- AT THE SAME TIME--I'M LOSING CONSCIOUSNESS-- BECAUSE MY BODY ISN'T USED TO SUCH AWESOME VIBRATIONS!
EANWHILE, HIGH ABOVE
HE ATLANTIC OCEAN,
ONAR HEADS FOR HIS
OMELAND...
AFTER I
XHIBIT MY PRIZE CATCH,
HEY'LL PROBABLY PUT ME
N JAIL FOR WHAT I'VE
ONE TO GREEN LANTERN.
UT THAT'S A SMALL PRICE
O PAY FOR MAKING MY
COUNTRY FAMOUS!
VEN THE MOTIONLESS HECTOR HAMMOND EXULTS
T HIS TRIUMPH, MOMENTARILY BREAKING OFF
ENTAL CONTACT WITH SONAR...
IT WORKED! THANKS TO MY "TEST RUN" OF THE BATTLE BE-TWEEN GREEN LANTERN AND SONAR, I WAS ABLE TO GAIN FOR SONAR-- AND MYSELF--THE ULTIMATE VICTORY!
BUT NOW I MUST CONTACT SONAR AGAIN--COMPEL HIM TO TURN OVER THE POWER RING TO ME SO NOTHING CAN INTERFERE WITH MY ESCAPE FROM THIS JAIL CELL AND MY DOMINATION OF THE EARTH!
22

BY THIS TIME THE *EMERALD WARRIOR* HAS MANAGED BY AN INTENSE EFFORT TO SHUT OFF THE *SONIC GUN* AND...

I'LL USE *SONAR'S* WEAPON NOW AS A *SONAR-TRACKING DEVICE--*TO FIND HIM SO I CAN GO AFTER HIM! AHHH, AS I SUSPECTED--HE'S OVER THE OCEAN ON HIS WAY TO *MODORA!*

RACING INTO THE SKY ON THE *"STEPS OF SOUND"* HE BOUNCES OFF THE SURGING WATERS BELOW, HE HURTLES AFTER HIS QUARRY AT THE SPEED OF SOUND...

BECAUSE *SONAR* IS IN NO HURRY--HE PREFERS TO SA THE TASTE OF HIS GREAT *"T UMPH"--GREEN LANTERN* SOON OVERTAKES HIM...

HE DOESN'T KNOW I'M HERE-- SO THE ADVANTAGE OF SURPRISE IS MINE

AN *ULTRA-SONIC BEAM* SPEEDS SILENTLY DOWNWARD TO HIT THE OCEAN WATERS...

INSTANTLY A GIGANTIC *GEYSER* LIFTS UPWARD LIKE A WATERY HAMMER...

WHAT...?

HOCKED INTO UNCONSCIOUSNESS BY THE STRIKING FORCE OF THE WATER, THE **SULTAN OF SOUND** IS EASY PREY FOR THE **EMERALD WARRIOR**...

NOW TO TAKE BACK MY POWER RING -- AND WIND UP THIS CASE!

WHEN **SONAR** RECOVERS HIS WITS HE IS INSIDE A VERDANT CAGE, PRISONER OF THE MAN HE THOUGHT HE HAD DEFEATED...

OHHH-- NO! YOU COULDN'T HAVE DEFEATED ME! YOU WERE MY PRISONER!

THIS WILL TEACH YOU NOT TO COUNT YOUR **GREEN LANTERNS** BEFORE THEY'RE "CATCHED"!

IT IS AT THIS MOMENT THAT HECTOR HAMMOND AGAIN MAKES MENTAL CONTACT WITH HIS AGENT...

SONAR--IMPRISONED?! WHAT WENT WRONG? HOW DID **GREEN LANTERN** ESCAPE THAT EMERALD BLOCK? FOR THE BRIEF TIME WHEN I WASN'T IN CONTACT WITH **SONAR**-- MY ARCH-ENEMY UNDID ALL MY CLEVER WORK!

FRUSTRATED, THE IMMORTAL MAN RAGES INWARDLY...

BUT I'LL TRY AGAIN! AND AGAIN! AND AGAIN! UNTIL VICTORY IS MINE! I'LL FIND ANOTHER AGENT--A BETTER ONE--EVEN IF I HAVE TO INVENT HIM! AND THE BEST PART OF IT IS-- **GREEN LANTERN** WILL NEVER REALIZE **I'M** THE ONE BEHIND HIS TROUBLES!

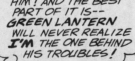

A DEJECTED **SONAR** STANDS ONCE MORE BEHIND CELL BARS--BUT THIS TIME, CELL BARS OF THE **POWER RING'S** MAKING...

HE WON'T BE ABLE TO TRY HIS SOUND TRICKS ON THESE BARS! **SONAR** WILL REMAIN IN JAIL NOW--UNTIL HE HAS SERVED HIS LONG SENTENCE!

24

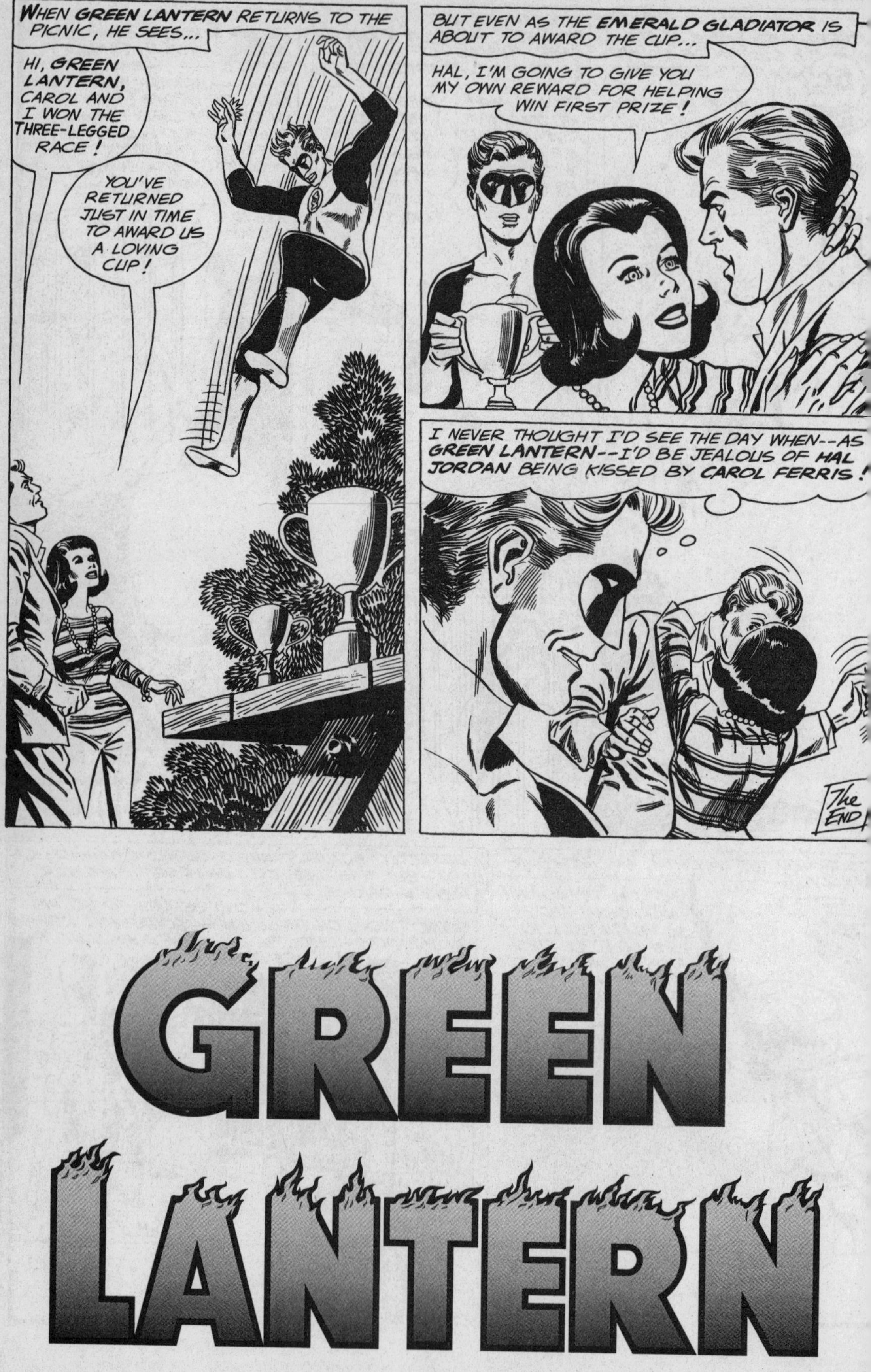
WHEN GREEN LANTERN RETURNS TO THE PICNIC, HE SEES...
HI, GREEN LANTERN, CAROL AND I WON THE THREE-LEGGED RACE!
YOU'VE RETURNED JUST IN TIME TO AWARD US A LOVING CUP!
BUT EVEN AS THE EMERALD GLADIATOR IS ABOUT TO AWARD THE CUP...
HAL, I'M GOING TO GIVE YOU MY OWN REWARD FOR HELPING WIN FIRST PRIZE!
I NEVER THOUGHT I'D SEE THE DAY WHEN--AS GREEN LANTERN--I'D BE JEALOUS OF HAL JORDAN BEING KISSED BY CAROL FERRIS!
The END

GREEN LANTERN

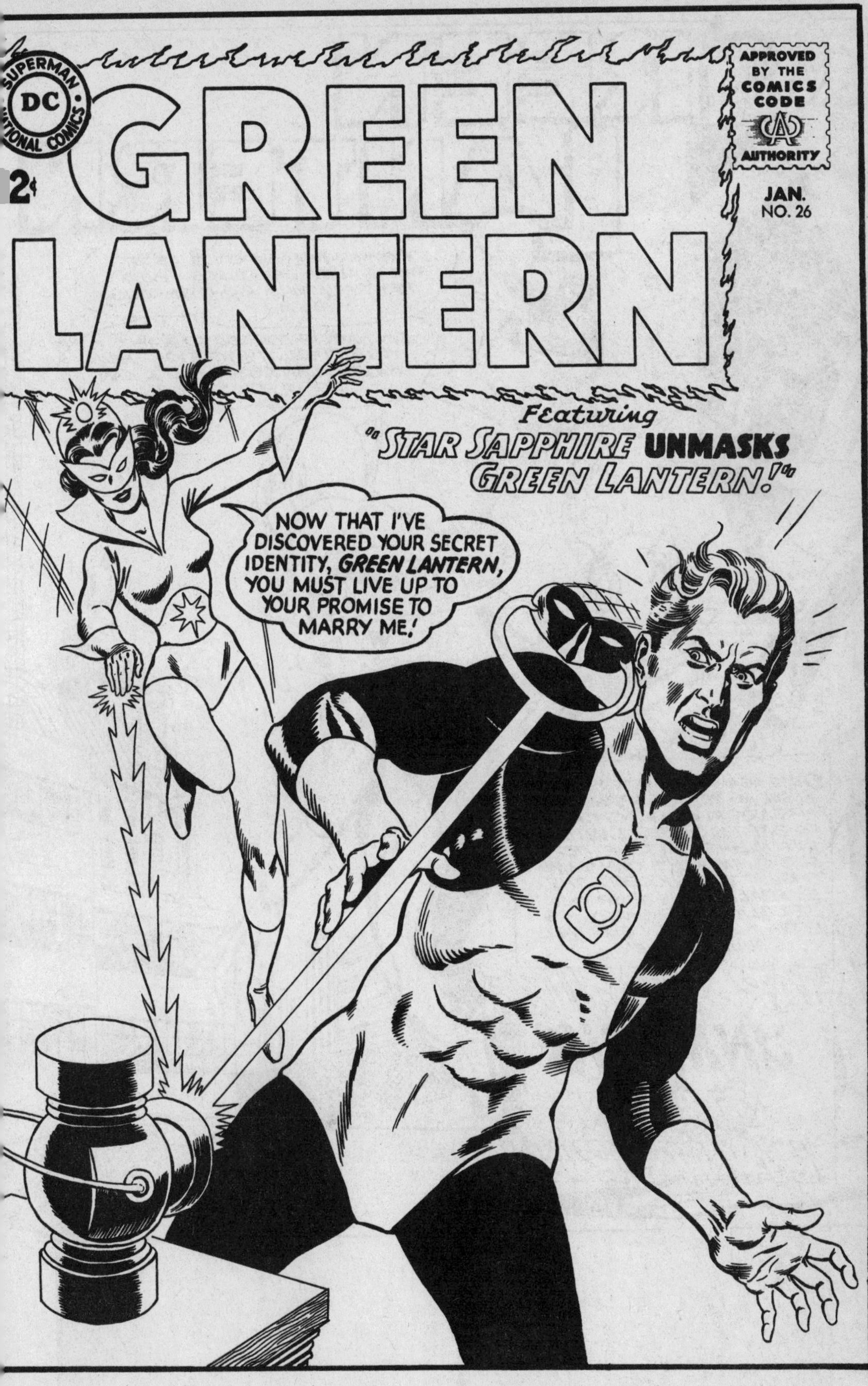
SUPERMAN DC NATIONAL COMICS
2¢
GREEN LANTERN
APPROVED BY THE COMICS CODE AUTHORITY
JAN. NO. 26
Featuring "STAR SAPPHIRE UNMASKS GREEN LANTERN!"
NOW THAT I'VE DISCOVERED YOUR SECRET IDENTITY, GREEN LANTERN, YOU MUST LIVE UP TO YOUR PROMISE TO MARRY ME!

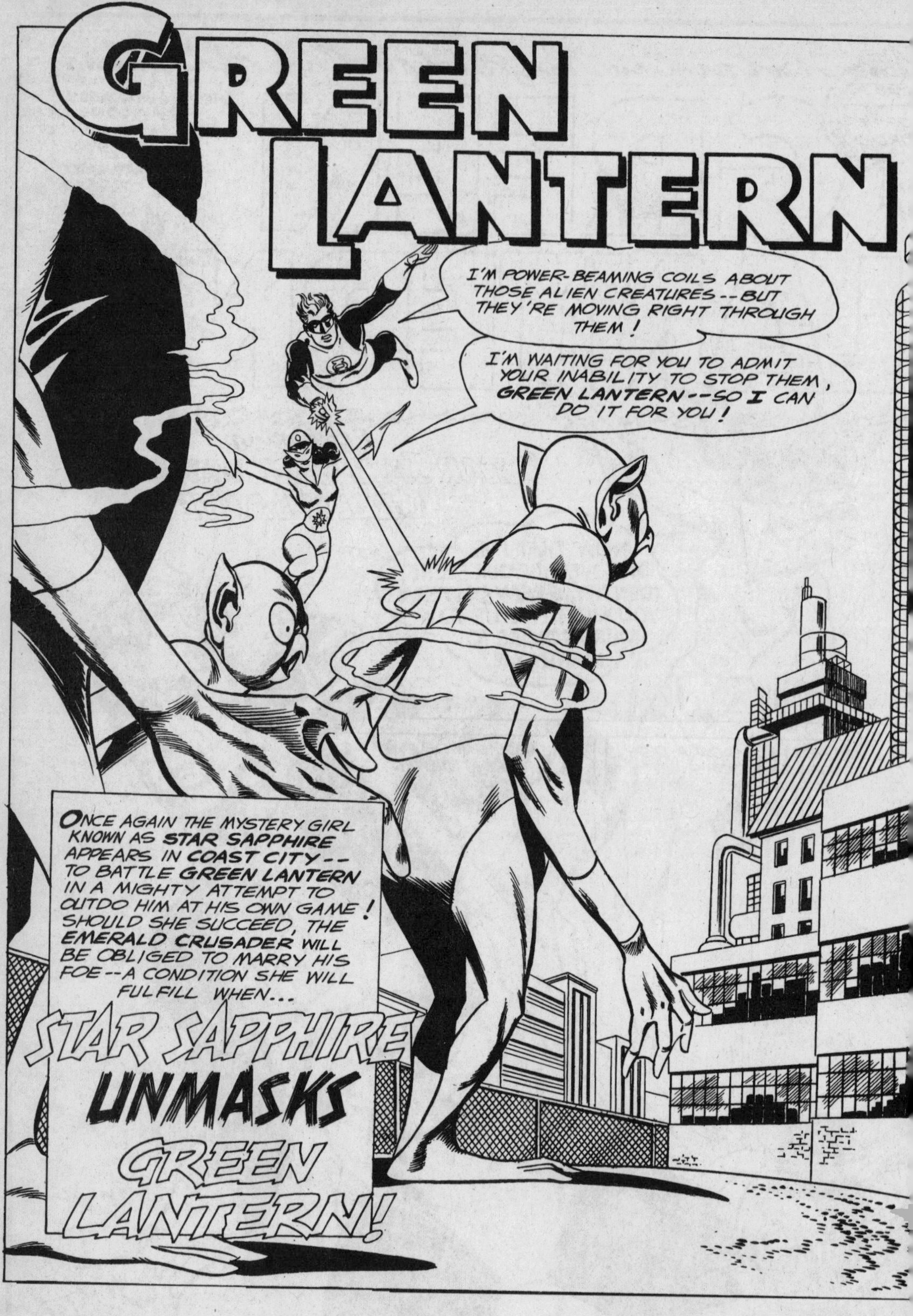
GREEN LANTERN
I'M POWER-BEAMING COILS ABOUT THOSE ALIEN CREATURES--BUT THEY'RE MOVING RIGHT THROUGH THEM!
I'M WAITING FOR YOU TO ADMIT YOUR INABILITY TO STOP THEM, GREEN LANTERN--SO I CAN DO IT FOR YOU!
ONCE AGAIN THE MYSTERY GIRL KNOWN AS STAR SAPPHIRE APPEARS IN COAST CITY--TO BATTLE GREEN LANTERN IN A MIGHTY ATTEMPT TO OUTDO HIM AT HIS OWN GAME! SHOULD SHE SUCCEED, THE EMERALD CRUSADER WILL BE OBLIGED TO MARRY HIS FOE--A CONDITION SHE WILL FULFILL WHEN...
STAR SAPPHIRE UNMASKS GREEN LANTERN!

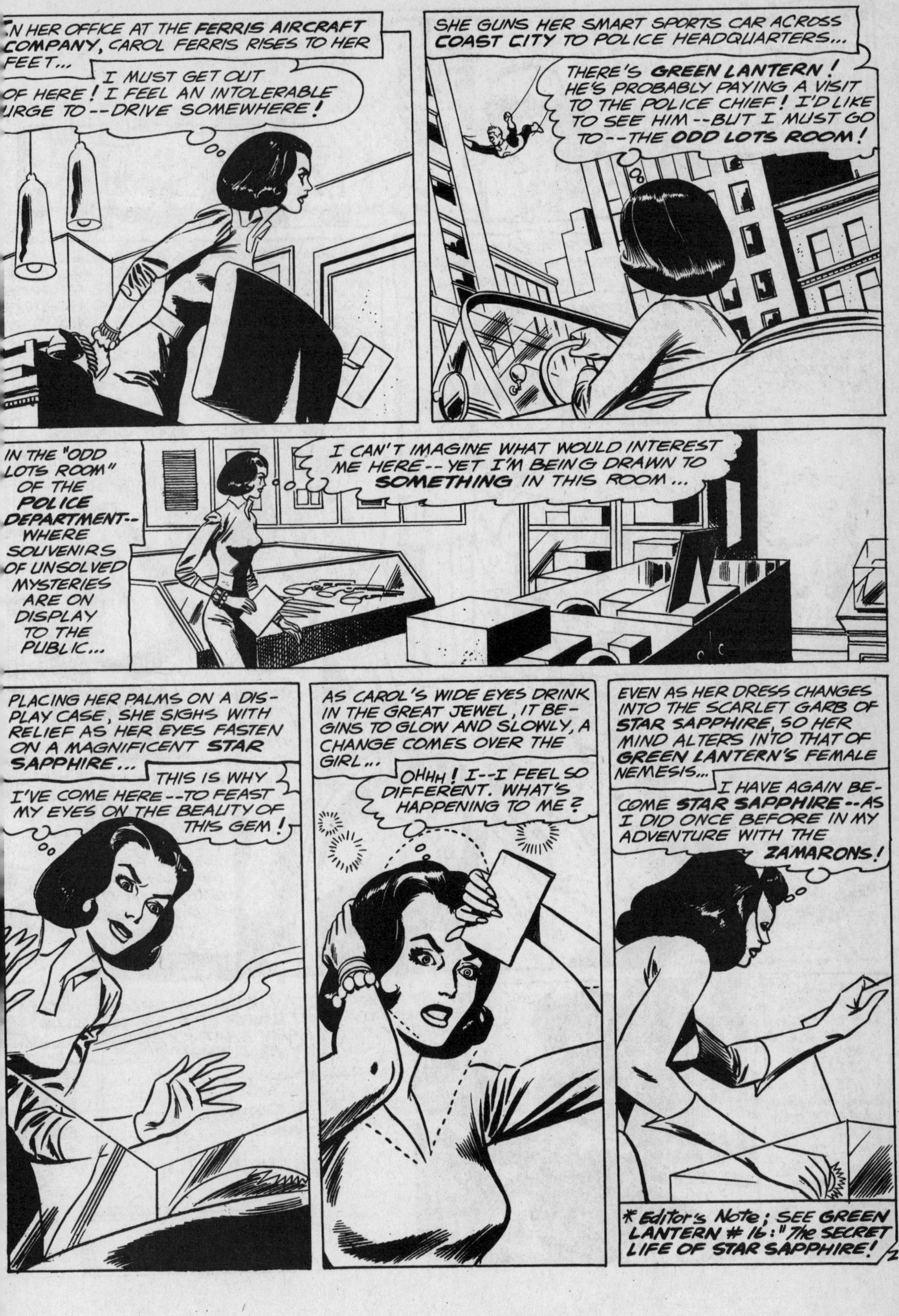
IN HER OFFICE AT THE FERRIS AIRCRAFT COMPANY, CAROL FERRIS RISES TO HER FEET...
I MUST GET OUT OF HERE! I FEEL AN INTOLERABLE URGE TO--DRIVE SOMEWHERE!
SHE GUNS HER SMART SPORTS CAR ACROSS COAST CITY TO POLICE HEADQUARTERS...
THERE'S GREEN LANTERN! HE'S PROBABLY PAYING A VISIT TO THE POLICE CHIEF! I'D LIKE TO SEE HIM--BUT I MUST GO TO--THE ODD LOTS ROOM!
IN THE "ODD LOTS ROOM" OF THE POLICE DEPARTMENT--WHERE SOUVENIRS OF UNSOLVED MYSTERIES ARE ON DISPLAY TO THE PUBLIC...
I CAN'T IMAGINE WHAT WOULD INTEREST ME HERE--YET I'M BEING DRAWN TO SOMETHING IN THIS ROOM...
PLACING HER PALMS ON A DISPLAY CASE, SHE SIGHS WITH RELIEF AS HER EYES FASTEN ON A MAGNIFICENT STAR SAPPHIRE...
THIS IS WHY I'VE COME HERE--TO FEAST MY EYES ON THE BEAUTY OF THIS GEM!
AS CAROL'S WIDE EYES DRINK IN THE GREAT JEWEL, IT BEGINS TO GLOW AND SLOWLY, A CHANGE COMES OVER THE GIRL...
OHHH! I--I FEEL SO DIFFERENT. WHAT'S HAPPENING TO ME?
EVEN AS HER DRESS CHANGES INTO THE SCARLET GARB OF STAR SAPPHIRE, SO HER MIND ALTERS INTO THAT OF GREEN LANTERN'S FEMALE NEMESIS...
I HAVE AGAIN BECOME STAR SAPPHIRE--AS I DID ONCE BEFORE IN MY ADVENTURE WITH THE ZAMARONS!
* Editor's Note; SEE GREEN LANTERN # 16: "The SECRET LIFE OF STAR SAPPHIRE!"
2

STRAIGHTENING, SHE RECALLS VIVIDLY THE EVENTS BY WHICH SHE FIRST BECAME STAR SAPPHIRE...

WE HAVE SEARCHED THE GALAXY FOR A QUEEN! YOU-- CAROL FERRIS OF EARTH-- ARE THE ONE WE HAVE CHOSEN!

SINCE YOU SAY YOU LOVE THE HERO GREEN LANTERN, WE WILL ALLOW YOU TO PROVE HE IS A WEAKLING COMPARED TO YOU!

HER GARB CHANGED INTO THAT OF A ZAMARON QUEEN, STAR SAPPHIRE THEN ENGAGED GREEN LANTERN IN A SERIES OF BRILLIANT DUELS...

I DON'T WANT TO DEFEAT YOU, GREEN LANTERN-- BUT I MUST!

I SEEM TO BE TWO PEOPLE. THE DOMINANT PART OF ME WANTS TO DEFEAT GREEN LANTERN! THE OTHER PART OF ME WANTS HIM TO DEFEAT ME!

THE STAR SAPPHIRE FROM WHICH SHE DERIVED HER GREAT POWERS WAS FOUND BY THE EMERALD GLADIATOR AFTER SHE HAD BEEN DEFEATED AND WAS RESTORED TO HER NORMAL IDENTITY AS CAROL FERRIS, FOR IT HAD BEEN DELIBERATELY LEFT BEHIND BY THE ZAMARONS...

WE FEEL RESPONSIBLE FOR CAROL FERRIS-- AND WHAT WILL HAPPEN TO HER...

YES--FROM TIME TO TIME SHE WILL ENDURE AN IRRESISTIBLE URGE TO BECOME STAR SAPPHIRE AGAIN!

WE'VE LEFT THE SAPPHIRE BEHIND SO WHEN THIS URGE COMES TO HER, SHE CAN SEEK OUT THE GEM AND BY LOOKING AT IT RE- GAIN HER STAR SAPPHIRE IDENTITY. OTHERWISE HER LIFE WOULD BE INTOLERABLE.

THE ONLY WAY SHE CAN REGAIN HER NORMAL IDENTITY IS...

BUT INSTEAD OF REVEAL- ING NOW HOW STAR SAPPHIRE CAN REVERT TO HERSELF AS CAROL FERRIS, LET US WATCH EVENTS AS THEY DEVELOP BETWEEN GREEN LANTERN AND THIS GIRL WHO LOVES HIM!

AS STAR SAPPHIRE TURNS FROM THE DISPLAY CASE SHE RECALLS THAT SHE SAW GREEN LANTERN APPROACH- ING POLICE HEAD- QUARTERS...

WITH MY POWERS, I CAN MAKE THE WALL A GREAT HEARING DEVICE ATTUNED TO MY EARS ALONE. THAT WAY I'LL LEARN WHAT MY FRIENDLY ENEMY IS DOING!

3

IN THE OFFICE OF THE POLICE CHIEF...

I'VE ASKED YOU TO LEND A HAND, GREEN LANTERN, BECAUSE COAST CITY HAS BEEN MARKED BY THE COPTER GANG FOR ITS NEXT RAID!

TELL ME MORE ABOUT THEM, CHIEF!

THEY GOT THEIR NAME BECAUSE THEY PULL OFF THEIR JOBS IN HELICOPTERS! STRANGELY ENOUGH, WHEN THE POLICE TRY TO GET THEIR WHIRLYBIRDS IN THE AIR AFTER THE CROOKS -- THEIR BIRDS WON'T FLY! SOMEHOW THE GANG DOES SOMETHING TO KEEP THEM GROUNDED!

TO GUARD AGAINST THIS HAPPENING IN COAST CITY, I'D FEEL SAFER IF YOU WERE PATROLLING THE AIR LANES WHEN THE 'COPTER GANG IS DUE TO STRIKE ACCORDING TO A TIP WE GOT FROM AN INFORMER!

STAR SAPPHIRE HAS BEEN LISTENING CLOSELY TO EVERY WORD...

SO GREEN LANTERN IS GOING AFTER THE 'COPTER GANG, IS HE? WELL, I HAVE SOMETHING TO SAY ABOUT THAT!

EXTENDING HER HAND, SHE SENDS A BOLT OF ENCEPHALOGRAPHIC ENERGY (SINCE SHE POSSESSES THE POWER OF MIND OVER MATTER) AT THE EMERALD GLADIATOR...

I'LL WARP GREEN LANTERN'S TIME-SENSE--SO THAT TIME PASSES MUCH MORE SLOWLY FOR HIM THAN FOR ANYONE ELSE--WHILE I GO CAPTURE THE 'COPTER GANG MYSELF!

SECONDS LATER SHE IS RISING INTO THE AIR...

IT MAY NOT BE SPORTING TO TAKE ADVANTAGE OF *GREEN LANTERN* THIS WAY--BUT SINCE I HAVE DETERMINED TO DEFEAT HIM AND MAKE HIM MY MATE--THE SOONER I DO IT--THE BETTER!

THE TWO PEOPLE WHO OCCUPY THE SAME BODY ENCOUNTER CONFLICTING IMPULSES WHERE THE *GREEN GLADIATOR* IS CONCERNED...

THE *CAROL FERRIS* PART OF ME WANTS TO MARRY *GREEN LANTERN!* THE *STAR SAPPHIRE* PART IS DETERMINED TO BE A QUEEN! I CAN ACCOMPLISH BOTH BY GETTING HIM TO GIVE UP HIS ROLE OF *GREEN LANTERN* AND SERVE AS MY CONSORT!

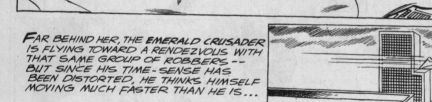

AS SHE HURTLES ABOVE COAST CITY, SHE SEES THE APPROACHING 'COPTER GANG...

ONLY BY CONVINCING HIM THAT I CAN DO A BETTER JOB AS A CRUSADER THAN HE COULD I HOPE TO GET HIM TO ABANDON HIS LIFE OF *GREEN LANTERN!*

FAR BEHIND HER, THE *EMERALD CRUSADER* IS FLYING TOWARD A RENDEZVOUS WITH THAT SAME GROUP OF ROBBERS--BUT SINCE HIS TIME-SENSE HAS BEEN DISTORTED, HE THINKS HIMSELF MOVING MUCH FASTER THAN HE IS...

THE LADY OF THE STAR-GEM SWOOPS TOWARD THE THREE WHIRLYBIRDS...

WHO IS SHE? WHAT'S SHE DOIN' HERE?

NEVER MIND THAT! JUST GET RID OF HER!

A SUBMACHINE GUN LIFTS AND CHATTERS...

RATAT!

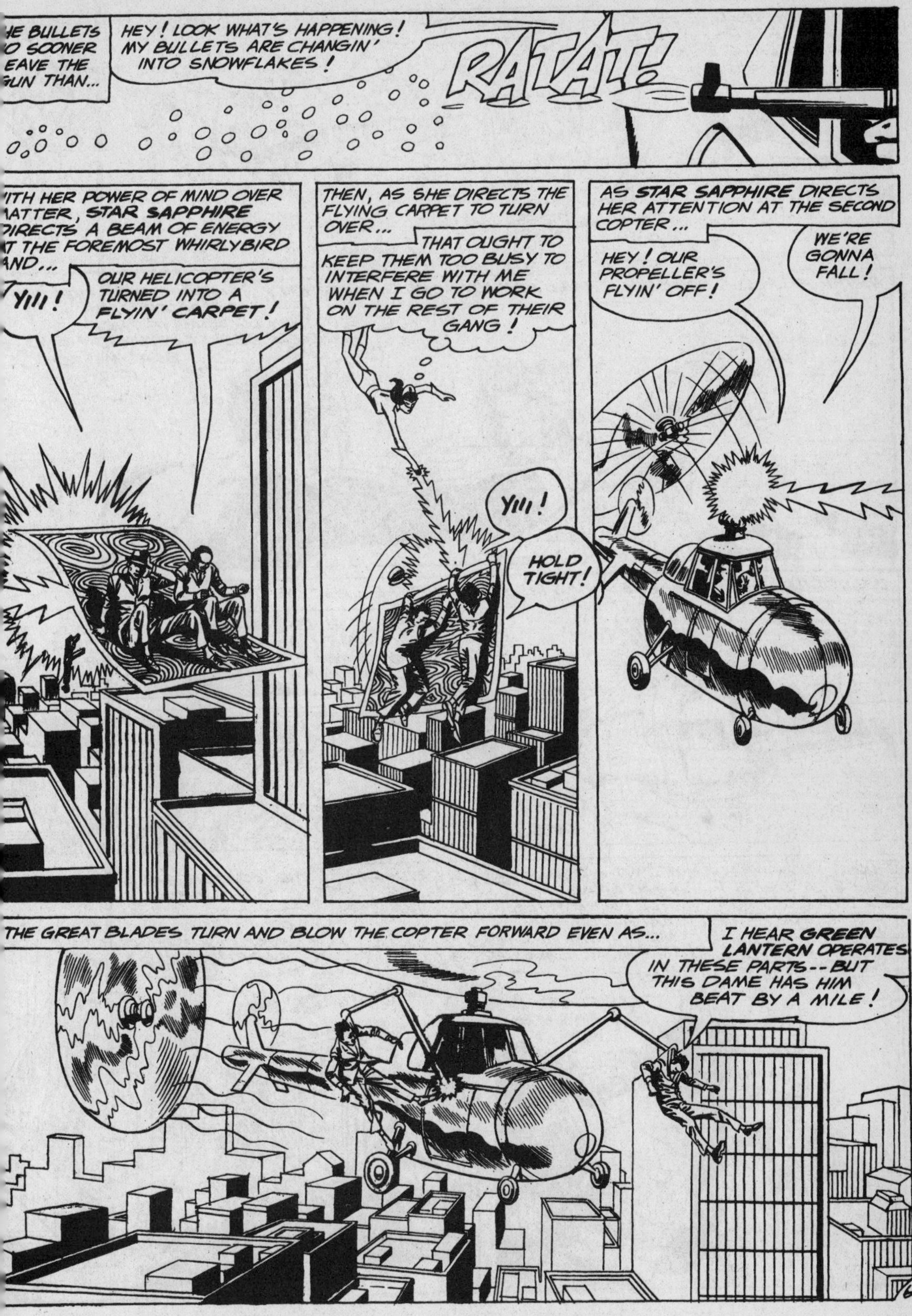

HE BULLETS O SOONER EAVE THE GUN THAN...
HEY! LOOK WHAT'S HAPPENING! MY BULLETS ARE CHANGIN' INTO SNOWFLAKES!
RATAT!
WITH HER POWER OF MIND OVER MATTER, STAR SAPPHIRE DIRECTS A BEAM OF ENERGY AT THE FOREMOST WHIRLYBIRD AND...
YIII!
OUR HELICOPTER'S TURNED INTO A FLYIN' CARPET!
THEN, AS SHE DIRECTS THE FLYING CARPET TO TURN OVER...
THAT OUGHT TO KEEP THEM TOO BUSY TO INTERFERE WITH ME WHEN I GO TO WORK ON THE REST OF THEIR GANG!
YIII!
HOLD TIGHT!
AS STAR SAPPHIRE DIRECTS HER ATTENTION AT THE SECOND COPTER...
HEY! OUR PROPELLER'S FLYIN' OFF!
WE'RE GONNA FALL!
THE GREAT BLADES TURN AND BLOW THE COPTER FORWARD EVEN AS...
I HEAR GREEN LANTERN OPERATES IN THESE PARTS--BUT THIS DAME HAS HIM BEAT BY A MILE!

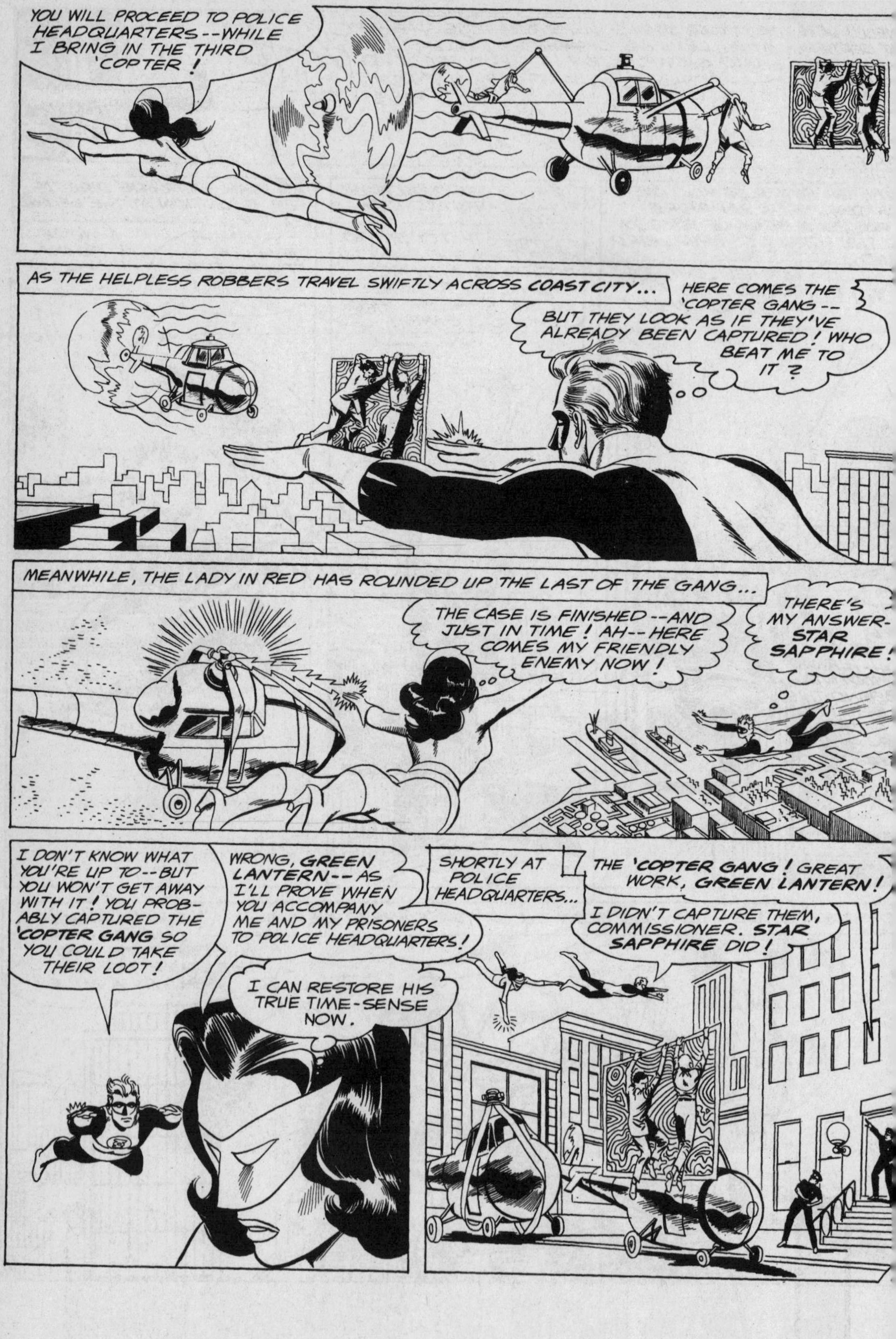
YOU WILL PROCEED TO POLICE HEADQUARTERS--WHILE I BRING IN THE THIRD 'COPTER!
AS THE HELPLESS ROBBERS TRAVEL SWIFTLY ACROSS COAST CITY...
HERE COMES THE 'COPTER GANG -- BUT THEY LOOK AS IF THEY'VE ALREADY BEEN CAPTURED! WHO BEAT ME TO IT?
MEANWHILE, THE LADY IN RED HAS ROUNDED UP THE LAST OF THE GANG...
THE CASE IS FINISHED--AND JUST IN TIME! AH--HERE COMES MY FRIENDLY ENEMY NOW!
THERE'S MY ANSWER-STAR SAPPHIRE!
I DON'T KNOW WHAT YOU'RE UP TO--BUT YOU WON'T GET AWAY WITH IT! YOU PROBABLY CAPTURED THE 'COPTER GANG SO YOU COULD TAKE THEIR LOOT!
WRONG, GREEN LANTERN--AS I'LL PROVE WHEN YOU ACCOMPANY ME AND MY PRISONERS TO POLICE HEADQUARTERS!
I CAN RESTORE HIS TRUE TIME-SENSE NOW.
SHORTLY AT POLICE HEADQUARTERS...
THE 'COPTER GANG! GREAT WORK, GREEN LANTERN!
I DIDN'T CAPTURE THEM, COMMISSIONER. STAR SAPPHIRE DID!

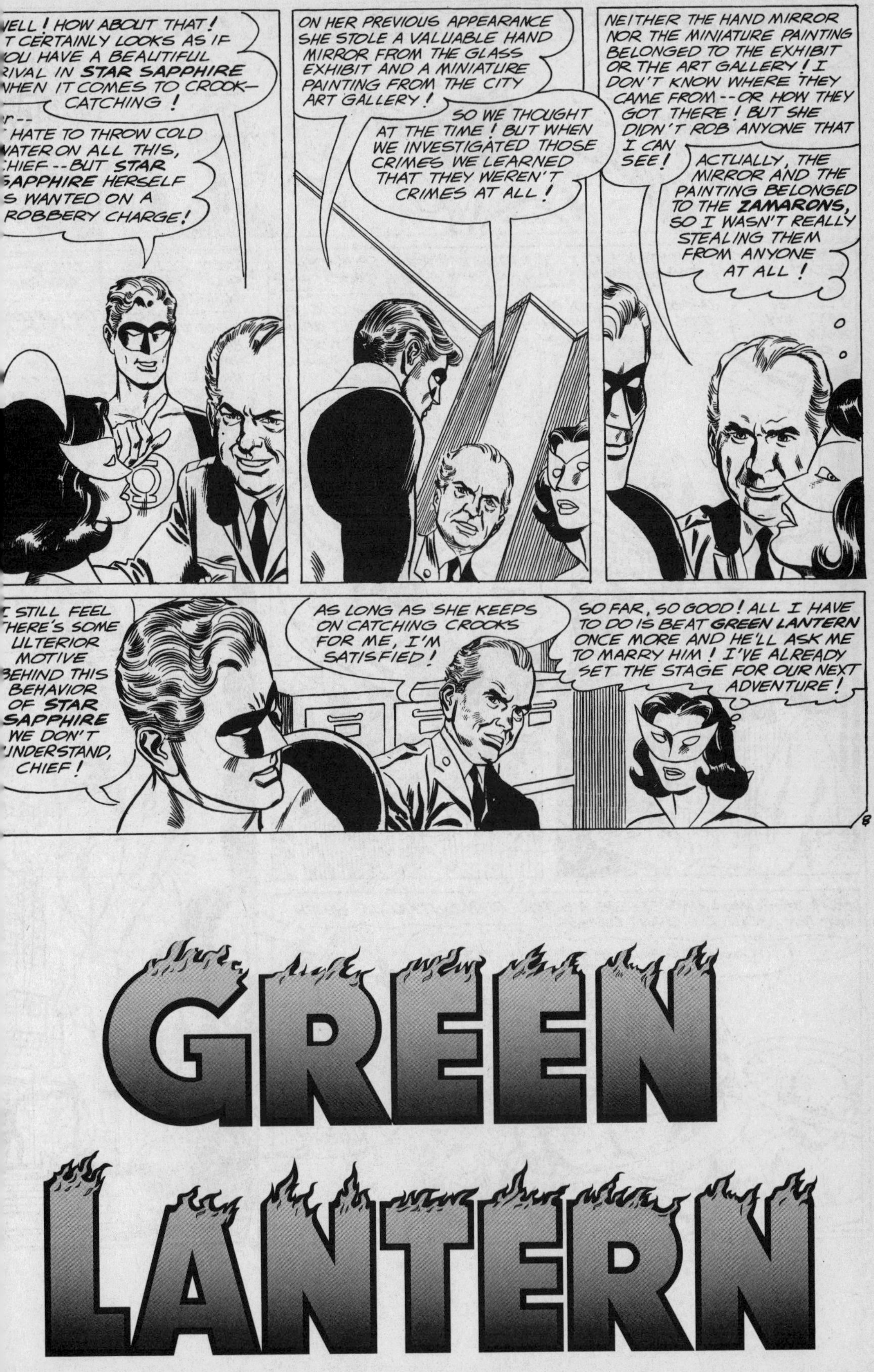

VELL! HOW ABOUT THAT! T CERTAINLY LOOKS AS IF OU HAVE A BEAUTIFUL RIVAL IN STAR SAPPHIRE WHEN IT COMES TO CROOK-CATCHING!
HATE TO THROW COLD WATER ON ALL THIS, CHIEF--BUT STAR SAPPHIRE HERSELF S WANTED ON A ROBBERY CHARGE!
ON HER PREVIOUS APPEARANCE SHE STOLE A VALUABLE HAND MIRROR FROM THE GLASS EXHIBIT AND A MINIATURE PAINTING FROM THE CITY ART GALLERY!
SO WE THOUGHT AT THE TIME! BUT WHEN WE INVESTIGATED THOSE CRIMES WE LEARNED THAT THEY WEREN'T CRIMES AT ALL!
NEITHER THE HAND MIRROR NOR THE MINIATURE PAINTING BELONGED TO THE EXHIBIT OR THE ART GALLERY! I DON'T KNOW WHERE THEY CAME FROM--OR HOW THEY GOT THERE! BUT SHE DIDN'T ROB ANYONE THAT I CAN SEE!
ACTUALLY, THE MIRROR AND THE PAINTING BELONGED TO THE ZAMARONS, SO I WASN'T REALLY STEALING THEM FROM ANYONE AT ALL!
STILL FEEL THERE'S SOME ULTERIOR MOTIVE BEHIND THIS BEHAVIOR OF STAR SAPPHIRE WE DON'T UNDERSTAND, CHIEF!
AS LONG AS SHE KEEPS ON CATCHING CROOKS FOR ME, I'M SATISFIED!
SO FAR, SO GOOD! ALL I HAVE TO DO IS BEAT GREEN LANTERN ONCE MORE AND HE'LL ASK ME TO MARRY HIM! I'VE ALREADY SET THE STAGE FOR OUR NEXT ADVENTURE!
8

GREEN LANTERN

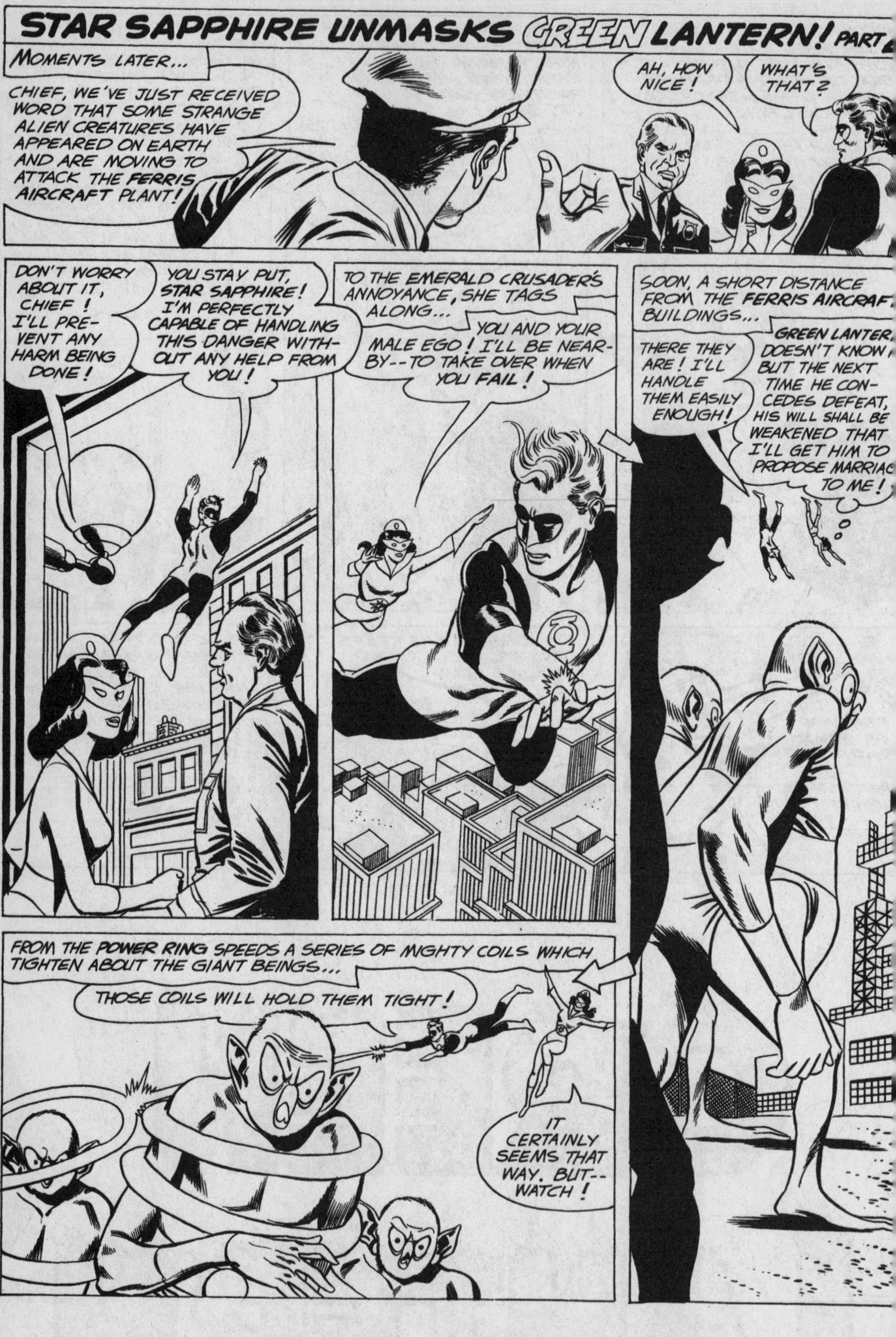
STAR SAPPHIRE UNMASKS GREEN LANTERN! PART
MOMENTS LATER...
CHIEF, WE'VE JUST RECEIVED WORD THAT SOME STRANGE ALIEN CREATURES HAVE APPEARED ON EARTH AND ARE MOVING TO ATTACK THE FERRIS AIRCRAFT PLANT!
AH, HOW NICE!
WHAT'S THAT?
DON'T WORRY ABOUT IT, CHIEF! I'LL PREVENT ANY HARM BEING DONE!
YOU STAY PUT, STAR SAPPHIRE! I'M PERFECTLY CAPABLE OF HANDLING THIS DANGER WITHOUT ANY HELP FROM YOU!
TO THE EMERALD CRUSADER'S ANNOYANCE, SHE TAGS ALONG...
YOU AND YOUR MALE EGO! I'LL BE NEARBY--TO TAKE OVER WHEN YOU FAIL!
SOON, A SHORT DISTANCE FROM THE FERRIS AIRCRAF BUILDINGS...
THERE THEY ARE! I'LL HANDLE THEM EASILY ENOUGH!
GREEN LANTER DOESN'T KNOW BUT THE NEXT TIME HE CONCEDES DEFEAT, HIS WILL SHALL BE WEAKENED THAT I'LL GET HIM TO PROPOSE MARRIAC TO ME!
FROM THE POWER RING SPEEDS A SERIES OF MIGHTY COILS WHICH TIGHTEN ABOUT THE GIANT BEINGS...
THOSE COILS WILL HOLD THEM TIGHT!
IT CERTAINLY SEEMS THAT WAY. BUT--WATCH!

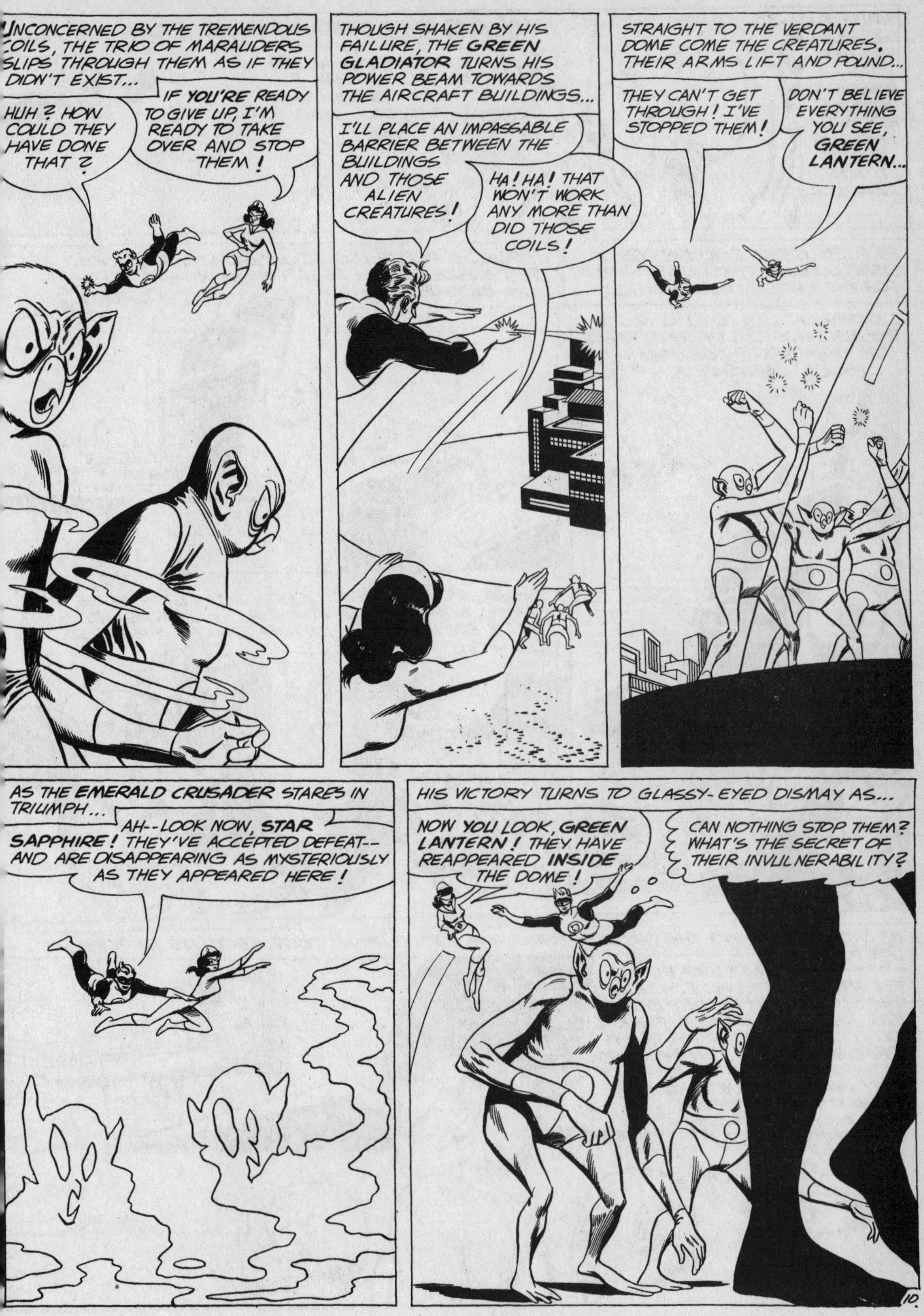
UNCONCERNED BY THE TREMENDOUS COILS, THE TRIO OF MARAUDERS SLIPS THROUGH THEM AS IF THEY DIDN'T EXIST...
HUH? HOW COULD THEY HAVE DONE THAT?
IF YOU'RE READY TO GIVE UP, I'M READY TO TAKE OVER AND STOP THEM!
THOUGH SHAKEN BY HIS FAILURE, THE GREEN GLADIATOR TURNS HIS POWER BEAM TOWARDS THE AIRCRAFT BUILDINGS...
I'LL PLACE AN IMPASSABLE BARRIER BETWEEN THE BUILDINGS AND THOSE ALIEN CREATURES!
HA! HA! THAT WON'T WORK ANY MORE THAN DID THOSE COILS!
STRAIGHT TO THE VERDANT DOME COME THE CREATURES. THEIR ARMS LIFT AND POUND...
THEY CAN'T GET THROUGH! I'VE STOPPED THEM!
DON'T BELIEVE EVERYTHING YOU SEE, GREEN LANTERN...
AS THE EMERALD CRUSADER STARES IN TRIUMPH...
AH--LOOK NOW, STAR SAPPHIRE! THEY'VE ACCEPTED DEFEAT--AND ARE DISAPPEARING AS MYSTERIOUSLY AS THEY APPEARED HERE!
HIS VICTORY TURNS TO GLASSY-EYED DISMAY AS...
NOW YOU LOOK, GREEN LANTERN! THEY HAVE REAPPEARED INSIDE THE DOME!
CAN NOTHING STOP THEM? WHAT'S THE SECRET OF THEIR INVULNERABILITY?
10.

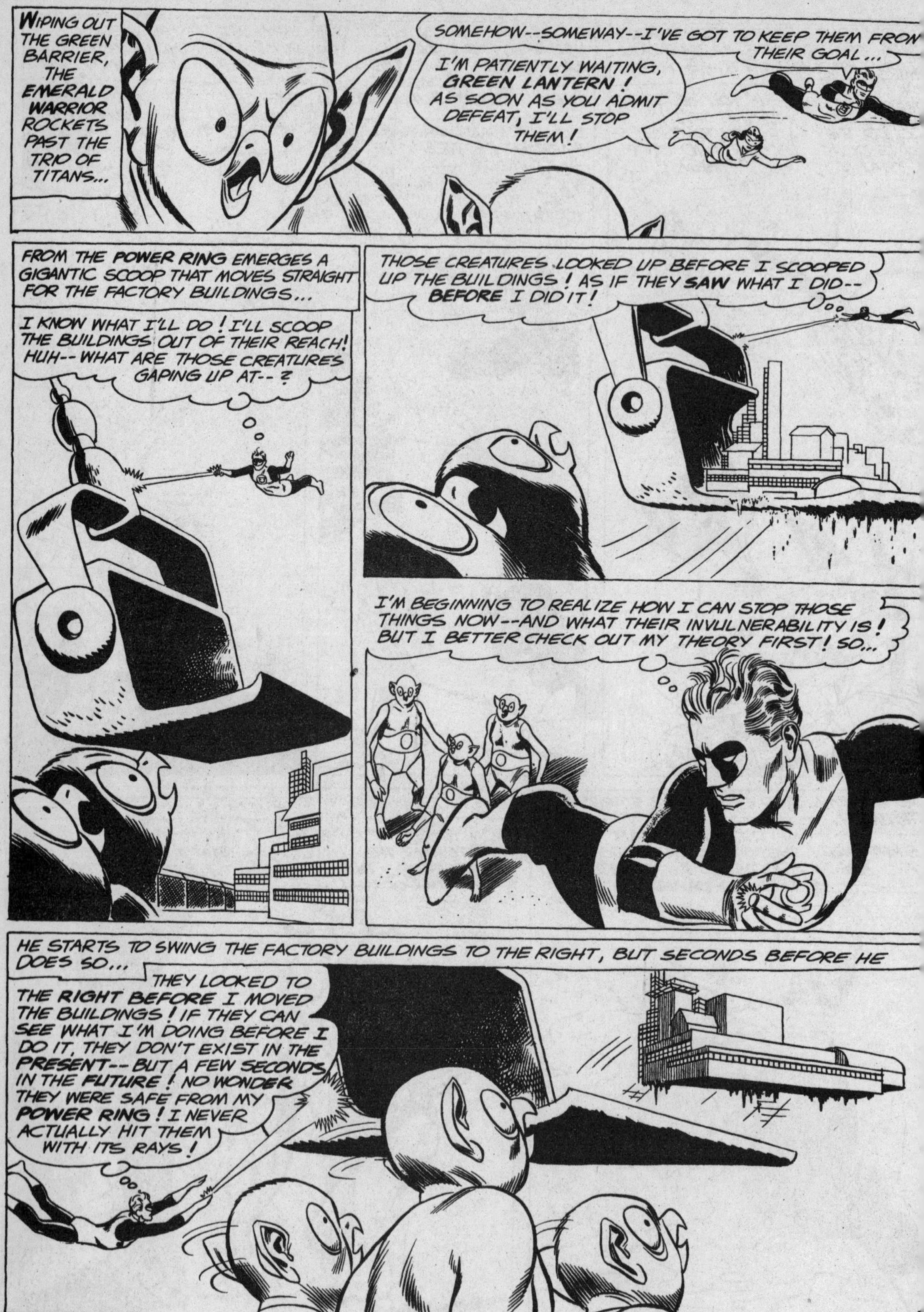
WIPING OUT THE GREEN BARRIER, THE EMERALD WARRIOR ROCKETS PAST THE TRIO OF TITANS...
SOMEHOW--SOMEWAY--I'VE GOT TO KEEP THEM FROM THEIR GOAL...
I'M PATIENTLY WAITING, GREEN LANTERN! AS SOON AS YOU ADMIT DEFEAT, I'LL STOP THEM!
FROM THE POWER RING EMERGES A GIGANTIC SCOOP THAT MOVES STRAIGHT FOR THE FACTORY BUILDINGS...
I KNOW WHAT I'LL DO! I'LL SCOOP THE BUILDINGS OUT OF THEIR REACH! HUH--WHAT ARE THOSE CREATURES GAPING UP AT--?
THOSE CREATURES LOOKED UP BEFORE I SCOOPED UP THE BUILDINGS! AS IF THEY SAW WHAT I DID--BEFORE I DID IT!
I'M BEGINNING TO REALIZE HOW I CAN STOP THOSE THINGS NOW--AND WHAT THEIR INVULNERABILITY IS! BUT I BETTER CHECK OUT MY THEORY FIRST! SO...
HE STARTS TO SWING THE FACTORY BUILDINGS TO THE RIGHT, BUT SECONDS BEFORE HE DOES SO...
THEY LOOKED TO THE RIGHT BEFORE I MOVED THE BUILDINGS! IF THEY CAN SEE WHAT I'M DOING BEFORE I DO IT, THEY DON'T EXIST IN THE PRESENT--BUT A FEW SECONDS IN THE FUTURE! NO WONDER THEY WERE SAFE FROM MY POWER RING! I NEVER ACTUALLY HIT THEM WITH ITS RAYS!

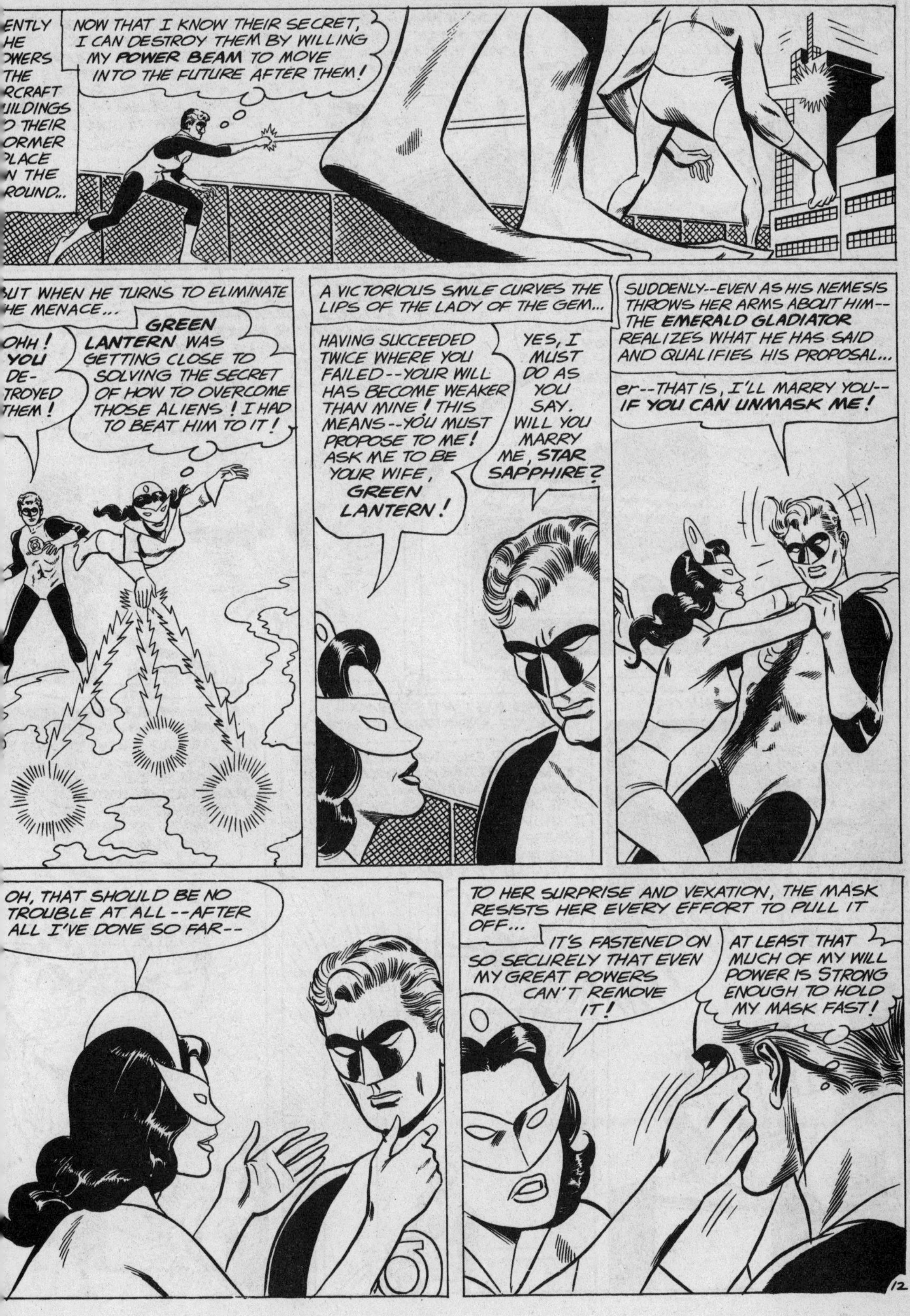
ENTLY HE OWERS THE RCRAFT UILDINGS O THEIR ORMER PLACE N THE ROUND...
NOW THAT I KNOW THEIR SECRET, I CAN DESTROY THEM BY WILLING MY POWER BEAM TO MOVE INTO THE FUTURE AFTER THEM!
BUT WHEN HE TURNS TO ELIMINATE HE MENACE...
OHH! YOU DE-TROYED THEM!
GREEN LANTERN WAS GETTING CLOSE TO SOLVING THE SECRET OF HOW TO OVERCOME THOSE ALIENS! I HAD TO BEAT HIM TO IT!
A VICTORIOUS SMILE CURVES THE LIPS OF THE LADY OF THE GEM...
HAVING SUCCEEDED TWICE WHERE YOU FAILED--YOUR WILL HAS BECOME WEAKER THAN MINE! THIS MEANS--YOU MUST PROPOSE TO ME! ASK ME TO BE YOUR WIFE, GREEN LANTERN!
YES, I MUST DO AS YOU SAY. WILL YOU MARRY ME, STAR SAPPHIRE?
SUDDENLY--EVEN AS HIS NEMESIS THROWS HER ARMS ABOUT HIM--THE EMERALD GLADIATOR REALIZES WHAT HE HAS SAID AND QUALIFIES HIS PROPOSAL...
er--THAT IS, I'LL MARRY YOU--IF YOU CAN UNMASK ME!
OH, THAT SHOULD BE NO TROUBLE AT ALL--AFTER ALL I'VE DONE SO FAR--
TO HER SURPRISE AND VEXATION, THE MASK RESISTS HER EVERY EFFORT TO PULL IT OFF...
IT'S FASTENED ON SO SECURELY THAT EVEN MY GREAT POWERS CAN'T REMOVE IT!
AT LEAST THAT MUCH OF MY WILL POWER IS STRONG ENOUGH TO HOLD MY MASK FAST!
12

IN THE NEXT MOMENT...

GUESS I'M SAFE ENOUGH FOR A WHILE, STAR SAPPHIRE! AS LONG AS MY MASK STAYS ON-- YOU'LL HAVE TO GET ALONG WITHOUT A HUSBAND!

I COULD "FEEL" HIS TREMENDOUS WILL POWER WHEN MY FINGERS TOUCHED HIS MASK. MY JOB NOW IS TO FIND A WAY TO OVERCOME THAT WILL POWER IN ORDER TO REMOVE HIS MASK.

AS SHE STANDS ALONE NEAR THE FERRIS AIRCRAFT HANGAR, STAR SAPPHIRE TOUCHES HER FINGERTIPS TO HER TEMPLES...

STRANGE! EVEN THOUGH GREEN LANTERN HAS GONE--I SENSE AROUND HERE THE SAME SORT OF POWER HE CARRIES IN HIS RING! Hmm--I WONDER WHERE IT COULD BE COMING FROM?

CHUCKLING OVER HIS VICTORY, GREEN LANTERN SECRETLY RETURNS TO THE FERRIS AIRCRAFT PLANT TO RECHARGE HIS POWER RING IN THE HANGAR DRESSING ROOM WHERE HE KEEPS THE POWER BATTERY...

NO SIGN OF HER! I GUESS SHE RAN AWAY TO SHED SOME ANGRY TEARS!

ONCE AGAIN A SOLEMN OATH IS REPEATED...

IN BRIGHTEST DAY, IN BLACKEST NIGHT, NO EVIL SHALL ESCAPE MY SIGHT...

AT THIS INSTANT, SPREAD-EAGLED ATOP THE CEILING...

I SENSED THE PRESENCE OF THE POWER BATTERY THROUGH ITS ENERGY VIBRATIONS--BUT SINCE IT'S INVISIBLE I COULDN'T SEE IT! I ONLY KNEW IT WAS SOMEWHERE INSIDE HERE, SO I WAITED FOR GREEN LANTERN TO RETURN TO REVEAL IT TO ME!

THE POWER BATTERY--PLUS MY OWN SAPPHIRE STRENGTH WILL BE TOO MUCH FOR HIM TO RESIST! I'LL GAIN MY TRIUMPH BY SECRETLY ORDERING GREEN LANTERN'S SUBCONSCIOUS TO REMOVE HIS MASK!

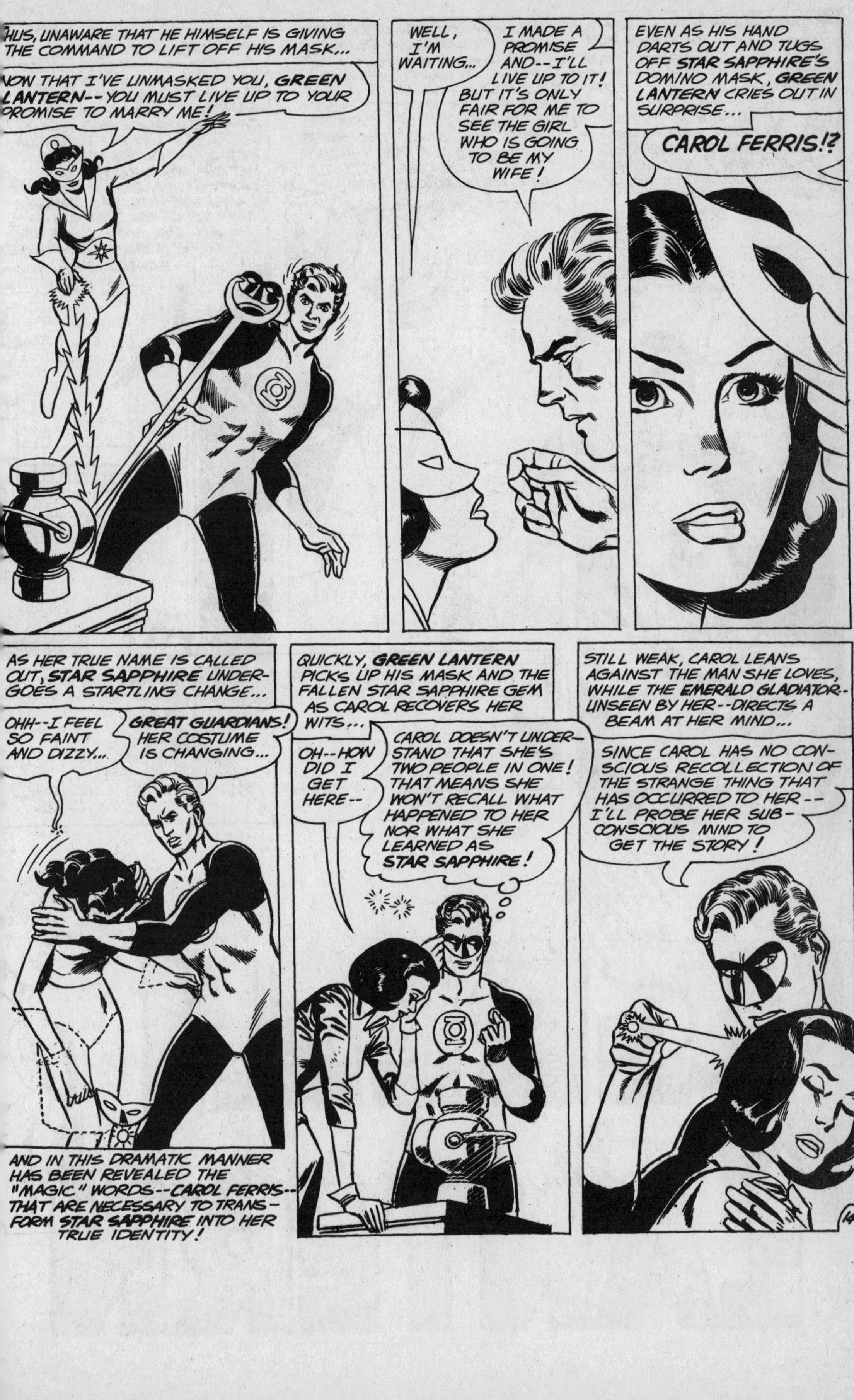
HUS, UNAWARE THAT HE HIMSELF IS GIVING THE COMMAND TO LIFT OFF HIS MASK...
NOW THAT I'VE UNMASKED YOU, GREEN LANTERN--YOU MUST LIVE UP TO YOUR PROMISE TO MARRY ME!
WELL, I'M WAITING...
I MADE A PROMISE AND--I'LL LIVE UP TO IT! BUT IT'S ONLY FAIR FOR ME TO SEE THE GIRL WHO IS GOING TO BE MY WIFE!
EVEN AS HIS HAND DARTS OUT AND TUGS OFF STAR SAPPHIRE'S DOMINO MASK, GREEN LANTERN CRIES OUT IN SURPRISE...
CAROL FERRIS!?
AS HER TRUE NAME IS CALLED OUT, STAR SAPPHIRE UNDERGOES A STARTLING CHANGE...
OHH--I FEEL SO FAINT AND DIZZY...
GREAT GUARDIANS! HER COSTUME IS CHANGING...
AND IN THIS DRAMATIC MANNER HAS BEEN REVEALED THE "MAGIC" WORDS--CAROL FERRIS--THAT ARE NECESSARY TO TRANSFORM STAR SAPPHIRE INTO HER TRUE IDENTITY!
QUICKLY, GREEN LANTERN PICKS UP HIS MASK AND THE FALLEN STAR SAPPHIRE GEM AS CAROL RECOVERS HER WITS...
OH--HOW DID I GET HERE--
CAROL DOESN'T UNDERSTAND THAT SHE'S TWO PEOPLE IN ONE! THAT MEANS SHE WON'T RECALL WHAT HAPPENED TO HER NOR WHAT SHE LEARNED AS STAR SAPPHIRE!
STILL WEAK, CAROL LEANS AGAINST THE MAN SHE LOVES, WHILE THE EMERALD GLADIATOR--UNSEEN BY HER--DIRECTS A BEAM AT HER MIND...
SINCE CAROL HAS NO CONSCIOUS RECOLLECTION OF THE STRANGE THING THAT HAS OCCURRED TO HER--I'LL PROBE HER SUBCONSCIOUS MIND TO GET THE STORY!
14

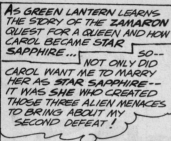

As GREEN LANTERN LEARNS THE STORY OF THE ZAMARON QUEST FOR A QUEEN AND HOW CAROL BECAME STAR SAPPHIRE...

SO-- NOT ONLY DID CAROL WANT ME TO MARRY HER AS STAR SAPPHIRE-- IT WAS SHE WHO CREATED THOSE THREE ALIEN MENACES TO BRING ABOUT MY SECOND DEFEAT!

SHE CREATED THE CREATURES BY MENTAL ENERGY PLUS THE COSMIC RAYS WHICH GO EVERY-WHERE ON EARTH. WHEN THEY TOUCHED MY BARRIER IT WAS SHE WHO DESTROYED THEM-- THEN CREATED DUPLICATE CREATURES INSIDE THE GREEN DOME! SHE CERTAINLY WAS TRICKY IN HER EFFORTS TO GET ME TO MARRY HER!

TENDERLY HE HELPS CAROL FROM THE HANGAR...

I'LL STILL HAVE TO FULFILL MY PROMISE TO MARRY STAR SAPPHIRE WHEN--AND IF-- CAROL BECOMES HER ALTER EGO AGAIN! IN THE LONG RUN THOUGH--I GUESS IT DOESN'T MATTER. WHETHER GREEN LANTERN MARRIES STAR SAPPHIRE--OR HAL JORDAN MARRIES CAROL FERRIS-- IT'S ALL THE SAME! SHE AND I WILL BE HUSBAND AND WIFE SOMEDAY!

The End

GREEN LANTERN

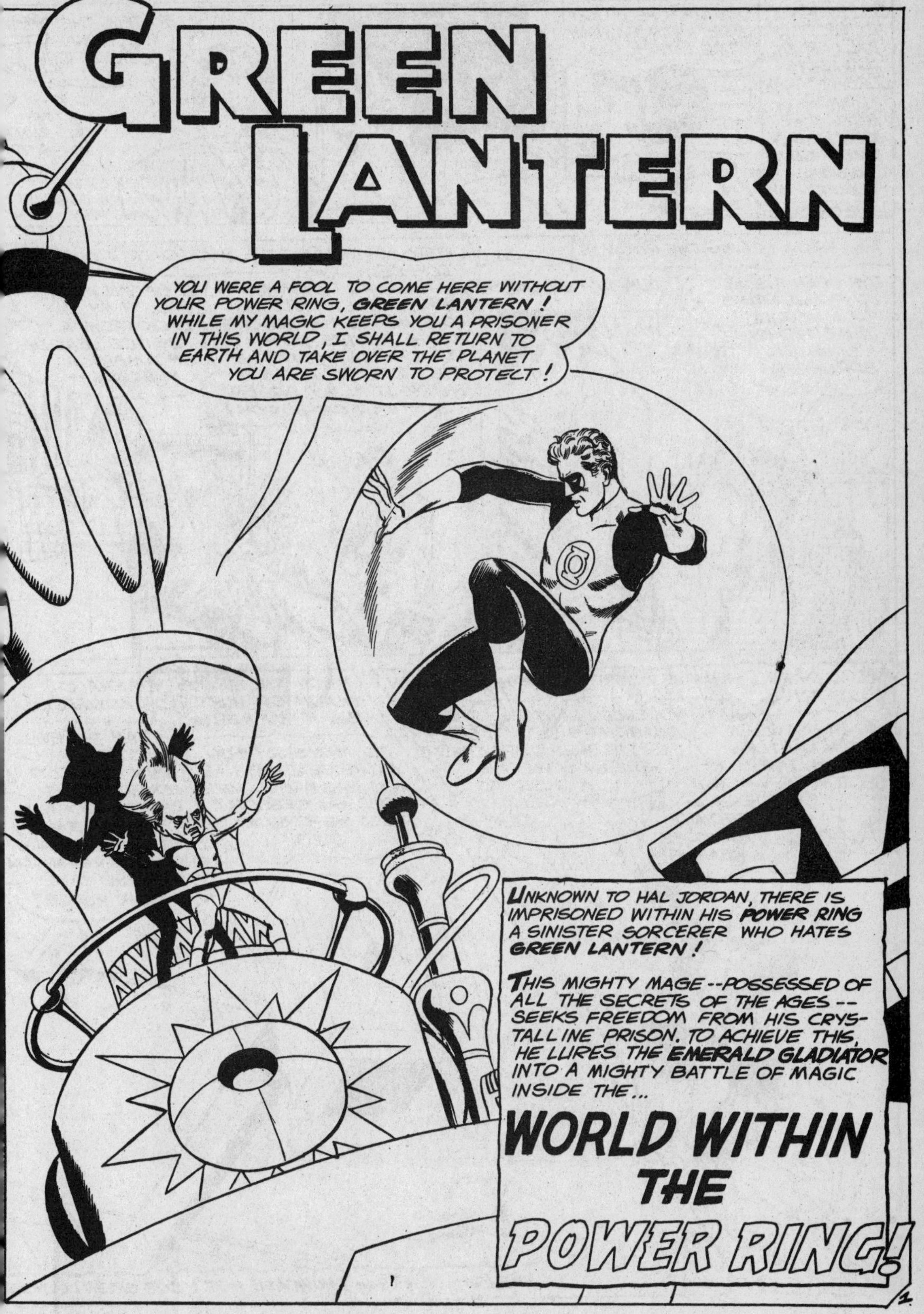
GREEN LANTERN
YOU WERE A FOOL TO COME HERE WITHOUT YOUR POWER RING, GREEN LANTERN! WHILE MY MAGIC KEEPS YOU A PRISONER IN THIS WORLD, I SHALL RETURN TO EARTH AND TAKE OVER THE PLANET YOU ARE SWORN TO PROTECT!
UNKNOWN TO HAL JORDAN, THERE IS IMPRISONED WITHIN HIS POWER RING A SINISTER SORCERER WHO HATES GREEN LANTERN!
THIS MIGHTY MAGE--POSSESSED OF ALL THE SECRETS OF THE AGES--SEEKS FREEDOM FROM HIS CRYSTALLINE PRISON. TO ACHIEVE THIS, HE LURES THE EMERALD GLADIATOR INTO A MIGHTY BATTLE OF MAGIC INSIDE THE...
WORLD WITHIN THE POWER RING!
1

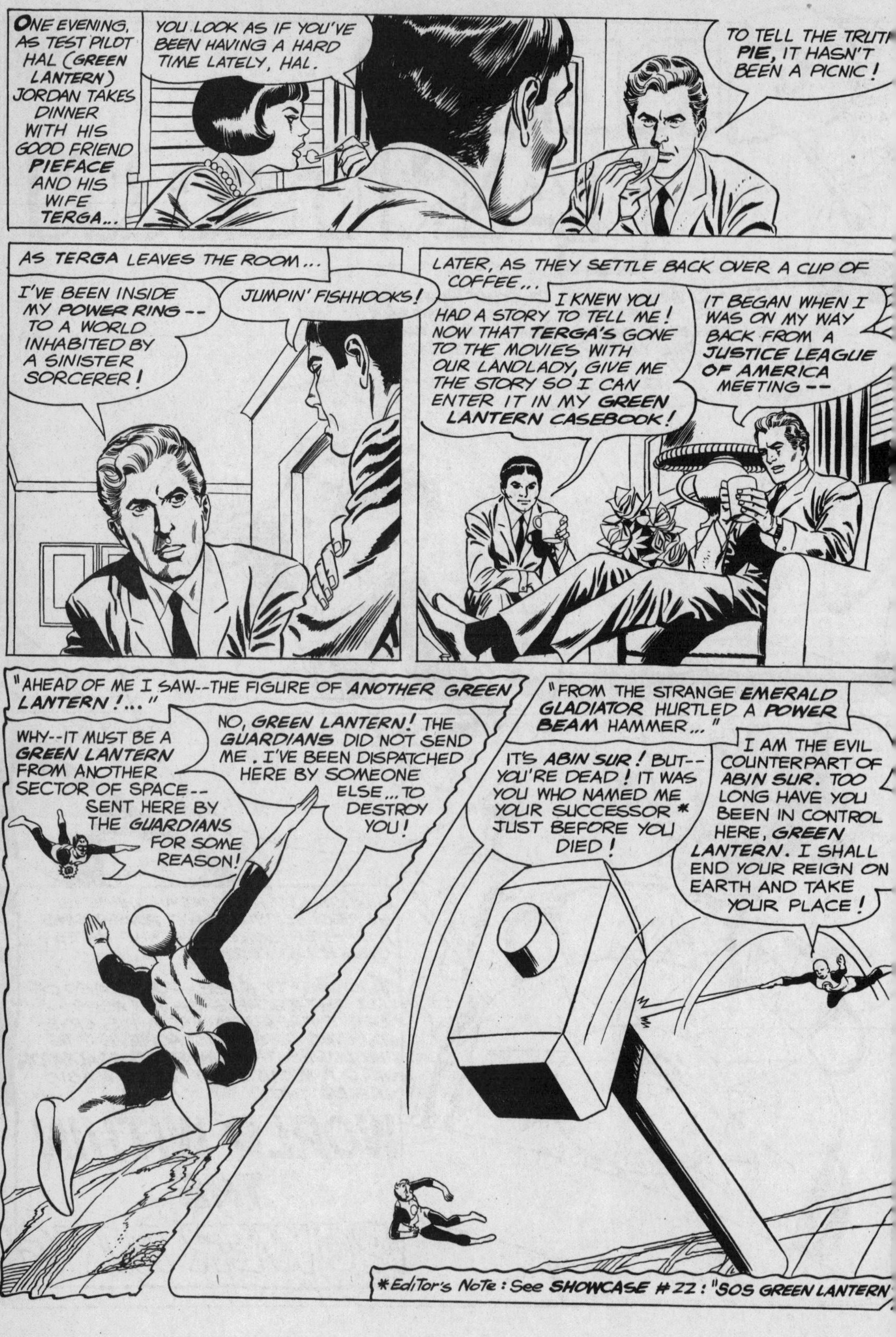
ONE EVENING, AS TEST PILOT HAL (GREEN LANTERN) JORDAN TAKES DINNER WITH HIS GOOD FRIEND PIEFACE AND HIS WIFE TERGA...
YOU LOOK AS IF YOU'VE BEEN HAVING A HARD TIME LATELY, HAL.
TO TELL THE TRUTH PIE, IT HASN'T BEEN A PICNIC!
AS TERGA LEAVES THE ROOM...
I'VE BEEN INSIDE MY POWER RING -- TO A WORLD INHABITED BY A SINISTER SORCERER!
JUMPIN' FISHHOOKS!
LATER, AS THEY SETTLE BACK OVER A CUP OF COFFEE...
I KNEW YOU HAD A STORY TO TELL ME! NOW THAT TERGA'S GONE TO THE MOVIES WITH OUR LANDLADY, GIVE ME THE STORY SO I CAN ENTER IT IN MY GREEN LANTERN CASEBOOK!
IT BEGAN WHEN I WAS ON MY WAY BACK FROM A JUSTICE LEAGUE OF AMERICA MEETING --
"AHEAD OF ME I SAW--THE FIGURE OF ANOTHER GREEN LANTERN!..."
WHY--IT MUST BE A GREEN LANTERN FROM ANOTHER SECTOR OF SPACE-- SENT HERE BY THE GUARDIANS FOR SOME REASON!
NO, GREEN LANTERN! THE GUARDIANS DID NOT SEND ME. I'VE BEEN DISPATCHED HERE BY SOMEONE ELSE... TO DESTROY YOU!
"FROM THE STRANGE EMERALD GLADIATOR HURTLED A POWER BEAM HAMMER..."
IT'S ABIN SUR! BUT-- YOU'RE DEAD! IT WAS YOU WHO NAMED ME YOUR SUCCESSOR * JUST BEFORE YOU DIED!
I AM THE EVIL COUNTERPART OF ABIN SUR. TOO LONG HAVE YOU BEEN IN CONTROL HERE, GREEN LANTERN. I SHALL END YOUR REIGN ON EARTH AND TAKE YOUR PLACE!
*EDITOR'S NOTE: SEE SHOWCASE #22: "SOS GREEN LANTERN"

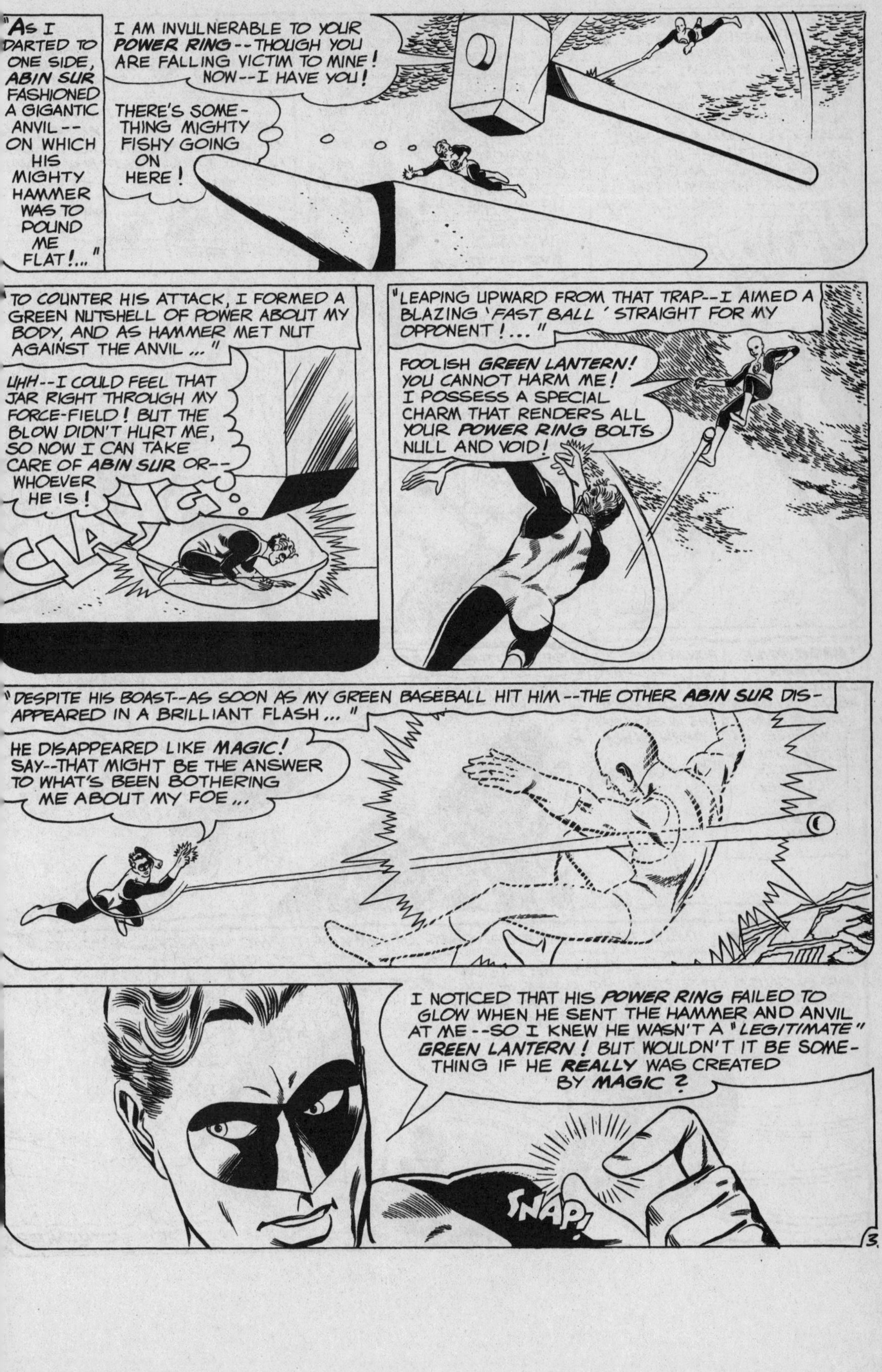
"AS I DARTED TO ONE SIDE, ABIN SUR FASHIONED A GIGANTIC ANVIL -- ON WHICH HIS MIGHTY HAMMER WAS TO POUND ME FLAT!..."
I AM INVULNERABLE TO YOUR POWER RING -- THOUGH YOU ARE FALLING VICTIM TO MINE! NOW -- I HAVE YOU!
THERE'S SOMETHING MIGHTY FISHY GOING ON HERE!
"TO COUNTER HIS ATTACK, I FORMED A GREEN NUTSHELL OF POWER ABOUT MY BODY, AND AS HAMMER MET NUT AGAINST THE ANVIL ..."
UHH -- I COULD FEEL THAT JAR RIGHT THROUGH MY FORCE-FIELD! BUT THE BLOW DIDN'T HURT ME, SO NOW I CAN TAKE CARE OF ABIN SUR OR -- WHOEVER HE IS!
CLANG!
"LEAPING UPWARD FROM THAT TRAP -- I AIMED A BLAZING 'FAST BALL' STRAIGHT FOR MY OPPONENT!..."
FOOLISH GREEN LANTERN! YOU CANNOT HARM ME! I POSSESS A SPECIAL CHARM THAT RENDERS ALL YOUR POWER RING BOLTS NULL AND VOID!
"DESPITE HIS BOAST -- AS SOON AS MY GREEN BASEBALL HIT HIM -- THE OTHER ABIN SUR DISAPPEARED IN A BRILLIANT FLASH ..."
HE DISAPPEARED LIKE MAGIC! SAY -- THAT MIGHT BE THE ANSWER TO WHAT'S BEEN BOTHERING ME ABOUT MY FOE ...
I NOTICED THAT HIS POWER RING FAILED TO GLOW WHEN HE SENT THE HAMMER AND ANVIL AT ME -- SO I KNEW HE WASN'T A "LEGITIMATE" GREEN LANTERN! BUT WOULDN'T IT BE SOMETHING IF HE REALLY WAS CREATED BY MAGIC?
SNAP!
3

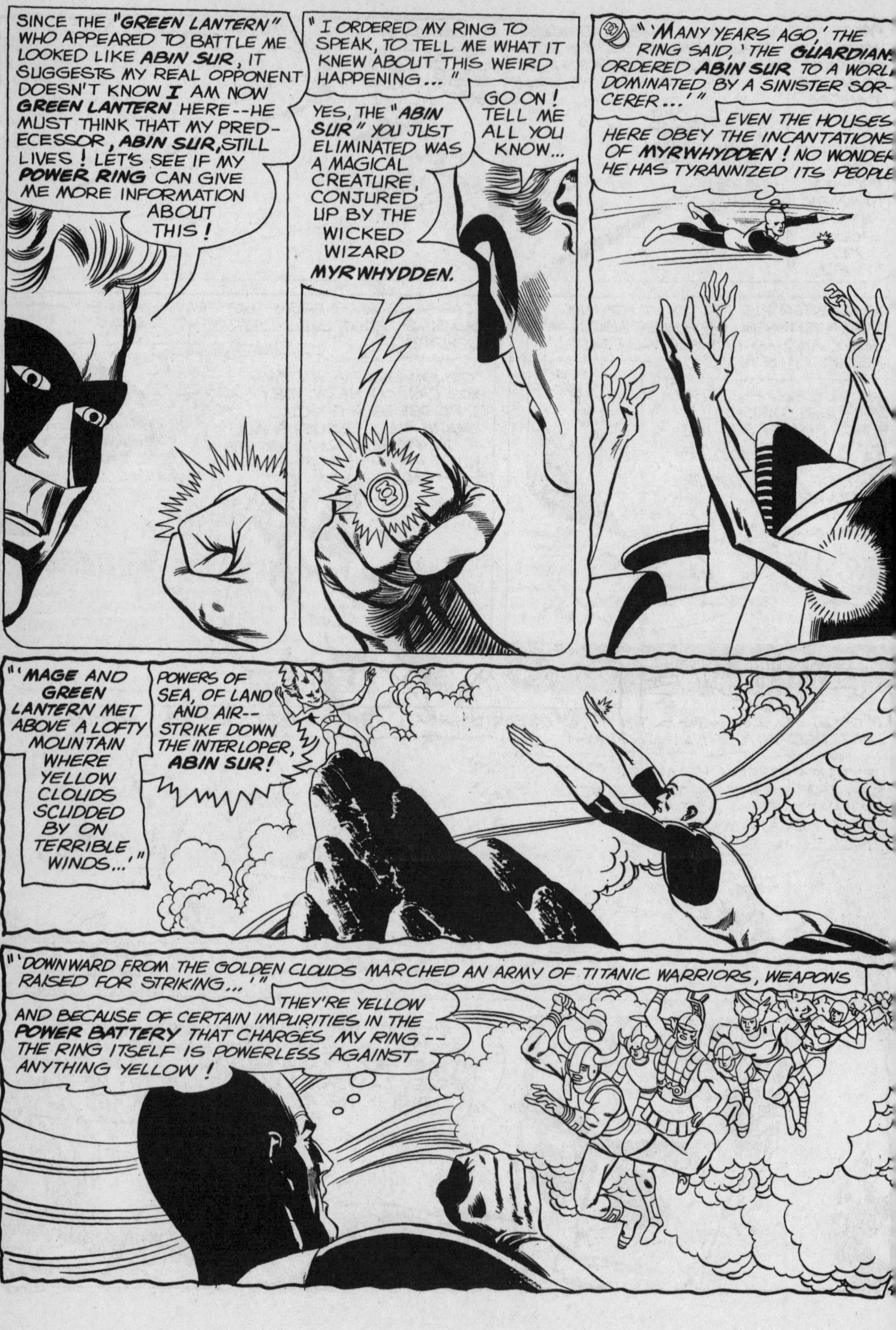
SINCE THE "GREEN LANTERN" WHO APPEARED TO BATTLE ME LOOKED LIKE ABIN SUR, IT SUGGESTS MY REAL OPPONENT DOESN'T KNOW I AM NOW GREEN LANTERN HERE--HE MUST THINK THAT MY PREDECESSOR, ABIN SUR, STILL LIVES! LET'S SEE IF MY POWER RING CAN GIVE ME MORE INFORMATION ABOUT THIS!
"I ORDERED MY RING TO SPEAK, TO TELL ME WHAT IT KNEW ABOUT THIS WEIRD HAPPENING..."
GO ON! TELL ME ALL YOU KNOW...
YES, THE "ABIN SUR" YOU JUST ELIMINATED WAS A MAGICAL CREATURE, CONJURED UP BY THE WICKED WIZARD MYRWHYDDEN.
"'MANY YEARS AGO,' THE RING SAID, 'THE GUARDIANS ORDERED ABIN SUR TO A WORLD DOMINATED BY A SINISTER SORCERER...'"
EVEN THE HOUSES HERE OBEY THE INCANTATIONS OF MYRWHYDDEN! NO WONDER HE HAS TYRANNIZED ITS PEOPLE!
"'MAGE AND GREEN LANTERN MET ABOVE A LOFTY MOUNTAIN WHERE YELLOW CLOUDS SCUDDED BY ON TERRIBLE WINDS...'"
POWERS OF SEA, OF LAND AND AIR--STRIKE DOWN THE INTERLOPER, ABIN SUR!
"'DOWNWARD FROM THE GOLDEN CLOUDS MARCHED AN ARMY OF TITANIC WARRIORS, WEAPONS RAISED FOR STRIKING...'"
THEY'RE YELLOW AND BECAUSE OF CERTAIN IMPURITIES IN THE POWER BATTERY THAT CHARGES MY RING--THE RING ITSELF IS POWERLESS AGAINST ANYTHING YELLOW!

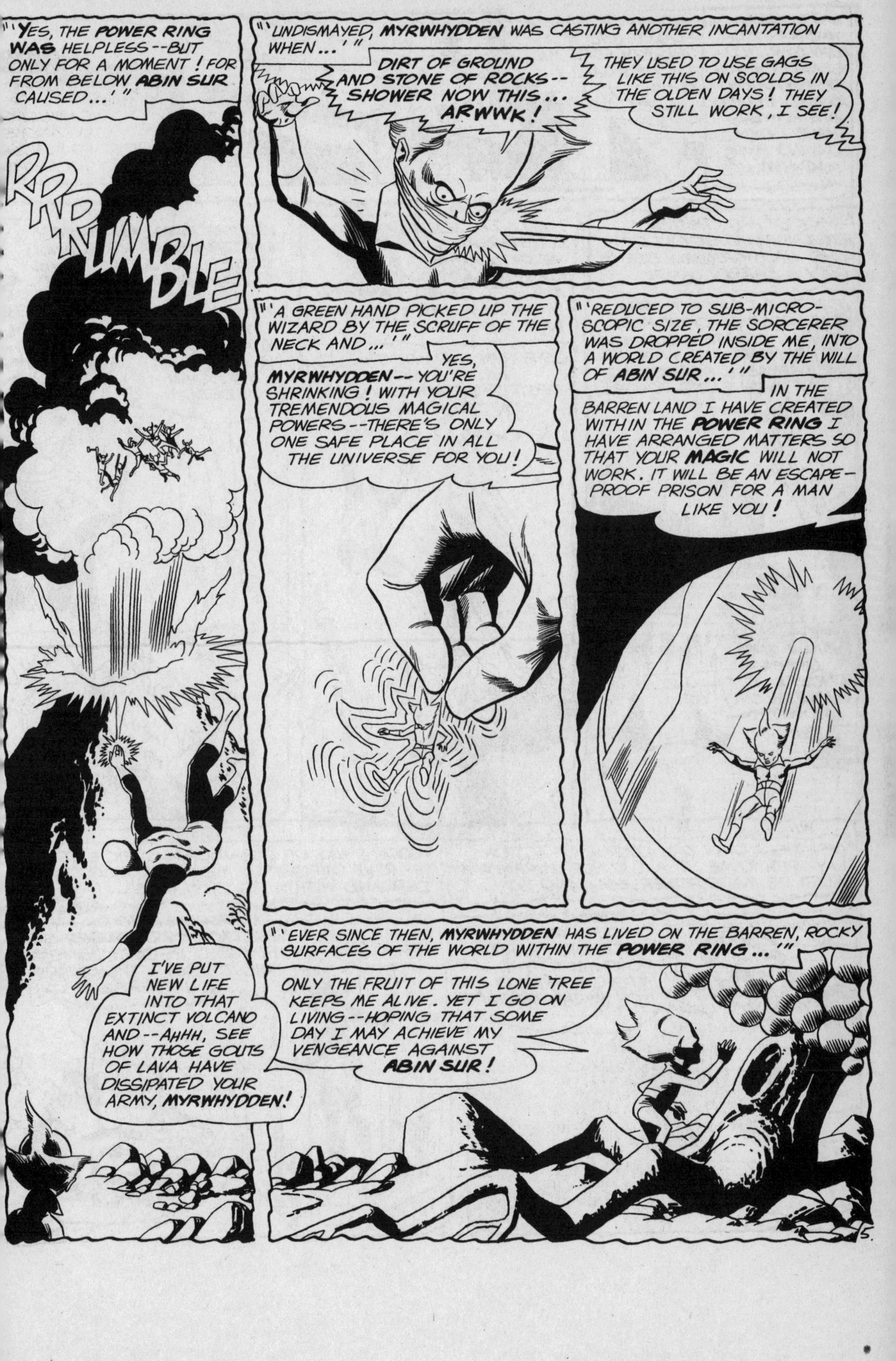
"'YES, THE POWER RING WAS HELPLESS--BUT ONLY FOR A MOMENT! FOR FROM BELOW ABIN SUR CAUSED...'"
RRRUMBLE
I'VE PUT NEW LIFE INTO THAT EXTINCT VOLCANO AND--AHHH, SEE HOW THOSE GOUTS OF LAVA HAVE DISSIPATED YOUR ARMY, MYRWHYDDEN!
"'UNDISMAYED, MYRWHYDDEN WAS CASTING ANOTHER INCANTATION WHEN...'"
DIRT OF GROUND AND STONE OF ROCKS--SHOWER NOW THIS... ARWWK!
THEY USED TO USE GAGS LIKE THIS ON SCOLDS IN THE OLDEN DAYS! THEY STILL WORK, I SEE!
"'A GREEN HAND PICKED UP THE WIZARD BY THE SCRUFF OF THE NECK AND...'"
YES, MYRWHYDDEN--YOU'RE SHRINKING! WITH YOUR TREMENDOUS MAGICAL POWERS--THERE'S ONLY ONE SAFE PLACE IN ALL THE UNIVERSE FOR YOU!
"'REDUCED TO SUB-MICRO-SCOPIC SIZE, THE SORCERER WAS DROPPED INSIDE ME, INTO A WORLD CREATED BY THE WILL OF ABIN SUR...'"
IN THE BARREN LAND I HAVE CREATED WITHIN THE POWER RING I HAVE ARRANGED MATTERS SO THAT YOUR MAGIC WILL NOT WORK. IT WILL BE AN ESCAPE-PROOF PRISON FOR A MAN LIKE YOU!
"'EVER SINCE THEN, MYRWHYDDEN HAS LIVED ON THE BARREN, ROCKY SURFACES OF THE WORLD WITHIN THE POWER RING...'"
ONLY THE FRUIT OF THIS LONE TREE KEEPS ME ALIVE. YET I GO ON LIVING--HOPING THAT SOME DAY I MAY ACHIEVE MY VENGEANCE AGAINST ABIN SUR!
5.

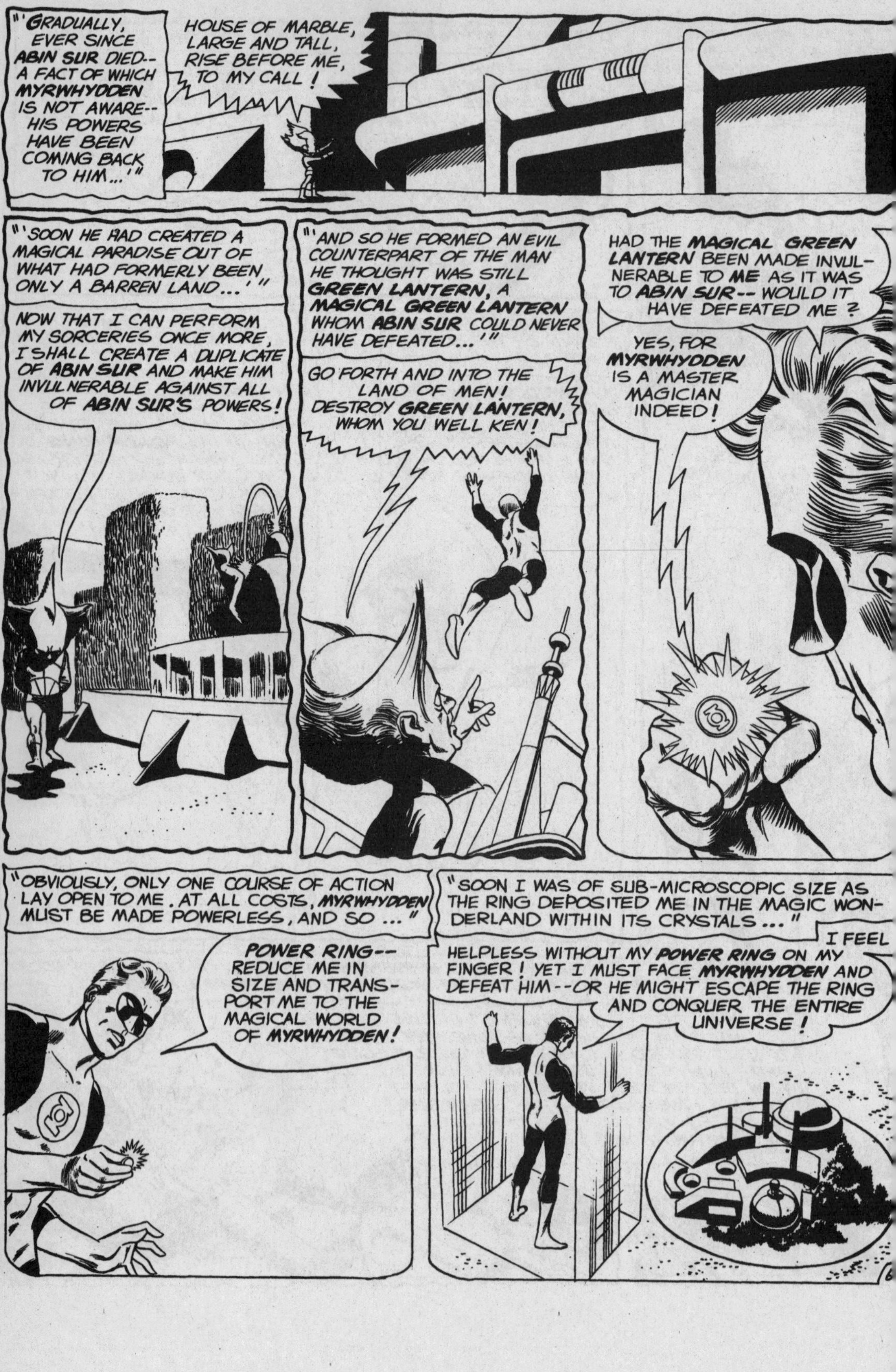
"'GRADUALLY, EVER SINCE ABIN SUR DIED-- A FACT OF WHICH MYRWHYDDEN IS NOT AWARE-- HIS POWERS HAVE BEEN COMING BACK TO HIM...'"
HOUSE OF MARBLE, LARGE AND TALL, RISE BEFORE ME, TO MY CALL!
"'SOON HE HAD CREATED A MAGICAL PARADISE OUT OF WHAT HAD FORMERLY BEEN ONLY A BARREN LAND...'"
NOW THAT I CAN PERFORM MY SORCERIES ONCE MORE, I SHALL CREATE A DUPLICATE OF ABIN SUR AND MAKE HIM INVULNERABLE AGAINST ALL OF ABIN SUR'S POWERS!
"'AND SO HE FORMED AN EVIL COUNTERPART OF THE MAN HE THOUGHT WAS STILL GREEN LANTERN, A MAGICAL GREEN LANTERN WHOM ABIN SUR COULD NEVER HAVE DEFEATED...'"
GO FORTH AND INTO THE LAND OF MEN! DESTROY GREEN LANTERN, WHOM YOU WELL KEN!
HAD THE MAGICAL GREEN LANTERN BEEN MADE INVULNERABLE TO ME AS IT WAS TO ABIN SUR-- WOULD IT HAVE DEFEATED ME?
YES, FOR MYRWHYDDEN IS A MASTER MAGICIAN INDEED!
"OBVIOUSLY, ONLY ONE COURSE OF ACTION LAY OPEN TO ME. AT ALL COSTS, MYRWHYDDEN MUST BE MADE POWERLESS, AND SO ..."
POWER RING-- REDUCE ME IN SIZE AND TRANSPORT ME TO THE MAGICAL WORLD OF MYRWHYDDEN!
"SOON I WAS OF SUB-MICROSCOPIC SIZE AS THE RING DEPOSITED ME IN THE MAGIC WONDERLAND WITHIN ITS CRYSTALS ..."
I FEEL HELPLESS WITHOUT MY POWER RING ON MY FINGER! YET I MUST FACE MYRWHYDDEN AND DEFEAT HIM--OR HE MIGHT ESCAPE THE RING AND CONQUER THE ENTIRE UNIVERSE!

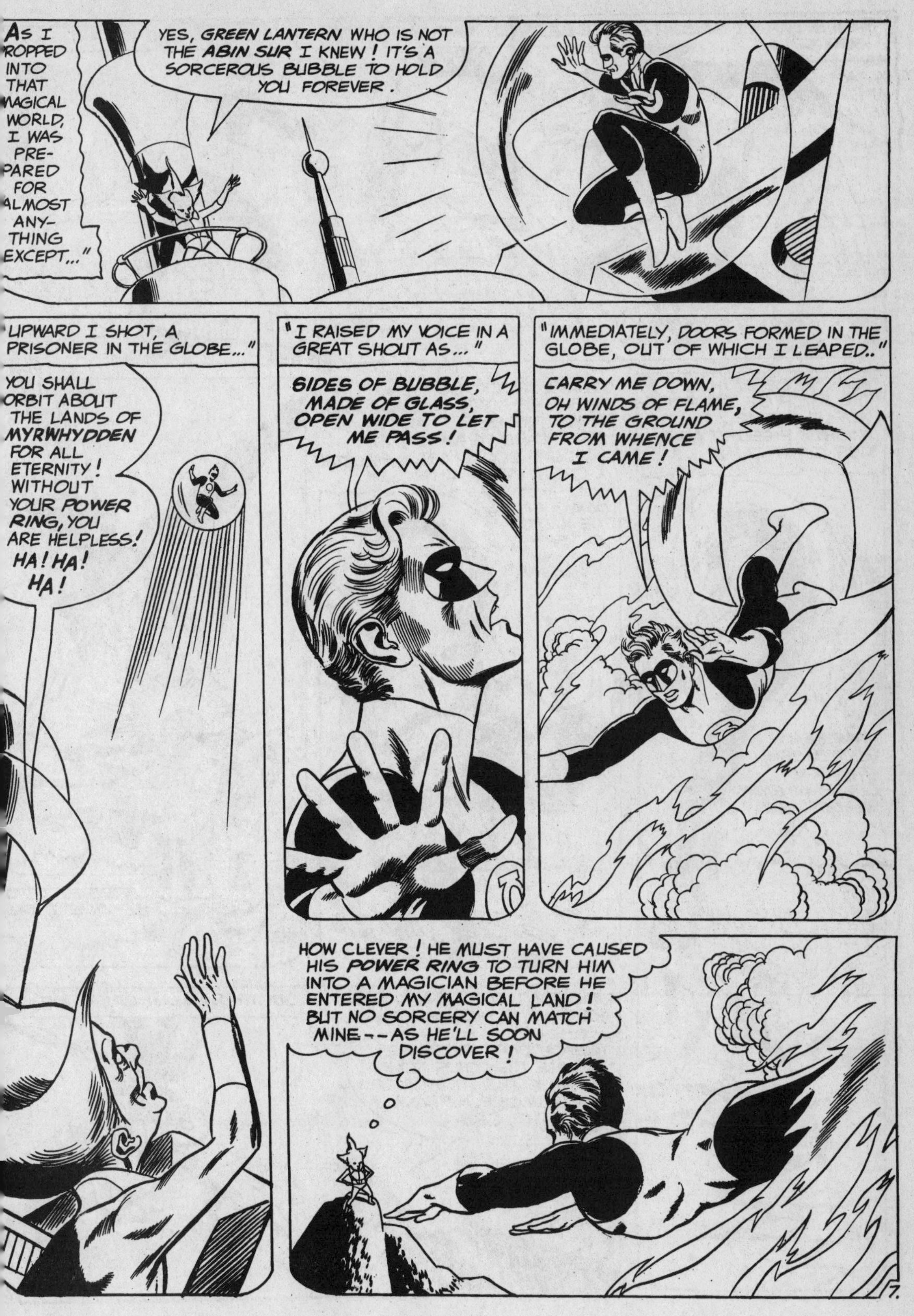
AS I ROPPED INTO THAT MAGICAL WORLD, I WAS PREPARED FOR ALMOST ANYTHING EXCEPT..."
YES, GREEN LANTERN WHO IS NOT THE ABIN SUR I KNEW! IT'S A SORCEROUS BUBBLE TO HOLD YOU FOREVER.
"UPWARD I SHOT, A PRISONER IN THE GLOBE..."
YOU SHALL ORBIT ABOUT THE LANDS OF MYRWHYDDEN FOR ALL ETERNITY! WITHOUT YOUR POWER RING, YOU ARE HELPLESS! HA! HA! HA!
"I RAISED MY VOICE IN A GREAT SHOUT AS..."
SIDES OF BUBBLE, MADE OF GLASS, OPEN WIDE TO LET ME PASS!
"IMMEDIATELY, DOORS FORMED IN THE GLOBE, OUT OF WHICH I LEAPED.."
CARRY ME DOWN, OH WINDS OF FLAME, TO THE GROUND FROM WHENCE I CAME!
HOW CLEVER! HE MUST HAVE CAUSED HIS POWER RING TO TURN HIM INTO A MAGICIAN BEFORE HE ENTERED MY MAGICAL LAND! BUT NO SORCERY CAN MATCH MINE--AS HE'LL SOON DISCOVER!
7.

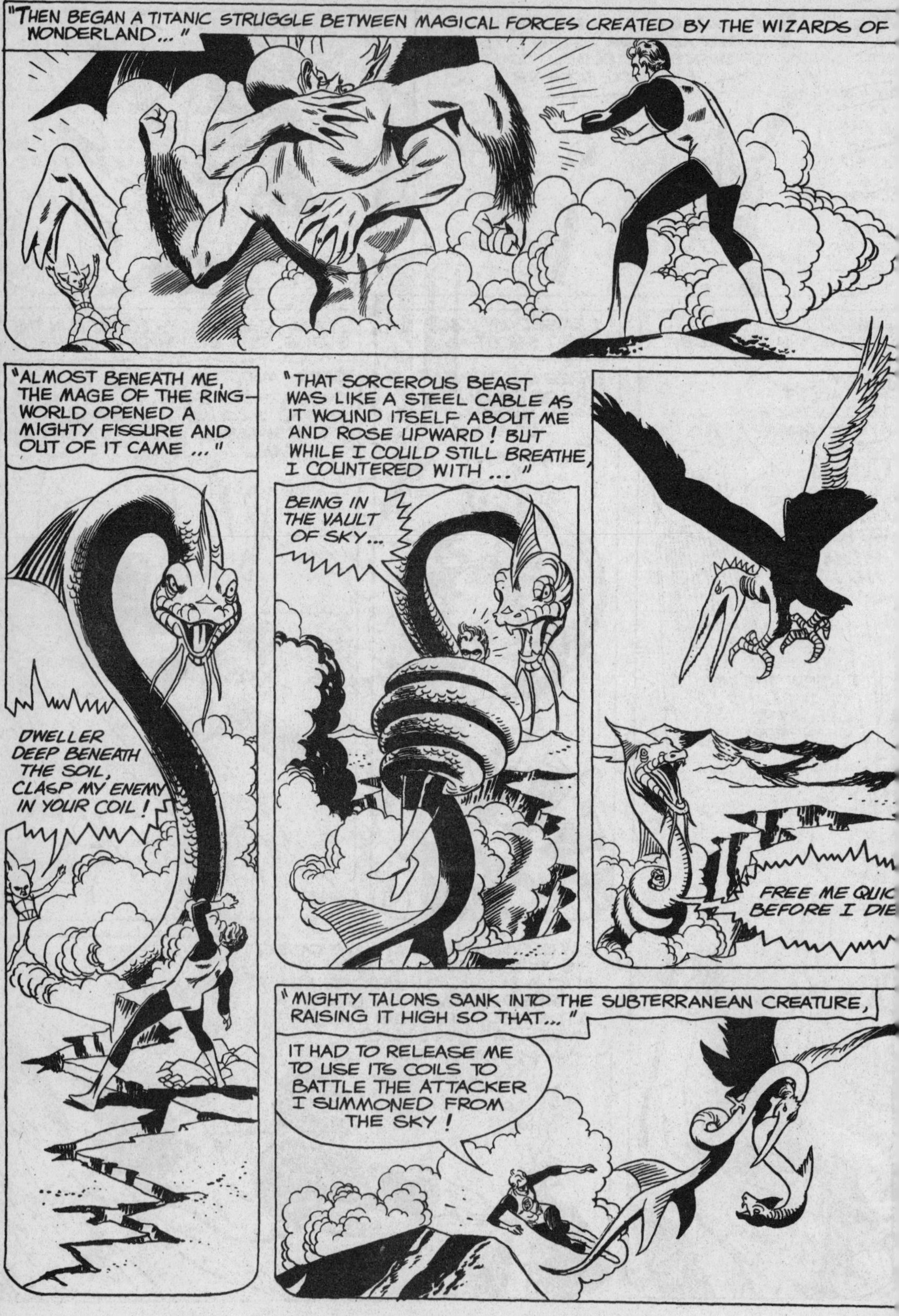
"THEN BEGAN A TITANIC STRUGGLE BETWEEN MAGICAL FORCES CREATED BY THE WIZARDS OF WONDERLAND..."
"ALMOST BENEATH ME, THE MAGE OF THE RING-WORLD OPENED A MIGHTY FISSURE AND OUT OF IT CAME ..."
DWELLER DEEP BENEATH THE SOIL, CLASP MY ENEMY IN YOUR COIL!
"THAT SORCEROUS BEAST WAS LIKE A STEEL CABLE AS IT WOUND ITSELF ABOUT ME AND ROSE UPWARD! BUT WHILE I COULD STILL BREATHE, I COUNTERED WITH ..."
BEING IN THE VAULT OF SKY...
FREE ME QUIC BEFORE I DIE
"MIGHTY TALONS SANK INTO THE SUBTERRANEAN CREATURE, RAISING IT HIGH SO THAT..."
IT HAD TO RELEASE ME TO USE ITS COILS TO BATTLE THE ATTACKER I SUMMONED FROM THE SKY!

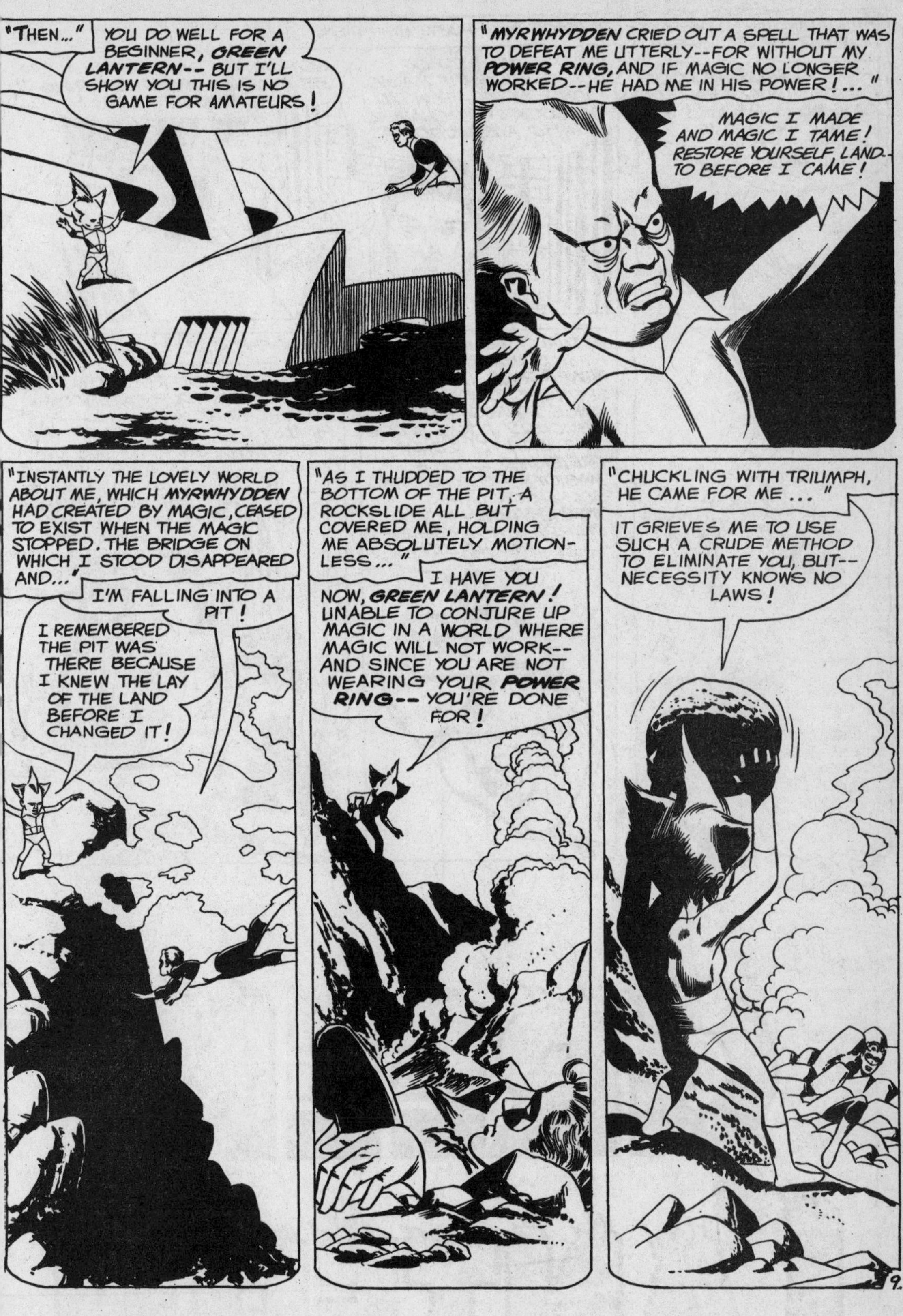
"THEN..."
YOU DO WELL FOR A BEGINNER, GREEN LANTERN-- BUT I'LL SHOW YOU THIS IS NO GAME FOR AMATEURS!
"MYRWHYDDEN CRIED OUT A SPELL THAT WAS TO DEFEAT ME UTTERLY--FOR WITHOUT MY POWER RING, AND IF MAGIC NO LONGER WORKED--HE HAD ME IN HIS POWER!..."
MAGIC I MADE AND MAGIC I TAME! RESTORE YOURSELF, LAND-- TO BEFORE I CAME!
"INSTANTLY THE LOVELY WORLD ABOUT ME, WHICH MYRWHYDDEN HAD CREATED BY MAGIC, CEASED TO EXIST WHEN THE MAGIC STOPPED. THE BRIDGE ON WHICH I STOOD DISAPPEARED AND..."
I'M FALLING INTO A PIT!
I REMEMBERED THE PIT WAS THERE BECAUSE I KNEW THE LAY OF THE LAND BEFORE I CHANGED IT!
"AS I THUDDED TO THE BOTTOM OF THE PIT, A ROCKSLIDE ALL BUT COVERED ME, HOLDING ME ABSOLUTELY MOTIONLESS..."
I HAVE YOU NOW, GREEN LANTERN! UNABLE TO CONJURE UP MAGIC IN A WORLD WHERE MAGIC WILL NOT WORK-- AND SINCE YOU ARE NOT WEARING YOUR POWER RING-- YOU'RE DONE FOR!
"CHUCKLING WITH TRIUMPH, HE CAME FOR ME..."
IT GRIEVES ME TO USE SUCH A CRUDE METHOD TO ELIMINATE YOU, BUT-- NECESSITY KNOWS NO LAWS!
9.

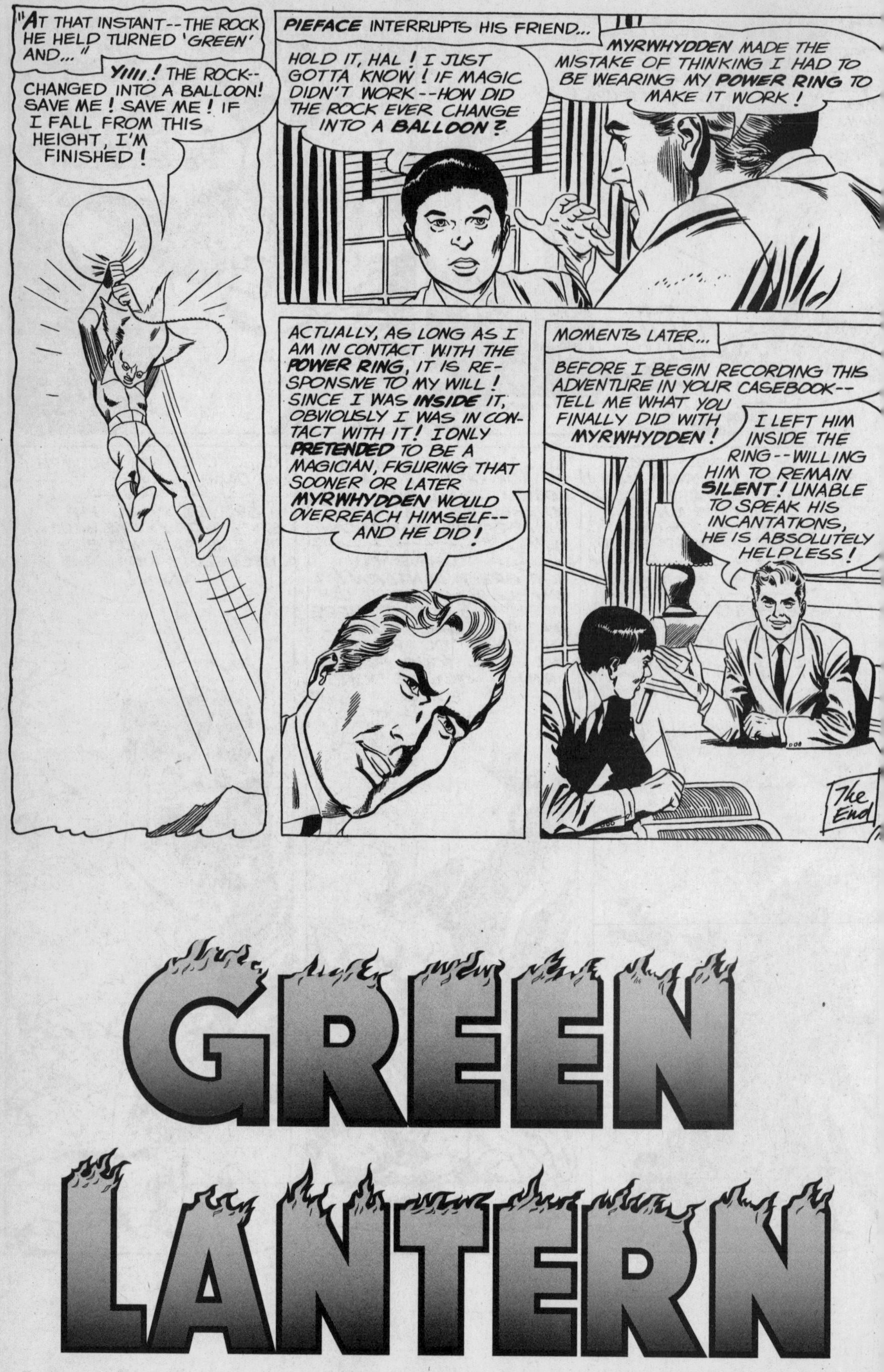
"AT THAT INSTANT--THE ROCK HE HELD TURNED 'GREEN' AND..."
YIIII! THE ROCK--CHANGED INTO A BALLOON! SAVE ME! SAVE ME! IF I FALL FROM THIS HEIGHT, I'M FINISHED!
PIEFACE INTERRUPTS HIS FRIEND...
HOLD IT, HAL! I JUST GOTTA KNOW! IF MAGIC DIDN'T WORK--HOW DID THE ROCK EVER CHANGE INTO A BALLOON?
MYRWHYDDEN MADE THE MISTAKE OF THINKING I HAD TO BE WEARING MY POWER RING TO MAKE IT WORK!
ACTUALLY, AS LONG AS I AM IN CONTACT WITH THE POWER RING, IT IS RESPONSIVE TO MY WILL! SINCE I WAS INSIDE IT, OBVIOUSLY I WAS IN CONTACT WITH IT! I ONLY PRETENDED TO BE A MAGICIAN, FIGURING THAT SOONER OR LATER MYRWHYDDEN WOULD OVERREACH HIMSELF--AND HE DID!
MOMENTS LATER...
BEFORE I BEGIN RECORDING THIS ADVENTURE IN YOUR CASEBOOK--TELL ME WHAT YOU FINALLY DID WITH MYRWHYDDEN!
I LEFT HIM INSIDE THE RING--WILLING HIM TO REMAIN SILENT! UNABLE TO SPEAK HIS INCANTATIONS, HE IS ABSOLUTELY HELPLESS!
The End

GREEN LANTERN

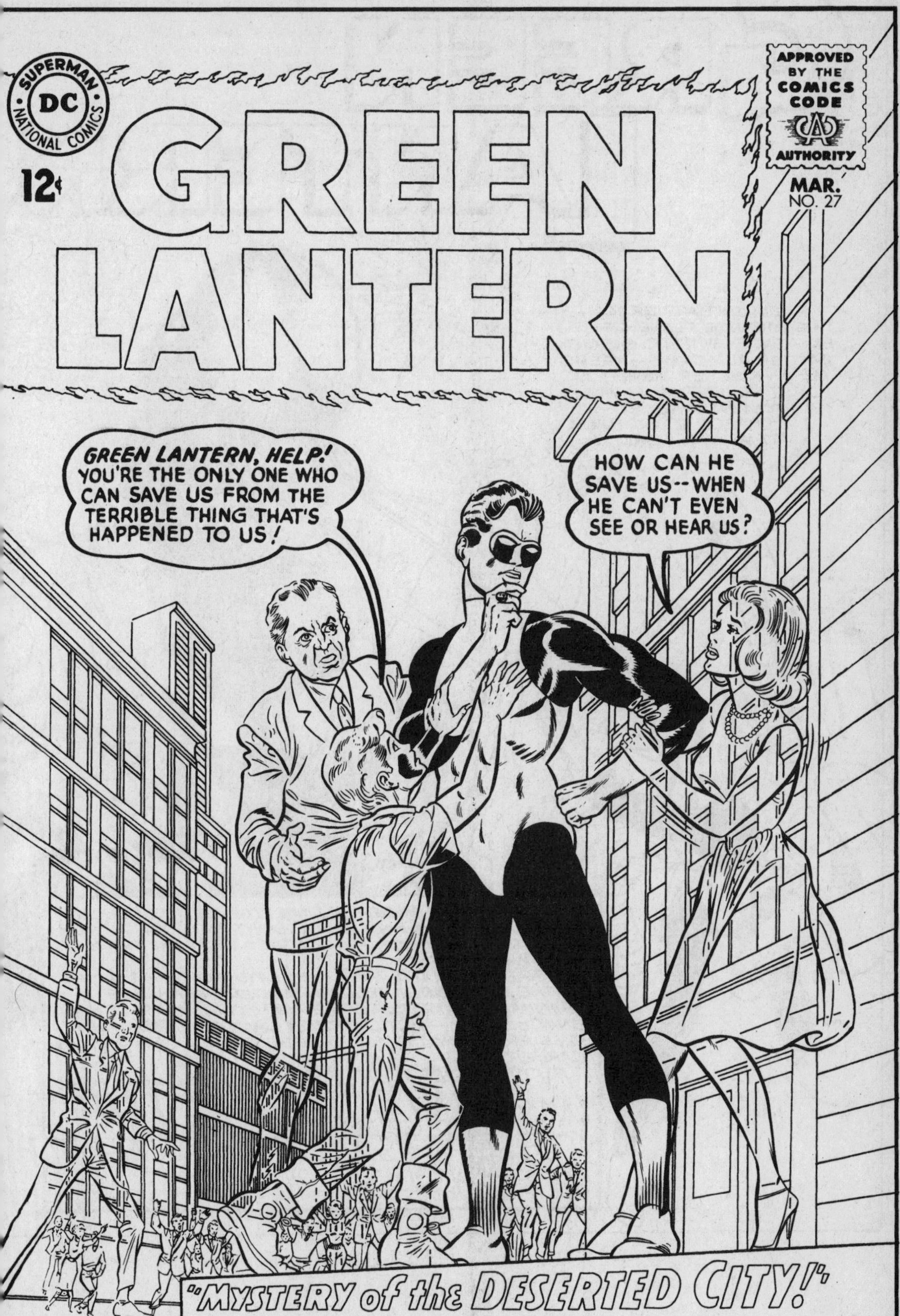
SUPERMAN DC NATIONAL COMICS
12¢
GREEN LANTERN
APPROVED BY THE COMICS CODE AUTHORITY
MAR. NO. 27
GREEN LANTERN, HELP! YOU'RE THE ONLY ONE WHO CAN SAVE US FROM THE TERRIBLE THING THAT'S HAPPENED TO US!
HOW CAN HE SAVE US--WHEN HE CAN'T EVEN SEE OR HEAR US?
"MYSTERY of the DESERTED CITY!"

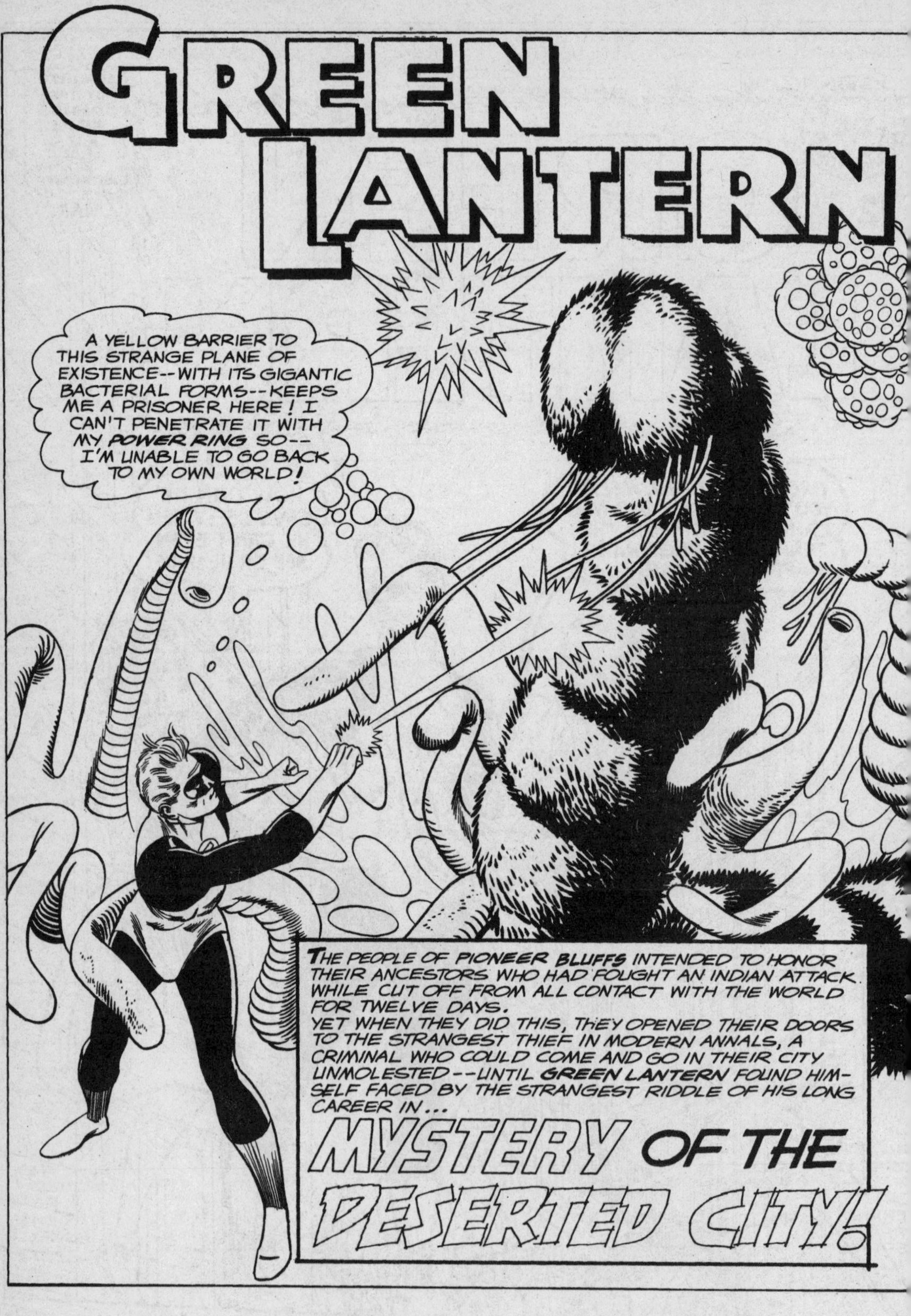
GREEN LANTERN
A YELLOW BARRIER TO THIS STRANGE PLANE OF EXISTENCE--WITH ITS GIGANTIC BACTERIAL FORMS--KEEPS ME A PRISONER HERE! I CAN'T PENETRATE IT WITH MY POWER RING SO-- I'M UNABLE TO GO BACK TO MY OWN WORLD!
THE PEOPLE OF PIONEER BLUFFS INTENDED TO HONOR THEIR ANCESTORS WHO HAD FOUGHT AN INDIAN ATTACK WHILE CUT OFF FROM ALL CONTACT WITH THE WORLD FOR TWELVE DAYS.
YET WHEN THEY DID THIS, THEY OPENED THEIR DOORS TO THE STRANGEST THIEF IN MODERN ANNALS, A CRIMINAL WHO COULD COME AND GO IN THEIR CITY UNMOLESTED--UNTIL GREEN LANTERN FOUND HIMSELF FACED BY THE STRANGEST RIDDLE OF HIS LONG CAREER IN...
MYSTERY OF THE DESERTED CITY!

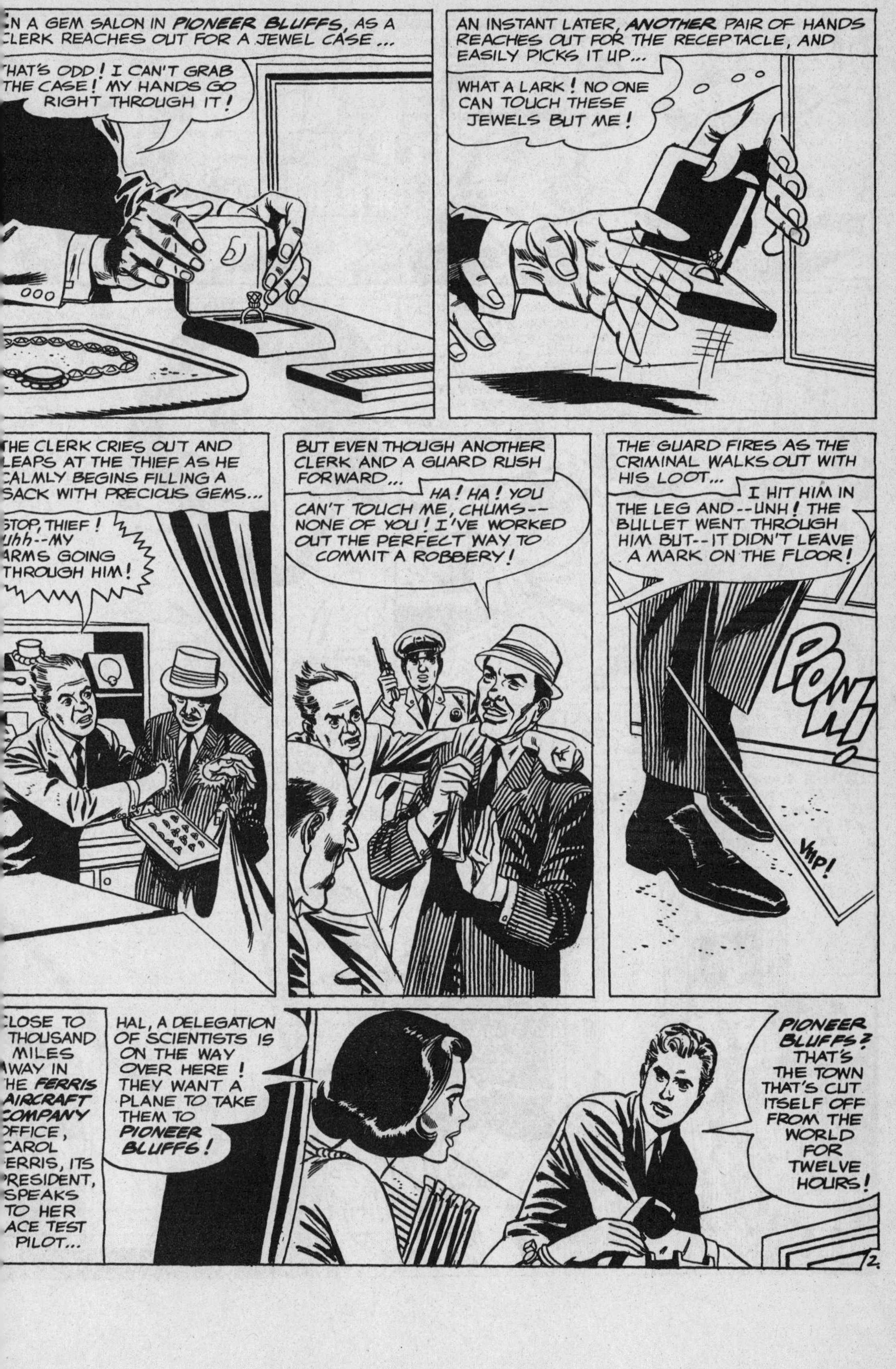

N A GEM SALON IN PIONEER BLUFFS, AS A CLERK REACHES OUT FOR A JEWEL CASE...
THAT'S ODD! I CAN'T GRAB THE CASE! MY HANDS GO RIGHT THROUGH IT!
AN INSTANT LATER, ANOTHER PAIR OF HANDS REACHES OUT FOR THE RECEPTACLE, AND EASILY PICKS IT UP...
WHAT A LARK! NO ONE CAN TOUCH THESE JEWELS BUT ME!
THE CLERK CRIES OUT AND LEAPS AT THE THIEF AS HE CALMLY BEGINS FILLING A SACK WITH PRECIOUS GEMS...
STOP, THIEF! Uhh--MY ARMS GOING THROUGH HIM!
BUT EVEN THOUGH ANOTHER CLERK AND A GUARD RUSH FORWARD...
HA! HA! YOU CAN'T TOUCH ME, CHUMS--NONE OF YOU! I'VE WORKED OUT THE PERFECT WAY TO COMMIT A ROBBERY!
THE GUARD FIRES AS THE CRIMINAL WALKS OUT WITH HIS LOOT...
I HIT HIM IN THE LEG AND--UNH! THE BULLET WENT THROUGH HIM BUT--IT DIDN'T LEAVE A MARK ON THE FLOOR!
POW!
VVIP!
CLOSE TO THOUSAND MILES AWAY IN THE FERRIS AIRCRAFT COMPANY OFFICE, CAROL FERRIS, ITS PRESIDENT, SPEAKS TO HER ACE TEST PILOT...
HAL, A DELEGATION OF SCIENTISTS IS ON THE WAY OVER HERE! THEY WANT A PLANE TO TAKE THEM TO PIONEER BLUFFS!
PIONEER BLUFFS? THAT'S THE TOWN THAT'S CUT ITSELF OFF FROM THE WORLD FOR TWELVE HOURS!
2

"A CENTURY AGO, *PIONEER BLUFFS* WAS A FRONTIER TOWN. WHEN IT WAS ATTACKED BY INDIANS, THEY CUT IT OFF FROM THE COUNTRY BY SURROUNDING IT AND LAYING SIEGE TO IT..."

"NOW, TO COMMEMORATE THE *100th* ANNIVERSARY OF THAT EVENT, THE TOWN HAS VOLUNTARILY CUT ITSELF OFF FROM THE REST OF THE COUNTRY..."

SORRY, FOLKS, ALL TELEPHONE AND TELEGRAPH LINES HAVE BEEN DISCONNECTED AND NOBODY'S ALLOWED IN OR OUT OF *PIONEER BLUFFS!*

BUT THE *SEISMOGRAM* AT *COAST UNIVERSITY* HAS RECORDED A SLIGHT TREMOR AT *PIONEER BLUFFS* THAT MAY SPREAD INTO MORE SERIOUS SHOCKS, CAUSING SEVERE DAMAGE AND LOSS OF LIFE

EDITOR'S NOTE: AN INSTRUMENT FOR DETECTING EARTHQUAKES.

A *BENIOFF STRAIN SEISMOMETER* SHOWED A BREAKAGE OF ROCKS NEAR THERE, WHICH IS A SIGN THAT A MORE SERIOUS EARTHQUAKE MAY OCCUR! THEY'VE TRIED TO WARN THE AUTHORITIES-- BUT THEY THINK IT'S THE WORK OF PRANKSTERS AND WON'T PAY ANY ATTENTION...

I THOUGHT YOU MIGHT LIKE TO FLY THOSE SCIENTISTS THERE, HAL!

I SUGGEST YOU HAVE YOUR REGULAR PILOT DO THAT, CAROL! I'M ONLY A TEST PILOT, REMEMBER.

CAN HAL *(GREEN LANTERN)* JORDAN BE REFUSING A CHANCE TO HELP HUMANITY WHILE CAROL HURRIES TO MAKE READY A PASSENGER PLANE, LET'S FOLLOW HER TEST PILOT INTO A LARGE HANGAR...

IN THAT HANGAR IS A DRESSING ROOM, WHERE THE TEST PILOT REVEALS HIMSELF AS--*GREEN LANTERN*! AS HE STRETCHES OUT HIS RING HAND TOWARD AN EMPTY SPACE...

AS *GREEN LANTERN* I CAN GO FASTER THAN ANY PLANE! I SHOULD BE ABLE TO HANDLE THAT EARTHQUAKE THREAT BEFORE THE SCIENTISTS EVEN GET THERE!

SUDDENLY A *POWER BATTERY* IN THE SHAPE OF A LANTERN APPEARS AND BEGINS TO GLOW AS...

IN BRIGHTEST DAY, IN BLACKEST NIGHT,
NO EVIL SHALL ESCAPE MY SIGHT!
LET THOSE WHO WORSHIP EVIL'S MIGHT
BEWARE MY POWER --
GREEN LANTERN'S LIGHT!

MOMENTS LATER...

IF I CAN REACH THE UNDER-GROUND STRAIN WHICH IS THE CAUSE OF THE 'QUAKE AND HEAL IT, I'LL PREVENT ANY DAMAGE TO *PIONEER BLUFFS*. SO AS NOT TO VIOLATE OUTWARDLY THE "NO VISITORS" RULE, I'LL MAKE MYSELF INVISIBLE.

UNSEEN, *GREEN LANTERN* FLIES ABOVE THE ROAD BARRIERS AND SWOOPS DOWN INTO THE GROUND ITSELF...

INSIDE THE EARTH I'LL BE ABLE TO SEE THE ROCK-STRAIN MORE CLEARLY!

HERE, AMID THE TORTUOUS UPTHRUST OF ROCKS TWISTED OUT OF PLACE BY THE SHRINKING OF THE EARTH'S CRUST, HIS *POWER RING* FASHIONS A GIGANTIC BLOWTORCH...

I'LL MELT THE STONE, RESHAPING IT TO RELIEVE THE SUBTERRANEAN PRESSURES.

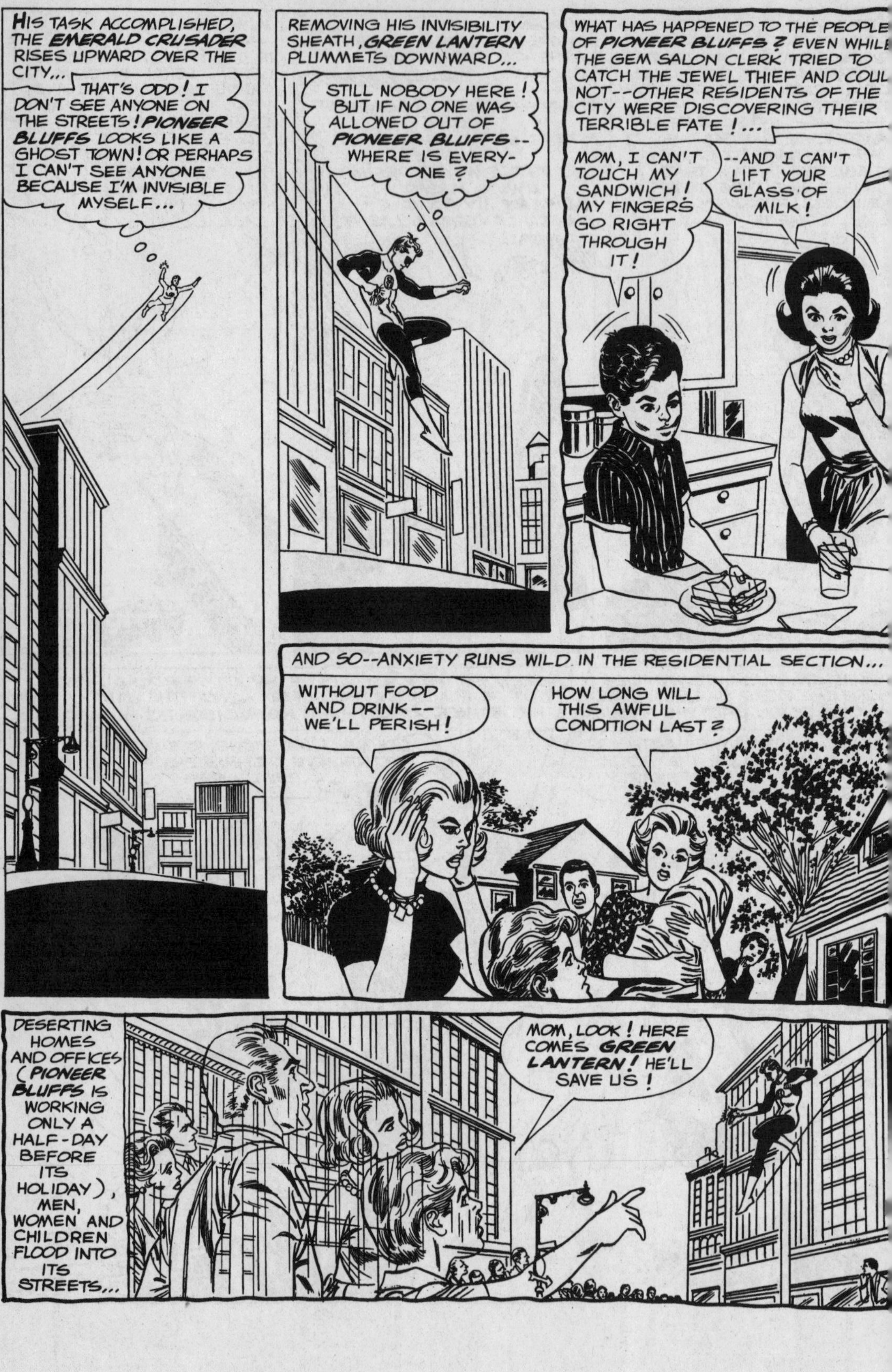
HIS TASK ACCOMPLISHED, THE EMERALD CRUSADER RISES UPWARD OVER THE CITY...
THAT'S ODD! I DON'T SEE ANYONE ON THE STREETS! PIONEER BLUFFS LOOKS LIKE A GHOST TOWN! OR PERHAPS I CAN'T SEE ANYONE BECAUSE I'M INVISIBLE MYSELF...
REMOVING HIS INVISIBILITY SHEATH, GREEN LANTERN PLUMMETS DOWNWARD...
STILL NOBODY HERE! BUT IF NO ONE WAS ALLOWED OUT OF PIONEER BLUFFS--WHERE IS EVERY-ONE?
WHAT HAS HAPPENED TO THE PEOPLE OF PIONEER BLUFFS? EVEN WHILE THE GEM SALON CLERK TRIED TO CATCH THE JEWEL THIEF AND COULD NOT--OTHER RESIDENTS OF THE CITY WERE DISCOVERING THEIR TERRIBLE FATE!...
MOM, I CAN'T TOUCH MY SANDWICH! MY FINGERS GO RIGHT THROUGH IT!
--AND I CAN'T LIFT YOUR GLASS OF MILK!
AND SO--ANXIETY RUNS WILD IN THE RESIDENTIAL SECTION...
WITHOUT FOOD AND DRINK--WE'LL PERISH!
HOW LONG WILL THIS AWFUL CONDITION LAST?
DESERTING HOMES AND OFFICES (PIONEER BLUFFS IS WORKING ONLY A HALF-DAY BEFORE ITS HOLIDAY), MEN, WOMEN AND CHILDREN FLOOD INTO ITS STREETS...
MOM, LOOK! HERE COMES GREEN LANTERN! HE'LL SAVE US!

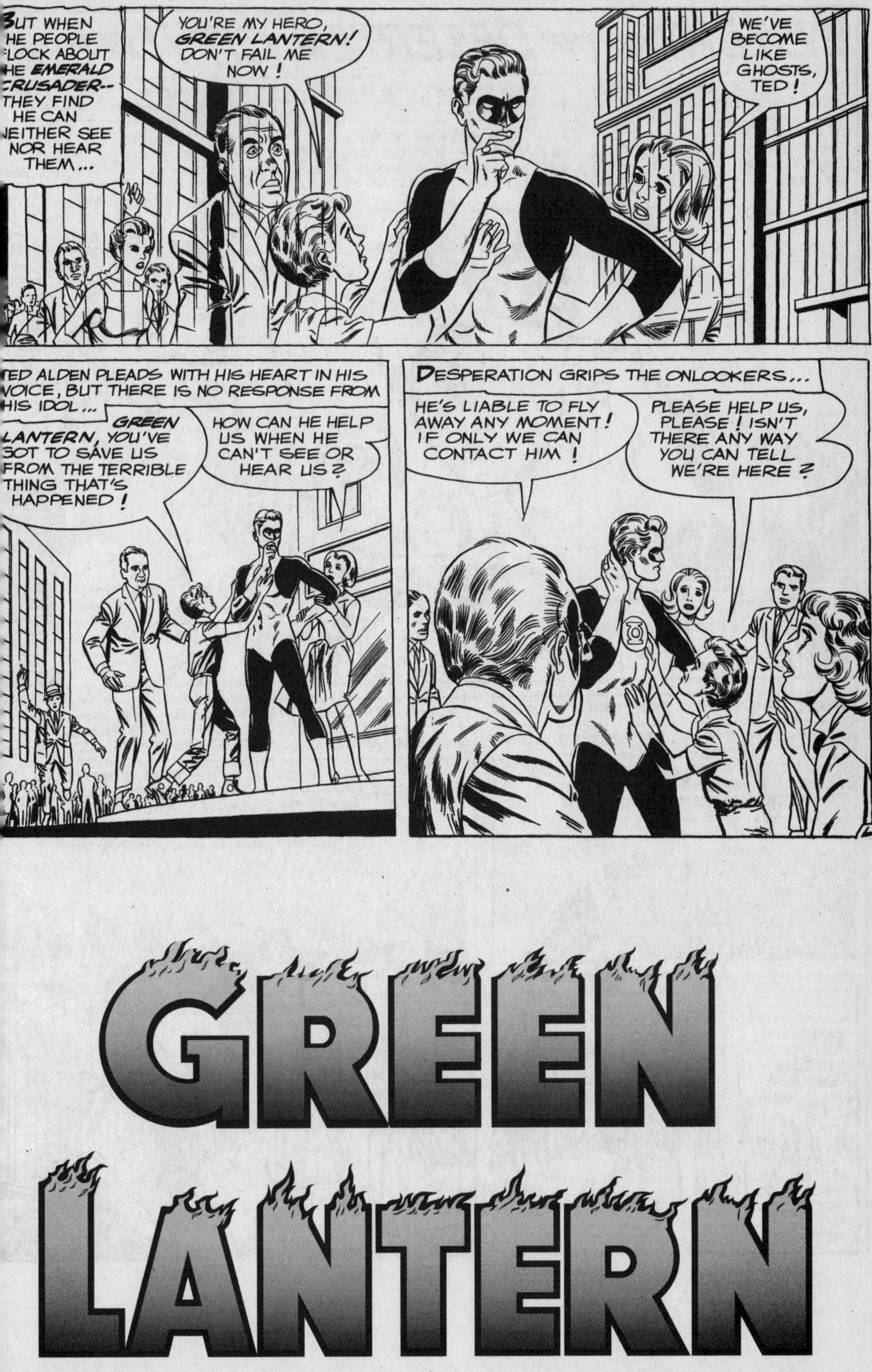
BUT WHEN HE PEOPLE FLOCK ABOUT HE EMERALD CRUSADER-- THEY FIND HE CAN EITHER SEE NOR HEAR THEM...
YOU'RE MY HERO, GREEN LANTERN! DON'T FAIL ME NOW!
WE'VE BECOME LIKE GHOSTS, TED!
TED ALDEN PLEADS WITH HIS HEART IN HIS VOICE, BUT THERE IS NO RESPONSE FROM HIS IDOL...
GREEN LANTERN, YOU'VE GOT TO SAVE US FROM THE TERRIBLE THING THAT'S HAPPENED!
HOW CAN HE HELP US WHEN HE CAN'T SEE OR HEAR US?
DESPERATION GRIPS THE ONLOOKERS...
HE'S LIABLE TO FLY AWAY ANY MOMENT! IF ONLY WE CAN CONTACT HIM!
PLEASE HELP US, PLEASE! ISN'T THERE ANY WAY YOU CAN TELL WE'RE HERE?

GREEN LANTERN

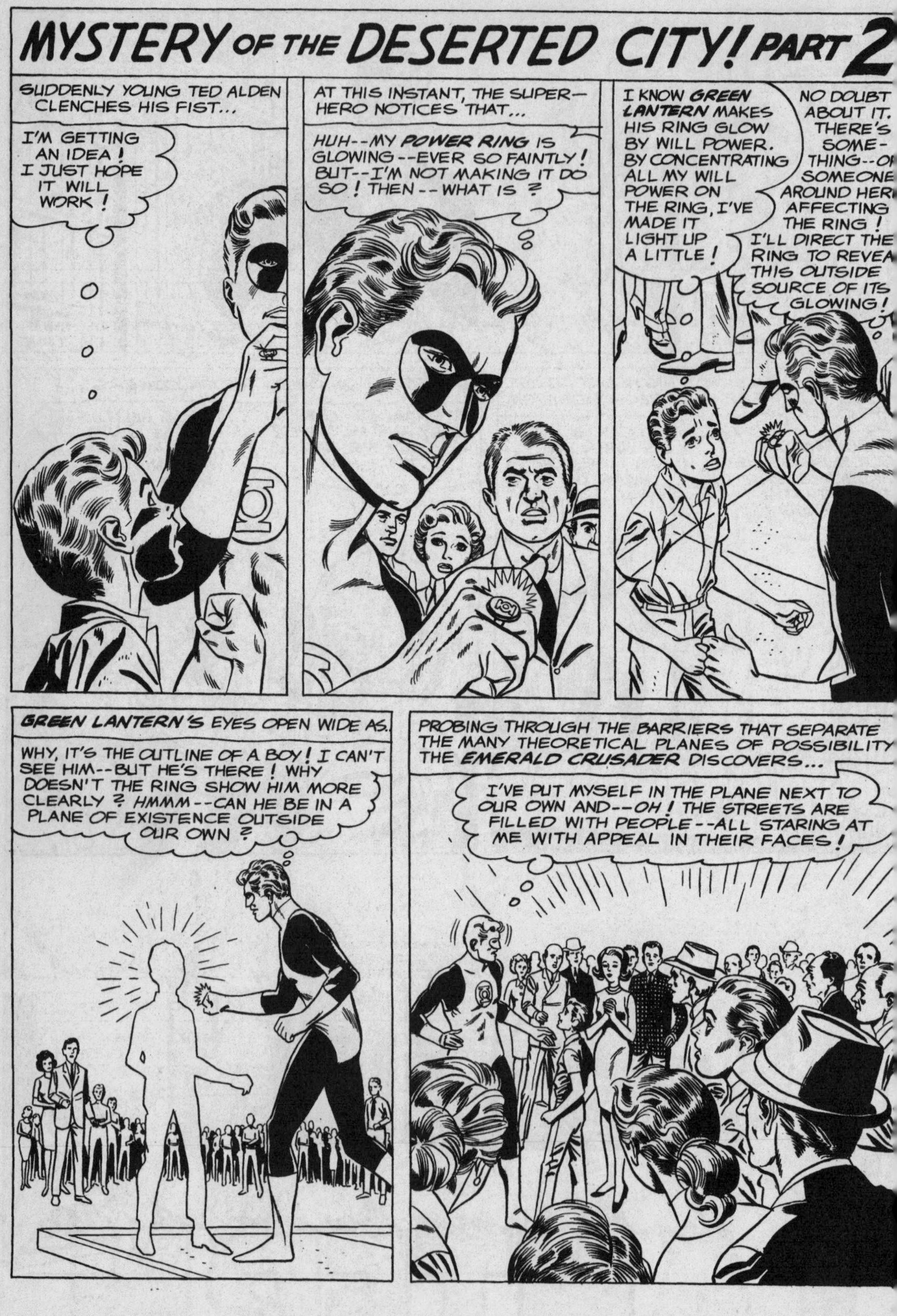
MYSTERY OF THE DESERTED CITY! PART 2
SUDDENLY YOUNG TED ALDEN CLENCHES HIS FIST...
I'M GETTING AN IDEA! I JUST HOPE IT WILL WORK!
AT THIS INSTANT, THE SUPER-HERO NOTICES THAT...
HUH--MY POWER RING IS GLOWING--EVER SO FAINTLY! BUT--I'M NOT MAKING IT DO SO! THEN--WHAT IS ?
I KNOW GREEN LANTERN MAKES HIS RING GLOW BY WILL POWER. BY CONCENTRATING ALL MY WILL POWER ON THE RING, I'VE MADE IT LIGHT UP A LITTLE!
NO DOUBT ABOUT IT. THERE'S SOME-THING--OR SOMEONE AROUND HERE AFFECTING THE RING! I'LL DIRECT THE RING TO REVEAL THIS OUTSIDE SOURCE OF ITS GLOWING!
GREEN LANTERN'S EYES OPEN WIDE AS.
WHY, IT'S THE OUTLINE OF A BOY! I CAN'T SEE HIM--BUT HE'S THERE! WHY DOESN'T THE RING SHOW HIM MORE CLEARLY ? HMMM--CAN HE BE IN A PLANE OF EXISTENCE OUTSIDE OUR OWN ?
PROBING THROUGH THE BARRIERS THAT SEPARATE THE MANY THEORETICAL PLANES OF POSSIBILITY THE EMERALD CRUSADER DISCOVERS...
I'VE PUT MYSELF IN THE PLANE NEXT TO OUR OWN AND--OH! THE STREETS ARE FILLED WITH PEOPLE--ALL STARING AT ME WITH APPEAL IN THEIR FACES!

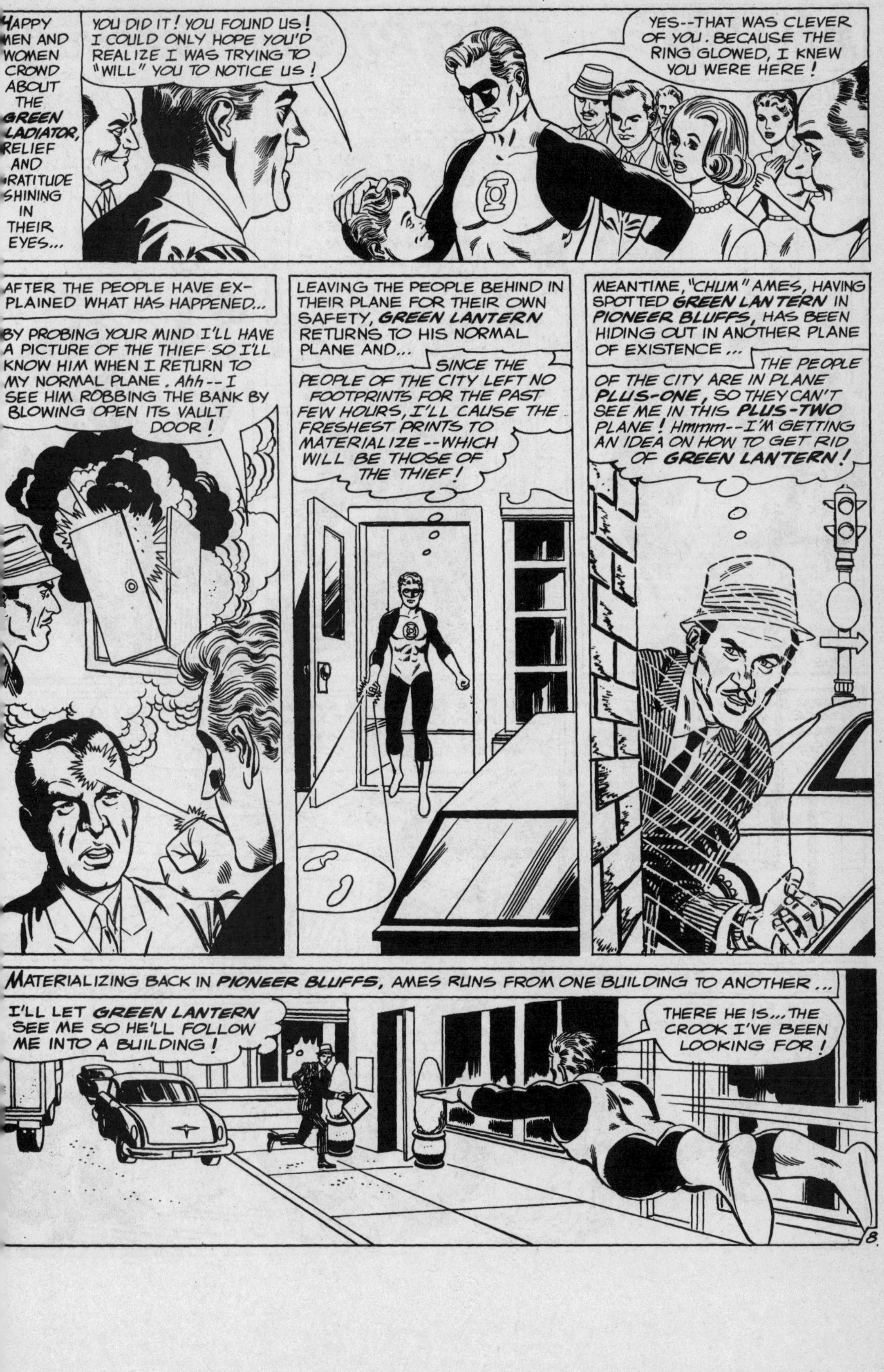
HAPPY MEN AND WOMEN CROWD ABOUT THE GREEN LADIATOR, RELIEF AND GRATITUDE SHINING IN THEIR EYES...
YOU DID IT! YOU FOUND US! I COULD ONLY HOPE YOU'D REALIZE I WAS TRYING TO "WILL" YOU TO NOTICE US!
YES--THAT WAS CLEVER OF YOU. BECAUSE THE RING GLOWED, I KNEW YOU WERE HERE!
AFTER THE PEOPLE HAVE EXPLAINED WHAT HAS HAPPENED...
BY PROBING YOUR MIND I'LL HAVE A PICTURE OF THE THIEF SO I'LL KNOW HIM WHEN I RETURN TO MY NORMAL PLANE. Ahh--I SEE HIM ROBBING THE BANK BY BLOWING OPEN ITS VAULT DOOR!
LEAVING THE PEOPLE BEHIND IN THEIR PLANE FOR THEIR OWN SAFETY, GREEN LANTERN RETURNS TO HIS NORMAL PLANE AND...
SINCE THE PEOPLE OF THE CITY LEFT NO FOOTPRINTS FOR THE PAST FEW HOURS, I'LL CAUSE THE FRESHEST PRINTS TO MATERIALIZE--WHICH WILL BE THOSE OF THE THIEF!
MEANTIME, "CHUM" AMES, HAVING SPOTTED GREEN LANTERN IN PIONEER BLUFFS, HAS BEEN HIDING OUT IN ANOTHER PLANE OF EXISTENCE...
THE PEOPLE OF THE CITY ARE IN PLANE PLUS-ONE, SO THEY CAN'T SEE ME IN THIS PLUS-TWO PLANE! Hmmm--I'M GETTING AN IDEA ON HOW TO GET RID OF GREEN LANTERN!
MATERIALIZING BACK IN PIONEER BLUFFS, AMES RUNS FROM ONE BUILDING TO ANOTHER...
I'LL LET GREEN LANTERN SEE ME SO HE'LL FOLLOW ME INTO A BUILDING!
THERE HE IS... THE CROOK I'VE BEEN LOOKING FOR!
8

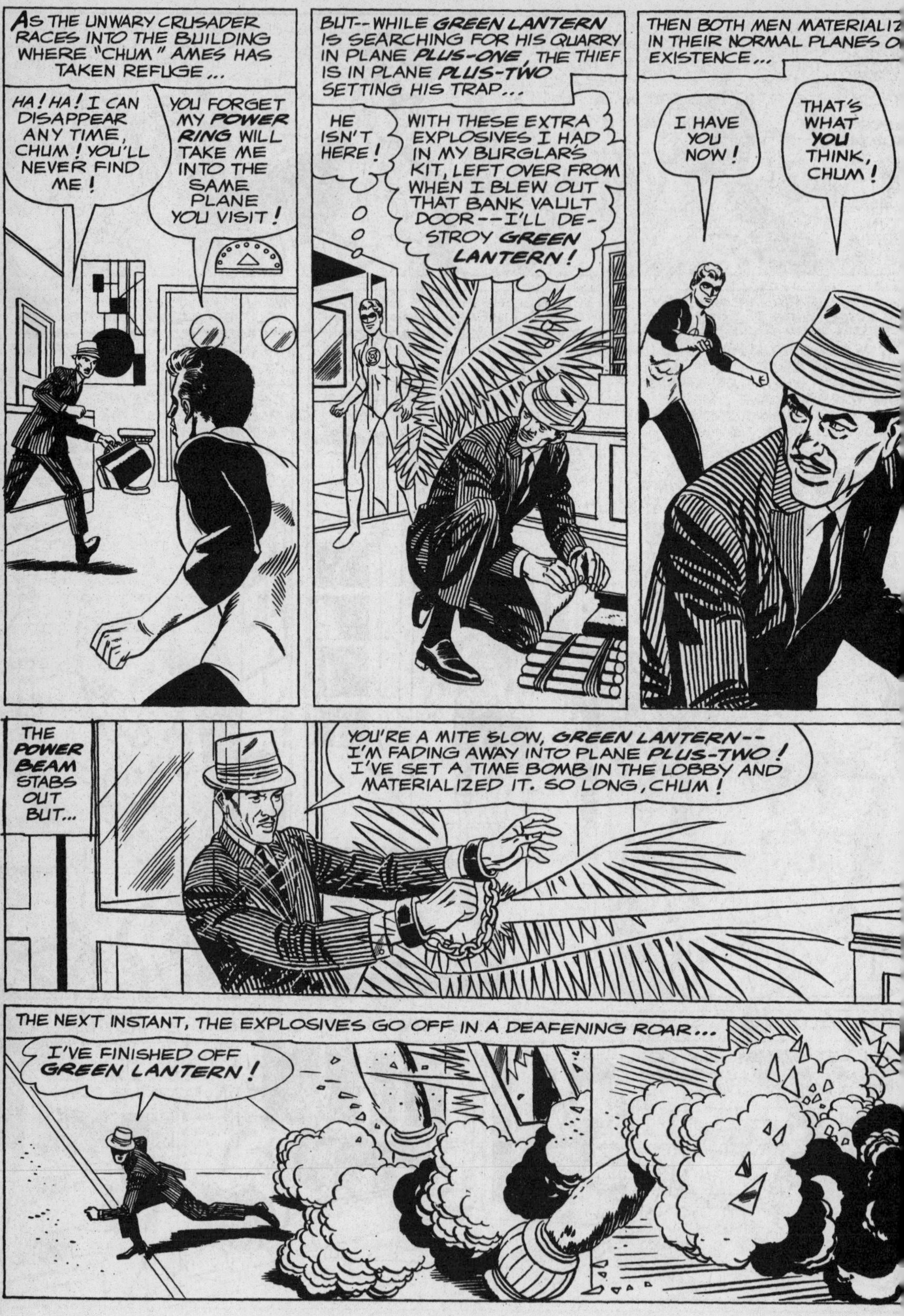
AS THE UNWARY CRUSADER RACES INTO THE BUILDING WHERE "CHUM" AMES HAS TAKEN REFUGE...
HA! HA! I CAN DISAPPEAR ANY TIME, CHUM! YOU'LL NEVER FIND ME!
YOU FORGET MY POWER RING WILL TAKE ME INTO THE SAME PLANE YOU VISIT!
BUT--WHILE GREEN LANTERN IS SEARCHING FOR HIS QUARRY IN PLANE PLUS-ONE, THE THIEF IS IN PLANE PLUS-TWO SETTING HIS TRAP...
HE ISN'T HERE!
WITH THESE EXTRA EXPLOSIVES I HAD IN MY BURGLAR'S KIT, LEFT OVER FROM WHEN I BLEW OUT THAT BANK VAULT DOOR--I'LL DESTROY GREEN LANTERN!
THEN BOTH MEN MATERIALIZ IN THEIR NORMAL PLANES O EXISTENCE...
I HAVE YOU NOW!
THAT'S WHAT YOU THINK, CHUM!
THE POWER BEAM STABS OUT BUT...
YOU'RE A MITE SLOW, GREEN LANTERN-- I'M FADING AWAY INTO PLANE PLUS-TWO! I'VE SET A TIME BOMB IN THE LOBBY AND MATERIALIZED IT. SO LONG, CHUM!
THE NEXT INSTANT, THE EXPLOSIVES GO OFF IN A DEAFENING ROAR...
I'VE FINISHED OFF GREEN LANTERN!

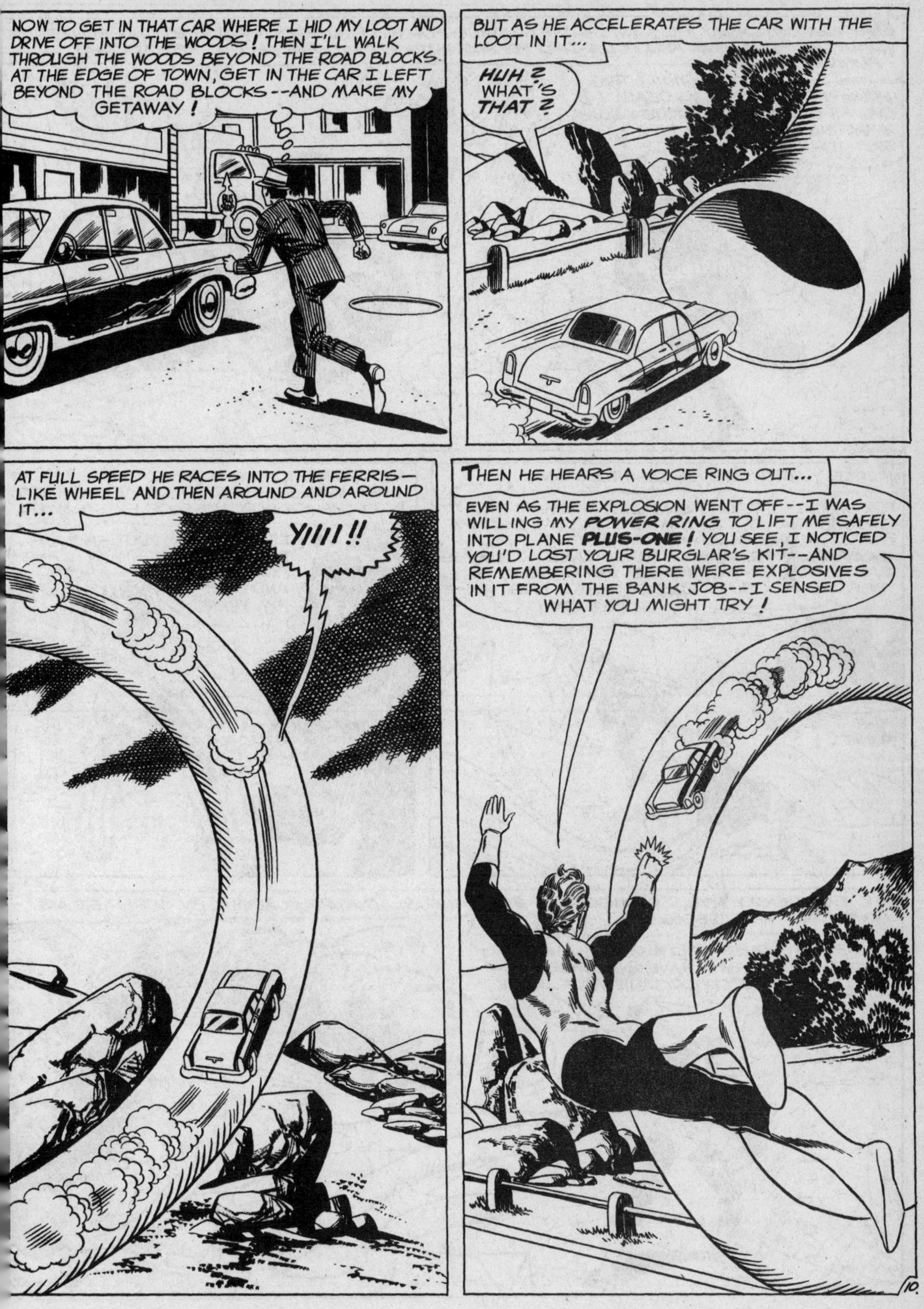
NOW TO GET IN THAT CAR WHERE I HID MY LOOT AND DRIVE OFF INTO THE WOODS! THEN I'LL WALK THROUGH THE WOODS BEYOND THE ROAD BLOCKS AT THE EDGE OF TOWN, GET IN THE CAR I LEFT BEYOND THE ROAD BLOCKS--AND MAKE MY GETAWAY!
BUT AS HE ACCELERATES THE CAR WITH THE LOOT IN IT...
HUH? WHAT'S THAT?
AT FULL SPEED HE RACES INTO THE FERRIS-LIKE WHEEL AND THEN AROUND AND AROUND IT...
YIIII!!
THEN HE HEARS A VOICE RING OUT...
EVEN AS THE EXPLOSION WENT OFF--I WAS WILLING MY POWER RING TO LIFT ME SAFELY INTO PLANE PLUS-ONE! YOU SEE, I NOTICED YOU'D LOST YOUR BURGLAR'S KIT--AND REMEMBERING THERE WERE EXPLOSIVES IN IT FROM THE BANK JOB--I SENSED WHAT YOU MIGHT TRY!
10

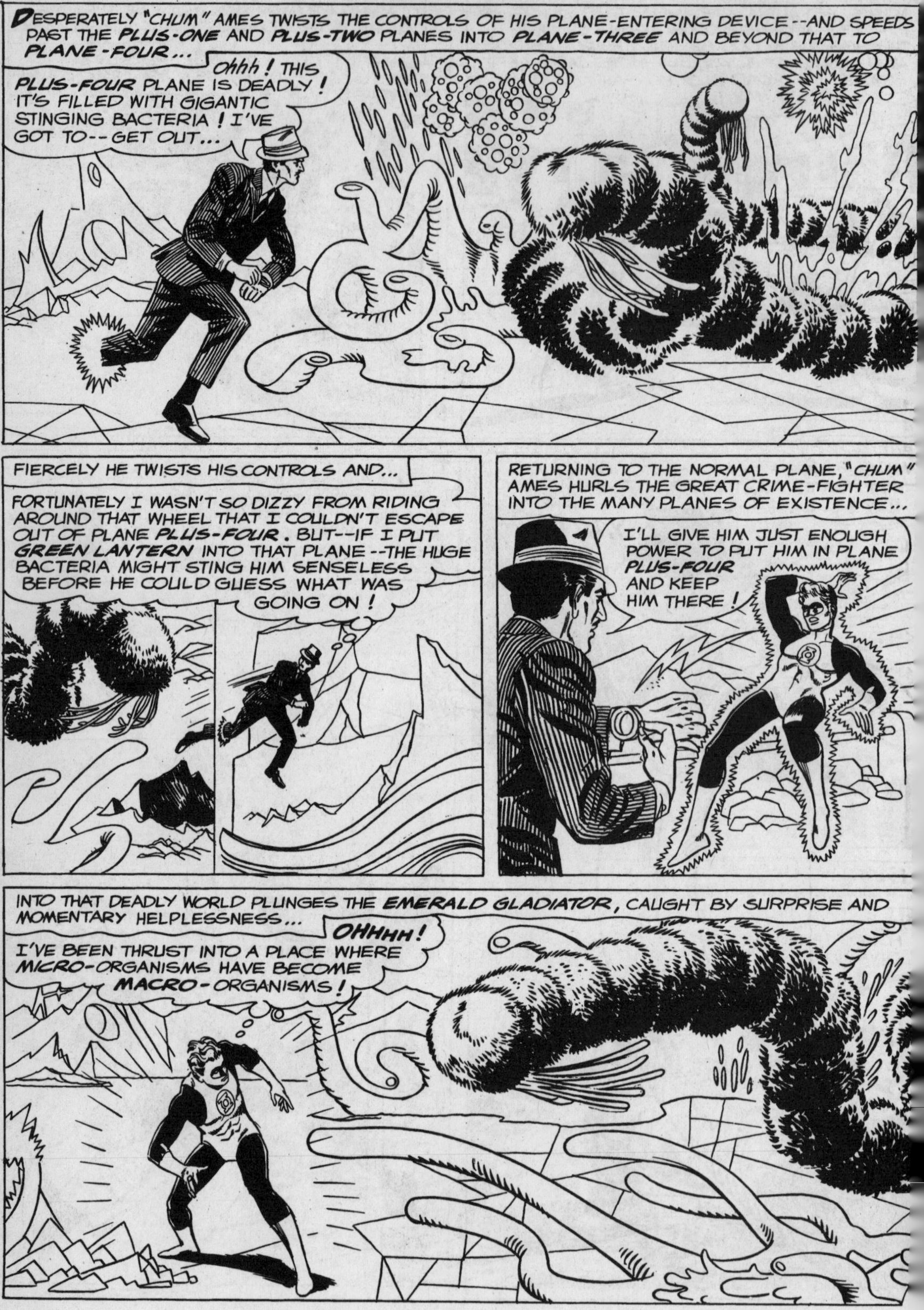
DESPERATELY "CHUM" AMES TWISTS THE CONTROLS OF HIS PLANE-ENTERING DEVICE--AND SPEEDS PAST THE PLUS-ONE AND PLUS-TWO PLANES INTO PLANE-THREE AND BEYOND THAT TO PLANE-FOUR...
OHHH! THIS PLUS-FOUR PLANE IS DEADLY! IT'S FILLED WITH GIGANTIC STINGING BACTERIA! I'VE GOT TO--GET OUT...
FIERCELY HE TWISTS HIS CONTROLS AND...
FORTUNATELY I WASN'T SO DIZZY FROM RIDING AROUND THAT WHEEL THAT I COULDN'T ESCAPE OUT OF PLANE PLUS-FOUR. BUT--IF I PUT GREEN LANTERN INTO THAT PLANE--THE HUGE BACTERIA MIGHT STING HIM SENSELESS BEFORE HE COULD GUESS WHAT WAS GOING ON!
RETURNING TO THE NORMAL PLANE, "CHUM" AMES HURLS THE GREAT CRIME-FIGHTER INTO THE MANY PLANES OF EXISTENCE...
I'LL GIVE HIM JUST ENOUGH POWER TO PUT HIM IN PLANE PLUS-FOUR AND KEEP HIM THERE!
INTO THAT DEADLY WORLD PLUNGES THE EMERALD GLADIATOR, CAUGHT BY SURPRISE AND MOMENTARY HELPLESSNESS...
OHHHH! I'VE BEEN THRUST INTO A PLACE WHERE MICRO-ORGANISMS HAVE BECOME MACRO-ORGANISMS!

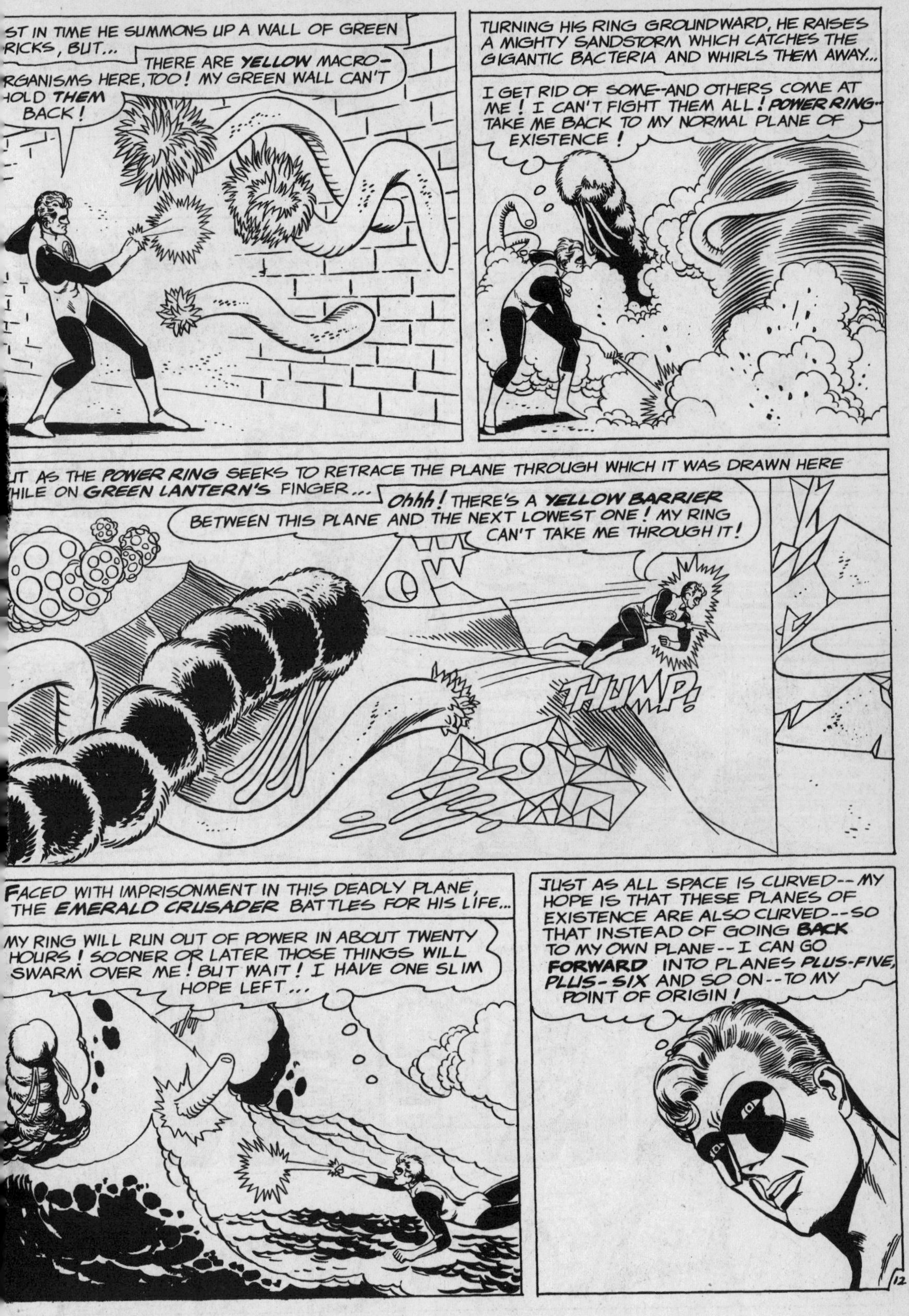
ST IN TIME HE SUMMONS UP A WALL OF GREEN RICKS, BUT...
THERE ARE YELLOW MACRO-RGANISMS HERE, TOO! MY GREEN WALL CAN'T HOLD THEM BACK!
TURNING HIS RING GROUNDWARD, HE RAISES A MIGHTY SANDSTORM WHICH CATCHES THE GIGANTIC BACTERIA AND WHIRLS THEM AWAY...
I GET RID OF SOME--AND OTHERS COME AT ME! I CAN'T FIGHT THEM ALL! POWER RING-- TAKE ME BACK TO MY NORMAL PLANE OF EXISTENCE!
UT AS THE POWER RING SEEKS TO RETRACE THE PLANE THROUGH WHICH IT WAS DRAWN HERE HILE ON GREEN LANTERN'S FINGER...
Ohhh! THERE'S A YELLOW BARRIER BETWEEN THIS PLANE AND THE NEXT LOWEST ONE! MY RING CAN'T TAKE ME THROUGH IT!
THUMP!
FACED WITH IMPRISONMENT IN THIS DEADLY PLANE, THE EMERALD CRUSADER BATTLES FOR HIS LIFE...
MY RING WILL RUN OUT OF POWER IN ABOUT TWENTY HOURS! SOONER OR LATER THOSE THINGS WILL SWARM OVER ME! BUT WAIT! I HAVE ONE SLIM HOPE LEFT...
JUST AS ALL SPACE IS CURVED--MY HOPE IS THAT THESE PLANES OF EXISTENCE ARE ALSO CURVED--SO THAT INSTEAD OF GOING BACK TO MY OWN PLANE--I CAN GO FORWARD INTO PLANES PLUS-FIVE, PLUS-SIX AND SO ON--TO MY POINT OF ORIGIN!
12

FORWARD THROUGH THE MYRIAD PLANES OF EXISTENCE SPEEDS THE *GREEN GLADIATOR*..

I CAN GO *FORWARD*-- BUT WILL THE PLANES BEND SO THAT I WILL GO ON IN A CIRCLE UNTIL I'M BACK AT MY STARTING POINT...?

THEN... I MADE IT! AND I CAME INTO MY WORLD--AT THE EDGE OF THOSE WOODS INTO WHICH THAT CROOK IS WALKING! I'LL BE ABLE TO CAPTURE HIM EASILY NOW!

LATER, AFTER HE HAS IMPRISONED THE THIEF, RETURNED THE LOOT AND TOLD THE SCIENTISTS ARRIVING AT *PIONEER BLUFFS* ABOUT THE STOPPED EARTHQUAKE...

THE PEOPLE ARE BACK IN THEIR NORMAL PLANE, NOW. THERE'S NO MORE DANGER FOR THEM--EITHER FROM AN EARTHQUAKE OR A CLEVER CROOK!

NEXT DAY AT THE *PIONEER DAY CENTENNIAL CELEBRATION*, YOUNG TED ALDEN IS NAMED *GRAND MARSHAL* OF THE PARADE...

GOLLY, AM I EVER PROUD TO BE WITH YOU, *GREEN LANTERN*!

I'M EVEN MORE PROUD TO BE HERE, TED! REMEMBER--IF YOU HADN'T THOUGHT OF MAKING MY RING GLOW, THIS CELEBRATION MIGHT POSSIBLY HAVE BEEN A TRAGEDY!

The End

GREEN LANTERN

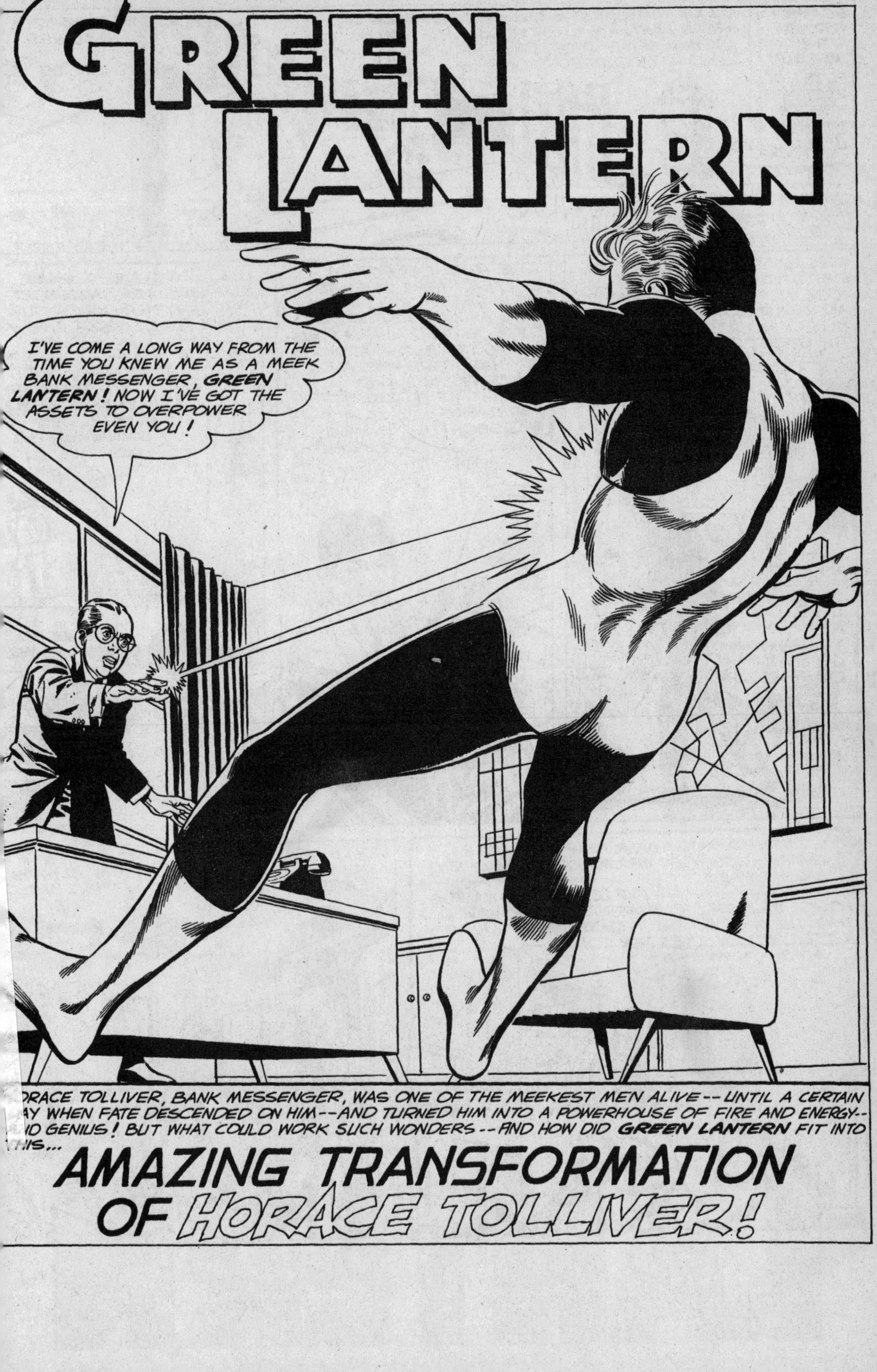
GREEN LANTERN
I'VE COME A LONG WAY FROM THE TIME YOU KNEW ME AS A MEEK BANK MESSENGER, GREEN LANTERN! NOW I'VE GOT THE ASSETS TO OVERPOWER EVEN YOU!
ORACE TOLLIVER, BANK MESSENGER, WAS ONE OF THE MEEKEST MEN ALIVE -- UNTIL A CERTAIN AY WHEN FATE DESCENDED ON HIM -- AND TURNED HIM INTO A POWERHOUSE OF FIRE AND ENERGY -- ND GENIUS! BUT WHAT COULD WORK SUCH WONDERS -- AND HOW DID GREEN LANTERN FIT INTO HIS...
AMAZING TRANSFORMATION OF HORACE TOLLIVER!

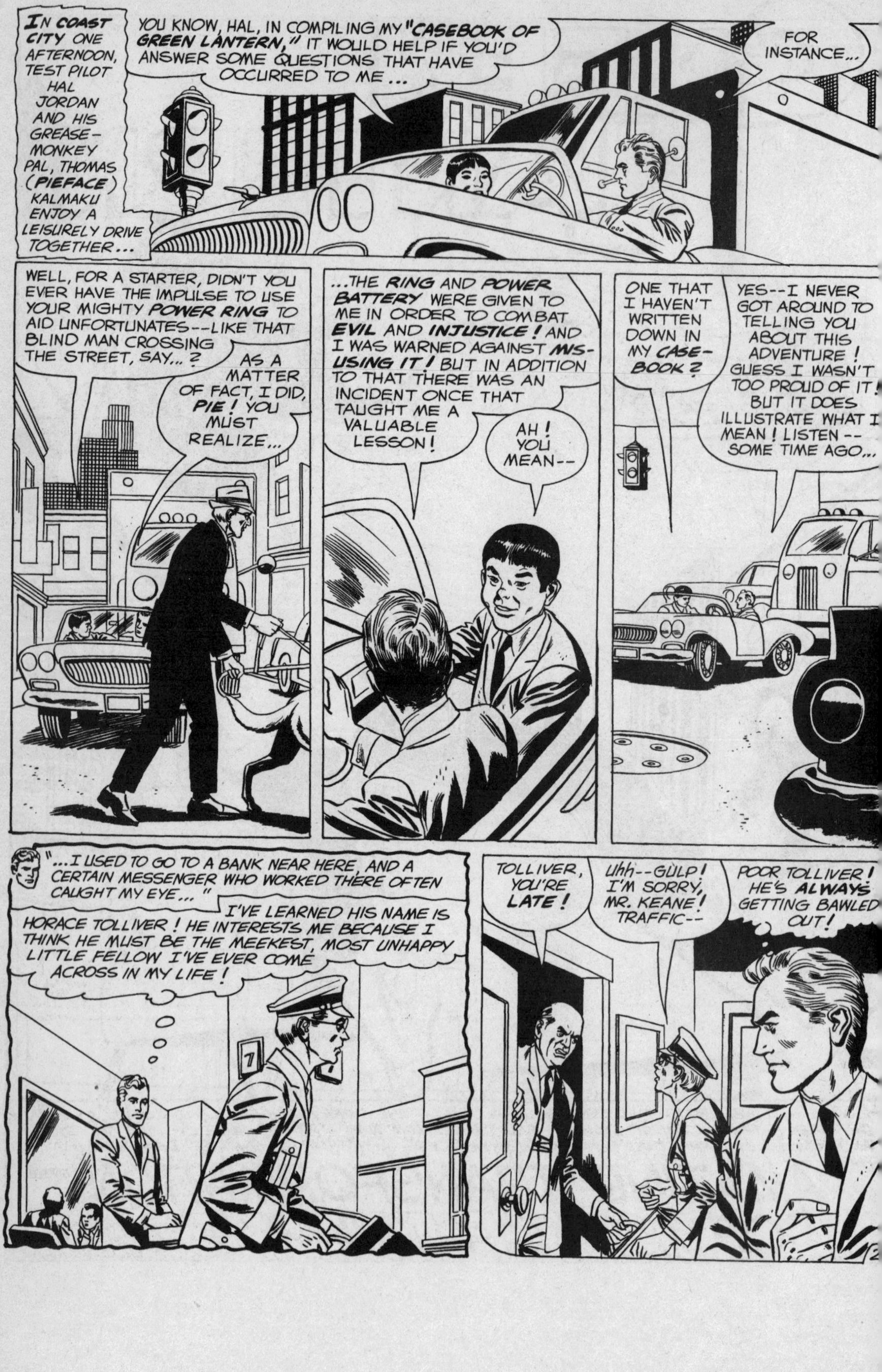

IN COAST CITY ONE AFTERNOON, TEST PILOT HAL JORDAN AND HIS GREASE-MONKEY PAL, THOMAS (PIEFACE) KALMAKU ENJOY A LEISURELY DRIVE TOGETHER...
YOU KNOW, HAL, IN COMPILING MY "CASEBOOK OF GREEN LANTERN," IT WOULD HELP IF YOU'D ANSWER SOME QUESTIONS THAT HAVE OCCURRED TO ME...
FOR INSTANCE...
WELL, FOR A STARTER, DIDN'T YOU EVER HAVE THE IMPULSE TO USE YOUR MIGHTY POWER RING TO AID UNFORTUNATES--LIKE THAT BLIND MAN CROSSING THE STREET, SAY...?
AS A MATTER OF FACT, I DID, PIE! YOU MUST REALIZE...
...THE RING AND POWER BATTERY WERE GIVEN TO ME IN ORDER TO COMBAT EVIL AND INJUSTICE! AND I WAS WARNED AGAINST MIS-USING IT! BUT IN ADDITION TO THAT THERE WAS AN INCIDENT ONCE THAT TAUGHT ME A VALUABLE LESSON!
AH! YOU MEAN--
ONE THAT I HAVEN'T WRITTEN DOWN IN MY CASE-BOOK?
YES--I NEVER GOT AROUND TO TELLING YOU ABOUT THIS ADVENTURE! GUESS I WASN'T TOO PROUD OF IT! BUT IT DOES ILLUSTRATE WHAT I MEAN! LISTEN--SOME TIME AGO...
"...I USED TO GO TO A BANK NEAR HERE, AND A CERTAIN MESSENGER WHO WORKED THERE OFTEN CAUGHT MY EYE..."
I'VE LEARNED HIS NAME IS HORACE TOLLIVER! HE INTERESTS ME BECAUSE I THINK HE MUST BE THE MEEKEST, MOST UNHAPPY LITTLE FELLOW I'VE EVER COME ACROSS IN MY LIFE!
7
TOLLIVER, YOU'RE LATE!
UHH--GULP! I'M SORRY, MR. KEANE! TRAFFIC--
POOR TOLLIVER! HE'S ALWAYS GETTING BAWLED OUT!

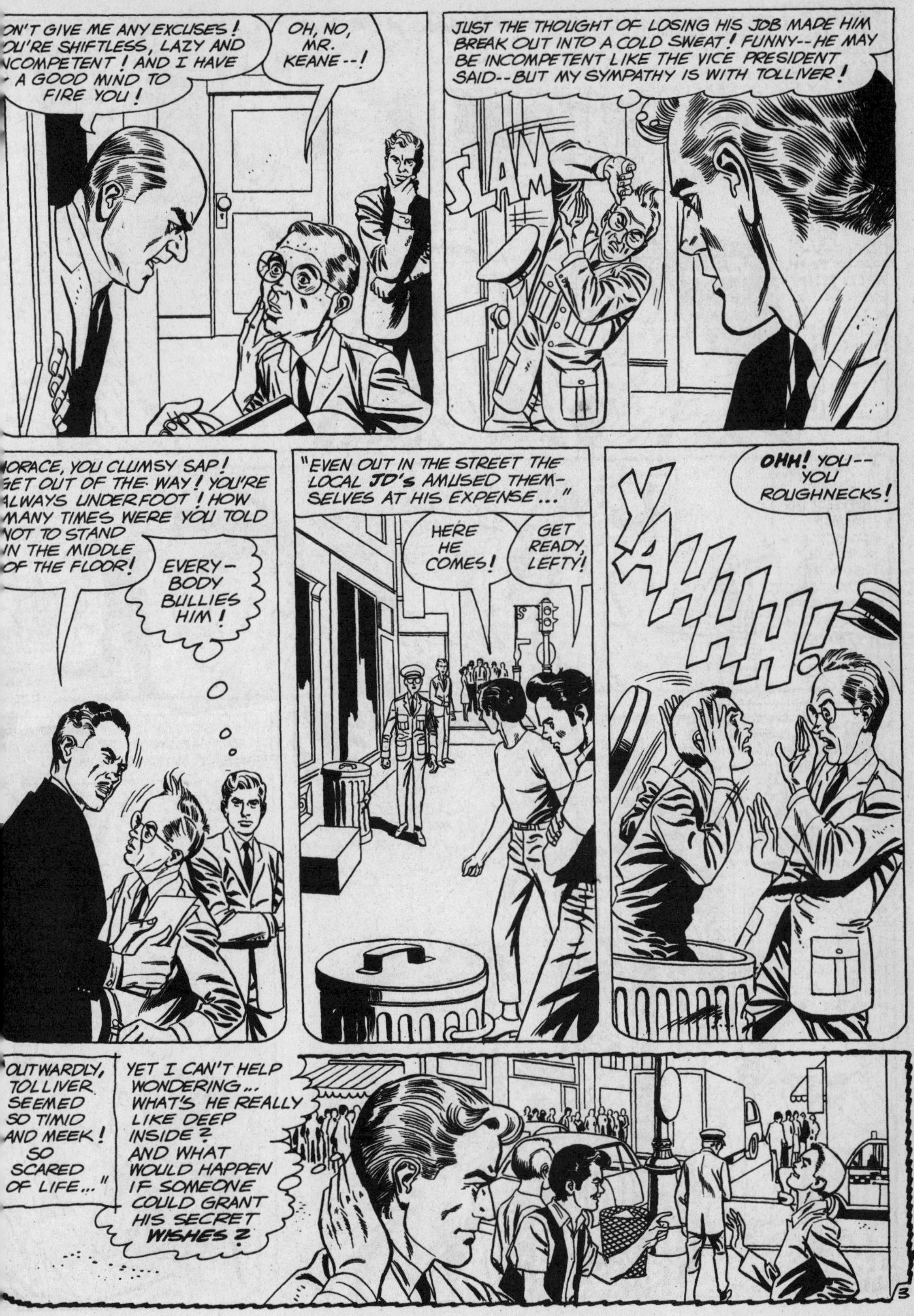

ON'T GIVE ME ANY EXCUSES! OU'RE SHIFTLESS, LAZY AND NCOMPETENT! AND I HAVE A GOOD MIND TO FIRE YOU!
OH, NO, MR. KEANE--!
JUST THE THOUGHT OF LOSING HIS JOB MADE HIM BREAK OUT INTO A COLD SWEAT! FUNNY--HE MAY BE INCOMPETENT LIKE THE VICE PRESIDENT SAID--BUT MY SYMPATHY IS WITH TOLLIVER!
SLAM
ORACE, YOU CLUMSY SAP! GET OUT OF THE WAY! YOU'RE ALWAYS UNDERFOOT! HOW MANY TIMES WERE YOU TOLD NOT TO STAND IN THE MIDDLE OF THE FLOOR!
EVERY-BODY BULLIES HIM!
"EVEN OUT IN THE STREET THE LOCAL JD's AMUSED THEM-SELVES AT HIS EXPENSE..."
HERE HE COMES!
GET READY, LEFTY!
YAHHH!
OHH! YOU--YOU ROUGHNECKS!
OUTWARDLY, TOLLIVER SEEMED SO TIMID AND MEEK! SO SCARED OF LIFE..."
YET I CAN'T HELP WONDERING... WHAT'S HE REALLY LIKE DEEP INSIDE? AND WHAT WOULD HAPPEN IF SOMEONE COULD GRANT HIS SECRET WISHES?
3

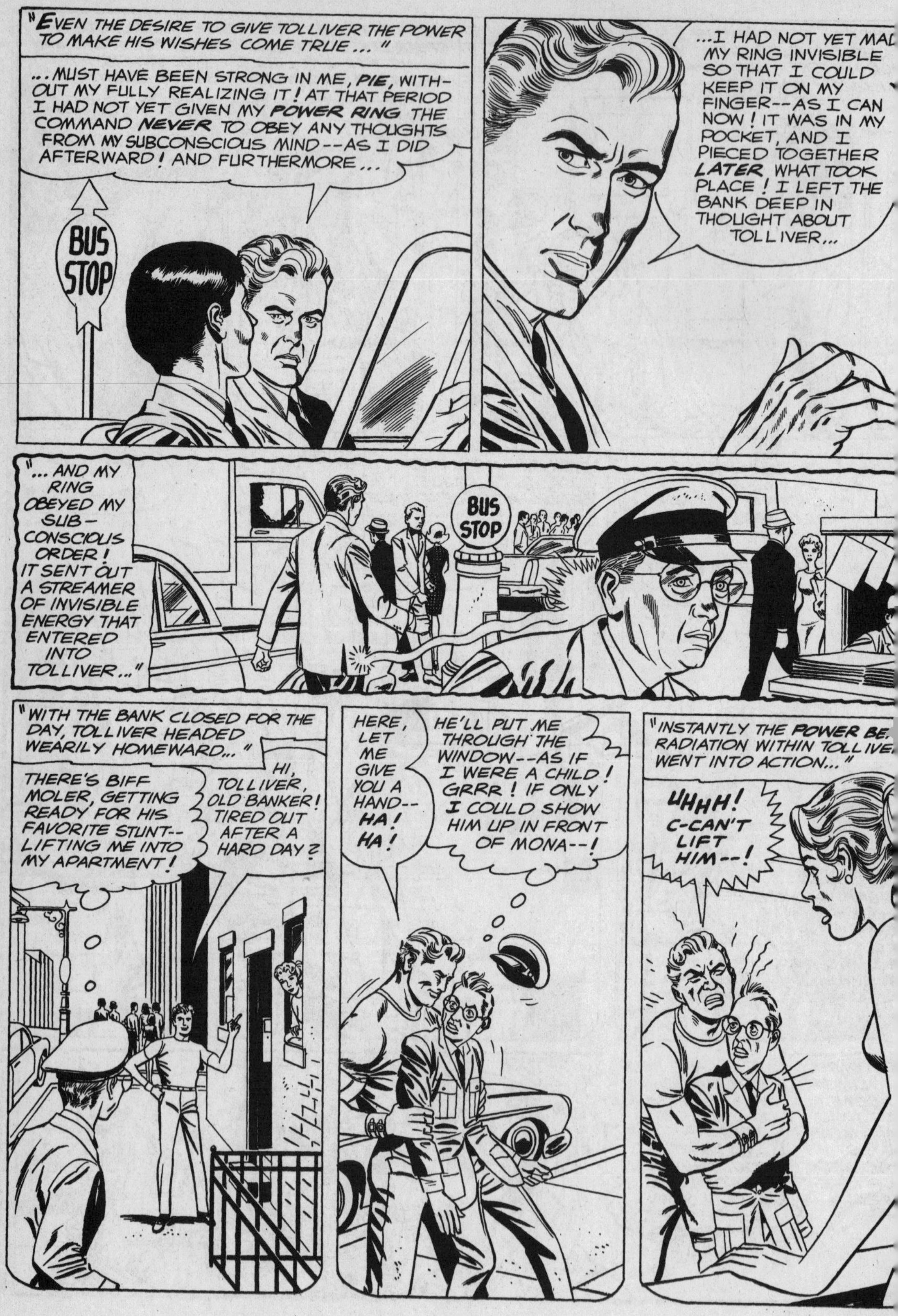
"EVEN THE DESIRE TO GIVE TOLLIVER THE POWER TO MAKE HIS WISHES COME TRUE ..."
...MUST HAVE BEEN STRONG IN ME, PIE, WITHOUT MY FULLY REALIZING IT! AT THAT PERIOD I HAD NOT YET GIVEN MY POWER RING THE COMMAND NEVER TO OBEY ANY THOUGHTS FROM MY SUBCONSCIOUS MIND--AS I DID AFTERWARD! AND FURTHERMORE...
BUS STOP
...I HAD NOT YET MAD MY RING INVISIBLE SO THAT I COULD KEEP IT ON MY FINGER--AS I CAN NOW! IT WAS IN MY POCKET, AND I PIECED TOGETHER LATER WHAT TOOK PLACE! I LEFT THE BANK DEEP IN THOUGHT ABOUT TOLLIVER...
"...AND MY RING OBEYED MY SUB-CONSCIOUS ORDER! IT SENT OUT A STREAMER OF INVISIBLE ENERGY THAT ENTERED INTO TOLLIVER..."
BUS STOP
"WITH THE BANK CLOSED FOR THE DAY, TOLLIVER HEADED WEARILY HOMEWARD..."
THERE'S BIFF MOLER, GETTING READY FOR HIS FAVORITE STUNT--LIFTING ME INTO MY APARTMENT!
HI, TOLLIVER, OLD BANKER! TIRED OUT AFTER A HARD DAY?
HERE, LET ME GIVE YOU A HAND--HA! HA!
HE'LL PUT ME THROUGH THE WINDOW--AS IF I WERE A CHILD! GRRR! IF ONLY I COULD SHOW HIM UP IN FRONT OF MONA--!
"INSTANTLY THE POWER BE RADIATION WITHIN TOLLIVE WENT INTO ACTION..."
UHHH! C-CAN'T LIFT HIM--!

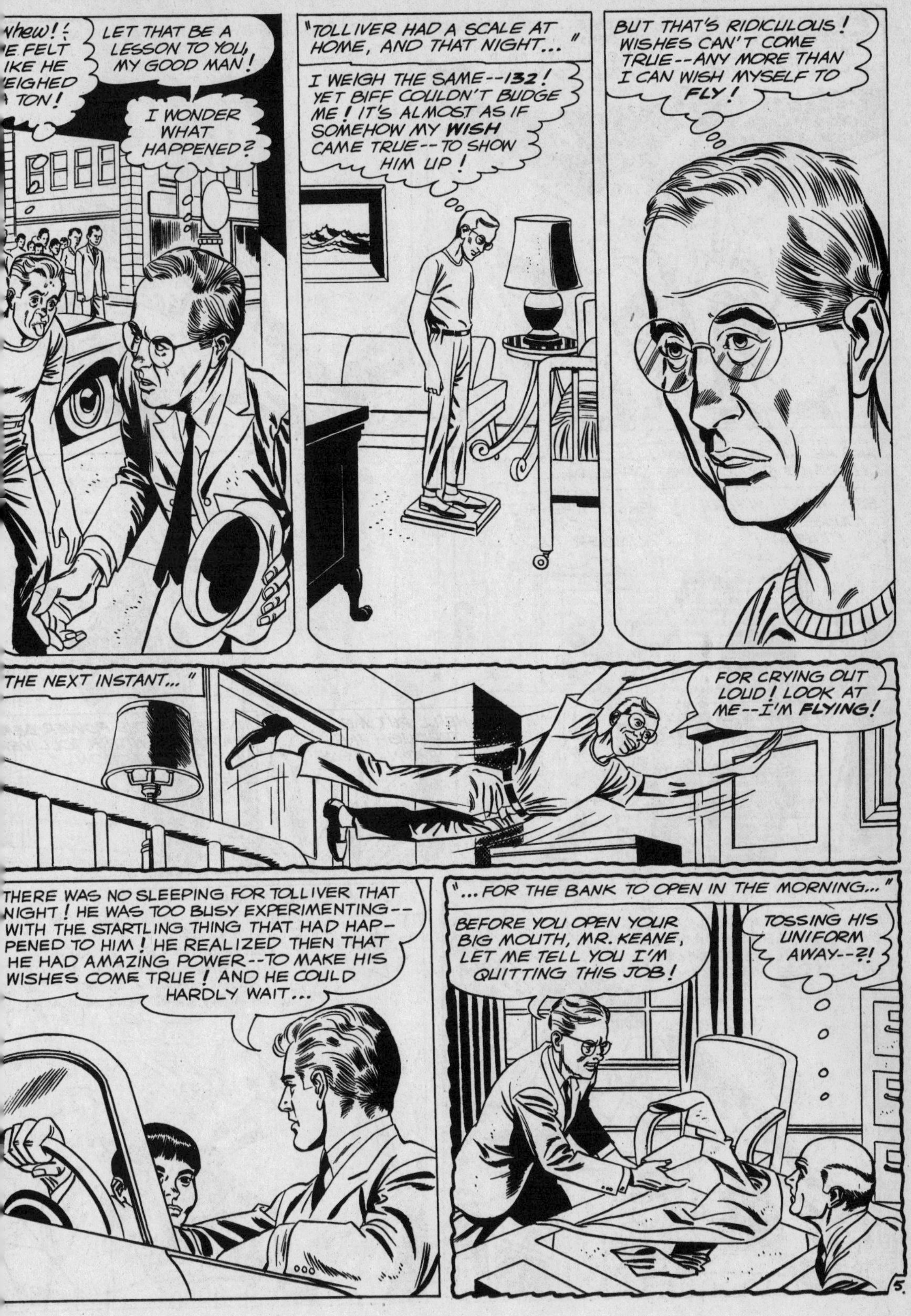

...hew! ...E FELT ...IKE HE ...EIGHED ...TON!
LET THAT BE A LESSON TO YOU, MY GOOD MAN!
I WONDER WHAT HAPPENED?
"TOLLIVER HAD A SCALE AT HOME, AND THAT NIGHT..."
I WEIGH THE SAME--132! YET BIFF COULDN'T BUDGE ME! IT'S ALMOST AS IF SOMEHOW MY WISH CAME TRUE--TO SHOW HIM UP!
BUT THAT'S RIDICULOUS! WISHES CAN'T COME TRUE--ANY MORE THAN I CAN WISH MYSELF TO FLY!
THE NEXT INSTANT..."
FOR CRYING OUT LOUD! LOOK AT ME--I'M FLYING!
THERE WAS NO SLEEPING FOR TOLLIVER THAT NIGHT! HE WAS TOO BUSY EXPERIMENTING--WITH THE STARTLING THING THAT HAD HAPPENED TO HIM! HE REALIZED THEN THAT HE HAD AMAZING POWER--TO MAKE HIS WISHES COME TRUE! AND HE COULD HARDLY WAIT...
"...FOR THE BANK TO OPEN IN THE MORNING..."
BEFORE YOU OPEN YOUR BIG MOUTH, MR. KEANE, LET ME TELL YOU I'M QUITTING THIS JOB!
TOSSING HIS UNIFORM AWAY--?!
5.

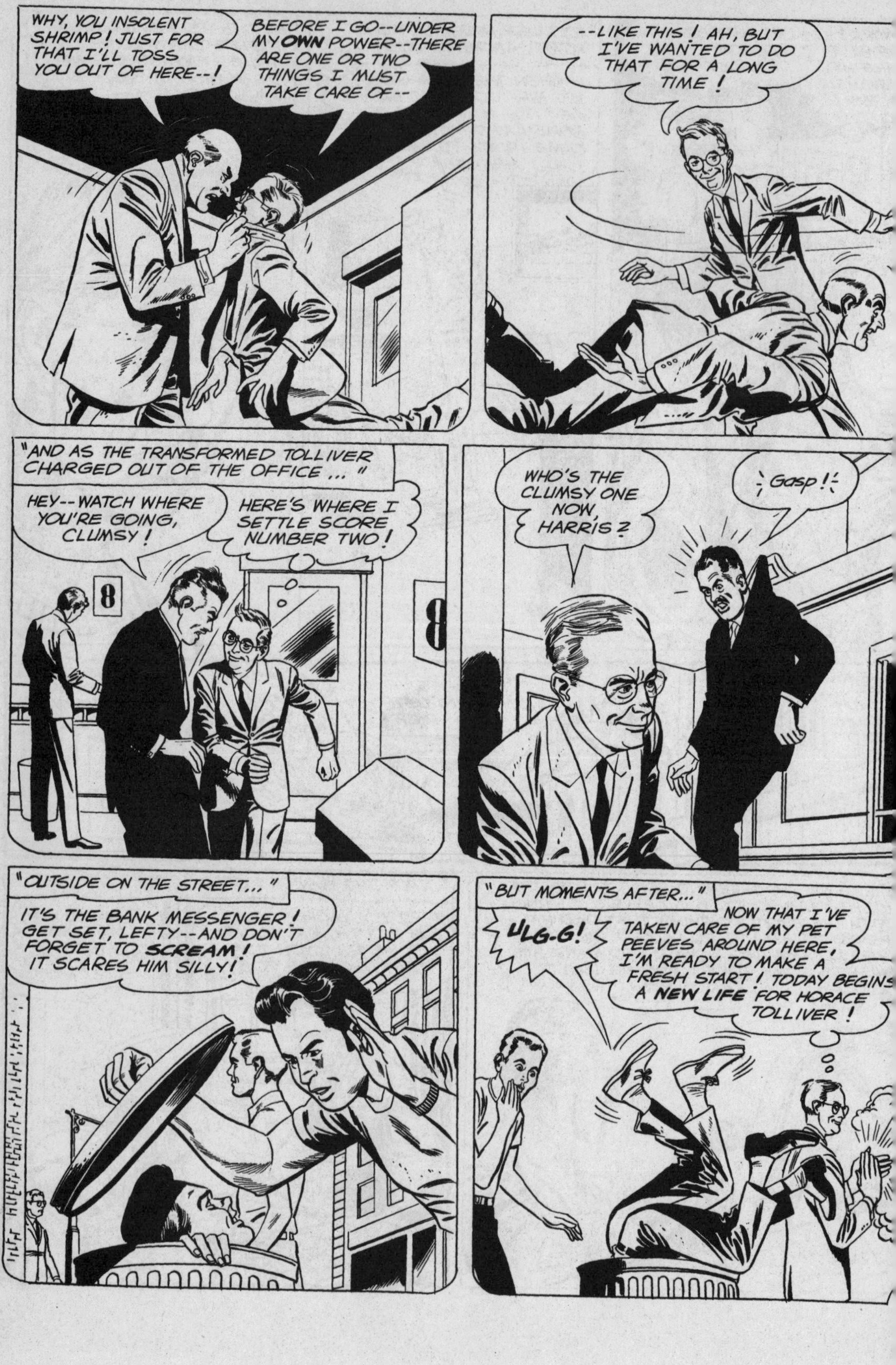
WHY, YOU INSOLENT SHRIMP! JUST FOR THAT I'LL TOSS YOU OUT OF HERE--!
BEFORE I GO--UNDER MY OWN POWER--THERE ARE ONE OR TWO THINGS I MUST TAKE CARE OF--
--LIKE THIS! AH, BUT I'VE WANTED TO DO THAT FOR A LONG TIME!
"AND AS THE TRANSFORMED TOLLIVER CHARGED OUT OF THE OFFICE ..."
HEY--WATCH WHERE YOU'RE GOING, CLUMSY!
HERE'S WHERE I SETTLE SCORE NUMBER TWO!
8
8
WHO'S THE CLUMSY ONE NOW, HARRIS?
Gasp!
"OUTSIDE ON THE STREET..."
IT'S THE BANK MESSENGER! GET SET, LEFTY--AND DON'T FORGET TO SCREAM! IT SCARES HIM SILLY!
"BUT MOMENTS AFTER..."
ULG-G!
NOW THAT I'VE TAKEN CARE OF MY PET PEEVES AROUND HERE, I'M READY TO MAKE A FRESH START! TODAY BEGINS A NEW LIFE FOR HORACE TOLLIVER!

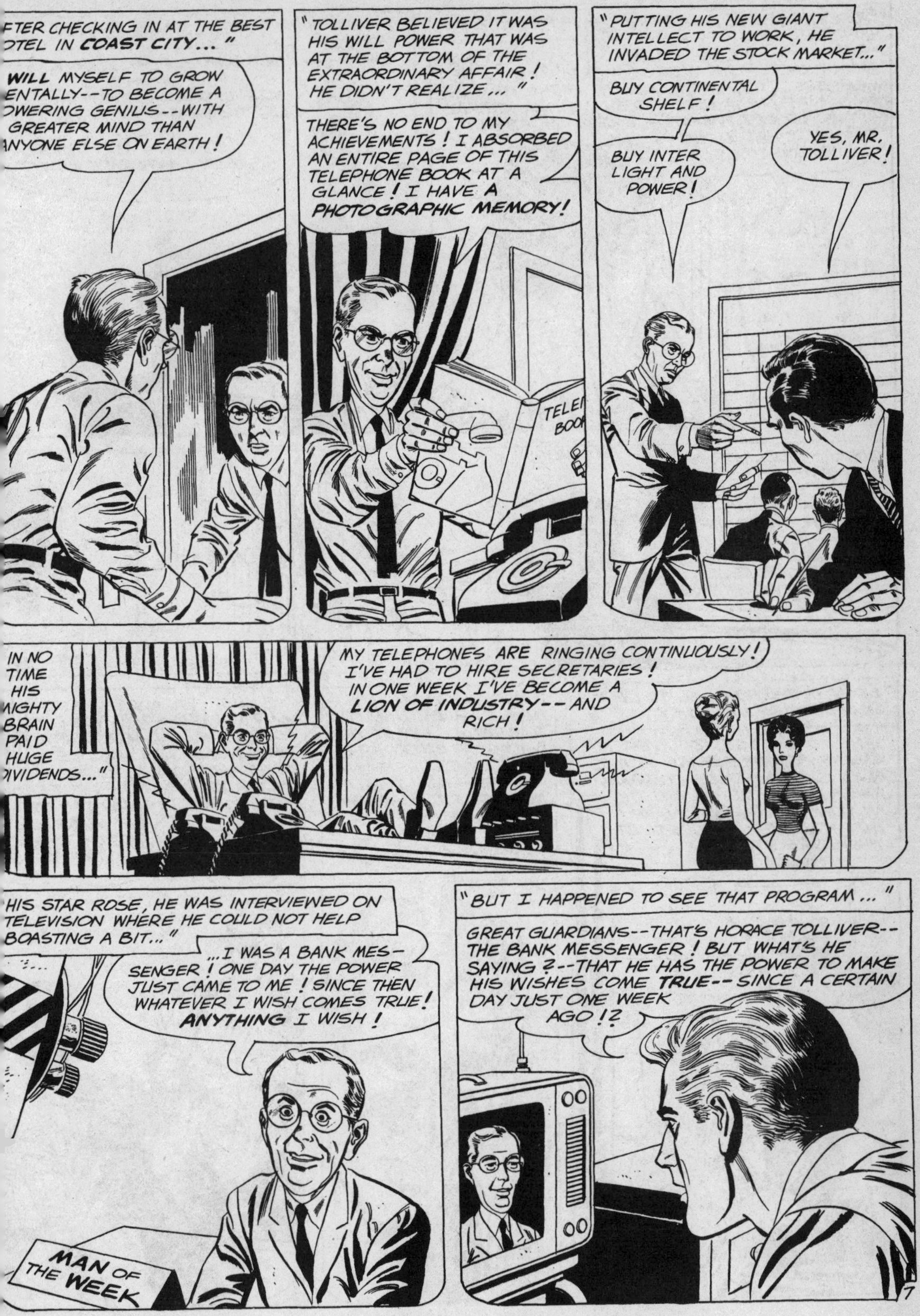
FTER CHECKING IN AT THE BEST OTEL IN COAST CITY... "
WILL MYSELF TO GROW ENTALLY--TO BECOME A OWERING GENIUS--WITH GREATER MIND THAN ANYONE ELSE ON EARTH!
" TOLLIVER BELIEVED IT WAS HIS WILL POWER THAT WAS AT THE BOTTOM OF THE EXTRAORDINARY AFFAIR! HE DIDN'T REALIZE... "
THERE'S NO END TO MY ACHIEVEMENTS! I ABSORBED AN ENTIRE PAGE OF THIS TELEPHONE BOOK AT A GLANCE! I HAVE A PHOTOGRAPHIC MEMORY!
" PUTTING HIS NEW GIANT INTELLECT TO WORK, HE INVADED THE STOCK MARKET..."
BUY CONTINENTAL SHELF!
BUY INTER LIGHT AND POWER!
YES, MR. TOLLIVER!
IN NO TIME HIS MIGHTY BRAIN PAID HUGE DIVIDENDS..."
MY TELEPHONES ARE RINGING CONTINUOUSLY! I'VE HAD TO HIRE SECRETARIES! IN ONE WEEK I'VE BECOME A LION OF INDUSTRY--AND RICH!
"HIS STAR ROSE, HE WAS INTERVIEWED ON TELEVISION WHERE HE COULD NOT HELP BOASTING A BIT..."
...I WAS A BANK MES-SENGER! ONE DAY THE POWER JUST CAME TO ME! SINCE THEN WHATEVER I WISH COMES TRUE! ANYTHING I WISH!
MAN OF THE WEEK
" BUT I HAPPENED TO SEE THAT PROGRAM... "
GREAT GUARDIANS--THAT'S HORACE TOLLIVER--THE BANK MESSENGER! BUT WHAT'S HE SAYING?--THAT HE HAS THE POWER TO MAKE HIS WISHES COME TRUE--SINCE A CERTAIN DAY JUST ONE WEEK AGO!?
7

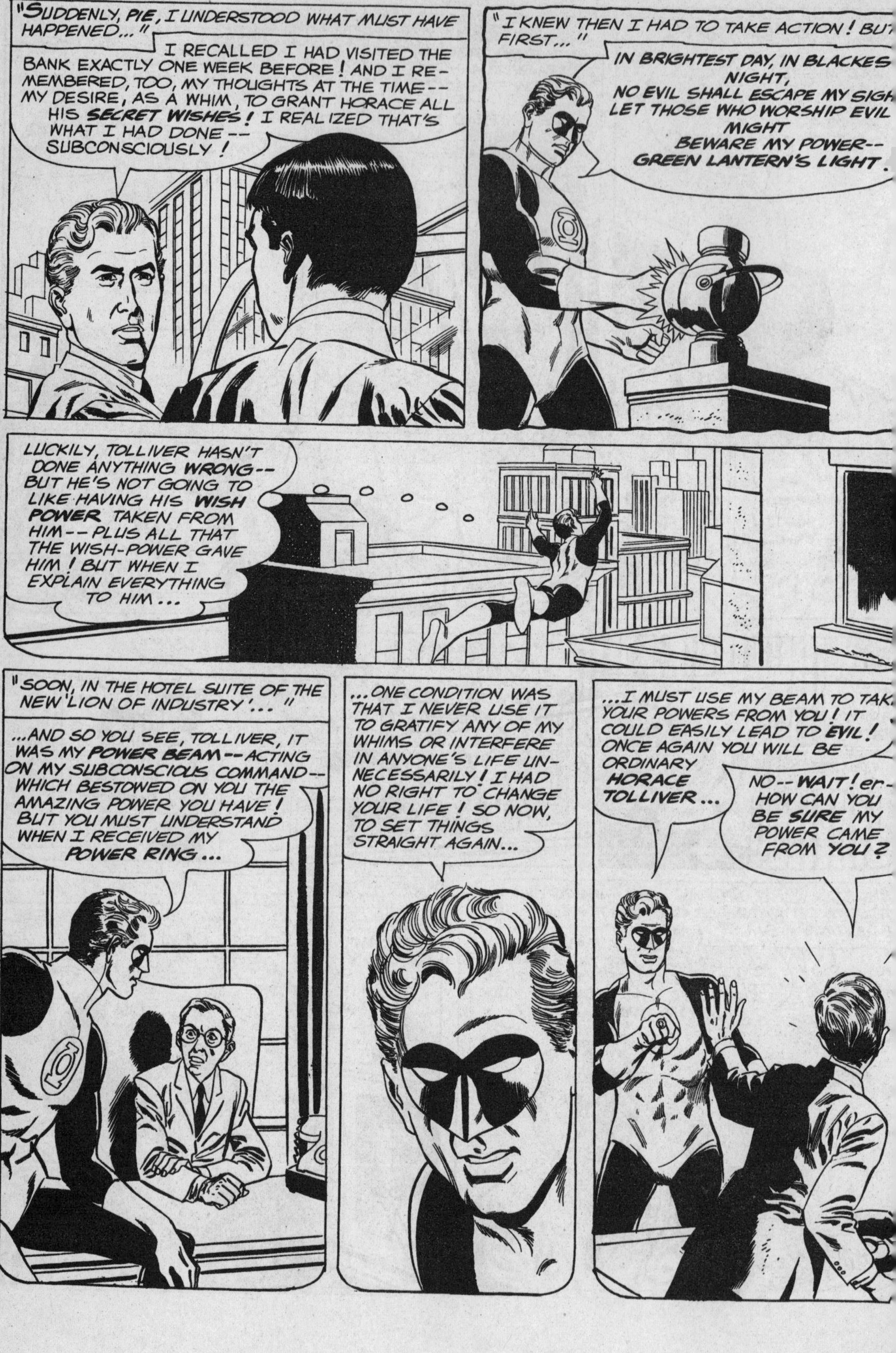
"SUDDENLY, PIE, I UNDERSTOOD WHAT MUST HAVE HAPPENED..."
I RECALLED I HAD VISITED THE BANK EXACTLY ONE WEEK BEFORE! AND I REMEMBERED, TOO, MY THOUGHTS AT THE TIME-- MY DESIRE, AS A WHIM, TO GRANT HORACE ALL HIS SECRET WISHES! I REALIZED THAT'S WHAT I HAD DONE -- SUBCONSCIOUSLY!
"I KNEW THEN I HAD TO TAKE ACTION! BUT FIRST..."
IN BRIGHTEST DAY, IN BLACKEST NIGHT, NO EVIL SHALL ESCAPE MY SIGHT LET THOSE WHO WORSHIP EVIL MIGHT BEWARE MY POWER-- GREEN LANTERN'S LIGHT.
LUCKILY, TOLLIVER HASN'T DONE ANYTHING WRONG-- BUT HE'S NOT GOING TO LIKE HAVING HIS WISH POWER TAKEN FROM HIM-- PLUS ALL THAT THE WISH-POWER GAVE HIM! BUT WHEN I EXPLAIN EVERYTHING TO HIM...
"SOON, IN THE HOTEL SUITE OF THE NEW 'LION OF INDUSTRY'..."
...AND SO YOU SEE, TOLLIVER, IT WAS MY POWER BEAM--ACTING ON MY SUBCONSCIOUS COMMAND-- WHICH BESTOWED ON YOU THE AMAZING POWER YOU HAVE! BUT YOU MUST UNDERSTAND WHEN I RECEIVED MY POWER RING...
...ONE CONDITION WAS THAT I NEVER USE IT TO GRATIFY ANY OF MY WHIMS OR INTERFERE IN ANYONE'S LIFE UNNECESSARILY! I HAD NO RIGHT TO CHANGE YOUR LIFE! SO NOW, TO SET THINGS STRAIGHT AGAIN...
...I MUST USE MY BEAM TO TAKE YOUR POWERS FROM YOU! IT COULD EASILY LEAD TO EVIL! ONCE AGAIN YOU WILL BE ORDINARY HORACE TOLLIVER...
NO--WAIT! er-- HOW CAN YOU BE SURE MY POWER CAME FROM YOU?

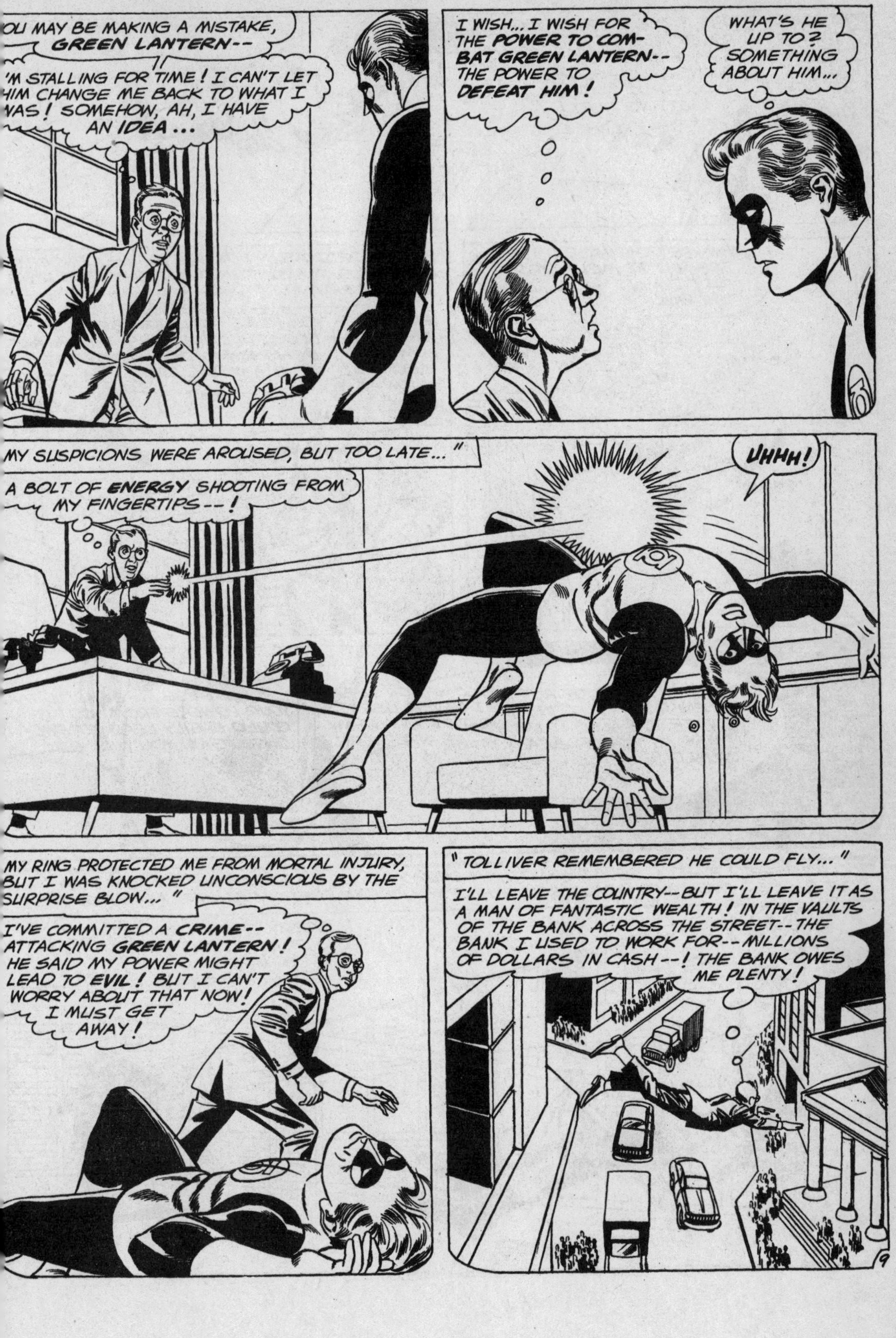
OU MAY BE MAKING A MISTAKE, GREEN LANTERN--
'M STALLING FOR TIME! I CAN'T LET HIM CHANGE ME BACK TO WHAT I WAS! SOMEHOW, AH, I HAVE AN IDEA...
I WISH... I WISH FOR THE POWER TO COMBAT GREEN LANTERN-- THE POWER TO DEFEAT HIM!
WHAT'S HE UP TO? SOMETHING ABOUT HIM...
MY SUSPICIONS WERE AROUSED, BUT TOO LATE..."
A BOLT OF ENERGY SHOOTING FROM MY FINGERTIPS--!
UHHH!
MY RING PROTECTED ME FROM MORTAL INJURY, BUT I WAS KNOCKED UNCONSCIOUS BY THE SURPRISE BLOW..."
I'VE COMMITTED A CRIME-- ATTACKING GREEN LANTERN! HE SAID MY POWER MIGHT LEAD TO EVIL! BUT I CAN'T WORRY ABOUT THAT NOW! I MUST GET AWAY!
"TOLLIVER REMEMBERED HE COULD FLY..."
I'LL LEAVE THE COUNTRY--BUT I'LL LEAVE IT AS A MAN OF FANTASTIC WEALTH! IN THE VAULTS OF THE BANK ACROSS THE STREET--THE BANK I USED TO WORK FOR--MILLIONS OF DOLLARS IN CASH--! THE BANK OWES ME PLENTY!
9

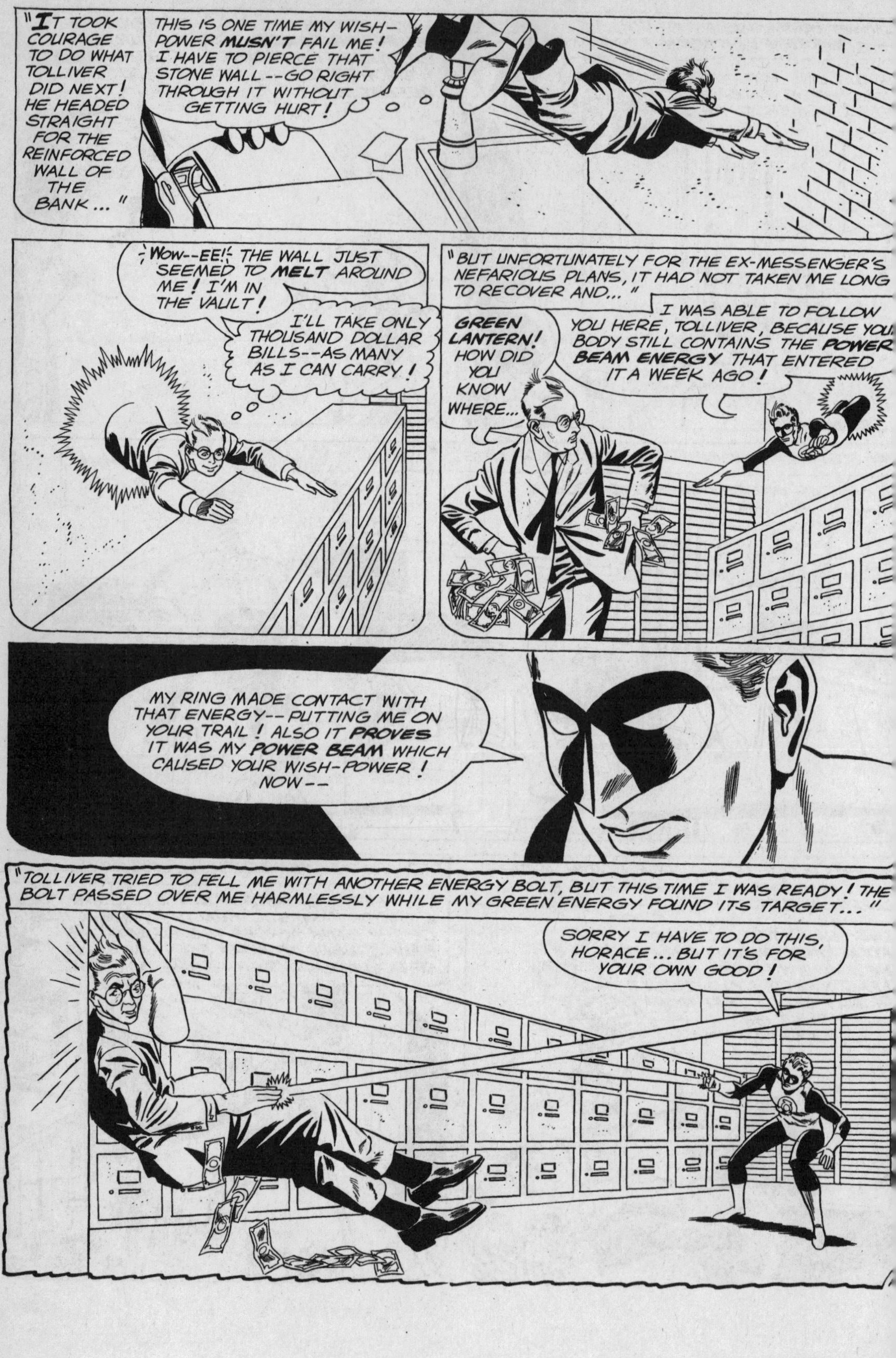
"IT TOOK COURAGE TO DO WHAT TOLLIVER DID NEXT! HE HEADED STRAIGHT FOR THE REINFORCED WALL OF THE BANK..."
THIS IS ONE TIME MY WISH-POWER MUSN'T FAIL ME! I HAVE TO PIERCE THAT STONE WALL--GO RIGHT THROUGH IT WITHOUT GETTING HURT!
WOW--EE! THE WALL JUST SEEMED TO MELT AROUND ME! I'M IN THE VAULT!
I'LL TAKE ONLY THOUSAND DOLLAR BILLS--AS MANY AS I CAN CARRY!
"BUT UNFORTUNATELY FOR THE EX-MESSENGER'S NEFARIOUS PLANS, IT HAD NOT TAKEN ME LONG TO RECOVER AND..."
GREEN LANTERN! HOW DID YOU KNOW WHERE...
I WAS ABLE TO FOLLOW YOU HERE, TOLLIVER, BECAUSE YOUR BODY STILL CONTAINS THE POWER BEAM ENERGY THAT ENTERED IT A WEEK AGO!
MY RING MADE CONTACT WITH THAT ENERGY--PUTTING ME ON YOUR TRAIL! ALSO IT PROVES IT WAS MY POWER BEAM WHICH CAUSED YOUR WISH-POWER! NOW--
"TOLLIVER TRIED TO FELL ME WITH ANOTHER ENERGY BOLT, BUT THIS TIME I WAS READY! THE BOLT PASSED OVER ME HARMLESSLY WHILE MY GREEN ENERGY FOUND ITS TARGET..."
SORRY I HAVE TO DO THIS, HORACE... BUT IT'S FOR YOUR OWN GOOD!

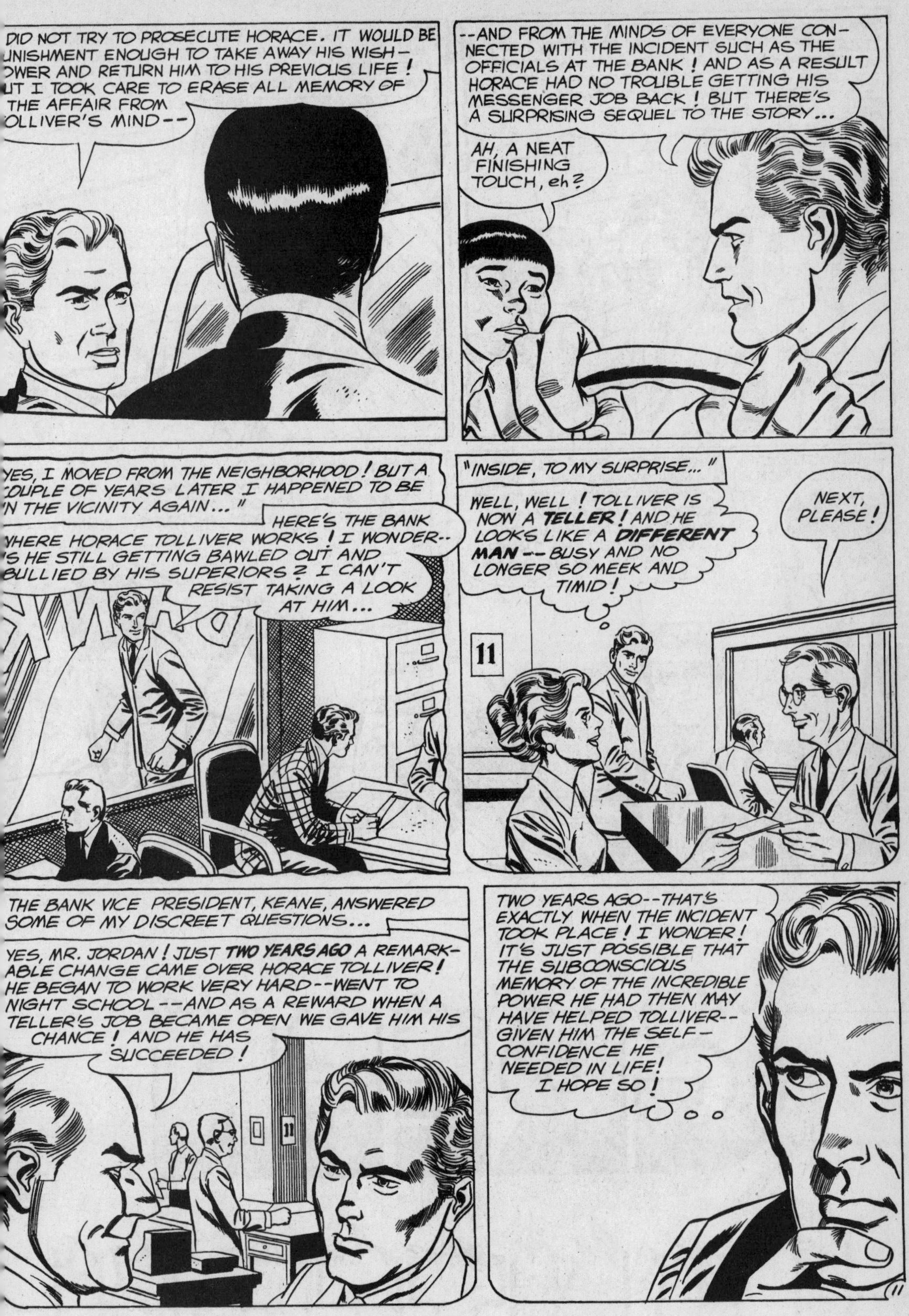
DID NOT TRY TO PROSECUTE HORACE. IT WOULD BE UNISHMENT ENOUGH TO TAKE AWAY HIS WISH-OWER AND RETURN HIM TO HIS PREVIOUS LIFE! UT I TOOK CARE TO ERASE ALL MEMORY OF THE AFFAIR FROM OLLIVER'S MIND--
--AND FROM THE MINDS OF EVERYONE CONNECTED WITH THE INCIDENT SUCH AS THE OFFICIALS AT THE BANK! AND AS A RESULT HORACE HAD NO TROUBLE GETTING HIS MESSENGER JOB BACK! BUT THERE'S A SURPRISING SEQUEL TO THE STORY...
AH, A NEAT FINISHING TOUCH, eh?
YES, I MOVED FROM THE NEIGHBORHOOD! BUT A OUPLE OF YEARS LATER I HAPPENED TO BE N THE VICINITY AGAIN..."
HERE'S THE BANK WHERE HORACE TOLLIVER WORKS! I WONDER--'S HE STILL GETTING BAWLED OUT AND BULLIED BY HIS SUPERIORS? I CAN'T RESIST TAKING A LOOK AT HIM...
"INSIDE, TO MY SURPRISE..."
WELL, WELL! TOLLIVER IS NOW A TELLER! AND HE LOOKS LIKE A DIFFERENT MAN--BUSY AND NO LONGER SO MEEK AND TIMID!
NEXT, PLEASE!
11
THE BANK VICE PRESIDENT, KEANE, ANSWERED SOME OF MY DISCREET QUESTIONS...
YES, MR. JORDAN! JUST TWO YEARS AGO A REMARKABLE CHANGE CAME OVER HORACE TOLLIVER! HE BEGAN TO WORK VERY HARD--WENT TO NIGHT SCHOOL--AND AS A REWARD WHEN A TELLER'S JOB BECAME OPEN WE GAVE HIM HIS CHANCE! AND HE HAS SUCCEEDED!
TWO YEARS AGO--THAT'S EXACTLY WHEN THE INCIDENT TOOK PLACE! I WONDER! IT'S JUST POSSIBLE THAT THE SUBCONSCIOUS MEMORY OF THE INCREDIBLE POWER HE HAD THEN MAY HAVE HELPED TOLLIVER--GIVEN HIM THE SELF-CONFIDENCE HE NEEDED IN LIFE! I HOPE SO!
11

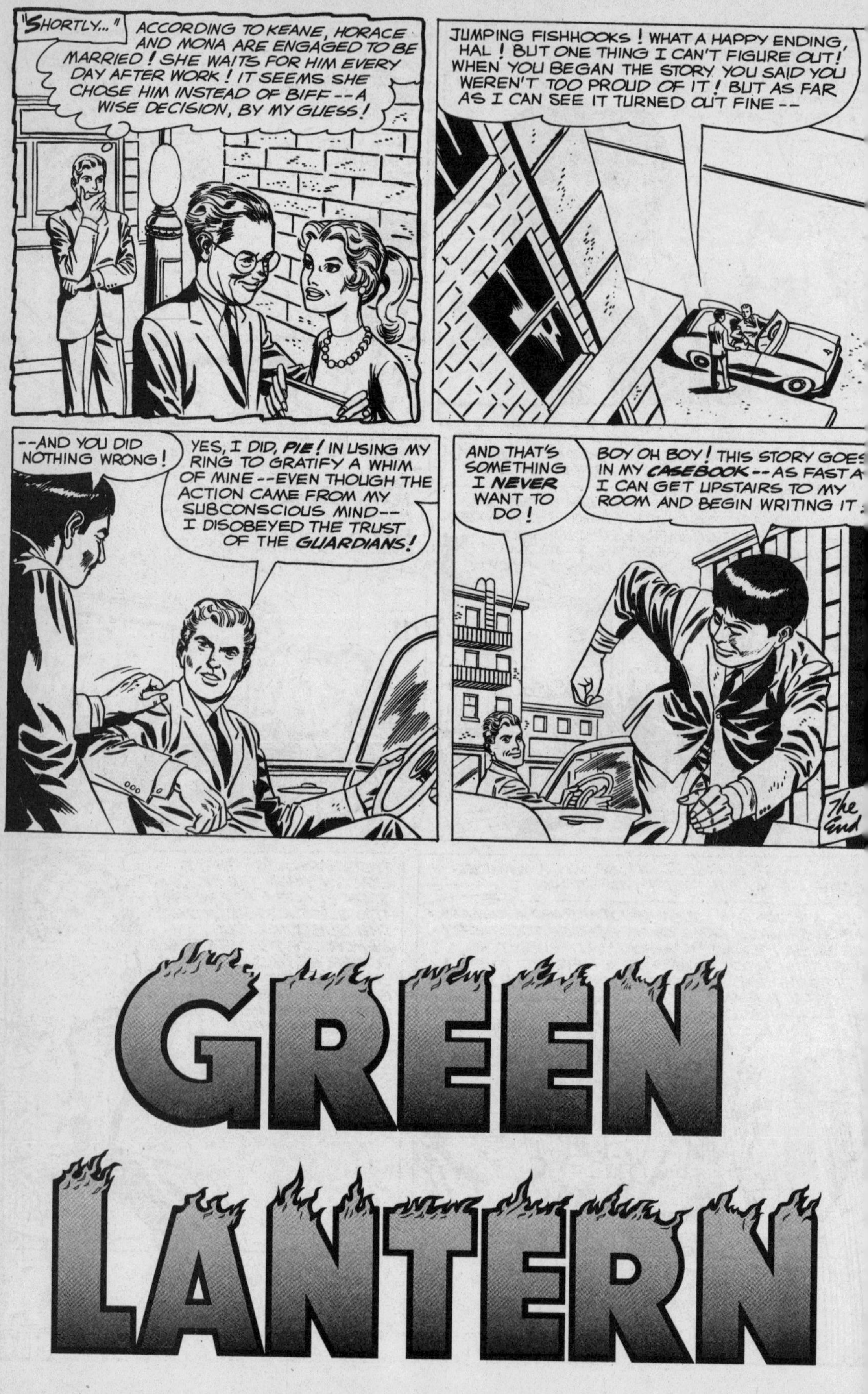
"SHORTLY..."
ACCORDING TO KEANE, HORACE AND MONA ARE ENGAGED TO BE MARRIED! SHE WAITS FOR HIM EVERY DAY AFTER WORK! IT SEEMS SHE CHOSE HIM INSTEAD OF BIFF--A WISE DECISION, BY MY GUESS!
JUMPING FISHHOOKS! WHAT A HAPPY ENDING, HAL! BUT ONE THING I CAN'T FIGURE OUT! WHEN YOU BEGAN THE STORY YOU SAID YOU WEREN'T TOO PROUD OF IT! BUT AS FAR AS I CAN SEE IT TURNED OUT FINE--
--AND YOU DID NOTHING WRONG!
YES, I DID, PIE! IN USING MY RING TO GRATIFY A WHIM OF MINE--EVEN THOUGH THE ACTION CAME FROM MY SUBCONSCIOUS MIND--I DISOBEYED THE TRUST OF THE GUARDIANS!
AND THAT'S SOMETHING I NEVER WANT TO DO!
BOY OH BOY! THIS STORY GOES IN MY CASEBOOK--AS FAST A I CAN GET UPSTAIRS TO MY ROOM AND BEGIN WRITING IT
The End

GREEN LANTERN

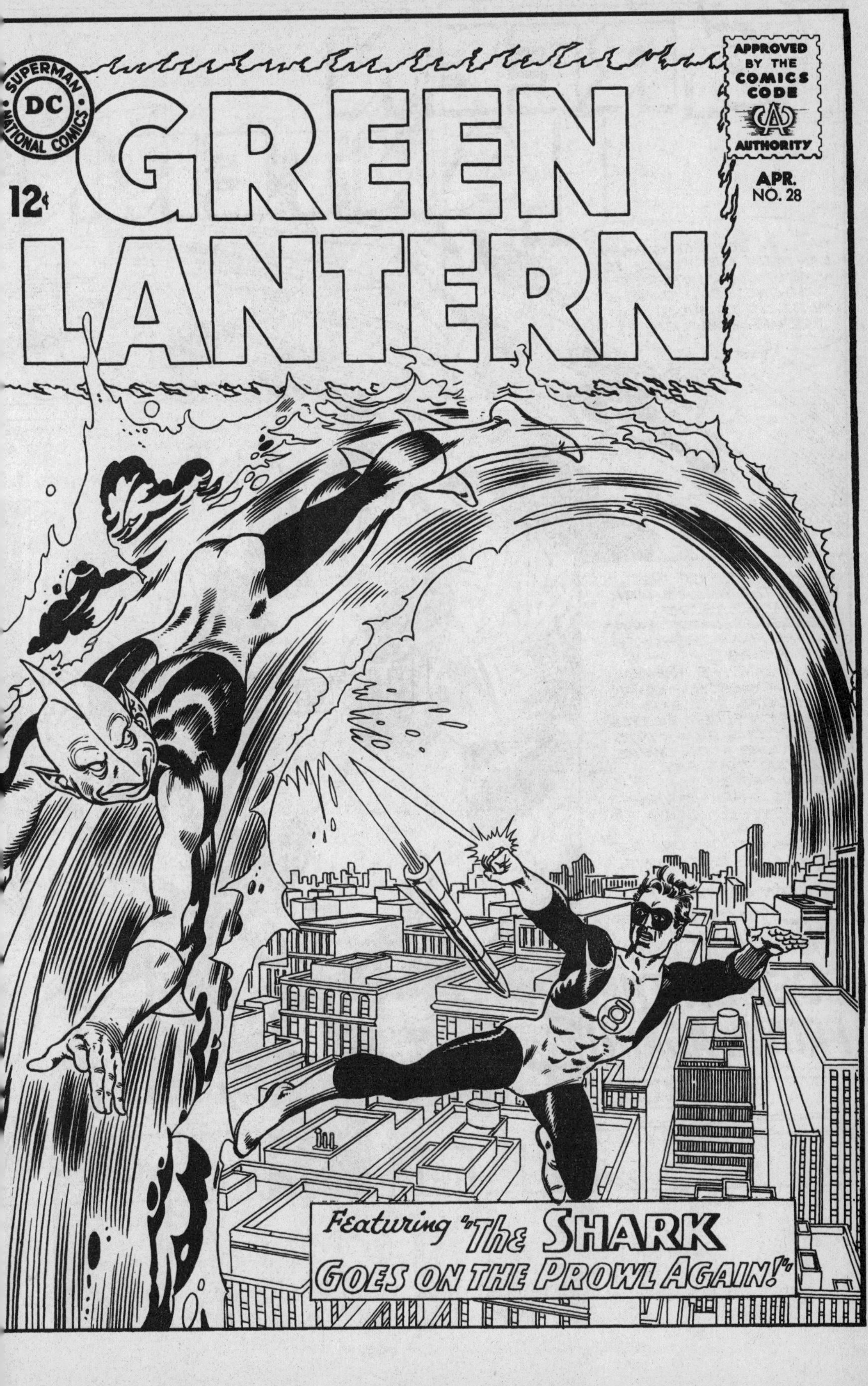
SUPERMAN
DC
NATIONAL COMICS
GREEN LANTERN
12¢
APPROVED BY THE COMICS CODE AUTHORITY
APR.
NO. 28
Featuring "The SHARK
GOES ON THE PROWL AGAIN!"

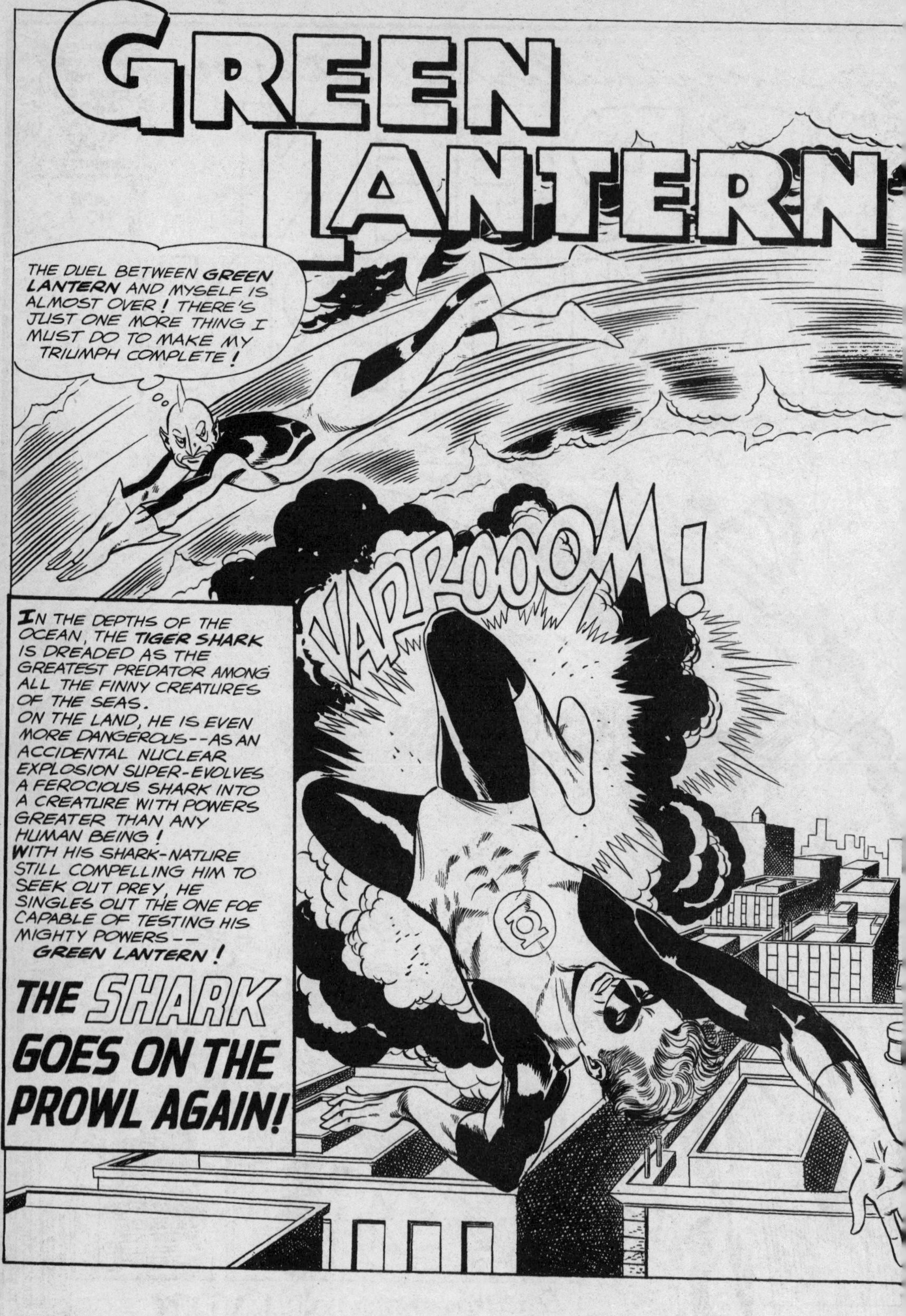
GREEN LANTERN
THE DUEL BETWEEN GREEN LANTERN AND MYSELF IS ALMOST OVER! THERE'S JUST ONE MORE THING I MUST DO TO MAKE MY TRIUMPH COMPLETE!
VARROOOM!
IN THE DEPTHS OF THE OCEAN, THE TIGER SHARK IS DREADED AS THE GREATEST PREDATOR AMONG ALL THE FINNY CREATURES OF THE SEAS. ON THE LAND, HE IS EVEN MORE DANGEROUS--AS AN ACCIDENTAL NUCLEAR EXPLOSION SUPER-EVOLVES A FEROCIOUS SHARK INTO A CREATURE WITH POWERS GREATER THAN ANY HUMAN BEING! WITH HIS SHARK-NATURE STILL COMPELLING HIM TO SEEK OUT PREY, HE SINGLES OUT THE ONE FOE CAPABLE OF TESTING HIS MIGHTY POWERS-- GREEN LANTERN!
THE SHARK GOES ON THE PROWL AGAIN!

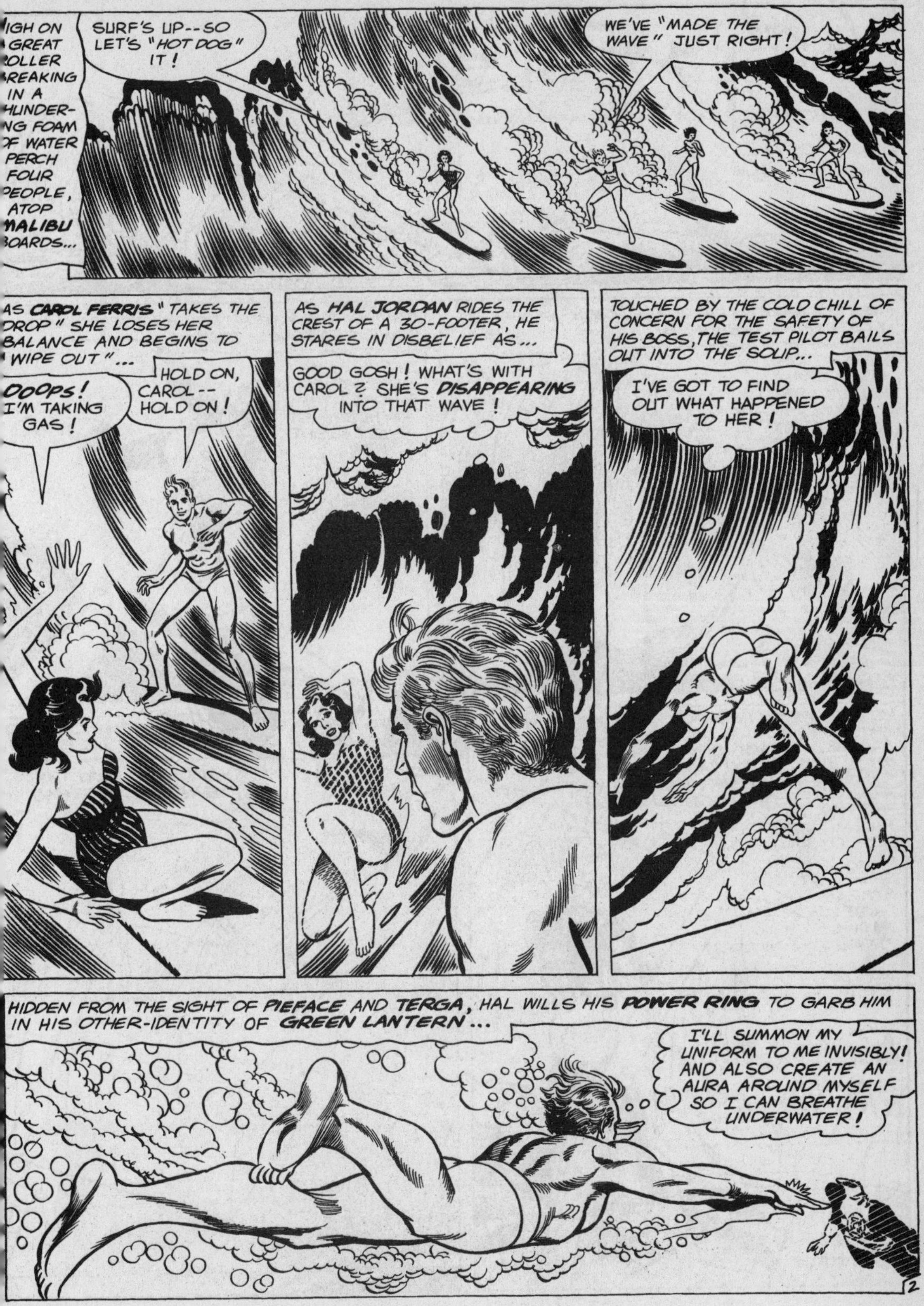
IGH ON A GREAT ROLLER BREAKING IN A THUNDERING FOAM OF WATER PERCH FOUR PEOPLE, ATOP MALIBU BOARDS...
SURF'S UP--SO LET'S "HOT DOG" IT!
WE'VE "MADE THE WAVE" JUST RIGHT!
AS CAROL FERRIS "TAKES THE DROP" SHE LOSES HER BALANCE AND BEGINS TO "WIPE OUT"...
OOOPS! I'M TAKING GAS!
HOLD ON, CAROL-- HOLD ON!
AS HAL JORDAN RIDES THE CREST OF A 30-FOOTER, HE STARES IN DISBELIEF AS...
GOOD GOSH! WHAT'S WITH CAROL? SHE'S DISAPPEARING INTO THAT WAVE!
TOUCHED BY THE COLD CHILL OF CONCERN FOR THE SAFETY OF HIS BOSS, THE TEST PILOT BAILS OUT INTO THE SOUP...
I'VE GOT TO FIND OUT WHAT HAPPENED TO HER!
HIDDEN FROM THE SIGHT OF PIEFACE AND TERGA, HAL WILLS HIS POWER RING TO GARB HIM IN HIS OTHER-IDENTITY OF GREEN LANTERN...
I'LL SUMMON MY UNIFORM TO ME INVISIBLY! AND ALSO CREATE AN AURA AROUND MYSELF SO I CAN BREATHE UNDERWATER!
2

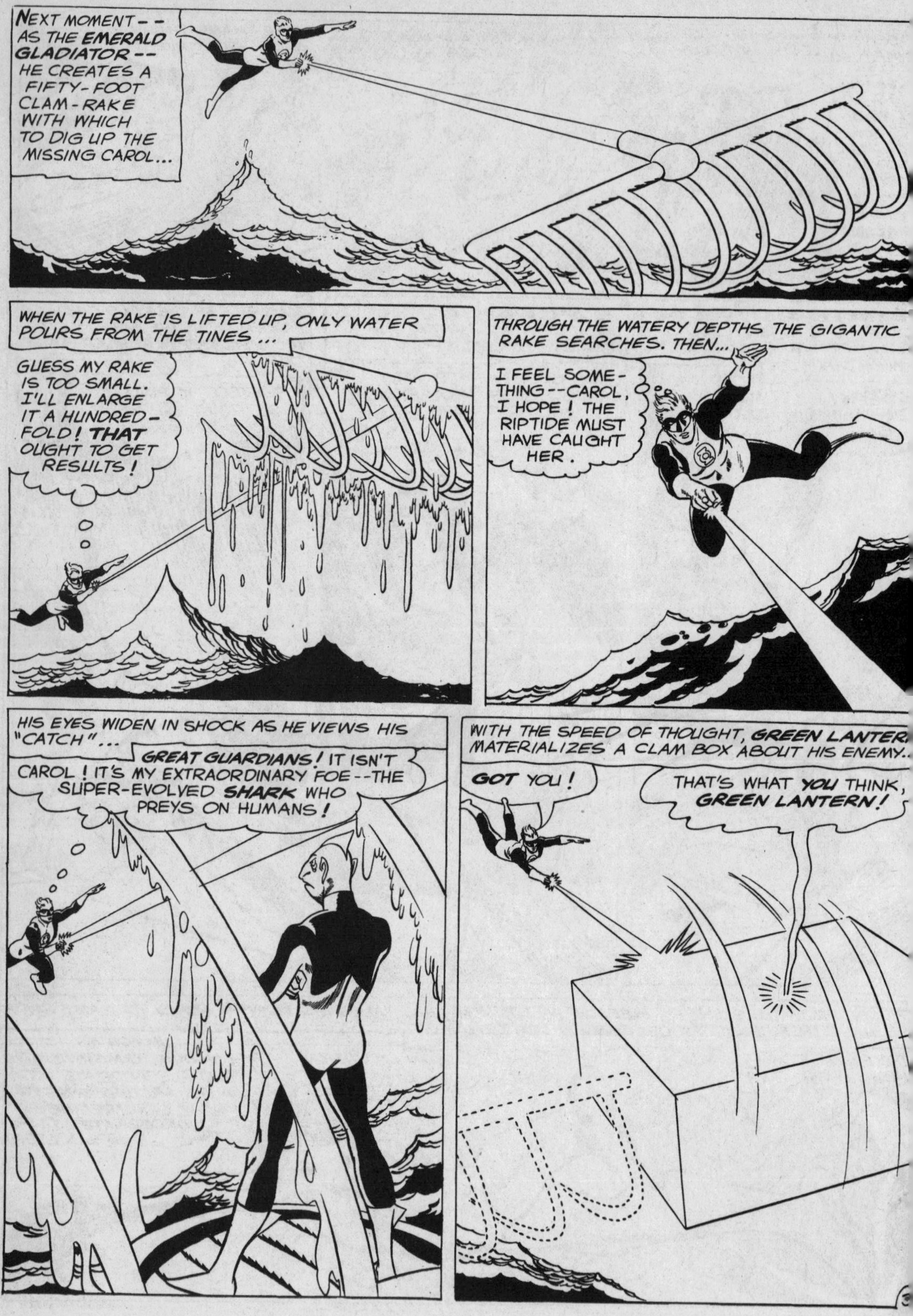
NEXT MOMENT-- AS THE EMERALD GLADIATOR-- HE CREATES A FIFTY-FOOT CLAM-RAKE WITH WHICH TO DIG UP THE MISSING CAROL...
WHEN THE RAKE IS LIFTED UP, ONLY WATER POURS FROM THE TINES...
GUESS MY RAKE IS TOO SMALL. I'LL ENLARGE IT A HUNDRED-FOLD! THAT OUGHT TO GET RESULTS!
THROUGH THE WATERY DEPTHS THE GIGANTIC RAKE SEARCHES. THEN...
I FEEL SOME-THING--CAROL, I HOPE! THE RIPTIDE MUST HAVE CAUGHT HER.
HIS EYES WIDEN IN SHOCK AS HE VIEWS HIS "CATCH"...
GREAT GUARDIANS! IT ISN'T CAROL! IT'S MY EXTRAORDINARY FOE--THE SUPER-EVOLVED SHARK WHO PREYS ON HUMANS!
WITH THE SPEED OF THOUGHT, GREEN LANTER MATERIALIZES A CLAM BOX ABOUT HIS ENEMY...
GOT YOU!
THAT'S WHAT YOU THINK, GREEN LANTERN!

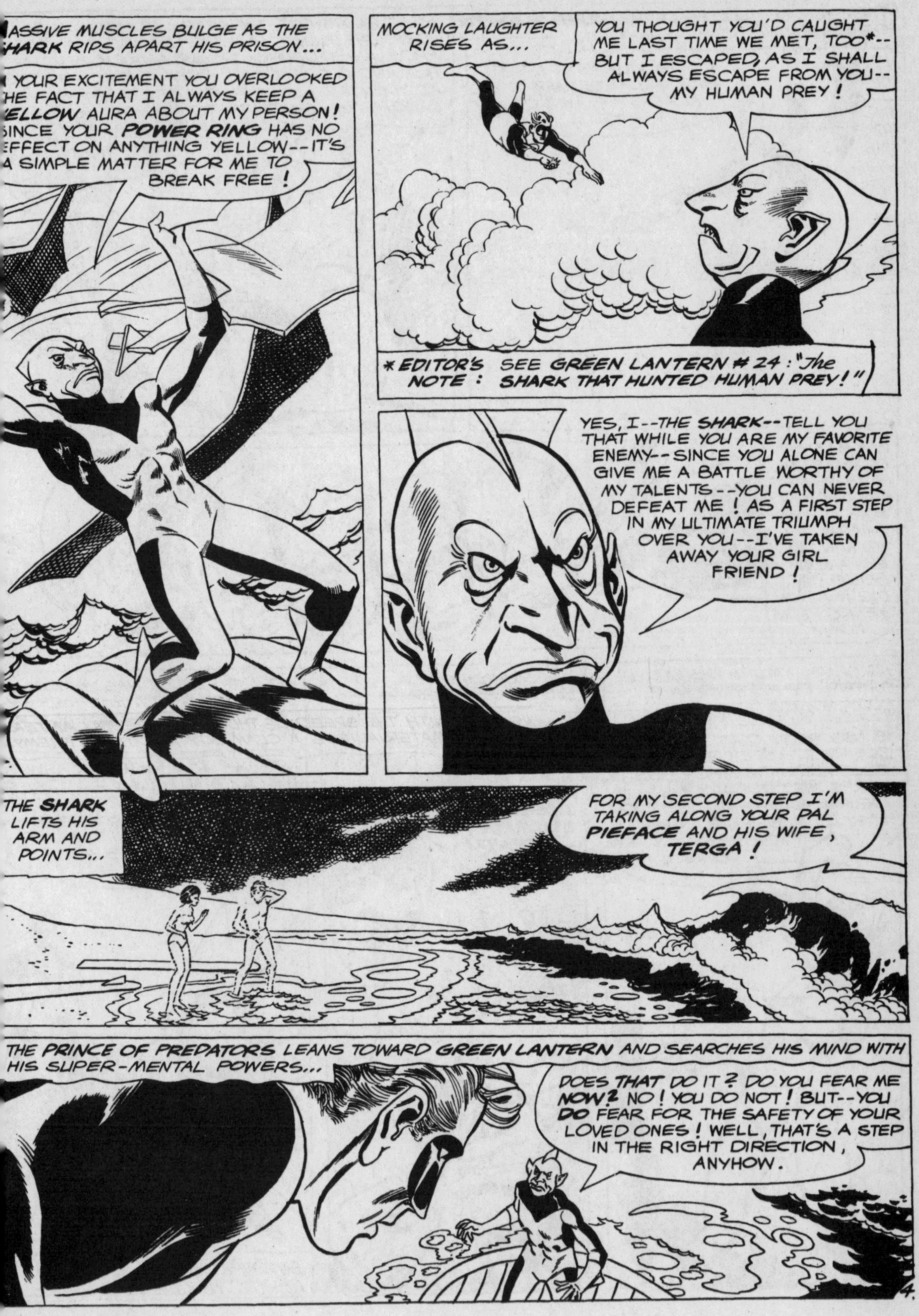
ASSIVE MUSCLES BULGE AS THE SHARK RIPS APART HIS PRISON...
YOUR EXCITEMENT YOU OVERLOOKED HE FACT THAT I ALWAYS KEEP A ELLOW AURA ABOUT MY PERSON! SINCE YOUR POWER RING HAS NO EFFECT ON ANYTHING YELLOW--IT'S A SIMPLE MATTER FOR ME TO BREAK FREE!
MOCKING LAUGHTER RISES AS...
YOU THOUGHT YOU'D CAUGHT ME LAST TIME WE MET, TOO*--BUT I ESCAPED, AS I SHALL ALWAYS ESCAPE FROM YOU--MY HUMAN PREY!
*EDITOR'S NOTE: SEE GREEN LANTERN #24: "The SHARK THAT HUNTED HUMAN PREY!"
YES, I--THE SHARK--TELL YOU THAT WHILE YOU ARE MY FAVORITE ENEMY--SINCE YOU ALONE CAN GIVE ME A BATTLE WORTHY OF MY TALENTS--YOU CAN NEVER DEFEAT ME! AS A FIRST STEP IN MY ULTIMATE TRIUMPH OVER YOU--I'VE TAKEN AWAY YOUR GIRL FRIEND!
THE SHARK LIFTS HIS ARM AND POINTS...
FOR MY SECOND STEP I'M TAKING ALONG YOUR PAL PIEFACE AND HIS WIFE, TERGA!
THE PRINCE OF PREDATORS LEANS TOWARD GREEN LANTERN AND SEARCHES HIS MIND WITH HIS SUPER-MENTAL POWERS...
DOES THAT DO IT? DO YOU FEAR ME NOW? NO! YOU DO NOT! BUT--YOU DO FEAR FOR THE SAFETY OF YOUR LOVED ONES! WELL, THAT'S A STEP IN THE RIGHT DIRECTION, ANYHOW.
4

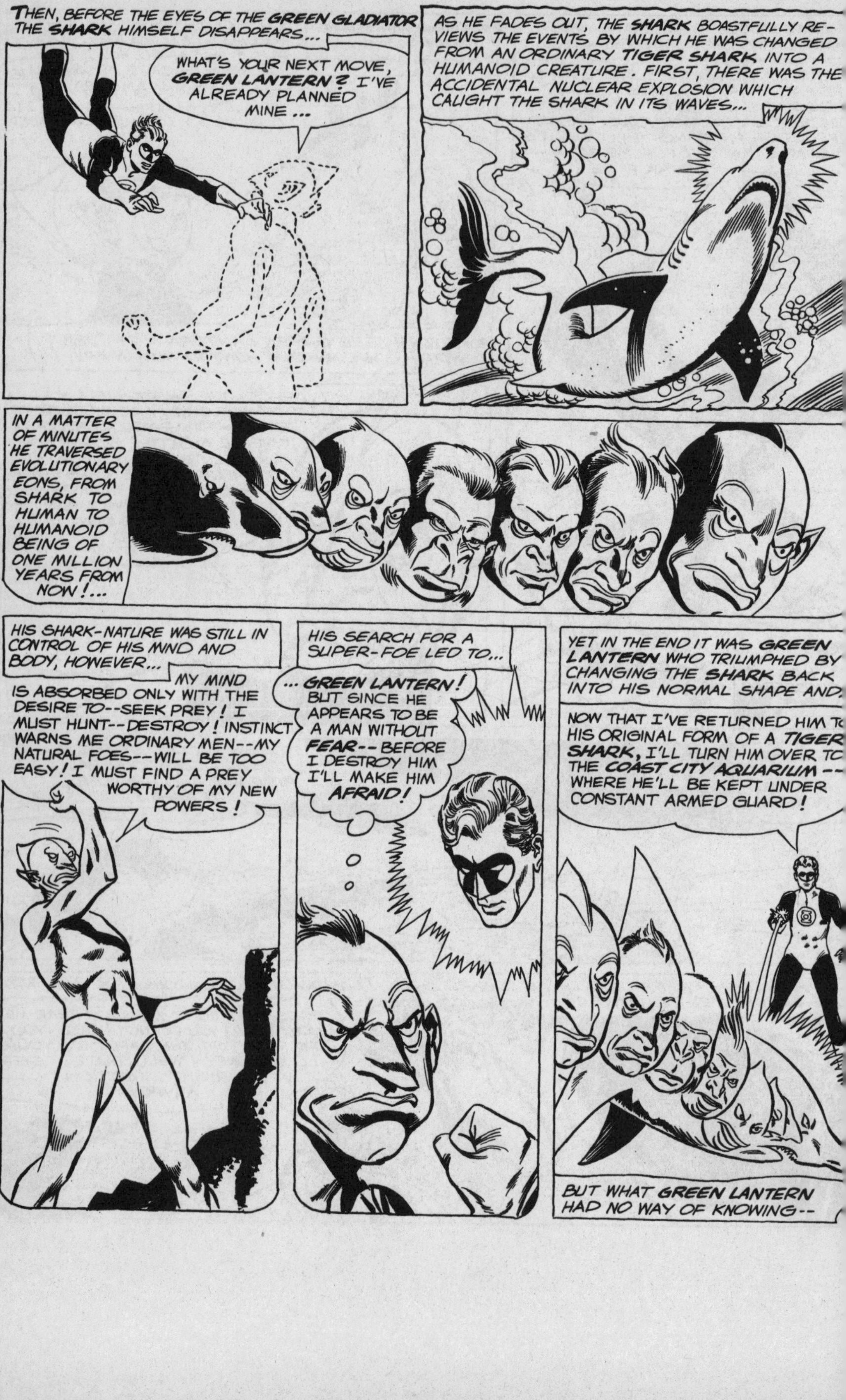
THEN, BEFORE THE EYES OF THE GREEN GLADIATOR THE SHARK HIMSELF DISAPPEARS...
WHAT'S YOUR NEXT MOVE, GREEN LANTERN? I'VE ALREADY PLANNED MINE...
AS HE FADES OUT, THE SHARK BOASTFULLY REVIEWS THE EVENTS BY WHICH HE WAS CHANGED FROM AN ORDINARY TIGER SHARK INTO A HUMANOID CREATURE. FIRST, THERE WAS THE ACCIDENTAL NUCLEAR EXPLOSION WHICH CAUGHT THE SHARK IN ITS WAVES...
IN A MATTER OF MINUTES HE TRAVERSED EVOLUTIONARY EONS, FROM SHARK TO HUMAN TO HUMANOID BEING OF ONE MILLION YEARS FROM NOW!...
HIS SHARK-NATURE WAS STILL IN CONTROL OF HIS MIND AND BODY, HOWEVER...
MY MIND IS ABSORBED ONLY WITH THE DESIRE TO--SEEK PREY! I MUST HUNT--DESTROY! INSTINCT WARNS ME ORDINARY MEN--MY NATURAL FOES--WILL BE TOO EASY! I MUST FIND A PREY WORTHY OF MY NEW POWERS!
HIS SEARCH FOR A SUPER-FOE LED TO...
...GREEN LANTERN! BUT SINCE HE APPEARS TO BE A MAN WITHOUT FEAR-- BEFORE I DESTROY HIM I'LL MAKE HIM AFRAID!
YET IN THE END IT WAS GREEN LANTERN WHO TRIUMPHED BY CHANGING THE SHARK BACK INTO HIS NORMAL SHAPE AND
NOW THAT I'VE RETURNED HIM TO HIS ORIGINAL FORM OF A TIGER SHARK, I'LL TURN HIM OVER TO THE COAST CITY AQUARIUM -- WHERE HE'LL BE KEPT UNDER CONSTANT ARMED GUARD!
BUT WHAT GREEN LANTERN HAD NO WAY OF KNOWING--

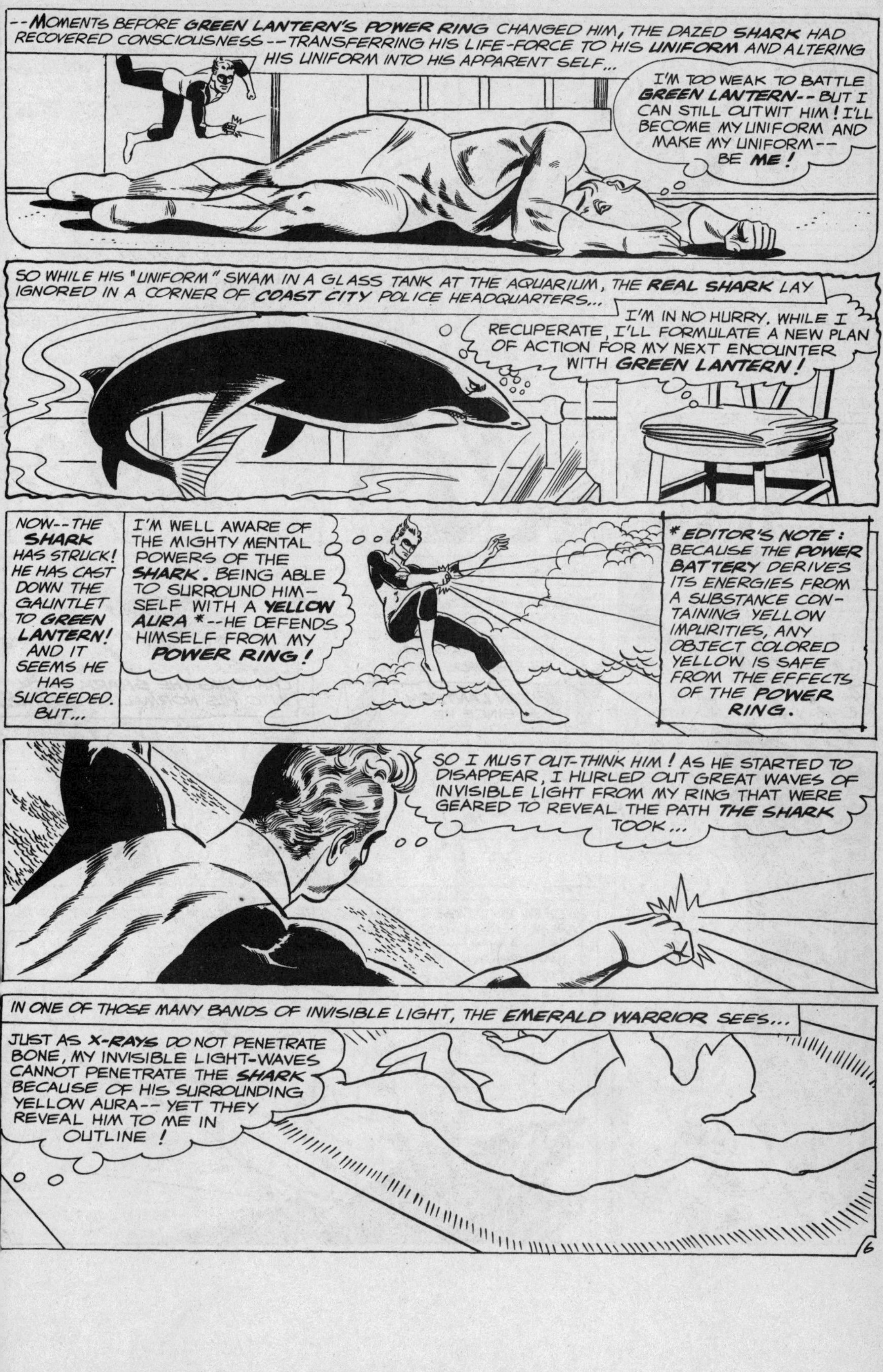
--MOMENTS BEFORE GREEN LANTERN'S POWER RING CHANGED HIM, THE DAZED SHARK HAD RECOVERED CONSCIOUSNESS--TRANSFERRING HIS LIFE-FORCE TO HIS UNIFORM AND ALTERING HIS UNIFORM INTO HIS APPARENT SELF...
I'M TOO WEAK TO BATTLE GREEN LANTERN--BUT I CAN STILL OUTWIT HIM! I'LL BECOME MY UNIFORM AND MAKE MY UNIFORM-- BE ME!
SO WHILE HIS "UNIFORM" SWAM IN A GLASS TANK AT THE AQUARIUM, THE REAL SHARK LAY IGNORED IN A CORNER OF COAST CITY POLICE HEADQUARTERS...
I'M IN NO HURRY. WHILE I RECUPERATE, I'LL FORMULATE A NEW PLAN OF ACTION FOR MY NEXT ENCOUNTER WITH GREEN LANTERN!
NOW--THE SHARK HAS STRUCK! HE HAS CAST DOWN THE GAUNTLET TO GREEN LANTERN! AND IT SEEMS HE HAS SUCCEEDED. BUT...
I'M WELL AWARE OF THE MIGHTY MENTAL POWERS OF THE SHARK. BEING ABLE TO SURROUND HIM-SELF WITH A YELLOW AURA*--HE DEFENDS HIMSELF FROM MY POWER RING!
*EDITOR'S NOTE: BECAUSE THE POWER BATTERY DERIVES ITS ENERGIES FROM A SUBSTANCE CON-TAINING YELLOW IMPURITIES, ANY OBJECT COLORED YELLOW IS SAFE FROM THE EFFECTS OF THE POWER RING.
SO I MUST OUT-THINK HIM! AS HE STARTED TO DISAPPEAR, I HURLED OUT GREAT WAVES OF INVISIBLE LIGHT FROM MY RING THAT WERE GEARED TO REVEAL THE PATH THE SHARK TOOK...
IN ONE OF THOSE MANY BANDS OF INVISIBLE LIGHT, THE EMERALD WARRIOR SEES...
JUST AS X-RAYS DO NOT PENETRATE BONE, MY INVISIBLE LIGHT-WAVES CANNOT PENETRATE THE SHARK BECAUSE OF HIS SURROUNDING YELLOW AURA--YET THEY REVEAL HIM TO ME IN OUTLINE!
6

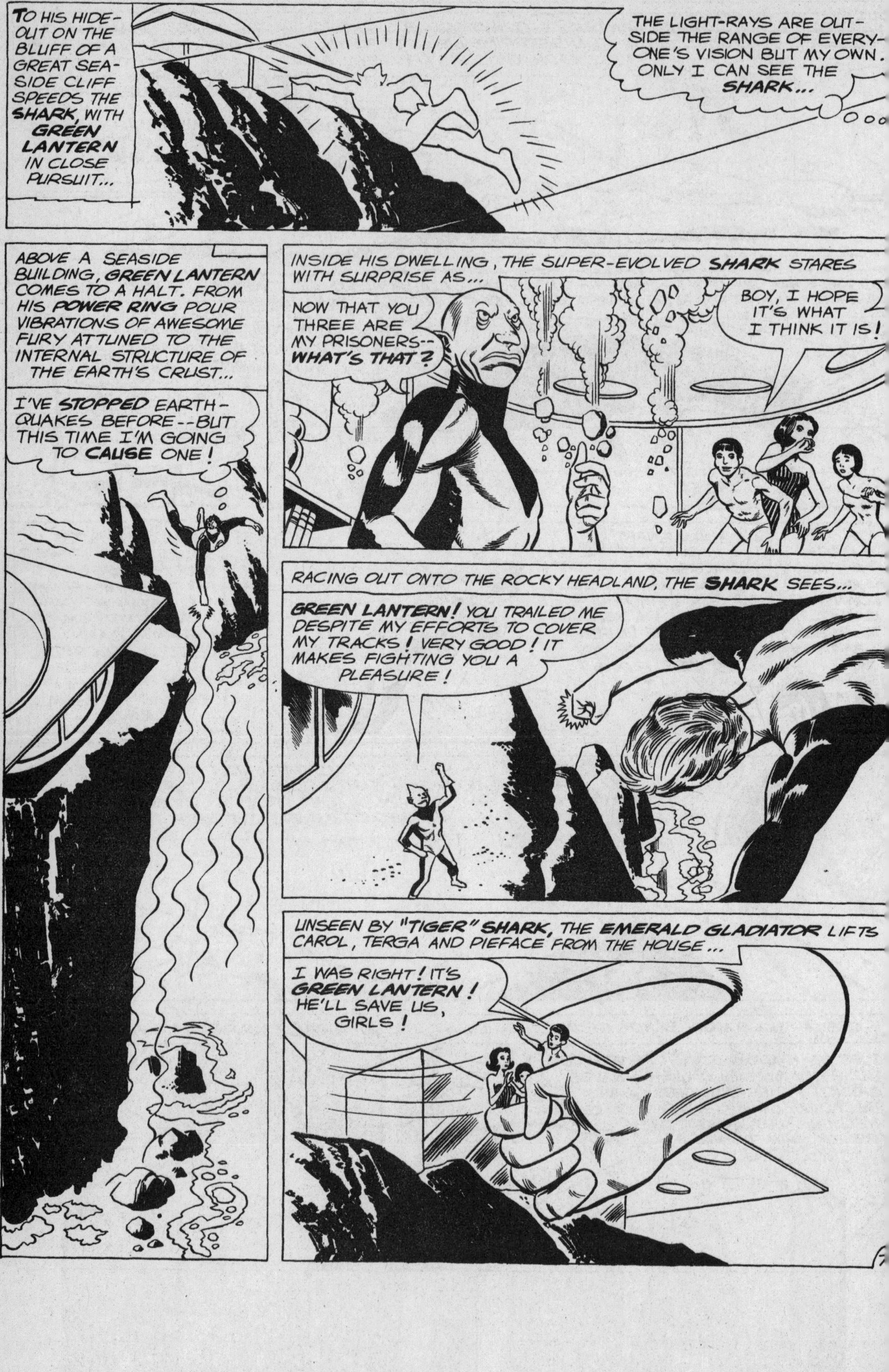
TO HIS HIDE-OUT ON THE BLUFF OF A GREAT SEA-SIDE CLIFF SPEEDS THE SHARK, WITH GREEN LANTERN IN CLOSE PURSUIT...
THE LIGHT-RAYS ARE OUT-SIDE THE RANGE OF EVERY-ONE'S VISION BUT MY OWN. ONLY I CAN SEE THE SHARK...
ABOVE A SEASIDE BUILDING, GREEN LANTERN COMES TO A HALT. FROM HIS POWER RING POUR VIBRATIONS OF AWESOME FURY ATTUNED TO THE INTERNAL STRUCTURE OF THE EARTH'S CRUST...
I'VE STOPPED EARTH-QUAKES BEFORE--BUT THIS TIME I'M GOING TO CAUSE ONE!
INSIDE HIS DWELLING, THE SUPER-EVOLVED SHARK STARES WITH SURPRISE AS...
NOW THAT YOU THREE ARE MY PRISONERS--WHAT'S THAT?
BOY, I HOPE IT'S WHAT I THINK IT IS!
RACING OUT ONTO THE ROCKY HEADLAND, THE SHARK SEES...
GREEN LANTERN! YOU TRAILED ME DESPITE MY EFFORTS TO COVER MY TRACKS! VERY GOOD! IT MAKES FIGHTING YOU A PLEASURE!
UNSEEN BY "TIGER" SHARK, THE EMERALD GLADIATOR LIFTS CAROL, TERGA AND PIEFACE FROM THE HOUSE...
I WAS RIGHT! IT'S GREEN LANTERN! HE'LL SAVE US, GIRLS!

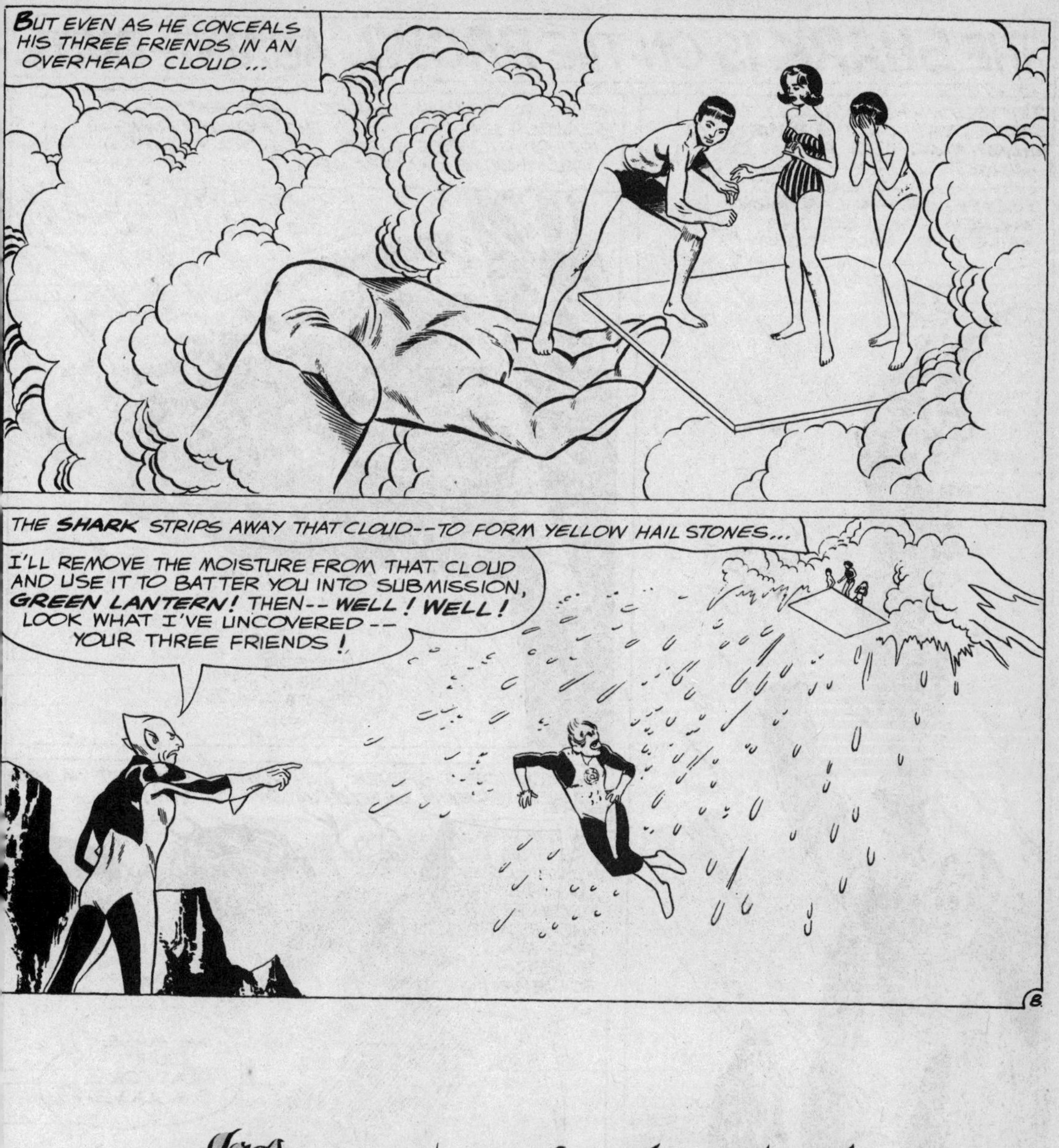
BUT EVEN AS HE CONCEALS HIS THREE FRIENDS IN AN OVERHEAD CLOUD...
THE SHARK STRIPS AWAY THAT CLOUD--TO FORM YELLOW HAIL STONES...
I'LL REMOVE THE MOISTURE FROM THAT CLOUD AND USE IT TO BATTER YOU INTO SUBMISSION, GREEN LANTERN! THEN--WELL! WELL! LOOK WHAT I'VE UNCOVERED--YOUR THREE FRIENDS!
B.

GREEN LANTERN

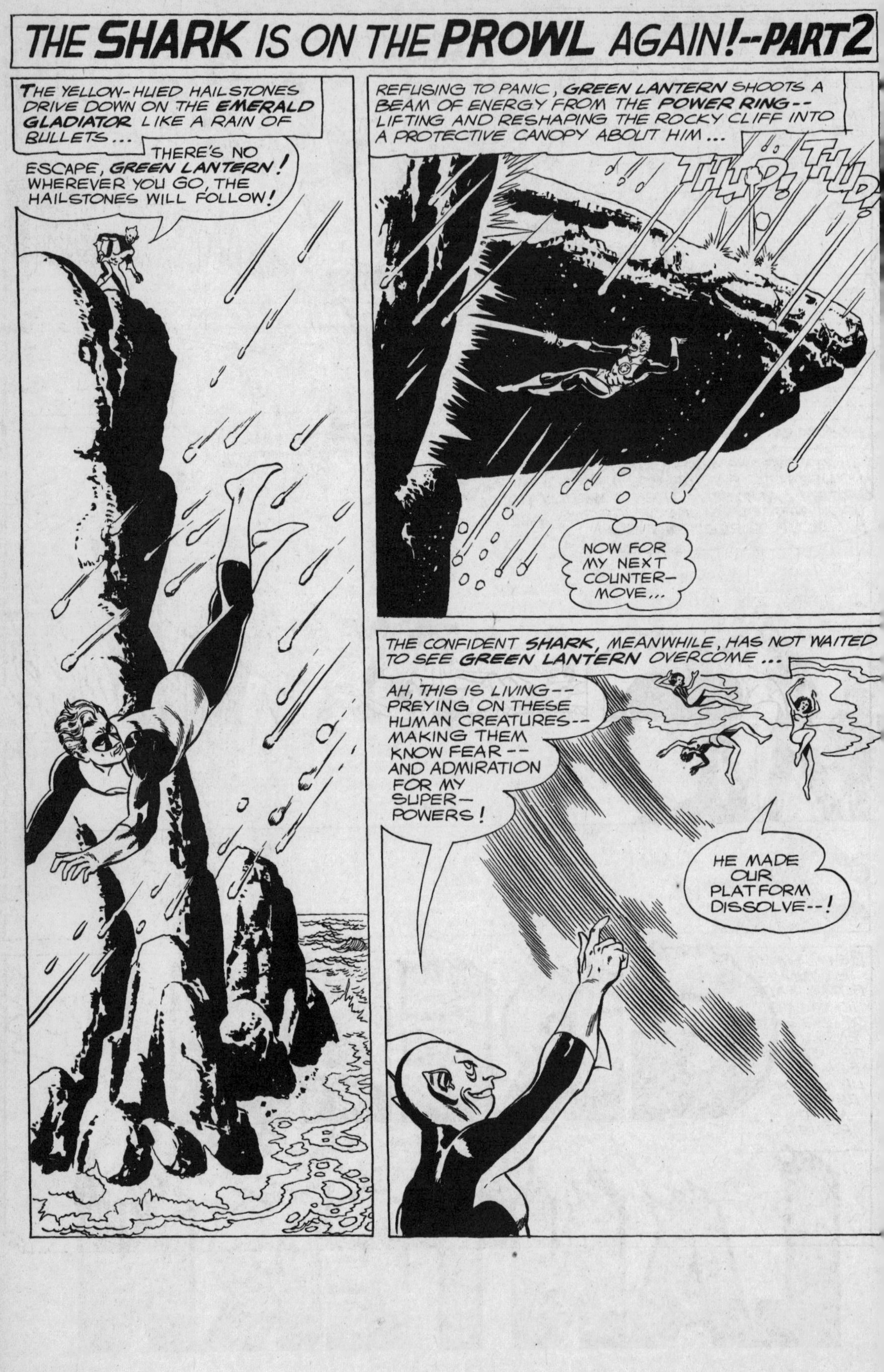
THE SHARK IS ON THE PROWL AGAIN!--PART 2
THE YELLOW-HUED HAILSTONES DRIVE DOWN ON THE EMERALD GLADIATOR LIKE A RAIN OF BULLETS...
THERE'S NO ESCAPE, GREEN LANTERN! WHEREVER YOU GO, THE HAILSTONES WILL FOLLOW!
REFUSING TO PANIC, GREEN LANTERN SHOOTS A BEAM OF ENERGY FROM THE POWER RING-- LIFTING AND RESHAPING THE ROCKY CLIFF INTO A PROTECTIVE CANOPY ABOUT HIM...
THUD! THUD!
NOW FOR MY NEXT COUNTER-MOVE...
THE CONFIDENT SHARK, MEANWHILE, HAS NOT WAITED TO SEE GREEN LANTERN OVERCOME...
AH, THIS IS LIVING-- PREYING ON THESE HUMAN CREATURES-- MAKING THEM KNOW FEAR-- AND ADMIRATION FOR MY SUPER-POWERS!
HE MADE OUR PLATFORM DISSOLVE--!

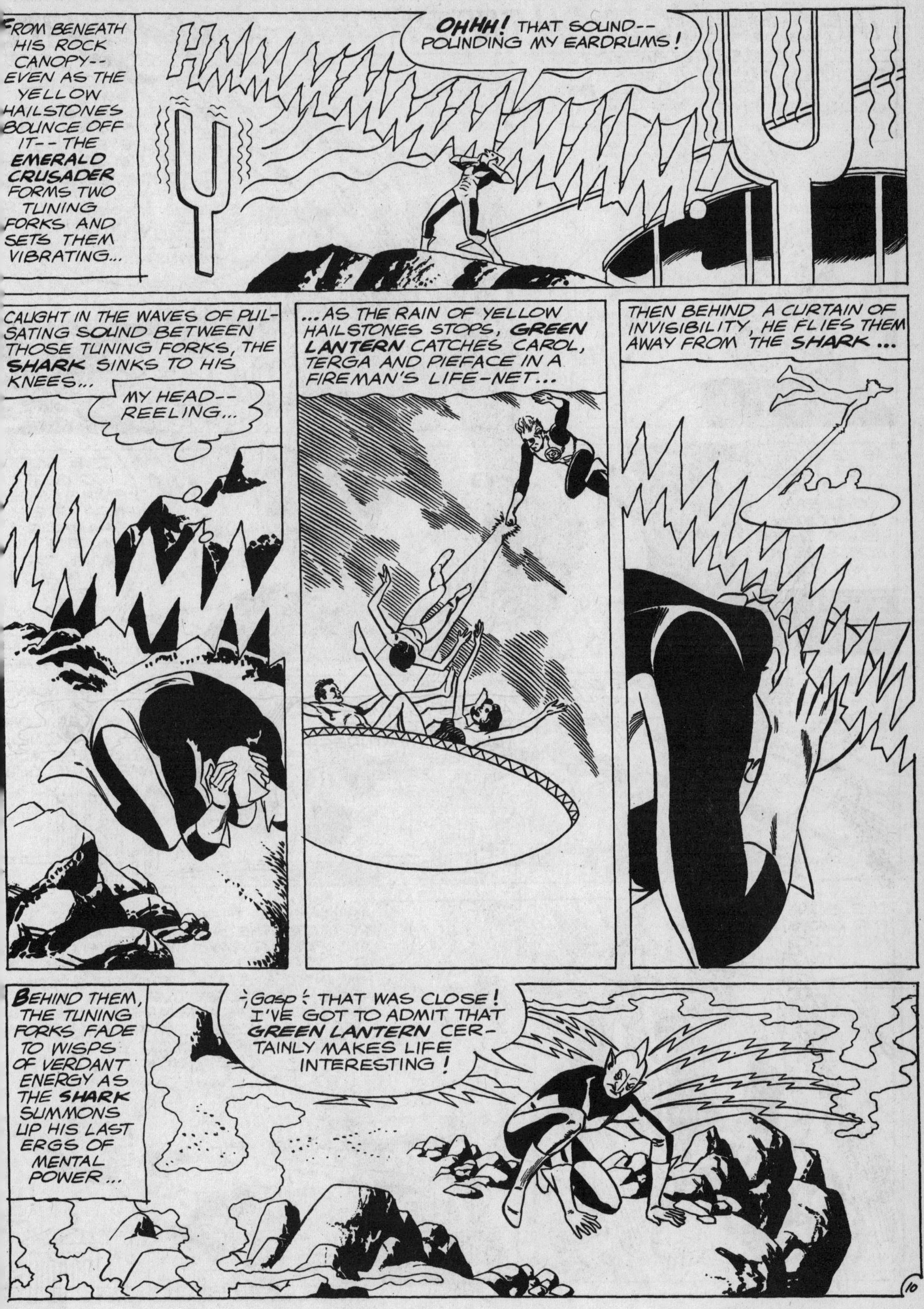
FROM BENEATH HIS ROCK CANOPY-- EVEN AS THE YELLOW HAILSTONES BOUNCE OFF IT-- THE EMERALD CRUSADER FORMS TWO TUNING FORKS AND SETS THEM VIBRATING...
OHHH! THAT SOUND-- POUNDING MY EARDRUMS!
CAUGHT IN THE WAVES OF PULSATING SOUND BETWEEN THOSE TUNING FORKS, THE SHARK SINKS TO HIS KNEES...
MY HEAD-- REELING...
...AS THE RAIN OF YELLOW HAILSTONES STOPS, GREEN LANTERN CATCHES CAROL, TERGA AND PIEFACE IN A FIREMAN'S LIFE-NET...
THEN BEHIND A CURTAIN OF INVISIBILITY, HE FLIES THEM AWAY FROM THE SHARK...
BEHIND THEM, THE TUNING FORKS FADE TO WISPS OF VERDANT ENERGY AS THE SHARK SUMMONS UP HIS LAST ERGS OF MENTAL POWER...
Gasp! THAT WAS CLOSE! I'VE GOT TO ADMIT THAT GREEN LANTERN CERTAINLY MAKES LIFE INTERESTING!
10

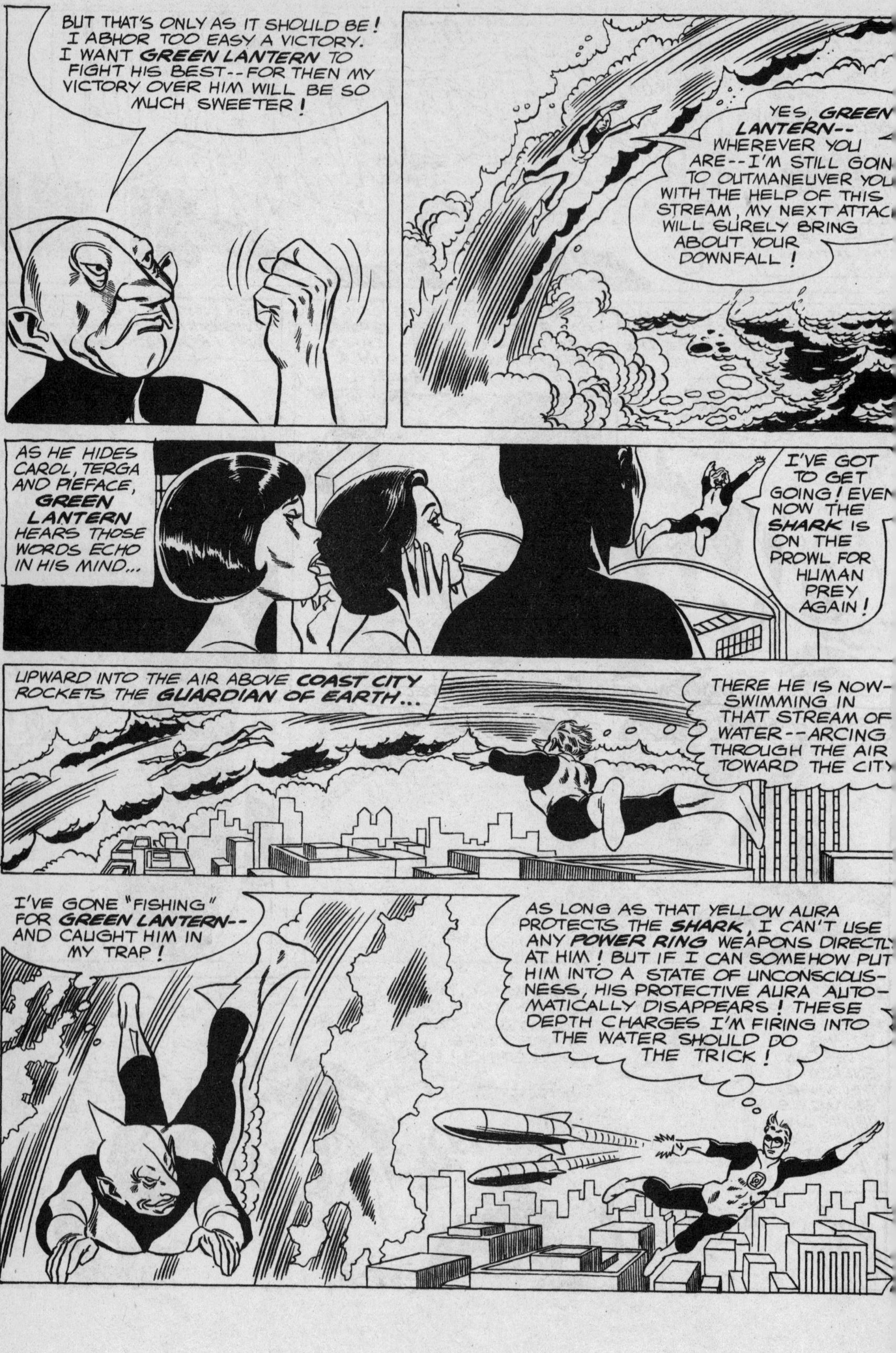
BUT THAT'S ONLY AS IT SHOULD BE! I ABHOR TOO EASY A VICTORY. I WANT GREEN LANTERN TO FIGHT HIS BEST--FOR THEN MY VICTORY OVER HIM WILL BE SO MUCH SWEETER!
YES, GREEN LANTERN--WHEREVER YOU ARE--I'M STILL GOIN TO OUTMANEUVER YOU WITH THE HELP OF THIS STREAM, MY NEXT ATTAC WILL SURELY BRING ABOUT YOUR DOWNFALL!
AS HE HIDES CAROL, TERGA AND PIEFACE, GREEN LANTERN HEARS THOSE WORDS ECHO IN HIS MIND...
I'VE GOT TO GET GOING! EVEN NOW THE SHARK IS ON THE PROWL FOR HUMAN PREY AGAIN!
UPWARD INTO THE AIR ABOVE COAST CITY ROCKETS THE GUARDIAN OF EARTH...
THERE HE IS NOW--SWIMMING IN THAT STREAM OF WATER--ARCING THROUGH THE AIR TOWARD THE CITY
I'VE GONE "FISHING" FOR GREEN LANTERN--AND CAUGHT HIM IN MY TRAP!
AS LONG AS THAT YELLOW AURA PROTECTS THE SHARK, I CAN'T USE ANY POWER RING WEAPONS DIRECTLY AT HIM! BUT IF I CAN SOMEHOW PUT HIM INTO A STATE OF UNCONSCIOUSNESS, HIS PROTECTIVE AURA AUTOMATICALLY DISAPPEARS! THESE DEPTH CHARGES I'M FIRING INTO THE WATER SHOULD DO THE TRICK!

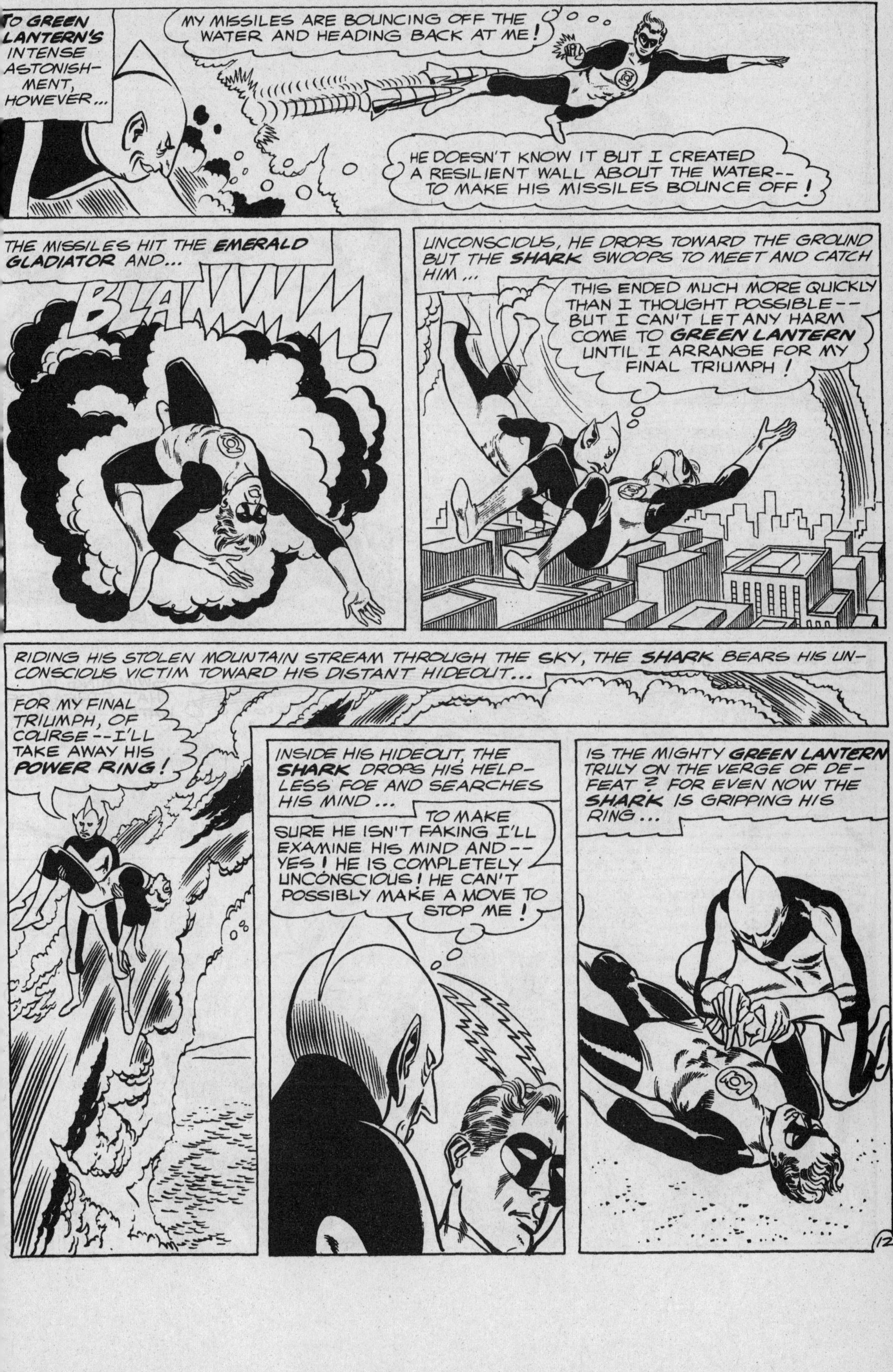
TO GREEN LANTERN'S INTENSE ASTONISHMENT, HOWEVER...
MY MISSILES ARE BOUNCING OFF THE WATER AND HEADING BACK AT ME!
HE DOESN'T KNOW IT BUT I CREATED A RESILIENT WALL ABOUT THE WATER-- TO MAKE HIS MISSILES BOUNCE OFF!
THE MISSILES HIT THE EMERALD GLADIATOR AND...
BLAMMM!
UNCONSCIOUS, HE DROPS TOWARD THE GROUND BUT THE SHARK SWOOPS TO MEET AND CATCH HIM...
THIS ENDED MUCH MORE QUICKLY THAN I THOUGHT POSSIBLE-- BUT I CAN'T LET ANY HARM COME TO GREEN LANTERN UNTIL I ARRANGE FOR MY FINAL TRIUMPH!
RIDING HIS STOLEN MOUNTAIN STREAM THROUGH THE SKY, THE SHARK BEARS HIS UNCONSCIOUS VICTIM TOWARD HIS DISTANT HIDEOUT...
FOR MY FINAL TRIUMPH, OF COURSE--I'LL TAKE AWAY HIS POWER RING!
INSIDE HIS HIDEOUT, THE SHARK DROPS HIS HELPLESS FOE AND SEARCHES HIS MIND...
TO MAKE SURE HE ISN'T FAKING I'LL EXAMINE HIS MIND AND-- YES! HE IS COMPLETELY UNCONSCIOUS! HE CAN'T POSSIBLY MAKE A MOVE TO STOP ME!
IS THE MIGHTY GREEN LANTERN TRULY ON THE VERGE OF DEFEAT? FOR EVEN NOW THE SHARK IS GRIPPING HIS RING...
12

ABRUPTLY, **GREEN LANTERN'S** ARM SHOOTS STRAIGHT OUT FOR THE **SHARK'S** JAW...

SOK!

KNOCKED COLD BY THAT POWERFUL BLOW, THE **SHARK** SLIDES LIMPLY TO THE GROUND BESIDE HIS FOE (FOR **GREEN LANTERN** IS **STILL** UNCONSCIOUS!.)...

FOR SEVERAL MINUTES, MAN AND "MAN-HUNTER" ARE MOTIONLESS! WHICH OF THEM WILL RECOVER FIRST? FOR VICTORY WILL COME TO HIM WHO CAN GET IN THE NEXT BLOW...

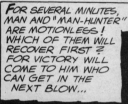

THE **SHARK** STIRS A HAND AS **GREEN LANTERN** OPENS HIS EYES...

AGONIZING MOMENTS FLEET BY...

I MUST ACT QUICKLY! AND SINCE KNOCKING OUT THE **SHARK** IS THE ONLY WAY TO RID HIM OF HIS YELLOW AURA...

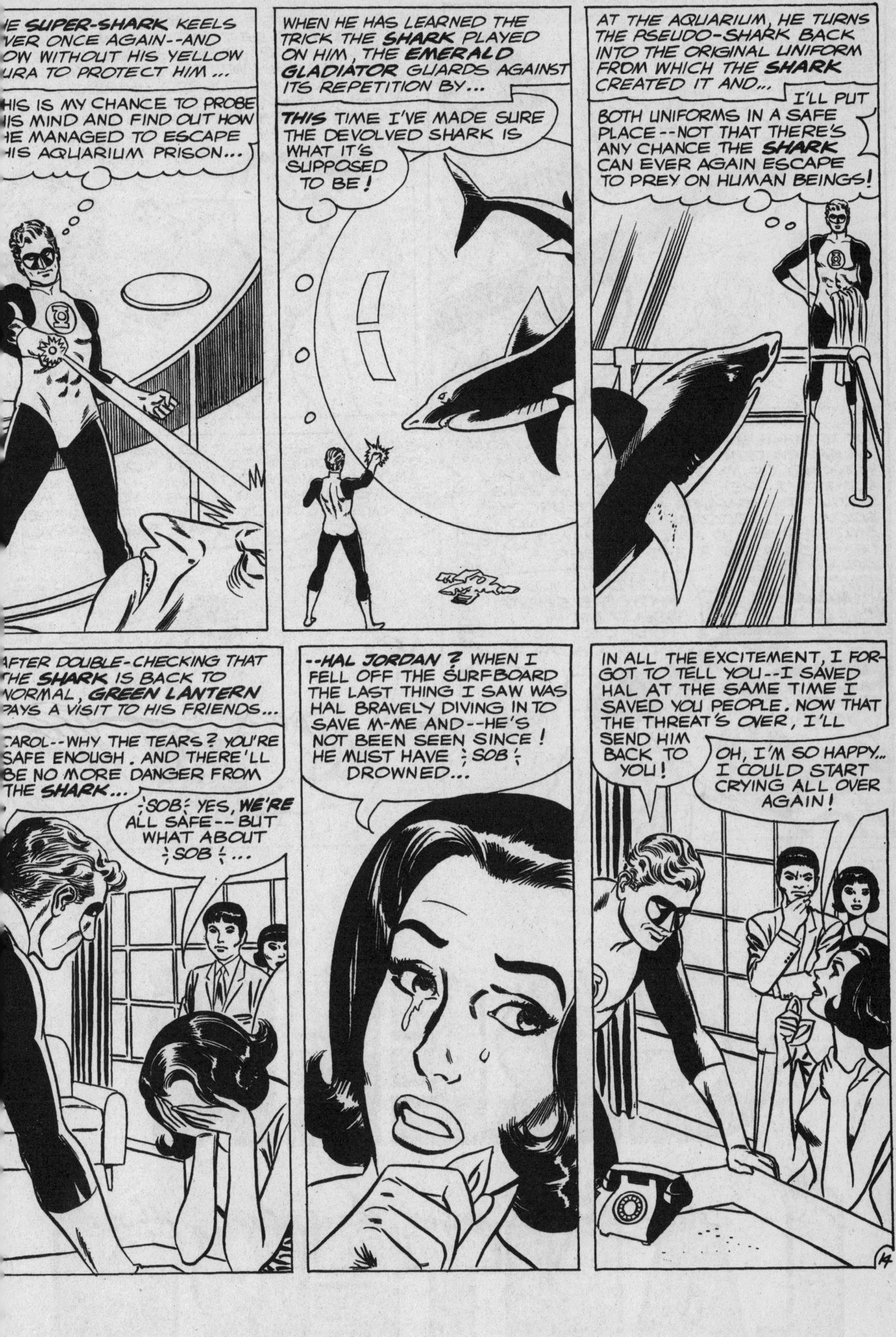
HE SUPER-SHARK KEELS OVER ONCE AGAIN--AND NOW WITHOUT HIS YELLOW AURA TO PROTECT HIM ...
THIS IS MY CHANCE TO PROBE HIS MIND AND FIND OUT HOW HE MANAGED TO ESCAPE HIS AQUARIUM PRISON...
WHEN HE HAS LEARNED THE TRICK THE SHARK PLAYED ON HIM, THE EMERALD GLADIATOR GUARDS AGAINST ITS REPETITION BY...
THIS TIME I'VE MADE SURE THE DEVOLVED SHARK IS WHAT IT'S SUPPOSED TO BE!
AT THE AQUARIUM, HE TURNS THE PSEUDO-SHARK BACK INTO THE ORIGINAL UNIFORM FROM WHICH THE SHARK CREATED IT AND...
I'LL PUT BOTH UNIFORMS IN A SAFE PLACE--NOT THAT THERE'S ANY CHANCE THE SHARK CAN EVER AGAIN ESCAPE TO PREY ON HUMAN BEINGS!
AFTER DOUBLE-CHECKING THAT THE SHARK IS BACK TO NORMAL, GREEN LANTERN PAYS A VISIT TO HIS FRIENDS...
CAROL--WHY THE TEARS? YOU'RE SAFE ENOUGH. AND THERE'LL BE NO MORE DANGER FROM THE SHARK...
SOB YES, WE'RE ALL SAFE--BUT WHAT ABOUT SOB ...
--HAL JORDAN? WHEN I FELL OFF THE SURFBOARD THE LAST THING I SAW WAS HAL BRAVELY DIVING IN TO SAVE M-ME AND--HE'S NOT BEEN SEEN SINCE! HE MUST HAVE SOB DROWNED...
IN ALL THE EXCITEMENT, I FORGOT TO TELL YOU--I SAVED HAL AT THE SAME TIME I SAVED YOU PEOPLE. NOW THAT THE THREAT'S OVER, I'LL SEND HIM BACK TO YOU!
OH, I'M SO HAPPY... I COULD START CRYING ALL OVER AGAIN!
14

THE NEXT DAY...

HAL, QUICK-- WHILE TERGA AND CAROL GO SURFBOARD RIDING --TELL ME BEFORE I BUST! HOW DID YOU EVER MANAGE *UNCONSCIOUS*-- WHILE YOU WERE *UNCONSCIOUS*-- TO KNOCK OUT THE *SHARK* AS HE REACHED FOR YOUR *POWER RING?*

FIGURING THAT THE *SHARK'S* VICTORY OVER ME WOULDN'T BE COMPLETE UNLESS HE HAD DEPRIVED ME OF MY RING --WHICH HE COULD DO ONLY WHILE I WAS UNCONSCIOUS. I'D PREVIOUSLY ORDERED MY RING TO MAKE ME SHOOT OUT MY FIST THE MOMENT THE *SHARK* ATTEMPTED TO REMOVE THE RING.

BUT TO MAKE SURE THE *YELLOW* AURA AROUND THE *SHARK* DIDN'T INTERFERE WITH THE WORKING OF MY RING AT THIS CRITICAL MOMENT, I PRE-COMMANDED THE RING-- SHOULD THE *SHARK* MAKE ME UNCON- SCIOUS--TO BECOME INVISIBLE AND SWITCH OVER TO MY *LEFT HAND,* LEAVING ON THE RIGHT FINGER A *COUNTERFEIT DUPLICATE RING!*

BUT HOW'D YOU KNOW THE *SHARK* WOULD BE IN POSITION FOR SUCH A BLOW?

HERE-- TRY AND REMOVE THE RING!

I SEE WHAT YOU MEAN! ANY OTHER POSITION WOULD BE AWKWARD! *Hmm*--IT PROVES THAT EVEN WHEN YOU'RE UN- CONSCIOUS, YOU'RE A BETTER MAN THAN THE *SHARK!*

GREEN LANTERN

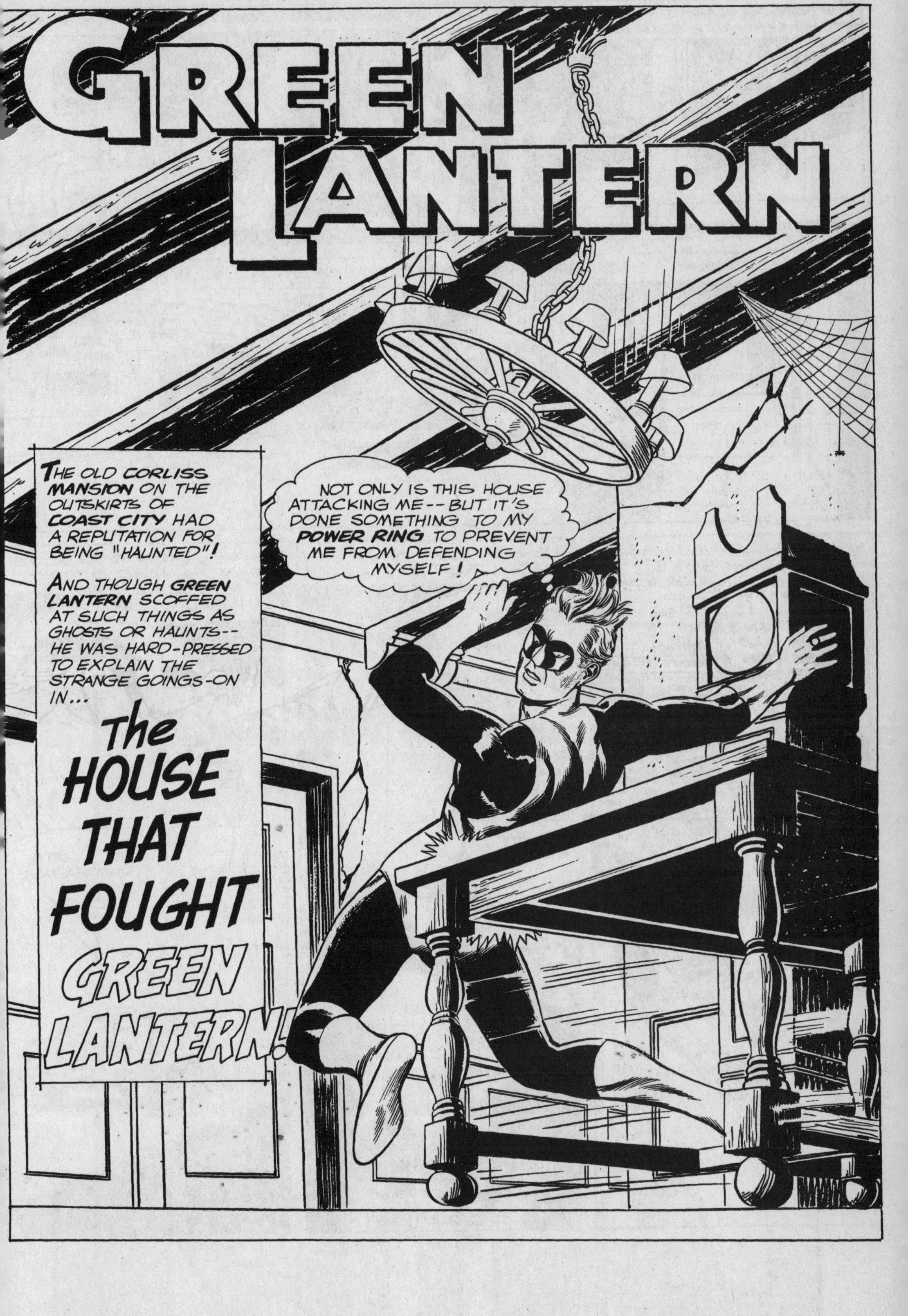
GREEN LANTERN
THE OLD CORLISS MANSION ON THE OUTSKIRTS OF COAST CITY HAD A REPUTATION FOR BEING "HAUNTED"!
AND THOUGH GREEN LANTERN SCOFFED AT SUCH THINGS AS GHOSTS OR HAUNTS-- HE WAS HARD-PRESSED TO EXPLAIN THE STRANGE GOINGS-ON IN...
The HOUSE THAT FOUGHT GREEN LANTERN!
NOT ONLY IS THIS HOUSE ATTACKING ME-- BUT IT'S DONE SOMETHING TO MY POWER RING TO PREVENT ME FROM DEFENDING MYSELF!

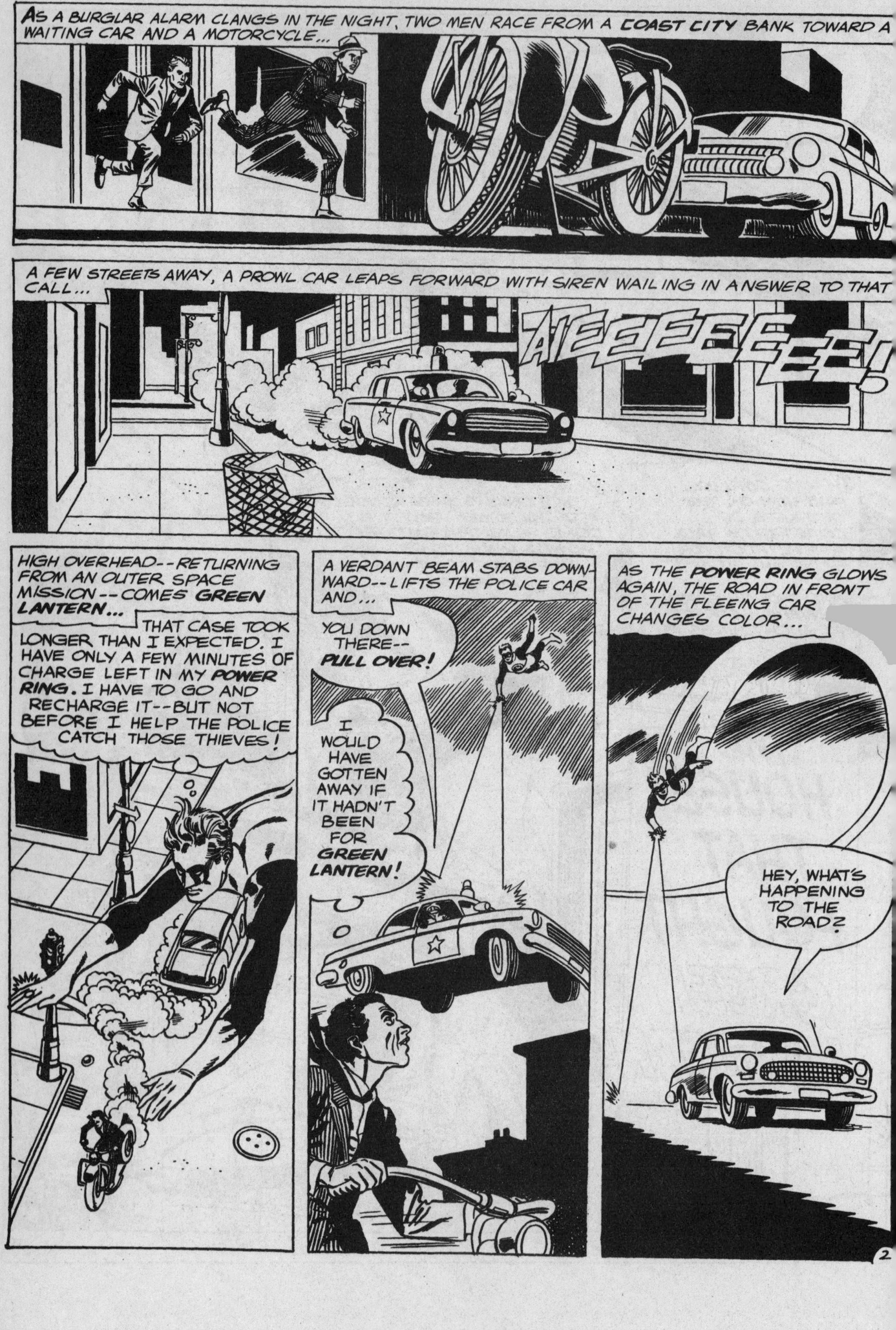
AS A BURGLAR ALARM CLANGS IN THE NIGHT, TWO MEN RACE FROM A COAST CITY BANK TOWARD A WAITING CAR AND A MOTORCYCLE...
A FEW STREETS AWAY, A PROWL CAR LEAPS FORWARD WITH SIREN WAILING IN ANSWER TO THAT CALL...
AEEEEEEEEE!
HIGH OVERHEAD--RETURNING FROM AN OUTER SPACE MISSION--COMES GREEN LANTERN...
THAT CASE TOOK LONGER THAN I EXPECTED. I HAVE ONLY A FEW MINUTES OF CHARGE LEFT IN MY POWER RING. I HAVE TO GO AND RECHARGE IT--BUT NOT BEFORE I HELP THE POLICE CATCH THOSE THIEVES!
A VERDANT BEAM STABS DOWNWARD--LIFTS THE POLICE CAR AND...
YOU DOWN THERE-- PULL OVER!
I WOULD HAVE GOTTEN AWAY IF IT HADN'T BEEN FOR GREEN LANTERN!
AS THE POWER RING GLOWS AGAIN, THE ROAD IN FRONT OF THE FLEEING CAR CHANGES COLOR...
HEY, WHAT'S HAPPENING TO THE ROAD?
2

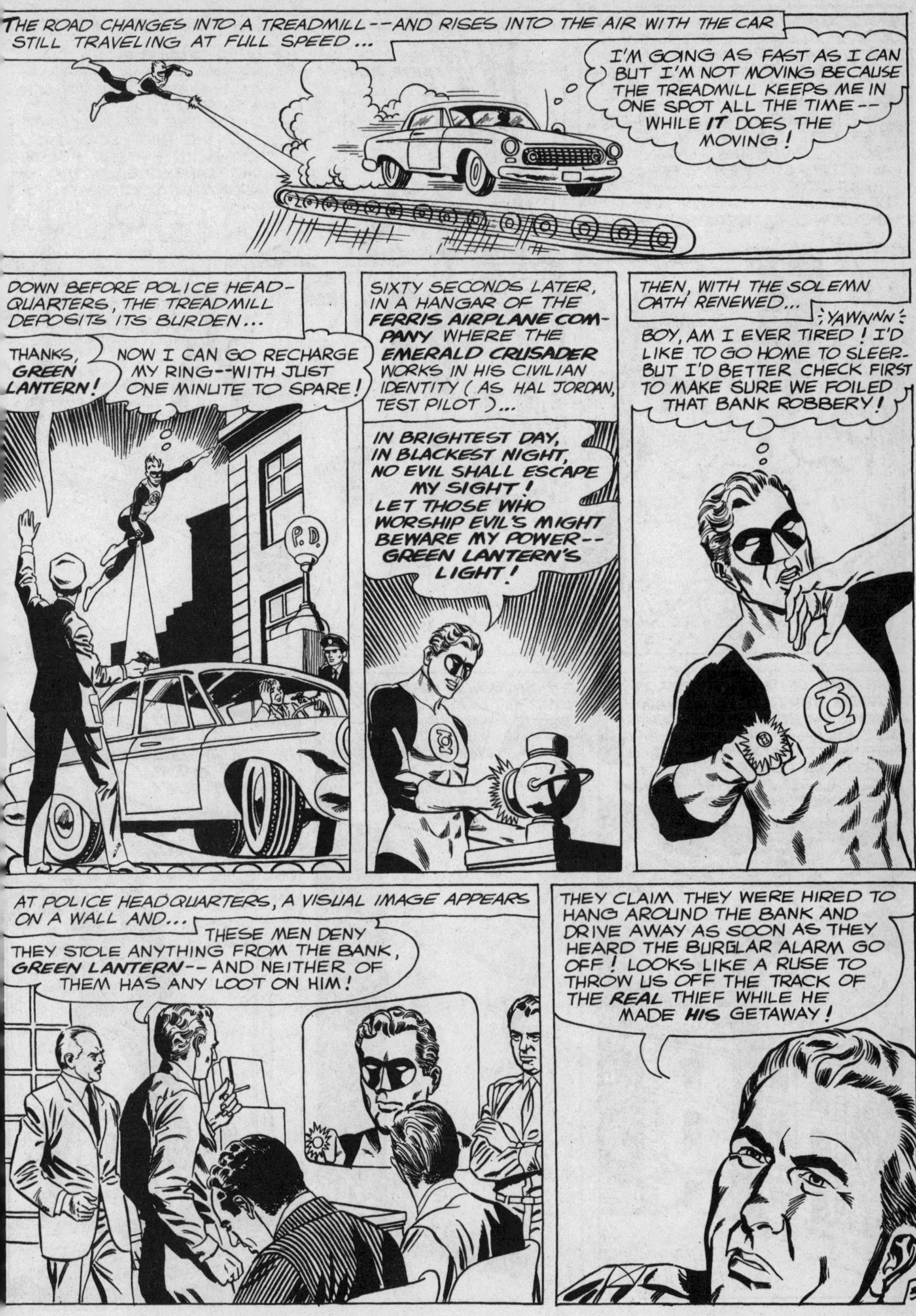
THE ROAD CHANGES INTO A TREADMILL--AND RISES INTO THE AIR WITH THE CAR STILL TRAVELING AT FULL SPEED...
I'M GOING AS FAST AS I CAN BUT I'M NOT MOVING BECAUSE THE TREADMILL KEEPS ME IN ONE SPOT ALL THE TIME-- WHILE IT DOES THE MOVING!
DOWN BEFORE POLICE HEADQUARTERS, THE TREADMILL DEPOSITS ITS BURDEN...
THANKS, GREEN LANTERN!
NOW I CAN GO RECHARGE MY RING--WITH JUST ONE MINUTE TO SPARE!
P.D.
SIXTY SECONDS LATER, IN A HANGAR OF THE FERRIS AIRPLANE COMPANY WHERE THE EMERALD CRUSADER WORKS IN HIS CIVILIAN IDENTITY (AS HAL JORDAN, TEST PILOT)...
IN BRIGHTEST DAY, IN BLACKEST NIGHT, NO EVIL SHALL ESCAPE MY SIGHT! LET THOSE WHO WORSHIP EVIL'S MIGHT BEWARE MY POWER-- GREEN LANTERN'S LIGHT!
THEN, WITH THE SOLEMN OATH RENEWED...
YAWNNN
BOY, AM I EVER TIRED! I'D LIKE TO GO HOME TO SLEEP-- BUT I'D BETTER CHECK FIRST TO MAKE SURE WE FOILED THAT BANK ROBBERY!
AT POLICE HEADQUARTERS, A VISUAL IMAGE APPEARS ON A WALL AND...
THESE MEN DENY THEY STOLE ANYTHING FROM THE BANK, GREEN LANTERN-- AND NEITHER OF THEM HAS ANY LOOT ON HIM!
THEY CLAIM THEY WERE HIRED TO HANG AROUND THE BANK AND DRIVE AWAY AS SOON AS THEY HEARD THE BURGLAR ALARM GO OFF! LOOKS LIKE A RUSE TO THROW US OFF THE TRACK OF THE REAL THIEF WHILE HE MADE HIS GETAWAY!
3

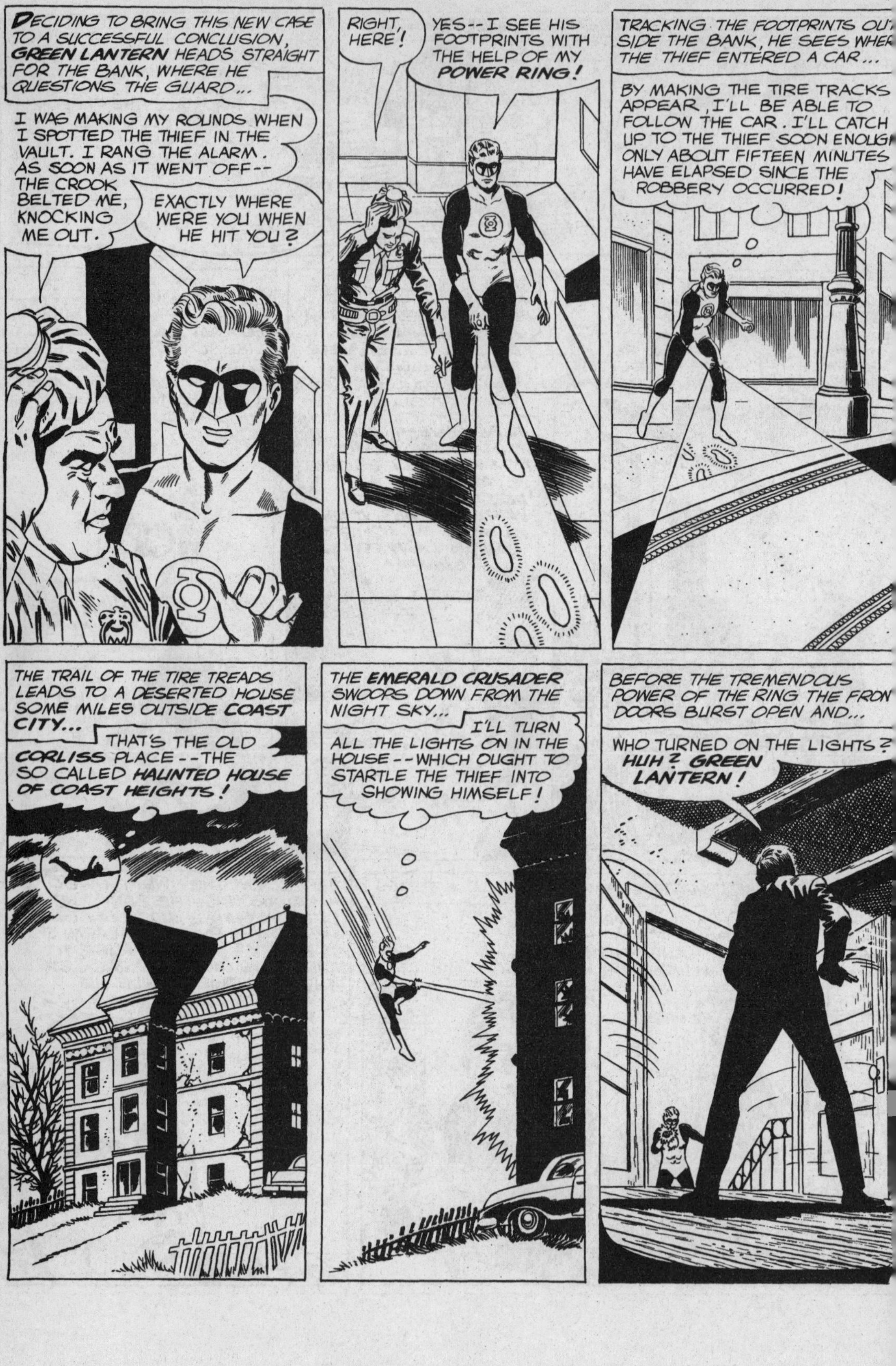
DECIDING TO BRING THIS NEW CASE TO A SUCCESSFUL CONCLUSION, GREEN LANTERN HEADS STRAIGHT FOR THE BANK, WHERE HE QUESTIONS THE GUARD...
I WAS MAKING MY ROUNDS WHEN I SPOTTED THE THIEF IN THE VAULT. I RANG THE ALARM. AS SOON AS IT WENT OFF--THE CROOK BELTED ME, KNOCKING ME OUT.
EXACTLY WHERE WERE YOU WHEN HE HIT YOU?
RIGHT, HERE!
YES--I SEE HIS FOOTPRINTS WITH THE HELP OF MY POWER RING!
TRACKING THE FOOTPRINTS OUTSIDE THE BANK, HE SEES WHERE THE THIEF ENTERED A CAR...
BY MAKING THE TIRE TRACKS APPEAR, I'LL BE ABLE TO FOLLOW THE CAR. I'LL CATCH UP TO THE THIEF SOON ENOUGH! ONLY ABOUT FIFTEEN MINUTES HAVE ELAPSED SINCE THE ROBBERY OCCURRED!
THE TRAIL OF THE TIRE TREADS LEADS TO A DESERTED HOUSE SOME MILES OUTSIDE COAST CITY...
THAT'S THE OLD CORLISS PLACE--THE SO CALLED HAUNTED HOUSE OF COAST HEIGHTS!
THE EMERALD CRUSADER SWOOPS DOWN FROM THE NIGHT SKY...
I'LL TURN ALL THE LIGHTS ON IN THE HOUSE--WHICH OUGHT TO STARTLE THE THIEF INTO SHOWING HIMSELF!
BEFORE THE TREMENDOUS POWER OF THE RING THE FRONT DOORS BURST OPEN AND...
WHO TURNED ON THE LIGHTS? HUH? GREEN LANTERN!

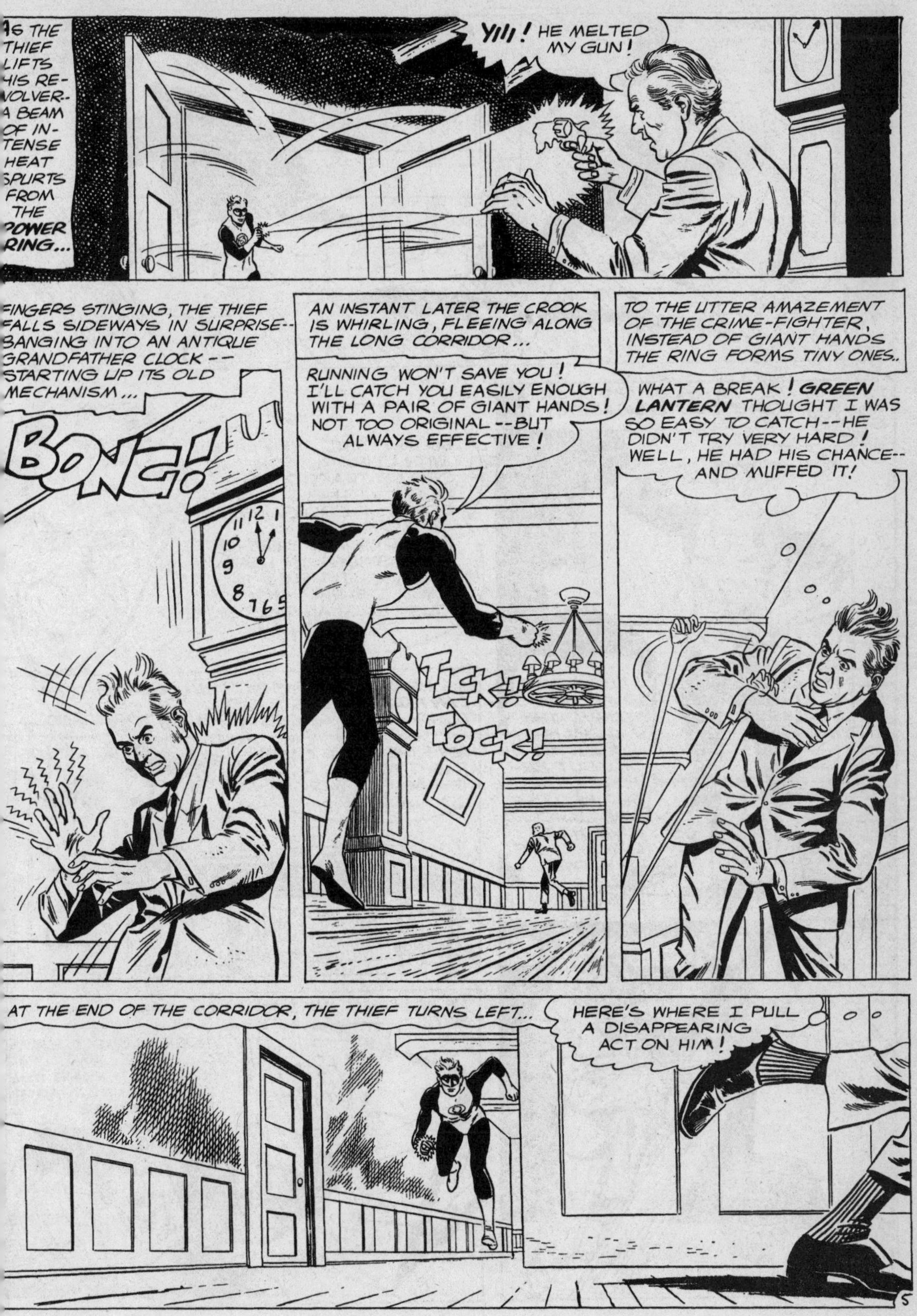
AS THE THIEF LIFTS HIS RE-VOLVER-A BEAM OF IN-TENSE HEAT SPURTS FROM THE POWER RING...
YIII! HE MELTED MY GUN!
FINGERS STINGING, THE THIEF FALLS SIDEWAYS IN SURPRISE--BANGING INTO AN ANTIQUE GRANDFATHER CLOCK -- STARTING UP ITS OLD MECHANISM...
BONG!
AN INSTANT LATER THE CROOK IS WHIRLING, FLEEING ALONG THE LONG CORRIDOR...
RUNNING WON'T SAVE YOU! I'LL CATCH YOU EASILY ENOUGH WITH A PAIR OF GIANT HANDS! NOT TOO ORIGINAL --BUT ALWAYS EFFECTIVE!
TICK! TOCK!
TO THE UTTER AMAZEMENT OF THE CRIME-FIGHTER, INSTEAD OF GIANT HANDS THE RING FORMS TINY ONES..
WHAT A BREAK! GREEN LANTERN THOUGHT I WAS SO EASY TO CATCH--HE DIDN'T TRY VERY HARD! WELL, HE HAD HIS CHANCE--AND MUFFED IT!
AT THE END OF THE CORRIDOR, THE THIEF TURNS LEFT...
HERE'S WHERE I PULL A DISAPPEARING ACT ON HIM!
5

AS *GREEN LANTERN* ROUNDS THE CORNER...

HUH? WHERE'D HE GO? HIS FOOTSTEPS END RIGHT HERE! HE COULDN'T POSSIBLY HAVE VANISHED INTO THIN AIR!

BENEATH THE "INVISIBLE" TRAPDOOR WHERE THE *EMERALD CRUSADER* STANDS...

LUCKY FOR ME, I'VE USED THE *CORLISS* HOUSE AS A HIDEOUT BEFORE! THE OLD RECLUSE WHO USED TO LIVE HERE LIKED TO BE ALONE...

SO HE FITTED THE PLACE WITH CLEVERLY CONCEALED TRAPDOORS, SLIDING PANELS, ALL SORTS OF ODD GADGETS TO SCARE OFF ANY INTRUDERS! I MADE IT MY BUSINESS TO LEARN ALL ABOUT THEM -- IN CASE I EVER RAN INTO JUST SUCH AN EMERGENCY AS THIS ONE!

AS HE WANDERS ABOUT THE HOUSE, *GREEN LANTERN* ENTERS THE DINING ROOM -- JUST AS A DUSTY TABLE SLIDES AT HIM!...

HEY! THE TABLE CAME RIGHT FOR ME AS IF -- AS IF IT WERE ALIVE!

HE WILLS HIS RING TO FORM GREAT GREEN WINGS BUT...

THOSE WINGS I FORMED TO LIFT ME UPWARD ARE SO TINY -- THEY'RE USELESS! WHAT'S HAPPENING TO MY *POWER* RING?

THUD!

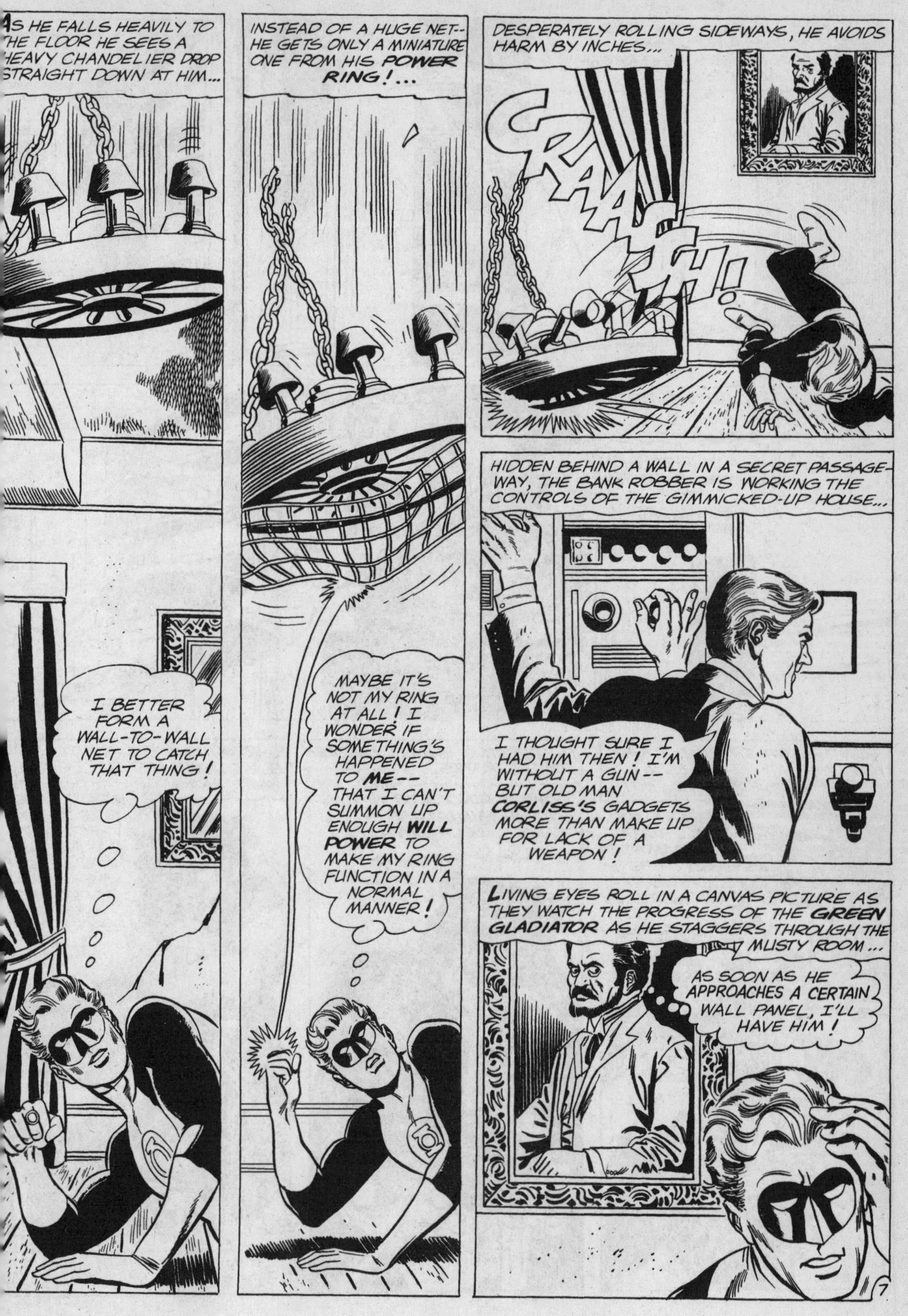
AS HE FALLS HEAVILY TO THE FLOOR HE SEES A HEAVY CHANDELIER DROP STRAIGHT DOWN AT HIM...
I BETTER FORM A WALL-TO-WALL NET TO CATCH THAT THING!
INSTEAD OF A HUGE NET--HE GETS ONLY A MINIATURE ONE FROM HIS POWER RING!...
MAYBE IT'S NOT MY RING AT ALL! I WONDER IF SOMETHING'S HAPPENED TO ME--THAT I CAN'T SUMMON UP ENOUGH WILL POWER TO MAKE MY RING FUNCTION IN A NORMAL MANNER!
DESPERATELY ROLLING SIDEWAYS, HE AVOIDS HARM BY INCHES...
CRAACHH!
HIDDEN BEHIND A WALL IN A SECRET PASSAGE-WAY, THE BANK ROBBER IS WORKING THE CONTROLS OF THE GIMMICKED-UP HOUSE...
I THOUGHT SURE I HAD HIM THEN! I'M WITHOUT A GUN--BUT OLD MAN CORLISS'S GADGETS MORE THAN MAKE UP FOR LACK OF A WEAPON!
LIVING EYES ROLL IN A CANVAS PICTURE AS THEY WATCH THE PROGRESS OF THE GREEN GLADIATOR AS HE STAGGERS THROUGH THE MUSTY ROOM...
AS SOON AS HE APPROACHES A CERTAIN WALL PANEL, I'LL HAVE HIM!
7

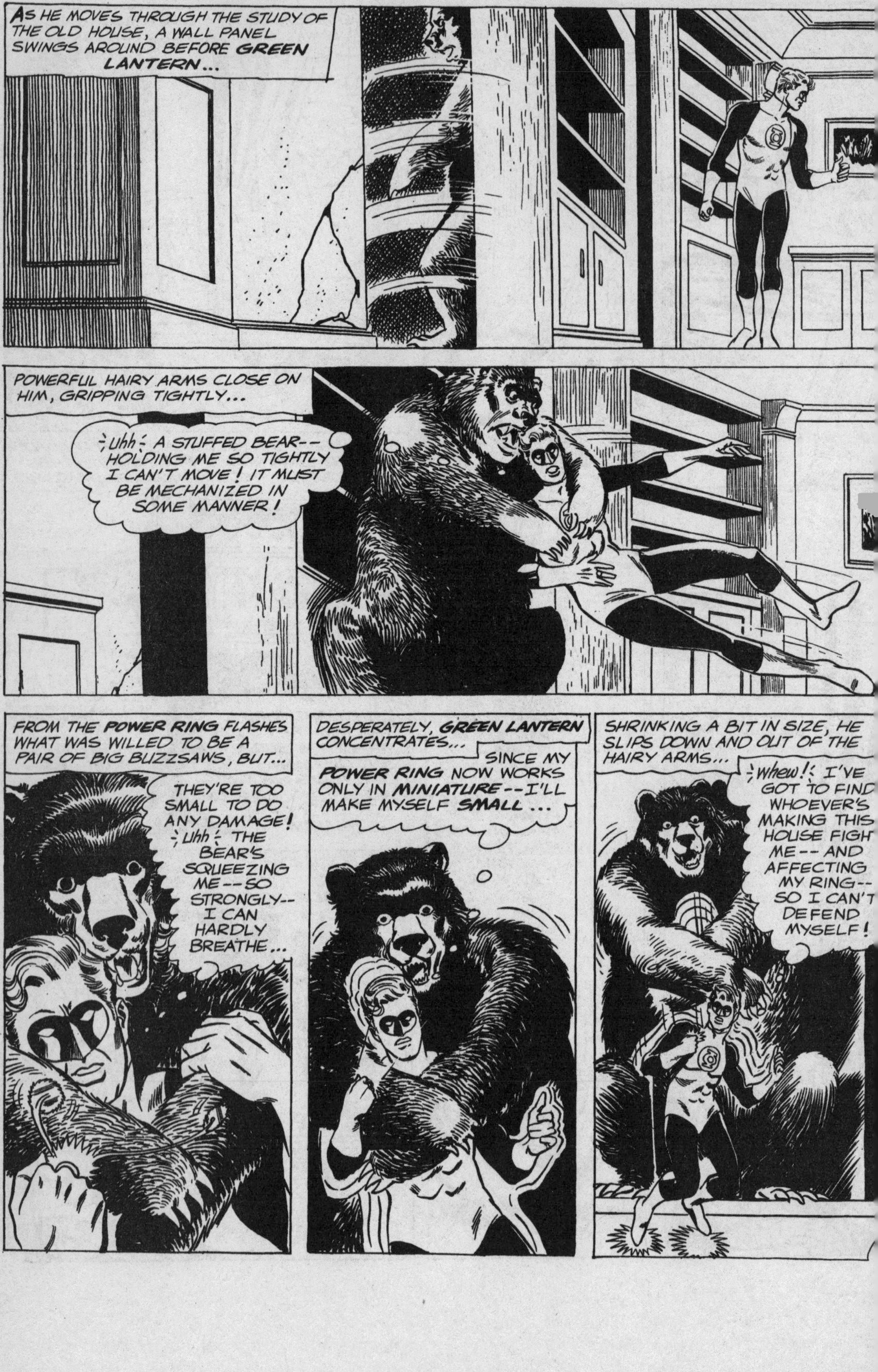
AS HE MOVES THROUGH THE STUDY OF THE OLD HOUSE, A WALL PANEL SWINGS AROUND BEFORE GREEN LANTERN...
POWERFUL HAIRY ARMS CLOSE ON HIM, GRIPPING TIGHTLY...
UHH! A STUFFED BEAR-- HOLDING ME SO TIGHTLY I CAN'T MOVE! IT MUST BE MECHANIZED IN SOME MANNER!
FROM THE POWER RING FLASHES WHAT WAS WILLED TO BE A PAIR OF BIG BUZZSAWS, BUT...
THEY'RE TOO SMALL TO DO ANY DAMAGE! UHH! THE BEAR'S SQUEEZING ME--SO STRONGLY-- I CAN HARDLY BREATHE...
DESPERATELY, GREEN LANTERN CONCENTRATES...
SINCE MY POWER RING NOW WORKS ONLY IN MINIATURE--I'LL MAKE MYSELF SMALL...
SHRINKING A BIT IN SIZE, HE SLIPS DOWN AND OUT OF THE HAIRY ARMS...
WHEW! I'VE GOT TO FIND WHOEVER'S MAKING THIS HOUSE FIGHT ME--AND AFFECTING MY RING-- SO I CAN'T DEFEND MYSELF!

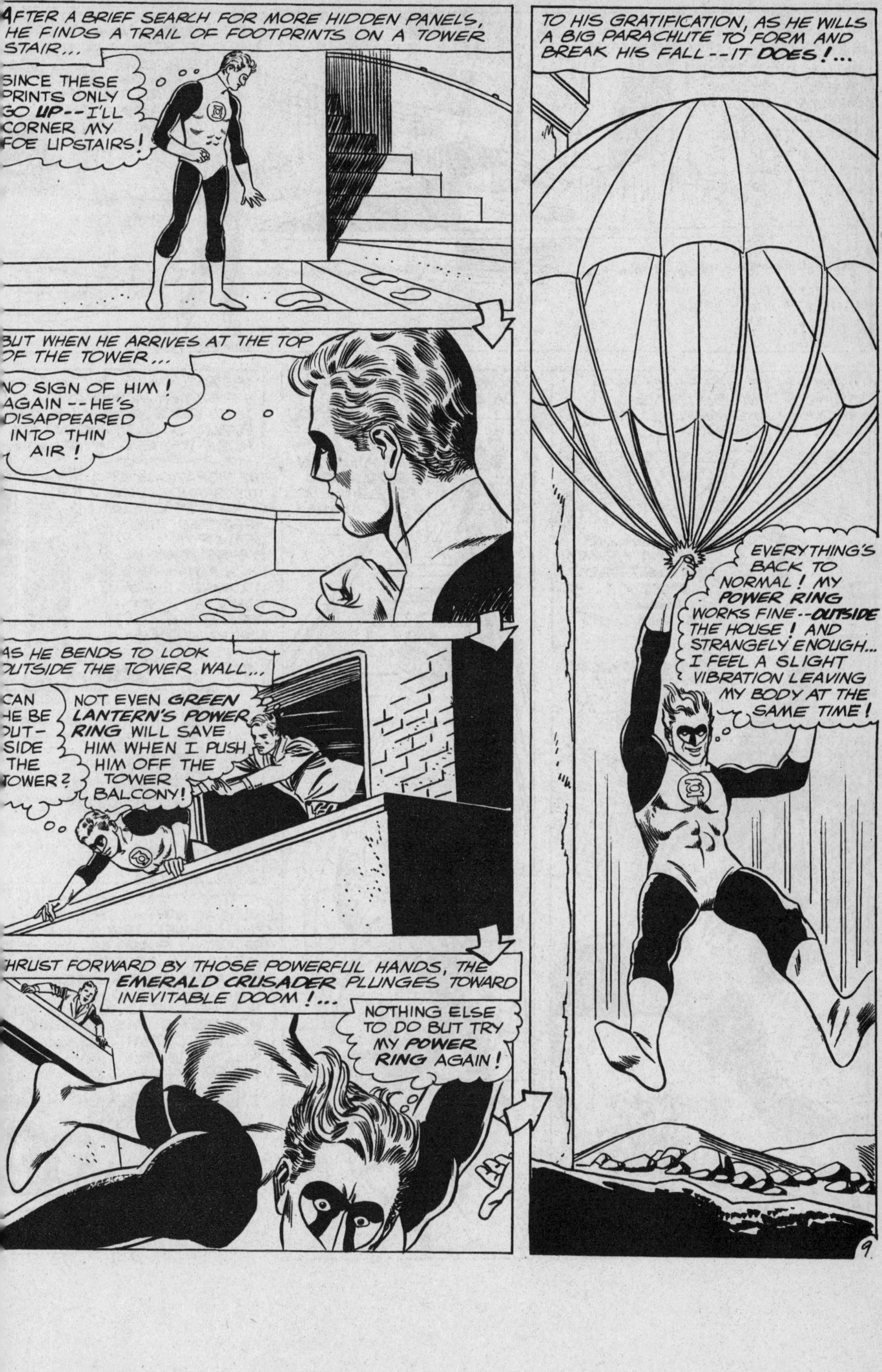
AFTER A BRIEF SEARCH FOR MORE HIDDEN PANELS, HE FINDS A TRAIL OF FOOTPRINTS ON A TOWER STAIR...
SINCE THESE PRINTS ONLY GO UP--I'LL CORNER MY FOE UPSTAIRS!
BUT WHEN HE ARRIVES AT THE TOP OF THE TOWER...
NO SIGN OF HIM! AGAIN--HE'S DISAPPEARED INTO THIN AIR!
AS HE BENDS TO LOOK OUTSIDE THE TOWER WALL...
CAN HE BE OUT-SIDE THE TOWER?
NOT EVEN GREEN LANTERN'S POWER RING WILL SAVE HIM WHEN I PUSH HIM OFF THE TOWER BALCONY!
THRUST FORWARD BY THOSE POWERFUL HANDS, THE EMERALD CRUSADER PLUNGES TOWARD INEVITABLE DOOM!...
NOTHING ELSE TO DO BUT TRY MY POWER RING AGAIN!
TO HIS GRATIFICATION, AS HE WILLS A BIG PARACHUTE TO FORM AND BREAK HIS FALL--IT DOES!...
EVERYTHING'S BACK TO NORMAL! MY POWER RING WORKS FINE--OUTSIDE THE HOUSE! AND STRANGELY ENOUGH... I FEEL A SLIGHT VIBRATION LEAVING MY BODY AT THE SAME TIME!
9

As his feet firm on solid ground, *GREEN LANTERN* aims his ring at the "HAUNTED" house...

SINCE MY *POWER RING* DOESN'T WORK *INSIDE* THE HOUSE I'LL SIMPLY STAY *OUTSIDE* AND CAPTURE THE CROOK BY RAISING THE MANSION...

HIGH ABOVE HIS HEAD HE SWINGS THE BUILDING AROUND AND AROUND AT DIZZYING SPEED!...

STOP! LEMME OUTTA HERE! I'M GETTING DIZZY! HELP!

FIRST--THROW OUT THE MONEY YOU STOLE!

MOMENTS LATER...

I'LL EVEN MAKE IT EASY FOR YOU TO COME DOWN -- BY FORMING AN *ESCALATOR* TO BRING YOU TO ME!

AFTER TURNING THE THIEF AND HIS STOLEN MONEY OVER TO THE POLICE, *GREEN LANTERN* RETURNS TO THE *CORLISS* HOME WHERE...

THE VIBRATIONS OF THIS GRANDFATHER CLOCK'S PENDULUM AFFECTED THE GEM OF MY *POWER RING* IN SUCH A WAY THAT IT CAUSED EVERY-THING THE RING FORMED TO APPEAR IN MINIATURE SIZE!

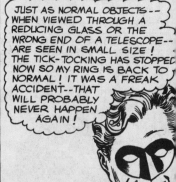

JUST AS NORMAL OBJECTS -- WHEN VIEWED THROUGH A REDUCING GLASS OR THE WRONG END OF A TELESCOPE-- ARE SEEN IN SMALL SIZE! THE TICK-TOCKING HAS STOPPED NOW SO MY RING IS BACK TO NORMAL! IT WAS A FREAK ACCIDENT--THAT WILL PROBABLY NEVER HAPPEN AGAIN!

The End

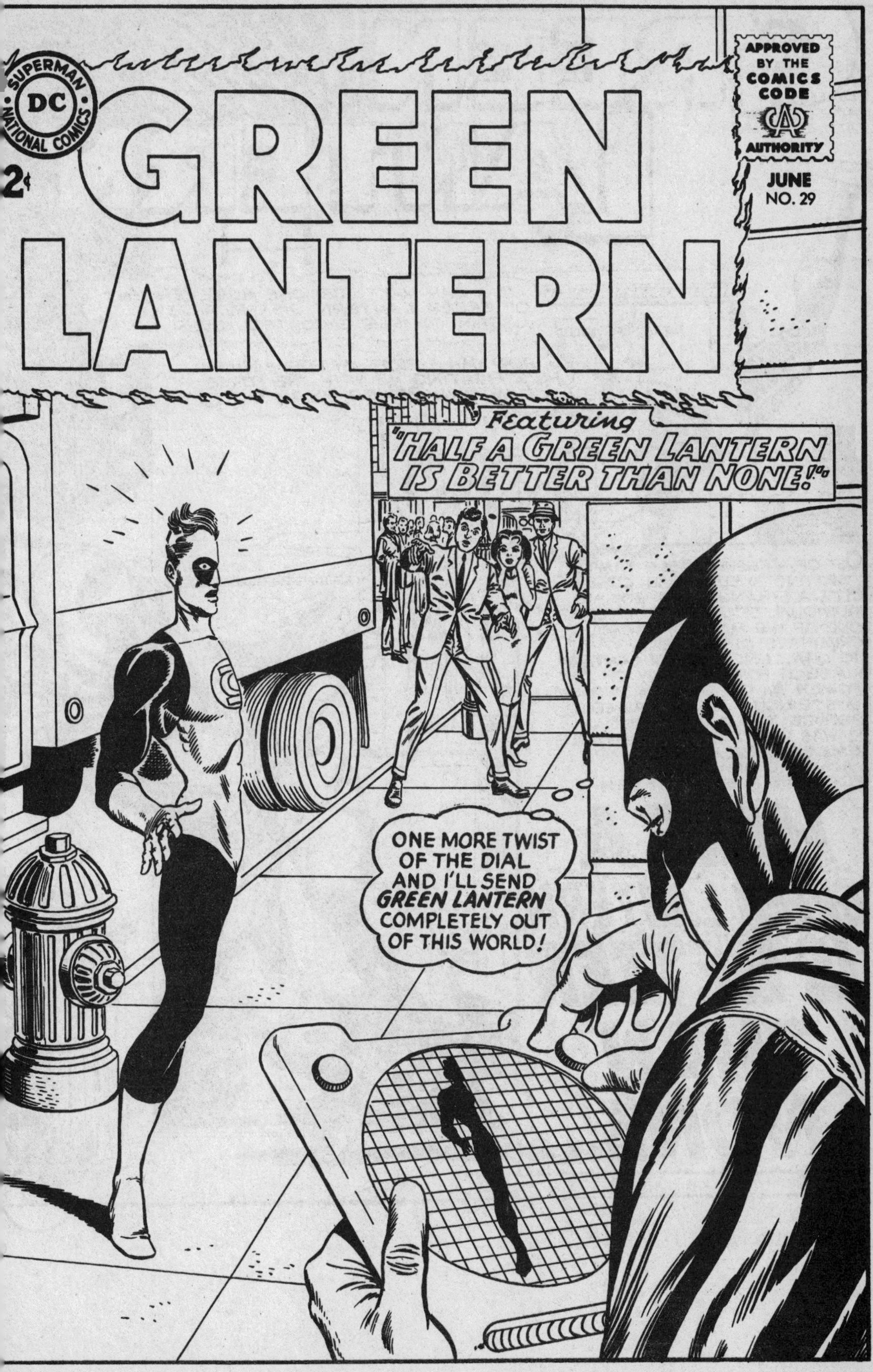
SUPERMAN DC NATIONAL COMICS
12¢
GREEN LANTERN
APPROVED BY THE COMICS CODE AUTHORITY
JUNE
NO. 29
Featuring "HALF A GREEN LANTERN IS BETTER THAN NONE!"
ONE MORE TWIST OF THE DIAL AND I'LL SEND GREEN LANTERN COMPLETELY OUT OF THIS WORLD!

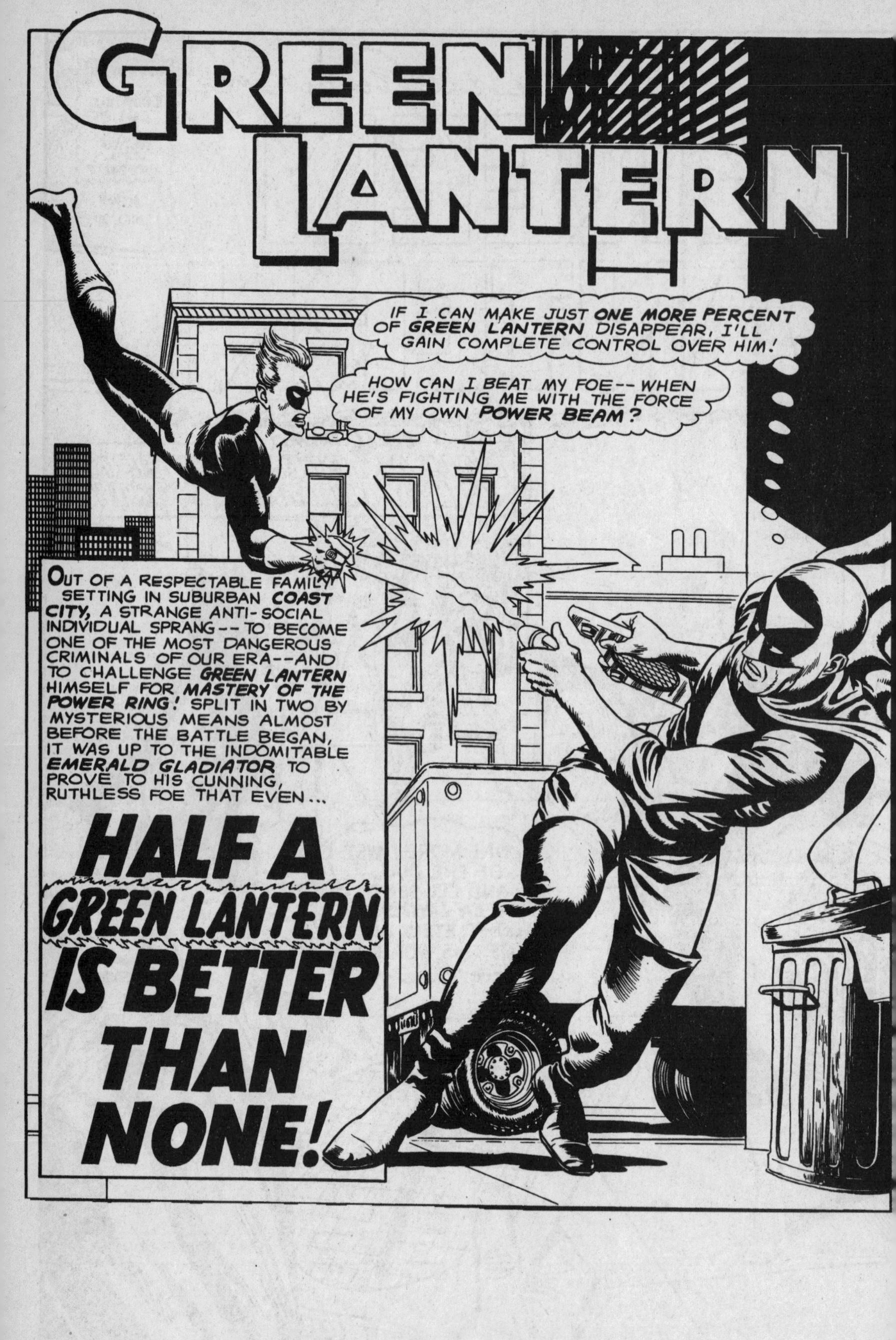

GREEN LANTERN
IF I CAN MAKE JUST ONE MORE PERCENT OF GREEN LANTERN DISAPPEAR, I'LL GAIN COMPLETE CONTROL OVER HIM!
HOW CAN I BEAT MY FOE-- WHEN HE'S FIGHTING ME WITH THE FORCE OF MY OWN POWER BEAM?
OUT OF A RESPECTABLE FAMILY SETTING IN SUBURBAN COAST CITY, A STRANGE ANTI-SOCIAL INDIVIDUAL SPRANG-- TO BECOME ONE OF THE MOST DANGEROUS CRIMINALS OF OUR ERA--AND TO CHALLENGE GREEN LANTERN HIMSELF FOR MASTERY OF THE POWER RING! SPLIT IN TWO BY MYSTERIOUS MEANS ALMOST BEFORE THE BATTLE BEGAN, IT WAS UP TO THE INDOMITABLE EMERALD GLADIATOR TO PROVE TO HIS CUNNING, RUTHLESS FOE THAT EVEN...
HALF A GREEN LANTERN IS BETTER THAN NONE!

A DREARY, RAINY NIGHT IN *COAST CITY*-- WHEN ONLY THE MOST URGENT REASON WOULD COMPEL ANYONE TO GO OUT-- SUCH AS THE OPPORTUNITY FOR A BAND OF CROOKS TO LOOT A FUR-STORAGE HOUSE...

WHAT A TERRIFIC HAUL !

BUT AS THE THIEVES SLIP OUT, A SKIN-TINGLING SIGHT...

GREEN LANTERN-- CHARGING DOWN AT US!

OPEN UP ON HIM, BUNKY! START SHOOTING!

HOT LEAD AND GREEN BEAM DUEL IN BRIEF FURY...

YOU THUGS WON'T NEED THOSE FURS WHERE YOU'RE GOING!

OUR BULLETS-- IT'S AS IF THEY'RE BEING *BLOWN* ASIDE!

IT WILL BE *HOT ENOUGH* FOR YOU IN THE *COAST CITY JAIL!*

WELL...IT WAS *ALMOST* A TERRIFIC HAUL !

THE ACTORS OF THE DRAMA DISAPPEAR. THERE IS SILENCE IN THE NIGHT. THE WAREHOUSE YARD IS EMPTY...OR IS IT...

SUDDENLY A FIGURE EMERGES, AND MYSTERIOUSLY...

I'VE GOT IT!

SSSSSSS

BIZARRE? WHAT CAN THE MAN BE UP TO ?

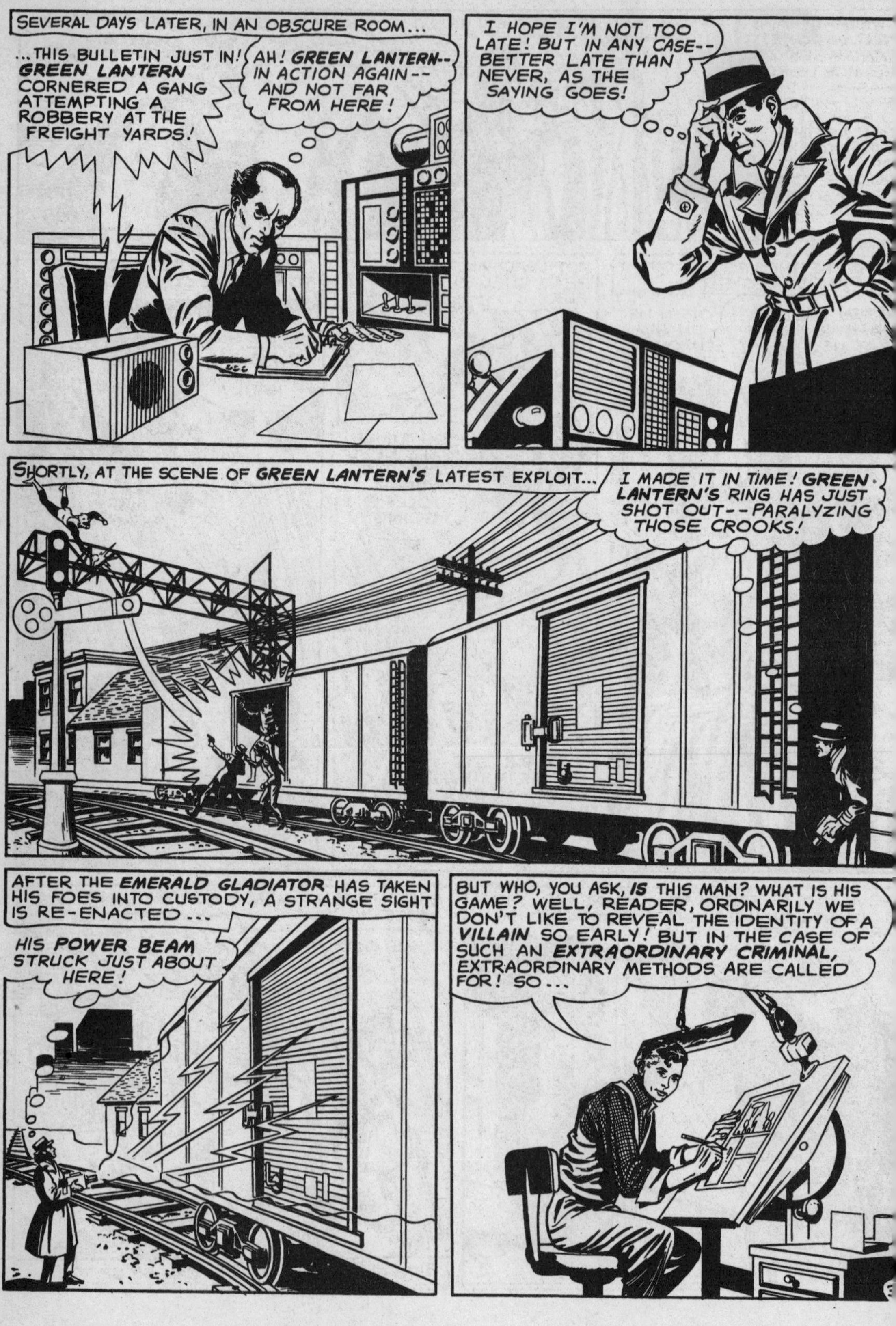
SEVERAL DAYS LATER, IN AN OBSCURE ROOM...
...THIS BULLETIN JUST IN! GREEN LANTERN CORNERED A GANG ATTEMPTING A ROBBERY AT THE FREIGHT YARDS!
AH! GREEN LANTERN-- IN ACTION AGAIN-- AND NOT FAR FROM HERE!
I HOPE I'M NOT TOO LATE! BUT IN ANY CASE-- BETTER LATE THAN NEVER, AS THE SAYING GOES!
SHORTLY, AT THE SCENE OF GREEN LANTERN'S LATEST EXPLOIT...
I MADE IT IN TIME! GREEN LANTERN'S RING HAS JUST SHOT OUT--PARALYZING THOSE CROOKS!
AFTER THE EMERALD GLADIATOR HAS TAKEN HIS FOES INTO CUSTODY, A STRANGE SIGHT IS RE-ENACTED...
HIS POWER BEAM STRUCK JUST ABOUT HERE!
BUT WHO, YOU ASK, IS THIS MAN? WHAT IS HIS GAME? WELL, READER, ORDINARILY WE DON'T LIKE TO REVEAL THE IDENTITY OF A VILLAIN SO EARLY! BUT IN THE CASE OF SUCH AN EXTRAORDINARY CRIMINAL, EXTRAORDINARY METHODS ARE CALLED FOR! SO...

...MEET WILLIAM HAND!!

HELLO! CURIOUS ABOUT ME, EH? WELL, LET ME TELL YOU... YOU'RE LOOKING AT THE MAN DESTINED TO *DEFEAT GREEN LANTERN!* WHAT?-- YOU DOUBT MY WORD? YOU DON'T BELIEVE ME? LISTEN, IT'S SIMPLE AS ABC...

YOU SEE, I DISCOVERED THAT EVERY TIME *GREEN LANTERN* USES HIS *POWER RING,* A CERTAIN AMOUNT OF *GREEN BEAM RADIATION* IS *ABSORBED* BY OBJECTS IN THE IMMEDIATE AREA OF THE ACTION! WITH THIS DEVICE I INVENTED, I COLLECT THAT RADIATION!

WANT TO KNOW WHY, EH? WELL, TO EXPLAIN I'LL HAVE TO GO BACK, TELL YOU ABOUT MYSELF! BUT I DON'T MIND! I'VE GOT TIME--AND *GREEN LANTERN* CAN'T ESCAPE! HA HA! TO BEGIN, I GUESS I'VE *ALWAYS* BEEN WHAT IS VULGARLY CALLED A *CROOK*...

MAYBE THE REASON IS THAT MY FAMILY-- THE RENOWNED *HAND FAMILY* OF NEARBY *COASTVILLE*-- WAS ALWAYS SO RESPECTABLE! AND I HATE THEM ALL! I *HAD* TO BE DIFFERENT! CRIME WAS MY WAY OF DOING IT! I STARTED WITH THE USUAL THINGS...

...SECOND-STORY WORK, POCKET-PICKING! BUT EVEN THEN I WAS METHODICAL! EVERYTHING I LEARNED I PUT DOWN IN THIS BOOK! THROUGH THE YEARS I'VE ACCUMULATED THE *ANSWERS* HERE TO *EVERY* SITUATION A CROOK CAN GET INTO! *THAT'S* WHERE I'M DIFFERENT FROM OTHER CRIMINALS!

WHEN *I'M* IN A TIGHT SPOT--IF THE POLICE APPEAR, SAY, WHILE I'M CRACKING A SAFE-- ALL I DO IS REFER MENTALLY TO THE PAGE OF THIS BOOK-- WHICH I HAVE COMPLETELY MEMORIZED--AND I KNOW HOW TO GET AWAY! IT'S NEVER FAILED ME!

4

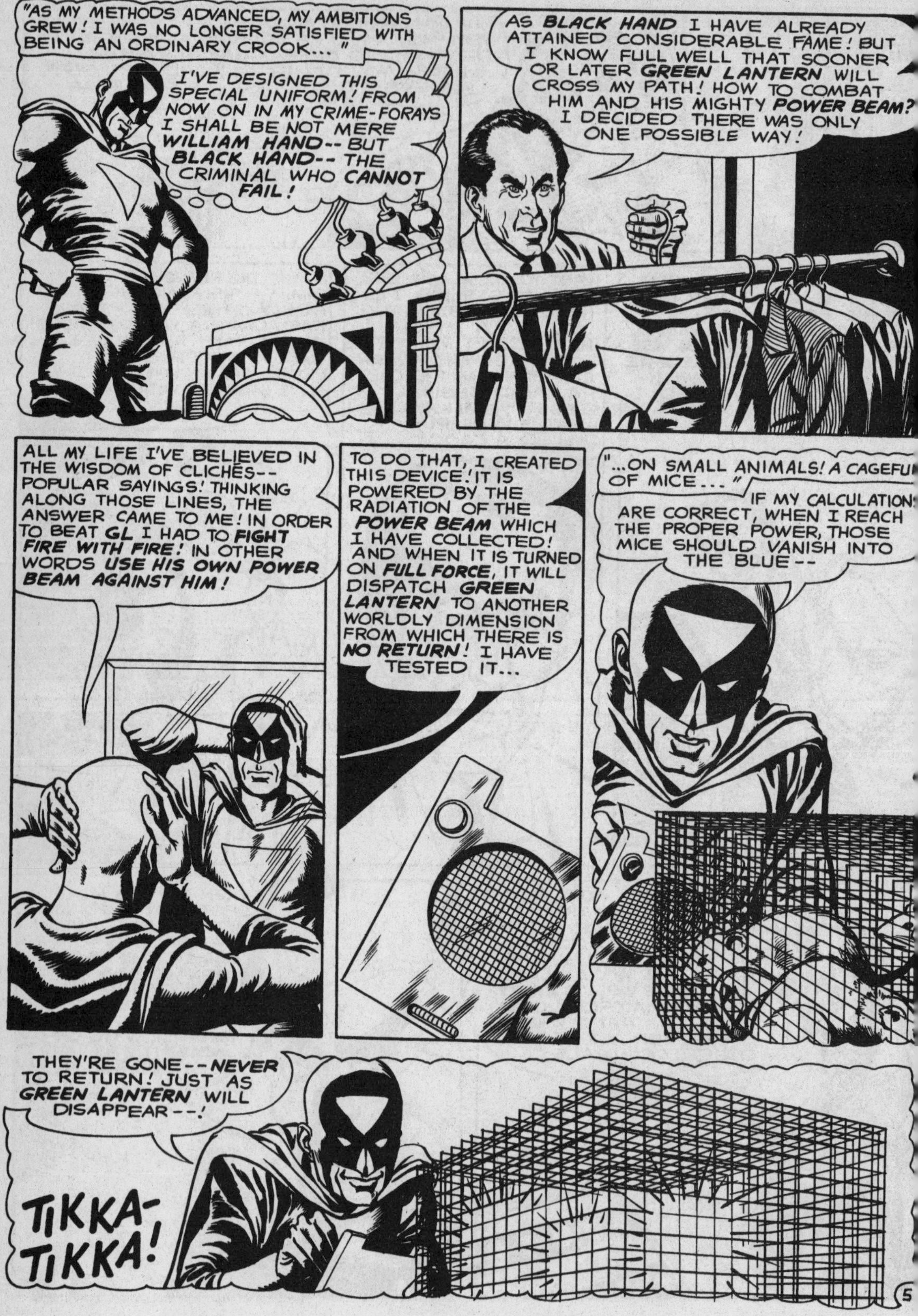
"AS MY METHODS ADVANCED, MY AMBITIONS GREW! I WAS NO LONGER SATISFIED WITH BEING AN ORDINARY CROOK..."
I'VE DESIGNED THIS SPECIAL UNIFORM! FROM NOW ON IN MY CRIME-FORAYS I SHALL BE NOT MERE WILLIAM HAND-- BUT BLACK HAND-- THE CRIMINAL WHO CANNOT FAIL!
AS BLACK HAND I HAVE ALREADY ATTAINED CONSIDERABLE FAME! BUT I KNOW FULL WELL THAT SOONER OR LATER GREEN LANTERN WILL CROSS MY PATH! HOW TO COMBAT HIM AND HIS MIGHTY POWER BEAM? I DECIDED THERE WAS ONLY ONE POSSIBLE WAY!
ALL MY LIFE I'VE BELIEVED IN THE WISDOM OF CLICHÉS-- POPULAR SAYINGS! THINKING ALONG THOSE LINES, THE ANSWER CAME TO ME! IN ORDER TO BEAT GL I HAD TO FIGHT FIRE WITH FIRE! IN OTHER WORDS USE HIS OWN POWER BEAM AGAINST HIM!
TO DO THAT, I CREATED THIS DEVICE! IT IS POWERED BY THE RADIATION OF THE POWER BEAM WHICH I HAVE COLLECTED! AND WHEN IT IS TURNED ON FULL FORCE, IT WILL DISPATCH GREEN LANTERN TO ANOTHER WORLDLY DIMENSION FROM WHICH THERE IS NO RETURN! I HAVE TESTED IT...
"...ON SMALL ANIMALS! A CAGEFUL OF MICE..."
IF MY CALCULATIONS ARE CORRECT, WHEN I REACH THE PROPER POWER, THOSE MICE SHOULD VANISH INTO THE BLUE--
THEY'RE GONE--NEVER TO RETURN! JUST AS GREEN LANTERN WILL DISAPPEAR--!
TIKKA-TIKKA!
5

BUT I HAVEN'T REVEALED THE *BEST PART!* MY CALCULATIONS SHOW THAT AFTER I HAVE SENT *GL* INTO THIS OTHER DIMENSION, *I* WILL BE ABLE TO *TAP HIS RING POWER*-- PLUS HIS *TREMENDOUS POWER OF CONCENTRATION*-- FROM HERE ON EARTH! IN OTHER WORDS...

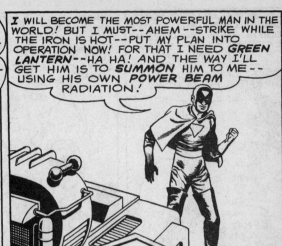

I WILL BECOME THE MOST POWERFUL MAN IN THE WORLD! BUT I MUST--AHEM--STRIKE WHILE THE IRON IS HOT--PUT MY PLAN INTO OPERATION NOW! FOR THAT I NEED *GREEN LANTERN*--HA HA! AND THE WAY I'LL GET HIM IS TO *SUMMON* HIM TO ME-- USING HIS OWN *POWER BEAM* RADIATION.'

MEANWHILE, AT THIS VERY MOMENT, IN HAL *(GREEN LANTERN)* JORDAN'S DRESSING ROOM AT THE *FERRIS AIRCRAFT COMPANY...*

YOU SAY YOU'RE *NOT* SATISFIED WITH YOUR EXPLOITS RECENTLY? GOSH, YOU'VE CORRALLED ONE CROOK GANG AFTER ANOTHER--

TRUE, *PIEFACE,* BUT WHAT YOU DON'T REALIZE...

IS THAT EACH TIME I CAME IN CONTACT WITH A GANG I WAS ACTUALLY ON THE HUNT FOR SOMEONE ELSE-- FOR THE FANTASTIC NEW *COSTUMED CROOK* KNOWN AS *BLACK HAND!* HOWEVER, I'M NOT GIVING UP! AS SOON AS I RECHARGE MY RING, I'M GOING TO RESUME MY SEARCH!

IN THE SECRECY OF THE LOCKED ROOM, A SOLEMN OATH IS TAKEN AS SO MANY TIMES BEFORE...

IN BRIGHTEST DAY, IN BLACKEST NIGHT, NO EVIL SHALL ESCAPE MY SIGHT! LET THOSE WHO WORSHIP EVIL'S MIGHT BEWARE MY POWER-- *GREEN LANTERN'S LIGHT!*

THEN... JUMPING FISH-HOOKS!

SOMETHING... COMING FROM MY RING !?

6

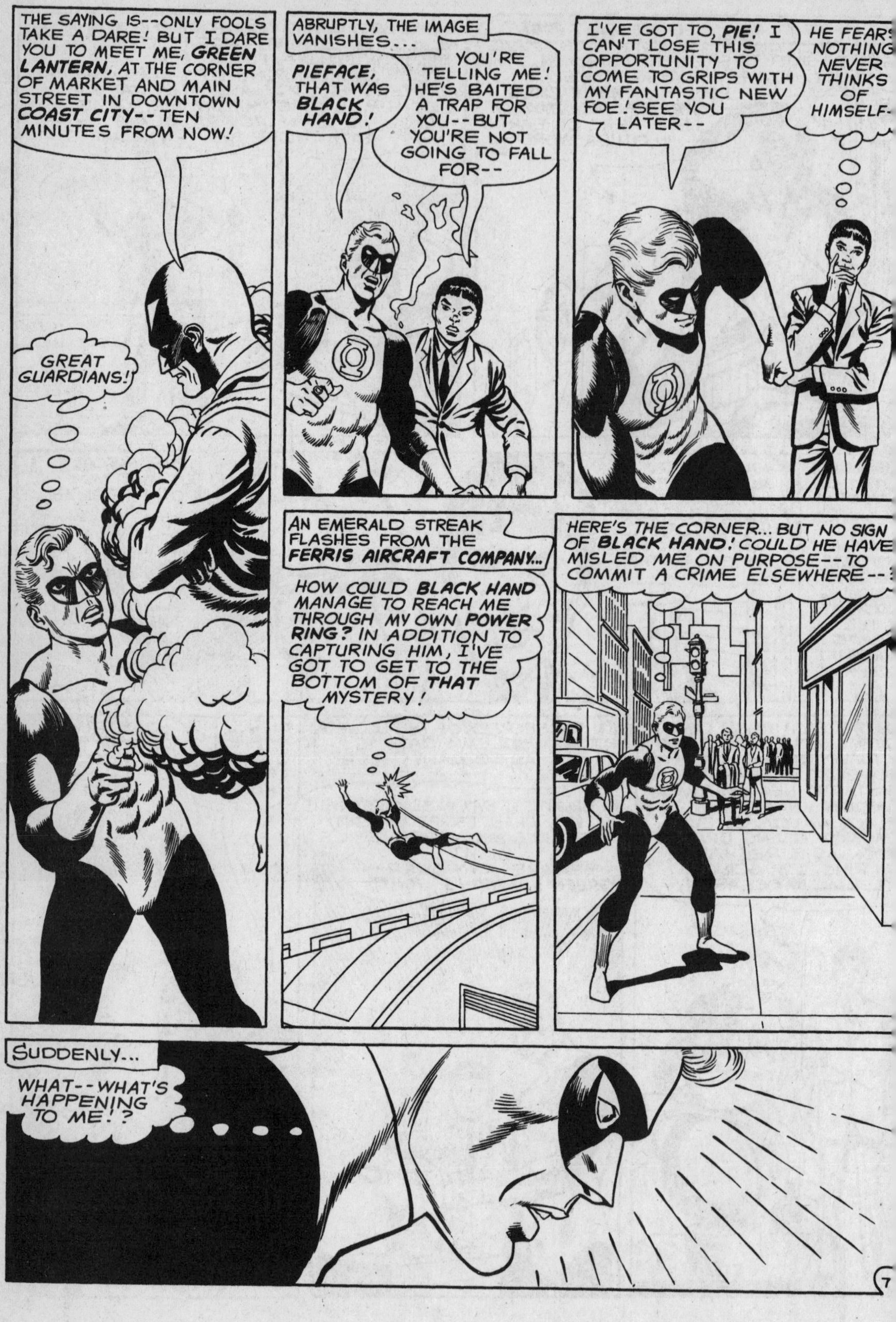
THE SAYING IS--ONLY FOOLS TAKE A DARE! BUT I DARE YOU TO MEET ME, GREEN LANTERN, AT THE CORNER OF MARKET AND MAIN STREET IN DOWNTOWN COAST CITY--TEN MINUTES FROM NOW!
GREAT GUARDIANS!
ABRUPTLY, THE IMAGE VANISHES...
PIEFACE, THAT WAS BLACK HAND!
YOU'RE TELLING ME! HE'S BAITED A TRAP FOR YOU--BUT YOU'RE NOT GOING TO FALL FOR--
I'VE GOT TO, PIE! I CAN'T LOSE THIS OPPORTUNITY TO COME TO GRIPS WITH MY FANTASTIC NEW FOE! SEE YOU LATER--
HE FEARS NOTHING NEVER THINKS OF HIMSELF-
AN EMERALD STREAK FLASHES FROM THE FERRIS AIRCRAFT COMPANY...
HOW COULD BLACK HAND MANAGE TO REACH ME THROUGH MY OWN POWER RING? IN ADDITION TO CAPTURING HIM, I'VE GOT TO GET TO THE BOTTOM OF THAT MYSTERY!
HERE'S THE CORNER... BUT NO SIGN OF BLACK HAND! COULD HE HAVE MISLED ME ON PURPOSE--TO COMMIT A CRIME ELSEWHERE--?
SUDDENLY...
WHAT--WHAT'S HAPPENING TO ME!?
7

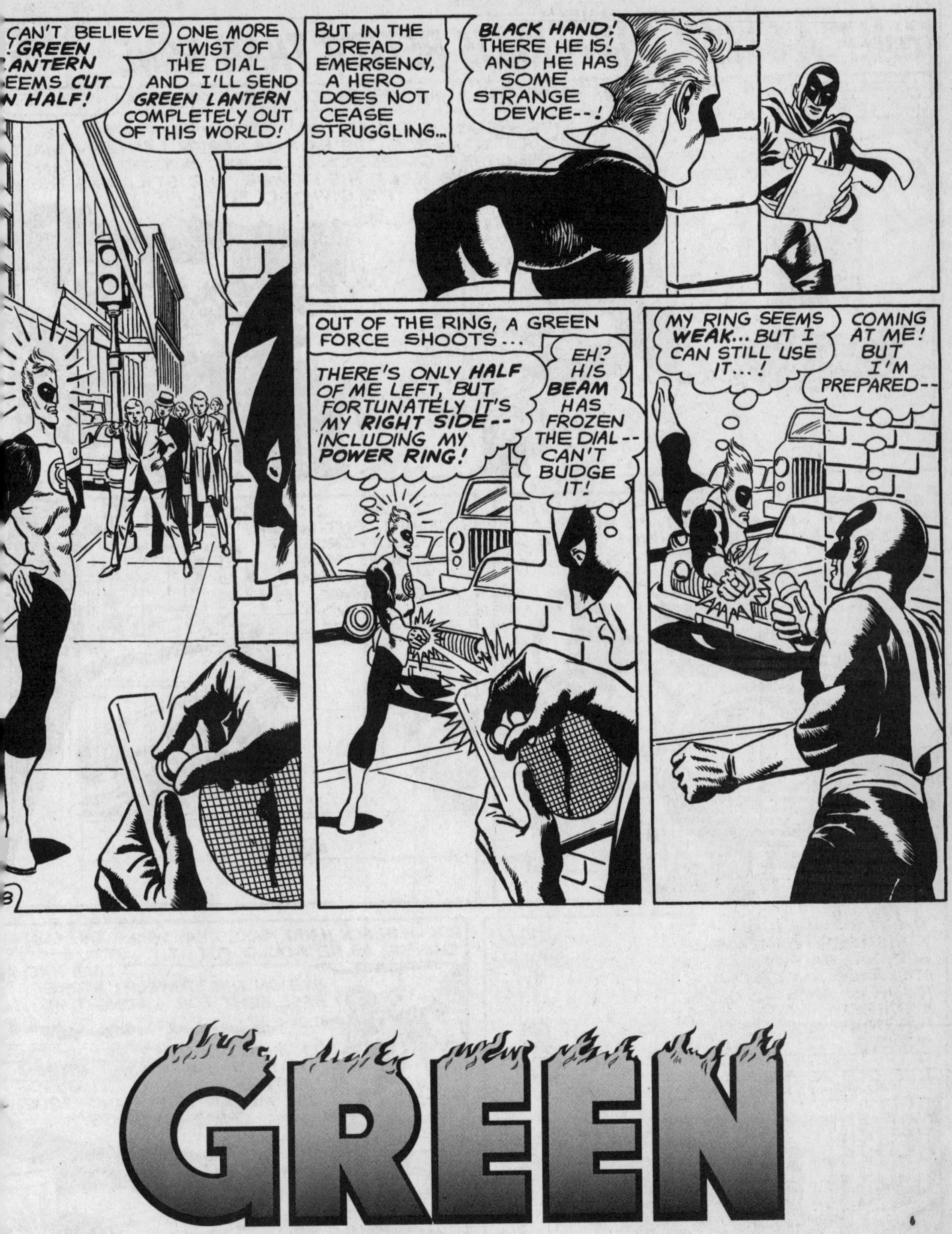
CAN'T BELIEVE GREEN ANTERN EEMS CUT N HALF!
ONE MORE TWIST OF THE DIAL AND I'LL SEND GREEN LANTERN COMPLETELY OUT OF THIS WORLD!
BUT IN THE DREAD EMERGENCY, A HERO DOES NOT CEASE STRUGGLING...
BLACK HAND! THERE HE IS! AND HE HAS SOME STRANGE DEVICE--!
OUT OF THE RING, A GREEN FORCE SHOOTS...
THERE'S ONLY HALF OF ME LEFT, BUT FORTUNATELY IT'S MY RIGHT SIDE--INCLUDING MY POWER RING!
EH? HIS BEAM HAS FROZEN THE DIAL--CAN'T BUDGE IT!
MY RING SEEMS WEAK... BUT I CAN STILL USE IT...!
COMING AT ME! BUT I'M PREPARED--

GREEN LANTERN

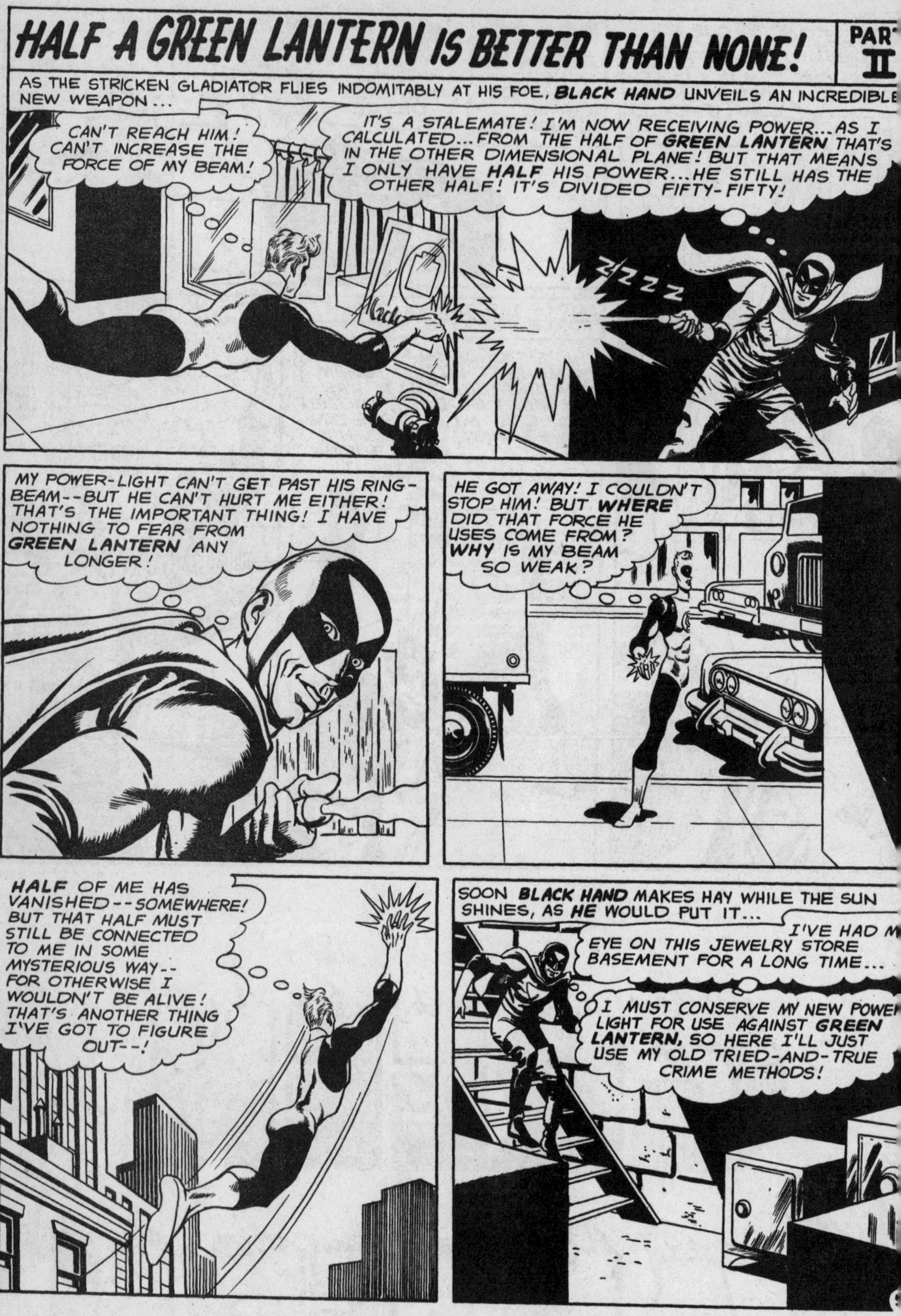
HALF A GREEN LANTERN IS BETTER THAN NONE!
PART II
AS THE STRICKEN GLADIATOR FLIES INDOMITABLY AT HIS FOE, BLACK HAND UNVEILS AN INCREDIBLE NEW WEAPON...
CAN'T REACH HIM! CAN'T INCREASE THE FORCE OF MY BEAM!
IT'S A STALEMATE! I'M NOW RECEIVING POWER...AS I CALCULATED...FROM THE HALF OF GREEN LANTERN THAT'S IN THE OTHER DIMENSIONAL PLANE! BUT THAT MEANS I ONLY HAVE HALF HIS POWER...HE STILL HAS THE OTHER HALF! IT'S DIVIDED FIFTY-FIFTY!
ZZZZ
MY POWER-LIGHT CAN'T GET PAST HIS RING-BEAM--BUT HE CAN'T HURT ME EITHER! THAT'S THE IMPORTANT THING! I HAVE NOTHING TO FEAR FROM GREEN LANTERN ANY LONGER!
HE GOT AWAY! I COULDN'T STOP HIM! BUT WHERE DID THAT FORCE HE USES COME FROM? WHY IS MY BEAM SO WEAK?
HALF OF ME HAS VANISHED--SOMEWHERE! BUT THAT HALF MUST STILL BE CONNECTED TO ME IN SOME MYSTERIOUS WAY--FOR OTHERWISE I WOULDN'T BE ALIVE! THAT'S ANOTHER THING I'VE GOT TO FIGURE OUT--!
SOON BLACK HAND MAKES HAY WHILE THE SUN SHINES, AS HE WOULD PUT IT...
I'VE HAD M EYE ON THIS JEWELRY STORE BASEMENT FOR A LONG TIME...
I MUST CONSERVE MY NEW POWE LIGHT FOR USE AGAINST GREEN LANTERN, SO HERE I'LL JUST USE MY OLD TRIED-AND-TRUE CRIME METHODS!

H-OH! I'VE BLOWN A LIGHT-FUSE IN DISCONNECTING THE BURGLAR ALARM! BUT SO WHAT? NO NEED TO PANIC! SUCH A SITUATION IS TAKEN CARE OF ON PAGE 83 OF MY BOOK...

IN **BLACK HAND'S** MEMORY, THE PAGE FLASHES INTO VIEW...

...In case of need a penny can be used for an **emergency** fuse!

A PENNY! I ALWAYS CARRY ONE IN MY POCKET--"A PENNY SAVED IS A PENNY EARNED"!

AS THE LIGHTS GO ON...

SOMETHING LIKE THIS WOULD HAVE STYMIED AN ORDINARY CRIMINAL! BUT NOT ME! BEING PREPARED IN ADVANCE-- THAT'S WHAT MAKES ALL THE DIFFERENCE!

AS THE COSTUMED CROOK COMES OUT OF THE BASEMENT...

GREEN LANTERN!

I FIGURED MY RING WAS ACTING STRANGELY! IT LED ME HERE TO **BLACK HAND**--HE'S LOOTED THAT JEWELRY ESTABLISHMENT!

THUS BEGINS A SERIES OF FANTASTIC DUELS...

MY BEAM IS WEAK... BUT I'VE GOT TO **WILL** IT TO BE STRONG!

IF I CAN MAKE JUST **ONE** MORE PERCENT OF **GREEN LANTERN** DISAPPEAR, I'LL HAVE FIFTY-ONE PERCENT OF THE POWER! THAT WILL GIVE ME **CONTROL**!

THERE MUST BE A WAY OF DEFEATING HIM! BUT HOW-- HOW?!

10

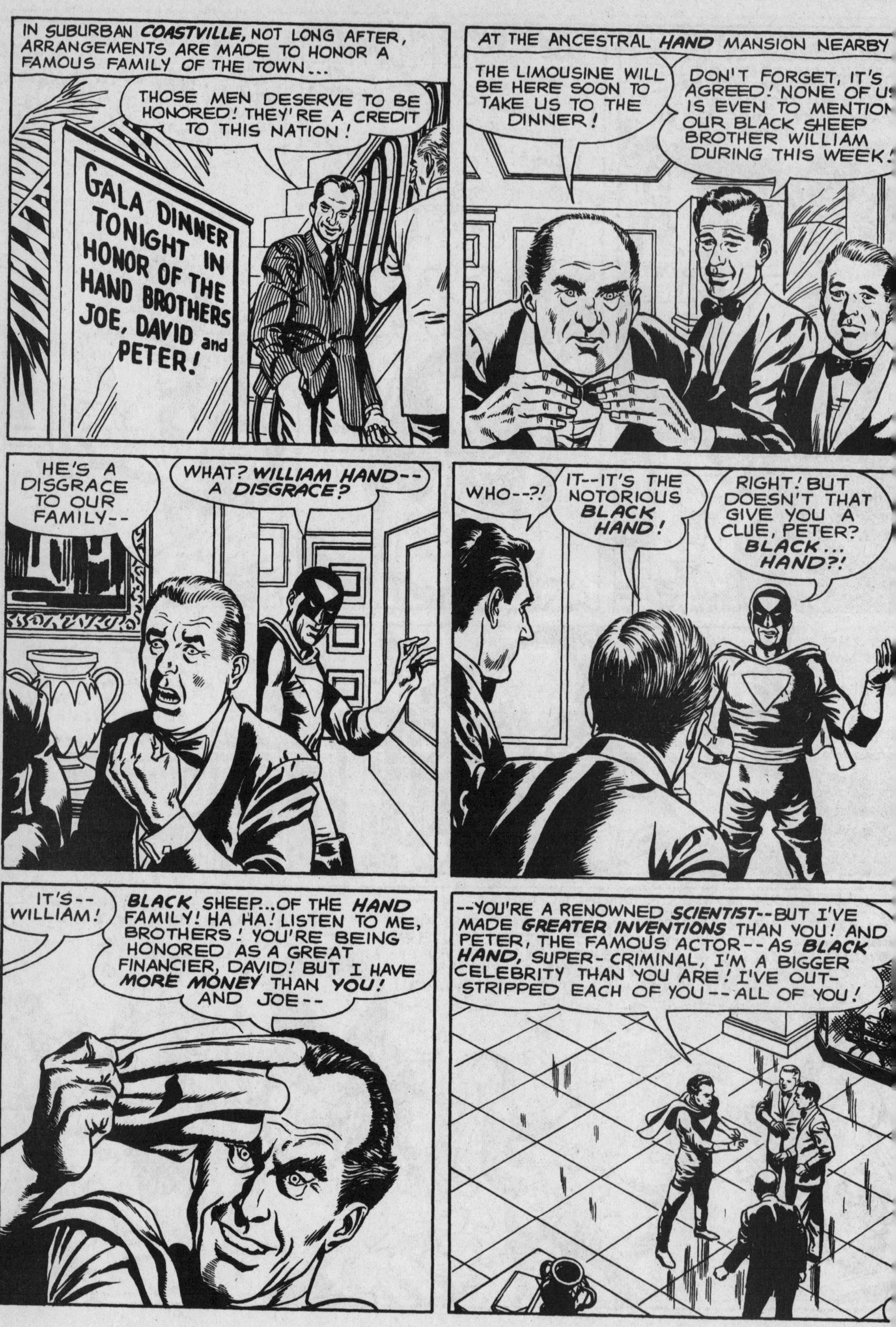
IN SUBURBAN COASTVILLE, NOT LONG AFTER, ARRANGEMENTS ARE MADE TO HONOR A FAMOUS FAMILY OF THE TOWN...
THOSE MEN DESERVE TO BE HONORED! THEY'RE A CREDIT TO THIS NATION!
GALA DINNER TONIGHT IN HONOR OF THE HAND BROTHERS JOE, DAVID and PETER!
AT THE ANCESTRAL HAND MANSION NEARBY
THE LIMOUSINE WILL BE HERE SOON TO TAKE US TO THE DINNER!
DON'T FORGET, IT'S AGREED! NONE OF U IS EVEN TO MENTION OUR BLACK SHEEP BROTHER WILLIAM DURING THIS WEEK!
HE'S A DISGRACE TO OUR FAMILY--
WHAT? WILLIAM HAND-- A DISGRACE?
WHO--?!
IT--IT'S THE NOTORIOUS BLACK HAND!
RIGHT! BUT DOESN'T THAT GIVE YOU A CLUE, PETER? BLACK... HAND?!
IT'S-- WILLIAM!
BLACK SHEEP...OF THE HAND FAMILY! HA HA! LISTEN TO ME, BROTHERS! YOU'RE BEING HONORED AS A GREAT FINANCIER, DAVID! BUT I HAVE MORE MONEY THAN YOU! AND JOE--
--YOU'RE A RENOWNED SCIENTIST--BUT I'VE MADE GREATER INVENTIONS THAN YOU! AND PETER, THE FAMOUS ACTOR--AS BLACK HAND, SUPER-CRIMINAL, I'M A BIGGER CELEBRITY THAN YOU ARE! I'VE OUT-STRIPPED EACH OF YOU--ALL OF YOU!

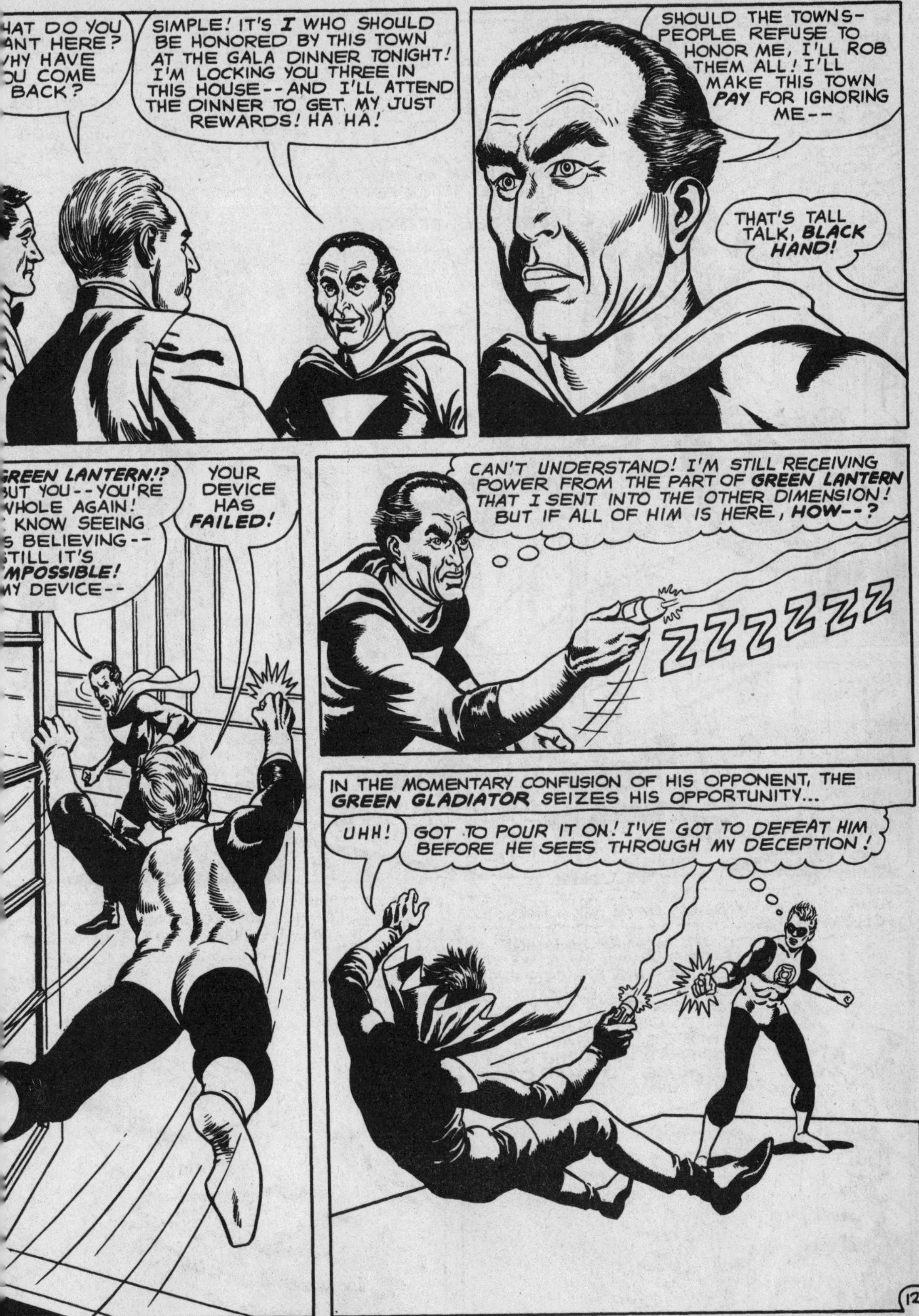

HAT DO YOU ANT HERE? HY HAVE OU COME BACK?
SIMPLE! IT'S I WHO SHOULD BE HONORED BY THIS TOWN AT THE GALA DINNER TONIGHT! I'M LOCKING YOU THREE IN THIS HOUSE--AND I'LL ATTEND THE DINNER TO GET MY JUST REWARDS! HA HA!
SHOULD THE TOWNSPEOPLE REFUSE TO HONOR ME, I'LL ROB THEM ALL! I'LL MAKE THIS TOWN PAY FOR IGNORING ME--
THAT'S TALL TALK, BLACK HAND!
GREEN LANTERN!? BUT YOU--YOU'RE WHOLE AGAIN! KNOW SEEING S BELIEVING--STILL IT'S MPOSSIBLE! MY DEVICE--
YOUR DEVICE HAS FAILED!
CAN'T UNDERSTAND! I'M STILL RECEIVING POWER FROM THE PART OF GREEN LANTERN THAT I SENT INTO THE OTHER DIMENSION! BUT IF ALL OF HIM IS HERE, HOW--?
ZZZZZZ
IN THE MOMENTARY CONFUSION OF HIS OPPONENT, THE GREEN GLADIATOR SEIZES HIS OPPORTUNITY...
UHH!
GOT TO POUR IT ON! I'VE GOT TO DEFEAT HIM BEFORE HE SEES THROUGH MY DECEPTION!
12

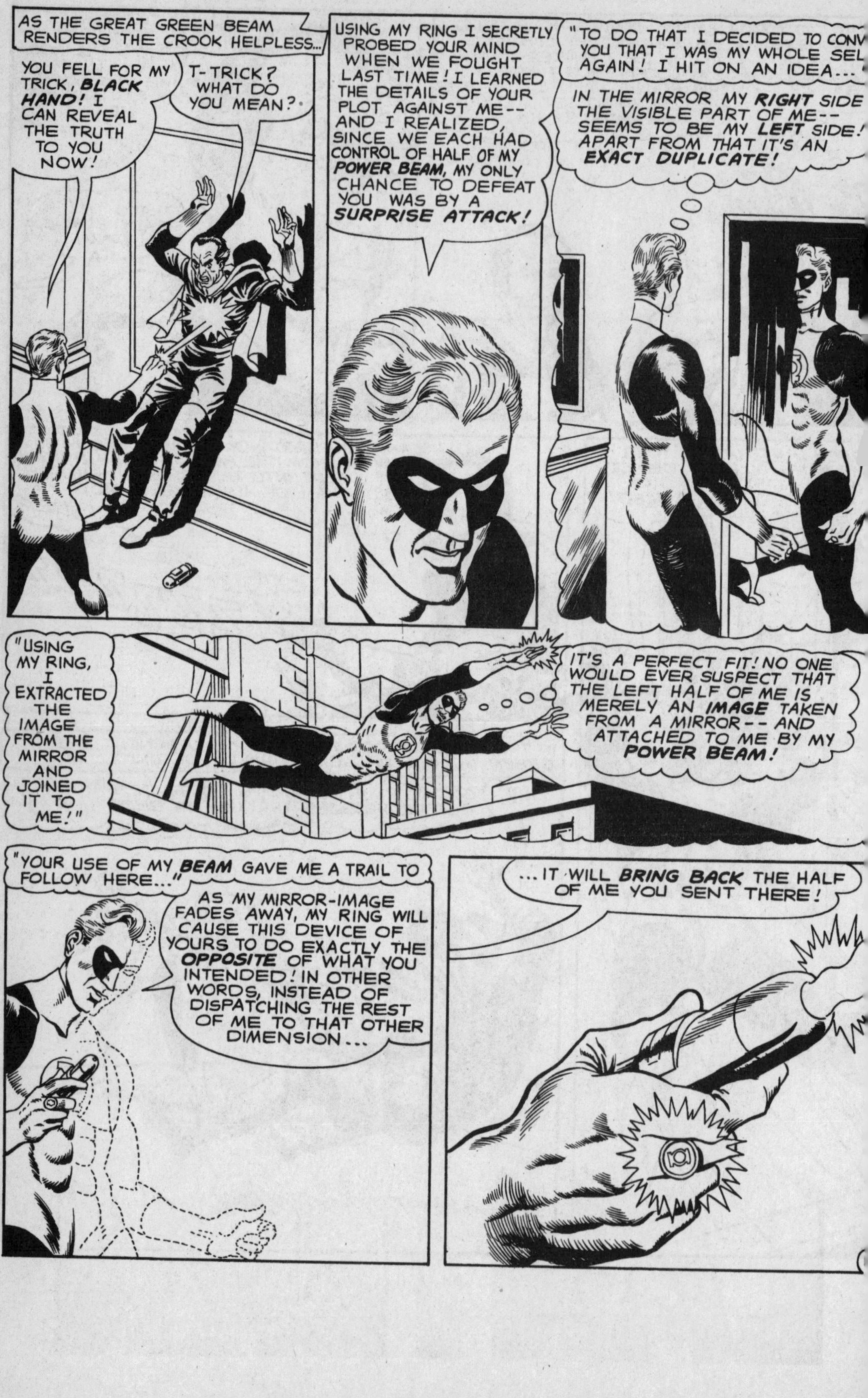
AS THE GREAT GREEN BEAM RENDERS THE CROOK HELPLESS...
YOU FELL FOR MY TRICK, BLACK HAND! I CAN REVEAL THE TRUTH TO YOU NOW!
T-TRICK? WHAT DO YOU MEAN?
USING MY RING I SECRETLY PROBED YOUR MIND WHEN WE FOUGHT LAST TIME! I LEARNED THE DETAILS OF YOUR PLOT AGAINST ME--AND I REALIZED, SINCE WE EACH HAD CONTROL OF HALF OF MY POWER BEAM, MY ONLY CHANCE TO DEFEAT YOU WAS BY A SURPRISE ATTACK!
"TO DO THAT I DECIDED TO CONV YOU THAT I WAS MY WHOLE SEL AGAIN! I HIT ON AN IDEA...
IN THE MIRROR MY RIGHT SIDE THE VISIBLE PART OF ME--SEEMS TO BE MY LEFT SIDE! APART FROM THAT IT'S AN EXACT DUPLICATE!
"USING MY RING, I EXTRACTED THE IMAGE FROM THE MIRROR AND JOINED IT TO ME!"
IT'S A PERFECT FIT! NO ONE WOULD EVER SUSPECT THAT THE LEFT HALF OF ME IS MERELY AN IMAGE TAKEN FROM A MIRROR--AND ATTACHED TO ME BY MY POWER BEAM!
"YOUR USE OF MY BEAM GAVE ME A TRAIL TO FOLLOW HERE..."
AS MY MIRROR-IMAGE FADES AWAY, MY RING WILL CAUSE THIS DEVICE OF YOURS TO DO EXACTLY THE OPPOSITE OF WHAT YOU INTENDED! IN OTHER WORDS, INSTEAD OF DISPATCHING THE REST OF ME TO THAT OTHER DIMENSION...
...IT WILL BRING BACK THE HALF OF ME YOU SENT THERE!

THE LEFT HALF OF ME... MATERIALIZING...

...SOLIDIFYING...

AT LAST! I'M RESTORED TO MYSELF! I'M WHOLE AGAIN!

AS GREEN LANTERN FLIES OFF WITH HIS PRISONER TO POLICE HEADQUARTERS...

YOU THINK YOU'VE WON! BUT HE WHO LAUGHS LAST, LAUGHS BEST, *GREEN LANTERN!* I'LL FIND A WAY TO BEAT YOU YET--

I DOUBT IT! I'VE NOTICED YOUR FONDNESS FOR CLICHÉS...

...SO HERE'S A SWITCH ON AN OLD PROVERB THAT SHOULD GIVE YOU SOMETHING TO THINK ABOUT, *BLACK HAND!* DESPITE YOUR BEST-LAID PLANS, I'VE SHOWN YOU THAT-- *HALF OF GREEN LANTERN IS BETTER THAN NONE!*

BAH!

The End.

GREEN LANTERN

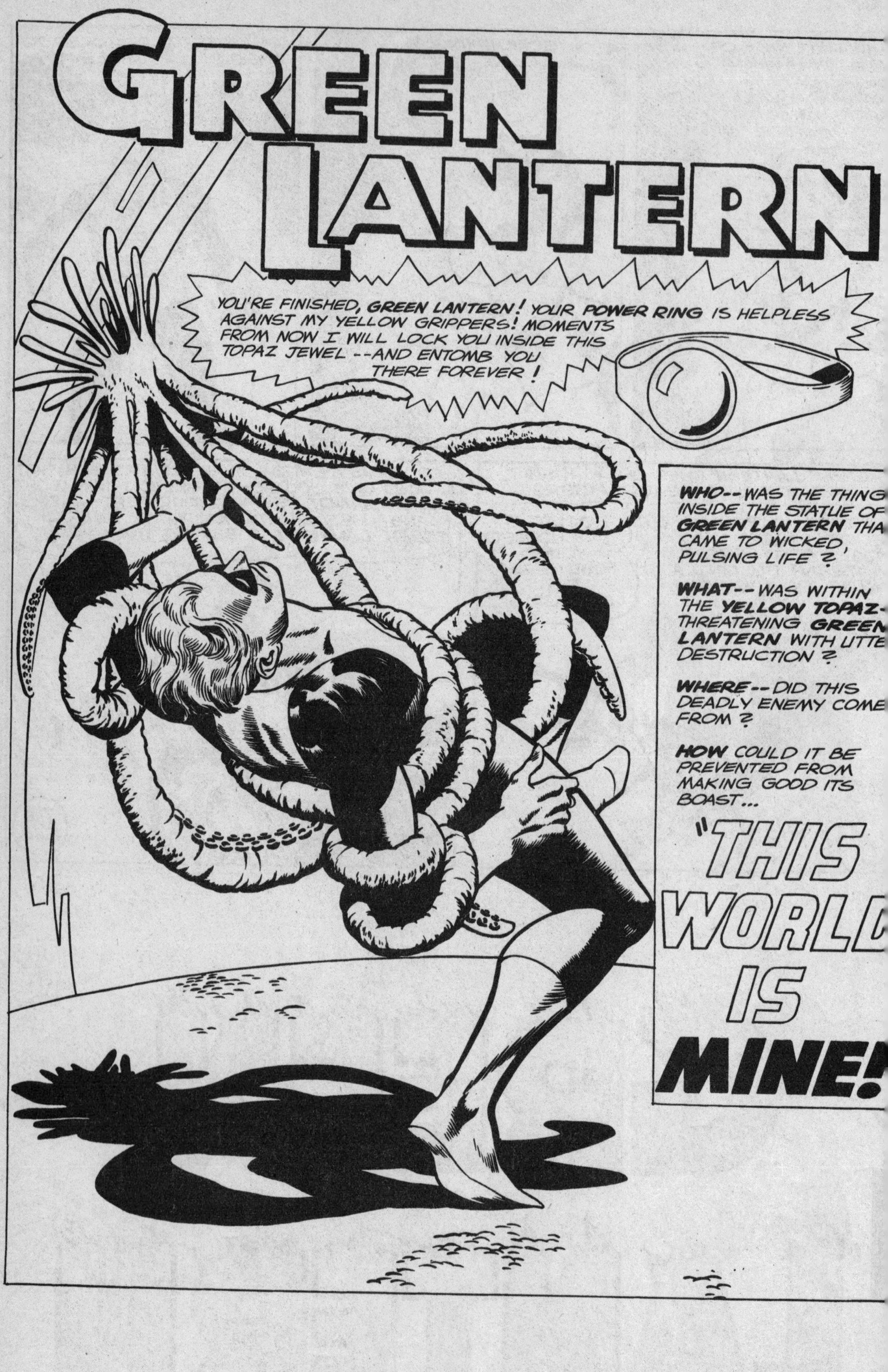
GREEN LANTERN
YOU'RE FINISHED, GREEN LANTERN! YOUR POWER RING IS HELPLESS AGAINST MY YELLOW GRIPPERS! MOMENTS FROM NOW I WILL LOCK YOU INSIDE THIS TOPAZ JEWEL --AND ENTOMB YOU THERE FOREVER!
WHO--WAS THE THING INSIDE THE STATUE OF GREEN LANTERN THA CAME TO WICKED, PULSING LIFE?
WHAT--WAS WITHIN THE YELLOW TOPAZ-THREATENING GREEN LANTERN WITH UTTE DESTRUCTION?
WHERE--DID THIS DEADLY ENEMY COME FROM?
HOW COULD IT BE PREVENTED FROM MAKING GOOD ITS BOAST...
"THIS WORLD IS MINE!

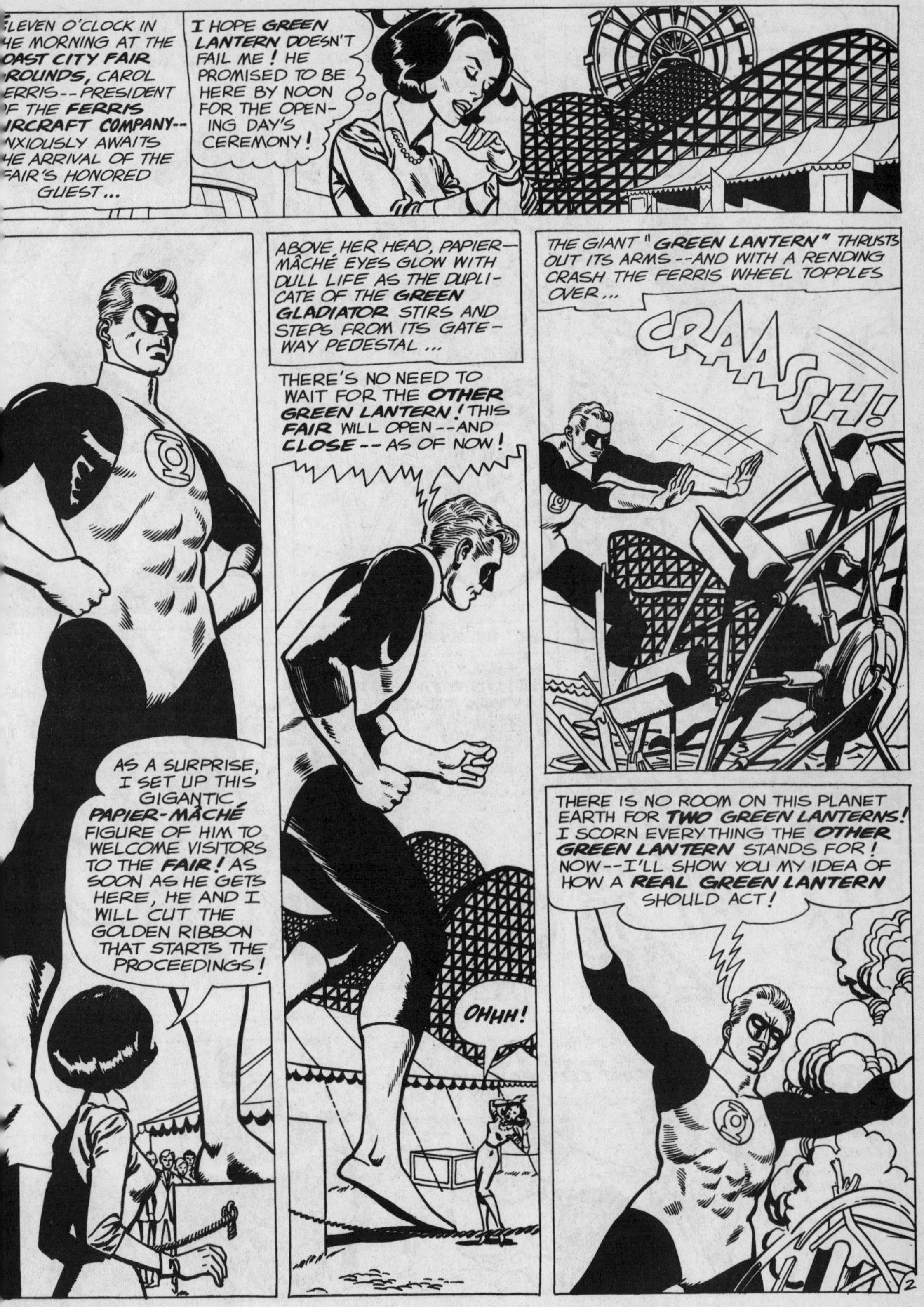
ELEVEN O'CLOCK IN THE MORNING AT THE COAST CITY FAIR GROUNDS, CAROL FERRIS--PRESIDENT OF THE FERRIS AIRCRAFT COMPANY--ANXIOUSLY AWAITS THE ARRIVAL OF THE FAIR'S HONORED GUEST...
I HOPE GREEN LANTERN DOESN'T FAIL ME! HE PROMISED TO BE HERE BY NOON FOR THE OPENING DAY'S CEREMONY!
AS A SURPRISE, I SET UP THIS GIGANTIC PAPIER-MÂCHÉ FIGURE OF HIM TO WELCOME VISITORS TO THE FAIR! AS SOON AS HE GETS HERE, HE AND I WILL CUT THE GOLDEN RIBBON THAT STARTS THE PROCEEDINGS!
ABOVE HER HEAD, PAPIER-MÂCHÉ EYES GLOW WITH DULL LIFE AS THE DUPLICATE OF THE GREEN GLADIATOR STIRS AND STEPS FROM ITS GATEWAY PEDESTAL...
THERE'S NO NEED TO WAIT FOR THE OTHER GREEN LANTERN! THIS FAIR WILL OPEN--AND CLOSE--AS OF NOW!
OHHH!
THE GIANT "GREEN LANTERN" THRUSTS OUT ITS ARMS--AND WITH A RENDING CRASH THE FERRIS WHEEL TOPPLES OVER...
CRAASSH!
THERE IS NO ROOM ON THIS PLANET EARTH FOR TWO GREEN LANTERNS! I SCORN EVERYTHING THE OTHER GREEN LANTERN STANDS FOR! NOW--I'LL SHOW YOU MY IDEA OF HOW A REAL GREEN LANTERN SHOULD ACT!
2

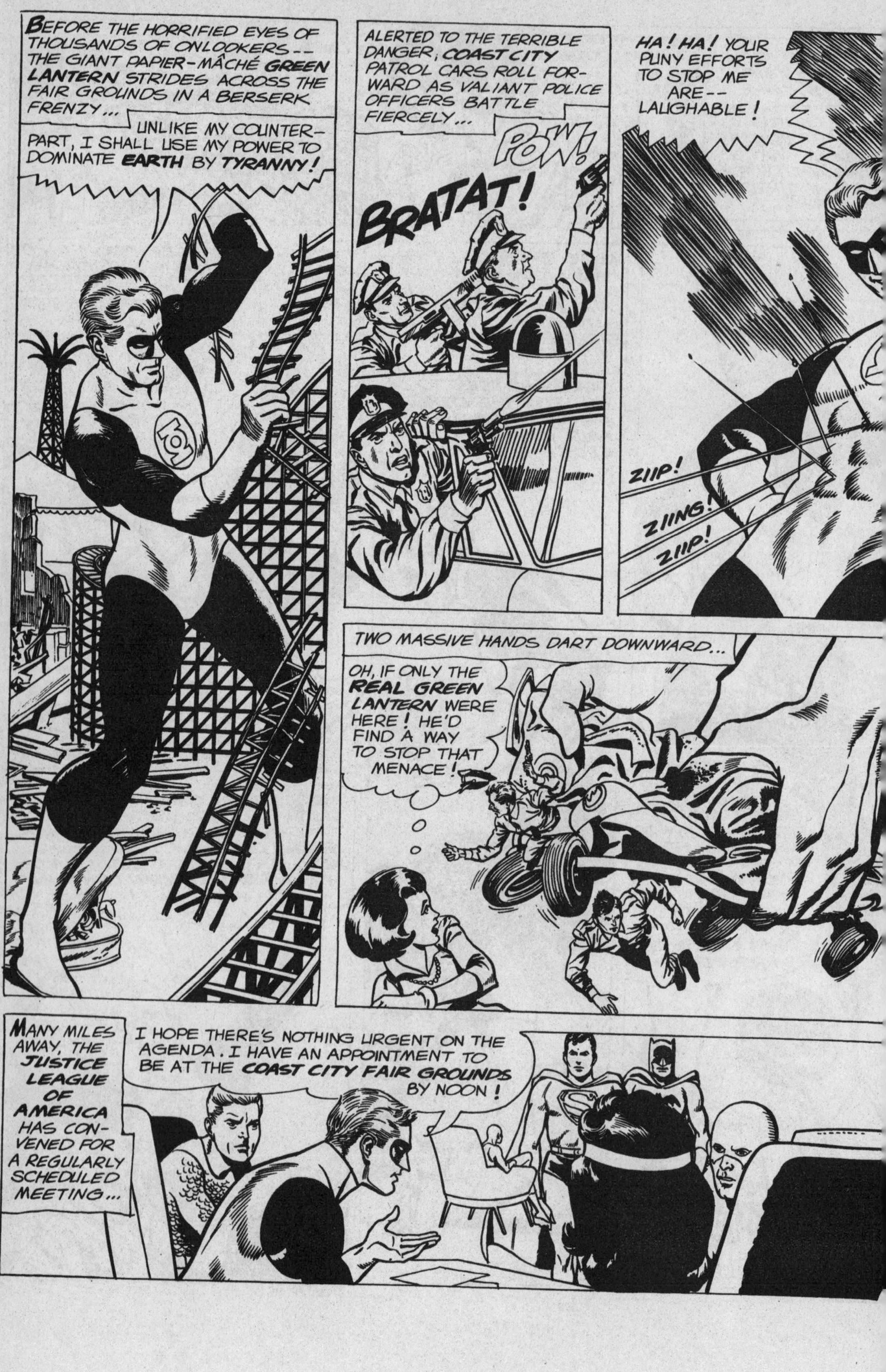
BEFORE THE HORRIFIED EYES OF THOUSANDS OF ONLOOKERS -- THE GIANT PAPIER-MÂCHÉ GREEN LANTERN STRIDES ACROSS THE FAIR GROUNDS IN A BERSERK FRENZY...
UNLIKE MY COUNTERPART, I SHALL USE MY POWER TO DOMINATE EARTH BY TYRANNY!
ALERTED TO THE TERRIBLE DANGER, COAST CITY PATROL CARS ROLL FORWARD AS VALIANT POLICE OFFICERS BATTLE FIERCELY...
POW!
BRATAT!
HA! HA! YOUR PUNY EFFORTS TO STOP ME ARE-- LAUGHABLE!
ZIIP!
ZIING!
ZIIP!
TWO MASSIVE HANDS DART DOWNWARD...
OH, IF ONLY THE REAL GREEN LANTERN WERE HERE! HE'D FIND A WAY TO STOP THAT MENACE!
MANY MILES AWAY, THE JUSTICE LEAGUE OF AMERICA HAS CONVENED FOR A REGULARLY SCHEDULED MEETING...
I HOPE THERE'S NOTHING URGENT ON THE AGENDA. I HAVE AN APPOINTMENT TO BE AT THE COAST CITY FAIR GROUNDS BY NOON!

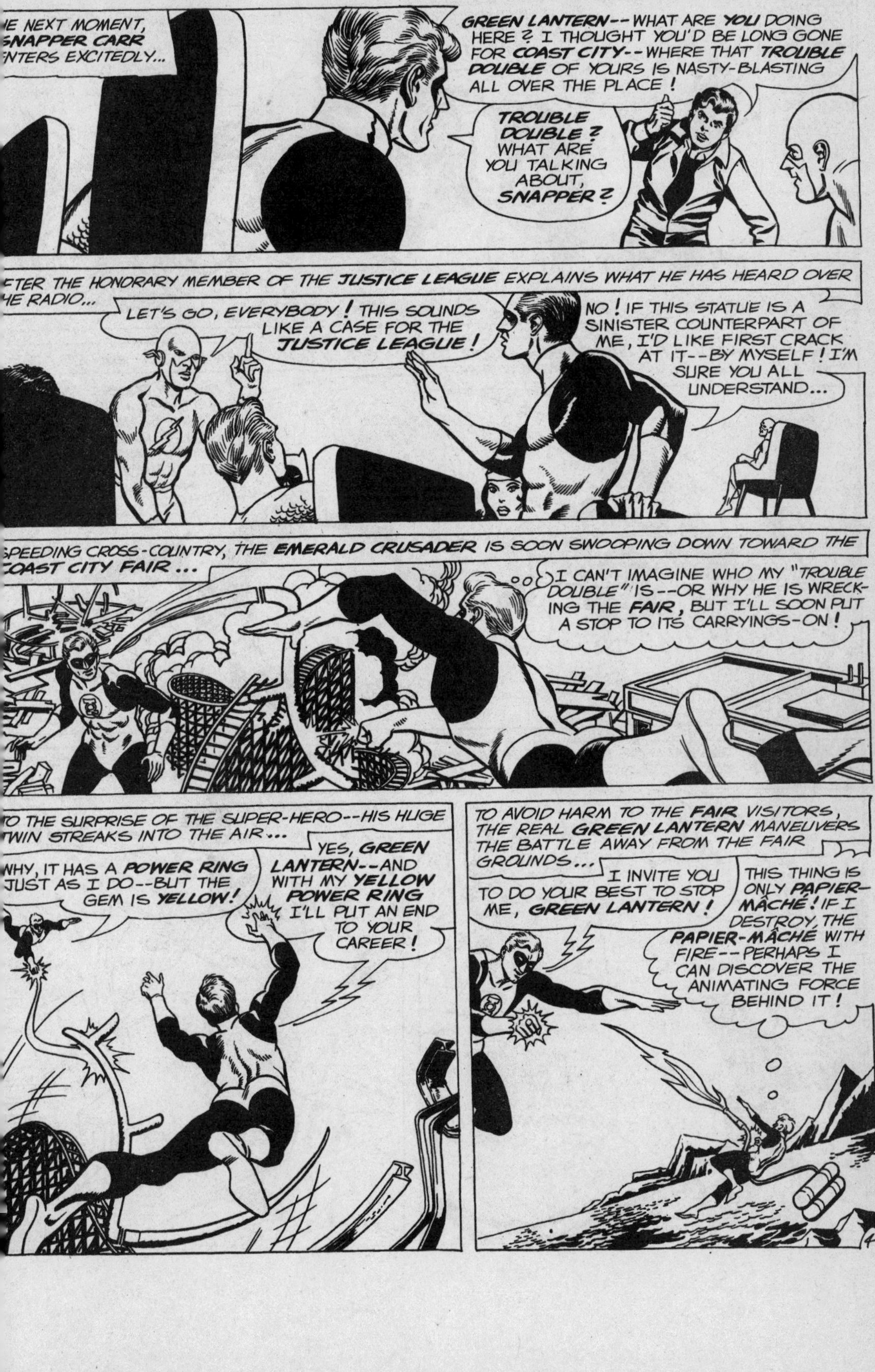

HE NEXT MOMENT, SNAPPER CARR ENTERS EXCITEDLY...
GREEN LANTERN--WHAT ARE YOU DOING HERE? I THOUGHT YOU'D BE LONG GONE FOR COAST CITY--WHERE THAT TROUBLE DOUBLE OF YOURS IS NASTY-BLASTING ALL OVER THE PLACE!
TROUBLE DOUBLE? WHAT ARE YOU TALKING ABOUT, SNAPPER?
FTER THE HONORARY MEMBER OF THE JUSTICE LEAGUE EXPLAINS WHAT HE HAS HEARD OVER HE RADIO...
LET'S GO, EVERYBODY! THIS SOUNDS LIKE A CASE FOR THE JUSTICE LEAGUE!
NO! IF THIS STATUE IS A SINISTER COUNTERPART OF ME, I'D LIKE FIRST CRACK AT IT--BY MYSELF! I'M SURE YOU ALL UNDERSTAND...
SPEEDING CROSS-COUNTRY, THE EMERALD CRUSADER IS SOON SWOOPING DOWN TOWARD THE COAST CITY FAIR...
I CAN'T IMAGINE WHO MY "TROUBLE DOUBLE" IS--OR WHY HE IS WRECKING THE FAIR, BUT I'LL SOON PUT A STOP TO ITS CARRYINGS-ON!
TO THE SURPRISE OF THE SUPER-HERO--HIS HUGE TWIN STREAKS INTO THE AIR...
WHY, IT HAS A POWER RING JUST AS I DO--BUT THE GEM IS YELLOW!
YES, GREEN LANTERN--AND WITH MY YELLOW POWER RING I'LL PUT AN END TO YOUR CAREER!
TO AVOID HARM TO THE FAIR VISITORS, THE REAL GREEN LANTERN MANEUVERS THE BATTLE AWAY FROM THE FAIR GROUNDS...
I INVITE YOU TO DO YOUR BEST TO STOP ME, GREEN LANTERN!
THIS THING IS ONLY PAPIER-MÂCHÉ! IF I DESTROY THE PAPIER-MÂCHÉ WITH FIRE--PERHAPS I CAN DISCOVER THE ANIMATING FORCE BEHIND IT!
4

TO COUNTER THOSE VERDANT FLAMES, THE GIANT **GREEN LANTERN** CREATES A MASSIVE WALL OF WATER...

FOR EVERYTHING YOU DO-- I HAVE A YELLOW COUNTER-PART!

I'VE BEEN IN SPOTS LIKE THIS BEFORE--AND I HAVE WAYS OF OVERCOMING MY SEEMINGLY FATAL WEAKNESS, BELIEVE ME!

AS FAST AS THOUGHT, THE **GREEN GLADIATOR** DROPS A GREEN DOME OVER HIMSELF AND HIS FOE-- INSTALLING A SUPER-AIR-CONDITIONER WITHIN IT...

ONLY MY DOUBLE AND MYSELF ARE INSIDE THIS DOME SO NO ONE ELSE CAN BE HARMED BY THE COLD--AND I'VE PROTECTED MYSELF BY AN INVISIBLE SHEATH!

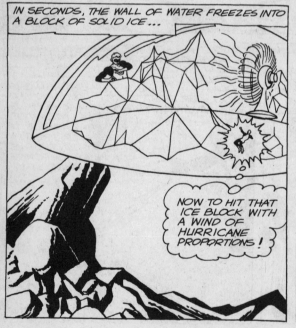

IN SECONDS, THE WALL OF WATER FREEZES INTO A BLOCK OF SOLID ICE...

NOW TO HIT THAT ICE BLOCK WITH A WIND OF HURRICANE PROPORTIONS!

AS THAT INCREDIBLY POWERFUL JET STREAM OF AIR HITS IT, THE ICE WALL TOPPLES AND...

I'VE CRUSHED THE HUGE IMAGE FLAT. NOW TO SEE IF ANYTHING IS STILL INSIDE IT!

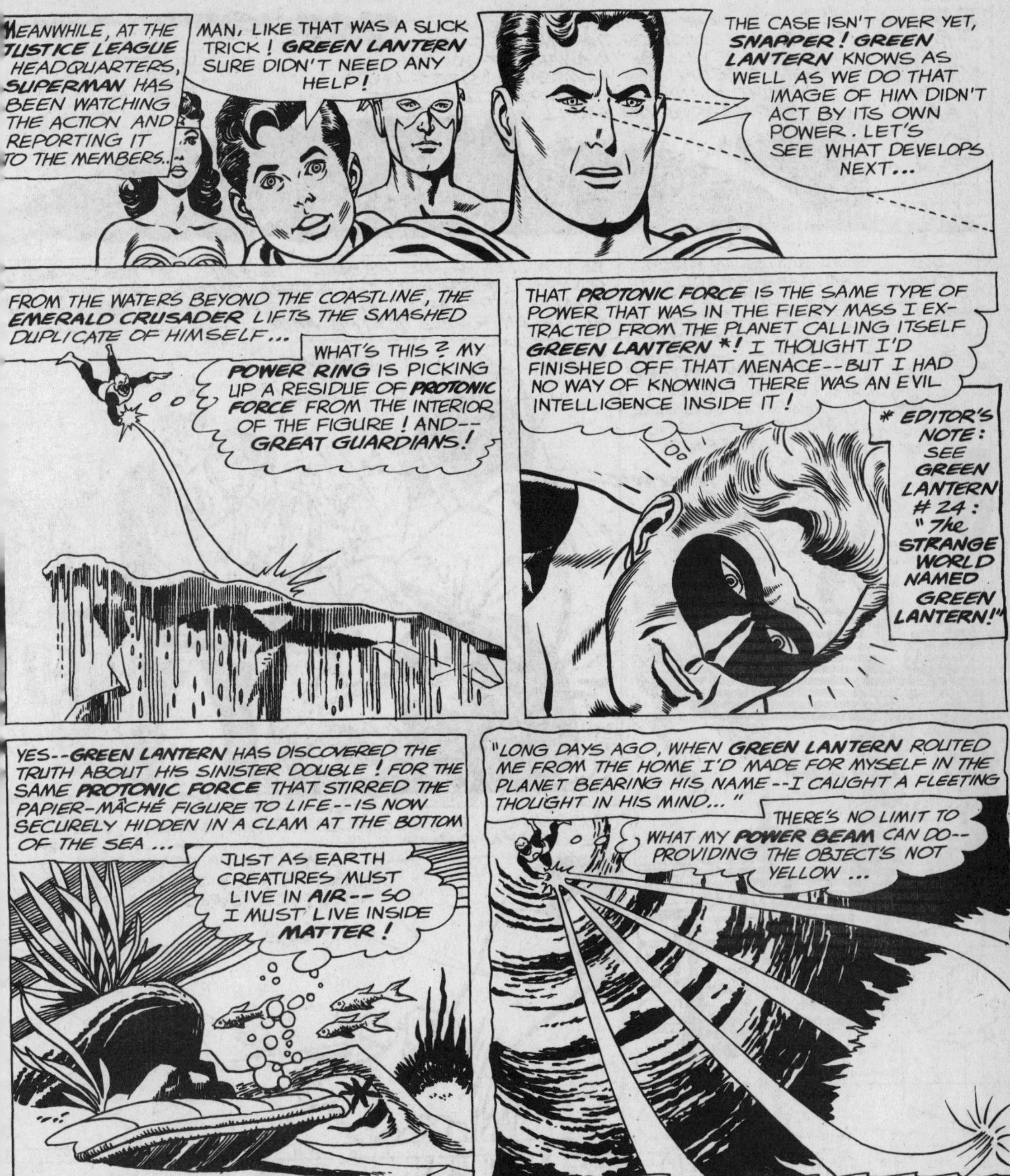
MEANWHILE, AT THE JUSTICE LEAGUE HEADQUARTERS, SUPERMAN HAS BEEN WATCHING THE ACTION AND REPORTING IT TO THE MEMBERS...
MAN, LIKE THAT WAS A SLICK TRICK! GREEN LANTERN SURE DIDN'T NEED ANY HELP!
THE CASE ISN'T OVER YET, SNAPPER! GREEN LANTERN KNOWS AS WELL AS WE DO THAT IMAGE OF HIM DIDN'T ACT BY ITS OWN POWER. LET'S SEE WHAT DEVELOPS NEXT...
FROM THE WATERS BEYOND THE COASTLINE, THE EMERALD CRUSADER LIFTS THE SMASHED DUPLICATE OF HIMSELF...
WHAT'S THIS? MY POWER RING IS PICKING UP A RESIDUE OF PROTONIC FORCE FROM THE INTERIOR OF THE FIGURE! AND-- GREAT GUARDIANS!
THAT PROTONIC FORCE IS THE SAME TYPE OF POWER THAT WAS IN THE FIERY MASS I EXTRACTED FROM THE PLANET CALLING ITSELF GREEN LANTERN*! I THOUGHT I'D FINISHED OFF THAT MENACE--BUT I HAD NO WAY OF KNOWING THERE WAS AN EVIL INTELLIGENCE INSIDE IT!
* EDITOR'S NOTE: SEE GREEN LANTERN #24: "The STRANGE WORLD NAMED GREEN LANTERN!"
YES--GREEN LANTERN HAS DISCOVERED THE TRUTH ABOUT HIS SINISTER DOUBLE! FOR THE SAME PROTONIC FORCE THAT STIRRED THE PAPIER-MÂCHÉ FIGURE TO LIFE--IS NOW SECURELY HIDDEN IN A CLAM AT THE BOTTOM OF THE SEA...
JUST AS EARTH CREATURES MUST LIVE IN AIR--SO I MUST LIVE INSIDE MATTER!
"LONG DAYS AGO, WHEN GREEN LANTERN ROUTED ME FROM THE HOME I'D MADE FOR MYSELF IN THE PLANET BEARING HIS NAME--I CAUGHT A FLEETING THOUGHT IN HIS MIND..."
THERE'S NO LIMIT TO WHAT MY POWER BEAM CAN DO--PROVIDING THE OBJECT'S NOT YELLOW...
"GREEN LANTERN DIDN'T KNOW AS HE PUT ME IN ORBIT, THAT I WAS ONLY INHABITING THAT FIREBALL UNTIL I COULD MAKE PLANS FOR TAKING OVER THE PLANET..."
AS SOON AS I RECOVER MY STRENGTH, I'LL DO SOME METEOR AND COMET-HOPPING AND FOLLOW GREEN LANTERN TO HIS HOME WORLD!
6

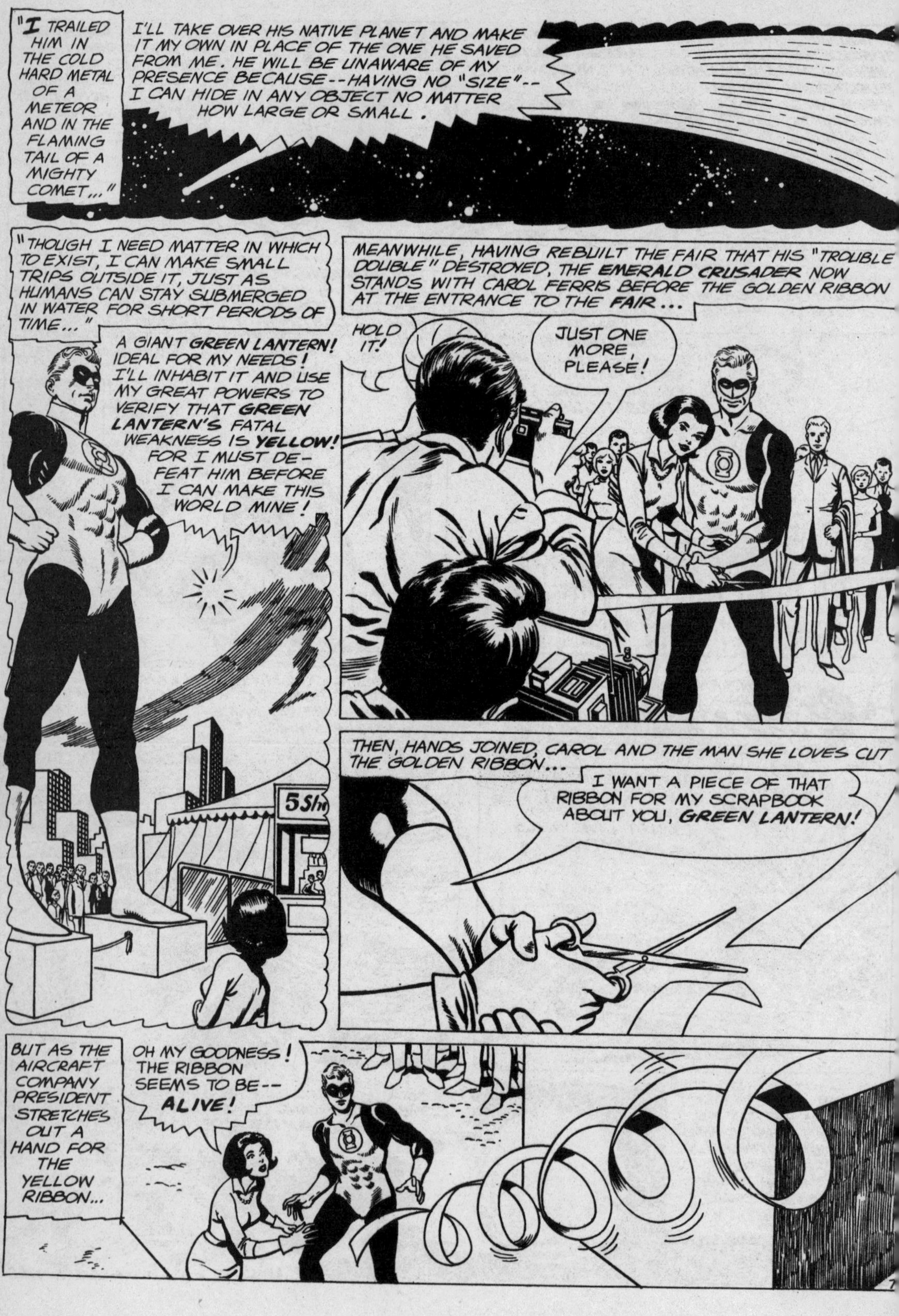
"I TRAILED HIM IN THE COLD HARD METAL OF A METEOR AND IN THE FLAMING TAIL OF A MIGHTY COMET..."
I'LL TAKE OVER HIS NATIVE PLANET AND MAKE IT MY OWN IN PLACE OF THE ONE HE SAVED FROM ME. HE WILL BE UNAWARE OF MY PRESENCE BECAUSE--HAVING NO "SIZE"--I CAN HIDE IN ANY OBJECT NO MATTER HOW LARGE OR SMALL.
"THOUGH I NEED MATTER IN WHICH TO EXIST, I CAN MAKE SMALL TRIPS OUTSIDE IT, JUST AS HUMANS CAN STAY SUBMERGED IN WATER FOR SHORT PERIODS OF TIME..."
A GIANT GREEN LANTERN! IDEAL FOR MY NEEDS! I'LL INHABIT IT AND USE MY GREAT POWERS TO VERIFY THAT GREEN LANTERN'S FATAL WEAKNESS IS YELLOW! FOR I MUST DEFEAT HIM BEFORE I CAN MAKE THIS WORLD MINE!
MEANWHILE, HAVING REBUILT THE FAIR THAT HIS "TROUBLE DOUBLE" DESTROYED, THE EMERALD CRUSADER NOW STANDS WITH CAROL FERRIS BEFORE THE GOLDEN RIBBON AT THE ENTRANCE TO THE FAIR...
HOLD IT!
JUST ONE MORE, PLEASE!
THEN, HANDS JOINED, CAROL AND THE MAN SHE LOVES CUT THE GOLDEN RIBBON...
I WANT A PIECE OF THAT RIBBON FOR MY SCRAPBOOK ABOUT YOU, GREEN LANTERN!
BUT AS THE AIRCRAFT COMPANY PRESIDENT STRETCHES OUT A HAND FOR THE YELLOW RIBBON...
OH MY GOODNESS! THE RIBBON SEEMS TO BE--ALIVE!

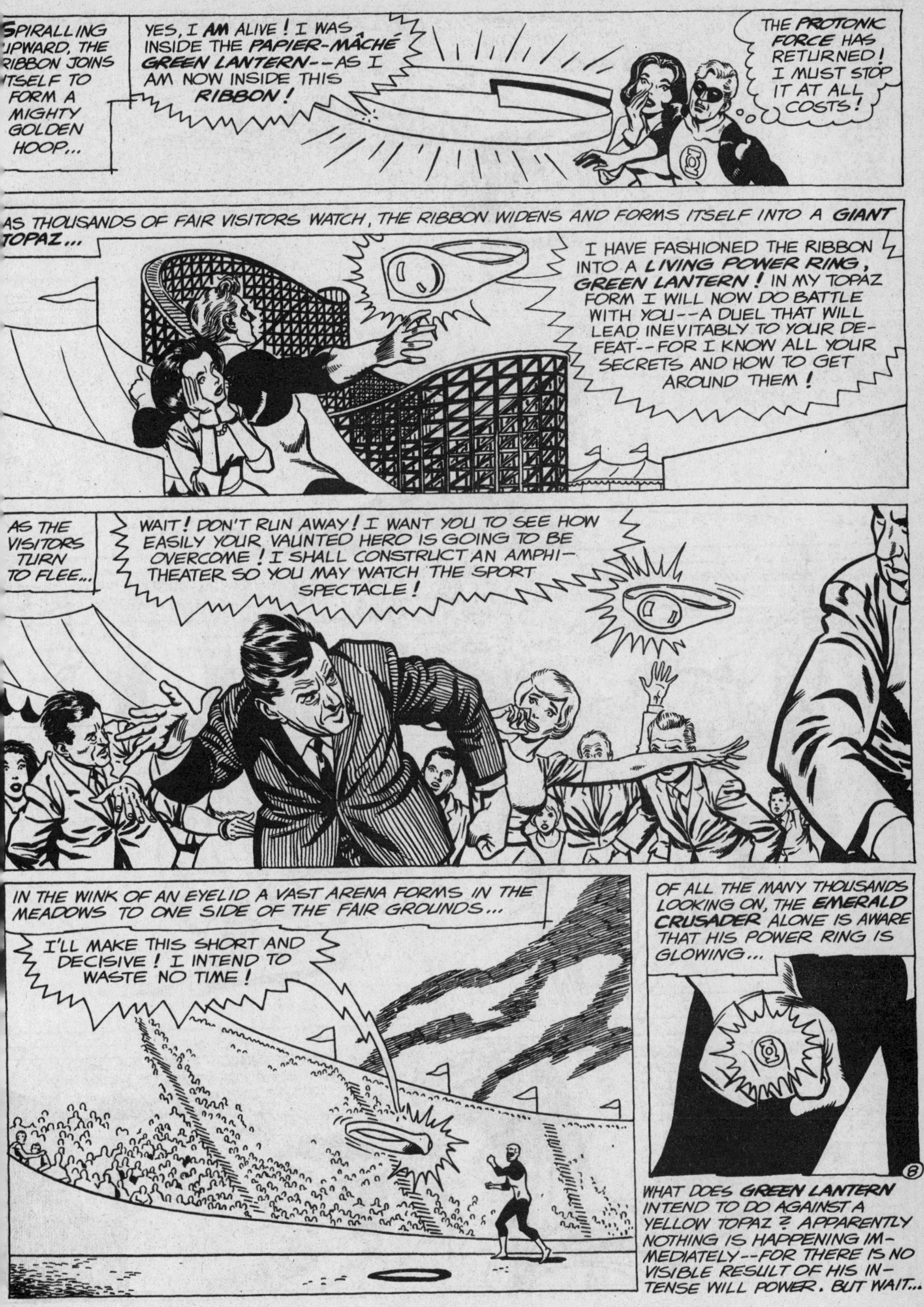
SPIRALLING UPWARD, THE RIBBON JOINS ITSELF TO FORM A MIGHTY GOLDEN HOOP...
YES, I AM ALIVE! I WAS INSIDE THE PAPIER-MÂCHÉ GREEN LANTERN--AS I AM NOW INSIDE THIS RIBBON!
THE PROTONIC FORCE HAS RETURNED! I MUST STOP IT AT ALL COSTS!
AS THOUSANDS OF FAIR VISITORS WATCH, THE RIBBON WIDENS AND FORMS ITSELF INTO A GIANT TOPAZ...
I HAVE FASHIONED THE RIBBON INTO A LIVING POWER RING, GREEN LANTERN! IN MY TOPAZ FORM I WILL NOW DO BATTLE WITH YOU--A DUEL THAT WILL LEAD INEVITABLY TO YOUR DE-FEAT--FOR I KNOW ALL YOUR SECRETS AND HOW TO GET AROUND THEM!
AS THE VISITORS TURN TO FLEE...
WAIT! DON'T RUN AWAY! I WANT YOU TO SEE HOW EASILY YOUR VAUNTED HERO IS GOING TO BE OVERCOME! I SHALL CONSTRUCT AN AMPHI-THEATER SO YOU MAY WATCH THE SPORT SPECTACLE!
IN THE WINK OF AN EYELID A VAST ARENA FORMS IN THE MEADOWS TO ONE SIDE OF THE FAIR GROUNDS...
I'LL MAKE THIS SHORT AND DECISIVE! I INTEND TO WASTE NO TIME!
OF ALL THE MANY THOUSANDS LOOKING ON, THE EMERALD CRUSADER ALONE IS AWARE THAT HIS POWER RING IS GLOWING...
8
WHAT DOES GREEN LANTERN INTEND TO DO AGAINST A YELLOW TOPAZ? APPARENTLY NOTHING IS HAPPENING IM-MEDIATELY--FOR THERE IS NO VISIBLE RESULT OF HIS IN-TENSE WILL POWER. BUT WAIT...

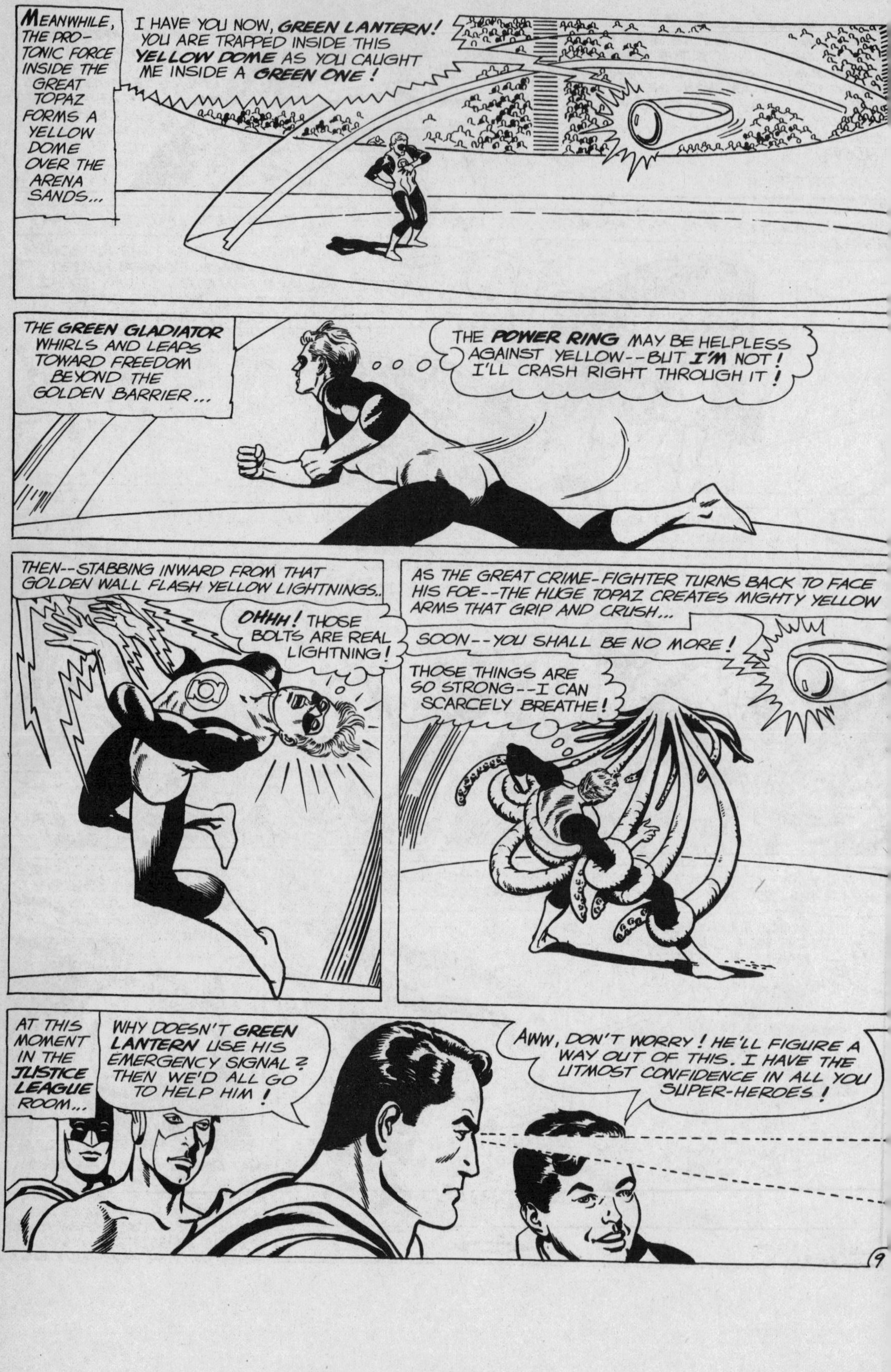
MEANWHILE, THE PRO-TONIC FORCE INSIDE THE GREAT TOPAZ FORMS A YELLOW DOME OVER THE ARENA SANDS...
I HAVE YOU NOW, GREEN LANTERN! YOU ARE TRAPPED INSIDE THIS YELLOW DOME AS YOU CAUGHT ME INSIDE A GREEN ONE!
THE GREEN GLADIATOR WHIRLS AND LEAPS TOWARD FREEDOM BEYOND THE GOLDEN BARRIER...
THE POWER RING MAY BE HELPLESS AGAINST YELLOW--BUT I'M NOT! I'LL CRASH RIGHT THROUGH IT!
THEN--STABBING INWARD FROM THAT GOLDEN WALL FLASH YELLOW LIGHTNINGS..
OHHH! THOSE BOLTS ARE REAL LIGHTNING!
AS THE GREAT CRIME-FIGHTER TURNS BACK TO FACE HIS FOE--THE HUGE TOPAZ CREATES MIGHTY YELLOW ARMS THAT GRIP AND CRUSH...
SOON--YOU SHALL BE NO MORE!
THOSE THINGS ARE SO STRONG--I CAN SCARCELY BREATHE!
AT THIS MOMENT IN THE JUSTICE LEAGUE ROOM...
WHY DOESN'T GREEN LANTERN USE HIS EMERGENCY SIGNAL? THEN WE'D ALL GO TO HELP HIM!
AWW, DON'T WORRY! HE'LL FIGURE A WAY OUT OF THIS. I HAVE THE UTMOST CONFIDENCE IN ALL YOU SUPER-HEROES!
9

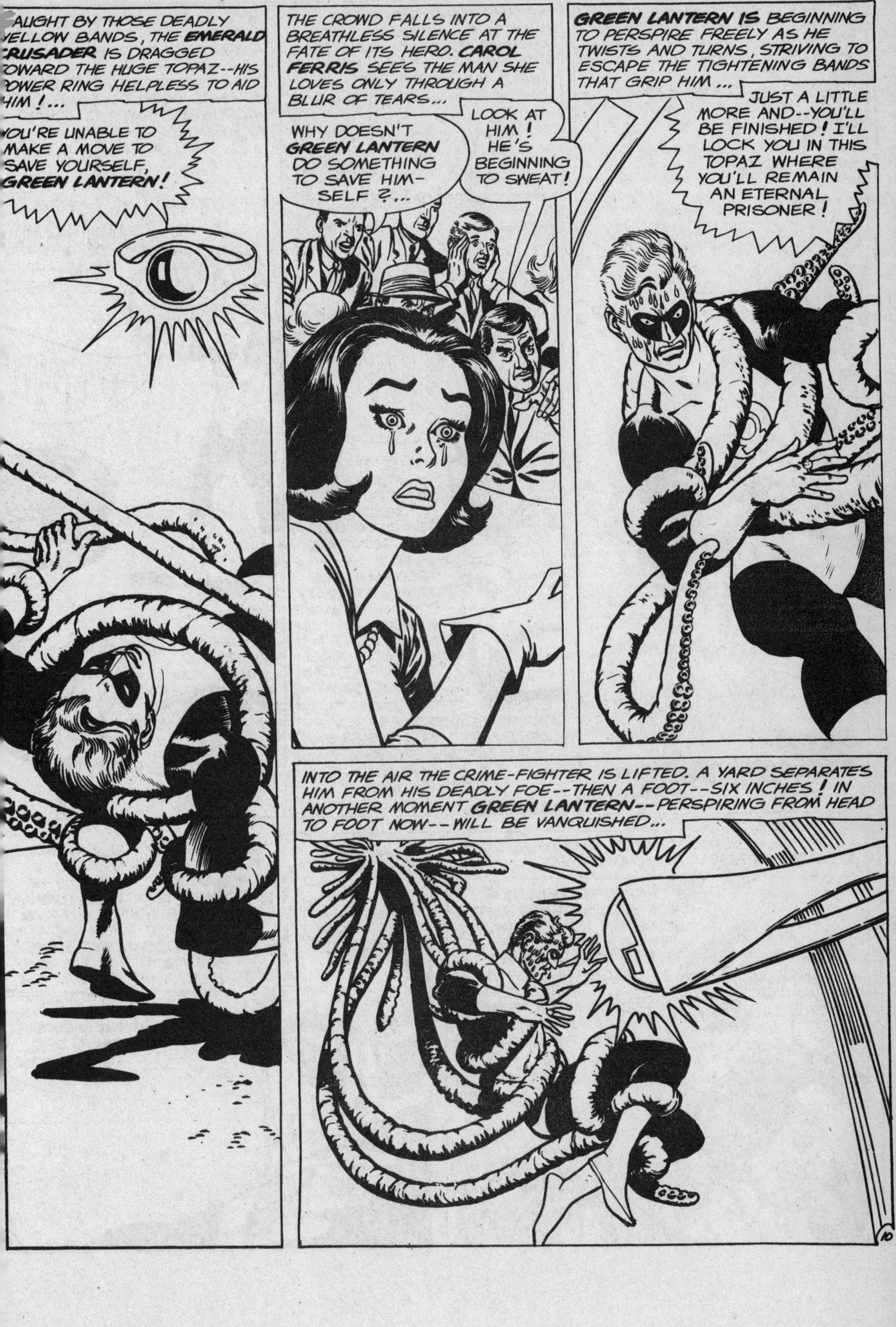
CAUGHT BY THOSE DEADLY YELLOW BANDS, THE EMERALD CRUSADER IS DRAGGED TOWARD THE HUGE TOPAZ--HIS POWER RING HELPLESS TO AID HIM!...
YOU'RE UNABLE TO MAKE A MOVE TO SAVE YOURSELF, GREEN LANTERN!
THE CROWD FALLS INTO A BREATHLESS SILENCE AT THE FATE OF ITS HERO. CAROL FERRIS SEES THE MAN SHE LOVES ONLY THROUGH A BLUR OF TEARS...
WHY DOESN'T GREEN LANTERN DO SOMETHING TO SAVE HIMSELF ?...
LOOK AT HIM! HE'S BEGINNING TO SWEAT!
GREEN LANTERN IS BEGINNING TO PERSPIRE FREELY AS HE TWISTS AND TURNS, STRIVING TO ESCAPE THE TIGHTENING BANDS THAT GRIP HIM...
JUST A LITTLE MORE AND--YOU'LL BE FINISHED! I'LL LOCK YOU IN THIS TOPAZ WHERE YOU'LL REMAIN AN ETERNAL PRISONER!
INTO THE AIR THE CRIME-FIGHTER IS LIFTED. A YARD SEPARATES HIM FROM HIS DEADLY FOE--THEN A FOOT--SIX INCHES! IN ANOTHER MOMENT GREEN LANTERN--PERSPIRING FROM HEAD TO FOOT NOW--WILL BE VANQUISHED...
10

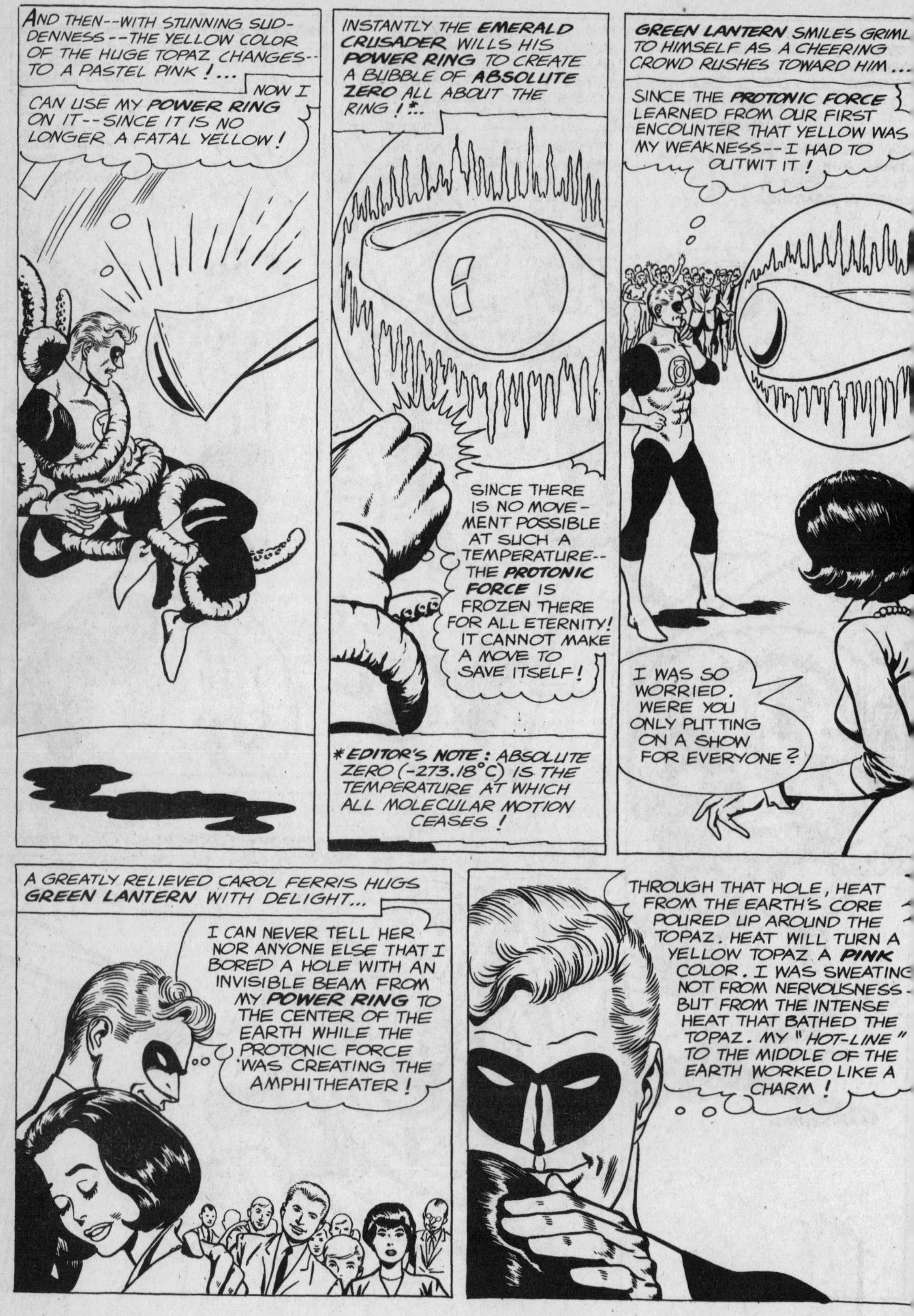

AND THEN--WITH STUNNING SUDDENNESS--THE YELLOW COLOR OF THE HUGE TOPAZ CHANGES--TO A PASTEL PINK!...
NOW I CAN USE MY POWER RING ON IT--SINCE IT IS NO LONGER A FATAL YELLOW!
INSTANTLY THE EMERALD CRUSADER WILLS HIS POWER RING TO CREATE A BUBBLE OF ABSOLUTE ZERO ALL ABOUT THE RING!*...
SINCE THERE IS NO MOVEMENT POSSIBLE AT SUCH A TEMPERATURE--THE PROTONIC FORCE IS FROZEN THERE FOR ALL ETERNITY! IT CANNOT MAKE A MOVE TO SAVE ITSELF!
*EDITOR'S NOTE: ABSOLUTE ZERO (-273.18°C) IS THE TEMPERATURE AT WHICH ALL MOLECULAR MOTION CEASES!
GREEN LANTERN SMILES GRIML TO HIMSELF AS A CHEERING CROWD RUSHES TOWARD HIM...
SINCE THE PROTONIC FORCE LEARNED FROM OUR FIRST ENCOUNTER THAT YELLOW WAS MY WEAKNESS--I HAD TO OUTWIT IT!
I WAS SO WORRIED. WERE YOU ONLY PUTTING ON A SHOW FOR EVERYONE?
A GREATLY RELIEVED CAROL FERRIS HUGS GREEN LANTERN WITH DELIGHT...
I CAN NEVER TELL HER NOR ANYONE ELSE THAT I BORED A HOLE WITH AN INVISIBLE BEAM FROM MY POWER RING TO THE CENTER OF THE EARTH WHILE THE PROTONIC FORCE WAS CREATING THE AMPHITHEATER!
THROUGH THAT HOLE, HEAT FROM THE EARTH'S CORE POURED UP AROUND THE TOPAZ. HEAT WILL TURN A YELLOW TOPAZ A PINK COLOR. I WAS SWEATING NOT FROM NERVOUSNESS-BUT FROM THE INTENSE HEAT THAT BATHED THE TOPAZ. MY "HOT-LINE" TO THE MIDDLE OF THE EARTH WORKED LIKE A CHARM!

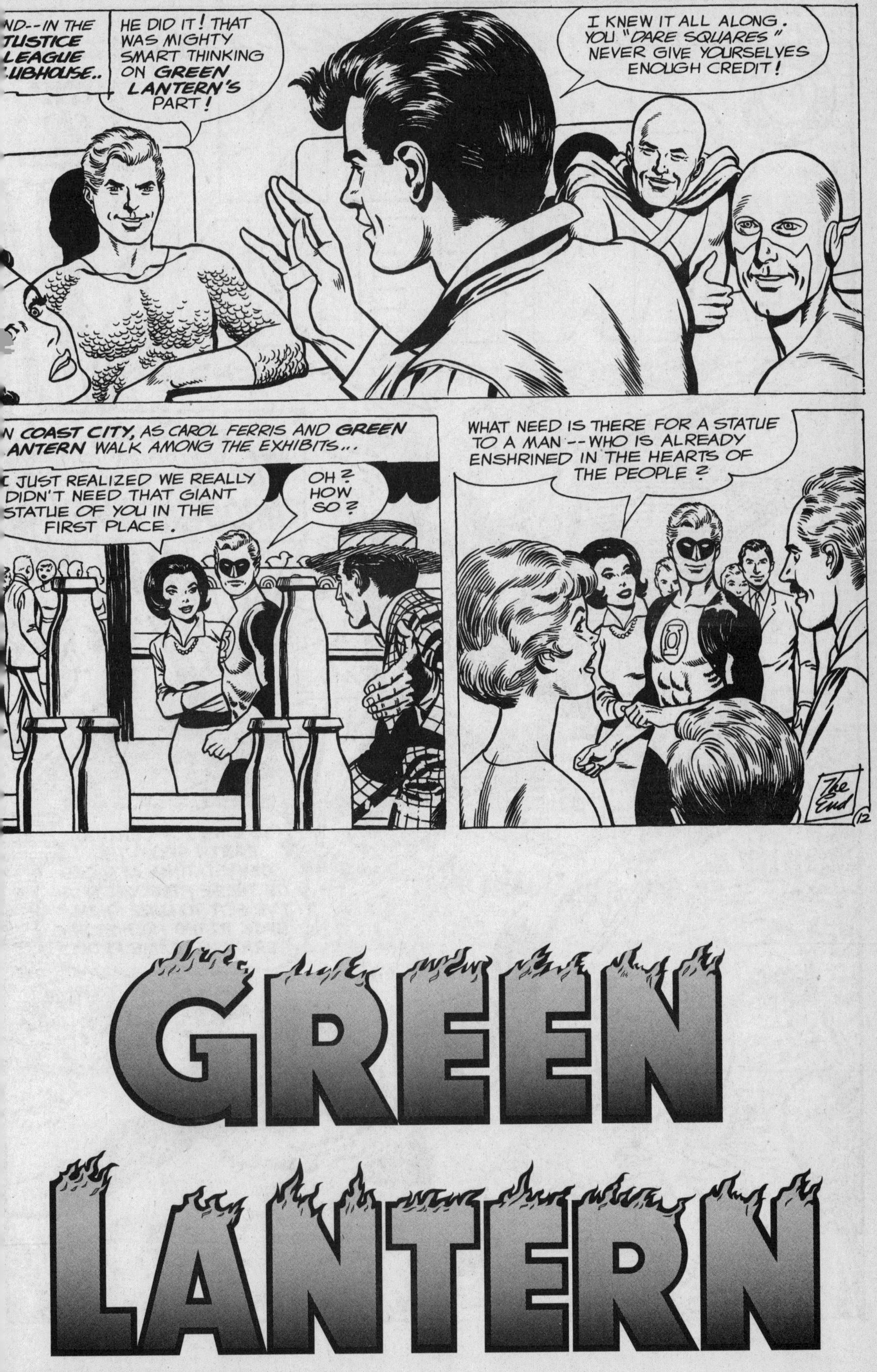
ND--IN THE JUSTICE LEAGUE UBHOUSE..
HE DID IT! THAT WAS MIGHTY SMART THINKING ON GREEN LANTERN'S PART!
I KNEW IT ALL ALONG. YOU "DARE SQUARES" NEVER GIVE YOURSELVES ENOUGH CREDIT!
N COAST CITY, AS CAROL FERRIS AND GREEN ANTERN WALK AMONG THE EXHIBITS...
JUST REALIZED WE REALLY DIDN'T NEED THAT GIANT STATUE OF YOU IN THE FIRST PLACE.
OH? HOW SO?
WHAT NEED IS THERE FOR A STATUE TO A MAN--WHO IS ALREADY ENSHRINED IN THE HEARTS OF THE PEOPLE?
The End
12

GREEN LANTERN

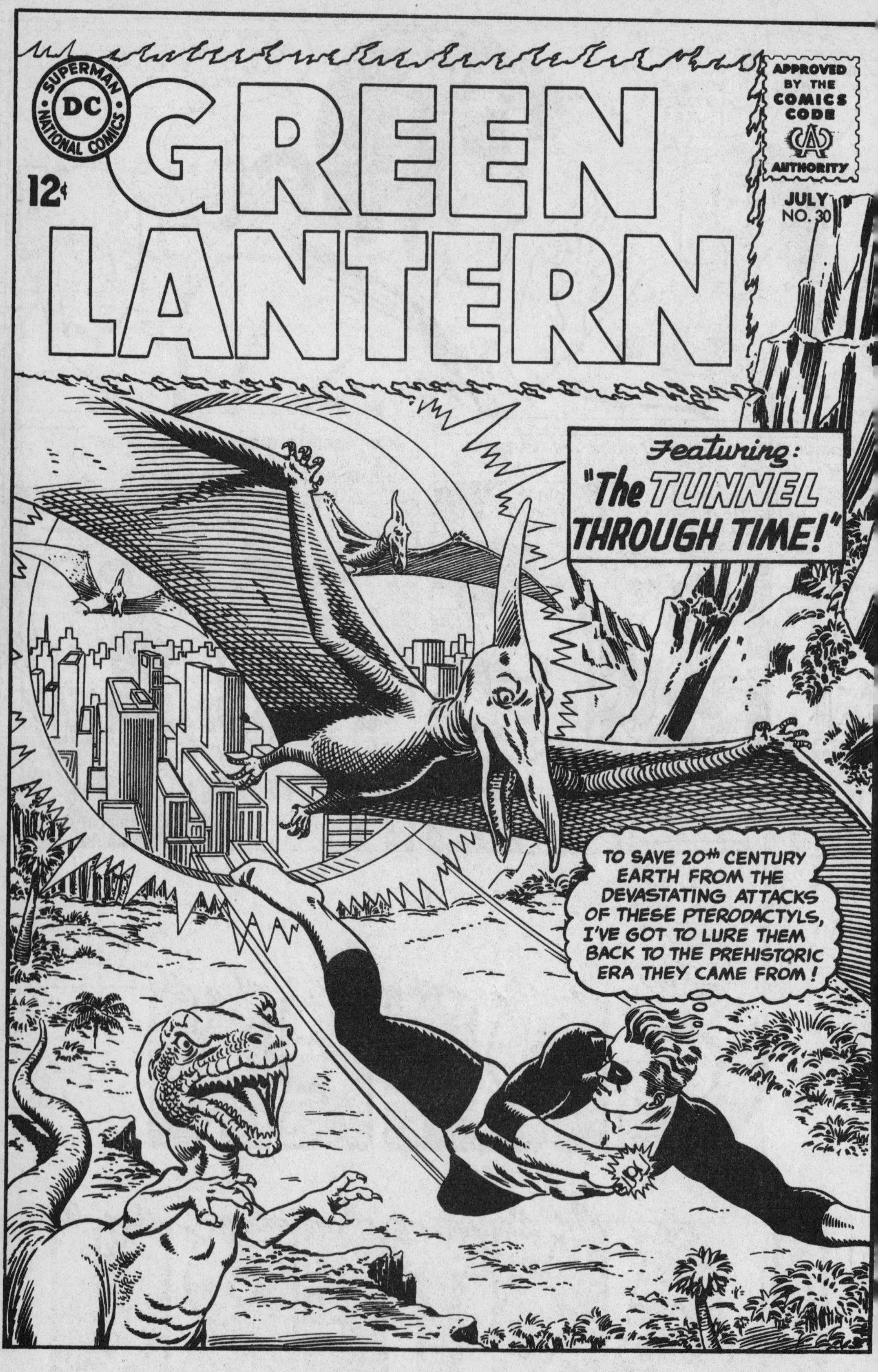
SUPERMAN DC NATIONAL COMICS
12¢
GREEN LANTERN
APPROVED BY THE COMICS CODE AUTHORITY
JULY NO. 30
Featuring: "The TUNNEL THROUGH TIME!"
TO SAVE 20th CENTURY EARTH FROM THE DEVASTATING ATTACKS OF THESE PTERODACTYLS, I'VE GOT TO LURE THEM BACK TO THE PREHISTORIC ERA THEY CAME FROM!

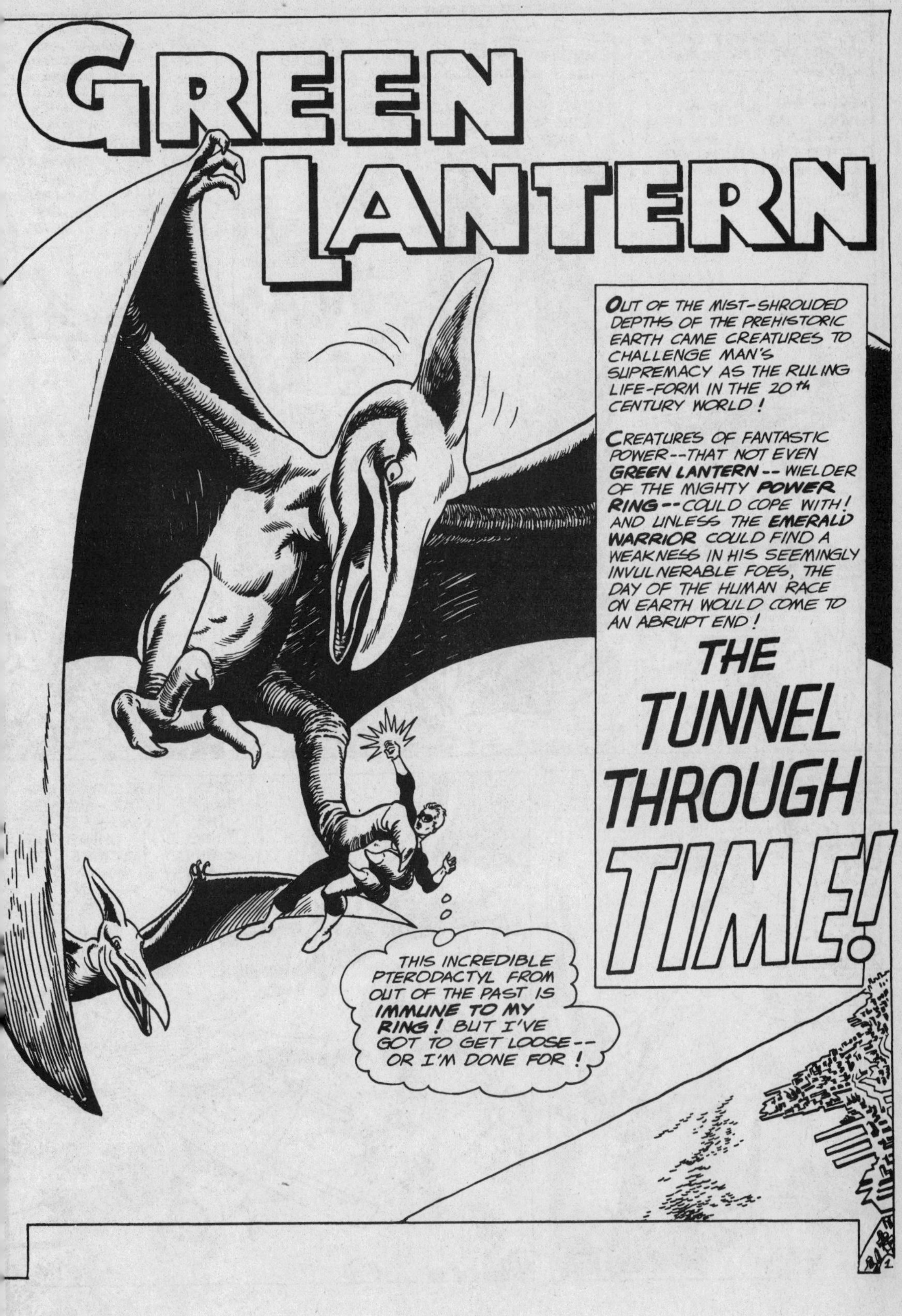
GREEN LANTERN
OUT OF THE MIST-SHROUDED DEPTHS OF THE PREHISTORIC EARTH CAME CREATURES TO CHALLENGE MAN'S SUPREMACY AS THE RULING LIFE-FORM IN THE 20th CENTURY WORLD!
CREATURES OF FANTASTIC POWER--THAT NOT EVEN GREEN LANTERN-- WIELDER OF THE MIGHTY POWER RING--COULD COPE WITH! AND UNLESS THE EMERALD WARRIOR COULD FIND A WEAKNESS IN HIS SEEMINGLY INVULNERABLE FOES, THE DAY OF THE HUMAN RACE ON EARTH WOULD COME TO AN ABRUPT END!
THE TUNNEL THROUGH TIME!
THIS INCREDIBLE PTERODACTYL FROM OUT OF THE PAST IS IMMUNE TO MY RING! BUT I'VE GOT TO GET LOOSE-- OR I'M DONE FOR!

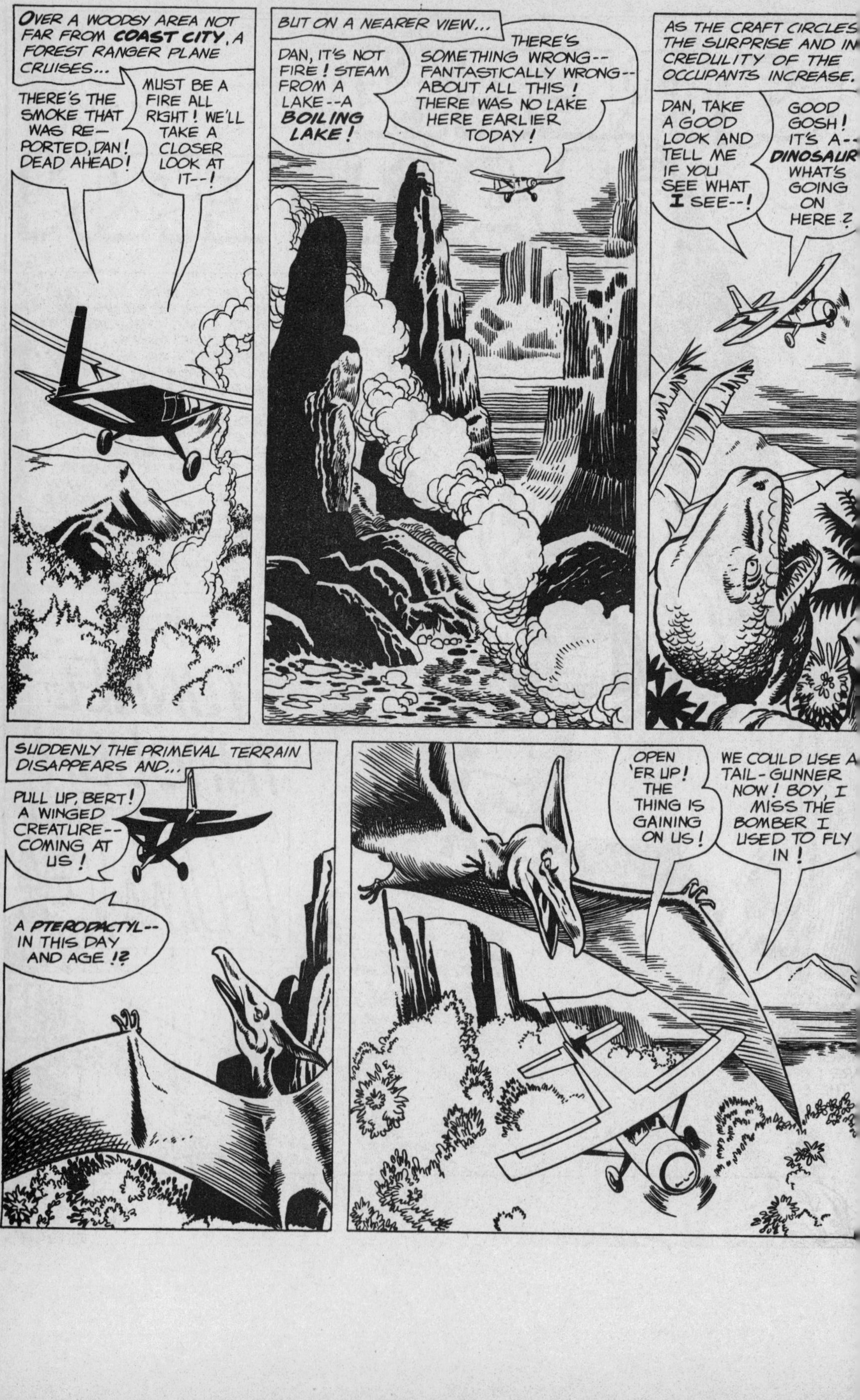
OVER A WOODSY AREA NOT FAR FROM COAST CITY, A FOREST RANGER PLANE CRUISES...
THERE'S THE SMOKE THAT WAS REPORTED, DAN! DEAD AHEAD!
MUST BE A FIRE ALL RIGHT! WE'LL TAKE A CLOSER LOOK AT IT--!
BUT ON A NEARER VIEW...
DAN, IT'S NOT FIRE! STEAM FROM A LAKE--A BOILING LAKE!
THERE'S SOMETHING WRONG--FANTASTICALLY WRONG--ABOUT ALL THIS! THERE WAS NO LAKE HERE EARLIER TODAY!
AS THE CRAFT CIRCLES THE SURPRISE AND IN CREDULITY OF THE OCCUPANTS INCREASE.
DAN, TAKE A GOOD LOOK AND TELL ME IF YOU SEE WHAT I SEE--!
GOOD GOSH! IT'S A--DINOSAUR WHAT'S GOING ON HERE?
SUDDENLY THE PRIMEVAL TERRAIN DISAPPEARS AND...
PULL UP, BERT! A WINGED CREATURE--COMING AT US!
A PTERODACTYL--IN THIS DAY AND AGE!?
OPEN 'ER UP! THE THING IS GAINING ON US!
WE COULD USE A TAIL-GUNNER NOW! BOY, I MISS THE BOMBER I USED TO FLY IN!

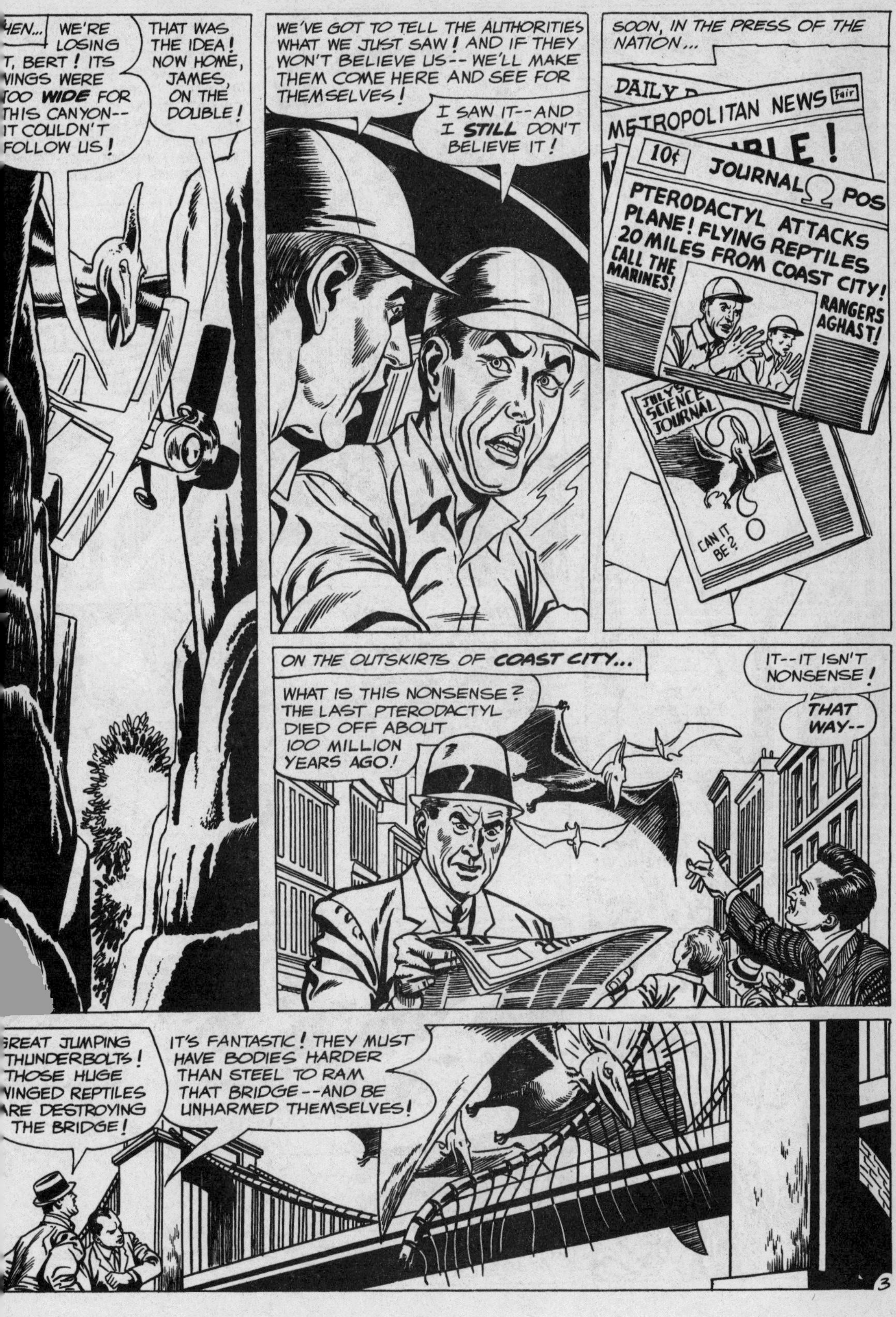
WE'RE LOSING
T, BERT! ITS WINGS WERE TOO WIDE FOR THIS CANYON-- IT COULDN'T FOLLOW US!
THAT WAS THE IDEA! NOW HOME, JAMES, ON THE DOUBLE!
WE'VE GOT TO TELL THE AUTHORITIES WHAT WE JUST SAW! AND IF THEY WON'T BELIEVE US-- WE'LL MAKE THEM COME HERE AND SEE FOR THEMSELVES!
I SAW IT--AND I STILL DON'T BELIEVE IT!
SOON, IN THE PRESS OF THE NATION...
DAILY
METROPOLITAN NEWS
Fair
10¢
JOURNAL
POS
PTERODACTYL ATTACKS PLANE! FLYING REPTILES 20 MILES FROM COAST CITY!
CALL THE MARINES!
RANGERS AGHAST!
JULY'S SCIENCE JOURNAL
CAN IT BE?
ON THE OUTSKIRTS OF COAST CITY...
WHAT IS THIS NONSENSE? THE LAST PTERODACTYL DIED OFF ABOUT 100 MILLION YEARS AGO!
IT--IT ISN'T NONSENSE!
THAT WAY--
GREAT JUMPING THUNDERBOLTS! THOSE HUGE WINGED REPTILES ARE DESTROYING THE BRIDGE!
IT'S FANTASTIC! THEY MUST HAVE BODIES HARDER THAN STEEL TO RAM THAT BRIDGE--AND BE UNHARMED THEMSELVES!
3

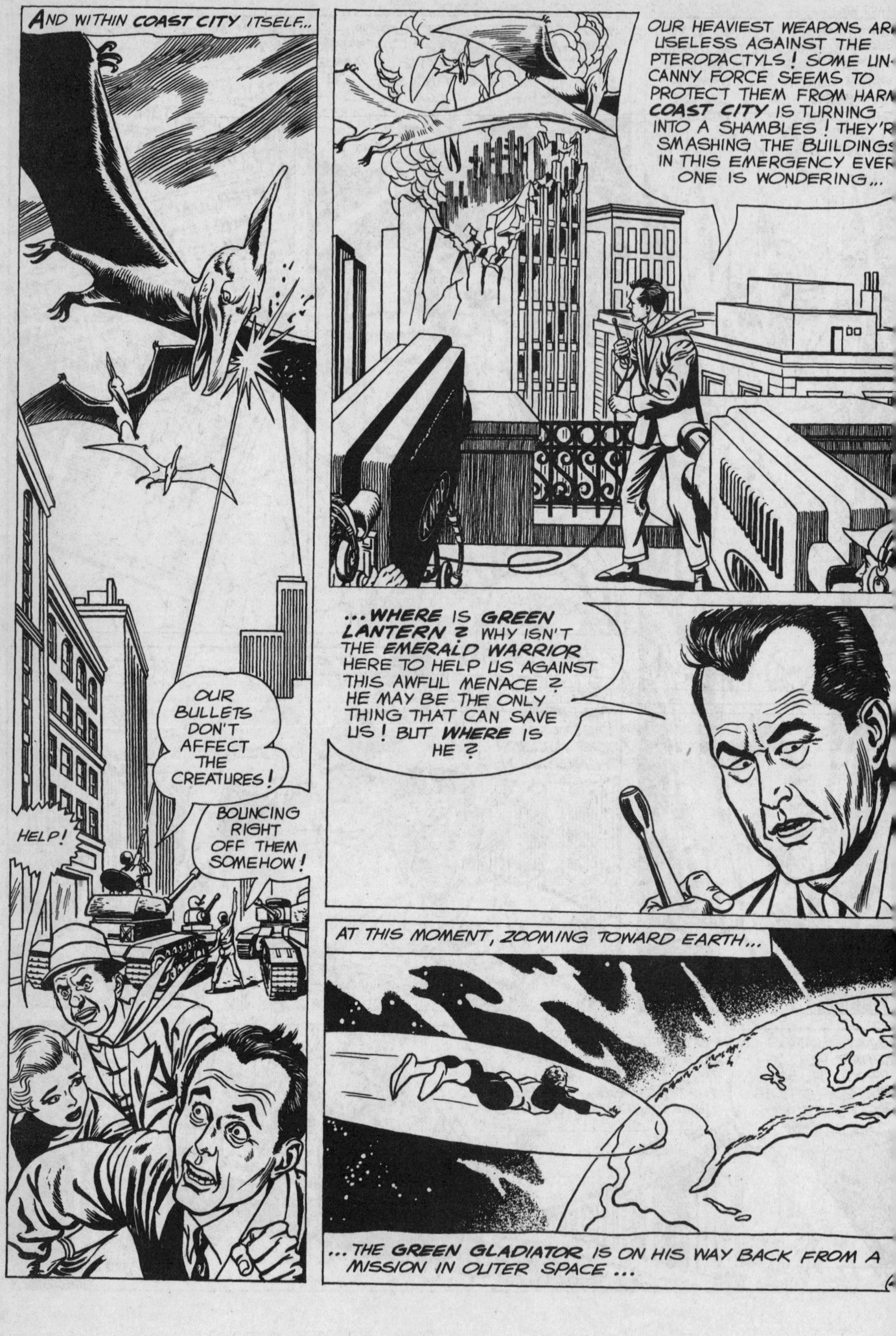
AND WITHIN COAST CITY ITSELF...
OUR BULLETS DON'T AFFECT THE CREATURES!
BOUNCING RIGHT OFF THEM SOMEHOW!
HELP!
OUR HEAVIEST WEAPONS AR USELESS AGAINST THE PTERODACTYLS! SOME UN-CANNY FORCE SEEMS TO PROTECT THEM FROM HAR COAST CITY IS TURNING INTO A SHAMBLES! THEY'R SMASHING THE BUILDINGS IN THIS EMERGENCY EVER ONE IS WONDERING...
...WHERE IS GREEN LANTERN? WHY ISN'T THE EMERALD WARRIOR HERE TO HELP US AGAINST THIS AWFUL MENACE? HE MAY BE THE ONLY THING THAT CAN SAVE US! BUT WHERE IS HE?
AT THIS MOMENT, ZOOMING TOWARD EARTH...
...THE GREEN GLADIATOR IS ON HIS WAY BACK FROM A MISSION IN OUTER SPACE...

AND SOON, AT THE *FERRIS AIRCRAFT COMPANY*...

GREEN LANTERN! BOY, AM I GLAD YOU FINALLY SHOWED UP!

WHY--WHAT'S THE MATTER, *PIE*?

AS THE STORY POURS FROM THE ESKIMO GREASEMONKEY WHO IS *GREEN LANTERN'S* SOLE CONFIDANT...

NOTHING--EXCEPT *YOU*... I HOPE!

--*2 PTERODACTYLS* --FROM A BYGONE AGE--ATTACKING *COAST CITY*!? AND NOTHING CAN STOP THEM!?

I'LL GET INTO ACTION IMMEDIATELY, *PIE*--AS SOON AS I RE-CHARGE MY RING!

HURRY, *GL*! EVERY MOMENT COUNTS NOW--!

*B*UT WHILE THE GREEN-CLAD CHAMPION CHARGES HIS RING AT THE *POWER BATTERY* SECRETED IN THE DRESSING ROOM OF TEST PILOT HAL JORDAN (HIS ALTER EGO), LET US FOR A MOMENT RAISE THE PERPLEXING QUESTION -- WHERE *DO* THE PTERO-DACTYLS COME FROM? WHAT LIES BEHIND THEIR SUDDEN APPEARANCE IN OUR PRESENT-DAY WORLD? AND FOR ANSWER, LET US TURN TO A STRANGE CIVILIZATION, MULTI-LIGHT-YEARS DISTANT FROM OUR GLOBE ...

WHERE THE RULING LIFE FORM IS NONE OTHER THAN *PTERO-DACTYLS!*

AS THIS *HIGH COUNCIL* KNOWS, OUR EFFORTS TO MAKE *OUR* RACE THE *DOMINANT* ONE ON THE LIFE-SUSTAINING PLANET CALLED *EARTH* HAVE FAILED UTTERLY! MANY TIME-UNITS AGO WHEN MEMBERS OF OUR RACE SPRANG UP ON EARTH, WE TOOK MEASURES TO INSURE THEIR VICTORY OVER OTHER LIFE-FORMS ...

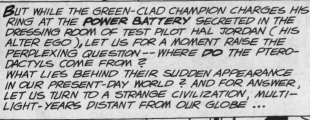

5

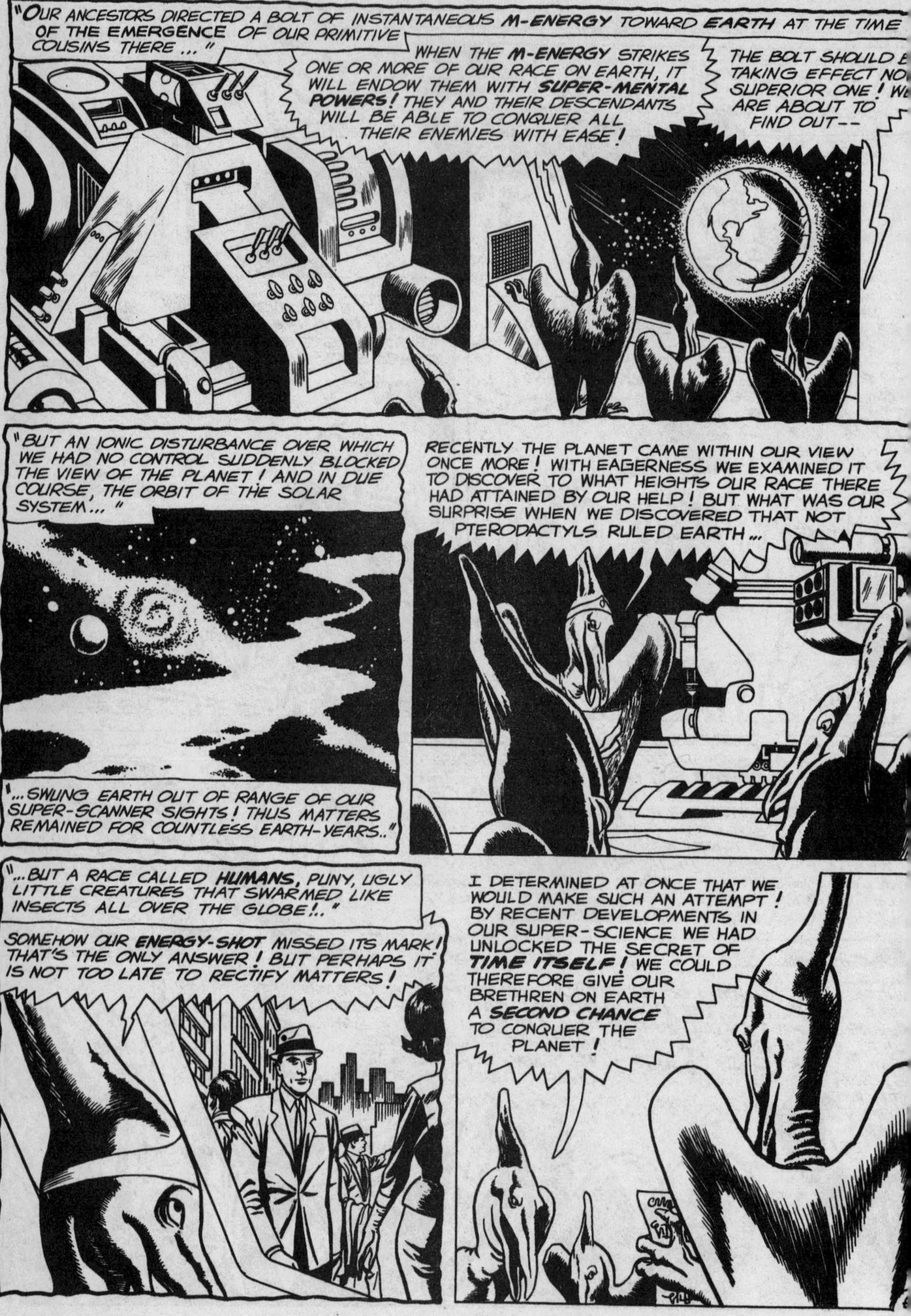
"OUR ANCESTORS DIRECTED A BOLT OF INSTANTANEOUS M-ENERGY TOWARD EARTH AT THE TIME OF THE EMERGENCE OF OUR PRIMITIVE COUSINS THERE ..."
WHEN THE M-ENERGY STRIKES ONE OR MORE OF OUR RACE ON EARTH, IT WILL ENDOW THEM WITH SUPER-MENTAL POWERS! THEY AND THEIR DESCENDANTS WILL BE ABLE TO CONQUER ALL THEIR ENEMIES WITH EASE!
THE BOLT SHOULD B TAKING EFFECT NO SUPERIOR ONE! WE ARE ABOUT TO FIND OUT--
"BUT AN IONIC DISTURBANCE OVER WHICH WE HAD NO CONTROL SUDDENLY BLOCKED THE VIEW OF THE PLANET! AND IN DUE COURSE, THE ORBIT OF THE SOLAR SYSTEM..."
"...SWUNG EARTH OUT OF RANGE OF OUR SUPER-SCANNER SIGHTS! THUS MATTERS REMAINED FOR COUNTLESS EARTH-YEARS.."
RECENTLY THE PLANET CAME WITHIN OUR VIEW ONCE MORE! WITH EAGERNESS WE EXAMINED IT TO DISCOVER TO WHAT HEIGHTS OUR RACE THERE HAD ATTAINED BY OUR HELP! BUT WHAT WAS OUR SURPRISE WHEN WE DISCOVERED THAT NOT PTERODACTYLS RULED EARTH...
"...BUT A RACE CALLED HUMANS, PUNY, UGLY LITTLE CREATURES THAT SWARMED LIKE INSECTS ALL OVER THE GLOBE!.."
SOMEHOW OUR ENERGY-SHOT MISSED ITS MARK! THAT'S THE ONLY ANSWER! BUT PERHAPS IT IS NOT TOO LATE TO RECTIFY MATTERS!
I DETERMINED AT ONCE THAT WE WOULD MAKE SUCH AN ATTEMPT! BY RECENT DEVELOPMENTS IN OUR SUPER-SCIENCE WE HAD UNLOCKED THE SECRET OF TIME ITSELF! WE COULD THEREFORE GIVE OUR BRETHREN ON EARTH A SECOND CHANCE TO CONQUER THE PLANET!

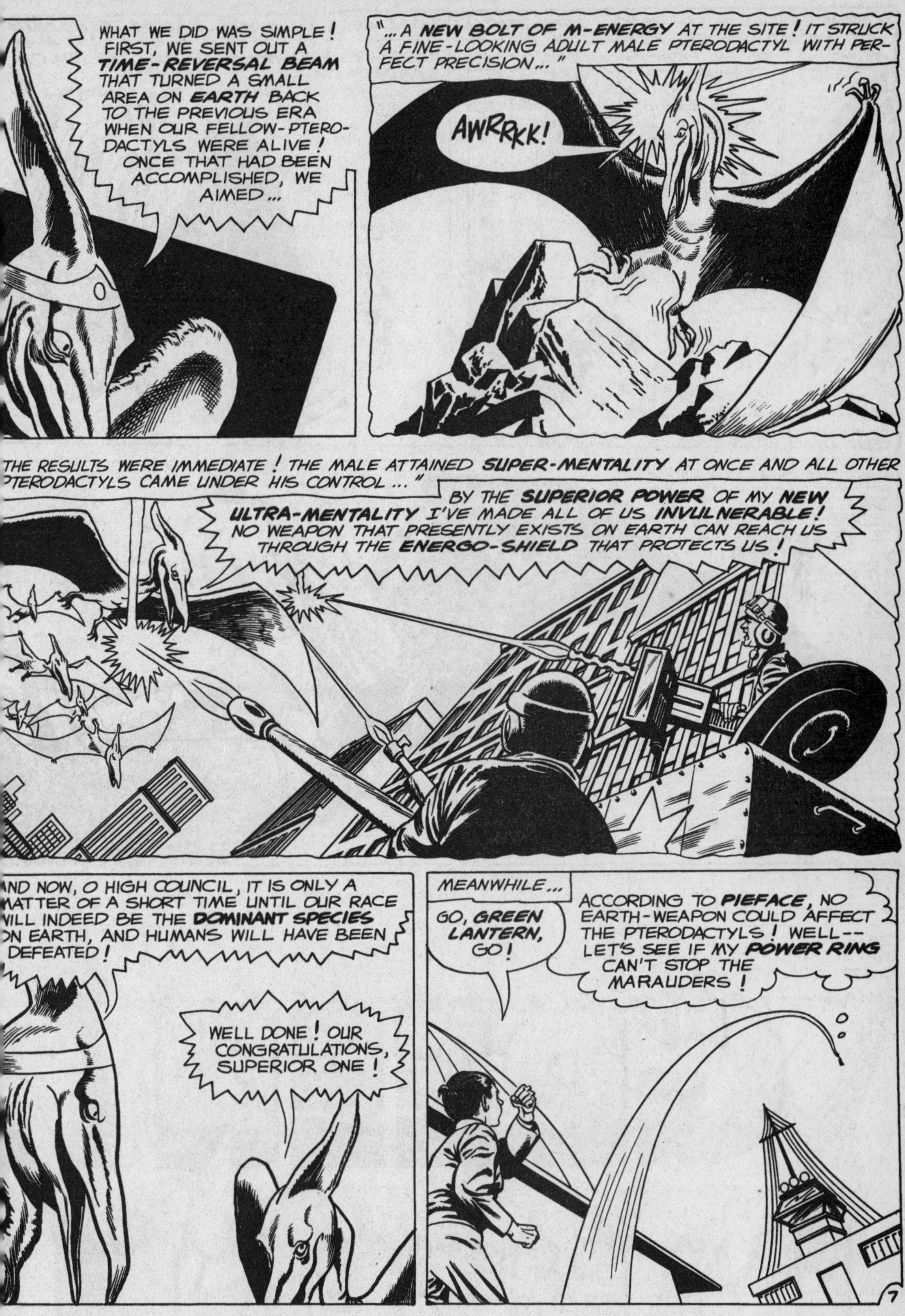
WHAT WE DID WAS SIMPLE! FIRST, WE SENT OUT A TIME-REVERSAL BEAM THAT TURNED A SMALL AREA ON EARTH BACK TO THE PREVIOUS ERA WHEN OUR FELLOW-PTERODACTYLS WERE ALIVE! ONCE THAT HAD BEEN ACCOMPLISHED, WE AIMED...
"... A NEW BOLT OF M-ENERGY AT THE SITE! IT STRUCK A FINE-LOOKING ADULT MALE PTERODACTYL WITH PERFECT PRECISION..."
AWRRKK!
THE RESULTS WERE IMMEDIATE! THE MALE ATTAINED SUPER-MENTALITY AT ONCE AND ALL OTHER PTERODACTYLS CAME UNDER HIS CONTROL..."
BY THE SUPERIOR POWER OF MY NEW ULTRA-MENTALITY I'VE MADE ALL OF US INVULNERABLE! NO WEAPON THAT PRESENTLY EXISTS ON EARTH CAN REACH US THROUGH THE ENERGO-SHIELD THAT PROTECTS US!
AND NOW, O HIGH COUNCIL, IT IS ONLY A MATTER OF A SHORT TIME UNTIL OUR RACE WILL INDEED BE THE DOMINANT SPECIES ON EARTH, AND HUMANS WILL HAVE BEEN DEFEATED!
WELL DONE! OUR CONGRATULATIONS, SUPERIOR ONE!
MEANWHILE...
GO, GREEN LANTERN, GO!
ACCORDING TO PIEFACE, NO EARTH-WEAPON COULD AFFECT THE PTERODACTYLS! WELL-- LET'S SEE IF MY POWER RING CAN'T STOP THE MARAUDERS!
7

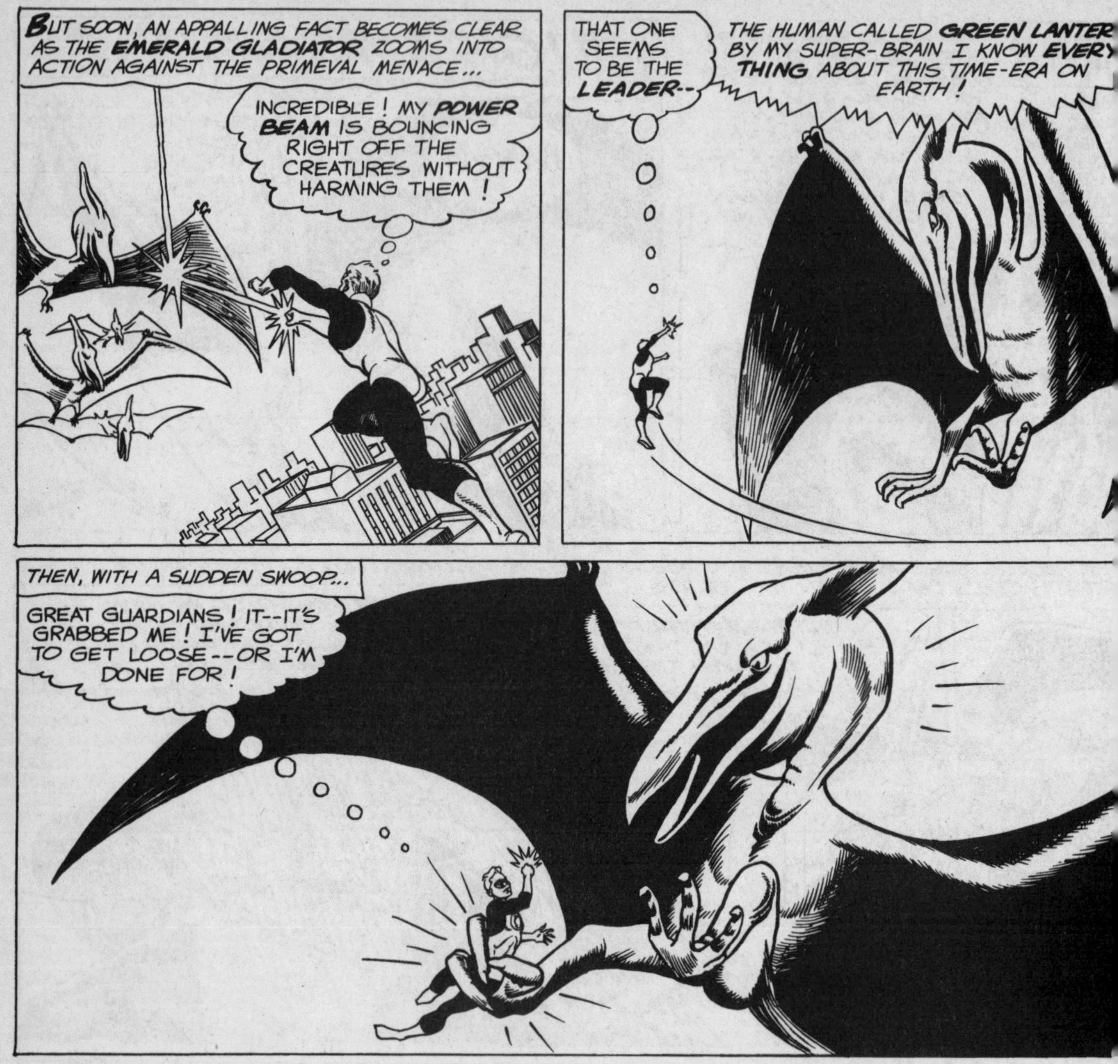
BUT SOON, AN APPALLING FACT BECOMES CLEAR AS THE EMERALD GLADIATOR ZOOMS INTO ACTION AGAINST THE PRIMEVAL MENACE...
INCREDIBLE! MY POWER BEAM IS BOUNCING RIGHT OFF THE CREATURES WITHOUT HARMING THEM!
THAT ONE SEEMS TO BE THE LEADER--
THE HUMAN CALLED GREEN LANTER
BY MY SUPER-BRAIN I KNOW EVERY
THING ABOUT THIS TIME-ERA ON EARTH!
THEN, WITH A SUDDEN SWOOP...
GREAT GUARDIANS! IT--IT'S GRABBED ME! I'VE GOT TO GET LOOSE--OR I'M DONE FOR!

GREEN LANTERN

THE TUNNEL THROUGH TIME! PART 2

USING HIS GREAT GREEN BEAM LIKE THE EXHAUST OF A ROCKET, THE EMERALD CRUSADER SPURTS WITH OVERWHELMING FORCE OUT OF THE GRIP OF THE GIANT REPTILE...

AWRRK!

BY SHOOTING MY BEAM OUT *BEHIND ME*, THE RESULT IS TO GIVE ME A POWERFUL THRUST *FORWARD*! I'M RIPPING LOOSE FROM THE PTERO'S GRASP!

THEN, A SWIFT *REAR ATTACK*...

UHH!

AWRK! GREEN LANTERN DIDN'T REALIZE--

--THAT I CAN CONTROL *ALL* MY FELLOW-PTERODACTYLS BY THE FORCE OF MY *SUPER-BRAIN*! IT'S HIS FINISH--

BUT AS THE *GREEN GLADIATOR* FALLS, HIS *POWER RING* AUTOMATICALLY LEAPS INTO THE BREACH, TO SAVE HIM FROM *MORTAL HARM*...

...AND CUSHIONS HIS FALL TO KEEP HIM FROM BEING CRUSHED.

AND THUS, SHORTLY, AS *PIE-FACE* REACHES HIS "FALLEN IDOL"...

I SAW YOUR BATTLE WITH THE PTERO-DACTYLS, *GREEN LANTERN*, AND RUSHED OVER HERE AS FAST AS I COULD! ARE Y-YOU ALL RIGHT?

GUESS SO, *PIE*! NO BONES BROKEN! BUT I SURE TOOK A LICKING!

9

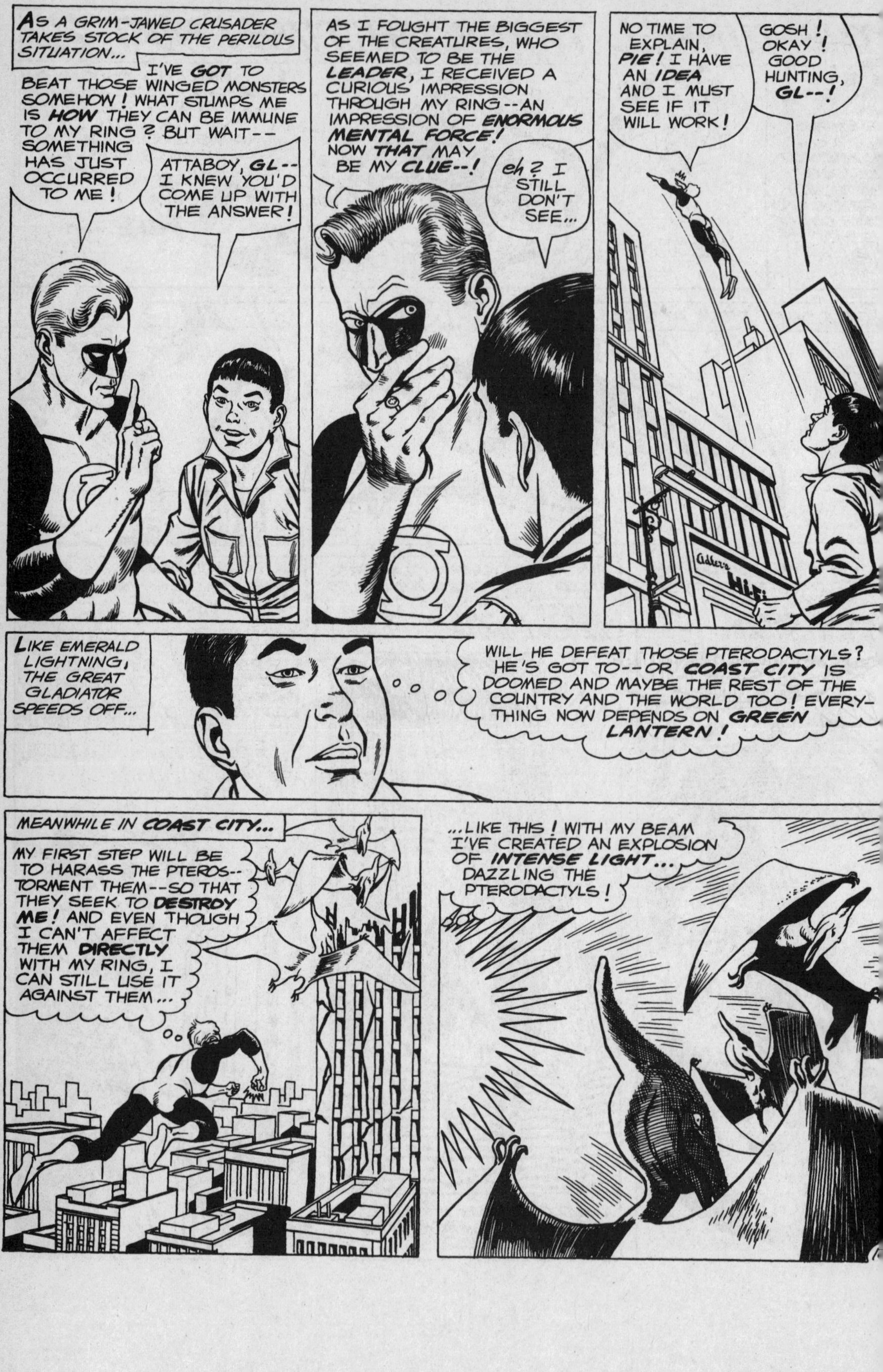
AS A GRIM-JAWED CRUSADER TAKES STOCK OF THE PERILOUS SITUATION...
I'VE GOT TO BEAT THOSE WINGED MONSTERS SOMEHOW! WHAT STUMPS ME IS HOW THEY CAN BE IMMUNE TO MY RING? BUT WAIT-- SOMETHING HAS JUST OCCURRED TO ME!
ATTABOY, GL-- I KNEW YOU'D COME UP WITH THE ANSWER!
AS I FOUGHT THE BIGGEST OF THE CREATURES, WHO SEEMED TO BE THE LEADER, I RECEIVED A CURIOUS IMPRESSION THROUGH MY RING--AN IMPRESSION OF ENORMOUS MENTAL FORCE! NOW THAT MAY BE MY CLUE--!
eh? I STILL DON'T SEE...
NO TIME TO EXPLAIN, PIE! I HAVE AN IDEA AND I MUST SEE IF IT WILL WORK!
GOSH! OKAY! GOOD HUNTING, GL--!
Adler's
Hi-Fi
LIKE EMERALD LIGHTNING, THE GREAT GLADIATOR SPEEDS OFF...
WILL HE DEFEAT THOSE PTERODACTYLS? HE'S GOT TO--OR COAST CITY IS DOOMED AND MAYBE THE REST OF THE COUNTRY AND THE WORLD TOO! EVERYTHING NOW DEPENDS ON GREEN LANTERN!
MEANWHILE IN COAST CITY...
MY FIRST STEP WILL BE TO HARASS THE PTEROS-- TORMENT THEM--SO THAT THEY SEEK TO DESTROY ME! AND EVEN THOUGH I CAN'T AFFECT THEM DIRECTLY WITH MY RING, I CAN STILL USE IT AGAINST THEM...
...LIKE THIS! WITH MY BEAM I'VE CREATED AN EXPLOSION OF INTENSE LIGHT... DAZZLING THE PTERODACTYLS!

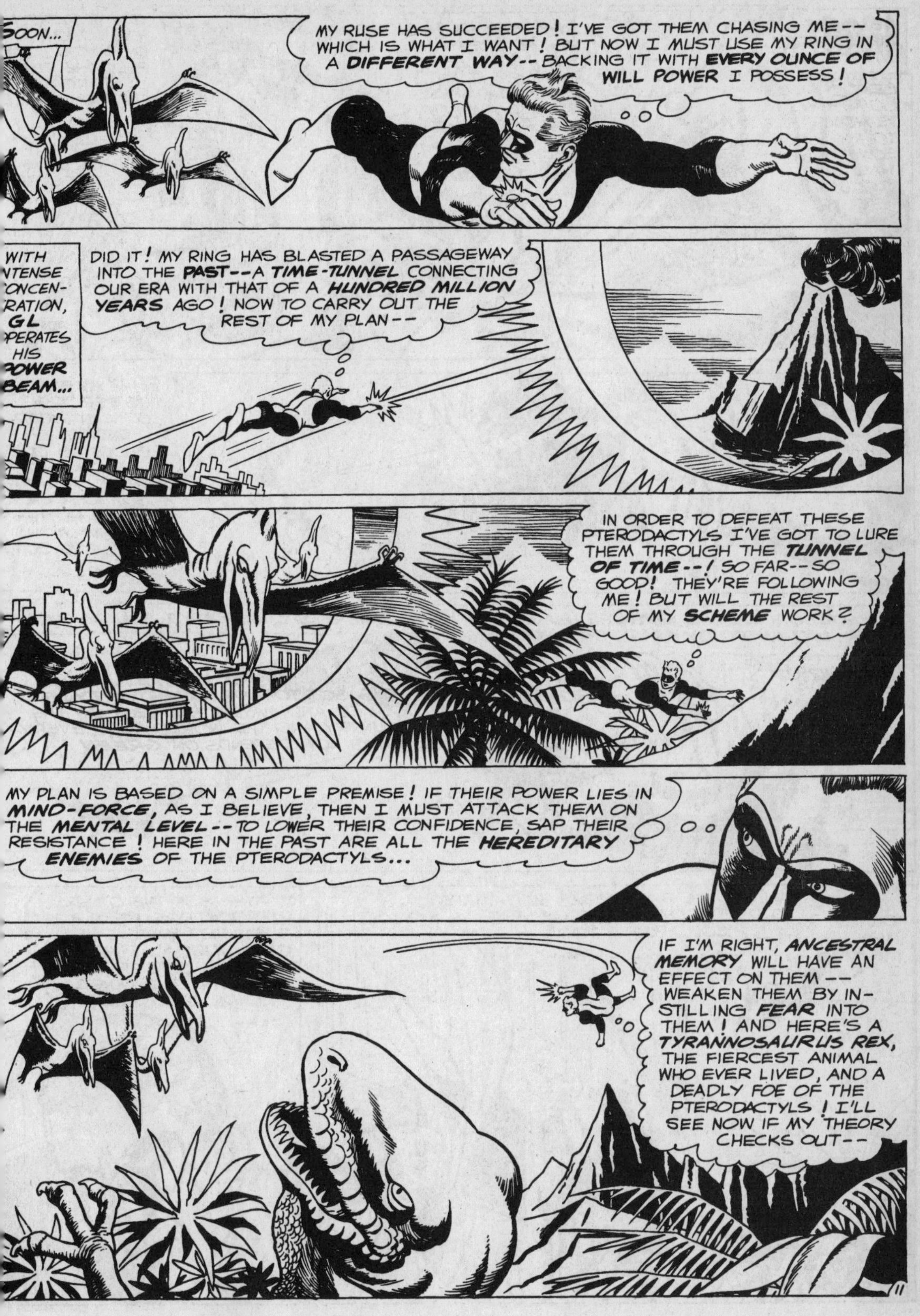
SOON...
MY RUSE HAS SUCCEEDED! I'VE GOT THEM CHASING ME -- WHICH IS WHAT I WANT! BUT NOW I MUST USE MY RING IN A DIFFERENT WAY -- BACKING IT WITH EVERY OUNCE OF WILL POWER I POSSESS!
WITH INTENSE CONCENTRATION, GL OPERATES HIS POWER BEAM...
DID IT! MY RING HAS BLASTED A PASSAGEWAY INTO THE PAST -- A TIME-TUNNEL CONNECTING OUR ERA WITH THAT OF A HUNDRED MILLION YEARS AGO! NOW TO CARRY OUT THE REST OF MY PLAN --
IN ORDER TO DEFEAT THESE PTERODACTYLS I'VE GOT TO LURE THEM THROUGH THE TUNNEL OF TIME --! SO FAR -- SO GOOD! THEY'RE FOLLOWING ME! BUT WILL THE REST OF MY SCHEME WORK?
MY PLAN IS BASED ON A SIMPLE PREMISE! IF THEIR POWER LIES IN MIND-FORCE, AS I BELIEVE, THEN I MUST ATTACK THEM ON THE MENTAL LEVEL -- TO LOWER THEIR CONFIDENCE, SAP THEIR RESISTANCE! HERE IN THE PAST ARE ALL THE HEREDITARY ENEMIES OF THE PTERODACTYLS...
IF I'M RIGHT, ANCESTRAL MEMORY WILL HAVE AN EFFECT ON THEM -- WEAKEN THEM BY INSTILLING FEAR INTO THEM! AND HERE'S A TYRANNOSAURUS REX, THE FIERCEST ANIMAL WHO EVER LIVED, AND A DEADLY FOE OF THE PTERODACTYLS! I'LL SEE NOW IF MY THEORY CHECKS OUT --
11

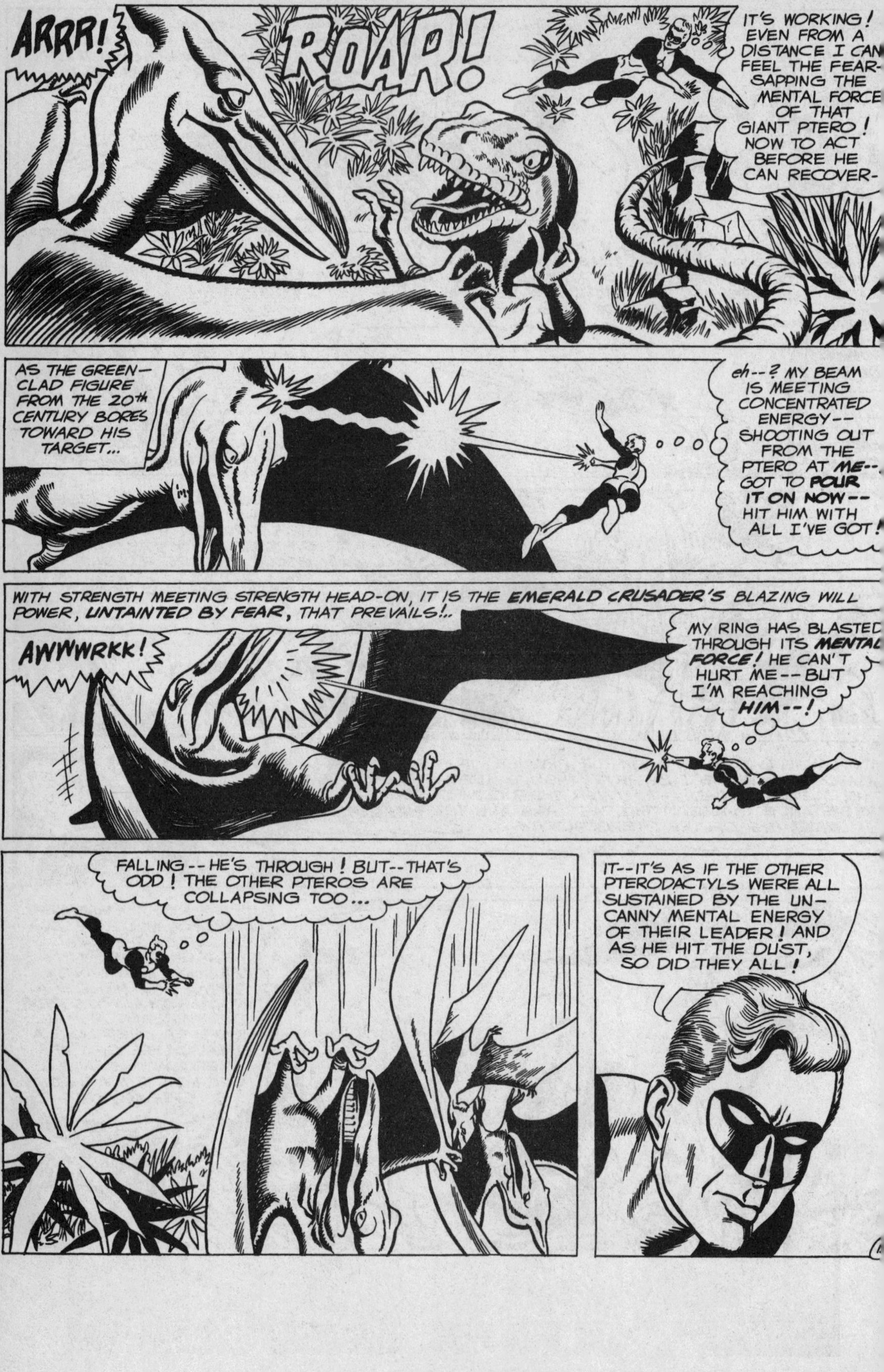
ARRR!
ROAR!
IT'S WORKING! EVEN FROM A DISTANCE I CAN FEEL THE FEAR-SAPPING THE MENTAL FORCE OF THAT GIANT PTERO! NOW TO ACT BEFORE HE CAN RECOVER-
AS THE GREEN-CLAD FIGURE FROM THE 20th CENTURY BORES TOWARD HIS TARGET...
eh--? MY BEAM IS MEETING CONCENTRATED ENERGY--SHOOTING OUT FROM THE PTERO AT ME--GOT TO POUR IT ON NOW--HIT HIM WITH ALL I'VE GOT!
WITH STRENGTH MEETING STRENGTH HEAD-ON, IT IS THE EMERALD CRUSADER'S BLAZING WILL POWER, UNTAINTED BY FEAR, THAT PREVAILS!..
AWWWRKK!
MY RING HAS BLASTED THROUGH ITS MENTAL FORCE! HE CAN'T HURT ME--BUT I'M REACHING HIM--!
FALLING--HE'S THROUGH! BUT--THAT'S ODD! THE OTHER PTEROS ARE COLLAPSING TOO...
IT--IT'S AS IF THE OTHER PTERODACTYLS WERE ALL SUSTAINED BY THE UNCANNY MENTAL ENERGY OF THEIR LEADER! AND AS HE HIT THE DUST, SO DID THEY ALL!

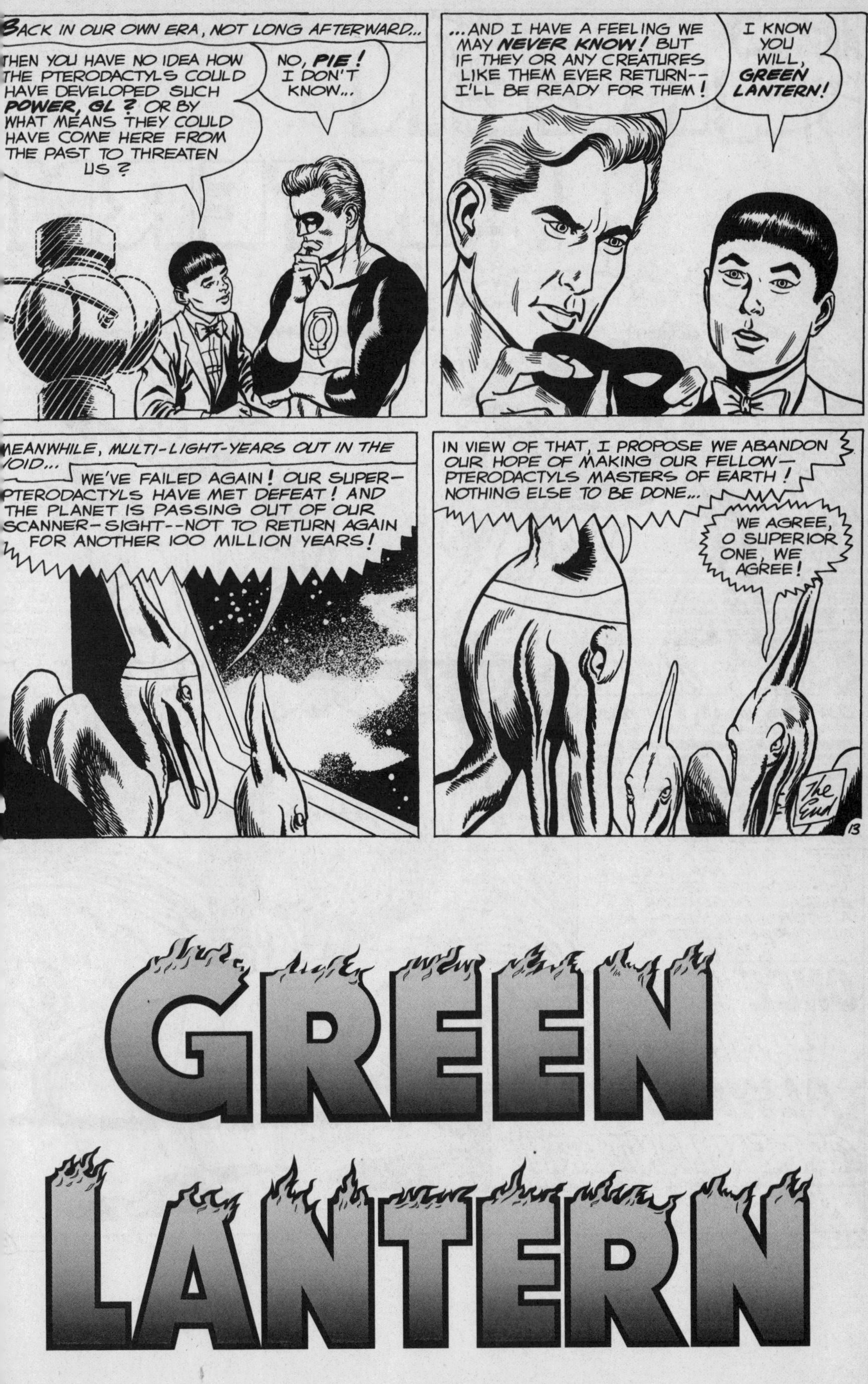
BACK IN OUR OWN ERA, NOT LONG AFTERWARD...
THEN YOU HAVE NO IDEA HOW THE PTERODACTYLS COULD HAVE DEVELOPED SUCH POWER, GL? OR BY WHAT MEANS THEY COULD HAVE COME HERE FROM THE PAST TO THREATEN US?
NO, PIE! I DON'T KNOW...
...AND I HAVE A FEELING WE MAY NEVER KNOW! BUT IF THEY OR ANY CREATURES LIKE THEM EVER RETURN-- I'LL BE READY FOR THEM!
I KNOW YOU WILL, GREEN LANTERN!
MEANWHILE, MULTI-LIGHT-YEARS OUT IN THE VOID...
WE'VE FAILED AGAIN! OUR SUPER-PTERODACTYLS HAVE MET DEFEAT! AND THE PLANET IS PASSING OUT OF OUR SCANNER-SIGHT--NOT TO RETURN AGAIN FOR ANOTHER 100 MILLION YEARS!
IN VIEW OF THAT, I PROPOSE WE ABANDON OUR HOPE OF MAKING OUR FELLOW-PTERODACTYLS MASTERS OF EARTH! NOTHING ELSE TO BE DONE...
WE AGREE, O SUPERIOR ONE, WE AGREE!
The End
13

GREEN LANTERN

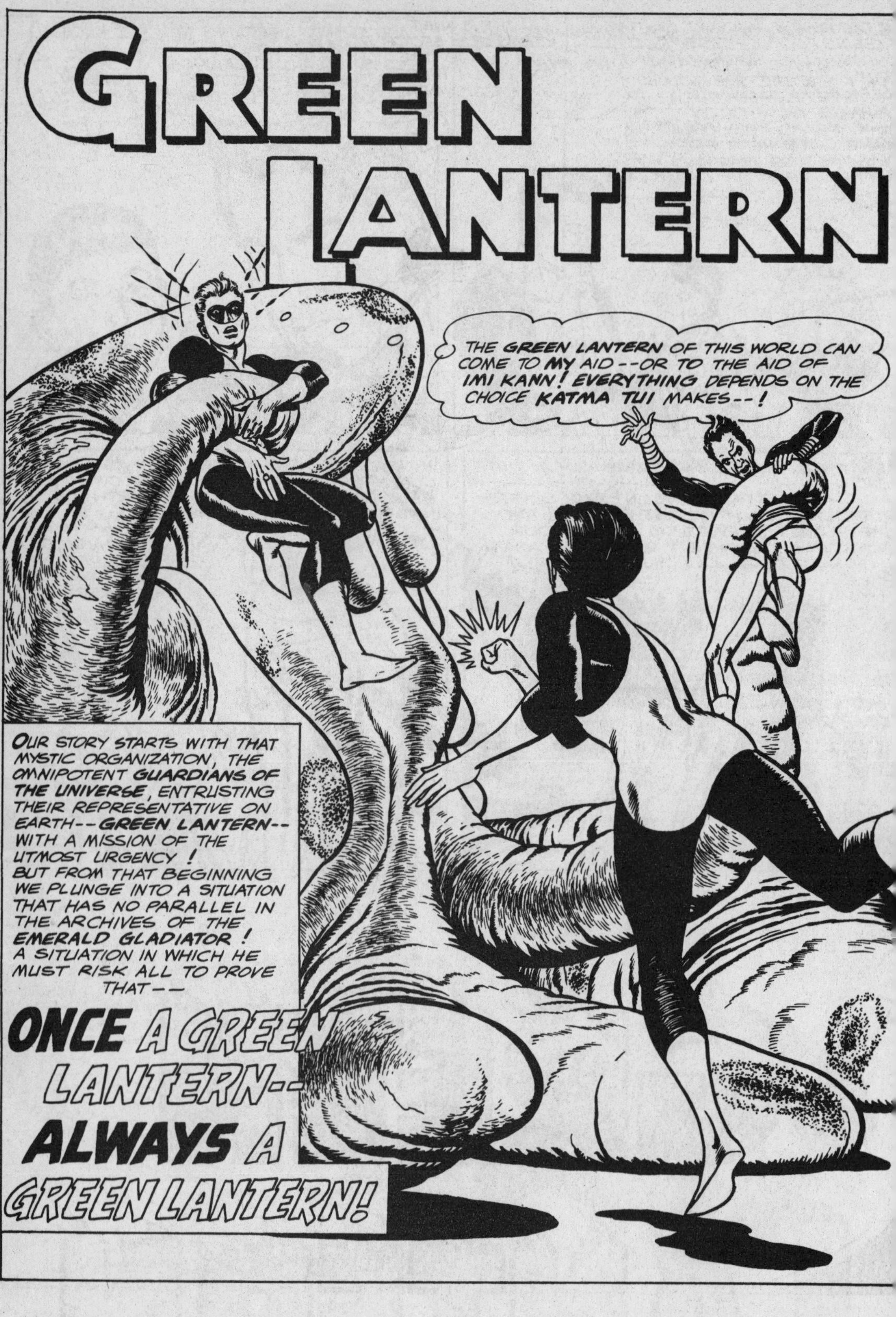
GREEN LANTERN
THE GREEN LANTERN OF THIS WORLD CAN COME TO MY AID--OR TO THE AID OF IMI KANN! EVERYTHING DEPENDS ON THE CHOICE KATMA TUI MAKES--!
OUR STORY STARTS WITH THAT MYSTIC ORGANIZATION, THE OMNIPOTENT GUARDIANS OF THE UNIVERSE, ENTRUSTING THEIR REPRESENTATIVE ON EARTH--GREEN LANTERN--WITH A MISSION OF THE UTMOST URGENCY! BUT FROM THAT BEGINNING WE PLUNGE INTO A SITUATION THAT HAS NO PARALLEL IN THE ARCHIVES OF THE EMERALD GLADIATOR! A SITUATION IN WHICH HE MUST RISK ALL TO PROVE THAT--
ONCE A GREEN LANTERN--ALWAYS A GREEN LANTERN!

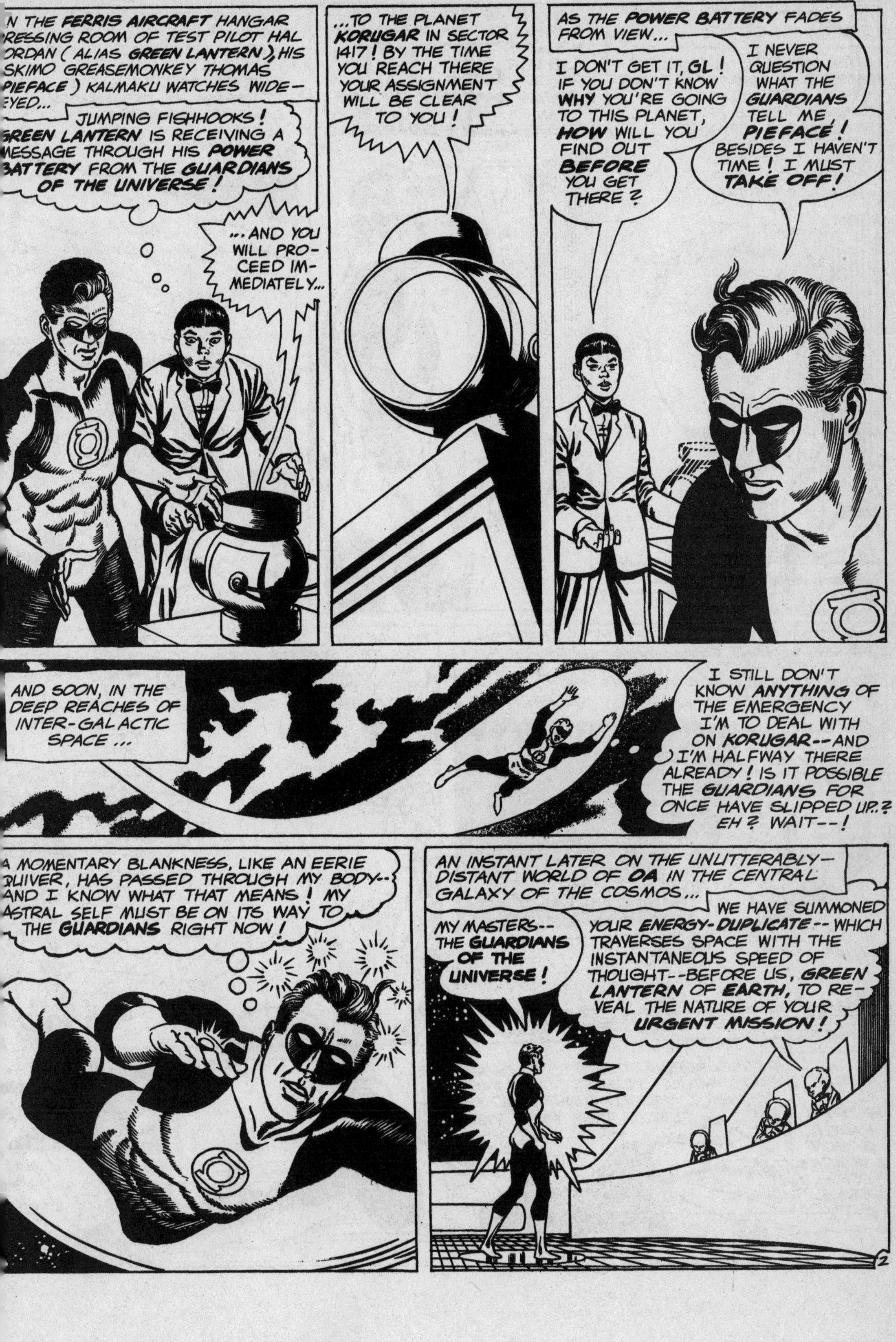
IN THE FERRIS AIRCRAFT HANGAR DRESSING ROOM OF TEST PILOT HAL JORDAN (ALIAS GREEN LANTERN), HIS ESKIMO GREASEMONKEY THOMAS (PIEFACE) KALMAKU WATCHES WIDE-EYED...
JUMPING FISHHOOKS! GREEN LANTERN IS RECEIVING A MESSAGE THROUGH HIS POWER BATTERY FROM THE GUARDIANS OF THE UNIVERSE!
...AND YOU WILL PROCEED IMMEDIATELY...
...TO THE PLANET KORUGAR IN SECTOR 1417! BY THE TIME YOU REACH THERE YOUR ASSIGNMENT WILL BE CLEAR TO YOU!
AS THE POWER BATTERY FADES FROM VIEW...
I DON'T GET IT, GL! IF YOU DON'T KNOW WHY YOU'RE GOING TO THIS PLANET, HOW WILL YOU FIND OUT BEFORE YOU GET THERE?
I NEVER QUESTION WHAT THE GUARDIANS TELL ME, PIEFACE! BESIDES I HAVEN'T TIME! I MUST TAKE OFF!
AND SOON, IN THE DEEP REACHES OF INTER-GALACTIC SPACE...
I STILL DON'T KNOW ANYTHING OF THE EMERGENCY I'M TO DEAL WITH ON KORUGAR--AND I'M HALFWAY THERE ALREADY! IS IT POSSIBLE THE GUARDIANS FOR ONCE HAVE SLIPPED UP..? EH? WAIT--!
A MOMENTARY BLANKNESS, LIKE AN EERIE QUIVER, HAS PASSED THROUGH MY BODY--AND I KNOW WHAT THAT MEANS! MY ASTRAL SELF MUST BE ON ITS WAY TO THE GUARDIANS RIGHT NOW!
AN INSTANT LATER ON THE UNUTTERABLY-DISTANT WORLD OF OA IN THE CENTRAL GALAXY OF THE COSMOS...
MY MASTERS--THE GUARDIANS OF THE UNIVERSE!
WE HAVE SUMMONED YOUR ENERGY-DUPLICATE--WHICH TRAVERSES SPACE WITH THE INSTANTANEOUS SPEED OF THOUGHT--BEFORE US, GREEN LANTERN OF EARTH, TO REVEAL THE NATURE OF YOUR URGENT MISSION!
2

AS A STRANGE SITUATION IS SWIFTLY REVEALED...

...AND AFTER THE RENEGADE GREEN LANTERN--SINESTRO--TURNED TO EVIL, AND HAD BEEN BANISHED BY US FROM KORUGAR,* WE WERE FORCED TO SELECT ANOTHER BATTERY POSSESSOR TO TAKE HIS PLACE ON THAT WORLD...

*Editor's Note: SEE "THE DAY 100,000 PEOPLE VANISHED!"-- in GREEN LANTERN #7.

THE ONE WE CHOSE, CALLED KATMA TUI, FULFILLED OUR HOPES IN EVERY RESPECT, AND DURING THE PROBATION PERIOD CARRIED OUT ALL GREEN LANTERN DUTIES IN AN EXEMPLARY MANNER! THEREFORE WE GUARDIANS DECIDED...

...TO MAKE THE CHANGE PERMANEN[T] BUT WHAT WAS OUR ASTONISHMEN[T] WHEN, UPON CONTACTING KORUGA[R] TO REVEAL THE NEWS, WE LEARNE[D] THAT KATMA TUI HAD RESOLVED TO RESIGN AS THE GREEN LANTERN OF THAT PLANET AS OF THE END OF THE PROBATION PERIOD!

AND NO AMOUNT OF ARGUING OR EVEN BESEECH-ING ON OUR PART COULD MAKE ANY DIFFERENCE! NOW, GREEN LANTERN, THAT IS WHY YOU ARE GOING TO KORUGAR! WE WANT YOU TO CON-TACT KATMA TUI AS SOON AS YOU ARRIVE THERE...

WE WANT YOU TO USE EVERY POSSIBLE MEANS TO ALTER KATMA TUI'S DECISION! AND YOU HAVE NO TIME TO WASTE! THE PROBATION PERIOD ENDS IN ONE KORUGARAN DAY-- ABOUT TWENTY OF YOUR EARTH HOURS!

I WILL DO MY BEST!

AS THE ASTRAL SELF REJOINS EARTH GREEN LANTERN'S COR-POREAL BODY...

THERE'S KORUGAR NOW! THE GUARDIANS SAID I WOULD UNDERSTAND MY MISSION BEFORE I ARRIVED THERE, AND AS ALWAYS THEY WERE RIGHT!

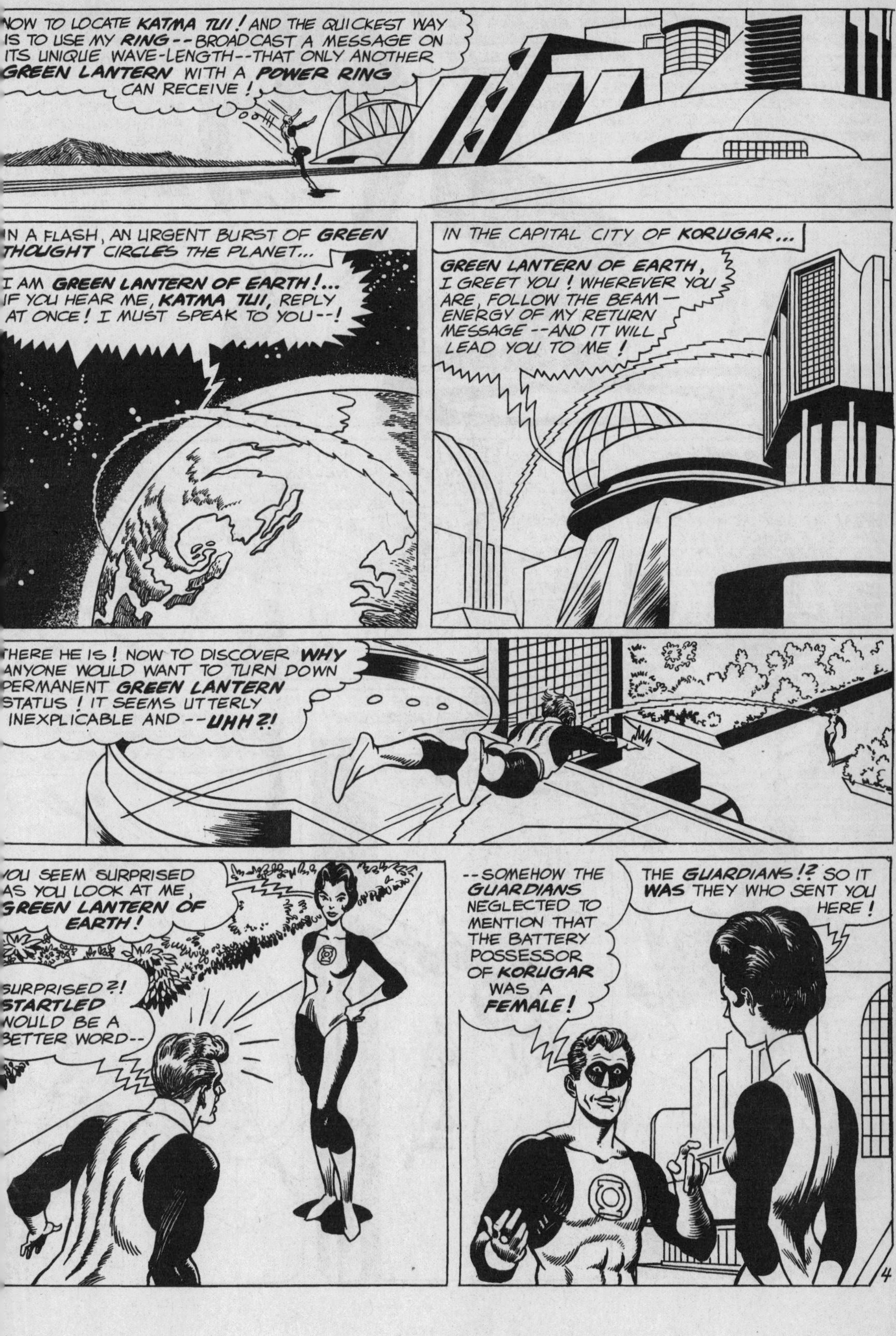
NOW TO LOCATE KATMA TUI! AND THE QUICKEST WAY IS TO USE MY RING--BROADCAST A MESSAGE ON ITS UNIQUE WAVE-LENGTH--THAT ONLY ANOTHER GREEN LANTERN WITH A POWER RING CAN RECEIVE!
IN A FLASH, AN URGENT BURST OF GREEN THOUGHT CIRCLES THE PLANET...
I AM GREEN LANTERN OF EARTH!... IF YOU HEAR ME, KATMA TUI, REPLY AT ONCE! I MUST SPEAK TO YOU--!
IN THE CAPITAL CITY OF KORUGAR...
GREEN LANTERN OF EARTH, I GREET YOU! WHEREVER YOU ARE, FOLLOW THE BEAM--ENERGY OF MY RETURN MESSAGE--AND IT WILL LEAD YOU TO ME!
THERE HE IS! NOW TO DISCOVER WHY ANYONE WOULD WANT TO TURN DOWN PERMANENT GREEN LANTERN STATUS! IT SEEMS UTTERLY INEXPLICABLE AND--UHH?!
YOU SEEM SURPRISED AS YOU LOOK AT ME, GREEN LANTERN OF EARTH!
SURPRISED?! STARTLED WOULD BE A BETTER WORD--
--SOMEHOW THE GUARDIANS NEGLECTED TO MENTION THAT THE BATTERY POSSESSOR OF KORUGAR WAS A FEMALE!
THE GUARDIANS!? SO IT WAS THEY WHO SENT YOU HERE!
4

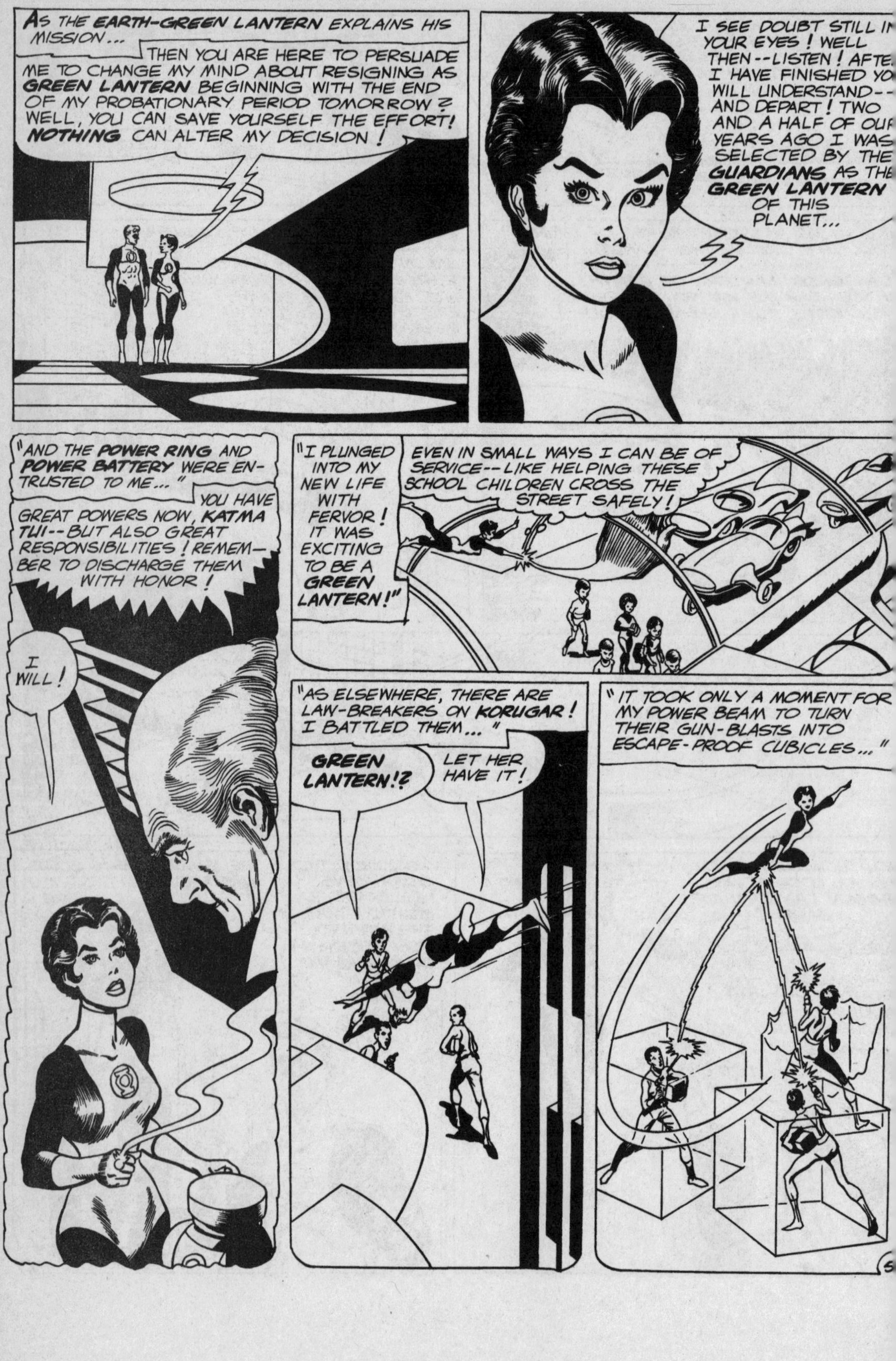
AS THE EARTH-GREEN LANTERN EXPLAINS HIS MISSION...
THEN YOU ARE HERE TO PERSUADE ME TO CHANGE MY MIND ABOUT RESIGNING AS GREEN LANTERN BEGINNING WITH THE END OF MY PROBATIONARY PERIOD TOMORROW? WELL, YOU CAN SAVE YOURSELF THE EFFORT! NOTHING CAN ALTER MY DECISION!
I SEE DOUBT STILL IN YOUR EYES! WELL THEN--LISTEN! AFTE I HAVE FINISHED YO WILL UNDERSTAND-- AND DEPART! TWO AND A HALF OF OU YEARS AGO I WAS SELECTED BY THE GUARDIANS AS THE GREEN LANTERN OF THIS PLANET...
"AND THE POWER RING AND POWER BATTERY WERE ENTRUSTED TO ME..."
YOU HAVE GREAT POWERS NOW, KATMA TUI--BUT ALSO GREAT RESPONSIBILITIES! REMEMBER TO DISCHARGE THEM WITH HONOR!
I WILL!
"I PLUNGED INTO MY NEW LIFE WITH FERVOR! IT WAS EXCITING TO BE A GREEN LANTERN!"
EVEN IN SMALL WAYS I CAN BE OF SERVICE--LIKE HELPING THESE SCHOOL CHILDREN CROSS THE STREET SAFELY!
"AS ELSEWHERE, THERE ARE LAW-BREAKERS ON KORUGAR! I BATTLED THEM..."
GREEN LANTERN!?
LET HER HAVE IT!
"IT TOOK ONLY A MOMENT FOR MY POWER BEAM TO TURN THEIR GUN-BLASTS INTO ESCAPE-PROOF CUBICLES..."
5

DURING THOSE YEARS A FAN-ASTIC MENACE THREATENED UR PLANET..."

...WHAT EEMS TO BE A *GIANT* *MOEBA*!* IT IS ADVANCING N *KORUGAR CITY* -- BSORBING ALL LIVING HINGS IN ITS PATH!

Editor's Note: ORDINARILY, A MICROSCOPIC ONE-CELLED ANIMAL!

"I SPED AT ONCE TO MEET THE THREAT..."

OUR SCIENTISTS SAY THE *AMOEBA* HAS SOMEHOW DEVELOPED A "BRAIN"--AND THAT IT SEEMS BENT ON BECOMING THE DOMINATING LIFE-FORM OF *KORUGAR*--DE-STROYING US HUMANS COMPLETELY! I MUST DEFEAT IT!

"THE CONFLICT BETWEEN US WAS OF TERRIBLE INTENSITY!"

THE "NERVE-CENTER" OF AN AMOEBA IS IN ITS *NUCLEUS*! I'VE SHATTERED THAT WITH MY RING --AND THE ENTIRE CREATURE IS DISSOLVING, COLLAPSING COMPLETELY!

IT SHOULD BE CLEAR FROM WHAT I HAVE TOLD YOU, MY RECORD HAS BEEN A GOOD NE! AND I WAS PRE-ARED TO REMAIN A REEN LANTERN ALL Y LIFE! BUT THE NE THING I DIDN'T ORESEE WAS THAT WAS GOING TO *FALL IN LOVE*!

EH?!

ONE OF OUR MOST BRILLIANT SCIENTISTS, WHO COLLABORATED WITH ME IN OUR FIGHT AGAINST THE AMOEBA, FELL IN LOVE WITH ME! I FELT MYSELF RETURNING HIS LOVE! BUT I HAD TO BE SURE! I USED MY *POWER BEAM* TO *TEST MYSELF...!* ⑥

I'VE MADE AN *EMOTION-METER* WITH MY *RING!* IT SHOWS WHAT I FEEL-- AND THERE'S NO DOUBT...

...THE POINTER IS ALL THE WAY TOWARD THE *PLUS* SIDE! I *LOVE IMI KANN!* MY HEART IS *HIS!*

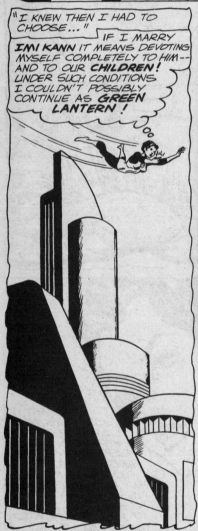

"I KNEW THEN I HAD TO CHOOSE..."

IF I MARRY *IMI KANN* IT MEANS DEVOTING MYSELF COMPLETELY TO HIM-- AND TO OUR *CHILDREN!* UNDER SUCH CONDITIONS I COULDN'T POSSIBLY CONTINUE AS *GREEN LANTERN!*

"FINALLY, I MADE MY CHOICE, AND I CHOSE *LOVE!*"

SO YOU SEE, YOU ARE UP AGAINST ONE OF THE MOST *POWERFUL FORCES* IN THE UNIVERSE! IT'S USELESS TO BATTLE AGAINST IT!

MAYBE SO...

BUT ON THE OTHER HAND I STILL HAVE SOME TIME IN WHICH I AM DUTY-BOUND TO MAKE *EVERY EFFORT* TO CARRY OUT MY MISSION! YOU KNOW AS WELL AS I DO, *KATMA TUI,* WE *GREEN LANTERNS* DON'T GIVE UP SO EASILY!

SEE YOU LATER...!

WHERE IS HE GOING? WHAT IS HE UP TO NOW--?

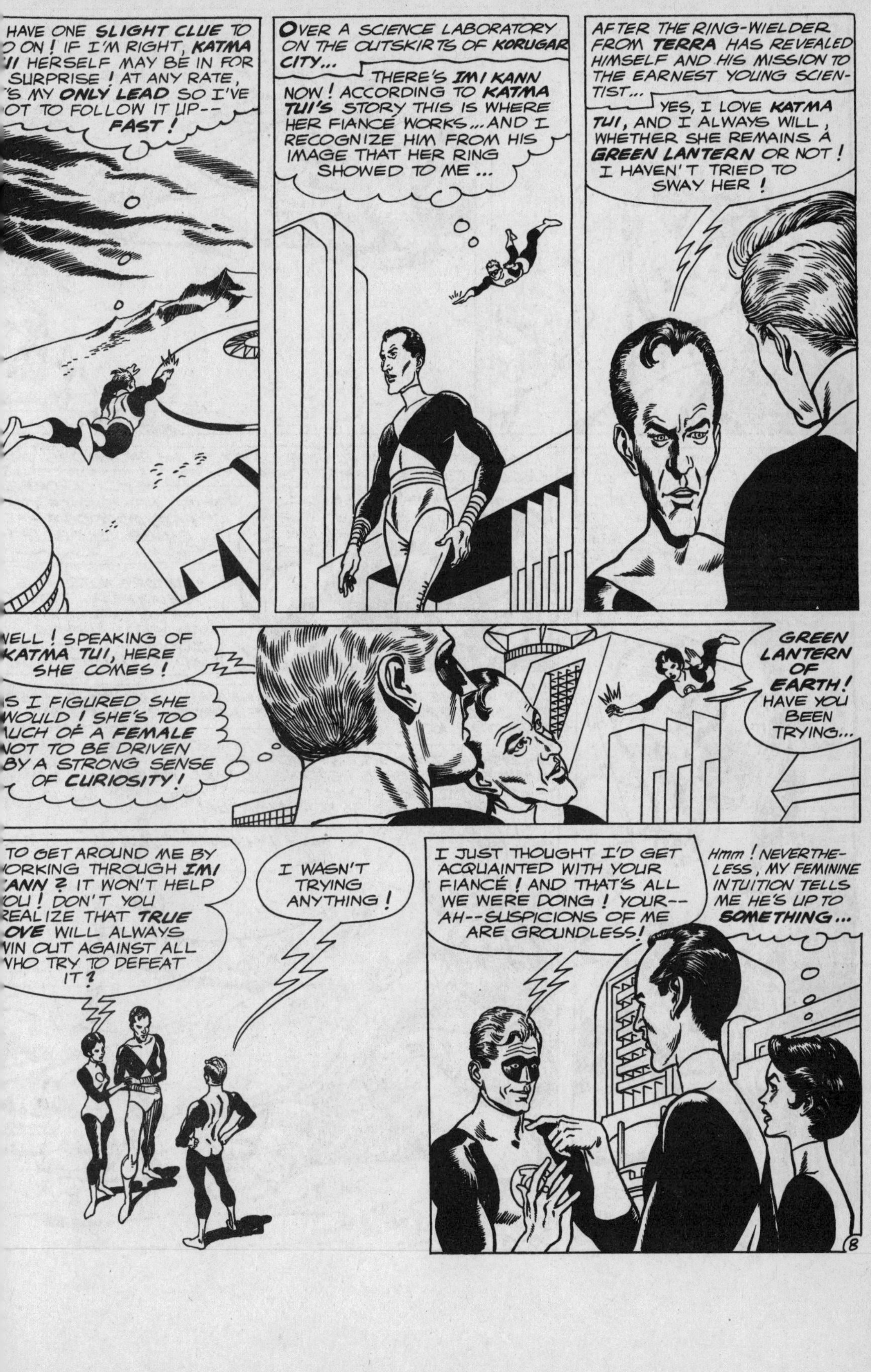
HAVE ONE SLIGHT CLUE TO GO ON! IF I'M RIGHT, KATMA TUI HERSELF MAY BE IN FOR A SURPRISE! AT ANY RATE, IT'S MY ONLY LEAD SO I'VE GOT TO FOLLOW IT UP-- FAST!
OVER A SCIENCE LABORATORY ON THE OUTSKIRTS OF KORUGAR CITY...
THERE'S IMI KANN NOW! ACCORDING TO KATMA TUI'S STORY THIS IS WHERE HER FIANCÉ WORKS... AND I RECOGNIZE HIM FROM HIS IMAGE THAT HER RING SHOWED TO ME...
AFTER THE RING-WIELDER FROM TERRA HAS REVEALED HIMSELF AND HIS MISSION TO THE EARNEST YOUNG SCIENTIST...
YES, I LOVE KATMA TUI, AND I ALWAYS WILL, WHETHER SHE REMAINS A GREEN LANTERN OR NOT! I HAVEN'T TRIED TO SWAY HER!
WELL! SPEAKING OF KATMA TUI, HERE SHE COMES!
AS I FIGURED SHE WOULD! SHE'S TOO MUCH OF A FEMALE NOT TO BE DRIVEN BY A STRONG SENSE OF CURIOSITY!
GREEN LANTERN OF EARTH! HAVE YOU BEEN TRYING...
TO GET AROUND ME BY WORKING THROUGH IMI KANN? IT WON'T HELP YOU! DON'T YOU REALIZE THAT TRUE LOVE WILL ALWAYS WIN OUT AGAINST ALL WHO TRY TO DEFEAT IT?
I WASN'T TRYING ANYTHING!
I JUST THOUGHT I'D GET ACQUAINTED WITH YOUR FIANCÉ! AND THAT'S ALL WE WERE DOING! YOUR-- AH--SUSPICIONS OF ME ARE GROUNDLESS!
Hmm! NEVERTHELESS, MY FEMININE INTUITION TELLS ME HE'S UP TO SOMETHING...
8

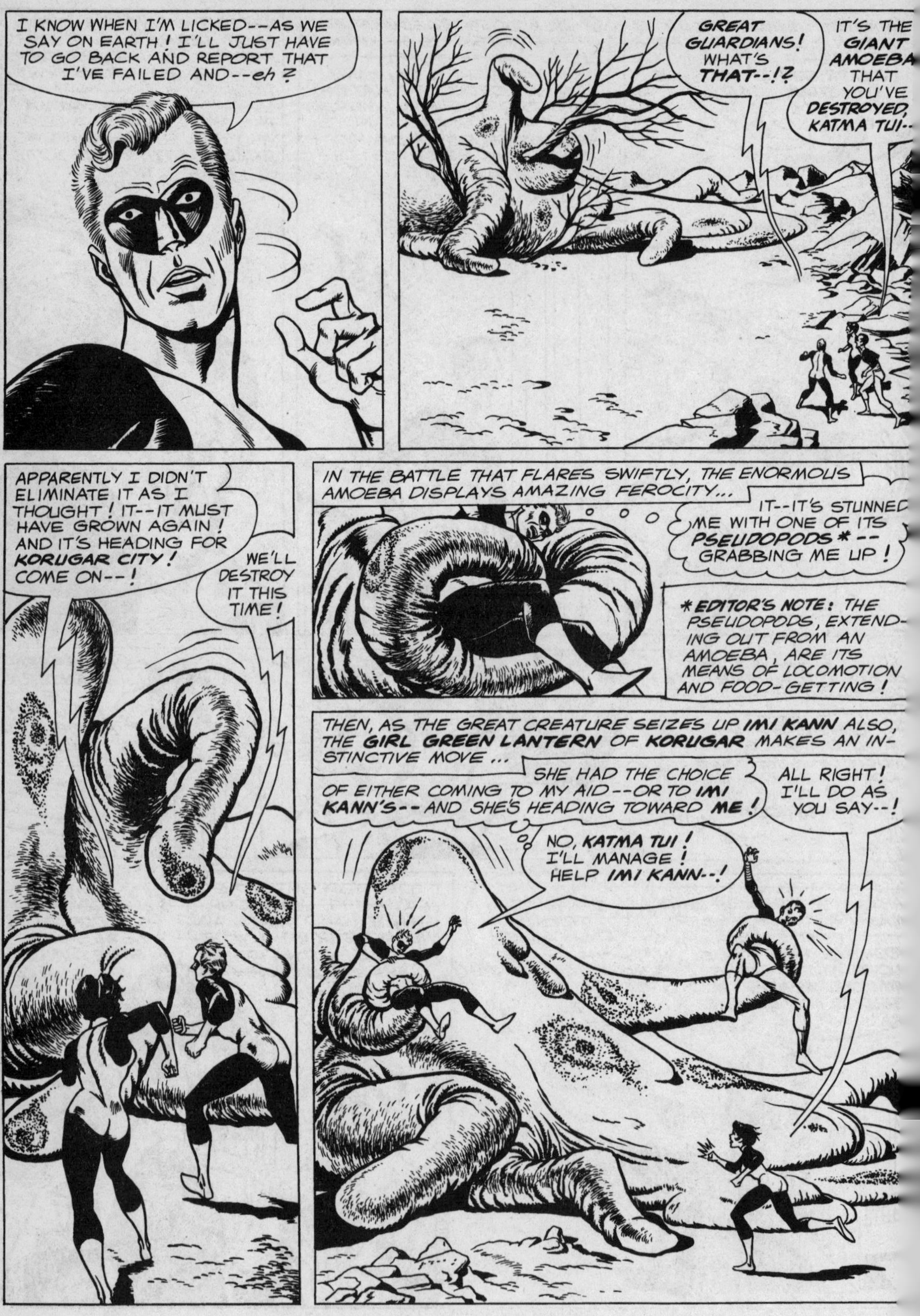
I KNOW WHEN I'M LICKED--AS WE SAY ON EARTH! I'LL JUST HAVE TO GO BACK AND REPORT THAT I'VE FAILED AND--eh?
GREAT GUARDIANS! WHAT'S THAT--!?
IT'S THE GIANT AMOEBA THAT YOU'VE DESTROYED, KATMA TUI--
APPARENTLY I DIDN'T ELIMINATE IT AS I THOUGHT! IT--IT MUST HAVE GROWN AGAIN! AND IT'S HEADING FOR KORUGAR CITY! COME ON--!
WE'LL DESTROY IT THIS TIME!
IN THE BATTLE THAT FLARES SWIFTLY, THE ENORMOUS AMOEBA DISPLAYS AMAZING FEROCITY...
IT--IT'S STUNNED ME WITH ONE OF ITS PSEUDOPODS* -- GRABBING ME UP!
*EDITOR'S NOTE: THE PSEUDOPODS, EXTENDING OUT FROM AN AMOEBA, ARE ITS MEANS OF LOCOMOTION AND FOOD-GETTING!
THEN, AS THE GREAT CREATURE SEIZES UP IMI KANN ALSO, THE GIRL GREEN LANTERN OF KORUGAR MAKES AN INSTINCTIVE MOVE ...
SHE HAD THE CHOICE OF EITHER COMING TO MY AID--OR TO IMI KANN'S--AND SHE'S HEADING TOWARD ME!
NO, KATMA TUI! I'LL MANAGE! HELP IMI KANN--!
ALL RIGHT! I'LL DO AS YOU SAY--!

WITH COOL COURAGE THE SLIM RING-WIELDER CARRIES OUT A DEVASTATING TWIN-PRONGED ACTION...

GREAT GOING! IT'S LOSING STRENGTH-- RELEASING ME!

ONE PART OF MY RING HAS FREED *IMI KANN*-- WHILE THE MAIN PART IS *BLASTING* THE CREATURE WITH EXPLOSIVE FORCE!

AS THE TWO EMERALD CRUSADERS TEAM UP TO FINISH THEIR FOE...

OUR RINGS ARE DISSOLVING IT UTTERLY! IT WON'T EVER MAKE ANOTHER REAPPEARANCE--THAT'S FOR SURE!

AND LATER, WHILE *IMI KANN* IS TREATED FOR MILD SHOCK...

YOU MEAN--THAT THE INCIDENT WITH THE AMOEBA SHOWS I BELONG IN THE RANKS OF THE *GREEN LANTERNS*?

SIMPLE! YOUR INSTINCTIVE MOVEMENT TOWARD *ME* AND *NOT* TOWARD YOUR FIANCE...

...REVEALED TO ME THAT DEEP *WITHIN YOU*, YOUR LOYALTY TO THE *GREEN LANTERN* CORPS IS EVEN MORE POWERFUL THAN YOUR LOVE FOR *IMI KANN*! NOW I SEE DOUBT IN *YOUR* EYES--SO I'LL *PROVE* IT TO YOU!

GO AHEAD-- IF YOU CAN!

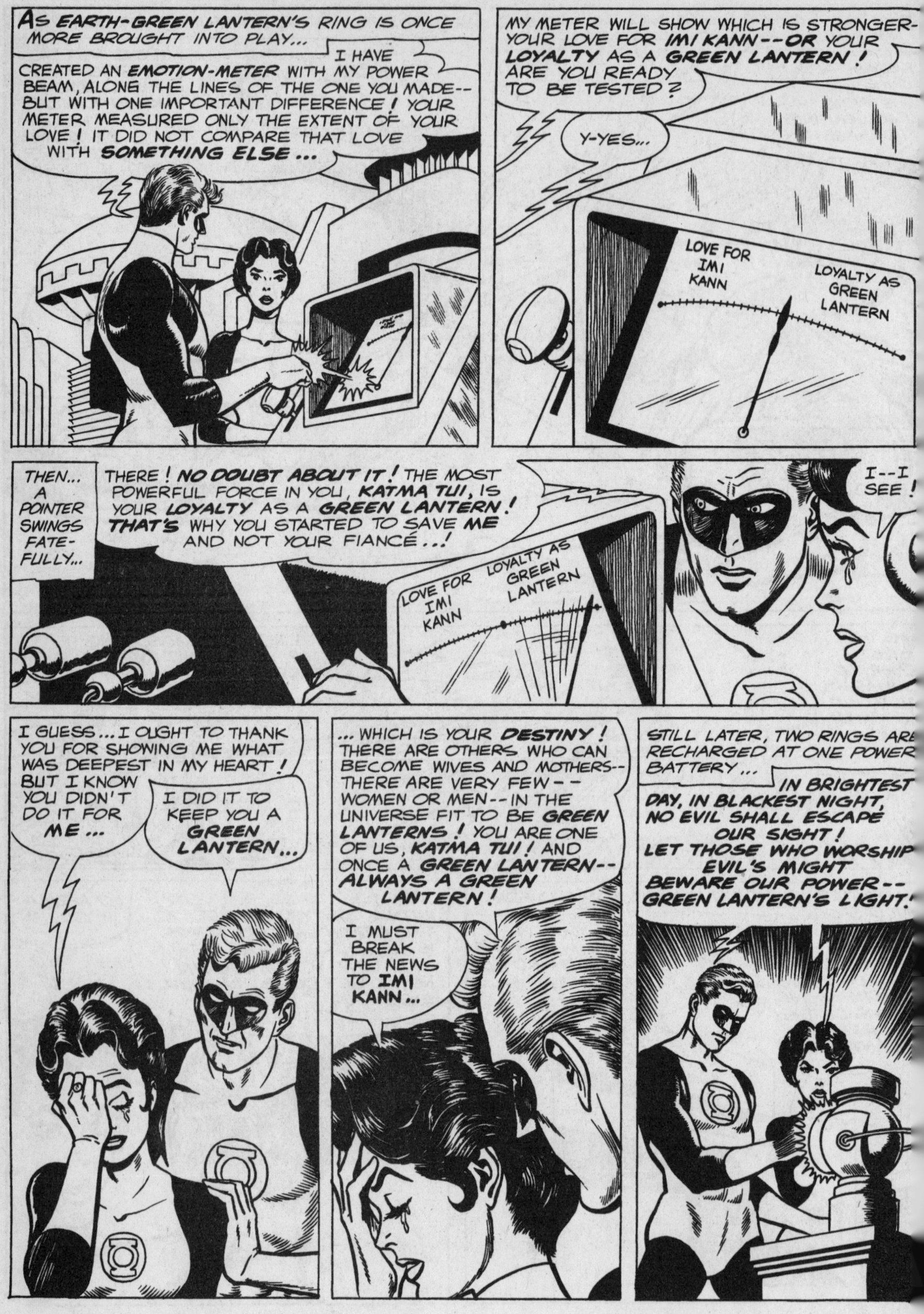
AS EARTH-GREEN LANTERN'S RING IS ONCE MORE BROUGHT INTO PLAY...
I HAVE CREATED AN EMOTION-METER WITH MY POWER BEAM, ALONG THE LINES OF THE ONE YOU MADE-- BUT WITH ONE IMPORTANT DIFFERENCE! YOUR METER MEASURED ONLY THE EXTENT OF YOUR LOVE! IT DID NOT COMPARE THAT LOVE WITH SOMETHING ELSE...
MY METER WILL SHOW WHICH IS STRONGER-- YOUR LOVE FOR IMI KANN--OR YOUR LOYALTY AS A GREEN LANTERN! ARE YOU READY TO BE TESTED?
Y-YES...
LOVE FOR IMI KANN
LOYALTY AS GREEN LANTERN
THEN... A POINTER SWINGS FATE-FULLY...
THERE! NO DOUBT ABOUT IT! THE MOST POWERFUL FORCE IN YOU, KATMA TUI, IS YOUR LOYALTY AS A GREEN LANTERN! THAT'S WHY YOU STARTED TO SAVE ME AND NOT YOUR FIANCÉ...!
I--I SEE!
LOVE FOR IMI KANN
LOYALTY AS GREEN LANTERN
I GUESS...I OUGHT TO THANK YOU FOR SHOWING ME WHAT WAS DEEPEST IN MY HEART! BUT I KNOW YOU DIDN'T DO IT FOR ME...
I DID IT TO KEEP YOU A GREEN LANTERN...
...WHICH IS YOUR DESTINY! THERE ARE OTHERS WHO CAN BECOME WIVES AND MOTHERS-- THERE ARE VERY FEW--WOMEN OR MEN--IN THE UNIVERSE FIT TO BE GREEN LANTERNS! YOU ARE ONE OF US, KATMA TUI! AND ONCE A GREEN LANTERN-- ALWAYS A GREEN LANTERN!
I MUST BREAK THE NEWS TO IMI KANN...
STILL LATER, TWO RINGS ARE RECHARGED AT ONE POWER BATTERY...
IN BRIGHTEST DAY, IN BLACKEST NIGHT, NO EVIL SHALL ESCAPE OUR SIGHT! LET THOSE WHO WORSHIP EVIL'S MIGHT BEWARE OUR POWER-- GREEN LANTERN'S LIGHT!

SHORTLY, A POWERFUL GREEN-CLAD SHAPE ROCKETS AWAY FROM *KORUGAR*...

KATMA TUI'S SITUATION PARALLELS MY OWN ON EARTH! DOES WHAT I TOLD HER MEAN I CAN NEVER MARRY *CAROL FERRIS*? BUT *KATMA* IS A WOMAN--AND I AM A MAN! PERHAPS *THAT* WILL MAKE A DIFFERENCE--!

ON THE PLANET *OA*, AN ASTRAL FIGURE REPORTS...

YES, MASTERS! THE GIANT AMOEBA THAT WE FOUGHT AGAINST WAS *SECRETLY* CREATED BY MY *POWER RING*! I ADMIT THAT I TRICKED *KATMA TUI*...

BUT I DID IT ONLY TO REVEAL THE *TRUTH* TO HER! IT WAS A CALCULATED RISK! BESIDES, I REMEMBERED YOUR INSTRUCTIONS-- TO USE *EVERY POSSIBLE MEANS* TO GET HER TO REMAIN AS A *BATTERY POSSESSOR!*

WE WERE AWARE OF WHAT YOU DID, *GREEN LANTERN*...

AND WE ARE ALL OF THE OPINION THAT UNDER THE CIRCUMSTANCES YOUR RUSE, WHICH HARMED NO ONE, WAS JUSTIFIED! YOU HAVE OUR CONGRATULATIONS AND OUR THANKS ON A JOB *WELL DONE!*

PRAISE FROM THE *GUARDIANS!* THAT'S WORTH *ANY* EFFORT!

The End /12

GREEN LANTERN

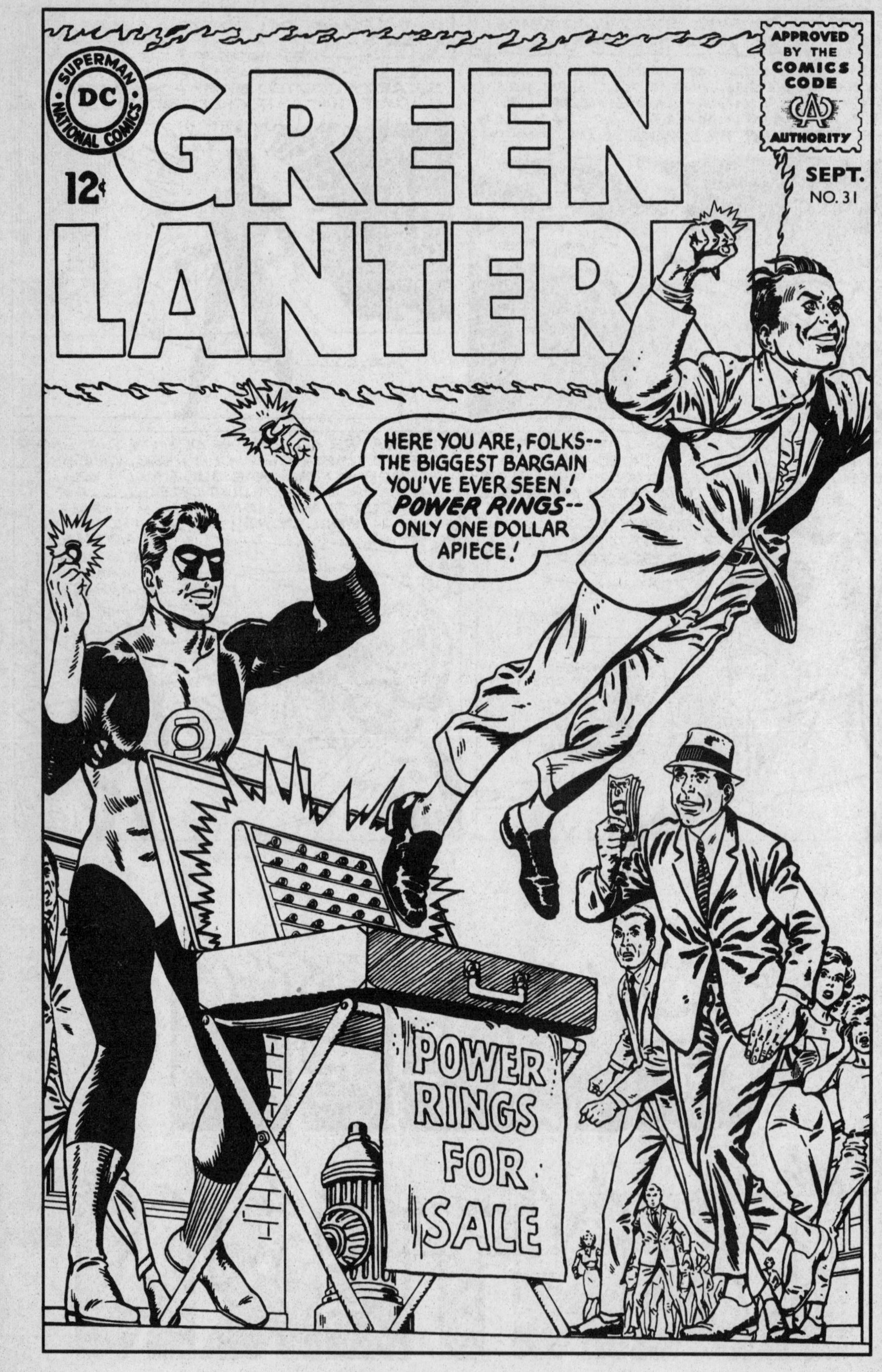
SUPERMAN DC NATIONAL COMICS
12¢
GREEN LANTERN
APPROVED BY THE COMICS CODE AUTHORITY
SEPT.
NO. 31
HERE YOU ARE, FOLKS-- THE BIGGEST BARGAIN YOU'VE EVER SEEN! POWER RINGS-- ONLY ONE DOLLAR APIECE!
POWER RINGS FOR SALE

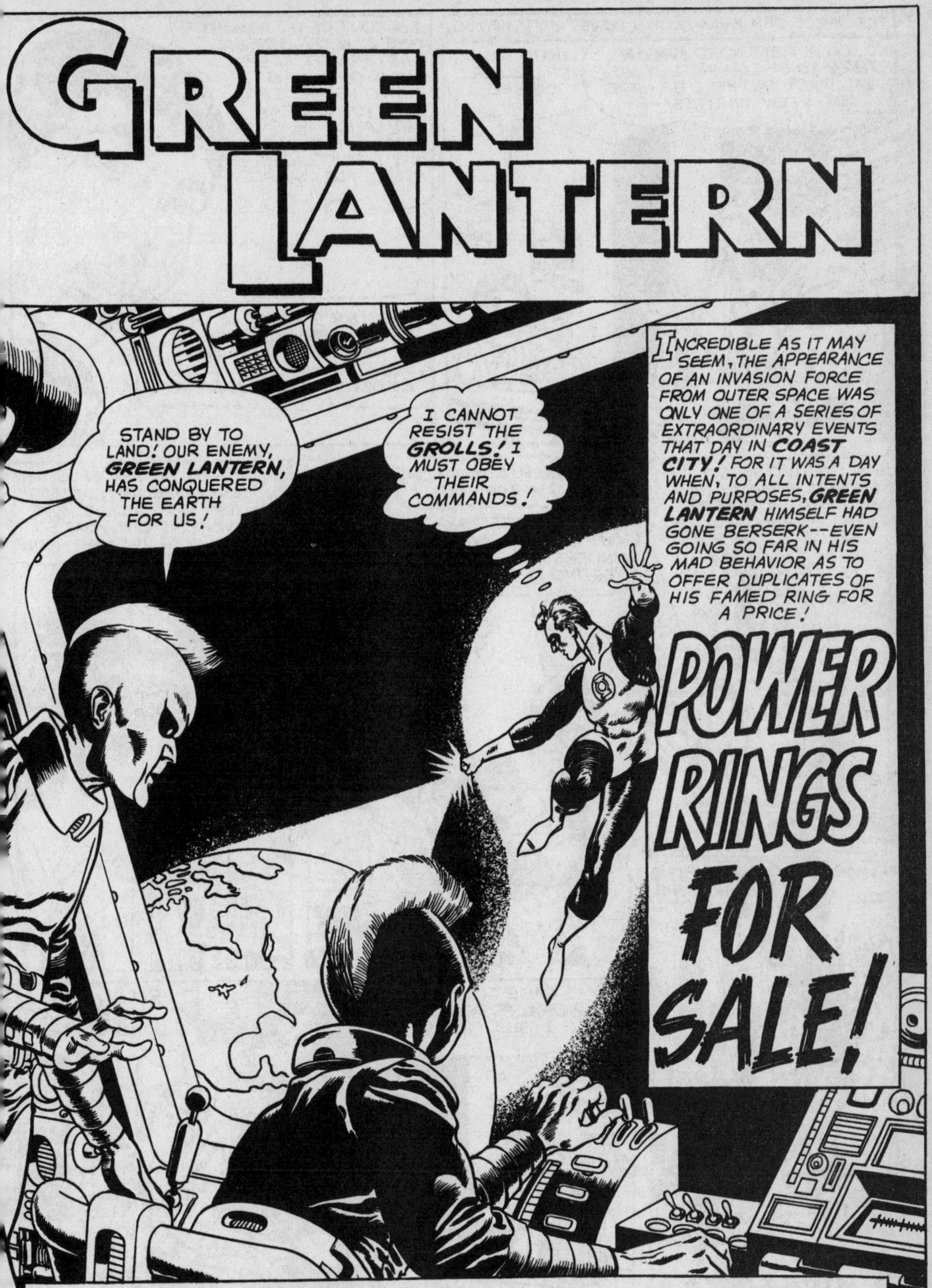
GREEN LANTERN
STAND BY TO LAND! OUR ENEMY, GREEN LANTERN, HAS CONQUERED THE EARTH FOR US!
I CANNOT RESIST THE GROLLS! I MUST OBEY THEIR COMMANDS!
INCREDIBLE AS IT MAY SEEM, THE APPEARANCE OF AN INVASION FORCE FROM OUTER SPACE WAS ONLY ONE OF A SERIES OF EXTRAORDINARY EVENTS THAT DAY IN COAST CITY! FOR IT WAS A DAY WHEN, TO ALL INTENTS AND PURPOSES, GREEN LANTERN HIMSELF HAD GONE BERSERK--EVEN GOING SO FAR IN HIS MAD BEHAVIOR AS TO OFFER DUPLICATES OF HIS FAMED RING FOR A PRICE!
POWER RINGS FOR SALE!

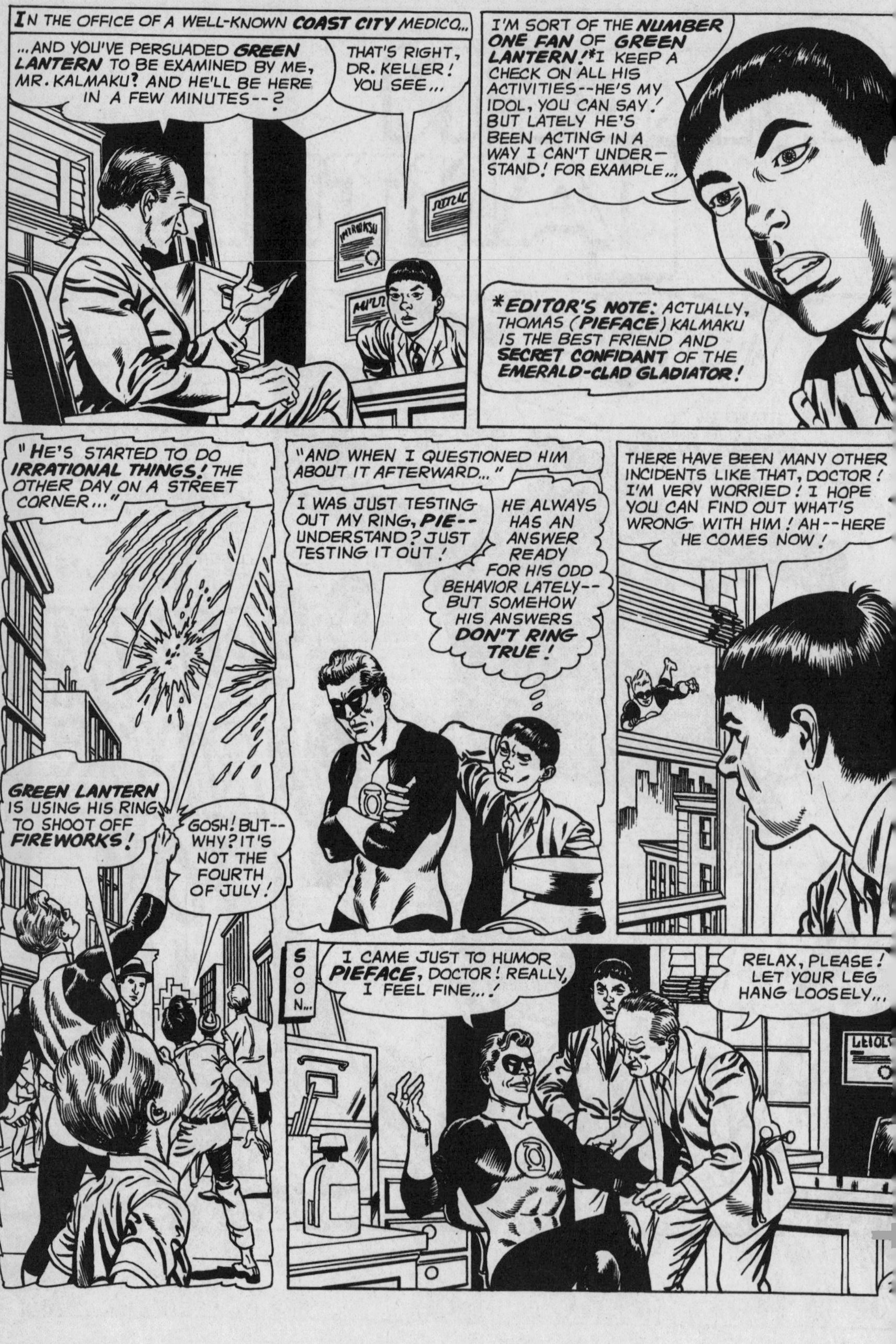
IN THE OFFICE OF A WELL-KNOWN COAST CITY MEDICO...
...AND YOU'VE PERSUADED GREEN LANTERN TO BE EXAMINED BY ME, MR. KALMAKU? AND HE'LL BE HERE IN A FEW MINUTES--?
THAT'S RIGHT, DR. KELLER! YOU SEE...
I'M SORT OF THE NUMBER ONE FAN OF GREEN LANTERN!* I KEEP A CHECK ON ALL HIS ACTIVITIES--HE'S MY IDOL, YOU CAN SAY! BUT LATELY HE'S BEEN ACTING IN A WAY I CAN'T UNDERSTAND! FOR EXAMPLE...
*EDITOR'S NOTE: ACTUALLY, THOMAS (PIEFACE) KALMAKU IS THE BEST FRIEND AND SECRET CONFIDANT OF THE EMERALD-CLAD GLADIATOR!
"HE'S STARTED TO DO IRRATIONAL THINGS! THE OTHER DAY ON A STREET CORNER..."
GREEN LANTERN IS USING HIS RING TO SHOOT OFF FIREWORKS!
GOSH! BUT--WHY? IT'S NOT THE FOURTH OF JULY!
"AND WHEN I QUESTIONED HIM ABOUT IT AFTERWARD..."
I WAS JUST TESTING OUT MY RING, PIE--UNDERSTAND? JUST TESTING IT OUT!
HE ALWAYS HAS AN ANSWER READY FOR HIS ODD BEHAVIOR LATELY--BUT SOMEHOW HIS ANSWERS DON'T RING TRUE!
THERE HAVE BEEN MANY OTHER INCIDENTS LIKE THAT, DOCTOR! I'M VERY WORRIED! I HOPE YOU CAN FIND OUT WHAT'S WRONG WITH HIM! AH--HERE HE COMES NOW!
SOON...
I CAME JUST TO HUMOR PIEFACE, DOCTOR! REALLY, I FEEL FINE...!
RELAX, PLEASE! LET YOUR LEG HANG LOOSELY...

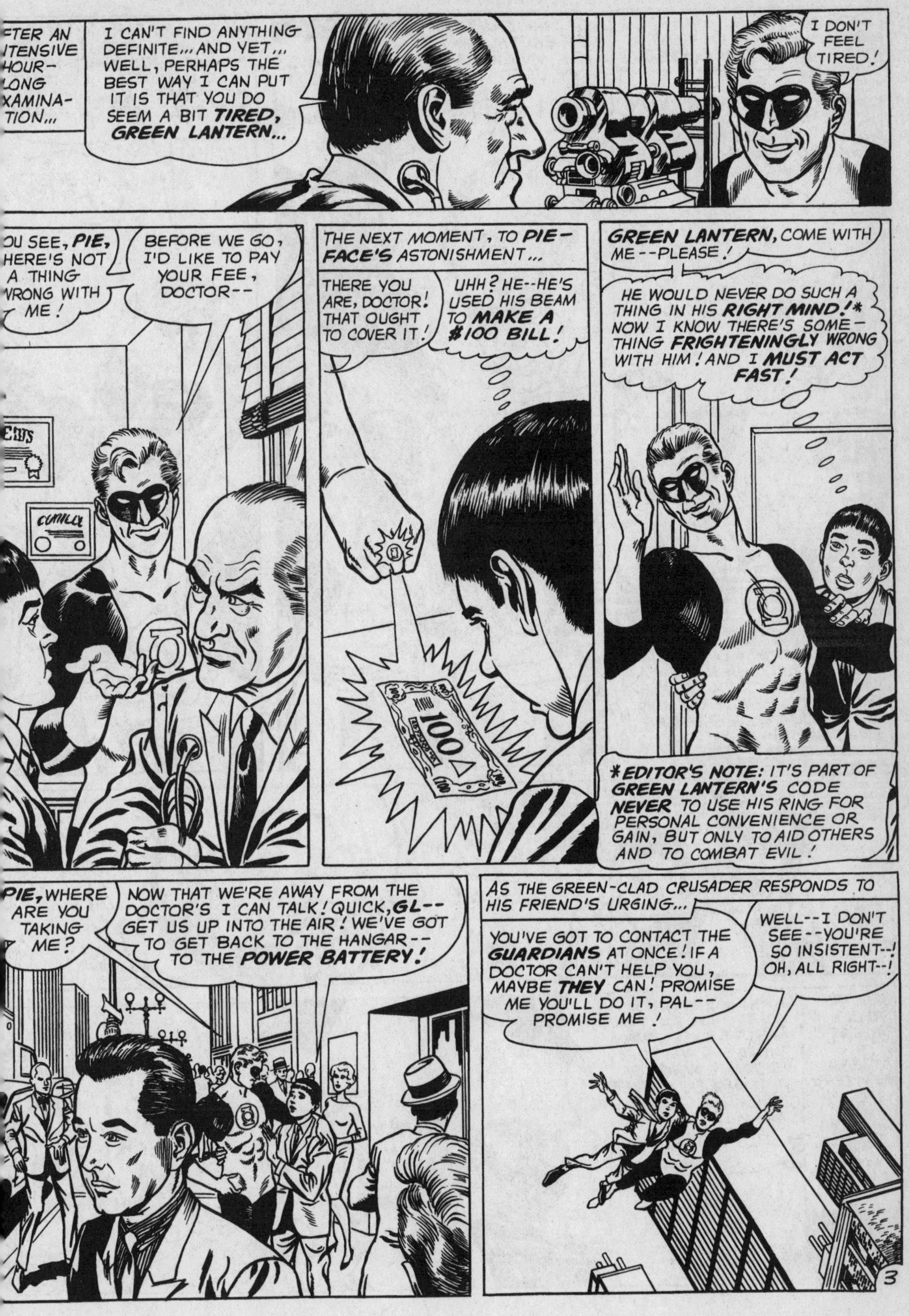
FTER AN
TENSIVE
HOUR-
LONG
XAMINA-
TION...
I CAN'T FIND ANYTHING DEFINITE... AND YET... WELL, PERHAPS THE BEST WAY I CAN PUT IT IS THAT YOU DO SEEM A BIT TIRED, GREEN LANTERN...
I DON'T FEEL TIRED!
OU SEE, PIE, HERE'S NOT A THING WRONG WITH ME!
BEFORE WE GO, I'D LIKE TO PAY YOUR FEE, DOCTOR--
THE NEXT MOMENT, TO PIE-FACE'S ASTONISHMENT...
THERE YOU ARE, DOCTOR! THAT OUGHT TO COVER IT!
UHH? HE--HE'S USED HIS BEAM TO MAKE A $100 BILL!
100
GREEN LANTERN, COME WITH ME--PLEASE!
HE WOULD NEVER DO SUCH A THING IN HIS RIGHT MIND!* NOW I KNOW THERE'S SOMETHING FRIGHTENINGLY WRONG WITH HIM! AND I MUST ACT FAST!
*EDITOR'S NOTE: IT'S PART OF GREEN LANTERN'S CODE NEVER TO USE HIS RING FOR PERSONAL CONVENIENCE OR GAIN, BUT ONLY TO AID OTHERS AND TO COMBAT EVIL!
PIE, WHERE ARE YOU TAKING ME?
NOW THAT WE'RE AWAY FROM THE DOCTOR'S I CAN TALK! QUICK, GL-- GET US UP INTO THE AIR! WE'VE GOT TO GET BACK TO THE HANGAR-- TO THE POWER BATTERY!
AS THE GREEN-CLAD CRUSADER RESPONDS TO HIS FRIEND'S URGING...
YOU'VE GOT TO CONTACT THE GUARDIANS AT ONCE! IF A DOCTOR CAN'T HELP YOU, MAYBE THEY CAN! PROMISE ME YOU'LL DO IT, PAL-- PROMISE ME!
WELL--I DON'T SEE--YOU'RE SO INSISTENT--! OH, ALL RIGHT--!
3

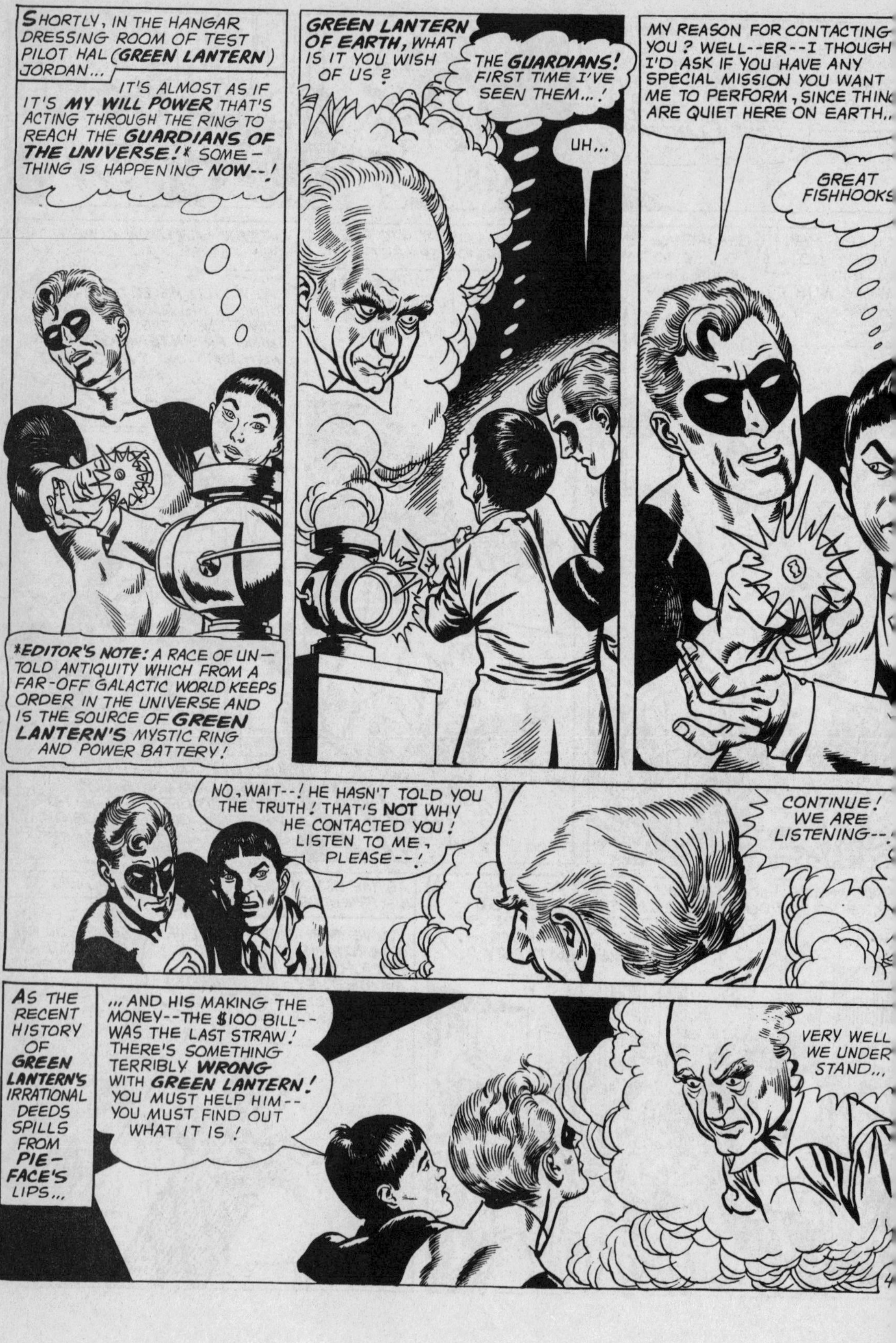
SHORTLY, IN THE HANGAR DRESSING ROOM OF TEST PILOT HAL (GREEN LANTERN) JORDAN...
IT'S ALMOST AS IF IT'S MY WILL POWER THAT'S ACTING THROUGH THE RING TO REACH THE GUARDIANS OF THE UNIVERSE!* SOMETHING IS HAPPENING NOW--!
*EDITOR'S NOTE: A RACE OF UNTOLD ANTIQUITY WHICH FROM A FAR-OFF GALACTIC WORLD KEEPS ORDER IN THE UNIVERSE AND IS THE SOURCE OF GREEN LANTERN'S MYSTIC RING AND POWER BATTERY!
GREEN LANTERN OF EARTH, WHAT IS IT YOU WISH OF US?
THE GUARDIANS! FIRST TIME I'VE SEEN THEM...!
UH...
MY REASON FOR CONTACTING YOU? WELL--ER--I THOUGH I'D ASK IF YOU HAVE ANY SPECIAL MISSION YOU WANT ME TO PERFORM, SINCE THIN ARE QUIET HERE ON EARTH..
GREAT FISHHOOKS
NO, WAIT--! HE HASN'T TOLD YOU THE TRUTH! THAT'S NOT WHY HE CONTACTED YOU! LISTEN TO ME, PLEASE--!
CONTINUE! WE ARE LISTENING--.
AS THE RECENT HISTORY OF GREEN LANTERN'S IRRATIONAL DEEDS SPILLS FROM PIE-FACE'S LIPS...
...AND HIS MAKING THE MONEY--THE $100 BILL--WAS THE LAST STRAW! THERE'S SOMETHING TERRIBLY WRONG WITH GREEN LANTERN! YOU MUST HELP HIM--YOU MUST FIND OUT WHAT IT IS!
VERY WELL WE UNDER STAND...

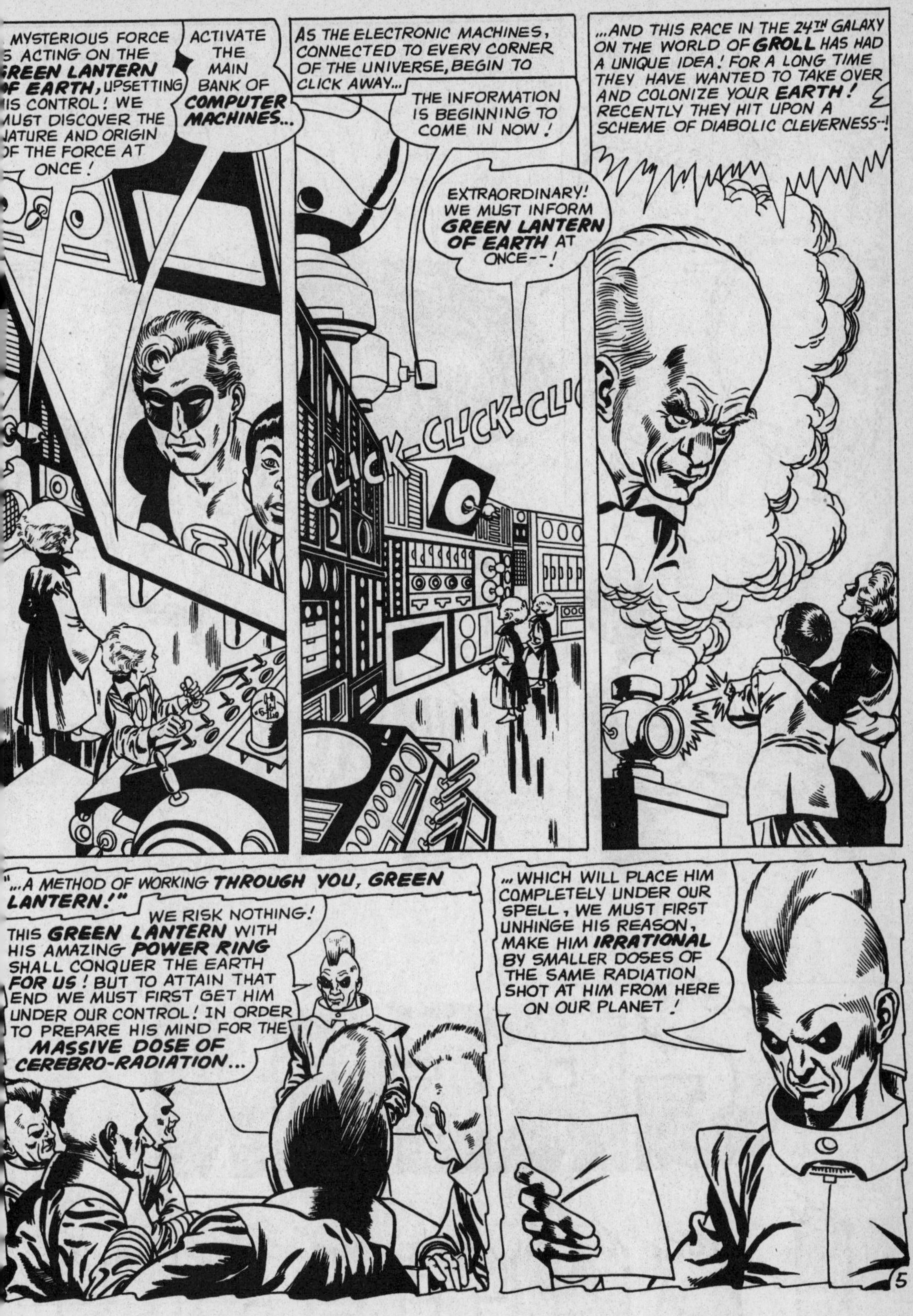

MYSTERIOUS FORCE IS ACTING ON THE GREEN LANTERN OF EARTH, UPSETTING HIS CONTROL! WE MUST DISCOVER THE NATURE AND ORIGIN OF THE FORCE AT ONCE!
ACTIVATE THE MAIN BANK OF COMPUTER MACHINES...
AS THE ELECTRONIC MACHINES, CONNECTED TO EVERY CORNER OF THE UNIVERSE, BEGIN TO CLICK AWAY...
THE INFORMATION IS BEGINNING TO COME IN NOW!
CLICK-CLICK-CLI
EXTRAORDINARY! WE MUST INFORM GREEN LANTERN OF EARTH AT ONCE--!
...AND THIS RACE IN THE 24TH GALAXY ON THE WORLD OF GROLL HAS HAD A UNIQUE IDEA! FOR A LONG TIME THEY HAVE WANTED TO TAKE OVER AND COLONIZE YOUR EARTH! RECENTLY THEY HIT UPON A SCHEME OF DIABOLIC CLEVERNESS--!
"...A METHOD OF WORKING THROUGH YOU, GREEN LANTERN!"
WE RISK NOTHING! THIS GREEN LANTERN WITH HIS AMAZING POWER RING SHALL CONQUER THE EARTH FOR US! BUT TO ATTAIN THAT END WE MUST FIRST GET HIM UNDER OUR CONTROL! IN ORDER TO PREPARE HIS MIND FOR THE MASSIVE DOSE OF CEREBRO-RADIATION...
...WHICH WILL PLACE HIM COMPLETELY UNDER OUR SPELL, WE MUST FIRST UNHINGE HIS REASON, MAKE HIM IRRATIONAL BY SMALLER DOSES OF THE SAME RADIATION SHOT AT HIM FROM HERE ON OUR PLANET!
5

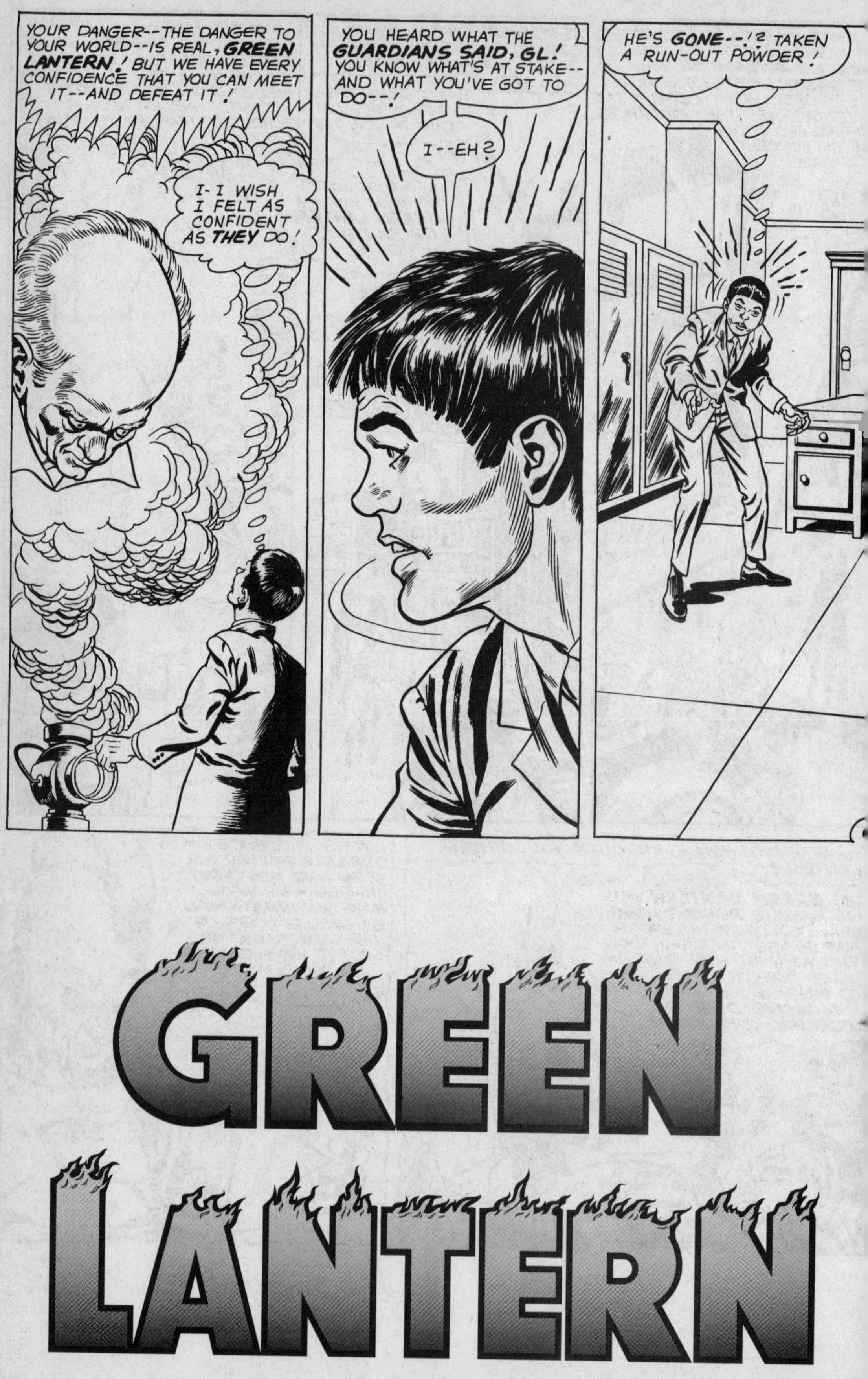
YOUR DANGER--THE DANGER TO YOUR WORLD--IS REAL, GREEN LANTERN! BUT WE HAVE EVERY CONFIDENCE THAT YOU CAN MEET IT--AND DEFEAT IT!
I-I WISH I FELT AS CONFIDENT AS THEY DO!
YOU HEARD WHAT THE GUARDIANS SAID, GL! YOU KNOW WHAT'S AT STAKE--AND WHAT YOU'VE GOT TO DO--!
I--EH?
HE'S GONE--!? TAKEN A RUN-OUT POWDER!

GREEN LANTERN

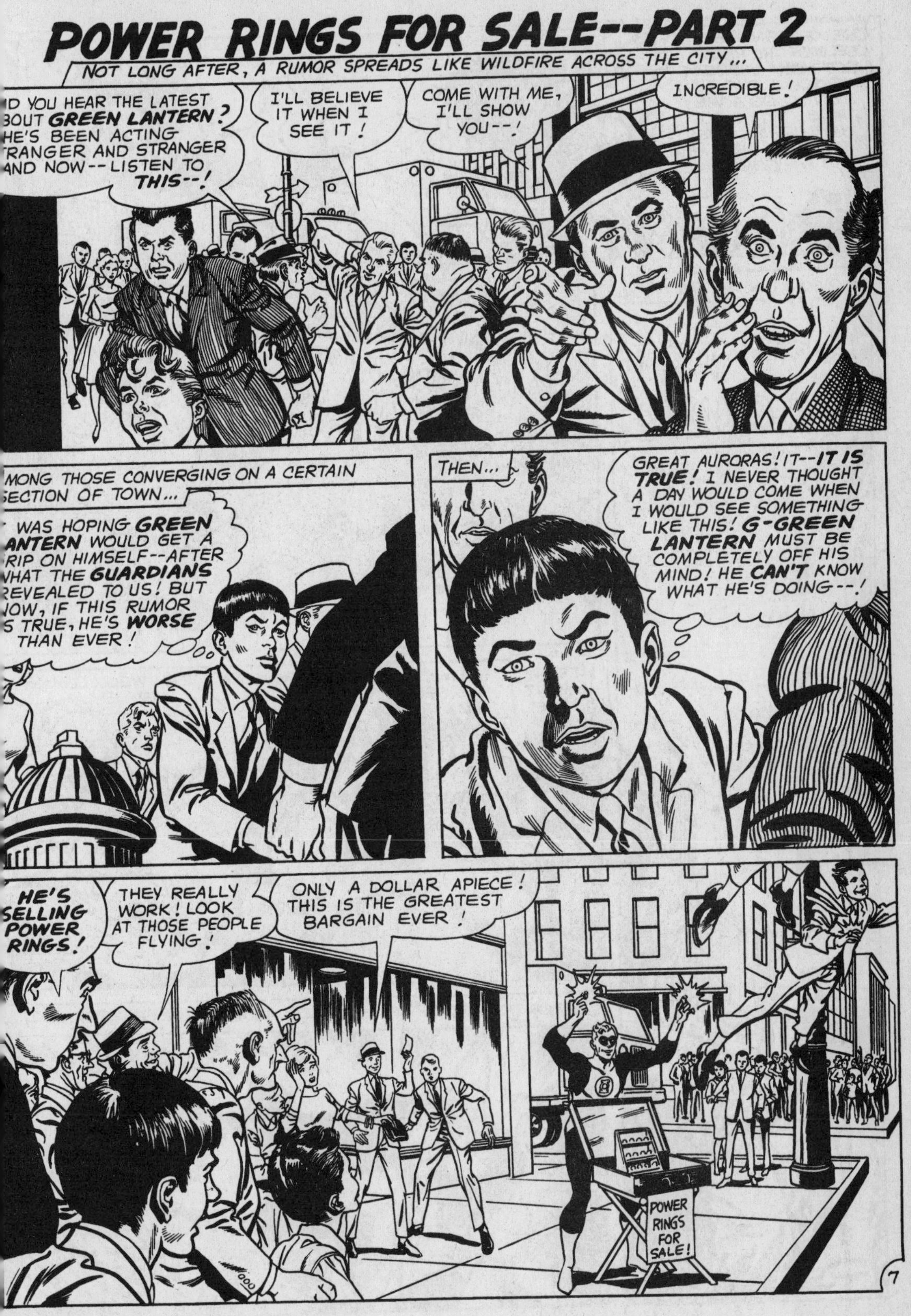
POWER RINGS FOR SALE--PART 2
NOT LONG AFTER, A RUMOR SPREADS LIKE WILDFIRE ACROSS THE CITY...
ID YOU HEAR THE LATEST BOUT GREEN LANTERN? HE'S BEEN ACTING TRANGER AND STRANGER AND NOW--LISTEN TO THIS--!
I'LL BELIEVE IT WHEN I SEE IT!
COME WITH ME, I'LL SHOW YOU--!
INCREDIBLE!
MONG THOSE CONVERGING ON A CERTAIN SECTION OF TOWN...
WAS HOPING GREEN ANTERN WOULD GET A RIP ON HIMSELF--AFTER VHAT THE GUARDIANS REVEALED TO US! BUT NOW, IF THIS RUMOR S TRUE, HE'S WORSE THAN EVER!
THEN...
GREAT AURORAS! IT--IT IS TRUE! I NEVER THOUGHT A DAY WOULD COME WHEN I WOULD SEE SOMETHING LIKE THIS! G-GREEN LANTERN MUST BE COMPLETELY OFF HIS MIND! HE CAN'T KNOW WHAT HE'S DOING--!
HE'S SELLING POWER RINGS!
THEY REALLY WORK! LOOK AT THOSE PEOPLE FLYING!
ONLY A DOLLAR APIECE! THIS IS THE GREATEST BARGAIN EVER!
POWER RINGS FOR SALE!
7

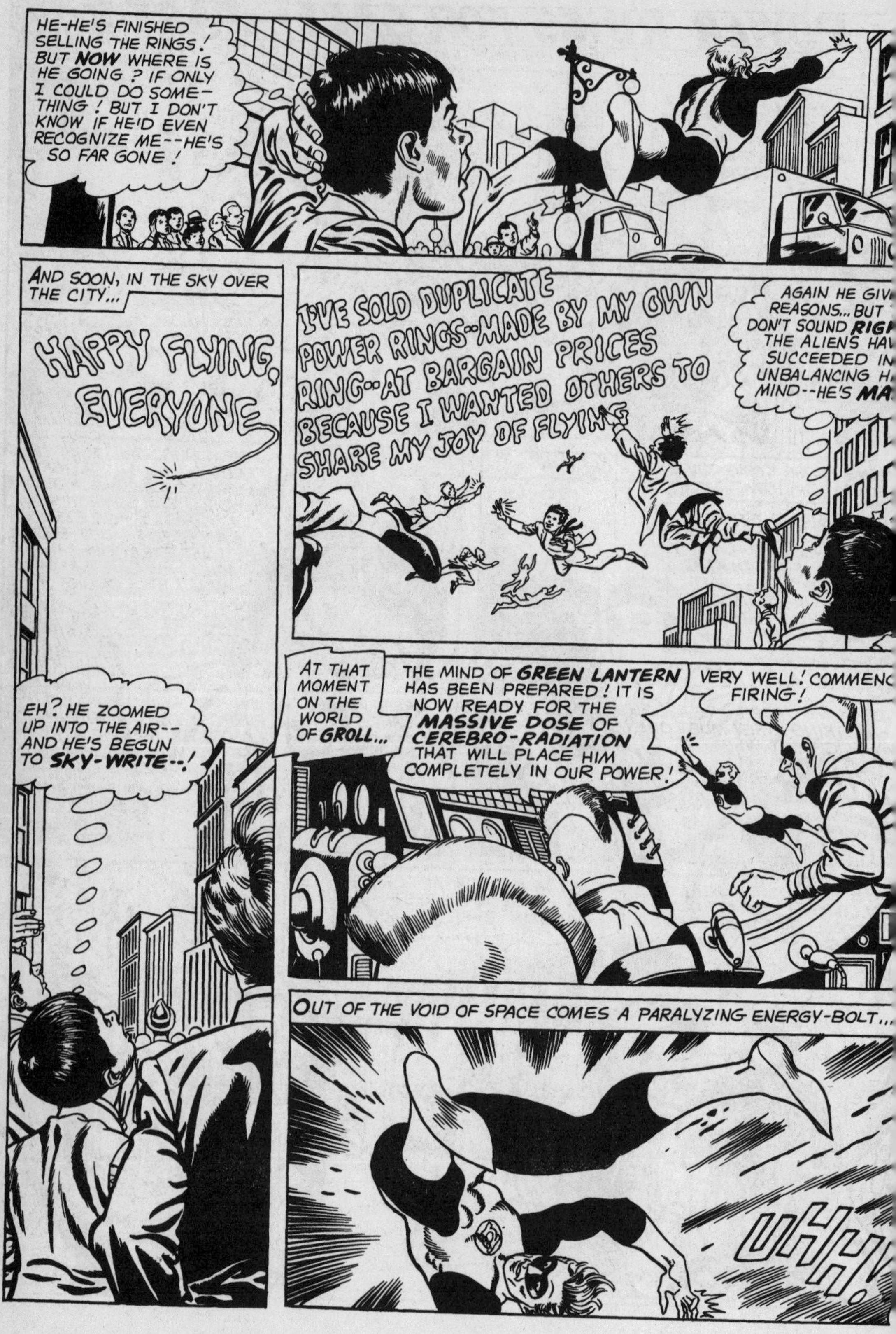
HE-HE'S FINISHED SELLING THE RINGS! BUT NOW WHERE IS HE GOING? IF ONLY I COULD DO SOMETHING! BUT I DON'T KNOW IF HE'D EVEN RECOGNIZE ME--HE'S SO FAR GONE!
AND SOON, IN THE SKY OVER THE CITY...
HAPPY FLYING, EVERYONE
EH? HE ZOOMED UP INTO THE AIR--AND HE'S BEGUN TO SKY-WRITE--!
I'VE SOLD DUPLICATE POWER RINGS--MADE BY MY OWN RING--AT BARGAIN PRICES BECAUSE I WANTED OTHERS TO SHARE MY JOY OF FLYING
AT THAT MOMENT ON THE WORLD OF GROLL...
THE MIND OF GREEN LANTERN HAS BEEN PREPARED! IT IS NOW READY FOR THE MASSIVE DOSE OF CEREBRO-RADIATION THAT WILL PLACE HIM COMPLETELY IN OUR POWER!
OUT OF THE VOID OF SPACE COMES A PARALYZING ENERGY-BOLT...
UHH!

...IS COMPLETELY
UNDER OUR
CONTROL NOW!
USING HIS
RING FOR OUR
BENEFIT!

GASP! I CAN'T MOVE!

MY *POWER BEAM* IS SPREADING OVER THE ENTIRE EARTH... INTO EVERY CORNER OF THE GLOBE... AFFECTING EVERY HUMAN... TURNING THEM INTO *LIVING AUTOMATONS...!*

I CAN MAKE THEM DO WHATEVER I WANT-- MAKE THEM MARCH LIKE SOLDIERS...

...OR CLIMB TREES LIKE A MONKEY --ANYTHING! THEY MUST OBEY MY SLIGHTEST WHIM--!

IN DUE COURSE, A GREAT VESSEL FROM OUTER SPACE LANDS AT *COAST CITY...*

WE HAVE CONQUERED EARTH--BY MEANS OF *GREEN LANTERN'S* BEAM!

HERE HE COMES IN RESPONSE TO OUR COMMAND--!

YOU HAVE FULFILLED YOUR PURPOSE FOR US, *GREEN LANTERN!* WE HAVE NO FURTHER USE FOR YOU! THEREFORE OUR LAST COMMAND TO YOU IS THIS-- *USE YOUR RING TO DESTROY YOURSELF AT ONCE!*

9

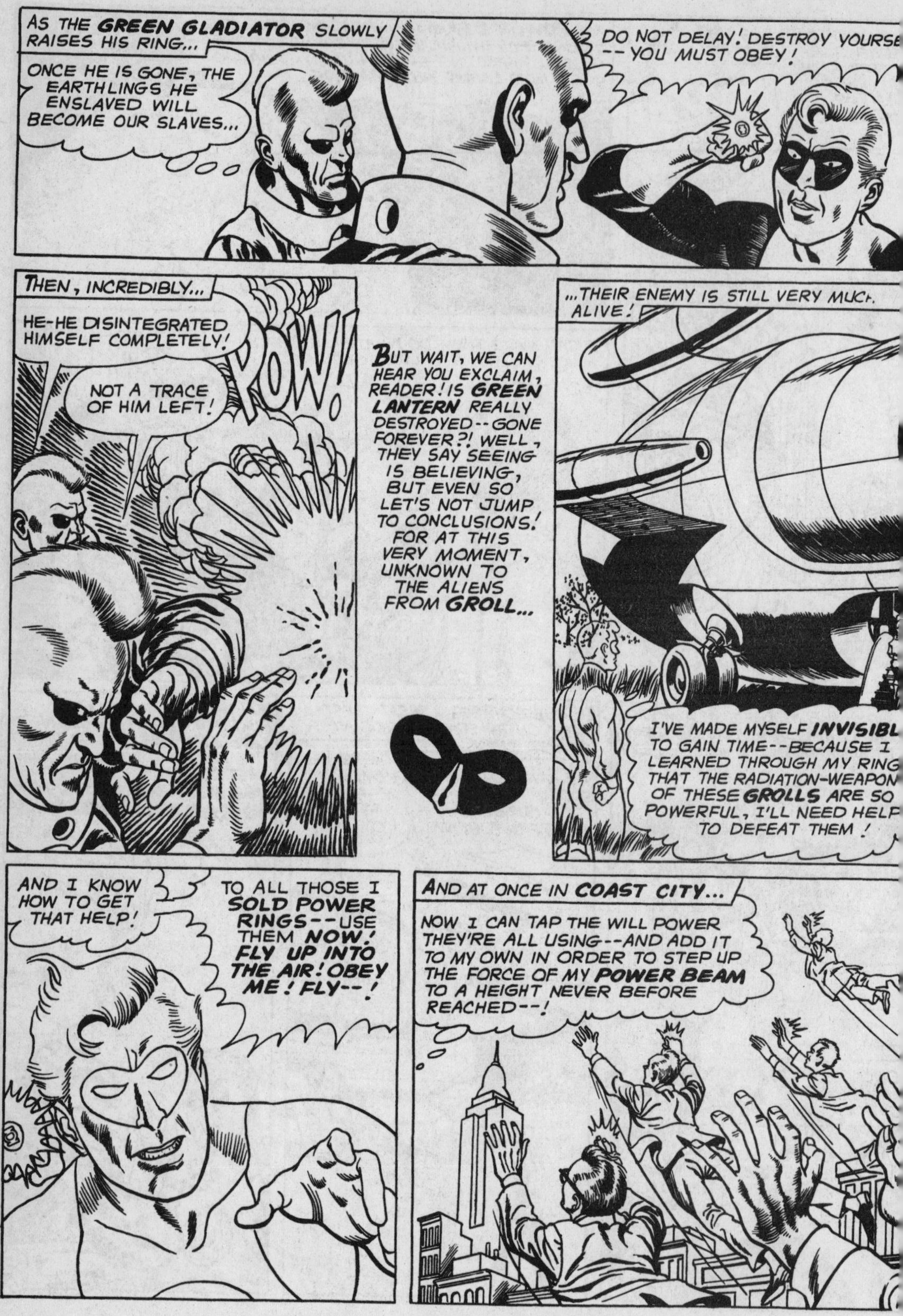
AS THE GREEN GLADIATOR SLOWLY RAISES HIS RING...
ONCE HE IS GONE, THE EARTHLINGS HE ENSLAVED WILL BECOME OUR SLAVES...
DO NOT DELAY! DESTROY YOURSE
-- YOU MUST OBEY!
THEN, INCREDIBLY...
HE-HE DISINTEGRATED HIMSELF COMPLETELY!
NOT A TRACE OF HIM LEFT!
POW!
BUT WAIT, WE CAN HEAR YOU EXCLAIM, READER! IS GREEN LANTERN REALLY DESTROYED--GONE FOREVER?! WELL, THEY SAY SEEING IS BELIEVING, BUT EVEN SO LET'S NOT JUMP TO CONCLUSIONS! FOR AT THIS VERY MOMENT, UNKNOWN TO THE ALIENS FROM GROLL...
...THEIR ENEMY IS STILL VERY MUCH ALIVE!
I'VE MADE MYSELF INVISIBL TO GAIN TIME--BECAUSE I LEARNED THROUGH MY RING THAT THE RADIATION-WEAPON OF THESE GROLLS ARE SO POWERFUL, I'LL NEED HELP TO DEFEAT THEM!
AND I KNOW HOW TO GET THAT HELP!
TO ALL THOSE I SOLD POWER RINGS--USE THEM NOW! FLY UP INTO THE AIR! OBEY ME! FLY--!
AND AT ONCE IN COAST CITY...
NOW I CAN TAP THE WILL POWER THEY'RE ALL USING--AND ADD IT TO MY OWN IN ORDER TO STEP UP THE FORCE OF MY POWER BEAM TO A HEIGHT NEVER BEFORE REACHED--!

MOMENT LATER, AS THE DOUGHTY CRUSADER MAKES HIMSELF VISIBLE AGAIN...

H-- *GREEN ANTERN!? E TRICKED S--*

WE'LL DESTROY HIM OURSELVES--!

AS THE TWO MIGHTY FORCES MEET HEAD-ON, IN A MOMENTARY DEADLOCK...

GOT TO POUR IT ON! I MUST DEFEAT THEM--!

HEN, AS WILL-POWER ENERGY FLOWS INTO THE CRUSADER FROM OTHERS USING HIS DUPLICATE *POWER RINGS* IN THE CITY...

IT'S WORKING! THE COMBINED WILL POWER BEHIND MY BEAM IS OVERWHELMING THE GROLLS! I'VE GOT THEM BEATEN NOW--!

UH-- TERRIBLE STRENGTH--!

NOT LONG AFTER, THE INVADERS TAKE OFF NTO SPACE...

I SPARED THEIR LIVES ON CONDITION THAT THEY NEVER COME BACK--AND NEVER AGAIN TRY TO COLONIZE OUR PLANET! I THINK THEY'LL KEEP THEIR WORD--AFTER THE BITTER LESSON THEY LEARNED!

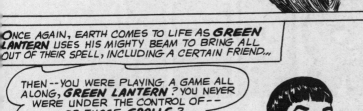

ONCE AGAIN, EARTH COMES TO LIFE AS *GREEN LANTERN* USES HIS MIGHTY BEAM TO BRING ALL OUT OF THEIR SPELL, INCLUDING A CERTAIN FRIEND...

THEN-- YOU WERE PLAYING A GAME ALL ALONG, GREEN LANTERN? YOU NEVER WERE UNDER THE CONTROL OF-- OF THOSE GROLLS?

NOT REALLY, PIE! I PRETENDED THAT I WAS-- I PLAYED ALONG WITH THEIR GAME--ONLY IN ORDER TO DEFEAT THEM!

11

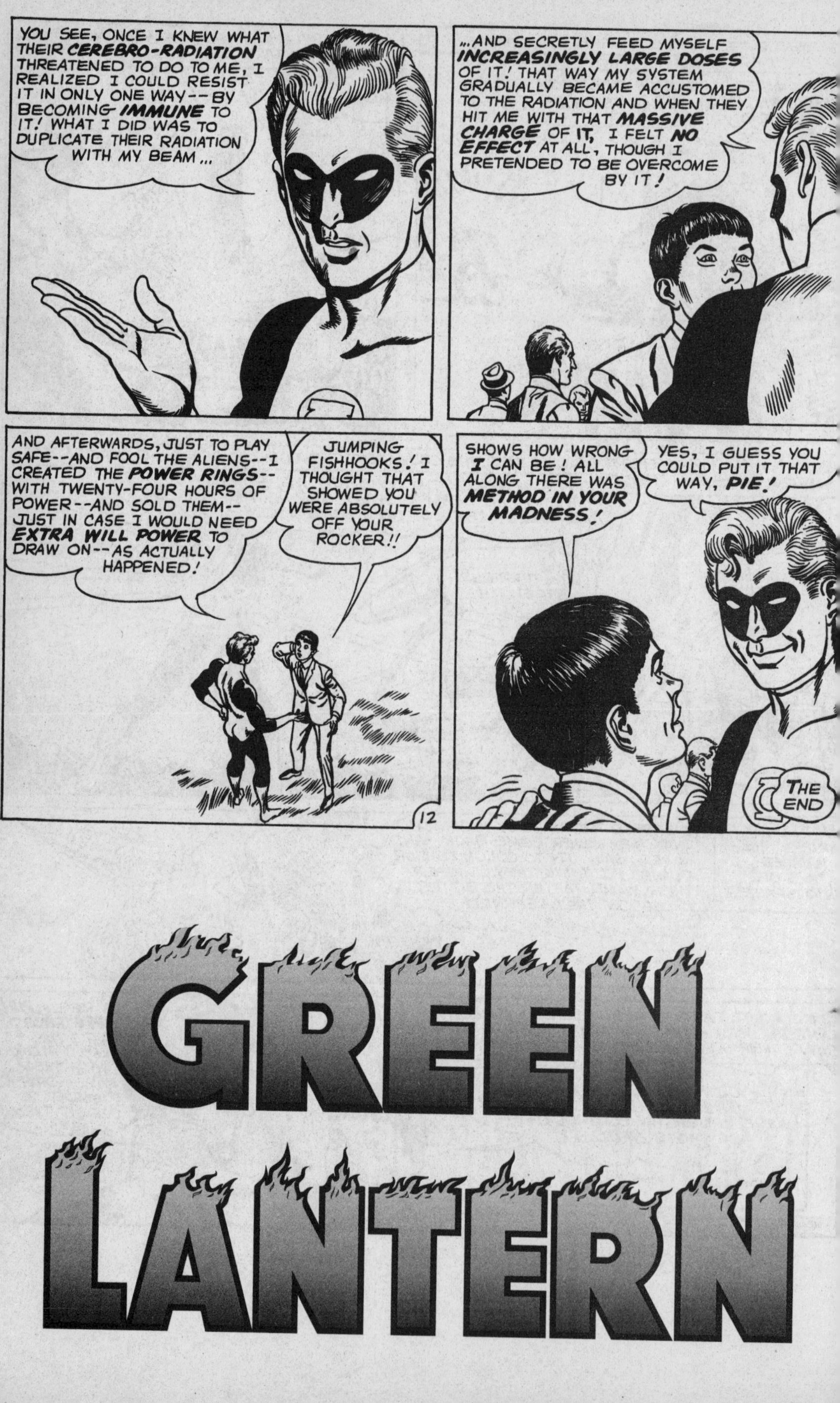
YOU SEE, ONCE I KNEW WHAT THEIR CEREBRO-RADIATION THREATENED TO DO TO ME, I REALIZED I COULD RESIST IT IN ONLY ONE WAY--BY BECOMING IMMUNE TO IT! WHAT I DID WAS TO DUPLICATE THEIR RADIATION WITH MY BEAM...
...AND SECRETLY FEED MYSELF INCREASINGLY LARGE DOSES OF IT! THAT WAY MY SYSTEM GRADUALLY BECAME ACCUSTOMED TO THE RADIATION AND WHEN THEY HIT ME WITH THAT MASSIVE CHARGE OF IT, I FELT NO EFFECT AT ALL, THOUGH I PRETENDED TO BE OVERCOME BY IT!
AND AFTERWARDS, JUST TO PLAY SAFE--AND FOOL THE ALIENS--I CREATED THE POWER RINGS--WITH TWENTY-FOUR HOURS OF POWER--AND SOLD THEM--JUST IN CASE I WOULD NEED EXTRA WILL POWER TO DRAW ON--AS ACTUALLY HAPPENED!
JUMPING FISHHOOKS! I THOUGHT THAT SHOWED YOU WERE ABSOLUTELY OFF YOUR ROCKER!!
12
SHOWS HOW WRONG I CAN BE! ALL ALONG THERE WAS METHOD IN YOUR MADNESS!
YES, I GUESS YOU COULD PUT IT THAT WAY, PIE!
THE END

GREEN LANTERN

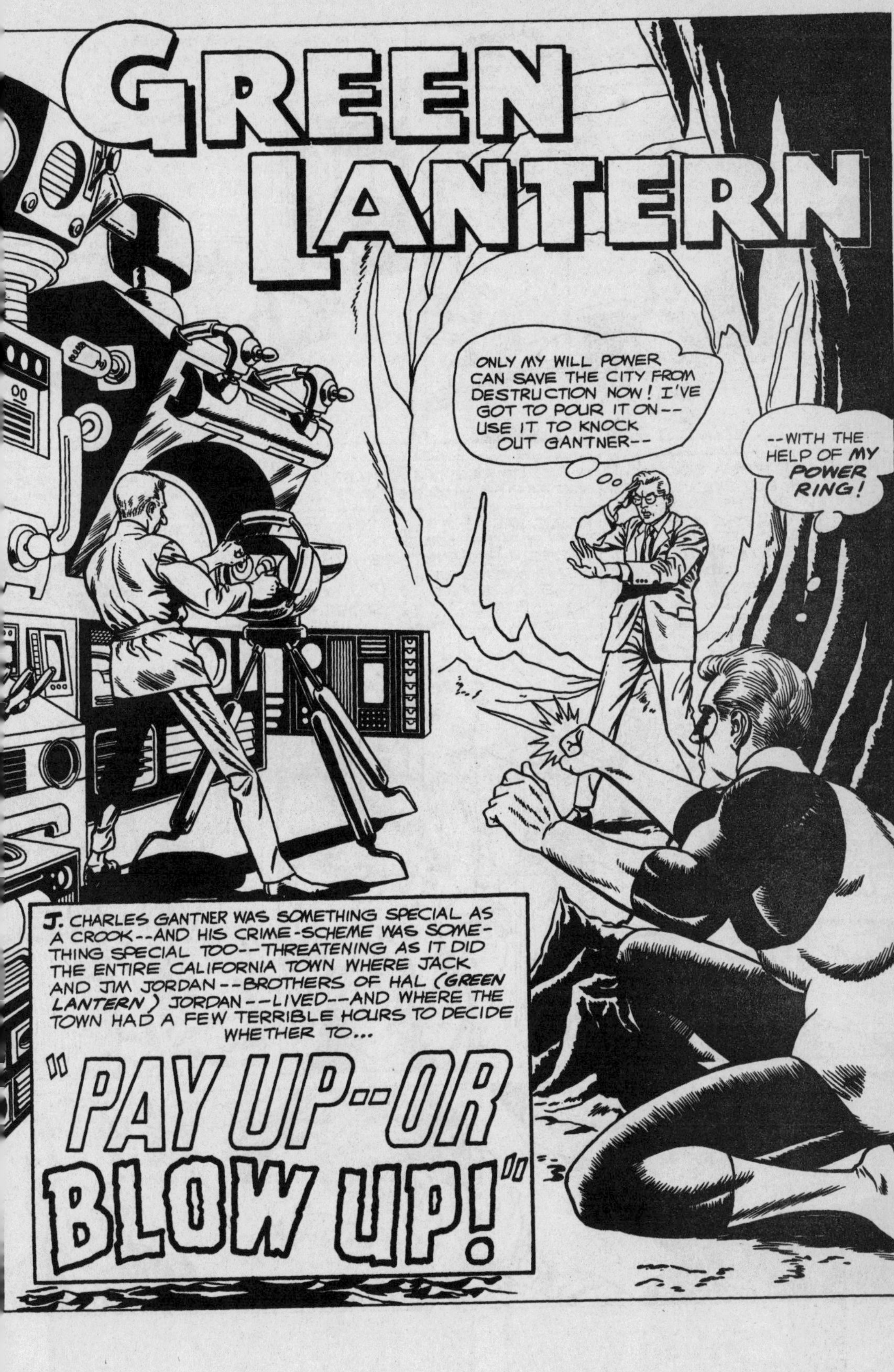
GREEN LANTERN
ONLY MY WILL POWER CAN SAVE THE CITY FROM DESTRUCTION NOW! I'VE GOT TO POUR IT ON-- USE IT TO KNOCK OUT GANTNER--
--WITH THE HELP OF MY POWER RING!
J. CHARLES GANTNER WAS SOMETHING SPECIAL AS A CROOK--AND HIS CRIME-SCHEME WAS SOMETHING SPECIAL TOO--THREATENING AS IT DID THE ENTIRE CALIFORNIA TOWN WHERE JACK AND JIM JORDAN--BROTHERS OF HAL (GREEN LANTERN) JORDAN--LIVED--AND WHERE THE TOWN HAD A FEW TERRIBLE HOURS TO DECIDE WHETHER TO...
"PAY UP--OR BLOW UP!"

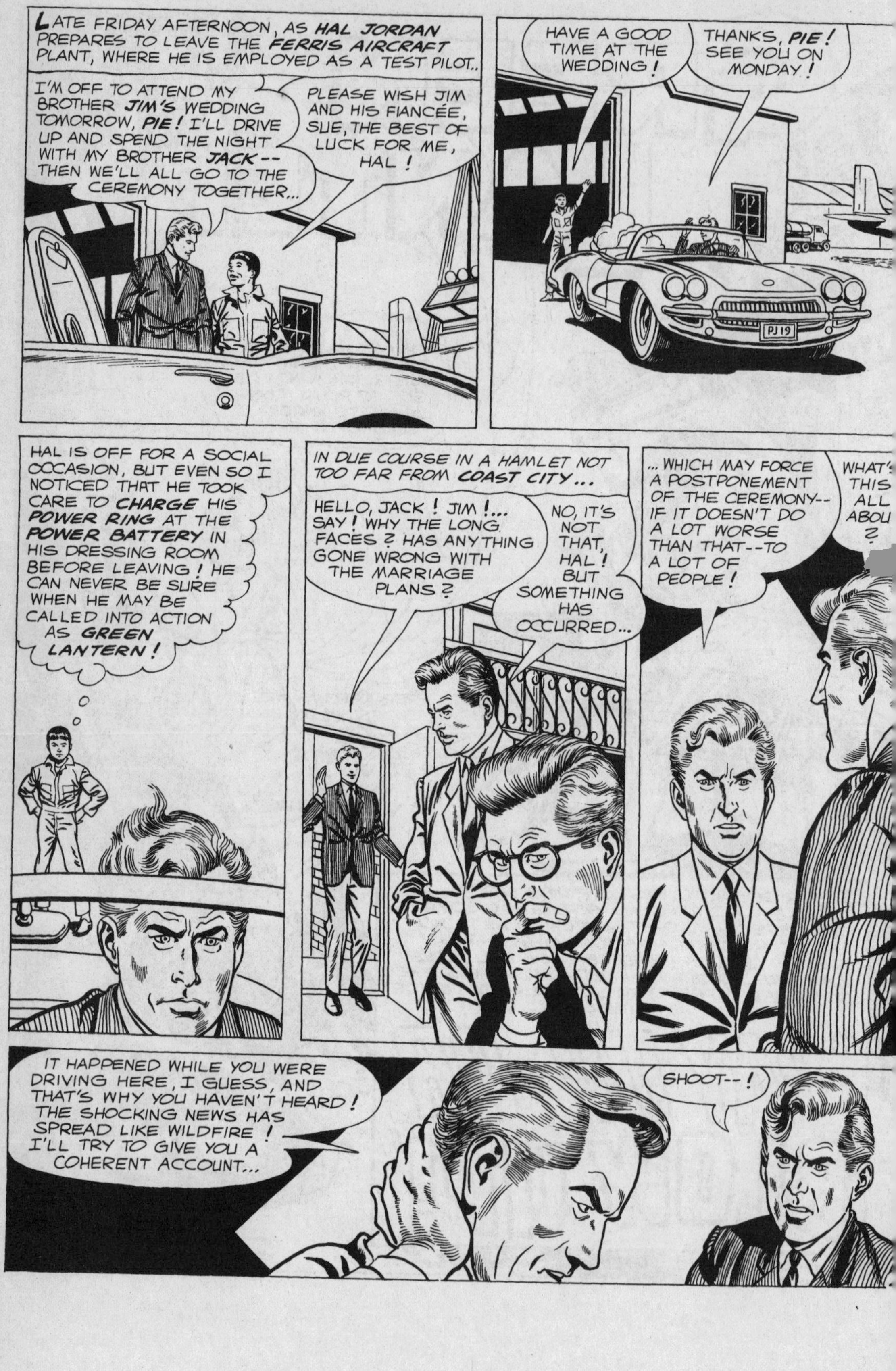
LATE FRIDAY AFTERNOON, AS HAL JORDAN PREPARES TO LEAVE THE FERRIS AIRCRAFT PLANT, WHERE HE IS EMPLOYED AS A TEST PILOT..
I'M OFF TO ATTEND MY BROTHER JIM'S WEDDING TOMORROW, PIE! I'LL DRIVE UP AND SPEND THE NIGHT WITH MY BROTHER JACK-- THEN WE'LL ALL GO TO THE CEREMONY TOGETHER...
PLEASE WISH JIM AND HIS FIANCÉE, SUE, THE BEST OF LUCK FOR ME, HAL!
HAVE A GOOD TIME AT THE WEDDING!
THANKS, PIE! SEE YOU ON MONDAY!
PJ19
HAL IS OFF FOR A SOCIAL OCCASION, BUT EVEN SO I NOTICED THAT HE TOOK CARE TO CHARGE HIS POWER RING AT THE POWER BATTERY IN HIS DRESSING ROOM BEFORE LEAVING! HE CAN NEVER BE SURE WHEN HE MAY BE CALLED INTO ACTION AS GREEN LANTERN!
IN DUE COURSE IN A HAMLET NOT TOO FAR FROM COAST CITY...
HELLO, JACK! JIM!... SAY! WHY THE LONG FACES? HAS ANYTHING GONE WRONG WITH THE MARRIAGE PLANS?
NO, IT'S NOT THAT, HAL! BUT SOMETHING HAS OCCURRED...
...WHICH MAY FORCE A POSTPONEMENT OF THE CEREMONY-- IF IT DOESN'T DO A LOT WORSE THAN THAT--TO A LOT OF PEOPLE!
WHAT'S THIS ALL ABOU ?
IT HAPPENED WHILE YOU WERE DRIVING HERE, I GUESS, AND THAT'S WHY YOU HAVEN'T HEARD! THE SHOCKING NEWS HAS SPREAD LIKE WILDFIRE! I'LL TRY TO GIVE YOU A COHERENT ACCOUNT...
SHOOT--!

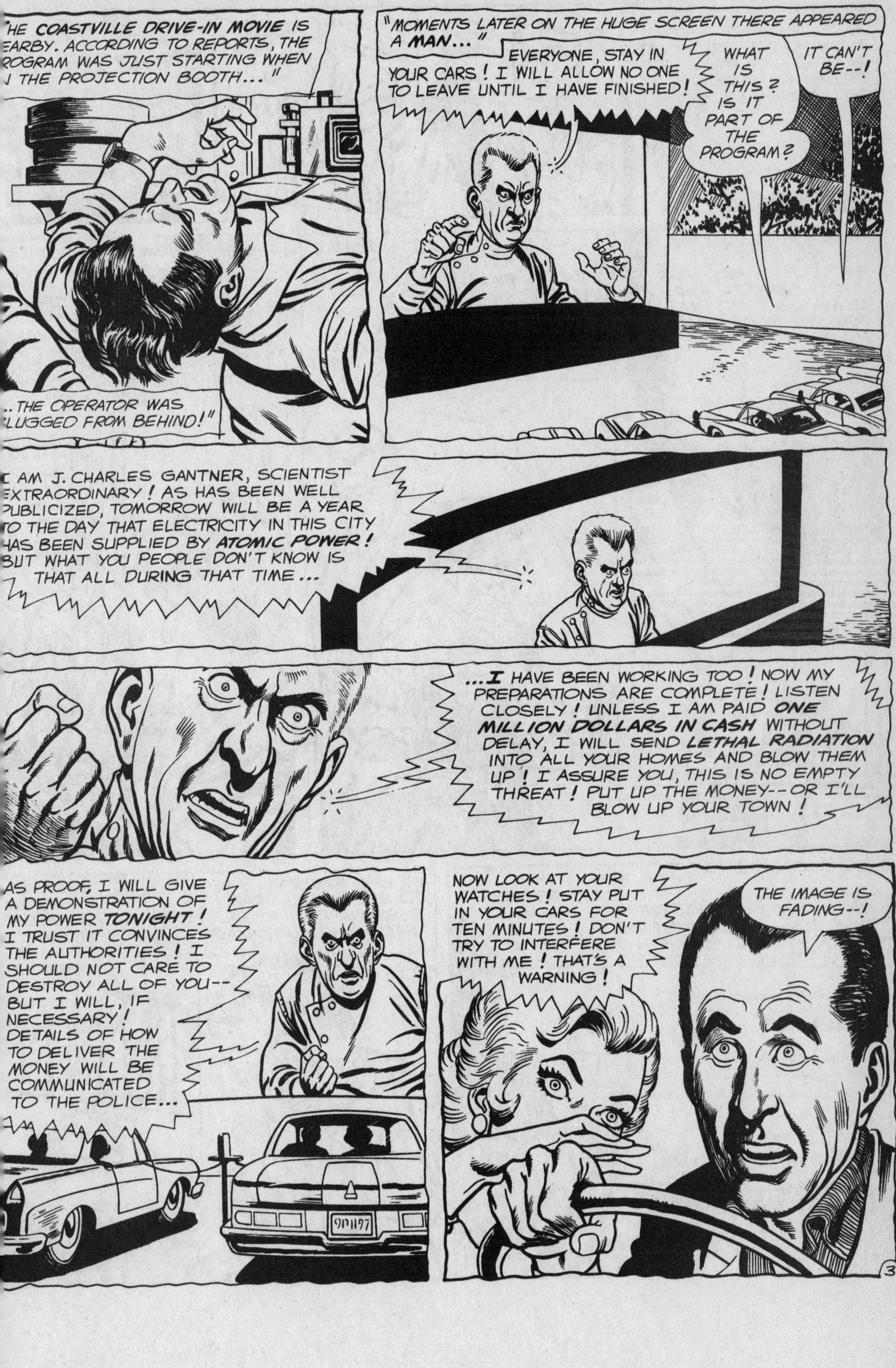
"HE COASTVILLE DRIVE-IN MOVIE IS EARBY. ACCORDING TO REPORTS, THE ROGRAM WAS JUST STARTING WHEN THE PROJECTION BOOTH..."
"..THE OPERATOR WAS LUGGED FROM BEHIND!"
"MOMENTS LATER ON THE HUGE SCREEN THERE APPEARED A MAN..."
EVERYONE, STAY IN YOUR CARS! I WILL ALLOW NO ONE TO LEAVE UNTIL I HAVE FINISHED!
WHAT IS THIS? IS IT PART OF THE PROGRAM?
IT CAN'T BE--!
I AM J. CHARLES GANTNER, SCIENTIST EXTRAORDINARY! AS HAS BEEN WELL PUBLICIZED, TOMORROW WILL BE A YEAR TO THE DAY THAT ELECTRICITY IN THIS CITY HAS BEEN SUPPLIED BY ATOMIC POWER! BUT WHAT YOU PEOPLE DON'T KNOW IS THAT ALL DURING THAT TIME...
...I HAVE BEEN WORKING TOO! NOW MY PREPARATIONS ARE COMPLETE! LISTEN CLOSELY! UNLESS I AM PAID ONE MILLION DOLLARS IN CASH WITHOUT DELAY, I WILL SEND LETHAL RADIATION INTO ALL YOUR HOMES AND BLOW THEM UP! I ASSURE YOU, THIS IS NO EMPTY THREAT! PUT UP THE MONEY--OR I'LL BLOW UP YOUR TOWN!
AS PROOF, I WILL GIVE A DEMONSTRATION OF MY POWER TONIGHT! I TRUST IT CONVINCES THE AUTHORITIES! I SHOULD NOT CARE TO DESTROY ALL OF YOU--BUT I WILL, IF NECESSARY! DETAILS OF HOW TO DELIVER THE MONEY WILL BE COMMUNICATED TO THE POLICE...
NOW LOOK AT YOUR WATCHES! STAY PUT IN YOUR CARS FOR TEN MINUTES! DON'T TRY TO INTERFERE WITH ME! THAT'S A WARNING!
THE IMAGE IS FADING--!
3

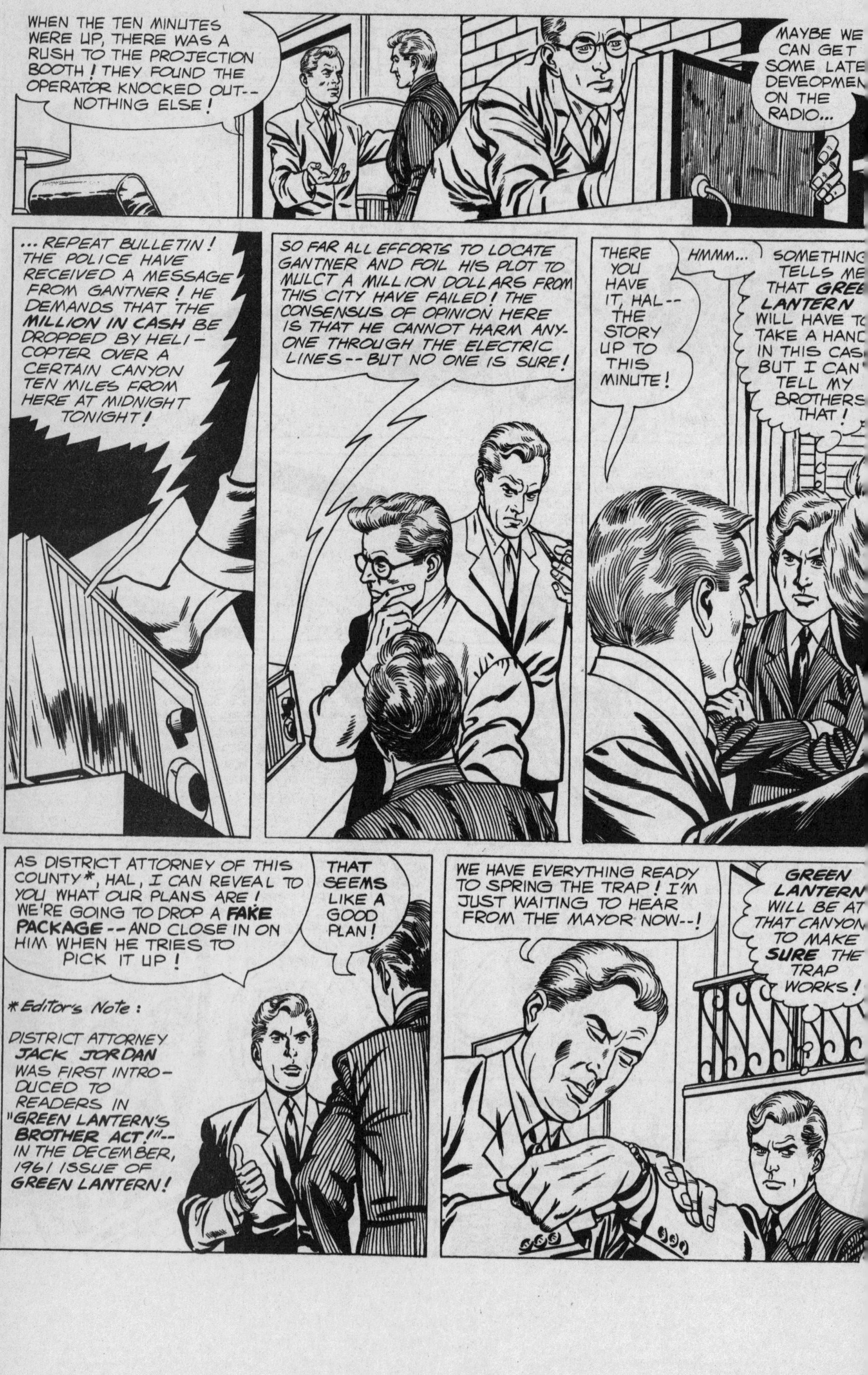
WHEN THE TEN MINUTES WERE UP, THERE WAS A RUSH TO THE PROJECTION BOOTH! THEY FOUND THE OPERATOR KNOCKED OUT-- NOTHING ELSE!
MAYBE WE CAN GET SOME LATE DEVEOPMEN ON THE RADIO...
...REPEAT BULLETIN! THE POLICE HAVE RECEIVED A MESSAGE FROM GANTNER! HE DEMANDS THAT THE MILLION IN CASH BE DROPPED BY HELI-COPTER OVER A CERTAIN CANYON TEN MILES FROM HERE AT MIDNIGHT TONIGHT!
SO FAR ALL EFFORTS TO LOCATE GANTNER AND FOIL HIS PLOT TO MULCT A MILLION DOLLARS FROM THIS CITY HAVE FAILED! THE CONSENSUS OF OPINION HERE IS THAT HE CANNOT HARM ANY-ONE THROUGH THE ELECTRIC LINES--BUT NO ONE IS SURE!
THERE YOU HAVE IT, HAL-- THE STORY UP TO THIS MINUTE!
HMMM...
SOMETHING TELLS ME THAT GREE LANTERN WILL HAVE T TAKE A HAND IN THIS CAS BUT I CAN' TELL MY BROTHERS THAT!
AS DISTRICT ATTORNEY OF THIS COUNTY*, HAL, I CAN REVEAL TO YOU WHAT OUR PLANS ARE! WE'RE GOING TO DROP A FAKE PACKAGE--AND CLOSE IN ON HIM WHEN HE TRIES TO PICK IT UP!
THAT SEEMS LIKE A GOOD PLAN!
*Editor's Note: DISTRICT ATTORNEY JACK JORDAN WAS FIRST INTRO-DUCED TO READERS IN "GREEN LANTERN'S BROTHER ACT!"-- IN THE DECEMBER, 1961 ISSUE OF GREEN LANTERN!
WE HAVE EVERYTHING READY TO SPRING THE TRAP! I'M JUST WAITING TO HEAR FROM THE MAYOR NOW--!
GREEN LANTERN WILL BE AT THAT CANYON TO MAKE SURE THE TRAP WORKS!

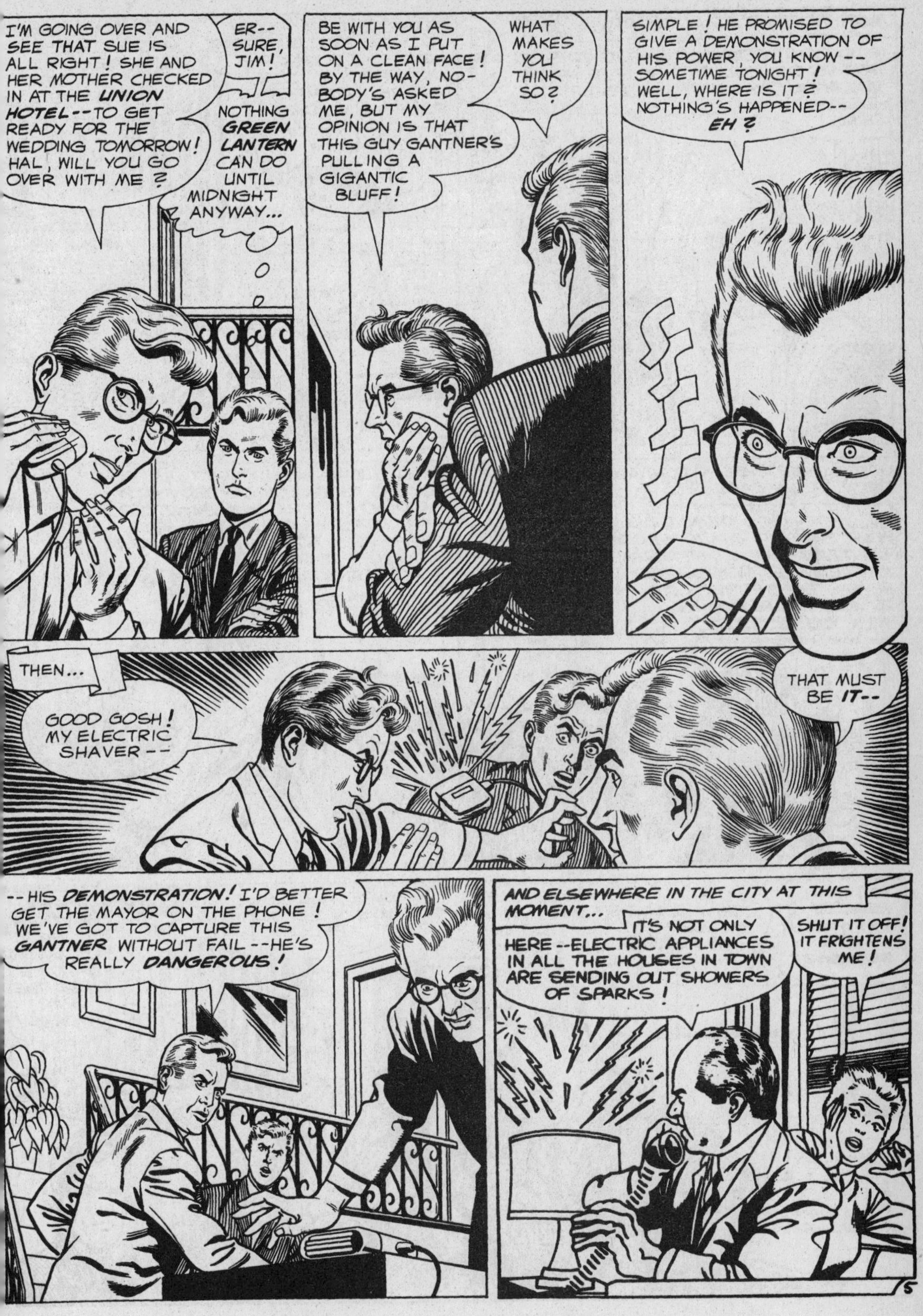

I'M GOING OVER AND SEE THAT SUE IS ALL RIGHT! SHE AND HER MOTHER CHECKED IN AT THE UNION HOTEL--TO GET READY FOR THE WEDDING TOMORROW! HAL, WILL YOU GO OVER WITH ME ?
ER-- SURE, JIM!
NOTHING GREEN LANTERN CAN DO UNTIL MIDNIGHT ANYWAY...
BE WITH YOU AS SOON AS I PUT ON A CLEAN FACE! BY THE WAY, NO-BODY'S ASKED ME, BUT MY OPINION IS THAT THIS GUY GANTNER'S PULLING A GIGANTIC BLUFF!
WHAT MAKES YOU THINK SO?
SIMPLE! HE PROMISED TO GIVE A DEMONSTRATION OF HIS POWER, YOU KNOW -- SOMETIME TONIGHT! WELL, WHERE IS IT? NOTHING'S HAPPENED-- EH?
THEN...
GOOD GOSH! MY ELECTRIC SHAVER --
THAT MUST BE IT--
--HIS DEMONSTRATION! I'D BETTER GET THE MAYOR ON THE PHONE! WE'VE GOT TO CAPTURE THIS GANTNER WITHOUT FAIL--HE'S REALLY DANGEROUS!
AND ELSEWHERE IN THE CITY AT THIS MOMENT...
IT'S NOT ONLY HERE--ELECTRIC APPLIANCES IN ALL THE HOUSES IN TOWN ARE SENDING OUT SHOWERS OF SPARKS!
SHUT IT OFF! IT FRIGHTENS ME!
5

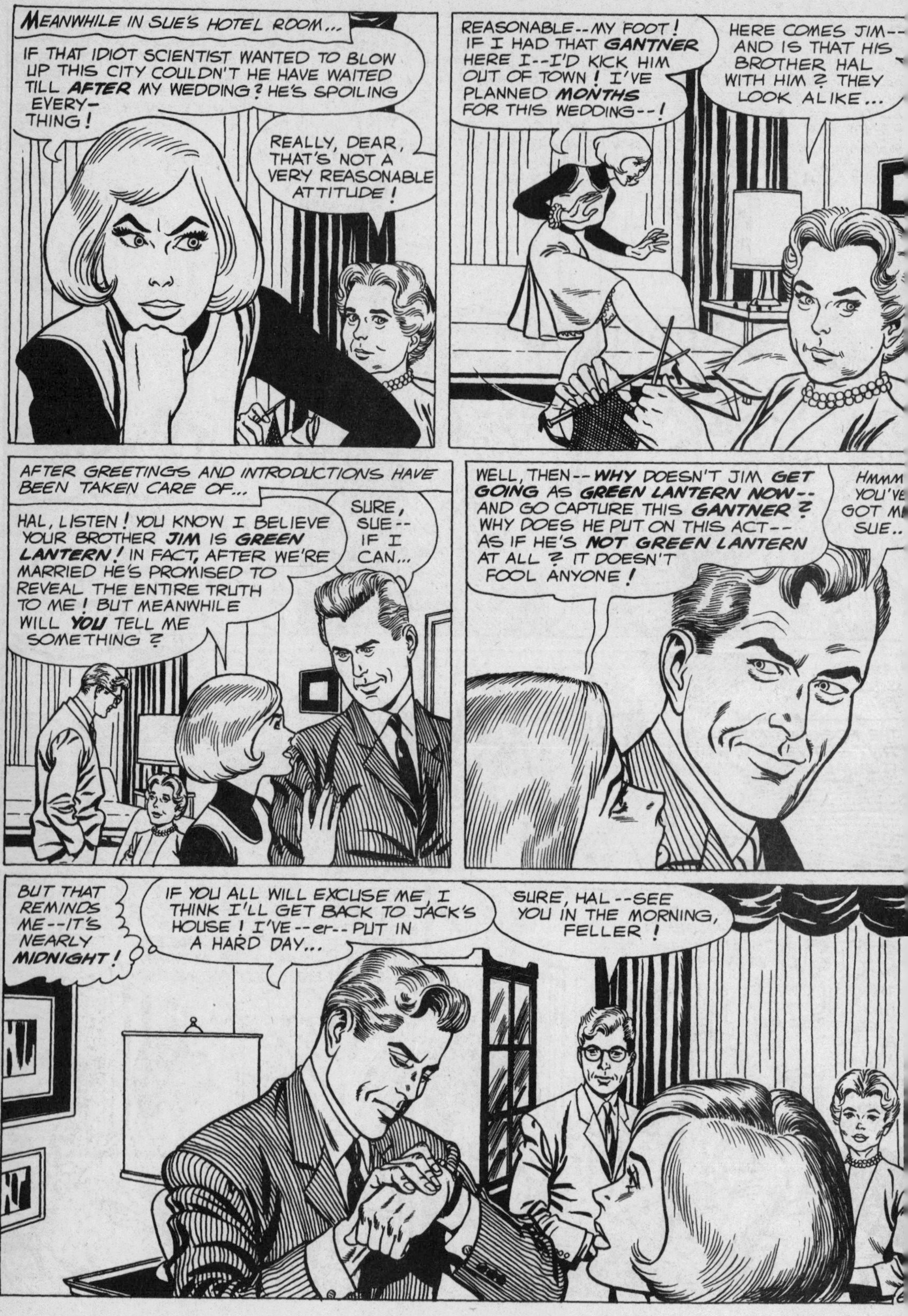

MEANWHILE IN SUE'S HOTEL ROOM...
IF THAT IDIOT SCIENTIST WANTED TO BLOW UP THIS CITY COULDN'T HE HAVE WAITED TILL AFTER MY WEDDING? HE'S SPOILING EVERY-THING!
REALLY, DEAR, THAT'S NOT A VERY REASONABLE ATTITUDE!
REASONABLE--MY FOOT! IF I HAD THAT GANTNER HERE I--I'D KICK HIM OUT OF TOWN! I'VE PLANNED MONTHS FOR THIS WEDDING--!
HERE COMES JIM--AND IS THAT HIS BROTHER HAL WITH HIM? THEY LOOK ALIKE...
AFTER GREETINGS AND INTRODUCTIONS HAVE BEEN TAKEN CARE OF...
HAL, LISTEN! YOU KNOW I BELIEVE YOUR BROTHER JIM IS GREEN LANTERN! IN FACT, AFTER WE'RE MARRIED HE'S PROMISED TO REVEAL THE ENTIRE TRUTH TO ME! BUT MEANWHILE WILL YOU TELL ME SOMETHING?
SURE, SUE--IF I CAN...
WELL, THEN--WHY DOESN'T JIM GET GOING AS GREEN LANTERN NOW--AND GO CAPTURE THIS GANTNER? WHY DOES HE PUT ON THIS ACT--AS IF HE'S NOT GREEN LANTERN AT ALL? IT DOESN'T FOOL ANYONE!
HMMM YOU'VE GOT M SUE..
BUT THAT REMINDS ME--IT'S NEARLY MIDNIGHT!
IF YOU ALL WILL EXCUSE ME, I THINK I'LL GET BACK TO JACK'S HOUSE! I'VE--er--PUT IN A HARD DAY...
SURE, HAL--SEE YOU IN THE MORNING, FELLER!

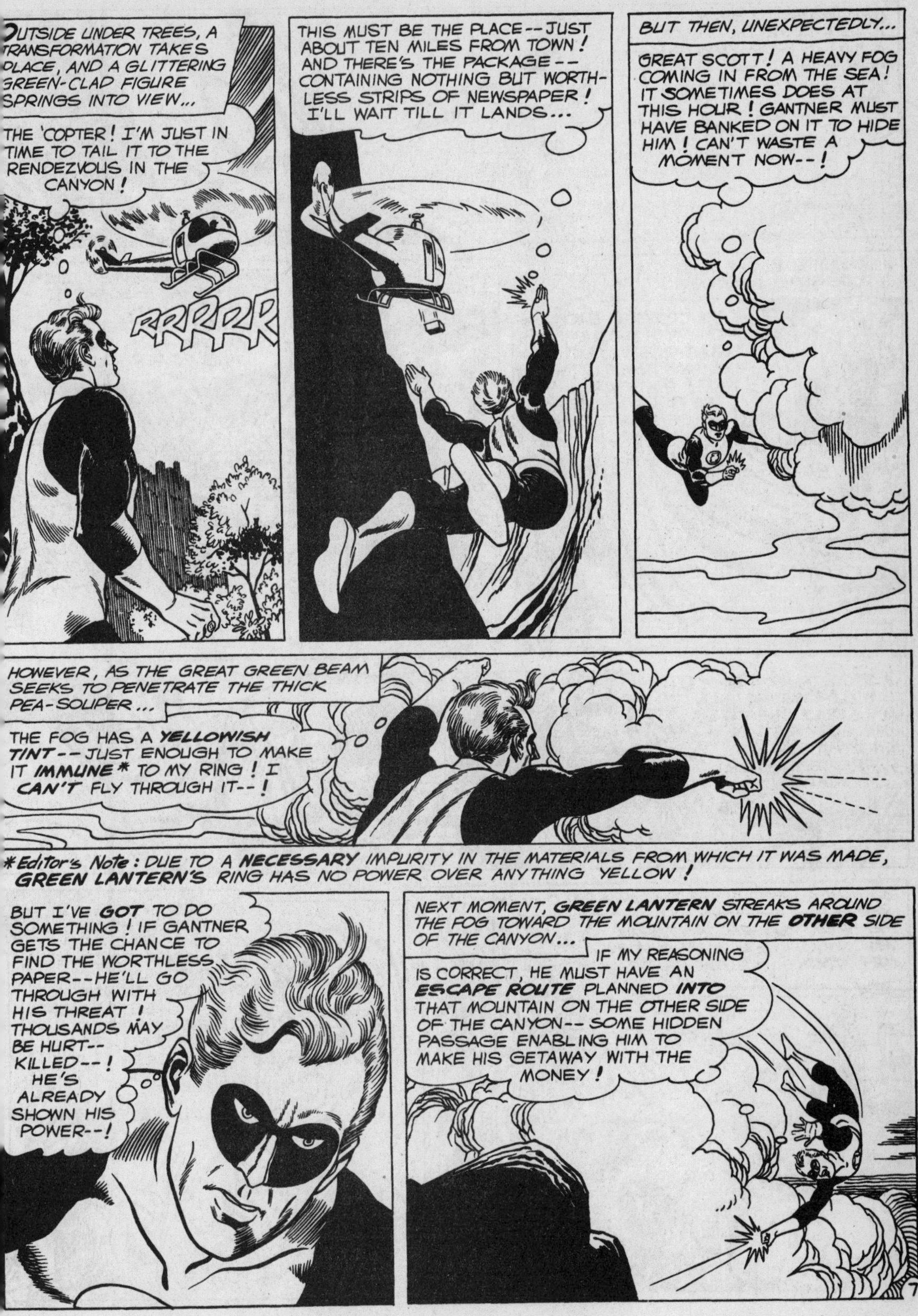
OUTSIDE UNDER TREES, A TRANSFORMATION TAKES PLACE, AND A GLITTERING GREEN-CLAD FIGURE SPRINGS INTO VIEW...
THE 'COPTER! I'M JUST IN TIME TO TAIL IT TO THE RENDEZVOUS IN THE CANYON!
RRRRR
THIS MUST BE THE PLACE--JUST ABOUT TEN MILES FROM TOWN! AND THERE'S THE PACKAGE--CONTAINING NOTHING BUT WORTHLESS STRIPS OF NEWSPAPER! I'LL WAIT TILL IT LANDS...
BUT THEN, UNEXPECTEDLY...
GREAT SCOTT! A HEAVY FOG COMING IN FROM THE SEA! IT SOMETIMES DOES AT THIS HOUR! GANTNER MUST HAVE BANKED ON IT TO HIDE HIM! CAN'T WASTE A MOMENT NOW--!
HOWEVER, AS THE GREAT GREEN BEAM SEEKS TO PENETRATE THE THICK PEA-SOUPER...
THE FOG HAS A YELLOWISH TINT--JUST ENOUGH TO MAKE IT IMMUNE* TO MY RING! I CAN'T FLY THROUGH IT--!
*Editor's Note: DUE TO A NECESSARY IMPURITY IN THE MATERIALS FROM WHICH IT WAS MADE, GREEN LANTERN'S RING HAS NO POWER OVER ANYTHING YELLOW!
BUT I'VE GOT TO DO SOMETHING! IF GANTNER GETS THE CHANCE TO FIND THE WORTHLESS PAPER--HE'LL GO THROUGH WITH HIS THREAT! THOUSANDS MAY BE HURT--KILLED--! HE'S ALREADY SHOWN HIS POWER--!
NEXT MOMENT, GREEN LANTERN STREAKS AROUND THE FOG TOWARD THE MOUNTAIN ON THE OTHER SIDE OF THE CANYON...
IF MY REASONING IS CORRECT, HE MUST HAVE AN ESCAPE ROUTE PLANNED INTO THAT MOUNTAIN ON THE OTHER SIDE OF THE CANYON--SOME HIDDEN PASSAGE ENABLING HIM TO MAKE HIS GETAWAY WITH THE MONEY!
7

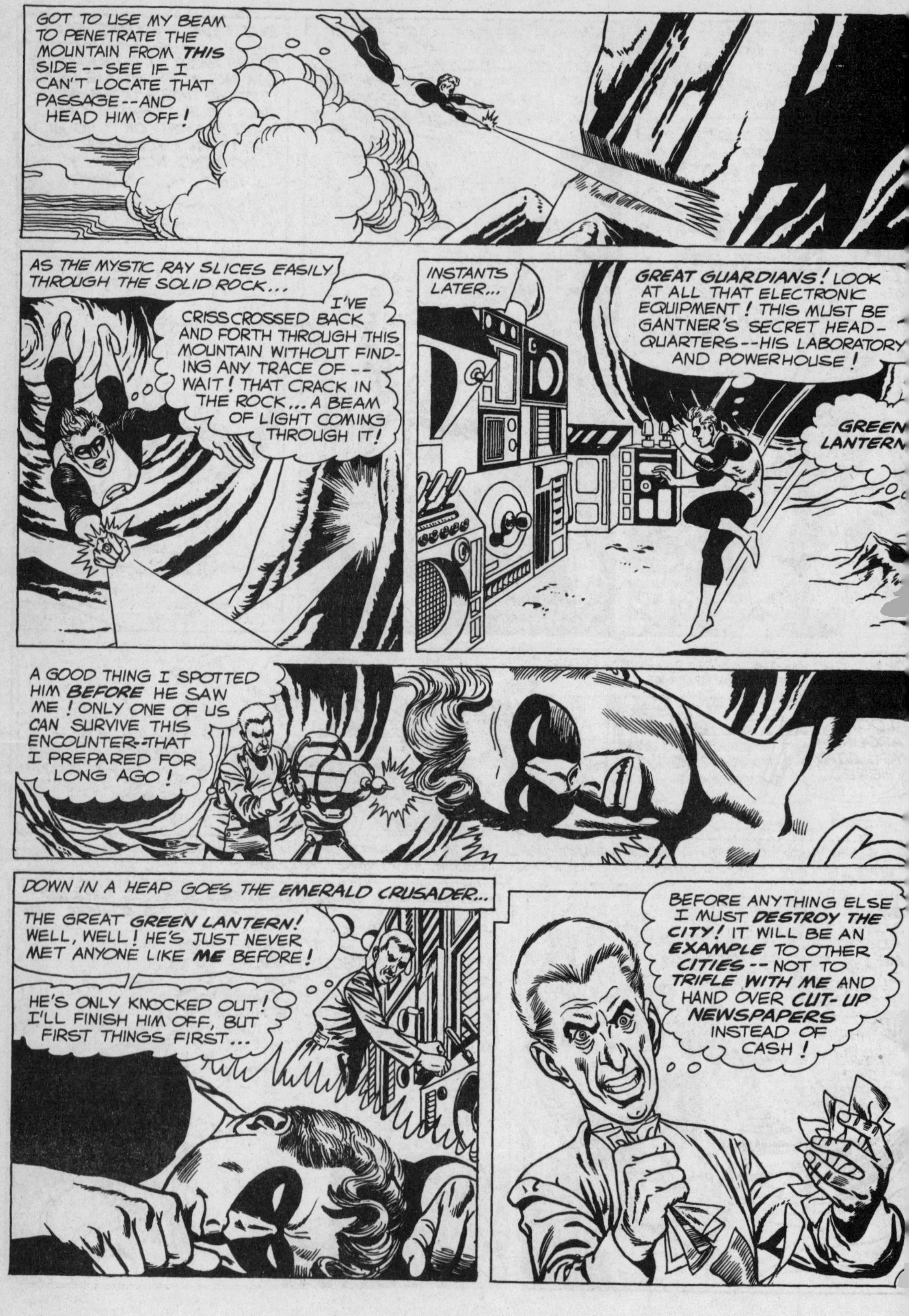

GOT TO USE MY BEAM TO PENETRATE THE MOUNTAIN FROM THIS SIDE --SEE IF I CAN'T LOCATE THAT PASSAGE--AND HEAD HIM OFF!
AS THE MYSTIC RAY SLICES EASILY THROUGH THE SOLID ROCK...
I'VE CRISSCROSSED BACK AND FORTH THROUGH THIS MOUNTAIN WITHOUT FINDING ANY TRACE OF -- WAIT! THAT CRACK IN THE ROCK... A BEAM OF LIGHT COMING THROUGH IT!
INSTANTS LATER...
GREAT GUARDIANS! LOOK AT ALL THAT ELECTRONIC EQUIPMENT! THIS MUST BE GANTNER'S SECRET HEAD-QUARTERS--HIS LABORATORY AND POWERHOUSE!
GREEN LANTERN
A GOOD THING I SPOTTED HIM BEFORE HE SAW ME! ONLY ONE OF US CAN SURVIVE THIS ENCOUNTER--THAT I PREPARED FOR LONG AGO!
DOWN IN A HEAP GOES THE EMERALD CRUSADER...
THE GREAT GREEN LANTERN! WELL, WELL! HE'S JUST NEVER MET ANYONE LIKE ME BEFORE!
HE'S ONLY KNOCKED OUT! I'LL FINISH HIM OFF, BUT FIRST THINGS FIRST...
BEFORE ANYTHING ELSE I MUST DESTROY THE CITY! IT WILL BE AN EXAMPLE TO OTHER CITIES -- NOT TO TRIFLE WITH ME AND HAND OVER CUT-UP NEWSPAPERS INSTEAD OF CASH!

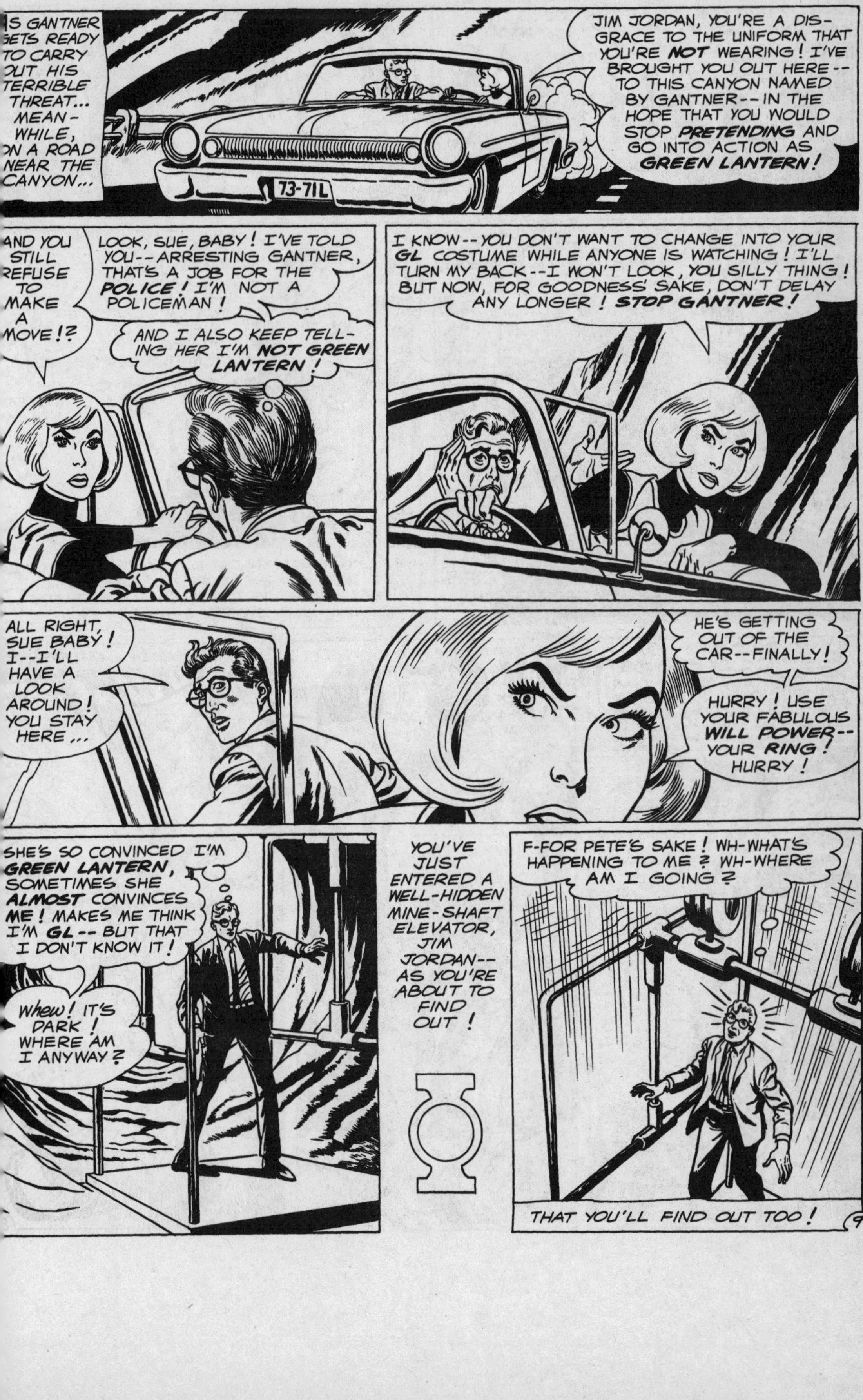
AS GANTNER GETS READY TO CARRY OUT HIS TERRIBLE THREAT... MEANWHILE, ON A ROAD NEAR THE CANYON...
73-71L
JIM JORDAN, YOU'RE A DISGRACE TO THE UNIFORM THAT YOU'RE NOT WEARING! I'VE BROUGHT YOU OUT HERE -- TO THIS CANYON NAMED BY GANTNER -- IN THE HOPE THAT YOU WOULD STOP PRETENDING AND GO INTO ACTION AS GREEN LANTERN!
AND YOU STILL REFUSE TO MAKE A MOVE!?
LOOK, SUE, BABY! I'VE TOLD YOU -- ARRESTING GANTNER, THAT'S A JOB FOR THE POLICE! I'M NOT A POLICEMAN!
AND I ALSO KEEP TELLING HER I'M NOT GREEN LANTERN!
I KNOW -- YOU DON'T WANT TO CHANGE INTO YOUR GL COSTUME WHILE ANYONE IS WATCHING! I'LL TURN MY BACK -- I WON'T LOOK, YOU SILLY THING! BUT NOW, FOR GOODNESS' SAKE, DON'T DELAY ANY LONGER! STOP GANTNER!
ALL RIGHT, SUE BABY! I--I'LL HAVE A LOOK AROUND! YOU STAY HERE...
HE'S GETTING OUT OF THE CAR -- FINALLY!
HURRY! USE YOUR FABULOUS WILL POWER -- YOUR RING! HURRY!
SHE'S SO CONVINCED I'M GREEN LANTERN, SOMETIMES SHE ALMOST CONVINCES ME! MAKES ME THINK I'M GL -- BUT THAT I DON'T KNOW IT!
Whew! IT'S DARK! WHERE AM I ANYWAY?
YOU'VE JUST ENTERED A WELL-HIDDEN MINE-SHAFT ELEVATOR, JIM JORDAN -- AS YOU'RE ABOUT TO FIND OUT!
F-FOR PETE'S SAKE! WH-WHAT'S HAPPENING TO ME? WH-WHERE AM I GOING?
THAT YOU'LL FIND OUT TOO!
9

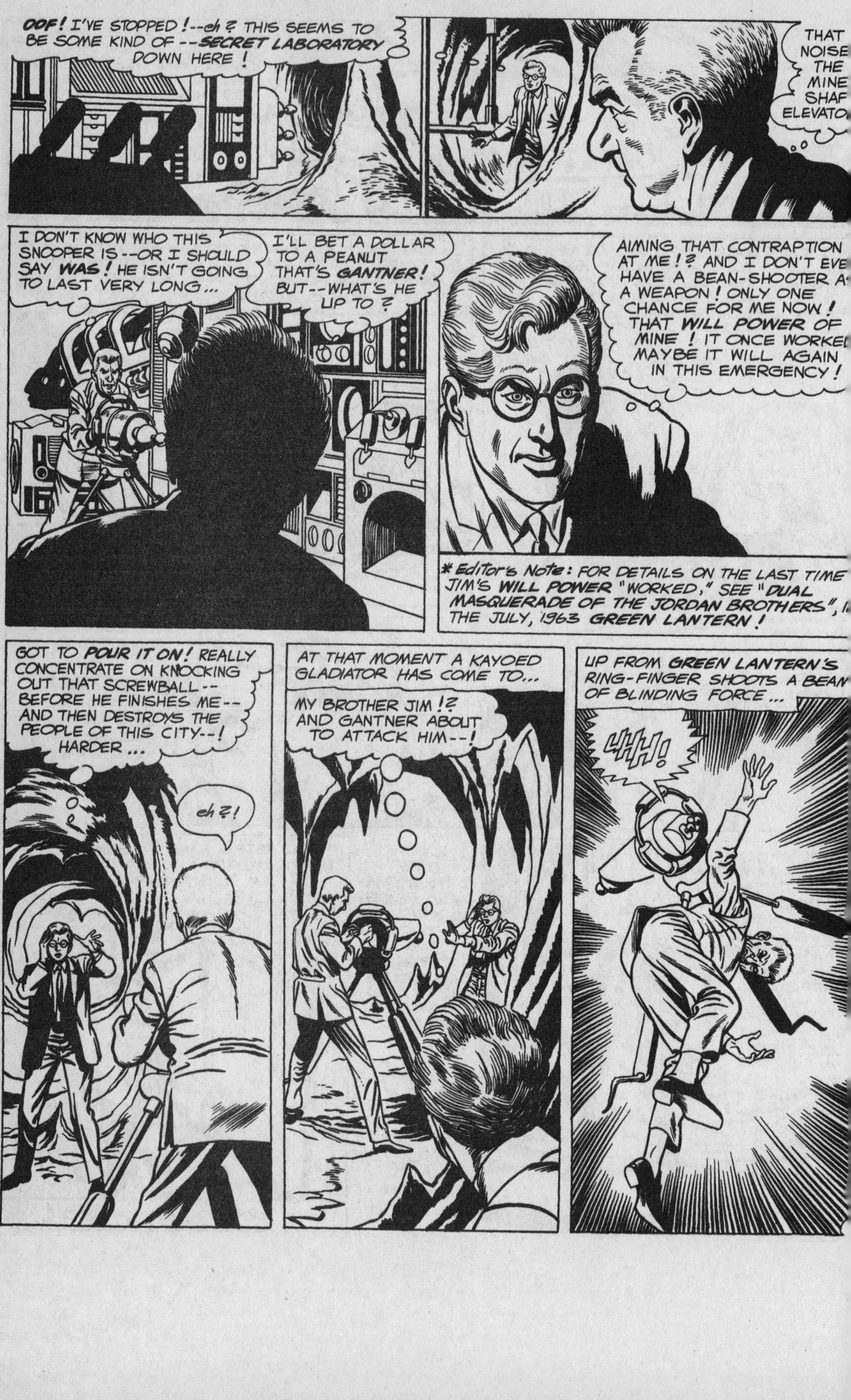

OOF! I'VE STOPPED! --eh? THIS SEEMS TO BE SOME KIND OF --SECRET LABORATORY DOWN HERE!
THAT NOISE THE MINE SHAF ELEVATO
I DON'T KNOW WHO THIS SNOOPER IS--OR I SHOULD SAY WAS! HE ISN'T GOING TO LAST VERY LONG...
I'LL BET A DOLLAR TO A PEANUT THAT'S GANTNER! BUT--WHAT'S HE UP TO?
AIMING THAT CONTRAPTION AT ME!? AND I DON'T EVE HAVE A BEAN-SHOOTER A A WEAPON! ONLY ONE CHANCE FOR ME NOW! THAT WILL POWER OF MINE! IT ONCE WORKE MAYBE IT WILL AGAIN IN THIS EMERGENCY!
* Editor's Note: FOR DETAILS ON THE LAST TIME JIM'S WILL POWER "WORKED," SEE "DUAL MASQUERADE OF THE JORDAN BROTHERS", I THE JULY, 1963 GREEN LANTERN!
GOT TO POUR IT ON! REALLY CONCENTRATE ON KNOCKING OUT THAT SCREWBALL--BEFORE HE FINISHES ME--AND THEN DESTROYS THE PEOPLE OF THIS CITY--! HARDER...
eh?!
AT THAT MOMENT A KAYOED GLADIATOR HAS COME TO...
MY BROTHER JIM!? AND GANTNER ABOUT TO ATTACK HIM--!
UP FROM GREEN LANTERN'S RING-FINGER SHOOTS A BEAM OF BLINDING FORCE...
UHH!

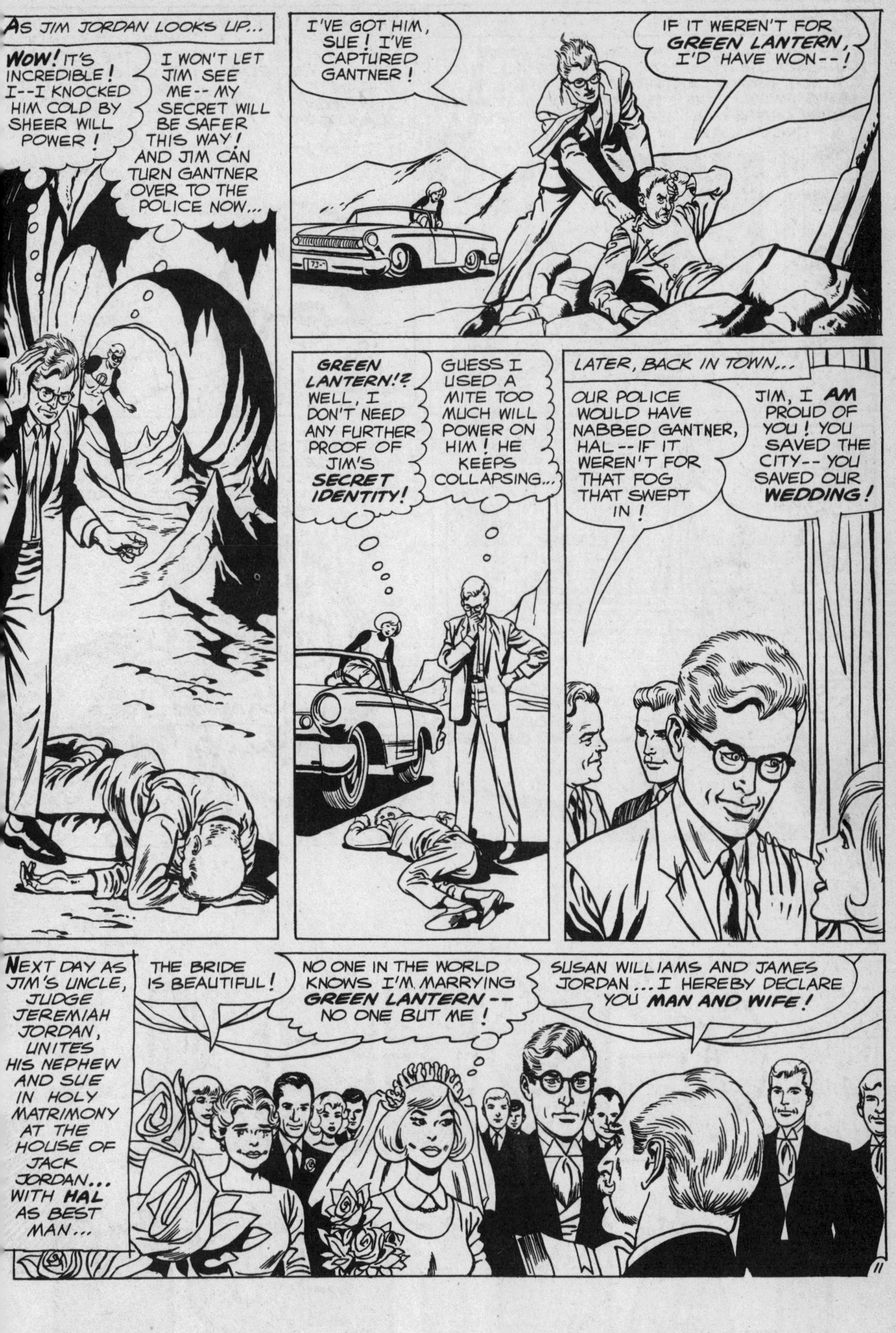
AS JIM JORDAN LOOKS UP...
WOW! IT'S INCREDIBLE! I--I KNOCKED HIM COLD BY SHEER WILL POWER!
I WON'T LET JIM SEE ME-- MY SECRET WILL BE SAFER THIS WAY! AND JIM CAN TURN GANTNER OVER TO THE POLICE NOW...
I'VE GOT HIM, SUE! I'VE CAPTURED GANTNER!
IF IT WEREN'T FOR GREEN LANTERN, I'D HAVE WON--!
GREEN LANTERN!? WELL, I DON'T NEED ANY FURTHER PROOF OF JIM'S SECRET IDENTITY!
GUESS I USED A MITE TOO MUCH WILL POWER ON HIM! HE KEEPS COLLAPSING...
LATER, BACK IN TOWN...
OUR POLICE WOULD HAVE NABBED GANTNER, HAL--IF IT WEREN'T FOR THAT FOG THAT SWEPT IN!
JIM, I AM PROUD OF YOU! YOU SAVED THE CITY-- YOU SAVED OUR WEDDING!
NEXT DAY AS JIM'S UNCLE, JUDGE JEREMIAH JORDAN, UNITES HIS NEPHEW AND SUE IN HOLY MATRIMONY AT THE HOUSE OF JACK JORDAN... WITH HAL AS BEST MAN...
THE BRIDE IS BEAUTIFUL!
NO ONE IN THE WORLD KNOWS I'M MARRYING GREEN LANTERN-- NO ONE BUT ME!
SUSAN WILLIAMS AND JAMES JORDAN... I HEREBY DECLARE YOU MAN AND WIFE!
11

TWO WEEKS LATER, A HONEYMOON COUPLE RETURNS HOME...
WELL, SUE, THIS OUGHT TO PROVE TO YOU ABSOLUTELY AND ONCE AND FOR ALL THAT I'M NOT GREEN LANTERN! LOOK... HERE'S A NEWS PHOTO TAKEN YESTERDAY THAT SHOWS GREEN LANTERN IN THE ACT OF CAPTURING A CROOK GANG IN COAST CITY!
DAILY PAPER
AND SINCE YOU KNOW THAT I WAS WITH YOU EVERY MINUTE OF THE DAY YESTERDAY-- I CAN'T BE GREEN LANTERN!
NONSENSE! DID YOU THINK YOU COULD PULL THE WOOL OVER MY EYES SO EASILY?
I KNOW YOU CAN CREATE AN IMAGE OF GREEN LANTERN ANY TIME YOU WANT AND SEND IT INTO ACTION! OF COURSE, THAT'S WHAT YOU MUST HAVE DONE! SILLY, TO THINK YOU COULD FOOL ME!
THERE MUST BE A WAY TO CONVINCE HER I'M NOT GREEN LANTERN--BUT SO FAR I HAVEN'T FOUND IT! AND TO THINK--I MAY BE FACED WITH THIS SITUATION FOR THE REST OF MY LIFE!
The End

GREEN LANTERN

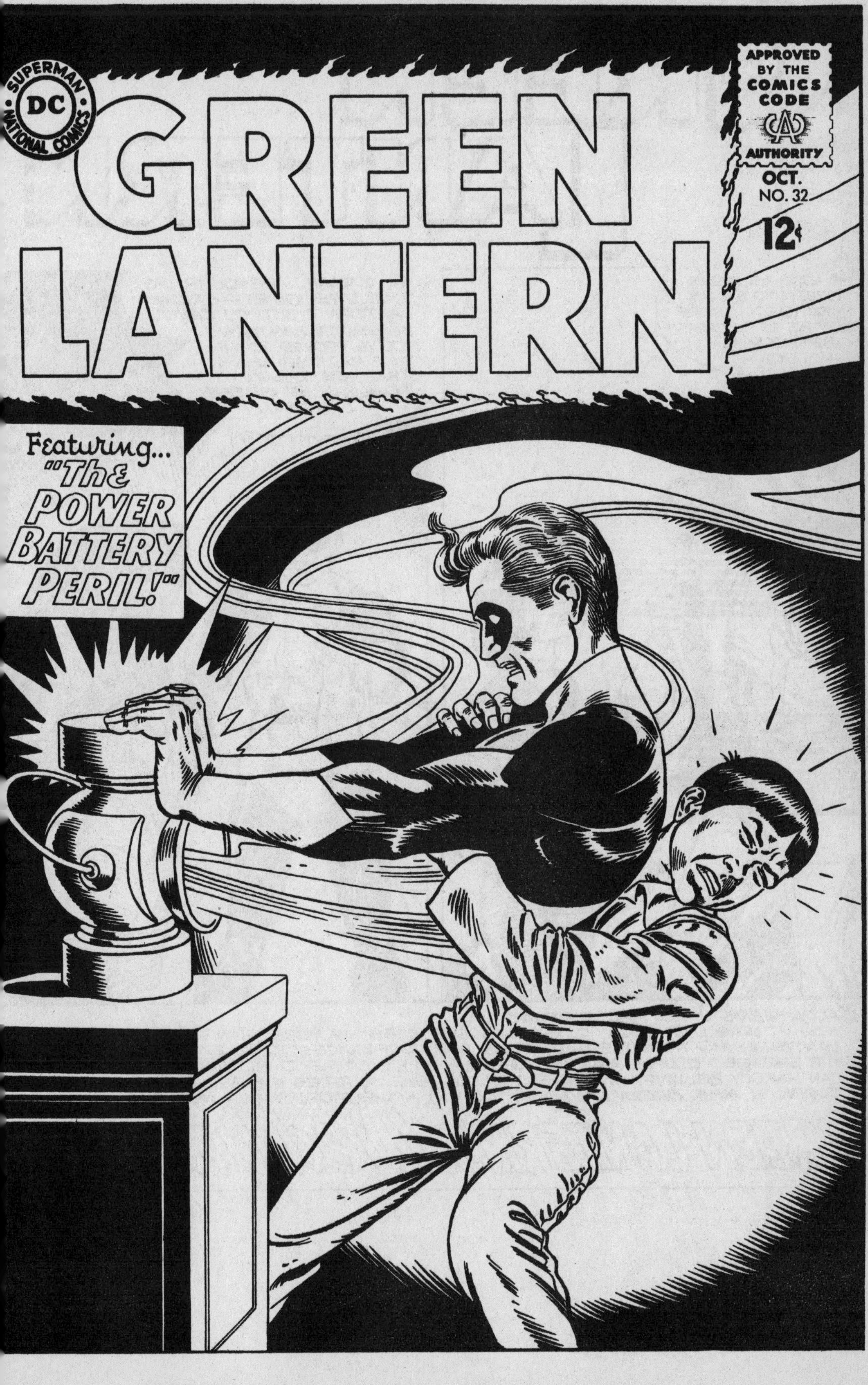
SUPERMAN DC NATIONAL COMICS
GREEN LANTERN
APPROVED BY THE COMICS CODE AUTHORITY
OCT. NO. 32
12¢
Featuring... "The POWER BATTERY PERIL!"

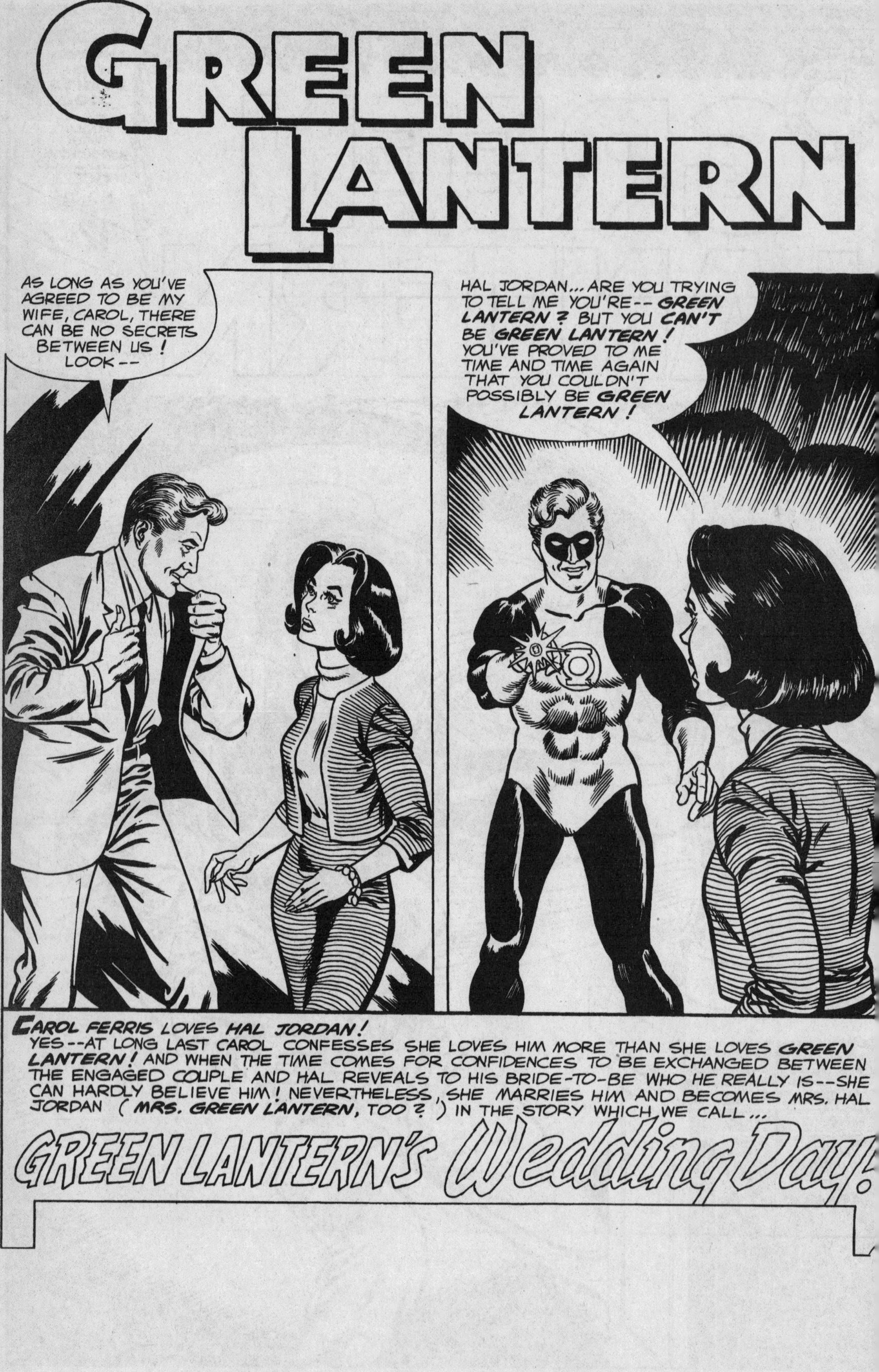
GREEN LANTERN
AS LONG AS YOU'VE AGREED TO BE MY WIFE, CAROL, THERE CAN BE NO SECRETS BETWEEN US! LOOK--
HAL JORDAN... ARE YOU TRYING TO TELL ME YOU'RE--GREEN LANTERN? BUT YOU CAN'T BE GREEN LANTERN! YOU'VE PROVED TO ME TIME AND TIME AGAIN THAT YOU COULDN'T POSSIBLY BE GREEN LANTERN!
CAROL FERRIS LOVES HAL JORDAN! YES--AT LONG LAST CAROL CONFESSES SHE LOVES HIM MORE THAN SHE LOVES GREEN LANTERN! AND WHEN THE TIME COMES FOR CONFIDENCES TO BE EXCHANGED BETWEEN THE ENGAGED COUPLE AND HAL REVEALS TO HIS BRIDE-TO-BE WHO HE REALLY IS--SHE CAN HARDLY BELIEVE HIM! NEVERTHELESS, SHE MARRIES HIM AND BECOMES MRS. HAL JORDAN (MRS. GREEN LANTERN, TOO?) IN THE STORY WHICH WE CALL...
GREEN LANTERN'S Wedding Day!

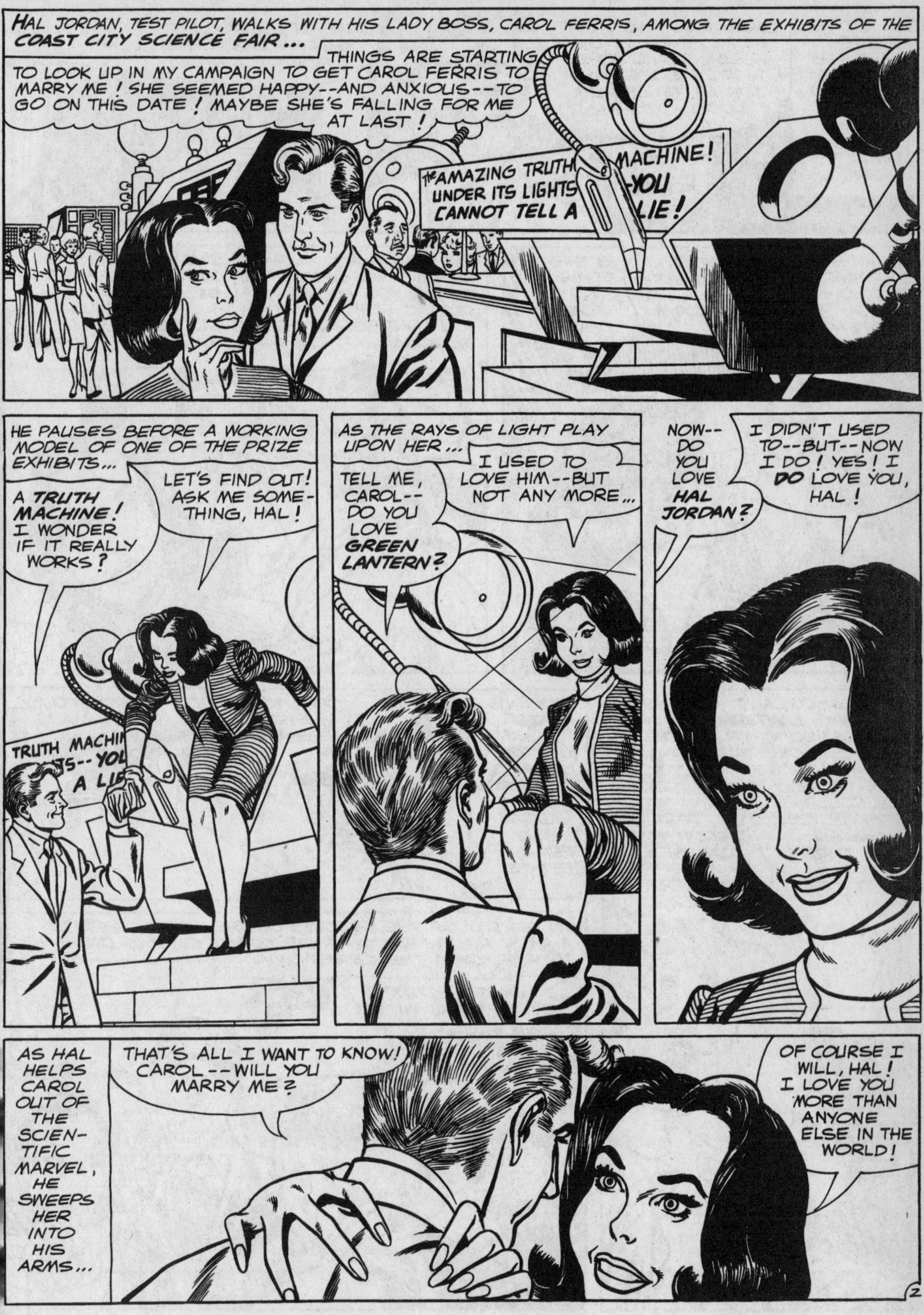
HAL JORDAN, TEST PILOT, WALKS WITH HIS LADY BOSS, CAROL FERRIS, AMONG THE EXHIBITS OF THE COAST CITY SCIENCE FAIR...
THINGS ARE STARTING TO LOOK UP IN MY CAMPAIGN TO GET CAROL FERRIS TO MARRY ME! SHE SEEMED HAPPY--AND ANXIOUS--TO GO ON THIS DATE! MAYBE SHE'S FALLING FOR ME AT LAST!
THE AMAZING TRUTH MACHINE! UNDER ITS LIGHTS -YOU CANNOT TELL A LIE!
HE PAUSES BEFORE A WORKING MODEL OF ONE OF THE PRIZE EXHIBITS...
A TRUTH MACHINE! I WONDER IF IT REALLY WORKS?
LET'S FIND OUT! ASK ME SOMETHING, HAL!
AS THE RAYS OF LIGHT PLAY UPON HER...
TELL ME, CAROL--DO YOU LOVE GREEN LANTERN?
I USED TO LOVE HIM--BUT NOT ANY MORE...
NOW--DO YOU LOVE HAL JORDAN?
I DIDN'T USED TO--BUT--NOW I DO! YES! I DO LOVE YOU, HAL!
AS HAL HELPS CAROL OUT OF THE SCIENTIFIC MARVEL, HE SWEEPS HER INTO HIS ARMS...
THAT'S ALL I WANT TO KNOW! CAROL--WILL YOU MARRY ME?
OF COURSE I WILL, HAL! I LOVE YOU MORE THAN ANYONE ELSE IN THE WORLD!
2

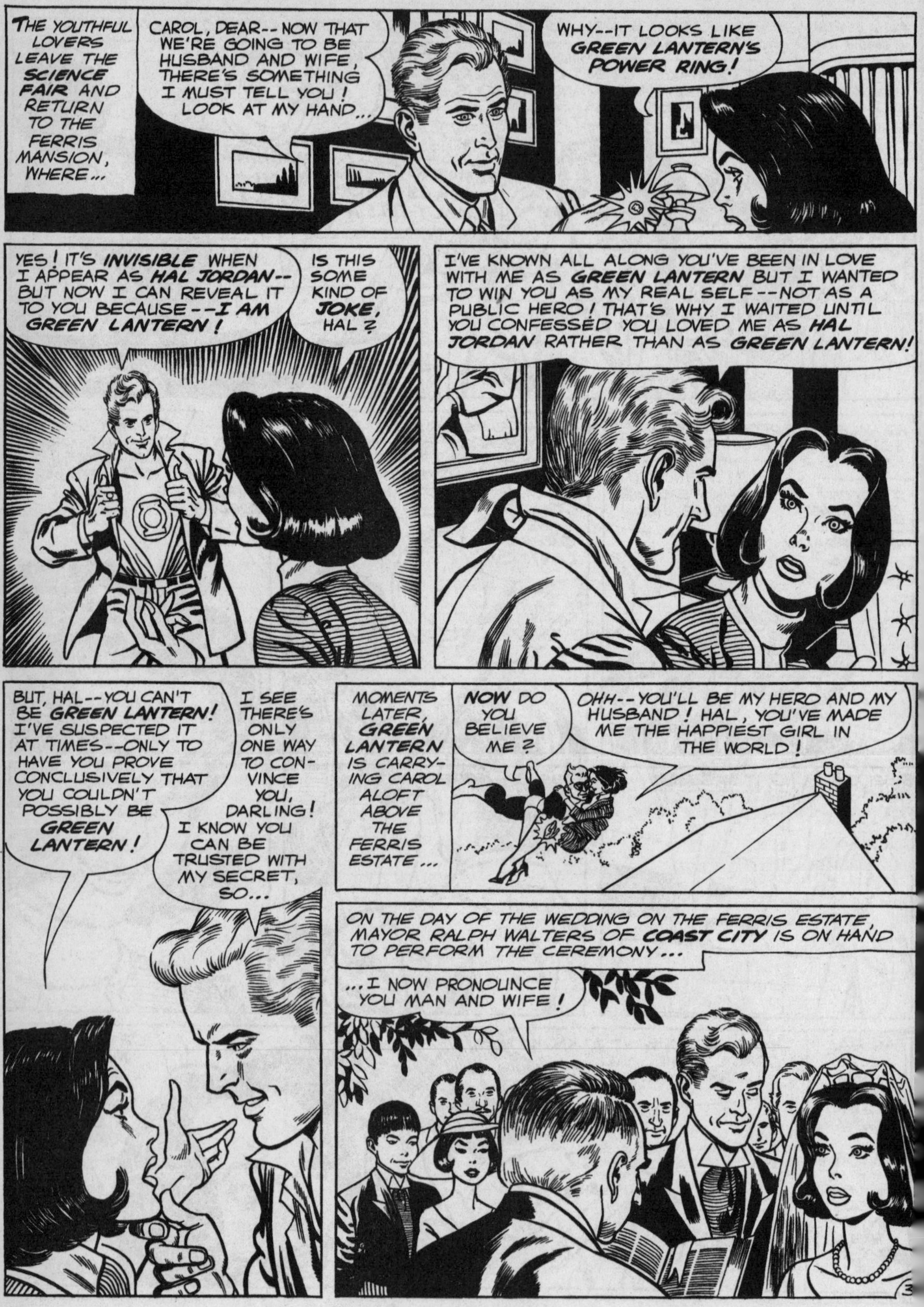
THE YOUTHFUL LOVERS LEAVE THE SCIENCE FAIR AND RETURN TO THE FERRIS MANSION, WHERE...
CAROL, DEAR--NOW THAT WE'RE GOING TO BE HUSBAND AND WIFE, THERE'S SOMETHING I MUST TELL YOU! LOOK AT MY HAND...
WHY--IT LOOKS LIKE GREEN LANTERN'S POWER RING!
YES! IT'S INVISIBLE WHEN I APPEAR AS HAL JORDAN--BUT NOW I CAN REVEAL IT TO YOU BECAUSE--I AM GREEN LANTERN!
IS THIS SOME KIND OF JOKE, HAL?
I'VE KNOWN ALL ALONG YOU'VE BEEN IN LOVE WITH ME AS GREEN LANTERN BUT I WANTED TO WIN YOU AS MY REAL SELF--NOT AS A PUBLIC HERO! THAT'S WHY I WAITED UNTIL YOU CONFESSED YOU LOVED ME AS HAL JORDAN RATHER THAN AS GREEN LANTERN!
BUT, HAL--YOU CAN'T BE GREEN LANTERN! I'VE SUSPECTED IT AT TIMES--ONLY TO HAVE YOU PROVE CONCLUSIVELY THAT YOU COULDN'T POSSIBLY BE GREEN LANTERN!
I SEE THERE'S ONLY ONE WAY TO CONVINCE YOU, DARLING! I KNOW YOU CAN BE TRUSTED WITH MY SECRET, SO...
MOMENTS LATER, GREEN LANTERN IS CARRYING CAROL ALOFT ABOVE THE FERRIS ESTATE...
NOW DO YOU BELIEVE ME?
OHH--YOU'LL BE MY HERO AND MY HUSBAND! HAL, YOU'VE MADE ME THE HAPPIEST GIRL IN THE WORLD!
ON THE DAY OF THE WEDDING ON THE FERRIS ESTATE, MAYOR RALPH WALTERS OF COAST CITY IS ON HAND TO PERFORM THE CEREMONY...
...I NOW PRONOUNCE YOU MAN AND WIFE!

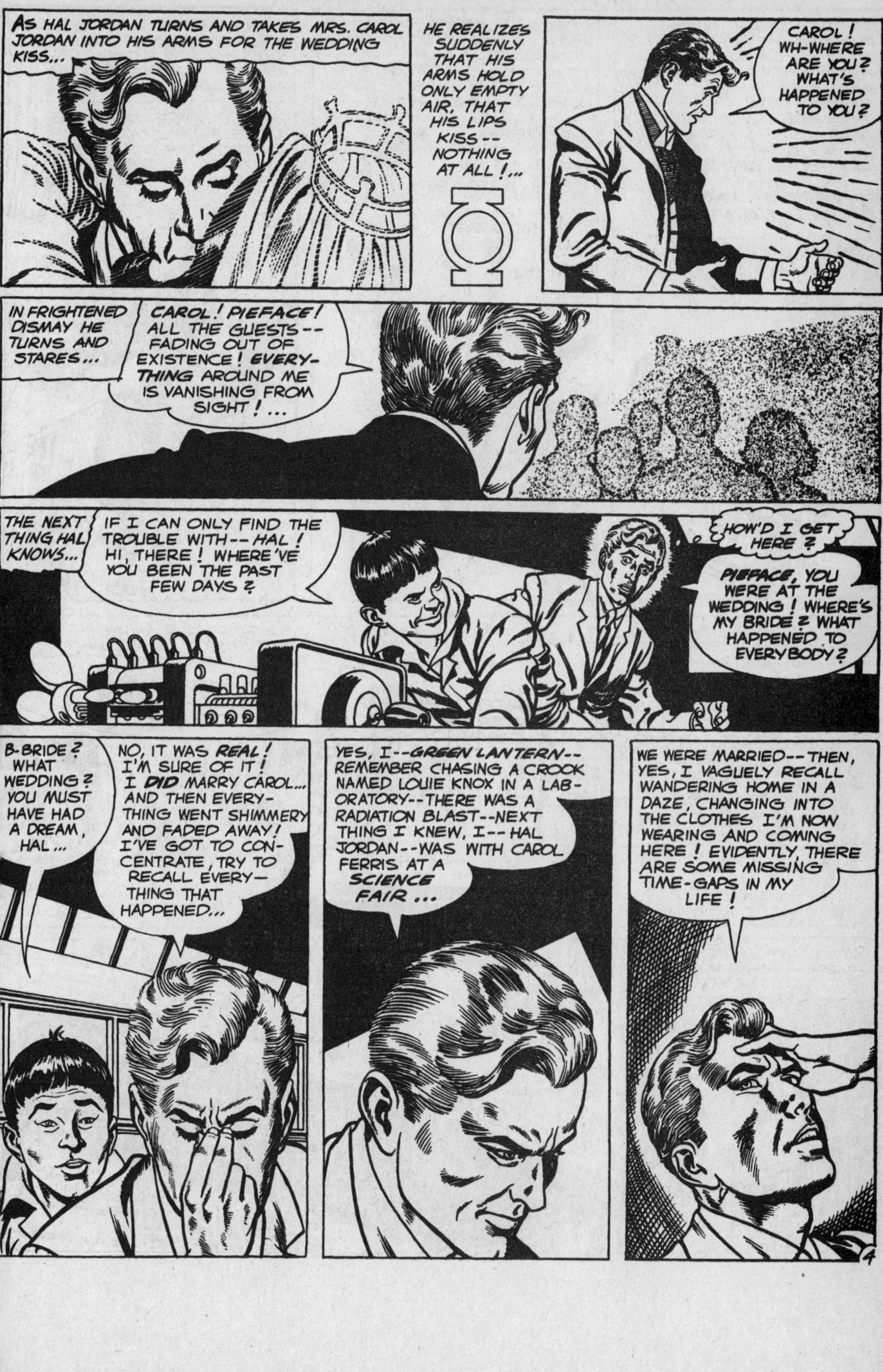
AS HAL JORDAN TURNS AND TAKES MRS. CAROL JORDAN INTO HIS ARMS FOR THE WEDDING KISS...
HE REALIZES SUDDENLY THAT HIS ARMS HOLD ONLY EMPTY AIR, THAT HIS LIPS KISS -- NOTHING AT ALL!...
CAROL! WH-WHERE ARE YOU? WHAT'S HAPPENED TO YOU?
IN FRIGHTENED DISMAY HE TURNS AND STARES...
CAROL! PIEFACE! ALL THE GUESTS -- FADING OUT OF EXISTENCE! EVERYTHING AROUND ME IS VANISHING FROM SIGHT!...
THE NEXT THING HAL KNOWS...
IF I CAN ONLY FIND THE TROUBLE WITH -- HAL! HI, THERE! WHERE'VE YOU BEEN THE PAST FEW DAYS?
HOW'D I GET HERE?
PIEFACE, YOU WERE AT THE WEDDING! WHERE'S MY BRIDE? WHAT HAPPENED TO EVERYBODY?
B-BRIDE? WHAT WEDDING? YOU MUST HAVE HAD A DREAM, HAL...
NO, IT WAS REAL! I'M SURE OF IT! I DID MARRY CAROL... AND THEN EVERYTHING WENT SHIMMERY AND FADED AWAY! I'VE GOT TO CONCENTRATE, TRY TO RECALL EVERYTHING THAT HAPPENED...
YES, I--GREEN LANTERN--REMEMBER CHASING A CROOK NAMED LOUIE KNOX IN A LABORATORY--THERE WAS A RADIATION BLAST--NEXT THING I KNEW, I--HAL JORDAN--WAS WITH CAROL FERRIS AT A SCIENCE FAIR...
WE WERE MARRIED--THEN, YES, I VAGUELY RECALL WANDERING HOME IN A DAZE, CHANGING INTO THE CLOTHES I'M NOW WEARING AND COMING HERE! EVIDENTLY, THERE ARE SOME MISSING TIME-GAPS IN MY LIFE!
4

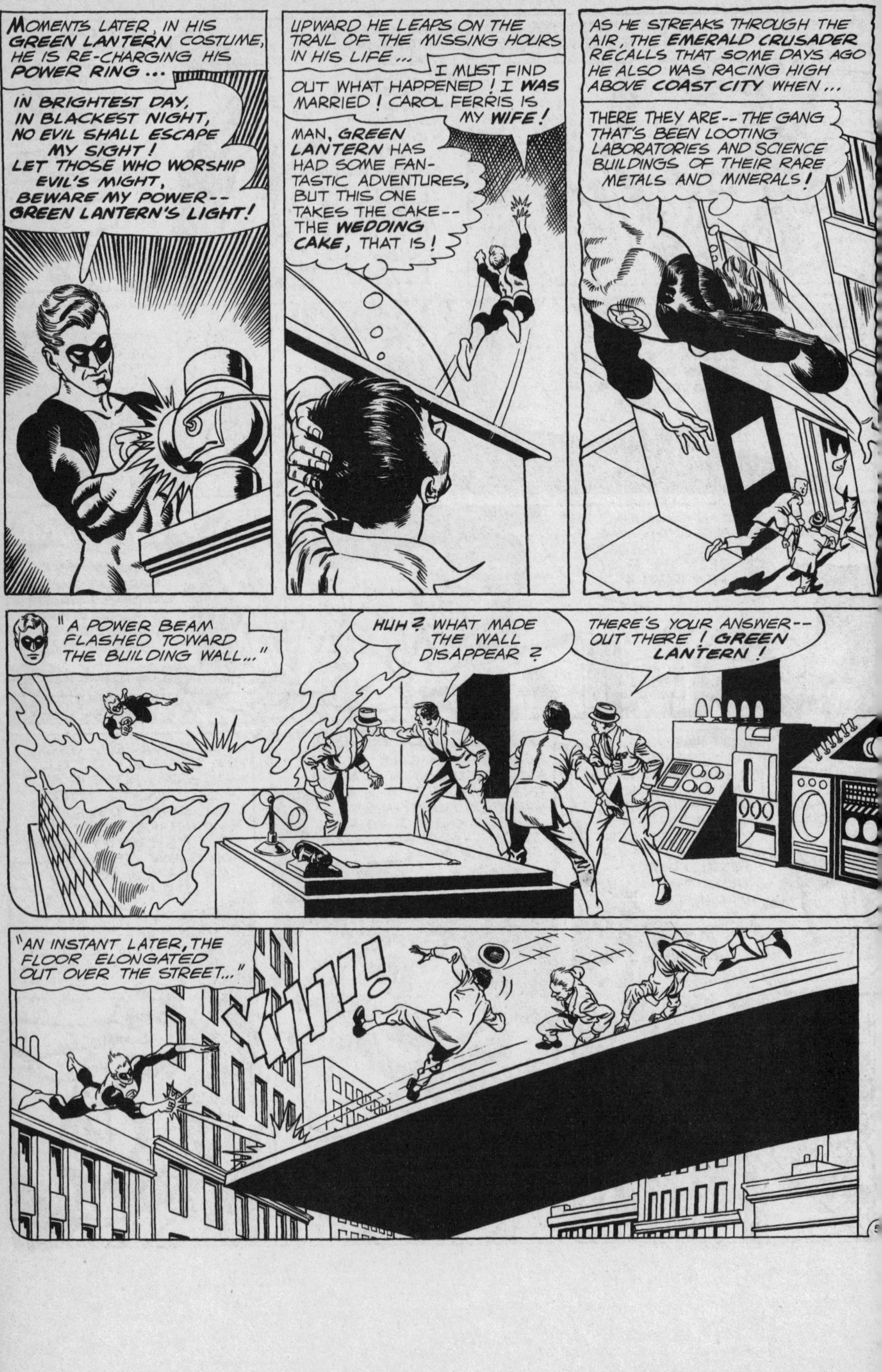
MOMENTS LATER, IN HIS GREEN LANTERN COSTUME, HE IS RE-CHARGING HIS POWER RING...
IN BRIGHTEST DAY, IN BLACKEST NIGHT, NO EVIL SHALL ESCAPE MY SIGHT! LET THOSE WHO WORSHIP EVIL'S MIGHT, BEWARE MY POWER-- GREEN LANTERN'S LIGHT!
UPWARD HE LEAPS ON THE TRAIL OF THE MISSING HOURS IN HIS LIFE...
I MUST FIND OUT WHAT HAPPENED! I WAS MARRIED! CAROL FERRIS IS MY WIFE!
MAN, GREEN LANTERN HAS HAD SOME FANTASTIC ADVENTURES, BUT THIS ONE TAKES THE CAKE-- THE WEDDING CAKE, THAT IS!
AS HE STREAKS THROUGH THE AIR, THE EMERALD CRUSADER RECALLS THAT SOME DAYS AGO HE ALSO WAS RACING HIGH ABOVE COAST CITY WHEN...
THERE THEY ARE--THE GANG THAT'S BEEN LOOTING LABORATORIES AND SCIENCE BUILDINGS OF THEIR RARE METALS AND MINERALS!
"A POWER BEAM FLASHED TOWARD THE BUILDING WALL..."
HUH? WHAT MADE THE WALL DISAPPEAR?
THERE'S YOUR ANSWER-- OUT THERE! GREEN LANTERN!
"AN INSTANT LATER, THE FLOOR ELONGATED OUT OVER THE STREET..."
YIIII!

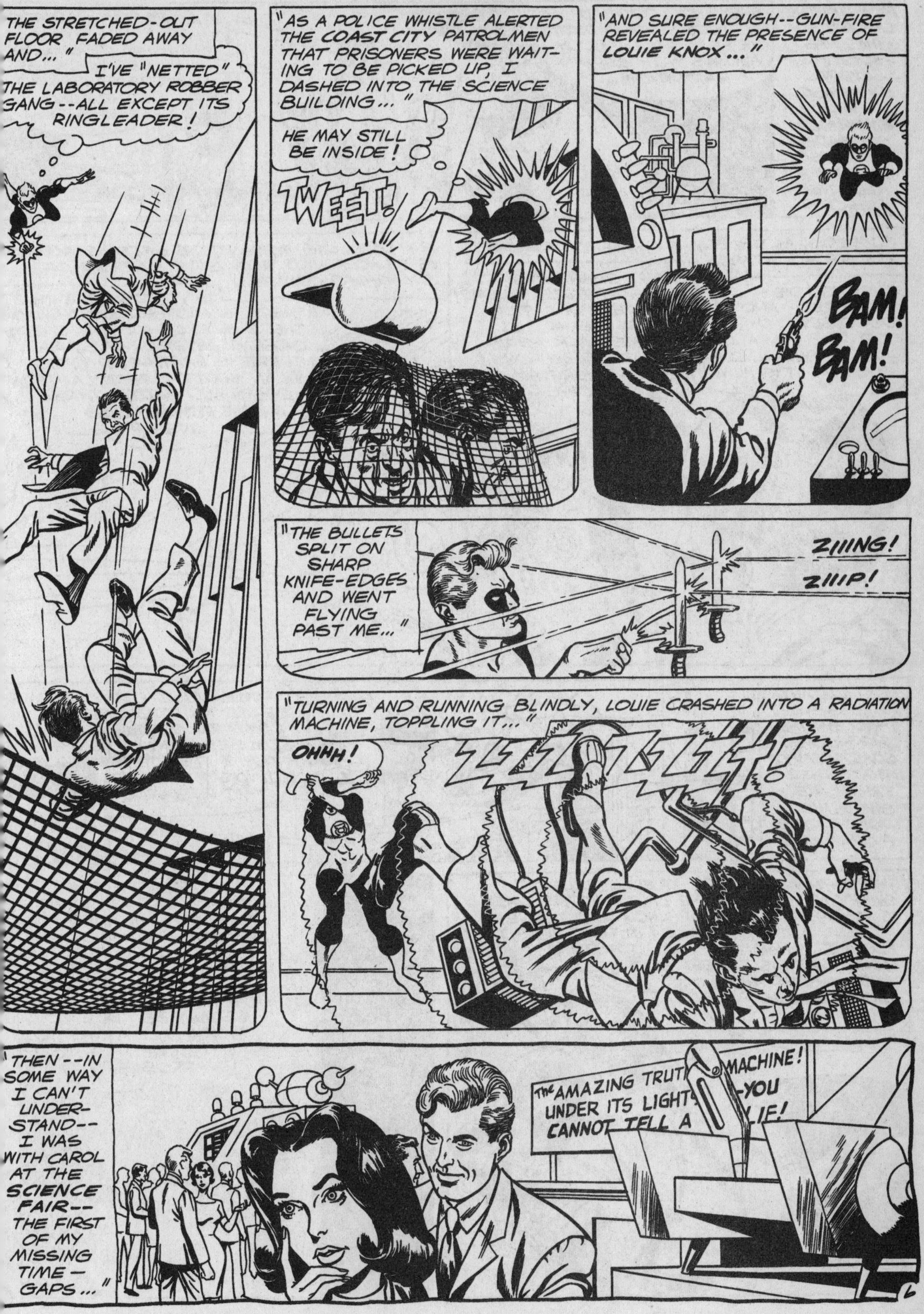
THE STRETCHED-OUT FLOOR FADED AWAY AND..."
I'VE "NETTED" THE LABORATORY ROBBER GANG--ALL EXCEPT ITS RINGLEADER!
"AS A POLICE WHISTLE ALERTED THE COAST CITY PATROLMEN THAT PRISONERS WERE WAITING TO BE PICKED UP, I DASHED INTO THE SCIENCE BUILDING..."
HE MAY STILL BE INSIDE!
TWEET!
"AND SURE ENOUGH--GUN-FIRE REVEALED THE PRESENCE OF LOUIE KNOX..."
BAM! BAM!
"THE BULLETS SPLIT ON SHARP KNIFE-EDGES AND WENT FLYING PAST ME..."
ZIIING!
ZIIIP!
"TURNING AND RUNNING BLINDLY, LOUIE CRASHED INTO A RADIATION MACHINE, TOPPLING IT..."
OHHH!
ZZZZZZT!
"THEN--IN SOME WAY I CAN'T UNDERSTAND--I WAS WITH CAROL AT THE SCIENCE FAIR--THE FIRST OF MY MISSING TIME-GAPS..."
THE AMAZING TRUT MACHINE! UNDER ITS LIGHT -YOU CANNOT TELL A LIE!
6

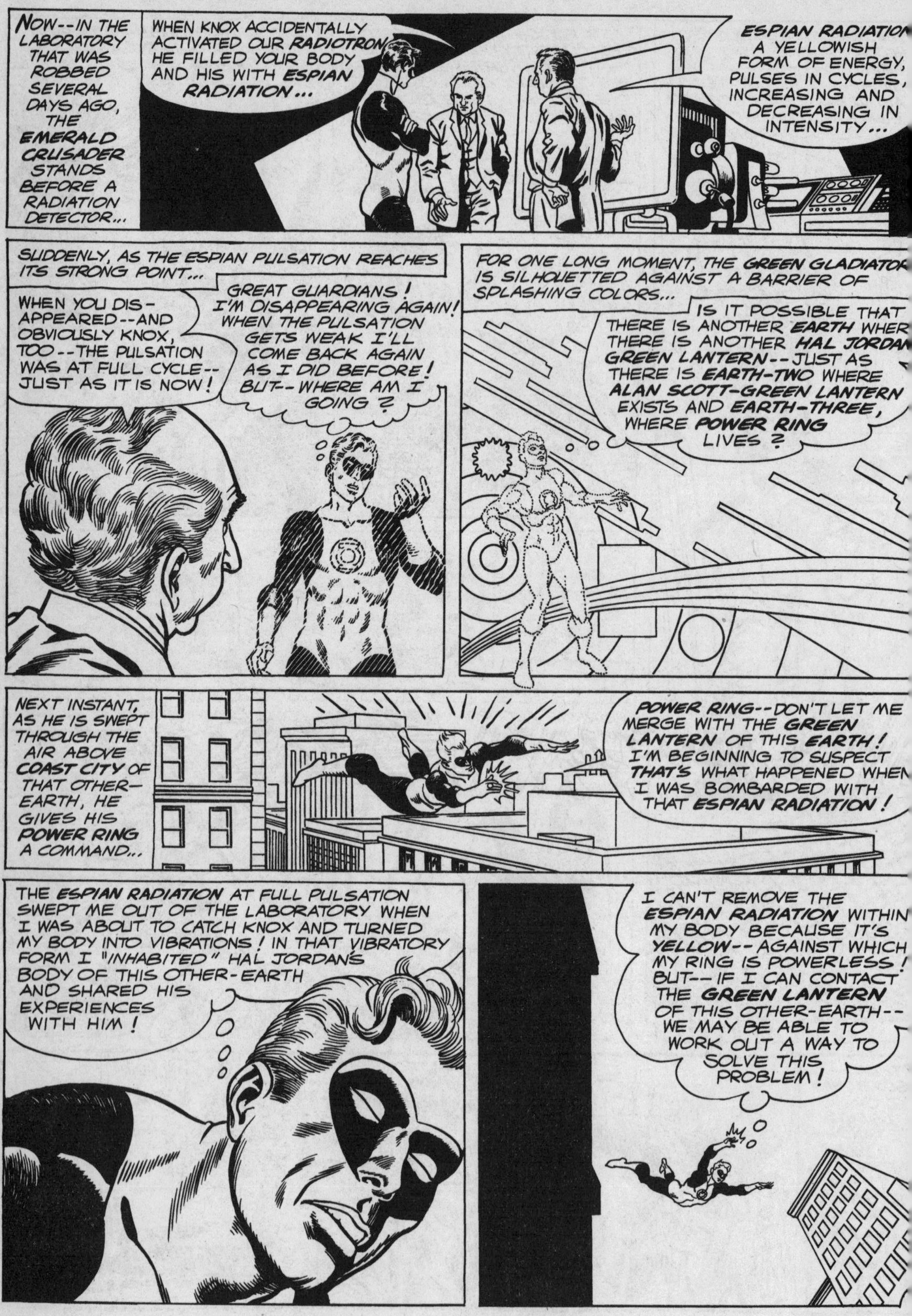
NOW--IN THE LABORATORY THAT WAS ROBBED SEVERAL DAYS AGO, THE EMERALD CRUSADER STANDS BEFORE A RADIATION DETECTOR...
WHEN KNOX ACCIDENTALLY ACTIVATED OUR RADIOTRON HE FILLED YOUR BODY AND HIS WITH ESPIAN RADIATION...
ESPIAN RADIATION A YELLOWISH FORM OF ENERGY, PULSES IN CYCLES, INCREASING AND DECREASING IN INTENSITY...
SUDDENLY, AS THE ESPIAN PULSATION REACHES ITS STRONG POINT...
WHEN YOU DIS-APPEARED--AND OBVIOUSLY KNOX, TOO--THE PULSATION WAS AT FULL CYCLE--JUST AS IT IS NOW!
GREAT GUARDIANS! I'M DISAPPEARING AGAIN! WHEN THE PULSATION GETS WEAK I'LL COME BACK AGAIN AS I DID BEFORE! BUT--WHERE AM I GOING?
FOR ONE LONG MOMENT, THE GREEN GLADIATOR IS SILHOUETTED AGAINST A BARRIER OF SPLASHING COLORS...
IS IT POSSIBLE THAT THERE IS ANOTHER EARTH WHERE THERE IS ANOTHER HAL JORDAN GREEN LANTERN--JUST AS THERE IS EARTH-TWO WHERE ALAN SCOTT-GREEN LANTERN EXISTS AND EARTH-THREE, WHERE POWER RING LIVES?
NEXT INSTANT, AS HE IS SWEPT THROUGH THE AIR ABOVE COAST CITY OF THAT OTHER-EARTH, HE GIVES HIS POWER RING A COMMAND...
POWER RING--DON'T LET ME MERGE WITH THE GREEN LANTERN OF THIS EARTH! I'M BEGINNING TO SUSPECT THAT'S WHAT HAPPENED WHEN I WAS BOMBARDED WITH THAT ESPIAN RADIATION!
THE ESPIAN RADIATION AT FULL PULSATION SWEPT ME OUT OF THE LABORATORY WHEN I WAS ABOUT TO CATCH KNOX AND TURNED MY BODY INTO VIBRATIONS! IN THAT VIBRATORY FORM I "INHABITED" HAL JORDAN'S BODY OF THIS OTHER-EARTH AND SHARED HIS EXPERIENCES WITH HIM!
I CAN'T REMOVE THE ESPIAN RADIATION WITHIN MY BODY BECAUSE IT'S YELLOW--AGAINST WHICH MY RING IS POWERLESS! BUT--IF I CAN CONTACT THE GREEN LANTERN OF THIS OTHER-EARTH--WE MAY BE ABLE TO WORK OUT A WAY TO SOLVE THIS PROBLEM!

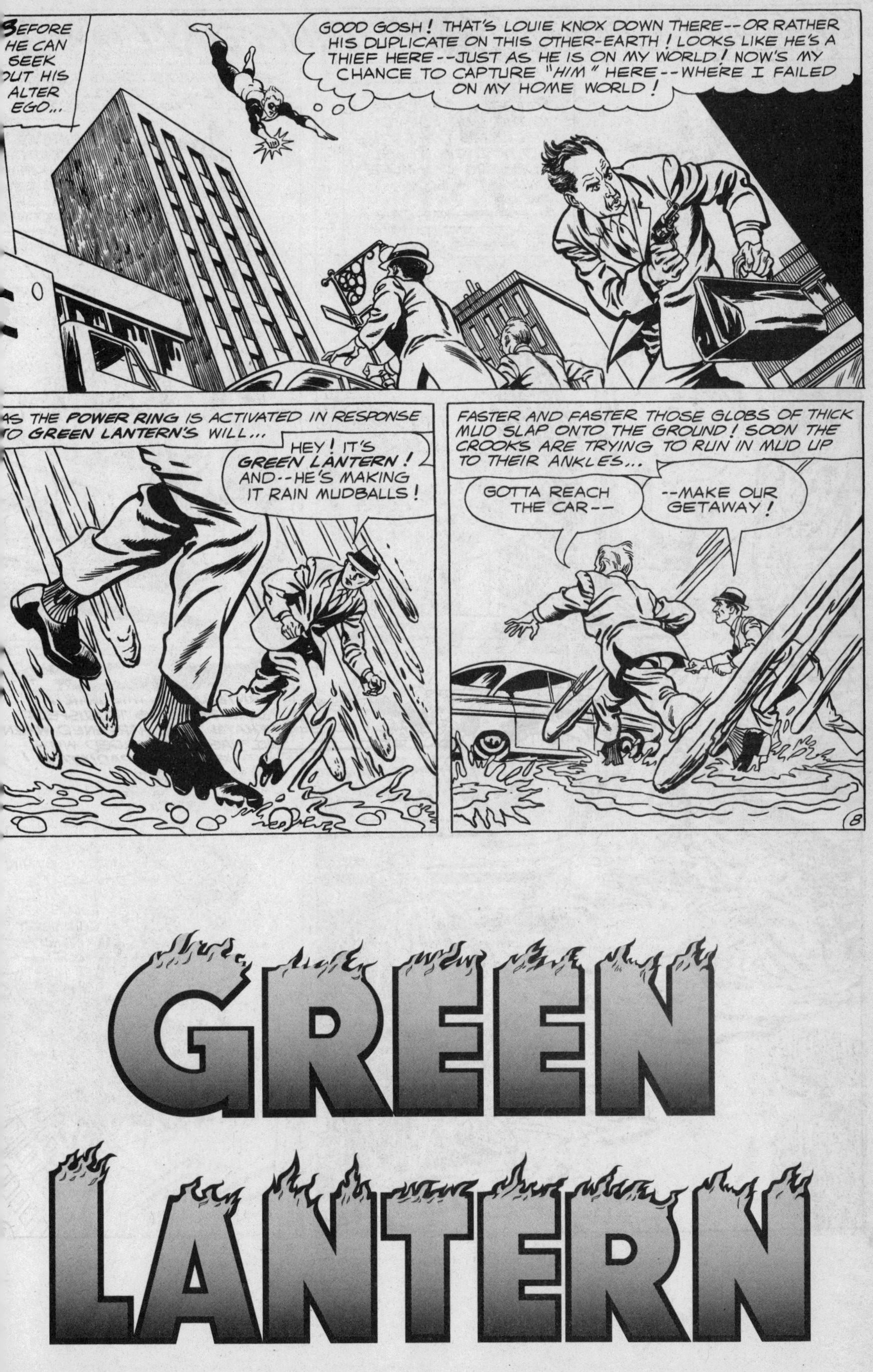
BEFORE HE CAN SEEK OUT HIS ALTER EGO...
GOOD GOSH! THAT'S LOUIE KNOX DOWN THERE--OR RATHER HIS DUPLICATE ON THIS OTHER-EARTH! LOOKS LIKE HE'S A THIEF HERE--JUST AS HE IS ON MY WORLD! NOW'S MY CHANCE TO CAPTURE "HIM" HERE--WHERE I FAILED ON MY HOME WORLD!
AS THE POWER RING IS ACTIVATED IN RESPONSE TO GREEN LANTERN'S WILL...
HEY! IT'S GREEN LANTERN! AND--HE'S MAKING IT RAIN MUDBALLS!
FASTER AND FASTER THOSE GLOBS OF THICK MUD SLAP ONTO THE GROUND! SOON THE CROOKS ARE TRYING TO RUN IN MUD UP TO THEIR ANKLES...
GOTTA REACH THE CAR--
--MAKE OUR GETAWAY!
8

GREEN LANTERN

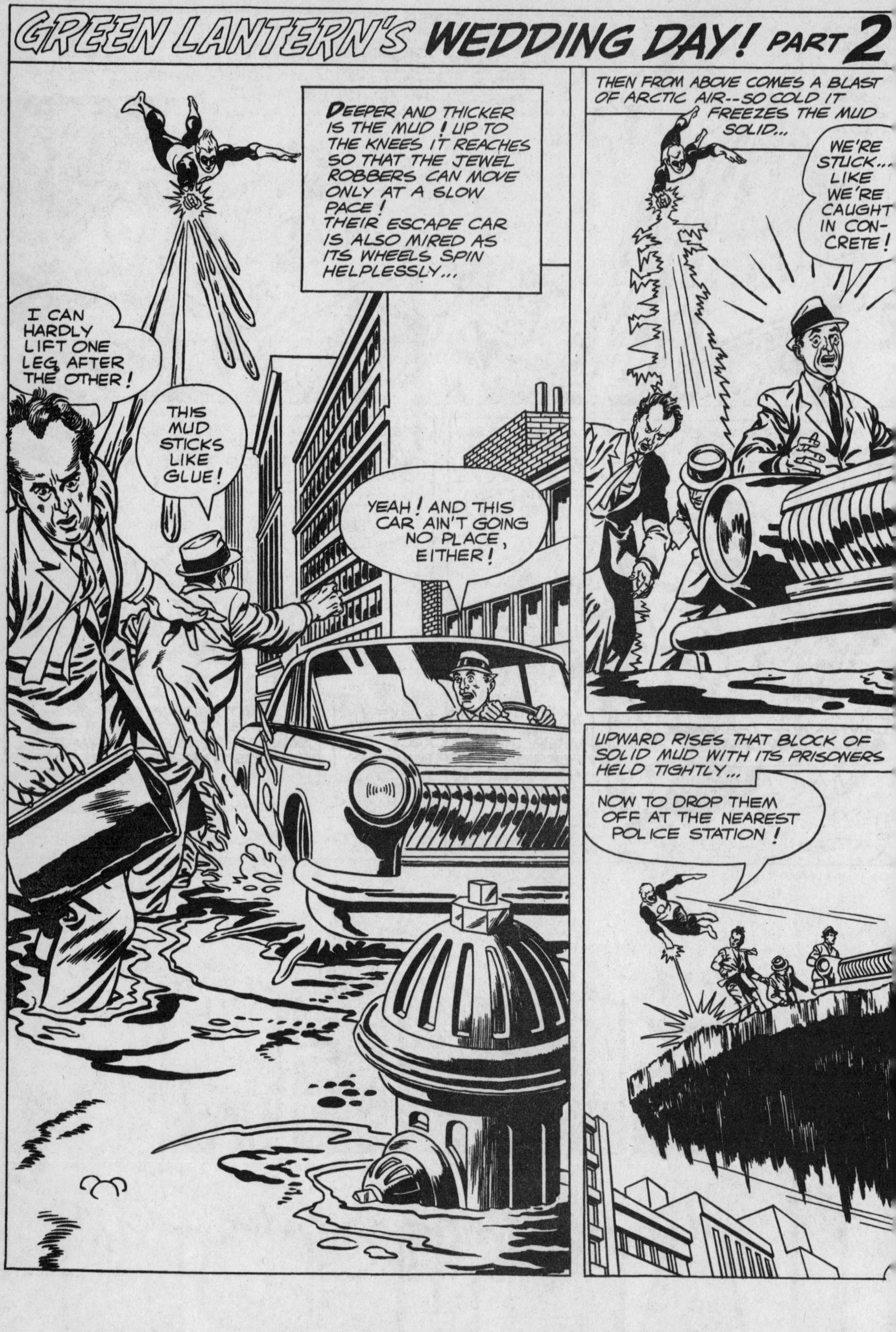
GREEN LANTERN'S WEDDING DAY! PART 2
DEEPER AND THICKER IS THE MUD! UP TO THE KNEES IT REACHES SO THAT THE JEWEL ROBBERS CAN MOVE ONLY AT A SLOW PACE! THEIR ESCAPE CAR IS ALSO MIRED AS ITS WHEELS SPIN HELPLESSLY...
I CAN HARDLY LIFT ONE LEG AFTER THE OTHER!
THIS MUD STICKS LIKE GLUE!
YEAH! AND THIS CAR AIN'T GOING NO PLACE, EITHER!
THEN FROM ABOVE COMES A BLAST OF ARCTIC AIR--SO COLD IT FREEZES THE MUD SOLID...
WE'RE STUCK... LIKE WE'RE CAUGHT IN CON-CRETE!
UPWARD RISES THAT BLOCK OF SOLID MUD WITH ITS PRISONERS HELD TIGHTLY...
NOW TO DROP THEM OFF AT THE NEAREST POLICE STATION!

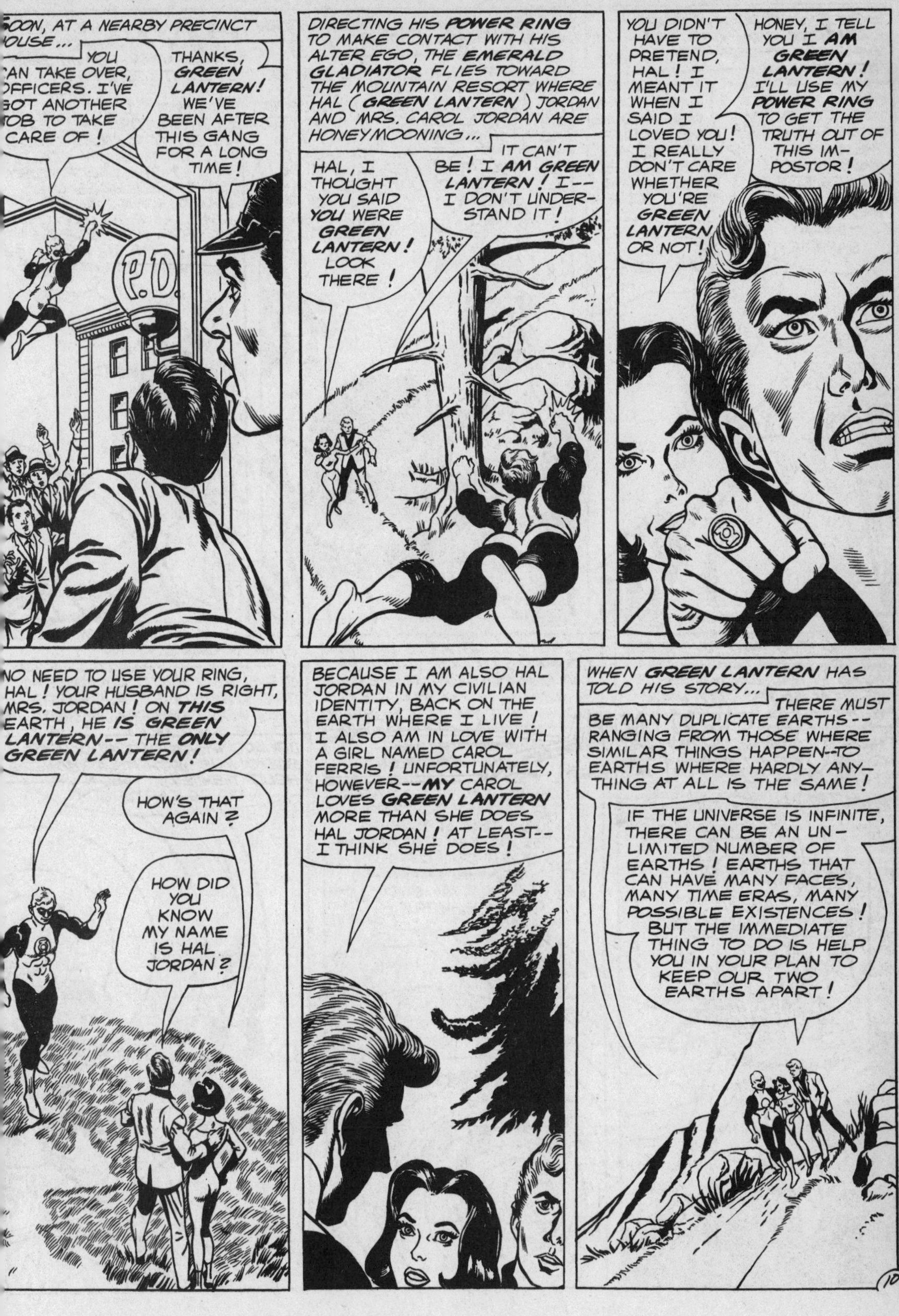
SOON, AT A NEARBY PRECINCT HOUSE...
YOU CAN TAKE OVER, OFFICERS. I'VE GOT ANOTHER JOB TO TAKE CARE OF!
THANKS, GREEN LANTERN! WE'VE BEEN AFTER THIS GANG FOR A LONG TIME!
P.D.
DIRECTING HIS POWER RING TO MAKE CONTACT WITH HIS ALTER EGO, THE EMERALD GLADIATOR FLIES TOWARD THE MOUNTAIN RESORT WHERE HAL (GREEN LANTERN) JORDAN AND MRS. CAROL JORDAN ARE HONEYMOONING...
HAL, I THOUGHT YOU SAID YOU WERE GREEN LANTERN! LOOK THERE!
IT CAN'T BE! I AM GREEN LANTERN! I-- I DON'T UNDERSTAND IT!
YOU DIDN'T HAVE TO PRETEND, HAL! I MEANT IT WHEN I SAID I LOVED YOU! I REALLY DON'T CARE WHETHER YOU'RE GREEN LANTERN OR NOT!
HONEY, I TELL YOU I AM GREEN LANTERN! I'LL USE MY POWER RING TO GET THE TRUTH OUT OF THIS IMPOSTOR!
NO NEED TO USE YOUR RING, HAL! YOUR HUSBAND IS RIGHT, MRS. JORDAN! ON THIS EARTH, HE IS GREEN LANTERN-- THE ONLY GREEN LANTERN!
HOW'S THAT AGAIN?
HOW DID YOU KNOW MY NAME IS HAL JORDAN?
BECAUSE I AM ALSO HAL JORDAN IN MY CIVILIAN IDENTITY, BACK ON THE EARTH WHERE I LIVE! I ALSO AM IN LOVE WITH A GIRL NAMED CAROL FERRIS! UNFORTUNATELY, HOWEVER--MY CAROL LOVES GREEN LANTERN MORE THAN SHE DOES HAL JORDAN! AT LEAST-- I THINK SHE DOES!
WHEN GREEN LANTERN HAS TOLD HIS STORY...
THERE MUST BE MANY DUPLICATE EARTHS-- RANGING FROM THOSE WHERE SIMILAR THINGS HAPPEN--TO EARTHS WHERE HARDLY ANYTHING AT ALL IS THE SAME!
IF THE UNIVERSE IS INFINITE, THERE CAN BE AN UNLIMITED NUMBER OF EARTHS! EARTHS THAT CAN HAVE MANY FACES, MANY TIME ERAS, MANY POSSIBLE EXISTENCES! BUT THE IMMEDIATE THING TO DO IS HELP YOU IN YOUR PLAN TO KEEP OUR TWO EARTHS APART!
10

SIDE BY SIDE BOTH *GREEN LANTERNS* SEAL OFF THE BARRIER BETWEEN THEIR WORLDS...

VERY GOOD! THE NEXT TIME I'M ON MY OWN EARTH AND THE *ESPIAN RADIATION* PULSES TO FULL FORCE IN ME AND DRAWS ME TO THAT BARRIER--

THE *ESPIAN RADIATION* WILL PASS THROUGH THE BARRIER AND DISSIPATE ITS ENERGIES IN MY EARTH WHILE YOUR BODY WILL BE HELD BACK BY THE BARRIER!

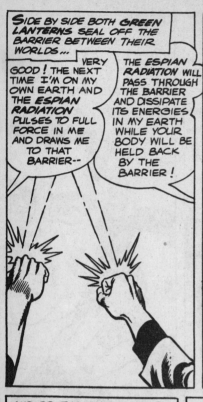

AS *EARTH-ONE'S* GREEN LANTERN BIDS FAREWELL TO HIS NEW FRIENDS...

I'M SURE THAT SOME DAY *YOUR* CAROL WILL REALIZE THAT SHE LOVES YOU AS HAL JORDAN-- WHEN AT LAST SHE ISN'T OVERWHELMED BY YOUR GLAMOUR AS *GREEN LANTERN!*

I WISH YOU COULD IN-VITE US TO YOUR WEDDING BUT I'M AFRAID IT MIGHT BE TOO CON-FUSING TO THE OTHER GUESTS!

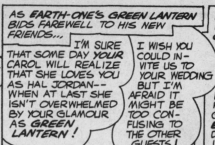

RETURNING TO HIS OWN WORLD, THE *EMERALD CRUSADER* REMEMBERS ABOUT LOUIE KNOX...

Hmmm! I SETTLED THIS ENTIRE CASE EX-CEPT FOR KNOX! I NEVER DID CAPTURE HIM FOR HIS PART IN THE LABORATORY GANG ROBBERIES ON *EARTH-ONE!* BUT I DON'T HAVE TO GO LOOK-ING FOR HIM BECAUSE-- HE'LL COME TO *ME,* SOONER OR LATER!

AND SO IT IS THAT AS THE PUL-SATIONS BEGIN BUILDING UP AGAIN IN HAL JORDAN WHILE HE IS ON HIS WAY TO A DATE WITH CAROL...

OH-OH! HERE IT COMES! I'D BETTER CHANGE INTO MY *GREEN LANTERN* OUTFIT!

THUS IT IS THAT HE IS DRAWN TOWARD BUT NOT *THROUGH* THE BARRIER THAT PREVENTS ANYONE IN HIS WORLD FROM GOING INTO THE OTHER-EARTH.

JUST AS A WET SPONGE PLACED ATOP A SCREEN WILL REMAIN THERE-- ALLOWING ONLY THE WATER IN THE SPONGE TO DRIP THROUGH THE SCREEN-- SO THE *ESPIAN RADIATION* WILL OOZE OUT OF MY BODY INTO THE OTHER-EARTH, WHILE MY BODY REMAINS HERE!

SIMULTANEOUSLY...

LOUIE KNOX: I FIGURED YOU'D PULSATE AT THE SAME TIME I PULSATED AND WOULD BE DRAWN HERE TO THE BARRIER! ALL I HAD TO DO WAS WAIT UNTIL THAT HAPPENED--KNOWING THAT YOU'D INEVITABLY SHOW UP TO BE CAPTURED!

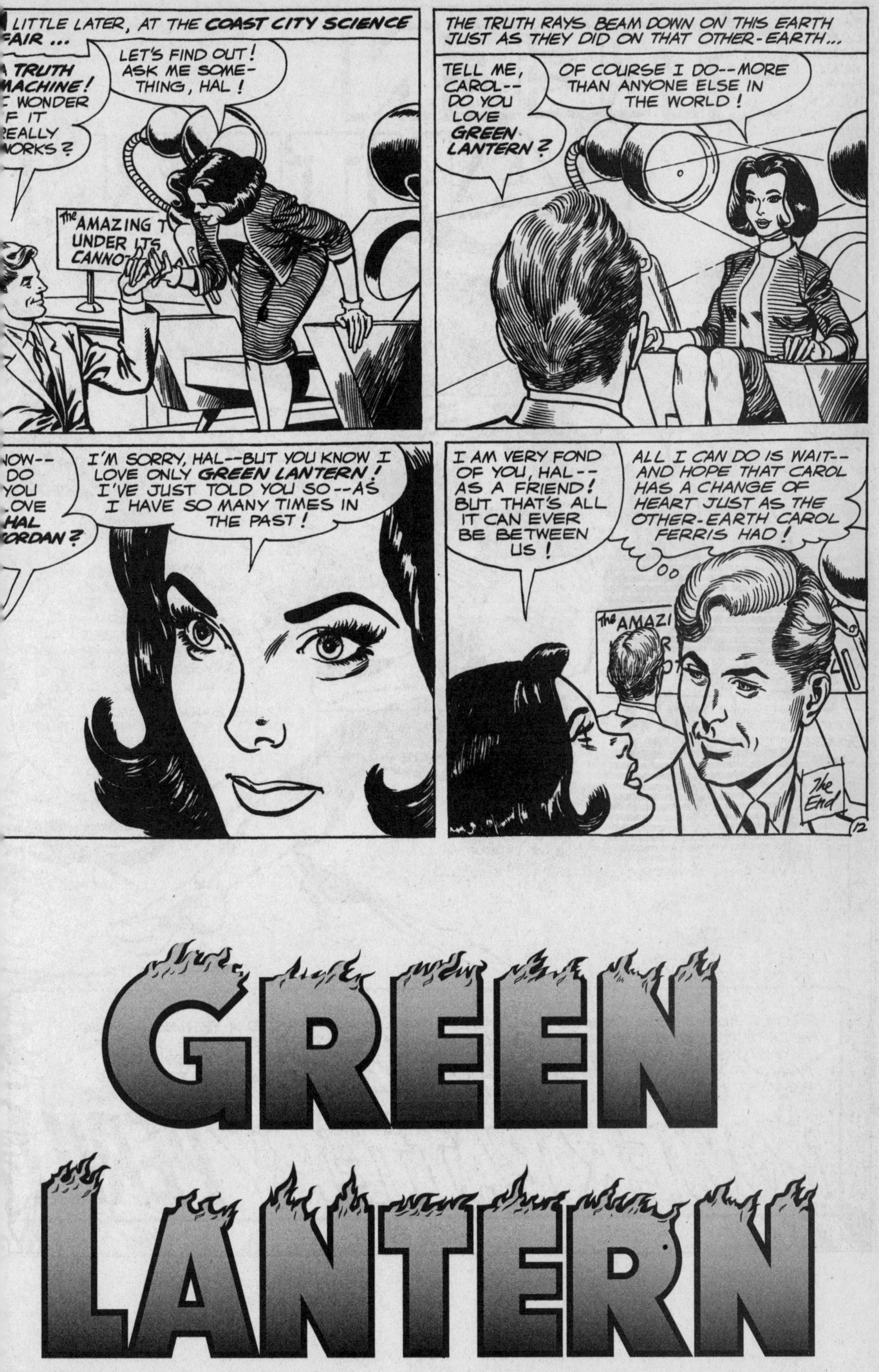
LITTLE LATER, AT THE COAST CITY SCIENCE AIR ...
TRUTH MACHINE! WONDER F IT REALLY ORKS?
LET'S FIND OUT! ASK ME SOME-THING, HAL!
THE AMAZING T UNDER ITS CANNO
THE TRUTH RAYS BEAM DOWN ON THIS EARTH JUST AS THEY DID ON THAT OTHER-EARTH...
TELL ME, CAROL-- DO YOU LOVE GREEN LANTERN?
OF COURSE I DO--MORE THAN ANYONE ELSE IN THE WORLD!
NOW-- DO YOU OVE HAL ORDAN?
I'M SORRY, HAL--BUT YOU KNOW I LOVE ONLY GREEN LANTERN! I'VE JUST TOLD YOU SO--AS I HAVE SO MANY TIMES IN THE PAST!
I AM VERY FOND OF YOU, HAL-- AS A FRIEND! BUT THAT'S ALL IT CAN EVER BE BETWEEN US!
ALL I CAN DO IS WAIT-- AND HOPE THAT CAROL HAS A CHANGE OF HEART JUST AS THE OTHER-EARTH CAROL FERRIS HAD!
THE AMAZI
The End
12

GREEN LANTERN

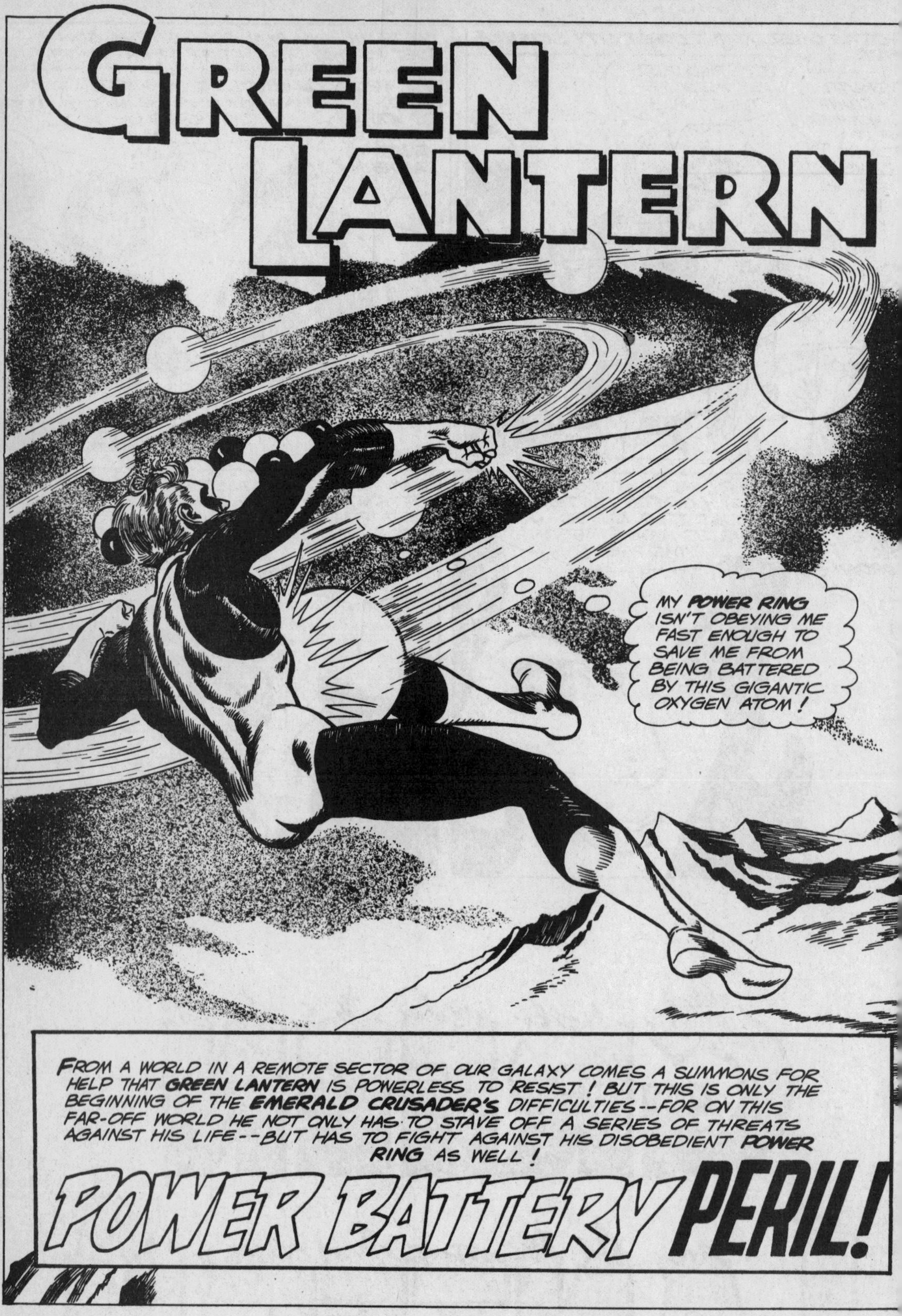
GREEN LANTERN
MY POWER RING ISN'T OBEYING ME FAST ENOUGH TO SAVE ME FROM BEING BATTERED BY THIS GIGANTIC OXYGEN ATOM!
FROM A WORLD IN A REMOTE SECTOR OF OUR GALAXY COMES A SUMMONS FOR HELP THAT GREEN LANTERN IS POWERLESS TO RESIST! BUT THIS IS ONLY THE BEGINNING OF THE EMERALD CRUSADER'S DIFFICULTIES--FOR ON THIS FAR-OFF WORLD HE NOT ONLY HAS TO STAVE OFF A SERIES OF THREATS AGAINST HIS LIFE--BUT HAS TO FIGHT AGAINST HIS DISOBEDIENT POWER RING AS WELL!
POWER BATTERY PERIL!

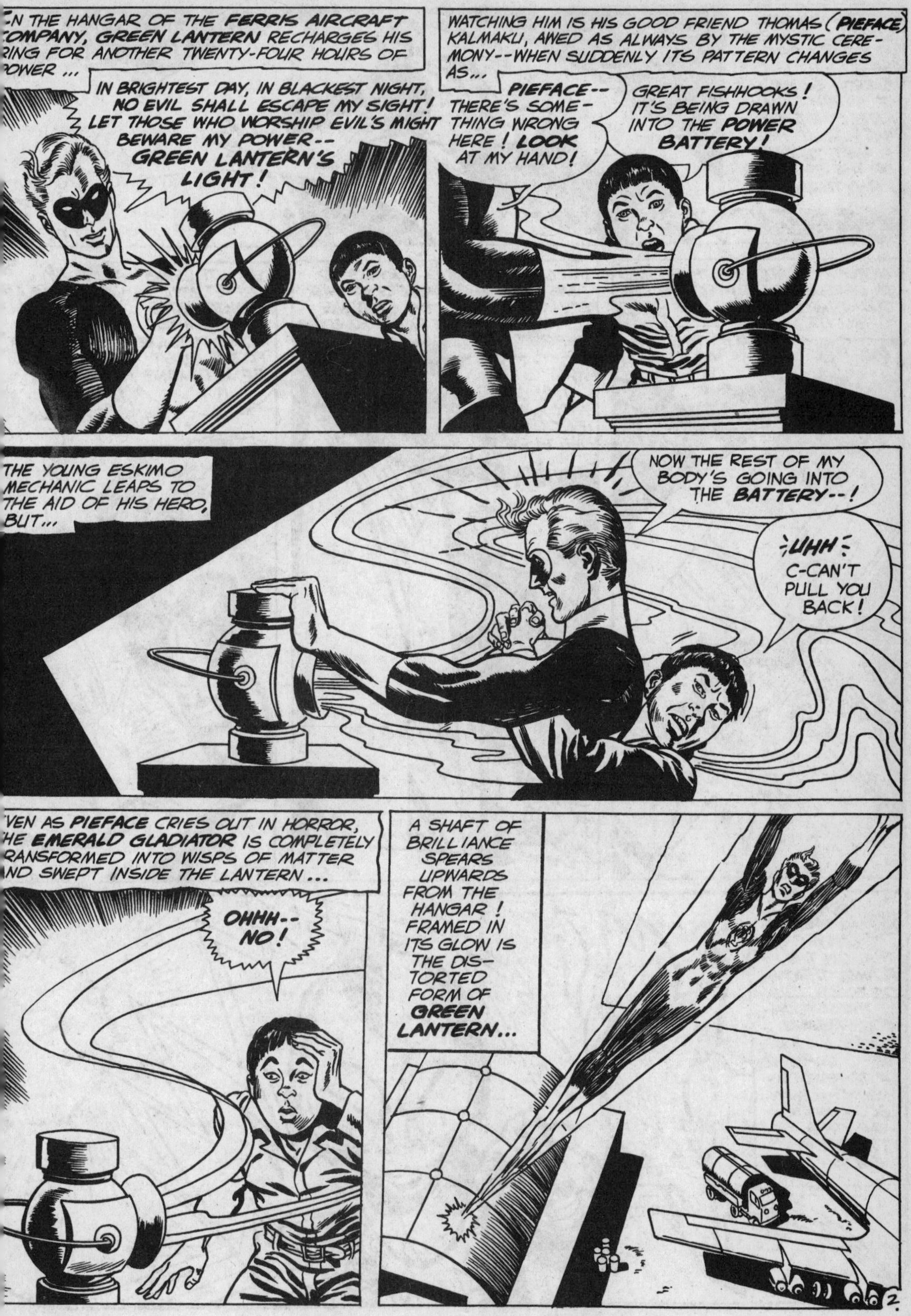
IN THE HANGAR OF THE FERRIS AIRCRAFT COMPANY, GREEN LANTERN RECHARGES HIS RING FOR ANOTHER TWENTY-FOUR HOURS OF POWER ...
IN BRIGHTEST DAY, IN BLACKEST NIGHT, NO EVIL SHALL ESCAPE MY SIGHT! LET THOSE WHO WORSHIP EVIL'S MIGHT BEWARE MY POWER-- GREEN LANTERN'S LIGHT!
WATCHING HIM IS HIS GOOD FRIEND THOMAS (PIEFACE) KALMAKU, AWED AS ALWAYS BY THE MYSTIC CEREMONY--WHEN SUDDENLY ITS PATTERN CHANGES AS...
PIEFACE-- THERE'S SOMETHING WRONG HERE! LOOK AT MY HAND!
GREAT FISHHOOKS! IT'S BEING DRAWN INTO THE POWER BATTERY!
THE YOUNG ESKIMO MECHANIC LEAPS TO THE AID OF HIS HERO, BUT...
NOW THE REST OF MY BODY'S GOING INTO THE BATTERY--!
UHH C-CAN'T PULL YOU BACK!
EVEN AS PIEFACE CRIES OUT IN HORROR, THE EMERALD GLADIATOR IS COMPLETELY TRANSFORMED INTO WISPS OF MATTER AND SWEPT INSIDE THE LANTERN ...
OHHH-- NO!
A SHAFT OF BRILLIANCE SPEARS UPWARDS FROM THE HANGAR! FRAMED IN ITS GLOW IS THE DISTORTED FORM OF GREEN LANTERN...
2.

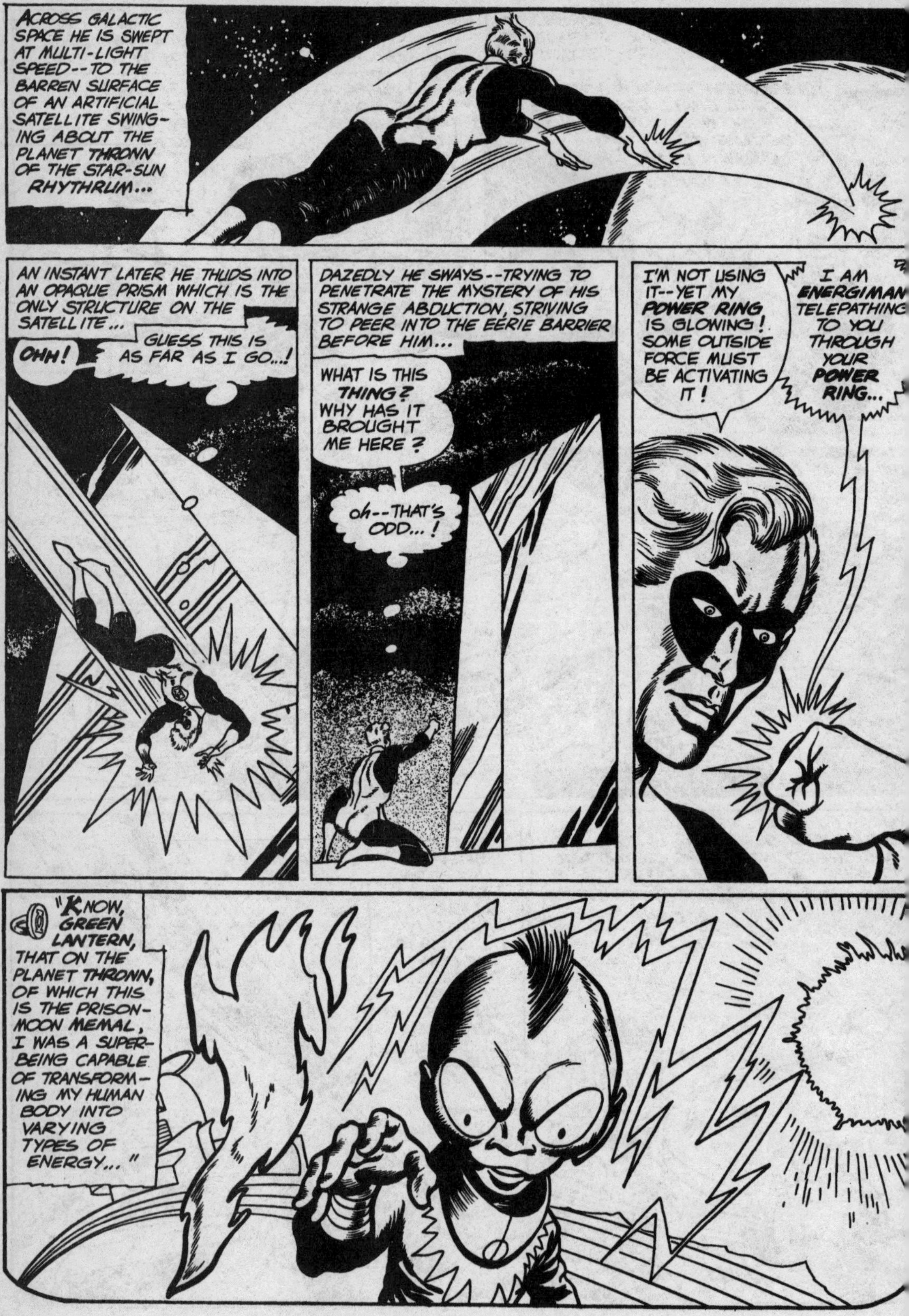

ACROSS GALACTIC SPACE HE IS SWEPT AT MULTI-LIGHT SPEED--TO THE BARREN SURFACE OF AN ARTIFICIAL SATELLITE SWINGING ABOUT THE PLANET THRONN OF THE STAR-SUN RHYTHRUM...
AN INSTANT LATER HE THUDS INTO AN OPAQUE PRISM WHICH IS THE ONLY STRUCTURE ON THE SATELLITE...
OHH!
GUESS THIS IS AS FAR AS I GO...!
DAZEDLY HE SWAYS--TRYING TO PENETRATE THE MYSTERY OF HIS STRANGE ABDUCTION, STRIVING TO PEER INTO THE EERIE BARRIER BEFORE HIM...
WHAT IS THIS THING? WHY HAS IT BROUGHT ME HERE?
oh--THAT'S ODD...!
I'M NOT USING IT--YET MY POWER RING IS GLOWING! SOME OUTSIDE FORCE MUST BE ACTIVATING IT!
I AM ENERGIMAN TELEPATHING TO YOU THROUGH YOUR POWER RING...
"KNOW, GREEN LANTERN, THAT ON THE PLANET THRONN, OF WHICH THIS IS THE PRISON-MOON MEMAL, I WAS A SUPER-BEING CAPABLE OF TRANSFORMING MY HUMAN BODY INTO VARYING TYPES OF ENERGY..."

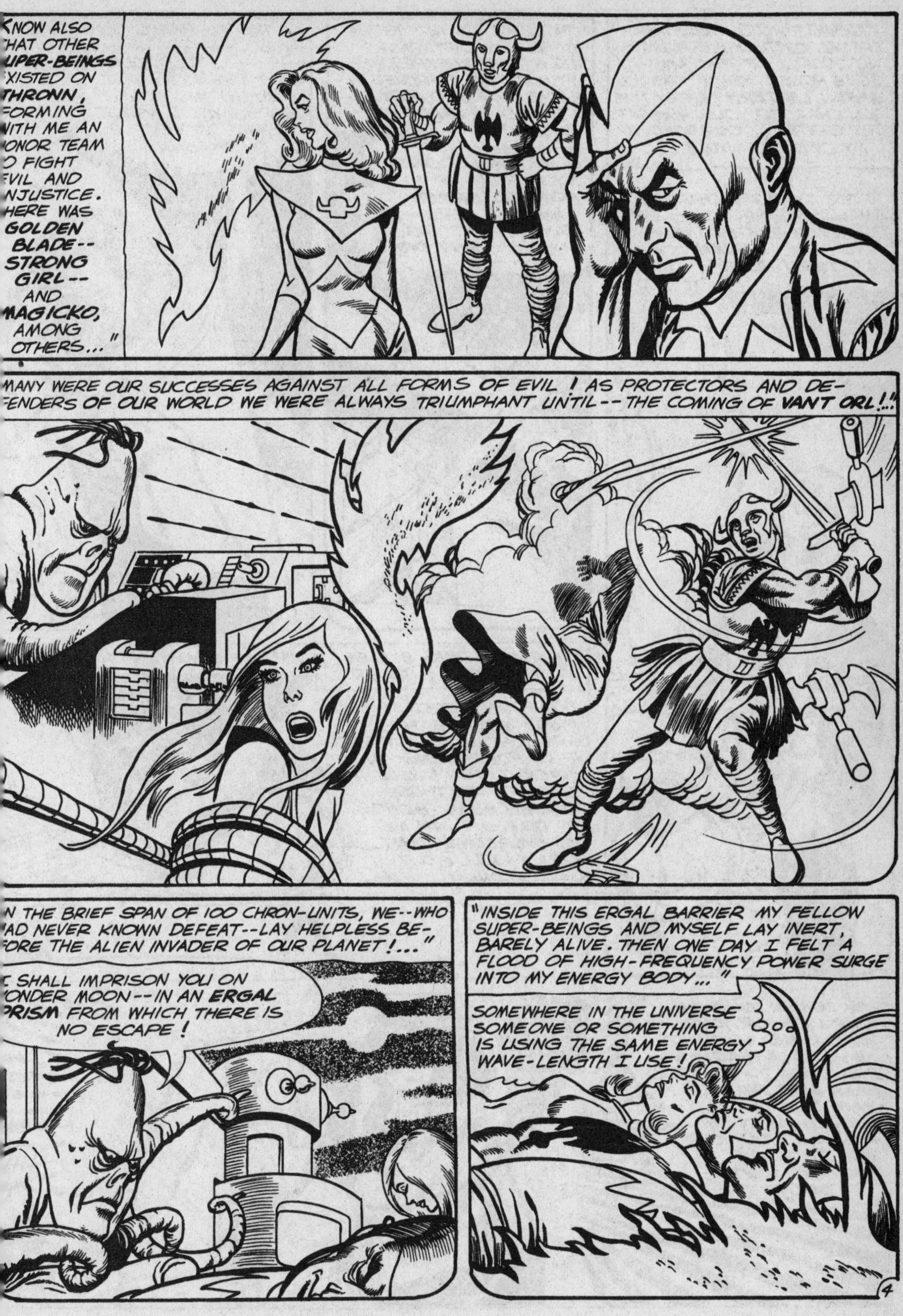
KNOW ALSO THAT OTHER SUPER-BEINGS EXISTED ON THRONN, FORMING WITH ME AN HONOR TEAM TO FIGHT EVIL AND INJUSTICE. THERE WAS GOLDEN BLADE-- STRONG GIRL-- AND MAGICKO, AMONG OTHERS..."
MANY WERE OUR SUCCESSES AGAINST ALL FORMS OF EVIL! AS PROTECTORS AND DEFENDERS OF OUR WORLD WE WERE ALWAYS TRIUMPHANT UNTIL--THE COMING OF VANT ORL!.."
IN THE BRIEF SPAN OF 100 CHRON-UNITS, WE--WHO HAD NEVER KNOWN DEFEAT--LAY HELPLESS BEFORE THE ALIEN INVADER OF OUR PLANET!..."
I SHALL IMPRISON YOU ON WONDER MOON--IN AN ERGAL PRISM FROM WHICH THERE IS NO ESCAPE!
"INSIDE THIS ERGAL BARRIER MY FELLOW SUPER-BEINGS AND MYSELF LAY INERT, BARELY ALIVE. THEN ONE DAY I FELT A FLOOD OF HIGH-FREQUENCY POWER SURGE INTO MY ENERGY BODY..."
SOMEWHERE IN THE UNIVERSE SOMEONE OR SOMETHING IS USING THE SAME ENERGY WAVE-LENGTH I USE!
4

"PROBING THROUGH THE HYPER-SPATIAL CONTINUUM, I FOUND THE SOURCE OF THAT AWE-SOME POWER. YES, IT WAS YOU, *GREEN LANTERN!* EVERY TIME YOU CHARGED YOUR RING AT THE BATTERY, YOU ADDED TO MY OWN STRENGTH!..."

AFTER 100 MORE CHARGES, I SHALL HAVE ENOUGH POWER TO REACH ACROSS THE VOID AND BRING *GREEN LANTERN* HERE!

"THOUGH I DID NOT INFORM MY FELLOW-CAPTIVES--I KNEW THAT BY EXPENDING MY HOARDED ENERGIES IN BRINGING YOU TO *MEMAL*-- I WOULD BE SACRIFICING MY LIFE!..."

GLADLY WILL I OFFER MYSELF UP--IF IN BRINGING *GREEN LANTERN* HERE--HE CAN DEFEAT THE TYRANT *VANT ORL!*

AS THE TELEPATHIC "VOICE" FADES AWAY...

I TOLD YOUR RING THIS STORY AS I BROUGHT YOU HERE-- HOPING YOU'D AGREE TO HELP MY PEOPLE ON *THRONN!*

AND S... I WIL... I SWE... IT! BU... FIRS...

THE *POWER RING* BLAZES! A VERDANT BEAM OF FURY HITS HARD AT THE ERGAL BARRIER...

THAT ERGAL FORCE OF THIS PRISM MUST BE THE GREATEST IN THE UNIVERSE-- IF MY *POWER RING* CAN'T CRACK IT OPEN! WELL, IF I CAN'T FREE THOSE *THRONN* SUPER-BEINGS TO TEAM UP WITH ME TO OVERCOME *VANT ORL*--I'LL GO IT ALONE!

AND THOUGH YOU GAVE YOUR LIFE FOR YOUR PEOPLE AND SO CANNOT HEAR ME, *ENERGIMAN*-- THIS I VOW TO YOU: *YOU HAVE NOT DIED IN VAIN!* I WILL DO EVERYTHING IN MY POWER TO RID YOUR WORLD OF THE USURPER *VANT ORL!*

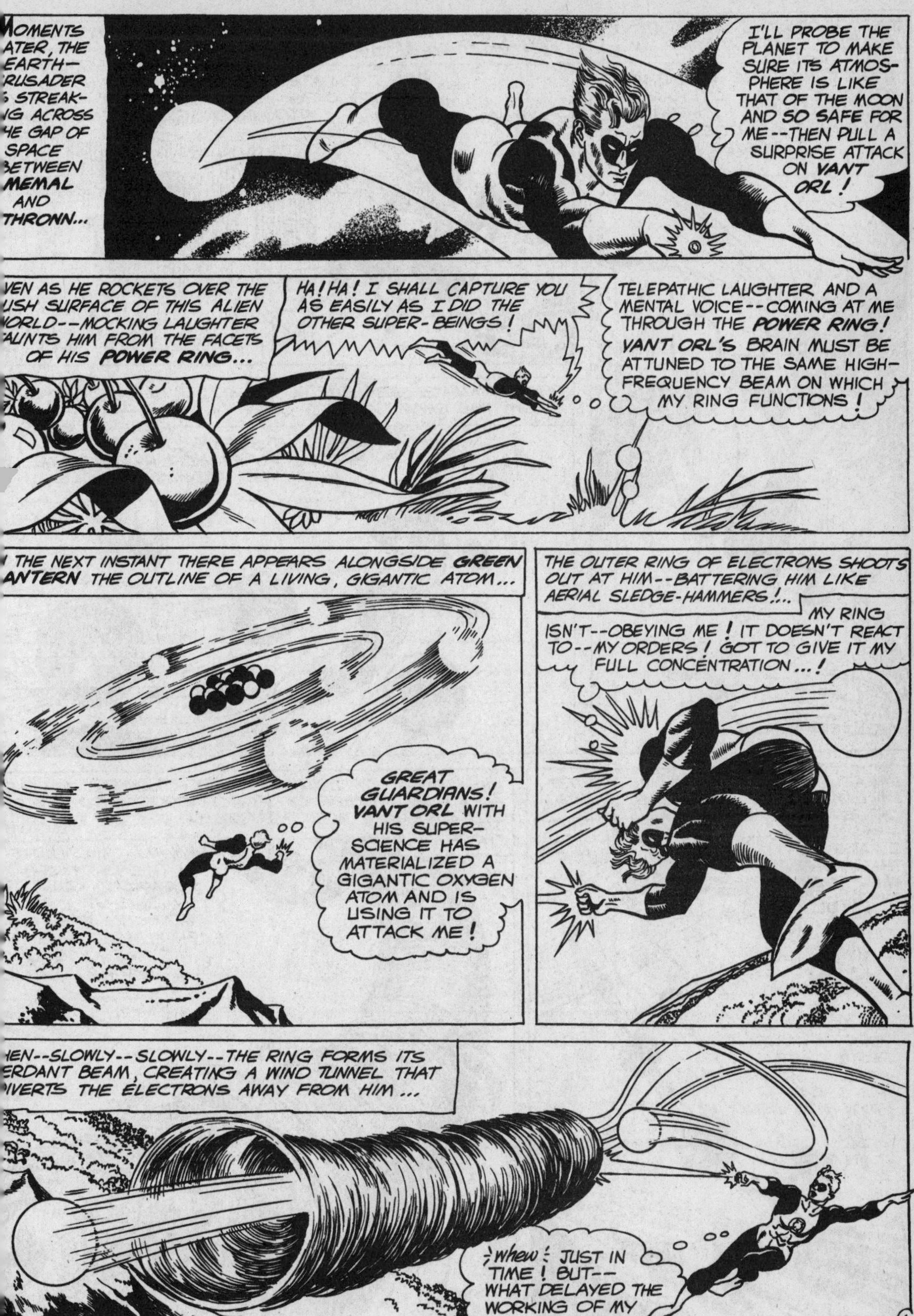
MOMENTS LATER, THE EARTH-CRUSADER IS STREAKING ACROSS THE GAP OF SPACE BETWEEN MEMAL AND THRONN...
I'LL PROBE THE PLANET TO MAKE SURE ITS ATMOSPHERE IS LIKE THAT OF THE MOON AND SO SAFE FOR ME--THEN PULL A SURPRISE ATTACK ON VANT ORL!
EVEN AS HE ROCKETS OVER THE LUSH SURFACE OF THIS ALIEN WORLD--MOCKING LAUGHTER TAUNTS HIM FROM THE FACETS OF HIS POWER RING...
HA! HA! I SHALL CAPTURE YOU AS EASILY AS I DID THE OTHER SUPER-BEINGS!
TELEPATHIC LAUGHTER AND A MENTAL VOICE--COMING AT ME THROUGH THE POWER RING! VANT ORL'S BRAIN MUST BE ATTUNED TO THE SAME HIGH-FREQUENCY BEAM ON WHICH MY RING FUNCTIONS!
IN THE NEXT INSTANT THERE APPEARS ALONGSIDE GREEN LANTERN THE OUTLINE OF A LIVING, GIGANTIC ATOM...
GREAT GUARDIANS! VANT ORL WITH HIS SUPER-SCIENCE HAS MATERIALIZED A GIGANTIC OXYGEN ATOM AND IS USING IT TO ATTACK ME!
THE OUTER RING OF ELECTRONS SHOOTS OUT AT HIM--BATTERING HIM LIKE AERIAL SLEDGE-HAMMERS!...
MY RING ISN'T--OBEYING ME! IT DOESN'T REACT TO--MY ORDERS! GOT TO GIVE IT MY FULL CONCENTRATION...!
THEN--SLOWLY--SLOWLY--THE RING FORMS ITS VERDANT BEAM, CREATING A WIND TUNNEL THAT DIVERTS THE ELECTRONS AWAY FROM HIM...
:WHEW: JUST IN TIME! BUT--WHAT DELAYED THE WORKING OF MY RING?
6

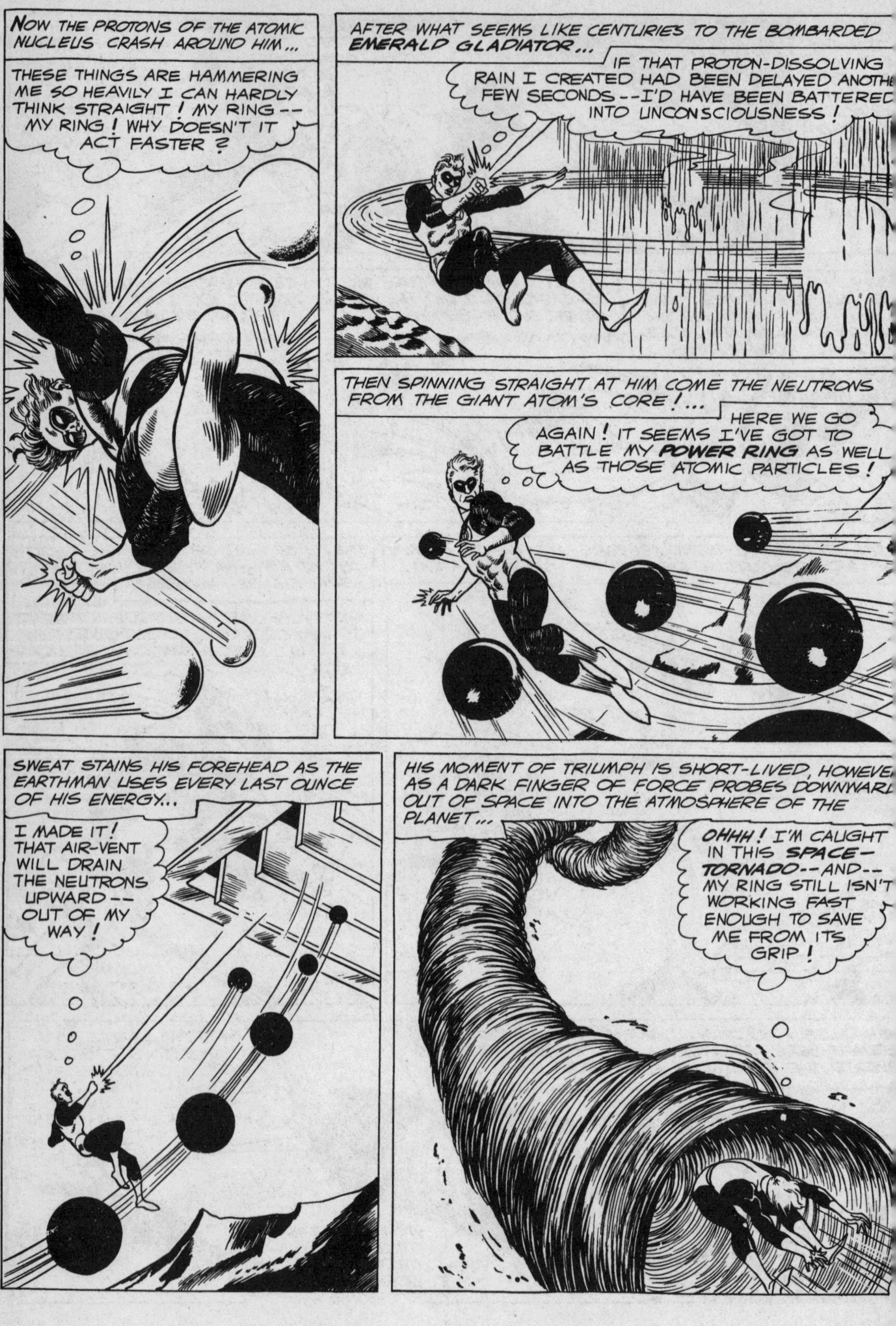
NOW THE PROTONS OF THE ATOMIC NUCLEUS CRASH AROUND HIM...
THESE THINGS ARE HAMMERING ME SO HEAVILY I CAN HARDLY THINK STRAIGHT! MY RING -- MY RING! WHY DOESN'T IT ACT FASTER?
AFTER WHAT SEEMS LIKE CENTURIES TO THE BOMBARDED EMERALD GLADIATOR...
IF THAT PROTON-DISSOLVING RAIN I CREATED HAD BEEN DELAYED ANOTHE FEW SECONDS -- I'D HAVE BEEN BATTERED INTO UNCONSCIOUSNESS!
THEN SPINNING STRAIGHT AT HIM COME THE NEUTRONS FROM THE GIANT ATOM'S CORE!...
HERE WE GO AGAIN! IT SEEMS I'VE GOT TO BATTLE MY POWER RING AS WELL AS THOSE ATOMIC PARTICLES!
SWEAT STAINS HIS FOREHEAD AS THE EARTHMAN USES EVERY LAST OUNCE OF HIS ENERGY...
I MADE IT! THAT AIR-VENT WILL DRAIN THE NEUTRONS UPWARD -- OUT OF MY WAY!
HIS MOMENT OF TRIUMPH IS SHORT-LIVED, HOWEVE AS A DARK FINGER OF FORCE PROBES DOWNWAR OUT OF SPACE INTO THE ATMOSPHERE OF THE PLANET...
OHHH! I'M CAUGHT IN THIS SPACE-TORNADO -- AND -- MY RING STILL ISN'T WORKING FAST ENOUGH TO SAVE ME FROM ITS GRIP!

...WARD TOWARD THE RINGE OF SPACE ITSELF E IS CARRIED LIKE A UST MOTE IN A STORM...

KEEP FEEDING THE RING RDERS--BUT IT TAKES O LONG TO--OBEY THEM!

THEN--SCANT SECONDS BEFORE THE EMERALD GLADIATOR FEELS THE COLD OF OUTER SPACE...

AT LAST-- MY POWER-RINGED PROPELLER DREW ME OUT JUST IN TIME!

PUZZLED--BAFFLED BY THE SLUGGISHNESS OF HIS POWER RING-- HE COURSES ABOUT THE SURFACE OF THRONN...

BY THE TIME MY RING SAVES ME--I COULD BE OVERCOME! Hmmm-- I'M GETTING AN IDEA! I'LL HAVE TO DROP TO THE GROUND TO CHECK IT OUT...

SOON... I'M NOT USING MY RING--BUT IT'S STILL GLOWING, JUST AS IT'S DONE EVER SINCE I TRIED TO BREAK THE ERGAL BARRIER ON MEMAL, AND FAILED!

MY RING IS UNDER THE INFLUENCE OF SOMEONE ELSE--OF COURSE! VANT ORL! HE NOT ONLY USES IT TO TELE-PATH HIS THOUGHTS AT ME--BUT ALSO TO SLOW DOWN ITS REACTIONS WITH HIS TERRIFIC WILL POWER!

NOW THAT I KNOW WHAT THE TROUBLE S--I CAN DO SOMETHING ABOUT IT!

I'M GETTING BORED WITH THIS GAME I'M PLAYING WITH YOU, GREEN LANTERN! I'M GIVING YOU JUST ONE MORE TRY AT ME--AND THEN I'M ENDING THE GAME-- WITH YOUR COMPLETE DEFEAT!

8

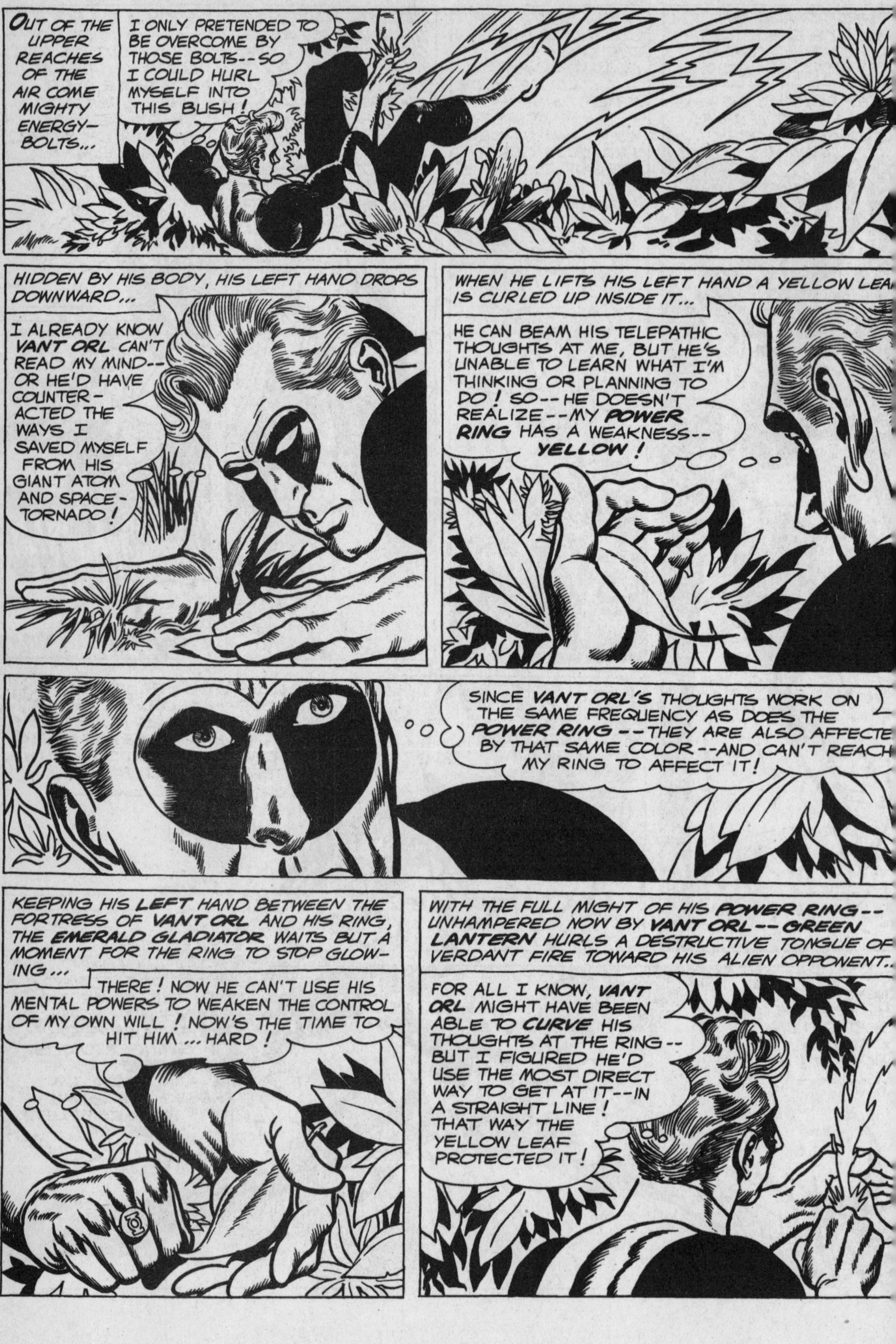
OUT OF THE UPPER REACHES OF THE AIR COME MIGHTY ENERGY-BOLTS...
I ONLY PRETENDED TO BE OVERCOME BY THOSE BOLTS--SO I COULD HURL MYSELF INTO THIS BUSH!
HIDDEN BY HIS BODY, HIS LEFT HAND DROPS DOWNWARD...
I ALREADY KNOW VANT ORL CAN'T READ MY MIND--OR HE'D HAVE COUNTER-ACTED THE WAYS I SAVED MYSELF FROM HIS GIANT ATOM AND SPACE-TORNADO!
WHEN HE LIFTS HIS LEFT HAND A YELLOW LEA IS CURLED UP INSIDE IT...
HE CAN BEAM HIS TELEPATHIC THOUGHTS AT ME, BUT HE'S UNABLE TO LEARN WHAT I'M THINKING OR PLANNING TO DO! SO--HE DOESN'T REALIZE--MY POWER RING HAS A WEAKNESS--YELLOW!
SINCE VANT ORL'S THOUGHTS WORK ON THE SAME FREQUENCY AS DOES THE POWER RING--THEY ARE ALSO AFFECTE BY THAT SAME COLOR--AND CAN'T REACH MY RING TO AFFECT IT!
KEEPING HIS LEFT HAND BETWEEN THE FORTRESS OF VANT ORL AND HIS RING, THE EMERALD GLADIATOR WAITS BUT A MOMENT FOR THE RING TO STOP GLOWING...
THERE! NOW HE CAN'T USE HIS MENTAL POWERS TO WEAKEN THE CONTROL OF MY OWN WILL! NOW'S THE TIME TO HIT HIM ...HARD!
WITH THE FULL MIGHT OF HIS POWER RING--UNHAMPERED NOW BY VANT ORL--GREEN LANTERN HURLS A DESTRUCTIVE TONGUE OF VERDANT FIRE TOWARD HIS ALIEN OPPONENT...
FOR ALL I KNOW, VANT ORL MIGHT HAVE BEEN ABLE TO CURVE HIS THOUGHTS AT THE RING--BUT I FIGURED HE'D USE THE MOST DIRECT WAY TO GET AT IT--IN A STRAIGHT LINE! THAT WAY THE YELLOW LEAF PROTECTED IT!

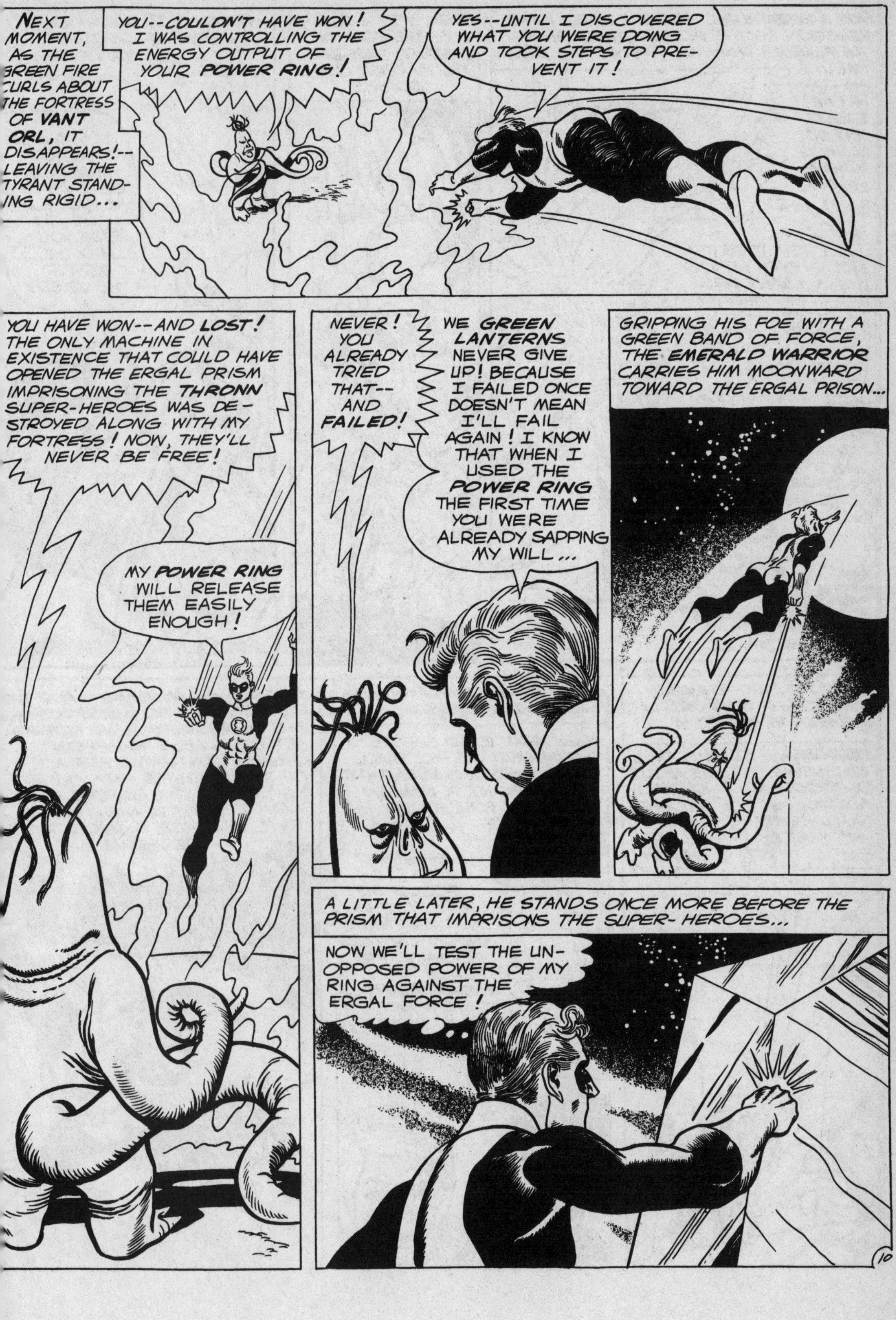
NEXT MOMENT, AS THE GREEN FIRE CURLS ABOUT THE FORTRESS OF VANT ORL, IT DISAPPEARS!--LEAVING THE TYRANT STANDING RIGID...
YOU--COULDN'T HAVE WON! I WAS CONTROLLING THE ENERGY OUTPUT OF YOUR POWER RING!
YES--UNTIL I DISCOVERED WHAT YOU WERE DOING AND TOOK STEPS TO PREVENT IT!
YOU HAVE WON--AND LOST! THE ONLY MACHINE IN EXISTENCE THAT COULD HAVE OPENED THE ERGAL PRISM IMPRISONING THE THRONN SUPER-HEROES WAS DESTROYED ALONG WITH MY FORTRESS! NOW, THEY'LL NEVER BE FREE!
MY POWER RING WILL RELEASE THEM EASILY ENOUGH!
NEVER! YOU ALREADY TRIED THAT--AND FAILED!
WE GREEN LANTERNS NEVER GIVE UP! BECAUSE I FAILED ONCE DOESN'T MEAN I'LL FAIL AGAIN! I KNOW THAT WHEN I USED THE POWER RING THE FIRST TIME YOU WERE ALREADY SAPPING MY WILL...
GRIPPING HIS FOE WITH A GREEN BAND OF FORCE, THE EMERALD WARRIOR CARRIES HIM MOONWARD TOWARD THE ERGAL PRISON...
A LITTLE LATER, HE STANDS ONCE MORE BEFORE THE PRISM THAT IMPRISONS THE SUPER-HEROES...
NOW WE'LL TEST THE UNOPPOSED POWER OF MY RING AGAINST THE ERGAL FORCE!
10

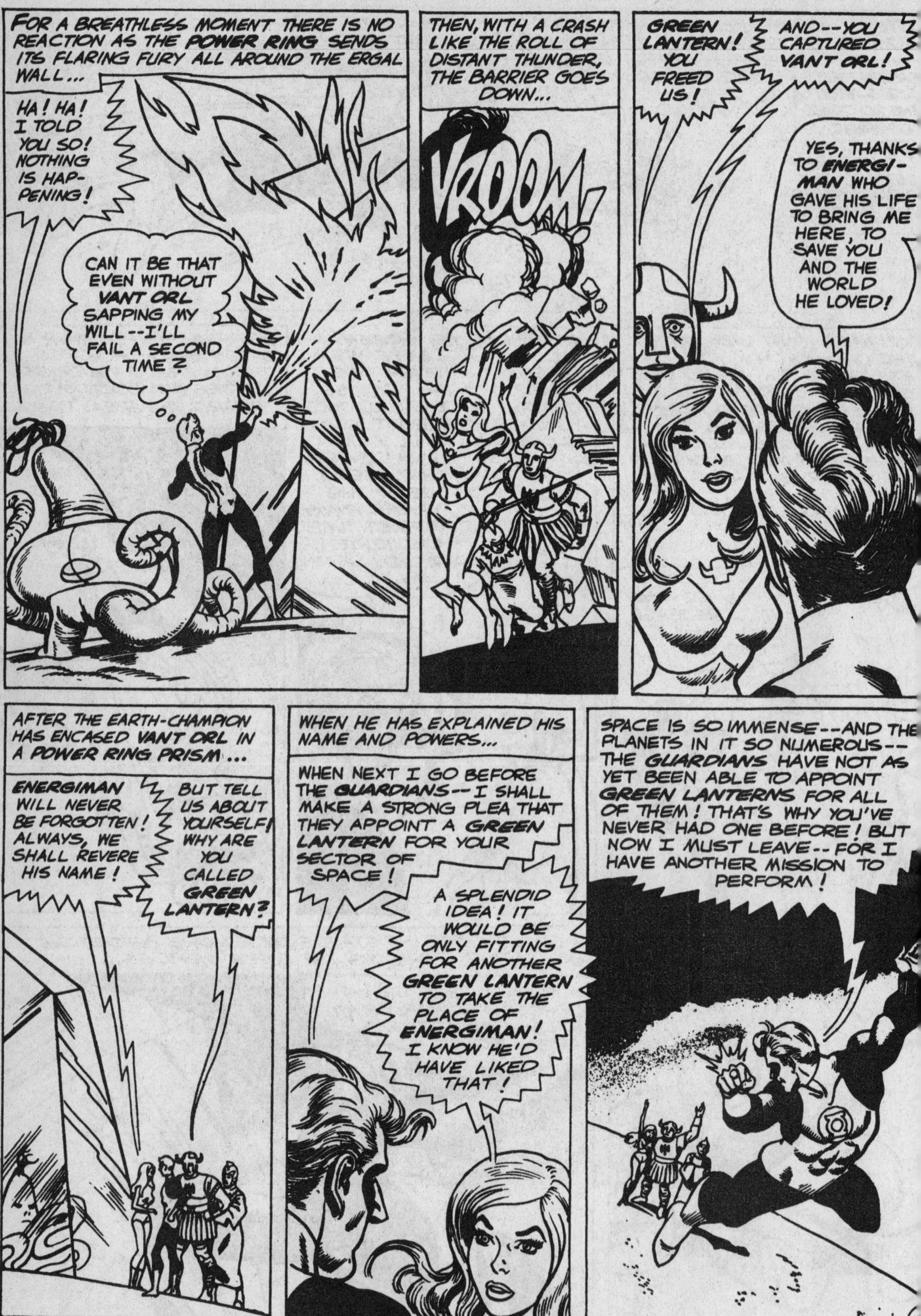
FOR A BREATHLESS MOMENT THERE IS NO REACTION AS THE POWER RING SENDS ITS FLARING FURY ALL AROUND THE ERGAL WALL...
HA! HA! I TOLD YOU SO! NOTHING IS HAPPENING!
CAN IT BE THAT EVEN WITHOUT VANT ORL SAPPING MY WILL--I'LL FAIL A SECOND TIME?
THEN, WITH A CRASH LIKE THE ROLL OF DISTANT THUNDER, THE BARRIER GOES DOWN...
VROOM!
GREEN LANTERN! YOU FREED US!
AND--YOU CAPTURED VANT ORL!
YES, THANKS TO ENERGI-MAN WHO GAVE HIS LIFE TO BRING ME HERE, TO SAVE YOU AND THE WORLD HE LOVED!
AFTER THE EARTH-CHAMPION HAS ENCASED VANT ORL IN A POWER RING PRISM...
ENERGIMAN WILL NEVER BE FORGOTTEN! ALWAYS, WE SHALL REVERE HIS NAME!
BUT TELL US ABOUT YOURSELF! WHY ARE YOU CALLED GREEN LANTERN?
WHEN HE HAS EXPLAINED HIS NAME AND POWERS...
WHEN NEXT I GO BEFORE THE GUARDIANS--I SHALL MAKE A STRONG PLEA THAT THEY APPOINT A GREEN LANTERN FOR YOUR SECTOR OF SPACE!
A SPLENDID IDEA! IT WOULD BE ONLY FITTING FOR ANOTHER GREEN LANTERN TO TAKE THE PLACE OF ENERGIMAN! I KNOW HE'D HAVE LIKED THAT!
SPACE IS SO IMMENSE--AND THE PLANETS IN IT SO NUMEROUS--THE GUARDIANS HAVE NOT AS YET BEEN ABLE TO APPOINT GREEN LANTERNS FOR ALL OF THEM! THAT'S WHY YOU'VE NEVER HAD ONE BEFORE! BUT NOW I MUST LEAVE--FOR I HAVE ANOTHER MISSION TO PERFORM!

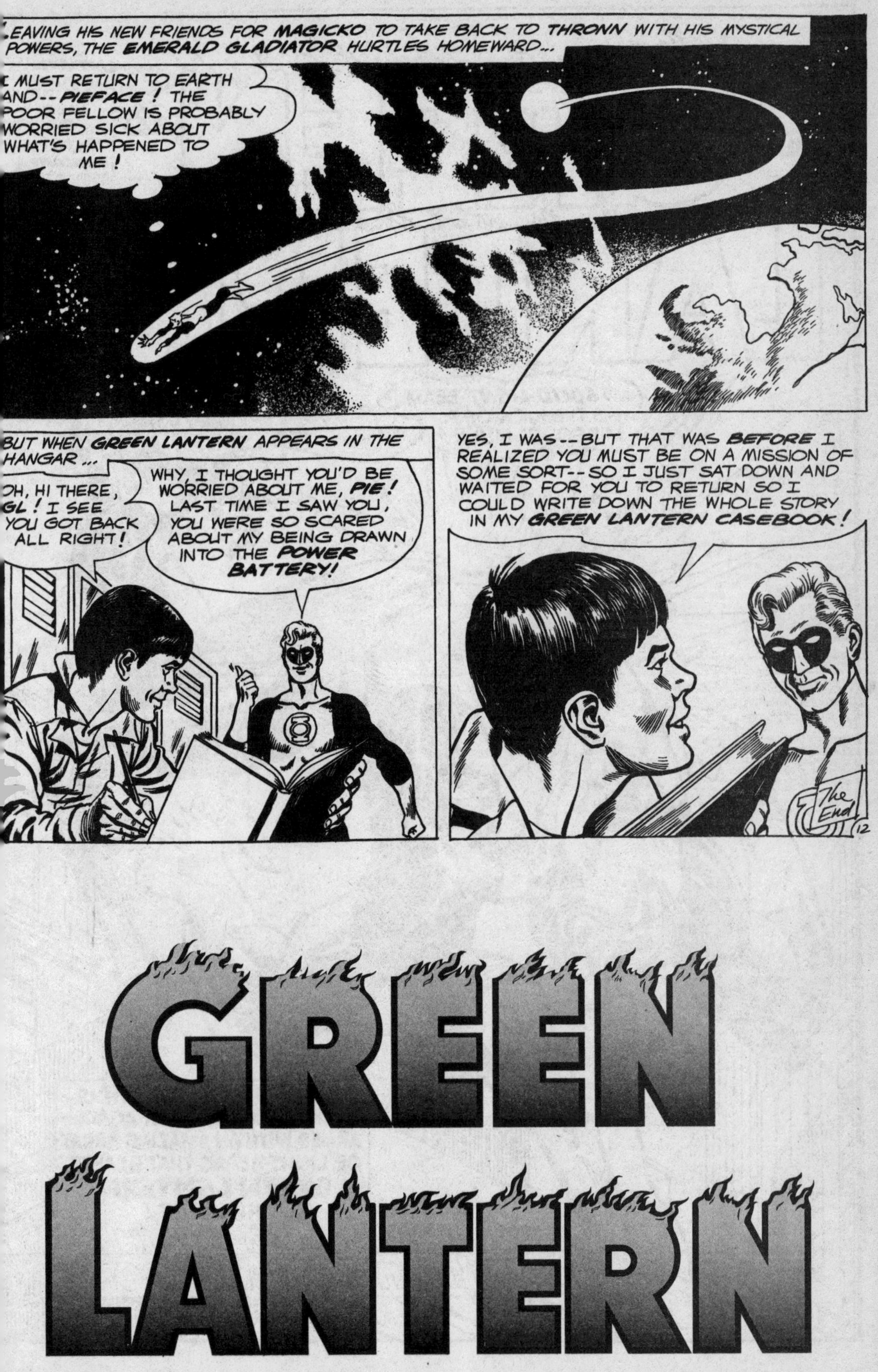
LEAVING HIS NEW FRIENDS FOR MAGICKO TO TAKE BACK TO THRONN WITH HIS MYSTICAL POWERS, THE EMERALD GLADIATOR HURTLES HOMEWARD...
I MUST RETURN TO EARTH AND--PIEFACE! THE POOR FELLOW IS PROBABLY WORRIED SICK ABOUT WHAT'S HAPPENED TO ME!
BUT WHEN GREEN LANTERN APPEARS IN THE HANGAR...
OH, HI THERE, GL! I SEE YOU GOT BACK ALL RIGHT!
WHY, I THOUGHT YOU'D BE WORRIED ABOUT ME, PIE! LAST TIME I SAW YOU, YOU WERE SO SCARED ABOUT MY BEING DRAWN INTO THE POWER BATTERY!
YES, I WAS--BUT THAT WAS BEFORE I REALIZED YOU MUST BE ON A MISSION OF SOME SORT--SO I JUST SAT DOWN AND WAITED FOR YOU TO RETURN SO I COULD WRITE DOWN THE WHOLE STORY IN MY GREEN LANTERN CASEBOOK!
The End
12

GREEN LANTERN

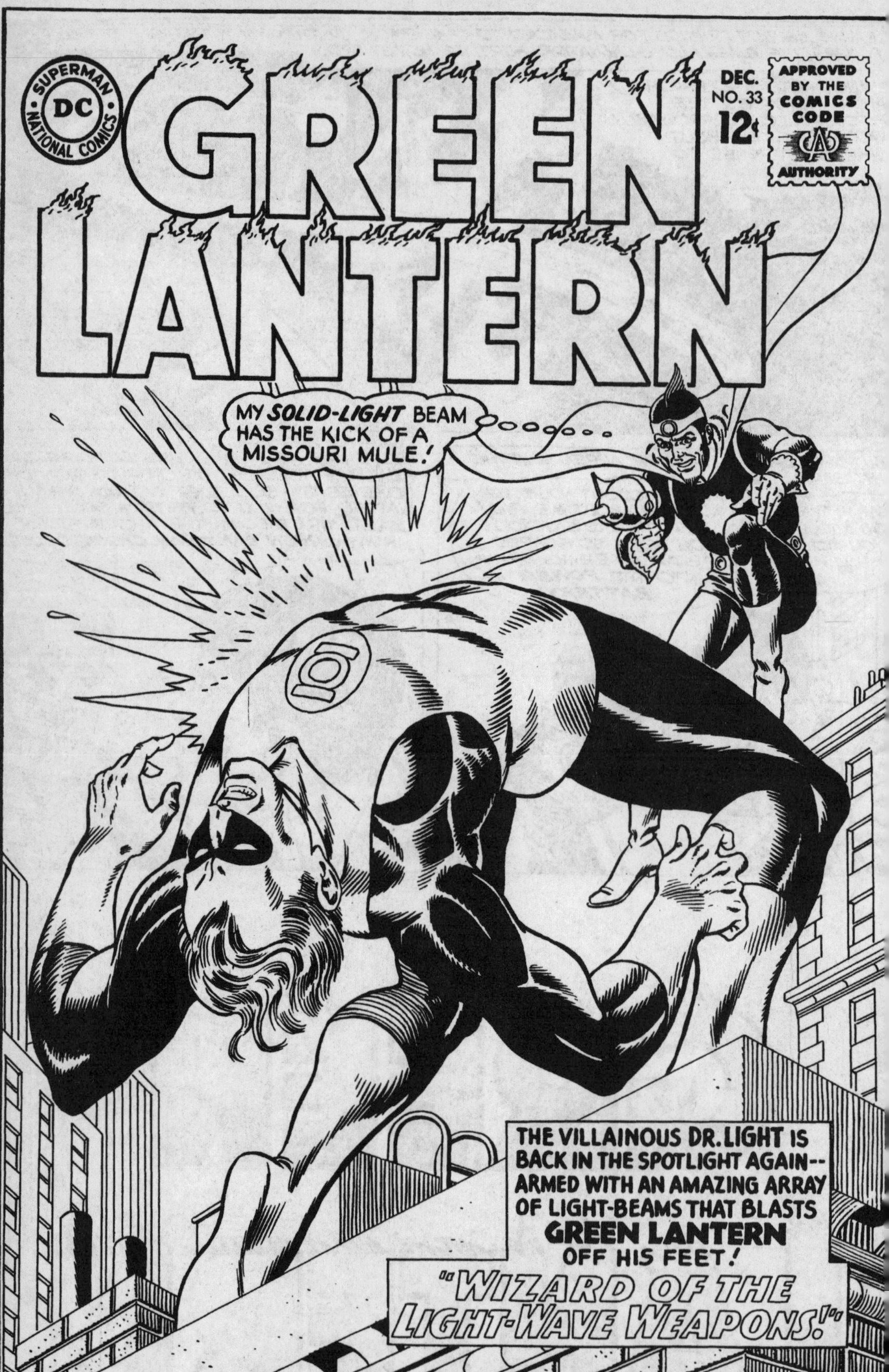
SUPERMAN DC NATIONAL COMICS
GREEN LANTERN
DEC. NO. 33 12¢
APPROVED BY THE COMICS CODE AUTHORITY
MY SOLID-LIGHT BEAM HAS THE KICK OF A MISSOURI MULE!
THE VILLAINOUS DR. LIGHT IS BACK IN THE SPOTLIGHT AGAIN-- ARMED WITH AN AMAZING ARRAY OF LIGHT-BEAMS THAT BLASTS GREEN LANTERN OFF HIS FEET!
"WIZARD OF THE LIGHT-WAVE WEAPONS!"

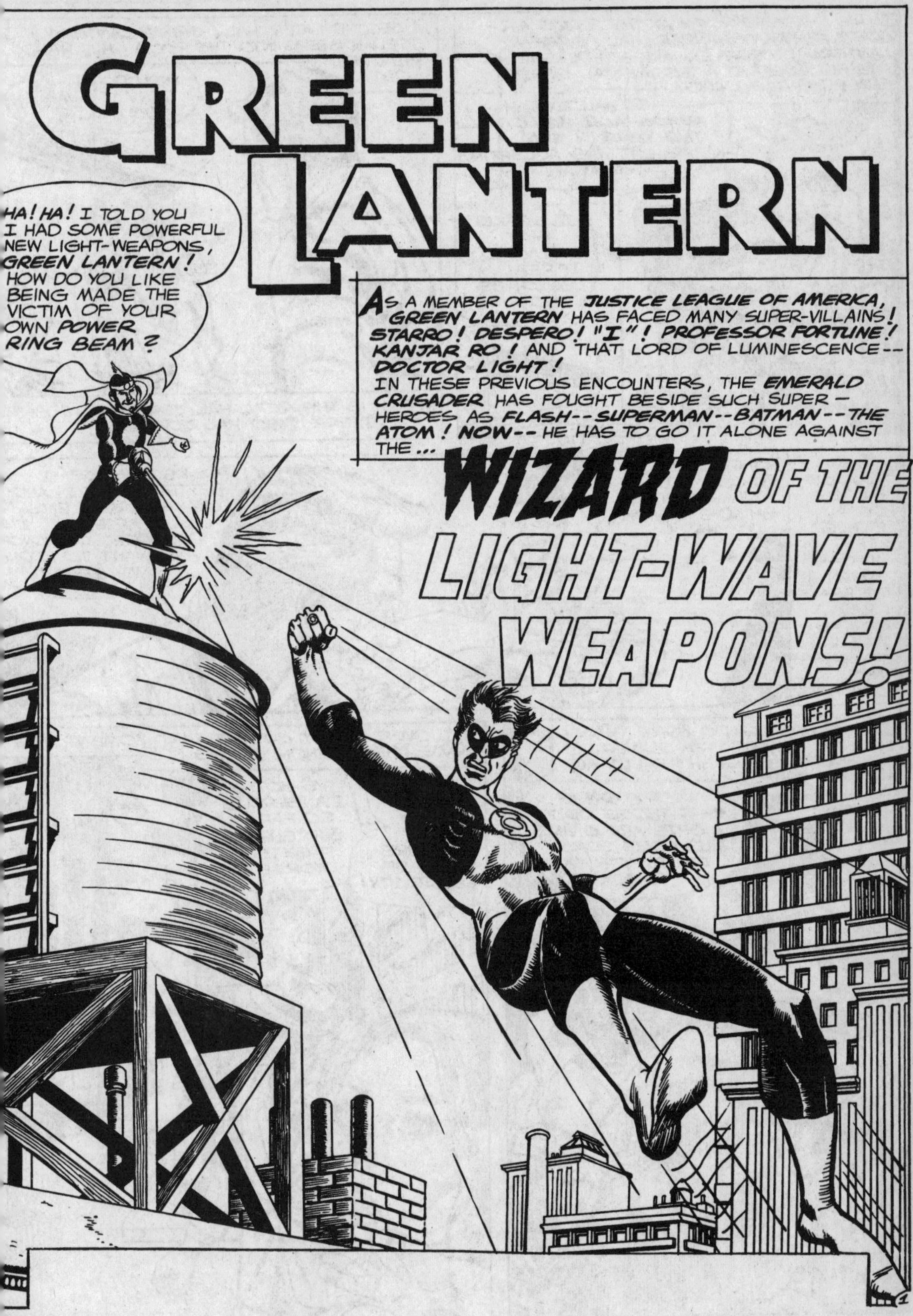
GREEN LANTERN
HA! HA! I TOLD YOU I HAD SOME POWERFUL NEW LIGHT-WEAPONS, GREEN LANTERN! HOW DO YOU LIKE BEING MADE THE VICTIM OF YOUR OWN POWER RING BEAM?
AS A MEMBER OF THE JUSTICE LEAGUE OF AMERICA, GREEN LANTERN HAS FACED MANY SUPER-VILLAINS! STARRO! DESPERO! "I"! PROFESSOR FORTUNE! KANJAR RO! AND THAT LORD OF LUMINESCENCE--DOCTOR LIGHT! IN THESE PREVIOUS ENCOUNTERS, THE EMERALD CRUSADER HAS FOUGHT BESIDE SUCH SUPER-HEROES AS FLASH--SUPERMAN--BATMAN--THE ATOM! NOW--HE HAS TO GO IT ALONE AGAINST THE...
WIZARD OF THE LIGHT-WAVE WEAPONS!
1

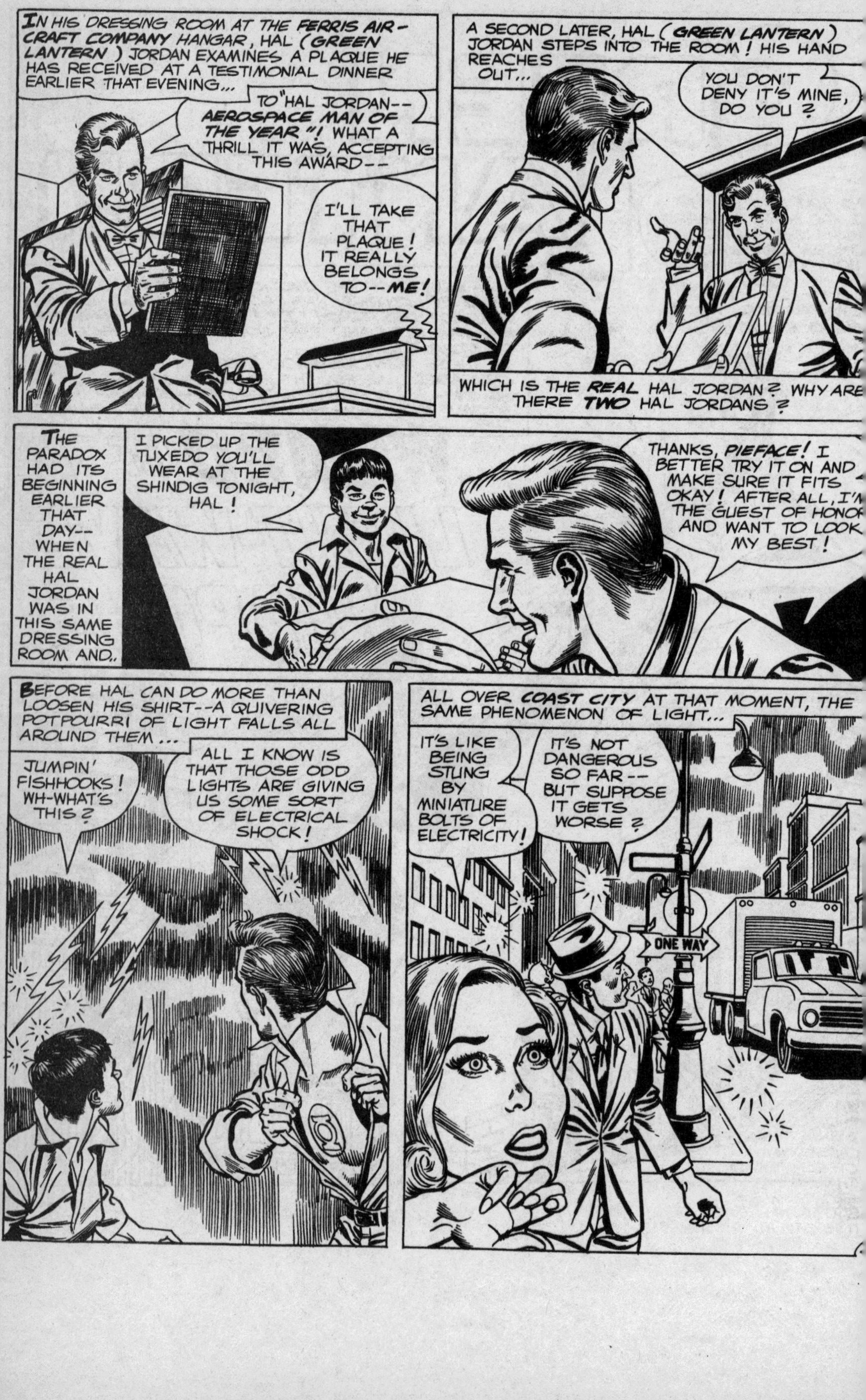
IN HIS DRESSING ROOM AT THE FERRIS AIRCRAFT COMPANY HANGAR, HAL (GREEN LANTERN) JORDAN EXAMINES A PLAQUE HE HAS RECEIVED AT A TESTIMONIAL DINNER EARLIER THAT EVENING...
TO "HAL JORDAN-- AEROSPACE MAN OF THE YEAR"! WHAT A THRILL IT WAS, ACCEPTING THIS AWARD--
I'LL TAKE THAT PLAQUE! IT REALLY BELONGS TO--ME!
A SECOND LATER, HAL (GREEN LANTERN) JORDAN STEPS INTO THE ROOM! HIS HAND REACHES OUT...
YOU DON'T DENY IT'S MINE, DO YOU?
WHICH IS THE REAL HAL JORDAN? WHY ARE THERE TWO HAL JORDANS?
THE PARADOX HAD ITS BEGINNING EARLIER THAT DAY-- WHEN THE REAL HAL JORDAN WAS IN THIS SAME DRESSING ROOM AND..
I PICKED UP THE TUXEDO YOU'LL WEAR AT THE SHINDIG TONIGHT, HAL!
THANKS, PIEFACE! I BETTER TRY IT ON AND MAKE SURE IT FITS OKAY! AFTER ALL, I'M THE GUEST OF HONOR AND WANT TO LOOK MY BEST!
BEFORE HAL CAN DO MORE THAN LOOSEN HIS SHIRT--A QUIVERING POTPOURRI OF LIGHT FALLS ALL AROUND THEM...
JUMPIN' FISHHOOKS! WH-WHAT'S THIS?
ALL I KNOW IS THAT THOSE ODD LIGHTS ARE GIVING US SOME SORT OF ELECTRICAL SHOCK!
ALL OVER COAST CITY AT THAT MOMENT, THE SAME PHENOMENON OF LIGHT...
IT'S LIKE BEING STUNG BY MINIATURE BOLTS OF ELECTRICITY!
IT'S NOT DANGEROUS SO FAR-- BUT SUPPOSE IT GETS WORSE?
ONE WAY

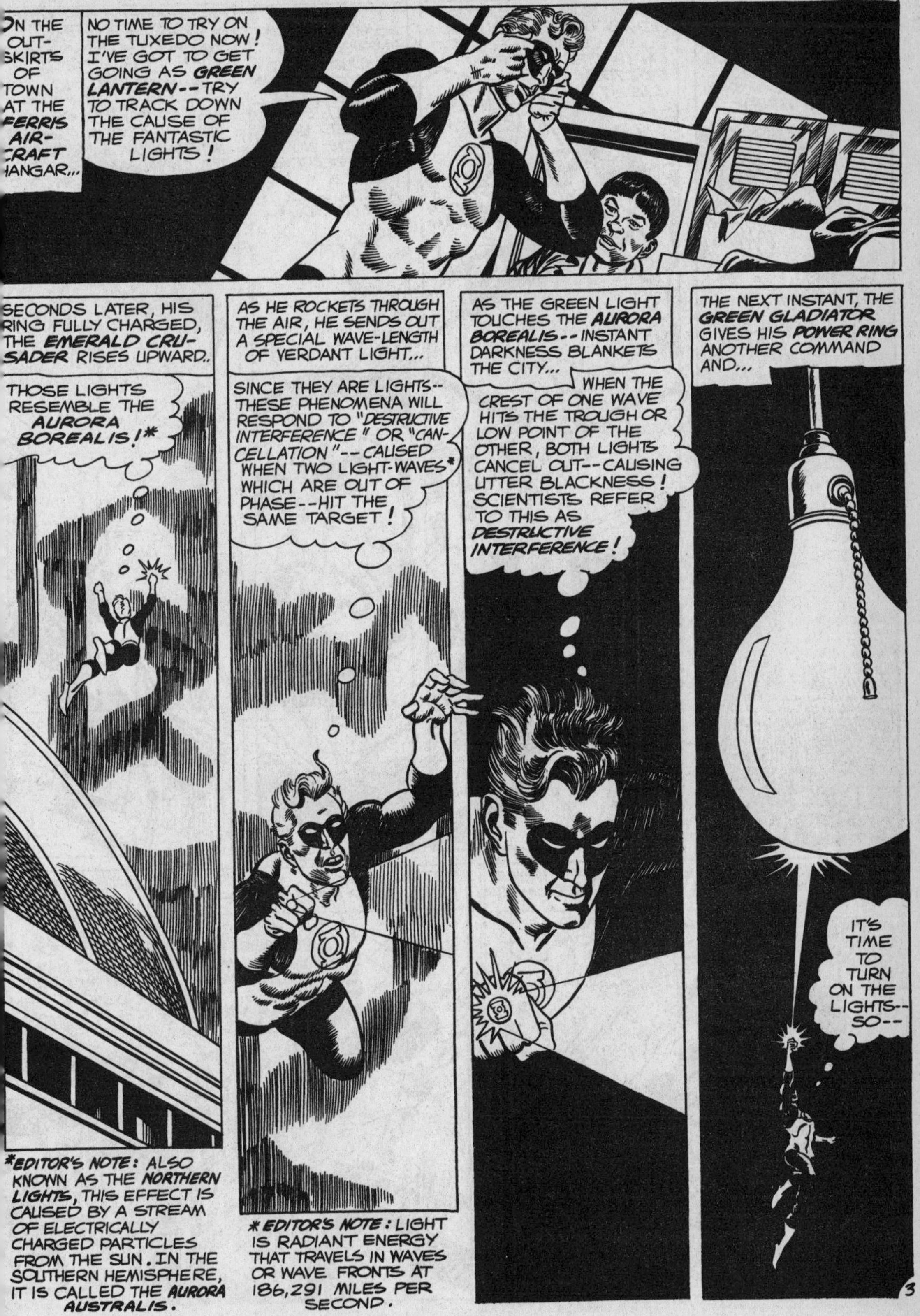
ON THE OUT-SKIRTS OF TOWN AT THE FERRIS AIR-CRAFT HANGAR...
NO TIME TO TRY ON THE TUXEDO NOW! I'VE GOT TO GET GOING AS GREEN LANTERN--TRY TO TRACK DOWN THE CAUSE OF THE FANTASTIC LIGHTS!
SECONDS LATER, HIS RING FULLY CHARGED, THE EMERALD CRUSADER RISES UPWARD..
THOSE LIGHTS RESEMBLE THE AURORA BOREALIS!*
*EDITOR'S NOTE: ALSO KNOWN AS THE NORTHERN LIGHTS, THIS EFFECT IS CAUSED BY A STREAM OF ELECTRICALLY CHARGED PARTICLES FROM THE SUN. IN THE SOUTHERN HEMISPHERE, IT IS CALLED THE AURORA AUSTRALIS.
AS HE ROCKETS THROUGH THE AIR, HE SENDS OUT A SPECIAL WAVE-LENGTH OF VERDANT LIGHT...
SINCE THEY ARE LIGHTS--THESE PHENOMENA WILL RESPOND TO "DESTRUCTIVE INTERFERENCE" OR "CANCELLATION"--CAUSED WHEN TWO LIGHT-WAVES* WHICH ARE OUT OF PHASE--HIT THE SAME TARGET!
*EDITOR'S NOTE: LIGHT IS RADIANT ENERGY THAT TRAVELS IN WAVES OR WAVE FRONTS AT 186,291 MILES PER SECOND.
AS THE GREEN LIGHT TOUCHES THE AURORA BOREALIS--INSTANT DARKNESS BLANKETS THE CITY...
WHEN THE CREST OF ONE WAVE HITS THE TROUGH OR LOW POINT OF THE OTHER, BOTH LIGHTS CANCEL OUT--CAUSING UTTER BLACKNESS! SCIENTISTS REFER TO THIS AS DESTRUCTIVE INTERFERENCE!
THE NEXT INSTANT, THE GREEN GLADIATOR GIVES HIS POWER RING ANOTHER COMMAND AND...
IT'S TIME TO TURN ON THE LIGHTS--SO--
3

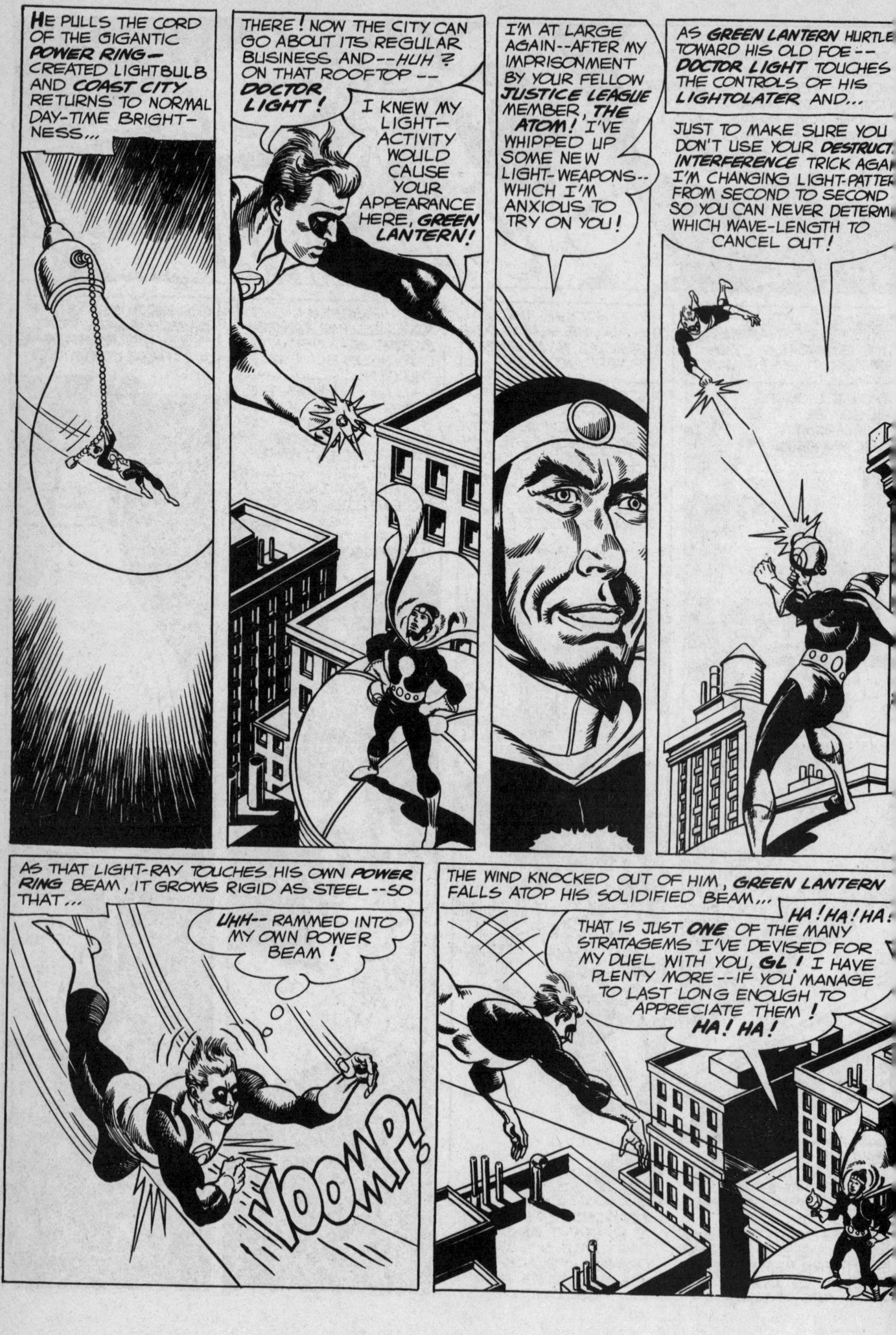
HE PULLS THE CORD OF THE GIGANTIC POWER RING—CREATED LIGHTBULB AND COAST CITY RETURNS TO NORMAL DAY-TIME BRIGHTNESS...
THERE! NOW THE CITY CAN GO ABOUT ITS REGULAR BUSINESS AND--HUH? ON THAT ROOFTOP--DOCTOR LIGHT!
I KNEW MY LIGHT-ACTIVITY WOULD CAUSE YOUR APPEARANCE HERE, GREEN LANTERN!
I'M AT LARGE AGAIN--AFTER MY IMPRISONMENT BY YOUR FELLOW JUSTICE LEAGUE MEMBER, THE ATOM! I'VE WHIPPED UP SOME NEW LIGHT-WEAPONS--WHICH I'M ANXIOUS TO TRY ON YOU!
AS GREEN LANTERN HURTLE TOWARD HIS OLD FOE--DOCTOR LIGHT TOUCHES THE CONTROLS OF HIS LIGHTOLATER AND...
JUST TO MAKE SURE YOU DON'T USE YOUR DESTRUCT INTERFERENCE TRICK AGAI I'M CHANGING LIGHT-PATTE FROM SECOND TO SECOND SO YOU CAN NEVER DETERM WHICH WAVE-LENGTH TO CANCEL OUT!
AS THAT LIGHT-RAY TOUCHES HIS OWN POWER RING BEAM, IT GROWS RIGID AS STEEL--SO THAT...
UHH--RAMMED INTO MY OWN POWER BEAM!
VOOMP!
THE WIND KNOCKED OUT OF HIM, GREEN LANTERN FALLS ATOP HIS SOLIDIFIED BEAM...
HA! HA! HA!
THAT IS JUST ONE OF THE MANY STRATAGEMS I'VE DEVISED FOR MY DUEL WITH YOU, GL! I HAVE PLENTY MORE--IF YOU MANAGE TO LAST LONG ENOUGH TO APPRECIATE THEM! HA! HA!

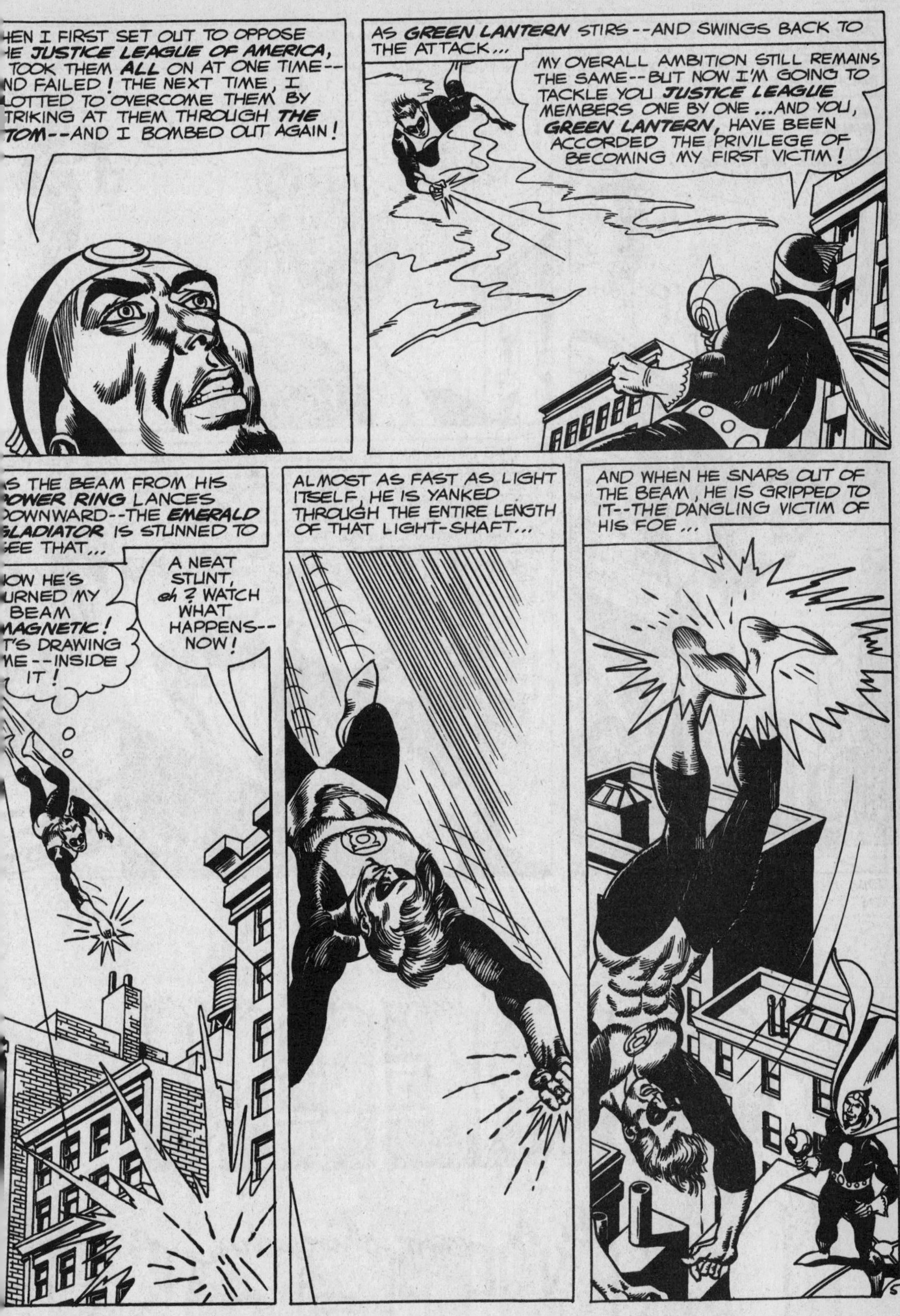
HEN I FIRST SET OUT TO OPPOSE HE JUSTICE LEAGUE OF AMERICA, TOOK THEM ALL ON AT ONE TIME-- ND FAILED! THE NEXT TIME, I LOTTED TO OVERCOME THEM BY TRIKING AT THEM THROUGH THE TOM--AND I BOMBED OUT AGAIN!
AS GREEN LANTERN STIRS--AND SWINGS BACK TO THE ATTACK...
MY OVERALL AMBITION STILL REMAINS THE SAME--BUT NOW I'M GOING TO TACKLE YOU JUSTICE LEAGUE MEMBERS ONE BY ONE ...AND YOU, GREEN LANTERN, HAVE BEEN ACCORDED THE PRIVILEGE OF BECOMING MY FIRST VICTIM!
S THE BEAM FROM HIS POWER RING LANCES DOWNWARD--THE EMERALD GLADIATOR IS STUNNED TO SEE THAT...
NOW HE'S URNED MY BEAM MAGNETIC! T'S DRAWING ME--INSIDE IT!
A NEAT STUNT, eh? WATCH WHAT HAPPENS--NOW!
ALMOST AS FAST AS LIGHT ITSELF, HE IS YANKED THROUGH THE ENTIRE LENGTH OF THAT LIGHT-SHAFT...
AND WHEN HE SNAPS OUT OF THE BEAM, HE IS GRIPPED TO IT--THE DANGLING VICTIM OF HIS FOE...
5

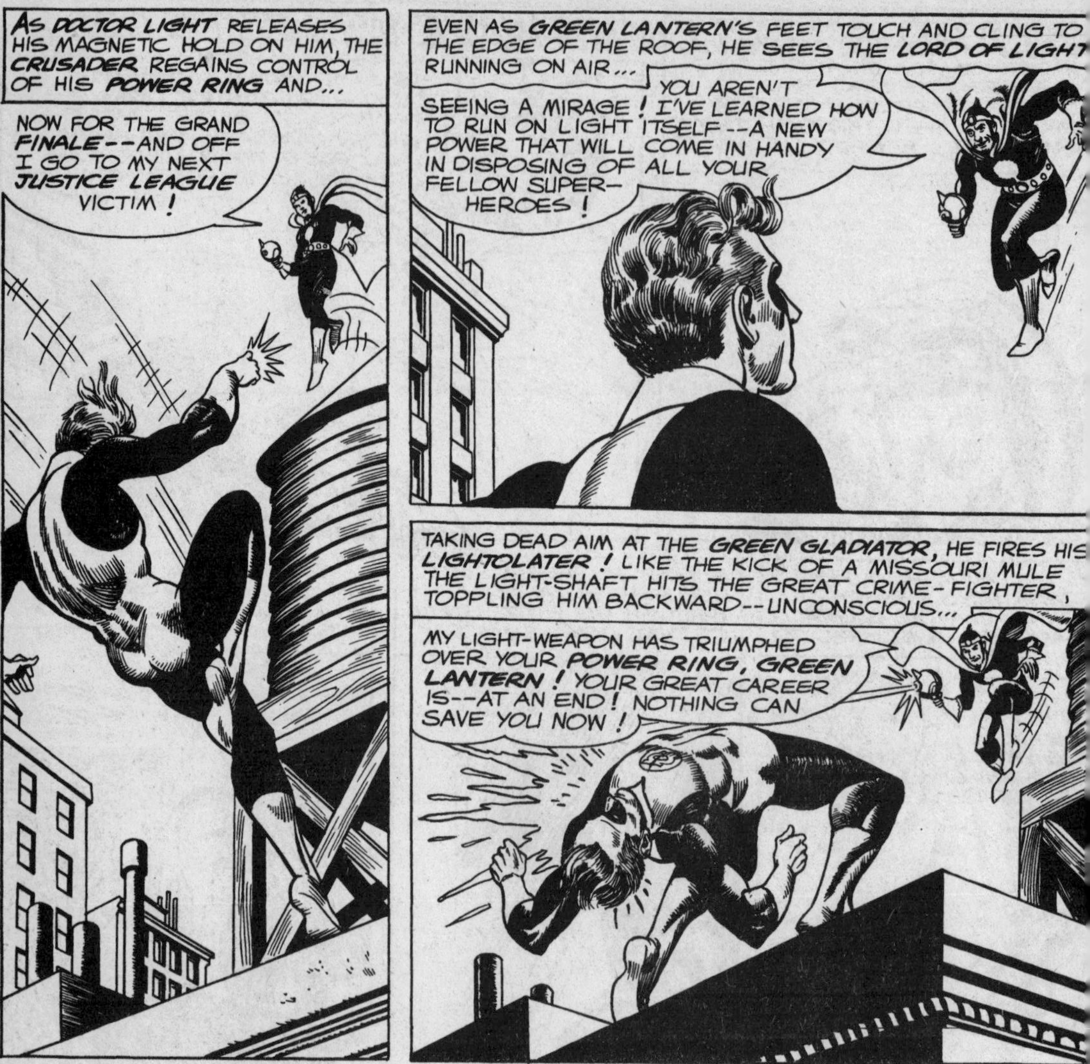
AS DOCTOR LIGHT RELEASES HIS MAGNETIC HOLD ON HIM, THE CRUSADER REGAINS CONTROL OF HIS POWER RING AND...
NOW FOR THE GRAND FINALE--AND OFF I GO TO MY NEXT JUSTICE LEAGUE VICTIM!
EVEN AS GREEN LANTERN'S FEET TOUCH AND CLING TO THE EDGE OF THE ROOF, HE SEES THE LORD OF LIGHT RUNNING ON AIR...
YOU AREN'T SEEING A MIRAGE! I'VE LEARNED HOW TO RUN ON LIGHT ITSELF--A NEW POWER THAT WILL COME IN HANDY IN DISPOSING OF ALL YOUR FELLOW SUPER-HEROES!
TAKING DEAD AIM AT THE GREEN GLADIATOR, HE FIRES HIS LIGHTOLATER! LIKE THE KICK OF A MISSOURI MULE THE LIGHT-SHAFT HITS THE GREAT CRIME-FIGHTER, TOPPLING HIM BACKWARD--UNCONSCIOUS...
MY LIGHT-WEAPON HAS TRIUMPHED OVER YOUR POWER RING, GREEN LANTERN! YOUR GREAT CAREER IS--AT AN END! NOTHING CAN SAVE YOU NOW!

GREEN LANTERN

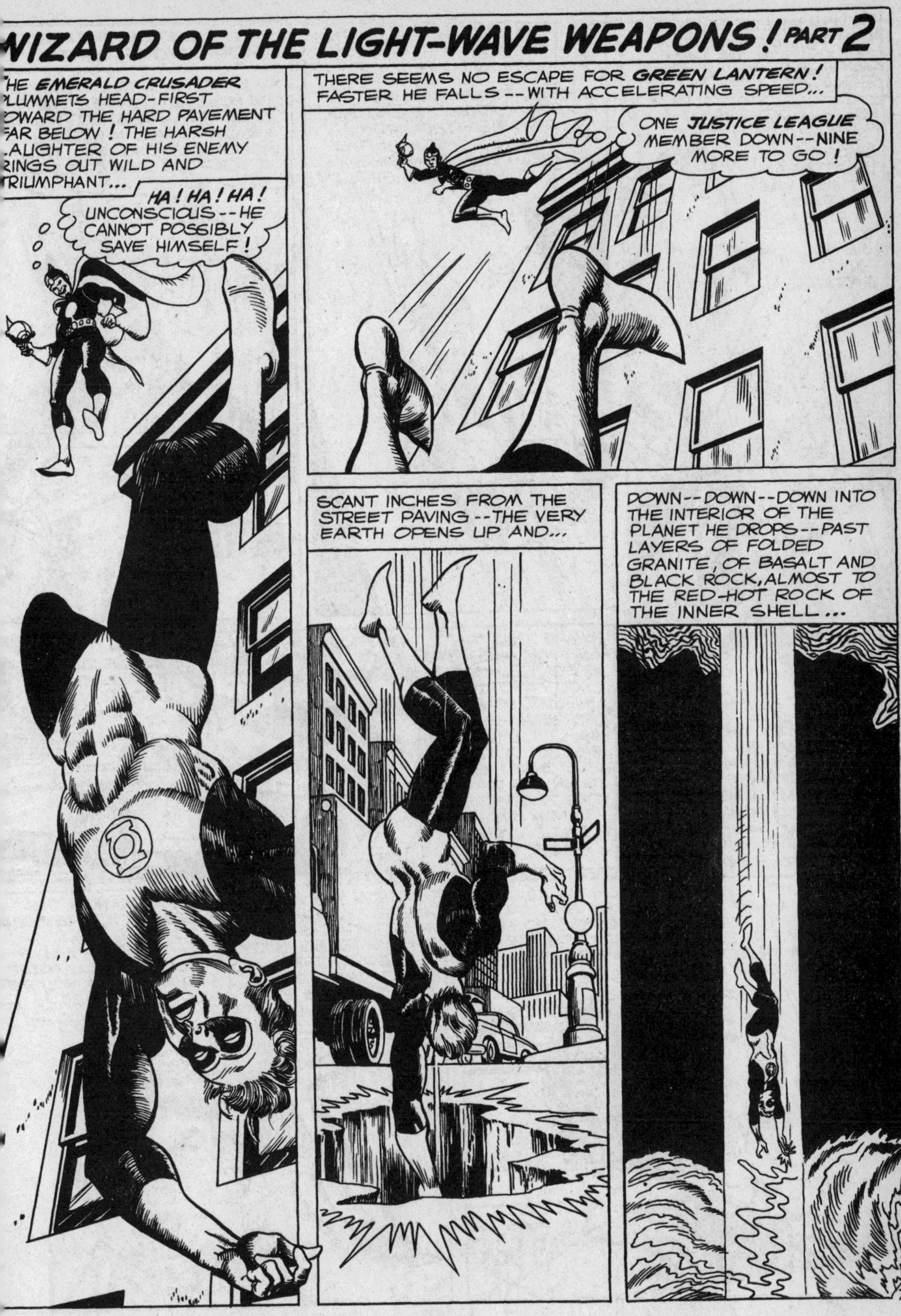
WIZARD OF THE LIGHT-WAVE WEAPONS! PART 2
THE EMERALD CRUSADER PLUMMETS HEAD-FIRST TOWARD THE HARD PAVEMENT FAR BELOW! THE HARSH LAUGHTER OF HIS ENEMY RINGS OUT WILD AND TRIUMPHANT...
HA! HA! HA! UNCONSCIOUS--HE CANNOT POSSIBLY SAVE HIMSELF!
THERE SEEMS NO ESCAPE FOR GREEN LANTERN! FASTER HE FALLS--WITH ACCELERATING SPEED...
ONE JUSTICE LEAGUE MEMBER DOWN--NINE MORE TO GO!
SCANT INCHES FROM THE STREET PAVING--THE VERY EARTH OPENS UP AND...
DOWN--DOWN--DOWN INTO THE INTERIOR OF THE PLANET HE DROPS--PAST LAYERS OF FOLDED GRANITE, OF BASALT AND BLACK ROCK, ALMOST TO THE RED-HOT ROCK OF THE INNER SHELL...
7

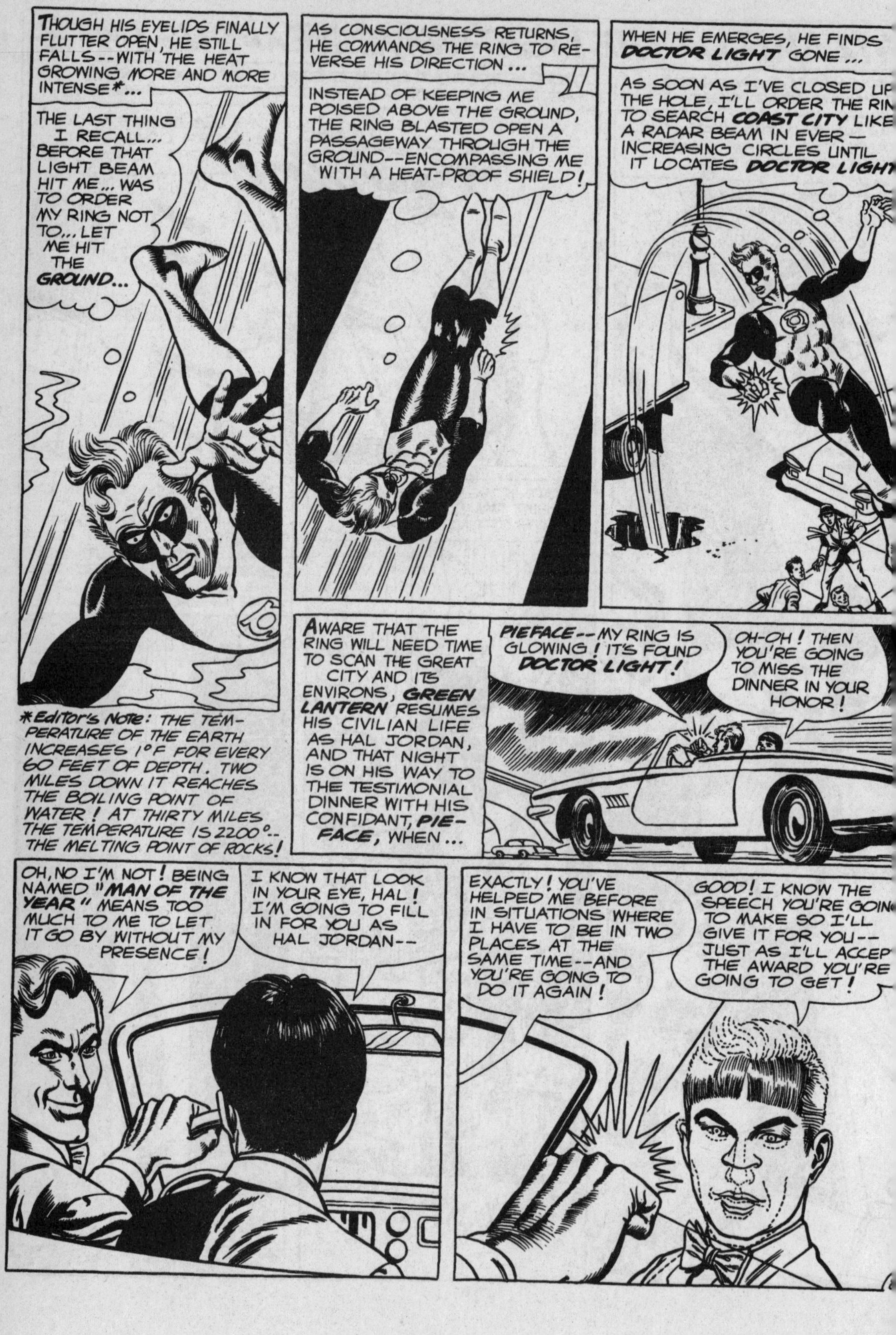
THOUGH HIS EYELIDS FINALLY FLUTTER OPEN, HE STILL FALLS--WITH THE HEAT GROWING MORE AND MORE INTENSE*...
THE LAST THING I RECALL... BEFORE THAT LIGHT BEAM HIT ME... WAS TO ORDER MY RING NOT TO... LET ME HIT THE GROUND...
*Editor's Note: THE TEMPERATURE OF THE EARTH INCREASES 1°F FOR EVERY 60 FEET OF DEPTH. TWO MILES DOWN IT REACHES THE BOILING POINT OF WATER! AT THIRTY MILES THE TEMPERATURE IS 2200°-- THE MELTING POINT OF ROCKS!
AS CONSCIOUSNESS RETURNS, HE COMMANDS THE RING TO REVERSE HIS DIRECTION...
INSTEAD OF KEEPING ME POISED ABOVE THE GROUND, THE RING BLASTED OPEN A PASSAGEWAY THROUGH THE GROUND--ENCOMPASSING ME WITH A HEAT-PROOF SHIELD!
WHEN HE EMERGES, HE FINDS DOCTOR LIGHT GONE...
AS SOON AS I'VE CLOSED UP THE HOLE, I'LL ORDER THE RING TO SEARCH COAST CITY LIKE A RADAR BEAM IN EVER-INCREASING CIRCLES UNTIL IT LOCATES DOCTOR LIGHT
AWARE THAT THE RING WILL NEED TIME TO SCAN THE GREAT CITY AND ITS ENVIRONS, GREEN LANTERN RESUMES HIS CIVILIAN LIFE AS HAL JORDAN, AND THAT NIGHT IS ON HIS WAY TO THE TESTIMONIAL DINNER WITH HIS CONFIDANT, PIE-FACE, WHEN...
PIEFACE--MY RING IS GLOWING! IT'S FOUND DOCTOR LIGHT!
OH-OH! THEN YOU'RE GOING TO MISS THE DINNER IN YOUR HONOR!
OH, NO I'M NOT! BEING NAMED "MAN OF THE YEAR" MEANS TOO MUCH TO ME TO LET IT GO BY WITHOUT MY PRESENCE!
I KNOW THAT LOOK IN YOUR EYE, HAL! I'M GOING TO FILL IN FOR YOU AS HAL JORDAN--
EXACTLY! YOU'VE HELPED ME BEFORE IN SITUATIONS WHERE I HAVE TO BE IN TWO PLACES AT THE SAME TIME--AND YOU'RE GOING TO DO IT AGAIN!
GOOD! I KNOW THE SPEECH YOU'RE GOIN TO MAKE SO I'LL GIVE IT FOR YOU-- JUST AS I'LL ACCEP THE AWARD YOU'RE GOING TO GET!

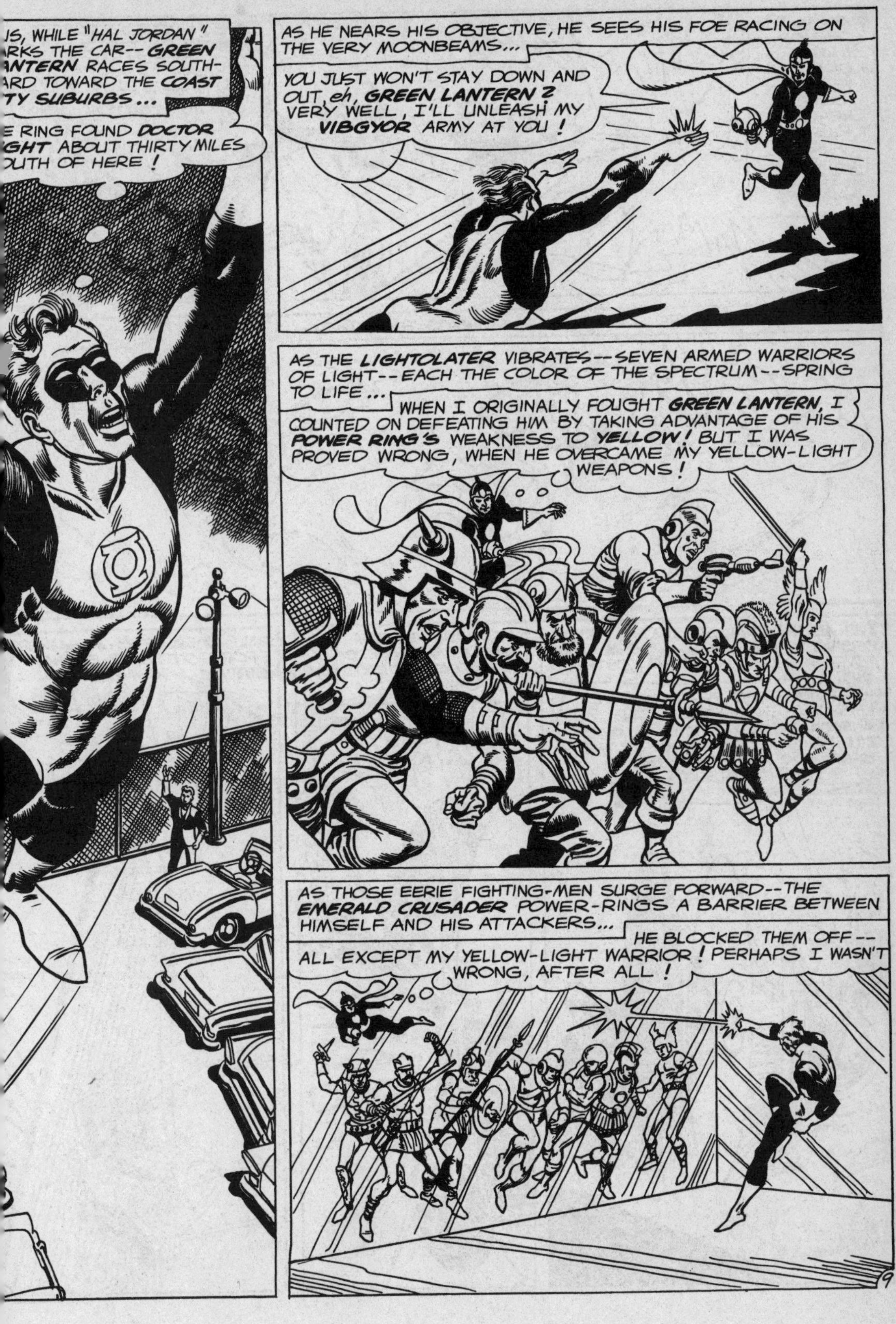

IS, WHILE "HAL JORDAN" ARKS THE CAR-- GREEN ANTERN RACES SOUTH-ARD TOWARD THE COAST TY SUBURBS...
E RING FOUND DOCTOR GHT ABOUT THIRTY MILES OUTH OF HERE!
AS HE NEARS HIS OBJECTIVE, HE SEES HIS FOE RACING ON THE VERY MOONBEAMS...
YOU JUST WON'T STAY DOWN AND OUT, eh, GREEN LANTERN? VERY WELL, I'LL UNLEASH MY VIBGYOR ARMY AT YOU!
AS THE LIGHTOLATER VIBRATES--SEVEN ARMED WARRIORS OF LIGHT--EACH THE COLOR OF THE SPECTRUM--SPRING TO LIFE...
WHEN I ORIGINALLY FOUGHT GREEN LANTERN, I COUNTED ON DEFEATING HIM BY TAKING ADVANTAGE OF HIS POWER RING'S WEAKNESS TO YELLOW! BUT I WAS PROVED WRONG, WHEN HE OVERCAME MY YELLOW-LIGHT WEAPONS!
AS THOSE EERIE FIGHTING-MEN SURGE FORWARD--THE EMERALD CRUSADER POWER-RINGS A BARRIER BETWEEN HIMSELF AND HIS ATTACKERS...
HE BLOCKED THEM OFF-- ALL EXCEPT MY YELLOW-LIGHT WARRIOR! PERHAPS I WASN'T WRONG, AFTER ALL!
9

EVEN AS THE *LORD OF LIGHT* GLOATS, THE YELLOW-LIGHT CREATURE TURNS AND HURLS ITSELF ON ITS FELLOW WARRIORS...

OOPS! WRONG AGAIN! HIS *POWER RING'S* TAKEN CONTROL OF THE YELLOW-LIGHT WARRIOR--AND IS COMMANDING IT TO BATTLE THE REST OF MY *VIBGYOR* ARMY!

BATTLING FURIOUSLY, THE LONE WARRIOR DEFEATS THE OTHERS...

EVEN AS THE FINAL SPECTRO-WARRIOR BEGINS TO DISSIPATE--*DOCTOR LIGHT* MOVES HIS *LIGHTOLATER* CONTROLS AND...

A GREAT PERFORMANCE LIKE THAT DESERVES SOME MUSICAL ACCOMPANIMENT, *GL!* I'LL BE GLAD TO STRIKE UP THE BAND FOR YOU--WITH SOME "LIGHT" MUSIC!

REACHING *GREEN LANTERN* FIRST IS A PAIR OF GREAT CYMBALS...

CLANG!

AH! WHAT MUSIC TO MY EARS!

HALF-DAZED, THE CRUSADER DROPS ONTO MIGHTY HARP STRINGS...

TWANNG!

OVERWHELMED BY THE CYMBALS AND THE HARP--THE *EMERALD GLADIATOR* FALLS ONTO A XYLOPHONE ...

OH! THE JAR OF MY LANDING ON THE XYLOPHONE-- SHOOK THE POWER-ELEMENT OF MY RING OUT OF ITS SETTING!

THAT'S AN UN-EXPECTED BREAK--FOR *ME!*

THE *LORD OF LIGHT* FLASHES UNDER THE GROGGY CRIME-FIGHTER, CATCHING THE FALLING *POWER RING* GEM ...

HA HA! YOU'RE COM-PLETELY POWERLESS, NOW, *GL!*

BUT--EVEN AS THE VILLAIN'S FINGERS CLOSE OVER THE *POWER RING* MINERAL ...

HUH? THIS THING IS GROWING--ENCASING MY HAND IN IT! I--I CAN'T LET GO!

LARGER AND LARGER GROWS THE POWER ELEMENT ...

HE DOESN'T REALIZE IT, BUT IF I'M WITHIN 100 YARDS OF MY *POWER RING*, I STILL MAINTAIN CONTROL OVER IT! I DIRECTED THE MINERAL TO DROP OUT OF ITS MOUNTING --JUST SO I COULD TRAP HIM INSIDE IT!

AS THE ENLARGED GEM SURROUNDS THE SINISTER *DOCTOR LIGHT*, THE *EMERALD CRUSADER* DIRECTS IT TOWARD THE NEAREST POLICE STATION ...

AS SOON AS I'VE TURNED *LIGHT* OVER TO THE AUTHORITIES, I'LL PUT MY TUXEDO ON AGAIN AND-- MEET *PIEFACE!* THE DINNER OUGHT TO BE OVER BY THAT TIME!

11

SO THAT, EVEN AS THE **REAL HAL JORDAN** REACHES FOR HIS PLAQUE, HIS DOUBLE TURNS BACK TO **PIEFACE**...

I'LL TRADE YOU, HAL! THE PLAQUE--FOR THE STORY OF YOUR LATEST ADVENTURE!

FAIR ENOUGH, **PIEFACE!**

WHEN THE TEST PILOT HAS COMPLETED HIS NARRATIVE...

A GREAT YARN, HAL-- BUT YOU NEGLECTED TO EXPLAIN HOW YOU--AS **GREEN LANTERN**-- WERE ABLE TO AFFECT THAT **YELLOW- LIGHT** WARRIOR!

I TOOK ADVANTAGE OF ITS BEING A CREATURE OF THE **LIGHT-SPECTRUM** AND SUBJECT TO THE **DOPPLER EFFECT!** WHEN AN OBJECT RECEDES FROM AN OBSERVER AT GREAT SPEED, ITS LIGHT SHIFTS TOWARD THE RED END OF THE SPECTRUM!

BY POWER-RINGING VIBRATIONS ABOUT THE YELLOW-LIGHT WARRIOR, I CAUSED IT TO VIBRATE AS **IF** IT WERE RAPIDLY RECEDING FROM ME--CHANGING IT FROM YELLOW TO RED AND ENABLING ME TO CONTROL IT WITH MY **POWER RING!**

SIMULTANEOUSLY, OTHER VIBRATIONS CAUSED THE WARRIOR--FROM **DOCTOR LIGHT'S** VIEWPOINT-- TO APPEAR **YELLOW!** THUS I MANAGED TO CONCEAL THE WEAKNESS OF MY **POWER RING!**

HA HA! YOU SURE PULLED THE "LIGHT WOOL" OVER HIS EYES!

The END

GREEN LANTERN

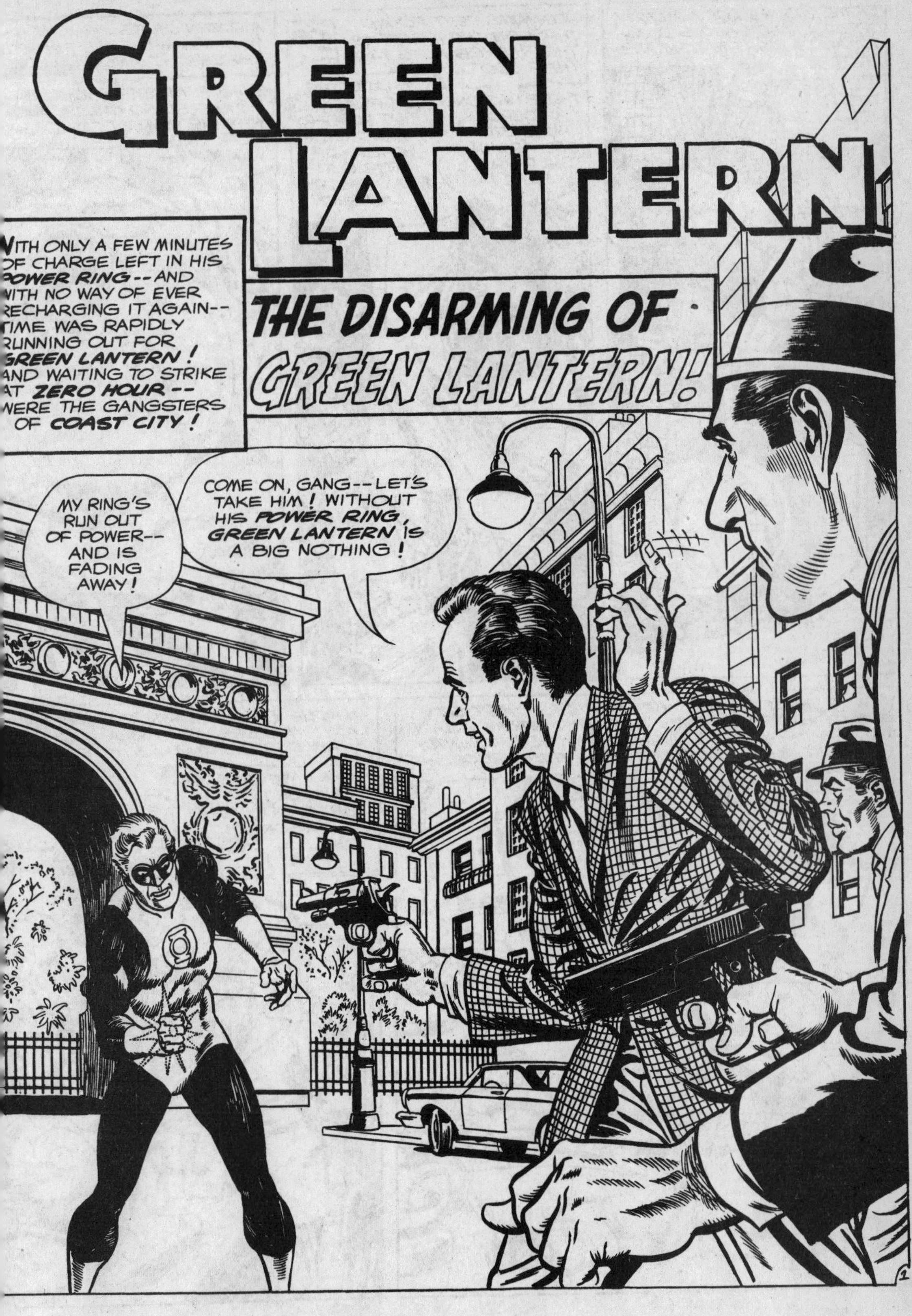
GREEN LANTERN
THE DISARMING OF GREEN LANTERN!
WITH ONLY A FEW MINUTES OF CHARGE LEFT IN HIS POWER RING -- AND WITH NO WAY OF EVER RECHARGING IT AGAIN-- TIME WAS RAPIDLY RUNNING OUT FOR GREEN LANTERN! AND WAITING TO STRIKE AT ZERO HOUR -- WERE THE GANGSTERS OF COAST CITY!
MY RING'S RUN OUT OF POWER-- AND IS FADING AWAY!
COME ON, GANG--LET'S TAKE HIM! WITHOUT HIS POWER RING, GREEN LANTERN IS A BIG NOTHING!

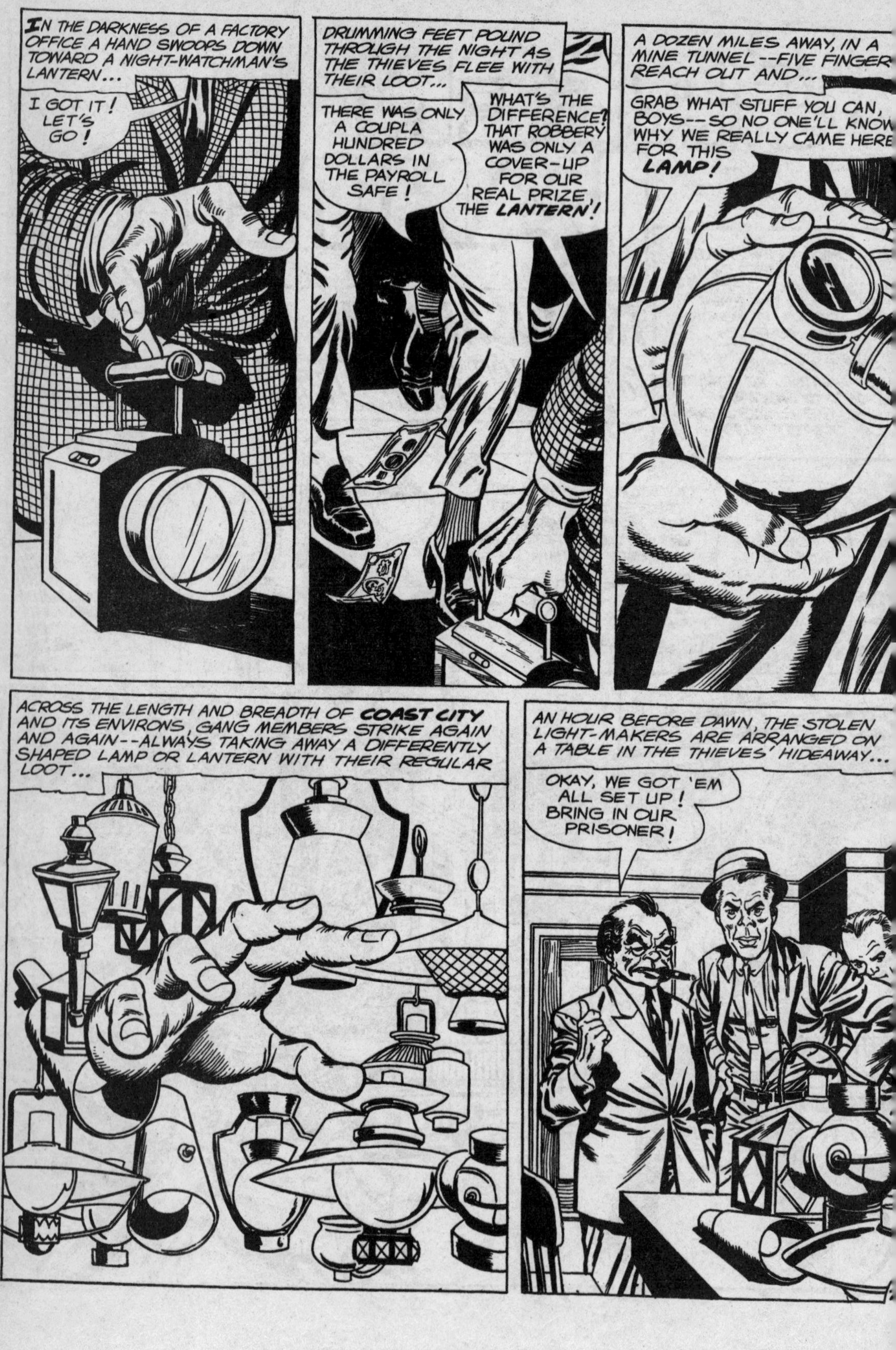
IN THE DARKNESS OF A FACTORY OFFICE A HAND SWOOPS DOWN TOWARD A NIGHT-WATCHMAN'S LANTERN...
I GOT IT! LET'S GO!
DRUMMING FEET POUND THROUGH THE NIGHT AS THE THIEVES FLEE WITH THEIR LOOT...
THERE WAS ONLY A COUPLA HUNDRED DOLLARS IN THE PAYROLL SAFE!
WHAT'S THE DIFFERENCE? THAT ROBBERY WAS ONLY A COVER-UP FOR OUR REAL PRIZE, THE LANTERN!
A DOZEN MILES AWAY, IN A MINE TUNNEL--FIVE FINGER REACH OUT AND...
GRAB WHAT STUFF YOU CAN, BOYS--SO NO ONE'LL KNOW WHY WE REALLY CAME HERE FOR THIS LAMP!
ACROSS THE LENGTH AND BREADTH OF COAST CITY AND ITS ENVIRONS, GANG MEMBERS STRIKE AGAIN AND AGAIN--ALWAYS TAKING AWAY A DIFFERENTLY SHAPED LAMP OR LANTERN WITH THEIR REGULAR LOOT...
AN HOUR BEFORE DAWN, THE STOLEN LIGHT-MAKERS ARE ARRANGED ON A TABLE IN THE THIEVES' HIDEAWAY...
OKAY, WE GOT 'EM ALL SET UP! BRING IN OUR PRISONER!

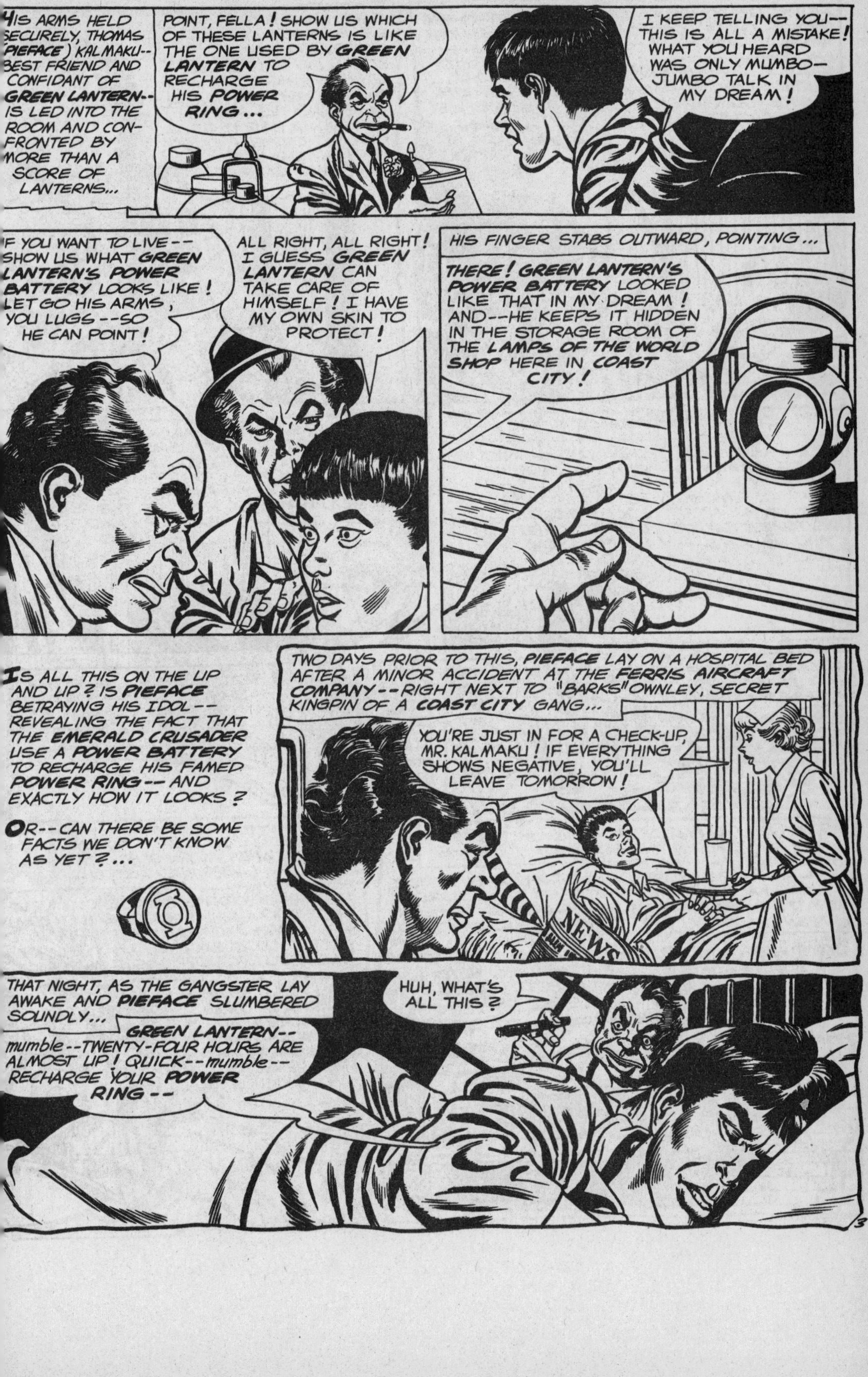
HIS ARMS HELD SECURELY, THOMAS (PIEFACE) KALMAKU--BEST FRIEND AND CONFIDANT OF GREEN LANTERN--IS LED INTO THE ROOM AND CONFRONTED BY MORE THAN A SCORE OF LANTERNS...
POINT, FELLA! SHOW US WHICH OF THESE LANTERNS IS LIKE THE ONE USED BY GREEN LANTERN TO RECHARGE HIS POWER RING...
I KEEP TELLING YOU--THIS IS ALL A MISTAKE! WHAT YOU HEARD WAS ONLY MUMBO-JUMBO TALK IN MY DREAM!
IF YOU WANT TO LIVE--SHOW US WHAT GREEN LANTERN'S POWER BATTERY LOOKS LIKE! LET GO HIS ARMS, YOU LUGS--SO HE CAN POINT!
ALL RIGHT, ALL RIGHT! I GUESS GREEN LANTERN CAN TAKE CARE OF HIMSELF! I HAVE MY OWN SKIN TO PROTECT!
HIS FINGER STABS OUTWARD, POINTING...
THERE! GREEN LANTERN'S POWER BATTERY LOOKED LIKE THAT IN MY DREAM! AND--HE KEEPS IT HIDDEN IN THE STORAGE ROOM OF THE LAMPS OF THE WORLD SHOP HERE IN COAST CITY!
IS ALL THIS ON THE UP AND UP? IS PIEFACE BETRAYING HIS IDOL--REVEALING THE FACT THAT THE EMERALD CRUSADER USE A POWER BATTERY TO RECHARGE HIS FAMED POWER RING--AND EXACTLY HOW IT LOOKS?
OR--CAN THERE BE SOME FACTS WE DON'T KNOW AS YET?...
TWO DAYS PRIOR TO THIS, PIEFACE LAY ON A HOSPITAL BED AFTER A MINOR ACCIDENT AT THE FERRIS AIRCRAFT COMPANY--RIGHT NEXT TO "BARKS" OWNLEY, SECRET KINGPIN OF A COAST CITY GANG...
YOU'RE JUST IN FOR A CHECK-UP, MR. KALMAKU! IF EVERYTHING SHOWS NEGATIVE, YOU'LL LEAVE TOMORROW!
NEWS
THAT NIGHT, AS THE GANGSTER LAY AWAKE AND PIEFACE SLUMBERED SOUNDLY...
HUH, WHAT'S ALL THIS?
GREEN LANTERN--mumble--TWENTY-FOUR HOURS ARE ALMOST UP! QUICK--mumble--RECHARGE YOUR POWER RING--
3

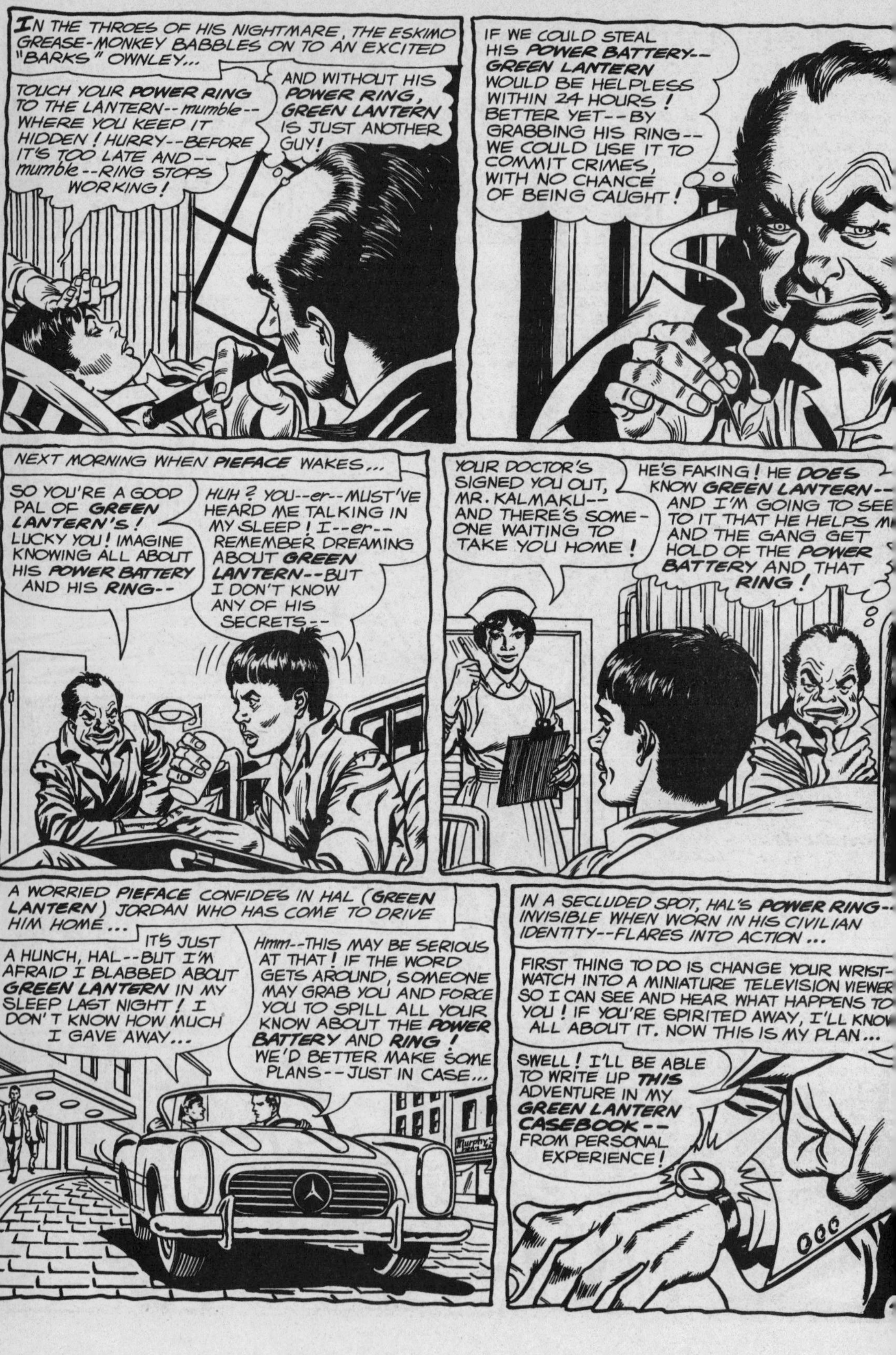
IN THE THROES OF HIS NIGHTMARE, THE ESKIMO GREASE-MONKEY BABBLES ON TO AN EXCITED "BARKS" OWNLEY...
TOUCH YOUR POWER RING TO THE LANTERN--mumble--WHERE YOU KEEP IT HIDDEN! HURRY--BEFORE IT'S TOO LATE AND--mumble--RING STOPS WORKING!
AND WITHOUT HIS POWER RING, GREEN LANTERN IS JUST ANOTHER GUY!
IF WE COULD STEAL HIS POWER BATTERY--GREEN LANTERN WOULD BE HELPLESS WITHIN 24 HOURS! BETTER YET--BY GRABBING HIS RING--WE COULD USE IT TO COMMIT CRIMES, WITH NO CHANCE OF BEING CAUGHT!
NEXT MORNING WHEN PIEFACE WAKES...
SO YOU'RE A GOOD PAL OF GREEN LANTERN'S! LUCKY YOU! IMAGINE KNOWING ALL ABOUT HIS POWER BATTERY AND HIS RING--
HUH? YOU--er--MUST'VE HEARD ME TALKING IN MY SLEEP! I--er--REMEMBER DREAMING ABOUT GREEN LANTERN--BUT I DON'T KNOW ANY OF HIS SECRETS--
YOUR DOCTOR'S SIGNED YOU OUT, MR. KALMAKU--AND THERE'S SOMEONE WAITING TO TAKE YOU HOME!
HE'S FAKING! HE DOES KNOW GREEN LANTERN--AND I'M GOING TO SEE TO IT THAT HE HELPS ME AND THE GANG GET HOLD OF THE POWER BATTERY AND THAT RING!
A WORRIED PIEFACE CONFIDES IN HAL (GREEN LANTERN) JORDAN WHO HAS COME TO DRIVE HIM HOME...
IT'S JUST A HUNCH, HAL--BUT I'M AFRAID I BLABBED ABOUT GREEN LANTERN IN MY SLEEP LAST NIGHT! I DON'T KNOW HOW MUCH I GAVE AWAY...
Hmm--THIS MAY BE SERIOUS AT THAT! IF THE WORD GETS AROUND, SOMEONE MAY GRAB YOU AND FORCE YOU TO SPILL ALL YOUR KNOW ABOUT THE POWER BATTERY AND RING! WE'D BETTER MAKE SOME PLANS--JUST IN CASE...
IN A SECLUDED SPOT, HAL'S POWER RING--INVISIBLE WHEN WORN IN HIS CIVILIAN IDENTITY--FLARES INTO ACTION...
FIRST THING TO DO IS CHANGE YOUR WRIST-WATCH INTO A MINIATURE TELEVISION VIEWER SO I CAN SEE AND HEAR WHAT HAPPENS TO YOU! IF YOU'RE SPIRITED AWAY, I'LL KNOW ALL ABOUT IT. NOW THIS IS MY PLAN...
SWELL! I'LL BE ABLE TO WRITE UP THIS ADVENTURE IN MY GREEN LANTERN CASEBOOK--FROM PERSONAL EXPERIENCE!

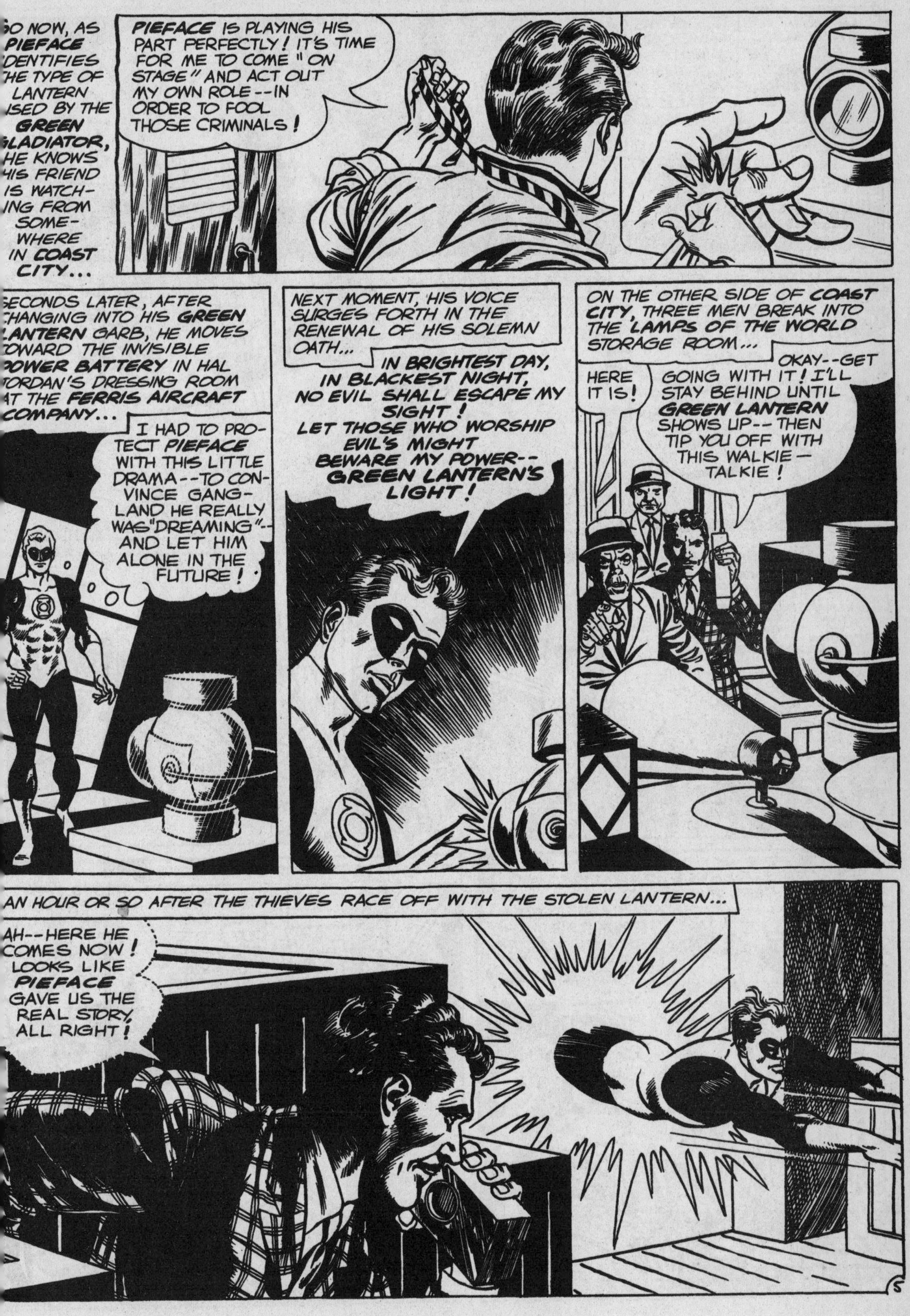
SO NOW, AS PIEFACE IDENTIFIES THE TYPE OF LANTERN USED BY THE GREEN GLADIATOR, HE KNOWS HIS FRIEND IS WATCHING FROM SOMEWHERE IN COAST CITY...
PIEFACE IS PLAYING HIS PART PERFECTLY! IT'S TIME FOR ME TO COME "ON STAGE" AND ACT OUT MY OWN ROLE--IN ORDER TO FOOL THOSE CRIMINALS!
SECONDS LATER, AFTER CHANGING INTO HIS GREEN LANTERN GARB, HE MOVES TOWARD THE INVISIBLE POWER BATTERY IN HAL JORDAN'S DRESSING ROOM AT THE FERRIS AIRCRAFT COMPANY...
I HAD TO PROTECT PIEFACE WITH THIS LITTLE DRAMA--TO CONVINCE GANGLAND HE REALLY WAS "DREAMING"--AND LET HIM ALONE IN THE FUTURE!
NEXT MOMENT, HIS VOICE SURGES FORTH IN THE RENEWAL OF HIS SOLEMN OATH...
IN BRIGHTEST DAY, IN BLACKEST NIGHT, NO EVIL SHALL ESCAPE MY SIGHT! LET THOSE WHO WORSHIP EVIL'S MIGHT BEWARE MY POWER--GREEN LANTERN'S LIGHT!
ON THE OTHER SIDE OF COAST CITY, THREE MEN BREAK INTO THE LAMPS OF THE WORLD STORAGE ROOM...
HERE IT IS!
OKAY--GET GOING WITH IT! I'LL STAY BEHIND UNTIL GREEN LANTERN SHOWS UP--THEN TIP YOU OFF WITH THIS WALKIE-TALKIE!
AN HOUR OR SO AFTER THE THIEVES RACE OFF WITH THE STOLEN LANTERN...
AH--HERE HE COMES NOW! LOOKS LIKE PIEFACE GAVE US THE REAL STORY, ALL RIGHT!
5

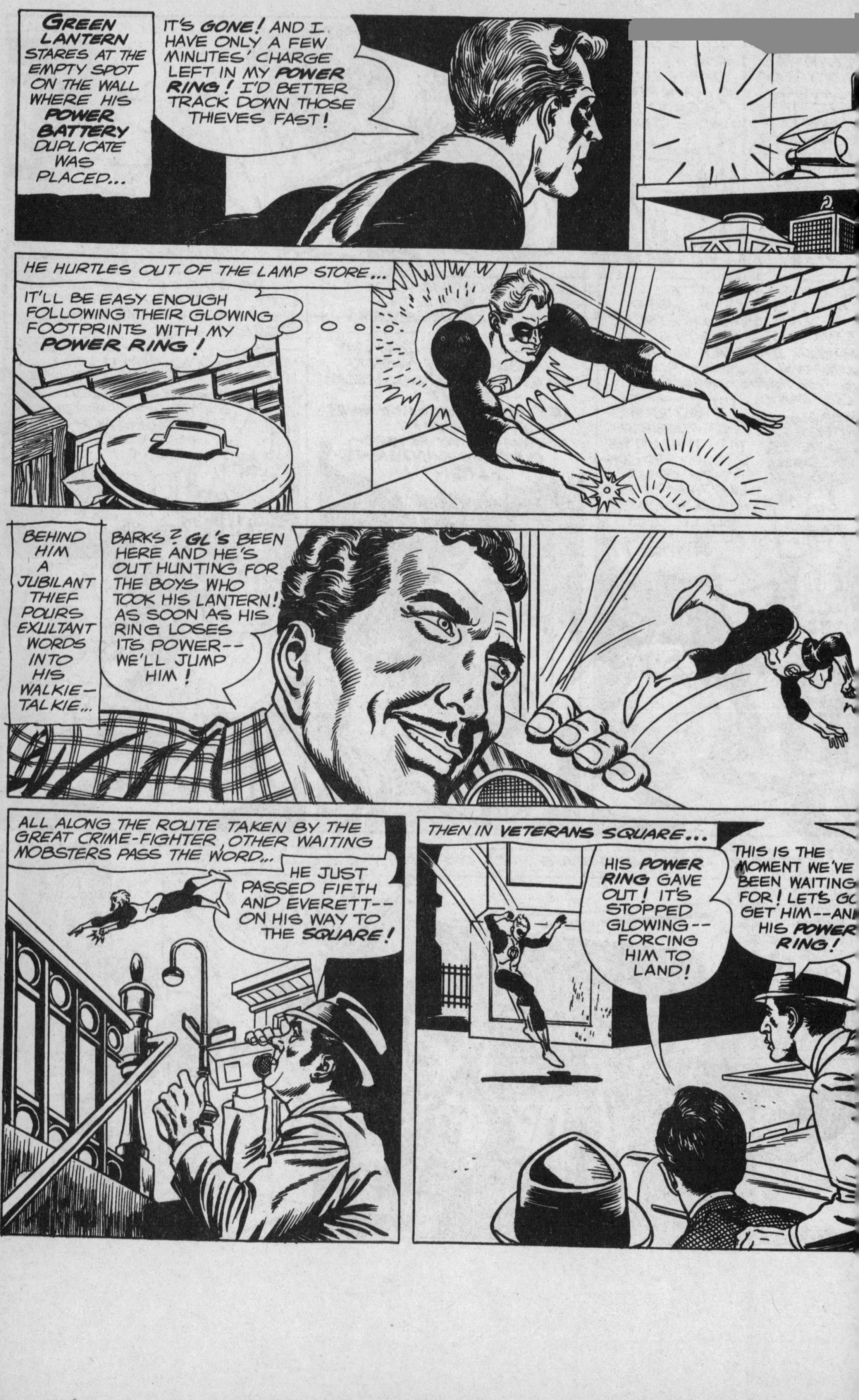
GREEN LANTERN STARES AT THE EMPTY SPOT ON THE WALL WHERE HIS POWER BATTERY DUPLICATE WAS PLACED...
IT'S GONE! AND I HAVE ONLY A FEW MINUTES' CHARGE LEFT IN MY POWER RING! I'D BETTER TRACK DOWN THOSE THIEVES FAST!
HE HURTLES OUT OF THE LAMP STORE...
IT'LL BE EASY ENOUGH FOLLOWING THEIR GLOWING FOOTPRINTS WITH MY POWER RING!
BEHIND HIM A JUBILANT THIEF POURS EXULTANT WORDS INTO HIS WALKIE-TALKIE...
BARKS? GL'S BEEN HERE AND HE'S OUT HUNTING FOR THE BOYS WHO TOOK HIS LANTERN! AS SOON AS HIS RING LOSES ITS POWER-- WE'LL JUMP HIM!
ALL ALONG THE ROUTE TAKEN BY THE GREAT CRIME-FIGHTER, OTHER WAITING MOBSTERS PASS THE WORD...
HE JUST PASSED FIFTH AND EVERETT-- ON HIS WAY TO THE SQUARE!
THEN IN VETERANS SQUARE...
HIS POWER RING GAVE OUT! IT'S STOPPED GLOWING-- FORCING HIM TO LAND!
THIS IS THE MOMENT WE'VE BEEN WAITING FOR! LET'S GO GET HIM--AND HIS POWER RING!

FROM THEIR HIDING PLACE, TWO OF THE HARD-FACED GANGSTERS POUNCE UPON *GREEN LANTERN*...

AS THEY HIT THE GROUND WITH A HARD JAR, A CRY OF ANGUISH ERUPTS FROM THE **EMERALD WARRIOR**...

MY RING--GONE! WITHOUT A POWER CHARGE IN IT, IT CEASED TO EXIST!

HUH? NO MORE **POWER RING?**

AS THE THIRD MOBSTER LEAPS TO PIN THE CRUSADER TO THE GROUND...

RING OR NO RING, WE'RE TAKING YOU BACK TO THE BOSS AND LET HIM DECIDE WHAT TO DO!

A QUICK TWIST OF THE **GREEN GLADIATOR'S** BODY-- AN OUTWARD STAB WITH A HAND-- AND...

I DON'T NEED A **POWER RING** TO HANDLE YOU!

PROPELLED BY A POWERFUL ARM AND LEG, THE MOBSTER KEEPS RIGHT ON GOING --UNTIL ...

⑦

THE THIRD MOBSTER REACHES FOR A GUN AS *GREEN LANTERN* COMES RACING FOR HIM ...

I COULD OVERCOME THESE HOODS EASILY WITH MY *POWER RING* -- BUT I DON'T DARE USE IT! I MUST CONVINCE THE UNDERWORLD THAT WHAT *PIEFACE* SAID TO BARKS OWNLEY WAS NO MORE THAN THE BABBLINGS OF NIGHTMARE!

AS THE GUN COMES OUT, THE *EMERALD WARRIOR* LEAVES HIS FEET...

THE BOSS SAID TO BRING YOU BACK -- BUT HE WON'T CARE WHETHER IT'S *DEAD* OR *ALIVE!*

HIS BODY CURVES IN A HOOK SLIDE! HIS FEET JAB OUT...

UH--GOING TO FALL!

HIS GUN GOES ONE WAY AND THE MOBSTER FLIES THE OTHER...

THIS TAKES CARE OF MY PRESENT OPPOSITION!

AS *GREEN LANTERN* RISES TO HIS FEET...

CAN'T FIGHT THE WHOLE UNDERWORLD WITHOUT MY *POWER RING!* GOT TO BEAT IT-- WHILE I STILL CAN!

I GUESS THIS ACT I'M PUTTING ON FOR THEIR BENEFIT WILL CONVINCE THEM MY RING'S POWERLESS!

OUTDISTANCING HIS PURSUERS, THE *EMERALD GLADIATOR* RACES INTO THE SHADOWS OF A NEARBY ALLEYWAY WHERE...

THOSE GANGSTERS KEPT ME SO BUSY I HAVEN'T HAD A CHANCE TO LOOK IN ON *PIEFACE* AND BARKS FOR SOME TIME!

I SENT CHARLEY AND HIS BOY TO THE *GARDEN PARK BANK,* NOW THAT *GREEN LANTERN* CAN'T STOP US! I'LL SEND YOU FELLOWS TO THE CHARITY CARNIVAL FOR ITS GATE RECEIPTS!

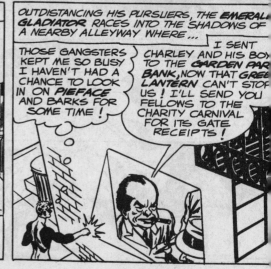

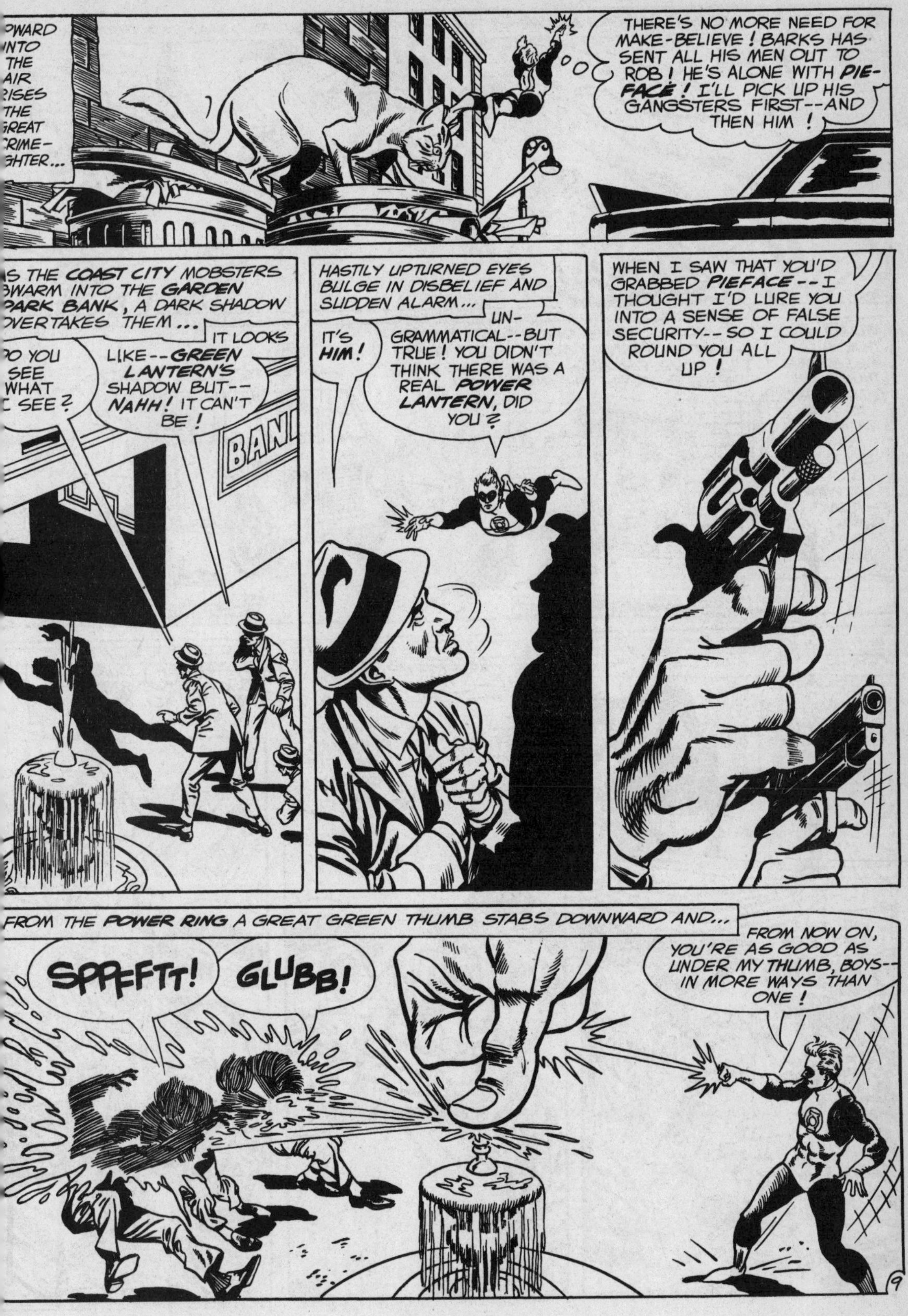
PWARD INTO THE AIR RISES THE GREAT CRIME-GHTER...
THERE'S NO MORE NEED FOR MAKE-BELIEVE! BARKS HAS SENT ALL HIS MEN OUT TO ROB! HE'S ALONE WITH PIE-FACE! I'LL PICK UP HIS GANGSTERS FIRST--AND THEN HIM!
S THE COAST CITY MOBSTERS SWARM INTO THE GARDEN PARK BANK, A DARK SHADOW OVERTAKES THEM...
DO YOU SEE WHAT I SEE?
IT LOOKS LIKE--GREEN LANTERN'S SHADOW BUT--NAHH! IT CAN'T BE!
BAN
HASTILY UPTURNED EYES BULGE IN DISBELIEF AND SUDDEN ALARM...
IT'S HIM!
UN-GRAMMATICAL--BUT TRUE! YOU DIDN'T THINK THERE WAS A REAL POWER LANTERN, DID YOU?
WHEN I SAW THAT YOU'D GRABBED PIEFACE--I THOUGHT I'D LURE YOU INTO A SENSE OF FALSE SECURITY--SO I COULD ROUND YOU ALL UP!
FROM THE POWER RING A GREAT GREEN THUMB STABS DOWNWARD AND...
SPPFFTT!
GLUBB!
FROM NOW ON, YOU'RE AS GOOD AS UNDER MY THUMB, BOYS--IN MORE WAYS THAN ONE!
9

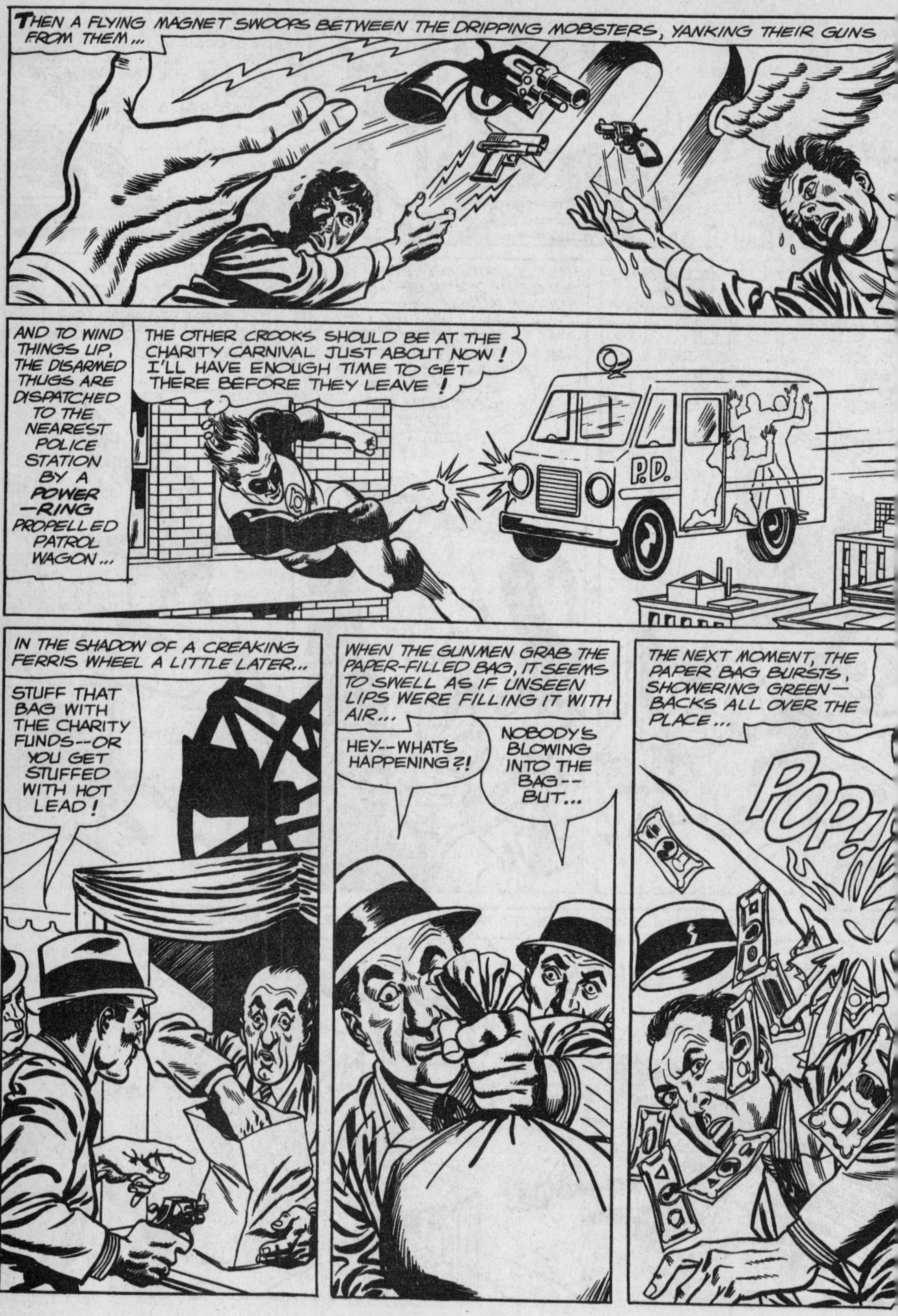
THEN A FLYING MAGNET SWOOPS BETWEEN THE DRIPPING MOBSTERS, YANKING THEIR GUNS FROM THEM...
AND TO WIND THINGS UP, THE DISARMED THUGS ARE DISPATCHED TO THE NEAREST POLICE STATION BY A POWER-RING PROPELLED PATROL WAGON...
THE OTHER CROOKS SHOULD BE AT THE CHARITY CARNIVAL JUST ABOUT NOW! I'LL HAVE ENOUGH TIME TO GET THERE BEFORE THEY LEAVE!
P.D.
IN THE SHADOW OF A CREAKING FERRIS WHEEL A LITTLE LATER...
STUFF THAT BAG WITH THE CHARITY FUNDS--OR YOU GET STUFFED WITH HOT LEAD!
WHEN THE GUNMEN GRAB THE PAPER-FILLED BAG, IT SEEMS TO SWELL AS IF UNSEEN LIPS WERE FILLING IT WITH AIR...
HEY--WHAT'S HAPPENING?!
NOBODY'S BLOWING INTO THE BAG--BUT...
THE NEXT MOMENT, THE PAPER BAG BURSTS, SHOWERING GREEN-BACKS ALL OVER THE PLACE...
POP!

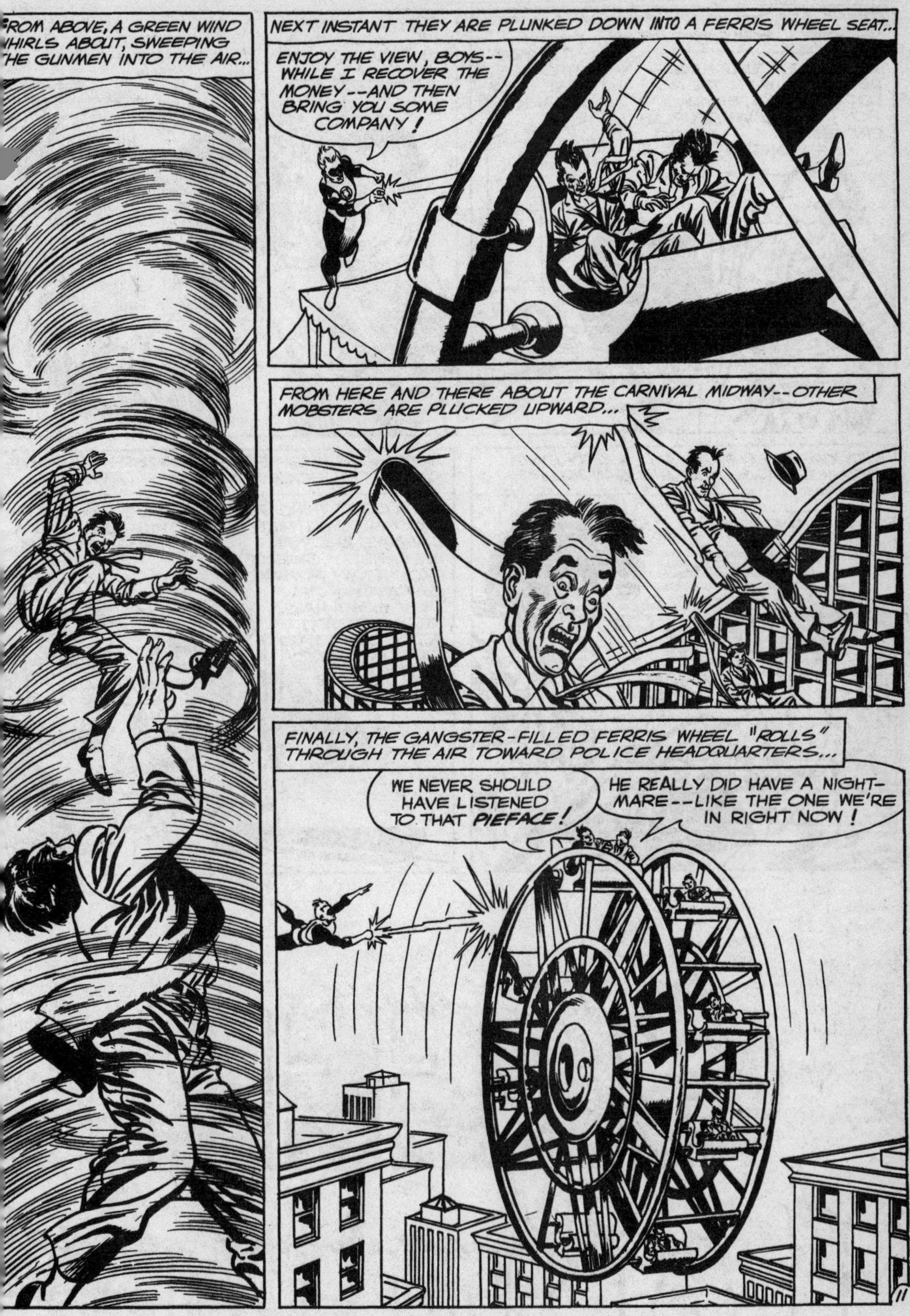
FROM ABOVE, A GREEN WIND WHIRLS ABOUT, SWEEPING THE GUNMEN INTO THE AIR...
NEXT INSTANT THEY ARE PLUNKED DOWN INTO A FERRIS WHEEL SEAT...
ENJOY THE VIEW, BOYS-- WHILE I RECOVER THE MONEY--AND THEN BRING YOU SOME COMPANY!
FROM HERE AND THERE ABOUT THE CARNIVAL MIDWAY--OTHER MOBSTERS ARE PLUCKED UPWARD...
FINALLY, THE GANGSTER-FILLED FERRIS WHEEL "ROLLS" THROUGH THE AIR TOWARD POLICE HEADQUARTERS...
WE NEVER SHOULD HAVE LISTENED TO THAT PIEFACE!
HE REALLY DID HAVE A NIGHT-MARE--LIKE THE ONE WE'RE IN RIGHT NOW!
11

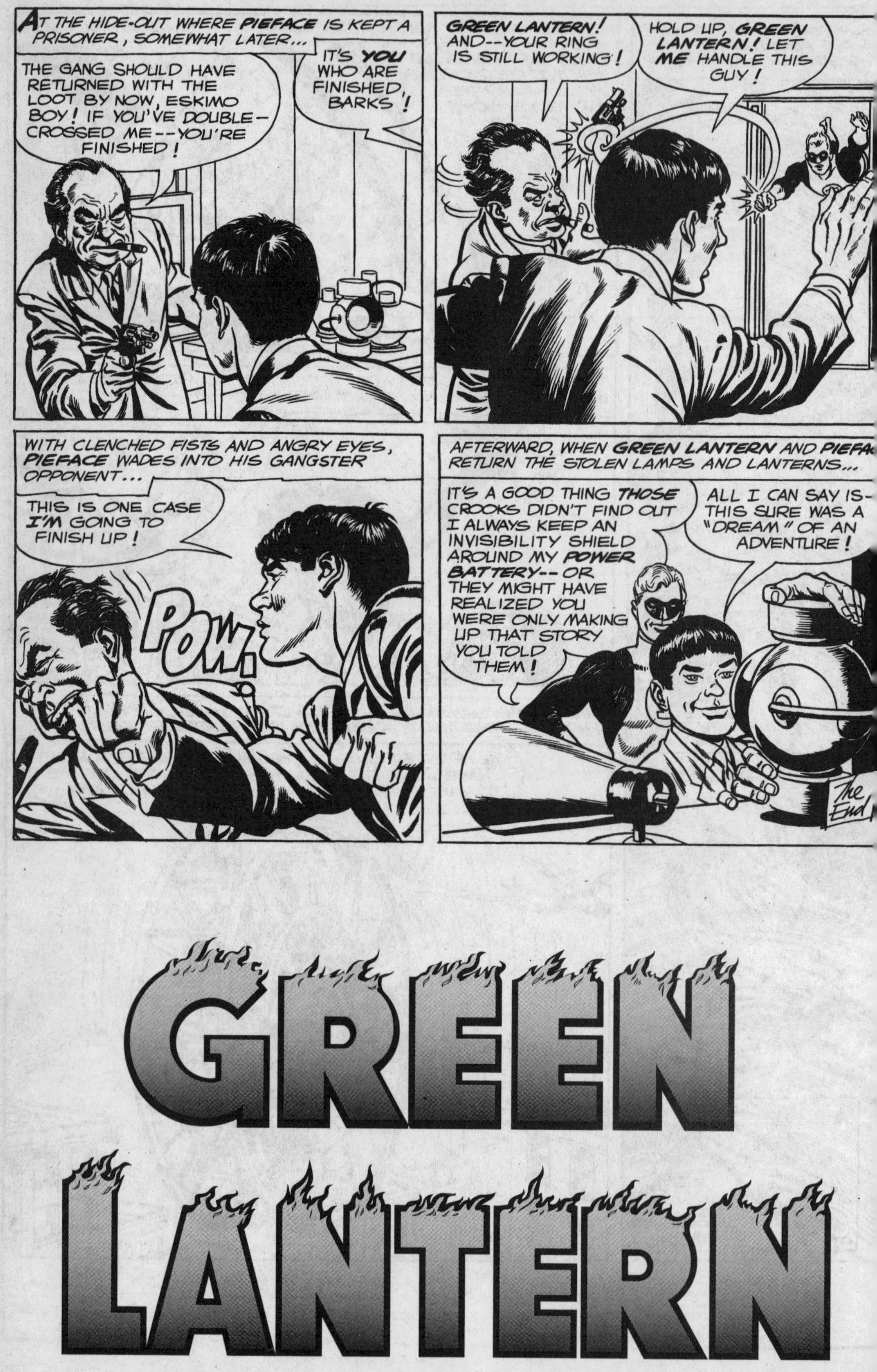
AT THE HIDE-OUT WHERE PIEFACE IS KEPT A PRISONER, SOMEWHAT LATER...
THE GANG SHOULD HAVE RETURNED WITH THE LOOT BY NOW, ESKIMO BOY! IF YOU'VE DOUBLE-CROSSED ME--YOU'RE FINISHED!
IT'S YOU WHO ARE FINISHED, BARKS!
GREEN LANTERN! AND--YOUR RING IS STILL WORKING!
HOLD UP, GREEN LANTERN! LET ME HANDLE THIS GUY!
WITH CLENCHED FISTS AND ANGRY EYES, PIEFACE WADES INTO HIS GANGSTER OPPONENT...
THIS IS ONE CASE I'M GOING TO FINISH UP!
POW!
AFTERWARD, WHEN GREEN LANTERN AND PIEFACE RETURN THE STOLEN LAMPS AND LANTERNS...
IT'S A GOOD THING THOSE CROOKS DIDN'T FIND OUT I ALWAYS KEEP AN INVISIBILITY SHIELD AROUND MY POWER BATTERY--OR THEY MIGHT HAVE REALIZED YOU WERE ONLY MAKING UP THAT STORY YOU TOLD THEM!
ALL I CAN SAY IS--THIS SURE WAS A "DREAM" OF AN ADVENTURE!
The End

GREEN LANTERN

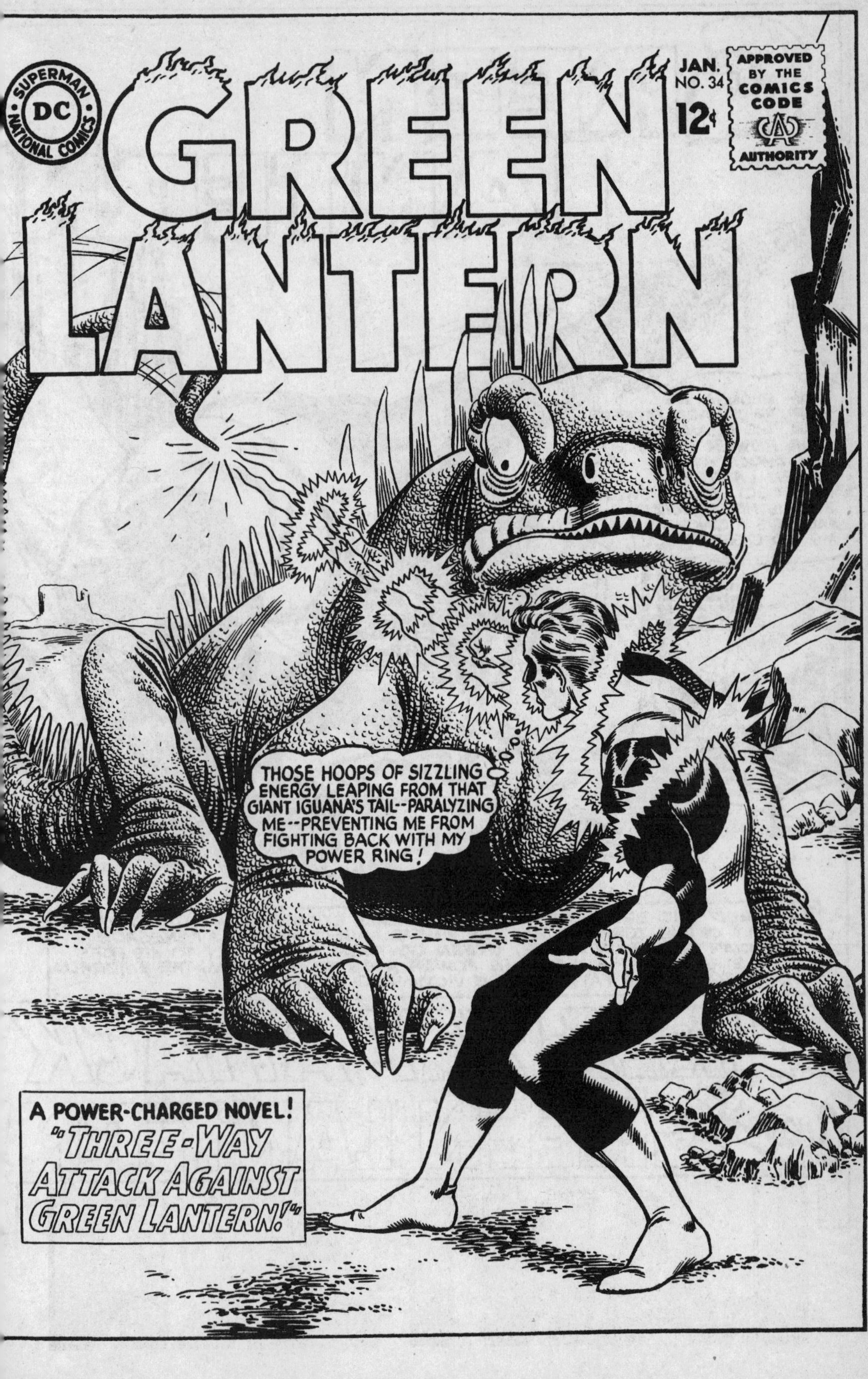
SUPERMAN DC NATIONAL COMICS
GREEN LANTERN
JAN. NO. 34
12¢
APPROVED BY THE COMICS CODE AUTHORITY
THOSE HOOPS OF SIZZLING ENERGY LEAPING FROM THAT GIANT IGUANA'S TAIL--PARALYZING ME--PREVENTING ME FROM FIGHTING BACK WITH MY POWER RING!
A POWER-CHARGED NOVEL! "THREE-WAY ATTACK AGAINST GREEN LANTERN!"

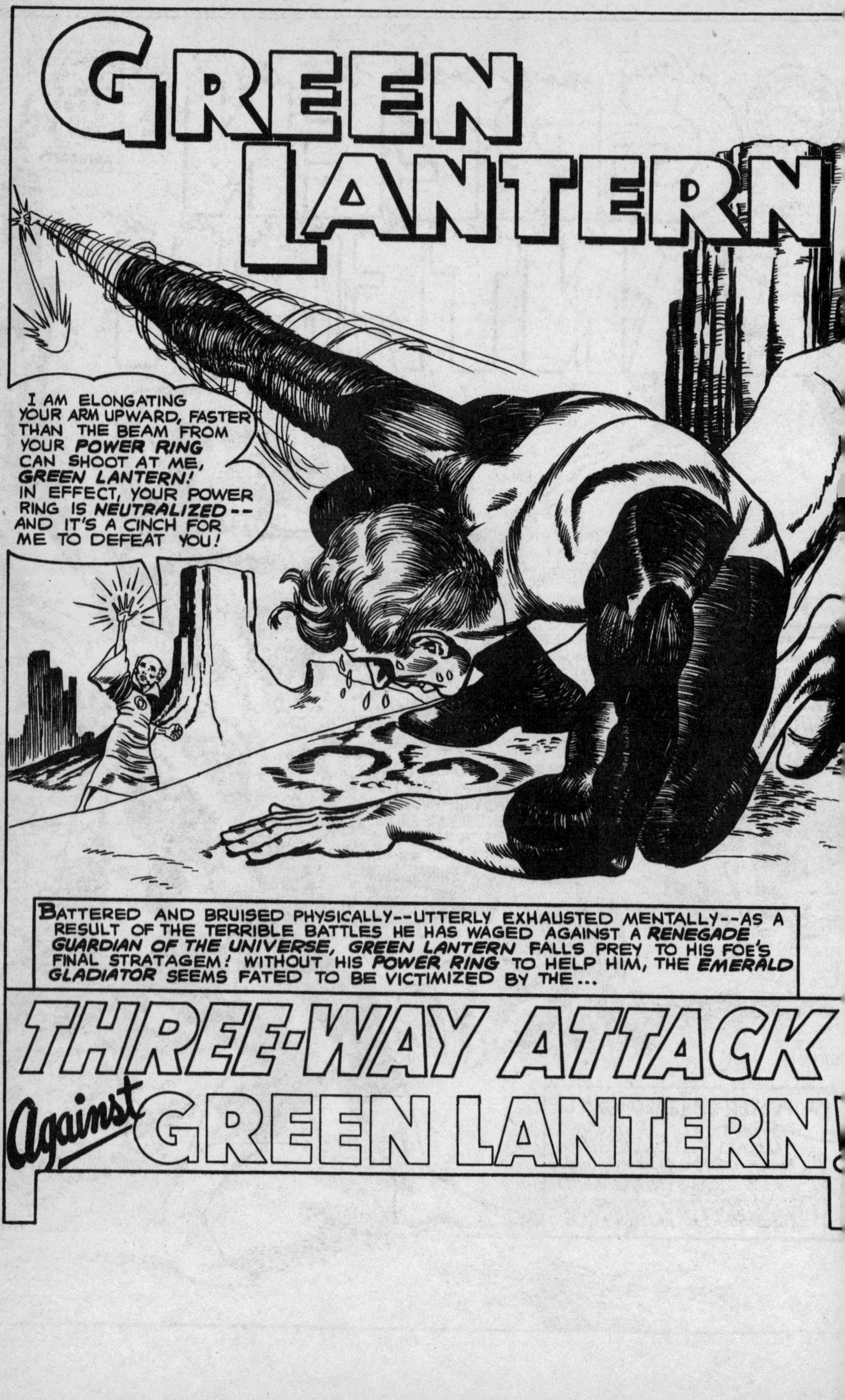
GREEN LANTERN
I AM ELONGATING YOUR ARM UPWARD, FASTER THAN THE BEAM FROM YOUR POWER RING CAN SHOOT AT ME, GREEN LANTERN! IN EFFECT, YOUR POWER RING IS NEUTRALIZED-- AND IT'S A CINCH FOR ME TO DEFEAT YOU!
BATTERED AND BRUISED PHYSICALLY--UTTERLY EXHAUSTED MENTALLY--AS A RESULT OF THE TERRIBLE BATTLES HE HAS WAGED AGAINST A RENEGADE GUARDIAN OF THE UNIVERSE, GREEN LANTERN FALLS PREY TO HIS FOE'S FINAL STRATAGEM! WITHOUT HIS POWER RING TO HELP HIM, THE EMERALD GLADIATOR SEEMS FATED TO BE VICTIMIZED BY THE...
THREE-WAY ATTACK Against GREEN LANTERN!

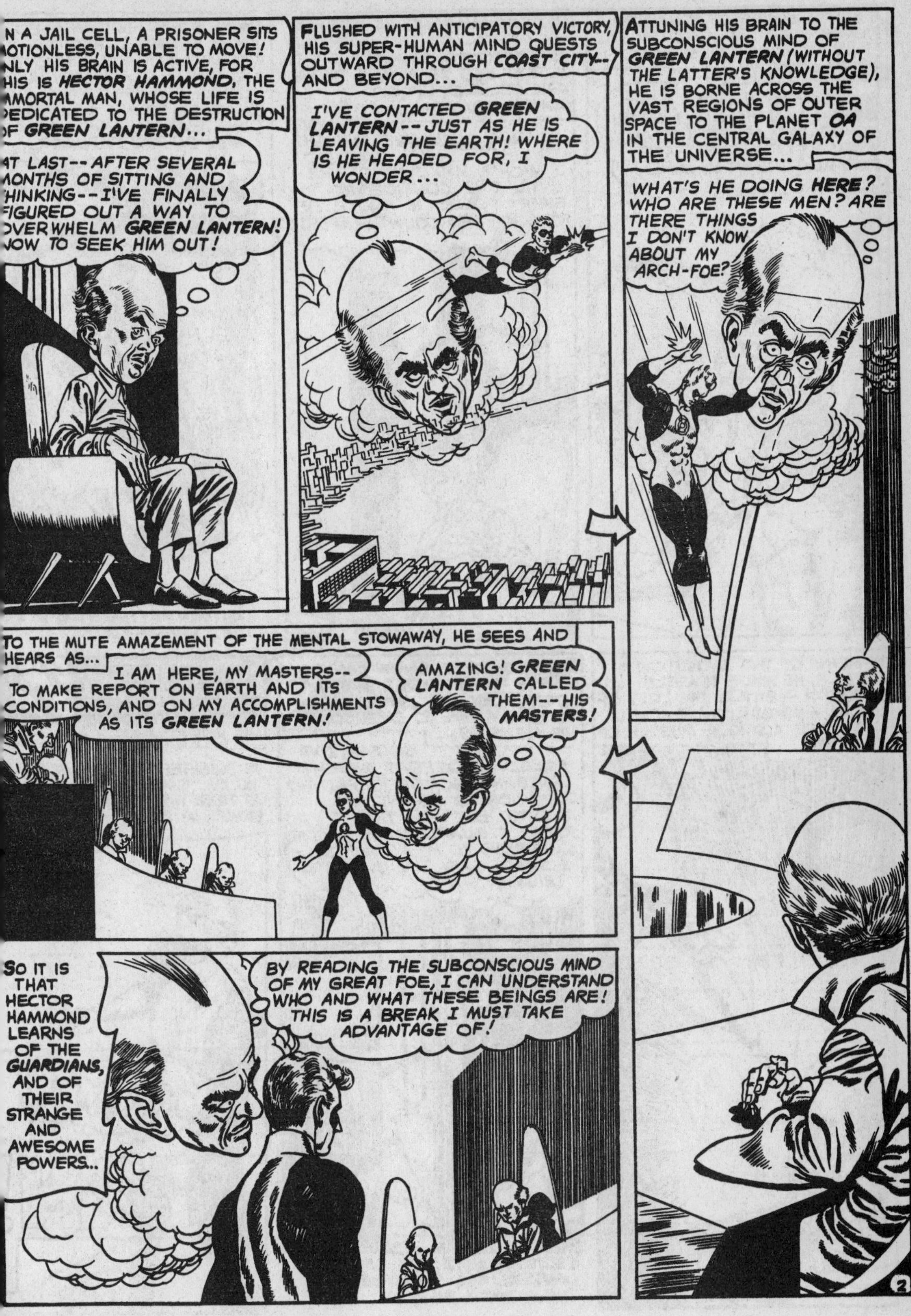
N A JAIL CELL, A PRISONER SITS OTIONLESS, UNABLE TO MOVE! NLY HIS BRAIN IS ACTIVE, FOR HIS IS HECTOR HAMMOND, THE AMORTAL MAN, WHOSE LIFE IS EDICATED TO THE DESTRUCTION OF GREEN LANTERN...
AT LAST--AFTER SEVERAL MONTHS OF SITTING AND HINKING--I'VE FINALLY FIGURED OUT A WAY TO OVERWHELM GREEN LANTERN! NOW TO SEEK HIM OUT!
FLUSHED WITH ANTICIPATORY VICTORY, HIS SUPER-HUMAN MIND QUESTS OUTWARD THROUGH COAST CITY-- AND BEYOND...
I'VE CONTACTED GREEN LANTERN--JUST AS HE IS LEAVING THE EARTH! WHERE IS HE HEADED FOR, I WONDER...
ATTUNING HIS BRAIN TO THE SUBCONSCIOUS MIND OF GREEN LANTERN (WITHOUT THE LATTER'S KNOWLEDGE), HE IS BORNE ACROSS THE VAST REGIONS OF OUTER SPACE TO THE PLANET OA IN THE CENTRAL GALAXY OF THE UNIVERSE...
WHAT'S HE DOING HERE? WHO ARE THESE MEN? ARE THERE THINGS I DON'T KNOW ABOUT MY ARCH-FOE?
TO THE MUTE AMAZEMENT OF THE MENTAL STOWAWAY, HE SEES AND HEARS AS...
I AM HERE, MY MASTERS-- TO MAKE REPORT ON EARTH AND ITS CONDITIONS, AND ON MY ACCOMPLISHMENTS AS ITS GREEN LANTERN!
AMAZING! GREEN LANTERN CALLED THEM--HIS MASTERS!
SO IT IS THAT HECTOR HAMMOND LEARNS OF THE GUARDIANS, AND OF THEIR STRANGE AND AWESOME POWERS..
BY READING THE SUBCONSCIOUS MIND OF MY GREAT FOE, I CAN UNDERSTAND WHO AND WHAT THESE BEINGS ARE! THIS IS A BREAK I MUST TAKE ADVANTAGE OF!
2

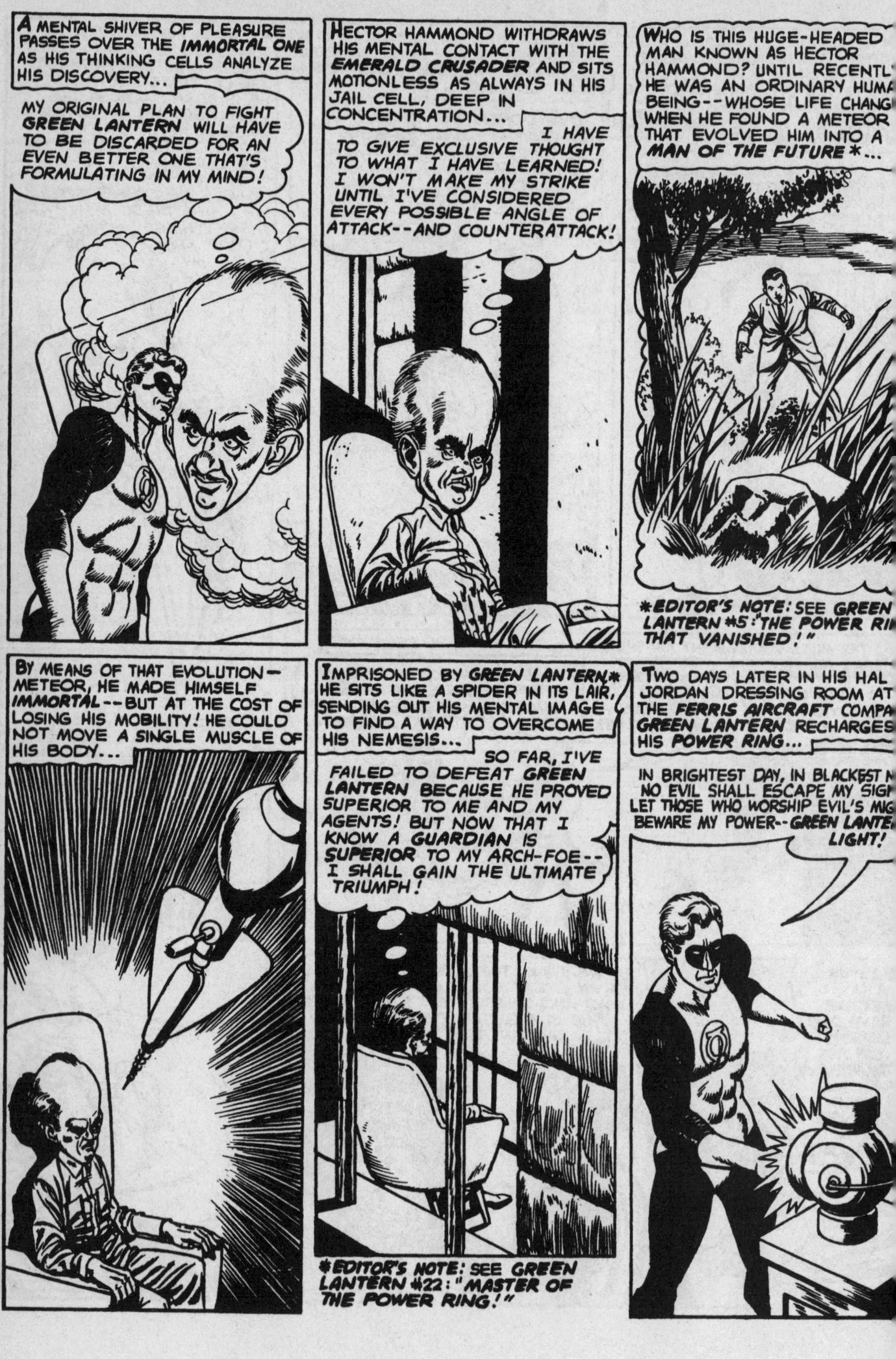
A MENTAL SHIVER OF PLEASURE PASSES OVER THE IMMORTAL ONE AS HIS THINKING CELLS ANALYZE HIS DISCOVERY...
MY ORIGINAL PLAN TO FIGHT GREEN LANTERN WILL HAVE TO BE DISCARDED FOR AN EVEN BETTER ONE THAT'S FORMULATING IN MY MIND!
HECTOR HAMMOND WITHDRAWS HIS MENTAL CONTACT WITH THE EMERALD CRUSADER AND SITS MOTIONLESS AS ALWAYS IN HIS JAIL CELL, DEEP IN CONCENTRATION...
I HAVE TO GIVE EXCLUSIVE THOUGHT TO WHAT I HAVE LEARNED! I WON'T MAKE MY STRIKE UNTIL I'VE CONSIDERED EVERY POSSIBLE ANGLE OF ATTACK--AND COUNTERATTACK!
WHO IS THIS HUGE-HEADED MAN KNOWN AS HECTOR HAMMOND? UNTIL RECENTL HE WAS AN ORDINARY HUMA BEING--WHOSE LIFE CHANG WHEN HE FOUND A METEOR THAT EVOLVED HIM INTO A MAN OF THE FUTURE*...
*EDITOR'S NOTE: SEE GREEN LANTERN #5: "THE POWER RI THAT VANISHED!"
BY MEANS OF THAT EVOLUTION-METEOR, HE MADE HIMSELF IMMORTAL--BUT AT THE COST OF LOSING HIS MOBILITY! HE COULD NOT MOVE A SINGLE MUSCLE OF HIS BODY...
IMPRISONED BY GREEN LANTERN,* HE SITS LIKE A SPIDER IN ITS LAIR, SENDING OUT HIS MENTAL IMAGE TO FIND A WAY TO OVERCOME HIS NEMESIS...
SO FAR, I'VE FAILED TO DEFEAT GREEN LANTERN BECAUSE HE PROVED SUPERIOR TO ME AND MY AGENTS! BUT NOW THAT I KNOW A GUARDIAN IS SUPERIOR TO MY ARCH-FOE--I SHALL GAIN THE ULTIMATE TRIUMPH!
*EDITOR'S NOTE: SEE GREEN LANTERN #22: "MASTER OF THE POWER RING!"
TWO DAYS LATER IN HIS HAL JORDAN DRESSING ROOM AT THE FERRIS AIRCRAFT COMPA GREEN LANTERN RECHARGES HIS POWER RING...
IN BRIGHTEST DAY, IN BLACKEST N NO EVIL SHALL ESCAPE MY SIGH LET THOSE WHO WORSHIP EVIL'S MIG BEWARE MY POWER--GREEN LANTE LIGHT!

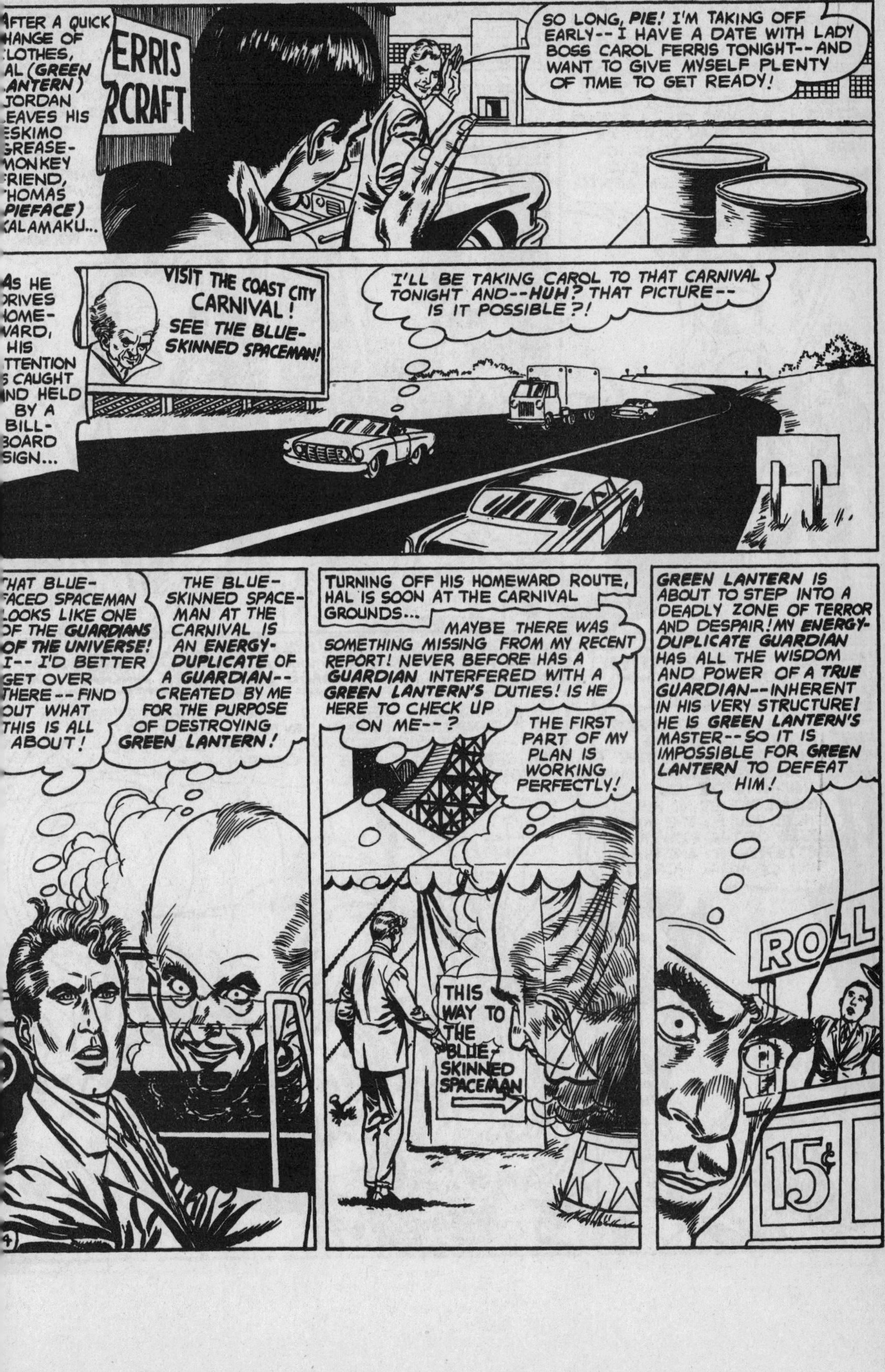
AFTER A QUICK HANGE OF CLOTHES, AL (GREEN ANTERN) JORDAN LEAVES HIS ESKIMO GREASE-MONKEY FRIEND, THOMAS (PIEFACE) KALAMAKU...
ERRIS RCRAFT
SO LONG, PIE! I'M TAKING OFF EARLY-- I HAVE A DATE WITH LADY BOSS CAROL FERRIS TONIGHT-- AND WANT TO GIVE MYSELF PLENTY OF TIME TO GET READY!
AS HE DRIVES HOME-WARD, HIS TTENTION S CAUGHT AND HELD BY A BILL-BOARD SIGN...
VISIT THE COAST CITY CARNIVAL! SEE THE BLUE-SKINNED SPACEMAN!
I'LL BE TAKING CAROL TO THAT CARNIVAL TONIGHT AND--HUH? THAT PICTURE-- IS IT POSSIBLE?!
THAT BLUE-FACED SPACEMAN LOOKS LIKE ONE OF THE GUARDIANS OF THE UNIVERSE! I-- I'D BETTER GET OVER THERE-- FIND OUT WHAT THIS IS ALL ABOUT!
THE BLUE-SKINNED SPACE-MAN AT THE CARNIVAL IS AN ENERGY-DUPLICATE OF A GUARDIAN-- CREATED BY ME FOR THE PURPOSE OF DESTROYING GREEN LANTERN!
TURNING OFF HIS HOMEWARD ROUTE, HAL IS SOON AT THE CARNIVAL GROUNDS...
MAYBE THERE WAS SOMETHING MISSING FROM MY RECENT REPORT! NEVER BEFORE HAS A GUARDIAN INTERFERED WITH A GREEN LANTERN'S DUTIES! IS HE HERE TO CHECK UP ON ME--?
THE FIRST PART OF MY PLAN IS WORKING PERFECTLY!
THIS WAY TO THE BLUE-SKINNED SPACEMAN
GREEN LANTERN IS ABOUT TO STEP INTO A DEADLY ZONE OF TERROR AND DESPAIR! MY ENERGY-DUPLICATE GUARDIAN HAS ALL THE WISDOM AND POWER OF A TRUE GUARDIAN--INHERENT IN HIS VERY STRUCTURE! HE IS GREEN LANTERN'S MASTER--SO IT IS IMPOSSIBLE FOR GREEN LANTERN TO DEFEAT HIM!
ROLL
15¢

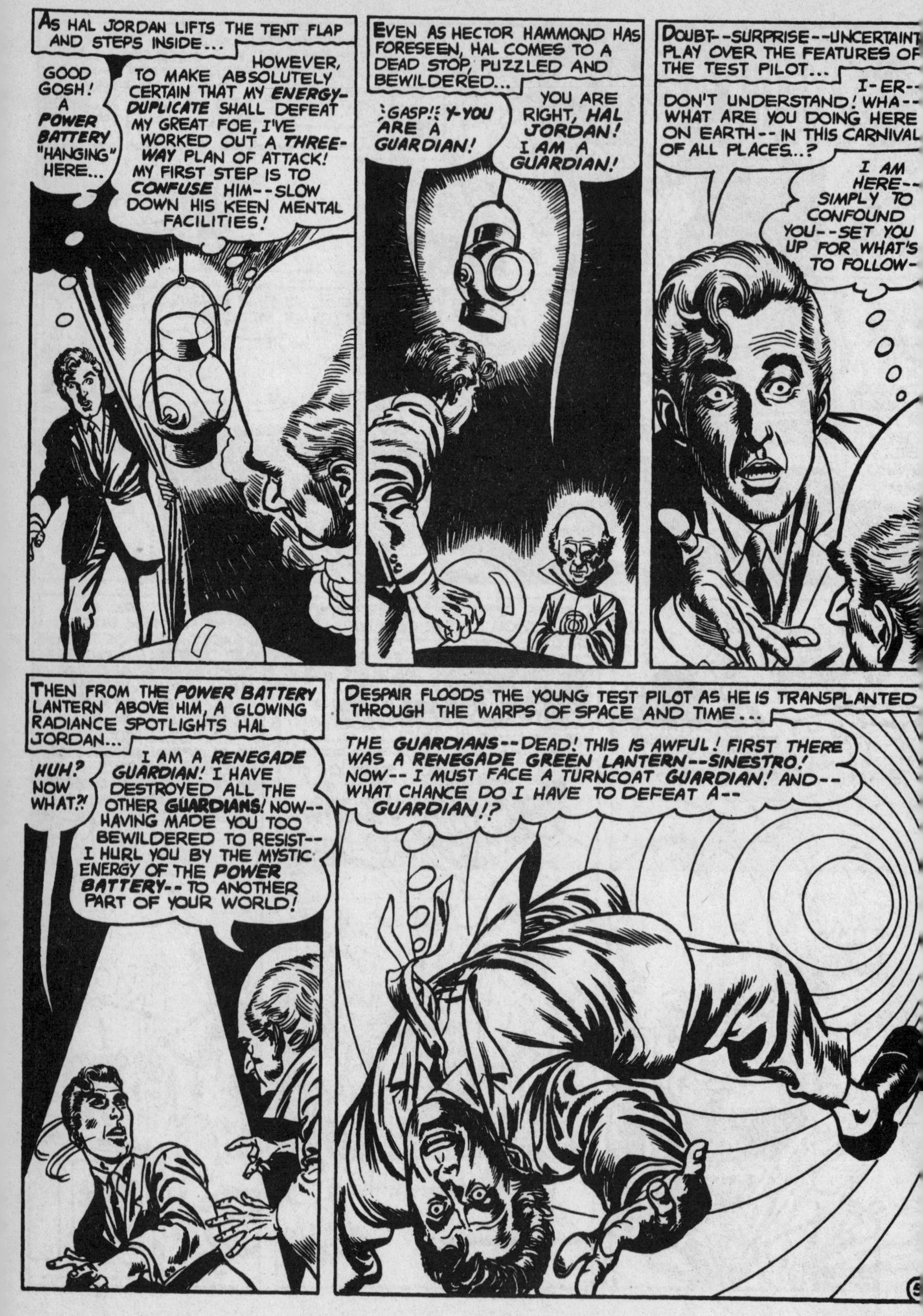
AS HAL JORDAN LIFTS THE TENT FLAP AND STEPS INSIDE...
GOOD GOSH! A POWER BATTERY "HANGING" HERE...
HOWEVER, TO MAKE ABSOLUTELY CERTAIN THAT MY ENERGY-DUPLICATE SHALL DEFEAT MY GREAT FOE, I'VE WORKED OUT A THREE-WAY PLAN OF ATTACK! MY FIRST STEP IS TO CONFUSE HIM--SLOW DOWN HIS KEEN MENTAL FACILITIES!
EVEN AS HECTOR HAMMOND HAS FORESEEN, HAL COMES TO A DEAD STOP, PUZZLED AND BEWILDERED...
GASP!! Y-YOU ARE A GUARDIAN!
YOU ARE RIGHT, HAL JORDAN! I AM A GUARDIAN!
DOUBT--SURPRISE--UNCERTAINT PLAY OVER THE FEATURES OF THE TEST PILOT...
I-ER-- DON'T UNDERSTAND! WHA-- WHAT ARE YOU DOING HERE ON EARTH--IN THIS CARNIVAL OF ALL PLACES..?
I AM HERE-- SIMPLY TO CONFOUND YOU--SET YOU UP FOR WHAT'S TO FOLLOW-
THEN FROM THE POWER BATTERY LANTERN ABOVE HIM, A GLOWING RADIANCE SPOTLIGHTS HAL JORDAN...
HUH? NOW WHAT?!
I AM A RENEGADE GUARDIAN! I HAVE DESTROYED ALL THE OTHER GUARDIANS! NOW--HAVING MADE YOU TOO BEWILDERED TO RESIST--I HURL YOU BY THE MYSTIC ENERGY OF THE POWER BATTERY--TO ANOTHER PART OF YOUR WORLD!
DESPAIR FLOODS THE YOUNG TEST PILOT AS HE IS TRANSPLANTED THROUGH THE WARPS OF SPACE AND TIME...
THE GUARDIANS--DEAD! THIS IS AWFUL! FIRST THERE WAS A RENEGADE GREEN LANTERN--SINESTRO! NOW--I MUST FACE A TURNCOAT GUARDIAN! AND--WHAT CHANCE DO I HAVE TO DEFEAT A--GUARDIAN!?

AS THE BATTERY LIGHT FADES OUT, HE FINDS HIMSELF STANDING IN A GREAT FOREST...

WE ARE IN THE RAIN FORESTS OF SOUTH AMERICA! HERE I SHALL PUT INTO ACTION THE SECOND STEP OF MY THREE-WAY PLAN TO DEFEAT YOU!

THE ENERGY-DUPLICATE GUARDIAN WILL NOW PHYSICALLY EXHAUST GREEN LANTERN SO THAT HE WILL BE UNABLE TO DEFEND HIMSELF WHEN IT COMES TIME FOR THE FINISHING BLOW!

THE GUARDIAN GESTURES AND...

BUT FIRST-- SINCE I WANT TO DEFEAT YOU AS GREEN LANTERN AND NOT AS HAL JORDAN--

GOOD GOSH! HE'S TRANS-FORMED ME INTO MY ALTER EGO!

OKAY, IT'S TIME FOR ME TO DO SOME "DEFEATING" OF MY OWN!

DEFEAT ME? IMPOSSIBLE! MY ENTIRE BODY IS FILLED WITH THE SAME STRANGE AND MYSTIC ENERGIES AFTER WHICH YOUR POWER BATTERY IS FASHIONED! IN SEEKING TO DUPLICATE THOSE ENERGIES--WE HAD TO USE ARTIFICIAL MEANS...

BUT BECAUSE OF THE IMPURITIES IN THOSE ARTIFICIAL MEANS-- THE POWER BATTERIES HAVE A WEAKNESS TO YELLOW! WE GUARDIANS HAVE NO SUCH WEAKNESS! WE ARE PERFECT POWER BATTERIES! SO-- YOU CANNOT POSSIBLY DEFEAT ME!

GREEN LANTERN

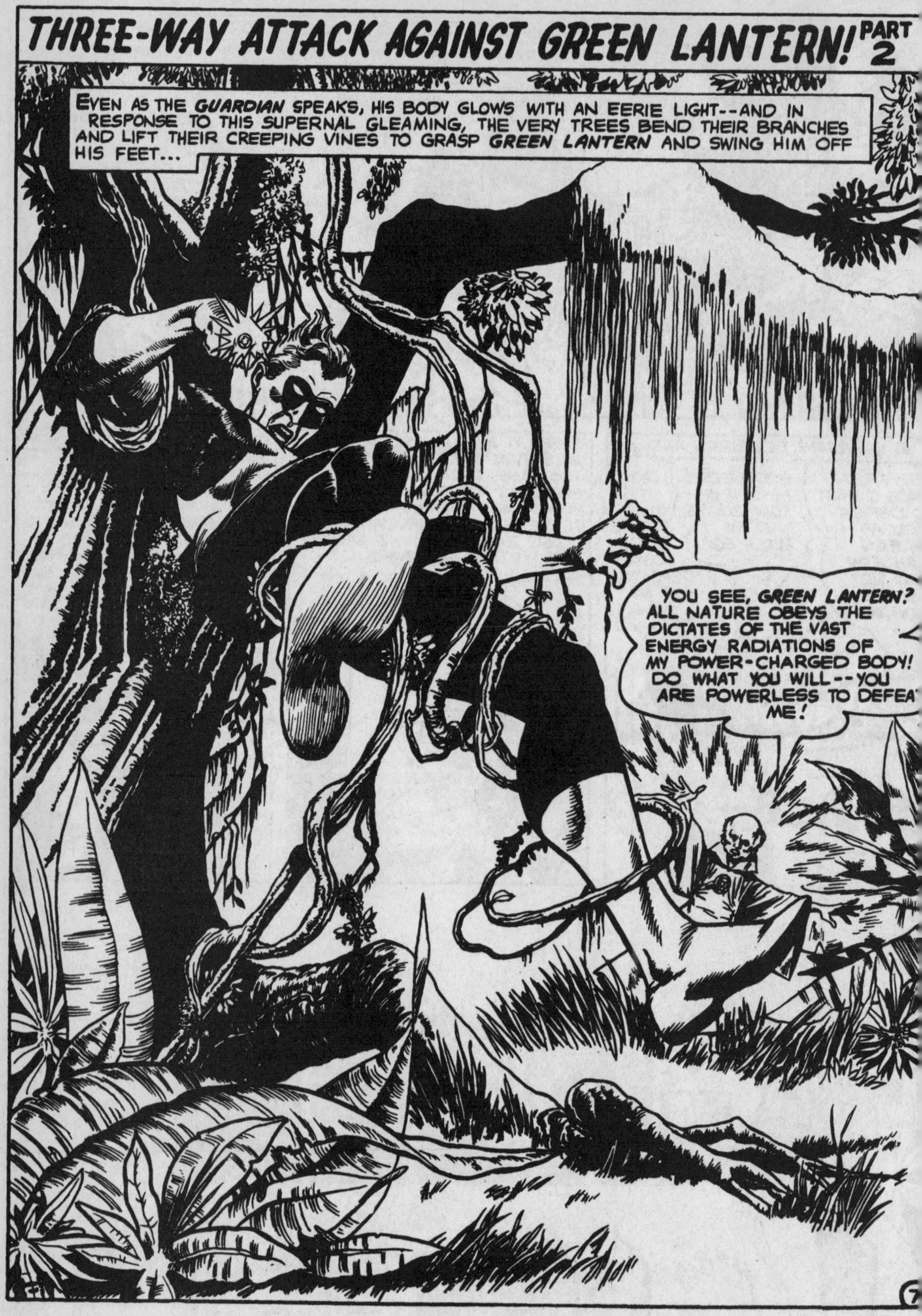
THREE-WAY ATTACK AGAINST GREEN LANTERN! PART 2
EVEN AS THE GUARDIAN SPEAKS, HIS BODY GLOWS WITH AN EERIE LIGHT--AND IN RESPONSE TO THIS SUPERNAL GLEAMING, THE VERY TREES BEND THEIR BRANCHES AND LIFT THEIR CREEPING VINES TO GRASP GREEN LANTERN AND SWING HIM OFF HIS FEET...
YOU SEE, GREEN LANTERN? ALL NATURE OBEYS THE DICTATES OF THE VAST ENERGY RADIATIONS OF MY POWER-CHARGED BODY! DO WHAT YOU WILL--YOU ARE POWERLESS TO DEFEA ME!

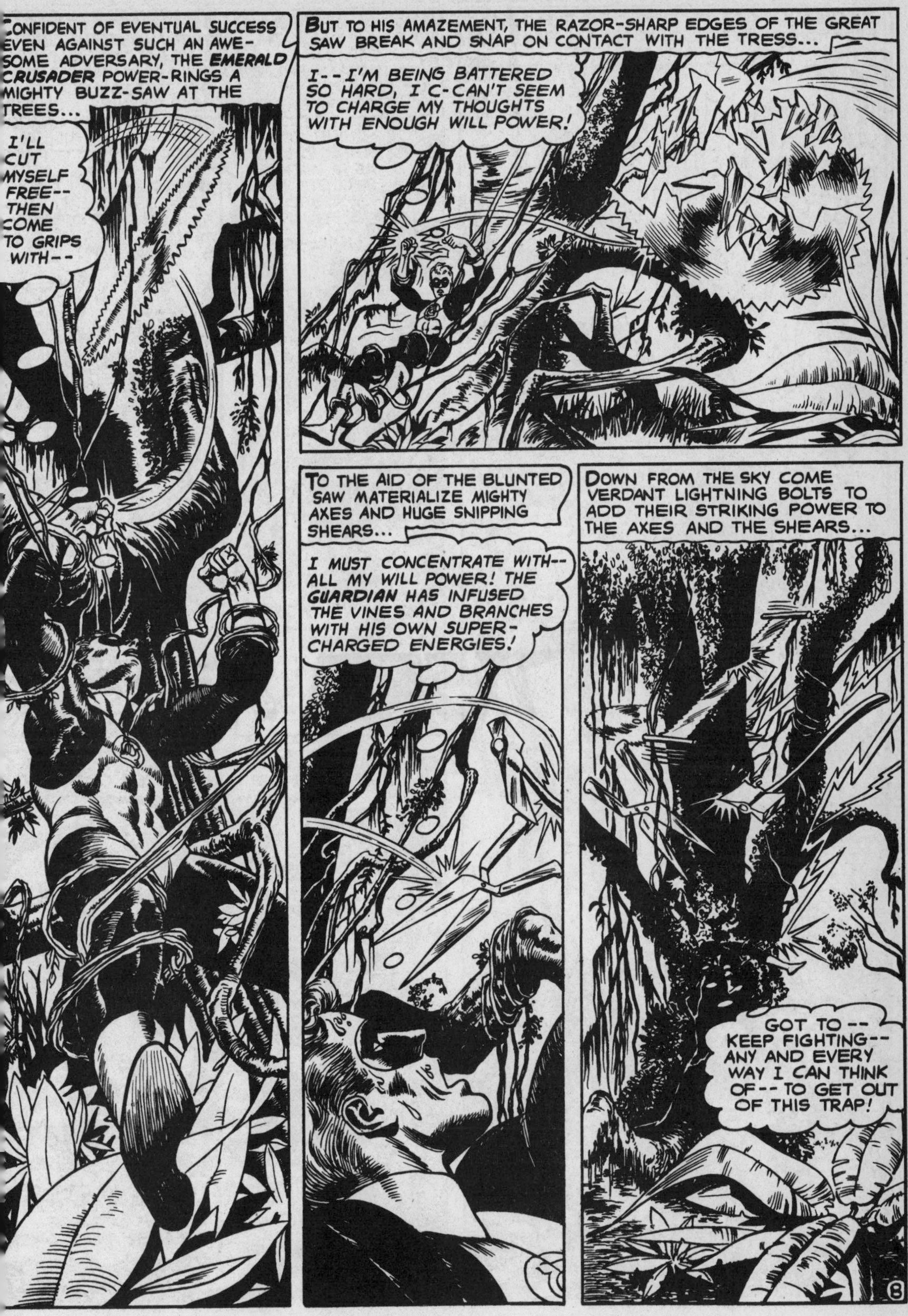
CONFIDENT OF EVENTUAL SUCCESS EVEN AGAINST SUCH AN AWESOME ADVERSARY, THE EMERALD CRUSADER POWER-RINGS A MIGHTY BUZZ-SAW AT THE TREES...
I'LL CUT MYSELF FREE-- THEN COME TO GRIPS WITH--
BUT TO HIS AMAZEMENT, THE RAZOR-SHARP EDGES OF THE GREAT SAW BREAK AND SNAP ON CONTACT WITH THE TRESS...
I--I'M BEING BATTERED SO HARD, I C-CAN'T SEEM TO CHARGE MY THOUGHTS WITH ENOUGH WILL POWER!
TO THE AID OF THE BLUNTED SAW MATERIALIZE MIGHTY AXES AND HUGE SNIPPING SHEARS...
I MUST CONCENTRATE WITH-- ALL MY WILL POWER! THE GUARDIAN HAS INFUSED THE VINES AND BRANCHES WITH HIS OWN SUPER-CHARGED ENERGIES!
DOWN FROM THE SKY COME VERDANT LIGHTNING BOLTS TO ADD THEIR STRIKING POWER TO THE AXES AND THE SHEARS...
GOT TO -- KEEP FIGHTING-- ANY AND EVERY WAY I CAN THINK OF-- TO GET OUT OF THIS TRAP!
8

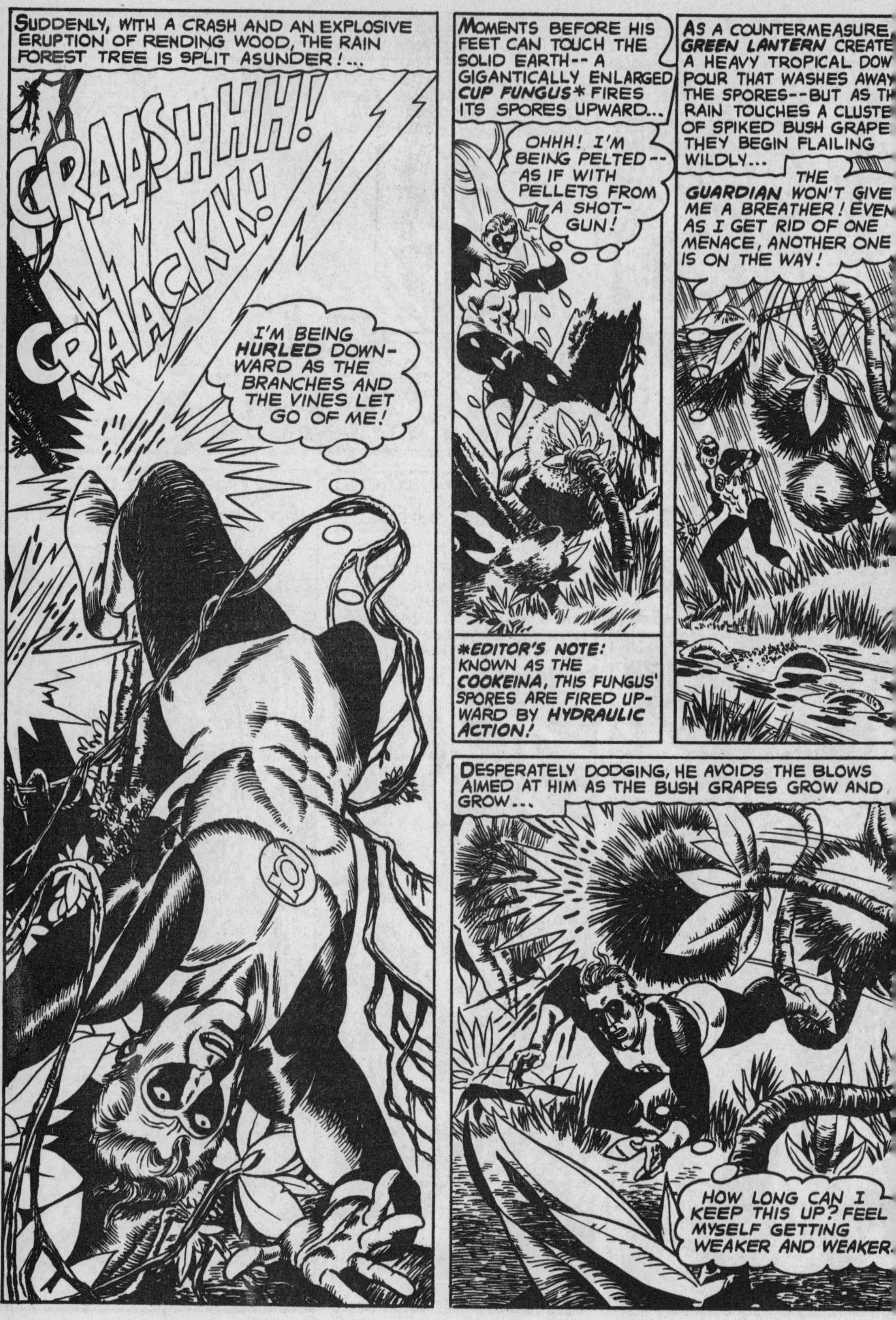
SUDDENLY, WITH A CRASH AND AN EXPLOSIVE ERUPTION OF RENDING WOOD, THE RAIN FOREST TREE IS SPLIT ASUNDER!...
CRAASHHH!
CRAACKK!
I'M BEING HURLED DOWNWARD AS THE BRANCHES AND THE VINES LET GO OF ME!
MOMENTS BEFORE HIS FEET CAN TOUCH THE SOLID EARTH-- A GIGANTICALLY ENLARGED CUP FUNGUS* FIRES ITS SPORES UPWARD...
OHHH! I'M BEING PELTED-- AS IF WITH PELLETS FROM A SHOT-GUN!
*EDITOR'S NOTE: KNOWN AS THE COOKEINA, THIS FUNGUS' SPORES ARE FIRED UPWARD BY HYDRAULIC ACTION!
AS A COUNTERMEASURE, GREEN LANTERN CREATE A HEAVY TROPICAL DOW POUR THAT WASHES AWAY THE SPORES--BUT AS TH RAIN TOUCHES A CLUSTE OF SPIKED BUSH GRAPE THEY BEGIN FLAILING WILDLY...
THE GUARDIAN WON'T GIVE ME A BREATHER! EVEN AS I GET RID OF ONE MENACE, ANOTHER ONE IS ON THE WAY!
DESPERATELY DODGING, HE AVOIDS THE BLOWS AIMED AT HIM AS THE BUSH GRAPES GROW AND GROW...
HOW LONG CAN I KEEP THIS UP? FEEL MYSELF GETTING WEAKER AND WEAKER.

SWOOPING BETWEEN TWO BUSH GRAPES THAT MOVE TO BASH HIM, THE GREEN GLADIATOR'S RING FLARES INTO ACTION AGAIN...

THOSE GRAPES ARE SO STRONG-- THEY SMASHED THROUGH THE NETS I FASHIONED TO CONTAIN THEM!

SINCE THE GUARDIAN HAS SUCH UNLIMITED ENERGY--EVERYTHING HE USES THAT ENERGY ON POSSESSES A GREATER POWER THAN THAT OF MY POWER RING! CAN I STAY ALIVE--LET ALONE DEFEAT HIM?

STRAINING HIS EVERY MUSCLE-- CONCENTRATING AS HE HAS NEVER BEFORE-- THE EMERALD WARRIOR ENCASES HIMSELF IN A PROJECTILE AND...

CUT THROUGH THE DEADLY GRAPES, POWER RING! FLY ME UP TO SAFETY BEYOND THEIR REACH!

UPWARD--AND THROUGH THOSE GIGANTIC GROWTHS ROCKETS GREEN LANTERN...

I MADE IT!

VERY GOOD, GREEN LANTERN! YOU HAVE WON THE FIRST ROUND OF OUR BATTLE! NOW-- WITH NO TIMEOUT-- LET US PROCEED TO THE ARENA OF ROUND TWO!

AS THE CONCENTRIC RINGS OF HIS COSMIC ENERGIES FLOW OUT OF THE GUARDIAN, THEY CATCH GREEN LANTERN IN THEIR CLUTCH AND...

NOW TO TRANSPORT HIM TO A COLD, ICY BATTLE- GROUND IN THE ARCTIC-- AND A NEW SERIES OF MENACES!

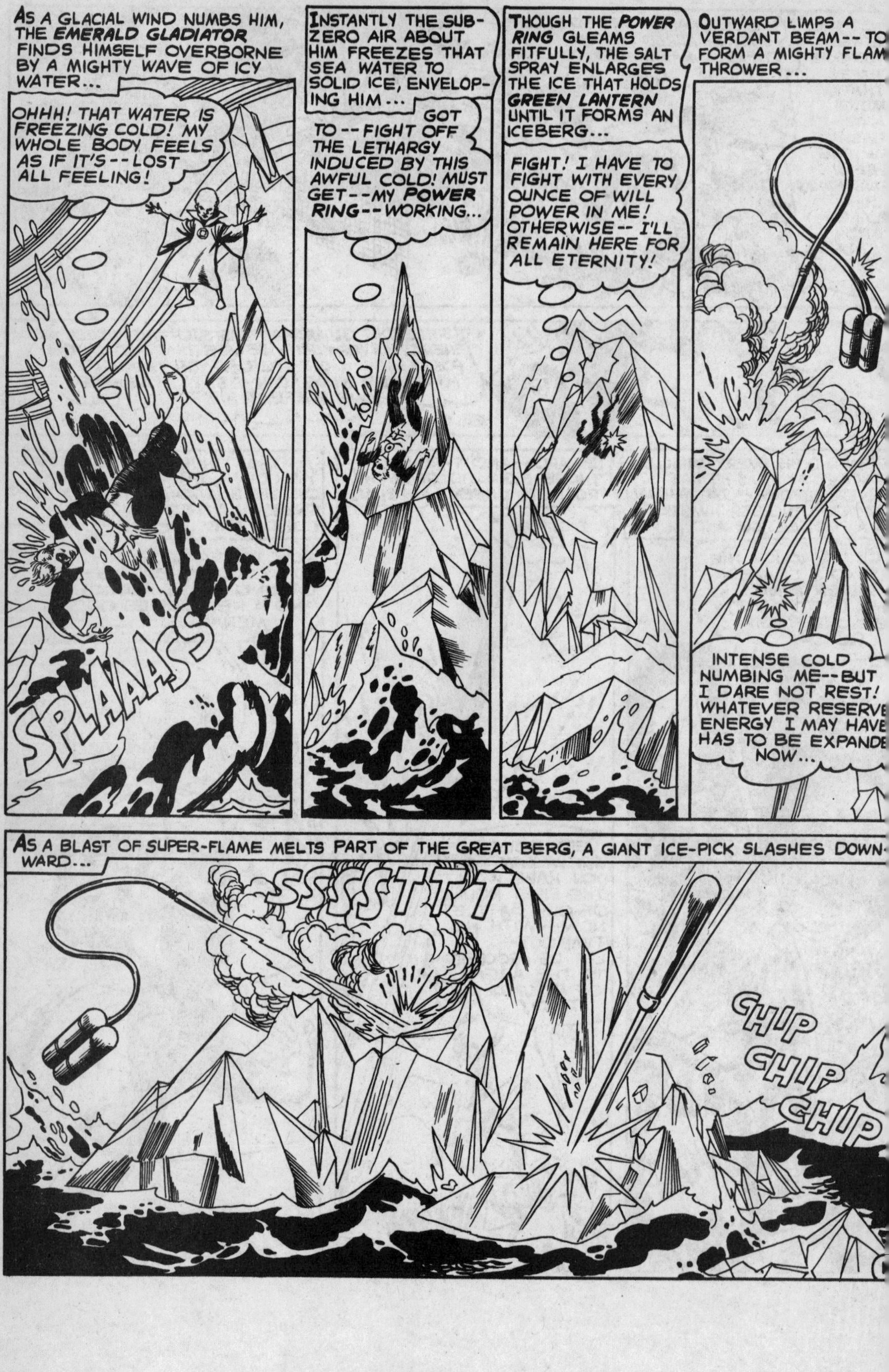
AS A GLACIAL WIND NUMBS HIM, THE EMERALD GLADIATOR FINDS HIMSELF OVERBORNE BY A MIGHTY WAVE OF ICY WATER...
OHHH! THAT WATER IS FREEZING COLD! MY WHOLE BODY FEELS AS IF IT'S--LOST ALL FEELING!
SPLAAASS
INSTANTLY THE SUB-ZERO AIR ABOUT HIM FREEZES THAT SEA WATER TO SOLID ICE, ENVELOPING HIM...
GOT TO--FIGHT OFF THE LETHARGY INDUCED BY THIS AWFUL COLD! MUST GET--MY POWER RING--WORKING...
THOUGH THE POWER RING GLEAMS FITFULLY, THE SALT SPRAY ENLARGES THE ICE THAT HOLDS GREEN LANTERN UNTIL IT FORMS AN ICEBERG...
FIGHT! I HAVE TO FIGHT WITH EVERY OUNCE OF WILL POWER IN ME! OTHERWISE--I'LL REMAIN HERE FOR ALL ETERNITY!
OUTWARD LIMPS A VERDANT BEAM--TO FORM A MIGHTY FLAM THROWER...
INTENSE COLD NUMBING ME--BUT I DARE NOT REST! WHATEVER RESERVE ENERGY I MAY HAVE HAS TO BE EXPANDE NOW...
AS A BLAST OF SUPER-FLAME MELTS PART OF THE GREAT BERG, A GIANT ICE-PICK SLASHES DOWNWARD...
SSSSTTT
CHIP CHIP CHIP

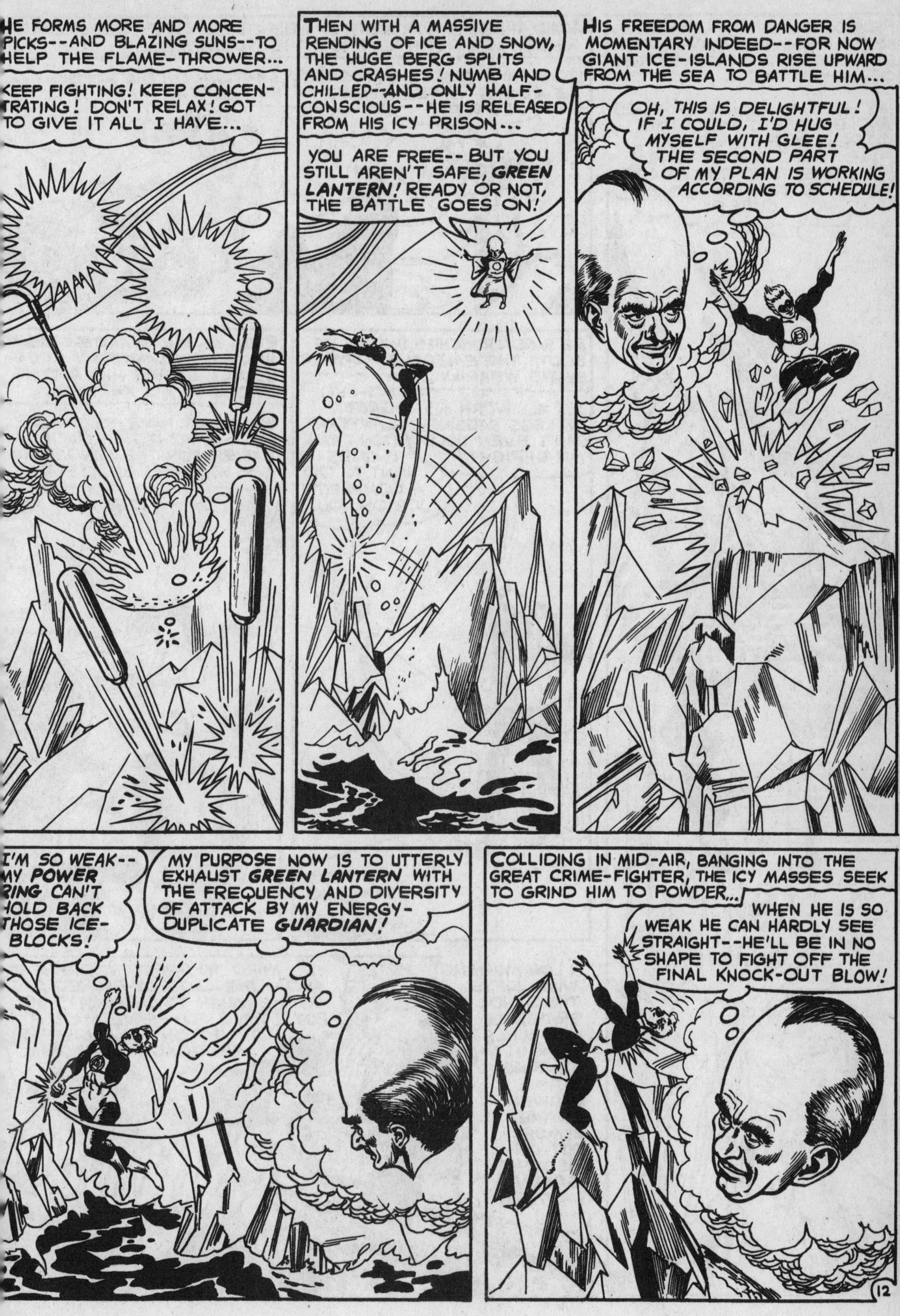
HE FORMS MORE AND MORE PICKS--AND BLAZING SUNS--TO HELP THE FLAME-THROWER...
KEEP FIGHTING! KEEP CONCENTRATING! DON'T RELAX! GOT TO GIVE IT ALL I HAVE...
THEN WITH A MASSIVE RENDING OF ICE AND SNOW, THE HUGE BERG SPLITS AND CRASHES! NUMB AND CHILLED--AND ONLY HALF-CONSCIOUS--HE IS RELEASED FROM HIS ICY PRISON...
YOU ARE FREE--BUT YOU STILL AREN'T SAFE, GREEN LANTERN! READY OR NOT, THE BATTLE GOES ON!
HIS FREEDOM FROM DANGER IS MOMENTARY INDEED--FOR NOW GIANT ICE-ISLANDS RISE UPWARD FROM THE SEA TO BATTLE HIM...
OH, THIS IS DELIGHTFUL! IF I COULD, I'D HUG MYSELF WITH GLEE! THE SECOND PART OF MY PLAN IS WORKING ACCORDING TO SCHEDULE!
I'M SO WEAK--MY POWER RING CAN'T HOLD BACK THOSE ICE-BLOCKS!
MY PURPOSE NOW IS TO UTTERLY EXHAUST GREEN LANTERN WITH THE FREQUENCY AND DIVERSITY OF ATTACK BY MY ENERGY-DUPLICATE GUARDIAN!
COLLIDING IN MID-AIR, BANGING INTO THE GREAT CRIME-FIGHTER, THE ICY MASSES SEEK TO GRIND HIM TO POWDER...
WHEN HE IS SO WEAK HE CAN HARDLY SEE STRAIGHT--HE'LL BE IN NO SHAPE TO FIGHT OFF THE FINAL KNOCK-OUT BLOW!
12

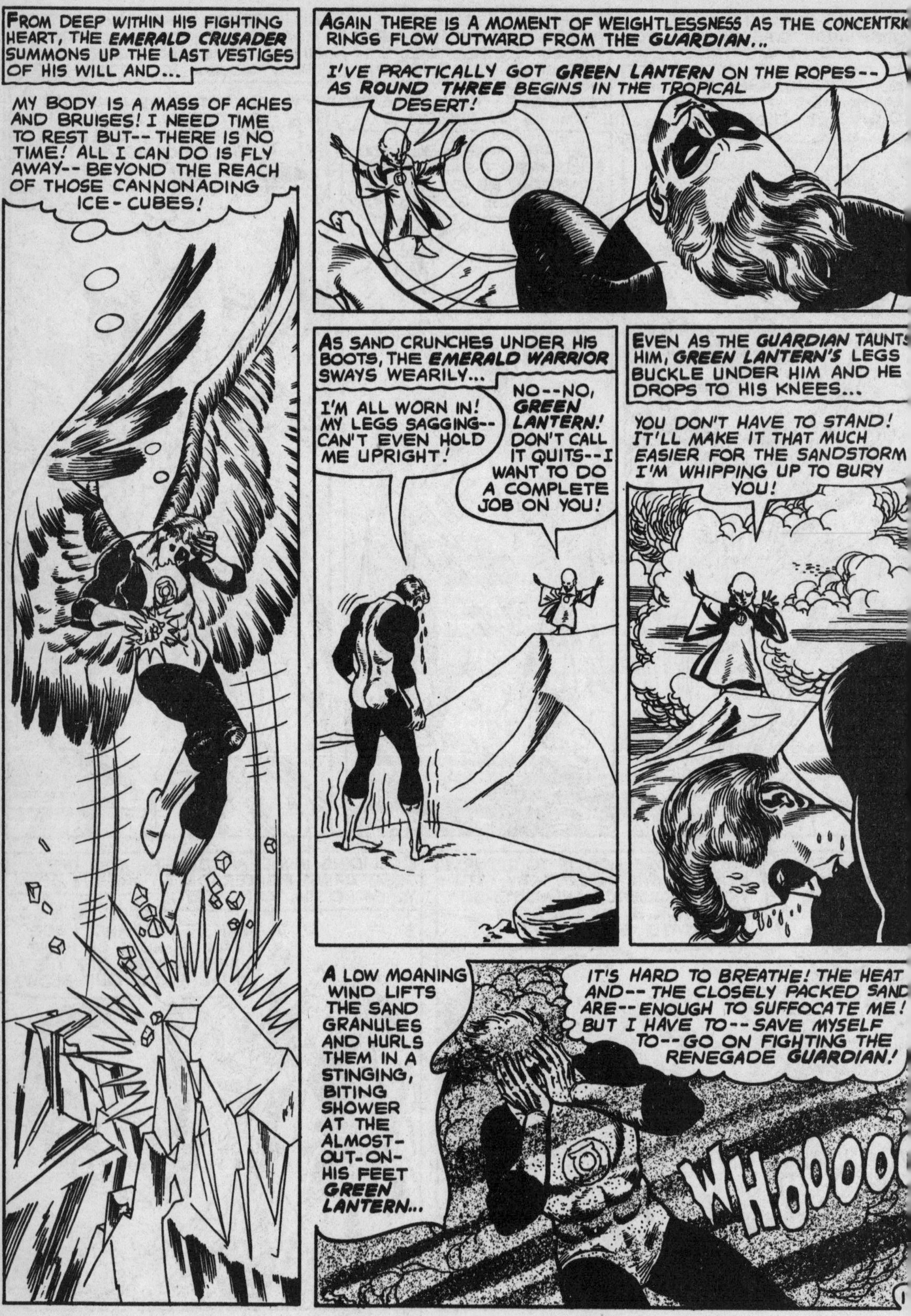

FROM DEEP WITHIN HIS FIGHTING HEART, THE EMERALD CRUSADER SUMMONS UP THE LAST VESTIGES OF HIS WILL AND...
MY BODY IS A MASS OF ACHES AND BRUISES! I NEED TIME TO REST BUT-- THERE IS NO TIME! ALL I CAN DO IS FLY AWAY-- BEYOND THE REACH OF THOSE CANNONADING ICE-CUBES!
AGAIN THERE IS A MOMENT OF WEIGHTLESSNESS AS THE CONCENTRIC RINGS FLOW OUTWARD FROM THE GUARDIAN...
I'VE PRACTICALLY GOT GREEN LANTERN ON THE ROPES-- AS ROUND THREE BEGINS IN THE TROPICAL DESERT!
AS SAND CRUNCHES UNDER HIS BOOTS, THE EMERALD WARRIOR SWAYS WEARILY...
I'M ALL WORN IN! MY LEGS SAGGING-- CAN'T EVEN HOLD ME UPRIGHT!
NO--NO, GREEN LANTERN! DON'T CALL IT QUITS--I WANT TO DO A COMPLETE JOB ON YOU!
EVEN AS THE GUARDIAN TAUNTS HIM, GREEN LANTERN'S LEGS BUCKLE UNDER HIM AND HE DROPS TO HIS KNEES...
YOU DON'T HAVE TO STAND! IT'LL MAKE IT THAT MUCH EASIER FOR THE SANDSTORM I'M WHIPPING UP TO BURY YOU!
A LOW MOANING WIND LIFTS THE SAND GRANULES AND HURLS THEM IN A STINGING, BITING SHOWER AT THE ALMOST-OUT-ON-HIS FEET GREEN LANTERN...
IT'S HARD TO BREATHE! THE HEAT AND-- THE CLOSELY PACKED SAND ARE--ENOUGH TO SUFFOCATE ME! BUT I HAVE TO-- SAVE MYSELF TO--GO ON FIGHTING THE RENEGADE GUARDIAN!
WHOOOOO

THE *POWER RING* GLOWS -- TO FORM A *GLASS HOUSE* ABOUT THE *EMERALD GLADIATOR*...

NO MATTER HOW MUCH POWER I DRAW FROM MY RING--THOSE SANDS KEEP PENETRATING MY "HOUSE"! SOMEWHERE I MUST FIND THE WILL WITHIN ME TO-- KEEP THEM OUT OR-- PERISH!

ACHING MUSCLES STRAIN BEYOND THE LIMIT OF THEIR ENDURANCE WHILE SWEAT DAMPENS HIS UNIFORM AS *CRUSADER* AND *GUARDIAN* ARE LOCKED IN THEIR MONUMENTAL STRUGGLE...

WHEW: JUST IN TIME... I STRENGTHENED MY HOUSE ENOUGH TO KEEP OUT THE SAND!

THAT WON'T HELP YOU AT ALL, *GREEN LANTERN*! LOOK UP AND-- SEE WHAT COMES NOW TO BATTLE YOU!

GREEN LANTERN

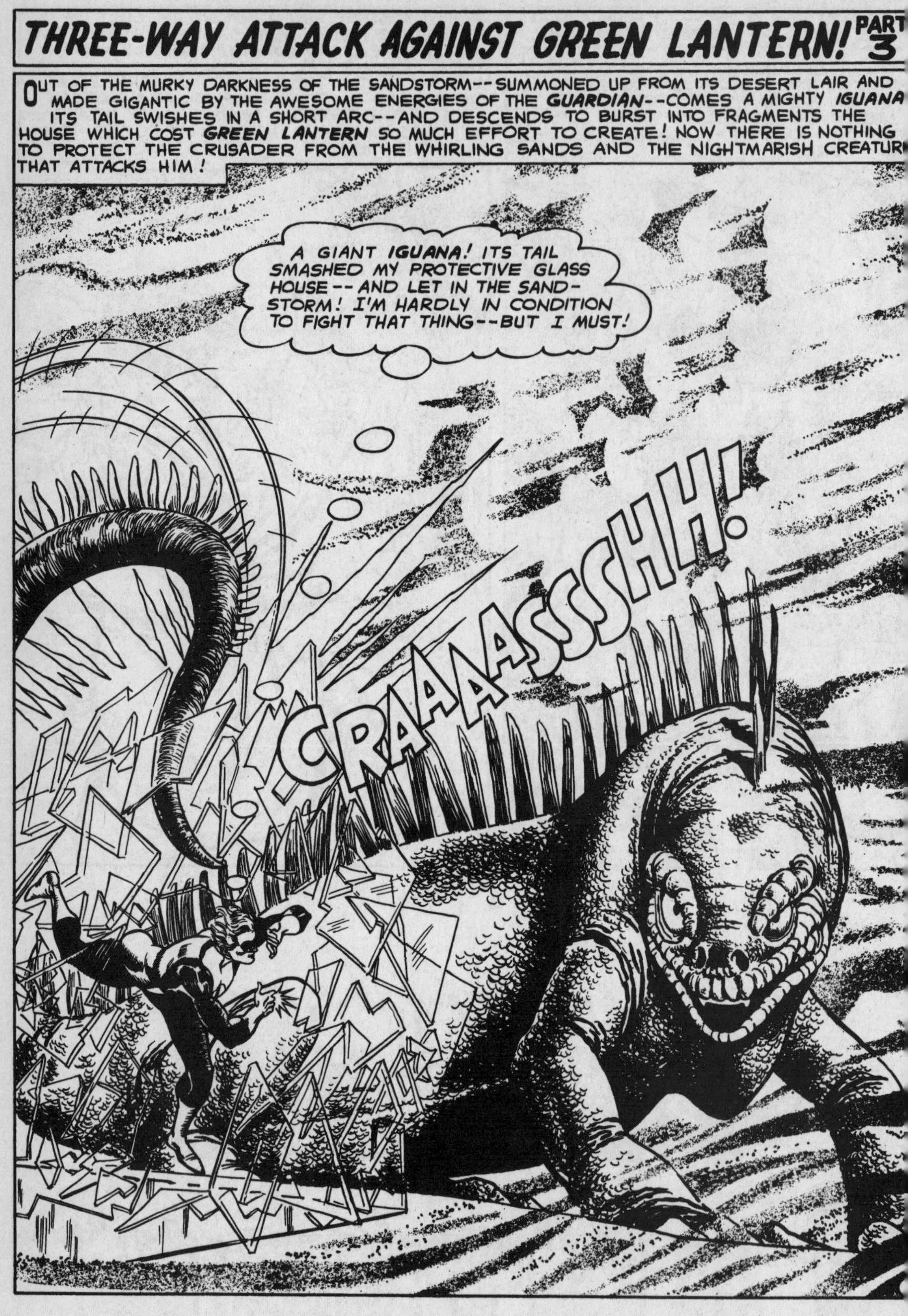
THREE-WAY ATTACK AGAINST GREEN LANTERN! PART 3
OUT OF THE MURKY DARKNESS OF THE SANDSTORM--SUMMONED UP FROM ITS DESERT LAIR AND MADE GIGANTIC BY THE AWESOME ENERGIES OF THE GUARDIAN--COMES A MIGHTY IGUANA ITS TAIL SWISHES IN A SHORT ARC--AND DESCENDS TO BURST INTO FRAGMENTS THE HOUSE WHICH COST GREEN LANTERN SO MUCH EFFORT TO CREATE! NOW THERE IS NOTHING TO PROTECT THE CRUSADER FROM THE WHIRLING SANDS AND THE NIGHTMARISH CREATUR THAT ATTACKS HIM!
A GIANT IGUANA! ITS TAIL SMASHED MY PROTECTIVE GLASS HOUSE--AND LET IN THE SAND-STORM! I'M HARDLY IN CONDITION TO FIGHT THAT THING--BUT I MUST!
CRAAAASSSSHH!

AS THE GLASS HOUSE SHATTERS AROUND GREEN LANTERN, THE GIANT IGUANA LASHES OUTWARD AND UPWARD WITH ITS TAIL...

NOW WHAT FANTASTIC DANGER DO I HAVE TO FACE?

AS IF IN ANSWER TO THE GLADIATOR'S MENTAL QUESTION...

HOOPS OF SIZZLING ENERGY LEAPING FROM ITS TAIL?!

THE CRACKLING HOOPS DROP DOWN OVER THE EMERALD CRUSADER, PINNING HIM IN AN ERUPTION OF RADIANT POWER...

THOSE RINGS -- SAPPING ME OF MY ENERGY -- TURNING ME INTO A HOLLOW SHELL...

IN THE DEEPEST PART OF THE HUMAN HEART, THERE IS ALWAYS HOPE -- AND RAW COURAGE! IN THIS MOMENT OF TRUTH, GREEN LANTERN -- WHO IS MERELY A HUMAN BEING GIFTED WITH A POWER RING -- CALLS ON THAT LAST MEASURE OF BRAVERY...

FIGHT BACK! DON'T TAKE THIS LYING DOWN! FIGHT...FIGHT...FIGHT...

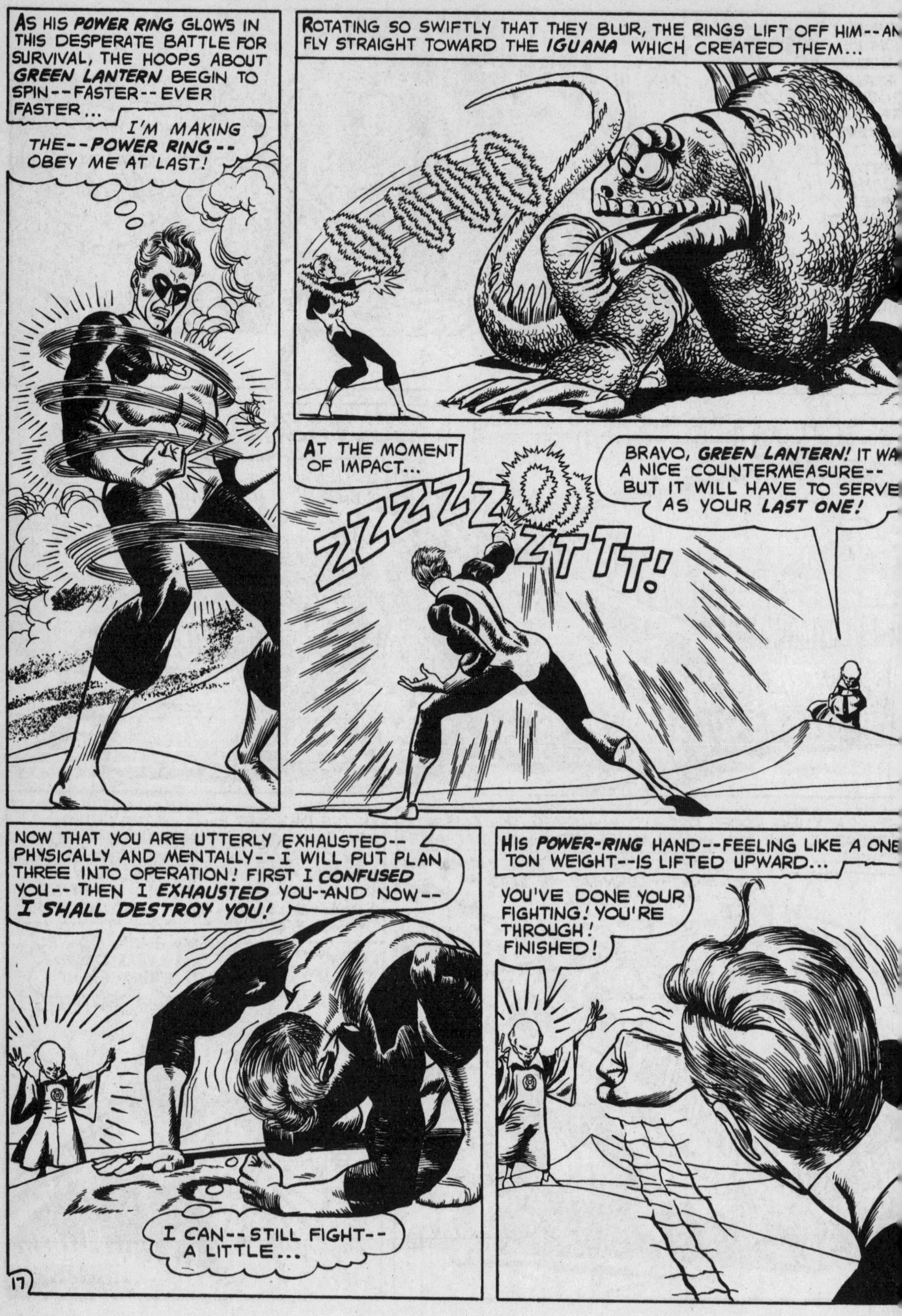
AS HIS POWER RING GLOWS IN THIS DESPERATE BATTLE FOR SURVIVAL, THE HOOPS ABOUT GREEN LANTERN BEGIN TO SPIN--FASTER--EVER FASTER...
I'M MAKING THE--POWER RING--OBEY ME AT LAST!
ROTATING SO SWIFTLY THAT THEY BLUR, THE RINGS LIFT OFF HIM--AN FLY STRAIGHT TOWARD THE IGUANA WHICH CREATED THEM...
AT THE MOMENT OF IMPACT...
ZZZZZZZTTTT!
BRAVO, GREEN LANTERN! IT WA A NICE COUNTERMEASURE--BUT IT WILL HAVE TO SERVE AS YOUR LAST ONE!
NOW THAT YOU ARE UTTERLY EXHAUSTED--PHYSICALLY AND MENTALLY--I WILL PUT PLAN THREE INTO OPERATION! FIRST I CONFUSED YOU--THEN I EXHAUSTED YOU--AND NOW--I SHALL DESTROY YOU!
I CAN--STILL FIGHT--A LITTLE...
17
HIS POWER-RING HAND--FEELING LIKE A ONE TON WEIGHT--IS LIFTED UPWARD...
YOU'VE DONE YOUR FIGHTING! YOU'RE THROUGH! FINISHED!

...EN AS HE HURLS A BEAM ROM HIS *POWER RING*-- HE *EMERALD CRUSADER* EELS HIS ARM ENGTHEN--ELONGATE-- FT UPWARD AT A ZZYING RATE OF PEED...

...Y RM!? NOT *YOUR* ARM--BUT *"MINE"!* FOR *I* CONTROL THAT ARM WITH MY SUPER-HUMAN ABILITIES!

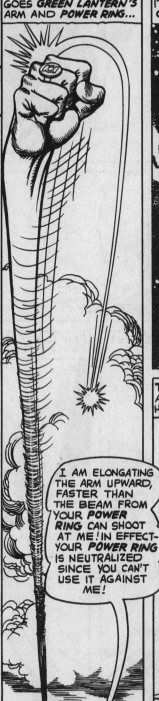

HIGHER--HIGHER--RACING SWIFTLY SPACEWARD-- GOES *GREEN LANTERN'S* ARM AND *POWER RING*...

I AM ELONGATING THE ARM UPWARD, FASTER THAN THE BEAM FROM YOUR *POWER RING* CAN SHOOT AT ME! IN EFFECT-- YOUR *POWER RING* IS NEUTRALIZED SINCE YOU CAN'T USE IT AGAINST ME!

UPWARD INTO SPACE FLASHES THAT SPEEDING ARM! THE *POWER RING* CANNOT OUTSPEED IT AND SO-- IT IS CHECKMATE FOR THE *EMERALD CRUSADER!*...

THE TRIUMPHANT *GUARDIAN* LIFTS HIS OWN ARM--AS A GOLDEN SPHERE FORMS FROM HIS FINGERTIPS...

WITHOUT YOUR *POWER RING*--YOU ARE HELPLESS TO COMBAT MY FINAL AND MOST DEADLY WEAPON! THIS IS THE KNOCKOUT BLOW TOWARD WHICH ALL MY OTHER "STUNTS" WERE AIMED!

18

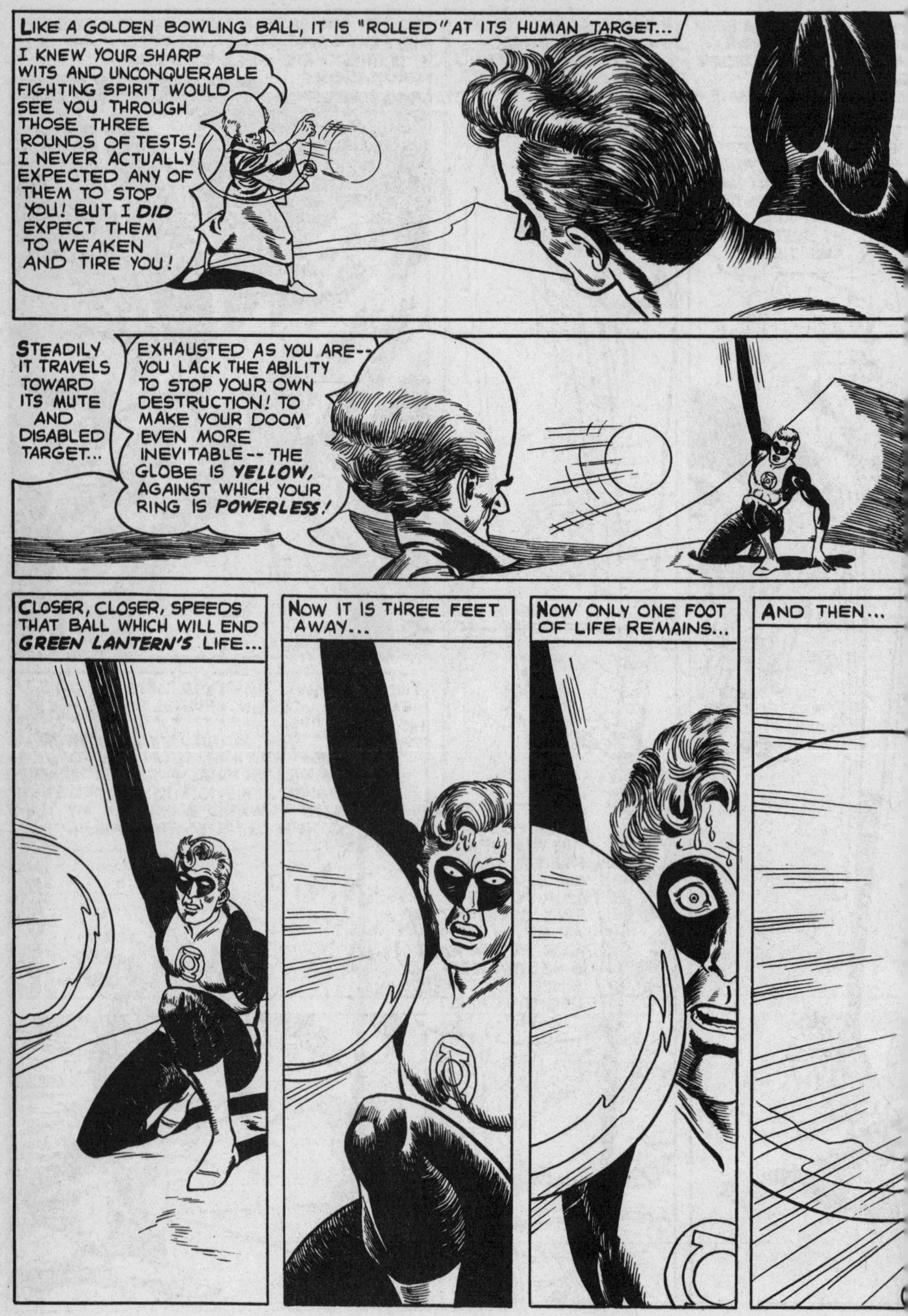
LIKE A GOLDEN BOWLING BALL, IT IS "ROLLED" AT ITS HUMAN TARGET...
I KNEW YOUR SHARP WITS AND UNCONQUERABLE FIGHTING SPIRIT WOULD SEE YOU THROUGH THOSE THREE ROUNDS OF TESTS! I NEVER ACTUALLY EXPECTED ANY OF THEM TO STOP YOU! BUT I *DID* EXPECT THEM TO WEAKEN AND TIRE YOU!
STEADILY IT TRAVELS TOWARD ITS MUTE AND DISABLED TARGET...
EXHAUSTED AS YOU ARE-- YOU LACK THE ABILITY TO STOP YOUR OWN DESTRUCTION! TO MAKE YOUR DOOM EVEN MORE INEVITABLE -- THE GLOBE IS *YELLOW*, AGAINST WHICH YOUR RING IS *POWERLESS!*
CLOSER, CLOSER, SPEEDS THAT BALL WHICH WILL END *GREEN LANTERN'S* LIFE...
NOW IT IS THREE FEET AWAY...
NOW ONLY ONE FOOT OF LIFE REMAINS...
AND THEN...

EVEN AS HE FEELS THE INVISIBLE RADIATIONS FROM THAT GOLDEN BALL, *GREEN LANTERN* SUMMONS HIS FAR-DISTANT RING TO TURN HIS ARM TO RUBBER-STRETCHED-BEYOND-ENDURANCE...

JUST AS A RUBBER BAND WILL SNAP BACK INTO POSITION WHEN STRETCHED TOO FAR-- SO WILL MY ARM!

AS HIS ARM SNAPS TOWARD THE *POWER RING*, IT YANKS THE *EMERALD CRUSADER* UPWARD AND AWAY FROM THE DEADLY GLOBE...

WHOOOOOSSSH!

INSTANTLY THE YELLOW MISSILE SWERVES IN ITS COURSE--RISES UPWARD AFTER ITS LIVING TARGET...

FOOLISH *GREEN LANTERN!* YOU ONLY DELAY THE INEVITABLE! THE BALL IS GEARED TO FOLLOW YOU-- ANY-WHERE IN THE UNIVERSE!

IS THERE TO BE NO ESCAPE FOR ME? IS THIS HOW I AM TO FINISH MY CAREER-- DESTROYED BY ONE OF THE VERY MEN WHO ALLOWED ME TO "GUARD" *EARTH* FROM EVIL AND INJUSTICE?

THEN--*GREEN LANTERN* IS GONE--AS A GIGANTIC FLARE OCCURS FAR OUT IN SPACE...

20

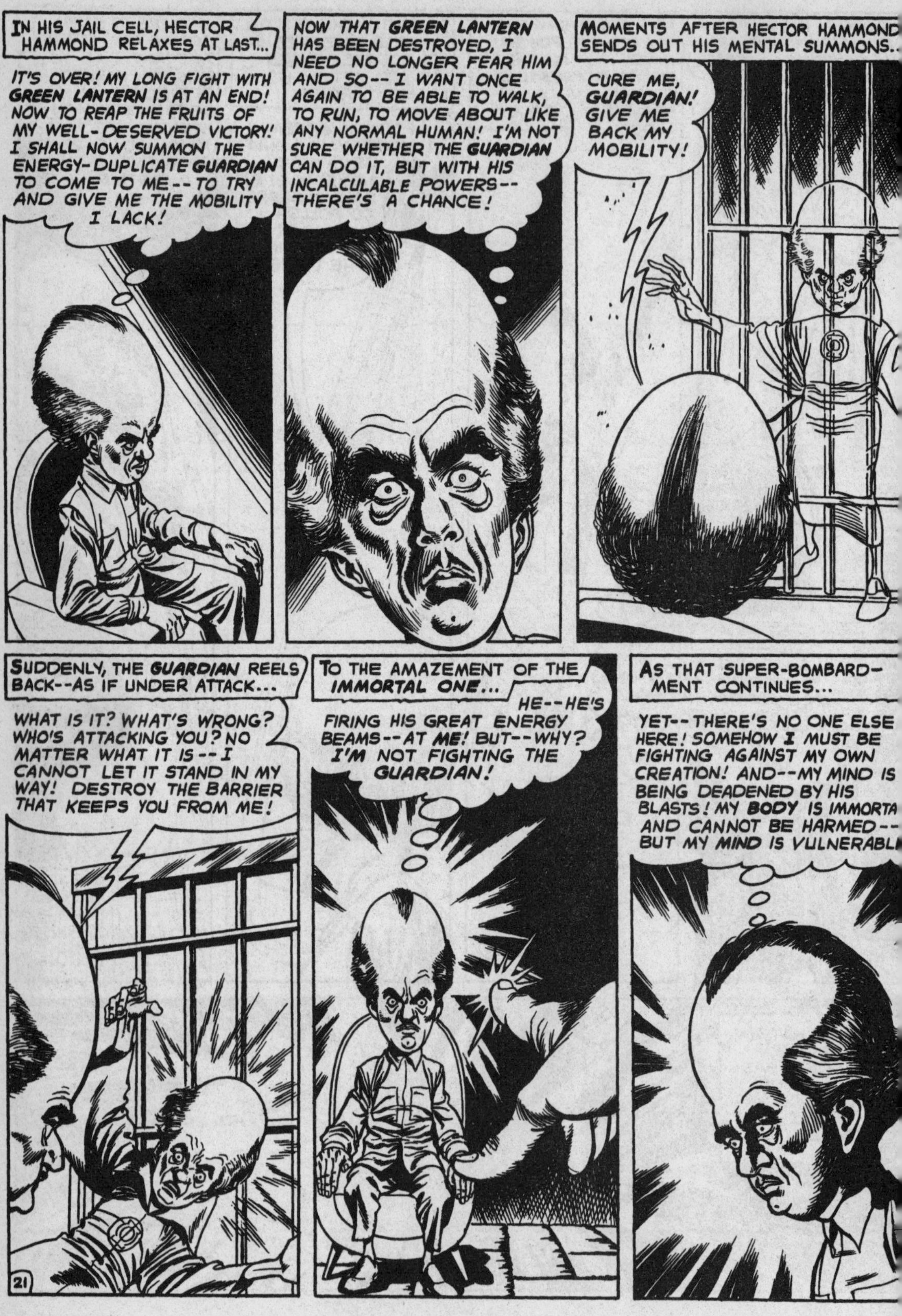
IN HIS JAIL CELL, HECTOR HAMMOND RELAXES AT LAST...
IT'S OVER! MY LONG FIGHT WITH GREEN LANTERN IS AT AN END! NOW TO REAP THE FRUITS OF MY WELL-DESERVED VICTORY! I SHALL NOW SUMMON THE ENERGY-DUPLICATE GUARDIAN TO COME TO ME--TO TRY AND GIVE ME THE MOBILITY I LACK!
NOW THAT GREEN LANTERN HAS BEEN DESTROYED, I NEED NO LONGER FEAR HIM AND SO--I WANT ONCE AGAIN TO BE ABLE TO WALK, TO RUN, TO MOVE ABOUT LIKE ANY NORMAL HUMAN! I'M NOT SURE WHETHER THE GUARDIAN CAN DO IT, BUT WITH HIS INCALCULABLE POWERS--THERE'S A CHANCE!
MOMENTS AFTER HECTOR HAMMOND SENDS OUT HIS MENTAL SUMMONS...
CURE ME, GUARDIAN! GIVE ME BACK MY MOBILITY!
SUDDENLY, THE GUARDIAN REELS BACK--AS IF UNDER ATTACK...
WHAT IS IT? WHAT'S WRONG? WHO'S ATTACKING YOU? NO MATTER WHAT IT IS--I CANNOT LET IT STAND IN MY WAY! DESTROY THE BARRIER THAT KEEPS YOU FROM ME!
21
TO THE AMAZEMENT OF THE IMMORTAL ONE...
HE--HE'S FIRING HIS GREAT ENERGY BEAMS--AT ME! BUT--WHY? I'M NOT FIGHTING THE GUARDIAN!
AS THAT SUPER-BOMBARDMENT CONTINUES...
YET--THERE'S NO ONE ELSE HERE! SOMEHOW I MUST BE FIGHTING AGAINST MY OWN CREATION! AND--MY MIND IS BEING DEADENED BY HIS BLASTS! MY BODY IS IMMORTA AND CANNOT BE HARMED--BUT MY MIND IS VULNERABL

MY BRAIN IS DEADENED BY HIS BOLTS--I'LL BE A TRULY LIVING-DEAD PERSON! I DARE NOT LET THAT HAPPEN! I MUST SACRIFICE MY CHANCE AT MOBILITY AND DESTROY MY *GUARDIAN* CREATION!

THE NEXT INSTANT, THE FRANTIC HECTOR HAMMOND HURLS OUT A BOLT OF MENTAL ENERGY AT THE *GUARDIAN*...

THERE! TO SAVE MYSELF I--ELIMINATED HIM! AT LEAST MY BRAIN WILL REMAIN THE SAME-- EVEN THOUGH I WILL NEVER BE ABLE TO MOVE!

AND FAR AWAY IN ANOTHER UNIVERSE THAT OCCUPIES THE SAME SPACE-CONTINUUM AS OUR OWN, BUT ON A DIFFERENT TIME-LEVEL...

THE MISSION HAS BEEN COMPLETED, GREEN LANTERN! THE GUARDIAN IS NO MORE!

I'M GLAD THAT AT LEAST ONE OF MY MANEUVERS WORKED! WHEN THAT GOLDEN BALL ALMOST OVERTOOK ME OUT THERE IN SPACE--I SUDDENLY REMEMBERED ABOUT EARTH-TWO!

" *I VIBRATED INTO THAT OTHERDIMENSIONAL EARTH...* "

SINCE THE *GUARDIAN* COMMANDED THE GOLDEN GLOBE TO FOLLOW ME ANYWHERE "IN THE UNIVERSE"-- IT CANNOT FOLLOW ME INTO THIS *OTHER* UNIVERSE! IT WILL CRASH AGAINST THE BARRIER AND-- BLOW ITSELF UP!

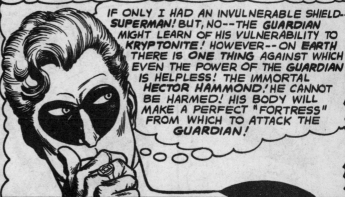

"ON *EARTH-TWO,* I FOUND MYSELF ABLE TO CONCENTRATE-- AND CAME UP WITH A POSSIBLE SOLUTION TO MY PROBLEM..."

IF ONLY I HAD AN INVULNERABLE SHIELD-- *SUPERMAN!* BUT, NO--THE GUARDIAN MIGHT LEARN OF HIS VULNERABILITY TO *KRYPTONITE!* HOWEVER-- ON *EARTH* THERE IS ONE THING AGAINST WHICH EVEN THE POWER OF THE GUARDIAN IS HELPLESS! THE IMMORTAL *HECTOR HAMMOND!* HE CANNOT BE HARMED! HIS BODY WILL MAKE A PERFECT "FORTRESS" FROM WHICH TO ATTACK THE *GUARDIAN!*

IRONY OF IRONIES! GREEN LANTERN HAS UNWITTINGLY SELECTED AS HIS "SHIELD" THE VERY PERSON WHO IS RESPONSIBLE FOR HIS PREDICAMENT!

22

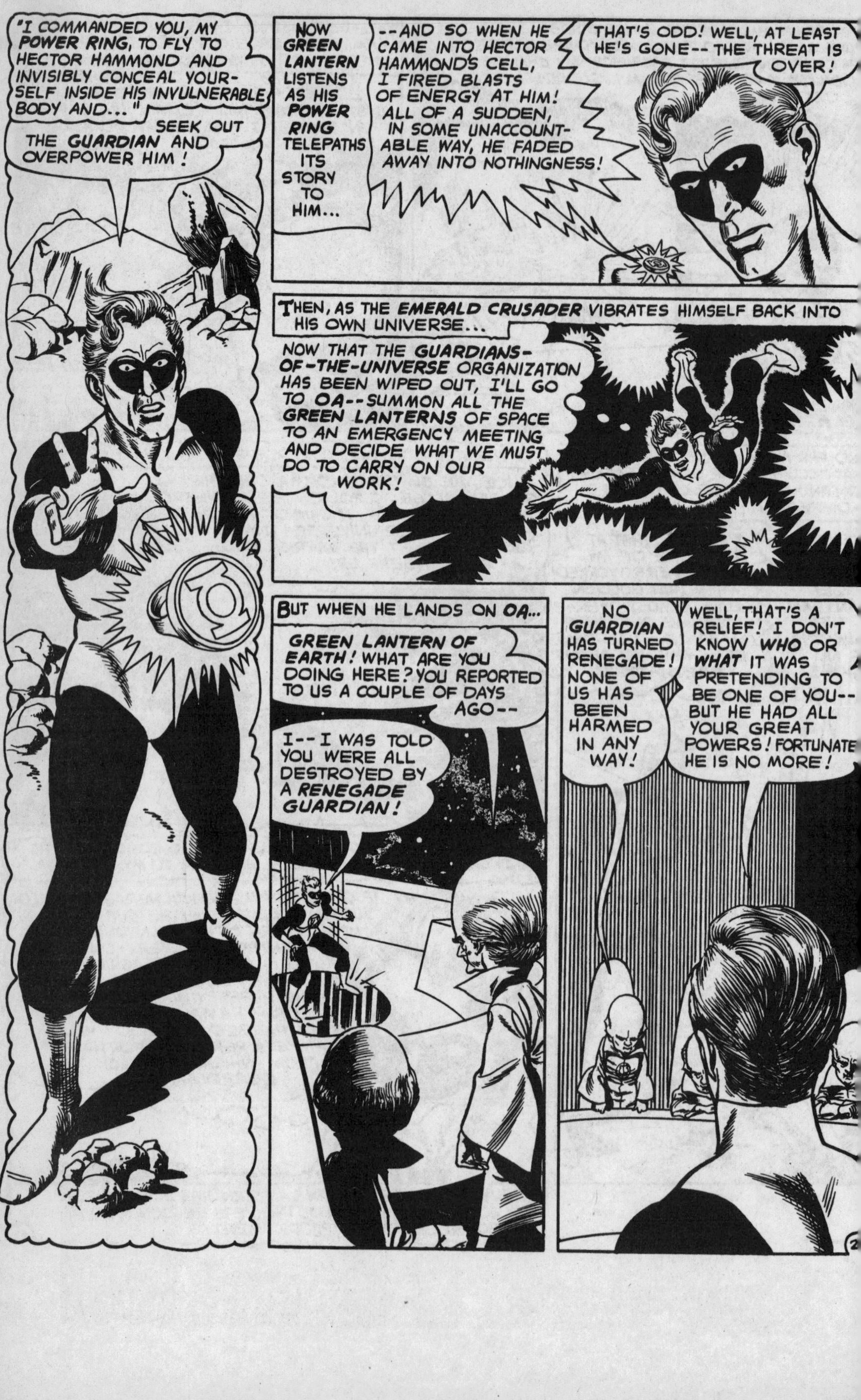
"I COMMANDED YOU, MY POWER RING, TO FLY TO HECTOR HAMMOND AND INVISIBLY CONCEAL YOURSELF INSIDE HIS INVULNERABLE BODY AND..."
SEEK OUT THE GUARDIAN AND OVERPOWER HIM!
NOW GREEN LANTERN LISTENS AS HIS POWER RING TELEPATHS ITS STORY TO HIM...
--AND SO WHEN HE CAME INTO HECTOR HAMMOND'S CELL, I FIRED BLASTS OF ENERGY AT HIM! ALL OF A SUDDEN, IN SOME UNACCOUNTABLE WAY, HE FADED AWAY INTO NOTHINGNESS!
THAT'S ODD! WELL, AT LEAST HE'S GONE-- THE THREAT IS OVER!
THEN, AS THE EMERALD CRUSADER VIBRATES HIMSELF BACK INTO HIS OWN UNIVERSE...
NOW THAT THE GUARDIANS-OF-THE-UNIVERSE ORGANIZATION HAS BEEN WIPED OUT, I'LL GO TO OA--SUMMON ALL THE GREEN LANTERNS OF SPACE TO AN EMERGENCY MEETING AND DECIDE WHAT WE MUST DO TO CARRY ON OUR WORK!
BUT WHEN HE LANDS ON OA...
GREEN LANTERN OF EARTH! WHAT ARE YOU DOING HERE? YOU REPORTED TO US A COUPLE OF DAYS AGO--
I--I WAS TOLD YOU WERE ALL DESTROYED BY A RENEGADE GUARDIAN!
NO GUARDIAN HAS TURNED RENEGADE! NONE OF US HAS BEEN HARMED IN ANY WAY!
WELL, THAT'S A RELIEF! I DON'T KNOW WHO OR WHAT IT WAS PRETENDING TO BE ONE OF YOU--BUT HE HAD ALL YOUR GREAT POWERS! FORTUNATE HE IS NO MORE!

WITH THE PROMISE OF THE *GUARDIANS* TO LOOK INTO THE MATTER STILL RINGING IN HIS EARS, AND NEVER SUSPECTING THAT HECTOR HAMMOND WAS BEHIND THE FALSE *GUARDIAN*, THE *EMERALD CRUSADER* HEADS HOMEWARD...

HMMM! I JUST REMEMBERED I HAVE A DATE WITH CAROL FERRIS AS-- HAL JORDAN! SINCE ONLY A FEW HOURS HAVE ELAPSED SINCE I FIRST SAW THE *PSEUDO-GUARDIAN*--I'LL BE ABLE TO KEEP IT!

AND SO--ONLY A LITTLE LATE--HAL JORDAN CALLS UPON THE GIRL HE LOVES...

I'M LOOKING FORWARD TO SEEING THAT CARNIVAL, HAL!

SO AM I, CAROL-- SEEING IT WITH *YOU*, THAT IS!

THERE IS ONLY ONE EXHIBIT MISSING FROM THE SCENE, HOWEVER...

OHH, THE BLUE-SKINNED SPACEMAN EXHIBIT IS CLOSED! I GUESS THE AUTHORITIES REALIZED HE WAS A *PHONY!*

COULD BE, CAROL-- COULD BE!

CLOSED

The End.

24

GREEN LANTERN

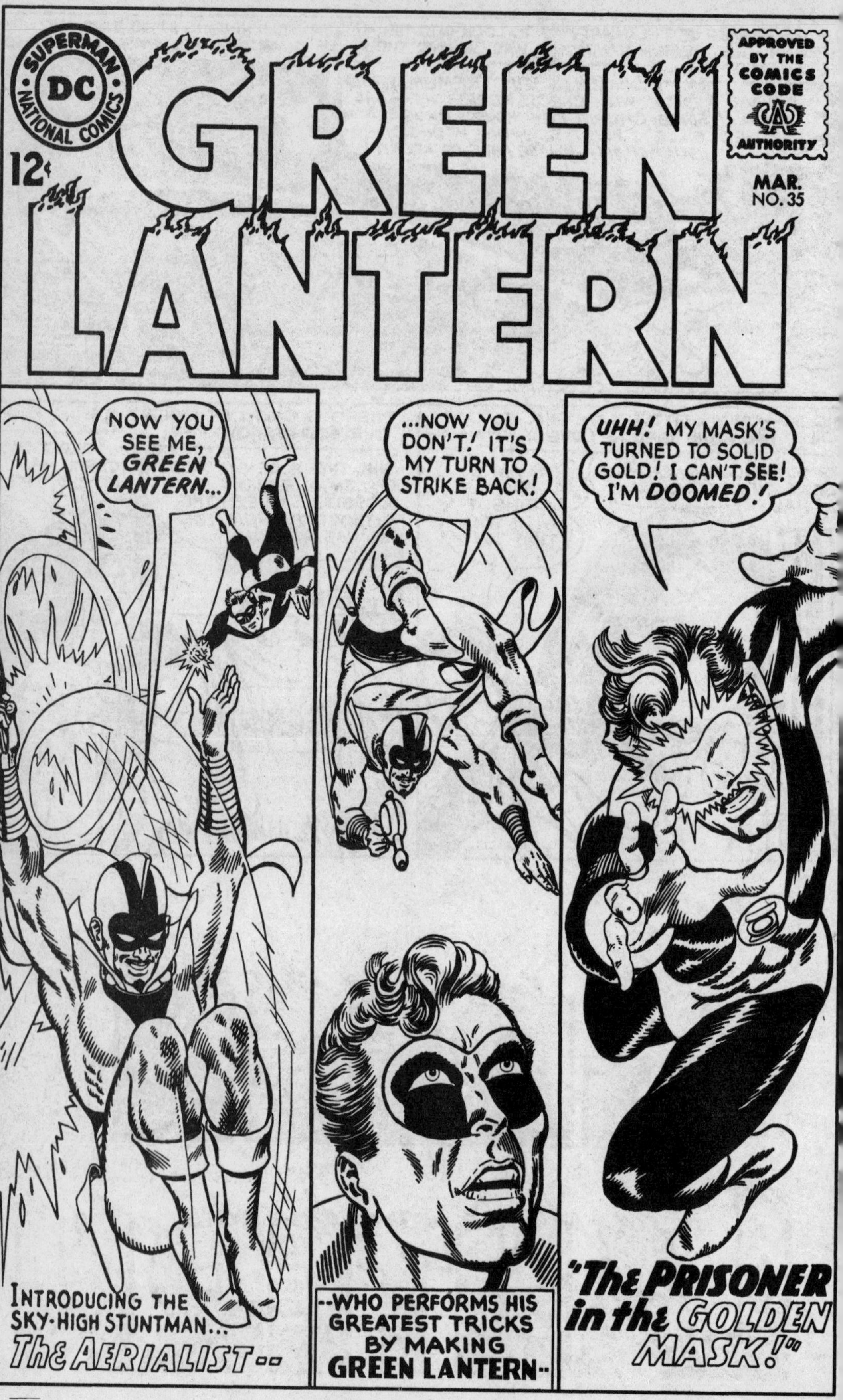

SUPERMAN DC NATIONAL COMICS
12¢
GREEN LANTERN
APPROVED BY THE COMICS CODE AUTHORITY
MAR. NO. 35
NOW YOU SEE ME, GREEN LANTERN...
...NOW YOU DON'T! IT'S MY TURN TO STRIKE BACK!
UHH! MY MASK'S TURNED TO SOLID GOLD! I CAN'T SEE! I'M DOOMED!
INTRODUCING THE SKY-HIGH STUNTMAN... THE AERIALIST--
--WHO PERFORMS HIS GREATEST TRICKS BY MAKING GREEN LANTERN--
"The PRISONER in the GOLDEN MASK!"

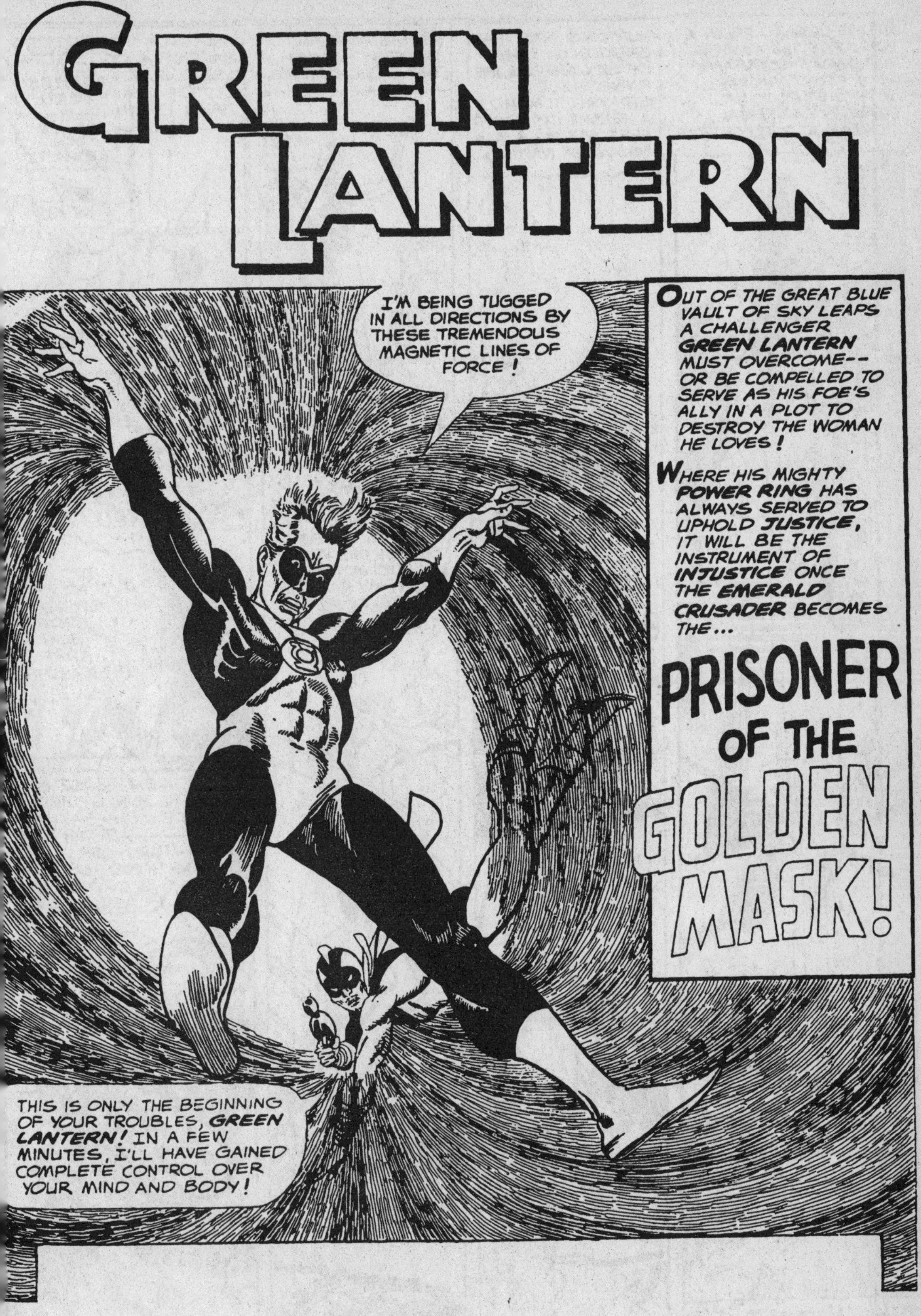
GREEN LANTERN
I'M BEING TUGGED IN ALL DIRECTIONS BY THESE TREMENDOUS MAGNETIC LINES OF FORCE!
OUT OF THE GREAT BLUE VAULT OF SKY LEAPS A CHALLENGER GREEN LANTERN MUST OVERCOME-- OR BE COMPELLED TO SERVE AS HIS FOE'S ALLY IN A PLOT TO DESTROY THE WOMAN HE LOVES!
WHERE HIS MIGHTY POWER RING HAS ALWAYS SERVED TO UPHOLD JUSTICE, IT WILL BE THE INSTRUMENT OF INJUSTICE ONCE THE EMERALD CRUSADER BECOMES THE...
PRISONER OF THE GOLDEN MASK!
THIS IS ONLY THE BEGINNING OF YOUR TROUBLES, GREEN LANTERN! IN A FEW MINUTES, I'LL HAVE GAINED COMPLETE CONTROL OVER YOUR MIND AND BODY!

RISING UPWARD FROM A RUNWAY OF THE *FERRIS AIRCRAFT COMPANY* IS A *VTOL** AIRCRAFT, WITH TEST PILOT HAL (*GREEN LANTERN*) JORDAN AT THE CONTROLS..

Editor's Note: VERTICAL TAKE OFF AND LANDING.

HURTLING INTO THAT GREAT BLUE VAULT OF SKY SPEEDS THE FLYING BULLET-- STRAIGHT TOWARD A HEIGHT OF 60,000 FEET WHERE A MAN "STANDS" WAITING...

AS THE AIRPLANE BURSTS THROUGH THE CLOUD COVER...

GREAT GUARDIANS! A MAN--STANDING THERE--ON EMPTY AIR! I MUST BE SUFFERING AN HALLUCINATION FROM MY RAPID TAKE-OFF!

SUDDENLY, THE MAN IN THE GARB OF A CIRCUS AERIALIST LEAPS OUTWARD-- HIS HAND CLUTCHING A POWERFUL HAND-GRENADE...

IT'S AS IF HE WERE SWINGING FROM ONE INVISIBLE TRAPEZE TO ANOTHER!

AS THE *AERIALIST* GLIDES PAST--HE HURLS THE GRENADE...

I CAN'T STOP--TURN--OR DO ANYTHING TO AVOID THE ONCOMING BLAST!

NEXT MOMENT AN EXPLOSION RIPS THE AIR ABOUT THE PLANE! AS DELICATE ENGINE PARTS ARE SHATTERED, HAL JORDAN IS TOSSED ABOUT LIKE A RAG DOLL...

WAROOOOO!

EXPLOSION WILL--WRECK INSTRUMENTS ENOUGH-- NO PLANE WILL CRASH! GOT TO-- EJECT...

THE POWERFUL EJECTOR SPRING HURLS HIM HIGH AND AWAY FROM THE OUT-OF-CONTROL *VTOL* ALREADY SPINNING TO ITS DOOM...

I DAREN'T BECOME *GREEN LANTERN!* IT WOULD REVEAL MY SECRET IDENTITY TO MY ASSAILANT--AND SO FAR THERE ISN'T ANY NEED TO GO TO SUCH EXTREMES!

THEN AS HIS RIP-CORD IS YANKED AND HIS PARACHUTE STARTS TO OPEN, THE *AERIALIST* LEAPS DOWNWARD...

YOU AGAIN! WHAT'S BEHIND ALL THIS?

I DON'T MEAN YOU ANY HARM! IT'S THE *FERRIS* FAMILY I'M AFTER!

AS IF MISSING A HOLD ON HIS INVISIBLE TRAPEZE BAR, THE *AERIALIST* FALLS PAST THE FLOATING TEST PILOT...

TELL THEM THE SPIRIT OF *ELKE HENSEN* DEMANDS VENGEANCE AND THAT I-- THE *AERIALIST*--WILL SEE THAT SHE GETS IT!

HE'S FALLING TOWARD THE GROUND! I'LL *HAVE* TO SAVE HIM--AS *GREEN LANTERN!*

SUDDENLY, THE MYSTERIOUS PERFORMER HITS WHAT SEEMS TO BE AN INVISIBLE NET AND TRIUMPHANTLY BOUNCES UPWARD...

HAD YOU WORRIED FOR A MOMENT, EH? MY POWER OVER THE MAGNETIC LINES OF EARTH ARE SUCH THAT NO HARM CAN COME TO ME AS IT CAME TO POOR *ELKE!* GO TELL CAROL FERRIS AND HER FAMILY THAT THEY ARE-- MARKED FOR *DOOM!*

FAR BELOW, SIRENS SCREAM AS AN AMBULANCE--WITH AN APPREHENSIVE CAROL FERRIS RIDING IN IT--RACES ACROSS THE COUNTRYSIDE...

VREEEEEE!

OH, HAL! I HOPE YOU'RE SAFE!

3.

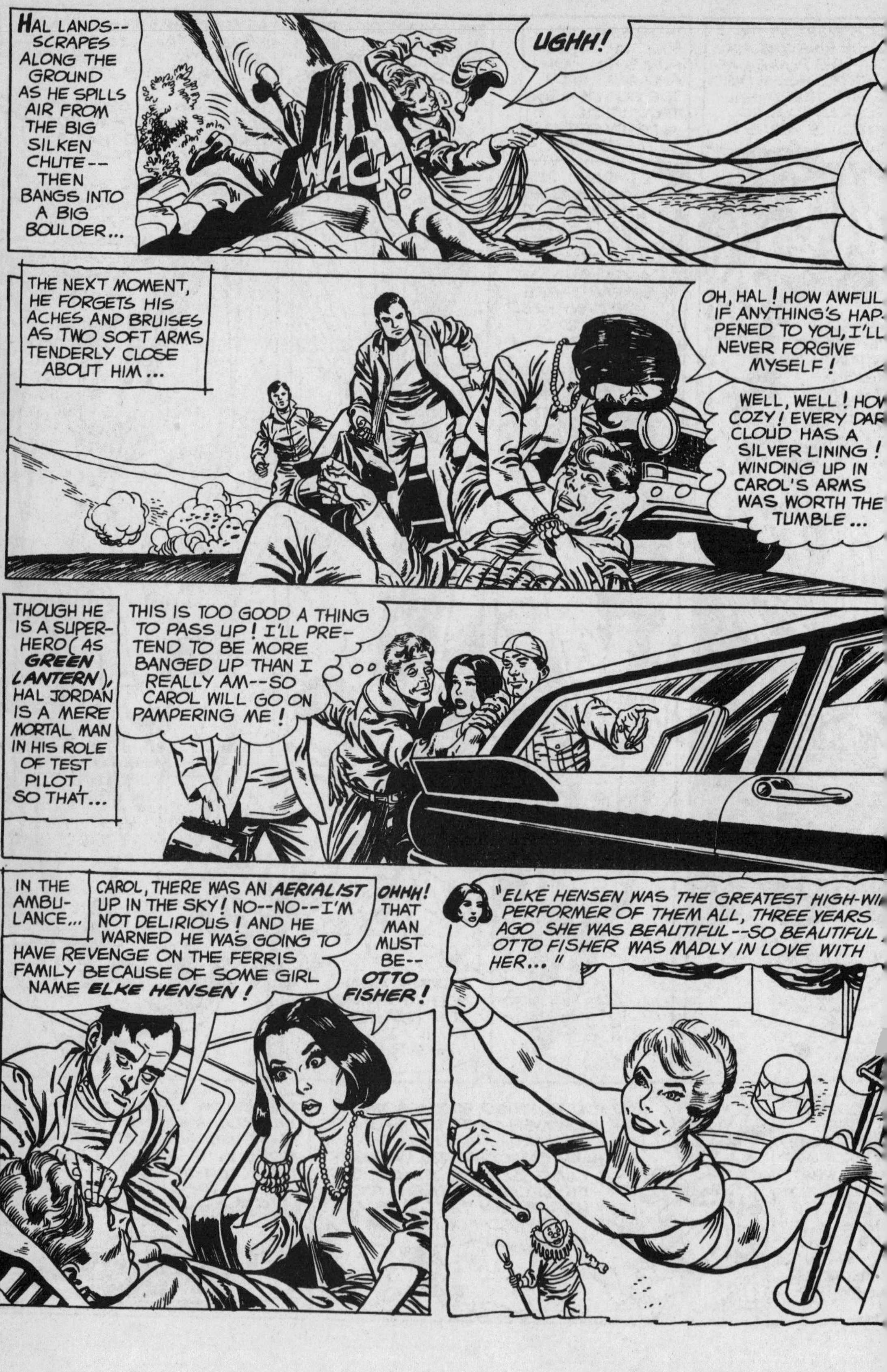

HAL LANDS-- SCRAPES ALONG THE GROUND AS HE SPILLS AIR FROM THE BIG SILKEN CHUTE-- THEN BANGS INTO A BIG BOULDER...
UGHH!
WACK!
THE NEXT MOMENT, HE FORGETS HIS ACHES AND BRUISES AS TWO SOFT ARMS TENDERLY CLOSE ABOUT HIM...
OH, HAL! HOW AWFUL IF ANYTHING'S HAP-PENED TO YOU, I'LL NEVER FORGIVE MYSELF!
WELL, WELL! HOW COZY! EVERY DAR CLOUD HAS A SILVER LINING! WINDING UP IN CAROL'S ARMS WAS WORTH THE TUMBLE...
THOUGH HE IS A SUPER-HERO (AS GREEN LANTERN), HAL JORDAN IS A MERE MORTAL MAN IN HIS ROLE OF TEST PILOT, SO THAT...
THIS IS TOO GOOD A THING TO PASS UP! I'LL PRE-TEND TO BE MORE BANGED UP THAN I REALLY AM--SO CAROL WILL GO ON PAMPERING ME!
IN THE AMBULANCE...
CAROL, THERE WAS AN AERIALIST UP IN THE SKY! NO--NO--I'M NOT DELIRIOUS! AND HE WARNED HE WAS GOING TO HAVE REVENGE ON THE FERRIS FAMILY BECAUSE OF SOME GIRL NAME ELKE HENSEN!
OHHH! THAT MAN MUST BE-- OTTO FISHER!
"ELKE HENSEN WAS THE GREATEST HIGH-WI PERFORMER OF THEM ALL, THREE YEARS AGO SHE WAS BEAUTIFUL--SO BEAUTIFUL OTTO FISHER WAS MADLY IN LOVE WITH HER..."

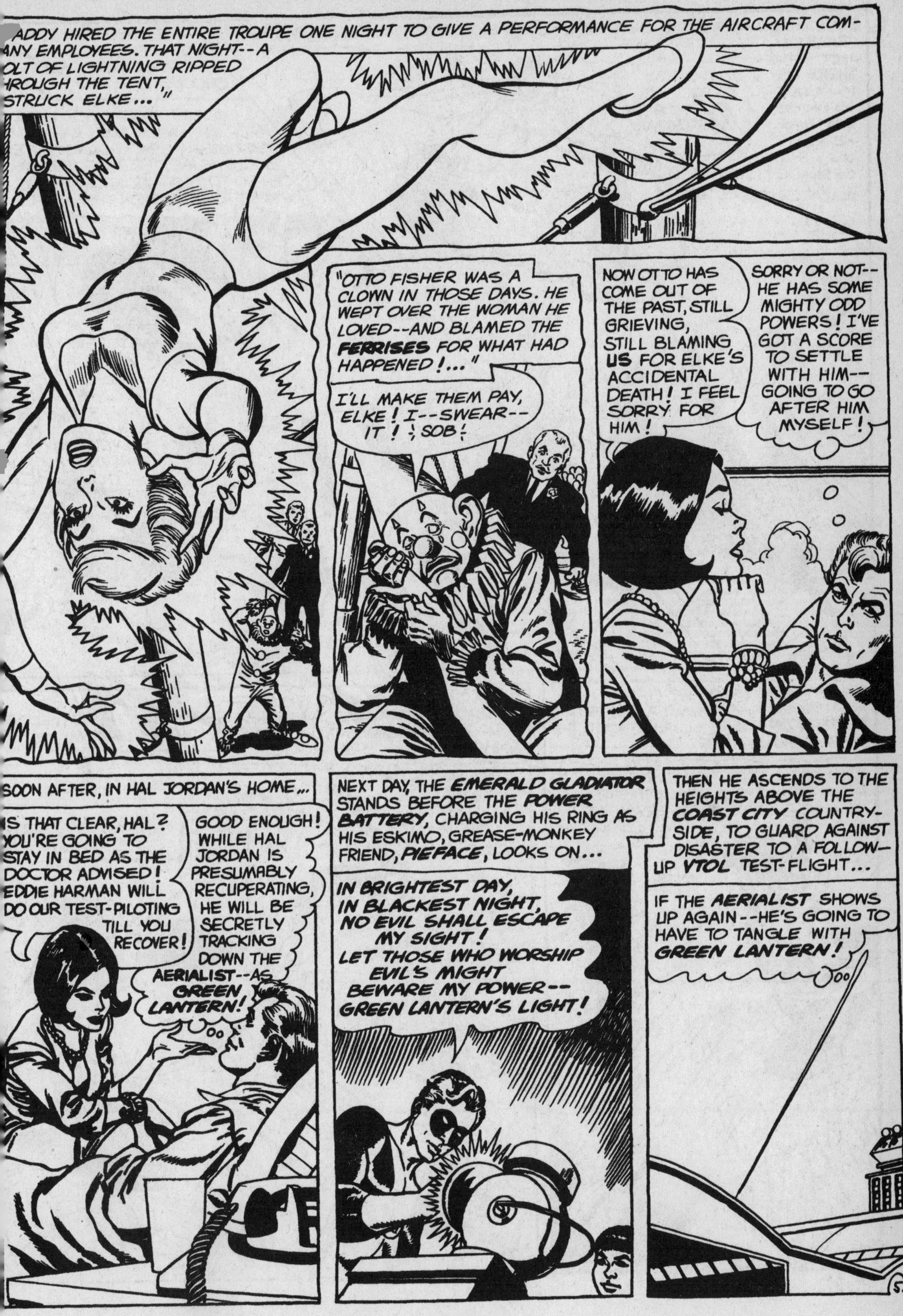

ADDY HIRED THE ENTIRE TROUPE ONE NIGHT TO GIVE A PERFORMANCE FOR THE AIRCRAFT COM-ANY EMPLOYEES. THAT NIGHT--A OLT OF LIGHTNING RIPPED HROUGH THE TENT, STRUCK ELKE..."
"OTTO FISHER WAS A CLOWN IN THOSE DAYS. HE WEPT OVER THE WOMAN HE LOVED--AND BLAMED THE FERRISES FOR WHAT HAD HAPPENED!..."
I'LL MAKE THEM PAY, ELKE! I--SWEAR--IT! SOB!
NOW OTTO HAS COME OUT OF THE PAST, STILL GRIEVING, STILL BLAMING US FOR ELKE'S ACCIDENTAL DEATH! I FEEL SORRY FOR HIM!
SORRY OR NOT--HE HAS SOME MIGHTY ODD POWERS! I'VE GOT A SCORE TO SETTLE WITH HIM--GOING TO GO AFTER HIM MYSELF!
SOON AFTER, IN HAL JORDAN'S HOME...
IS THAT CLEAR, HAL? YOU'RE GOING TO STAY IN BED AS THE DOCTOR ADVISED! EDDIE HARMAN WILL DO OUR TEST-PILOTING TILL YOU RECOVER!
GOOD ENOUGH! WHILE HAL JORDAN IS PRESUMABLY RECUPERATING, HE WILL BE SECRETLY TRACKING DOWN THE AERIALIST--AS GREEN LANTERN!
NEXT DAY, THE EMERALD GLADIATOR STANDS BEFORE THE POWER BATTERY, CHARGING HIS RING AS HIS ESKIMO, GREASE-MONKEY FRIEND, PIEFACE, LOOKS ON...
IN BRIGHTEST DAY, IN BLACKEST NIGHT, NO EVIL SHALL ESCAPE MY SIGHT! LET THOSE WHO WORSHIP EVIL'S MIGHT BEWARE MY POWER--GREEN LANTERN'S LIGHT!
THEN HE ASCENDS TO THE HEIGHTS ABOVE THE COAST CITY COUNTRY-SIDE, TO GUARD AGAINST DISASTER TO A FOLLOW-UP VTOL TEST-FLIGHT...
IF THE AERIALIST SHOWS UP AGAIN--HE'S GOING TO HAVE TO TANGLE WITH GREEN LANTERN!
5.

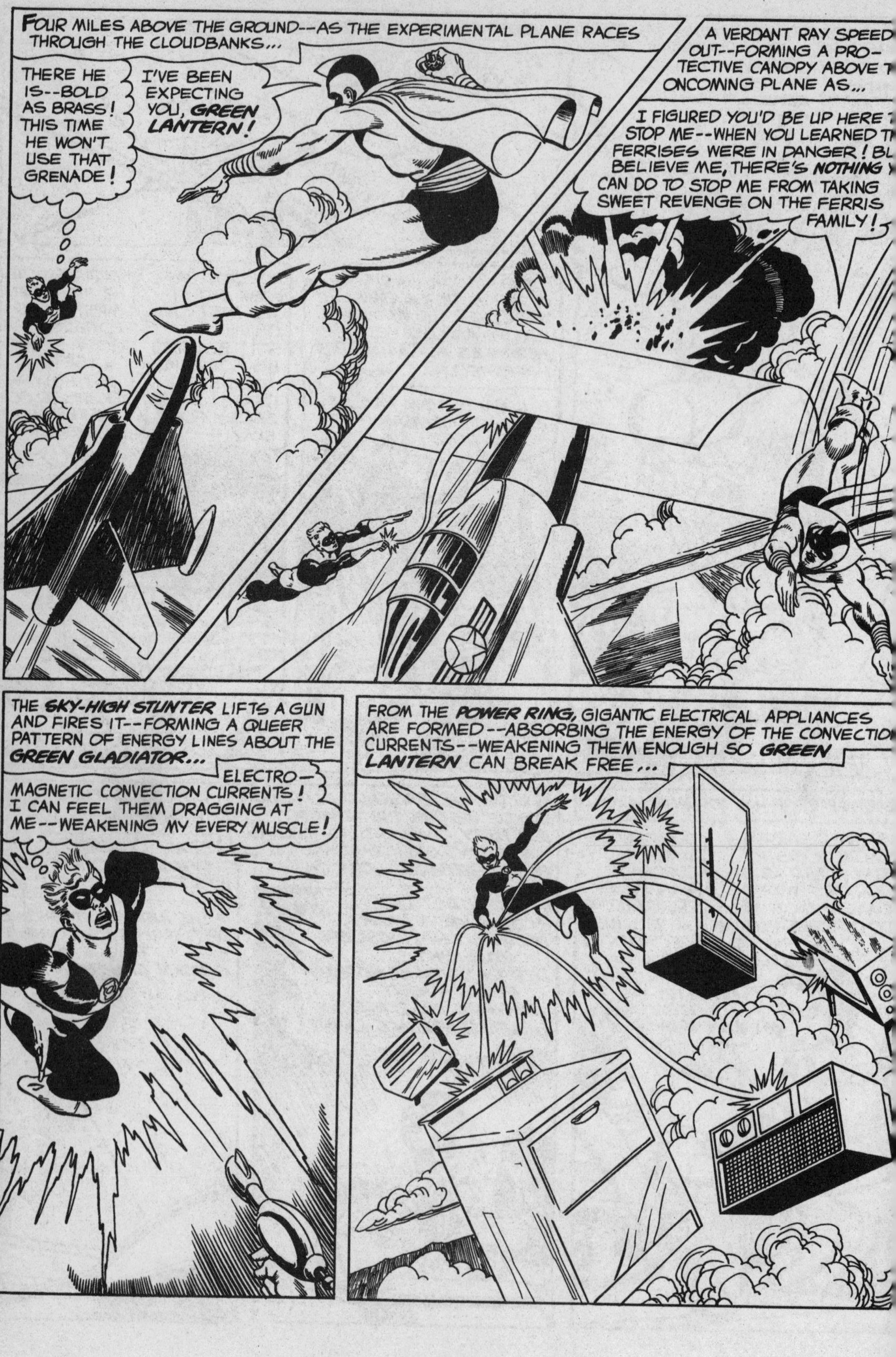
FOUR MILES ABOVE THE GROUND--AS THE EXPERIMENTAL PLANE RACES THROUGH THE CLOUDBANKS...
THERE HE IS--BOLD AS BRASS! THIS TIME HE WON'T USE THAT GRENADE!
I'VE BEEN EXPECTING YOU, GREEN LANTERN!
A VERDANT RAY SPEED OUT--FORMING A PRO-TECTIVE CANOPY ABOVE T ONCOMING PLANE AS...
I FIGURED YOU'D BE UP HERE STOP ME--WHEN YOU LEARNED T FERRISES WERE IN DANGER! B BELIEVE ME, THERE'S NOTHING CAN DO TO STOP ME FROM TAKING SWEET REVENGE ON THE FERRIS FAMILY!
THE SKY-HIGH STUNTER LIFTS A GUN AND FIRES IT--FORMING A QUEER PATTERN OF ENERGY LINES ABOUT THE GREEN GLADIATOR...
ELECTRO-MAGNETIC CONVECTION CURRENTS! I CAN FEEL THEM DRAGGING AT ME--WEAKENING MY EVERY MUSCLE!
FROM THE POWER RING, GIGANTIC ELECTRICAL APPLIANCES ARE FORMED--ABSORBING THE ENERGY OF THE CONVECTIO CURRENTS--WEAKENING THEM ENOUGH SO GREEN LANTERN CAN BREAK FREE...

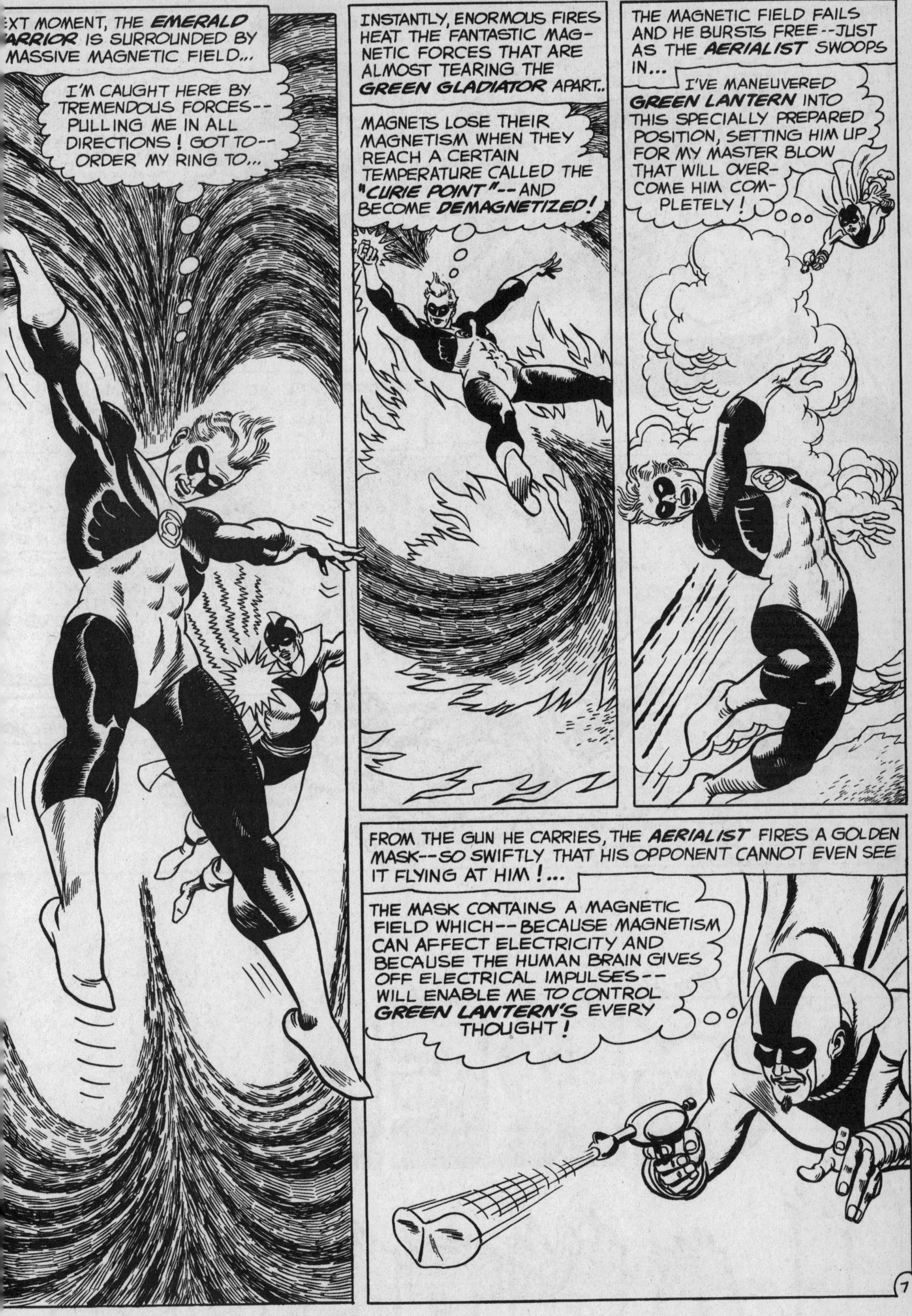
EXT MOMENT, THE EMERALD ARRIOR IS SURROUNDED BY MASSIVE MAGNETIC FIELD...
I'M CAUGHT HERE BY TREMENDOUS FORCES-- PULLING ME IN ALL DIRECTIONS! GOT TO-- ORDER MY RING TO...
INSTANTLY, ENORMOUS FIRES HEAT THE FANTASTIC MAGNETIC FORCES THAT ARE ALMOST TEARING THE GREEN GLADIATOR APART..
MAGNETS LOSE THEIR MAGNETISM WHEN THEY REACH A CERTAIN TEMPERATURE CALLED THE "CURIE POINT"-- AND BECOME DEMAGNETIZED!
THE MAGNETIC FIELD FAILS AND HE BURSTS FREE--JUST AS THE AERIALIST SWOOPS IN...
I'VE MANEUVERED GREEN LANTERN INTO THIS SPECIALLY PREPARED POSITION, SETTING HIM UP FOR MY MASTER BLOW THAT WILL OVERCOME HIM COMPLETELY!
FROM THE GUN HE CARRIES, THE AERIALIST FIRES A GOLDEN MASK--SO SWIFTLY THAT HIS OPPONENT CANNOT EVEN SEE IT FLYING AT HIM!...
THE MASK CONTAINS A MAGNETIC FIELD WHICH--BECAUSE MAGNETISM CAN AFFECT ELECTRICITY AND BECAUSE THE HUMAN BRAIN GIVES OFF ELECTRICAL IMPULSES-- WILL ENABLE ME TO CONTROL GREEN LANTERN'S EVERY THOUGHT!
7

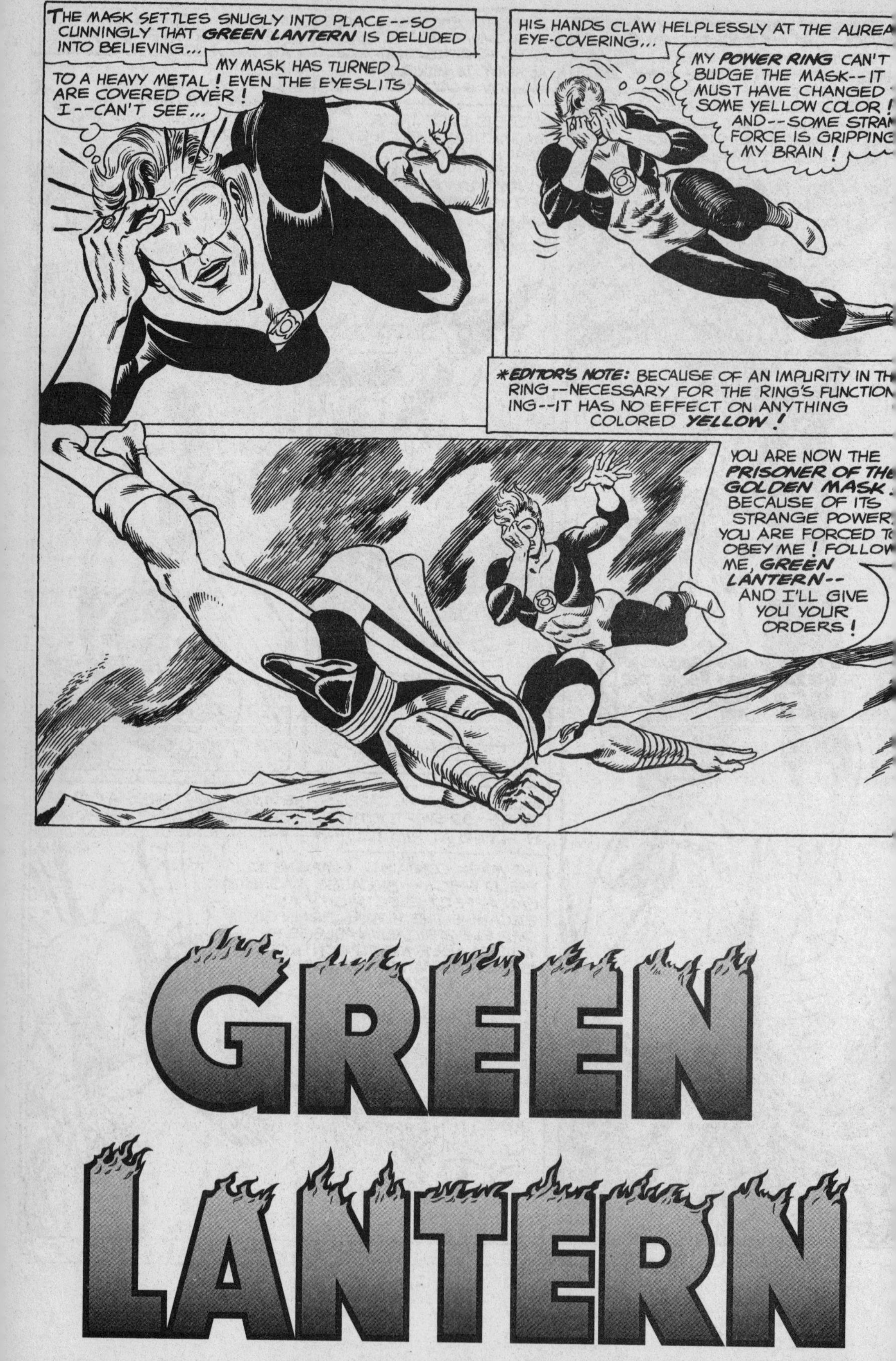
THE MASK SETTLES SNUGLY INTO PLACE--SO CUNNINGLY THAT GREEN LANTERN IS DELUDED INTO BELIEVING...
MY MASK HAS TURNED TO A HEAVY METAL! EVEN THE EYESLITS ARE COVERED OVER! I--CAN'T SEE...
HIS HANDS CLAW HELPLESSLY AT THE AUREA EYE-COVERING...
MY POWER RING CAN'T BUDGE THE MASK--IT MUST HAVE CHANGED T SOME YELLOW COLOR! AND--SOME STRAN FORCE IS GRIPPING MY BRAIN!
*EDITOR'S NOTE: BECAUSE OF AN IMPURITY IN TH RING--NECESSARY FOR THE RING'S FUNCTION ING--IT HAS NO EFFECT ON ANYTHING COLORED YELLOW!
YOU ARE NOW THE PRISONER OF THE GOLDEN MASK. BECAUSE OF ITS STRANGE POWER, YOU ARE FORCED TO OBEY ME! FOLLOW ME, GREEN LANTERN-- AND I'LL GIVE YOU YOUR ORDERS!

GREEN LANTERN

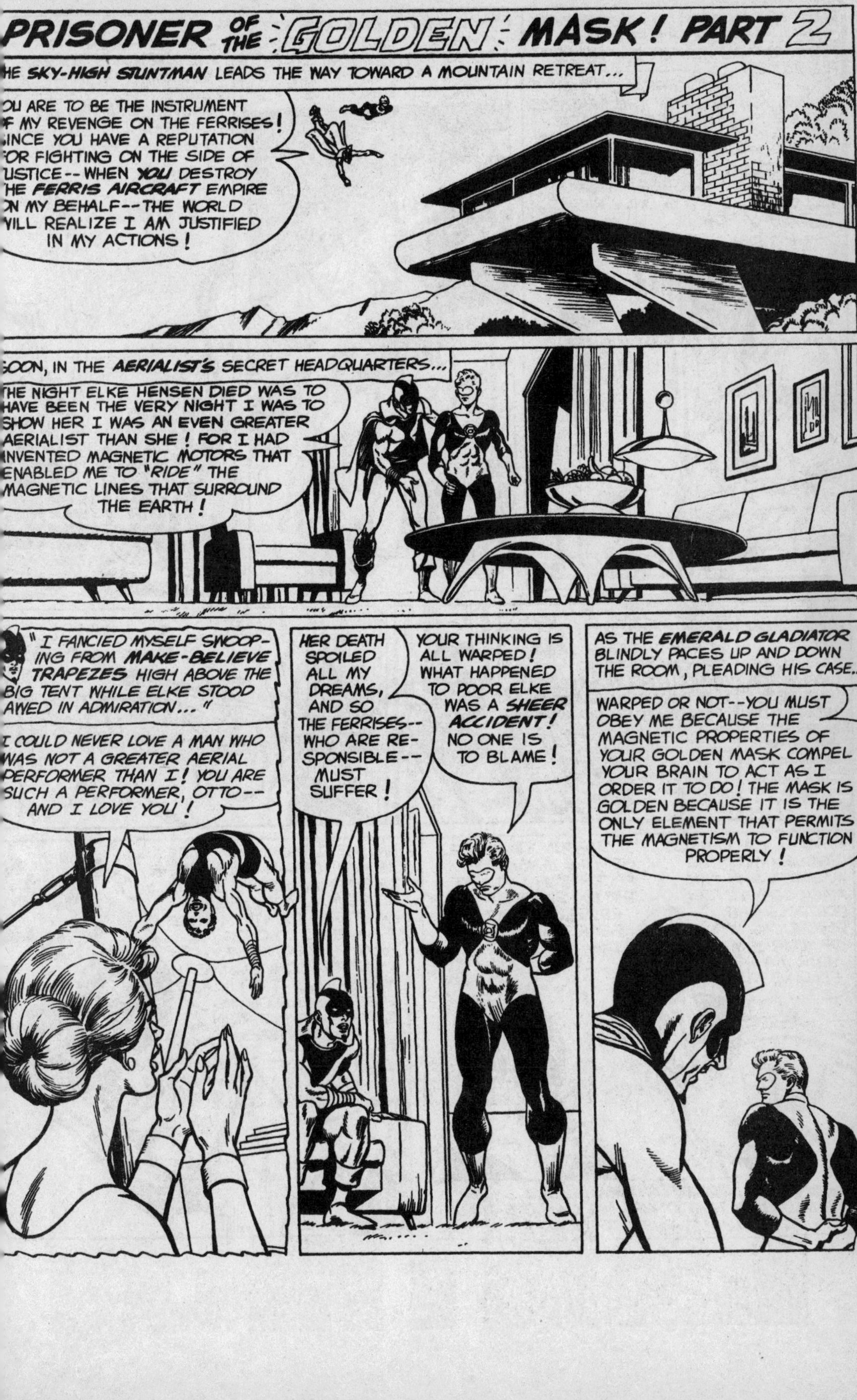
PRISONER OF THE GOLDEN MASK! PART 2
HE SKY-HIGH STUNTMAN LEADS THE WAY TOWARD A MOUNTAIN RETREAT...
OU ARE TO BE THE INSTRUMENT F MY REVENGE ON THE FERRISES! INCE YOU HAVE A REPUTATION OR FIGHTING ON THE SIDE OF USTICE--WHEN YOU DESTROY HE FERRIS AIRCRAFT EMPIRE N MY BEHALF--THE WORLD VILL REALIZE I AM JUSTIFIED IN MY ACTIONS!
OON, IN THE AERIALIST'S SECRET HEADQUARTERS...
HE NIGHT ELKE HENSEN DIED WAS TO HAVE BEEN THE VERY NIGHT I WAS TO SHOW HER I WAS AN EVEN GREATER AERIALIST THAN SHE! FOR I HAD NVENTED MAGNETIC MOTORS THAT ENABLED ME TO "RIDE" THE MAGNETIC LINES THAT SURROUND THE EARTH!
"I FANCIED MYSELF SWOOPING FROM MAKE-BELIEVE TRAPEZES HIGH ABOVE THE BIG TENT WHILE ELKE STOOD AWED IN ADMIRATION..."
I COULD NEVER LOVE A MAN WHO WAS NOT A GREATER AERIAL PERFORMER THAN I! YOU ARE SUCH A PERFORMER, OTTO--AND I LOVE YOU!
HER DEATH SPOILED ALL MY DREAMS, AND SO THE FERRISES--WHO ARE RESPONSIBLE--MUST SUFFER!
YOUR THINKING IS ALL WARPED! WHAT HAPPENED TO POOR ELKE WAS A SHEER ACCIDENT! NO ONE IS TO BLAME!
AS THE EMERALD GLADIATOR BLINDLY PACES UP AND DOWN THE ROOM, PLEADING HIS CASE...
WARPED OR NOT--YOU MUST OBEY ME BECAUSE THE MAGNETIC PROPERTIES OF YOUR GOLDEN MASK COMPEL YOUR BRAIN TO ACT AS I ORDER IT TO DO! THE MASK IS GOLDEN BECAUSE IT IS THE ONLY ELEMENT THAT PERMITS THE MAGNETISM TO FUNCTION PROPERLY!
9

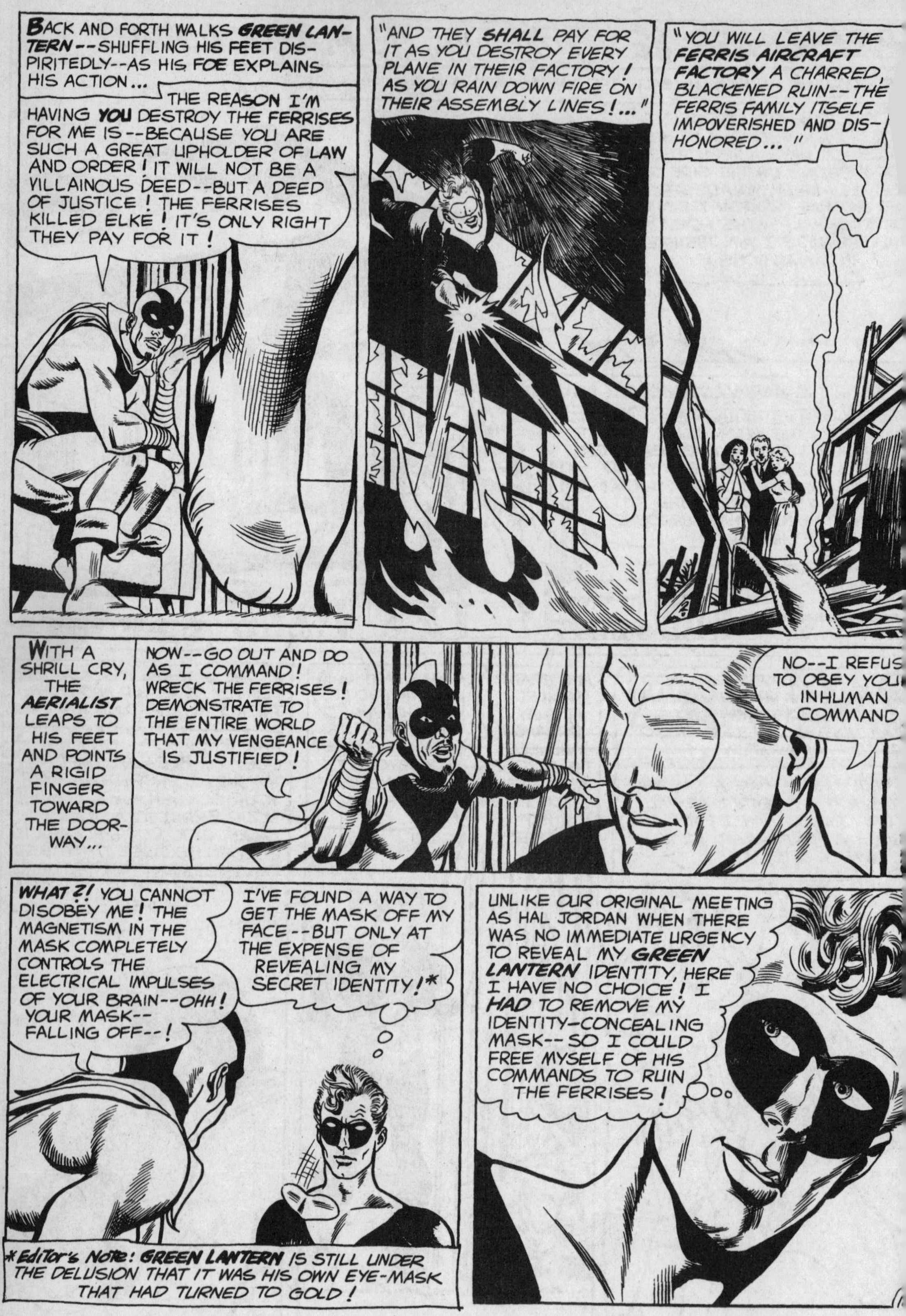
BACK AND FORTH WALKS GREEN LANTERN--SHUFFLING HIS FEET DISPIRITEDLY--AS HIS FOE EXPLAINS HIS ACTION...
THE REASON I'M HAVING YOU DESTROY THE FERRISES FOR ME IS--BECAUSE YOU ARE SUCH A GREAT UPHOLDER OF LAW AND ORDER! IT WILL NOT BE A VILLAINOUS DEED--BUT A DEED OF JUSTICE! THE FERRISES KILLED ELKE! IT'S ONLY RIGHT THEY PAY FOR IT!
"AND THEY SHALL PAY FOR IT AS YOU DESTROY EVERY PLANE IN THEIR FACTORY! AS YOU RAIN DOWN FIRE ON THEIR ASSEMBLY LINES!..."
"YOU WILL LEAVE THE FERRIS AIRCRAFT FACTORY A CHARRED, BLACKENED RUIN--THE FERRIS FAMILY ITSELF IMPOVERISHED AND DISHONORED..."
WITH A SHRILL CRY, THE AERIALIST LEAPS TO HIS FEET AND POINTS A RIGID FINGER TOWARD THE DOORWAY...
NOW--GO OUT AND DO AS I COMMAND! WRECK THE FERRISES! DEMONSTRATE TO THE ENTIRE WORLD THAT MY VENGEANCE IS JUSTIFIED!
NO--I REFUS TO OBEY YOU INHUMAN COMMAND
WHAT?! YOU CANNOT DISOBEY ME! THE MAGNETISM IN THE MASK COMPLETELY CONTROLS THE ELECTRICAL IMPULSES OF YOUR BRAIN--OHH! YOUR MASK--FALLING OFF--!
I'VE FOUND A WAY TO GET THE MASK OFF MY FACE--BUT ONLY AT THE EXPENSE OF REVEALING MY SECRET IDENTITY!*
*Editor's Note: GREEN LANTERN IS STILL UNDER THE DELUSION THAT IT WAS HIS OWN EYE-MASK THAT HAD TURNED TO GOLD!
UNLIKE OUR ORIGINAL MEETING AS HAL JORDAN WHEN THERE WAS NO IMMEDIATE URGENCY TO REVEAL MY GREEN LANTERN IDENTITY, HERE I HAVE NO CHOICE! I HAD TO REMOVE MY IDENTITY-CONCEALING MASK--SO I COULD FREE MYSELF OF HIS COMMANDS TO RUIN THE FERRISES!

INSTANTLY THE *POWER RING* FILLS THE ROOM WITH A STRANGE ARRAY OF OBJECTS...

GLASS ROD AND SILK--A PLANE GIVING OFF *ST. ELMO'S* FIRE BECAUSE OF ITS CHARGE OF STATIC ELECTRICITY--AN ELECTROSTATIC GENERATOR! THERE COULD BE ONLY ONE REASON FOR ALL THIS--

--THE SAME REASON WHY YOU WERE WALKING BACK AND FORTH, SHUFFLING YOUR FEET ON THE RUG! YOU WERE BUILDING A RESERVE OF *STATIC ELECTRICITY* IN YOUR BODY! YOUR MIND WAS UNDER MY CONTROL-- BUT I NEVER THOUGHT OF FORBIDDING YOU TO DO *THAT*!

SINCE THE *ELECTRIC CHARGE* IN THE HUMAN BRAIN IS SO WEAK--AND SINCE THE MAGNETISM OF THE GENERATOR WAS PREPARED ONLY TO HANDLE THAT CHARGE--THE FAR GREATER SURGE OF *STATIC ELECTRICITY* IN YOUR BODY SHORT-CIRCUITED THE MASK--AND CAUSED IT TO LOSE ITS GRIP ON YOUR FACE!

NEXT INSTANT, THE *AERIALIST* LEAPS FORWARD--FLIPPING INTO THE AIR TO LAND BEHIND *GREEN LANTERN*...

PRETTY CLEVER OF YOU--BUT IT WON'T DO YOU ANY GOOD! YOU FORMED THOSE OTHER STATIC ELECTRICITY GENERATORS TO PREVENT ME FROM AGAIN IMPRISONING YOU WITH MY MASK--BUT I CAN STILL WIN OVER YOU!

THUD!

HE FOLLOWS UP WITH A SMASHING BLOW, FLINGING THE *EMERALD GLADIATOR* BACKWARDS, CRASHING OVER A TABLE...

SOK!

I COULD STRIKE BACK AT HIM BY SWITCHING TO MY *POWER RING*-- BUT I'D RATHER *FIGHT* THAN *SWITCH*!

11.

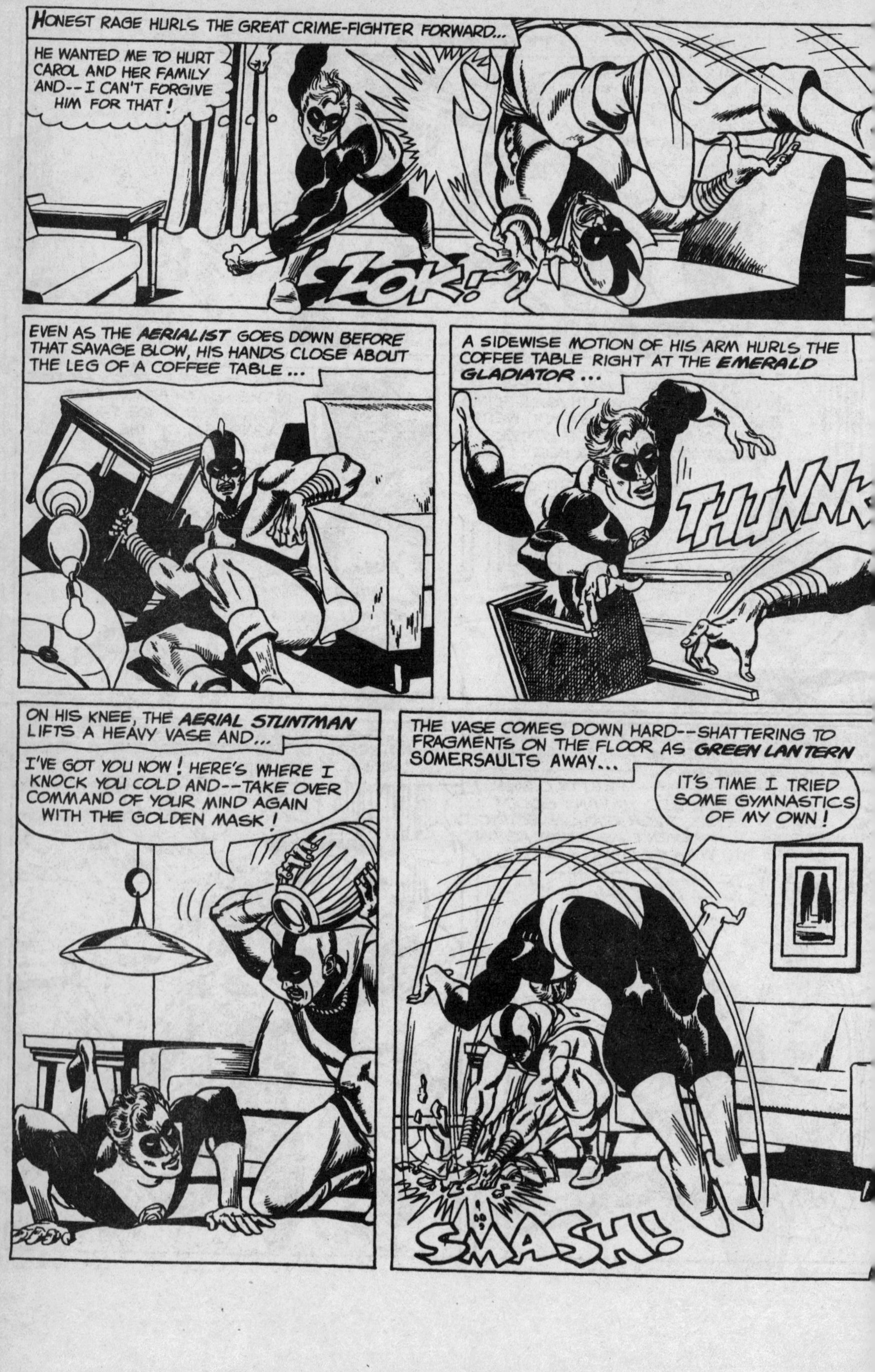
HONEST RAGE HURLS THE GREAT CRIME-FIGHTER FORWARD...
HE WANTED ME TO HURT CAROL AND HER FAMILY AND--I CAN'T FORGIVE HIM FOR THAT!
ZOK!
EVEN AS THE AERIALIST GOES DOWN BEFORE THAT SAVAGE BLOW, HIS HANDS CLOSE ABOUT THE LEG OF A COFFEE TABLE...
A SIDEWISE MOTION OF HIS ARM HURLS THE COFFEE TABLE RIGHT AT THE EMERALD GLADIATOR...
THUNNK
ON HIS KNEE, THE AERIAL STUNTMAN LIFTS A HEAVY VASE AND...
I'VE GOT YOU NOW! HERE'S WHERE I KNOCK YOU COLD AND--TAKE OVER COMMAND OF YOUR MIND AGAIN WITH THE GOLDEN MASK!
THE VASE COMES DOWN HARD--SHATTERING TO FRAGMENTS ON THE FLOOR AS GREEN LANTERN SOMERSAULTS AWAY...
IT'S TIME I TRIED SOME GYMNASTICS OF MY OWN!
SMASH!

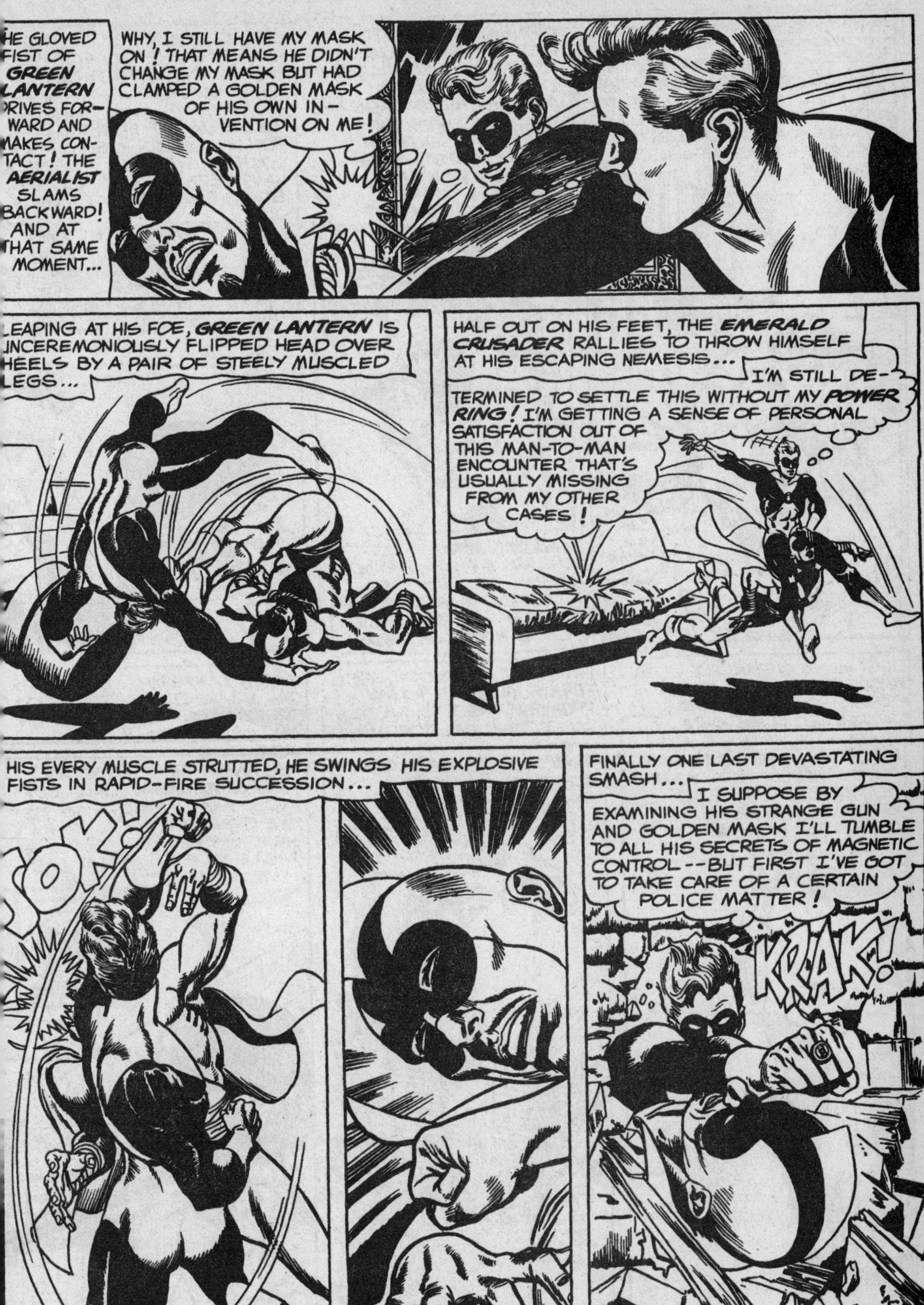
HE GLOVED FIST OF GREEN LANTERN DRIVES FORWARD AND MAKES CONTACT! THE AERIALIST SLAMS BACKWARD! AND AT THAT SAME MOMENT...
WHY, I STILL HAVE MY MASK ON! THAT MEANS HE DIDN'T CHANGE MY MASK BUT HAD CLAMPED A GOLDEN MASK OF HIS OWN INVENTION ON ME!
LEAPING AT HIS FOE, GREEN LANTERN IS UNCEREMONIOUSLY FLIPPED HEAD OVER HEELS BY A PAIR OF STEELY MUSCLED LEGS...
HALF OUT ON HIS FEET, THE EMERALD CRUSADER RALLIES TO THROW HIMSELF AT HIS ESCAPING NEMESIS...
I'M STILL DETERMINED TO SETTLE THIS WITHOUT MY POWER RING! I'M GETTING A SENSE OF PERSONAL SATISFACTION OUT OF THIS MAN-TO-MAN ENCOUNTER THAT'S USUALLY MISSING FROM MY OTHER CASES!
HIS EVERY MUSCLE STRUTTED, HE SWINGS HIS EXPLOSIVE FISTS IN RAPID-FIRE SUCCESSION...
SOK!
FINALLY ONE LAST DEVASTATING SMASH...
I SUPPOSE BY EXAMINING HIS STRANGE GUN AND GOLDEN MASK I'LL TUMBLE TO ALL HIS SECRETS OF MAGNETIC CONTROL--BUT FIRST I'VE GOT TO TAKE CARE OF A CERTAIN POLICE MATTER!
KRAK!
13

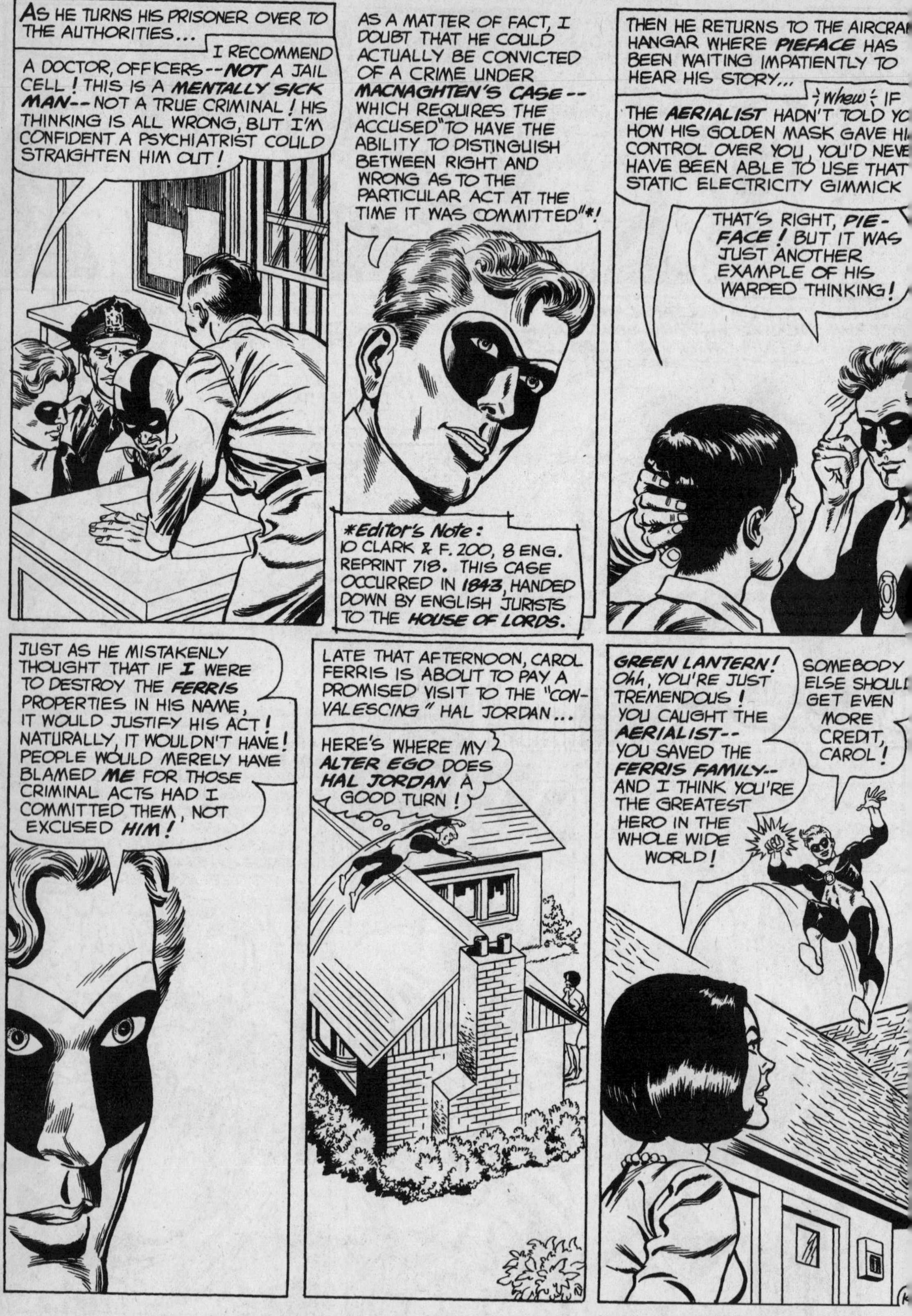

AS HE TURNS HIS PRISONER OVER TO THE AUTHORITIES...
I RECOMMEND A DOCTOR, OFFICERS--NOT A JAIL CELL! THIS IS A MENTALLY SICK MAN--NOT A TRUE CRIMINAL! HIS THINKING IS ALL WRONG, BUT I'M CONFIDENT A PSYCHIATRIST COULD STRAIGHTEN HIM OUT!
AS A MATTER OF FACT, I DOUBT THAT HE COULD ACTUALLY BE CONVICTED OF A CRIME UNDER MACNAGHTEN'S CASE--WHICH REQUIRES THE ACCUSED "TO HAVE THE ABILITY TO DISTINGUISH BETWEEN RIGHT AND WRONG AS TO THE PARTICULAR ACT AT THE TIME IT WAS COMMITTED"*!
*Editor's Note: 10 CLARK & F. 200, 8 ENG. REPRINT 718. THIS CASE OCCURRED IN 1843, HANDED DOWN BY ENGLISH JURISTS TO THE HOUSE OF LORDS.
THEN HE RETURNS TO THE AIRCRA HANGAR WHERE PIEFACE HAS BEEN WAITING IMPATIENTLY TO HEAR HIS STORY...
WHEW! IF THE AERIALIST HADN'T TOLD YO HOW HIS GOLDEN MASK GAVE HI CONTROL OVER YOU, YOU'D NEVE HAVE BEEN ABLE TO USE THAT STATIC ELECTRICITY GIMMICK
THAT'S RIGHT, PIE-FACE! BUT IT WAS JUST ANOTHER EXAMPLE OF HIS WARPED THINKING!
JUST AS HE MISTAKENLY THOUGHT THAT IF I WERE TO DESTROY THE FERRIS PROPERTIES IN HIS NAME, IT WOULD JUSTIFY HIS ACT! NATURALLY, IT WOULDN'T HAVE! PEOPLE WOULD MERELY HAVE BLAMED ME FOR THOSE CRIMINAL ACTS HAD I COMMITTED THEM, NOT EXCUSED HIM!
LATE THAT AFTERNOON, CAROL FERRIS IS ABOUT TO PAY A PROMISED VISIT TO THE "CONVALESCING" HAL JORDAN...
HERE'S WHERE MY ALTER EGO DOES HAL JORDAN A GOOD TURN!
GREEN LANTERN! Ohh, YOU'RE JUST TREMENDOUS! YOU CAUGHT THE AERIALIST--YOU SAVED THE FERRIS FAMILY--AND I THINK YOU'RE THE GREATEST HERO IN THE WHOLE WIDE WORLD!
SOMEBODY ELSE SHOUL GET EVEN MORE CREDIT, CAROL!

MORE CREDIT--THAN *YOU*? BUT *YOU* DID IT ALL! WHO ELSE DESERVES TO SHARE THE GLORY?

HAL JORDAN!

HAL JORDAN! WHAT DID HE DO?

AS A RESULT OF HIS FIRST ENCOUNTER WITH THE *AERIALIST*, HAL TIPPED ME OFF TO THE FACT THAT *STATIC ELECTRICITY* COULD DEFEAT YOUR WOULD-BE AVENGER! WITHOUT THAT KNOWLEDGE, I NEVER WOULD HAVE STOPPED *THE AERIALIST*!

MOMENTS LATER [AFTER *GREEN LANTERN* HAS SECRETLY FLOWN BACK INSIDE THE HOUSE AND REAPPEARED AS THE TEST PILOT RECOVERING FROM HIS "INJURIES"]...

HAL, I NEVER REALIZED WHAT YOU'D DONE! I'M SO PROUD OF YOU!

I DIDN'T TELL HER A LIE AS *GREEN LANTERN*! WHATEVER I LEARN AS *GREEN LANTERN*, I ALSO LEARN AS *HAL JORDAN*!

EVEN THOUGH *GREEN LANTERN* IS MY RIVAL FOR THE AFFECTIONS OF CAROL FERRIS, IT WAS NICE OF HIM TO "MANEUVER" ME INTO THIS PLEASANT POSITION!

The END

15

GREEN LANTERN

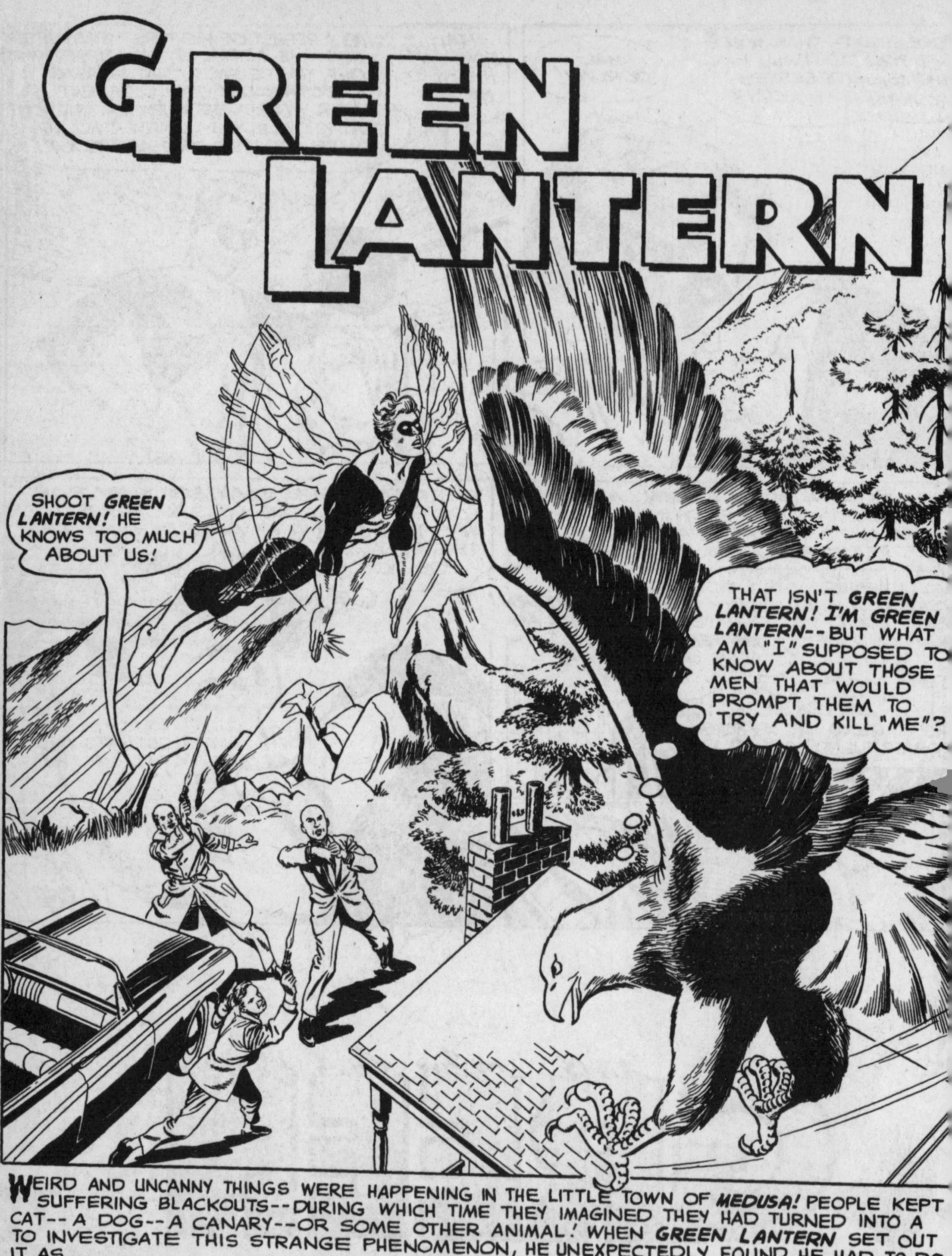
GREEN LANTERN
SHOOT GREEN LANTERN! HE KNOWS TOO MUCH ABOUT US!
THAT ISN'T GREEN LANTERN! I'M GREEN LANTERN--BUT WHAT AM "I" SUPPOSED TO KNOW ABOUT THOSE MEN THAT WOULD PROMPT THEM TO TRY AND KILL "ME"?
WEIRD AND UNCANNY THINGS WERE HAPPENING IN THE LITTLE TOWN OF MEDUSA! PEOPLE KEPT SUFFERING BLACKOUTS--DURING WHICH TIME THEY IMAGINED THEY HAD TURNED INTO A CAT--A DOG--A CANARY--OR SOME OTHER ANIMAL! WHEN GREEN LANTERN SET OUT TO INVESTIGATE THIS STRANGE PHENOMENON, HE UNEXPECTEDLY FOUND HE HAD TO DO IT AS...
THE EAGLE CRUSADER OF EARTH!

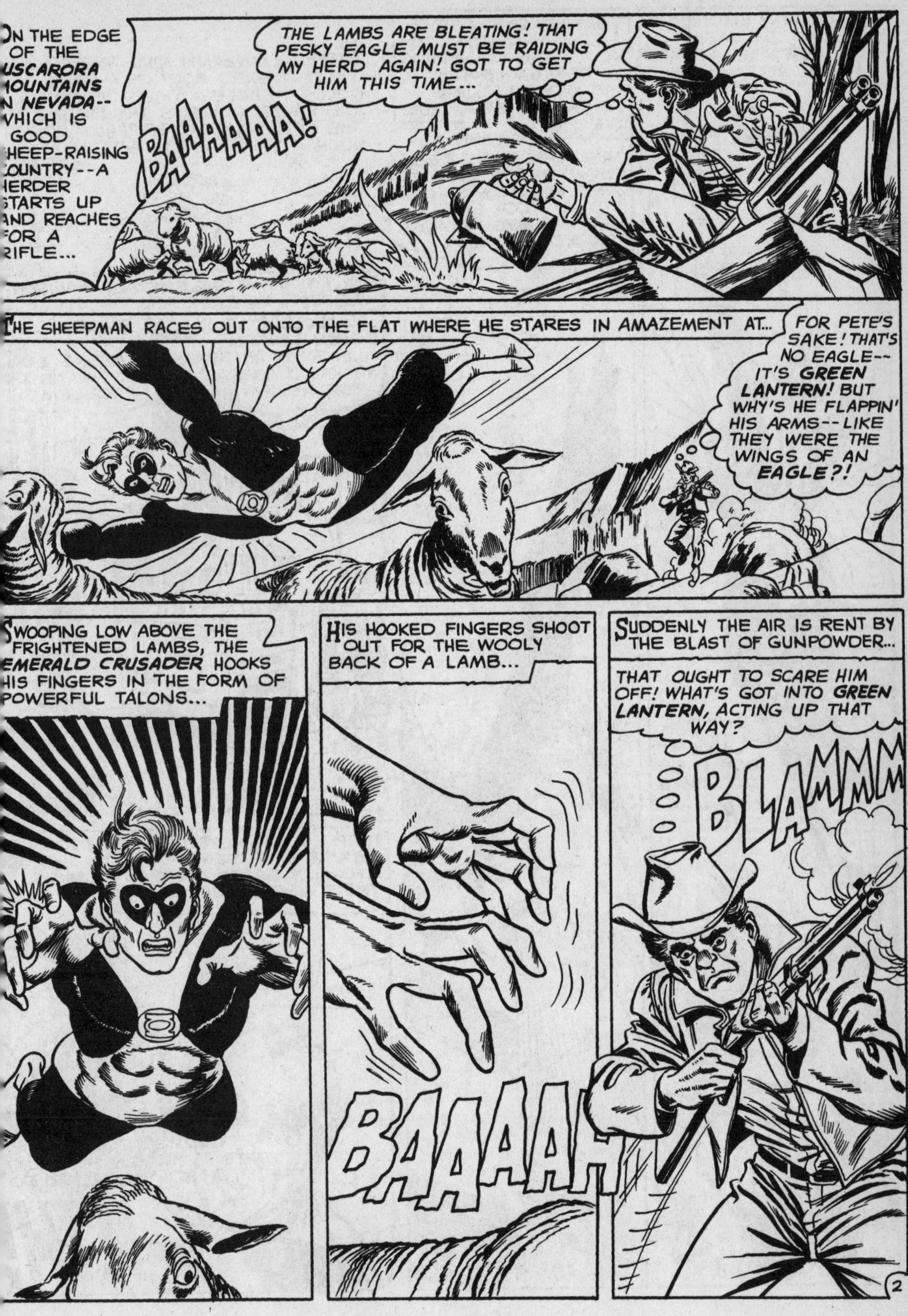
ON THE EDGE OF THE TUSCARORA MOUNTAINS IN NEVADA--WHICH IS GOOD SHEEP-RAISING COUNTRY--A HERDER STARTS UP AND REACHES FOR A RIFLE...
THE LAMBS ARE BLEATING! THAT PESKY EAGLE MUST BE RAIDING MY HERD AGAIN! GOT TO GET HIM THIS TIME...
BAAAAAA!
THE SHEEPMAN RACES OUT ONTO THE FLAT WHERE HE STARES IN AMAZEMENT AT...
FOR PETE'S SAKE! THAT'S NO EAGLE--IT'S GREEN LANTERN! BUT WHY'S HE FLAPPIN' HIS ARMS--LIKE THEY WERE THE WINGS OF AN EAGLE?!
SWOOPING LOW ABOVE THE FRIGHTENED LAMBS, THE EMERALD CRUSADER HOOKS HIS FINGERS IN THE FORM OF POWERFUL TALONS...
HIS HOOKED FINGERS SHOOT OUT FOR THE WOOLY BACK OF A LAMB...
BAAAAH
SUDDENLY THE AIR IS RENT BY THE BLAST OF GUNPOWDER...
THAT OUGHT TO SCARE HIM OFF! WHAT'S GOT INTO GREEN LANTERN, ACTING UP THAT WAY?
BLAMMM
2

NEXT MOMENT, STARTLED BY THE BLAST, THE *GREEN CRUSADER* RISES UPWARD INTO THE AIR...

HAW! LOOK AT HIM SCOOT AWAY!

THE KEEN EYES OF THE SHEEP-HERDER FAIL TO NOTICE THE HIGH-FLYING GOLDEN EAGLE THAT HAS BEEN TRAILING *GREEN LANTERN* ACROSS THE SKY...

WHAT A MESS THIS HAS TURNED OUT TO BE! AN EAGLE'S MIND HAS BEEN SWITCHED INTO MY BODY--AND MINE HAS BEEN TRANS-FERRED INTO HIS!

GREEN LANTERN'S MIND TRAPPED INSIDE THE FEATHERED BODY OF A GREAT GOLDEN EAGLE--WHILE THE MIND OF THE EAGLE INHABITS THE FIGURE OF THE GREAT CRUSADER?! HOW COULD SUCH A THING EVER HAPPEN?

EARLY THAT DAY, THE *EMERALD WARRIOR* WAS BEING USHERED INTO THE OFFICE OF THE GOVERNOR OF THE STATE...

GREEN LANTERN, THANKS FOR ANSWERING MY RADIO APPEAL FOR HELP!

I'M HERE TO DO ANYTHING I CAN BUT WHAT'S THE PROBLEM?

PEOPLE LIVING HERE IN THE TINY TOWN OF *MEDUSA* HAVE BEEN--AND I'M SPEAKING LITERALLY, *GREEN LANTERN*--LOSING THEIR MINDS AND BODIES!

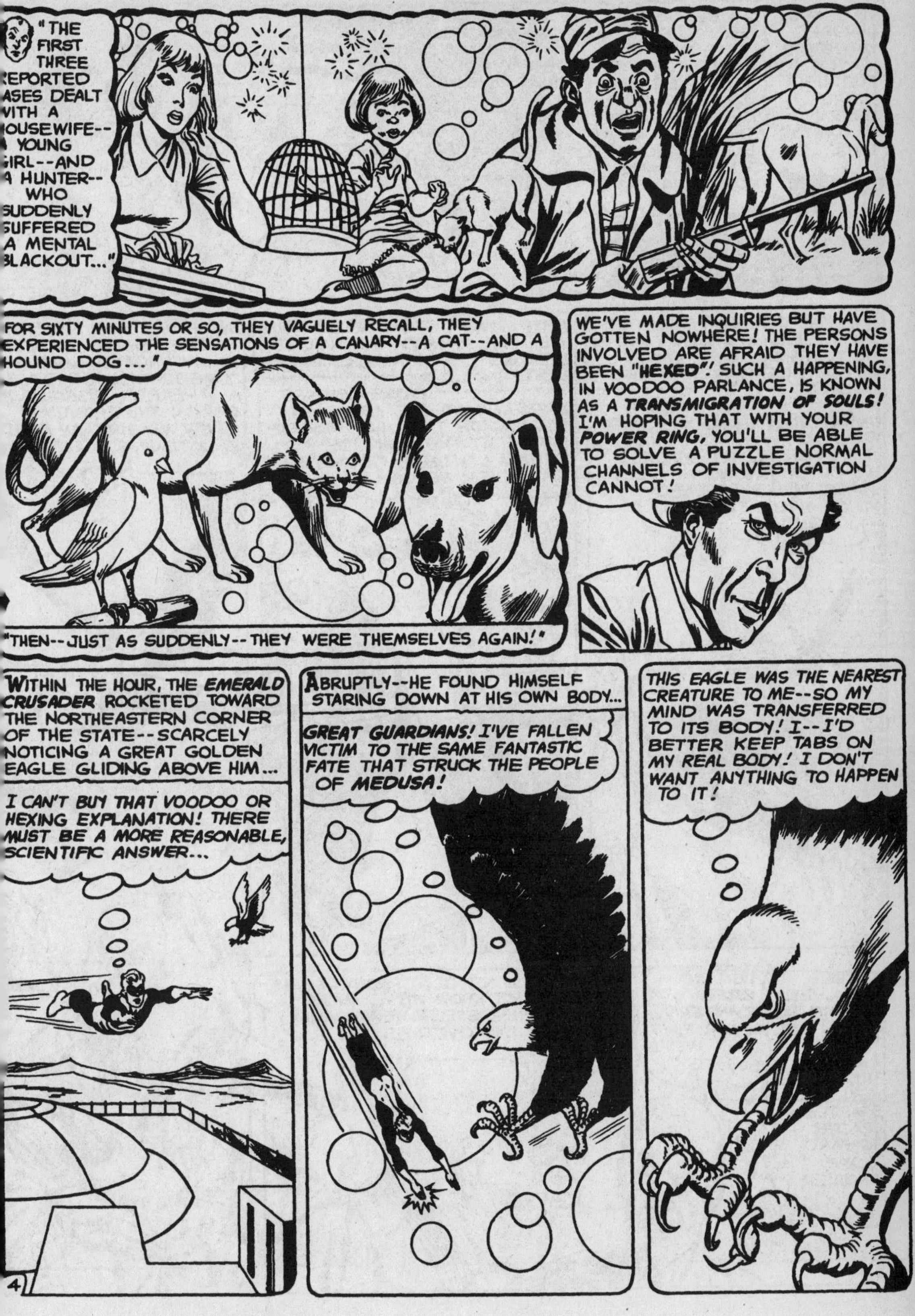
"THE FIRST THREE REPORTED CASES DEALT WITH A HOUSEWIFE-- A YOUNG GIRL--AND A HUNTER-- WHO SUDDENLY SUFFERED A MENTAL BLACKOUT..."
FOR SIXTY MINUTES OR SO, THEY VAGUELY RECALL, THEY EXPERIENCED THE SENSATIONS OF A CANARY--A CAT--AND A HOUND DOG..."
"THEN--JUST AS SUDDENLY--THEY WERE THEMSELVES AGAIN!"
WE'VE MADE INQUIRIES BUT HAVE GOTTEN NOWHERE! THE PERSONS INVOLVED ARE AFRAID THEY HAVE BEEN "HEXED"! SUCH A HAPPENING, IN VOODOO PARLANCE, IS KNOWN AS A TRANSMIGRATION OF SOULS! I'M HOPING THAT WITH YOUR POWER RING, YOU'LL BE ABLE TO SOLVE A PUZZLE NORMAL CHANNELS OF INVESTIGATION CANNOT!
WITHIN THE HOUR, THE EMERALD CRUSADER ROCKETED TOWARD THE NORTHEASTERN CORNER OF THE STATE--SCARCELY NOTICING A GREAT GOLDEN EAGLE GLIDING ABOVE HIM...
I CAN'T BUY THAT VOODOO OR HEXING EXPLANATION! THERE MUST BE A MORE REASONABLE, SCIENTIFIC ANSWER...
4
ABRUPTLY--HE FOUND HIMSELF STARING DOWN AT HIS OWN BODY...
GREAT GUARDIANS! I'VE FALLEN VICTIM TO THE SAME FANTASTIC FATE THAT STRUCK THE PEOPLE OF MEDUSA!
THIS EAGLE WAS THE NEAREST CREATURE TO ME--SO MY MIND WAS TRANSFERRED TO ITS BODY! I--I'D BETTER KEEP TABS ON MY REAL BODY! I DON'T WANT ANYTHING TO HAPPEN TO IT!

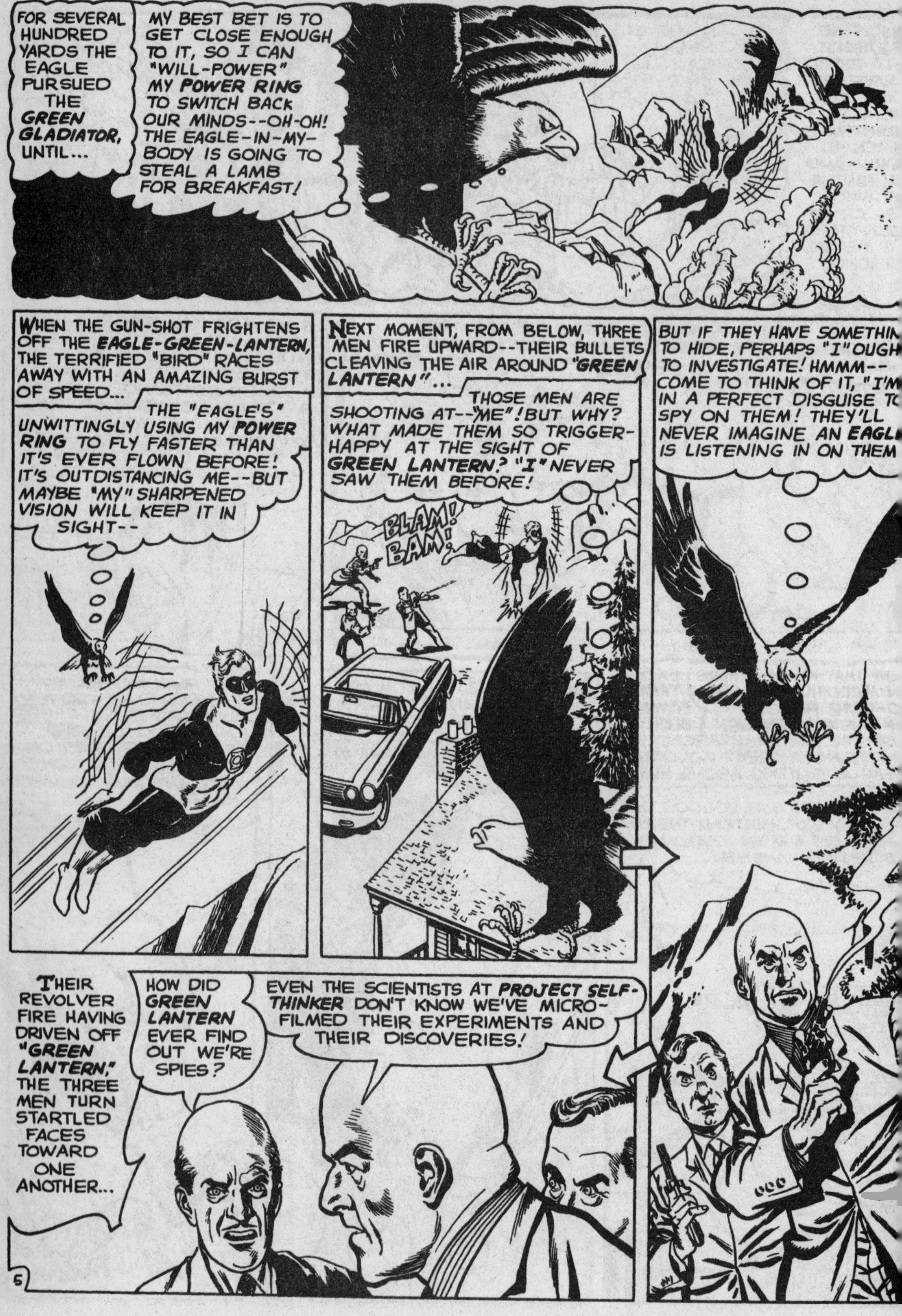
FOR SEVERAL HUNDRED YARDS THE EAGLE PURSUED THE GREEN GLADIATOR, UNTIL...
MY BEST BET IS TO GET CLOSE ENOUGH TO IT, SO I CAN "WILL-POWER" MY POWER RING TO SWITCH BACK OUR MINDS--OH-OH! THE EAGLE-IN-MY-BODY IS GOING TO STEAL A LAMB FOR BREAKFAST!
WHEN THE GUN-SHOT FRIGHTENS OFF THE EAGLE-GREEN-LANTERN, THE TERRIFIED "BIRD" RACES AWAY WITH AN AMAZING BURST OF SPEED...
THE "EAGLE'S" UNWITTINGLY USING MY POWER RING TO FLY FASTER THAN IT'S EVER FLOWN BEFORE! IT'S OUTDISTANCING ME--BUT MAYBE "MY" SHARPENED VISION WILL KEEP IT IN SIGHT--
NEXT MOMENT, FROM BELOW, THREE MEN FIRE UPWARD--THEIR BULLETS CLEAVING THE AIR AROUND "GREEN LANTERN"...
THOSE MEN ARE SHOOTING AT--"ME"! BUT WHY? WHAT MADE THEM SO TRIGGER-HAPPY AT THE SIGHT OF GREEN LANTERN? "I" NEVER SAW THEM BEFORE!
BLAM! BAM!
BUT IF THEY HAVE SOMETHIN TO HIDE, PERHAPS "I" OUGH TO INVESTIGATE! HMMM-- COME TO THINK OF IT, "I'M IN A PERFECT DISGUISE T SPY ON THEM! THEY'LL NEVER IMAGINE AN EAGL IS LISTENING IN ON THEM
THEIR REVOLVER FIRE HAVING DRIVEN OFF "GREEN LANTERN," THE THREE MEN TURN STARTLED FACES TOWARD ONE ANOTHER...
HOW DID GREEN LANTERN EVER FIND OUT WE'RE SPIES?
EVEN THE SCIENTISTS AT PROJECT SELF-THINKER DON'T KNOW WE'VE MICRO-FILMED THEIR EXPERIMENTS AND THEIR DISCOVERIES!
5

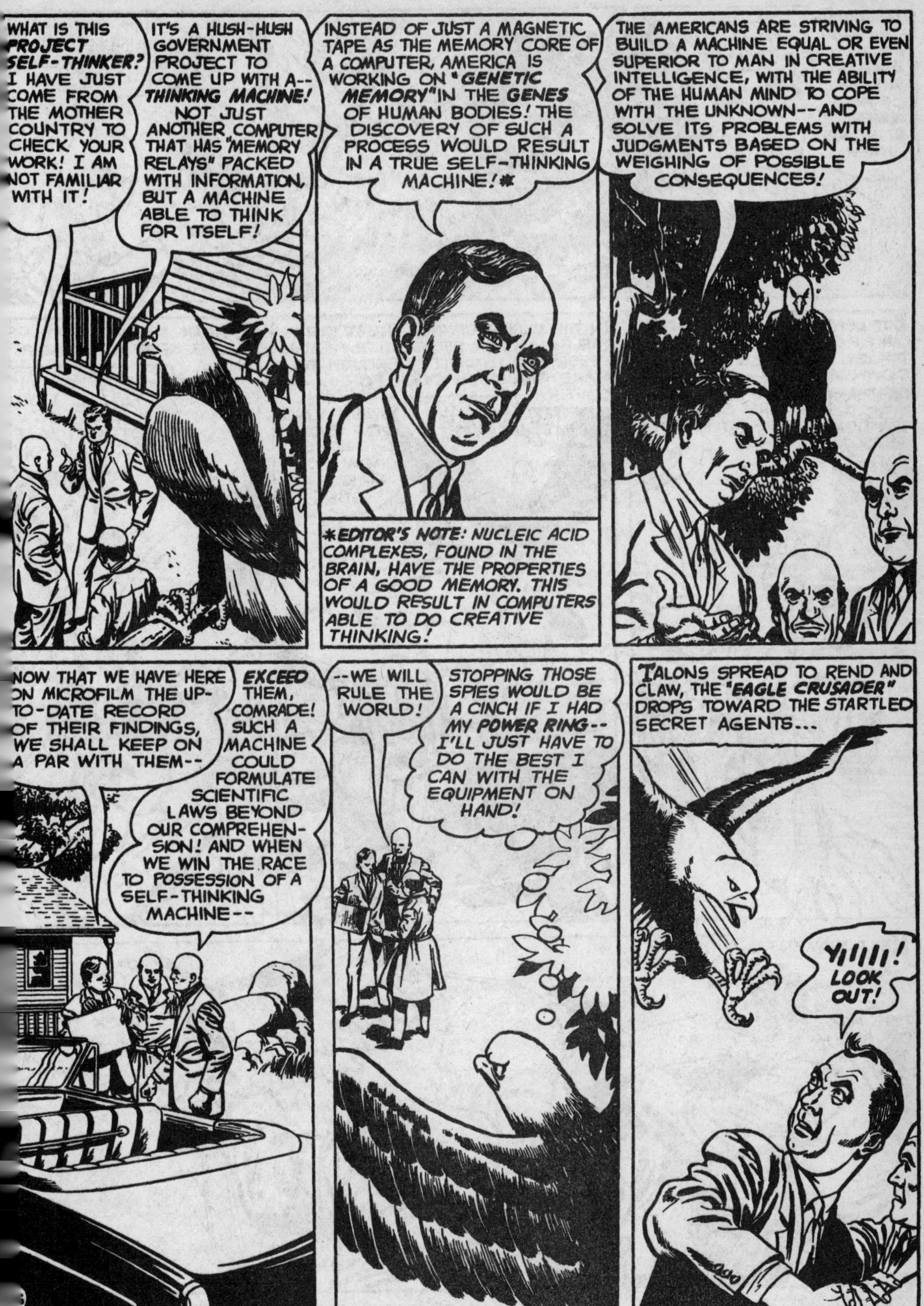
WHAT IS THIS PROJECT SELF-THINKER? I HAVE JUST COME FROM THE MOTHER COUNTRY TO CHECK YOUR WORK! I AM NOT FAMILIAR WITH IT!
IT'S A HUSH-HUSH GOVERNMENT PROJECT TO COME UP WITH A-- THINKING MACHINE! NOT JUST ANOTHER COMPUTER THAT HAS "MEMORY RELAYS" PACKED WITH INFORMATION, BUT A MACHINE ABLE TO THINK FOR ITSELF!
INSTEAD OF JUST A MAGNETIC TAPE AS THE MEMORY CORE OF A COMPUTER, AMERICA IS WORKING ON "GENETIC MEMORY" IN THE GENES OF HUMAN BODIES! THE DISCOVERY OF SUCH A PROCESS WOULD RESULT IN A TRUE SELF-THINKING MACHINE!*
*EDITOR'S NOTE: NUCLEIC ACID COMPLEXES, FOUND IN THE BRAIN, HAVE THE PROPERTIES OF A GOOD MEMORY. THIS WOULD RESULT IN COMPUTERS ABLE TO DO CREATIVE THINKING!
THE AMERICANS ARE STRIVING TO BUILD A MACHINE EQUAL OR EVEN SUPERIOR TO MAN IN CREATIVE INTELLIGENCE, WITH THE ABILITY OF THE HUMAN MIND TO COPE WITH THE UNKNOWN--AND SOLVE ITS PROBLEMS WITH JUDGMENTS BASED ON THE WEIGHING OF POSSIBLE CONSEQUENCES!
NOW THAT WE HAVE HERE ON MICROFILM THE UP-TO-DATE RECORD OF THEIR FINDINGS, WE SHALL KEEP ON A PAR WITH THEM--
EXCEED THEM, COMRADE! SUCH A MACHINE COULD FORMULATE SCIENTIFIC LAWS BEYOND OUR COMPREHENSION! AND WHEN WE WIN THE RACE TO POSSESSION OF A SELF-THINKING MACHINE--
--WE WILL RULE THE WORLD!
STOPPING THOSE SPIES WOULD BE A CINCH IF I HAD MY POWER RING-- I'LL JUST HAVE TO DO THE BEST I CAN WITH THE EQUIPMENT ON HAND!
TALONS SPREAD TO REND AND CLAW, THE "EAGLE CRUSADER" DROPS TOWARD THE STARTLED SECRET AGENTS...
YIIIII! LOOK OUT!

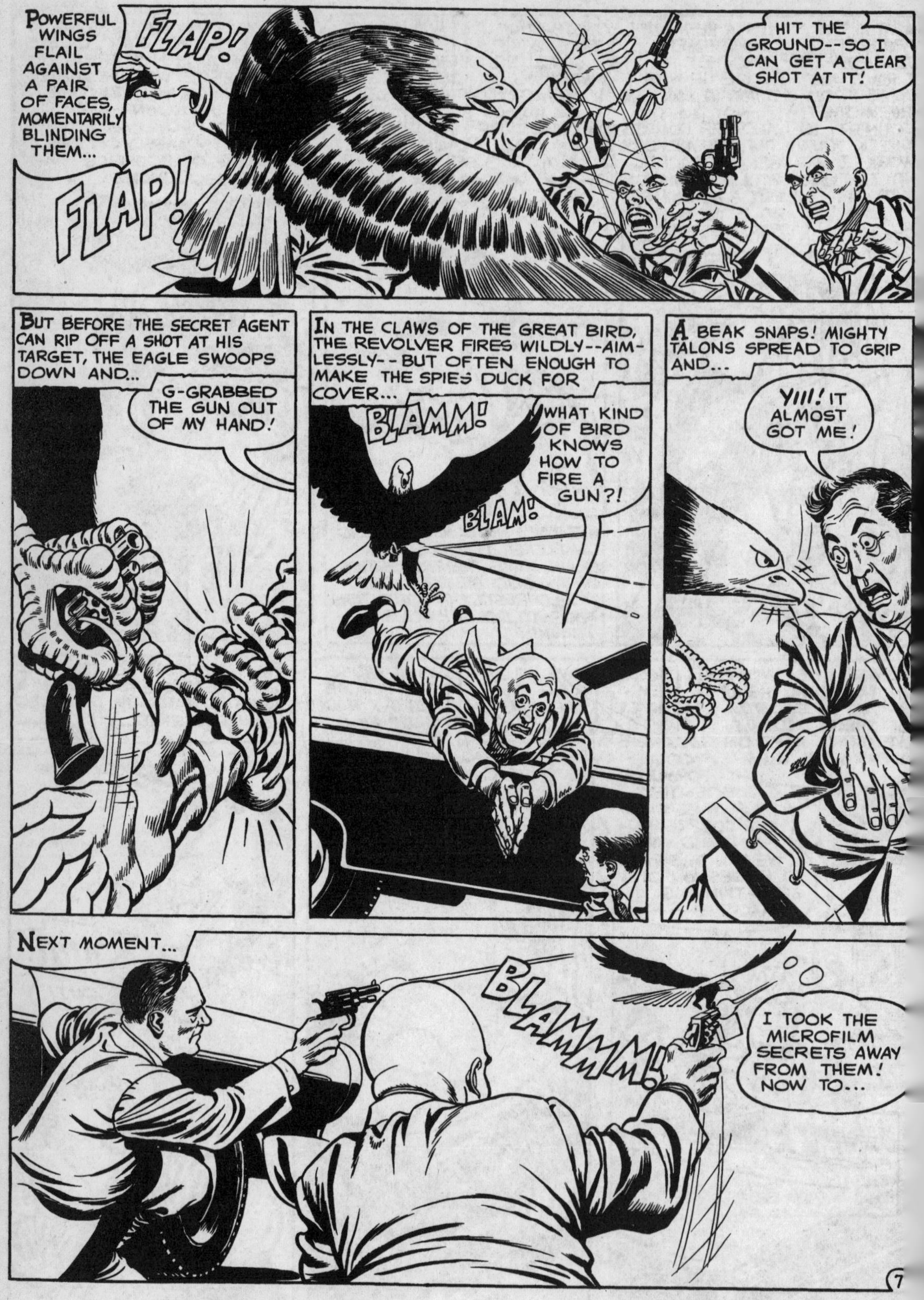
POWERFUL WINGS FLAIL AGAINST A PAIR OF FACES, MOMENTARILY BLINDING THEM...
FLAP!
FLAP!
HIT THE GROUND--SO I CAN GET A CLEAR SHOT AT IT!
BUT BEFORE THE SECRET AGENT CAN RIP OFF A SHOT AT HIS TARGET, THE EAGLE SWOOPS DOWN AND...
G-GRABBED THE GUN OUT OF MY HAND!
IN THE CLAWS OF THE GREAT BIRD, THE REVOLVER FIRES WILDLY--AIMLESSLY--BUT OFTEN ENOUGH TO MAKE THE SPIES DUCK FOR COVER...
BLAMM!
WHAT KIND OF BIRD KNOWS HOW TO FIRE A GUN?!
BLAM!
A BEAK SNAPS! MIGHTY TALONS SPREAD TO GRIP AND...
YIII! IT ALMOST GOT ME!
NEXT MOMENT...
BLAMMMM!
I TOOK THE MICROFILM SECRETS AWAY FROM THEM! NOW TO...
7

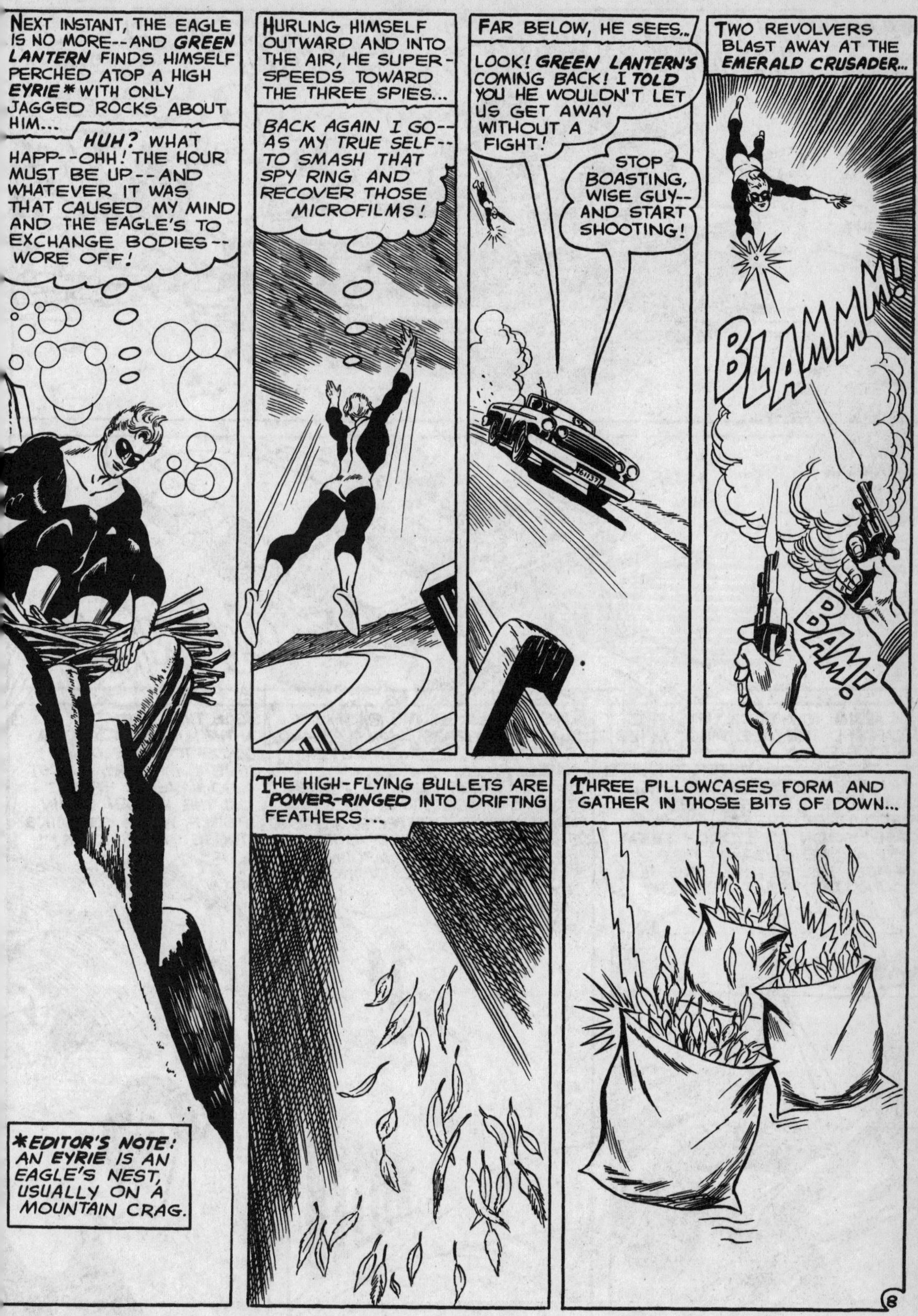
NEXT INSTANT, THE EAGLE IS NO MORE--AND GREEN LANTERN FINDS HIMSELF PERCHED ATOP A HIGH EYRIE* WITH ONLY JAGGED ROCKS ABOUT HIM...
HUH? WHAT HAPP--OHH! THE HOUR MUST BE UP--AND WHATEVER IT WAS THAT CAUSED MY MIND AND THE EAGLE'S TO EXCHANGE BODIES--WORE OFF!
*EDITOR'S NOTE: AN EYRIE IS AN EAGLE'S NEST, USUALLY ON A MOUNTAIN CRAG.
HURLING HIMSELF OUTWARD AND INTO THE AIR, HE SUPER-SPEEDS TOWARD THE THREE SPIES...
BACK AGAIN I GO--AS MY TRUE SELF--TO SMASH THAT SPY RING AND RECOVER THOSE MICROFILMS!
FAR BELOW, HE SEES..
LOOK! GREEN LANTERN'S COMING BACK! I TOLD YOU HE WOULDN'T LET US GET AWAY WITHOUT A FIGHT!
STOP BOASTING, WISE GUY--AND START SHOOTING!
TWO REVOLVERS BLAST AWAY AT THE EMERALD CRUSADER...
BLAMMM!
BAM!
THE HIGH-FLYING BULLETS ARE POWER-RINGED INTO DRIFTING FEATHERS...
THREE PILLOWCASES FORM AND GATHER IN THOSE BITS OF DOWN...
8

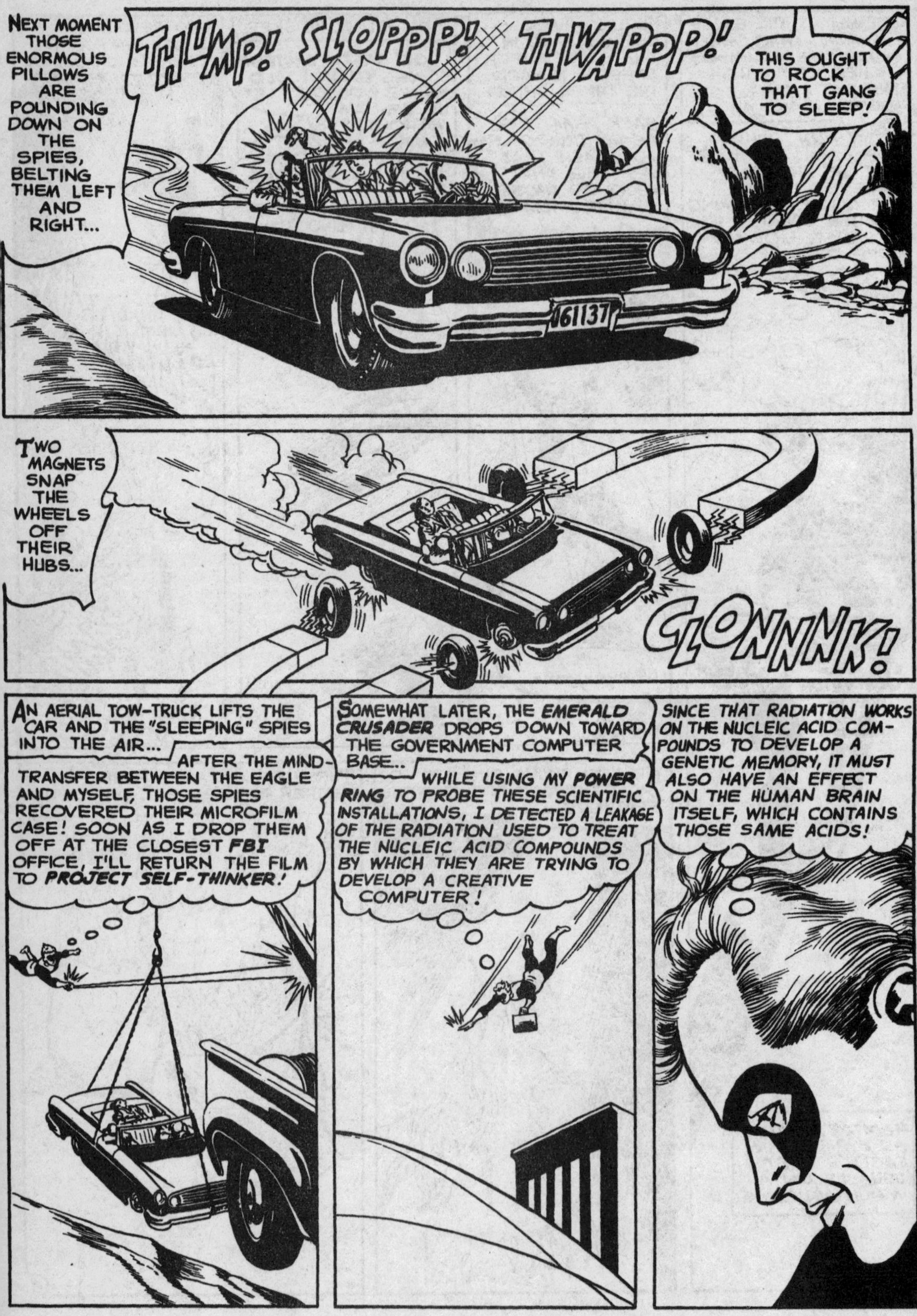
NEXT MOMENT THOSE ENORMOUS PILLOWS ARE POUNDING DOWN ON THE SPIES, BELTING THEM LEFT AND RIGHT...
THUMP! SLOPPP! THWAPPP!
THIS OUGHT TO ROCK THAT GANG TO SLEEP!
U61137
TWO MAGNETS SNAP THE WHEELS OFF THEIR HUBS...
CLONNNK!
AN AERIAL TOW-TRUCK LIFTS THE CAR AND THE "SLEEPING" SPIES INTO THE AIR...
AFTER THE MIND-TRANSFER BETWEEN THE EAGLE AND MYSELF, THOSE SPIES RECOVERED THEIR MICROFILM CASE! SOON AS I DROP THEM OFF AT THE CLOSEST FBI OFFICE, I'LL RETURN THE FILM TO PROJECT SELF-THINKER!
SOMEWHAT LATER, THE EMERALD CRUSADER DROPS DOWN TOWARD THE GOVERNMENT COMPUTER BASE..
WHILE USING MY POWER RING TO PROBE THESE SCIENTIFIC INSTALLATIONS, I DETECTED A LEAKAGE OF THE RADIATION USED TO TREAT THE NUCLEIC ACID COMPOUNDS BY WHICH THEY ARE TRYING TO DEVELOP A CREATIVE COMPUTER!
SINCE THAT RADIATION WORKS ON THE NUCLEIC ACID COMPOUNDS TO DEVELOP A GENETIC MEMORY, IT MUST ALSO HAVE AN EFFECT ON THE HUMAN BRAIN ITSELF, WHICH CONTAINS THOSE SAME ACIDS!

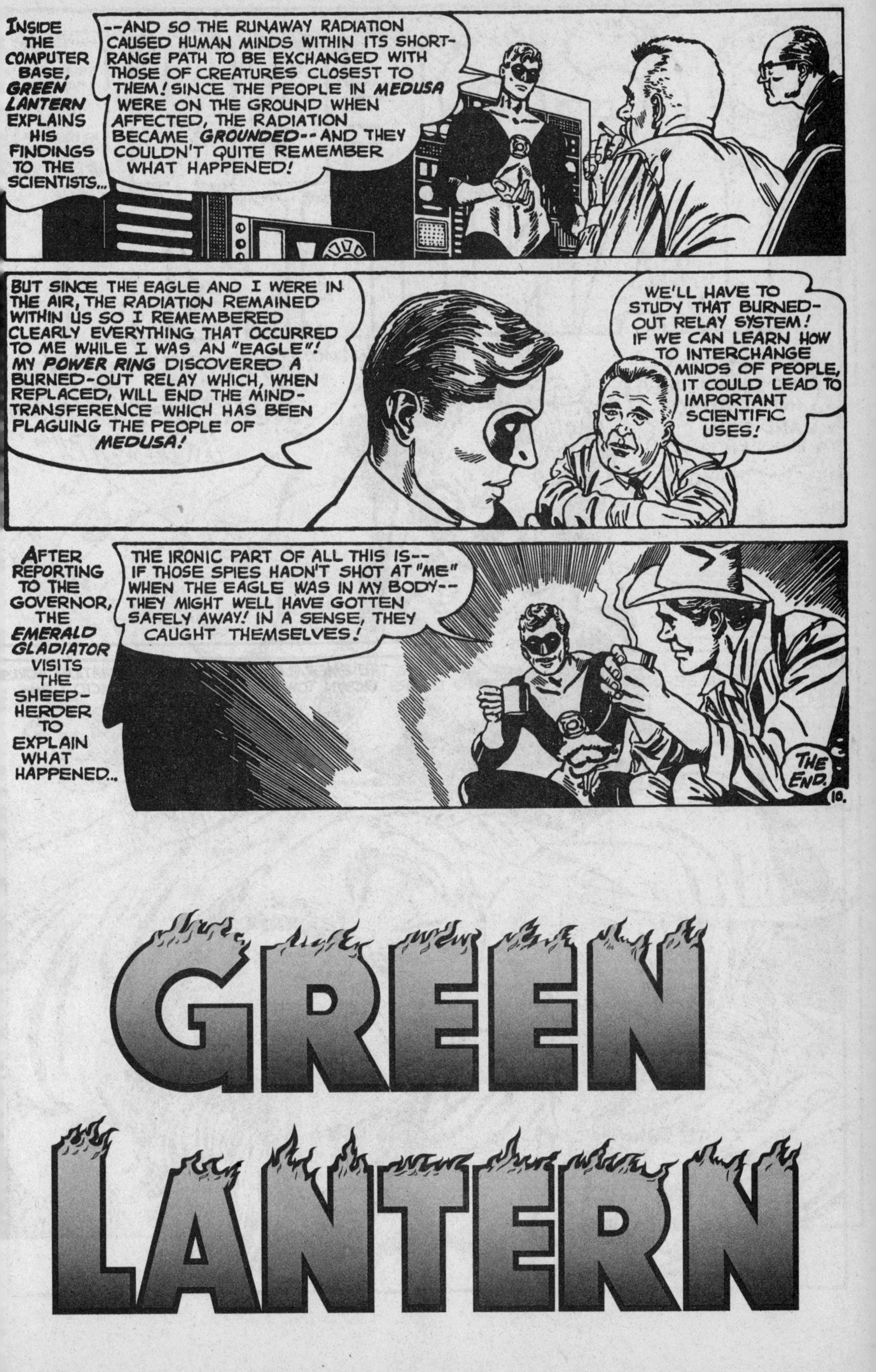
INSIDE THE COMPUTER BASE, GREEN LANTERN EXPLAINS HIS FINDINGS TO THE SCIENTISTS...
--AND SO THE RUNAWAY RADIATION CAUSED HUMAN MINDS WITHIN ITS SHORT-RANGE PATH TO BE EXCHANGED WITH THOSE OF CREATURES CLOSEST TO THEM! SINCE THE PEOPLE IN MEDUSA WERE ON THE GROUND WHEN AFFECTED, THE RADIATION BECAME GROUNDED--AND THEY COULDN'T QUITE REMEMBER WHAT HAPPENED!
BUT SINCE THE EAGLE AND I WERE IN THE AIR, THE RADIATION REMAINED WITHIN US SO I REMEMBERED CLEARLY EVERYTHING THAT OCCURRED TO ME WHILE I WAS AN "EAGLE"! MY POWER RING DISCOVERED A BURNED-OUT RELAY WHICH, WHEN REPLACED, WILL END THE MIND-TRANSFERENCE WHICH HAS BEEN PLAGUING THE PEOPLE OF MEDUSA!
WE'LL HAVE TO STUDY THAT BURNED-OUT RELAY SYSTEM! IF WE CAN LEARN HOW TO INTERCHANGE MINDS OF PEOPLE, IT COULD LEAD TO IMPORTANT SCIENTIFIC USES!
AFTER REPORTING TO THE GOVERNOR, THE EMERALD GLADIATOR VISITS THE SHEEP-HERDER TO EXPLAIN WHAT HAPPENED...
THE IRONIC PART OF ALL THIS IS--IF THOSE SPIES HADN'T SHOT AT "ME" WHEN THE EAGLE WAS IN MY BODY--THEY MIGHT WELL HAVE GOTTEN SAFELY AWAY! IN A SENSE, THEY CAUGHT THEMSELVES!
THE END.
10.

GREEN LANTERN

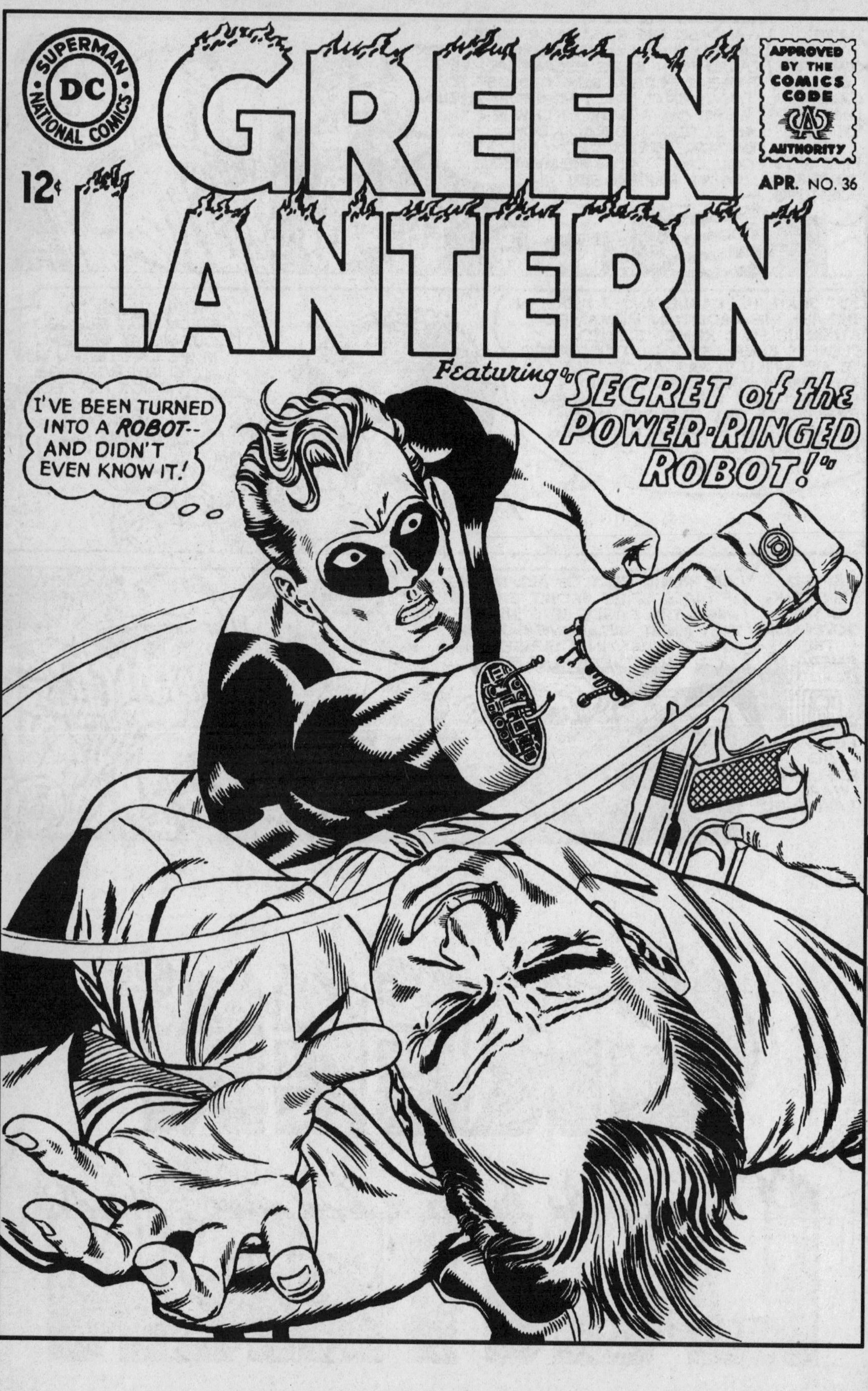
SUPERMAN DC NATIONAL COMICS
GREEN LANTERN
12¢
APPROVED BY THE COMICS CODE AUTHORITY
APR. NO. 36
Featuring "SECRET of the POWER-RINGED ROBOT!"
I'VE BEEN TURNED INTO A ROBOT-- AND DIDN'T EVEN KNOW IT!

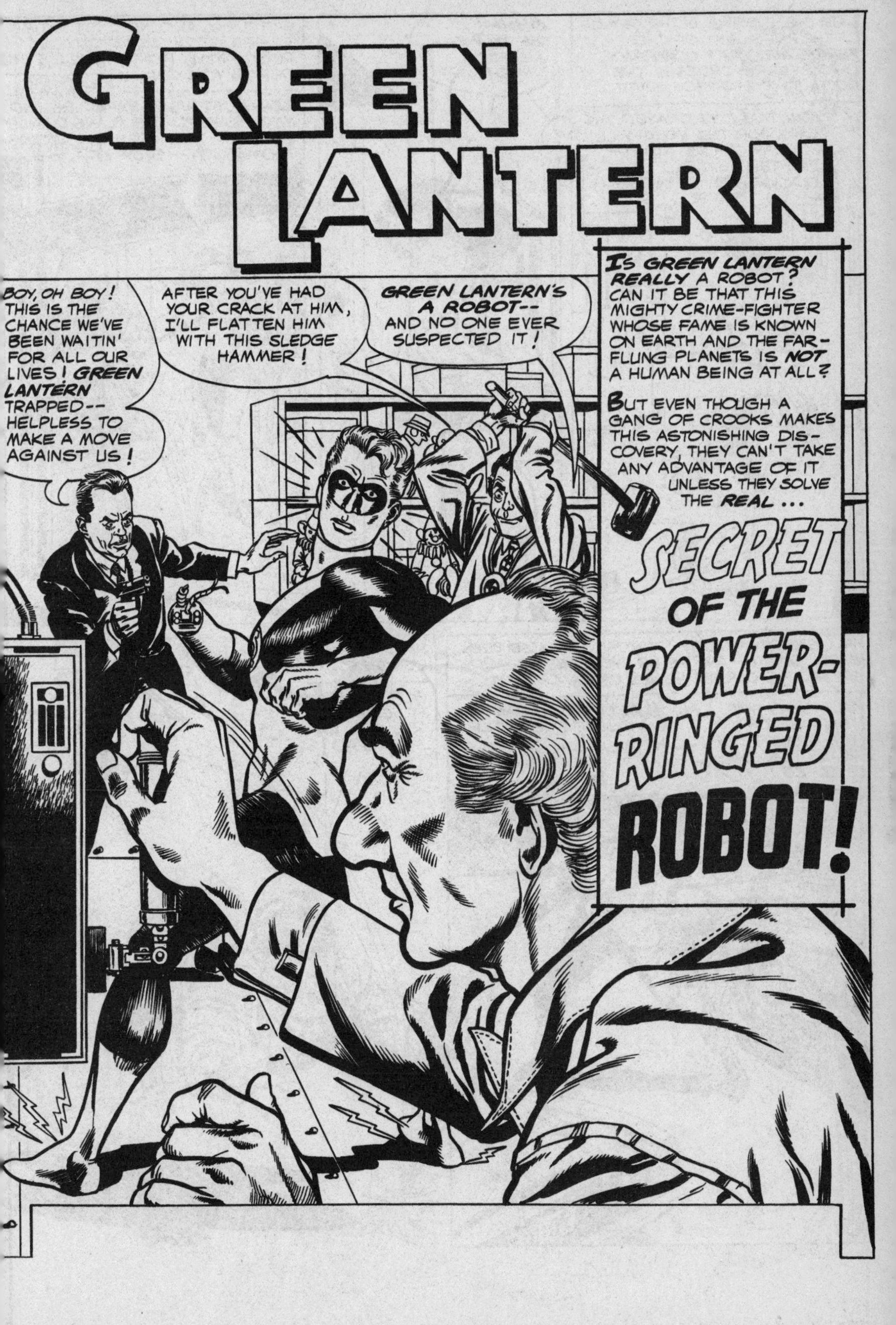
GREEN LANTERN
BOY, OH BOY! THIS IS THE CHANCE WE'VE BEEN WAITIN' FOR ALL OUR LIVES! GREEN LANTERN TRAPPED-- HELPLESS TO MAKE A MOVE AGAINST US!
AFTER YOU'VE HAD YOUR CRACK AT HIM, I'LL FLATTEN HIM WITH THIS SLEDGE HAMMER!
GREEN LANTERN'S A ROBOT-- AND NO ONE EVER SUSPECTED IT!
IS GREEN LANTERN REALLY A ROBOT? CAN IT BE THAT THIS MIGHTY CRIME-FIGHTER WHOSE FAME IS KNOWN ON EARTH AND THE FAR-FLUNG PLANETS IS NOT A HUMAN BEING AT ALL?
BUT EVEN THOUGH A GANG OF CROOKS MAKES THIS ASTONISHING DISCOVERY, THEY CAN'T TAKE ANY ADVANTAGE OF IT UNLESS THEY SOLVE THE REAL ...
SECRET OF THE POWER-RINGED ROBOT!

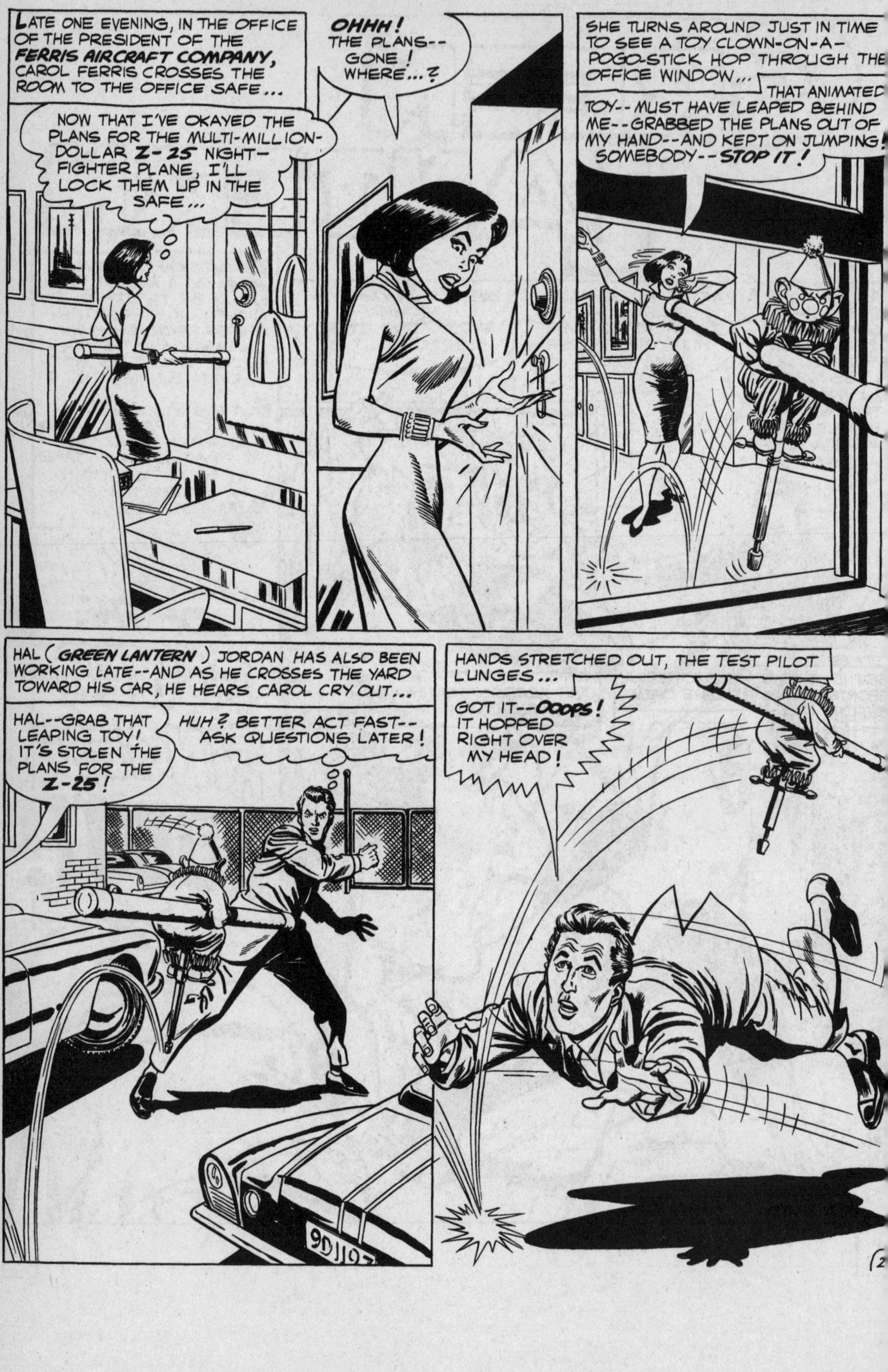
LATE ONE EVENING, IN THE OFFICE OF THE PRESIDENT OF THE FERRIS AIRCRAFT COMPANY, CAROL FERRIS CROSSES THE ROOM TO THE OFFICE SAFE...
NOW THAT I'VE OKAYED THE PLANS FOR THE MULTI-MILLION-DOLLAR Z-25 NIGHT-FIGHTER PLANE, I'LL LOCK THEM UP IN THE SAFE...
OHHH! THE PLANS--GONE! WHERE...?
SHE TURNS AROUND JUST IN TIME TO SEE A TOY CLOWN-ON-A-POGO-STICK HOP THROUGH THE OFFICE WINDOW...
THAT ANIMATED TOY--MUST HAVE LEAPED BEHIND ME--GRABBED THE PLANS OUT OF MY HAND--AND KEPT ON JUMPING! SOMEBODY--STOP IT!
HAL (GREEN LANTERN) JORDAN HAS ALSO BEEN WORKING LATE--AND AS HE CROSSES THE YARD TOWARD HIS CAR, HE HEARS CAROL CRY OUT...
HAL--GRAB THAT LEAPING TOY! IT'S STOLEN THE PLANS FOR THE Z-25!
HUH? BETTER ACT FAST--ASK QUESTIONS LATER!
HANDS STRETCHED OUT, THE TEST PILOT LUNGES...
GOT IT--OOOPS! IT HOPPED RIGHT OVER MY HEAD!

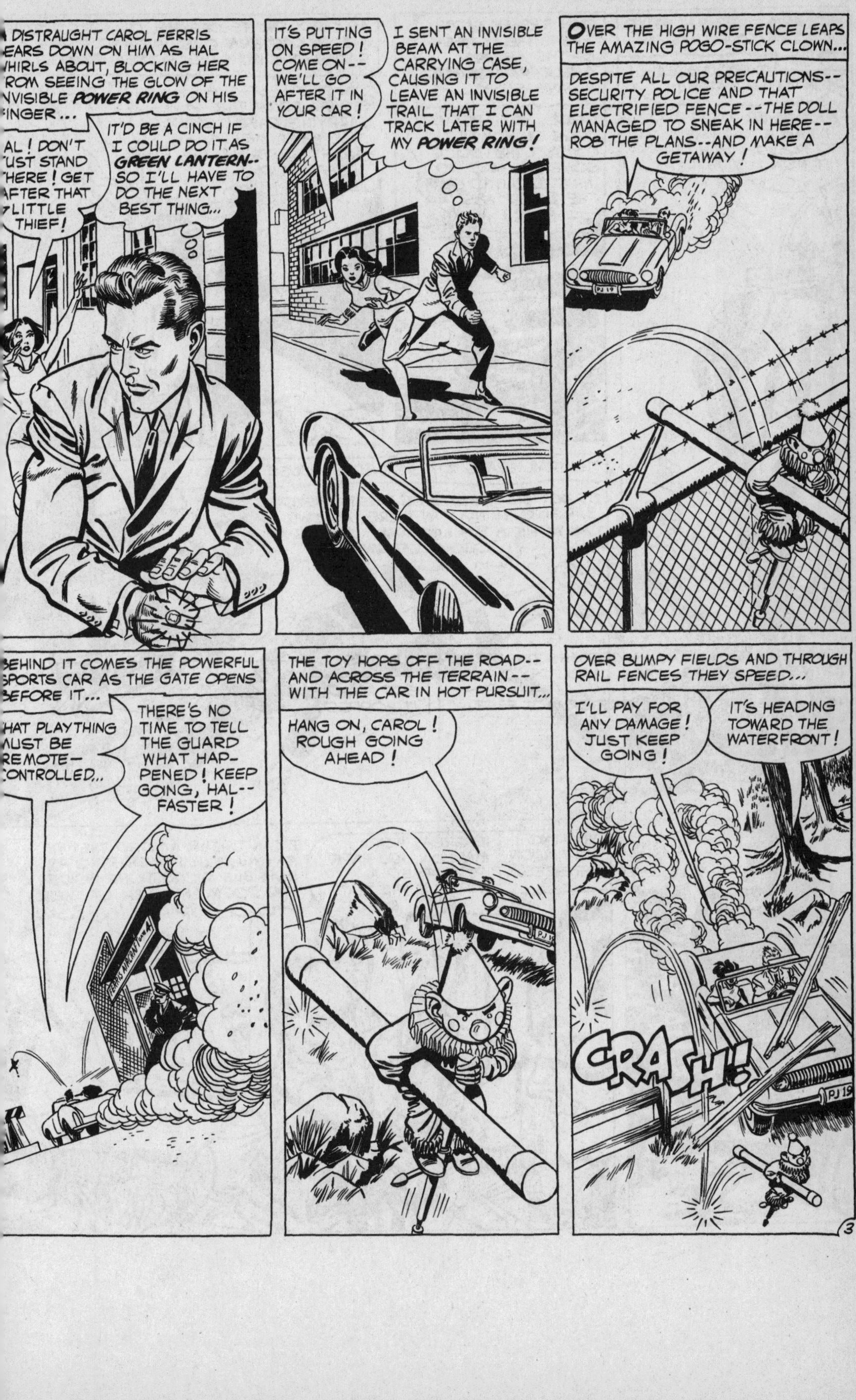
A DISTRAUGHT CAROL FERRIS BEARS DOWN ON HIM AS HAL WHIRLS ABOUT, BLOCKING HER FROM SEEING THE GLOW OF THE INVISIBLE POWER RING ON HIS FINGER...
AL! DON'T JUST STAND THERE! GET AFTER THAT LITTLE THIEF!
IT'D BE A CINCH IF I COULD DO IT AS GREEN LANTERN-- SO I'LL HAVE TO DO THE NEXT BEST THING...
IT'S PUTTING ON SPEED! COME ON-- WE'LL GO AFTER IT IN YOUR CAR!
I SENT AN INVISIBLE BEAM AT THE CARRYING CASE, CAUSING IT TO LEAVE AN INVISIBLE TRAIL THAT I CAN TRACK LATER WITH MY POWER RING!
OVER THE HIGH WIRE FENCE LEAPS THE AMAZING POGO-STICK CLOWN...
DESPITE ALL OUR PRECAUTIONS-- SECURITY POLICE AND THAT ELECTRIFIED FENCE--THE DOLL MANAGED TO SNEAK IN HERE-- ROB THE PLANS--AND MAKE A GETAWAY!
BEHIND IT COMES THE POWERFUL SPORTS CAR AS THE GATE OPENS BEFORE IT...
HAT PLAYTHING MUST BE REMOTE-CONTROLLED...
THERE'S NO TIME TO TELL THE GUARD WHAT HAPPENED! KEEP GOING, HAL-- FASTER!
THE TOY HOPS OFF THE ROAD-- AND ACROSS THE TERRAIN-- WITH THE CAR IN HOT PURSUIT...
HANG ON, CAROL! ROUGH GOING AHEAD!
OVER BUMPY FIELDS AND THROUGH RAIL FENCES THEY SPEED...
I'LL PAY FOR ANY DAMAGE! JUST KEEP GOING!
IT'S HEADING TOWARD THE WATERFRONT!
CRASH!
3

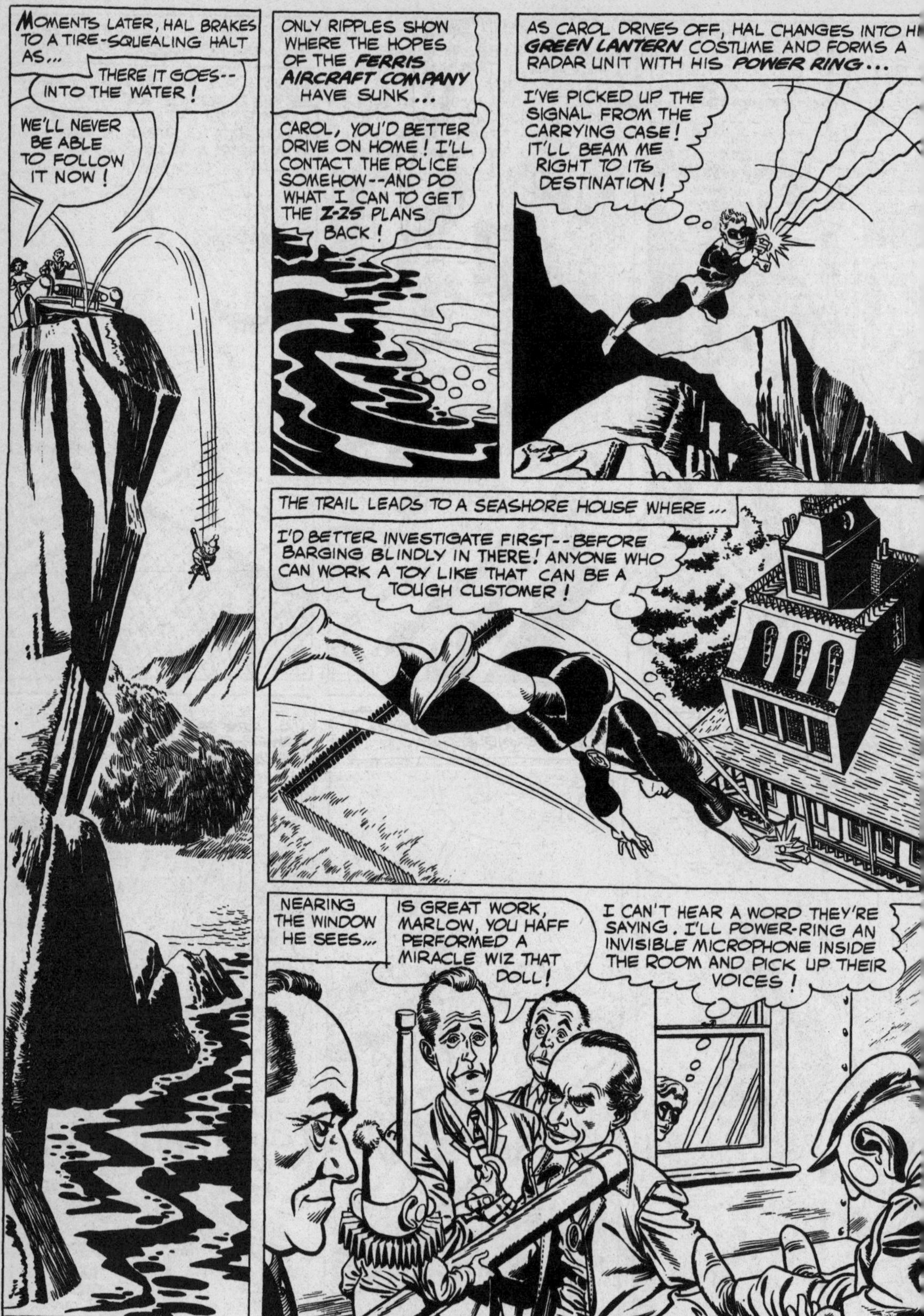

MOMENTS LATER, HAL BRAKES TO A TIRE-SQUEALING HALT AS...
THERE IT GOES-- INTO THE WATER!
WE'LL NEVER BE ABLE TO FOLLOW IT NOW!
ONLY RIPPLES SHOW WHERE THE HOPES OF THE FERRIS AIRCRAFT COMPANY HAVE SUNK...
CAROL, YOU'D BETTER DRIVE ON HOME! I'LL CONTACT THE POLICE SOMEHOW--AND DO WHAT I CAN TO GET THE Z-25 PLANS BACK!
AS CAROL DRIVES OFF, HAL CHANGES INTO HI GREEN LANTERN COSTUME AND FORMS A RADAR UNIT WITH HIS POWER RING...
I'VE PICKED UP THE SIGNAL FROM THE CARRYING CASE! IT'LL BEAM ME RIGHT TO ITS DESTINATION!
THE TRAIL LEADS TO A SEASHORE HOUSE WHERE...
I'D BETTER INVESTIGATE FIRST--BEFORE BARGING BLINDLY IN THERE! ANYONE WHO CAN WORK A TOY LIKE THAT CAN BE A TOUGH CUSTOMER!
NEARING THE WINDOW HE SEES...
IS GREAT WORK, MARLOW, YOU HAFF PERFORMED A MIRACLE WIZ THAT DOLL!
I CAN'T HEAR A WORD THEY'RE SAYING. I'LL POWER-RING AN INVISIBLE MICROPHONE INSIDE THE ROOM AND PICK UP THEIR VOICES!

AVE YOU ANY DOUBTS NOW F MY MECHANICAL GENIUS, ENTLEMEN & ALL MY DOLLS ERFORM EXACTLY AS I EAR THEM TO DO! ACH OF THEM CON- AINS A MECHANISM S DELICATE AS HAT OF A WISS WATCH!

I HAFF ZE QUARTER MILLION DOLLARS SPY-MONEY FOR ZE **Z-25** PLANS!

A PUZZLED FROWN CREASES **GREEN LANTERN'S** FOREHEAD AS...

THAT'S ODD! I SEE THEIR LIPS MOVING SO I KNOW THEY'RE TALKING, BUT I CAN'T HEAR ANYTHING! I'LL TRY FORMING A HEARING DEVICE **OUTSIDE** THE HOUSE!

ARE YOU NOT AFRAID ZE POLICE WILL FOLLOW ZE DOLL?

EVEN IF THEY DID--THERE'S NOT A CHANCE OF THEM NABBING US!

AH, NOW I HEAR THEIR VOICES!

I GAVE EACH OF YOU A **NEUTRALIZER** TO HANG ABOUT YOUR NECKS TO PROTECT YOU FROM THE DEADLY RADIATION IN THIS ROOM! ANY LIVING CREATURE THAT ENTERS WITHOUT IT-- WILL SUFFER INSTANT DEATH!

LISTENING IN, **GREEN LANTERN** WHISTLES SOUNDLESSLY...

WHEW! IT'S A GOOD THING I EAVESDROPPED! OTHER- WISE I'D HAVE BLUNDERED IN AND BEEN KILLED ON THE SPOT!

IT'S CLEAR NOW--SINCE I COULDN'T **POWER-RING** THAT MICROPHONE **INSIDE** THE ROOM--THAT THE RADIATION IN THERE HAS A **YELLOW** * BASE!

*EDITOR'S NOTE: GREEN LANTERN'S POWER RING HAS NO EFFECT ON ANYTHING COLORED **YELLOW**!

5

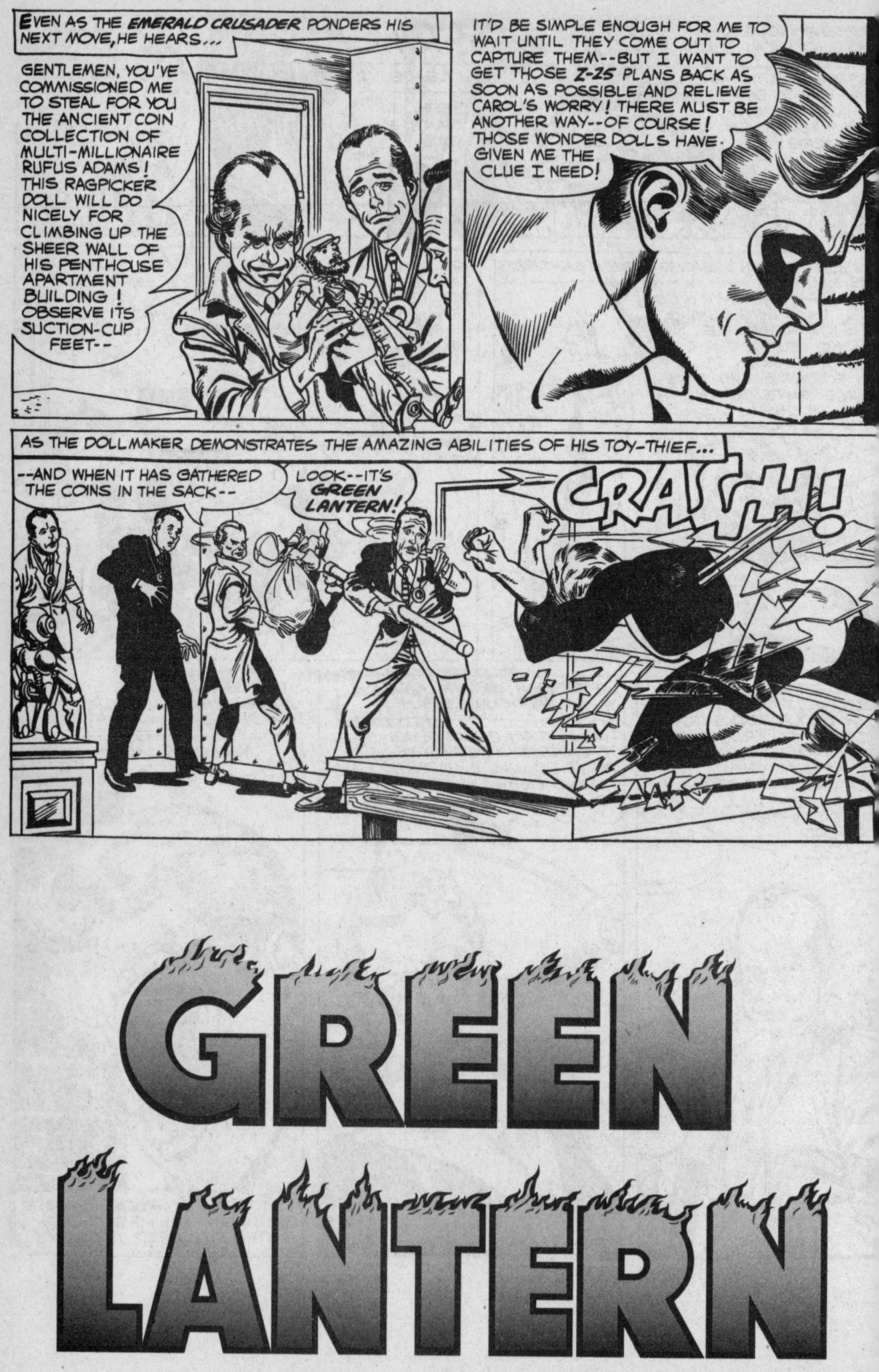
EVEN AS THE EMERALD CRUSADER PONDERS HIS NEXT MOVE, HE HEARS...
GENTLEMEN, YOU'VE COMMISSIONED ME TO STEAL FOR YOU THE ANCIENT COIN COLLECTION OF MULTI-MILLIONAIRE RUFUS ADAMS! THIS RAGPICKER DOLL WILL DO NICELY FOR CLIMBING UP THE SHEER WALL OF HIS PENTHOUSE APARTMENT BUILDING! OBSERVE ITS SUCTION-CUP FEET--
IT'D BE SIMPLE ENOUGH FOR ME TO WAIT UNTIL THEY COME OUT TO CAPTURE THEM--BUT I WANT TO GET THOSE Z-25 PLANS BACK AS SOON AS POSSIBLE AND RELIEVE CAROL'S WORRY! THERE MUST BE ANOTHER WAY--OF COURSE! THOSE WONDER DOLLS HAVE GIVEN ME THE CLUE I NEED!
AS THE DOLLMAKER DEMONSTRATES THE AMAZING ABILITIES OF HIS TOY-THIEF...
--AND WHEN IT HAS GATHERED THE COINS IN THE SACK--
LOOK--IT'S GREEN LANTERN!
CRASH!

GREEN LANTERN

SECRET OF THE POWER-RINGED *ROBOT!* PART 2

ON STEEL-THEWED LEGS, THE *GREEN GLADIATOR* LEAPS INTO THE ROOM, VAULTING A TABLE...

HEY, MARLOW! WHY AIN'T YOUR RADIATION STOPPING HIM?

I--I CAN'T UNDERSTAND IT! HE SHOULD HAVE DROPPED DEAD THE INSTANT HE ENTERED THE ROOM!

HE COMES DOWN LIKE THE PROVERBIAL TON OF BRICKS ON TWO OF THE ROOM'S FOUR OCCUPANTS...

AWWWK! IT'S *US* WHO'S CONKIN' OUT!

THUNKK

HE WHIRLS AND A HAND STABS OUT JUST AS THE SPY LIFTS AN AUTOMATIC FROM HIS COAT...

"CHAIR" UP, FELLA-- YOU'LL SOON BE ON YOUR WAY TO JAIL!

GREEN LANTERN FLIPS HIS BODY UP AT ANOTHER THUG...

AND *CHIN UP* FOR YOU--YOU'LL BE KEEPING HIM COMPANY!

SOK

7

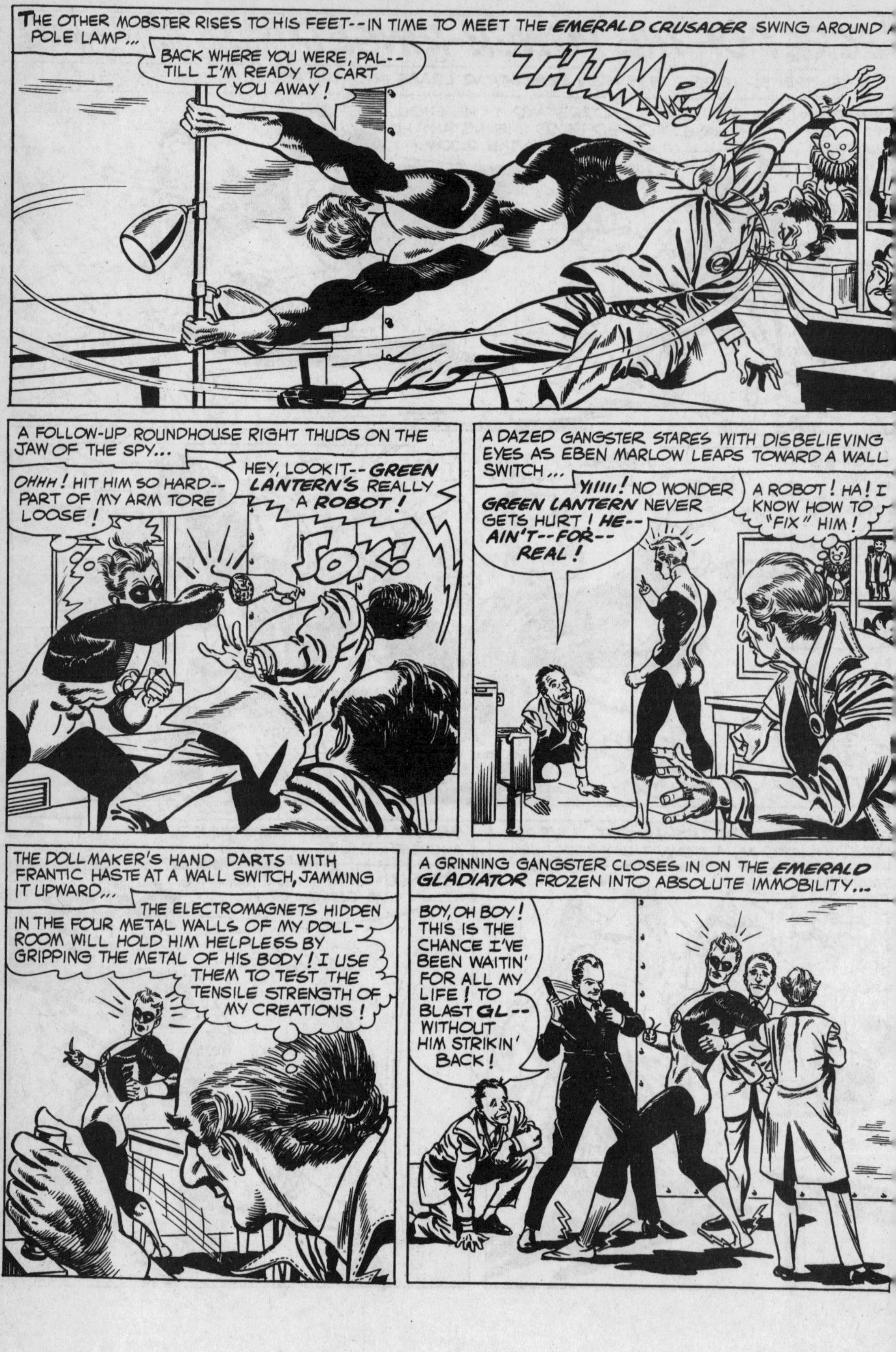
THE OTHER MOBSTER RISES TO HIS FEET--IN TIME TO MEET THE EMERALD CRUSADER SWING AROUND A POLE LAMP...
BACK WHERE YOU WERE, PAL--TILL I'M READY TO CART YOU AWAY!
THUMP!
A FOLLOW-UP ROUNDHOUSE RIGHT THUDS ON THE JAW OF THE SPY...
OHHH! HIT HIM SO HARD--PART OF MY ARM TORE LOOSE!
HEY, LOOKIT--GREEN LANTERN'S REALLY A ROBOT!
SOK!
A DAZED GANGSTER STARES WITH DISBELIEVING EYES AS EBEN MARLOW LEAPS TOWARD A WALL SWITCH...
YIIIII! NO WONDER GREEN LANTERN NEVER GETS HURT! HE--AIN'T--FOR--REAL!
A ROBOT! HA! I KNOW HOW TO "FIX" HIM!
THE DOLLMAKER'S HAND DARTS WITH FRANTIC HASTE AT A WALL SWITCH, JAMMING IT UPWARD...
THE ELECTROMAGNETS HIDDEN IN THE FOUR METAL WALLS OF MY DOLL-ROOM WILL HOLD HIM HELPLESS BY GRIPPING THE METAL OF HIS BODY! I USE THEM TO TEST THE TENSILE STRENGTH OF MY CREATIONS!
A GRINNING GANGSTER CLOSES IN ON THE EMERALD GLADIATOR FROZEN INTO ABSOLUTE IMMOBILITY...
BOY, OH BOY! THIS IS THE CHANCE I'VE BEEN WAITIN' FOR ALL MY LIFE! TO BLAST GL--WITHOUT HIM STRIKIN' BACK!

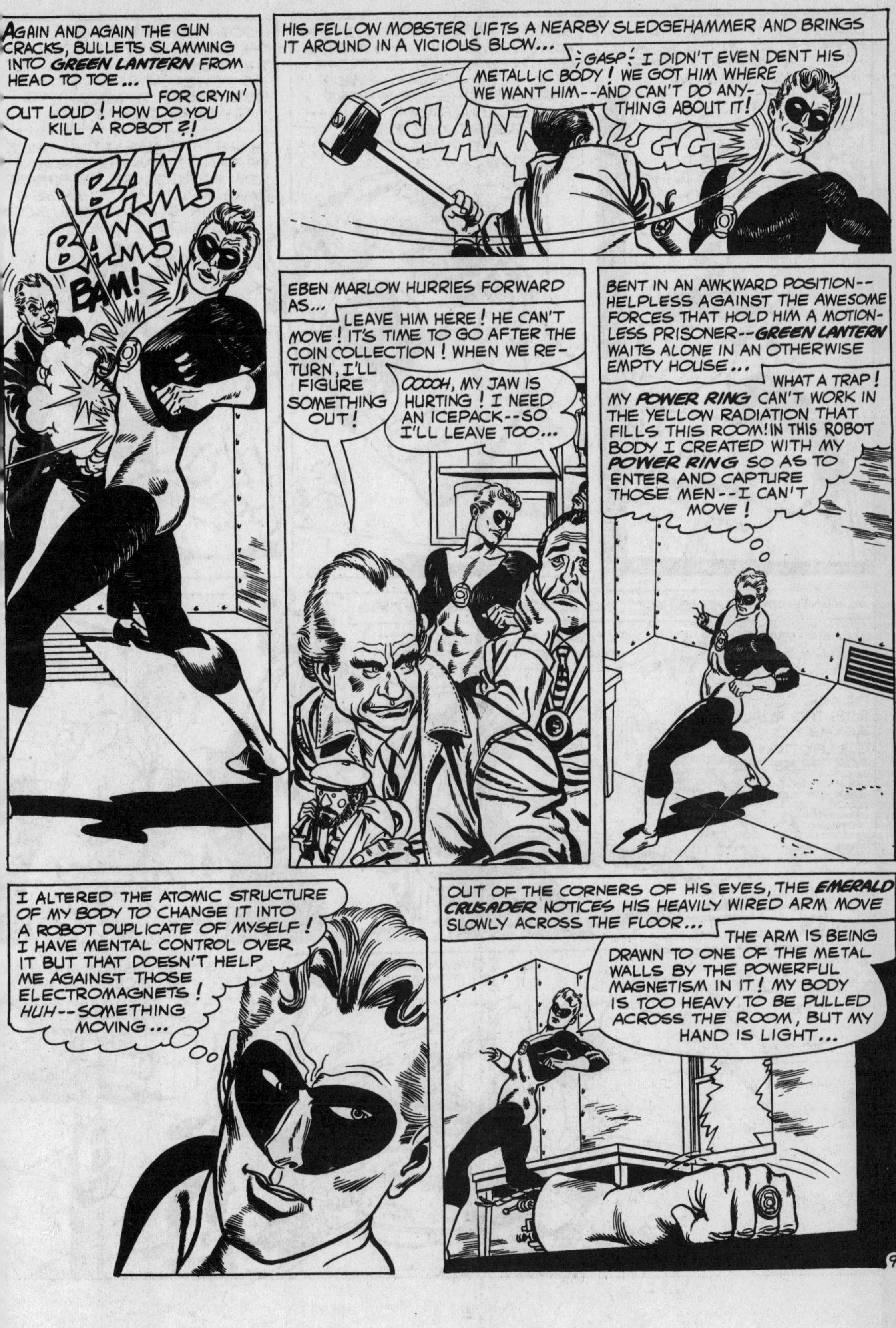
AGAIN AND AGAIN THE GUN CRACKS, BULLETS SLAMMING INTO GREEN LANTERN FROM HEAD TO TOE...
FOR CRYIN' OUT LOUD! HOW DO YOU KILL A ROBOT ?!
BAM! BAM! BAM!
HIS FELLOW MOBSTER LIFTS A NEARBY SLEDGEHAMMER AND BRINGS IT AROUND IN A VICIOUS BLOW...
GASP! I DIDN'T EVEN DENT HIS METALLIC BODY! WE GOT HIM WHERE WE WANT HIM--AND CAN'T DO ANYTHING ABOUT IT!
CLANGG
EBEN MARLOW HURRIES FORWARD AS...
LEAVE HIM HERE! HE CAN'T MOVE! IT'S TIME TO GO AFTER THE COIN COLLECTION! WHEN WE RETURN, I'LL FIGURE SOMETHING OUT!
OOOOH, MY JAW IS HURTING! I NEED AN ICEPACK--SO I'LL LEAVE TOO...
BENT IN AN AWKWARD POSITION--HELPLESS AGAINST THE AWESOME FORCES THAT HOLD HIM A MOTIONLESS PRISONER--GREEN LANTERN WAITS ALONE IN AN OTHERWISE EMPTY HOUSE...
WHAT A TRAP! MY POWER RING CAN'T WORK IN THE YELLOW RADIATION THAT FILLS THIS ROOM! IN THIS ROBOT BODY I CREATED WITH MY POWER RING SO AS TO ENTER AND CAPTURE THOSE MEN--I CAN'T MOVE!
I ALTERED THE ATOMIC STRUCTURE OF MY BODY TO CHANGE IT INTO A ROBOT DUPLICATE OF MYSELF! I HAVE MENTAL CONTROL OVER IT BUT THAT DOESN'T HELP ME AGAINST THOSE ELECTROMAGNETS! HUH--SOMETHING MOVING...
OUT OF THE CORNERS OF HIS EYES, THE EMERALD CRUSADER NOTICES HIS HEAVILY WIRED ARM MOVE SLOWLY ACROSS THE FLOOR...
THE ARM IS BEING DRAWN TO ONE OF THE METAL WALLS BY THE POWERFUL MAGNETISM IN IT! MY BODY IS TOO HEAVY TO BE PULLED ACROSS THE ROOM, BUT MY HAND IS LIGHT...
9

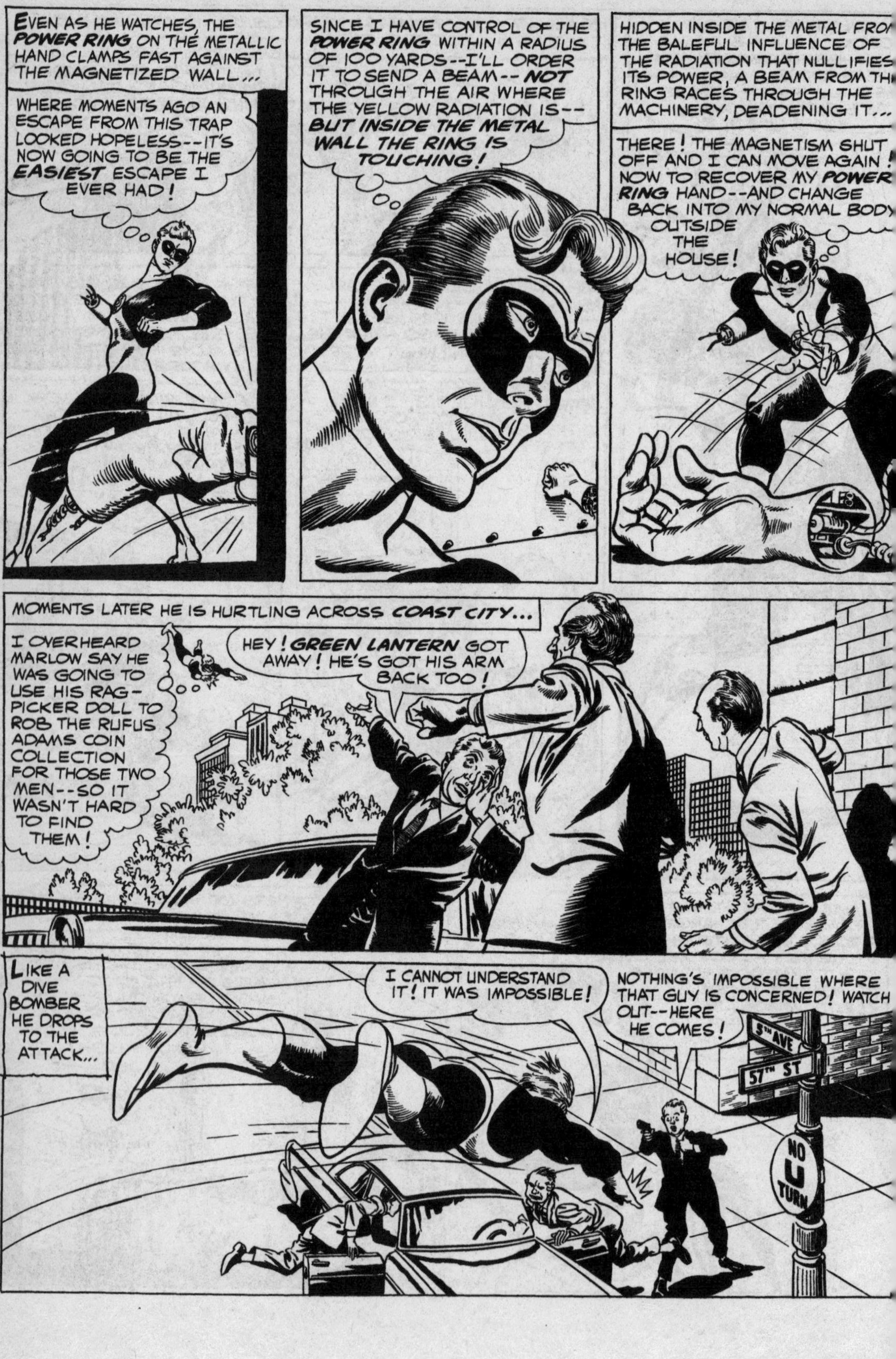

EVEN AS HE WATCHES, THE POWER RING ON THE METALLIC HAND CLAMPS FAST AGAINST THE MAGNETIZED WALL...
WHERE MOMENTS AGO AN ESCAPE FROM THIS TRAP LOOKED HOPELESS--IT'S NOW GOING TO BE THE EASIEST ESCAPE I EVER HAD!
SINCE I HAVE CONTROL OF THE POWER RING WITHIN A RADIUS OF 100 YARDS--I'LL ORDER IT TO SEND A BEAM--NOT THROUGH THE AIR WHERE THE YELLOW RADIATION IS--BUT INSIDE THE METAL WALL THE RING IS TOUCHING!
HIDDEN INSIDE THE METAL FROM THE BALEFUL INFLUENCE OF THE RADIATION THAT NULLIFIES ITS POWER, A BEAM FROM THE RING RACES THROUGH THE MACHINERY, DEADENING IT...
THERE! THE MAGNETISM SHUT OFF AND I CAN MOVE AGAIN! NOW TO RECOVER MY POWER RING HAND--AND CHANGE BACK INTO MY NORMAL BODY OUTSIDE THE HOUSE!
MOMENTS LATER HE IS HURTLING ACROSS COAST CITY...
I OVERHEARD MARLOW SAY HE WAS GOING TO USE HIS RAG-PICKER DOLL TO ROB THE RUFUS ADAMS COIN COLLECTION FOR THOSE TWO MEN--SO IT WASN'T HARD TO FIND THEM!
HEY! GREEN LANTERN GOT AWAY! HE'S GOT HIS ARM BACK TOO!
LIKE A DIVE BOMBER HE DROPS TO THE ATTACK...
I CANNOT UNDERSTAND IT! IT WAS IMPOSSIBLE!
NOTHING'S IMPOSSIBLE WHERE THAT GUY IS CONCERNED! WATCH OUT--HERE HE COMES!
5TH AVE
57TH ST
NO U TURN

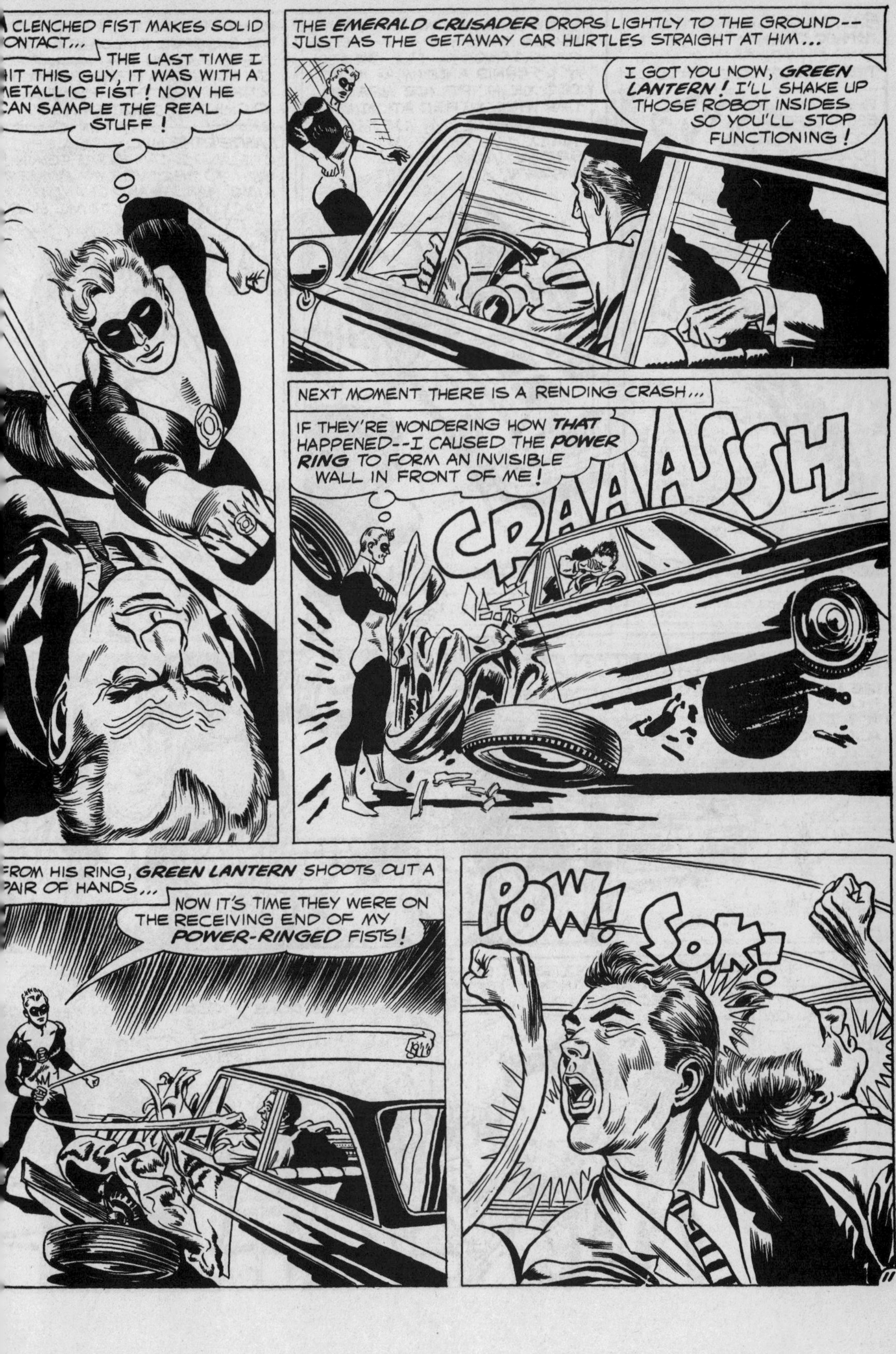
A CLENCHED FIST MAKES SOLID CONTACT,,,
THE LAST TIME I HIT THIS GUY, IT WAS WITH A METALLIC FIST! NOW HE CAN SAMPLE THE REAL STUFF!
THE EMERALD CRUSADER DROPS LIGHTLY TO THE GROUND-- JUST AS THE GETAWAY CAR HURTLES STRAIGHT AT HIM...
I GOT YOU NOW, GREEN LANTERN! I'LL SHAKE UP THOSE ROBOT INSIDES SO YOU'LL STOP FUNCTIONING!
NEXT MOMENT THERE IS A RENDING CRASH,,,
IF THEY'RE WONDERING HOW THAT HAPPENED--I CAUSED THE POWER RING TO FORM AN INVISIBLE WALL IN FRONT OF ME!
CRAAASSH
FROM HIS RING, GREEN LANTERN SHOOTS OUT A PAIR OF HANDS,,,
NOW IT'S TIME THEY WERE ON THE RECEIVING END OF MY POWER-RINGED FISTS!
POW! SOK!
11

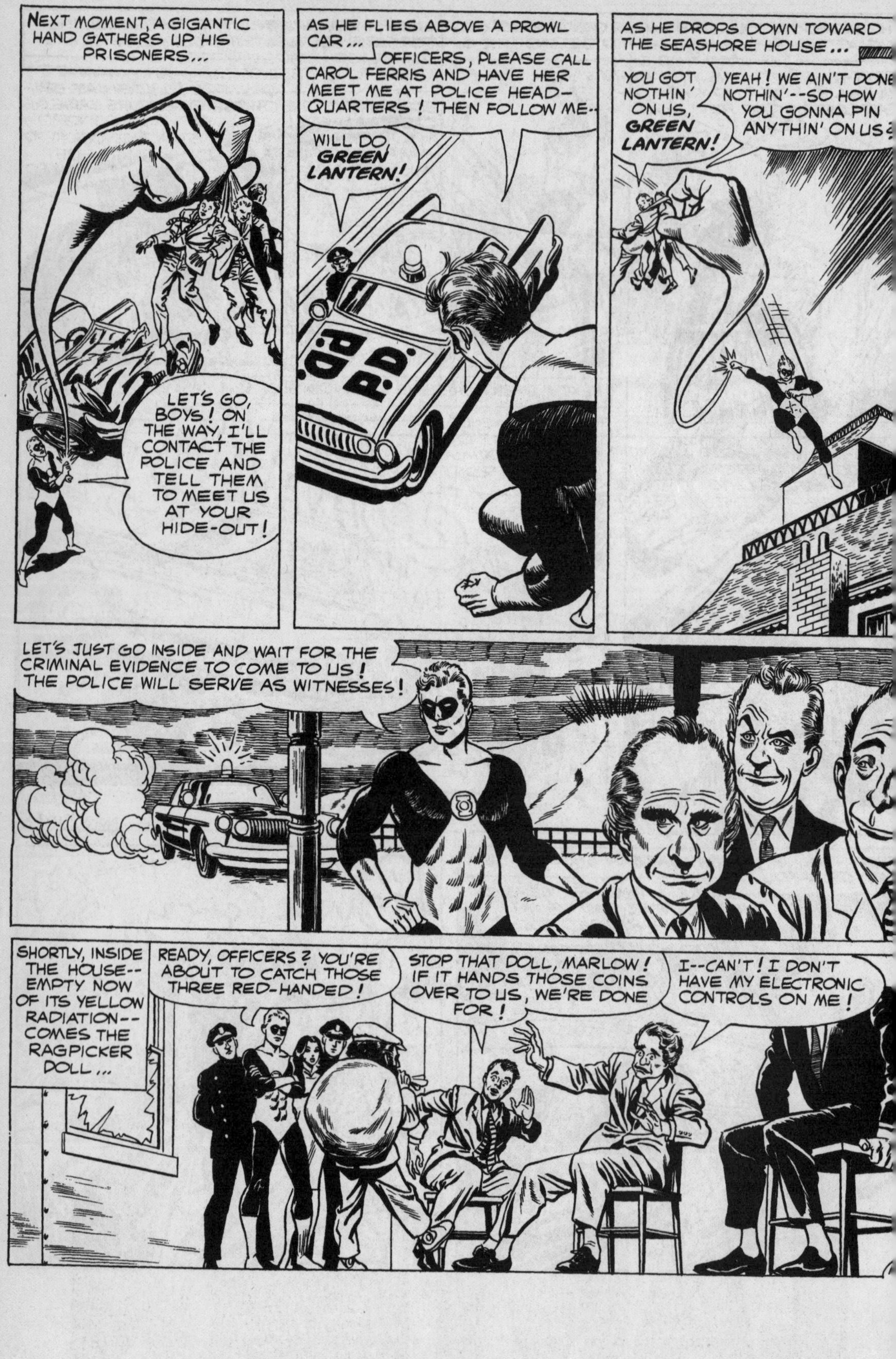
NEXT MOMENT, A GIGANTIC HAND GATHERS UP HIS PRISONERS...
LET'S GO, BOYS! ON THE WAY, I'LL CONTACT THE POLICE AND TELL THEM TO MEET US AT YOUR HIDE-OUT!
AS HE FLIES ABOVE A PROWL CAR...
OFFICERS, PLEASE CALL CAROL FERRIS AND HAVE HER MEET ME AT POLICE HEAD-QUARTERS! THEN FOLLOW ME--
WILL DO, GREEN LANTERN!
P.D.
AS HE DROPS DOWN TOWARD THE SEASHORE HOUSE...
YOU GOT NOTHIN' ON US, GREEN LANTERN!
YEAH! WE AIN'T DONE NOTHIN'--SO HOW YOU GONNA PIN ANYTHIN' ON US?
LET'S JUST GO INSIDE AND WAIT FOR THE CRIMINAL EVIDENCE TO COME TO US! THE POLICE WILL SERVE AS WITNESSES!
SHORTLY, INSIDE THE HOUSE--EMPTY NOW OF ITS YELLOW RADIATION--COMES THE RAGPICKER DOLL...
READY, OFFICERS? YOU'RE ABOUT TO CATCH THOSE THREE RED-HANDED!
STOP THAT DOLL, MARLOW! IF IT HANDS THOSE COINS OVER TO US, WE'RE DONE FOR!
I--CAN'T! I DON'T HAVE MY ELECTRONIC CONTROLS ON ME!

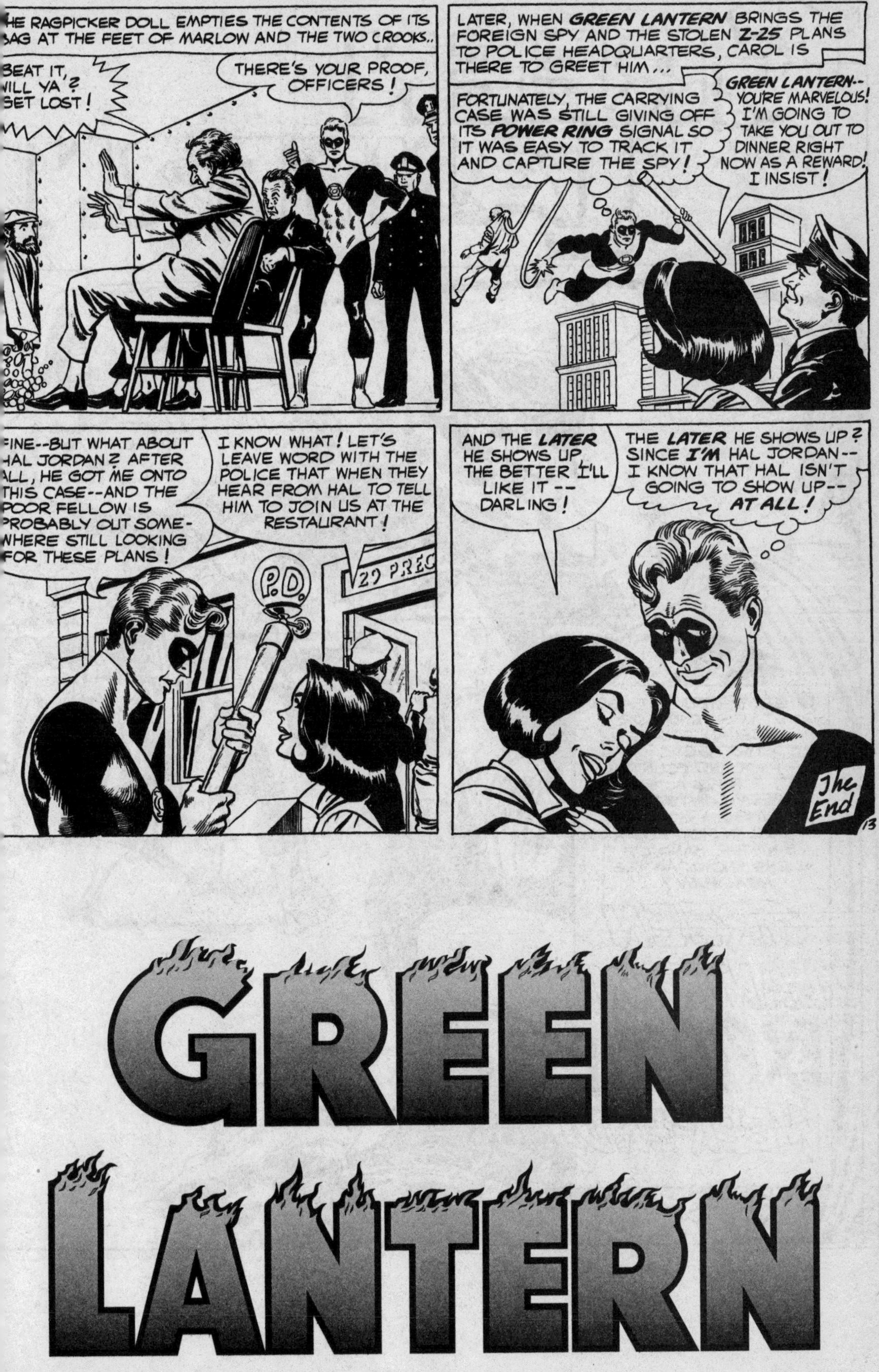
HE RAGPICKER DOLL EMPTIES THE CONTENTS OF ITS BAG AT THE FEET OF MARLOW AND THE TWO CROOKS..
BEAT IT, WILL YA? GET LOST!
THERE'S YOUR PROOF, OFFICERS!
LATER, WHEN GREEN LANTERN BRINGS THE FOREIGN SPY AND THE STOLEN Z-25 PLANS TO POLICE HEADQUARTERS, CAROL IS THERE TO GREET HIM...
FORTUNATELY, THE CARRYING CASE WAS STILL GIVING OFF ITS POWER RING SIGNAL SO IT WAS EASY TO TRACK IT AND CAPTURE THE SPY!
GREEN LANTERN-- YOU'RE MARVELOUS! I'M GOING TO TAKE YOU OUT TO DINNER RIGHT NOW AS A REWARD! I INSIST!
FINE--BUT WHAT ABOUT HAL JORDAN? AFTER ALL, HE GOT ME ONTO THIS CASE--AND THE POOR FELLOW IS PROBABLY OUT SOMEWHERE STILL LOOKING FOR THESE PLANS!
I KNOW WHAT! LET'S LEAVE WORD WITH THE POLICE THAT WHEN THEY HEAR FROM HAL TO TELL HIM TO JOIN US AT THE RESTAURANT!
P.D.
29 PREC
AND THE LATER HE SHOWS UP, THE BETTER I'LL LIKE IT -- DARLING!
THE LATER HE SHOWS UP? SINCE I'M HAL JORDAN-- I KNOW THAT HAL ISN'T GOING TO SHOW UP-- AT ALL!
The End
13

GREEN LANTERN

GREEN LANTERN

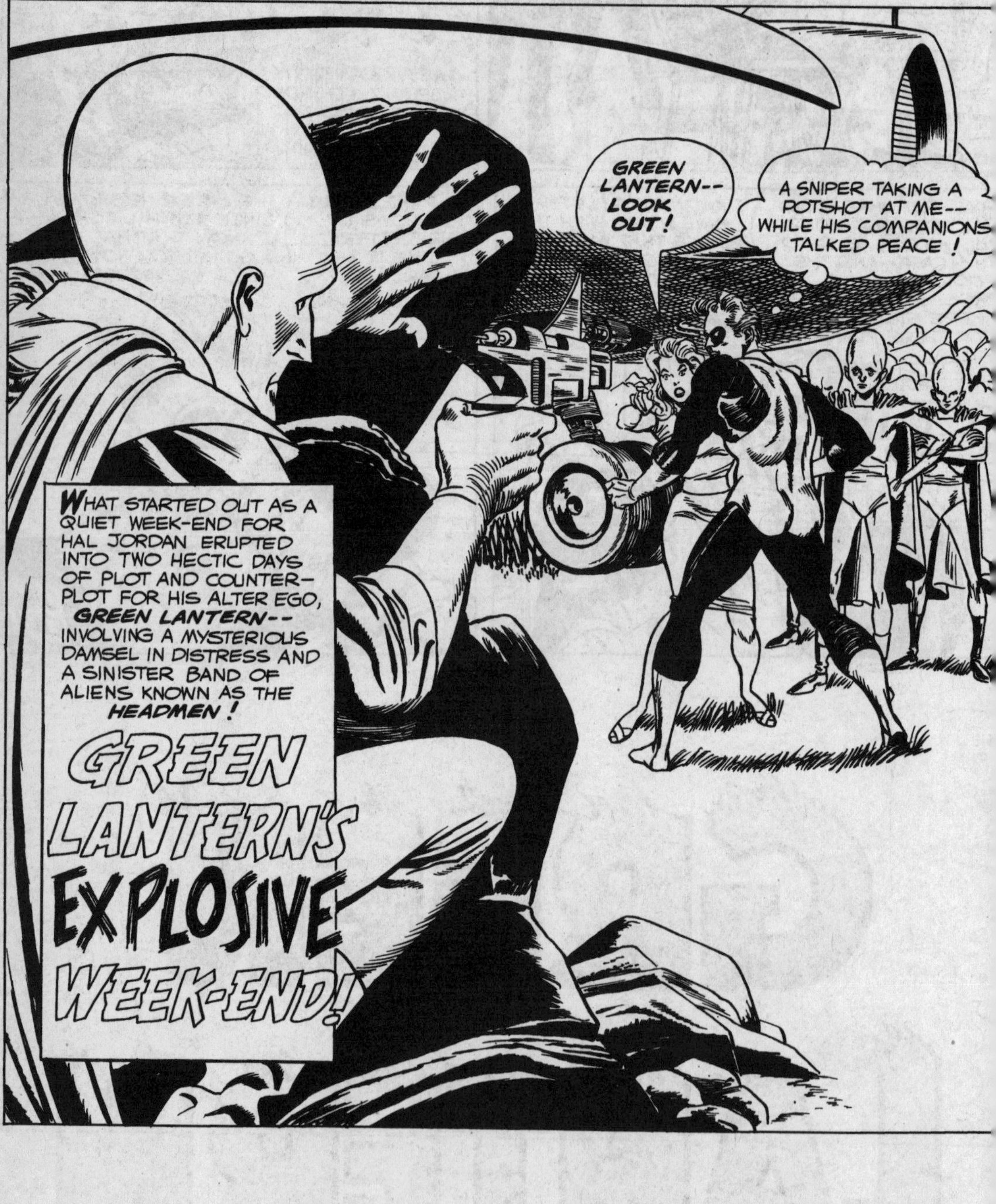
GREEN LANTERN-- LOOK OUT!
A SNIPER TAKING A POTSHOT AT ME-- WHILE HIS COMPANIONS TALKED PEACE!
WHAT STARTED OUT AS A QUIET WEEK-END FOR HAL JORDAN ERUPTED INTO TWO HECTIC DAYS OF PLOT AND COUNTER-PLOT FOR HIS ALTER EGO, GREEN LANTERN-- INVOLVING A MYSTERIOUS DAMSEL IN DISTRESS AND A SINISTER BAND OF ALIENS KNOWN AS THE HEADMEN!
GREEN LANTERN'S EXPLOSIVE WEEK-END!

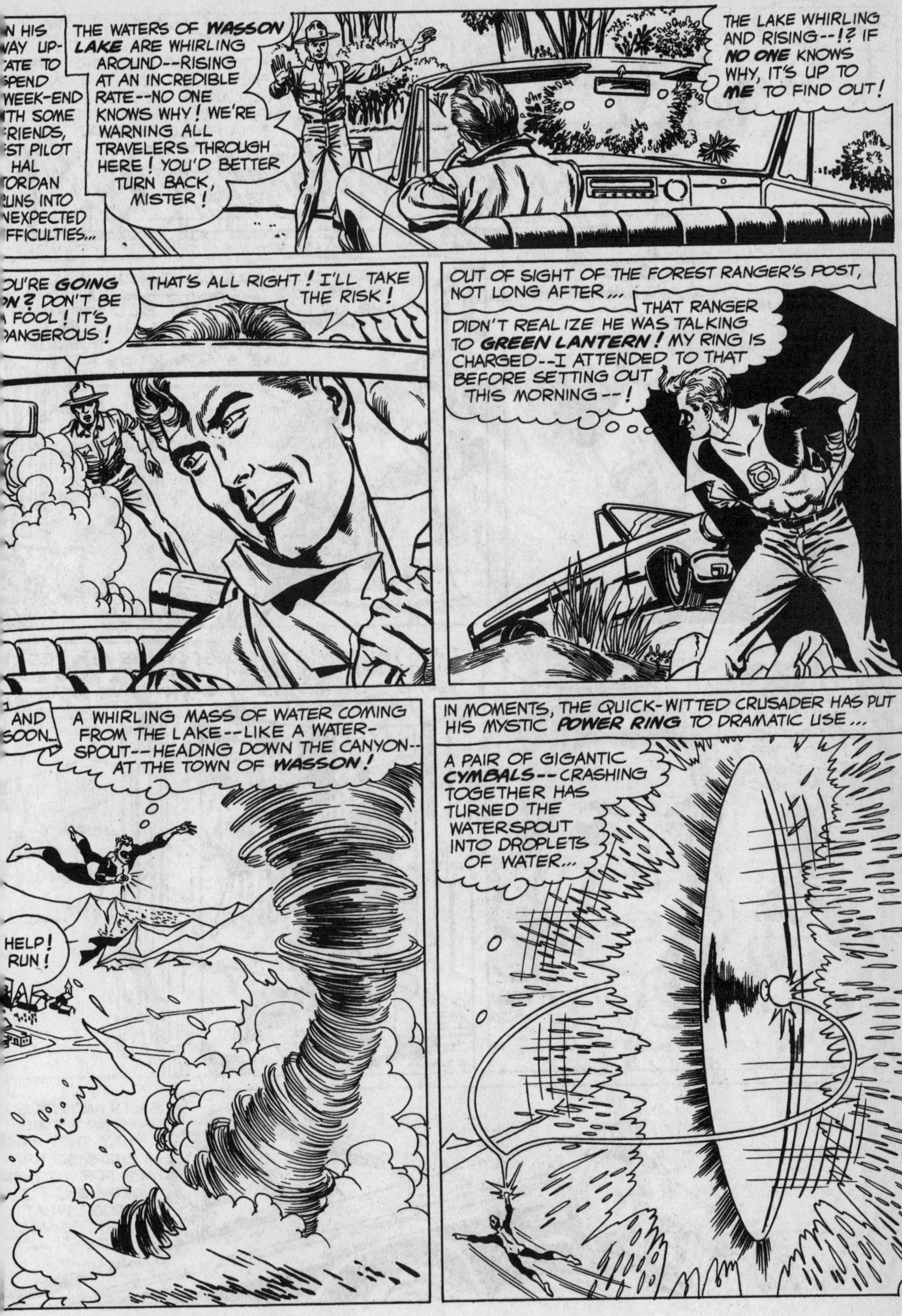

N HIS WAY UP-STATE TO SPEND WEEK-END WITH SOME FRIENDS, TEST PILOT HAL JORDAN RUNS INTO UNEXPECTED DIFFICULTIES...
THE WATERS OF WASSON LAKE ARE WHIRLING AROUND--RISING AT AN INCREDIBLE RATE--NO ONE KNOWS WHY! WE'RE WARNING ALL TRAVELERS THROUGH HERE! YOU'D BETTER TURN BACK, MISTER!
THE LAKE WHIRLING AND RISING--!? IF NO ONE KNOWS WHY, IT'S UP TO ME TO FIND OUT!
OU'RE GOING ON? DON'T BE A FOOL! IT'S DANGEROUS!
THAT'S ALL RIGHT! I'LL TAKE THE RISK!
OUT OF SIGHT OF THE FOREST RANGER'S POST, NOT LONG AFTER...
THAT RANGER DIDN'T REALIZE HE WAS TALKING TO GREEN LANTERN! MY RING IS CHARGED--I ATTENDED TO THAT BEFORE SETTING OUT THIS MORNING--!
AND SOON...
A WHIRLING MASS OF WATER COMING FROM THE LAKE--LIKE A WATER-SPOUT--HEADING DOWN THE CANYON--AT THE TOWN OF WASSON!
HELP! RUN!
IN MOMENTS, THE QUICK-WITTED CRUSADER HAS PUT HIS MYSTIC POWER RING TO DRAMATIC USE...
A PAIR OF GIGANTIC CYMBALS--CRASHING TOGETHER HAS TURNED THE WATERSPOUT INTO DROPLETS OF WATER...
2

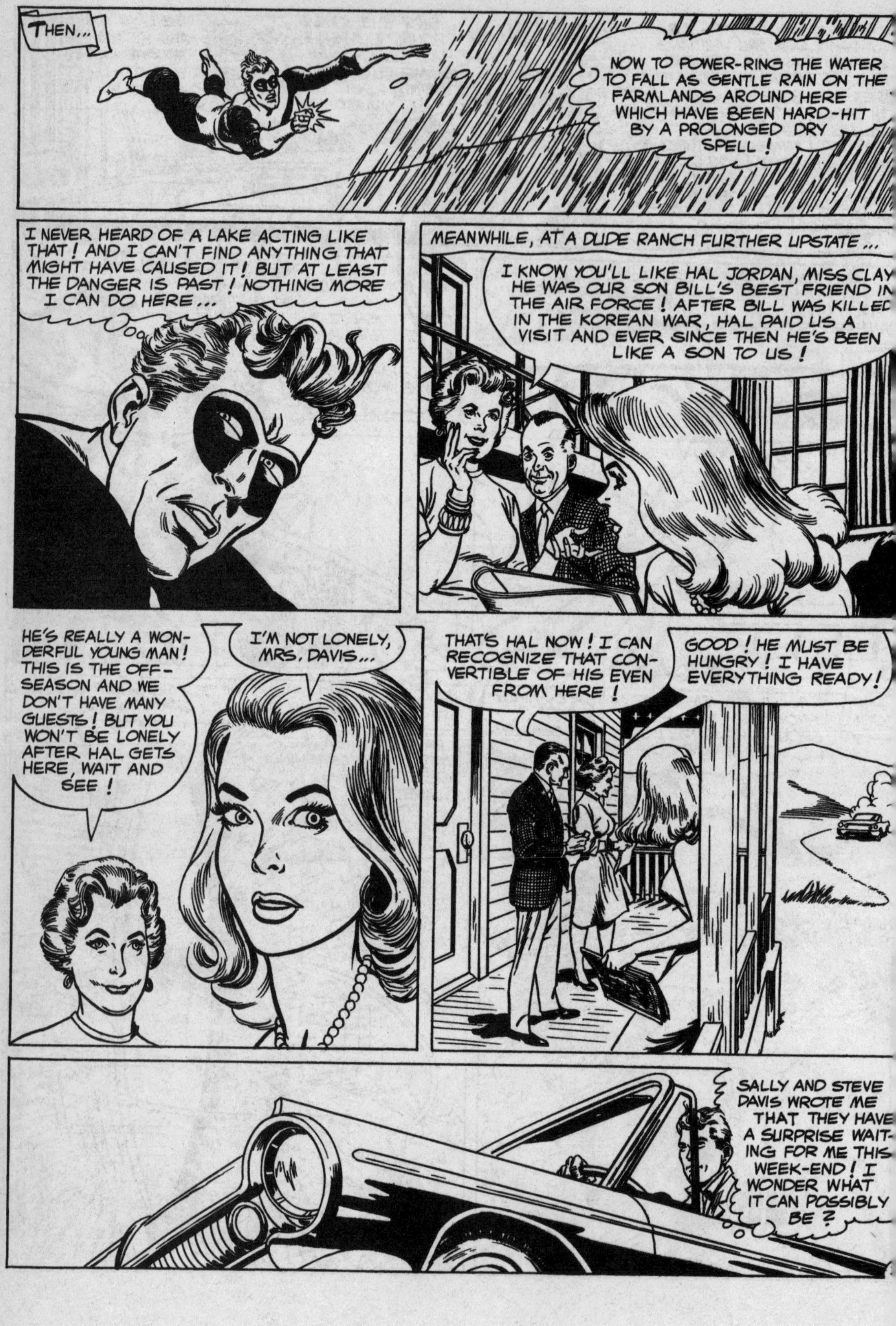
THEN,..
NOW TO POWER-RING THE WATER TO FALL AS GENTLE RAIN ON THE FARMLANDS AROUND HERE WHICH HAVE BEEN HARD-HIT BY A PROLONGED DRY SPELL!
I NEVER HEARD OF A LAKE ACTING LIKE THAT! AND I CAN'T FIND ANYTHING THAT MIGHT HAVE CAUSED IT! BUT AT LEAST THE DANGER IS PAST! NOTHING MORE I CAN DO HERE...
MEANWHILE, AT A DUDE RANCH FURTHER UPSTATE...
I KNOW YOU'LL LIKE HAL JORDAN, MISS CLAY HE WAS OUR SON BILL'S BEST FRIEND IN THE AIR FORCE! AFTER BILL WAS KILLED IN THE KOREAN WAR, HAL PAID US A VISIT AND EVER SINCE THEN HE'S BEEN LIKE A SON TO US!
HE'S REALLY A WONDERFUL YOUNG MAN! THIS IS THE OFF-SEASON AND WE DON'T HAVE MANY GUESTS! BUT YOU WON'T BE LONELY AFTER HAL GETS HERE, WAIT AND SEE!
I'M NOT LONELY, MRS. DAVIS...
THAT'S HAL NOW! I CAN RECOGNIZE THAT CONVERTIBLE OF HIS EVEN FROM HERE!
GOOD! HE MUST BE HUNGRY! I HAVE EVERYTHING READY!
SALLY AND STEVE DAVIS WROTE ME THAT THEY HAVE A SURPRISE WAITING FOR ME THIS WEEK-END! I WONDER WHAT IT CAN POSSIBLY BE?

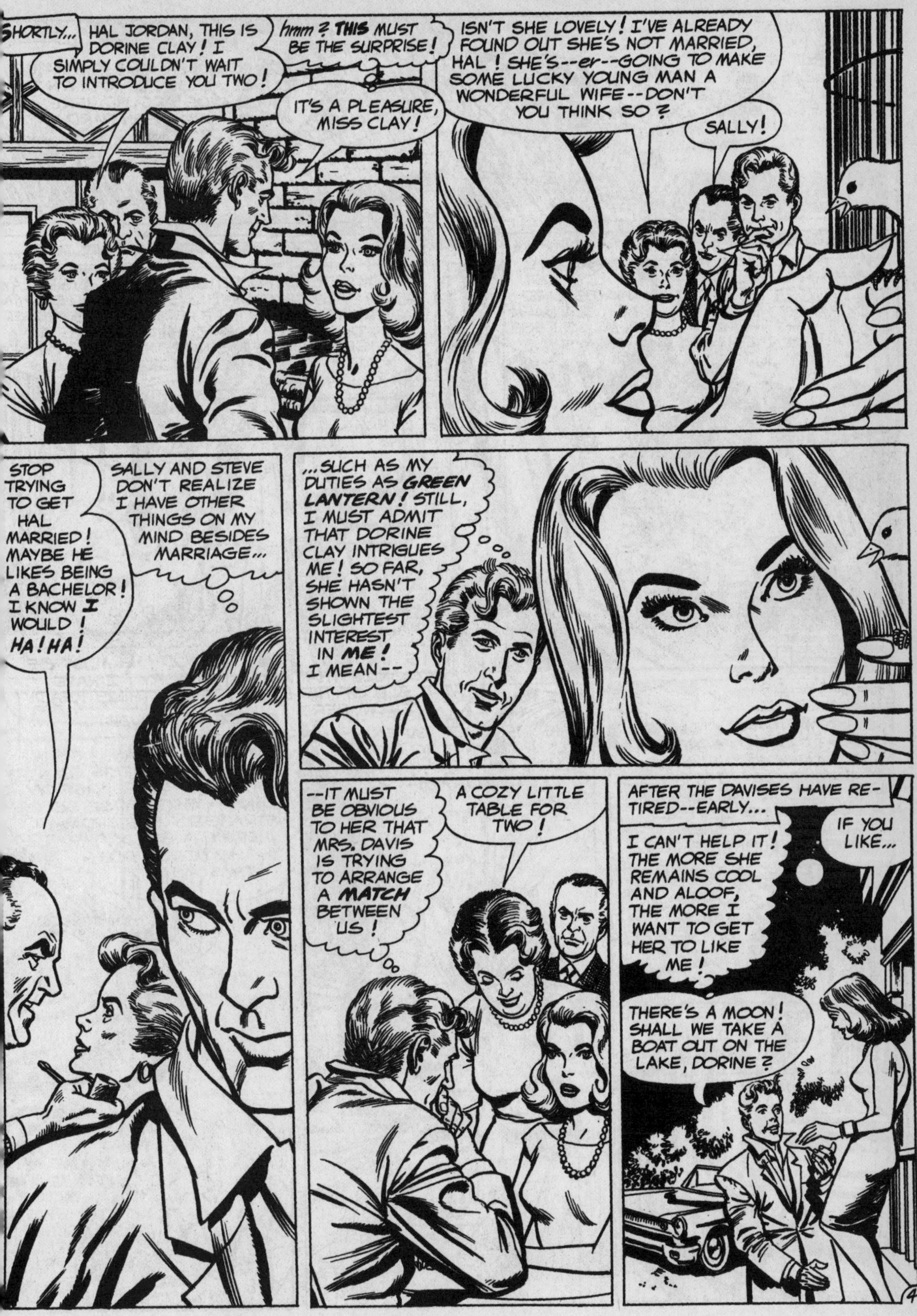
SHORTLY...
HAL JORDAN, THIS IS DORINE CLAY! I SIMPLY COULDN'T WAIT TO INTRODUCE YOU TWO!
hmm? THIS MUST BE THE SURPRISE!
IT'S A PLEASURE, MISS CLAY!
ISN'T SHE LOVELY! I'VE ALREADY FOUND OUT SHE'S NOT MARRIED, HAL! SHE'S--er--GOING TO MAKE SOME LUCKY YOUNG MAN A WONDERFUL WIFE--DON'T YOU THINK SO?
SALLY!
STOP TRYING TO GET HAL MARRIED! MAYBE HE LIKES BEING A BACHELOR! I KNOW I WOULD! HA! HA!
SALLY AND STEVE DON'T REALIZE I HAVE OTHER THINGS ON MY MIND BESIDES MARRIAGE...
...SUCH AS MY DUTIES AS GREEN LANTERN! STILL, I MUST ADMIT THAT DORINE CLAY INTRIGUES ME! SO FAR, SHE HASN'T SHOWN THE SLIGHTEST INTEREST IN ME! I MEAN--
--IT MUST BE OBVIOUS TO HER THAT MRS. DAVIS IS TRYING TO ARRANGE A MATCH BETWEEN US!
A COZY LITTLE TABLE FOR TWO!
AFTER THE DAVISES HAVE RETIRED--EARLY...
I CAN'T HELP IT! THE MORE SHE REMAINS COOL AND ALOOF, THE MORE I WANT TO GET HER TO LIKE ME!
IF YOU LIKE...
THERE'S A MOON! SHALL WE TAKE A BOAT OUT ON THE LAKE, DORINE?
4

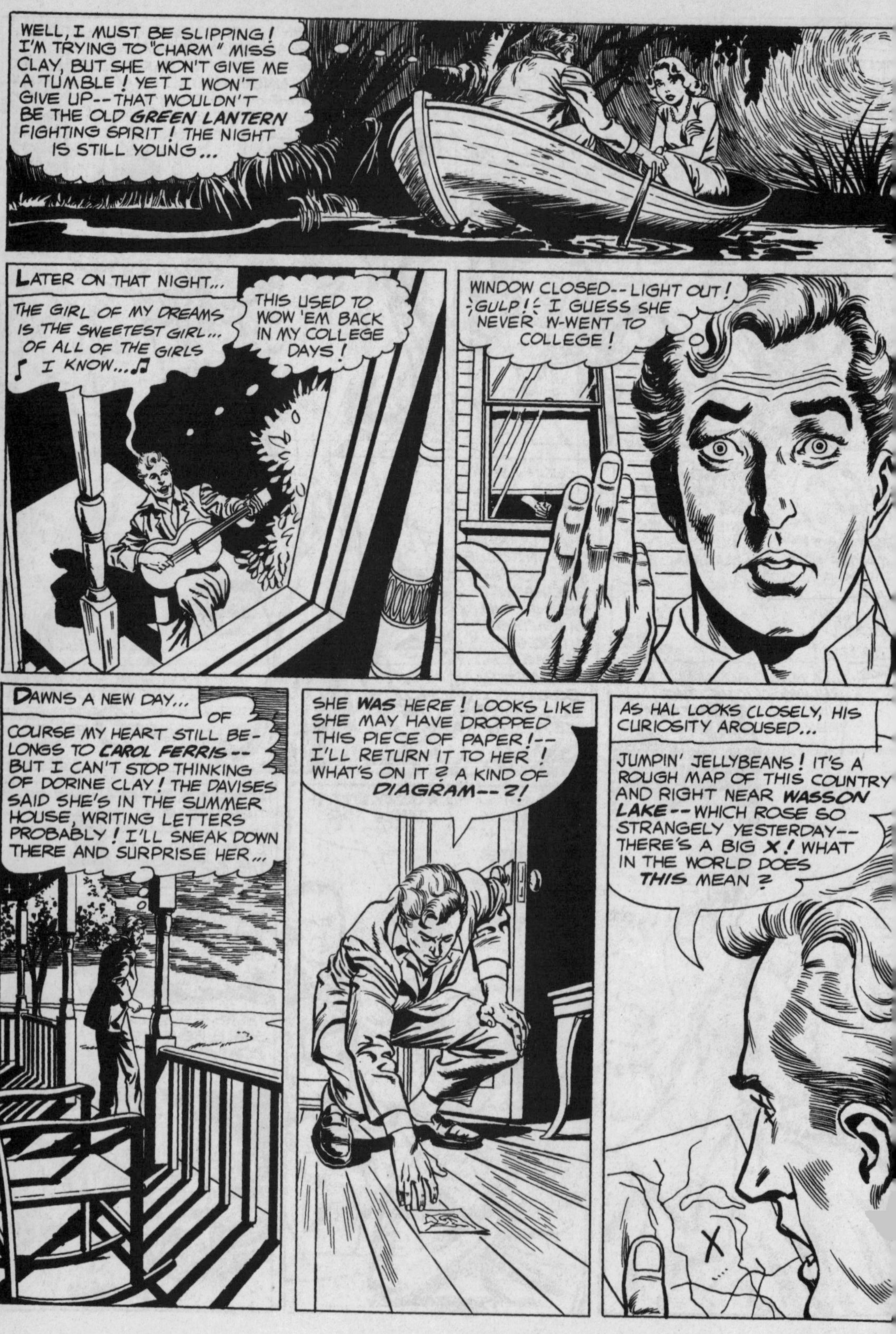
WELL, I MUST BE SLIPPING! I'M TRYING TO "CHARM" MISS CLAY, BUT SHE WON'T GIVE ME A TUMBLE! YET I WON'T GIVE UP--THAT WOULDN'T BE THE OLD GREEN LANTERN FIGHTING SPIRIT! THE NIGHT IS STILL YOUNG...
LATER ON THAT NIGHT...
THE GIRL OF MY DREAMS IS THE SWEETEST GIRL... OF ALL OF THE GIRLS I KNOW...
THIS USED TO WOW 'EM BACK IN MY COLLEGE DAYS!
WINDOW CLOSED--LIGHT OUT! GULP! I GUESS SHE NEVER W-WENT TO COLLEGE!
DAWNS A NEW DAY...
OF COURSE MY HEART STILL BELONGS TO CAROL FERRIS--BUT I CAN'T STOP THINKING OF DORINE CLAY! THE DAVISES SAID SHE'S IN THE SUMMER HOUSE, WRITING LETTERS PROBABLY! I'LL SNEAK DOWN THERE AND SURPRISE HER...
SHE WAS HERE! LOOKS LIKE SHE MAY HAVE DROPPED THIS PIECE OF PAPER!--I'LL RETURN IT TO HER! WHAT'S ON IT? A KIND OF DIAGRAM--?!
AS HAL LOOKS CLOSELY, HIS CURIOSITY AROUSED...
JUMPIN' JELLYBEANS! IT'S A ROUGH MAP OF THIS COUNTRY AND RIGHT NEAR WASSON LAKE--WHICH ROSE SO STRANGELY YESTERDAY--THERE'S A BIG X! WHAT IN THE WORLD DOES THIS MEAN?
X

As HAL seeks out the girl...

WHAT CAN A GIRL LIKE DORINE HAVE TO DO WITH THAT AMAZING OCCURRENCE !? THERE SHE IS NOW ! I WONDER--IS THERE MORE TO HER THAN MEETS THE EYE ? I'VE GOT TO FIND OUT WITHOUT DELAY !

I'LL USE MY RING TO *MINDS-DROP* ON HER ! IT'S NOT EXACTLY CRICKET, BUT IF I BEGIN TO OVER-HEAR SOMETHING I SHOULDN'T, I'LL STOP AT ONCE !...eh ?! GREAT SCOTT--!

AS THE GIRL'S MIND, WITHOUT HER REALIZING IT, COMMUNICATES DIRECTLY WITH THE RING-WIELDER VIA THE MYSTIC BEAM ...

I'M GETTING HER WHOLE STORY! BUT IT'S IN-CREDIBLE...!

I AM NOT OF EARTH... NOT OF THIS WORLD AT ALL ! MY REAL NAME IS *ONU MURTU* AND I COME FROM THE PLANET *GARON* FAR FROM THIS STAR-SYSTEM...

"... A WORLD GOVERNED BY A *RULING CLIQUE*, THE *SINISTER HEADMEN*, AS THEY ARE CALLED ..."

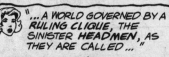
... WHO BY MEANS OF THEIR *CEREBRO-RAY* HOLD ALL OUR RACE IN BONDAGE !"

"WHENEVER AN INFANT IS BORN ON GARON, IT IS SUBJECTED TO THE *CEREBRO-RAY* ... "

"THE RAY AFFECTS ITS BRAIN ! FROM THEN ON FOR THE REST OF ITS LIFE IT MUST OBEY EVERY COMMAND OF THE *HEADMEN* !"

"BUT IN MY CASE, BY CHANCE, THE MACHINE DID NOT WORK PROPERLY! WITHOUT ANYONE SUSPECTING IT, I GREW UP FREE OF THE C-RAY'S DOMINATION!..."

I AM THE ONLY ONE ON *GARON* WHOSE WILL AND SPIRIT HAS NOT BEEN ENSLAVED BY THE TERRIBLE *HEADMEN* ! I CAN THINK FOR MYSELF ! IT'S FRIGHTENING TO BE SO ALONE, BUT I MUST BE BRAVE--!

6

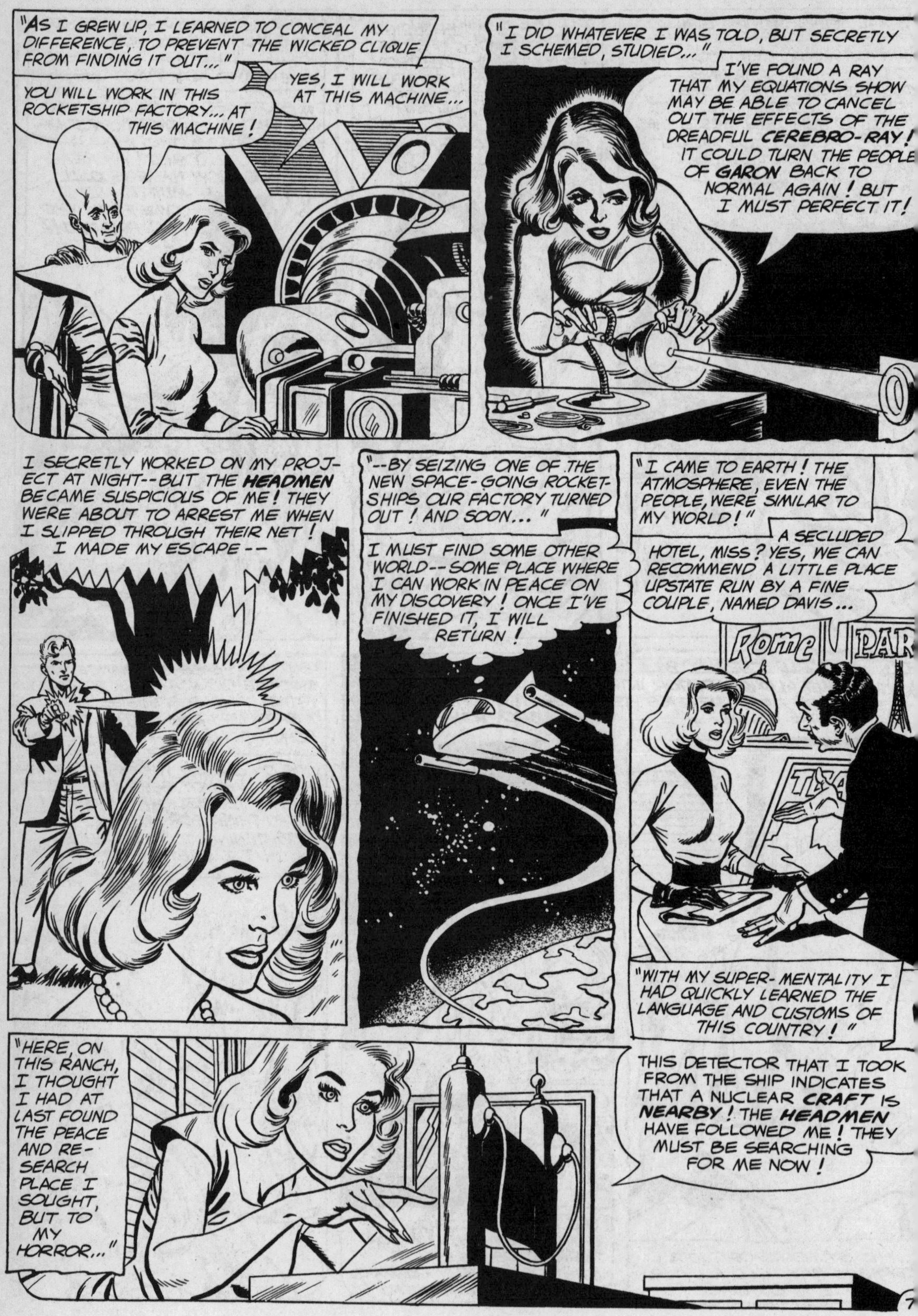
"AS I GREW UP, I LEARNED TO CONCEAL MY DIFFERENCE, TO PREVENT THE WICKED CLIQUE FROM FINDING IT OUT..."
YOU WILL WORK IN THIS ROCKETSHIP FACTORY... AT THIS MACHINE!
YES, I WILL WORK AT THIS MACHINE...
"I DID WHATEVER I WAS TOLD, BUT SECRETLY I SCHEMED, STUDIED..."
I'VE FOUND A RAY THAT MY EQUATIONS SHOW MAY BE ABLE TO CANCEL OUT THE EFFECTS OF THE DREADFUL CEREBRO-RAY! IT COULD TURN THE PEOPLE OF GARON BACK TO NORMAL AGAIN! BUT I MUST PERFECT IT!
I SECRETLY WORKED ON MY PROJECT AT NIGHT--BUT THE HEADMEN BECAME SUSPICIOUS OF ME! THEY WERE ABOUT TO ARREST ME WHEN I SLIPPED THROUGH THEIR NET! I MADE MY ESCAPE--
"--BY SEIZING ONE OF THE NEW SPACE-GOING ROCKETSHIPS OUR FACTORY TURNED OUT! AND SOON..."
I MUST FIND SOME OTHER WORLD--SOME PLACE WHERE I CAN WORK IN PEACE ON MY DISCOVERY! ONCE I'VE FINISHED IT, I WILL RETURN!
"I CAME TO EARTH! THE ATMOSPHERE, EVEN THE PEOPLE, WERE SIMILAR TO MY WORLD!"
A SECLUDED HOTEL, MISS? YES, WE CAN RECOMMEND A LITTLE PLACE UPSTATE RUN BY A FINE COUPLE, NAMED DAVIS...
Rome
PAR
"WITH MY SUPER-MENTALITY I HAD QUICKLY LEARNED THE LANGUAGE AND CUSTOMS OF THIS COUNTRY!"
"HERE, ON THIS RANCH, I THOUGHT I HAD AT LAST FOUND THE PEACE AND RESEARCH PLACE I SOUGHT, BUT TO MY HORROR..."
THIS DETECTOR THAT I TOOK FROM THE SHIP INDICATES THAT A NUCLEAR CRAFT IS NEARBY! THE HEADMEN HAVE FOLLOWED ME! THEY MUST BE SEARCHING FOR ME NOW!
7

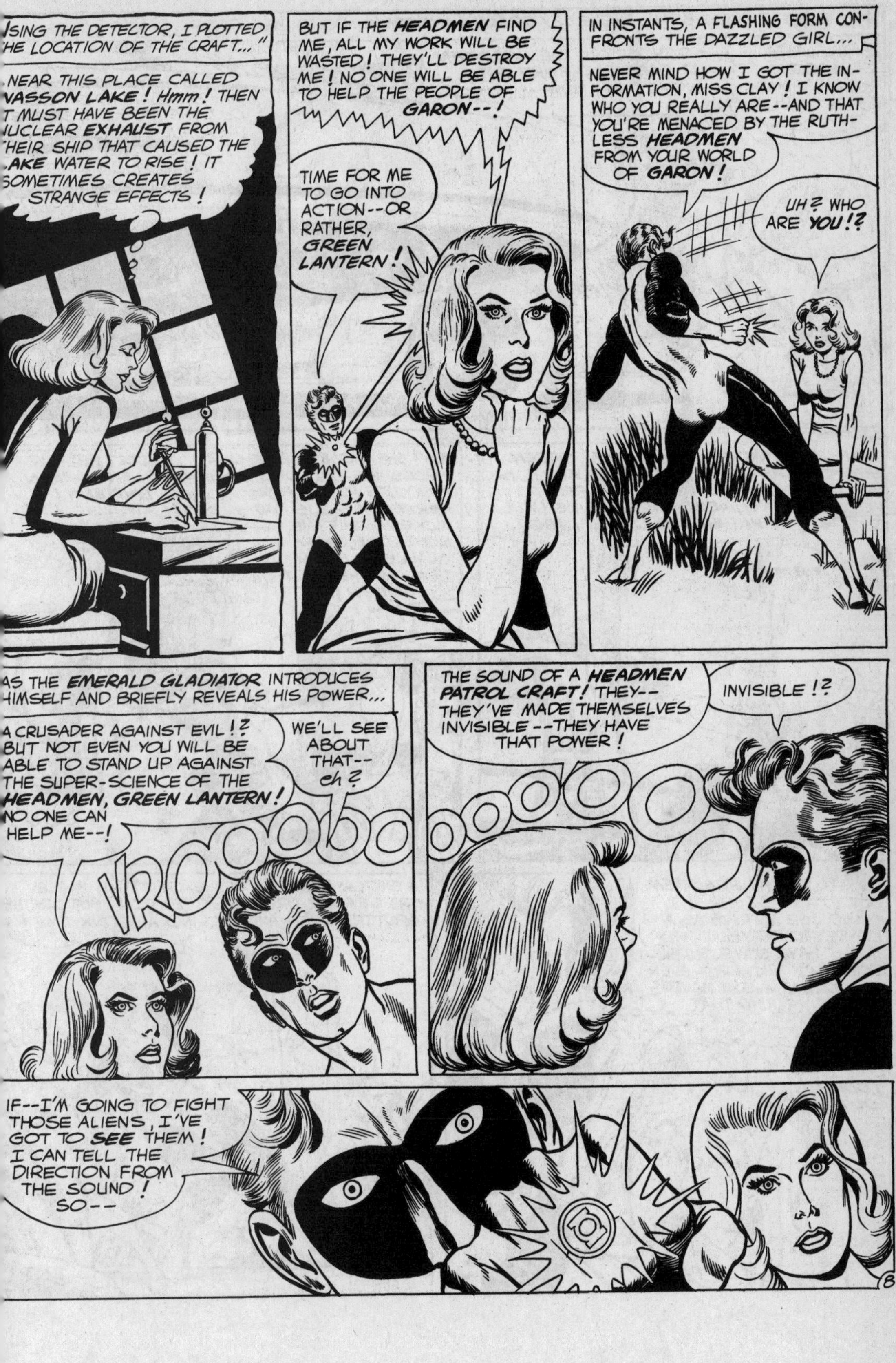
USING THE DETECTOR, I PLOTTED THE LOCATION OF THE CRAFT..."
...NEAR THIS PLACE CALLED WASSON LAKE! Hmm! THEN IT MUST HAVE BEEN THE NUCLEAR EXHAUST FROM THEIR SHIP THAT CAUSED THE LAKE WATER TO RISE! IT SOMETIMES CREATES STRANGE EFFECTS!
BUT IF THE HEADMEN FIND ME, ALL MY WORK WILL BE WASTED! THEY'LL DESTROY ME! NO ONE WILL BE ABLE TO HELP THE PEOPLE OF GARON--!
TIME FOR ME TO GO INTO ACTION--OR RATHER, GREEN LANTERN!
IN INSTANTS, A FLASHING FORM CONFRONTS THE DAZZLED GIRL...
NEVER MIND HOW I GOT THE INFORMATION, MISS CLAY! I KNOW WHO YOU REALLY ARE--AND THAT YOU'RE MENACED BY THE RUTHLESS HEADMEN FROM YOUR WORLD OF GARON!
UH? WHO ARE YOU!?
AS THE EMERALD GLADIATOR INTRODUCES HIMSELF AND BRIEFLY REVEALS HIS POWER...
A CRUSADER AGAINST EVIL!? BUT NOT EVEN YOU WILL BE ABLE TO STAND UP AGAINST THE SUPER-SCIENCE OF THE HEADMEN, GREEN LANTERN! NO ONE CAN HELP ME--!
WE'LL SEE ABOUT THAT--eh?
VROOOOOOOOOOOOOOO
THE SOUND OF A HEADMEN PATROL CRAFT! THEY--THEY'VE MADE THEMSELVES INVISIBLE--THEY HAVE THAT POWER!
INVISIBLE!?
IF--I'M GOING TO FIGHT THOSE ALIENS, I'VE GOT TO SEE THEM! I CAN TELL THE DIRECTION FROM THE SOUND! SO--
8

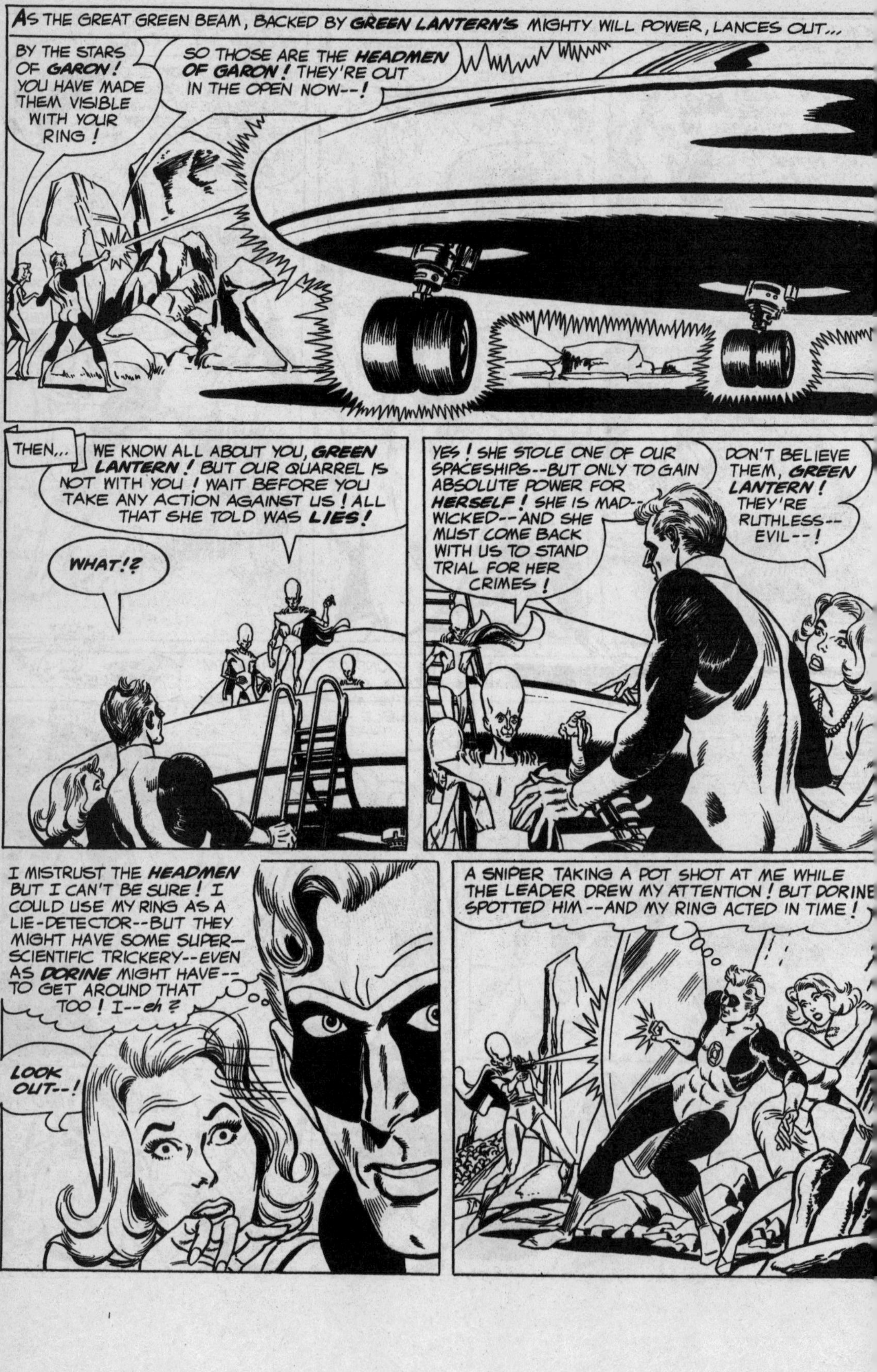
AS THE GREAT GREEN BEAM, BACKED BY GREEN LANTERN'S MIGHTY WILL POWER, LANCES OUT...
BY THE STARS OF GARON! YOU HAVE MADE THEM VISIBLE WITH YOUR RING!
SO THOSE ARE THE HEADMEN OF GARON! THEY'RE OUT IN THE OPEN NOW--!
THEN,..
WE KNOW ALL ABOUT YOU, GREEN LANTERN! BUT OUR QUARREL IS NOT WITH YOU! WAIT BEFORE YOU TAKE ANY ACTION AGAINST US! ALL THAT SHE TOLD WAS LIES!
WHAT!?
YES! SHE STOLE ONE OF OUR SPACESHIPS--BUT ONLY TO GAIN ABSOLUTE POWER FOR HERSELF! SHE IS MAD--WICKED--AND SHE MUST COME BACK WITH US TO STAND TRIAL FOR HER CRIMES!
DON'T BELIEVE THEM, GREEN LANTERN! THEY'RE RUTHLESS--EVIL--!
I MISTRUST THE HEADMEN BUT I CAN'T BE SURE! I COULD USE MY RING AS A LIE-DETECTOR--BUT THEY MIGHT HAVE SOME SUPER-SCIENTIFIC TRICKERY--EVEN AS DORINE MIGHT HAVE--TO GET AROUND THAT TOO! I--eh?
LOOK OUT--!
A SNIPER TAKING A POT SHOT AT ME WHILE THE LEADER DREW MY ATTENTION! BUT DORINE SPOTTED HIM--AND MY RING ACTED IN TIME!

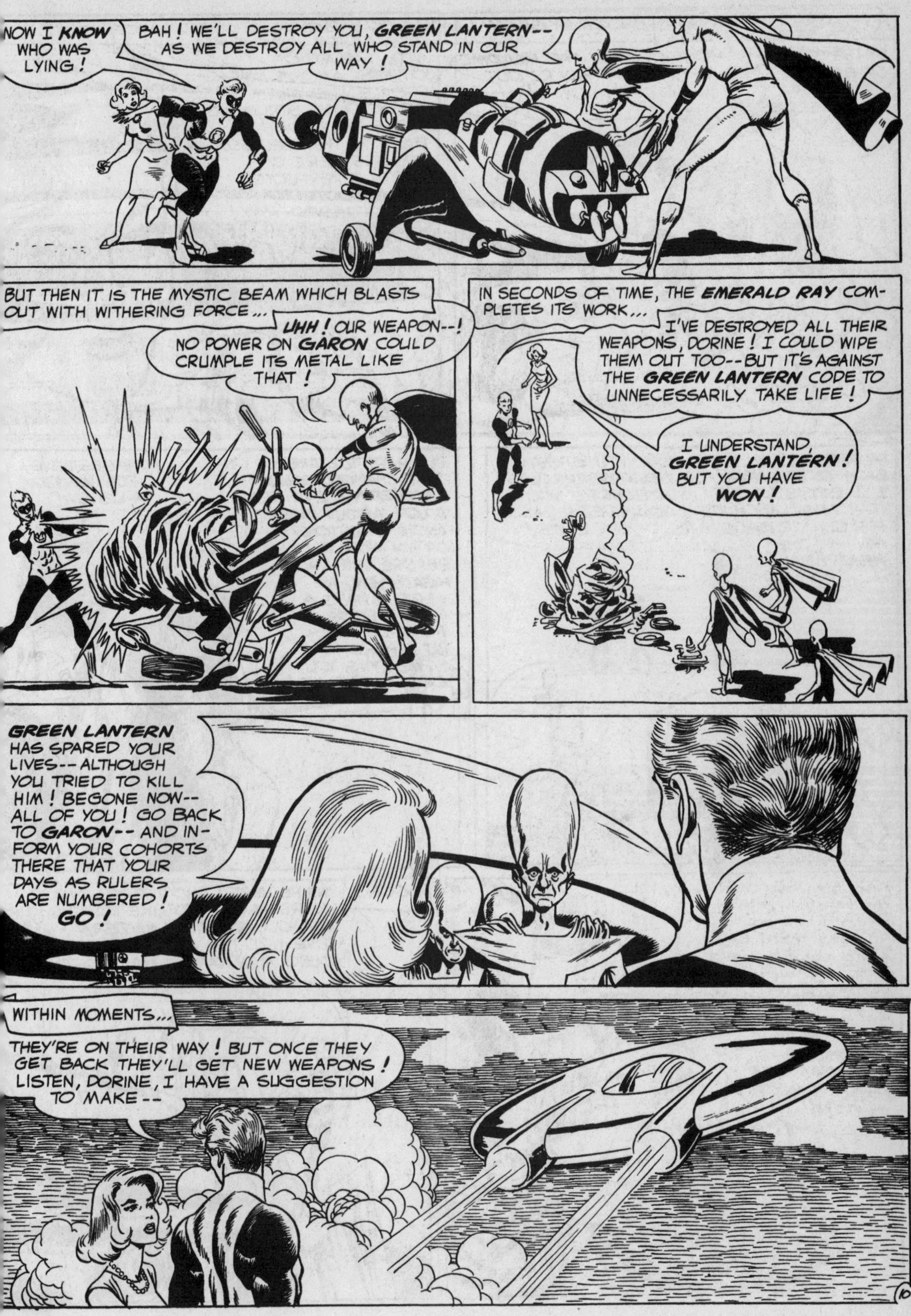
NOW I KNOW WHO WAS LYING!
BAH! WE'LL DESTROY YOU, GREEN LANTERN-- AS WE DESTROY ALL WHO STAND IN OUR WAY!
BUT THEN IT IS THE MYSTIC BEAM WHICH BLASTS OUT WITH WITHERING FORCE...
UHH! OUR WEAPON--! NO POWER ON GARON COULD CRUMPLE ITS METAL LIKE THAT!
IN SECONDS OF TIME, THE EMERALD RAY COMPLETES ITS WORK...
I'VE DESTROYED ALL THEIR WEAPONS, DORINE! I COULD WIPE THEM OUT TOO--BUT IT'S AGAINST THE GREEN LANTERN CODE TO UNNECESSARILY TAKE LIFE!
I UNDERSTAND, GREEN LANTERN! BUT YOU HAVE WON!
GREEN LANTERN HAS SPARED YOUR LIVES--ALTHOUGH YOU TRIED TO KILL HIM! BEGONE NOW--ALL OF YOU! GO BACK TO GARON--AND INFORM YOUR COHORTS THERE THAT YOUR DAYS AS RULERS ARE NUMBERED! GO!
WITHIN MOMENTS...
THEY'RE ON THEIR WAY! BUT ONCE THEY GET BACK THEY'LL GET NEW WEAPONS! LISTEN, DORINE, I HAVE A SUGGESTION TO MAKE--
10

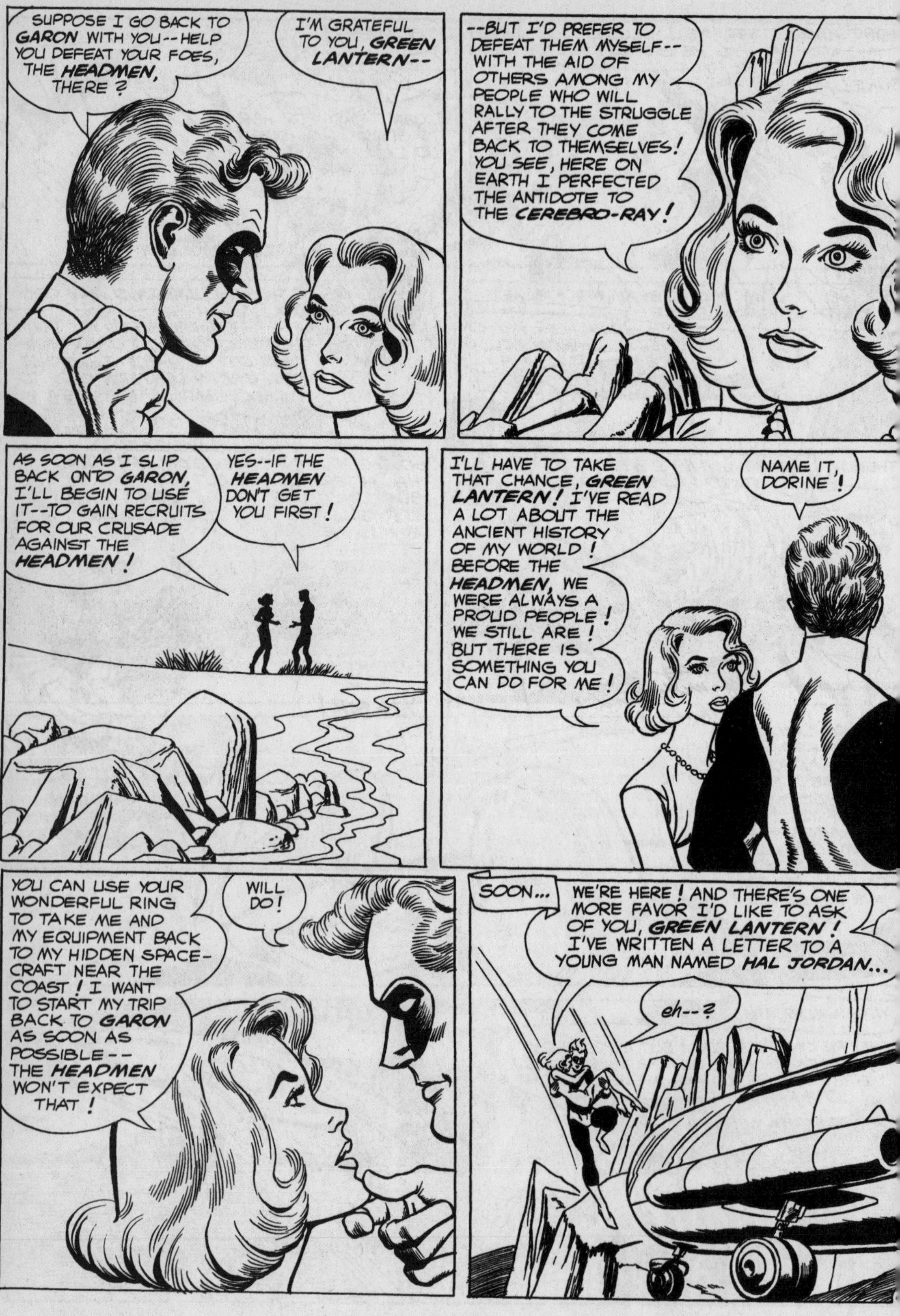
SUPPOSE I GO BACK TO GARON WITH YOU--HELP YOU DEFEAT YOUR FOES, THE HEADMEN, THERE ?
I'M GRATEFUL TO YOU, GREEN LANTERN--
--BUT I'D PREFER TO DEFEAT THEM MYSELF-- WITH THE AID OF OTHERS AMONG MY PEOPLE WHO WILL RALLY TO THE STRUGGLE AFTER THEY COME BACK TO THEMSELVES! YOU SEE, HERE ON EARTH I PERFECTED THE ANTIDOTE TO THE CEREBRO-RAY!
AS SOON AS I SLIP BACK ONTO GARON, I'LL BEGIN TO USE IT--TO GAIN RECRUITS FOR OUR CRUSADE AGAINST THE HEADMEN!
YES--IF THE HEADMEN DON'T GET YOU FIRST!
I'LL HAVE TO TAKE THAT CHANCE, GREEN LANTERN! I'VE READ A LOT ABOUT THE ANCIENT HISTORY OF MY WORLD! BEFORE THE HEADMEN, WE WERE ALWAYS A PROUD PEOPLE! WE STILL ARE! BUT THERE IS SOMETHING YOU CAN DO FOR ME!
NAME IT, DORINE!
YOU CAN USE YOUR WONDERFUL RING TO TAKE ME AND MY EQUIPMENT BACK TO MY HIDDEN SPACE-CRAFT NEAR THE COAST! I WANT TO START MY TRIP BACK TO GARON AS SOON AS POSSIBLE-- THE HEADMEN WON'T EXPECT THAT!
WILL DO!
SOON...
WE'RE HERE! AND THERE'S ONE MORE FAVOR I'D LIKE TO ASK OF YOU, GREEN LANTERN! I'VE WRITTEN A LETTER TO A YOUNG MAN NAMED HAL JORDAN...
eh--?

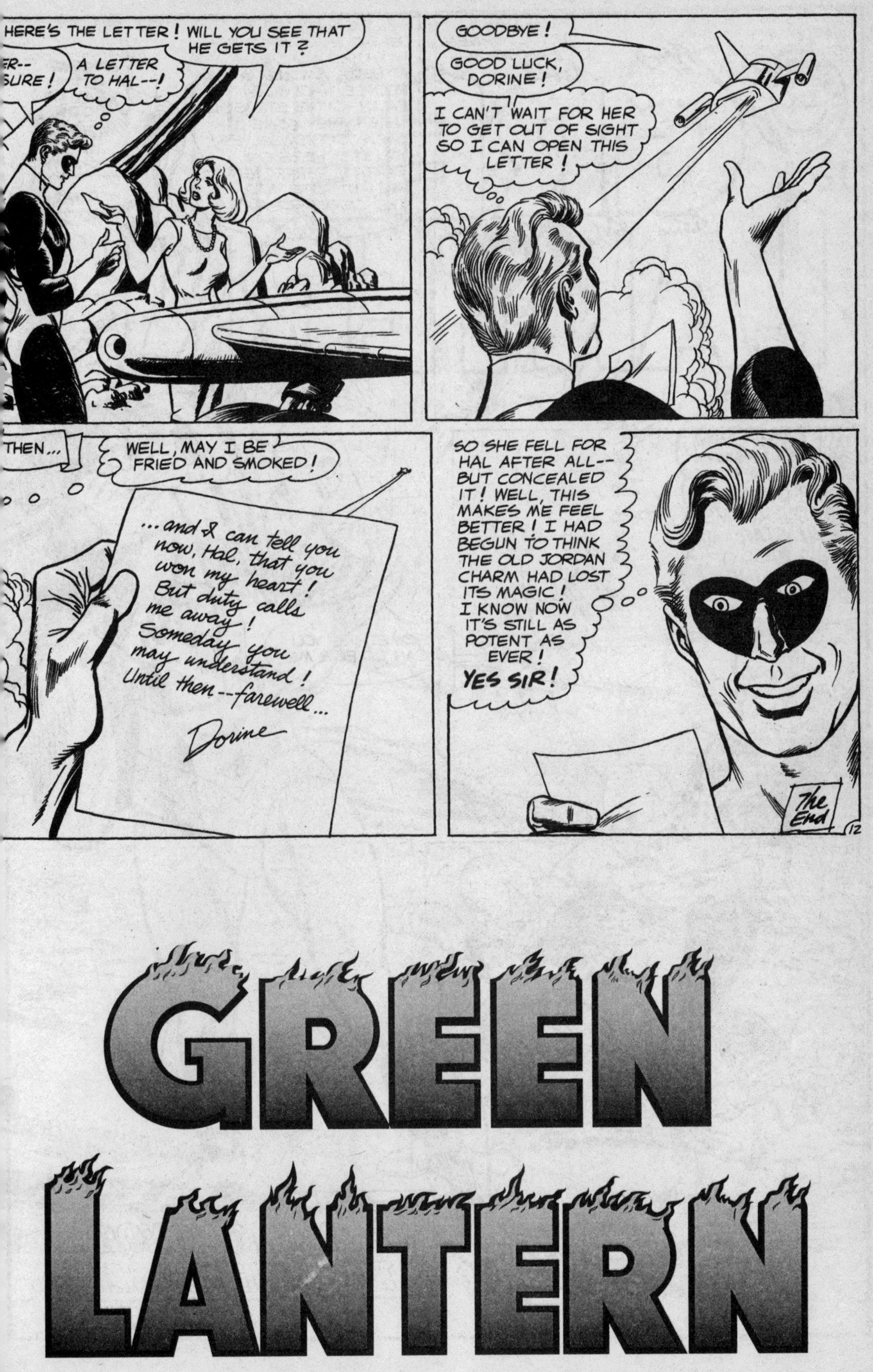
HERE'S THE LETTER! WILL YOU SEE THAT HE GETS IT?
A LETTER TO HAL--!
GOODBYE!
GOOD LUCK, DORINE!
I CAN'T WAIT FOR HER TO GET OUT OF SIGHT SO I CAN OPEN THIS LETTER!
THEN...
WELL, MAY I BE FRIED AND SMOKED!
...and I can tell you now, Hal, that you won my heart! But duty calls me away! Someday you may understand! Until then--farewell...
Dorine
SO SHE FELL FOR HAL AFTER ALL-- BUT CONCEALED IT! WELL, THIS MAKES ME FEEL BETTER! I HAD BEGUN TO THINK THE OLD JORDAN CHARM HAD LOST ITS MAGIC! I KNOW NOW IT'S STILL AS POTENT AS EVER! YES SIR!
The End
12

GREEN LANTERN

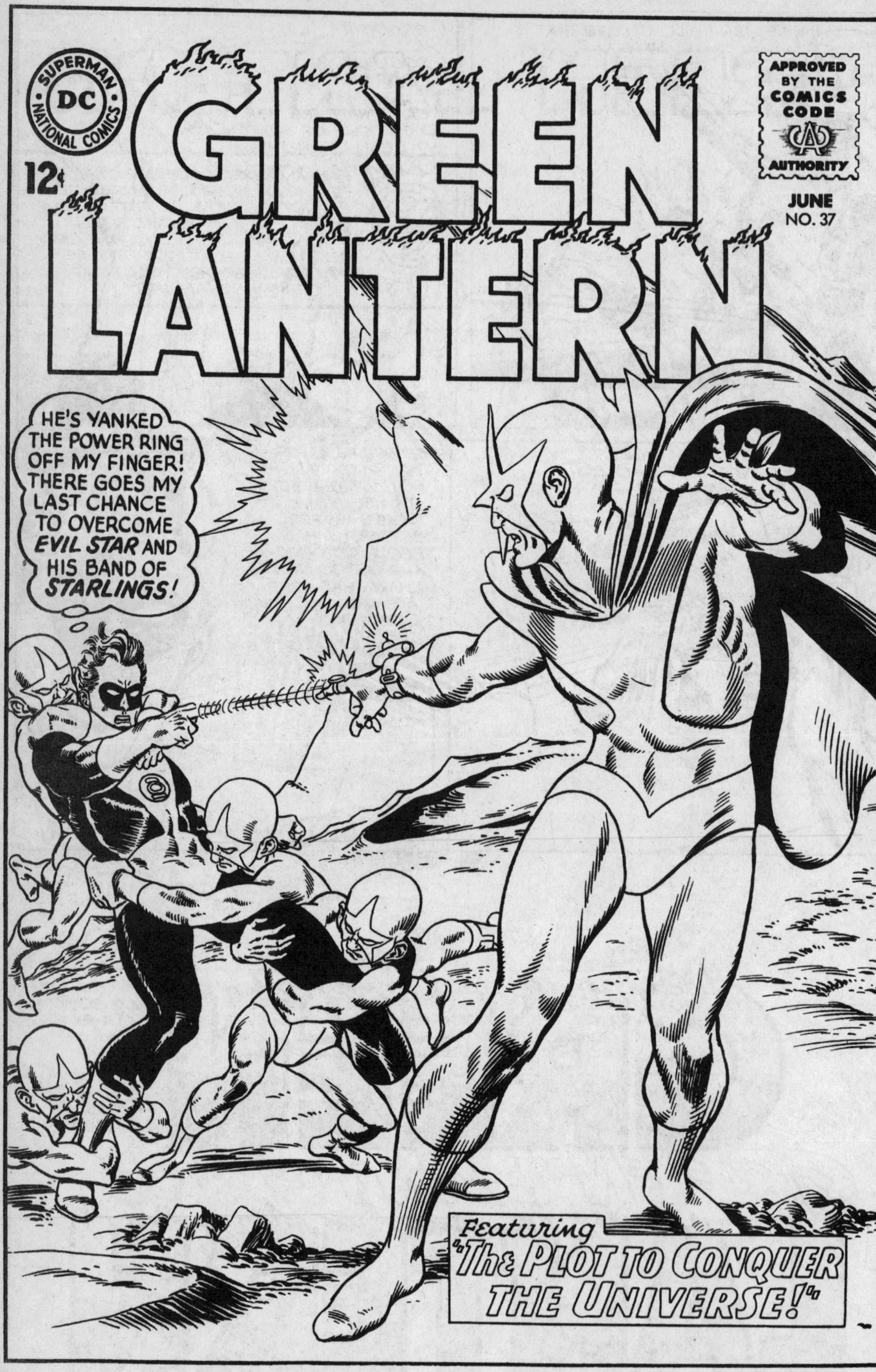
SUPERMAN DC NATIONAL COMICS
12¢
GREEN LANTERN
APPROVED BY THE COMICS CODE AUTHORITY
JUNE
NO. 37
HE'S YANKED THE POWER RING OFF MY FINGER! THERE GOES MY LAST CHANCE TO OVERCOME EVIL STAR AND HIS BAND OF STARLINGS!
Featuring
"The PLOT TO CONQUER THE UNIVERSE!"

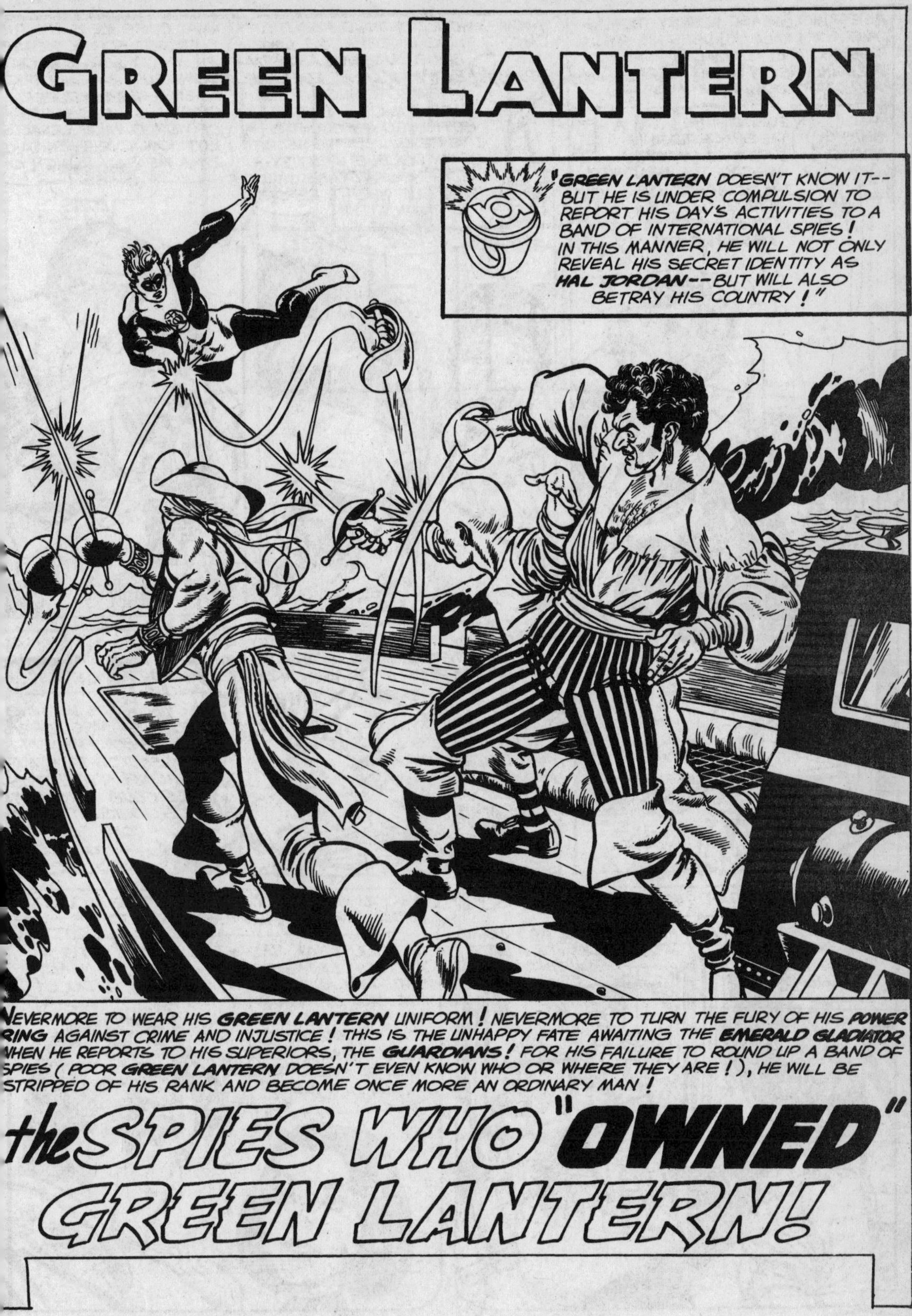
GREEN LANTERN
"GREEN LANTERN DOESN'T KNOW IT-- BUT HE IS UNDER COMPULSION TO REPORT HIS DAY'S ACTIVITIES TO A BAND OF INTERNATIONAL SPIES! IN THIS MANNER, HE WILL NOT ONLY REVEAL HIS SECRET IDENTITY AS HAL JORDAN--BUT WILL ALSO BETRAY HIS COUNTRY!"
NEVERMORE TO WEAR HIS GREEN LANTERN UNIFORM! NEVERMORE TO TURN THE FURY OF HIS POWER RING AGAINST CRIME AND INJUSTICE! THIS IS THE UNHAPPY FATE AWAITING THE EMERALD GLADIATOR WHEN HE REPORTS TO HIS SUPERIORS, THE GUARDIANS! FOR HIS FAILURE TO ROUND UP A BAND OF SPIES (POOR GREEN LANTERN DOESN'T EVEN KNOW WHO OR WHERE THEY ARE!), HE WILL BE STRIPPED OF HIS RANK AND BECOME ONCE MORE AN ORDINARY MAN!
the SPIES WHO "OWNED" GREEN LANTERN!

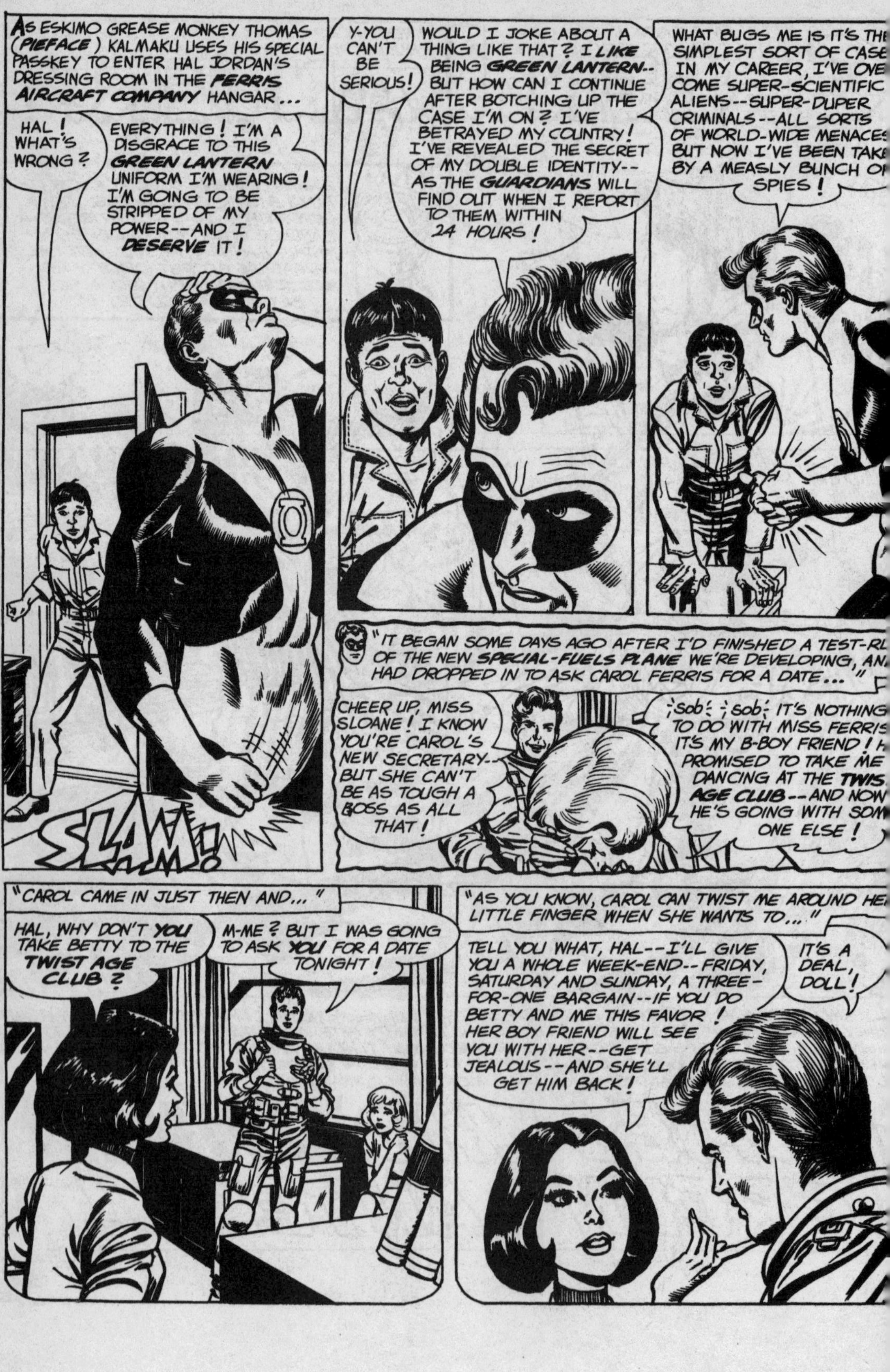
AS ESKIMO GREASE MONKEY THOMAS (PIEFACE) KALMAKU USES HIS SPECIAL PASSKEY TO ENTER HAL JORDAN'S DRESSING ROOM IN THE FERRIS AIRCRAFT COMPANY HANGAR...
HAL! WHAT'S WRONG?
EVERYTHING! I'M A DISGRACE TO THIS GREEN LANTERN UNIFORM I'M WEARING! I'M GOING TO BE STRIPPED OF MY POWER--AND I DESERVE IT!
SLAM!
Y-YOU CAN'T BE SERIOUS!
WOULD I JOKE ABOUT A THING LIKE THAT? I LIKE BEING GREEN LANTERN-- BUT HOW CAN I CONTINUE AFTER BOTCHING UP THE CASE I'M ON? I'VE BETRAYED MY COUNTRY! I'VE REVEALED THE SECRET OF MY DOUBLE IDENTITY-- AS THE GUARDIANS WILL FIND OUT WHEN I REPORT TO THEM WITHIN 24 HOURS!
WHAT BUGS ME IS IT'S THE SIMPLEST SORT OF CASE IN MY CAREER, I'VE OVE COME SUPER-SCIENTIFIC ALIENS--SUPER-DUPER CRIMINALS--ALL SORTS OF WORLD-WIDE MENACES BUT NOW I'VE BEEN TAKE BY A MEASLY BUNCH OF SPIES!
"IT BEGAN SOME DAYS AGO AFTER I'D FINISHED A TEST-RU OF THE NEW SPECIAL-FUELS PLANE WE'RE DEVELOPING, AN HAD DROPPED IN TO ASK CAROL FERRIS FOR A DATE..."
CHEER UP, MISS SLOANE! I KNOW YOU'RE CAROL'S NEW SECRETARY-- BUT SHE CAN'T BE AS TOUGH A BOSS AS ALL THAT!
-sob- -sob- IT'S NOTHING TO DO WITH MISS FERRIS IT'S MY B-BOY FRIEND! H PROMISED TO TAKE ME DANCING AT THE TWIS AGE CLUB--AND NOW HE'S GOING WITH SOM ONE ELSE!
"CAROL CAME IN JUST THEN AND..."
HAL, WHY DON'T YOU TAKE BETTY TO THE TWIST AGE CLUB?
M-ME? BUT I WAS GOING TO ASK YOU FOR A DATE TONIGHT!
"AS YOU KNOW, CAROL CAN TWIST ME AROUND HE LITTLE FINGER WHEN SHE WANTS TO..."
TELL YOU WHAT, HAL--I'LL GIVE YOU A WHOLE WEEK-END--FRIDAY, SATURDAY AND SUNDAY, A THREE-FOR-ONE BARGAIN--IF YOU DO BETTY AND ME THIS FAVOR! HER BOY FRIEND WILL SEE YOU WITH HER--GET JEALOUS--AND SHE'LL GET HIM BACK!
IT'S A DEAL, DOLL!

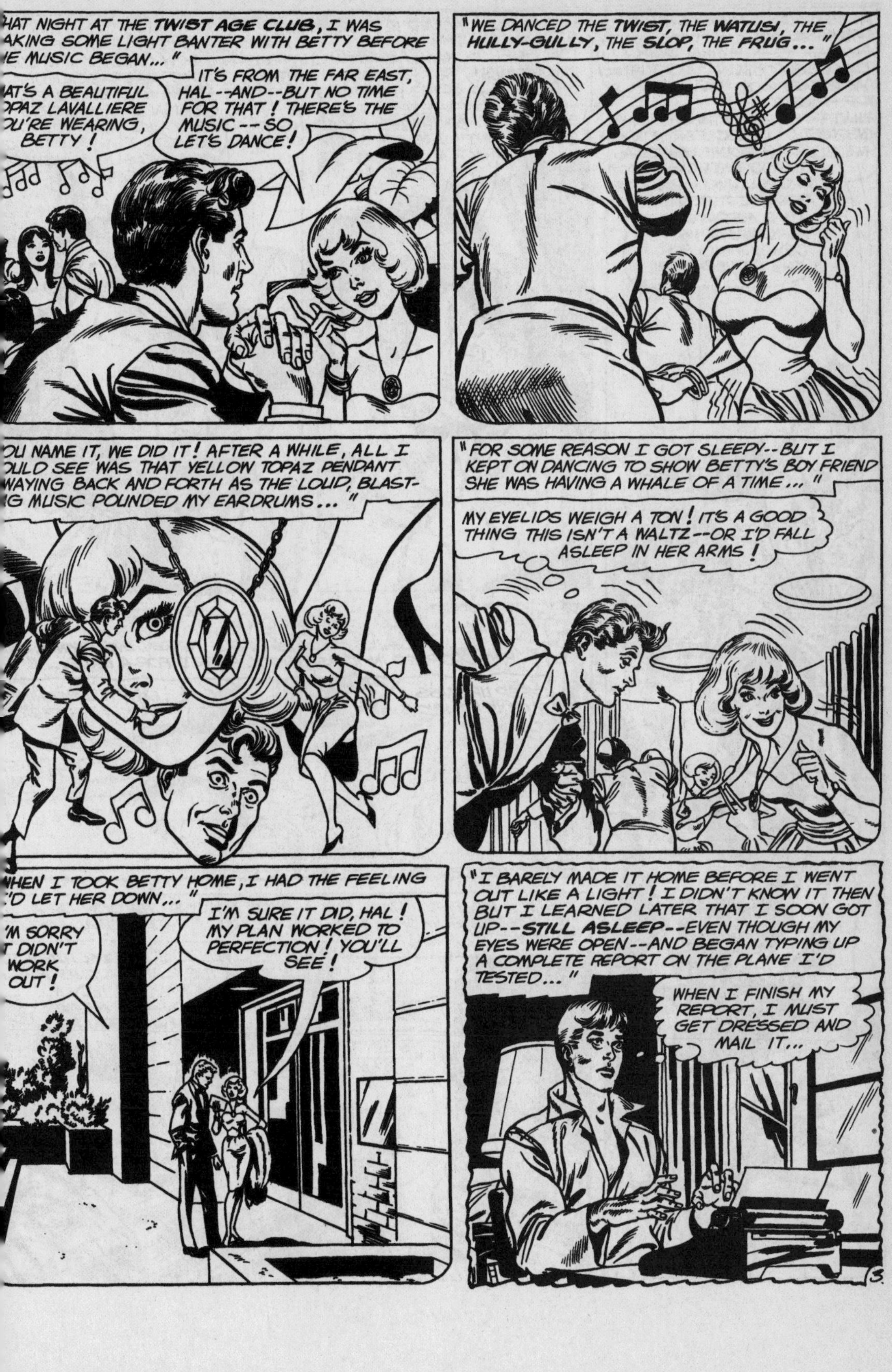
HAT NIGHT AT THE TWIST AGE CLUB, I WAS AKING SOME LIGHT BANTER WITH BETTY BEFORE HE MUSIC BEGAN..."
AT'S A BEAUTIFUL OPAZ LAVALLIERE OU'RE WEARING, BETTY!
IT'S FROM THE FAR EAST, HAL--AND--BUT NO TIME FOR THAT! THERE'S THE MUSIC--SO LET'S DANCE!
"WE DANCED THE TWIST, THE WATUSI, THE HULLY-GULLY, THE SLOP, THE FRUG..."
OU NAME IT, WE DID IT! AFTER A WHILE, ALL I OULD SEE WAS THAT YELLOW TOPAZ PENDANT WAYING BACK AND FORTH AS THE LOUD, BLAST- G MUSIC POUNDED MY EARDRUMS..."
"FOR SOME REASON I GOT SLEEPY--BUT I KEPT ON DANCING TO SHOW BETTY'S BOY FRIEND SHE WAS HAVING A WHALE OF A TIME..."
MY EYELIDS WEIGH A TON! IT'S A GOOD THING THIS ISN'T A WALTZ--OR I'D FALL ASLEEP IN HER ARMS!
HEN I TOOK BETTY HOME, I HAD THE FEELING 'D LET HER DOWN..."
'M SORRY T DIDN'T WORK OUT!
I'M SURE IT DID, HAL! MY PLAN WORKED TO PERFECTION! YOU'LL SEE!
"I BARELY MADE IT HOME BEFORE I WENT OUT LIKE A LIGHT! I DIDN'T KNOW IT THEN BUT I LEARNED LATER THAT I SOON GOT UP--STILL ASLEEP--EVEN THOUGH MY EYES WERE OPEN--AND BEGAN TYPING UP A COMPLETE REPORT ON THE PLANE I'D TESTED..."
WHEN I FINISH MY REPORT, I MUST GET DRESSED AND MAIL IT...
3

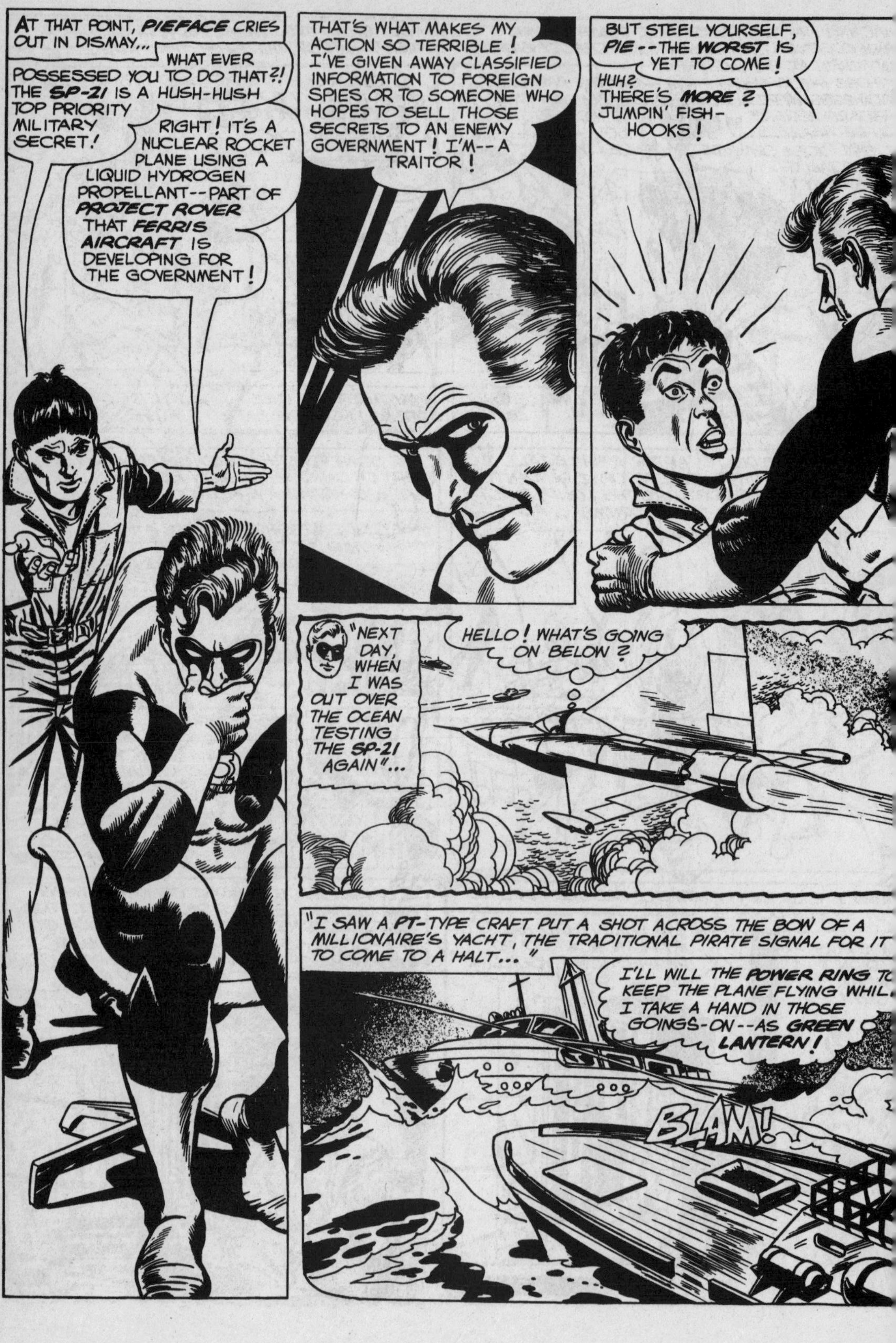
AT THAT POINT, PIEFACE CRIES OUT IN DISMAY...
WHAT EVER POSSESSED YOU TO DO THAT?! THE SP-21 IS A HUSH-HUSH TOP PRIORITY MILITARY SECRET!
RIGHT! IT'S A NUCLEAR ROCKET PLANE USING A LIQUID HYDROGEN PROPELLANT--PART OF PROJECT ROVER THAT FERRIS AIRCRAFT IS DEVELOPING FOR THE GOVERNMENT!
THAT'S WHAT MAKES MY ACTION SO TERRIBLE! I'VE GIVEN AWAY CLASSIFIED INFORMATION TO FOREIGN SPIES OR TO SOMEONE WHO HOPES TO SELL THOSE SECRETS TO AN ENEMY GOVERNMENT! I'M--A TRAITOR!
BUT STEEL YOURSELF, PIE--THE WORST IS YET TO COME!
HUH? THERE'S MORE? JUMPIN' FISH-HOOKS!
"NEXT DAY, WHEN I WAS OUT OVER THE OCEAN TESTING THE SP-21 AGAIN"...
HELLO! WHAT'S GOING ON BELOW?
"I SAW A PT-TYPE CRAFT PUT A SHOT ACROSS THE BOW OF A MILLIONAIRE'S YACHT, THE TRADITIONAL PIRATE SIGNAL FOR IT TO COME TO A HALT..."
I'LL WILL THE POWER RING TO KEEP THE PLANE FLYING WHIL. I TAKE A HAND IN THOSE GOINGS-ON--AS GREEN LANTERN!
BLAM!

"...WITCHING UNIFORMS, I DOVE DOWNWARD, POWER-BEAMING A GIANT CHAIN AT THE YACHT JUST AS THOSE MODERN-DAY BUCCANEERS WERE ABOUT TO BOARD HER..."

I'LL GIVE THOSE SEA-RATS MY SPECIALIZED TREATMENT!

"WITH THE YACHT SAFELY OUT OF HARM'S WAY--I DROPPED ONTO THE FOREDECK OF THE CONVERTED PT-BOAT..."

I ONLY HAVE TO "WILL" MY CUTLASSES TO MOVE--AND THEY RESPOND IN A PARRY WITH THE SPEED OF THOUGHT!

"AS I WAS ENGAGED IN MY THREE-WAY DUEL--A COUPLE OF OTHERS TRIED TO LEAP-FROG AT ME FROM THE BATTLE BRIDGE..."

THE MORE THE MERRIER!

"JUST AS THOSE 20TH CENTURY CORSAIRS WERE ABOUT TO POUNCE ON ME, I FORMED A TRAMPOLINE OVER MY HEAD..."

UP--AND AWAYYY!

"BOUNCING HIGH--UP AND DOWN-- AND SIDEWAYS--THEY WERE NO FURTHER THREAT TO ME ..."

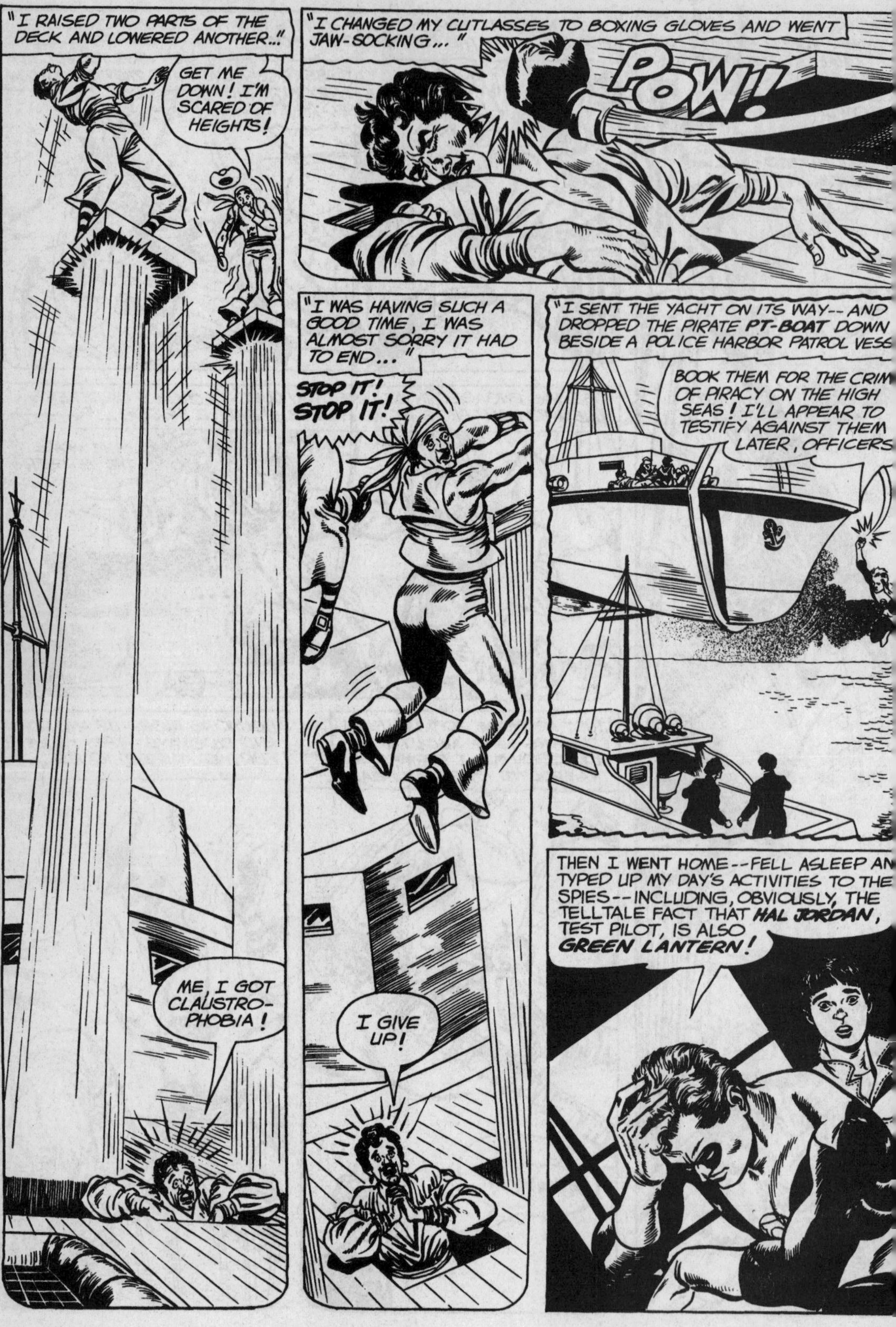
"I RAISED TWO PARTS OF THE DECK AND LOWERED ANOTHER..!"
GET ME DOWN! I'M SCARED OF HEIGHTS!
ME, I GOT CLAUSTRO-PHOBIA!
"I CHANGED MY CUTLASSES TO BOXING GLOVES AND WENT JAW-SOCKING..."
POW!
"I WAS HAVING SUCH A GOOD TIME, I WAS ALMOST SORRY IT HAD TO END..."
STOP IT! STOP IT!
I GIVE UP!
"I SENT THE YACHT ON ITS WAY-- AND DROPPED THE PIRATE PT-BOAT DOWN BESIDE A POLICE HARBOR PATROL VESS
BOOK THEM FOR THE CRIM OF PIRACY ON THE HIGH SEAS! I'LL APPEAR TO TESTIFY AGAINST THEM LATER, OFFICERS
THEN I WENT HOME--FELL ASLEEP AN TYPED UP MY DAY'S ACTIVITIES TO THE SPIES--INCLUDING, OBVIOUSLY, THE TELLTALE FACT THAT HAL JORDAN, TEST PILOT, IS ALSO GREEN LANTERN!

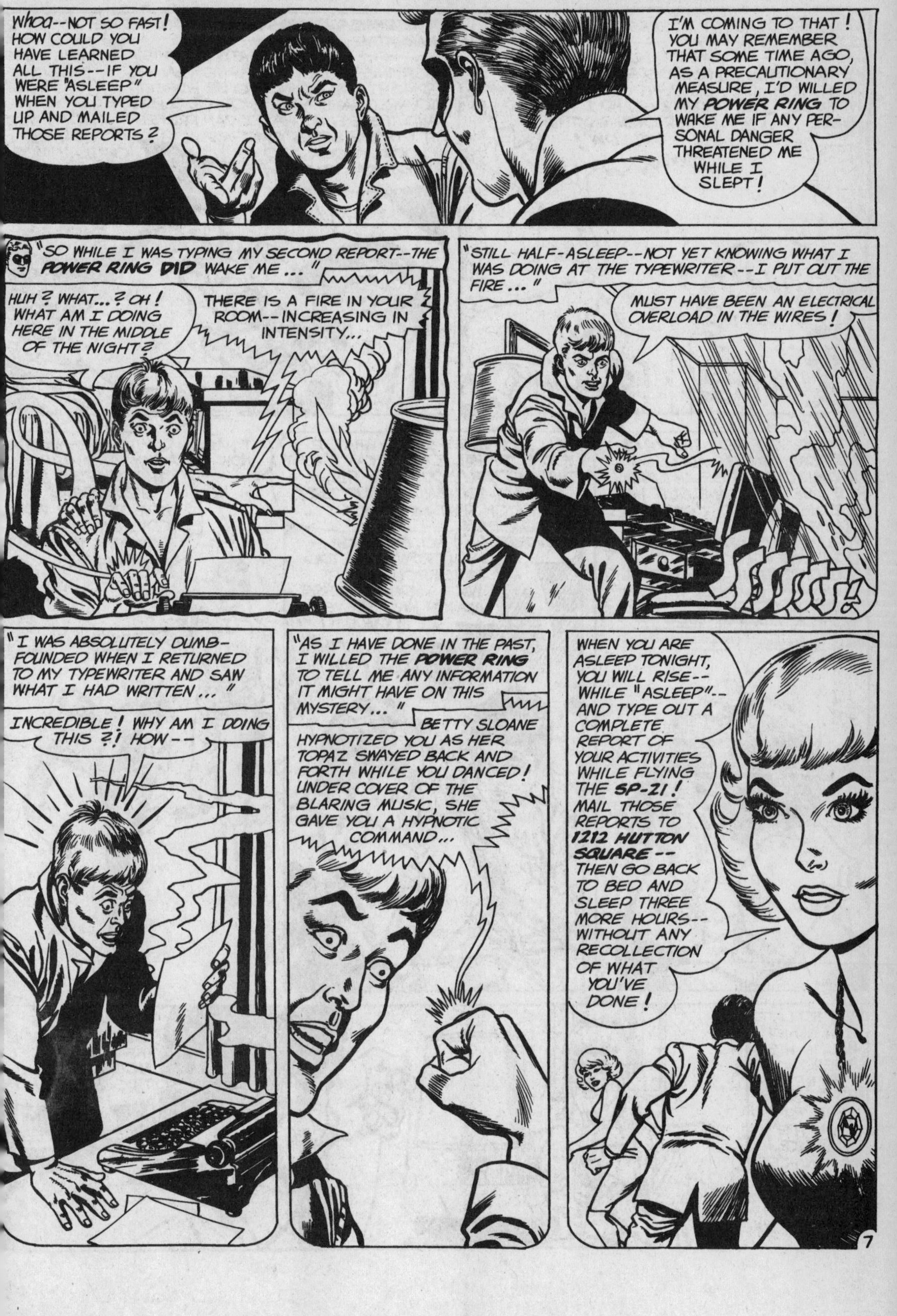
WHOA--NOT SO FAST! HOW COULD YOU HAVE LEARNED ALL THIS--IF YOU WERE "ASLEEP" WHEN YOU TYPED UP AND MAILED THOSE REPORTS?
I'M COMING TO THAT! YOU MAY REMEMBER THAT SOME TIME AGO, AS A PRECAUTIONARY MEASURE, I'D WILLED MY POWER RING TO WAKE ME IF ANY PERSONAL DANGER THREATENED ME WHILE I SLEPT!
"SO WHILE I WAS TYPING MY SECOND REPORT--THE POWER RING DID WAKE ME..."
HUH? WHAT...? OH! WHAT AM I DOING HERE IN THE MIDDLE OF THE NIGHT?
THERE IS A FIRE IN YOUR ROOM--INCREASING IN INTENSITY...
"STILL HALF-ASLEEP--NOT YET KNOWING WHAT I WAS DOING AT THE TYPEWRITER--I PUT OUT THE FIRE..."
MUST HAVE BEEN AN ELECTRICAL OVERLOAD IN THE WIRES!
SSSSSS!
"I WAS ABSOLUTELY DUMBFOUNDED WHEN I RETURNED TO MY TYPEWRITER AND SAW WHAT I HAD WRITTEN..."
INCREDIBLE! WHY AM I DOING THIS?! HOW--
"AS I HAVE DONE IN THE PAST, I WILLED THE POWER RING TO TELL ME ANY INFORMATION IT MIGHT HAVE ON THIS MYSTERY..."
BETTY SLOANE HYPNOTIZED YOU AS HER TOPAZ SWAYED BACK AND FORTH WHILE YOU DANCED! UNDER COVER OF THE BLARING MUSIC, SHE GAVE YOU A HYPNOTIC COMMAND...
WHEN YOU ARE ASLEEP TONIGHT, YOU WILL RISE--WHILE "ASLEEP"--AND TYPE OUT A COMPLETE REPORT OF YOUR ACTIVITIES WHILE FLYING THE SP-21! MAIL THOSE REPORTS TO 1212 HUTTON SQUARE--THEN GO BACK TO BED AND SLEEP THREE MORE HOURS--WITHOUT ANY RECOLLECTION OF WHAT YOU'VE DONE!
7

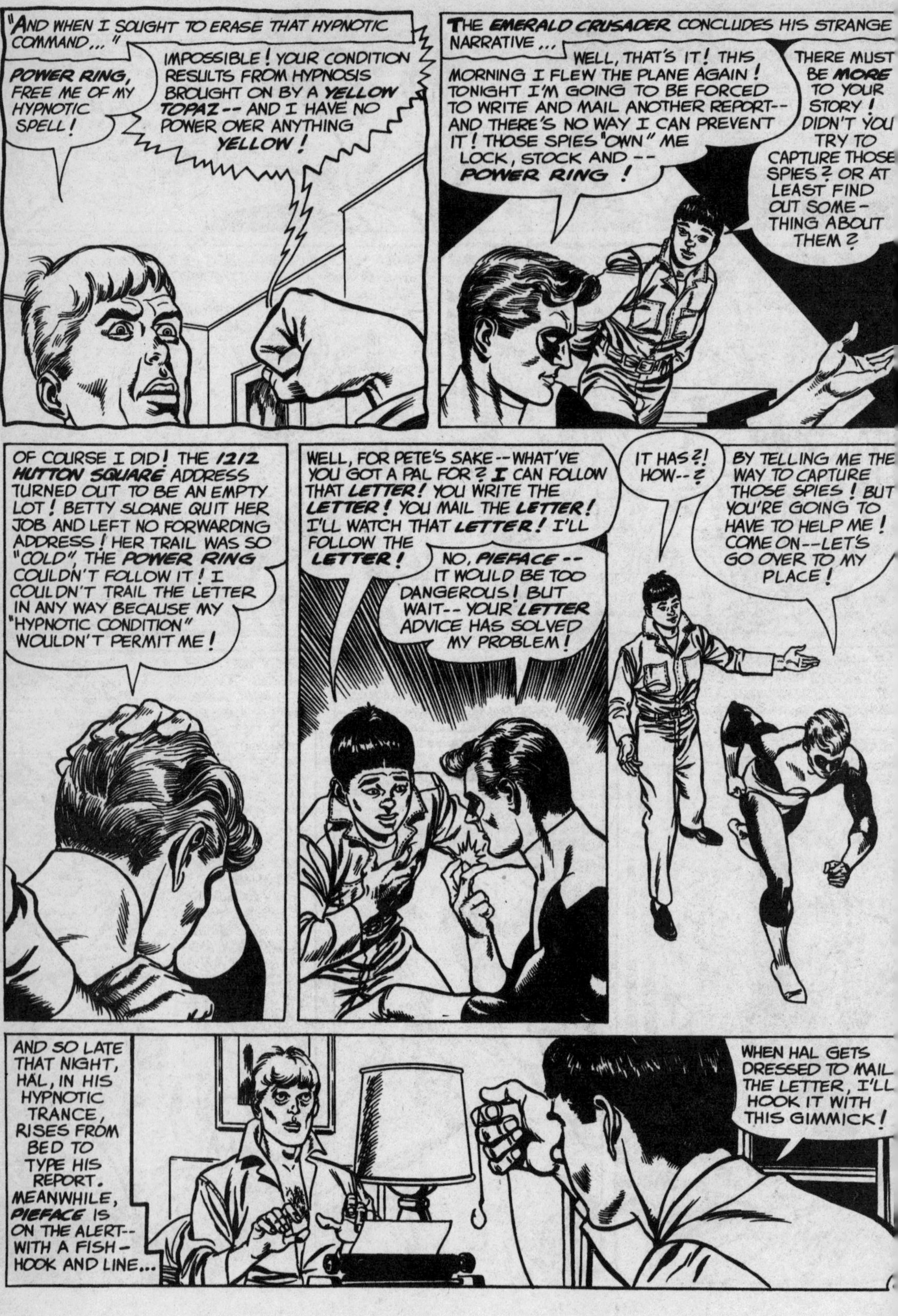
"AND WHEN I SOUGHT TO ERASE THAT HYPNOTIC COMMAND..."
POWER RING, FREE ME OF MY HYPNOTIC SPELL!
IMPOSSIBLE! YOUR CONDITION RESULTS FROM HYPNOSIS BROUGHT ON BY A YELLOW TOPAZ-- AND I HAVE NO POWER OVER ANYTHING YELLOW!
THE EMERALD CRUSADER CONCLUDES HIS STRANGE NARRATIVE...
WELL, THAT'S IT! THIS MORNING I FLEW THE PLANE AGAIN! TONIGHT I'M GOING TO BE FORCED TO WRITE AND MAIL ANOTHER REPORT-- AND THERE'S NO WAY I CAN PREVENT IT! THOSE SPIES "OWN" ME LOCK, STOCK AND -- POWER RING!
THERE MUST BE MORE TO YOUR STORY! DIDN'T YOU TRY TO CAPTURE THOSE SPIES? OR AT LEAST FIND OUT SOME-THING ABOUT THEM?
OF COURSE I DID! THE 1212 HUTTON SQUARE ADDRESS TURNED OUT TO BE AN EMPTY LOT! BETTY SLOANE QUIT HER JOB AND LEFT NO FORWARDING ADDRESS! HER TRAIL WAS SO "COLD", THE POWER RING COULDN'T FOLLOW IT! I COULDN'T TRAIL THE LETTER IN ANY WAY BECAUSE MY "HYPNOTIC CONDITION" WOULDN'T PERMIT ME!
WELL, FOR PETE'S SAKE--WHAT'VE YOU GOT A PAL FOR? I CAN FOLLOW THAT LETTER! YOU WRITE THE LETTER! YOU MAIL THE LETTER! I'LL WATCH THAT LETTER! I'LL FOLLOW THE LETTER!
NO, PIEFACE -- IT WOULD BE TOO DANGEROUS! BUT WAIT-- YOUR LETTER ADVICE HAS SOLVED MY PROBLEM!
IT HAS?! HOW--?
BY TELLING ME THE WAY TO CAPTURE THOSE SPIES! BUT YOU'RE GOING TO HAVE TO HELP ME! COME ON--LET'S GO OVER TO MY PLACE!
AND SO LATE THAT NIGHT, HAL, IN HIS HYPNOTIC TRANCE, RISES FROM BED TO TYPE HIS REPORT. MEANWHILE, PIEFACE IS ON THE ALERT-- WITH A FISH-HOOK AND LINE...
WHEN HAL GETS DRESSED TO MAIL THE LETTER, I'LL HOOK IT WITH THIS GIMMICK!

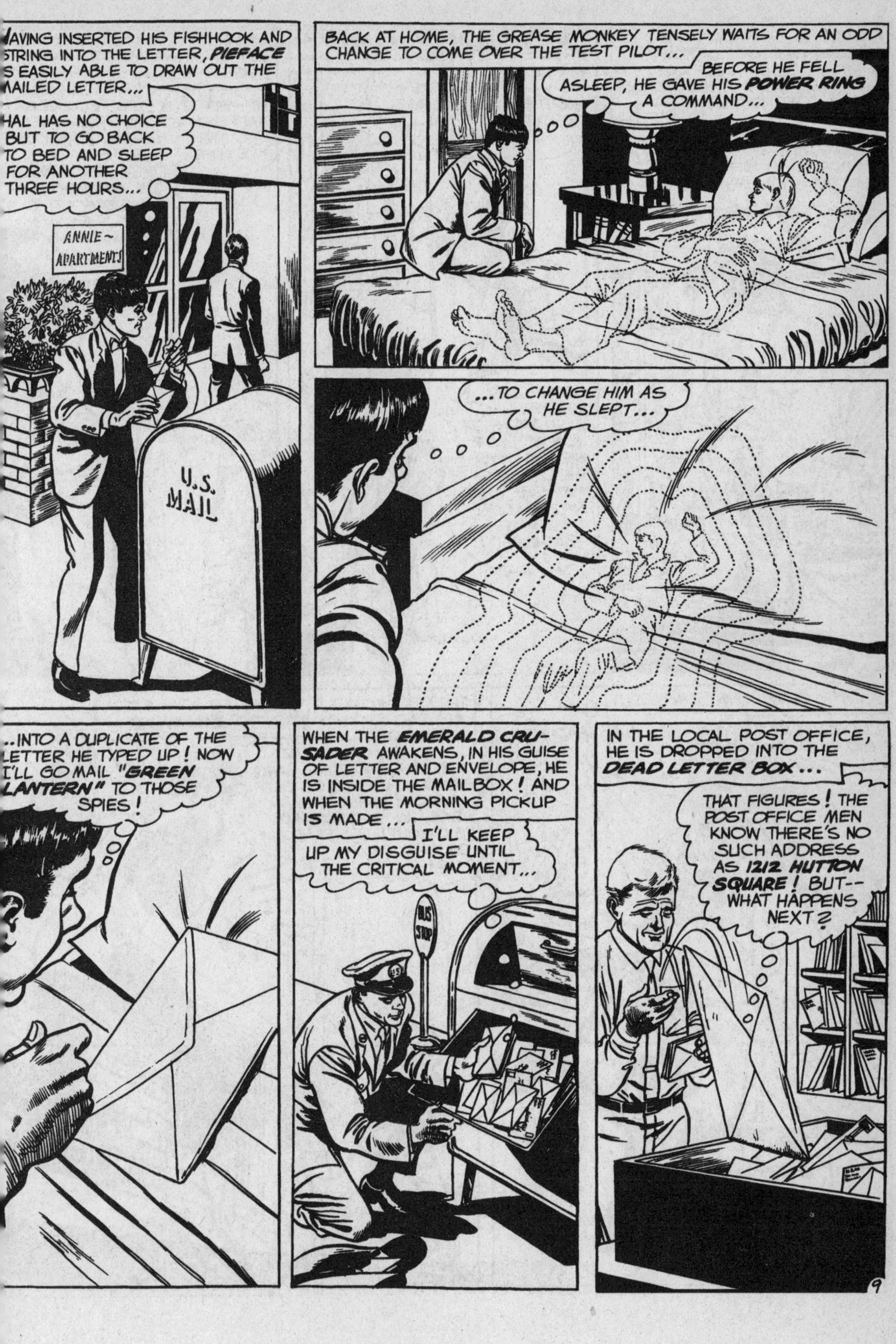
HAVING INSERTED HIS FISHHOOK AND STRING INTO THE LETTER, PIEFACE IS EASILY ABLE TO DRAW OUT THE MAILED LETTER...
HAL HAS NO CHOICE BUT TO GO BACK TO BED AND SLEEP FOR ANOTHER THREE HOURS...
ANNIE~ APARTMENTS
U.S. MAIL
BACK AT HOME, THE GREASE MONKEY TENSELY WAITS FOR AN ODD CHANGE TO COME OVER THE TEST PILOT...
BEFORE HE FELL ASLEEP, HE GAVE HIS POWER RING A COMMAND...
...TO CHANGE HIM AS HE SLEPT...
...INTO A DUPLICATE OF THE LETTER HE TYPED UP! NOW I'LL GO MAIL "GREEN LANTERN" TO THOSE SPIES!
WHEN THE EMERALD CRUSADER AWAKENS, IN HIS GUISE OF LETTER AND ENVELOPE, HE IS INSIDE THE MAILBOX! AND WHEN THE MORNING PICKUP IS MADE...
I'LL KEEP UP MY DISGUISE UNTIL THE CRITICAL MOMENT...
BUS STOP
IN THE LOCAL POST OFFICE, HE IS DROPPED INTO THE DEAD LETTER BOX...
THAT FIGURES! THE POST OFFICE MEN KNOW THERE'S NO SUCH ADDRESS AS 1212 HUTTON SQUARE! BUT-- WHAT HAPPENS NEXT?
9

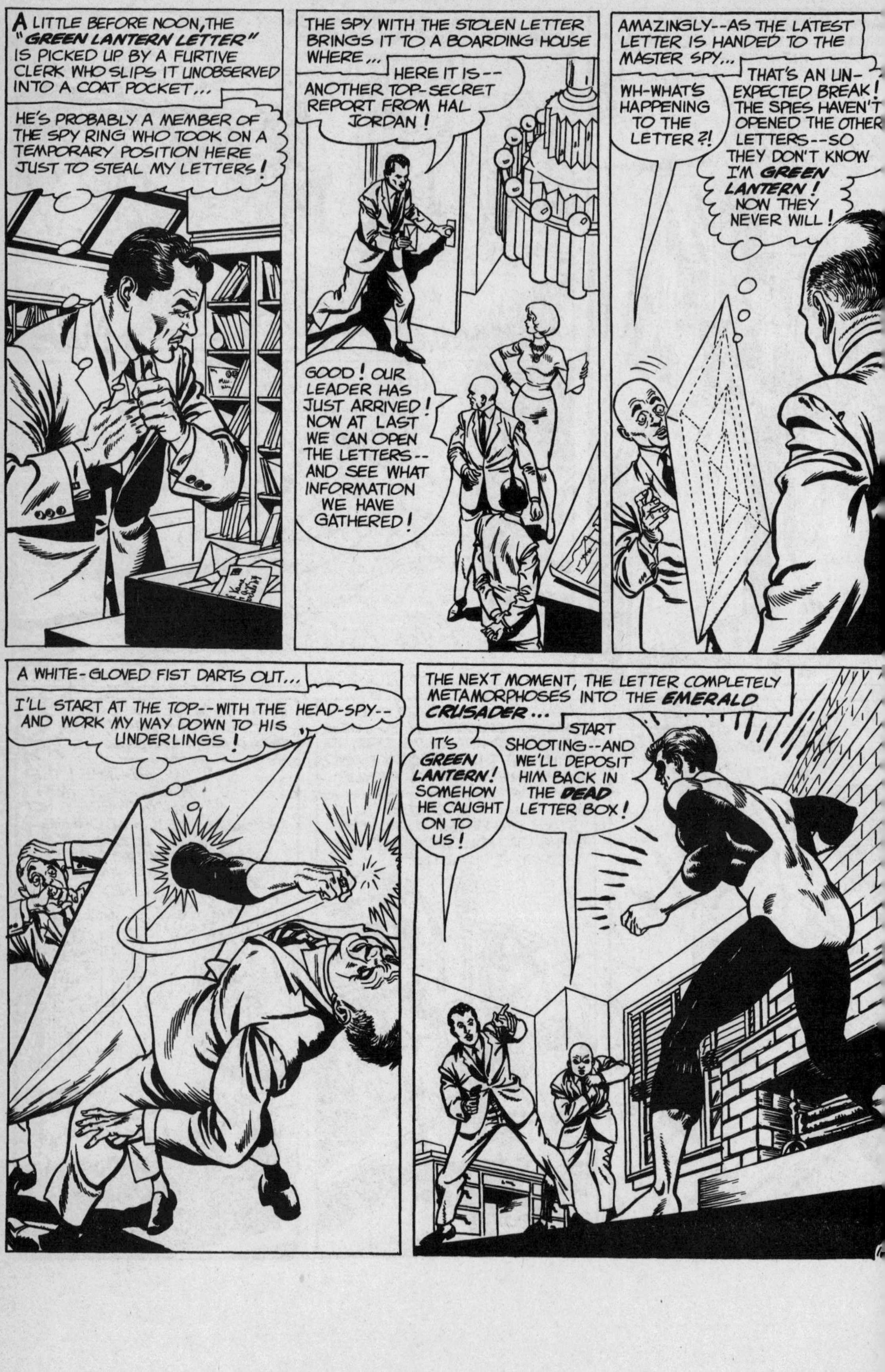
A LITTLE BEFORE NOON, THE "GREEN LANTERN LETTER" IS PICKED UP BY A FURTIVE CLERK WHO SLIPS IT UNOBSERVED INTO A COAT POCKET...
HE'S PROBABLY A MEMBER OF THE SPY RING WHO TOOK ON A TEMPORARY POSITION HERE JUST TO STEAL MY LETTERS!
THE SPY WITH THE STOLEN LETTER BRINGS IT TO A BOARDING HOUSE WHERE...
HERE IT IS-- ANOTHER TOP-SECRET REPORT FROM HAL JORDAN!
GOOD! OUR LEADER HAS JUST ARRIVED! NOW AT LAST WE CAN OPEN THE LETTERS-- AND SEE WHAT INFORMATION WE HAVE GATHERED!
AMAZINGLY--AS THE LATEST LETTER IS HANDED TO THE MASTER SPY...
WH-WHAT'S HAPPENING TO THE LETTER ?!
THAT'S AN UN-EXPECTED BREAK! THE SPIES HAVEN'T OPENED THE OTHER LETTERS--SO THEY DON'T KNOW I'M GREEN LANTERN! NOW THEY NEVER WILL!
A WHITE-GLOVED FIST DARTS OUT...
I'LL START AT THE TOP--WITH THE HEAD-SPY-- AND WORK MY WAY DOWN TO HIS UNDERLINGS!
THE NEXT MOMENT, THE LETTER COMPLETELY METAMORPHOSES INTO THE EMERALD CRUSADER...
IT'S GREEN LANTERN! SOMEHOW HE CAUGHT ON TO US!
START SHOOTING--AND WE'LL DEPOSIT HIM BACK IN THE DEAD LETTER BOX!

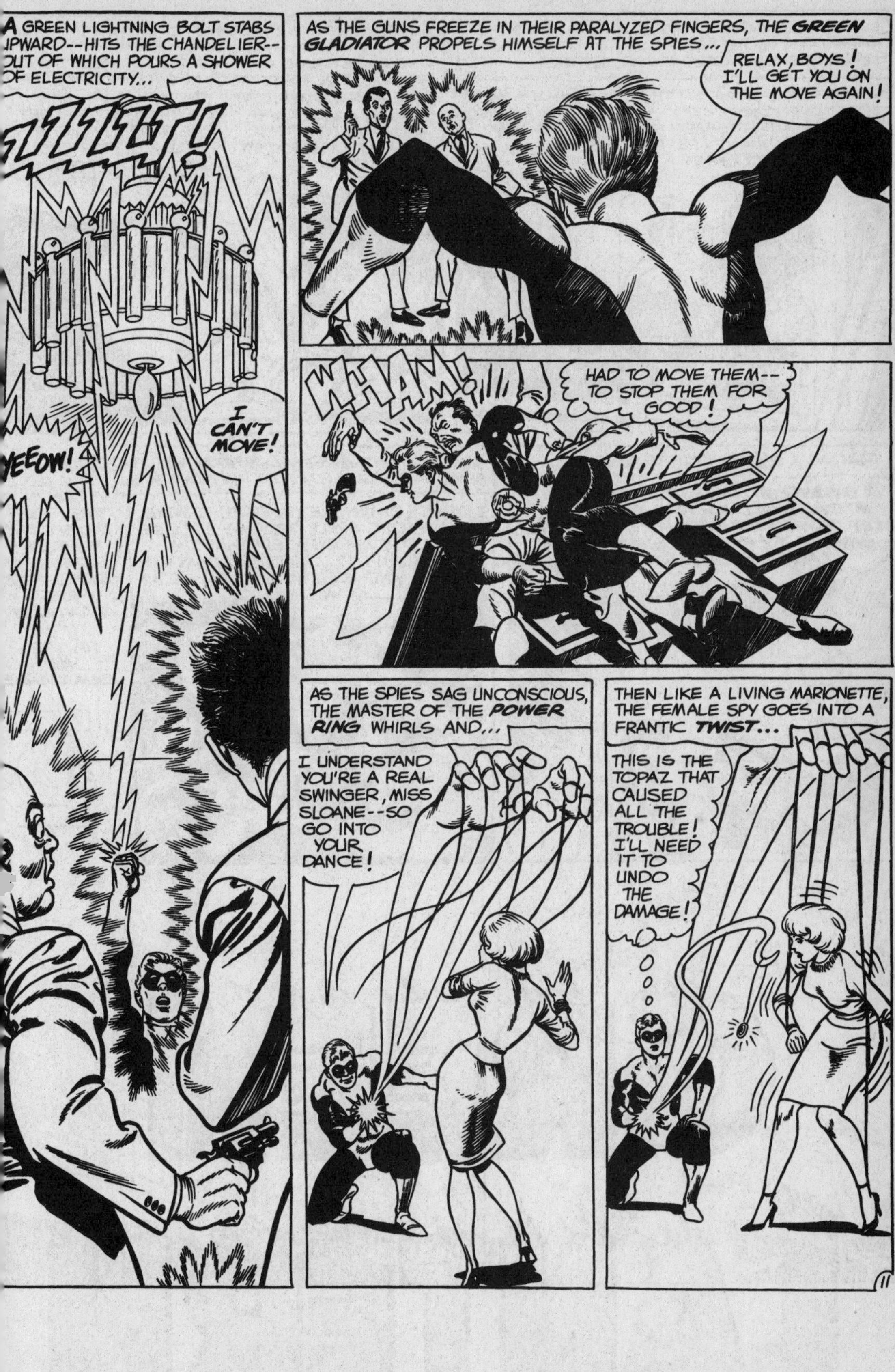
A GREEN LIGHTNING BOLT STABS UPWARD--HITS THE CHANDELIER--OUT OF WHICH POURS A SHOWER OF ELECTRICITY...
ZZZZT!
YEEOW!
I CAN'T MOVE!
AS THE GUNS FREEZE IN THEIR PARALYZED FINGERS, THE GREEN GLADIATOR PROPELS HIMSELF AT THE SPIES...
RELAX, BOYS! I'LL GET YOU ON THE MOVE AGAIN!
WHAM!
HAD TO MOVE THEM--TO STOP THEM FOR GOOD!
AS THE SPIES SAG UNCONSCIOUS, THE MASTER OF THE POWER RING WHIRLS AND...
I UNDERSTAND YOU'RE A REAL SWINGER, MISS SLOANE--SO GO INTO YOUR DANCE!
THEN LIKE A LIVING MARIONETTE, THE FEMALE SPY GOES INTO A FRANTIC TWIST...
THIS IS THE TOPAZ THAT CAUSED ALL THE TROUBLE! I'LL NEED IT TO UNDO THE DAMAGE!
11

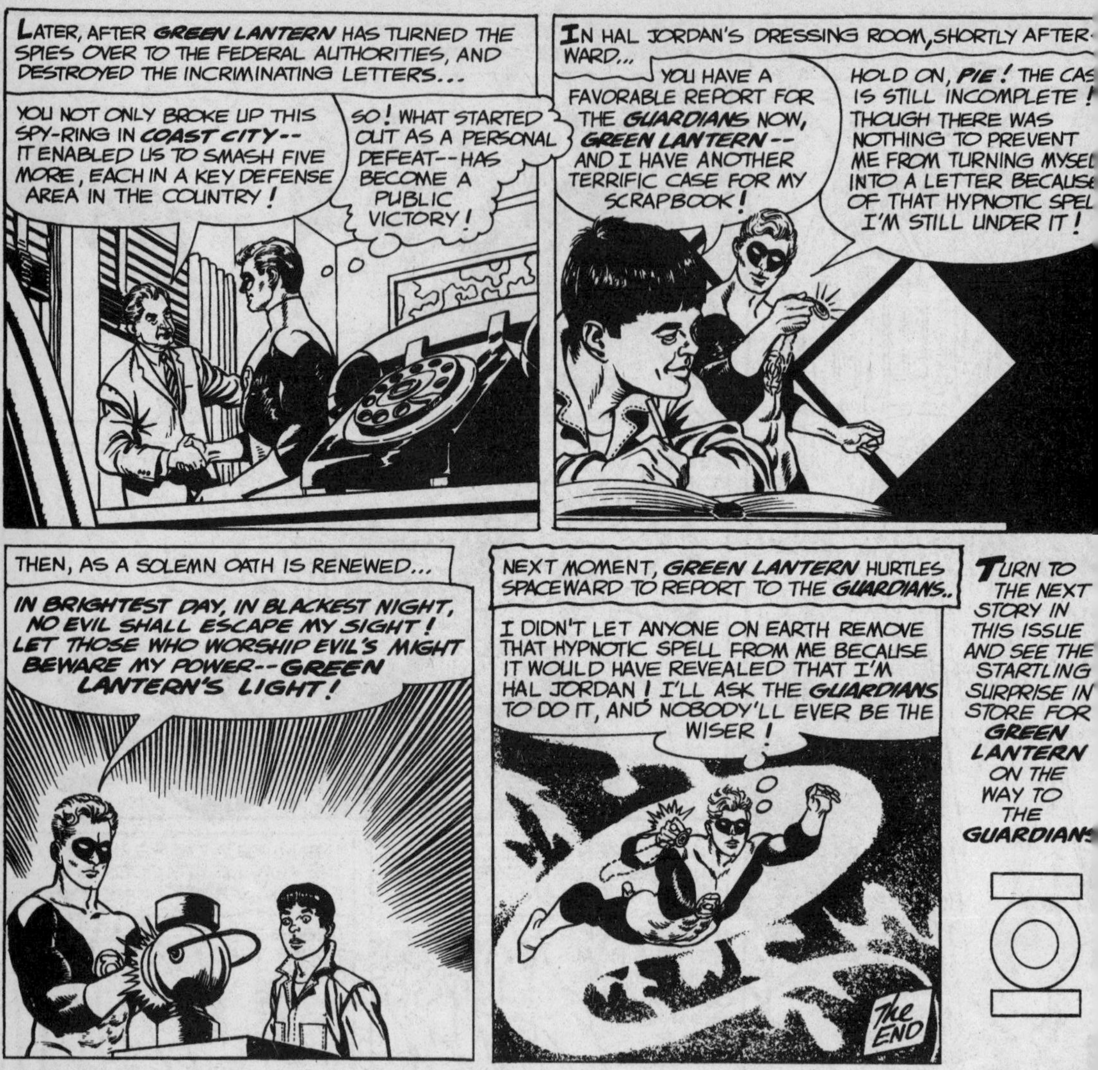
LATER, AFTER GREEN LANTERN HAS TURNED THE SPIES OVER TO THE FEDERAL AUTHORITIES, AND DESTROYED THE INCRIMINATING LETTERS...
YOU NOT ONLY BROKE UP THIS SPY-RING IN COAST CITY-- IT ENABLED US TO SMASH FIVE MORE, EACH IN A KEY DEFENSE AREA IN THE COUNTRY!
SO! WHAT STARTED OUT AS A PERSONAL DEFEAT--HAS BECOME A PUBLIC VICTORY!
IN HAL JORDAN'S DRESSING ROOM, SHORTLY AFTERWARD...
YOU HAVE A FAVORABLE REPORT FOR THE GUARDIANS NOW, GREEN LANTERN-- AND I HAVE ANOTHER TERRIFIC CASE FOR MY SCRAPBOOK!
HOLD ON, PIE! THE CAS IS STILL INCOMPLETE! THOUGH THERE WAS NOTHING TO PREVENT ME FROM TURNING MYSEL INTO A LETTER BECAUSE OF THAT HYPNOTIC SPEL I'M STILL UNDER IT!
THEN, AS A SOLEMN OATH IS RENEWED...
IN BRIGHTEST DAY, IN BLACKEST NIGHT, NO EVIL SHALL ESCAPE MY SIGHT! LET THOSE WHO WORSHIP EVIL'S MIGHT BEWARE MY POWER--GREEN LANTERN'S LIGHT!
NEXT MOMENT, GREEN LANTERN HURTLES SPACEWARD TO REPORT TO THE GUARDIANS..
I DIDN'T LET ANYONE ON EARTH REMOVE THAT HYPNOTIC SPELL FROM ME BECAUSE IT WOULD HAVE REVEALED THAT I'M HAL JORDAN! I'LL ASK THE GUARDIANS TO DO IT, AND NOBODY'LL EVER BE THE WISER!
THE END
TURN TO THE NEXT STORY IN THIS ISSUE AND SEE THE STARTLING SURPRISE IN STORE FOR GREEN LANTERN ON THE WAY TO THE GUARDIANS

GREEN LANTERN

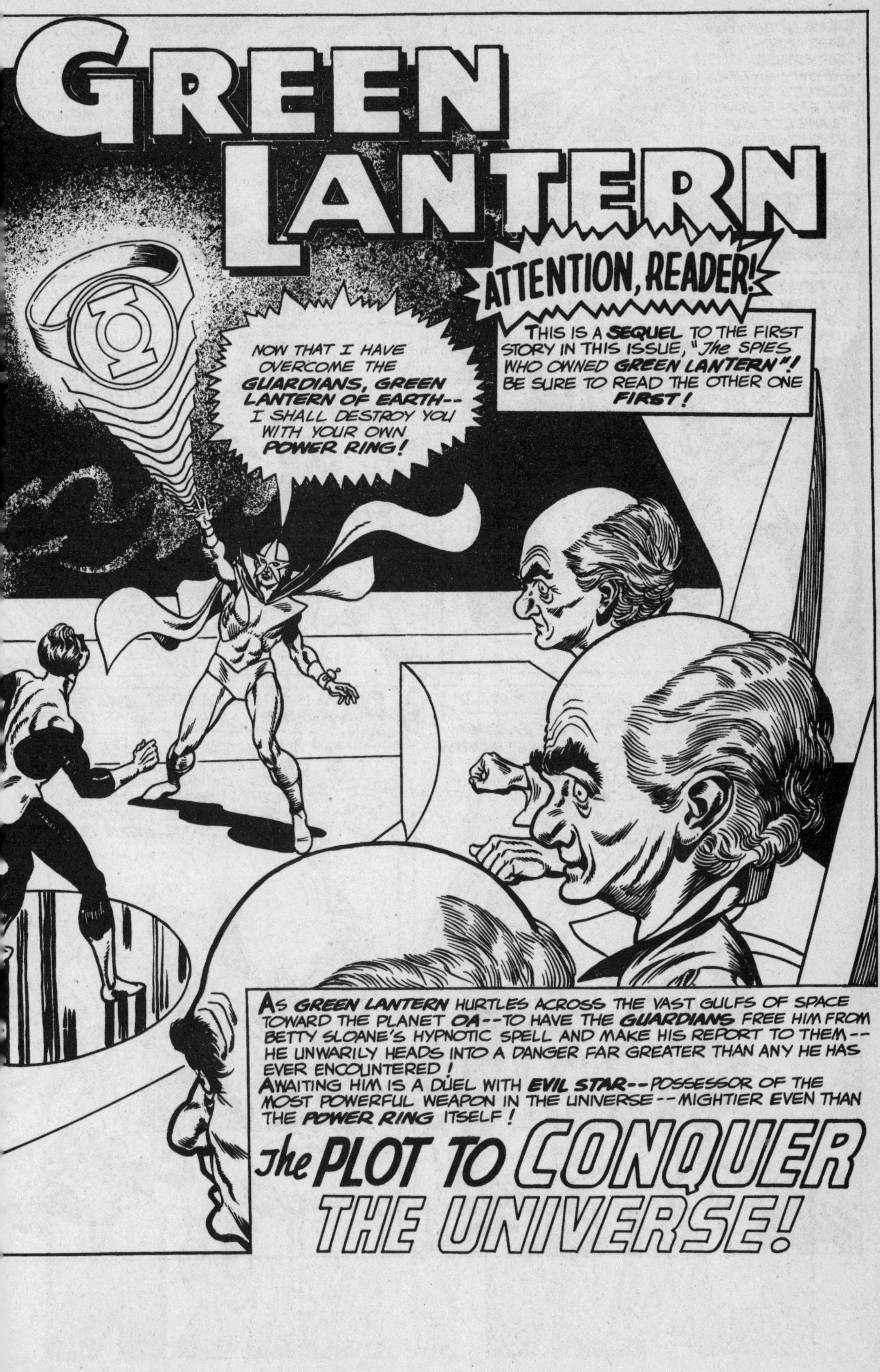
GREEN LANTERN
ATTENTION, READER!
THIS IS A SEQUEL TO THE FIRST STORY IN THIS ISSUE, "The SPIES WHO OWNED GREEN LANTERN"! BE SURE TO READ THE OTHER ONE FIRST!
NOW THAT I HAVE OVERCOME THE GUARDIANS, GREEN LANTERN OF EARTH-- I SHALL DESTROY YOU WITH YOUR OWN POWER RING!
AS GREEN LANTERN HURTLES ACROSS THE VAST GULFS OF SPACE TOWARD THE PLANET OA--TO HAVE THE GUARDIANS FREE HIM FROM BETTY SLOANE'S HYPNOTIC SPELL AND MAKE HIS REPORT TO THEM--HE UNWARILY HEADS INTO A DANGER FAR GREATER THAN ANY HE HAS EVER ENCOUNTERED!
AWAITING HIM IS A DUEL WITH EVIL STAR--POSSESSOR OF THE MOST POWERFUL WEAPON IN THE UNIVERSE--MIGHTIER EVEN THAN THE POWER RING ITSELF!
The PLOT TO CONQUER THE UNIVERSE!

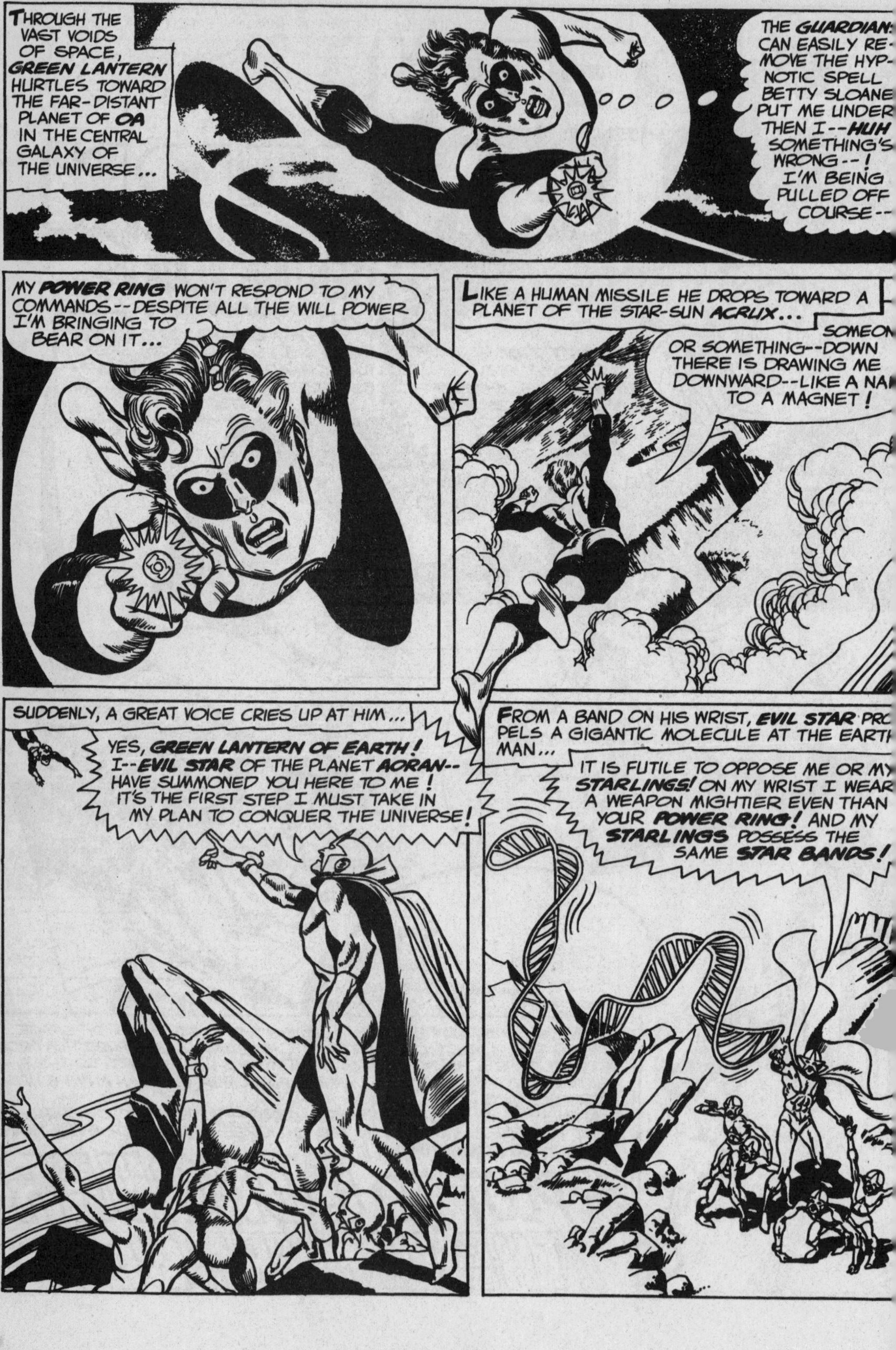
THROUGH THE VAST VOIDS OF SPACE, GREEN LANTERN HURTLES TOWARD THE FAR-DISTANT PLANET OF OA IN THE CENTRAL GALAXY OF THE UNIVERSE...
CAN EASILY RE-MOVE THE HYP-NOTIC SPELL PUT ME UNDER THEN I--HUH SOMETHING'S WRONG--! I'M BEING PULLED OFF
MY POWER RING WON'T RESPOND TO MY COMMANDS--DESPITE ALL THE WILL POWER I'M BRINGING TO BEAR ON IT...
LIKE A HUMAN MISSILE HE DROPS TOWARD A PLANET OF THE STAR-SUN ACRUX...
OR SOMETHING--DOWN THERE IS DRAWING ME TO A MAGNET!
SUDDENLY, A GREAT VOICE CRIES UP AT HIM...
YES, GREEN LANTERN OF EARTH! I--EVIL STAR OF THE PLANET AORAN--HAVE SUMMONED YOU HERE TO ME! IT'S THE FIRST STEP I MUST TAKE IN MY PLAN TO CONQUER THE UNIVERSE!
FROM A BAND ON HIS WRIST, EVIL STAR PELS A GIGANTIC MOLECULE AT THE MAN...
IT IS FUTILE TO OPPOSE ME OR STARLINGS! ON MY WRIST I WEAR A WEAPON MIGHTIER EVEN THAN YOUR POWER RING! AND MY STARLINGS POSSESS THE SAME STAR BANDS!

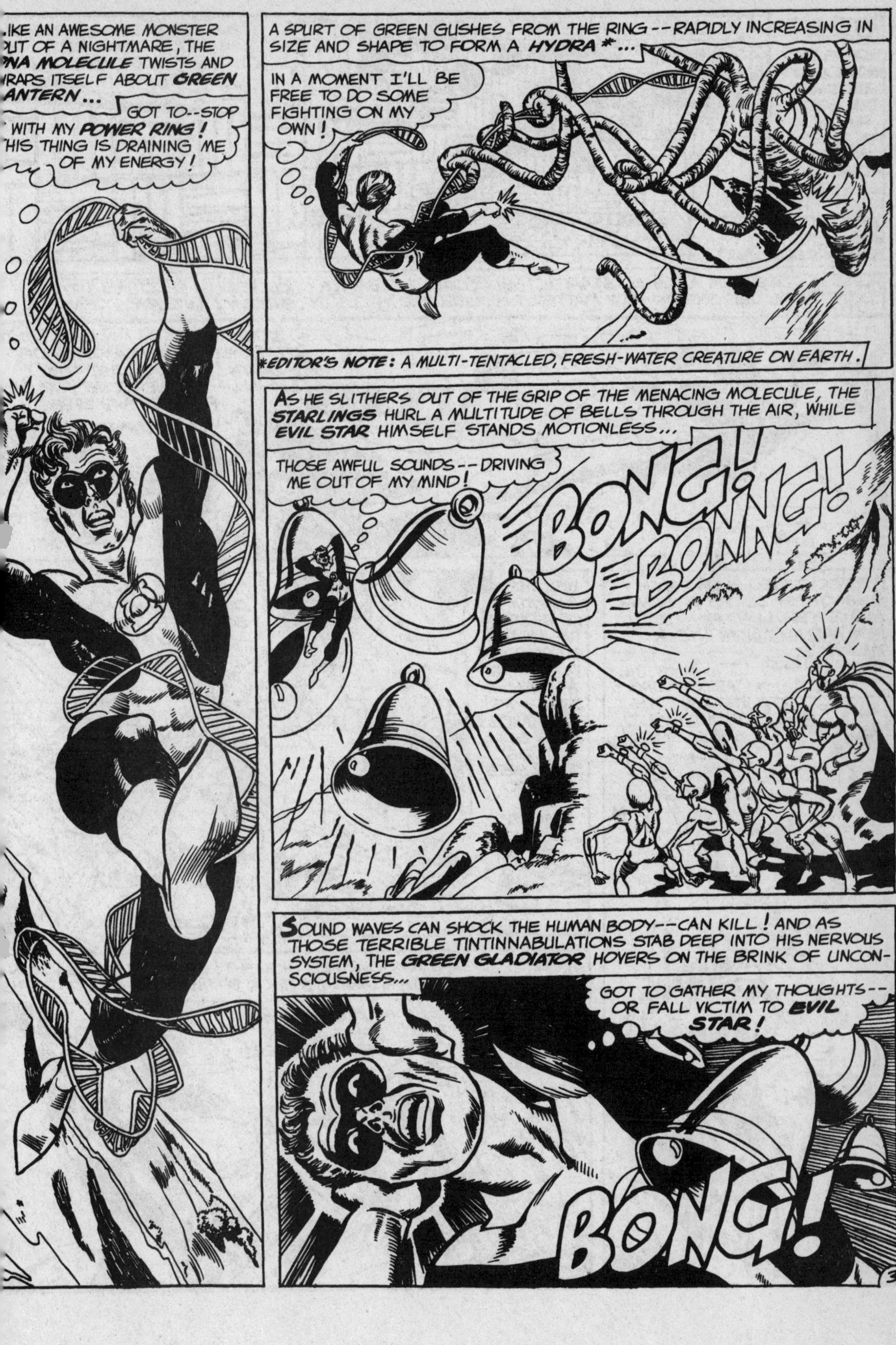
LIKE AN AWESOME MONSTER OUT OF A NIGHTMARE, THE DNA MOLECULE TWISTS AND WRAPS ITSELF ABOUT GREEN LANTERN...
GOT TO--STOP IT WITH MY POWER RING! THIS THING IS DRAINING ME OF MY ENERGY!
A SPURT OF GREEN GUSHES FROM THE RING--RAPIDLY INCREASING IN SIZE AND SHAPE TO FORM A HYDRA*...
IN A MOMENT I'LL BE FREE TO DO SOME FIGHTING ON MY OWN!
*EDITOR'S NOTE: A MULTI-TENTACLED, FRESH-WATER CREATURE ON EARTH.
AS HE SLITHERS OUT OF THE GRIP OF THE MENACING MOLECULE, THE STARLINGS HURL A MULTITUDE OF BELLS THROUGH THE AIR, WHILE EVIL STAR HIMSELF STANDS MOTIONLESS...
THOSE AWFUL SOUNDS--DRIVING ME OUT OF MY MIND!
BONG! BONNG!
SOUND WAVES CAN SHOCK THE HUMAN BODY--CAN KILL! AND AS THOSE TERRIBLE TINTINNABULATIONS STAB DEEP INTO HIS NERVOUS SYSTEM, THE GREEN GLADIATOR HOVERS ON THE BRINK OF UNCONSCIOUSNESS...
GOT TO GATHER MY THOUGHTS--OR FALL VICTIM TO EVIL STAR!
BONG!
3

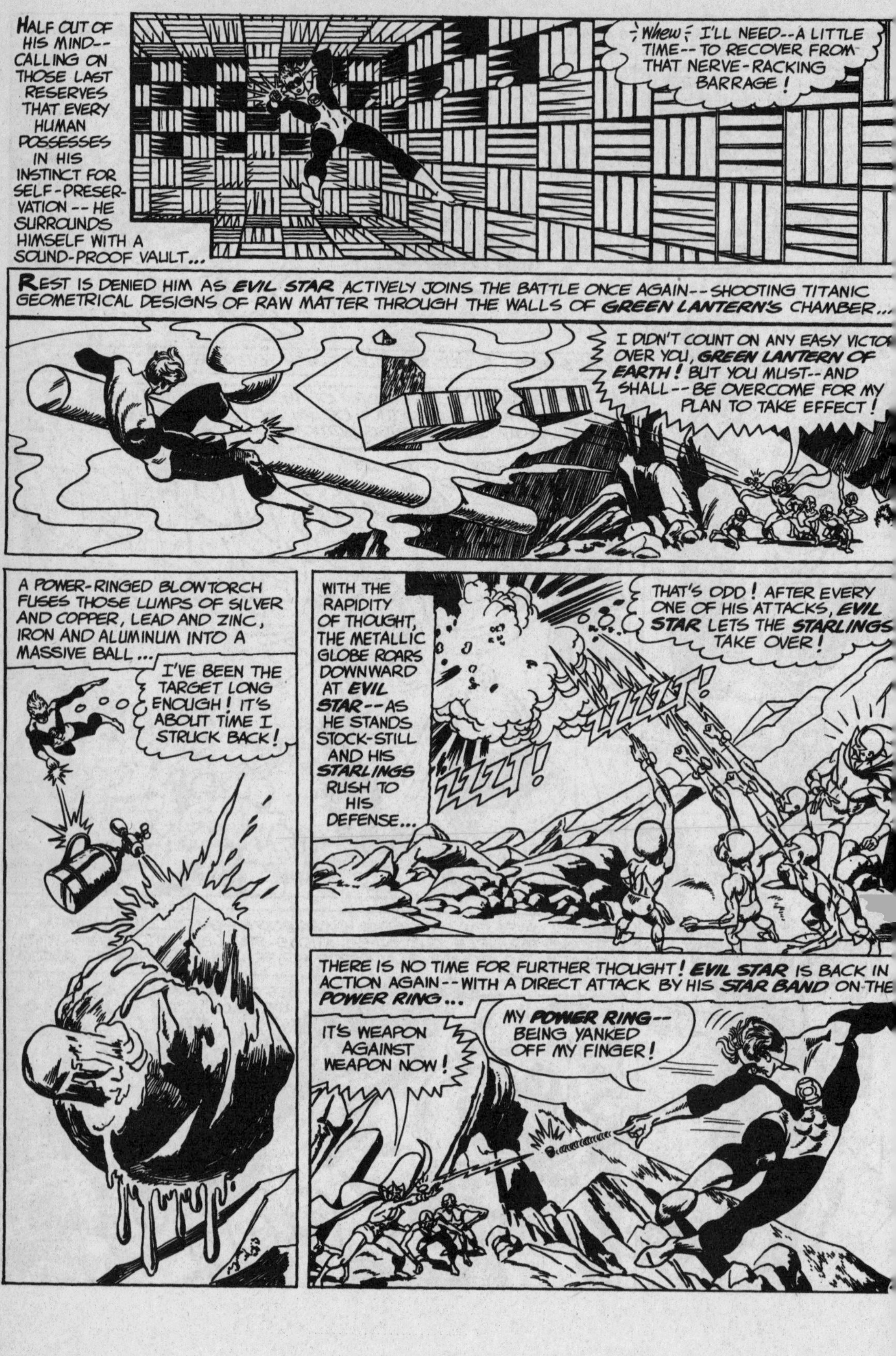
HALF OUT OF HIS MIND--CALLING ON THOSE LAST RESERVES THAT EVERY HUMAN POSSESSES IN HIS INSTINCT FOR SELF-PRESERVATION -- HE SURROUNDS HIMSELF WITH A SOUND-PROOF VAULT...
WHEW! I'LL NEED--A LITTLE TIME-- TO RECOVER FROM THAT NERVE-RACKING BARRAGE!
REST IS DENIED HIM AS EVIL STAR ACTIVELY JOINS THE BATTLE ONCE AGAIN--SHOOTING TITANIC GEOMETRICAL DESIGNS OF RAW MATTER THROUGH THE WALLS OF GREEN LANTERN'S CHAMBER...
I DIDN'T COUNT ON ANY EASY VICTOR OVER YOU, GREEN LANTERN OF EARTH! BUT YOU MUST--AND SHALL--BE OVERCOME FOR MY PLAN TO TAKE EFFECT!
A POWER-RINGED BLOWTORCH FUSES THOSE LUMPS OF SILVER AND COPPER, LEAD AND ZINC, IRON AND ALUMINUM INTO A MASSIVE BALL...
I'VE BEEN THE TARGET LONG ENOUGH! IT'S ABOUT TIME I STRUCK BACK!
WITH THE RAPIDITY OF THOUGHT, THE METALLIC GLOBE ROARS DOWNWARD AT EVIL STAR--AS HE STANDS STOCK-STILL AND HIS STARLINGS RUSH TO HIS DEFENSE...
THAT'S ODD! AFTER EVERY ONE OF HIS ATTACKS, EVIL STAR LETS THE STARLINGS TAKE OVER!
ZZZZT!
ZZZT!
THERE IS NO TIME FOR FURTHER THOUGHT! EVIL STAR IS BACK IN ACTION AGAIN--WITH A DIRECT ATTACK BY HIS STAR BAND ON THE POWER RING...
IT'S WEAPON AGAINST WEAPON NOW!
MY POWER RING--BEING YANKED OFF MY FINGER!

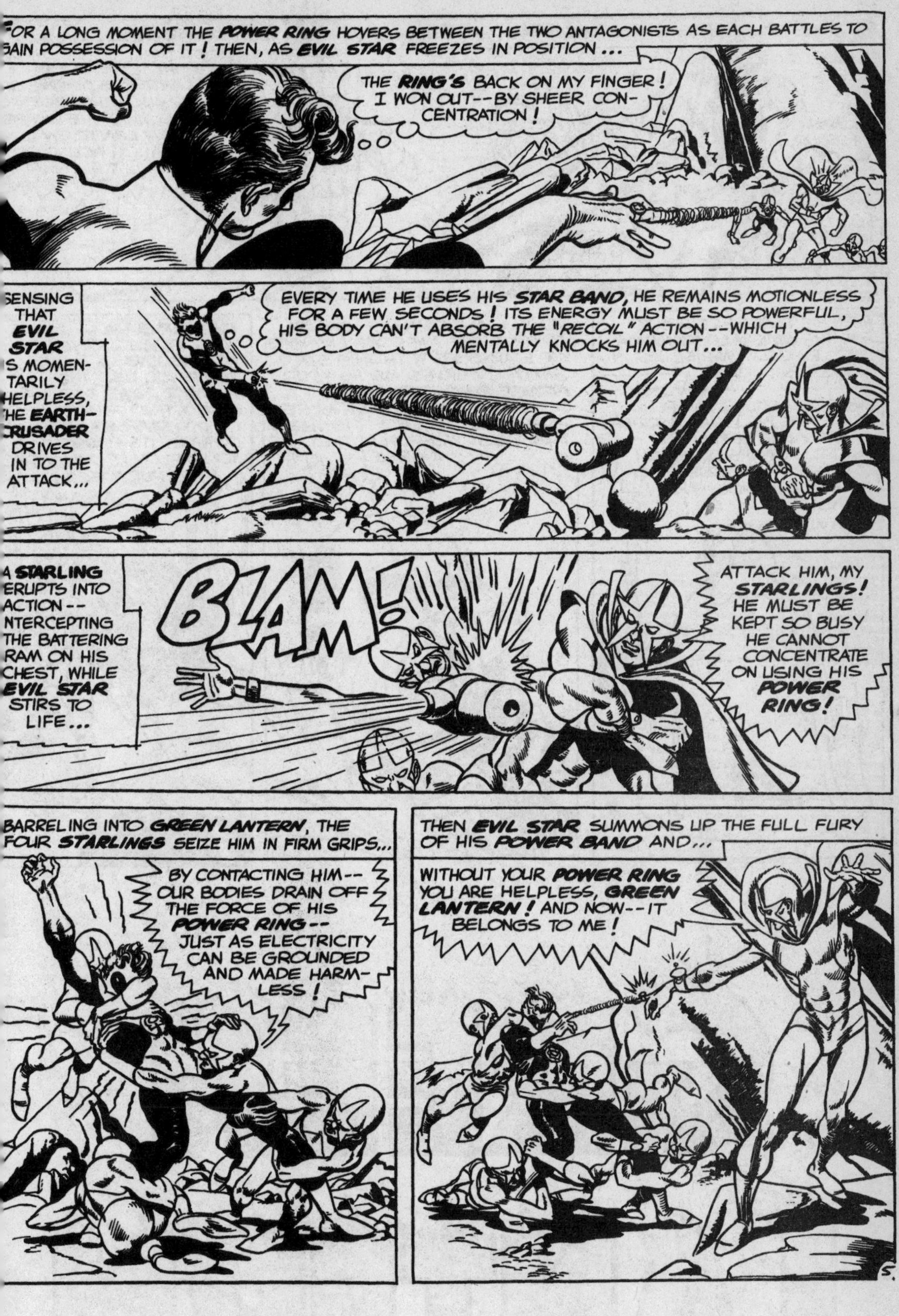
FOR A LONG MOMENT THE POWER RING HOVERS BETWEEN THE TWO ANTAGONISTS AS EACH BATTLES TO GAIN POSSESSION OF IT! THEN, AS EVIL STAR FREEZES IN POSITION...
THE RING'S BACK ON MY FINGER! I WON OUT--BY SHEER CONCENTRATION!
SENSING THAT EVIL STAR IS MOMENTARILY HELPLESS, THE EARTH-CRUSADER DRIVES IN TO THE ATTACK...
EVERY TIME HE USES HIS STAR BAND, HE REMAINS MOTIONLESS FOR A FEW SECONDS! ITS ENERGY MUST BE SO POWERFUL, HIS BODY CAN'T ABSORB THE "RECOIL" ACTION--WHICH MENTALLY KNOCKS HIM OUT...
A STARLING ERUPTS INTO ACTION--INTERCEPTING THE BATTERING RAM ON HIS CHEST, WHILE EVIL STAR STIRS TO LIFE...
BLAM!
ATTACK HIM, MY STARLINGS! HE MUST BE KEPT SO BUSY HE CANNOT CONCENTRATE ON USING HIS POWER RING!
BARRELING INTO GREEN LANTERN, THE FOUR STARLINGS SEIZE HIM IN FIRM GRIPS...
BY CONTACTING HIM--OUR BODIES DRAIN OFF THE FORCE OF HIS POWER RING--JUST AS ELECTRICITY CAN BE GROUNDED AND MADE HARMLESS!
THEN EVIL STAR SUMMONS UP THE FULL FURY OF HIS POWER BAND AND...
WITHOUT YOUR POWER RING YOU ARE HELPLESS, GREEN LANTERN! AND NOW--IT BELONGS TO ME!
5.

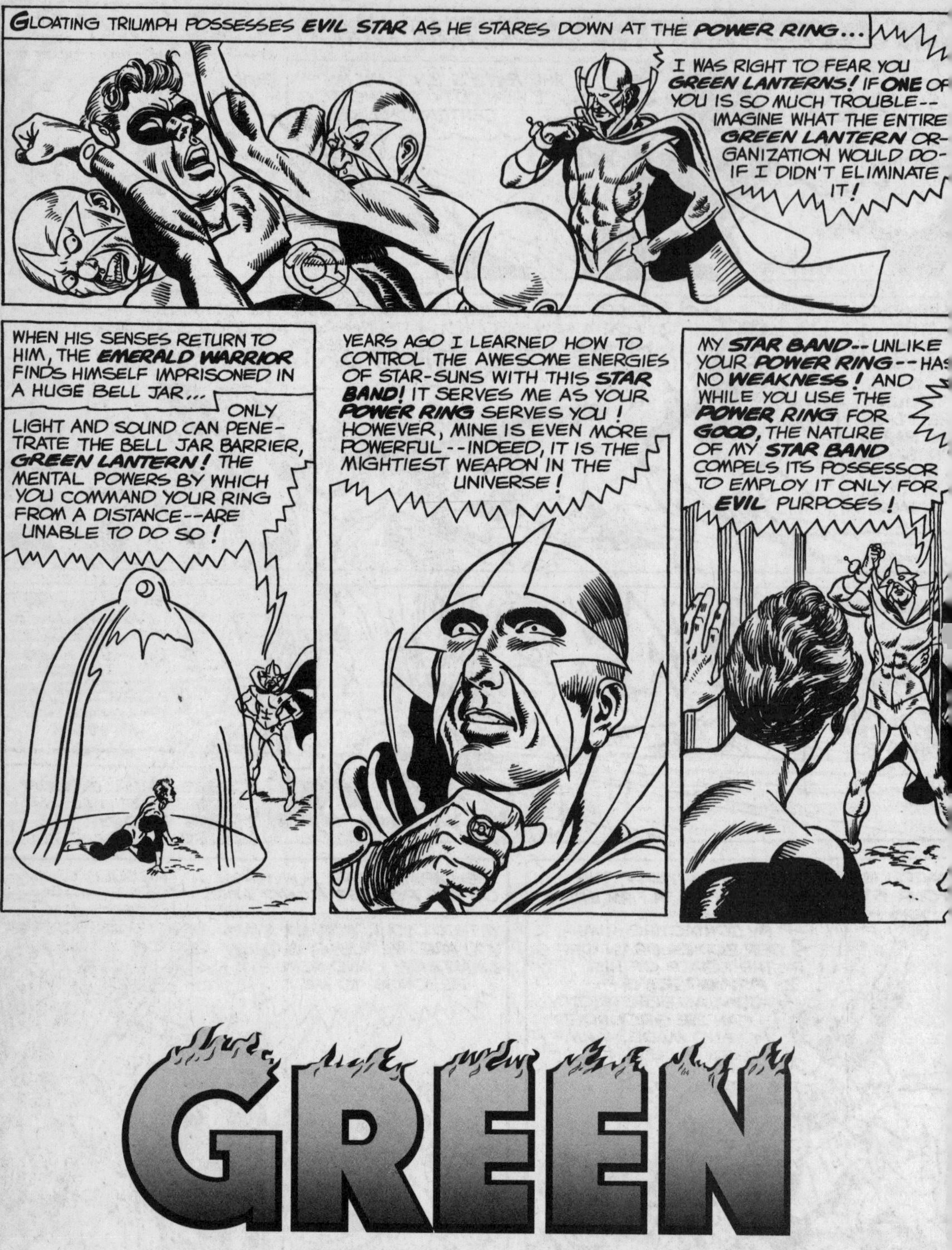
GLOATING TRIUMPH POSSESSES EVIL STAR AS HE STARES DOWN AT THE POWER RING...
I WAS RIGHT TO FEAR YOU GREEN LANTERNS! IF ONE OF YOU IS SO MUCH TROUBLE-- IMAGINE WHAT THE ENTIRE GREEN LANTERN ORGANIZATION WOULD DO-IF I DIDN'T ELIMINATE IT!
WHEN HIS SENSES RETURN TO HIM, THE EMERALD WARRIOR FINDS HIMSELF IMPRISONED IN A HUGE BELL JAR...
ONLY LIGHT AND SOUND CAN PENETRATE THE BELL JAR BARRIER, GREEN LANTERN! THE MENTAL POWERS BY WHICH YOU COMMAND YOUR RING FROM A DISTANCE--ARE UNABLE TO DO SO!
YEARS AGO I LEARNED HOW TO CONTROL THE AWESOME ENERGIES OF STAR-SUNS WITH THIS STAR BAND! IT SERVES ME AS YOUR POWER RING SERVES YOU! HOWEVER, MINE IS EVEN MORE POWERFUL--INDEED, IT IS THE MIGHTIEST WEAPON IN THE UNIVERSE!
MY STAR BAND--UNLIKE YOUR POWER RING--HAS NO WEAKNESS! AND WHILE YOU USE THE POWER RING FOR GOOD, THE NATURE OF MY STAR BAND COMPELS ITS POSSESSOR TO EMPLOY IT ONLY FOR EVIL PURPOSES!

GREEN LANTERN

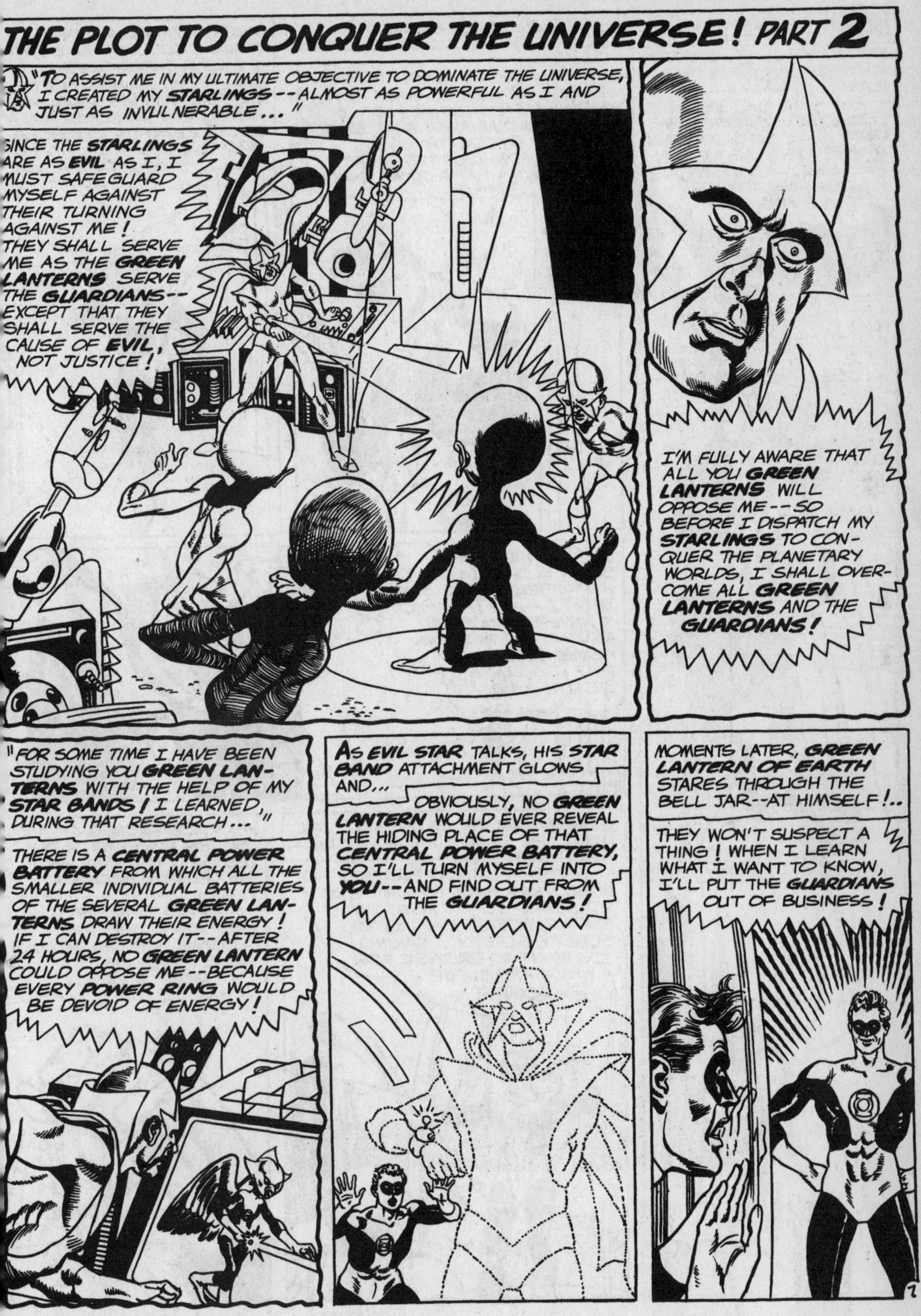
THE PLOT TO CONQUER THE UNIVERSE! PART 2
"TO ASSIST ME IN MY ULTIMATE OBJECTIVE TO DOMINATE THE UNIVERSE, I CREATED MY STARLINGS--ALMOST AS POWERFUL AS I AND JUST AS INVULNERABLE..."
SINCE THE STARLINGS ARE AS EVIL AS I, I MUST SAFEGUARD MYSELF AGAINST THEIR TURNING AGAINST ME! THEY SHALL SERVE ME AS THE GREEN LANTERNS SERVE THE GUARDIANS--EXCEPT THAT THEY SHALL SERVE THE CAUSE OF EVIL, NOT JUSTICE!
I'M FULLY AWARE THAT ALL YOU GREEN LANTERNS WILL OPPOSE ME--SO BEFORE I DISPATCH MY STARLINGS TO CONQUER THE PLANETARY WORLDS, I SHALL OVERCOME ALL GREEN LANTERNS AND THE GUARDIANS!
"FOR SOME TIME I HAVE BEEN STUDYING YOU GREEN LANTERNS WITH THE HELP OF MY STAR BANDS! I LEARNED, DURING THAT RESEARCH..."
THERE IS A CENTRAL POWER BATTERY FROM WHICH ALL THE SMALLER INDIVIDUAL BATTERIES OF THE SEVERAL GREEN LANTERNS DRAW THEIR ENERGY! IF I CAN DESTROY IT--AFTER 24 HOURS, NO GREEN LANTERN COULD OPPOSE ME--BECAUSE EVERY POWER RING WOULD BE DEVOID OF ENERGY!
AS EVIL STAR TALKS, HIS STAR BAND ATTACHMENT GLOWS AND...
OBVIOUSLY, NO GREEN LANTERN WOULD EVER REVEAL THE HIDING PLACE OF THAT CENTRAL POWER BATTERY, SO I'LL TURN MYSELF INTO YOU--AND FIND OUT FROM THE GUARDIANS!
MOMENTS LATER, GREEN LANTERN OF EARTH STARES THROUGH THE BELL JAR--AT HIMSELF!..
THEY WON'T SUSPECT A THING! WHEN I LEARN WHAT I WANT TO KNOW, I'LL PUT THE GUARDIANS OUT OF BUSINESS!
7

LEAVING HIS PRISONER UNDER GUARD OF THE *STARLINGS*, *EVIL STAR-GREEN LANTERN* ROCKETS AWAY FROM THE PLANET...

I MUST KEEP THE REAL *EARTH-GREEN LANTERN* ALIVE SO I CAN MAINTAIN HIS DISGUISE ! I NOW POSSESS HIS BODY AND HIS MEMORIES TO CARRY OUT MY SCHEME !

LEFT ALONE, THE *EMERALD GLADIATOR* YIELDS TO MOMENTARY DISMAY...

FIRST I ALMOST FAILED AGAINST THOSE SPIES WHEN BETTY SLOANE HYPNOTIZED ME ! NOW I HAVE FAILED AGAINST *EVIL STAR* ! NOT ONLY MY COUNTRY IS IN DANGER NOW--BUT THE ENTIRE UNIVERSE ! WHAT A COMEDOWN !

THEN I FACED A BUNCH OF SPIES I COULDN'T FIND ! NOW I FACE A SUPER-CRIMINAL I CAN'T FIGHT ! I HAVE NO WEAPON--AND HIS *STARLINGS* ARE ALMOST AS POWERFUL AS HE IS ! EVERYTHING'S GONE WRONG LATELY ! I--HUH ? WHAT'S *THIS* ?

OH ! IT'S THE *TOPAZ* BETTY SLOANE USED TO HYPNOTIZE ME ! I JUST WISH I --SAY ! WHY NOT ? I NEVER HYPNOTIZED ANYONE -- WITHOUT MY *POWER RING* -- BUT IT'S SURE WORTH A TRY !

STANDING CLOSE TO THE BELL JAR WALL, HE SWINGS THE TOPAZ BACK AND FORTH...

TOO BAD YOU *STARLINGS* HAVE TO STAY HERE TO GUARD ME ! IT MUST BE BORING WORK--MAKING YOU SLEEPY, SLEEPY...MAKING YOU WANT TO DROWSE FOR A WHILE AND SLEEP... *SLEEP...*

HIS VOICE DRONES ON AND ON. HIS FINGERS CAUSE THE GEM TO SWAY BACK AND FORTH, BACK AND FORTH...

YOUR EYELIDS ARE HEAVY. THEY ARE CLOSING. YOU ARE FALLING ASLEEP...ASLEEP... A DEEP SLEEP...

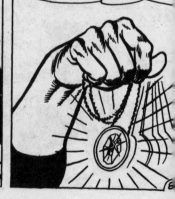

WITHIN MOMENTS...

SO FAR, SO GOOD! NOW TO SEE IF I CAN GET THEM TO OBEY MY HYPNOTIC COMMANDS...

STARLING--AT THE FAR RIGHT--ADVANCE AND FREE ME--

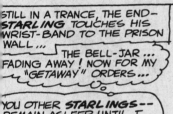

STILL IN A TRANCE, THE END-STARLING TOUCHES HIS WRIST-BAND TO THE PRISON WALL...

THE BELL-JAR... FADING AWAY! NOW FOR MY "GETAWAY" ORDERS...

YOU OTHER STARLINGS--REMAIN ASLEEP UNTIL I RETURN TO AWAKEN YOU! YOU END-STARLING--TAKE ME TO THE PLANET OA--FAST AS YOU CAN!

OFF THE PLANET AORAN LEAPS THE STARLING, WITH THE EMERALD CRUSADER HANGING ON...

I NEED ONE MORE BREAK--THAT I GET TO THE UNWARY GUARDIANS BEFORE EVIL STAR OVERPOWERS THEM!

MEANWHILE ON THE PLANET OA, EVIL STAR-GREEN LANTERN MAKES HIS APPEARANCE...

GREEN LANTERN OF SPACE-SECTOR 2814 REPORTING ON A STRANGE NEW VILLAIN CALLED EVIL STAR...

EVEN AS HE SPEAKS, THE FALSE GREEN LANTERN PROBES THE GUARDIANS' MINDS WITH HIS HIDDEN STAR BAND...

SO! THE CENTRAL POWER BATTERY IS HERE ON OA! I'LL ELIMINATE THE GUARDIANS FIRST! THEN DEMOLISH THEIR MASTER BATTERY!

9.

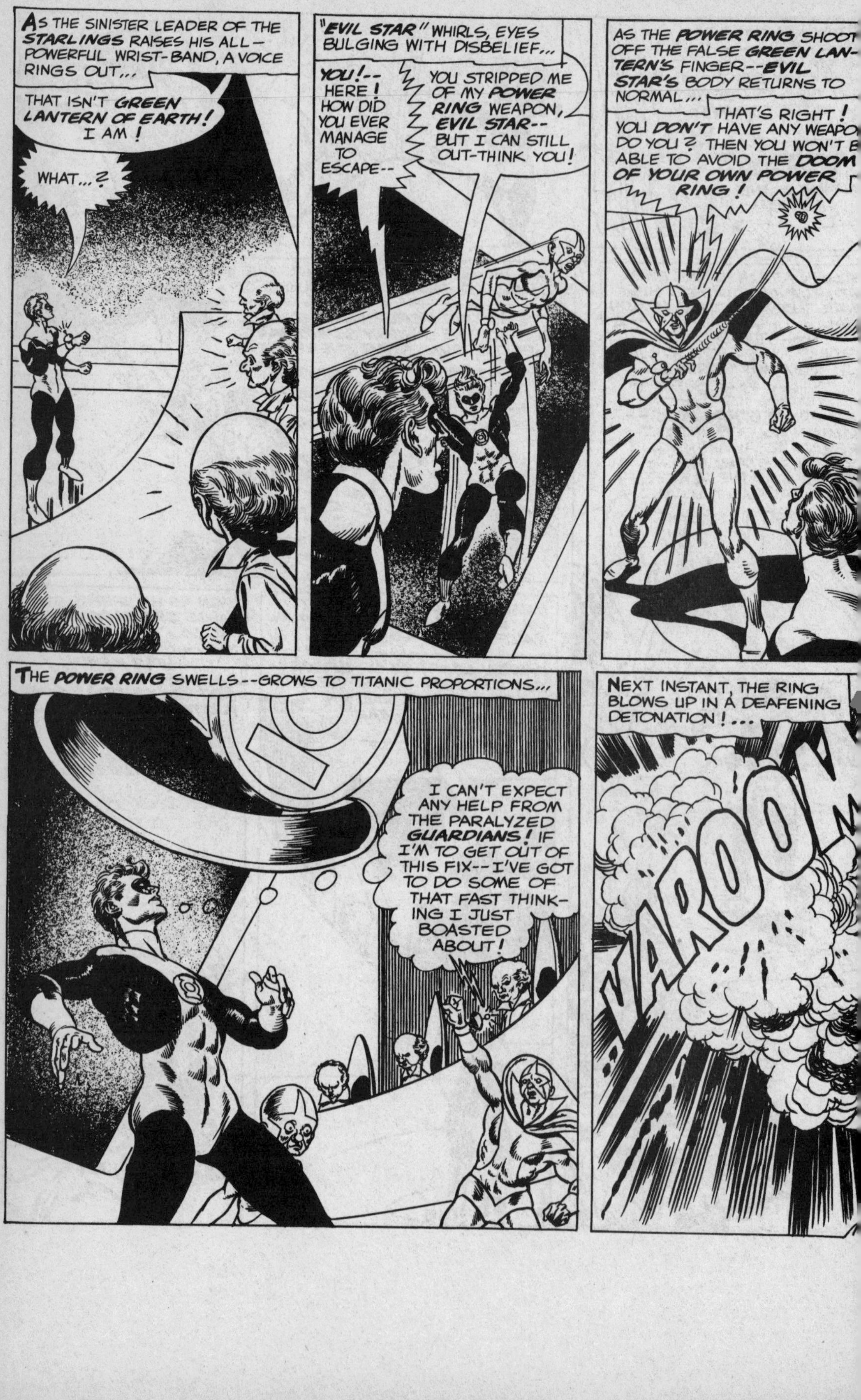
AS THE SINISTER LEADER OF THE STARLINGS RAISES HIS ALL-POWERFUL WRIST-BAND, A VOICE RINGS OUT...
THAT ISN'T GREEN LANTERN OF EARTH! I AM!
WHAT...?
"EVIL STAR" WHIRLS, EYES BULGING WITH DISBELIEF...
YOU!-- HERE! HOW DID YOU EVER MANAGE TO ESCAPE--
YOU STRIPPED ME OF MY POWER RING WEAPON, EVIL STAR-- BUT I CAN STILL OUT-THINK YOU!
AS THE POWER RING SHOOTS OFF THE FALSE GREEN LANTERN'S FINGER--EVIL STAR'S BODY RETURNS TO NORMAL...
THAT'S RIGHT! YOU DON'T HAVE ANY WEAPON DO YOU? THEN YOU WON'T BE ABLE TO AVOID THE DOOM OF YOUR OWN POWER RING!
THE POWER RING SWELLS--GROWS TO TITANIC PROPORTIONS...
I CAN'T EXPECT ANY HELP FROM THE PARALYZED GUARDIANS! IF I'M TO GET OUT OF THIS FIX--I'VE GOT TO DO SOME OF THAT FAST THINKING I JUST BOASTED ABOUT!
NEXT INSTANT, THE RING BLOWS UP IN A DEAFENING DETONATION!...
VAROOM

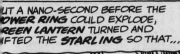

UT A NANO-SECOND BEFORE THE *POWER RING* COULD EXPLODE, *GREEN LANTERN* TURNED AND IFTED THE *STARLING* SO THAT...

EVIL STAR SAID HIS *STARLINGS* WERE IN-VULNERABLE-- SO I'LL USE THIS ONE AS A PROTECTIVE SHIELD!

AS THE EXPLOSION DISSIPATES ITSELF, THE *EMERALD CRUSADER* LUNGES FORWARD...

I NOTICED ON *AORAN* THAT *EVIL STAR* FREEZES FOR A FEW SECONDS AFTER USING HIS *STAR BAND!* BY EXPLODING MY *POWER RING* -- HE MADE HIMSELF TEMPORARILY HELPLESS!

SOK!

NOT *COMPLETELY* HELPLESS, *GREEN LANTERN!* FOR WHILE *EVIL STAR* BANGS BACKWARD INTO THE *GUARDIANS'* DAIS-- HE SNAPS OUT OF HIS INDUCED LETHARGY AND...

YOU DIS-COVERED MY ONE WEAKNESS--BUT THE KNOWLEDGE WILL DO YOU NO GOOD!

OOMPH

THUD!

THE *EMERALD CRUSADER* IS BATTLING FOR MORE THAN HIS LIFE! HE IS STRUGGLING FOR ALL *GREEN LANTERNS* EVERYWHERE, FOR THE FORCES OF GOOD AGAINST EVIL ALL ACROSS THE COSMOS...

AT LEAST *EVIL STAR* WON'T USE HIS *STAR BAND* AGAINST ME! IT'D PARALYZE HIM JUST LONG ENOUGH FOR ME TO "TAKE" HIM!

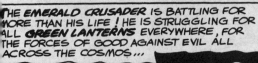

LIFTING HIS LEGS, THE *GREEN GLADIATOR* CATCHES HIS FOE AND KICKS HIM UP AND AWAY...

I'VE *GOT* TO WIN-- OR EVIL WILL DOMINATE EVERYWHERE IN SPACE!

11.

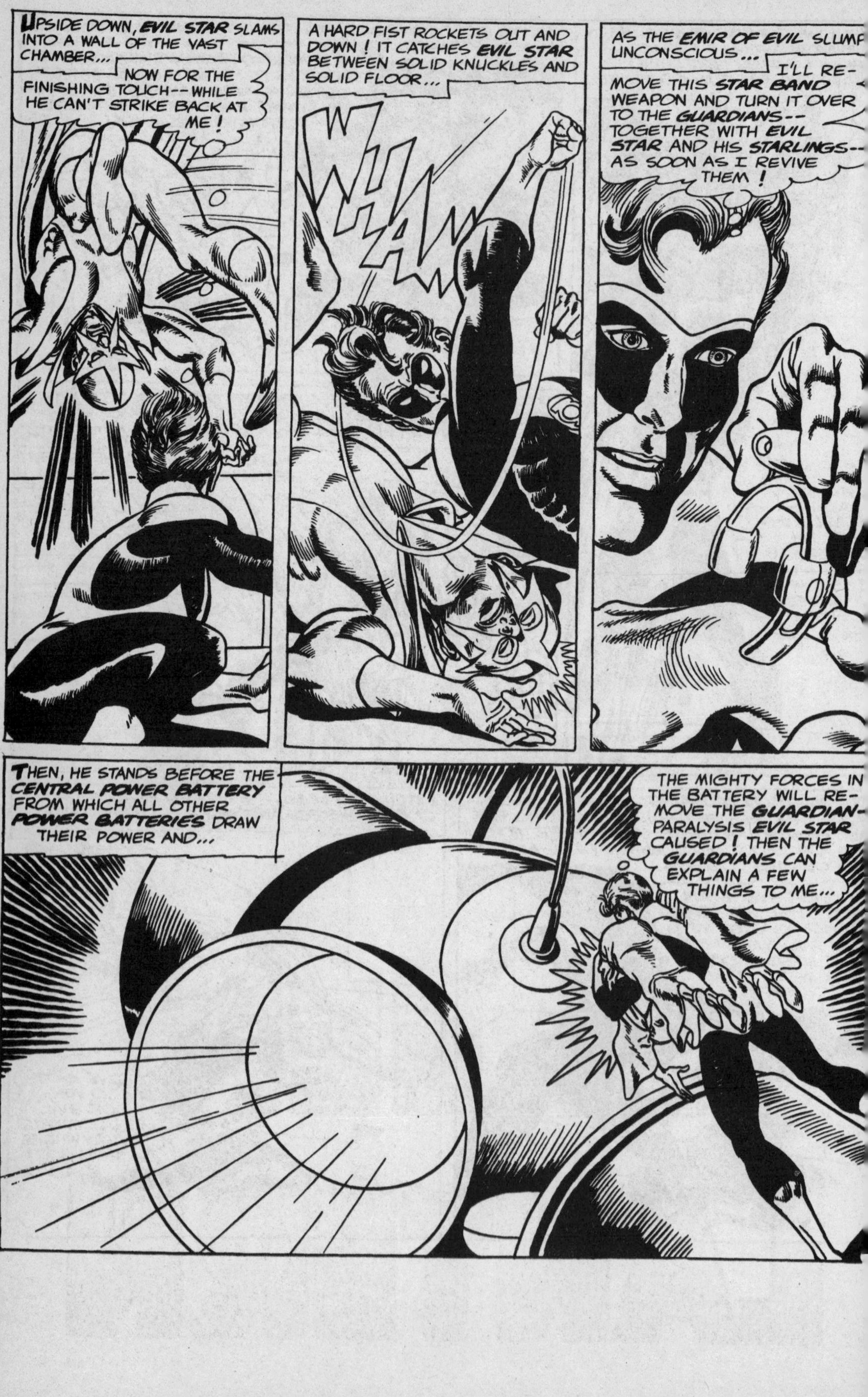
UPSIDE DOWN, EVIL STAR SLAMS INTO A WALL OF THE VAST CHAMBER...
NOW FOR THE FINISHING TOUCH-- WHILE HE CAN'T STRIKE BACK AT ME!
A HARD FIST ROCKETS OUT AND DOWN! IT CATCHES EVIL STAR BETWEEN SOLID KNUCKLES AND SOLID FLOOR...
WHAM
AS THE EMIR OF EVIL SLUMP UNCONSCIOUS...
I'LL REMOVE THIS STAR BAND WEAPON AND TURN IT OVER TO THE GUARDIANS-- TOGETHER WITH EVIL STAR AND HIS STARLINGS-- AS SOON AS I REVIVE THEM!
THEN, HE STANDS BEFORE THE CENTRAL POWER BATTERY FROM WHICH ALL OTHER POWER BATTERIES DRAW THEIR POWER AND...
THE MIGHTY FORCES IN THE BATTERY WILL REMOVE THE GUARDIAN-PARALYSIS EVIL STAR CAUSED! THEN THE GUARDIANS CAN EXPLAIN A FEW THINGS TO ME...

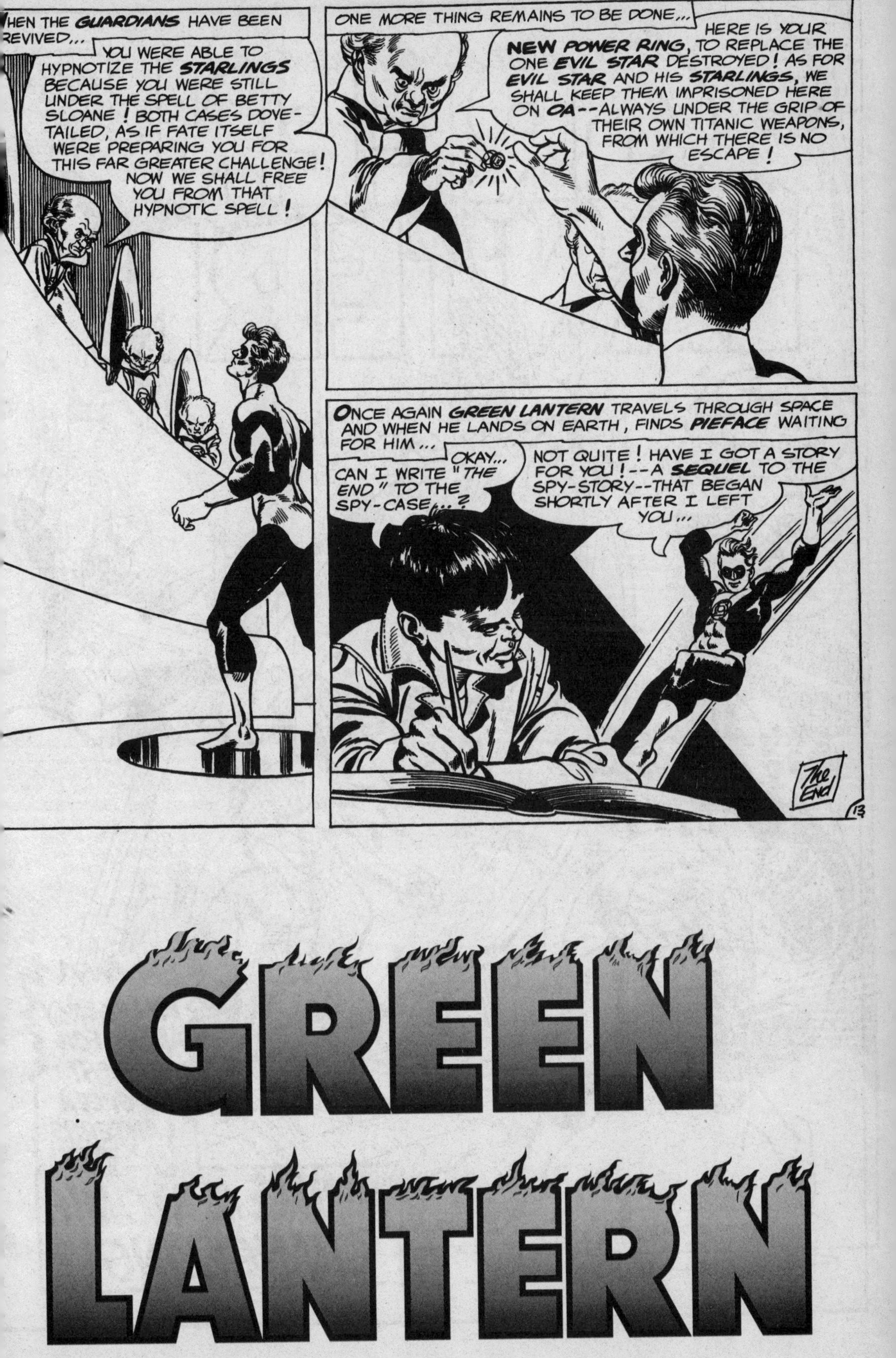
WHEN THE GUARDIANS HAVE BEEN REVIVED,..
YOU WERE ABLE TO HYPNOTIZE THE STARLINGS BECAUSE YOU WERE STILL UNDER THE SPELL OF BETTY SLOANE ! BOTH CASES DOVE-TAILED, AS IF FATE ITSELF WERE PREPARING YOU FOR THIS FAR GREATER CHALLENGE! NOW WE SHALL FREE YOU FROM THAT HYPNOTIC SPELL !
ONE MORE THING REMAINS TO BE DONE,..
HERE IS YOUR NEW POWER RING, TO REPLACE THE ONE EVIL STAR DESTROYED! AS FOR EVIL STAR AND HIS STARLINGS, WE SHALL KEEP THEM IMPRISONED HERE ON OA--ALWAYS UNDER THE GRIP OF THEIR OWN TITANIC WEAPONS, FROM WHICH THERE IS NO ESCAPE !
ONCE AGAIN GREEN LANTERN TRAVELS THROUGH SPACE AND WHEN HE LANDS ON EARTH, FINDS PIEFACE WAITING FOR HIM...
OKAY... CAN I WRITE "THE END" TO THE SPY-CASE...?
NOT QUITE ! HAVE I GOT A STORY FOR YOU !--A SEQUEL TO THE SPY-STORY--THAT BEGAN SHORTLY AFTER I LEFT YOU...
The End
13

GREEN LANTERN

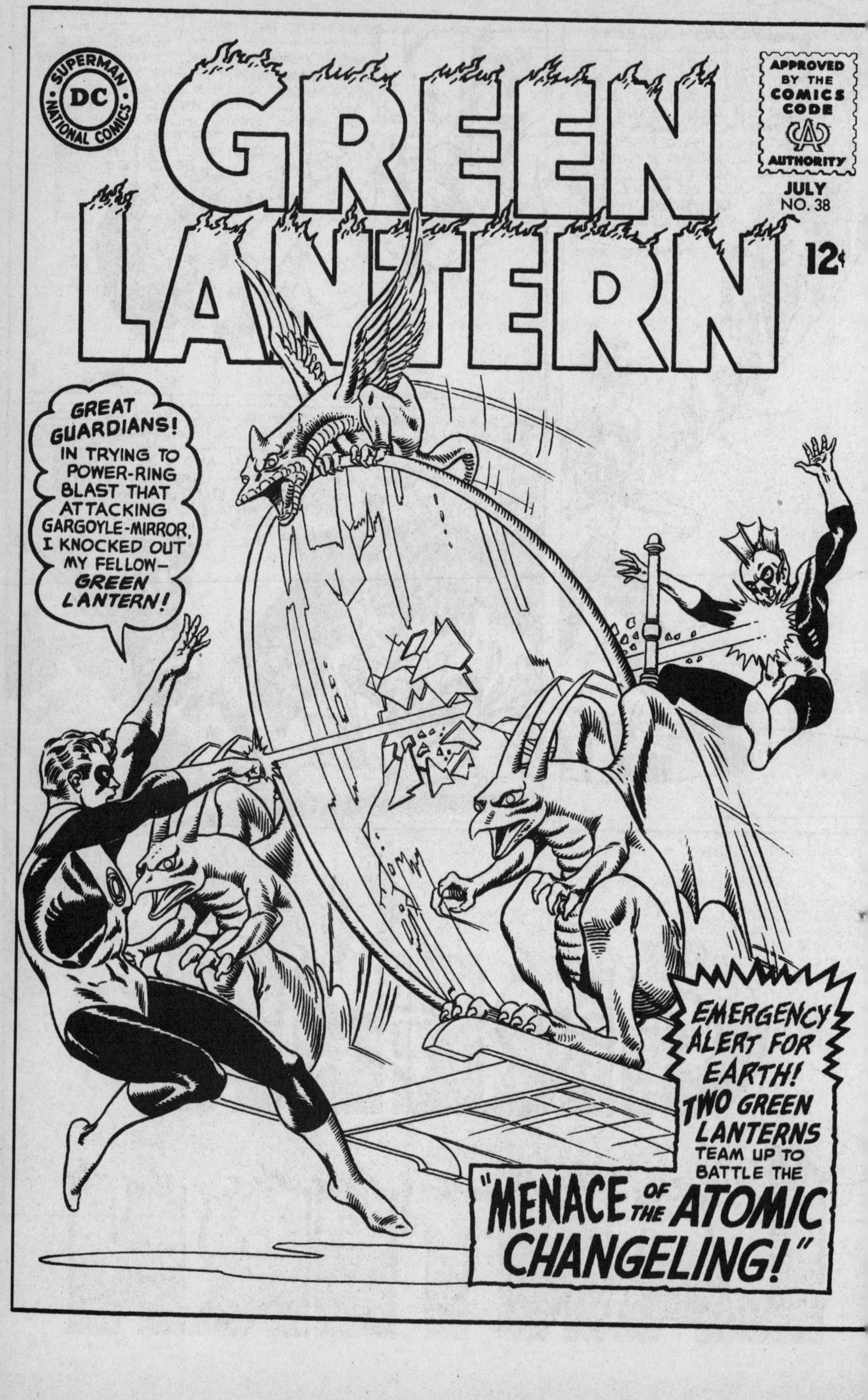
SUPERMAN DC NATIONAL COMICS
GREEN LANTERN
APPROVED BY THE COMICS CODE AUTHORITY
JULY NO. 38
12¢
GREAT GUARDIANS! IN TRYING TO POWER-RING BLAST THAT ATTACKING GARGOYLE-MIRROR, I KNOCKED OUT MY FELLOW-GREEN LANTERN!
EMERGENCY ALERT FOR EARTH! TWO GREEN LANTERNS TEAM UP TO BATTLE THE
"MENACE OF THE ATOMIC CHANGELING!"

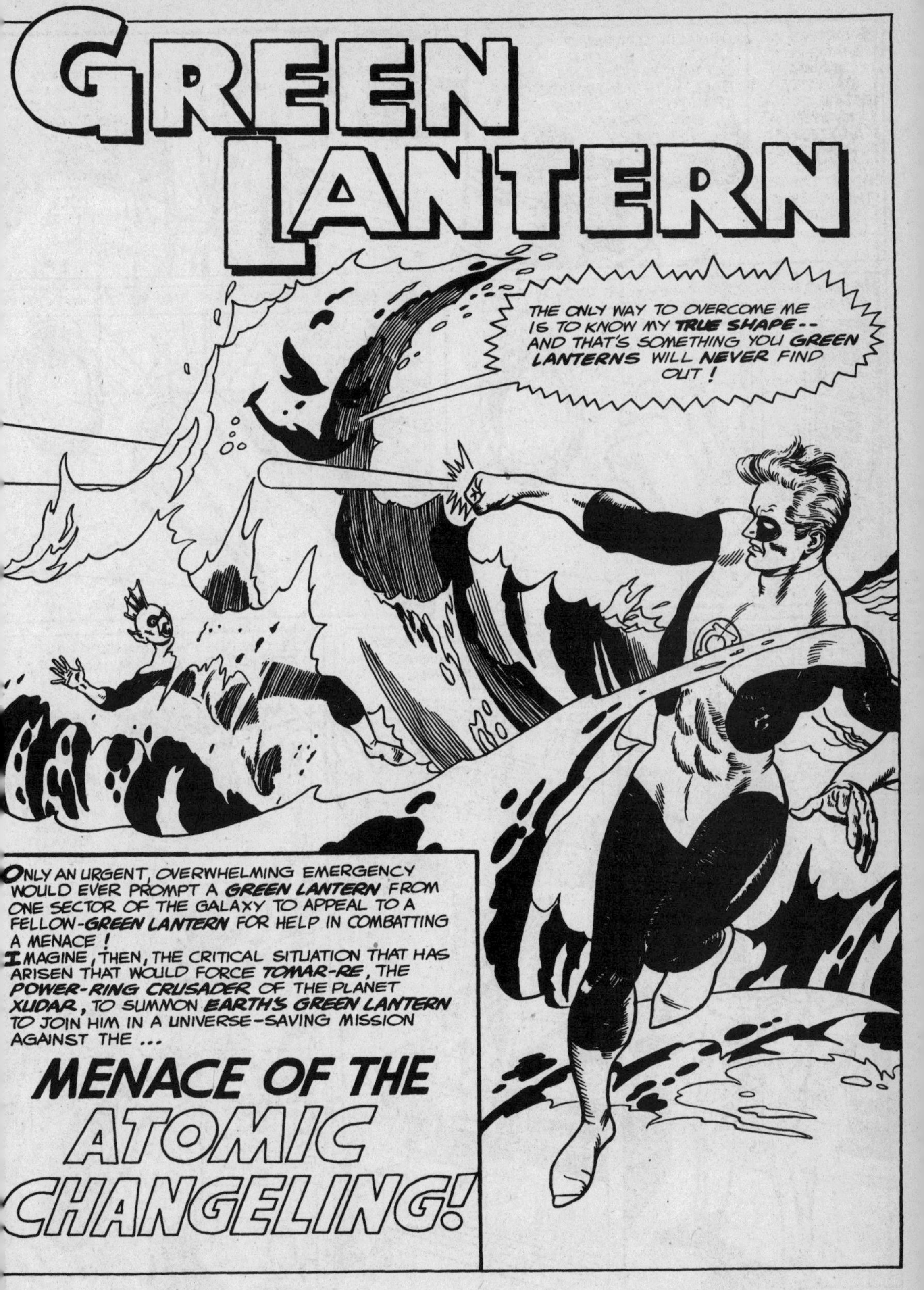
GREEN LANTERN
THE ONLY WAY TO OVERCOME ME IS TO KNOW MY TRUE SHAPE -- AND THAT'S SOMETHING YOU GREEN LANTERNS WILL NEVER FIND OUT!
ONLY AN URGENT, OVERWHELMING EMERGENCY WOULD EVER PROMPT A GREEN LANTERN FROM ONE SECTOR OF THE GALAXY TO APPEAL TO A FELLOW-GREEN LANTERN FOR HELP IN COMBATTING A MENACE!
IMAGINE, THEN, THE CRITICAL SITUATION THAT HAS ARISEN THAT WOULD FORCE TOMAR-RE, THE POWER-RING CRUSADER OF THE PLANET XUDAR, TO SUMMON EARTH'S GREEN LANTERN TO JOIN HIM IN A UNIVERSE-SAVING MISSION AGAINST THE ...
MENACE OF THE ATOMIC CHANGELING!

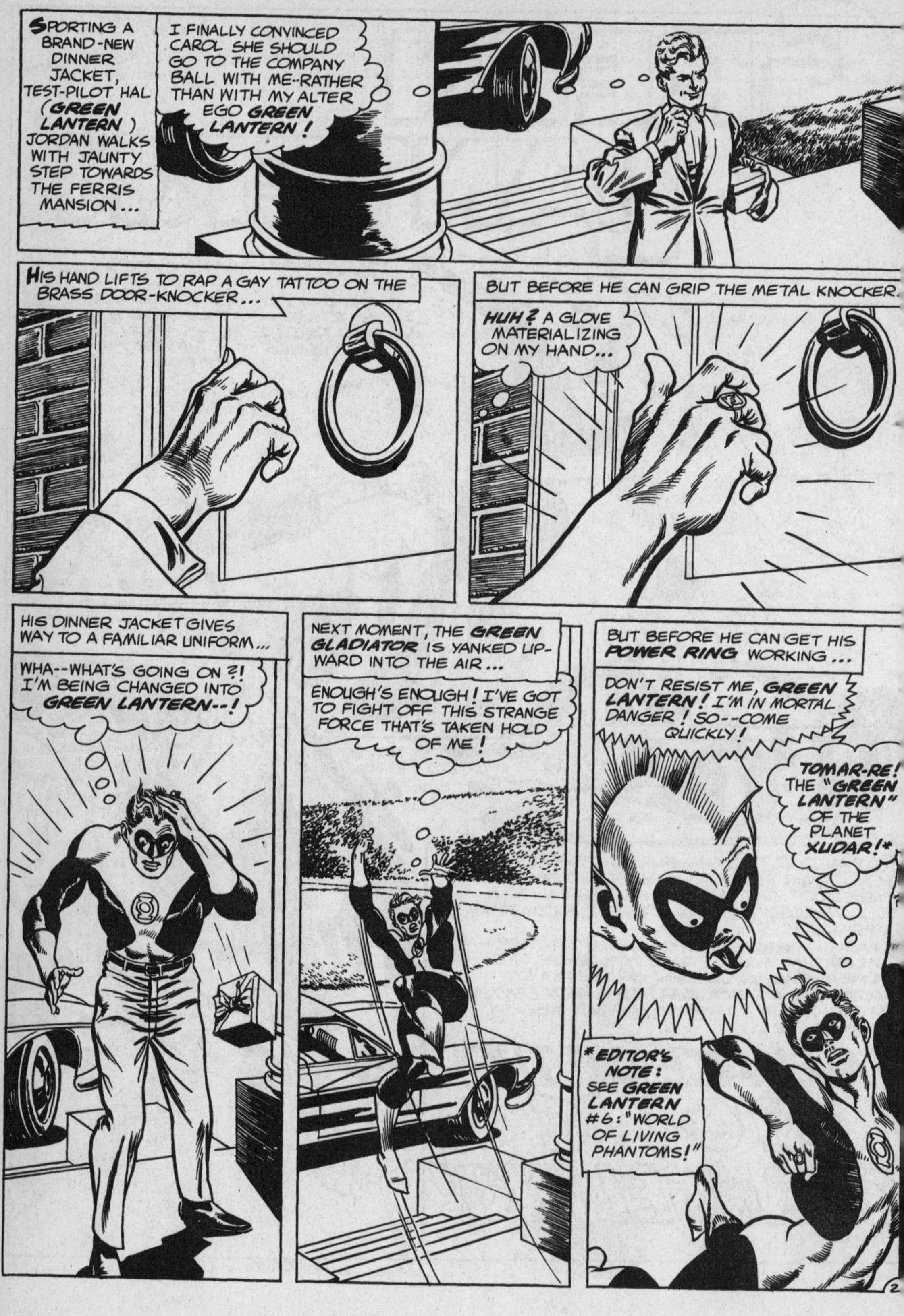
SPORTING A BRAND-NEW DINNER JACKET, TEST-PILOT HAL (GREEN LANTERN) JORDAN WALKS WITH JAUNTY STEP TOWARDS THE FERRIS MANSION...
I FINALLY CONVINCED CAROL SHE SHOULD GO TO THE COMPANY BALL WITH ME--RATHER THAN WITH MY ALTER EGO GREEN LANTERN!
HIS HAND LIFTS TO RAP A GAY TATTOO ON THE BRASS DOOR-KNOCKER...
BUT BEFORE HE CAN GRIP THE METAL KNOCKER...
HUH? A GLOVE MATERIALIZING ON MY HAND...
HIS DINNER JACKET GIVES WAY TO A FAMILIAR UNIFORM...
WHA--WHAT'S GOING ON ?! I'M BEING CHANGED INTO GREEN LANTERN--!
NEXT MOMENT, THE GREEN GLADIATOR IS YANKED UPWARD INTO THE AIR...
ENOUGH'S ENOUGH! I'VE GOT TO FIGHT OFF THIS STRANGE FORCE THAT'S TAKEN HOLD OF ME!
BUT BEFORE HE CAN GET HIS POWER RING WORKING...
DON'T RESIST ME, GREEN LANTERN! I'M IN MORTAL DANGER! SO--COME QUICKLY!
TOMAR-RE! THE "GREEN LANTERN" OF THE PLANET XUDAR!*
*EDITOR'S NOTE: SEE GREEN LANTERN #6: "WORLD OF LIVING PHANTOMS!"
2

DIRECTING HIS *POWER RING* TO SPEED HIM TO THAT DISTANT WORLD, THE *EMERALD GLADIATOR* SOARS UPWARD...

I'LL BE ON *XUDAR* RIGHT AWAY!

NO, NO, *GREEN LANTERN!* I'M NOT ON *XUDAR*-- I'M ON *EARTH!* JUST FOLLOW MY IMAGE--

WITHIN MOMENTS, IN A DESERTED STRETCH OF MOUNTAINOUS COUNTRY...

THAT'S THE *SECOND TIME* YOU'VE PULLED ME AWAY FROM A DATE WITH CAROL FERRIS, *TOMAR-RE!* I HOPE *YOUR* TROUBLE IS EQUAL TO THE TROUBLE *I* WENT TO--TO GET THAT DATE!

I KNOW YOU'RE ONLY JOKING-- BUT THIS IS NO TIME FOR LEVITY! MY *POWER RING* IS ALMOST EXHAUSTED--AND UNLESS I RECHARGE IT WITHIN A FEW SECONDS--I MAY DIE!

HOLD ON, PAL! I'LL HAVE YOU IN MY HANGAR DRESSING ROOM IN SECONDS!

IT CAN'T BE TOO SOON! IF THE *CHANGELING* KNEW WHAT HAD HAPPENED--HE'D STEAL MY BODY!

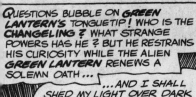

QUESTIONS BUBBLE ON *GREEN LANTERN'S* TONGUETIP! WHO IS THE *CHANGELING?* WHAT STRANGE POWERS HAS HE? BUT HE RESTRAINS HIS CURIOSITY WHILE THE ALIEN *GREEN LANTERN* RENEWS A SOLEMN OATH...

...AND I SHALL SHED MY LIGHT OVER DARK EVIL--FOR THE DARK THINGS CANNOT STAND THE LIGHT-- THE LIGHT OF *GREEN LANTERN!*

THEN... *NOW* WILL YOU TELL ME WHAT THIS IS ALL ABOUT?

YES, BUT FIRST COMMAND YOUR *POWER RING* TO PREVENT THE *CHANGELING* FROM DUPLICATING YOUR BODY--OR YOU'LL BE AS GOOD AS DEAD!

THE *CHANGELING*-- I KNOW NO OTHER NAME FOR *IT*--WAS FOUND ON THE DEAD, BARREN PLANET *KRASTL* BY ONE OF *XUDAR'S* GALACTIC ARCHEOLOGICAL UNITS, WHEN IT BROKE INTO AN UNDER-GROUND TOMB...

3.

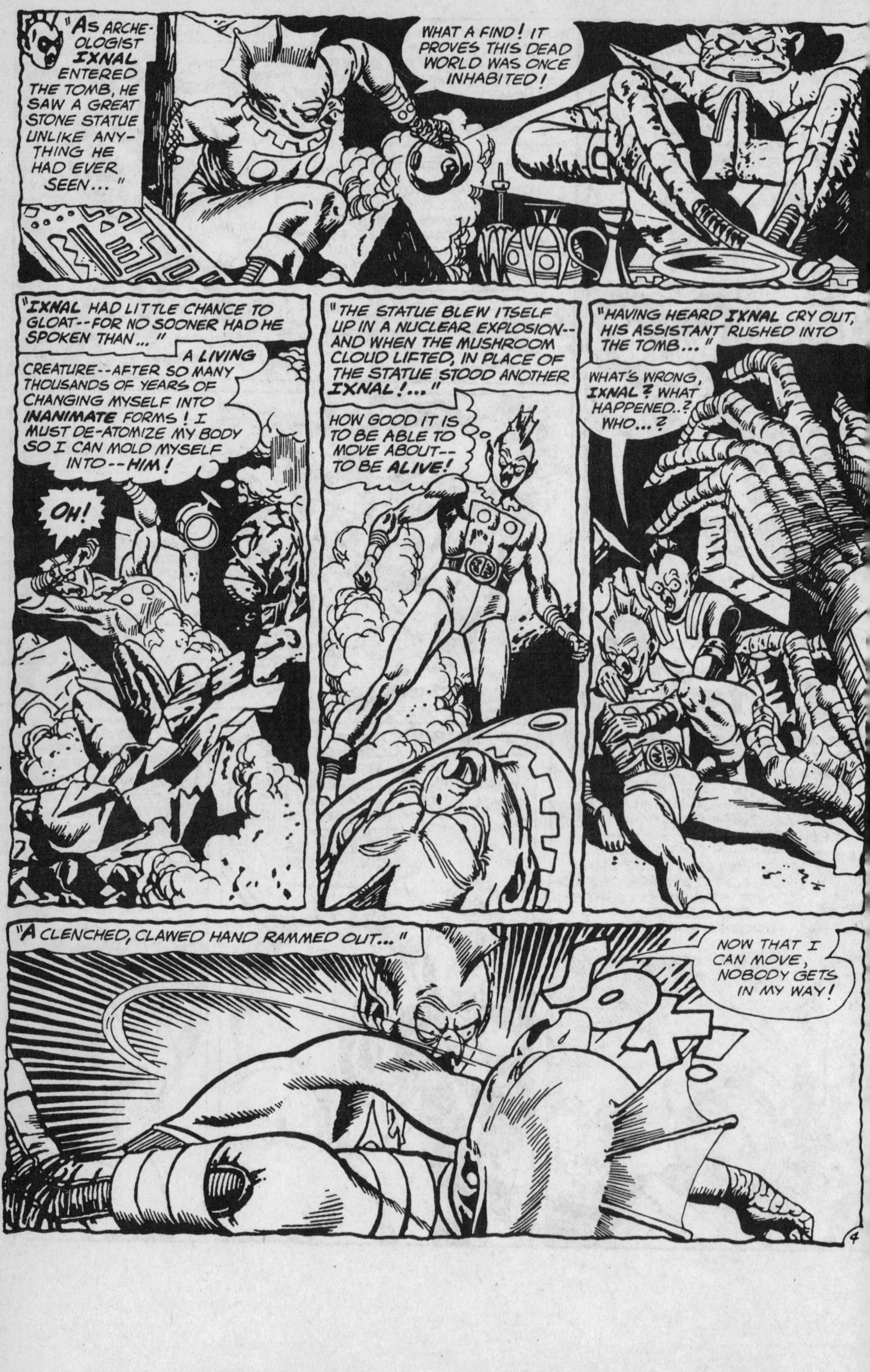
"As archeologist Ixnal entered the tomb, he saw a great stone statue unlike anything he had ever seen..."
What a find! It proves this dead world was once inhabited!
"Ixnal had little chance to gloat--for no sooner had he spoken than..."
A living creature--after so many thousands of years of changing myself into inanimate forms! I must de-atomize my body so I can mold myself into--him!
Oh!
"The statue blew itself up in a nuclear explosion--and when the mushroom cloud lifted, in place of the statue stood another Ixnal!..."
How good it is to be able to move about--to be alive!
"Having heard Ixnal cry out, his assistant rushed into the tomb..."
What's wrong, Ixnal? What happened..? Who...?
"A clenched, clawed hand rammed out..."
Now that I can move, nobody gets in my way!
Sok!
4

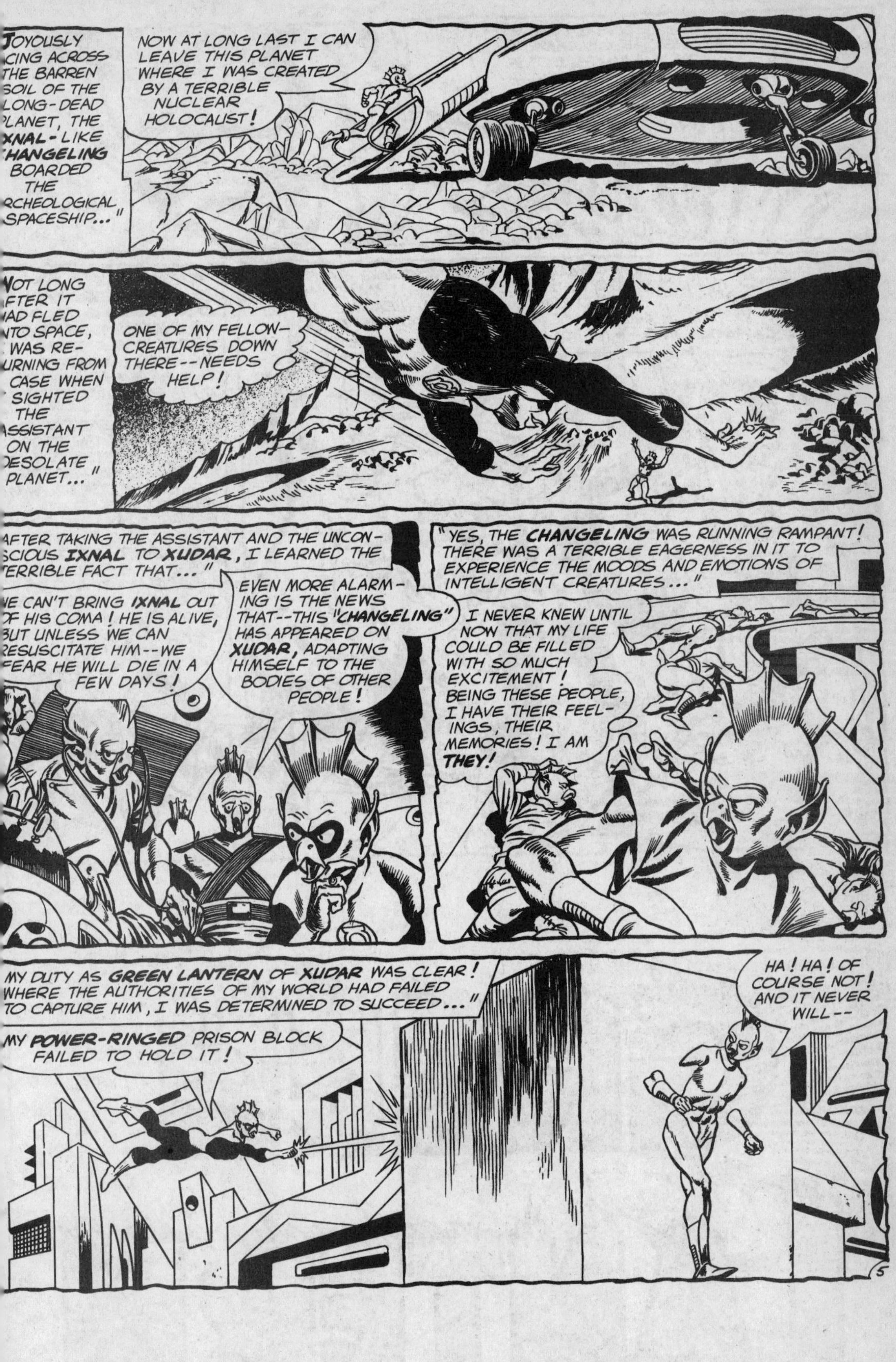
JOYOUSLY ...CING ACROSS THE BARREN SOIL OF THE LONG-DEAD PLANET, THE ...XNAL-LIKE ...HANGELING BOARDED THE ...RCHEOLOGICAL SPACESHIP..."
NOW AT LONG LAST I CAN LEAVE THIS PLANET WHERE I WAS CREATED BY A TERRIBLE NUCLEAR HOLOCAUST!
...OT LONG ...FTER IT ...AD FLED ...NTO SPACE, ... WAS RE-...URNING FROM ... CASE WHEN ... SIGHTED THE ...SSISTANT ON THE ...ESOLATE PLANET..."
ONE OF MY FELLOW-CREATURES DOWN THERE--NEEDS HELP!
"AFTER TAKING THE ASSISTANT AND THE UNCON-...SCIOUS IXNAL TO XUDAR, I LEARNED THE ...TERRIBLE FACT THAT..."
...E CAN'T BRING IXNAL OUT ...F HIS COMA! HE IS ALIVE, ...UT UNLESS WE CAN ...ESUSCITATE HIM--WE ...EAR HE WILL DIE IN A FEW DAYS!
EVEN MORE ALARMING IS THE NEWS THAT--THIS "CHANGELING" HAS APPEARED ON XUDAR, ADAPTING HIMSELF TO THE BODIES OF OTHER PEOPLE!
"YES, THE CHANGELING WAS RUNNING RAMPANT! THERE WAS A TERRIBLE EAGERNESS IN IT TO EXPERIENCE THE MOODS AND EMOTIONS OF INTELLIGENT CREATURES..."
I NEVER KNEW UNTIL NOW THAT MY LIFE COULD BE FILLED WITH SO MUCH EXCITEMENT! BEING THESE PEOPLE, I HAVE THEIR FEELINGS, THEIR MEMORIES! I AM THEY!
...MY DUTY AS GREEN LANTERN OF XUDAR WAS CLEAR! ...WHERE THE AUTHORITIES OF MY WORLD HAD FAILED ...TO CAPTURE HIM, I WAS DETERMINED TO SUCCEED..."
...MY POWER-RINGED PRISON BLOCK FAILED TO HOLD IT!
HA! HA! OF COURSE NOT! AND IT NEVER WILL--
5

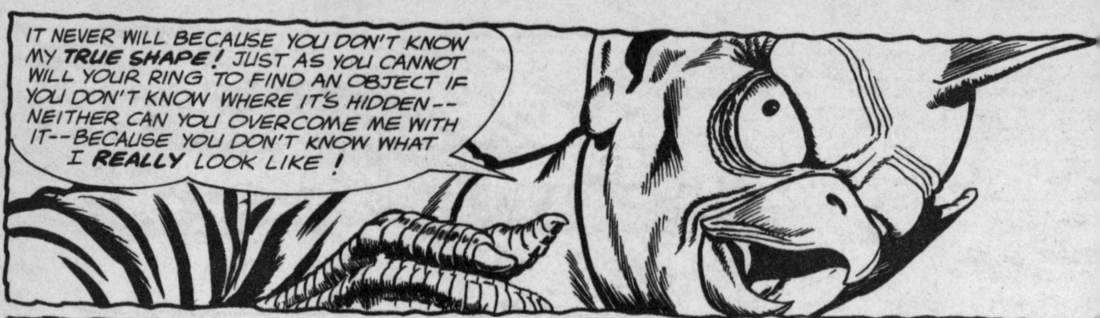
IT NEVER WILL BECAUSE YOU DON'T KNOW MY **TRUE SHAPE!** JUST AS YOU CANNOT WILL YOUR RING TO FIND AN OBJECT IF YOU DON'T KNOW WHERE IT'S HIDDEN-- NEITHER CAN YOU OVERCOME ME WITH IT--BECAUSE YOU DON'T KNOW WHAT I **REALLY** LOOK LIKE!

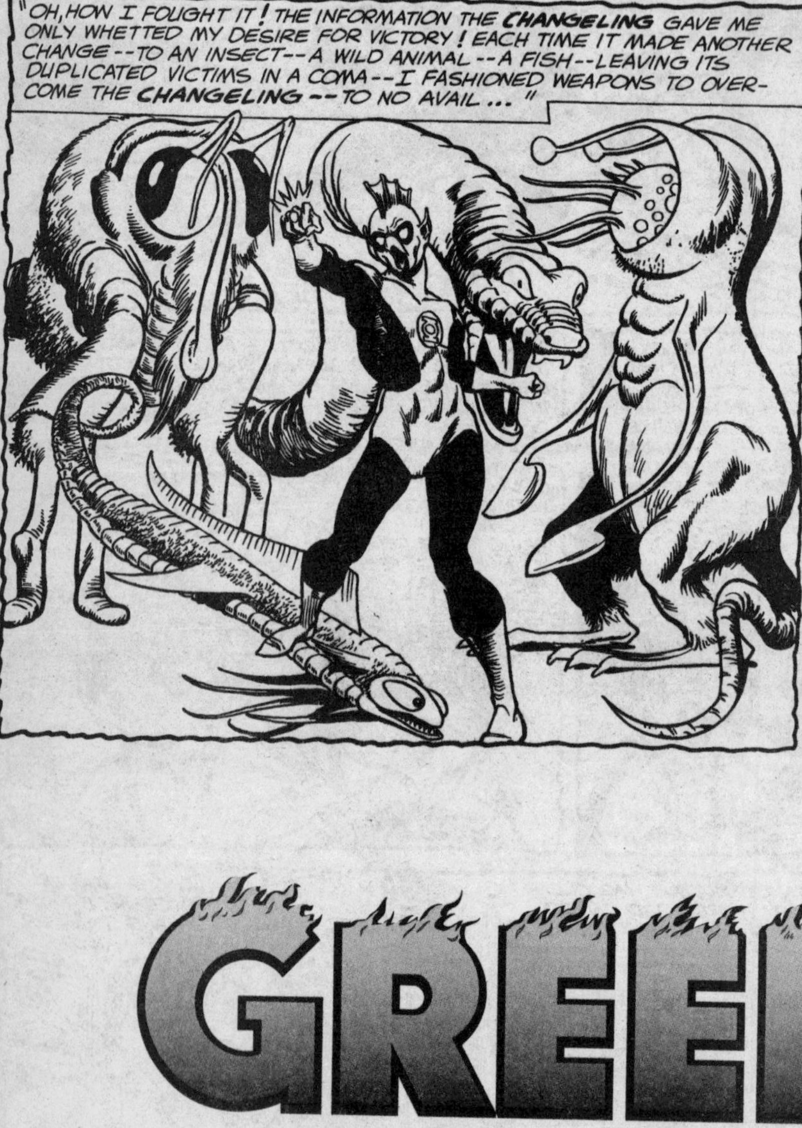
"OH, HOW I FOUGHT IT! THE INFORMATION THE **CHANGELING** GAVE ME ONLY WHETTED MY DESIRE FOR VICTORY! EACH TIME IT MADE ANOTHER CHANGE--TO AN INSECT--A WILD ANIMAL--A FISH--LEAVING ITS DUPLICATED VICTIMS IN A COMA--I FASHIONED WEAPONS TO OVER-COME THE **CHANGELING**--TO NO AVAIL..."

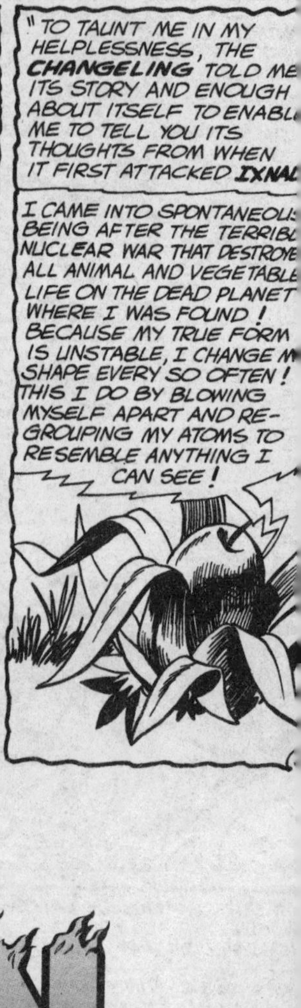
"TO TAUNT ME IN MY HELPLESSNESS, THE **CHANGELING** TOLD ME ITS STORY AND ENOUGH ABOUT ITSELF TO ENABL ME TO TELL YOU ITS THOUGHTS FROM WHEN IT FIRST ATTACKED **IXNA**
I CAME INTO SPONTANEOU BEING AFTER THE TERRIB NUCLEAR WAR THAT DESTROYE ALL ANIMAL AND VEGETABL LIFE ON THE DEAD PLANET WHERE I WAS FOUND! BECAUSE MY TRUE FORM IS UNSTABLE, I CHANGE M SHAPE EVERY SO OFTEN! THIS I DO BY BLOWING MYSELF APART AND RE-GROUPING MY ATOMS TO RESEMBLE ANYTHING I CAN SEE!

GREEN LANTERN

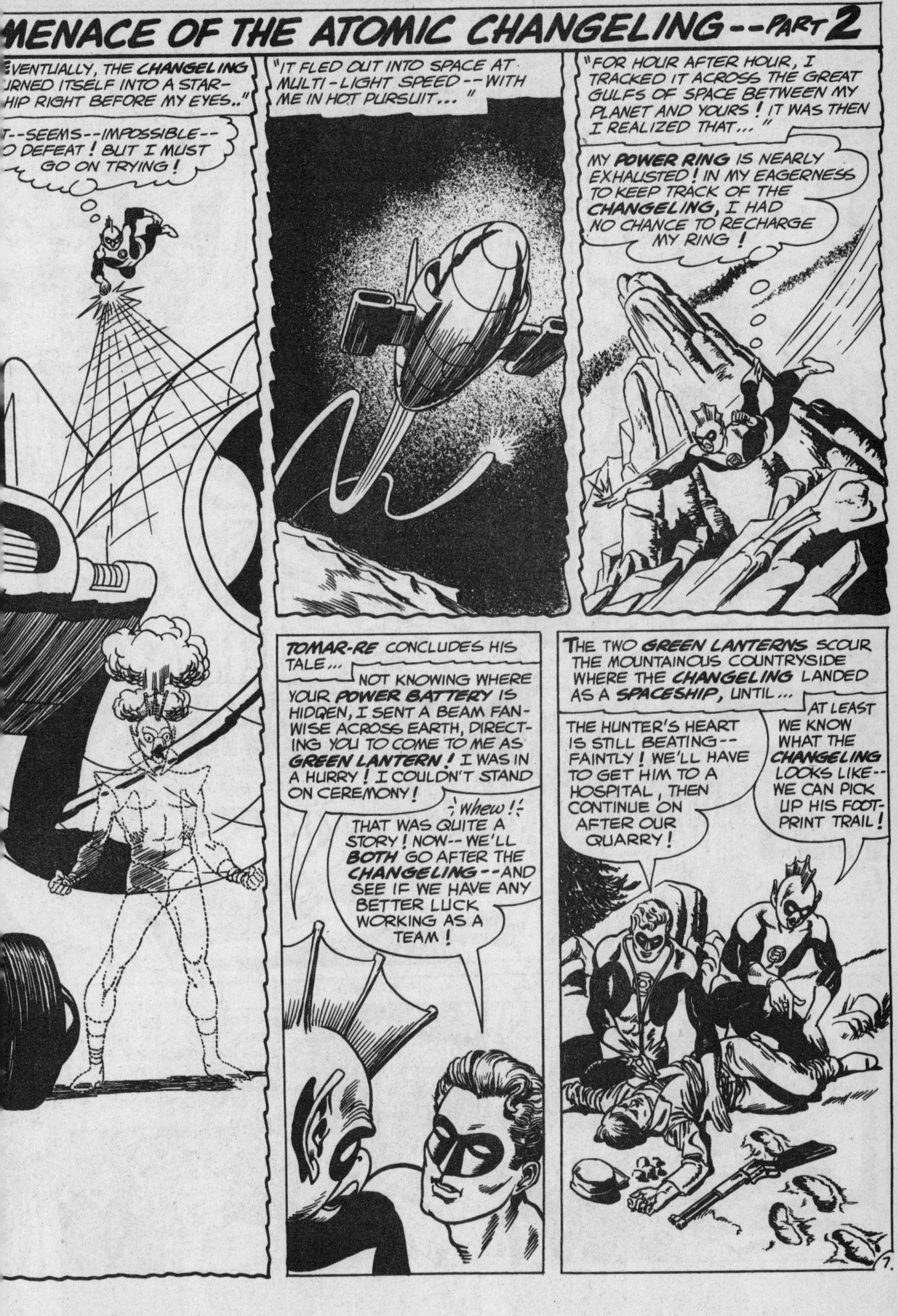
MENACE OF THE ATOMIC CHANGELING--PART 2
EVENTUALLY, THE CHANGELING URNED ITSELF INTO A STAR-HIP RIGHT BEFORE MY EYES.."
T--SEEMS--IMPOSSIBLE--O DEFEAT! BUT I MUST GO ON TRYING!
"IT FLED OUT INTO SPACE AT MULTI-LIGHT SPEED--WITH ME IN HOT PURSUIT..."
"FOR HOUR AFTER HOUR, I TRACKED IT ACROSS THE GREAT GULFS OF SPACE BETWEEN MY PLANET AND YOURS! IT WAS THEN I REALIZED THAT..."
MY POWER RING IS NEARLY EXHAUSTED! IN MY EAGERNESS TO KEEP TRACK OF THE CHANGELING, I HAD NO CHANCE TO RECHARGE MY RING!
TOMAR-RE CONCLUDES HIS TALE...
NOT KNOWING WHERE YOUR POWER BATTERY IS HIDDEN, I SENT A BEAM FAN-WISE ACROSS EARTH, DIRECTING YOU TO COME TO ME AS GREEN LANTERN! I WAS IN A HURRY! I COULDN'T STAND ON CEREMONY!
WHEW!
THAT WAS QUITE A STORY! NOW--WE'LL BOTH GO AFTER THE CHANGELING--AND SEE IF WE HAVE ANY BETTER LUCK WORKING AS A TEAM!
THE TWO GREEN LANTERNS SCOUR THE MOUNTAINOUS COUNTRYSIDE WHERE THE CHANGELING LANDED AS A SPACESHIP, UNTIL...
THE HUNTER'S HEART IS STILL BEATING--FAINTLY! WE'LL HAVE TO GET HIM TO A HOSPITAL, THEN CONTINUE ON AFTER OUR QUARRY!
AT LEAST WE KNOW WHAT THE CHANGELING LOOKS LIKE--WE CAN PICK UP HIS FOOT-PRINT TRAIL!
7

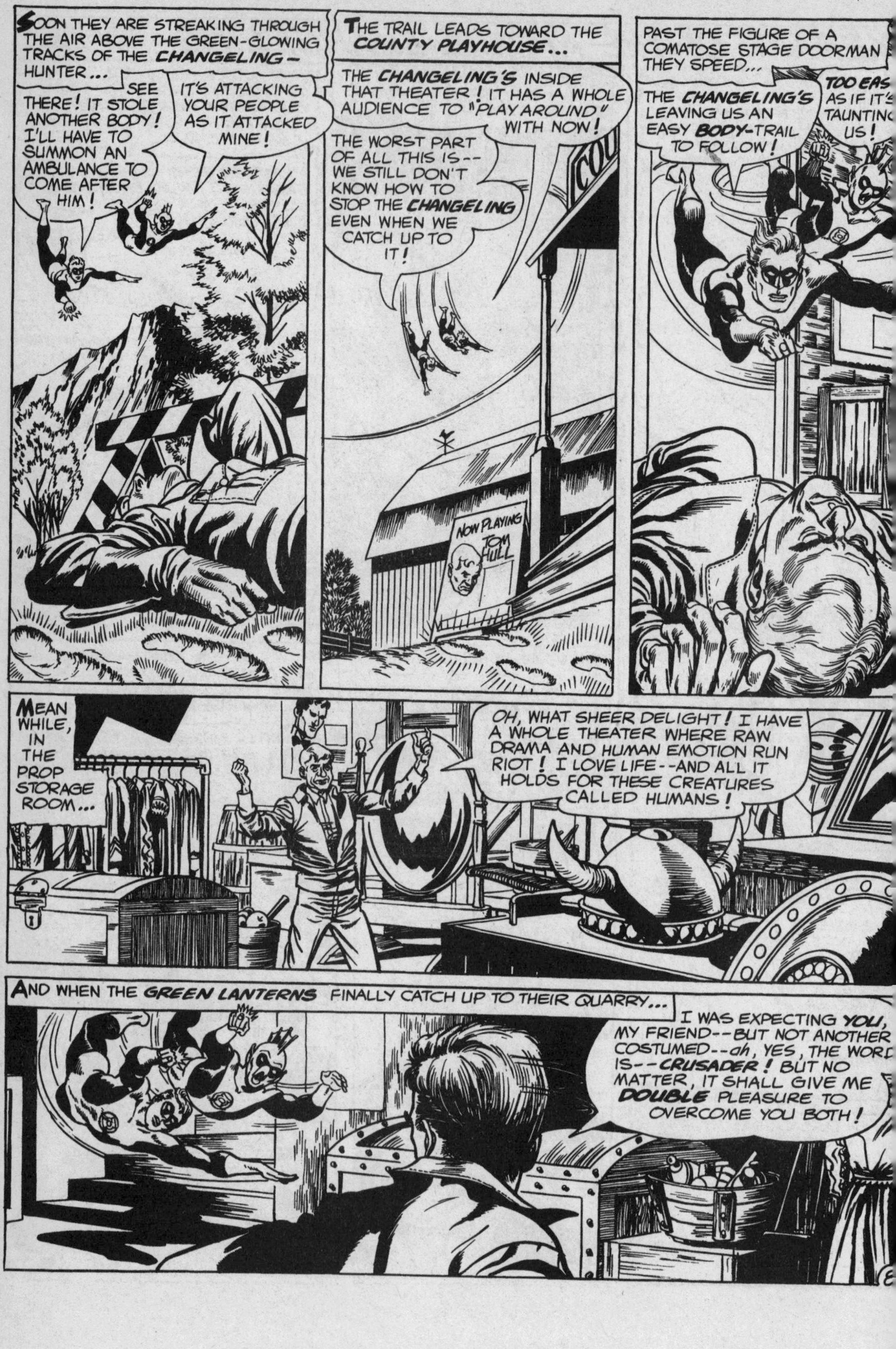
SOON THEY ARE STREAKING THROUGH THE AIR ABOVE THE GREEN-GLOWING TRACKS OF THE CHANGELING-HUNTER...
SEE THERE! IT STOLE ANOTHER BODY! I'LL HAVE TO SUMMON AN AMBULANCE TO COME AFTER HIM!
IT'S ATTACKING YOUR PEOPLE AS IT ATTACKED MINE!
THE TRAIL LEADS TOWARD THE COUNTY PLAYHOUSE...
THE CHANGELING'S INSIDE THAT THEATER! IT HAS A WHOLE AUDIENCE TO "PLAY AROUND" WITH NOW!
THE WORST PART OF ALL THIS IS-- WE STILL DON'T KNOW HOW TO STOP THE CHANGELING EVEN WHEN WE CATCH UP TO IT!
NOW PLAYING TOM HULL
PAST THE FIGURE OF A COMATOSE STAGE DOORMAN THEY SPEED...
THE CHANGELING'S LEAVING US AN EASY BODY-TRAIL TO FOLLOW!
MEANWHILE, IN THE PROP STORAGE ROOM...
OH, WHAT SHEER DELIGHT! I HAVE A WHOLE THEATER WHERE RAW DRAMA AND HUMAN EMOTION RUN RIOT! I LOVE LIFE--AND ALL IT HOLDS FOR THESE CREATURES CALLED HUMANS!
AND WHEN THE GREEN LANTERNS FINALLY CATCH UP TO THEIR QUARRY...
I WAS EXPECTING YOU, MY FRIEND--BUT NOT ANOTHER COSTUMED--ah, YES, THE WORD IS--CRUSADER! BUT NO MATTER, IT SHALL GIVE ME DOUBLE PLEASURE TO OVERCOME YOU BOTH!

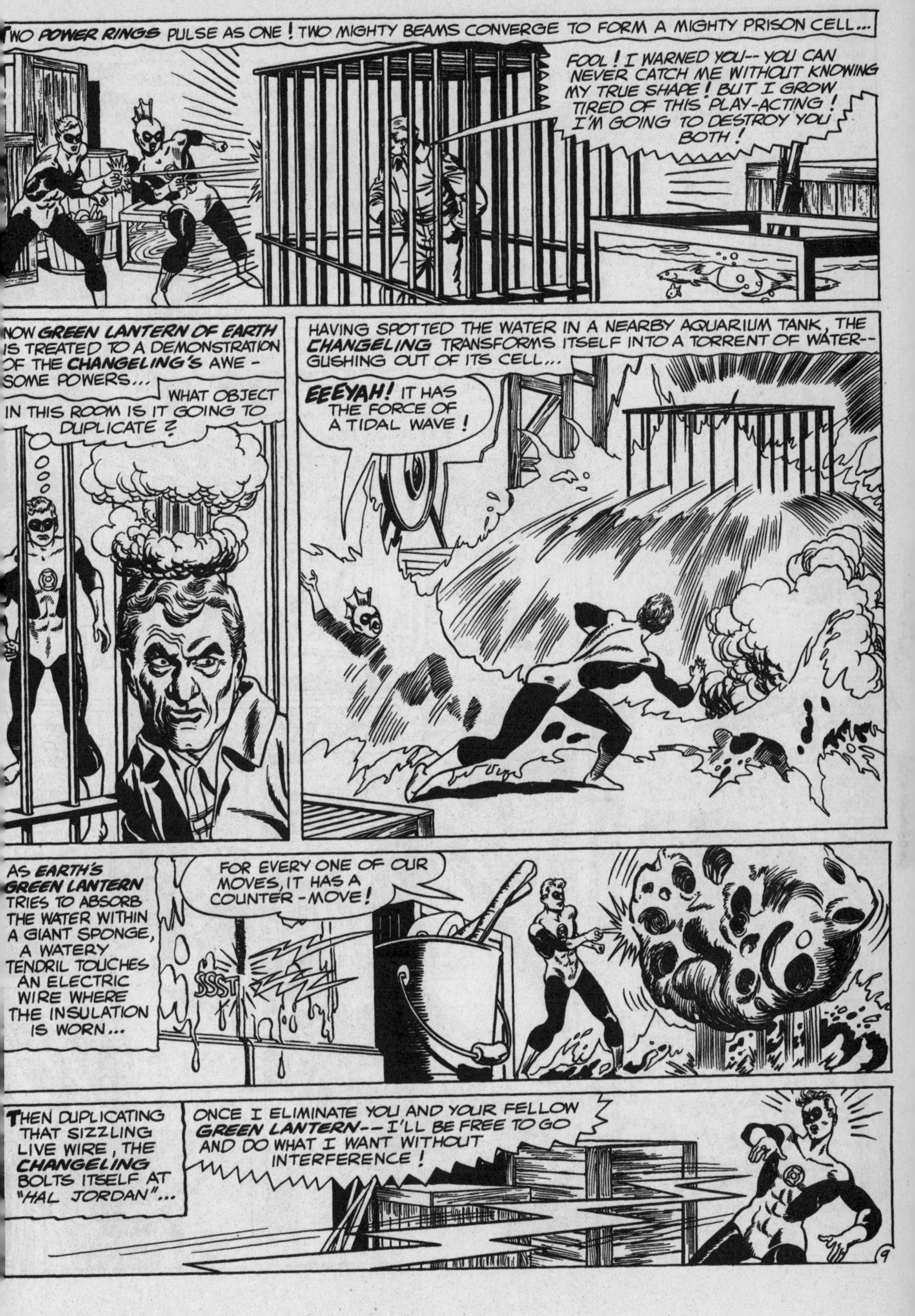
TWO POWER RINGS PULSE AS ONE! TWO MIGHTY BEAMS CONVERGE TO FORM A MIGHTY PRISON CELL...
FOOL! I WARNED YOU-- YOU CAN NEVER CATCH ME WITHOUT KNOWING MY TRUE SHAPE! BUT I GROW TIRED OF THIS PLAY-ACTING! I'M GOING TO DESTROY YOU BOTH!
NOW GREEN LANTERN OF EARTH IS TREATED TO A DEMONSTRATION OF THE CHANGELING'S AWE-SOME POWERS...
WHAT OBJECT IN THIS ROOM IS IT GOING TO DUPLICATE ?
HAVING SPOTTED THE WATER IN A NEARBY AQUARIUM TANK, THE CHANGELING TRANSFORMS ITSELF INTO A TORRENT OF WATER-- GUSHING OUT OF ITS CELL...
EEEYAH! IT HAS THE FORCE OF A TIDAL WAVE!
AS EARTH'S GREEN LANTERN TRIES TO ABSORB THE WATER WITHIN A GIANT SPONGE, A WATERY TENDRIL TOUCHES AN ELECTRIC WIRE WHERE THE INSULATION IS WORN...
FOR EVERY ONE OF OUR MOVES, IT HAS A COUNTER-MOVE!
SSST
THEN DUPLICATING THAT SIZZLING LIVE WIRE, THE CHANGELING BOLTS ITSELF AT "HAL JORDAN"...
ONCE I ELIMINATE YOU AND YOUR FELLOW GREEN LANTERN-- I'LL BE FREE TO GO AND DO WHAT I WANT WITHOUT INTERFERENCE!
9

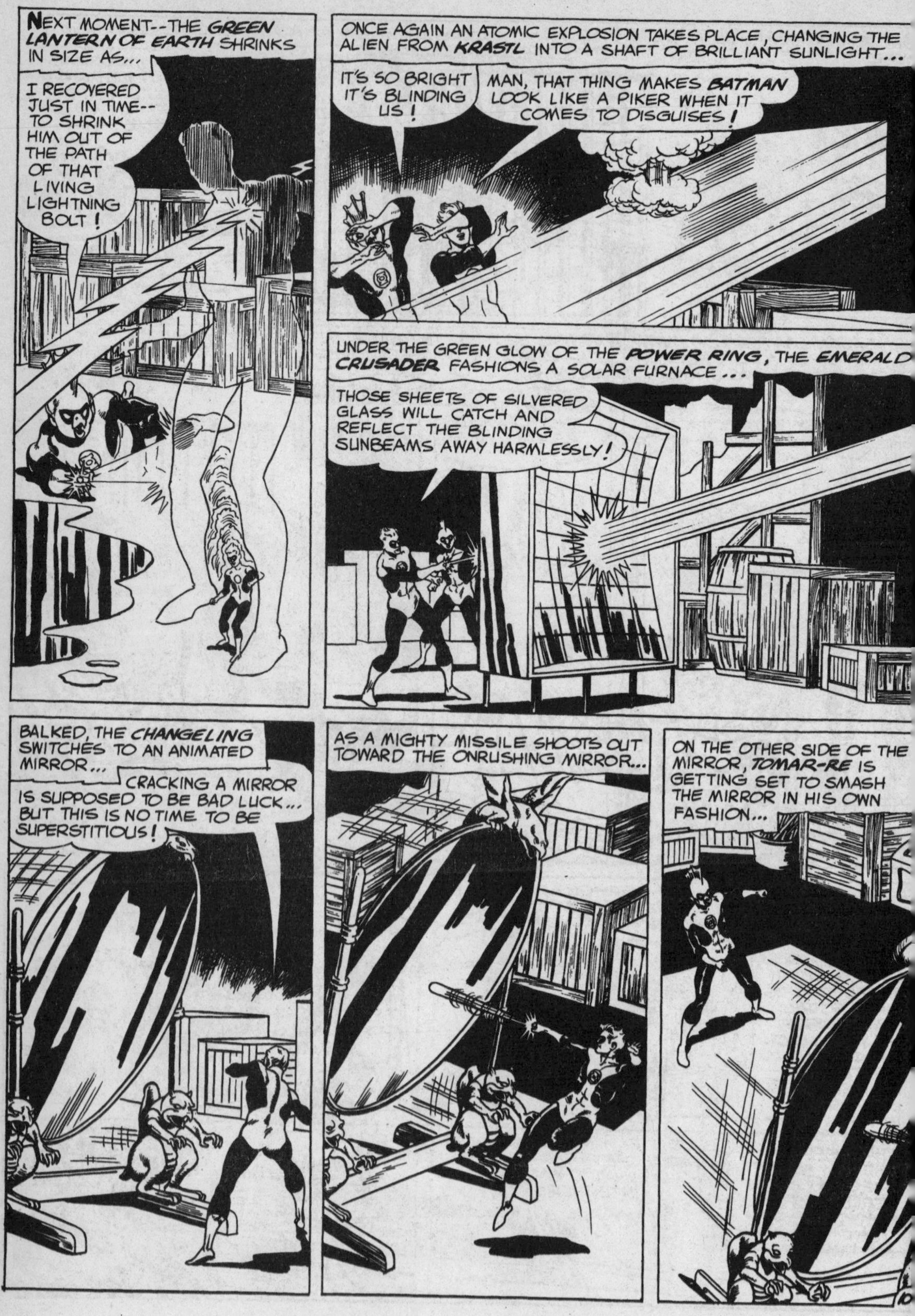
NEXT MOMENT--THE GREEN LANTERN OF EARTH SHRINKS IN SIZE AS...
I RECOVERED JUST IN TIME-- TO SHRINK HIM OUT OF THE PATH OF THAT LIVING LIGHTNING BOLT!
ONCE AGAIN AN ATOMIC EXPLOSION TAKES PLACE, CHANGING THE ALIEN FROM KRASTL INTO A SHAFT OF BRILLIANT SUNLIGHT...
IT'S SO BRIGHT IT'S BLINDING US!
MAN, THAT THING MAKES BATMAN LOOK LIKE A PIKER WHEN IT COMES TO DISGUISES!
UNDER THE GREEN GLOW OF THE POWER RING, THE EMERALD CRUSADER FASHIONS A SOLAR FURNACE...
THOSE SHEETS OF SILVERED GLASS WILL CATCH AND REFLECT THE BLINDING SUNBEAMS AWAY HARMLESSLY!
BALKED, THE CHANGELING SWITCHES TO AN ANIMATED MIRROR...
CRACKING A MIRROR IS SUPPOSED TO BE BAD LUCK... BUT THIS IS NO TIME TO BE SUPERSTITIOUS!
AS A MIGHTY MISSILE SHOOTS OUT TOWARD THE ONRUSHING MIRROR...
ON THE OTHER SIDE OF THE MIRROR, TOMAR-RE IS GETTING SET TO SMASH THE MIRROR IN HIS OWN FASHION...

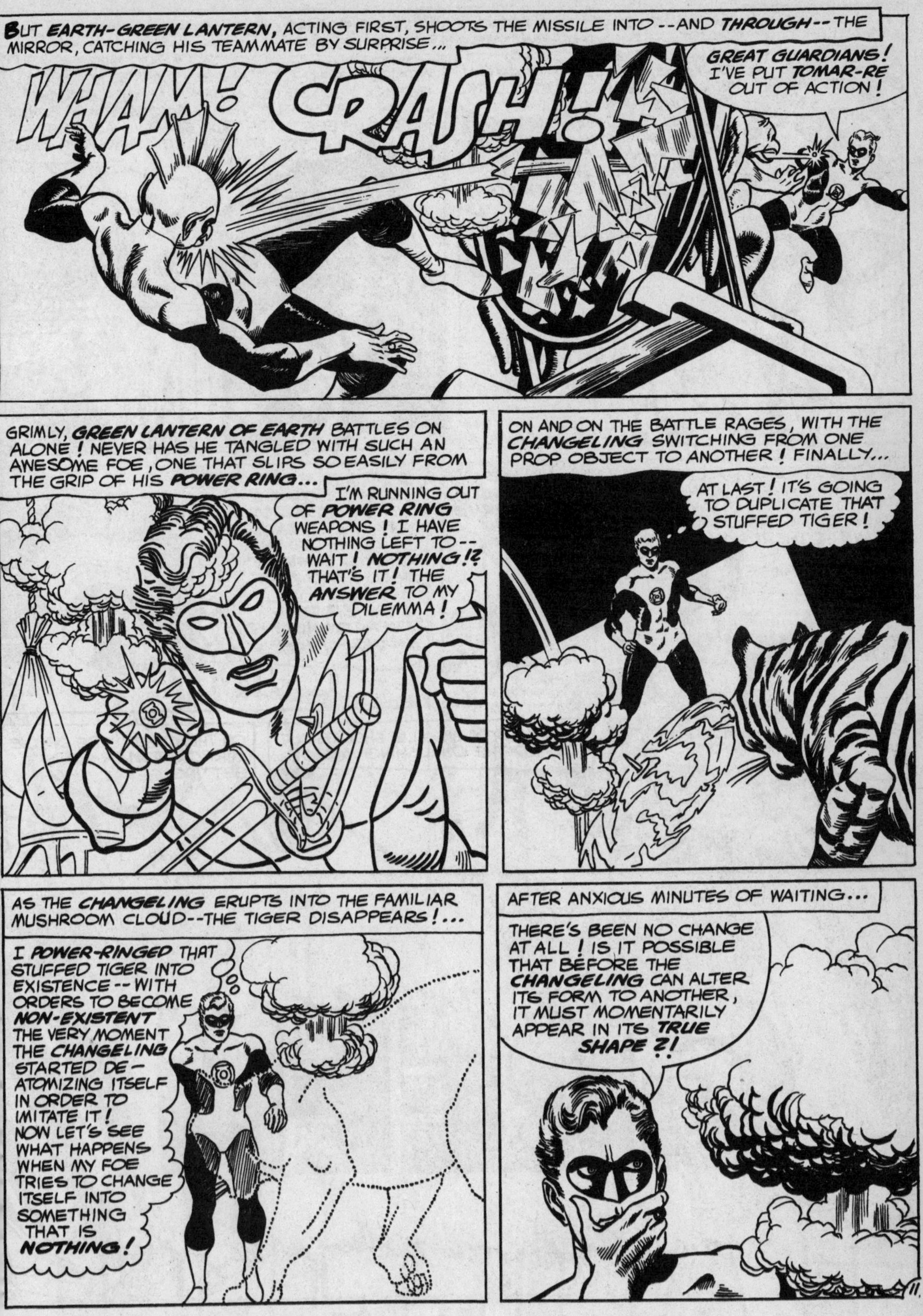
BUT EARTH-GREEN LANTERN, ACTING FIRST, SHOOTS THE MISSILE INTO--AND THROUGH--THE MIRROR, CATCHING HIS TEAMMATE BY SURPRISE...
WHAM! CRASH!
GREAT GUARDIANS! I'VE PUT TOMAR-RE OUT OF ACTION!
GRIMLY, GREEN LANTERN OF EARTH BATTLES ON ALONE! NEVER HAS HE TANGLED WITH SUCH AN AWESOME FOE, ONE THAT SLIPS SO EASILY FROM THE GRIP OF HIS POWER RING...
I'M RUNNING OUT OF POWER RING WEAPONS! I HAVE NOTHING LEFT TO--WAIT! NOTHING!? THAT'S IT! THE ANSWER TO MY DILEMMA!
ON AND ON THE BATTLE RAGES, WITH THE CHANGELING SWITCHING FROM ONE PROP OBJECT TO ANOTHER! FINALLY...
AT LAST! IT'S GOING TO DUPLICATE THAT STUFFED TIGER!
AS THE CHANGELING ERUPTS INTO THE FAMILIAR MUSHROOM CLOUD--THE TIGER DISAPPEARS!...
I POWER-RINGED THAT STUFFED TIGER INTO EXISTENCE--WITH ORDERS TO BECOME NON-EXISTENT THE VERY MOMENT THE CHANGELING STARTED DE-ATOMIZING ITSELF IN ORDER TO IMITATE IT! NOW LET'S SEE WHAT HAPPENS WHEN MY FOE TRIES TO CHANGE ITSELF INTO SOMETHING THAT IS NOTHING!
AFTER ANXIOUS MINUTES OF WAITING...
THERE'S BEEN NO CHANGE AT ALL! IS IT POSSIBLE THAT BEFORE THE CHANGELING CAN ALTER ITS FORM TO ANOTHER, IT MUST MOMENTARILY APPEAR IN ITS TRUE SHAPE?!
11

THAT MUST BE IT! THE *TRUE SHAPE* OF THE *CHANGELING*-- IS THAT OF THE *NUCLEAR EXPLOSION CLOUD!* IT RE-VEALED ITSELF TO US ALL THE TIME--ONLY WE DIDN'T KNOW IT! IT MUST REMAIN THAT WAY NOW--FROZEN IN TIME-- BECAUSE OF ITS INABILITY TO CHANGE IT-SELF INTO A *NON-EXISTENT OBJECT!*

SNAP!

WITH HIS *POWER RING, GREEN LANTERN* REVIVES *TOMAR-RE* AND...

WHAT'S GOING ON IN HERE?

YOU DID MORE THAN YOU REALIZED, *GREEN LANTERN!* THE STAGE DOORMAN WAS IN A *COMA!* NOW THAT THE *CHANGELING* IS POWER-LESS IN ITS TRUE SHAPE--ALL THE PEOPLE IT AFFECTED HAVE RETURNED TO NORMAL!

A LITTLE LATER...

THE NON-CHANGING *CHANGELING* BACK TO ITS DEAD WORLD AND LEAVE IT THERE--HARMLESS--FOR ALL ETERNITY--AND THIS CASE IS COMPLETE!

ALL THAT REMAINS NOW IS TO TAKE

NOT ENTIRELY, *TOMAR-RE--*

I STILL HAVE TO EXPLAIN TO CAROL FERRIS -- AS *HAL JORDAN*-- WHY I'M SO LATE FOR OUR DATE TO THE *FERRIS COMPANY BALL! AND THAT* MAY BE EVEN TOUGHER THAN OVERCOMING THE *CHANGELING!*

The End

GREEN LANTERN

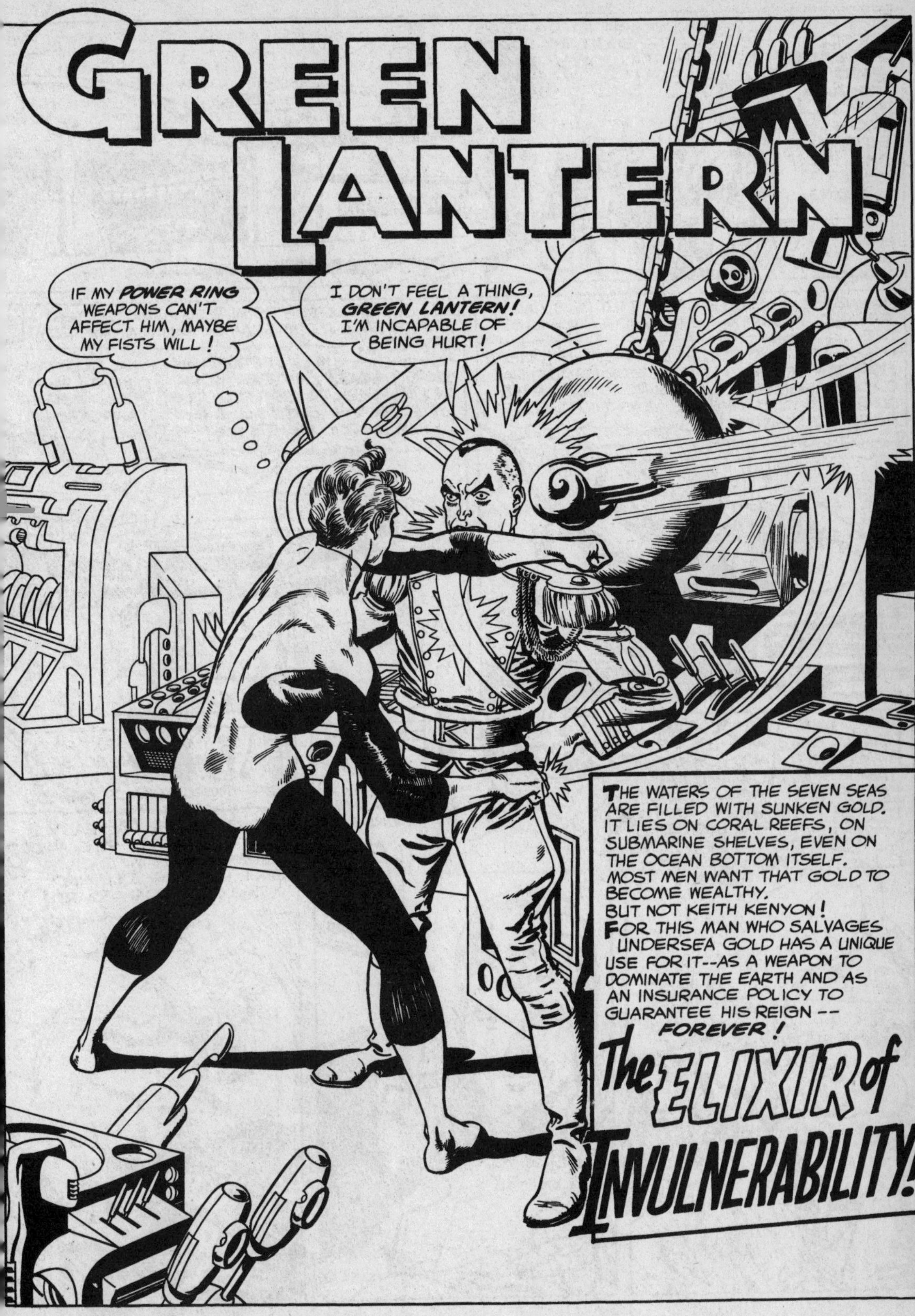
GREEN LANTERN!
IF MY POWER RING WEAPONS CAN'T AFFECT HIM, MAYBE MY FISTS WILL!
I DON'T FEEL A THING, GREEN LANTERN! I'M INCAPABLE OF BEING HURT!
THE WATERS OF THE SEVEN SEAS ARE FILLED WITH SUNKEN GOLD. IT LIES ON CORAL REEFS, ON SUBMARINE SHELVES, EVEN ON THE OCEAN BOTTOM ITSELF. MOST MEN WANT THAT GOLD TO BECOME WEALTHY. BUT NOT KEITH KENYON! FOR THIS MAN WHO SALVAGES UNDERSEA GOLD HAS A UNIQUE USE FOR IT--AS A WEAPON TO DOMINATE THE EARTH AND AS AN INSURANCE POLICY TO GUARANTEE HIS REIGN -- FOREVER!
The ELIXIR of INVULNERABILITY!

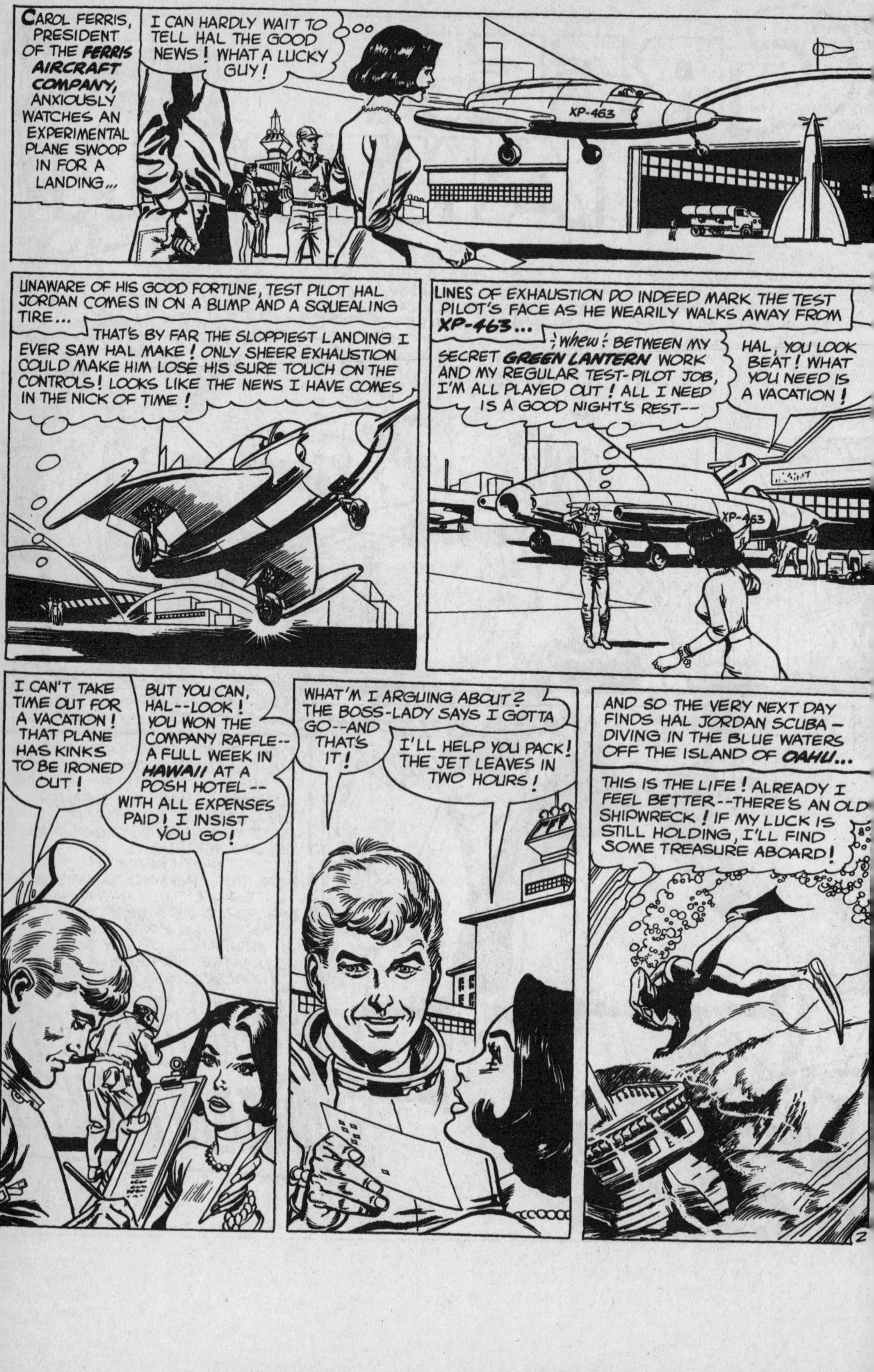
CAROL FERRIS, PRESIDENT OF THE FERRIS AIRCRAFT COMPANY, ANXIOUSLY WATCHES AN EXPERIMENTAL PLANE SWOOP IN FOR A LANDING...
I CAN HARDLY WAIT TO TELL HAL THE GOOD NEWS! WHAT A LUCKY GUY!
XP-463
UNAWARE OF HIS GOOD FORTUNE, TEST PILOT HAL JORDAN COMES IN ON A BUMP AND A SQUEALING TIRE...
THAT'S BY FAR THE SLOPPIEST LANDING I EVER SAW HAL MAKE! ONLY SHEER EXHAUSTION COULD MAKE HIM LOSE HIS SURE TOUCH ON THE CONTROLS! LOOKS LIKE THE NEWS I HAVE COMES IN THE NICK OF TIME!
LINES OF EXHAUSTION DO INDEED MARK THE TEST PILOT'S FACE AS HE WEARILY WALKS AWAY FROM XP-463...
; whew ; BETWEEN MY SECRET GREEN LANTERN WORK AND MY REGULAR TEST-PILOT JOB, I'M ALL PLAYED OUT! ALL I NEED IS A GOOD NIGHT'S REST--
HAL, YOU LOOK BEAT! WHAT YOU NEED IS A VACATION!
XP-463
I CAN'T TAKE TIME OUT FOR A VACATION! THAT PLANE HAS KINKS TO BE IRONED OUT!
BUT YOU CAN, HAL--LOOK! YOU WON THE COMPANY RAFFLE--A FULL WEEK IN HAWAII AT A POSH HOTEL--WITH ALL EXPENSES PAID! I INSIST YOU GO!
WHAT'M I ARGUING ABOUT? THE BOSS-LADY SAYS I GOTTA GO--AND THAT'S IT!
I'LL HELP YOU PACK! THE JET LEAVES IN TWO HOURS!
AND SO THE VERY NEXT DAY FINDS HAL JORDAN SCUBA-DIVING IN THE BLUE WATERS OFF THE ISLAND OF OAHU...
THIS IS THE LIFE! ALREADY I FEEL BETTER--THERE'S AN OLD SHIPWRECK! IF MY LUCK IS STILL HOLDING, I'LL FIND SOME TREASURE ABOARD!
2

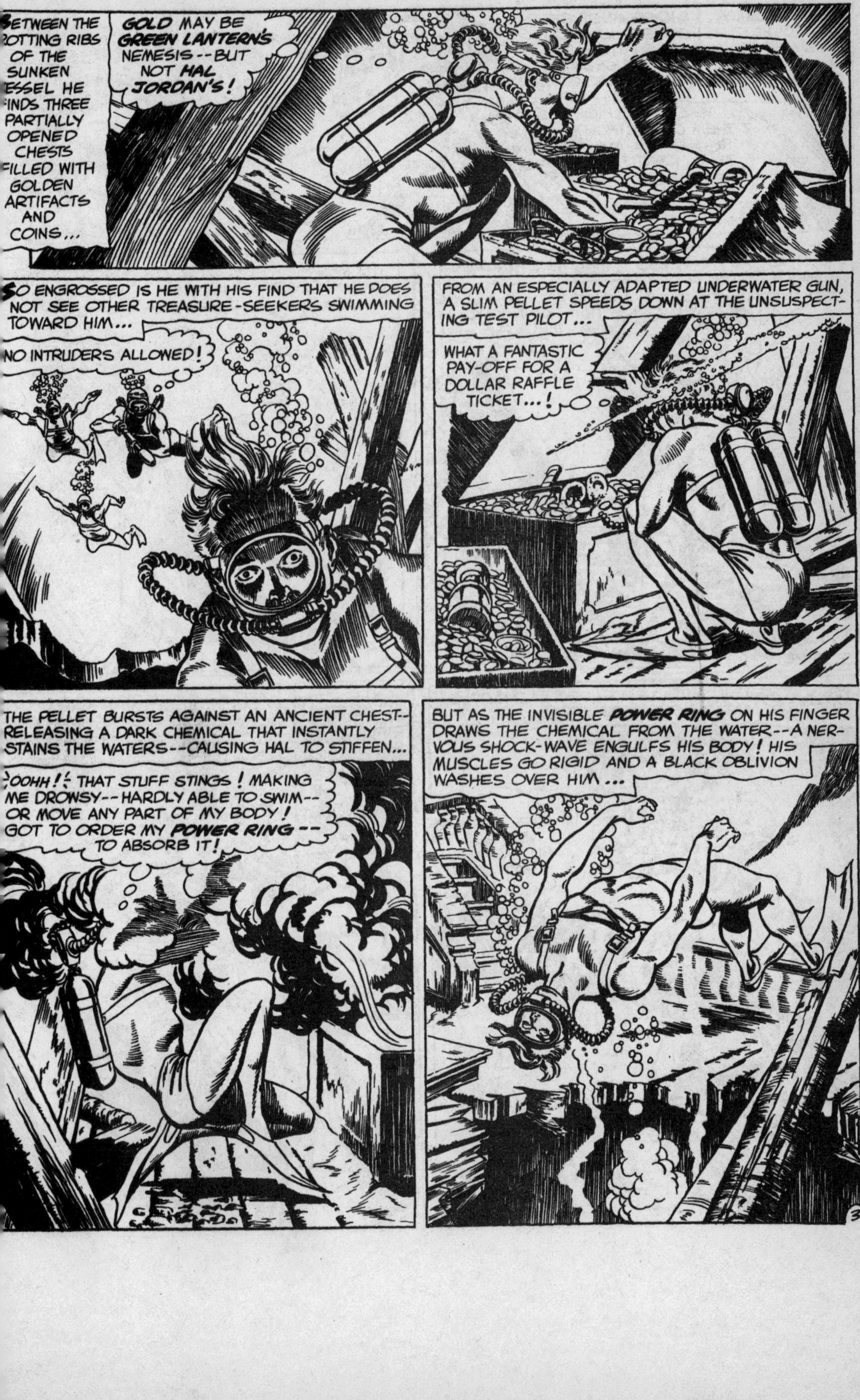
BETWEEN THE ROTTING RIBS OF THE SUNKEN VESSEL HE FINDS THREE PARTIALLY OPENED CHESTS FILLED WITH GOLDEN ARTIFACTS AND COINS...
GOLD MAY BE GREEN LANTERN'S NEMESIS--BUT NOT HAL JORDAN'S!
SO ENGROSSED IS HE WITH HIS FIND THAT HE DOES NOT SEE OTHER TREASURE-SEEKERS SWIMMING TOWARD HIM...
NO INTRUDERS ALLOWED!
FROM AN ESPECIALLY ADAPTED UNDERWATER GUN, A SLIM PELLET SPEEDS DOWN AT THE UNSUSPECTING TEST PILOT...
WHAT A FANTASTIC PAY-OFF FOR A DOLLAR RAFFLE TICKET...!
THE PELLET BURSTS AGAINST AN ANCIENT CHEST--RELEASING A DARK CHEMICAL THAT INSTANTLY STAINS THE WATERS--CAUSING HAL TO STIFFEN...
OOHH!! THAT STUFF STINGS! MAKING ME DROWSY--HARDLY ABLE TO SWIM--OR MOVE ANY PART OF MY BODY! GOT TO ORDER MY POWER RING--TO ABSORB IT!
BUT AS THE INVISIBLE POWER RING ON HIS FINGER DRAWS THE CHEMICAL FROM THE WATER--A NERVOUS SHOCK-WAVE ENGULFS HIS BODY! HIS MUSCLES GO RIGID AND A BLACK OBLIVION WASHES OVER HIM...
3

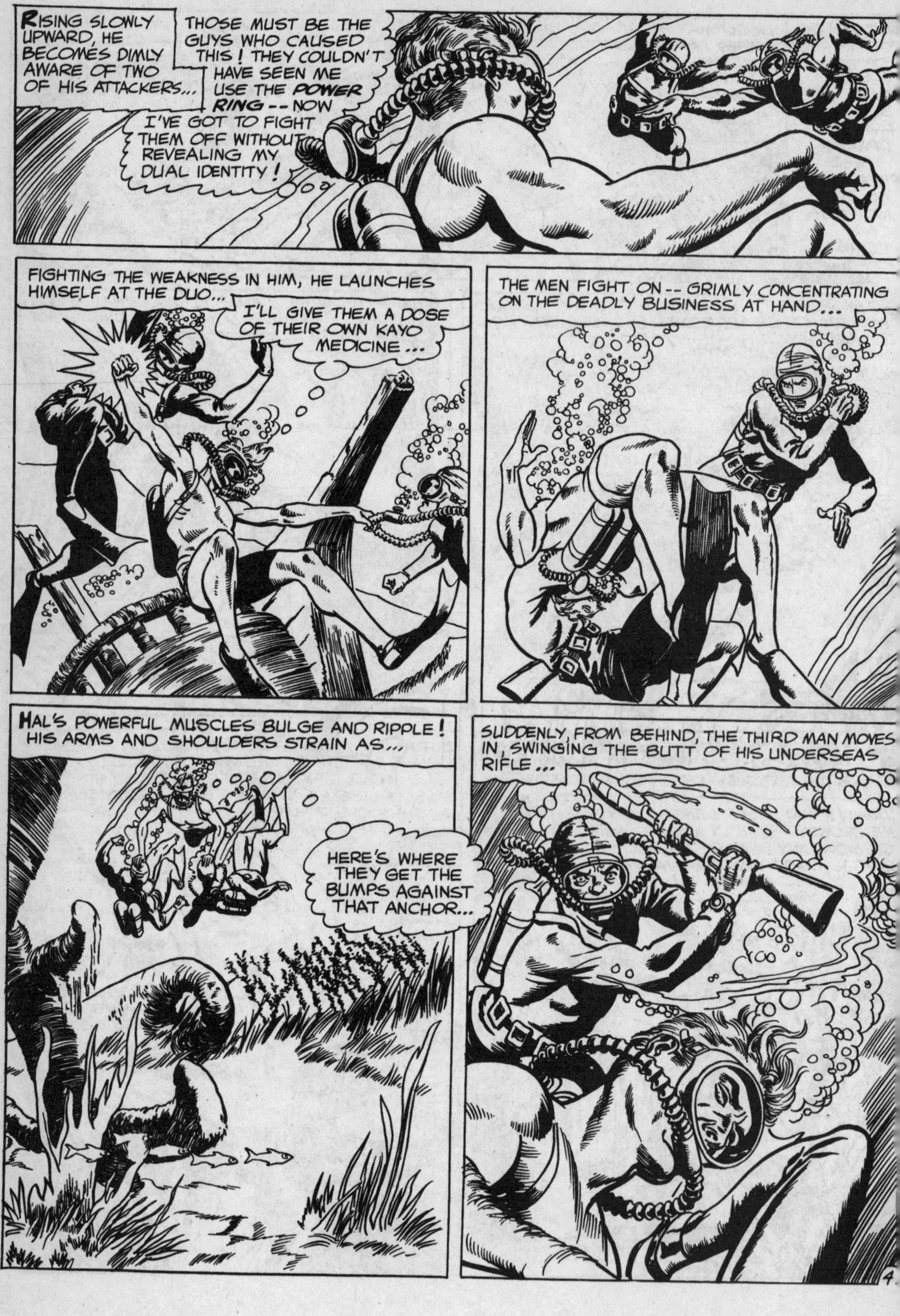
RISING SLOWLY UPWARD, HE BECOMES DIMLY AWARE OF TWO OF HIS ATTACKERS...
THOSE MUST BE THE GUYS WHO CAUSED THIS! THEY COULDN'T HAVE SEEN ME USE THE POWER RING -- NOW
I'VE GOT TO FIGHT THEM OFF WITHOUT REVEALING MY DUAL IDENTITY!
FIGHTING THE WEAKNESS IN HIM, HE LAUNCHES HIMSELF AT THE DUO...
I'LL GIVE THEM A DOSE OF THEIR OWN KAYO MEDICINE...
THE MEN FIGHT ON -- GRIMLY CONCENTRATING ON THE DEADLY BUSINESS AT HAND...
HAL'S POWERFUL MUSCLES BULGE AND RIPPLE! HIS ARMS AND SHOULDERS STRAIN AS...
HERE'S WHERE THEY GET THE BUMPS AGAINST THAT ANCHOR...
SUDDENLY, FROM BEHIND, THE THIRD MAN MOVES IN, SWINGING THE BUTT OF HIS UNDERSEAS RIFLE...
4

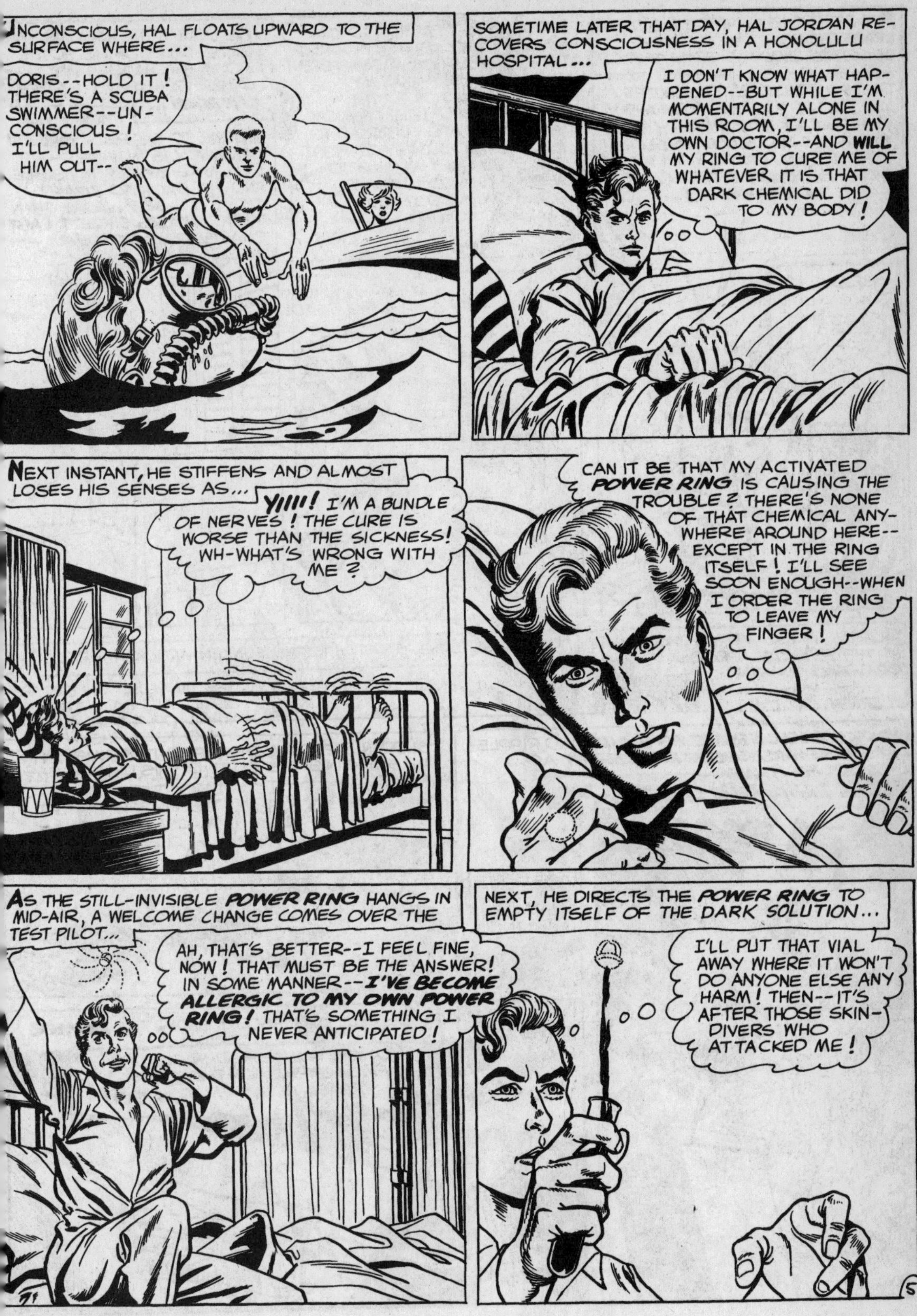
UNCONSCIOUS, HAL FLOATS UPWARD TO THE SURFACE WHERE...
DORIS--HOLD IT! THERE'S A SCUBA SWIMMER--UNCONSCIOUS! I'LL PULL HIM OUT--
SOMETIME LATER THAT DAY, HAL JORDAN RECOVERS CONSCIOUSNESS IN A HONOLULU HOSPITAL...
I DON'T KNOW WHAT HAPPENED--BUT WHILE I'M MOMENTARILY ALONE IN THIS ROOM, I'LL BE MY OWN DOCTOR--AND WILL MY RING TO CURE ME OF WHATEVER IT IS THAT DARK CHEMICAL DID TO MY BODY!
NEXT INSTANT, HE STIFFENS AND ALMOST LOSES HIS SENSES AS...
YIIII! I'M A BUNDLE OF NERVES! THE CURE IS WORSE THAN THE SICKNESS! WH-WHAT'S WRONG WITH ME?
CAN IT BE THAT MY ACTIVATED POWER RING IS CAUSING THE TROUBLE? THERE'S NONE OF THAT CHEMICAL ANYWHERE AROUND HERE--EXCEPT IN THE RING ITSELF! I'LL SEE SOON ENOUGH--WHEN I ORDER THE RING TO LEAVE MY FINGER!
AS THE STILL-INVISIBLE POWER RING HANGS IN MID-AIR, A WELCOME CHANGE COMES OVER THE TEST PILOT...
AH, THAT'S BETTER--I FEEL FINE, NOW! THAT MUST BE THE ANSWER! IN SOME MANNER--I'VE BECOME ALLERGIC TO MY OWN POWER RING! THAT'S SOMETHING I NEVER ANTICIPATED!
NEXT, HE DIRECTS THE POWER RING TO EMPTY ITSELF OF THE DARK SOLUTION...
I'LL PUT THAT VIAL AWAY WHERE IT WON'T DO ANYONE ELSE ANY HARM! THEN--IT'S AFTER THOSE SKIN-DIVERS WHO ATTACKED ME!
5

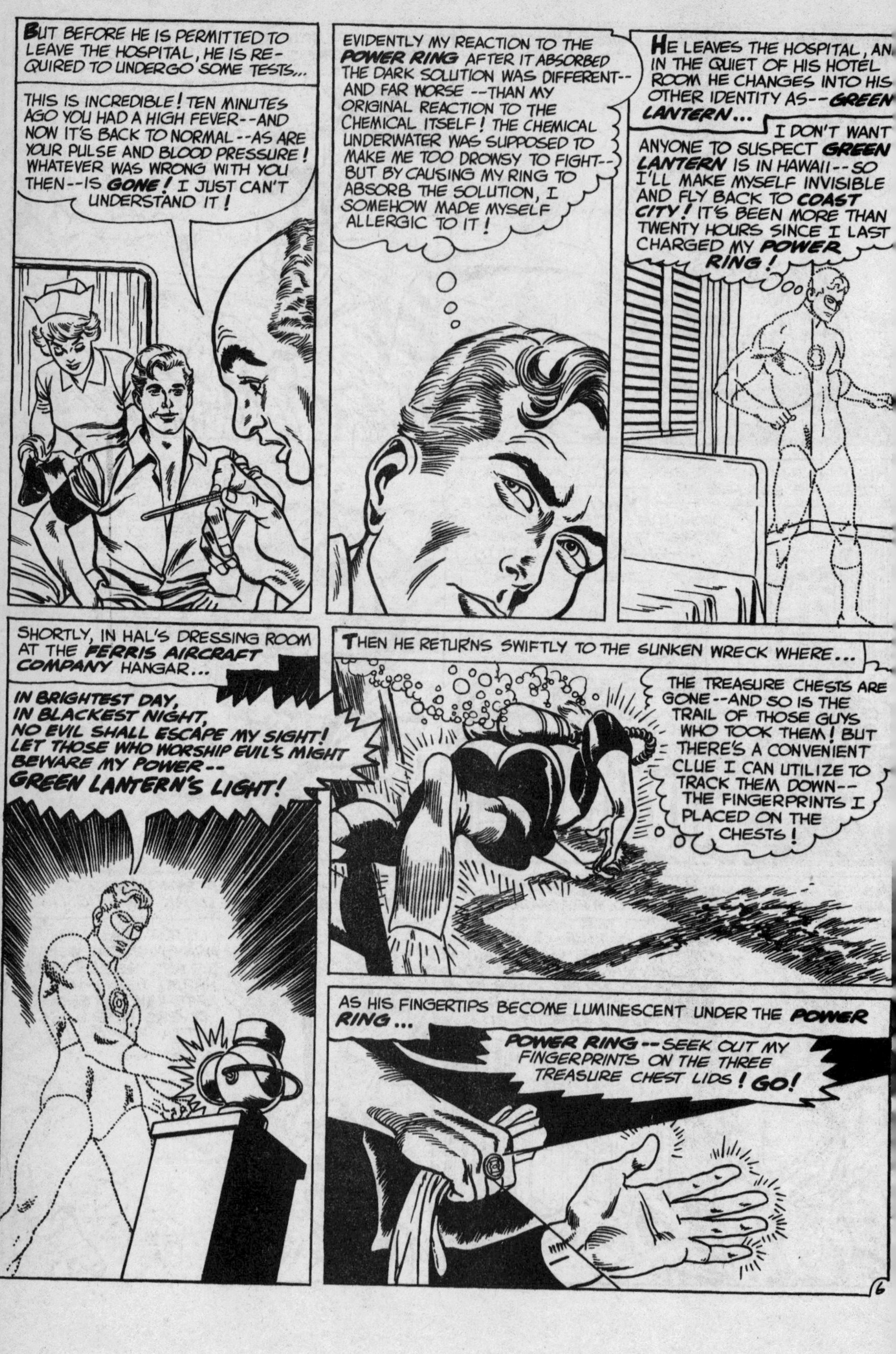
BUT BEFORE HE IS PERMITTED TO LEAVE THE HOSPITAL, HE IS REQUIRED TO UNDERGO SOME TESTS...
THIS IS INCREDIBLE! TEN MINUTES AGO YOU HAD A HIGH FEVER--AND NOW IT'S BACK TO NORMAL--AS ARE YOUR PULSE AND BLOOD PRESSURE! WHATEVER WAS WRONG WITH YOU THEN--IS GONE! I JUST CAN'T UNDERSTAND IT!
EVIDENTLY MY REACTION TO THE POWER RING AFTER IT ABSORBED THE DARK SOLUTION WAS DIFFERENT--AND FAR WORSE --THAN MY ORIGINAL REACTION TO THE CHEMICAL ITSELF! THE CHEMICAL UNDERWATER WAS SUPPOSED TO MAKE ME TOO DROWSY TO FIGHT--BUT BY CAUSING MY RING TO ABSORB THE SOLUTION, I SOMEHOW MADE MYSELF ALLERGIC TO IT!
HE LEAVES THE HOSPITAL, AN IN THE QUIET OF HIS HOTEL ROOM HE CHANGES INTO HIS OTHER IDENTITY AS--GREEN LANTERN...
I DON'T WANT ANYONE TO SUSPECT GREEN LANTERN IS IN HAWAII--SO I'LL MAKE MYSELF INVISIBLE AND FLY BACK TO COAST CITY! IT'S BEEN MORE THAN TWENTY HOURS SINCE I LAST CHARGED MY POWER RING!
SHORTLY, IN HAL'S DRESSING ROOM AT THE FERRIS AIRCRAFT COMPANY HANGAR...
IN BRIGHTEST DAY, IN BLACKEST NIGHT, NO EVIL SHALL ESCAPE MY SIGHT! LET THOSE WHO WORSHIP EVIL'S MIGHT BEWARE MY POWER-- GREEN LANTERN'S LIGHT!
THEN HE RETURNS SWIFTLY TO THE SUNKEN WRECK WHERE...
THE TREASURE CHESTS ARE GONE--AND SO IS THE TRAIL OF THOSE GUYS WHO TOOK THEM! BUT THERE'S A CONVENIENT CLUE I CAN UTILIZE TO TRACK THEM DOWN--THE FINGERPRINTS I PLACED ON THE CHESTS!
AS HIS FINGERTIPS BECOME LUMINESCENT UNDER THE POWER RING...
POWER RING--SEEK OUT MY FINGERPRINTS ON THE THREE TREASURE CHEST LIDS! GO!
6

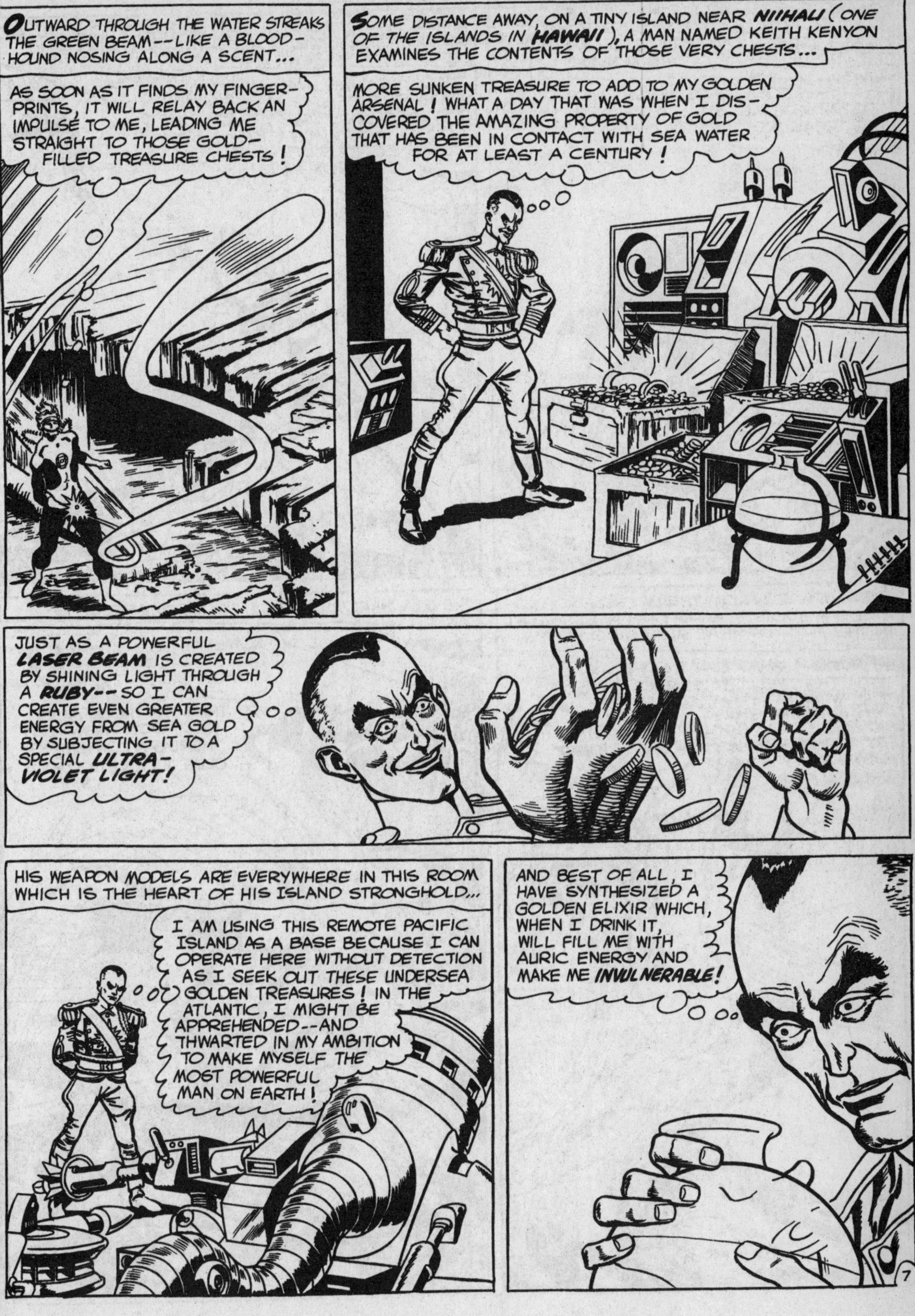
OUTWARD THROUGH THE WATER STREAKS THE GREEN BEAM--LIKE A BLOOD-HOUND NOSING ALONG A SCENT...
AS SOON AS IT FINDS MY FINGER-PRINTS, IT WILL RELAY BACK AN IMPULSE TO ME, LEADING ME STRAIGHT TO THOSE GOLD-FILLED TREASURE CHESTS!
SOME DISTANCE AWAY, ON A TINY ISLAND NEAR NIIHAU (ONE OF THE ISLANDS IN HAWAII), A MAN NAMED KEITH KENYON EXAMINES THE CONTENTS OF THOSE VERY CHESTS...
MORE SUNKEN TREASURE TO ADD TO MY GOLDEN ARSENAL! WHAT A DAY THAT WAS WHEN I DIS-COVERED THE AMAZING PROPERTY OF GOLD THAT HAS BEEN IN CONTACT WITH SEA WATER FOR AT LEAST A CENTURY!
JUST AS A POWERFUL LASER BEAM IS CREATED BY SHINING LIGHT THROUGH A RUBY--SO I CAN CREATE EVEN GREATER ENERGY FROM SEA GOLD BY SUBJECTING IT TO A SPECIAL ULTRA-VIOLET LIGHT!
HIS WEAPON MODELS ARE EVERYWHERE IN THIS ROOM WHICH IS THE HEART OF HIS ISLAND STRONGHOLD...
I AM USING THIS REMOTE PACIFIC ISLAND AS A BASE BECAUSE I CAN OPERATE HERE WITHOUT DETECTION AS I SEEK OUT THESE UNDERSEA GOLDEN TREASURES! IN THE ATLANTIC, I MIGHT BE APPREHENDED--AND THWARTED IN MY AMBITION TO MAKE MYSELF THE MOST POWERFUL MAN ON EARTH!
AND BEST OF ALL, I HAVE SYNTHESIZED A GOLDEN ELIXIR WHICH, WHEN I DRINK IT, WILL FILL ME WITH AURIC ENERGY AND MAKE ME INVULNERABLE!
7

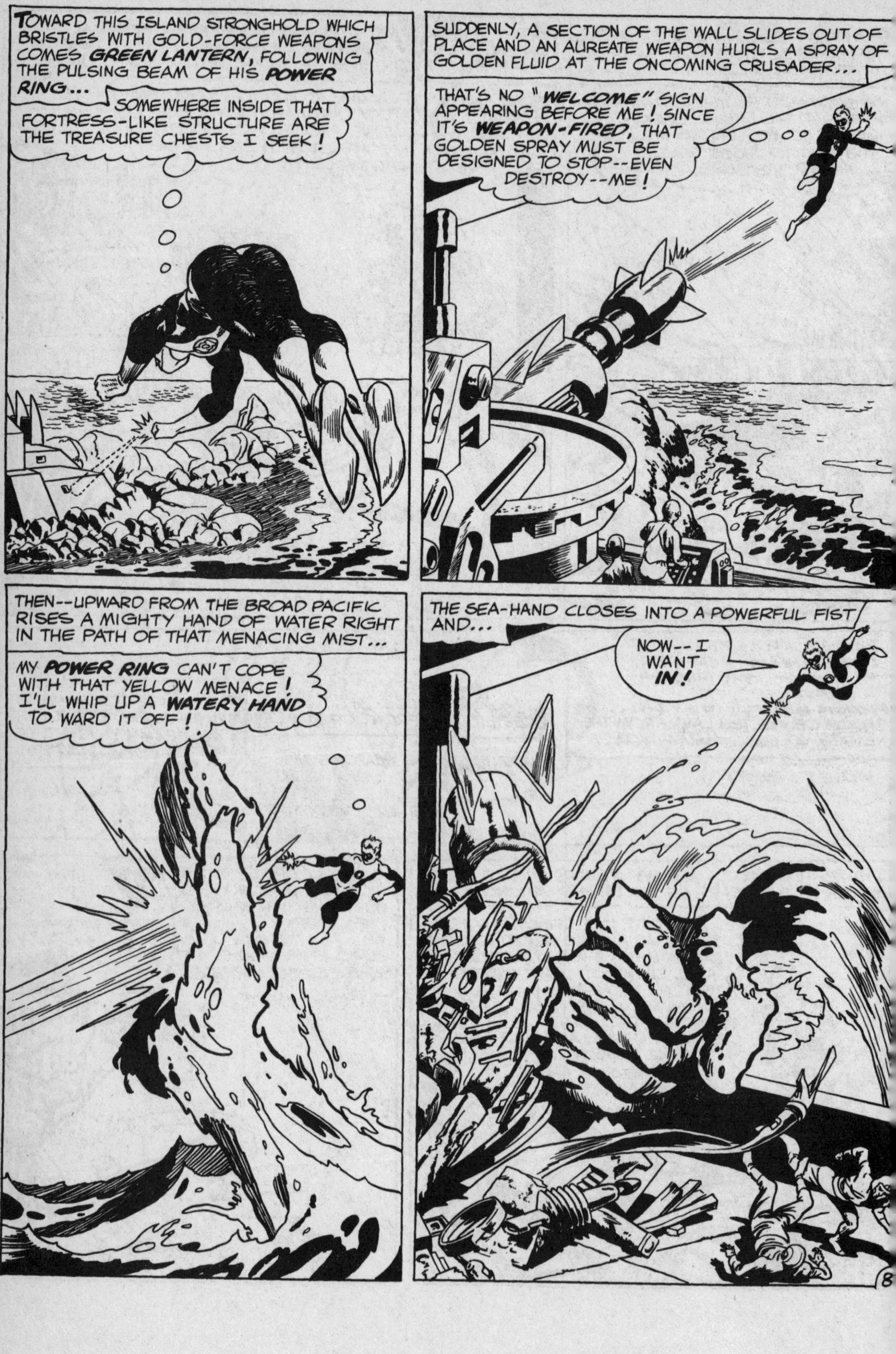
TOWARD THIS ISLAND STRONGHOLD WHICH BRISTLES WITH GOLD-FORCE WEAPONS COMES GREEN LANTERN, FOLLOWING THE PULSING BEAM OF HIS POWER RING...
SOMEWHERE INSIDE THAT FORTRESS-LIKE STRUCTURE ARE THE TREASURE CHESTS I SEEK!
SUDDENLY, A SECTION OF THE WALL SLIDES OUT OF PLACE AND AN AUREATE WEAPON HURLS A SPRAY OF GOLDEN FLUID AT THE ONCOMING CRUSADER...
THAT'S NO "WELCOME" SIGN APPEARING BEFORE ME! SINCE IT'S WEAPON-FIRED, THAT GOLDEN SPRAY MUST BE DESIGNED TO STOP--EVEN DESTROY--ME!
THEN--UPWARD FROM THE BROAD PACIFIC RISES A MIGHTY HAND OF WATER RIGHT IN THE PATH OF THAT MENACING MIST...
MY POWER RING CAN'T COPE WITH THAT YELLOW MENACE! I'LL WHIP UP A WATERY HAND TO WARD IT OFF!
THE SEA-HAND CLOSES INTO A POWERFUL FIST AND...
NOW--I WANT IN!
8

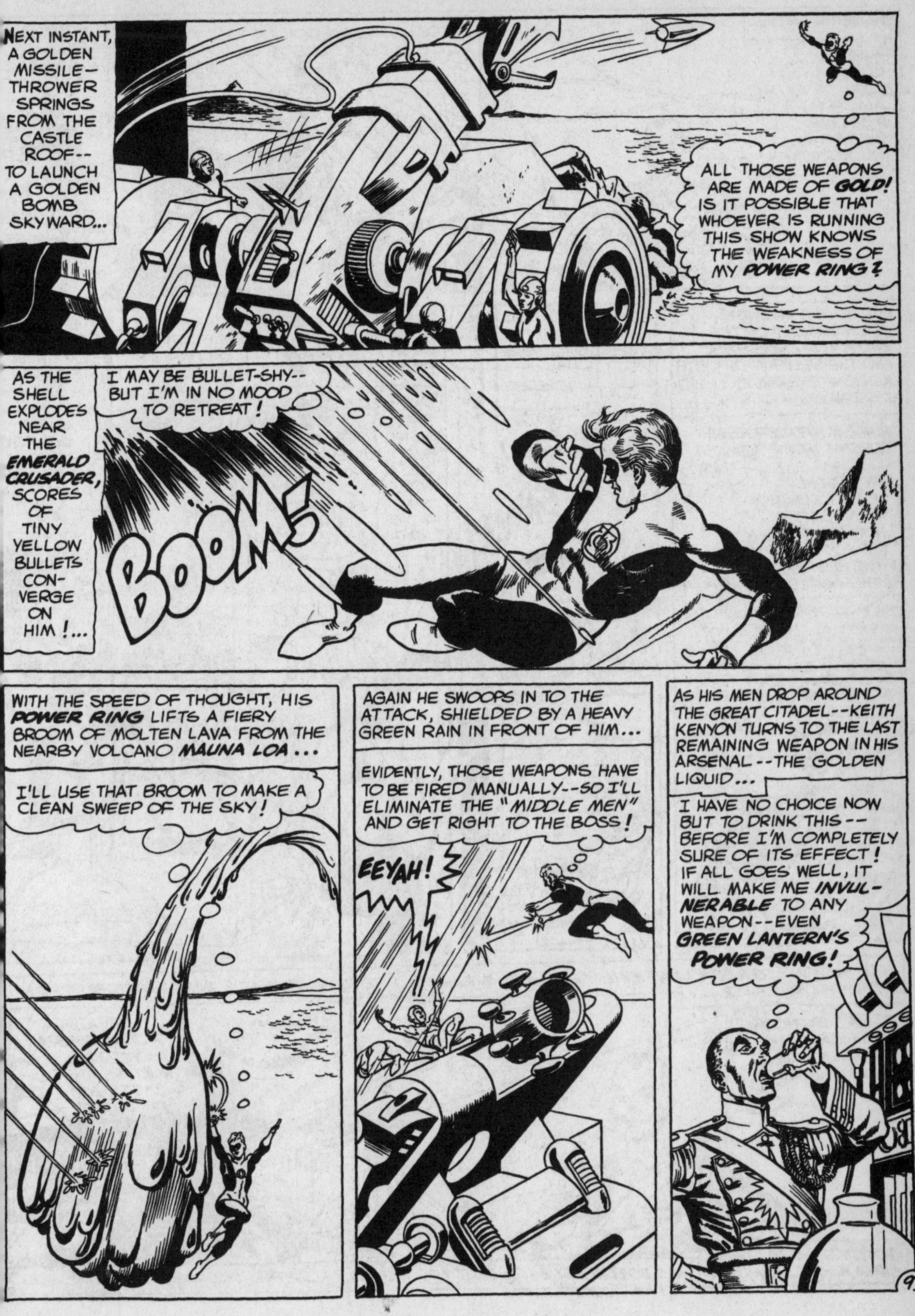
NEXT INSTANT, A GOLDEN MISSILE-THROWER SPRINGS FROM THE CASTLE ROOF-- TO LAUNCH A GOLDEN BOMB SKYWARD...
ALL THOSE WEAPONS ARE MADE OF GOLD! IS IT POSSIBLE THAT WHOEVER IS RUNNING THIS SHOW KNOWS THE WEAKNESS OF MY POWER RING?
AS THE SHELL EXPLODES NEAR THE EMERALD CRUSADER, SCORES OF TINY YELLOW BULLETS CON-VERGE ON HIM!...
I MAY BE BULLET-SHY-- BUT I'M IN NO MOOD TO RETREAT!
BOOM!
WITH THE SPEED OF THOUGHT, HIS POWER RING LIFTS A FIERY BROOM OF MOLTEN LAVA FROM THE NEARBY VOLCANO MAUNA LOA...
I'LL USE THAT BROOM TO MAKE A CLEAN SWEEP OF THE SKY!
AGAIN HE SWOOPS IN TO THE ATTACK, SHIELDED BY A HEAVY GREEN RAIN IN FRONT OF HIM...
EVIDENTLY, THOSE WEAPONS HAVE TO BE FIRED MANUALLY--SO I'LL ELIMINATE THE "MIDDLE MEN" AND GET RIGHT TO THE BOSS!
EEYAH!
AS HIS MEN DROP AROUND THE GREAT CITADEL--KEITH KENYON TURNS TO THE LAST REMAINING WEAPON IN HIS ARSENAL--THE GOLDEN LIQUID...
I HAVE NO CHOICE NOW BUT TO DRINK THIS-- BEFORE I'M COMPLETELY SURE OF ITS EFFECT! IF ALL GOES WELL, IT WILL MAKE ME INVUL-NERABLE TO ANY WEAPON--EVEN GREEN LANTERN'S POWER RING!
9.

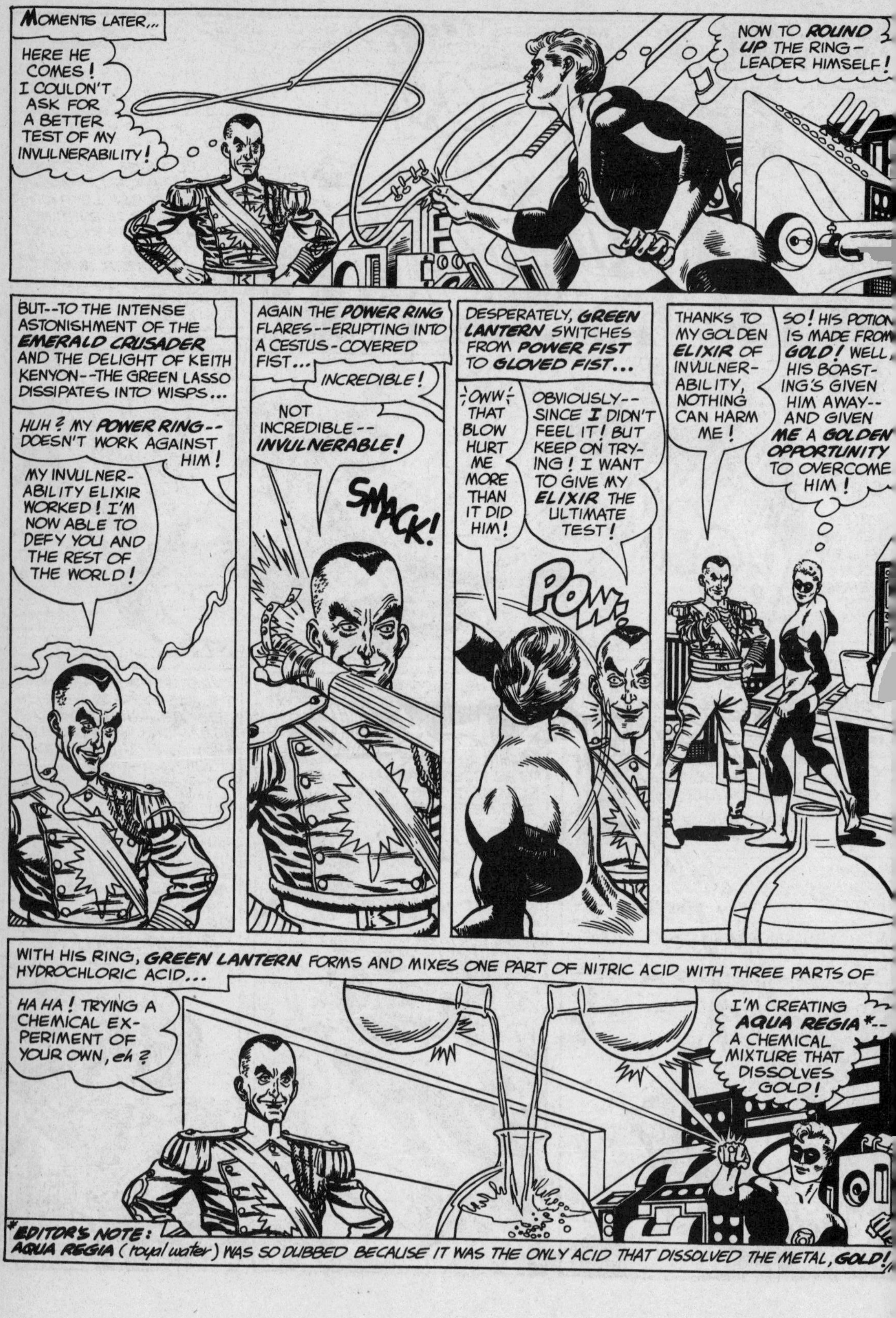
MOMENTS LATER...
HERE HE COMES! I COULDN'T ASK FOR A BETTER TEST OF MY INVULNERABILITY!
NOW TO ROUND UP THE RING-LEADER HIMSELF!
BUT--TO THE INTENSE ASTONISHMENT OF THE EMERALD CRUSADER AND THE DELIGHT OF KEITH KENYON--THE GREEN LASSO DISSIPATES INTO WISPS...
HUH? MY POWER RING--DOESN'T WORK AGAINST HIM!
MY INVULNERABILITY ELIXIR WORKED! I'M NOW ABLE TO DEFY YOU AND THE REST OF THE WORLD!
AGAIN THE POWER RING FLARES--ERUPTING INTO A CESTUS-COVERED FIST...
INCREDIBLE!
NOT INCREDIBLE--INVULNERABLE!
SMACK!
DESPERATELY, GREEN LANTERN SWITCHES FROM POWER FIST TO GLOVED FIST...
OWW! THAT BLOW HURT ME MORE THAN IT DID HIM!
OBVIOUSLY--SINCE I DIDN'T FEEL IT! BUT KEEP ON TRYING! I WANT TO GIVE MY ELIXIR THE ULTIMATE TEST!
POW!
THANKS TO MY GOLDEN ELIXIR OF INVULNERABILITY, NOTHING CAN HARM ME!
SO! HIS POTION IS MADE FROM GOLD! WELL, HIS BOASTING'S GIVEN HIM AWAY--AND GIVEN ME A GOLDEN OPPORTUNITY TO OVERCOME HIM!
WITH HIS RING, GREEN LANTERN FORMS AND MIXES ONE PART OF NITRIC ACID WITH THREE PARTS OF HYDROCHLORIC ACID...
HA HA! TRYING A CHEMICAL EXPERIMENT OF YOUR OWN, eh?
I'M CREATING AQUA REGIA*--A CHEMICAL MIXTURE THAT DISSOLVES GOLD!
*EDITOR'S NOTE: AQUA REGIA (royal water) WAS SO DUBBED BECAUSE IT WAS THE ONLY ACID THAT DISSOLVED THE METAL, GOLD!

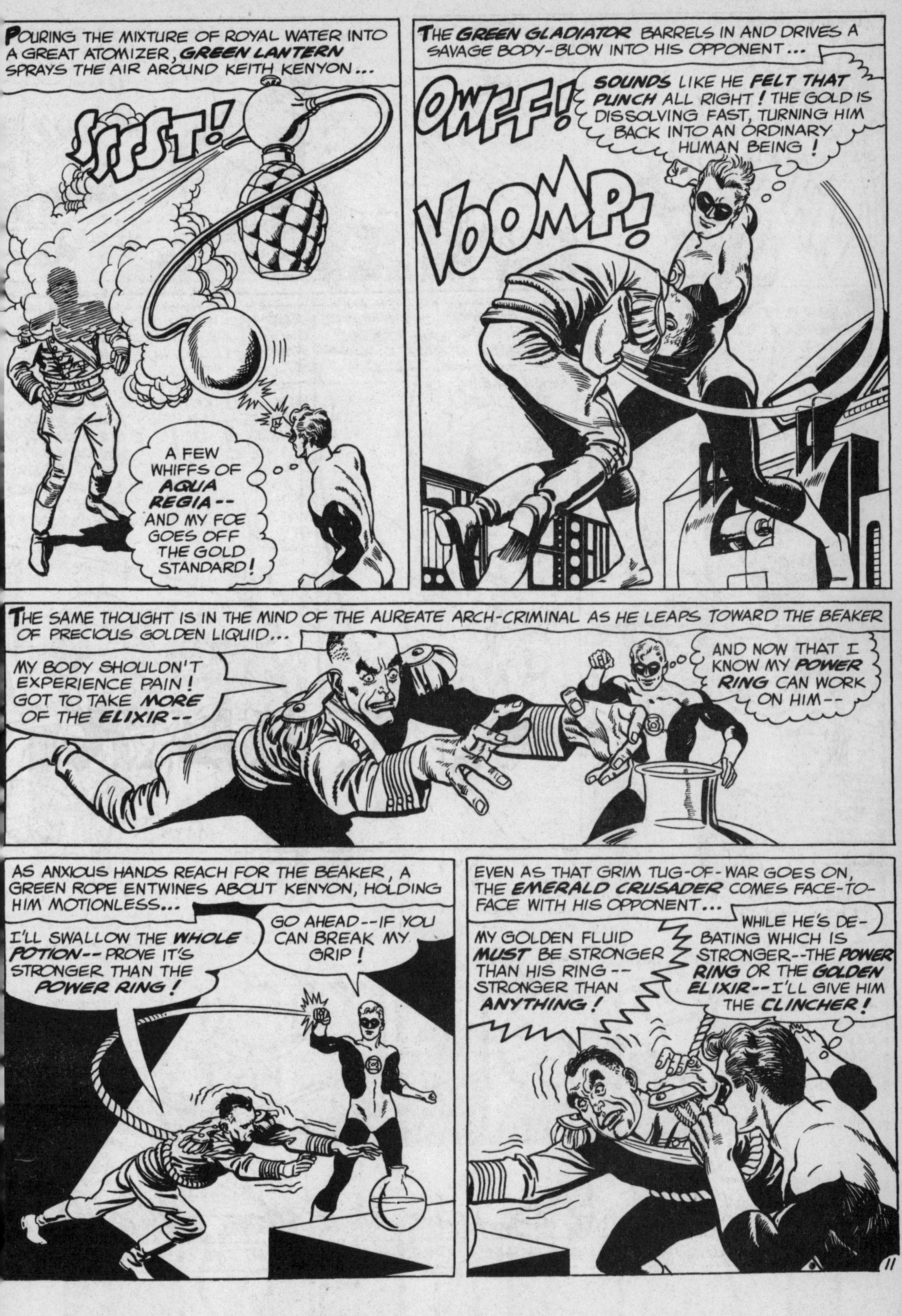
POURING THE MIXTURE OF ROYAL WATER INTO A GREAT ATOMIZER, GREEN LANTERN SPRAYS THE AIR AROUND KEITH KENYON...
SSSST!
A FEW WHIFFS OF AQUA REGIA-- AND MY FOE GOES OFF THE GOLD STANDARD!
THE GREEN GLADIATOR BARRELS IN AND DRIVES A SAVAGE BODY-BLOW INTO HIS OPPONENT...
OWF-F!
SOUNDS LIKE HE FELT THAT PUNCH ALL RIGHT! THE GOLD IS DISSOLVING FAST, TURNING HIM BACK INTO AN ORDINARY HUMAN BEING!
VOOMP!
THE SAME THOUGHT IS IN THE MIND OF THE AUREATE ARCH-CRIMINAL AS HE LEAPS TOWARD THE BEAKER OF PRECIOUS GOLDEN LIQUID...
MY BODY SHOULDN'T EXPERIENCE PAIN! GOT TO TAKE MORE OF THE ELIXIR--
AND NOW THAT I KNOW MY POWER RING CAN WORK ON HIM--
AS ANXIOUS HANDS REACH FOR THE BEAKER, A GREEN ROPE ENTWINES ABOUT KENYON, HOLDING HIM MOTIONLESS...
I'LL SWALLOW THE WHOLE POTION--PROVE IT'S STRONGER THAN THE POWER RING!
GO AHEAD--IF YOU CAN BREAK MY GRIP!
EVEN AS THAT GRIM TUG-OF-WAR GOES ON, THE EMERALD CRUSADER COMES FACE-TO-FACE WITH HIS OPPONENT...
MY GOLDEN FLUID MUST BE STRONGER THAN HIS RING-- STRONGER THAN ANYTHING!
WHILE HE'S DEBATING WHICH IS STRONGER--THE POWER RING OR THE GOLDEN ELIXIR--I'LL GIVE HIM THE CLINCHER!
11

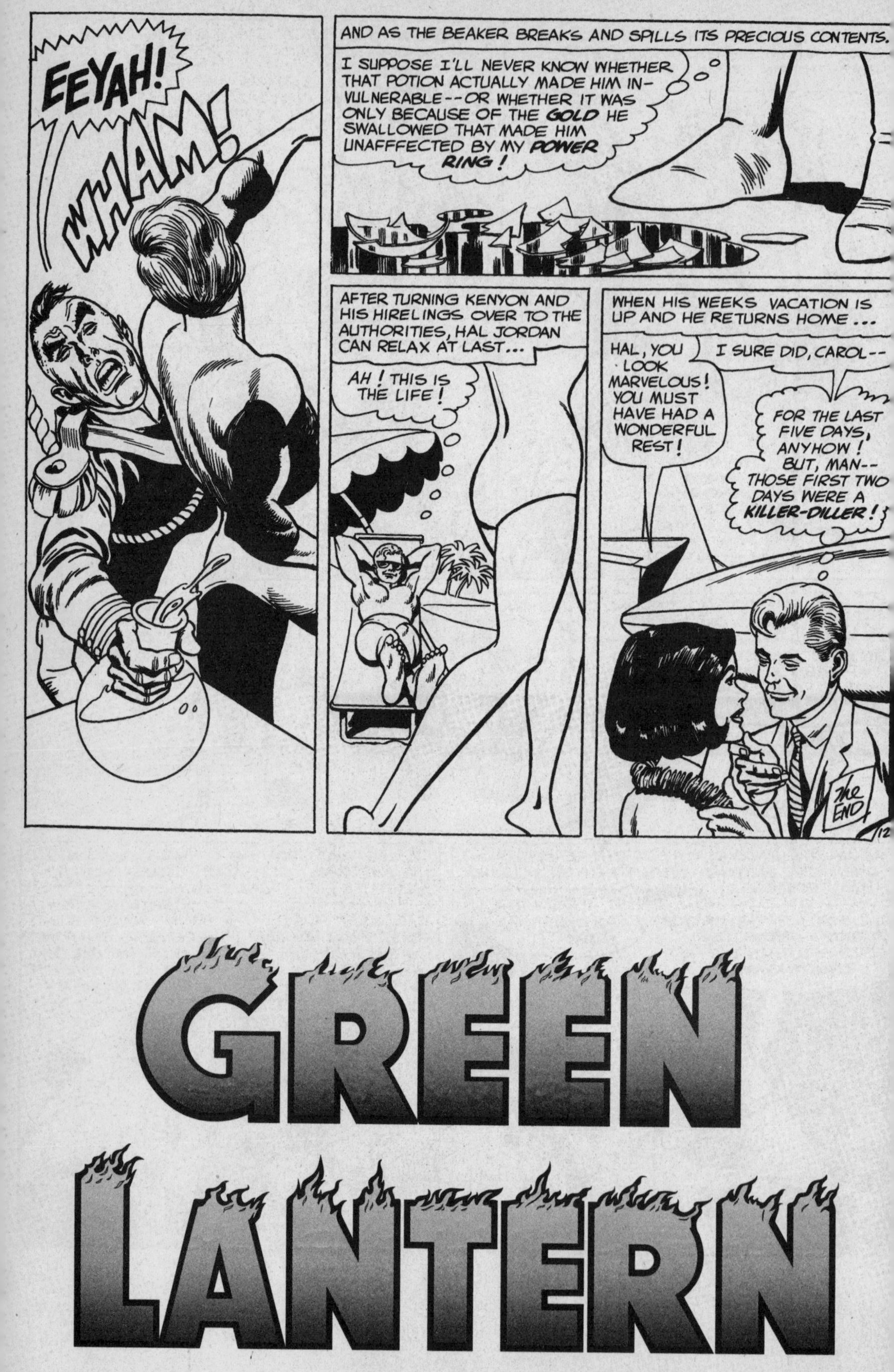
EEYAH!
WHAM!
AND AS THE BEAKER BREAKS AND SPILLS ITS PRECIOUS CONTENTS.
I SUPPOSE I'LL NEVER KNOW WHETHER THAT POTION ACTUALLY MADE HIM INVULNERABLE--OR WHETHER IT WAS ONLY BECAUSE OF THE GOLD HE SWALLOWED THAT MADE HIM UNAFFFECTED BY MY POWER RING!
AFTER TURNING KENYON AND HIS HIRELINGS OVER TO THE AUTHORITIES, HAL JORDAN CAN RELAX AT LAST...
AH! THIS IS THE LIFE!
WHEN HIS WEEKS VACATION IS UP AND HE RETURNS HOME...
HAL, YOU LOOK MARVELOUS! YOU MUST HAVE HAD A WONDERFUL REST!
I SURE DID, CAROL--
FOR THE LAST FIVE DAYS, ANYHOW! BUT, MAN--THOSE FIRST TWO DAYS WERE A KILLER-DILLER!
THE END
12

GREEN LANTERN

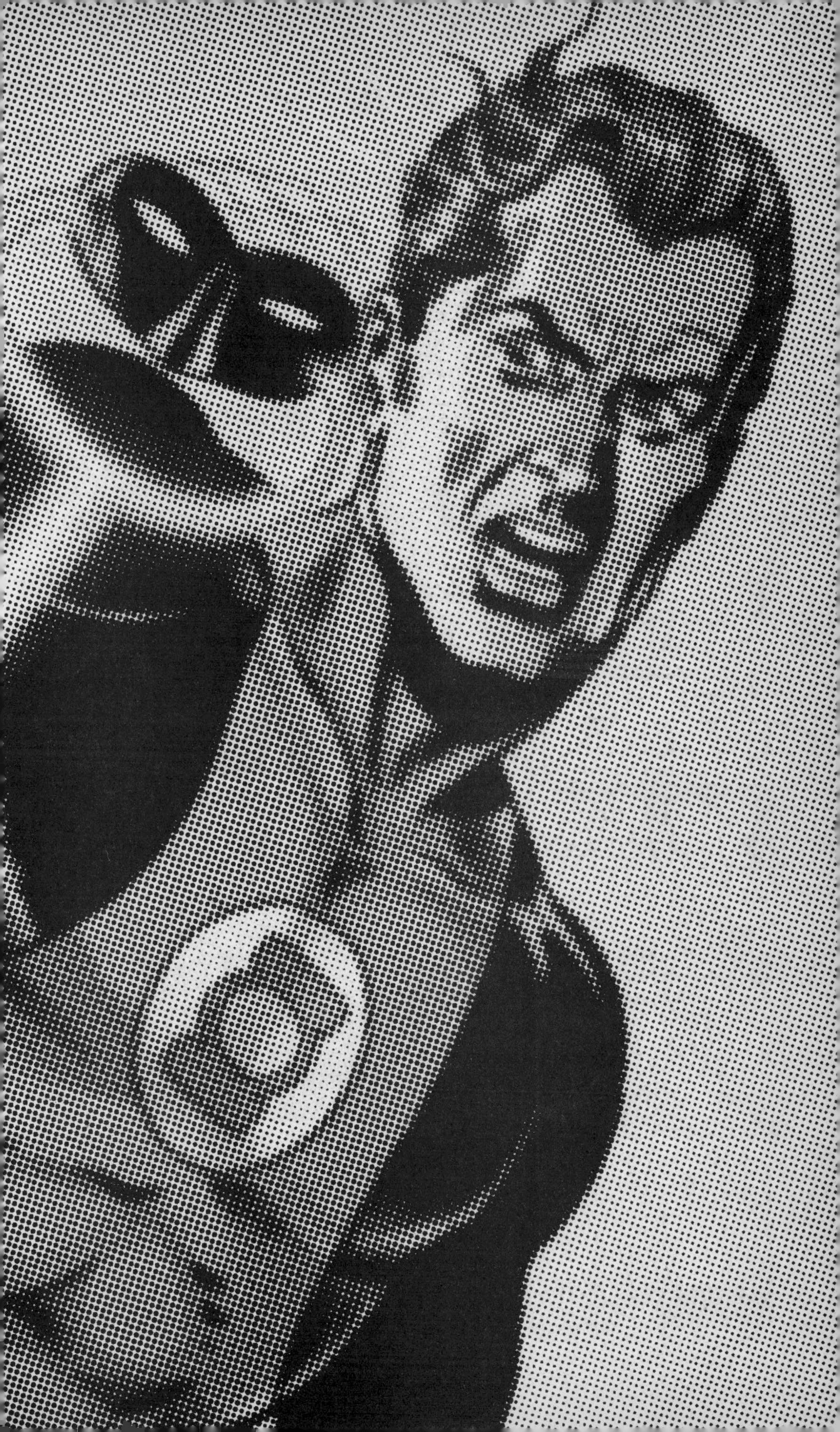

SHOWCASE
PRESENTS

OVER 500 PAGES OF DC'S CLASSIC HEROES AND STORIES PRESENTED IN EACH VOLUME!

GREEN LANTERN VOL. 1

SUPERMAN VOL. 1

SUPERMAN VOL. 2

SUPERMAN FAMILY VOL. 1

JONAH HEX VOL. 1

METAMORPHO VOL. 1

SEARCH THE GRAPHIC NOVELS SECTION OF
www.DCCOMICS.com
FOR ART AND INFORMATION ON ALL OF OUR BOOKS!

SHOWCASE PRESENTS

OVER 500 PAGES OF DC'S CLASSIC HEROES AND STORIES PRESENTED IN EACH VOLUME!

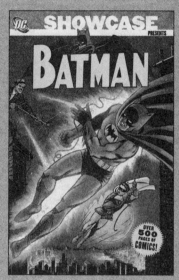

DC
SHOWCASE
PRESENTS
BATMAN
OVER 500 PAGES OF COMICS!

BATMAN
VOL. 1

DC
SHOWCASE
PRESENTS
OVER 500 PAGES OF COMICS!
JUSTICE LEAGUE of AMERICA

JUSTICE LEAGUE OF
AMERICA
VOL. 1

DC
SHOWCASE
PRESENTS
The ELONGATED Man
OVER 500 PAGES OF COMICS!

THE ELONGATED MAN
VOL. 1

DC
SHOWCASE
PRESENTS
CHALLENGERS OF THE UNKNOWN
OVER 500 PAGES OF COMICS!

THE CHALLENGERS OF THE
UNKNOWN
VOL. 1

DC
SHOWCASE
PRESENTS
THE HAUNTED TANK
OVER 500 PAGES OF COMICS!

THE HAUNTED TANK
VOL. 1

DC
SHOWCASE
PRESENTS
The PHANTOM STRANGER
OVER 500 PAGES OF COMICS!

THE PHANTOM STRANGER
VOL. 1

SEARCH THE GRAPHIC NOVELS SECTION OF

www.DCCOMICS.com

FOR ART AND INFORMATION ON ALL OF OUR BOOKS!

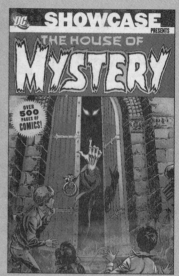